The New York City Opera

Martin L. Sokol

Macmillan Publishing Co., Inc.

NEW YORK

Collier Macmillan Publishers

LONDON

WITHDRAWN

The New York City Opera

AN AMERICAN

ADVENTURE

Copyright © 1981 by Martin L. Sokol
New York City Opera Annals 1944 through Spring 1979
copyright © 1981 by George Louis Mayer

Macmillan Publishing Co., Inc.
866 Third Avenue, New York, N.Y. 10022
Collier Macmillan Canada, Ltd.

Library of Congress Cataloging in Publication Data
Sokol, Martin L.
    The New York City Opera, 1943–1981.
    Includes index.
    1. New York City Opera—History.   I. Title.
ML1711.8.N3N58   782.1′06′07471   81–11781
ISBN 0–02–612280–4   AACR2

10 9 8 7 6 5 4 3 2 1

Designed by Jack Meserole

Printed in the United States of America

*The New York City Opera Company—indeed, the
entire complex of City Center performing companies—
could not have come into existence without the genius of
Morton Baum. And if, by chance, they had come about,
they could never have weathered the financial and
political trials of the early years without his presence.*

*It is to the memory of Morton Baum that this book
is reverently dedicated.*

Contents

Appendices

Annals of THE NEW YORK CITY OPERA   215

List of Illustrations

ix

In Praise of Morton Baum

Excerpts from a eulogy

written by Dr. Judah Cahn

and

delivered by Leonard Bernstein

He possessed the vision of a prophet, the soul of an artist, and above all else, the humility to understand that he was privileged to pursue goals that were greater than his own importance.

From his earliest youth he was a devoted servant of the arts. The culmination of that service was the opportunity to join in the creation of what became known as the "City Center." To some, the dream of a City Center of Music and Drama was an enterprise. To Morton it was a sacred task to implement a vision of putting great artistic achievements within the reach of the people of New York City—his birthplace, his home, and for him the most fascinating place in all the world.

He set out to accomplish this task, not in the spirit of a patron bestowing beneficence nor in a spirit of condescension that asked people to be satisfied with less than the best because they could not afford better. He would not—he could not—compromise with his own artistic integrity. Slowly and painfully, he helped create a multifaceted institution of artistic achievements that has become world-renowned.

He loved music with a compelling passion and was granted the gift of expressing that love as a pianist. To him the piano was not only a musical instrument, it was the expression of his whole being. His fingers built sets, sang roles, conducted orchestras, all created in his own mind, and through a highly personal magic, transmitted them to the minds of his listeners.

He was a phenomenon with which mankind is infrequently blessed. He served as a living witness of the spiritual heights to which man can aspire and reach.

Remarks added by Mr. Leonard Bernstein

As one who knew and loved him, who owed so much to him, who was so helped by him in my early years, who was perennially warmed by his enthusiasm and love, let me join Rabbi Cahn in saying—may the soul of Morton Baum rest in peace. *Amen.*

Preface

Some readers may find my approach to this book unconventional. Histories have been written about many opera companies, and the traditional point of view has been to focus on the performances themselves—the so-called public aspect of the company. When I was first asked to write this book, my original thought was to follow that well-established pattern; however, almost immediately thereafter, I met Lester Baum whose brother, Morton, had been the dominant force at City Opera from the company's origin until his untimely death in 1968. Morton had, himself, been at work on a book about all the City Center companies, including the New York City Opera, and Lester was kind enough to furnish me with Morton's draft manuscript, as well as his correspondence files in toto. I therefore had a gold mine of information at hand, most of it material that had never been made public, and so I decided to approach this book from a totally different direction—that of organization and management decisions and the many colorful factors that led to the company's creation, rather than of its performances. Much of what follows has never appeared in print, and I sincerely hope that this volume will clarify the various mysteries and half-truths that operaphiles have wondered about for years. My feeling about the validity of this approach was reinforced by the inclusion of a complete annals—a list of all performances given by the company in New York, along with dates and casts.

I cannot begin to thank everyone who has helped, but three people stand out in bold relief. They are Lester Baum, for his confidence in making Morton's papers available; Regina Fiorito, who provided an incredible amount of moral support as well as research, photographic editing, text preparation, and the painstaking task of typing and proofreading the manuscript; and Michael Edelson, who not only supplied several of the photographs used but also played devil's advocate, challenging every word of the text while it was still in manuscript form. In addition, I must express my deepest thanks to the company's various directors and to John S. White, the recently retired Managing Director; the cost of preparing the annals, which so enhance the reference value of this book, was most generously underwritten by Caroline Newhouse; Craig Macdonald of the City Center, Lincoln Kirstein, George Balanchine, Hans Sondheimer, and Thomas Martin as well as dozens of singers, both past and present, contributed additional information; Fred Fehl, whose many photographs appear in these pages; William Nudorf of the New York City Opera Guild; George Mayer, who prepared the bulk of the annals; Ruth M. Hider, Catherine Parsons, and the staff of the New York City Opera Company; Dr. Judah Cahn, whose moving eulogy to Morton Baum, delivered by Leonard Bernstein, appears in these pages; Thomas F. Kelley, Manager of the New York State Theater, and his assistant, Jacqueline Mooney; and Jane Cullen, my editor at Macmillan, whose patience and assistance have been considerable.

To these people and many others, I express my most profound thanks.

MARTIN L. SOKOL
June 1981

1

Prelude

The forty-two recipients of this telegram were so diverse professionally that the group had every appearance of having been chosen at random. There were union representatives, theatrical personalities, educators, members of the press, various city officials, philanthropists, and investors, all invited to participate in one of the greatest artistic ventures of our country's history. At the time, however, no one could have foreseen the eventual scope of the project inaugurated by the terse message. Had they realized the enormity of the undertaking, perhaps more people would have attended the mayor's meeting, despite the very short advance notice. As it was, exactly half of the invited guests appeared at City Hall on March 5.

It was Newbold Morris, president of the city council, who had called the meeting, using La Guardia's name to promote the greatest possible response. For some time, he and Morton Baum had been actively involved in trying to establish a varied theatrical enterprise of high quality that would not severely strain the budgets of the less than affluent, and after examining a host of alternatives, they finally arrived at one that seemed practical. The time had now come to translate their idea into reality, but they needed a great deal of assistance, and the roster of those chosen for the initial meeting, despite its almost casual appearance, was carefully narrowed down from more than 150 names that had come under consideration.

Broadway theater ticket prices averaged about $2.50 in 1943. Although hardly excessive by today's standards, in 1943 tomatoes cost 13¢ a pound, oranges were 45¢ a dozen, and a ten-room apartment with four baths, in one of the most elite sections of New York, was available for $225 a month. The "help wanted" advertisements in the *New York Times* offered $16 weekly to waiters, $25 to bookkeepers, and $50 to pharmacists; and a ten-inch string of cultured pearls secured by a gold clasp could be purchased from Bloomingdale's department store for $10. In that economy, few people could afford the luxury of theater, opera, or concerts.

This was not the first time that New York's municipal government had become concerned with the problem. It had arisen some thirty years earlier during the administration of Mayor William J. Gaynor (1910–13), who, upon the recommendation of a committee formed to investigate the situation, attempted to create a civic theater in Central Park. Architectural plans were drafted and estimates submitted, but ultimately, the Board of Aldermen refused to allocate funds for this purpose. Today, cultural institutions have public financing available on many levels, from local through federal—although the amounts allocated are still woefully inadequate and come nowhere near the running costs involved—but in 1912, the concept of municipal theater was quite radical. It is both interesting and frustrating to speculate on the probable development of the arts in America if Gaynor's plan had succeeded. His successors showed no interest in the question. Whether political expedience prevented them from embracing a losing cause, or whether the cause itself was considered unimportant, is a matter of conjecture, but it was not until La Guardia assumed the city's executive authority that it again became prominent.

Between 1874 and 1933, with only occasional lapses, all of New York City's mayors had been controlled by the corrupt political machinery of Tammany Hall. La Guardia had twice tried to change that—in 1921 when he sought the mayoralty but failed to win the Republican primary from Henry H. Curran, and in 1929 when he was solidly defeated by the incumbent Democratic mayor, Jimmy Walker. In 1932 he suffered his most stunning blow at the hands of Tammany when, after serving in Congress for five terms, he was defeated for reelection by the machine-sponsored James Lanzetta. His political career appeared to be at an end. So it was nothing short of miraculous when, like the phoenix rising from its own ashes, Fiorello Henry La Guardia was inaugurated as mayor of New York in January 1934, after a year of heavy campaigning.

It was not as a Republican that La Guardia had triumphed, though, but as a candidate of the Fusion party, one of the leaders of which was a young attorney named Morton Baum. He could not have succeeded, however, without a certain amount of GOP support, and this came from the "silk-stocking" Republican Club, whose president was Newbold Morris.

Involvement in both public life and music were prominent features of the Baum household. Lester Baum, Morton's brother and a New York State senator for many years, had mastered the violin, and their sister Evelyn had undertaken extensive vocal training. Morton was an excellent pianist, and many people felt that he could have had a successful musical career, had he so chosen. Morton also had an uncanny ability for finance, and after his election to the Board of Aldermen in 1934, he distinguished himself as the author of various tax bills when the payment of unemployment relief nearly forced the city into bankruptcy in 1935. La Guardia appointed him to the office of Special Tax Counsel, a position which he retained until 1938, when he resumed private legal practice. Thus, it was perfectly natural that Morton Baum, with his love and knowledge of music, finances, and politics would become one of the prime movers in city-sponsored theater.

Newbold Morris's background was deeply rooted in American history. One of his ancestors was Lewis Morris (1726–98), a signer of the Declaration of Independence, a member of the Second Continental Congress, and a major-general of the New York militia during the Revolution. An earlier Lewis Morris (1671–1746) was instrumental in establishing New Jersey as a colony separate from New York in 1738, and in addition to holding the office of chief justice of both colonies, he was New Jersey's first governor. The Morris family was therefore held in great esteem, and Newbold was a popular member of New York's social set.

Upon assuming his new office, La Guardia immediately appointed Morris assistant corporation counsel, and in 1934, he was chosen to fill a vacancy that arose among the Board of Aldermen. It was here that he met Morton Baum and they became close friends, their personal affection cemented by the mutual love of music that made them frequent companions at concert and opera. In 1937, La Guardia was nominated for a second term, and Morris was the candidate for president of the city council. Both men won an easy victory. By the time City Center came up for official discussions in 1942 and 1943, the already powerful triumvirate of La Guardia, Baum, and Morris was further strengthened by the enthusiastic support of City Comptroller Joseph D. McGoldrick, a former professor of economics at Columbia University.

In 1878, the world-famous soprano Adelina Patti embarked on a cross-country concert tour. Her accompanist and arranger was a twenty-nine-year-old Italian musician named Achille Luigi Carlo La Guardia. Enamored of America, Achille decided to make his home in New York and followed the time-honored tradition of returning to the Old World to find a bride. In Trieste, he met and married Irene Coen, a member of that city's Jewish community. The couple returned to New York in 1880, and on December 11, 1882, at 7 Varick Street in Greenwich Village, their first son, Fiorello, was born. Three years later, Achille enlisted in the Eleventh Infantry Regiment of the U. S. Army as chief musician. In 1892, he received a permanent assignment at Whipple Barracks in Prescott, a town in the Arizona Territory. It was here that Fiorello spent his formative years, remaining until 1898. Achille's most fervent hope was that his son would become a second John Philip Sousa, and toward this end he provided thorough training on the cornet and supplementary lessons on the banjo. Achille also instructed his daughter Gemma, and her instruments were the violin, piano, and mandolin. Music was as integral a part of the La Guardia home as food, air, and water.

Very early in his political career, La Guardia espoused the cause of the man in the street—"the little guy." Perhaps this stemmed from his own early experiences in Prescott, where his Italian ancestry won him the label of "dago" and his father's military rank (sergeant) prevented him from socializing with children of the officers. Like Morton Baum's, La Guardia's background provided a strong interest in theater—particularly music—for the masses.

New York City, like the rest of the country, was in difficult straits when La Guardia began his twelve-year reign as mayor. The Depression had brought about poverty and unemployment, and despite his desire to enhance the city's intellectual life, more urgent problems required his attention. Nonetheless, in 1936 he managed to persuade the board of education to establish the High School of Music and Art for talented students. In addition, he created the Municipal Acts Committee, which, under the leadership of Mrs. Henry Breckenridge, was to investigate the cultural picture and make recommendations for its improvement. They did so, but the economic situation prevented the mayor from implementing Mrs. Breckenridge's suggestions. Deeply frustrated, she submitted her resignation in 1937, and, for the time being, the local government withdrew from this area completely.

When the federal Works Progress Administration (WPA) was launched in 1938, its purpose was to create jobs in diverse areas for those who were unemployed. One of its subdivisions was the Federal Music Project, and La Guardia designated Newbold Morris as the liaison between New York City and Horace Johnson, the federal WPA music administrator. With an enthusiasm born of true love, Morris plunged into the task and arranged a series of concerts by the WPA orchestra that took place at Radio City and later at Carnegie Hall. The admission fee to these concerts was a nominal 25¢, and a substantial following developed, demonstrating that there was a sincere interest on the part of the public in affordable classical music. Morris never forgot this, and in the years to come, high-quality entertainment at modest cost became one of his principal causes.

The same phenomenon was manifested in the world of drama. Off-Broadway shows flourished, stimulated by the WPA theater projects. In 1939, Elmer Rice, a noted playwright with a strong public consciousness, sponsored a six-month run of Robert Sherwood's *Abe Lincoln in Illinois*, a prize-winning play that had been very popular on Broadway. The top admission price was $1, and, although Rice lost some money on the venture, he was convinced that this was due entirely to the small size of the theater used.

These then were the forces at work by the start of 1940—a public in search of low-priced, high-quality entertainment, federal funding in the form of WPA grants, a mayor eager to enhance the city's cultural life, and two dedicated, knowledgeable, and extremely capable workers in the persons of Newbold Morris and Morton Baum.

Midway between Sixth and Seventh avenues on the north side of Fifty-fifth Street, there was a large mosquelike building known as Mecca Temple. Built at a cost of $3.5 million, it looked like a discarded set from some bizarre Arabian Nights film. The vast dome of terra-cotta tile was surmounted by an immense scimitar and crescent, and the interior bore the inscription, in huge bas-relief lettering *"Es Salaam Aleikum"* (Arabic for "Peace be with you"). This had been the home of the Shriners, or more accurately, The Ancient Order of Nobles of the Mystic Shrine. The cornerstone had been put into place on October 13, 1923, by Judge Arthur S. Tompkins, and a little over a year later, on December 29, 1924, the building had its official dedication "to the cause of human service" in the name of "the great Jehovah." The opening ceremonies were attended by the mayors of fifty cities and some 3,500 spectators, and by the end of the day, over 8,000 Shriners had participated in the events, which included a parade and a musical program by tenor Ralph Errole, who had made his Metropolitan Opera debut a month earlier. The building consisted of an auditorium and stage, dressing rooms, scenery lofts and offices, and underneath the auditorium, a large ballroom. It was a strange structure, both inside and out—garish and florid, with slit windows, tall, narrow doors, and Moorish decor. The lighting was poor, the floors uncarpeted, and echoes reverberated throughout the stone hallways.

With the advent of the Depression, Mecca Temple was badly hit. Mortgage payments fell into arrears, as did real estate taxes due the city, and by 1939, the accumulated back payments totaled $560,000. The bank which held the first mortgage foreclosed and sold its interest to a Mr. Verchleiser, the lessee of the ballroom. He attempted to rent the theater to various performing groups, but his income from this was insufficient to sustain the huge financial burden, and in 1942, legal title to the building passed to New York City because of nonpayment of taxes. The structure proved to be a white elephant for many reasons. To begin with, it was suitable only as a theater, but its distance from the Broadway theatrical district was a serious drawback. The small off-Broadway houses with their seating capacities of one or two hundred could sustain themselves away from the mainstream, but a theater seating several thousand was another matter entirely. Then, because of its size, the building was very costly to operate; and finally, it was in so dilapidated a condition that a substantial investment would be required to make it operable.

Nonetheless, something had to be done. The city now owned the property, which, if it continued to deteriorate, would severely depreciate the values of neighboring real estate. La Guardia assigned to none other than Newbold Morris the task of putting Mecca Temple to constructive use. In midwinter of 1942, he and Morton Baum went to reexamine the property. They found a large stage, well equipped, and a seating capacity of 2,692, which could easily be increased. Additionally, the sight lines were good from all seats and although the house was large, it possessed a surprising intimacy due to its being wide rather than deep.

It was at this point that the dreams of the past merged with the problems of the present. Why not have a theater, operated by the city, that would offer opera, ballet, drama, and concerts at prices within the reach of the public? As lawyers well trained in government, both men knew that it would be necessary to find some legal precedent enabling the city to create and support a "Bureau of Performing Arts," but an exhaustive search of the statutes showed that this would be a dead end. The mechanism did not exist that would permit the city to run a theater. It gradually evolved that a private nonprofit corporation would have to be formed to assume this responsibility. Its members should consist of public-spirited citizens and representatives of organizations devoted to the performing arts, who would be willing to underwrite any losses incurred by the venture. The city could not contribute financially, but, since the site was to be used for the betterment of the community, it was proposed that the city enter into a long-term $1-per-year lease with the corporation, and that it also effect the necessary repairs and improvements, which as owner of the building, it could do. The plan was presented to an interested but skeptical La Guardia, who decided that it was at least worth investigating, and on March 3, 1943, Newbold Morris, under La Guardia's name, announced the inaugural meeting. The following is a complete list of people invited to attend the conference; the names of those who were present are preceded by an asterisk.

*Luigi Antonini	*ILGWU*
*Morton Baum	
Mrs. August Belmont	*Metropolitan Opera Association*
*Bernard Conal	*CIO*
*Howard S. Cullman	*Broadway investor*
Olin Downes	*New York Times*
David Dubinsky	*ILGWU*
*John Erskine	*Metropolitan Opera Association*
*William Feinberg	*American Federation of Musicians, Local 802*
Marshall Field	*Philharmonic Society*
*John Golden	*Theatrical producer*
Edmond A. Guggenheim	*Guggenheim Foundation*
Adolph Held	*Workmen's Circle*
*Ira A. Hirschmann	*New Friends of Music*
Mrs. Lytle Hull	*The New Opera Company*
Ernest Hutcheson	*Juilliard School of Music*
George S. Kaufman	*Playwrights' Producing Company*
*Fiorello H. La Guardia	
Erich Leinsdorf	*Cleveland Symphony Orchestra*
Bert Lytell	*Actors' Equity*
*Joseph D. McGoldrick	*Comptroller*
*Newbold Morris	
Robert Moses	*Commissioner of Parks*
*Paul Moss	*Commissioner of Licenses*
*Morris S. Novik	*Radio station WNYC*

*Jacob Potofsky	*Amalgamated Clothing Workers of America*
Mrs. Ruth Pratt	*Philharmonic Society*
*Mrs. Arthur M. Reis	*League of Composers*
*Elmer Rice	*Playwrights' Producing Company*
John D. Rockefeller, Jr.	*Philanthropist*
*Alex Rose	*United Hatters Cap and Millinery Workers*
*Jacob Rosenberg	*American Federation of Musicians, Local 802*
J. Robert Rubin	*Loews, Inc.*
*George Sloan	*Metropolitan Opera Association*
*Lee Thompson Smith	*New York City Bureau of Real Estate*
Deems Taylor	*ASCAP*
Mrs. Myron Taylor	*League of Composers*
Thomas D. Thacker	*Corporation counsel*
*Lawrence Tibbett	*American Guild of Musical Artists*
*Oscar Wagner	*Juilliard School of Music*
Gerald Warburg	*Cellist, conductor, and composer*
*Mrs. Herbert Witherspoon	*American Guild of Musical Artists*
Maurice Wertheim	*Theatre Guild, Inc.*

The meeting began with a few words of greeting from La Guardia, who then turned it over to Newbold Morris. After describing the city's acquisition of Mecca Temple, he outlined the plan formulated by himself and Morton Baum, and called upon the assemblage for their support. Enthusiasm ran high, and virtually everyone present pledged complete cooperation. Thus, the City Center of Music and Drama was born.

2

The Birth of
City Center

MAYOR LA GUARDIA delegated to Newbold Morris full
authority and responsibility for the organization of the new arts center.
His only admonition was that the enterprise must be self-sustaining, since
no direct financial aid from the city could be expected. He reaffirmed that
the city would make the building available at the nominal rental of $1
per year and would effect whatever repairs were necessary, a pledge that
would ultimately prove a very sore point.

Morris went about his task immediately. His initial step was the
creation of three committees—Organization and Business Planning, Scope
and Program, and Finance and Participation, headed respectively by
Howard S. Cullman, Newbold Morris, and Joseph D. McGoldrick. Prior
to the first committee meeting, Aymar Embury, a respected architect with
the city's Board of Estimate, had been asked to investigate and report on
the building. His findings resulted in two separate proposals. The first
of these called for immediate repairs to plumbing and electrical fixtures,
combined with repainting and general housecleaning, at an estimated cost
of $12,000. The more ambitious plan involved extensive remodeling of
the house and the creation of a new ceiling, which would cost about
$250,000, to improve acoustics.

These reports were presented at the March 18 meeting of the Scope
and Program committee, consisting of Sigmund Spaeth (a popular author
and lecturer on classical music), Newbold Morris, Mrs. Reis, Ernest
Hutcheson, Olin Downes, Mrs. Witherspoon, Elmer Rice, John Erskine,
and Mrs. Hull. All had very thorough credentials and solid achievements

9

behind them, but there was a distinct lack of balance, as eight of the nine present were oriented toward music, with only Elmer Rice representing theater.

The committee then went on to formulate a basic operating procedure. Suggestions for types of presentations included opera, ballet, operetta, symphonic concerts, choral programs, and drama, although no specific works were yet considered. The most significant accomplishment of the meeting was the decision to function not as a producing organization but rather as a booking house. Performing groups already in existence were to be presented at reduced ticket prices, which would still show a profit due to the large seating capacity of the theater. Among the groups to be invited would be the Playwrights' Producing Company, the New Opera Company, and various shows upon the completion of their Broadway engagements.

Until the organization had legal status, public solicitation of funds was impossible, and there was no way of predicting finances with any degree of accuracy. Morris felt that the committee could go no further at this point, and the meeting was adjourned.

With outside commitments keeping Howard Cullman away from New York for several weeks, on April 1, 1943, Morris called a joint meeting of the Organization and Business Planning and the Finance and Participation committees. Morton Baum presided in lieu of Cullman, and an operating budget was drawn up. Maintenance costs for fuel, electricity, and the appropriate operating personnel were estimated at $40,000 per year; managerial and administrative employees were to receive an additional $20,000, and another $20,000 was earmarked for much needed restoration of the stage. Expected income for the same period was $60,000 for the auditorium (based on 10 percent of gross ticket sales with an average admission price of $1, and forty weeks of production), $12,000 for rental of the ballroom, and $8,000 for rental of office space in the building. If these figures proved to be realistic, the company would succeed in getting through the first year without a deficit. Money was desperately needed at the outset, however, to get started, and since the estimated expenses exactly equaled the anticipated revenue, a certain amount of capital was required as a cushion against unforeseen contingencies. Morris realized that very few people would make substantial donations to a new theatrical venture, so he wisely decided to ask for loans. In a very short time he acquired pledges totaling $62,250. In addition, he received unsolicited contributions amounting to $10,600, giving the company a working fund of $72,850 (see Table I, page 201, for a complete list of initial guarantors).

The organization plan decided upon was a nonprofit corporation to be known as City Center of Music and Drama, Inc. There would be forty-six incorporators who would represent the organization in perpetuity, since no stock would be issued, and no part of the corporation would be traded. Furthermore, the company would be run by a board of directors, who would serve without compensation. There would be not less than five nor more than twenty-five directors, and the term of office would be one year. The forty-six incorporators consisted largely of the group at the initial meeting in the mayor's office, supplemented by the guarantors and a few additional people from the theatrical world (see Table II, page 202, for a complete list of incorporators).

The papers of incorporation were approved by the Supreme Court of New York on July 21, giving the City Center its eagerly awaited official existence. La Guardia immediately released the following statement to the press:

New York has become, by force of circumstances, the world center for creative and interpretive art. It is my belief that there are as many as a million of our fellow citizens in this city who do not have the opportunity of enjoying the best dramatic and musical productions, simply because the prevailing box-office prices are out of range of their personal incomes. Trade unions, whose representatives have signed the certificate of incorporation, have a total membership of more than half a million men and women.

The new Corporation is organized to meet a demand for cultural entertainment at popular prices.

It is my hope that we will carry on a 40-week season each year with a diversified program to include music, drama, ballet and allied forms of stage entertainment.

I have long cherished a dream of a center of cultural activity to be enjoyed by all the people of our city. The old Mecca Temple, which is now owned by the people of New York, can in my opinion be put to no more useful purpose.

Institutions of this kind have flourished in the old world. I believe that the American people are not only prepared but eagerly awaiting leadership in this field. If New York leads the way, our example will be followed in our sister cities and American life will become spiritually enriched in the post-war years to come.

The very next day a meeting was held to elect the board of directors and officers. As expected, Newbold Morris was named chairman of the board, and La Guardia president of the corporation. Other positions were filled by Gerald Warburg (vice-president), Mrs. Arthur Reis (secretary), and Almerindo Portfolio of the city comptroller's office (who was not a member of the board) as treasurer.

So far, progress had been very rapid. Only twenty weeks had elapsed since the initial meeting on March 5. The company now encountered its first major blow. Lee Thompson Smith, director of real estate for the city, advised Morris that he had received a rental offer of $2,300 per month for the building, and that he could in no way justify his acceptance of a lesser revenue. Coincidentally, this was almost exactly the amount of taxes due on the building, based upon its official evaluation of $1 million.

Morton Baum was drawn into the controversy as a substitute for Morris, who as a city official was not permitted to enter into negotiations against the city. Both men were justifiably outraged, partly because they felt betrayed, and partly because their projected budget left the company with no surplus whatever. This breach of faith on the part of the city would result in an annual deficit of about $25,000. It appeared that the city, having acquired the building through a tax default, was now determined to start collecting revenue without any sense of concern over the future of the City Center. Furthermore, the tax amount was derived from an unrealistic estimate. Although the city claimed that the building was worth $1 million, it had been unable to sell it to a prospective private buyer in 1942 for $450,000. According to Morton Baum's private notes, Morris directed him to accept the terms, lest the entire enterprise fall apart. Despite the severity of the situation, Morris felt sure that somehow the difficulty could be overcome, and he did not want to jeopardize the Center's very existence.

Whatever loose affiliation there was between the City Center and New York City was proving very costly. On the one hand, the city was providing neither financial aid nor a reasonable rental rate; on the other, the participation of the mayor and the fact that the theater was city-owned led most people to believe that it was municipally supported, which substantially increased the difficulty of getting any future private funding.

A second problem then arose, again with the city. Mayor La Guardia refused to make the promised repairs, on the grounds of wartime shortages of essential materials. Here, however, Baum stood his ground firmly. Thoroughly outraged by a second breach of faith on the part of the mayor, he refused to take occupancy of the building until it was put into proper condition, and after some haggling that delayed the scheduled opening by two months, the city agreed to make good on this commitment.

With all of the organizational details now resolved, the board was able to turn its attention to artistic matters. Morris appointed Howard Cullman chairman of the program committee, which had to settle, more or less immediately, the vital appointments of a managing director and a house manager. For this latter position, Macklin Marrow[1] proposed Ben Ketcham, who had served for many years with the Schuberts' theatrical empire, and with the Lewissohn Stadium concerts. The board readily approved the choice, and Mr. Ketcham was engaged. The managing director was more difficult to find. Various suggestions were made, but all were turned down for one reason or another.

Cullman also proposed the appointment of Jean Dalrymple as press director. She had begun her theatrical career as John Golden's secretary, and after a short apprenticeship became personal representative for a number of highly acclaimed artists, including Grace Moore, Lily Pons, André Kostelanetz, Bidu Sayao, and José Iturbi. She was invited to meet the board, created a strong positive impression, and was engaged.

On August 5, Morris wrote to those who had pledged loans, asking if one half the amount could be furnished without delay. Only the CIO reneged on its promise; the others all responded promptly, and $28,625 was received (in addition to the donations of $10,600), so that the company had about $40,000 cash on hand.

September came, and there was still no agreement on a managing director. It was Jean Dalrymple who proposed Harry Friedgut for the job. He had been director of the Mosque Theater in Newark and had built up large audiences for his concert series there. Morris brought him to meet La Guardia, who liked his background, and urged the board to engage him immediately—particularly in view of time pressures. Mr. Friedgut accepted the position on September 11, and his official employment began on October 4.

With these obstacles overcome, the company's initial structure was set and, in a surge of excitement, they embarked upon the next phase of operations.

---

1. Macklin Marrow, particularly prominent as president of MGM Records, was one of the original directors of the City Center.

3
The Origins of Opera

OPERA for the average man in the street was by no means a unique concept in 1943. In fact, from its very earliest days opera had always found a broad base of support and appreciation. If anything, the New York City Opera was a culmination, not a beginning. To understand the role of the City Opera there is no better way than to know the history of opera itself.

During the final years of the sixteenth century, a group of Florentine intellectuals frequently came together to discuss music, literature, and drama. Known as the "Camerata," they consisted of Giovanni Bardi, Jacopo Corsi, Vincenzo Galilei (father of the astronomer Galileo), Giulio Caccini, Jacopo Peri, Emilio de' Cavalieri, and Ottavio Rinuccini. One of their objectives was to restore the forms of Greek drama, particularly the dramatic use of music. They drew their inspiration from two Hellenic philosophers, Aristoxenus and Plato. The former stated in one of his treatises that song should be patterned after speech; the latter wrote, "Let music be first of all language and rhythm, and secondly tone, and not vice-versa." These ideas were in clear conflict with the polyphonic music[1] of the period, and they gradually evolved a new form, the single-voiced melody in which the words were clear and recognizable. In 1590 Cavalli used this new style for a series of musical scenes, or pastorals, and a short

---

1. "Polyphony: a texture arising from the simultaneous combination of two or more melodic lines." *Dictionary of Music,* Theodore Karp (New York: Dell Publishing Company, Inc., 1973).

time later Galilei applied it to *The Lamentations of Jeremiah*. It was Peri's lot to apply it to a dramatic presentation entitled *Dafne*, with words by Rinuccini, first performed at the Corsi Palace during Carnival of 1597. This date causes much confusion because the Julian calendar was still in use in Florence at that time. Carnival began in December and lasted into early March, but the new year began on March 1, rather than January 1, so that Carnival of 1597 in the Julian calendar refers to December 1597 or January or February 1598 in the Gregorian.

We now know considerably more about Greek drama than did the Camerata, and although they failed to re-create that which they sought, they did succeed in inventing a new form: opera.[2] Because all of the music of *Dafne* is lost to us, some regard Peri's *Euridice* (first performed on October 6, 1600) as the earliest opera, but, for the purist, that distinction is held by *Dafne*. This new form was popular with the aristocracy, whose support of it led many other composers to attempt the medium—Caccini, Gagliano, and most importantly, Claudio Monteverdi. Opera spread throughout the courts of Europe with no significant change until 1637, when Francesco Monelli's *L'Andromeda* inaugurated Venice's Teatro Tron di San Cassiano, the world's first public opera house. The reaction of the Venetians can be gauged by the fact that by 1700, nine additional opera houses were built in that city, and more than 350 different works were produced.[3]

The English poet John Milton was witness to another significant milestone. In a letter from Florence to Lucas Holstenius dated March 30, 1639, he refers to a performance he had seen of *Chi Soffre, Speri* by Virgilio Mazzocchi and Marco Marazzoli. This was the first comic opera. Its text was written by Giulio Rospigliosi, who on June 20, 1667, became Pope Clement IX. During most of the seventeenth century, performances alternated between private court theaters and those accessible to the public, which were, however, supported by the ruling families. From the very outset, as today, opera was unable to pay its way, despite its popularity, because of the tremendous expenses that make it the most costly of all theatrical entertainment.

More and more European musicians were drawn into composing for the stage—Jean-Baptiste Lully, Alessandro Stradella, John Blow, Alessan-

2. "Opera: a stage work that is sung throughout or in greater part, normally to an orchestral accompaniment." Ibid.

3. Included among the early operas first produced in Venice are two of Monteverdi's that have been in the New York City Opera repertoire, *Il Ritorno d'Ulisse in Patria* (Teatro Tron di San Cassiano, February 1641) and *L'Incoronazione di Poppea* (Teatro Grimani dei Santi Giovanni e Paolo, autumn 1642).

dro Scarlatti, Leonardo da Vinci, Henry Purcell, George Friedrich Handel, and Antonio Vivaldi, to name just a few.

Opera first reached London during September of 1656, when *The Siege of Rhodes*, with text by Sir William D'Avenant, was presented at Rutland House. Five composers collaborated on the music, and the libretto, published at the time of the premiere, contained the following preface written by D'Avenant:

> The Musick was compos'd and both the Vocal and Instrumental is exercis'd by the most transcendent of England in that Art, and perhaps not unequal to the best Masters abroad; but being Recitative, and therefore unpractis'd here; though of great reputation amongst other Nations, the very attempt of it is an obligation to our own.

At the end of the libretto, the list of composers is given as follows:

The Composition of Vocal Musick was perform'd

	First Entry			Mr. Henry Lawes	
	Second Entry			Capt. Henry Cook	
The	Third Entry		by	Capt. Henry Cook	
	Fourth Entry			Mr. Matthew Lock	
	Fifth Entry			Mr. Henry Lawes	

The Instrumental Musick was compos'd by
Dr. Charles Coleman, and Mr. George Hudson.

About forty years later, in the preface to Purcell's *The Fairy Queen*, we find the statement "That Sir William Davenant's *Siege of Rhodes* was the first Opera we ever had in England, no Man can deny; and is indeed a perfect Opera. . . ."

The English took to the new form immediately, and opera flourished in London. In 1711, Handel, the outstanding composer of his day, settled there after traveling throughout Germany and Italy and established The Royal Academy of Music, which was inaugurated on April 13, 1720— surprisingly with the opera of another composer, Giovanni Porta's *Numitore*. He later made up for this by composing a dozen operas for the Royal Academy before its ultimate collapse.

In 1725, Allan Ramsay brought forth *The Gentle Shepherd*, which introduced a new form, the ballad-opera (also called "people's opera" at the time). It consisted of a spoken comedy, generally satirical, with incidental music and songs. The texts were newly written to fit the dramatic context, while the melodies were made up of folk songs and popular ballads. The subject matter dealt with common people (as opposed to the mythological and high-ranking characters of traditional opera), the dialogue was colloquial, and the music was familiar and therefore easily accessible. The ballad-opera was an immediate success, and within three years the most famous of all works in the genre was produced, *The Beggar's Opera*, with words by John Gay and music arranged by John Christopher Pepusch. From a letter of Gay, we know that of the sixty-nine individual tunes in the work, twenty-eight are early English, fifteen early Irish, five early Scottish, and three French; the remaining eighteen are by individual composers, including Purcell, Handel, and Bononcini, among others. *The Beggar's Opera* was first performed on February 9, 1728, and ran for sixty-two nights, a record unequaled in London for almost a century. This overwhelming success inspired Ramsay to rework *The Gentle Shepherd*, and the four songs included in the original version were now expanded to twenty-one.

A wave of ballad-operas followed, while the popularity of grand opera waned in London, and in 1728 the Royal Academy went into bankruptcy. The following year saw the initial production of *Flora; or Hob in the Well*, a work arranged by Colley Cibber that would undoubtedly have passed into obscurity, except that on February 18, 1735, it became the first opera produced in the American colonies—not in a theater but in a courtroom in Charleston, South Carolina. The *South Carolina Gazette* of February 8, 1735, carried the following advertisement: "On Tuesday the 18th inst. will be presented at the Courtroom the opera of *Flora, or Hob in the Well*, with the Dance of the two Pierrots, and a new Pantomime entertainment, called *The Adventures of Harlequin Scaramouch. . . .*"

Not long after that, music came to New York, a bustling metropolis of about forty thousand people. It is not known for certain whether the concert of January 12, 1736, was the first to take place in that city, but it is the first on record. Information about the initial operatic performance there is equally sketchy. A production of *The Beggar's Opera* occurred on December 3, 1750, and it is believed that some seven months earlier, on April 30, the ballad-opera *The Mock Doctor* by Seedo was performed; it was at least scheduled for production, but there seems to be no verification of the event. The locale of these performances was the Theatre in Nassau Street, a room converted by the addition of a platform, a few benches, and a chandelier made from a barrel hoop through which several nails were driven to support candles. This was the sole source of light, and the tallow dripped on the heads of those in the best seats. The situation was improved in 1753, when Lewis Hallam opened his Nassau Street Theatre, the first theater in New York built expressly for the purpose of entertainment, or the site of the old makeshift one. The initial offering was a play *The Conscious Lovers*, followed by the ballad-farce *Damon and Phillida*. New York, like London, took to the ballad-opera, and performances were given more or less regularly for the next four decades.

Then, in 1767, two major events took place. The more significant was the publication of the ballad-opera *The Disappointment; or The Force of Credulity* by Andrew Barton. This was the first opera of American origin, but since it insulted several prominent Philadelphians, no public performance took place. The other important event was the production on December 21, 1767, of Arne's *Thomas and Sally*, New York's first exposure to a through-composed work, as opposed to a pastiche. Several others followed—*The Chaplet* by William Boyce (March 14, 1768) and *The Fairies*, based on Shakespeare's *A Midsummer Night's Dream*, by John Christopher Smith (May 29, 1786)—alternating with a variety of ballad-operas.

Until now, every opera presented in New York had been of English origin, but on November 17, 1786, French opera made its bow with Grétry's *Les Deux Avares*, which was, however, performed in an English translation. June 1 of the following year saw his *Zémire and Azor* performed the same way, as was Monsigny's *Le Déserteur* exactly one week later. Most European opera companies perform in the local language; it is only in the English-speaking countries that the original text is the rule rather than the exception. It is therefore particularly interesting to note that New York's introduction to foreign opera was in the vernacular.

The first non-English–language performance here was of a now forgotten work, *Le Tonnelier* by Nicolas Audinot, on October 7, 1790. Several other French operas were performed in the original language during the next two months by a group of French performers en route to the newly created opera company in New Orleans.

Although it had now been almost sixty years since the first operatic performance in the colonies, every presentation to date had been a work of European origin. This finally changed on March 3, 1794, when New York's John Street Theatre presented James Hewitt's *Tammany; or The Indian Chief*, the first opera expressly commissioned for an American audience, and, significantly, setting forth American subject matter. Some consider this the first American opera, since it was composed in the newly independent United States. However, many exclude it from this category because Hewitt was English and had only recently arrived. In 1796 two more works were composed here, and again, in both cases, the composers were European. These works were *The Archers; or The Mountaineers of Switzerland* by Benjamin Carr (April 18, 1796) and *Edwin and Angelina;*

or The Banditti [*sic*] by Victor Pelissier (December 19, 1796). *The Temple of Minerva* by Francis Hopkinson (1781) was advertised as an oratorio; in fact, it was not until William Henry Fry's *Leonora* in 1845 (June 4) that we had a publicly performed grand opera by a native American.

Ballad-operas continued with regularity, interspersed with an occasional French *opéra-comique*,[4] until 1825, when Manuel García's troupe arrived in New York. It was with the performance of Rossini's *Barber of Seville* on November 29, 1825, that the history of grand opera[5] in New York may be said to have truly begun.

4. *Opéra-comique:* A form of opera, generally dealing with simply treated and light-hearted subject matter. Its characteristic, from the point of view of form, is the substantial use of spoken dialogue.

5. "Grand Opera: opera without spoken dialogue." (Karp, op. cit.)

4
Opera Comes to New York

W H E N the packet ship *New York* docked here on Sunday evening, November 6, 1825, its passenger list boasted the first family of Italian opera, the Garcías.

The head of the clan, Manuel del Pópolo Vicente García, was born in Seville in 1775 and entered the local cathedral choir while still a young child. By the time he was seventeen, he had already established a reputation as singer, actor, conductor, and composer. Another sixteen years were to pass, however, before he entered the operatic world. His debut, which took place in Paris on February 11, 1808, as Gualtieri in Ferdinando Paër's *Griselda*, was so successful that there was no doubt about the proper outlet for his varied talents. Three years later he went to Italy, where he became so firmly established that Rossini, the reigning operatic composer of the day, created two of his most florid tenor roles with García in mind—Count Almaviva in *The Barber of Seville* and Norfolk in *Elisabetta, Regina d'Inghilterra*. He returned to Paris and became the idol of that city, and then in 1823 went to London, where he opened a highly successful school of singing.

His wife, Joaquina Sitchès García, was a lyric soprano whose career was without any particular distinction, but the tenor's fame was equaled—perhaps surpassed—by that of their two daughters. The older, baptized Marietta Felicità, was born in Paris in 1808. By the time she was five, the family was living in Naples, where she made her operatic debut portraying a child in what was rapidly becoming a García vehicle—Paer's *Griselda*. Her adult debut was in London twelve years later in that other García war-

20

horse, *The Barber of Seville*. Her major successes occurred after 1828 under her married name, Maria Malibran.

Her younger sister Pauline was born in 1821, also in Paris. She studied voice with her parents and piano with Franz Liszt. In 1837 she appeared in Brussels, then extensively throughout Europe until 1841, when she married the manager of the Théâtre des Italiens, Louis Viardot. She became the principal contralto of the Paris Opéra, where, in 1849, she sang the role of Fidès in the first performance of Meyerbeer's *Le Prophète*. After her retirement in 1863, she wrote plays, poems, and several operas to libretti by the famous Russian author, Ivan Turgenev, whose mistress she had become.

Manuel's son, Manuel Patricio Rodriguez García, was born in Madrid in 1805. He was a baritone who did not give his career a chance to mature, as he retired before his thirtieth birthday in order to teach voice. Among his pupils were Jennie Lind and Mathilde Marchesi (who herself became a famous teacher, with such students as Emma Calvé, Emma Eames, Etelka Gerster, Mary Garden, Nellie Melba, and Frances Alda). It was he who wrote the first scientific treatises on the physiology of the human voice, and he is known to the medical community as the inventor of the laryngoscope. He died in London three and a half months after his 101st birthday.

This was the family entrusted to introduce grand opera to Americans. It would be difficult to imagine a more auspicious beginning.

The debt of gratitude goes, however, to a man barely remembered today—a wealthy wine merchant named Dominick Lynch. Devoutly fond of music, particularly opera, and with sufficient means to indulge his love, he approached Stephen Price, manager of the Park Theatre, and persuaded him to present an operatic troupe that Lynch would underwrite. He thereupon journeyed to London and engaged the Garcías (four of the five—Pauline was only three years old), as well as ten other singers for the venture. The others in the company were Mme. Barbieri, soprano; Giovanni Crivelli, tenor; Felix Angrisani, bass; and Paolo Rosich, bass. The remaining six arrived, but, for some unknown reason, they did not appear in any performances. They were Señor and Señora Ferri, Don Fabian, Giuseppe Pasta, Giovanni Cardini, and Cristoforo Constantino.

The first public announcement of the company's plans was published in the *New-York Evening Post* of November 17, 1825, and the editorial page contained a letter signed "Musoeus" explaining the origins of opera along with a description of its structure. The orchestra of twenty-five pieces was recruited locally, and had the following distribution: seven violins, two violas, three cellos, two basses, two flutes, two clarinets, one bassoon, two horns, two trumpets, one kettledrum, and one piano. The conductor, Nathaniel De Luce, was also the principal violinist.

The opening performance, on November 29, was *The Barber of Seville*, with all four Garcías participating—Manuel senior as Almaviva, Manuel junior as Figaro, Maria as Rosina, and Joaquina as Berta. Bartolo and Basilio were sung by Rosich and Angrisani respectively, and Crivelli portrayed Fiorello. It is possible that the six artists whose names do not appear in any cast list constituted the chorus.

The following day, this review appeared in the *New-York Evening Post*:

In what language shall we speak of an entertainment so novel in this country, but which has so long ranked as the most elegant and refined among the amusements of the higher classes of the old world? All have obtained a general idea of the opera from report. But report can give but a faint idea of it. Until it is seen, it will never be believed that a play can be conducted in recitative or singing and yet appear nearly as natural as the ordinary drama. . . . There were no less than six whom we would esteem in the ordinary comedy, performers of the first order, considered merely as actors and independently of their vocal powers. Their style or manner of acting differs widely from any to which we have been accustomed. In the male performers you are struck with the variety, novelty and passion of their expressive, characteristic and unceasing gesticulation. The female performers, on the contrary, appear to us to have less action, though quite as much expression as any we had ever before seen. There is indeed in their style of acting a most remarkable chasteness and propriety; never violating good taste nor exceeding the strictest bounds of female decorum.

García's troupe remained for almost a year before closing on September 30, 1826. During most of that time they performed on Tuesday and Saturday evenings, but during July and the first part of August, 1826, the schedule was stepped up to three performances weekly: Mondays, Wednesdays, and Fridays. In all, they gave eighty performances of nine operas, two of them with music by García senior and words by his basso Rosich. Their complete repertoire was:

Rossini:	*The Barber of Seville*	24 performances
Rossini:	*Tancredi*	14 performances
Rossini:	*Otello*	11 performances
Mozart:	*Don Giovanni*	9 performances
García:	*La Figlia dell'Aria*[1]	6 performances

1. This has the same plot as Rossini's *Semiramide* and has been inaccurately reported by many writers as the more famous work.

Rossini:	*La Cenerentola*	6 performances
Rossini:	*Il Turco in Italia*	4 performances
Zingarelli:	*Giulietta e Romeo*	3 performances
García:	*L'Amante Astuto*	2 performances
Concert consisting of segments of		
	Otello and *Barber*	1 performance

In addition to the two García operas, both world premieres, the *Dictionnaire des Opéras* by Clément and Larousse and the *Opern-Handbuch* by Hugo Riemann list six other operas of García's as having been performed in New York in about 1827. An exhaustive search of the newspapers of that period failed to show any reference to these works, and one can safely assume that the anthologists were in error. The operas in question are *I Banditi, La Buona Famiglia, Don Chisciotti, La Gioventù di Enrico V, Il Lupo d'Ostenda* and *Le Tre Sultane.*

Although the initial enthusiasm was very high, it tapered off quickly. The opening-night crowd paid a total of $2,980 for tickets; the next highest paid admission was $1,962—roughly two-thirds, and the poorest attendance netted a mere $250. Ticket prices ranged from 25¢ in the gallery to $2 in boxes, and libretti were on sale at the incredible price of 37¾¢ each. Over the course of the ten months, total paid attendance was $56,685, an average of $708.50 per performance.

At the end of the engagement, the entire troupe went to Mexico City, except for Maria, who had taken out time between performances to marry a New York merchant, Eugene Malibran, on March 23. She learned English and began to appear in ballad-operas at the Bowery Theatre, receiving a fee of $500 per performance. The magnitude of this sum becomes apparent when you consider the average box-office receipts of her father's company. She also sang on Sundays at Grace Church—in the *choir!* The marriage was short-lived, and Maria left America after her farewell concert of October 29, 1827.

New York had experienced a lengthy season of Italian opera. After García left, a French group from New Orleans came in to fill the void. They opened on July 13, 1827, with Nicolo's *Cendrillon*, and brought a repertoire of about thirty operas, which they presented over the course of the next three and a half months. With their departure, ballad-opera recaptured the public's main interest.

Lorenzo da Ponte (1749–1838) is considered one of the greatest of Italian librettists (*Marriage of Figaro, Don Giovanni, Così fan Tutte*). He was, however, perpetually in trouble of one sort or another. Various intrigues and scandals had led to his banishment from Venice in 1780, and although he was able to secure the position of court poet in Vienna, he was forced to leave in 1793 when Joseph II died, as he was out of favor with the rest of the Viennese court. He thereupon went to London, but in 1805 debts and threats of imprisonment necessitated a highly secretive departure for the United States, where he became a professor of Italian at Columbia University.

In 1832, da Ponte took a positive step toward promoting opera in New York by the formation of his own company and the construction of the Italian Opera House, the first theater built expressly to feature opera, at Church and Leonard streets. It opened on November 18, 1833, with Rossini's *La Gazza Ladra*, and in its one and a half years of existence, before being razed by fire in 1835, it was the scene of many operas by Rossini, Bellini, and such lesser composers as Salvioni and Pacini. Many operatic groups continued to come and go, but da Ponte's company was the first resident organization in the city.

The next resident company of note was that of Edward P. Fry at the Astor Place Opera House. He was the brother of William Henry Fry, whose *Leonora* was the first opera produced by a native American composer. Fry's artistic standards left a great deal to be desired, and Max Maretzek in his *Crotchets and Quavers* provides a graphic and amusing description of his first exposure to Fry's Italian Opera Company. This extract is taken from a letter dated July 25, 1855, from Maretzek to his friend Hector Berlioz:

The orchestra consisted of about thirty-six performers on their individual instruments. They had a leader, Signor Lietti, who did not apparently consider it necessary to indicate the movement by beating the time. On the contrary, he was occupied in playing the first violin part, fully unconscious of the other instruments in the orchestra. But I wrong him. In order to guide them, he was possessed with the monomania of playing more loudly and vigorously upon his fiddle than any of his subordinates. He trampled on the floor as though he had been determined to work a path through the deal planking, and made a series of most grotesque faces with his nose, mouth and eyes. If you have ever seen a Nuremberg nut-cracker in full operation, you will enter into my feelings as my eyes were riveted on what appeared to me the extraordinary mechanism of this individual. In the mean time, the other fiddlers not being willing to allow Signor Lietti's violin a greater preponderance of sound, exerted themselves with a purely musical ferocity, which you have never seen equalled. I have, (although it must be owned, not often) upon this side of the Atlantic. It was necessary, however, that Lietti should be heard by the wind-instruments. He therefore began to *scrape* his fiddle. For a moment I actually imagined that he had succeeded. But until then, I had not been aware that "diabolical possession" had survived the time of the Apostles. It has, my dear Berlioz, and the players upon stringed instruments are indisputably subject to it. Rossini, had he listened to them, would have been of my opinion. After the first eighty bars of the allegro movement, you would, had you been there, upon shutting your eyes, have undoubtedly believed that you were surrounded by a series of saw-mills in vigorous operation. Under such circumstances, the leader could not of course be heard. They soon came out of time (how could they keep it?) and confusion ensued. Everybody felt himself individually called upon to restore order. A squeak from the *piccolo* would be heard, followed by a loud squall from all the wind-instruments, trying to indicate a place for re-union. Then came a broadside from the trombones and horns, to restrain the already too far advanced violins. It was in vain. The screech from the first trumpet was of no use. Even the kettle-drum player, who began to beat the right time *fortissimo* on his instrument, was totally unable to stay the confusion. Each one went his own way, and made his own speed. Rossini's delicate overture was treated by them, as history tells us that some unfortunate criminals were treated in the Middle Ages. These were tied by arm and leg to the hind-quarters of four wild horses, which were then driven by the scourge in different directions. It will be needless to hint to a man of your erudition, what followed upon this proceeding.

At last, struggling and worn out, one after the other, some few completely distanced, and Signor Lietti by no means first in, they terminated the overture. The audience bestowed upon them a round of applause, and the leader demonstrated by three low bows, his intense satisfaction both with himself and the public.

Lest one get the impression that the orchestra was the only weak link in Fry's company, Maretzek goes on to describe a performance of Verdi's *Ernani*.

I have intimated that *Sylva* rushed upon the stage. But can you imagine in what guise the unhappy Castrone brought him before the audience? No! you cannot. The decency of your imagination altogether disowns such a possibility, and I feel that I shall be obliged to tell you.

As I prepare to do so, although alone at my writing-table, a crimson blush overspreads my modest face.

It creeps across my body, and along mine arms, until it even dyes my fingers. They involuntarily redden like newly-pulled radishes, as I recall that incident to my memory.

He (could I hide my face I would do so, Berlioz, did I not luckily remember that you cannot see it) had forgotten what the Erse or Northern Scotch, though which it is I have suffered myself to forget, call their "gallygaskins." In our own more fastidiously refined language, upon this continent, they are most generally and generically classified as the "unmentionables." There he stood representing the Spanish idea of an Inexorable Fate, clad in a black velvet doublet, but with a pair of flesh-colored and closely-woven silk inexpressibles upon his nether man. The horn, that fatal horn, hung from his neck, in a position which it would be absolutely impossible for me consistently with propriety to indicate upon paper. Certainly, it was in anything but its right place. Some of the ladies who were present, rose and quitted the theatre. Others shrank back in their seats, and veiled their eyes with the feathery ridges of their fans, or the delicate lace of their handkerchiefs. Even the self-possessed and resolute *prima donna* reddened through her well-laid-on rouge, and dropped her eyelids over her bold eyes, while the Conductor for once forgets the impassibility imposed upon him by his position, and hurries up the Orchestra to the end. At length *Sylva* offers to *Ernani* the dagger. In his eagerness to put an end to himself, and escape the ridicule of which he felt conscious, the latter clutches at it. But, alas! the blade remains in *Sylva's* hand, and the lucklessly unconscious *Ernani*, a martyr to misplaced confidence, is obliged to dispatch himself with the scabbard. After this, the curtain falls where it always does, leaving *Ernani* without its drapery, and close to the foot-lights. The dead body sits up, and gazes around it in speechless consternation. An universal and irrepressible titter is heard throughout the whole house. In its agony it rises, and runs off from before the audience.

Maretzek (born Maximilian Mareczek on June 28, 1821, in Brno, Moravia, now part of Czechoslovakia) began his academic life as a medical student, but neither this nor law, his second course of study, interested him. He thereupon became a student of musical composition, and his first opera, *Hamlet* had an eminently successful premiere in Brno. He was only nineteen at the time, and his future seemed promising indeed. Appointments as conductor of various European opera companies followed, and 1842 found him in Paris, where he struck up friendships with Meyerbeer, Berlioz, Chopin, and Liszt. Two years later he accepted a position with Covent Garden as chorus master and assistant conductor, and in 1847 he was hired by Adolph Jullien to participate in a new opera company at Drury Lane. Jullien was incompetent, and his company collapsed almost immediately after opening night, leaving the staff stranded and unpaid. Thus, when Fry offered Maretzek a position with his company in New York, he was only too happy to accept. He arrived here in 1848 and found the conditions described in the letter to Berlioz.

At the end of that first season, for reasons that are perfectly obvious, the proprietors and shareholders of the theater removed Fry and turned the reins over to Maretzek. As an impresario he was volatile, colorful, and successful. Among the works he introduced to the New York public were such operas as *La Traviata, Rigoletto,* and *Roméo et Juliette,* and his singers included Adelina Patti, Enrico Tamberlick, and Pauline Lucca.

On October 2, 1854, a new opera house, the Academy of Music at Irving Place and Fourteenth Street, was inaugurated with a performance of *Norma* starring Giulia Grisi and Giovanni Mario, two of the world's leading singers. The manager was none other than Maretzek, whose ideas were frequently at odds with those of the stockholders. So were everyone else's, for that matter, for during the first three years of the Academy's existence it had five different managers. Some of these came and went with the regularity of a metronome, and Maretzek found himself alternately director of the company and, during adverse times, head of a competing organization. Regardless of who managed the company at any particular time, however, one fact is certain. Until the advent of the Metropolitan Opera in 1883, the Academy had no serious rivals.

The high-water mark of its thirty-year duration came in 1878 with the engagement of "Colonel" James Henry Mapleson of Her Majesty's Theatre in London. During the eight years of his directorship he functioned as head of various English companies as well, crossing the Atlantic with the ease of a commuter.

For his first season here, he embarked from London on August 31, 1878, with a staff of 140 employees, including sixty solo singers and a complete corps de ballet. En route to New York, he stopped in Ireland to give a few performances, and arrived here early in October with his entourage of stars, including Minnie Hauk, Etelka Gerster, Italo Campanini, and the conductor Luigi Arditi (whose "Il Bacio" figured prominently in every soprano recital of the time). During his American regime, Mapleson presented such other celebrities as Victor Capoul, Giuseppe del Puente, Emma Fursch-Madi, Felia Litvinne, Emma Nevada, Lillian Nordica, Adelina Patti, Sofia Scalchi, and Zelia Trebelli, and operas he introduced included Boito's *Mefistofele* and Bizet's *Carmen.*

During the middle of the nineteenth century, a newly monied class arose from America's industrial expansion. In many cases the wealth stemmed from the recent lucrative railroad networks that formed to span the continent. Steel and banking were stimulated by construction and trade, producing additional financial magnates. However, money and society are not necessarily compatible, and New York's long-established elite were none too eager to welcome the *nouveaux-riches* into their midst. Since opera was one of the marks of social and cultural acceptability, the new breed was most anxious to acquire boxes at the Academy of Music. The "old guard" was unwilling to relinquish any, however, and consequently none became available.

The newcomers did the only thing possible under the circumstances— they built their own theater, naming it the Metropolitan Opera House. It was completed during the summer of 1883 at a total cost of $1,732,978.71, and on October 22 of that year, the company was inaugurated with a performance of *Faust* starring Christine Nilsson, Sofia Scalchi, Italo Campanini, Giuseppe del Puente, and Franco Novara—four of them former stars of the Academy of Music. Mapleson's company could not possibly survive, because the Met had far more money and was able to lure away the Academy's outstanding artists. After two more feeble seasons, Mapleson threw in the towel, and the Met emerged supreme and unrivaled. There is no point in recounting its history here, as it has been told in literature in great detail and from many viewpoints. Now, almost one hundred years later, it is still going strong.

One other organization must be mentioned in closing, if we are to have a fairly realistic picture of the development of opera in New York. This is Oscar Hammerstein's short-lived Manhattan Opera Company, which flourished from 1906 to 1910. During those four years, Hammerstein presented a glittering roster of artists—Nellie Melba, Luisa Tetrazzini, Giovanni Zenatello, John McCormack, Mary Garden, Maurice Renaud, Alessandro Bonci . . . and on, and on. His repertoire was provocative and stimulating and included the American premieres of *Thaïs. Louise, Pelléas et Mélisande, Hérodiade*, and *Elektra*. So keen was the competition that the Met's director, Heinrich Conried, was forced to resign and the company was drastically reorganized. Why Hammerstein withdrew amid the success was a mystery at the time, but we have since learned that the directors of the Metropolitan paid him in excess of one million dollars in exchange for his pledge to withdraw from opera for ten years.

Briefly then, this was the growth of opera in New York. It had come a long way from the South Carolina courtroom where *Flora* was first produced.

5

An Opera Company for the People

W I T H the City Center fully organized and the building being readied for its public opening on December 11, the company began active negotiations for worthwhile presentations. Only then did the directors realize that the concept of using the theater as a booking house was unworkable. The idea was acceptable, but there were several practical obstacles to impede its realization. To present a Broadway production, they would have to do so immediately after its closing, since within a very short time, perhaps only a few days, the cast would be dispersed. At this late point they learned that most theatrical leases carried a clause prohibiting the rerun of a show until at least six weeks after its initial closing. It seems nothing short of incredible that something so basic could have been overlooked by a board that included a dozen theatrical personalities. Furthermore, almost all successful productions closed at about the same time—just before the summer—so that even without this restrictive clause, they would be able to get one or two shows at most per year.

Fortunately several board members having excellent personal contacts were able to secure the services of a few major talents for far less than their usual fees. Gertrude Lawrence agreed to appear in Rachel Crothers's *Susan and God* for the week of December 13 to 18, Walter Hampden was scheduled for Sidney Kingsley's *The Patriots* from December 20 to 25, and the two-man revue consisting of tap dancer Paul Draper and harmonica virtuoso Larry Adler was booked for December 30 through January 2. This was an excellent start artistically, but the City Center suddenly found itself in the position it had tried to avoid—that of being a producing organization.

From the outset, opera was very high on the list of priorities, and the board now turned its attention in that direction. The operatic situation in New York had been changing for about a decade, due in large measure to conditions brought about by the war in Europe. Over the course of a few years, New York had seen the arrival of thousands of immigrants, many of them from operatic centers of Europe such as Berlin, Vienna, and Munich. Earlier immigration waves were based on economic need, and those who arrived here were for the most part poor and with little education to speak of. They had not had the means in their native lands to enjoy the arts, and so there was no particular craving for opera or theater. But here was a different situation. Although most of the new refugees arrived in America penniless, their previous lives in Europe had provided heavy cultural exposure, and they constituted a large potential audience for inexpensive music-drama. Additionally, their backgrounds made them knowledgeable, and therefore critical, so that the standards of performance would have to be quite high.

Another factor brought about by the war was the emergence of the American singer. Since its very first season, the Metropolitan had engaged native artists, performers such as Alwina Valleria, Louise Homer, Geraldine Farrar, and Riccardo Martin; but by and large, these artists had first to establish European reputations before a Met audience would accept them. The company wanted to engage only stars for leading roles, and in this country there were few opportunities to become a star. Unlike Europe, we did not have a network of small companies where the performer could work his way up as his art matured. This desire for established stars changed to a slight extent in 1918 when the Met engaged Rosa Ponselle, the first American-born, American-trained singer to appear there in leading roles. Her spectacular success opened the door for other native artists such as Lawrence Tibbett, Frederick Jagel, and Grace Moore, but until the 1930s, the roster of Met soloists remained overwhelmingly European or European-trained.

In the early 1930s the Depression forced the Met to tighten its belt, and much of the importation of talent came to an end. There were still many foreign names present—Pinza, Martinelli, Bori, Rethberg, Melchior, to cite a few—but these were people who, although not American by birth, had chosen to make their homes here. The new wave of international talent, singers like Suzanne Balguérie, Gianna Pederzini, Marcel Wittrisch, and Alessandro Ziliani, did not reach our shores at all, and such stalwarts as Giacomo Lauri-Volpi and Tancredi Pasero now restricted their activities to Europe. A bit later, when increasing political tensions abroad made transatlantic travel difficult, more and more American singers came to the fore; first of all because they were confined to their native soil, and secondly, because the younger European artists were notably absent and their roles had to be filled by whatever talent was available. We now began to see artists such as Risë Stevens, Helen Traubel, Jan Peerce, Leonard Warren, and Robert Weede with ever increasing frequency.

American performers got a further boost when the Juilliard Foundation came to the financial assistance of the Met. A substantial donation was made on condition that the Met institute popular-priced seasons, which they presented in late spring of 1936 and 1937. Because of reduced ticket prices superimposed on an already aching economy, the Met was forced to hire many young Americans who might otherwise not have been heard. Although these series were short-lived they established two very important facts—that there was a large audience for popular-priced opera, and that there was no shortage of local talent.

In 1940, an unusual situation arose concerning the Metropolitan Opera. The opera house itself was owned by a private corporation, the Metropolitan Real Estate Company, which had leased the building since its construction in 1882 to the performing organization, the Metropolitan Opera Association. In order to gain a much needed tax exemption, it became necessary for the association to purchase the building, as the tax law explicitly stated that eligibility for exemption was contingent upon the building's being owned and operated by a nonprofit educational institution. A fund-raising drive was instituted by George Sloan, one of the directors of the Met, and $1 million was raised to finance the purchase. La Guardia, however, rejected the exemption because "an educational institution, to warrant exemption, must do things for the public, and that, the Met does not."

Morton Baum thereupon devised an intricate but fascinating plan, which he presented at a meeting with Morris, Sloan, Charles Spofford (another director of the Metropolitan), and Horace Johnson of the WPA. The idea was to have the Met furnish free use of its theater, scenery, and costumes; the WPA City Orchestra and Chorus would be made available by the federal government, which was already paying its salaries; young American artists would be secured for a four-week season each spring, and productions would be offered to the public at modest charge. Any deficit would be underwritten by a private group to be organized by Morris, but it was highly unlikely that such a loss would develop.

The plan seemed perfect. Everyone would gain by it, most of all the public. An operating budget was submitted to Edward Ziegler, assistant general manager of the Met in charge of finance, who received it enthusiastically. Everything seemed workable until the plan was squelched, most unexpectedly, by the federal government. They declared that WPA relief recipients would not be permitted to work with any existing commercial groups, not even nonprofit organizations. The entire scheme was thereupon abandoned, but a short time later, when George Sloan became president of the Met, Baum was invited to become a director, and for ten years he served on the finance committee.

Although this particular plan failed, both Baum and Morris were by now too deeply committed to the idea of opera for the broad public to let it drop. Baum then devised another plan. A nonprofit group would be incorporated under the name Radio City Opera Company, which would lease the now razed Center Theater for two nine-week periods—September 23 to November 27, 1940, and March 15 to May 15, 1941. Performances would take place every evening, and there would be Saturday and Sunday matinees as well, for a total of 164 presentations during the two seasons. If the venture were successful, he contemplated a tour for the second year that would embrace Boston, Philadelphia, Newark, Pittsburgh, and Chicago.

The initial repertoire would consist of *Carmen, Faust, Madama Butterfly, Aida, La Bohème, Rigoletto, Lohengrin, Cavalleria Rusticana, Pagliacci, Tristan und Isolde,* and *Boris Godunov,* and the artistic staff would include conductors Alexander Smallens, Fritz Mahler, Georges Sebastian, and Fritz Stiedry, and singers Paul Althouse, Florence Easton, Edwina Eustis, Lucy Monroe, Rose Pauly, Jan Peerce, and Robert Weede.

When budgets were set down in detail, the average weekly running cost was calculated at $18,075 with an anticipated income of $22,400. This was obviously a much riskier scheme than the one involving the Metropolitan, and, since it also required an initial investment of $21,650, it was discarded as impractical.

Now the City Center board came face to face with the problem. Clearly they felt that opera had an important place among their offerings. It was, in fact, the principal interest of both Morris and Baum, the two most influential members of the board. The major difficulty was the acquisition of a company. New York had three resident operatic organizations at the time—the Metropolitan, the Mascagni Opera Guild, and Alfredo Salmaggi's popular-priced company (at the time named the "99-cent Grand Opera Company").

The Salmaggi and Mascagni groups were immediately dismissed as being below the desired standards. Morton Baum, as a director of the

Metropolitan, approached its general manager, Edward Johnson, trying to enter into some sort of arrangement with the Met, but this was totally unfeasible economically. The Met's previous encounter with popular-priced opera, the spring seasons of 1936 and 1937, had resulted in a deficit of $69,274.13, and that was at the Metropolitan Opera House, which was substantially larger than the City Center (3,612 seats as opposed to 2,692). The only remaining alternative was The New Opera Company, a group started in 1941 under the artistic direction of former concert pianist Yolanda Mero-Irion. Its founder, financial backer, and president was Mrs. Lytle Hull. The company had done fine work and had presented a highly diversified repertoire but, despite both critical and public acclaim, it failed financially, providing still another example of opera's inability to function at a profit. Music critic Harold C. Schonberg once observed that "the human mind has not yet conceived a way to spend money faster than sponsoring a season of opera."[1]

The New Opera Company's repertoire had included Verdi's *Macbeth*, Tchaikovsky's *Pique-Dame*, Mussorgsky's *Fair at Sorotchinsk*, Walter Damrosch's *Opera Cloak* (world premiere), Offenbach's *La Vie Parisienne* and Johann Strauss's *Die Fledermaus*. Among the artists were such performers as Mimi Benzell, Mary Henderson, Winifred Heidt, Florence Kirk, Martha Lipton, Virginia MacWatters, Regina Resnik, Ina Souez, Hugh Thompson, and Jennie Tourel; choreographers George Balanchine and Leonid Massine; conductors Paul Breisach, Fritz Busch, Emil Cooper, Walter Damrosch, Antal Dorati, Erich Wolfgang Korngold, and Fritz Stiedry; and one of their dancers was a young man named José Limón. Despite this imposing array of talent, the company was unable to make ends meet. Rather than disband, they turned their energies to lighter works, and currently in production was Lehár's *Merry Widow* with Jan Kiepura and Marta Eggerth. Operetta proved to be quite lucrative, and finally tasting financial success, they were unwilling to return to opera on any large scale, although they did subsequently venture an occasional operatic production (Hindemith's *Hin und Zurück*, Pergolesi's *La Serva Padrona*, and Wolf-Ferrari's *Secret of Suzanne*, all chamber works requiring minimal resources).

This failure to acquire a company placed the City Center board in a difficult position. In order to present opera, they would have to start their own troupe, and this was totally impractical. The need for a large chorus and orchestra (considerably larger than that required by either operetta or musical comedy), a roster of first-rate singers, musical and dramatic pro-

1. Schonberg, *The Great Conductors* (New York: Simon and Schuster, 1967).

duction staffs, dancers, costumes, and scenery combined to make opera the most costly of all theatrical media. One glance at the financial statements of either the Metropolitan or the New Opera Company would confirm the futility of trying to produce opera with limited capital, particularly in the framework of a policy that dictated low ticket prices. Nevertheless, the board felt the obligation to make inexpensive operatic productions available to the people of New York, and so they decided to accept the inevitable loss, hoping that other City Center offerings would be sufficiently profitable to avert total economic disaster.[2]

Shortly after the initial March 5 meeting, the following statement appeared in the *New York Times*: "The success of the Mecca Temple proposal will rest upon the initiative, the sound horse sense, the experienced judgment of the right people, if they can be found and their efforts coordinated for the project" (March 14, 1943; Section 2, page 7). Sixty-three hopeful candidates wrote to Mayor La Guardia seeking appointments.

Among them was a Hungarian-born conductor named László Halász,[3] whose background seemed to include just those qualities necessary for starting an opera company from the ground up. His past achievements made a deep impression upon La Guardia, who suggested an exploratory meeting. Imagine Halasz's surprise when "The Little Flower" greeted him in Hungarian, one of the many languages the mayor spoke fluently. La Guardia was completely won over for a variety of reasons. One of these, he later told Halasz, was that of all sixty-three applicants, Halasz was the only one with no political connections.

The board of directors was conducting its own search for the appropriate director, and by coincidence Jean Dalrymple suggested Halasz's name. She had come to know his work a few years earlier when several of her clients (most notably Grace Moore and Dusolina Giannini) had performed under his direction. Newbold Morris had complete confidence in Dalrymple, and when her recommendation was reinforced by La Guardia's, there was no doubt that the City Center had found its man.

On October 13, 1943, the appointment of Laszlo Halasz as artistic and musical director was approved by the board, and on November 1 the information was released to the public.

---

2. From Morton Baum's private papers.

3. In Europe, Halasz used accent marks on his name, but when he arrived in the United States, eager to become Americanized, he dropped them. We have therefore, used the accents only when referring to his European career and life.

6

Laszlo Halasz— The Right Man at the Right Time

THE DIRECTOR of the newly formed opera company was no stranger to the medium, having been previously employed by several major houses both here and abroad. Furthermore, his experience covered the administrative as well as the artistic end of operatic production, an ideal combination—in fact, an essential combination for a company with financial strictures necessitating a very limited staff.

Halász was born in Debrecen, near Budapest, on June 6, 1905. He was the nephew of Téodore Szanto, a well-known pianist and composer who was sufficiently impressed by young László's innate musical talent to encourage him to pursue a musical career. Upon completion of his academic curriculum, Halász entered the Liszt Academy in Budapest, where he studied under the outstanding quartet of teachers—Béla Bartók, Ernst von Dohnanyi, Zoltán Kodály, and Leo Weiner. His education embraced all aspects of music, but it was piano that most appealed to him, and he specialized in those areas that would lead to a career as a concert pianist. During the course of these studies, however, he found himself increasingly drawn toward conducting.

He made his professional debut as a pianist in 1928, and so rapidly did he achieve renown that by 1930 his name appeared in commercial endorsements for a major piano manufacturer, August Förster. Nevertheless, he readily accepted a position as assistant conductor with the Royal Hungarian State Opera (now known as the Budapest Hungarian National Theatre) when it was offered to him in 1928. His work with this organization provided invaluable experience in opera, and also served to bring him

35

to the attention of George Szell, who was then the director of the German Opera[1] in Prague. When the Budapest contract expired in 1930, Halász accepted a similar position in the Czech capital, but continued concertizing in eastern Europe for an additional year.

Finally, in 1931, he decided to devote himself exclusively to conducting. In 1932 he joined the traveling Sakharoff Ballet as its musical director, and a European tour that year was followed by an offer from the Vienna Volksoper, where he first appeared in 1933 conducting a performance of Kienzl's *Der Evangelimann*. He remained at the Volksoper until 1936, and during this time he also made a number of guest appearances in Italy and Hungary. Perhaps the most significant engagement of this phase of his career was at Salzburg, where he served as assistant conductor to Bruno Walter and Arturo Toscanini.

In 1936, the National Broadcasting Company, hoping to induce Toscanini to return to the United States, created the NBC Symphony Orchestra expressly for him. Halasz, who came along as his assistant, still recalls the maestro's words—"Eh, Ungaro—tu vieni con me!" ("Hey, Hungarian—you're coming with me!") By now, however, the theater was in Halasz's blood, and he was not happy with his NBC position, which involved him almost exclusively with symphonic music. He mentioned this to Toscanini, who recommended him to the Saint Louis Opera Company, where he was engaged as chorus master. Later that year, Leo Blech was scheduled to conduct Wagner's *Tristan und Isolde* but was unable to reach St. Louis in time, and Halasz was asked to step in. This performance, on December 1, 1937, offers an interesting parallel with the debut of his mentor Toscanini who, in Buenos Aires on June 25, 1886, wielded the baton for the first time when scheduled conductor Carlo Superti withdrew from a performance of *Aida* at the last minute. Halasz's debut was a triumph, and he was invited to join the Civic Grand Opera Company of Philadelphia as the head of its German wing.

In 1939, the Saint Louis Opera Company was reorganized as the Saint Louis Grand Opera Association. Halasz was asked to return, this time in the esteemed position of artistic and musical director. Under his leadership, the company put on twenty-six performances, achieving new heights of musico-dramatic excellence. Reed Hynds, reviewing the initial performance in the *St. Louis Star-Times* wrote the following:

The St. Louis Grand Opera Association got off to a brilliant start in Municipal Auditorium last night with a production of Wagner's *Die Walkuere*,

1. Renamed the Smetana Theatre in 1948.

which for dignity, pathos and poetry left nothing to be desired. The house was crowded, with some standees, and most in the audience were as enthusiastic as they were fashionably dressed.

Under Laszlo Halasz, who has had so much to do with forming the new opera company, *Die Walkuere* was fused into an artistic entity which was more than the sum of its parts. From 8:30 until a quarter past midnight the family troubles of the Nibelungs exerted a compelling emotional force.

The opera was full and well rounded, Halasz wielding a strong but flexible control which not only brought out the music's essential vitality but revealed a sense of style in matters of form and rhythm. There was nothing of stop-and-go playing in this performance, the slowly mounting climaxes being carefully built along a single line and the quiet interludes managed with a fine understanding of mood.

The review ends: "All in all, this first production of the Saint Louis Grand Opera Association was the finest of its kind the city has enjoyed, in recent years at least, and holds bright promise for the future."

The stage direction was entrusted to Dr. Ernst Lert, whose very substantial credits included seven years at La Scala in Milan. In the same review, Mr. Hynds observed:

And the opera was acted as well as sung. The cast, under the direction of Dr. Ernst Lert, gave each role unique dramatic validity, so that one forgot these singers were Lauritz Melchior, Marjorie Lawrence, Fred Destal and Irene Jessner, remembering only that they were—respectively—Siegmund, Brunnhilde, Wotan, and Sieglinde. Around them swirled the magic mists of a mythology of heroes, but they were tangible and alive.

Apparently, not everyone shared Hynds's enthusiasm for Dr. Lert's work, for when Halasz and Lert had presided over *Die Walküre* in Philadelphia on March 22, 1938, critic Samuel L. Laciar wrote:

Dr. Lert apparently had his own ideas as to the staging of the opera and carried them out to the last degree. But the staging and the scenery were somewhat radical. The chief "motif" was a "hairpin" ramp, which, in the final act, was a double one. Dr. Lert's conceptions must be accorded respect because of his wide experience, but, on the other hand, no composer of opera, not excepting Meyerbeer and Verdi, has given such specific stage directions as Wagner, whose fundamental belief was in a union of the arts, which included the staging.

Last evening's staging violated almost every stage direction of the composer and it would be interesting to know what would become of a conductor who took such liberties with the music as Dr. Lert did in the stage instructions and, according to Wagner one is as important as the other.

Adverse commentary from Philadelphia notwithstanding, the music critics of St. Louis accorded consistently excellent reviews to Dr. Lert. Tensions developed between him and Halasz, however, and toward the end of his second St. Louis season, Lert resigned, informing the press that Halasz had "sabotaged" his productions and that he and Halasz were "artistically incompatible."[2]

Most of the operas and many of the singers presented to the St. Louis audience were later heard with the New York City Opera. Since these productions are significant in Halasz's development as an operatic impresario, and since they are not chronicled anywhere, a detailed listing is included at the end of this chapter.

Among Halasz's many gifts was an incredible energy. Seemingly, the word *procrastinate* was totally alien to him, and although there are countless examples of his immediate and complete immersion in the job at hand, one will suffice to illustrate his modus operandi. Upon his return to St. Louis in 1939, he arrived on February 13, scheduled chorus auditions for February 14 to 17, and began rehearsing the chorus on February 18. It was this commitment that enabled him to succeed where others had failed, but it also engendered a great deal of resentment from associates who regarded him as a relentless slave driver. However, like Toscanini, he only expected as much from his colleagues as he gave of himself.

There was one serious bone of contention between the St. Louis board of directors and Halasz. They wanted big-name artists for leading roles, while he preferred working with lesser lights. He felt that the most important element in producing a good performance was a tremendous amount of rehearshal, so that voice, words, music, and stage action became knitted into an integral entity. With name singers, he was not able to achieve this. The celebrity artists would arrive in town one or two days before a performance, perhaps consent to one rehearsal, and then claim immunity from further preparation based upon their fame. This was not always true, of course; there was an occasional exception, such as Marjorie Lawrence or Ezio Pinza, but by and large Halasz's hands were

---

2. *St. Louis Post-Dispatch*, November 21, 1939. Ironically, when Halasz was dismissed by the New York City Opera Company twelve years later, the word "sabotage" was again used prominently. This time, the case reached the law courts, and Halasz was completely vindicated by the jury.

tied. He had many productional innovations in mind, but with only limited rehearsal time, he had to rely upon the old clichés.

About a year before the Halasz-Lert blowup, the two men were interviewed for the *St. Louis Star-Times*:[3]

To them, it is nonsensical to think of grand opera as a play with incidental music, or a concert with incidental acting. Both feel that opera, far from being an artistic freak—a curious hybrid of the arts—is, when given a decent chance, a satisfyingly complete form.

They are quick to admit that this is seldom achieved. More often than not, they pointed out, the emphasis is on the singing. A few stars are engaged and their luster is supposed to make up for the unnaturalness of the action, the drab old settings, the untrained chorus, the lack of ensemble in the whole effort. Halasz and Dr. Lert say simply, "It's not thought out."

"The job," Halasz said, "is to combine all of the elements so that they contribute to one effect. That effect is a realistic experience obtained through music and drama. There should be a perfect synthesis, with every detail relevant and no one aspect dominating. The acting must be convincing, with the music reinforcing it at every point."

First requirement of such a program is thorough rehearsal. Unlike the Metropolitan, which does not require stars to rehearse operas in the regular repertoire, and which gives the stage director scant opportunity to rehearse any of his effects, the St. Louis directors believe that only through rehearsal is a fine sense of ensemble obtained.

In addition to the problem of rehearsals, the established prima donna could also demand huge fees, and as a result, the new Saint Louis opera company required unusually heavy private subsidy. In spring 1942 several of the organization's major sponsors entered the armed forces, and the company was forced to suspend its activities. During the period from 1937 through 1942, Halasz also undertook numerous guest appearances. In New York, he conducted the federal WPA orchestra and the Pepsi-Cola band, which gave free concerts in Central Park; he appeared with Alfredo Salmaggi's group at the time that it was known as The Hippodrome Opera Company; and there were assignments with the resident operatic groups of Chicago and Philadelphia. Three of these undertakings stand out in relief from the rest. One was to be the American premiere of Kodály's *Háry János*, which was to take place at the New York World's Fair. There were ten performances scheduled between July 3 and July 13, 1939, of which Halasz was engaged to conduct nine, while the composer, who came to

3. *St. Louis Star-Times*, April 5, 1939.

America specifically for this production, was to conduct the tenth. At the last minute, despite Kodály's presence in New York, the scheduled production was canceled. However, Halasz's reunion with his old professor from the Budapest conservatory was a joyous occasion, and the two men remained close friends until Kodály's death in 1967. For the production, Halasz had managed to acquire the services of Imre Palló[4] in the title role. Palló was Hungary's leading baritone, and had been featured as Háry János in the opera's world premiere in 1926. Coincidentally, his son is New York City Opera conductor Imre Pallo, one of the brightest young lights on the operatic horizon.

The second outstanding event of this period was a pair of concerts with the Concert Orchestra of New York. This was a newly formed group that was inaugurated on April 13, 1942, with a program featuring soprano Elisabeth Schumann and conducted by Otto Klemperer. On April 20, Halasz conducted Wagner's *Siegfried Idyll*, the overture to Rossini's *La Scala di Seta*, and the second act of *Don Giovanni* starring Anne Roselle, Maria Maximovitch, Margit Bokor, Jess Walters, Gerhard Pechner, Felix Knight, and Carlos Alexander. One week later, on the twenty-seventh, Halasz's program consisted of Schubert's Symphony no. 2 in B Major combined with an English language version of Gluck's *Orpheus and Eurydice*. The title roles were sung by Amy Ellerman and Florence Henders, and Bokor returned to sing the short but gratifying part of Amor.

A definite pattern in Halasz's tastes was emerging. He had always felt that opera should be accessible to the broad public—not only financially accessible but artistically so. Toward this end, he was particularly concerned about its dramatic integrity. Young lovers, for example, should be young; a femme fatale like Carmen should be physically attractive; and the stage action should be as convincing in opera as in the dramatic theater. The other major factor in popularizing opera was to make it comprehensible to the audience, and he was one of the leading pioneers and exponents of opera in English (*Martha* and *Falstaff* at St. Louis, and now the *Orpheus* in New York).

One of the major innovations planned for the Saint Louis opera was Rossini's *Barber of Seville* in an English translation by George Mead and Louis Garden. The company became insolvent before the production could take place, but Halasz decided to run it as a mass-appeal show. Under the title *Once Over Lightly*, it opened in Washington, D.C., on

4. Imre Palló, Sr., whose career was almost exclusively European, used the accent mark over the final letter of his name; his son and namesake, whose career is American, does not use the accent mark.

August 14, 1942, receiving critical acclaim. The cast, which comprised many of his St. Louis singers, included:

> *Rosina* . . . . Grace Panvini
> *Berta* . . . . Eleanor Knapp
> *Almaviva* . . . . Felix Knight
> *Figaro* . . . . Carlo Morelli
> *Bartolo* . . . . Louis d'Angelo
> *Basilio* . . . . Harold Kravitt
> *Fiorello* . . . . Stefan Kozakevich

A few months later, on November 19, it opened at New York's Alvin Theater with Igor Gorin and John de Surra alternating as Figaro, Grace Panvini and Frances Watkins as the two Rosinas, Felix Knight as Almaviva, and Richard Wentworth, Carlos Alexander, Ardelle Warner, and Myron Szandrowsky as Bartolo, Basilio, Berta, and Fiorello. The critical reaction to *Once Over Lightly* was summed up by the *New York Journal-American* music critic Grena Bennett, who said:

Once Over Lightly, an Americanized version of our old friend *The Barber of Seville*, was produced last night at the Alvin Theater and is, without exception, one of the most delightful and worthwhile entertainments now before the public.

It has everything that makes for a pleasant evening—beautiful music that falls easily on the ear; an excellent cast of singers; a capital English translation of which every word in the text came clearly over the footlights; comedy that had real humor and no suggestion; a stunning set of stage scenes; a good orchestra; and a capable conductor.

Nothing was left undone by Saul Colin, the producer, to make *Once Over Lightly* a top-notch attraction not only to theatregoers but also to lovers of opera.

Many attempts have been made to pour old wine into new bottles, but this writer cannot remember so successful a transformation of an ancient lyric work made so compact by the cautious deletions of the blue pencil and the incorporation of modern quips in the translated text, as is the case with last evening's musical play.

So far as the artists are concerned, there was not a weak spot in the cast.

Miss Bennett concluded: "All in all, it was a swell show and everyone in the large audience had a good time."

The next month, after *Once Over Lightly* ended its engagement, Halasz joined the American Symphony Orchestra, a group of thirty-seven instrumentalists organized by the USO to promote the morale of servicemen.

With mezzo-soprano Elen Longone (formerly Eleanor La Mance of the Metropolitan and Saint Louis Opera companies), they toured U.S. military camps and hospitals at a grueling pace. Starting in Harrisburg, Pennsylvania, on December 18, 1942, they concluded in Clarksville, Tennessee, on June 2, 1943. During the 167 days, Halasz conducted 225 concerts and 23 rehearsals, played to a total audience of about 175,000, and traveled 12,000 miles! He displayed the same zeal at the end of the year when he plunged into the enormous task of creating the New York City Opera Company. On October 25, 1943—less than two weeks after his appointment, and before news of it was made public—he inserted the following advertisement into the *New York Times*:

CITY CENTER SEEKS OPERA SINGERS

The City Center of Music and Drama, Inc., has announced completion of plans for organizing a choral ensemble to take part in operatic productions for presentation at the New York City Center, 133 West Fifty-fifth Street. Applicants for auditions may apply for application forms by letter or personally at 130 West Fifty-sixth Street. Auditions will be held singly, by appointment.

Over 1,000 responded, of whom fifty were ultimately chosen. The next few weeks were frantic, proposing repertoire, preparing budgets, auditioning singers, dancers, and musical and production staff members, and rehearsing. The City Center became a beehive of activity.

This dynamo was the man chosen to start the opera company, and there was probably no one better qualified to do so!

Halasz at the Saint Louis Opera Company

Laszlo Halasz as conductor before the reorganization:

December 1, 1937

Wagner: TRISTAN UND ISOLDE

Isolde	Kirsten Flagstad
Brangaene	Sonia Sharnova
Tristan	Paul Althouse
Kurwenal	Francis Row
King Marke	John Gurney
Melot	E. A. Dammrich
A Shepherd	Guy Golterman, Jr.
A Sailor's Voice	E. A. Dammrich

Halasz at the Saint Louis Grand Opera Association.
Laszlo Halasz as conductor and artistic and musical director:

April 17, 1939

Wagner: DIE WALKÜRE

Brünnhilde	Marjorie Lawrence
Sieglinde	Irene Jessner
Fricka	Hertha Glatz
Siegmund	Lauritz Melchior
Wotan	Fred Destal
Hunding	Deszo Ernster

Helmwige .... Florence Kirk
Gerhilde .... Leone Foley
Ortlinde .... Janice Deutsch
Waltraute .... Alice Meyer
Siegrüne .... Helen Wright
Rossweisse ... Nancy Hitch Fordyce
Grimgerde .... Florence Timmerhoff
Schwertleite .... Dolores Klute

April 21, 1939

Verdi: OTELLO

Desdemona .... Irene Jessner
Emilia .... Hertha Glatz
Otello .... Giovanni Martinelli
Iago .... Fred Destal
Cassio .... Nicola Massue
Roderigo ...... Gerald Whittington
Lodovico .... Lorenzo Alvary
Montano .... Charles Galloway
A Herald .... Millard Allen

April 24, 1939

Gounod: FAUST

Marguerite .... Lucy Monroe
Siébel .... Florence Kirk
Marthe .... Hertha Glatz
Faust .... Charles Kullman
Valentin .... Robert Weede
Méphistophélès .... Ezio Pinza
Wagner .... Nord Vernellj

October 14, 1939

Verdi: AÏDA

Aïda .... Rose Bampton
Amneris .... Bruna Castagna
A Priestess .... Dorothy Bott
Radames .... Frederick Jagel
Amonasro .... Fred Destal
Ramfis .... John Gurney
The King of Egypt .. Lorenzo Alvary
A Messenger .... Robert Ramsey

October 21, 1939

Puccini: LA BOHÈME

Mimi .... Jarmila Novotna
            (replacing Bidu Sayao)
Musetta .... Silvia Brema
Rodolfo .... Nino Martini

Marcello .... Carlo Morelli
Schaunard .... Jeffrey Gould
Colline .... Lorenzo Alvary
Benoit .... Pompilio Malatesta
Alcindoro ...... Pompilio Malatesta
Parpignol .... Jack Moeller
A Sergeant .... Millard Allen
A Customs
    Officer .... Dickinson Eastham

November 14, 1939

Menotti: AMELIA GOES TO THE BALL

Amelia .... Florence Kirk
Her Friend ... Nancy Hitch Fordyce
The Husband .... Robert Weede
The Lover .... Giulio Gari
The Police Chief ... Lorenzo Alvary
Three Maids .... Violet New
                     Helen Wright
                Florence Timmerhoff

followed by

Leoncavallo: I PAGLIACCI

Nedda .... Margit Bokor
            (replacing Livia Dobay)
Canio .... Giovanni Martinelli
Tonio .... John Charles Thomas
Silvio .... Robert Weede
Beppe .... Karl Laufkoetter

November 20, 1939

Wagner: SIEGFRIED

Brünnhilde ..... Marjorie Lawrence
Erda .... Enid Szantho
A Forest Bird .... June Hoertel
Siegfried .... Lauritz Melchior
The Wanderer .... Fred Destal
Mime .... Karl Laufkoetter
Alberich .... Oscar Lassner
Fafner .... Lorenzo Alvary

April 19, 1940

Verdi: RIGOLETTO

Gilda ....Bidu Sayao
Maddalena .... Hertha Glatz
The Duke .... Jan Kiepura
Rigoletto .... Carlo Morelli

Sparafucile .... Lorenzo Alvary
Monterone .... Carlos Alexander
Borsa .... Giuseppe Cavadore
Marullo .... Joseph Garnier
Ceprano .... Nathan Newman
Countess Ceprano ...... Violet New
Giovanna .... Leone Foley
A Page .... Annora Kelledy
A Guard .... James Porteous

April 25, 1940

Bizet: CARMEN

Carmen .... Majorie Lawrence
Micaëla .... Sylvia Brema
Don José .... Jan Kiepura
Escamillo .... Ezio Pinza
Zuniga .... Lorenzo Alvary
Frasquita .... Florence Kirk
Mercédès .... Elizabeth Brown
Remendado .... Giuseppe Cavadore
Dancaïro .... Carlos Alexander
Morales .... Carlos Alexander

April 29, 1940

Massenet: MANON

Manon .... Grace Moore
Des Grieux .... Raoul Jobin
Lescaut .... George Cehanovsky
Count Des Grieux .. Lorenzo Alvary
Guillot .... Giuseppe Cavadore
De Brétigny ...... Carlos Alexander
Pousette .... Silvia Brema
Javotte .... Rose Inghram
Rosette .... Elizabeth Brown
An Innkeeper ..... Nathan Newman
A Servant .... Helen Wright
Two Guards .... Russell Yaeger
Joseph Garnier

September 28, 1940 (in Havana, Cuba)

Massenet: MANON

Manon .... Grace Moore
Des Grieux .... Raoul Jobin
Lescaut .... Federico Ginrod
Count Des Grieux .. Lorenzo Alvary
Guillot .... Giuseppe Cavadore
De Brétigny ...... Carlos Alexander
Pousette .... Rose Inghram

Javotte .... Alice Meyer
Rosette .... Helen Wright
An Innkeeper ..... Nathan Newman
Two Guards .... Millard Allen
Dickinson Eastham

September 30, 1940 (in Havana, Cuba)

Mascagni: CAVALLERIA RUSTICANA

Santuzza .... Marianna Genitch
Lola .... Rose Inghram
Mama
Lucia ...... Florence Timmerhoff
Turiddu .... Armand Tokatyan
Alfio .... Federico Ginrod

followed by

Leoncavallo: I PAGLIACCI

Nedda .... Vivian della Chiesa
Canio .... Giovanni Martinelli
Tonio .... Carlos Alexander
Silvio .... Carlo Morelli
Beppe .... Giuseppe Cavadore

October 1, 1940 (in Havana, Cuba)

Puccini: LA BOHÈME

Mimi .... Grace Moore
Musetta .... Vivian della Chiesa
Rodolfo .... Armand Tokatyan
Marcello .... Carlo Morelli
Schaunard .... Carlos Alexander
Colline .... Lorenzo Alvary
Benoit .... Giuseppe Cavadore
Alcindoro ...... Giuseppe Cavadore
Parpignol .... Jack Moeller
A Sergeant .... Millard Allen
Customs Officer ..... Dick Eastham

October 3, 1940 (in Havana, Cuba)

Verdi: OTELLO

Desdemona ..... Vivian della Chiesa
Emilia .... Helen Wright
Otello .... Giovanni Martinelli
Iago .... Carlo Morelli
Cassio .... Giuseppe Cavadore
Roderigo .... Carlos Alexander
Lodovico .... Lorenzo Alvary
Montano ....Nathan Newman
A Herald .... Millard Allen

April 16, 1941

Mozart: DON GIOVANNI

Donna Anna .... Anne Roselle
Donna Elvira ... Vivian della Chiesa
Zerlina .... Margit Bokor
Don Giovanni .... Ezio Pinza
Leporello .... Lorenzo Alvary
Don Ottavio .... Tito Schipa
Masetto .... Carlos Alexander
The Commend-
atore .... Nicola Moscona

April 21, 1941

Thomas: MIGNON

Mignon .... Gladys Swarthout
Philine .... Christina Carroll
Wilhelm
Meister .... Armand Tokatyan
Lothario .... Nicola Moscona
Frederic .... Rose Inghram
Laërte .... Giuseppe Cavadore
Jarno .... Carlos Alexander
Antonio .... Nathan Newman

April 24, 1941

Verdi: LA TRAVIATA

Violetta .... Helen Jepson
Flora .... Rose Inghram
Annina .... Helen Wright
Alfredo .... James Melton
Giorgio Germont ..... Carlo Morelli
Gaston .... Giuseppe Cavadore
Baron Douphol ... Carlos Alexander
Marquis
d'Obigny .... Nathan Newman
Doctor Grenvil .. Dickinson Eastham

April 26, 1941

Mascagni: CAVALLERIA RUSTICANA

Santuzza .... Dusolina Giannini
Lola .... Rose Inghram
Mamma
Lucia ...... Florence Timmerhoff
Turiddu .... Kurt Baum
Alfio .... Alexander Sved

followed by

Leoncavallo: I PAGLIACCI

Nedda .... Vivian della Chiesa
Canio .... Giovanni Martinelli
Tonio .... Alexander Sved
Silvio .... George Czaplicki
Beppe .... Guiseppe Cavadore

September 25, 1941 (in Havana, Cuba)

Verdi: RIGOLETTO

Gilda .... Lucille Meusel
Maddalena ...... Maria Pisarewska
Giovanna ...... Lolita Pérez Moreno
Countess
Ceprano .... Lolita Pérez Moreno
The Duke of Mantua .... Jan Peerce
      (replacing Jussi Bjoerling)
Rigoletto ...... Francesco Valentino
Sparafucile .... John Gurney
Monterone .... Victor Morales
Borsa .... Armando Finzi
Marullo .... Romano Splinger
Ceprano .... José Berg

September 27, 1941 (in Havana, Cuba)

Puccini: TOSCA

Tosca .... Dusolina Giannini
Mario Cavaradossi .. Norbert Ardelli
Baron Scarpia .... Carlo Morelli
Angelotti .... John Gurney
A Sacristan ...... Carlos Alexander
Spoletta .... Armando Finzi
Sciarrone .... José Berg

September 30, 1941 (in Havana, Cuba)

Gounod: FAUST

Marguerite .... Eleanor Steber
Siébel .... Lolita Pérez Moreno
Marthe .... Maria Pisarewska
Faust .... Charles Kullman
Valentin .... Carlo Morelli
Méphistophélès .... Ezio Pinza
Wagner .... Carlos Alexander

October 2, 1941 (in Havana, Cuba)

Puccini: MADAMA BUTTERFLY

Cio-Cio-San .... Enya González
Suzuki .... Maria Pisarewska
B. F. Pinkerton ...... James Melton
Sharpless ...... Franesco Valentino
Goro .... J. Vázquez
The Bonze .... Armando Finzi
Yamadori .... Romano Splinger
Kate
    Pinkerton ... Lolita Pérez Moreno

October 18, 1941

Flotow: MARTHA
(in the English adaptation of
Ann Ronell and Vicki Baum)

Lady Harriet .... Helen Jepson
Nancy .... Hertha Glatz
Lionel .... James Melton
Plunkett .... Douglas Beattie
Sir Tristram ...... Gerhard Pechner
The Sheriff .... Nathan Newman
Three Maids .. Florence Timmerhoff
            Betty Billings
            Helen Nightingale

October 20, 1941 (in Evansville, Indiana)

Flotow: MARTHA
(in the English adaptation of
Ann Ronell and Vicki Baum)

Lady Harriett .... Helen Jepson
Nancy .... Hertha Glatz

Lionel .... Felix Knight
Plunkett .... Douglas Beattie
Sir Tristram ...... Gerhard Pechner
The Sheriff .... Nathan Newman
Three Maids .. Florence Timmerhoff
            Betty Billings
            Helen Nightingale

October 25, 1941

Puccini: TOSCA

Tosca .... Grace Moore
Mario Cavaradossi ..... Kurt Baum
Baron Scarpia .... Carlo Morelli
Angelotti .... Douglas Beattie
A Sacristan ...... Gerhard Pechner
Spoletta .... Santo Gullotta
Sciarrone .... Nathan Newman
A Jailer .... James Porteous

November 10, 1941

Verdi: FALSTAFF
(in the English translation of
W. Beatty Kingston)

Mistress Ford ... Dusolina Giannini
Mistress Page .... Hertha Glatz
Anne Page .... Christina Carroll
Dame Quickly ..... Sonia Sharnova
Falstaff ...... John Charles Thomas
Ford .... Mark Harell
Fenton ....Felix Knight
Bardolph .... Robert Long
        (replacing Anthony Marlowe)
Pistol .... Douglas Beattie
Dr. Caius .... Monas Harlan

7

A Different World
of Opera

B E F O R E we continue with the story of the New York City Opera, a brief digression is necessary. The past few decades have witnessed unprecedented changes in the international operatic picture, due to three postwar developments—the long-playing record, the home tape recorder, and jet travel.

LPs have made it commercially feasible to expand the recorded repertoire in an extravagant fashion. There are currently several hundred complete operas available commercially, and if one includes the numerous "pirate" labels (to which every dedicated operaphile has access) the list swells to over one thousand! In the entire seventy-year period between the first recorded sound and the appearance of the LP, only about fifty operas had been recorded in their entirety. Most of those existed in one or two versions; occasionally, there might be as many as three. By way of contrast, there are dozens of operas on LPs that exist in twenty or more performances.[1] Additionally, the price of a complete opera, which was once prohibitive, is now within the reach of all. For example, in 1936, depending upon the version chosen and whether or not discount prices could be found, *Aida* cost about $25 or $30—the better part of a week's wages; today one can, with little difficulty, obtain a complete recording on a budget label for as little as $3.

1. As an illustration, Verdi's *Ballo in Maschera* and *Otello* each had one recording on 78 rpm. On LP, there have been twenty-four *Ballo*s and twenty-two *Otello*s. An even more dramatic point is made by the operas of Rossini. Only one of his operas, *The Barber of Seville,* had been available on 78 rpm, but thirty have been issued on LP—twenty of them commercially!

47

With the advent of home tape recorders, combined with broadcasts from the Metropolitan, New York City, Chicago, Houston, San Francisco, and San Diego opera companies (to say nothing of those of the many operatic disc-jockeys), an investment of two or three dollars in tape will make available almost any opera one can name, with many choices of performers. All of this has had a profound impact upon the opera-going habits of the public.

To begin with, audiences are far more sophisticated today than in the past. Hundreds of operas that were once deemed great novelties are now more or less familiar fare. Except for the small group of works that had been recorded in complete versions on 78 rpm, one might have had the opportunity to hear a particular opera once every few years; now, in most cases, it can be heard at will. The results of this have been made manifest in several ways. For example, curiosity has been stimulated, and there is greater demand for novelty. Thus, the repertoire has expanded significantly. Thirty years ago, it would have seemed all but impossible actually to see a stage production of a Monteverdi opera. Yet, within the past few decades, the City Opera has presented three.[2] For years, the only Rossini opera one could count on seeing was *The Barber of Seville*, but since the LP, New York audiences have also been treated to stage productions of *Cenerentola*, *The Italian in Algiers*, *The Siege of Corinth*, *The Turk in Italy*, *Otello*, and *Le Comte Ory*. Concert performances have increased the list to include *La Pietra del Paragone*, *Moses*, *Semiramide*, *William Tell*, *La Gazza Ladra*, *Tancredi*, and others

When we look at the repertoire presented by the New York City Opera in its earliest years, it does not seem overly adventurous by today's standards; but at the time, productions of operas such as *Martha*, *Manon Lescaut*, *Andrea Chénier*, *Eugène Onegin*, and *The Bartered Bride* raised many an eyebrow, and left people with a "what-will-they-think-of-next" feeling. Try to picture, if you will, any American opera company offering the following repertoire today:

Bizet:	*Carmen*
	Don Procopio
Floyd:	*Susannah*
Gounod:	*Faust*
Massenet:	*Hérodiade*
Meyerbeer:	*Robert le Diable*
Moore:	*The Ballad of Baby Doe*

2. *Orfeo* (1960); *L'Incoronazione di Poppea* (1973); *Il Ritorno d'Ulisse in Patria* (1976).

Mozart:	*Don Giovanni*
Puccini:	*La Bohème*
	Tosca
	Le Villi
Reyer:	*Sigurd*
Ricci:	*Crispino e la Comare*
Rossini:	*Armida*
Strauss:	*Der Rosenkavalier*
Tchaikowsky:	*Mazeppa*
Verdi:	*Aïda*
	Stiffelio
	La Traviata
Wagner:	*Das Liebesverbot*

Such a schedule would approximate the impact of the early City Opera seasons.

If today's audiences have become more demanding in repertoire, they have also required higher production standards. The ability to hear the opera of one's choice sung by Montserrat Caballé, Maria Callas, Beverly Sills, or Joan Sutherland, partnered by José Carreras, Placido Domingo, Nicolai Gedda, or Luciano Pavarotti on recordings has done much to dispel the desire to attend performances, unless the productions themselves offer an outstanding theatrical experience. Routine traditional staging is not adequate to satisfy today's audience. In addition, Americans can frequently see excellent drama because of television, and the demand for quality productions has increased geometrically. Fast travel has made major talents available to theaters throughout the world. Specialization in roles has grown, because a singer may now perform a small handful of parts for many different companies during the course of a season, rather than being limited to one or two companies and being forced, by economic necessity, to perform a more varied repertoire.

All these factors must be borne in mind when one examines the early history of any opera company; thus, the formative years of the New York City Opera should be viewed in light of the standards of the 1940s.

8

Opening Night

W I T H Halasz installed as director of the opera company, the board was now fully commited to what they had been so anxious to avoid— being a production company, and in the most costly of all theatrical forms. It is true that only one week of performances was planned at this point, but even that could result in a loss of many thousands of dollars. Alexander Pope's "fools rush in where angels fear to tread" never seemed more appropriate.

The uncertainty about the future of the opera company was demonstrated by La Guardia when he told Halasz, half in jest and half in earnest, that he was engaging him for one week with an option on his services for three years.

If the board of directors had their doubts, Halasz did not. His years of experience assured him that the company would succeed, and drawing upon his seemingly unlimited energy, he went about the job of achieving the impossible. The week of February 21 to 27, 1944, was set aside for the opera company, and Halasz had four months in which to build a staff, prepare estimates and budgets, decide upon repertoire, audition singers, instrumentalists, and dancers, acquire scenery, costumes and props, and rehearse the first season's operas.

Days and evenings were set aside for auditions, while paperwork was brought home as a replacement for sleep. The choice of repertoire was critical to the success of the company, and Halasz felt that three was the proper number of operas for one week of production. Fewer works would mean less of an investment, but also reduced public interest and probably

Morton Baum, founding director, chairman of the executive committee and chairman of the board until his death in February 1968. He was the personification of the New York City Center. (COURTESY LESTER BAUM)

Laszlo Halasz, the company's first general director (1943–1951). (COURTESY LASZLO HALASZ)

Joseph Rosenstock, the second general director (1951–1956). (COLLECTION OF THE AUTHOR)

Erich Leinsdorf, the third general director (1956). (COLLECTION OF THE AUTHOR)

Julius Rudel, the fourth general director (1957–1979). (COURTESY JULIUS RUDEL)

Beverly Sills, the fifth general director (1979–), radiant as Massenet's Manon. (FRED FEHL)

Laszlo Halasz being congratulated by Mayor Fiorello La Guardia upon his appointment as artistic director of the newly formed opera company. (COURTESY LASZLO HALASZ)

The first performance, February 21, 1944. This is a scene from Act II of *Tosca*. The three principal artists are in the foreground: George Czaplicki as Baron Scarpia, Mario Berini as Mario Cavaradossi, and Dusolina Giannini as Floria Tosca. Behind them are Emanuel Kazaras (Sciaronne) and Hubert Norville (Spoletta). (A. F. SOZIO/NEW YORK CITY OPERA ARCHIVES)

Jennie Tourel was the company's first Carmen; she later went on to international fame. (A. F. SOZIO/NEW YORK CITY OPERA ARCHIVES)

Opera's classic double bill of *Cavalleria* and *Pagliacci* came into the repertoire during the second season. Dusolina Giannini, who inaugurated the company as Tosca, was also its first Santuzza. (COURTESY DUSOLINA GIANNINI)

Camilla Williams is remembered today for her thrilling *Butterfly,* but she sang a variety of other roles as well, including Nedda in *Pagliacci.* Here she is with Giuseppe Valdengo as Tonio. (FRED FEHL)

Dorothy Kirsten was another of the company's luminaries in the early years. Puccini's *Manon Lescaut* was revived for her after an absence from the New York stage of about fifteen years. This scene is Manon's dancing lesson, observed by Geronte (Ralph Telasko, seated) and Lescaut (John de Surra, behind him). (FRED FEHL)

When the company first introduced Gounod's *Faust,* the title role was sung by two tenors—one as the aged philosopher, the other, the rejuvenated lover. When the old Faust drank his elixir of youth, he fell to his knees behind the desk, and immediately the youthful Faust sprang up, clean-shaven, dashing, and ardent —thus eliminating an awkward costume change. The transformation took only a split second. Here we see Giulio Gari as the old Faust, Rudolf Petrak as his young counterpart. (COSMO-SILEO/NEW YORK CITY OPERA ARCHIVES)

Puccini's *Madama Butterfly* had been dropped by all American opera companies during World War II. When it was first produced by City Opera on May 15, 1946, management had some fears about its reception. As it turned out, the public accepted it back into the repertoire like a long-lost friend. Camilla Williams and Margery Mayer are seen above in Act II. (FRED FEHL)

Virginia Haskins as Zerlina and James Pease in the title role introduced *Don Giovanni* to City Opera audiences in 1948. Since then, it has been performed on the average of one season in three. (FRED FEHL)

A major coup of the Halasz years was the acquisition of Maggie Teyte's services for Mélisande. A specialist in Debussy's music, she was generally considered, at that time, the world's outstanding interpreter of the part. Pelléas was sung initially by Fernand Martel (above), subsequently by Theodor Uppman. (BEN GREENHAUS/NEW YORK CITY OPERA ARCHIVES)

Gian Carlo Menotti's *Old Maid and the Thief* was the company's first American opera. By 1980 almost fifty American works had been presented—more than one-fourth of the company's total repertoire. Here we see Virginia MacWatters, the Laetitia of the original production. (FRED FEHL)

The first performance of *Aida* boasted Chilean tenor Ramon Vinay as Radames. He later went on to international stardom, and will be remembered as Toscanini's preferred Otello. The artists in the foreground are Lawrence Winters as Amonasro, Vinay, Suzy Morris (Newbold Morris's sister-in-law) as Amneris, and Oscar Natzka as Ramfis. (FRED FEHL)

On March 31, 1949 the company gave its first world premiere, William Grant Still's *Troubled Island*. Robert Weede was the sometimes violent emperor, Dessalines. (BEN MANCUSO/NEW YORK CITY OPERA ARCHIVES)

(LEFT) Millions of opera lovers have been both entertained and enlightened by the wit and erudition of coach/musicologist Alberta Masiello. Few realize, however, that she began her professional career as a mezzo-soprano with City Opera. Here she is seen as Carmen, one of her roles under Halasz. (BRUNO/NEW YORK CITY OPERA ARCHIVES)

Amelia Goes to the Ball was dropped after two seasons, but its companion piece, *The Old Maid and the Thief,* was retained in the repertoire, now doubled with Menotti's *The Medium*. This touching scene from the original production of *The Medium* shows Evelyn Keller as Monica and Leo Coleman as the mute, Toby. (NEW YORK CITY OPERA ARCHIVES)

This is the opera that ultimately led to Halasz's dismissal, Tamkin's *The Dybbuk*. First performed on October 4, 1951, it was the company's second world premiere. This is the exorcism scene, terrifying in its intensity. Leah, center stage with her back to the audience, was Patricia Neway. Performing the exorcism was Rabbi Azrael, sung by baritone Mack Harrell. (BEN MANCUSO, COSMO-SILEO/NEW YORK CITY OPERA ARCHIVES)

In this photograph by world-renowned *Life* photographer Philippe Halsman, company director Laszlo Halasz is surrounded by seven of his divas. They are (clockwise from top) Frances Bible as Cherubino, Virginia Haskins as Zerlina, Wilma Spence as Tosca, Marguerite Piazza as Amelia (in *Amelia Goes to the Ball*), Brenda Lewis as Salome, Ann Ayars as Violetta, and Dorothy MacNeil as Musetta. (PHILIPPE HALSMAN)

In this scene from Act III of Alban Berg's *Wozzeck,* Margaret (Edith Evans) is on the right with Wozzeck (Marko Rothmueller). One of the leading interpreters of the title role, Rothmueller was in the Covent Garden and Buenos Aires premieres of Berg's opera. (NEW YORK CITY OPERA ARCHIVES)

Joseph Rosenstock conferring with three of his main staff members in 1952. From left to right: Rosenstock, John S. White, Julius Rudel, and Thomas Martin. (FREDERICK MELTON/NEW YORK CITY OPERA ARCHIVES)

Of the twenty works introduced by Rosenstock, *Cenerentola* has been second in popularity only to *Fledermaus.* From the initial *Cenerentola* production, we see Riccardo Manning and Frances Bible (Prince Ramiro and Cinderella) in the final scene. (FRIEDMAN-ABELES/NEW YORK CITY OPERA ARCHIVES)

Hansel and Gretel was in the repertoire for only three seasons—a great pity because it was a thoroughly delightful production. The photograph above shows Frances Bible and Laurel Hurley in the title roles. (TALBOT/NEW YORK CITY OPERA ARCHIVES)

The witch in the first *Hansel* performance was Claramae Turner. For later presentations, the well-known British comedienne Anna Russell (above) was engaged. (MICHAEL MYERBERG PRODUCTIONS/ NEW YORK CITY OPERA ARCHIVES)

Phyllis Curtin had a spectacular debut singing three roles in Gottfried von Einem's *The Trial*—Fräulein Burstner, the court attendant's wife, and Leni. Here we see her in the first two of the three parts. (TALBOT/NEW YORK CITY OPERA ARCHIVES)

Hollywood director Otto Preminger was engaged to stage *The Trial*. Here he and Maestro Rosenstock are discussing the score. (TALBOT/NEW YORK CITY OPERA ARCHIVES)

Collaborators on *The Tender Land*—Thomas Schippers (conductor), Aaron Copland (composer), Jerome Robbins (director), and librettist Horace Everett. (TALBOT/NEW YORK CITY OPERA ARCHIVES)

diminished ticket sales; conversely, more than three would increase audience enthusiasm but at far too great a cost for the stringent budget.

Since the original purpose of the company was to provide opera to the general public at affordable prices, Halasz felt that the principal concentration should be on standard repertoire, those works that, over the years, had consistently pleased the greatest number of people. At the same time, to attract attention and acquire an individual identity, the company had to provide a certain number of novelties. This first season, he felt, should consist of one unfamiliar and two standard operas.

At the time that the St. Louis company became inactive, they offered, as a gesture of friendship toward Halasz, to make any of their scenery and costumes available to him for just a token fee. If he limited his City Center repertoire to those operas that had been performed by his St. Louis company, the cost of scenery and costumes could be reduced to transportation expenses, any minor repairs that might be necessary, and a very nominal stipend to St. Louis.

One other factor went into planning the first set of operas—language. Halasz had always shown a strong tendency toward opera in the vernacular—*Amelia Goes to the Ball*, *Martha*, *Falstaff*, and the Broadway adaptation of *Barber of Seville* had amply proven this preference. He now felt that *every* City Opera season should have at least one work in English and one work outside the standard repertoire. The Ann Ronell–Vicki Baum version of *Martha* satisfied both of these conditions, and since the scenery and costumes were available from St. Louis, Flotow's most popular opera, which had last been heard in New York in 1928, was a logical choice. A desire for linguistic variety resulted in the selection of one French and one Italian work for the remaining operas. The French should most certainly be *Carmen*, one of the most durable of all favorites, but for the Italian, he had mixed feelings—either Puccini's *Tosca* or a double-bill of opera's Siamese twins, *Cavalleria Rusticana* and *Pagliacci*.

He therefore submitted estimated costs for the four productions to the board, and agreed to abide by their preference for the Italian offering.

In going through the early City Opera documents, these cost estimates were among the most interesting of the papers in the files, fascinating because of the thoroughness and precision involved. The following tabulation is for the *Carmen* production, and demonstrates the care required for proper budgeting.

The reason for the large differential between the first and subsequent performances is that all rehearsal costs were assigned to the premiere. This is both justifiable and proper, since a lone performance would require the same rehearsal time as would a series.

	FIRST PERFORMANCE	REPEAT
1. Staff Expenses		
Artistic and music director	$ 500.00	$ 150.00
Stage director	200.00	50.00
Chorus master	75.00	20.00
Assistant conductor	100.00	20.00
Assistant to stage director	75.00	20.00
Designer–lighting chief	60.00	—
SUBTOTAL	$ 1,010.00	$ 260.00
2. Artists and Ensemble Expenses		
a. Cast fees		
Carmen	$ 125.00	$ 100.00
Don José	150.00	100.00
Escamillo	125.00	100.00
Micaëla	55.00	50.00
Zuniga	50.00	50.00
Frasquita	40.00	40.00
Mercédès	40.00	40.00
Dancairo	50.00	50.00
Remendado	50.00	40.00
Morales	40.00	35.00
SUBTOTAL	$ 725.00	$ 605.00
b. Orchestra		
47 men, 10 hours rehearsal	$ 940.00	$ —
47 men per performance	564.00	564.00
SUBTOTAL	$ 1,504.00	$ 564.00
c. Chorus, ballet, and supers		
48 choristers, rehearsal	$ 720.00	$ —
48 choristers, performance	384.00	384.00
16 children, rehearsal	48.00	—
16 children, performance	32.00	32.00
14 dancers, rehearsal	210.00	—
14 dancers, performance	112.00	112.00
2 solo dancers, rehearsal	40.00	—
2 solo dancers, performance	60.00	60.00
20 supers, rehearsal	14.00	—
20 supers, performance	32.00	32.00
SUBTOTAL	$ 1,652.00	$ 620.00
ARTISTS AND ENSEMBLE SUBTOTAL	$ 3,881.00	$ 1,789.00

	FIRST PERFORMANCE	REPEAT
3. *Stage Department Expense*		
a. *Stagehands*		
15 men, rehearsal	$ 210.00	$ —
3 senior men, rehearsal	54.00	—
15 men, dress rehearsal	120.00	—
3 senior men, dress rehearsal	30.00	—
15 men, performance	116.25	116.25
3 senior men, performance	24.75	24.75
SUBTOTAL	$ 555.00	$ 141.00
b. *Makeup man*		
Rehearsal	$ 35.00	$ —
Performance	15.00	15.00
SUBTOTAL	$ 50.00	$ 15.00
c. *Dressers*		
4 dressers, rehearsal	$ 20.00	$ —
Head and assistant, performance	25.00	25.00
3 additional dressers, performance	13.50	13.50
SUBTOTAL	$ 58.50	$ 38.50
d. *Scenery*		
Shipping	$ 350.00	$ —
Touch-up	125.00	—
Rental to St. Louis	50.00	50.00
SUBTOTAL	$ 525.00	$ 50.00
e. *Costumes*		
Shipping	$ 90.00	$ —
Repairs and rental	90.00	90.00
SUBTOTAL	$ 180.00	$ 90.00
f. *Properties*		
Acquisitions	$ 35.00	$ —
Rental	40.00	40.00
SUBTOTAL	$ 75.00	$ 40.00
g. *Electrical equipment*		
Acquisitions	$ 30.00	$ —
Rental	30.00	30.00
SUBTOTAL	$ 60.00	$ 30.00
h. *Rental of drapes, cyclorama, etc.*	$ 70.00	$ 70.00
STAGE DEPARTMENT SUBTOTAL	$ 1,573.50	$ 474.50
4. *Music materials*	$ 35.00	$ 35.00
5. *Unforseen incidentals*	$ 200.00	$ 100.00
TOTAL	$ 6,699.50	$ 2,658.50

The costs for the other productions, arrived at in similar fashion, were:

	FIRST PERFORMANCE	REPEAT
Martha	$ 5,752.00	$ 2,266.00
Tosca	5,739.00	2,335.00
Cavalleria and *Pagliacci*	5,836.50	2,482.50

In addition, any performances beyond the third would result in a 10 percent saving, because singers would be willing to accept the lower fees once roles had been mastered, and miscellaneous expenses would be virtually eliminated.

The incredible accuracy of Halasz's calculations was not known until the season's end, when the aggregate of the actual costs was found to be $30,462.73, while the estimate was $32,413.90—a difference of only 6 percent.

The board had selected *Tosca* as the third offering and, indeed, this was the opera chosen to inaugurate the company. The week's activity would result in eight performances, one each night, with a matinee on Saturday, and there would be two performances of *Tosca* and three of each of the other operas.

The City Center had opened its doors to the public on December 11, 1943, with a concert by the New York Philharmonic conducted by Artur Rodzinski. The featured work was Gershwin's "An American in Paris," and baritone Lawrence Tibbett, who had generously donated his services as soloist sang "The Star Spangled Banner" and "Vision fugitive" from Massenet's *Hérodiade*. The date coincided with La Guardia's sixty-first birthday, and one of the highlights of the evening was the orchestra's rendition of "Happy Birthday" with Tibbett and all of the audience joining in.

During the next ten weeks, various plays and reviews commanded the theater's evening hours, while the stage was used during the day for auditions and rehearsals. From the more than one thousand singers who responded to Halasz's *New York Times* advertisement (see page 42) and some of his former St. Louis performers, he began to mold a company. The pianist for many of the hopeful singers was a recent graduate of the David Mannes School of Music, twenty-two-year-old Julius Rudel, who had been contracted for this, his first major professional job, at a salary of $50 weekly, in the capacity of "musical assistant."

A few of the soloists engaged were familiar to New York audiences from their previous association with the New Opera Company—Martha Lipton, Regina Resnik, Hugh Thompson, and Jennie Tourel; some, such as Norbert Ardelli and George Czaplicki, had appeared with the Saint Louis Opera Company after successful European careers; but most of the artists of that initial season were young Americans who were being given their first chance. The one "star" name on the roster was Dusolina Giannini, whose credits included La Scala, Salzburg, Covent Garden, the Berlin State, and Metropolitan Opera companies. A long career with the Victor Talking Machine Company (she began in 1924, before Victor affiliated itself with RCA) and its European counterpart, His Master's Voice, supplied the glamor and prestige so important in establishing the City Opera. Giannini had formerly sung under Halasz's direction on several occasions, in *Tosca*, *Cavalleria Rusticana*, and *Falstaff*. A native Philadelphian who, like so many other American artists had first to establish her credentials abroad, she was enthusiastic in her support of an organization that would assist the American singer on home soil.

As rehearsals moved into high gear, the board of directors made a dramatic decision, one that would set a precedent for many years to come. Despite the persistent fears of a potential economic disaster, an extra *Martha* was scheduled as a student matinee at reduced ticket prices. As a public service, the board was willing to put critically needed funds into a performance that would inevitably have to lose money, due to the lower admission cost. The initial season, then, would consist of *Tosca* (2/21); *Martha* (2/22); *Tosca* (2/23); *Carmen* (2/24); *Martha* (2/25); *Carmen* (2/26 matinee); *Martha* (2/26 evening); *Martha* (2/27 student matinee); and *Carmen* (2/27 evening). Halasz was to conduct all performances of *Carmen* and *Tosca* and the first *Martha*; James Sample, the other conductor on his staff, was entrusted with all of the *Martha* repeats.

The rehearsal schedule was grueling, because there was very little time to whip the season into shape, and it was made much more difficult by the use of many singers with little or no experience. If inexperience was a detriment, however, the enthusiasm of youth more than compensated, and as rehearsals progressed, everything began to fall into place. Because it was the opening work, and because it featured Giannini, *Tosca* would receive the greatest press attention, and the company put its best foot forward. The role of the hero, Mario Cavaradossi, was assigned to Russian-born, California-reared Mario Berini, a veteran of Radio City Music Hall who only a short time earlier, on October 9, had been featured in the world premiere of Italo Montemezzi's *L'Incantesimo*, one of the first operas composed for radio. George Czaplicki, a former star of the Warsaw Opera and a film idol in his native Poland, was to portray Scarpia.

Both *Tosca* and *Carmen* were in the current Metropolitan repertoire, and so comparisons were to be expected. Far from being intimidated by this, Halasz welcomed the opportunity, sure of his group's ability to compete successfully. *Tosca* was certainly in capable hands, but *Carmen* was equally favored by the presence of Jennie Tourel, who had not yet made a major name in this country, although she had previously appeared at the Met (one *Carmen* and one *Mignon*) during the economy-priced season of 1937. At Paris's Opéra-Comique, she had portrayed Bizet's gypsy temptress more than two hundred times, so she brought both authority and experience to her characterization. No, Halasz was not afraid of comparisons.

February 21 finally arrived. The sense of anticipation was nerve-wracking for many of the cast. Debuts and opening nights are difficult enough under the best of circumstances, but the inauguration of a new company—the mixture of fear and hope, anxiety and assurance, elation and apprehension—provides an emotional euphoria that few can imagine, and fewer still are privileged to experience. The excitement was barely less on the audience's side of the footlights. For some, it was simply a bargain-priced performance, but quite a few seemed to sense that they were witnessing, and truly participating in, a genuine historic event.

At eight-sixteen the house lights darkened. Halasz mounted the podium to an accompaniment of roaring applause. He raised his baton, remained poised for a moment, then brought it down sharply. Five crashing chords rang out. A new opera company was born!

9
Growing Pains

THE FIRST SEASON came and went very quickly. Nine performances in one week scarcely gave company members a chance to draw a breath, but when it was all over, they could well be pleased with their achievement. The reviews for *Martha* were mixed, with several members of the press particularly dissatisfied with the English adaptation. Arthur V. Berger, writing in the *New York Sun,* declared that "Flotow sounded almost like Sullivan in this version, but there was no Gilbert to supply the satire and intrigue necessary in this light operatic style to sustain the interest." *Carmen* was generally well received, although it was felt in some quarters that Tourel's approach was too tame. "She suggests the calculating minx rather than the fatalistically impelled Gypsy and she is far too well-manicured in appearance," according to Jerome D. Bohm, *New York Herald-Tribune. Tosca,* however, was an unqualified success, and one critic (Oscar Thompson, *New York Sun*) reported that George Czaplicki was the finest Scarpia since Antonio Scotti. As for the expected comparisons with the Metropolitan Opera, Halasz was completely justified in his self-assurance; the City Opera was the undisputed victor. *Time* magazine (March 6, 1944) summed up the season as follows:

When he was through he produced a *Tosca*, a *Martha* and a *Carmen* that set a new standard of quality in the popular-priced operatic field. Critics rated *Tosca* (with Soprano Dusolina Giannini and Baritone George Czaplicki) a notch higher than the Metropolitan's recent job (in which Soprano Grace Moore and Baritone Lawrence Tibbett substituted U.S. ham for Italian Salami).

The City Center's *Carmen* featured one of the best Carmens in a decade: dusky Jennie Tourel. . . . Her Carmen (a role she claims to have sung about 200 times) was full of Gallic spice and neat as a championship billiard game. The City Center's *Martha*, a bid to the Broadway trade, looked and sounded more like musical comedy than opera. So did its star: dark-haired, convent-bred Ethel Barrymore Colt (daughter of actress Ethel Barrymore and the late Russell Colt of Bristol, R.I.), who had arrived at opera after a fling at Broadway drama (*L'Aiglon*, *Cradle Song*) and the nightclub circuit (Spivy's Roof).

There were mishaps, to be sure. During the opening performance, the guns of the firing squad in the last act failed to go off, and Mario Cavaradossi fell to the ground for no apparent reason. One member of the audience wryly observed that this was the first *Tosca* in history in which the tenor died of a heart attack. At one of the *Carmen* performances, the audience was amused by the antics of a soldier who tried valiantly but unsuccessfully to slip his sabre into his scabbard the wrong way. But these things were of little consequence. What was important was that audiences were getting Cadillac quality opera at Ford prices of 75¢ to $2, plus 10 percent wartime tax.

Not only was the season an artistic success, but the deficit was extremely small. Box-office revenue after taxes provided an income of $30,143.72; libretto sales yielded an additional $190.19, so that the total intake was $30,333.91 against expenditures of $30,462.73—a loss of $128.82—for nine performances. These figures, of course, include only production costs. The financial statements show a substantially higher loss ($19,396.55) because they incorporate a pro-rata portion of the running expenses of the entire enterprise (rent, insurance, building maintenance, staff, etc.).

The near equality of cost and income almost defied belief. This incredibly foolhardy venture, producing opera, could be made economically self-sufficient while maintaining high quality and low admission prices. Halasz had clearly worked a miracle, and the board not only decided to offer a second opera season, but went so far as to double the length of the first. The period allocated was from May 1 to 14, 1944.

Unfortunately, Halasz lost three of his more important singers between these first two seasons—Martha Lipton and Hugh Thompson, both of whom were signed by the Met, and Jennie Tourel, who returned there after an eight-year absence. Thus began a problem that has plagued the company to this very day. The City Opera, whose budget has always been a mere fraction of the Met's, could never compete with the salaries offered by the larger house, nor could it vie with the prestige of a company that has boasted Enrico Caruso, Feodor Chaliapin, Geraldine Farrar, Titta Ruffo, Luisa Tetrazzini, and countless other performers of immortal stature. The majority of the leading American singers at the Met today have come via the City Opera—artists such as Mignon Dunn, Cornell MacNeil, Sherrill Milnes, Tatiana Troyanos, Shirley Verrett, and many others. Nor have these discoveries and losses been limited to native artists. José Carreras, Gilda Cruz-Romo, and Placido Domingo (and in the past Enzo Mascherini, Giuseppe Valdengo, and Ramon Vinay, to cite just a few) were all City Opera alumni at the time they joined the Met. Of course, there have been those who, like John Alexander and Beverly Sills, continued to sing at both houses, but they have been the exceptions rather than the rule.

Returning to 1944, however, Halasz had just two months to prepare his second season. Undaunted, he added three new productions to the repertoire—*La Bohème*, *Cavalleria*, and *Pagliacci*, and *La Traviata*—while holding over his initial season's offerings. Each of the new works featured at least one major debut, and the critical reception was undiminished.

The season began with *Carmen*, in which Dusolina Giannini took over Jennie Tourel's role, to unanimous acclaim. Harriett Johnson was representative of the press when she wrote: "Miss Giannini's Carmen had a bold and fiery (if rather youthful) quality, without being vulgar, and she played the part like a singing actress instead of an operatic soprano. Her voice, at the same time, had an exciting breadth of color, but her portrayal, rightly, was on playing a part rather than singing a role." Of the overall conception, she said: "Musical and artistic director Laszlo Halasz deserves credit for standing behind this kind of opera theatre rather than being content with turning out slick, routine productions."

Next, after a familiarly cast *Tosca*, was the company's initial *La Bohème*. The two sopranos, Irma Gonzalez (Mimi) and Natalie Bodanya (Musetta), were both new to the company, while tenor Mario Berini was appearing in his third City Opera premiere. Bodanya had been at the Met from 1936 to 1942, so her work was well known to the critics. The adjectives generally applied were "appealing," "charming," "lovely," and "vivacious," as they had been when she sang the role at the Met six years earlier. The real accolades were saved for Gonzalez, whose success seemed to presage a major international career.

The following night saw the company's first *Cavalleria* and *Pagliacci*, with Giannini as the unfortunate heroine of the first opera and Norina Greco, a former Metropolitan Aida, in the second.

If Irma Gonzalez somehow failed to achieve the stardom expected of her, the season's last major debutante, Dorothy Kirsten, more than made up for it. The former telephone operator from Montclair, New Jersey, was with the company for three seasons before being lured away by the Met, and during that time she created the leading soprano parts in *La Traviata, Manon Lescaut,* and *Faust.* Immediately hailed as a major find, she helped to ensure the artistic success of the company.

Now, with a repertoire of half a dozen operas, a noteworthy roster of artists, and a supportive press, the company was beginning to assume major proportions. Nonetheless, this second season was not successful at the box office. The first season's revenue had averaged $3,349.30 per performance; now it dropped to $2,692.50, a reduction of almost 20 percent. The reason was twofold. The season coincided with the New York appearance of Fortune Gallo's touring San Carlo Opera Company. Under normal circumstances, the competition would have been no more than a very minor problem. New York found itself in the midst of an unseasonably hot spell, however, and the City Center was not air-conditioned, while the Center Theater, which housed Gallo's troupe, was. Since the City Center did not yet have a subscription plan, tickets were purchased individually for each performance, and frequently at the last minute. Thus, weather became an important factor in ticket sales, and many of New York's opera-hungry population favored the cooler house.

A few days after the season's end, the board of directors held their first annual meeting, the most significant aspect of which was the decision not to renew Harry Friedgut's contract. They felt that as managing director he was not doing as good a job as they had anticipated, and this led to a particularly ugly situation that was described in a letter from Howard Cullman to Newbold Morris. Dated July 27, 1944, it says, in part:

I understand Harry Friedgut has gone in the managerial field, and I wish him good luck providing he does not try to embarrass us or pull any tricks. He evidently is trying to sign up all the young singers that Halasz uses in the opera under his management, with a proviso that they cannot sing at the City Center, which makes no sense. Among those he seemingly has signed up is John Hammill, with the provision that he cannot sing at the City Center, and he is one of our outstanding tenors. If we are going to treat Friedgut decently—and I want to, and we have—I think there is such a thing as reciprocity, but why he should go out to sabotage Halasz and the City Center makes no sense. I think you or the mayor should promptly have a talk with him. After all, we developed a lot of good singers—not to have Friedgut wreak vengeance on Halasz and try to take them away from us. In many years I have been in many enterprises and have made many mistakes, both on management and other situations. I felt that Friedgut was not the right director, did not get along well with the Board, antagonized those he should have been friendly to in the amusement business, and why there should be an international feud because we want another individual to operate the City Center makes no sense. It is simply a question of terminating a contract, which is not unique, either at City Hall or Broadway.

While a revelation of internal strife or dissatisfaction can in no way be detrimental thirty years after the fact, it can have a devastating effect at the time, and so, for the sake of public appearance, Friedgut had "resigned" his position, and Newbold Morris had accepted the resignation "with deep regret."

The problem of finding a replacement for Harry Friedgut was solved in a constructive, although high-handed, manner by Mayor La Guardia. His commissioner of licenses was Paul Moss, to whom he assigned, in addition to his regular duties, the task of assisting the president of the City Center on a part-time, nonsalaried basis. In effect, although his title was "assistant to the president," Moss's function was identical to Friedgut's. He had a theatrical background, having owned and operated a chain of motion picture and vaudeville houses for most of his life, and as the city's license commissioner since 1934, he exercised supervisory jurisdiction over theaters, movie houses, and ticket brokers, thereby providing a wealth of contacts. Moss was a good man for the job, and the saving of a fair-sized salary was a great boon for the company. The only negative feature, and a minor one at that, was that it reinforced the detrimental image of a municipally managed organization, which made fund-raising so difficult.

Moss's chief limitation was an absolute lack of knowledge about opera. Painfully aware of his shortcomings in this area, he appealed to Morton Baum, asking him to oversee the operation of the opera company. Baum agreed, and with his knowledge of finance, law, business, and music, he became the closest thing possible to a one-man board of directors, with the final word in all matters, monetary or artistic.

The third season was scheduled to run for two and a half weeks, from November 9 through 26. The opening opera would be Puccini's *Manon Lescaut*, a company first, which was being introduced primarily as a vehicle for Dorothy Kirsten. The company had temporarily lost Giannini; Kirsten and Gonzalez were now the main attractions.

The other new item in the repertoire was Johannn Strauss's *Gypsy Baron*, brought in to replace *Martha*, which was faring badly at the box office.

So far, the only part that luck had played in the company's history was an adverse one—the spring hot spell. Now, fortune smiled upon them.

The Philadelphia Opera Company, a seven-year-old organization that had been producing operas in English with reasonable success, had entered into a contract with Sol Hurok, who was gonig to take their *Merry Widow* on a twenty-week cross-country tour. Hurok had already signed contracts and made firm commitments to local impresarios when, without warning, the Philadelphia company went into bankruptcy. This left Hurok in a most embarassing position, and when Baum contacted him to offer the City Opera's *Gypsy Baron* as a substitute, Hurok was delighted, and the necessary legal documents were promptly drawn up and signed. For the Center, it meant a sizable guaranteed income and, at least as important, a great deal of prestige. Because of the esteem in which Hurok was held, appearing under his aegis was, in a sense, a coming of age. In addition, the company would be known nationally, and this might pave the way for future tours as well.

The Hurok contract guaranteed payment of $9,000 weekly to the City Center for the length of the tour. The Center would pay all operating costs out of that, but even the most conservative estimates showed a net profit of $25,000. In actual fact, the profit was not that great. Many illnesses on the road necessitated cast changes, additional rehearsals, and extra travel expenses for substitute artists, and the final figures showed a net gain of $16,119.76.

The tour opened in Hartford, Connecticut, on October 9, 1944, and closed in Pittsburgh on February 24, 1945, 128 performances later—128 performances and ten thousand miles of travel in 139 days! A performer's life was not an easy one.

One month after the tour started, the local season began. St. Louis did not have scenery specifically designed for *Manon Lescaut*, but they did have sets and costumes for Massenet's *Manon* that were, with only minor changes, suitable to the Puccini work. On opening night, Newbold Morris made a speech between Acts I and II in which he stated enthusiastically, but incorrectly, that the evening's tenor, William Horne, was the first American to sing the part of Des Grieux in New York.[1]

The critics were only lukewarm about the opera, although lavish in their praise of Kirsten, Horne, and Halasz, who was conducting. The public, however, greeted the work lovingly, and the company had another hit on its hands.

On November 11, there was a very important conducting debut, that

1. It had been sung at the Metropolitan by Brooklyn-born Frederick Jagel on February 8, 1930.

of Jean Paul Morel, considered by many to be second only to Pierre Monteux in the realm of French opera. His career at the Opéra-Comique had been cut short by the war, but he continued it at the Teatro Municipal in Rio de Janeiro and the Palacio de Bellas Artes in Mexico City before joining the City Opera staff.

The next two Saturdays, November 18 and 25, were the occasions of two other conducting debuts—Thomas Philipp Martin and Julius Rudel. Martin, born in Vienna, had previously worked with Halasz at the St. Louis Opera Company as choral director. In the years to come, working as a team, he and his wife, Ruth, would be known as America's leading translators of opera into English. Their *Marriage of Figaro* in particular is generally regarded as the outstanding example of the genre.

Rudel, like Martin, made his conducting debut leading *The Gypsy Baron*. He subsequently became the company's fourth general director, and at the time of his departure from the company (1980), the only member whose association dated back to the inaugural season.

The two-week period following the opera company's scheduled appearances had not been filled, and rather than have the house dark, the board decided to try a run of *The Gypsy Baron*. As a result, by the end of the third season, the total number of performances of opera at the City Center had grown to sixty-one.

Although there were three seasons during 1944, an operating pattern was now established between Baum and Halasz that would provide for two seasons each year—one in the fall preceding the Metropolitan Opera's season, and one in the spring after the Met closed its doors. This same pattern is still followed, although both companies have extended the lengths of their seasons significantly, so that there is now a period of several weeks annually during which their schedules overlap.

The City Opera continued to mount novelties over the years—*Eugène Onegin, Werther, Turandot, Salome, The Bartered Bride*, and a host of others. In addition, the standard repertoire was augmented to include *Rigoletto, Madama Butterfly, The Marriage of Figaro, Don Giovanni, Der Rosenkavalier*, etc. Many artists who would later become important figures in the operatic world secured their first major engagements with the City Opera—Eugene Conley, Frank Guarrera, Brenda Lewis, Gertrude Ribla, Frances Yeend, and others too numerous to mention.

In retrospect, with the advantage of hindsight, half a dozen events stand out in bold relief as being particularly noteworthy.

Of all the firsts to which the City Opera may lay claim, one of the finest is the debut of the black baritone Todd Duncan on September 28,

1945, as Tonio in *Pagliacci*. With his City Opera debut, Duncan became the first of his race to sing a leading role with a major American company, anticipating the Met's belated elimination of racial barriers by a decade.[2]

Another outstanding and propitious event, although certainly no one could have known it at the time, was the engagement of John S. White by the company in spring 1946. White had arrived in New York from Vienna in 1938. At about that time Morton Baum, who had always been a devout music lover, decided to learn French, Italian, and German to further enhance his enjoyment of opera. A friend of his who, having known White in Austria, was aware of his extraordinary linguistic abilities, brought the two men together, and a strong friendship blossomed. White subsequently served in the army, but when he was discharged in 1945, he resumed contact with Baum, who tried to find a position for him with City Opera. At Baum's suggestion, Halasz engaged White as the company's first language coach. Over the years, he has served in a variety of functions, on both the artistic end, as a stage director, and the administrative. Until very recently he was the company's managing director, with tremendous authority in all matters concerning the plans and running of the organization, and currently (1981), although retired, he is still retained as a consultant.

Halasz was always partial to the operas of Richard Strauss, and he considers the City Opera production of *Ariadne auf Naxos* to be the high-water mark of his directorship. *Ariadne* had been produced in New York at an earlier date, December 5, 1934, but this was a student production at the Juilliard School of Music. The first professional performance here was City Opera's, on October 10, 1946. The cast was superb— Ella Flesch in the title role, Vasso Argyris as Bacchus, Ralph Herbert as Harlequin, and particularly, as Zerbinetta, Virginia MacWatters, who demonstrated a voice of crystal clarity and limpid beauty, combined with a coloratura flexibility that left the listener in awe. Halasz feels that with the *Ariadne* production the company took its place alongside the major opera companies of the world.

He had always championed the young American singer, and probably did more to encourage native talent than anyone else up to that time. Yet he was realistic enough to know that box office was closely tied in with a certain mystique and glamour that could, for the most part, be supplied only by foreign artists. Accordingly, he made a practice of engaging several outstanding European performers each season. Aside from providing this glamour that was so necessary a part of Halasz's operational plan, the

2. Marian Anderson, the first black singer to appear at the Met, made her debut on January 7, 1955, as Ulrica in Verdi's *Un Ballo in Maschera*.

imported singers generally came with a great deal of experience, some of which could be imparted to the newcomers to the field. Nevertheless, his engagement of non-Americans became a source of great irritation to several members of the company. In the years of breast-beating chauvinism that followed World War II, certain views prevailed that would be totally unacceptable by today's standards. Indicative of the attitudes of some members of the company was a letter sent to Morton Baum by a member of the chorus, whose contract was not renewed at the time it expired:

Dear Mr. Baum:

You, as a member of the board of "City Center", should know the following I feel. I have spoken to you & think that you are a just person—

I have just written to Mr. Halasz to demand an answer as to why I have been excluded from the Spring Season of City Center—I will quote what I have written to him—

"It seems to me that as an American of *300 years on American Soil* ancestry, I would have infinitely more right to this job than some newly arrived refugee to this country, & as far as voice goes, you as a good musician must admit (if you will be honest) that my voice was second to none in the company, let alone the chorus. That you consider me too tall is perhaps because others are so short! You have but to ask any member of your board if my stage appearance was not as good as anyone's. You know also I have never been late for rehearsals & have been absolutely trustworthy. When I was ill last season, I worked like a slave to learn those 39 pages of "Eugene Onegin" with the result that anyone of my neighbors in the alto section will tell you that I knew it better than they did.

"So, Mr. Halasz I demand an answer as to why without a word you have replaced me with one of your friends—Justice is Justice. I will write to the Mayor & all the papers in N.Y. as the story of City Center & how it works should be told if you do not answer. It is not for the money but for my own satisfaction & pride—why should you behave like this to me who have been in City Center from the beginning & have a Conservatory Diploma French & Italian & the finest training three countries could give? Besides a musical background of centuries second to none.

"I have never complained at your injustice in never giving me an opportunity for a small role, though others are glad to get me. I have realized I could never rise higher with you in power, but it was a job & I live in N.Y. & pay taxes here & this is above all, more my country than some whippersnapper's just off the boat yesterday. I have a right to earn my bread in this country. That I was educated with no expense spared was because my father had an income of about the same as you, Mr. Halasz, but we lost all in the Depression —that I was born in the Social Register is a tribute to breeding & not to money & I have found that unfortunately being a lady & speaking grammatically has been more of a handicap than otherwise in a career."

This ends Mr. Baum what I have just written Mr. Halasz. The truth of which is easy to verify. That I feel deeply hurt is beyond the point.

One of the most important events of this period was the 1948 tour to Chicago. From its earliest days, the company had given occasional out-of-house performances—a *Rigoletto* here, a *Madama Butterfly* there; and of course there was the extended *Gypsy Baron* tour under Hurok. But this was the company's first organized tour under its own leadership. With this extended trip to Chicago, consisting of eighteen performances between December 1 and December 19, and with its unprecedented use of native talent, the company was starting to take on the aspects of an American opera company, rather than a local New York organization. In years to come, it would champion American opera as well as American artists, through grants, commissions, and frequency of performances.

The year 1949 was an eventful one for the company. The spring season was witness to its first world premiere, *Troubled Island* by composer William Grant Still, with libretto by Langston Hughes. The performance took place on March 31, and featured an extremely strong cast, led by Robert Weede, Marie Powers, and Oscar Natzka. Two minor roles were sung by Frances Bible, a mezzo-soprano of outstanding talent. The opera was not successful, however, and remained in the repertoire for only one season, but it is important as the first of many American premieres that would eventually be offered.

During the fall, on November 1, Sergei Prokofiev's *Love for Three Oranges* was the unlikely choice for a new addition to the repertoire. A work commissioned by the Chicago Opera in 1921, it had never achieved success anywhere. Its music was totally unfamiliar except for the processional march, and that was known only because it was chosen as the theme song for the popular radio series "The F.B.I. in Peace and War." It was as odd a choice as possible, but it became one of the most popular operas in the repertoire. During this and the next four seasons, until Halasz's departure from the company, it became the company's most frequently performed opera, almost always to sold-out houses.

This, then, is a cross-sectional view of Laszlo Halasz's New York City Center Opera Company—progressive, dynamic, and imaginative. In the few years of its existence, it went from a fear-filled dream to a respected and vital company, whose blend of theater and music would leave an indelible impression on all other domestic companies. The effect of its production standards was profound. Opera would never be the same again.

10

The Flying Baton

DURING the 1951 tour season, on November 24, Halasz was conducting Puccini's *Madama Butterfly* at the Chicago Opera House. Since the cast was a familiar one, nothing unusual was anticipated that evening. However, during the last act, the baton left Halasz's hand and fell at the feet of first cellist Suzette Forgues.[1] The concertmaster, Albert Bruening, later claimed that it had been thrown at him. At the time, however, the incident went unnoticed; Ms. Forgues returned the baton to Halasz, and the performance continued without a missed beat. Several days (and performances) later, Jean Paul Morel was about to conduct a *Carmen* when James C. Petrillo, president of the American Federation of Musicians, Local 802, arrived backstage and demanded that Halasz publicly apologize to Bruening for "throwing" his baton, or there would be no performance that night. Halasz, hastily summoned from his hotel, met with Petrillo in the presence of the full orchestra. The union leader reiterated his demands, but Halasz explained that there was no reason to apologize, since the baton had merely slipped. Petrillo was adamant, and Halasz equally so, creating a stalemate. Finally, the awkward situation was resolved by Petrillo's asking, "If you had thrown the baton, would you apologize?" To which Halasz replied, "Yes, if I had thrown the baton, I would apologize, but since I did not throw the baton, I refuse to apologize." Petrillo deemed this sufficient, and within minutes, the familiar opening chords of *Carmen* resounded throughout the house. The incident appeared

1. Halasz and Ms. Forgues, a former student of the great cellist Emanuel Feuermann, were married on July 22, 1953.

to be resolved, but Petrillo was later quoted by the *New York Times* as saying, "If that guy throws one more baton or anything else, out he goes. I'll throw him out myself."

In a field replete with artistic personality clashes, this incident seems trivial, possibly even humorous, but it was symptomatic of the dissension growing between Halasz and certain members of his company. As a footnote, during that very same *Carmen* performance the baton left Morel's hand twice, but nobody complained.

In retrospect, the seed of Halasz's problems had taken root earlier that year, when he locked horns with the board of directors over what he considered his artistic province. In his role as company director he was constantly examining scores with an eye toward new productions. In the past, these had included William Grant Still's *Troubled Island* (world premiere) and the American stage premiere of Richard Strauss's *Ariadne auf Naxos*. The score that now arrested Halasz's attention was *The Dybbuk* by David and Alex Tamkin, based on the immortal play by Sholom Ansky. For the spring 1951 season, the board had agreed on two new productions, Verdi's *Falstaff* and the world premiere of *The Dybbuk*. Toward the end of 1950, the City Center board found its financial situation even more precarious than usual due to a $50,000 loss incurred by the ballet company resulting from an unsuccessful English tour, the outbreak of the Korean War, and a costly new production of *Die Meistersinger*. In addition, the City Center Drama division, which could normally be counted upon to offset other losses, had experienced difficulties that cut its profit of $80,000 (1949) to about $10,000 (1950). As a result, the board revised its plans, and the directors instructed Halasz to cancel all new productions. He argued that it was just such new productions that kept public interest high. Without them, although there would be a smaller capital outlay, the savings would be outweighed by the reduced box-office receipts. Finally a compromise measure was reached. *The Dybbuk* would be presented in the spring, but *Falstaff* would be deferred. Halasz proceeded along these lines.

On January 16, 1951, the board of directors convened for their monthly meeting and the prime topic of conversation was, of course, the financial plight. Halasz had been asked to attend that meeting, and he was told that *The Dybbuk*, like *Falstaff*, must be dropped. Other economies were also to be put into effect. There were to be no European artists during the spring 1951 season as their transatlantic transportation costs taxed the budget too heavily; *Der Rosenkavalier*, *Tales of Hoffmann*, and *Turandot*, all very expensive to perform because of the large cast and chorus requirements, would be eliminated; and if Halasz felt so strongly that a new production was needed, he could do Massenet's *Manon*, using the scenery and costumes that had been previously utilized for Puccini's *Manon Lescaut*.

He objected strenuously, pointing out that numerous commitments for *The Dybbuk* had already been made, and, even if they were withdrawn, many people would be legally entitled to receive payment. Moreover, it would all be a great source of embarrassment to both the institution and himself. Nonetheless, the board was unyielding; their attitude was summed up by Howard Cullman, who declared that "a moral commitment to the composer was not too important"![2]

The debate continued, and it became progressively apparent that some members of the board felt that *The Dybbuk* was a poor choice. When the music was criticized Halasz pointed out that no one there could be familiar with it as the work had never been performed. Apparently, there was some confusion between the Tamkin opera and another setting of the dybbuk legend, by Lodovico Rocca, that had been presented in Detroit and at Carnegie Hall in 1936. In the midst of this discussion, according to the minutes, "Mrs. Reis stated that Mr. Halasz should be asked to submit new works to the board before he makes commitments to do them, in order to get the opinion of the members, to which Mr. Morris agreed."

Halasz felt that his artistic decisions, after twenty years of experience and demonstrably sound judgment, should not be subject to the whim of a board of directors consisting primarily of dilettantes. Returning to the theater, he drafted this letter:

Dear Mr. Morris:

Once in a while in our lives we arrive at crossroads where practical thinking and our conscience come into conflict. The recent resolution of the Board has put me in just such a situation. I have to justify three loyalties—one is to the institution to which we have all given so much; another is to our audiences which are the moving spirit of all our accomplishments and a third is my own conscience.

I have gone along with the necessary curtailment of expenses in cutting *Rosenkavalier*, *Turandot*, and *Tales of Hoffmann* from our repertoire, in reduction of the roster, and deferring the production of *Falstaff*, but I simply cannot reconcile cancellation of *The Dybbuk* for which artistic plans and production commitments have been made and which represents that last link to a first rate and progressive theatre. From the bottom of my heart I feel if all these "economies" were carried out the artistic standing and pioneering status

2. Minutes of the meeting of the executive committee on January 16, 1951

of our institution—which has taken years to build—would deteriorate to such a point that I cannot be instrumental in carrying thru these orders.

I well realize that the reasons for these decisions were strictly dictated by the unfortunate financial condition of our institution, but I am convinced that the lowering of the artistic standards will only further and not relieve these problems.

As to the solution of the present predicament, we need funds which can and should be gotten (1) by raising of the price of our best seats to the level which will correspond with the actual value given, (2) by public contributions. The basis for both of these is our uncompromising adherence to the standard and principles which we have achieved, or even improvement of them, for which there is ample space.

To explain all my thoughts to the Board was not possible in the short minutes I was granted; to carry thru the Board's decision against my honest convictions to the contrary would involve bad faith on my part: therefore I must ask you to relieve me of my duties.

I want to thank you for the wonderful association which you have made possible during the past seven years and I wish to assure you that I will be available in any explanatory capacity to anyone who will take over the directorship of the opera company. I hope that time will prove I am wrong but at this moment I am so convinced to the contrary that I am compelled to take the painful step I am taking.

Two days later he met with his staff, described his encounter with the board, and asked them to present a united front by signing the following letter, which he had prepared:

We, the undersigned members of the staff of the New York City Opera Company have heard, to our great consternation, a report from Mr. Halasz that the Board of Directors of the City Center of Music and Drama has requested the management of the opera company to further curtail the repertory by eliminating another new production from its spring season. It is our firm conviction that this demand would imply a distinct lowering of the artistic standard this institution has reached in its seven-year-old history and in which new productions have played the most important part. We want to stress that we fully understand the financial strain under which the City Center Opera has to work and we have tried to achieve maximum artistic results within a practically unparalleled low budget. Further restricting as recommended by the Board would be in conflict with our artistic conscience. Should the decision of the Board with its consequences prove to be irrevocable, we would, to our utmost regret, and in solidarity with Mr. Halasz, feel ourselves compelled to ask to be relieved from our obligations in connection with the coming opera season.

The staff supported Halasz, and the letter was signed by Thomas Martin, Jean Paul Morel, Joseph Rosenstock, Julius Rudel, Lee Shaynen, and John S. White.

Upon receipt of these resignations, Baum immediately called a meeting of those involved, explained that *The Dybbuk* cancellation was due solely to financial, not artistic, reasons, and that it would be mounted in the fall of 1951, finances permitting. Then he issued an ultimatum. The spring season would go on with or without these seven men. If necessary, he, Morton Baum, would assume direction of the company. However, he would allow any of the men to withdraw their resignations, but this must be done within twenty-four hours. They all agreed to stay, and Halasz was permitted to save face by stating that, with *The Dybbuk* promised for the fall, the reasons for his resignation no longer existed. From that point on, however, Halasz's City Opera career was doomed. He had engaged in a test of strength against the directorate and lost.

The spring season, which opened on March 14 with the company's fifth performance of *Die Meistersinger*, proved relatively unexciting. It consisted of standard City Opera fare—*Madama Butterfly, Carmen, Love for Three Oranges, La Bohème,* etc. Despite the board's original decision, *Tales of Hoffmann* was held over, but for only two performances. The one novelty was *Manon*, which entered the repertoire on March 22, and was presented three times with the four principal parts shared by Ann Ayars and Eva Likova as Manon, David Poleri and Rudolph Petrak as Des Grieux, Carlton Gauld and Norman Scott as the Count, and Ralph Herbert and James Pease as Lescaut. All performances were conducted by Jean Morel, and one of the many highlights of the evening was the dancing of Marina Svetlova.

About the premiere, *New York World Telegram and Sun* critic Louis Biancolli wrote:

Acting on the principle that the best gifts come in small packages, the City Center opera staged a compact and brilliant revival of Massenet's *Manon* last night.

There was proof all through the production that the center is the perfect house for so intimate and concentrated an opera as *Manon*—and equal proof that Mr. Halasz's company is the perfect little huddle of artists for such a house.

The performance positively shone with freshness. The sets were beautiful, and the costumes looked as if they were worth a king's ransom—which is remarkable, considering that Mr. Halasz's budget is so tiny it would be lost in one pigeonhole of the Metropolitan box office.

Biancolli concluded his review: "The whole production was another dazzling feather in Mr. Halasz's growing cap. I'd like to refer to his company as the 'Little Met' with the proviso that 'Little' be accepted as referring only to size."

The balance of the season was routine, with no other outstanding successes or failures, closing on April 22 with the company's seventeenth *Aïda*.

At this point, a serious situation arose involving Mary Kreste, one of the mezzo-sopranos. She had been part of the City Opera since its inception, first as a chorister, then later as a soloist alternating minor roles (such as Mamma Lucia in *Cavalleria Rusticana* and Annina in *La Traviata*) with somewhat larger ones (Suzuki in *Madama Butterfly*, Hérodias in *Salome*, and Marcellina in *Marriage of Figaro*). In all, she had appeared as a soloist 172 times. With the close of the spring season, her then current contract had expired, and since there were no options in force, Halasz instructed Rudel, his musical assistant, to negotiate a new contract along similar lines, but with a slight salary increase. Specifically, she had earned $100 per week during the spring of 1949, and $110 during the next two seasons. Halasz was now offering $118 weekly and essentially the same repertoire as before. Rudel met her on May 4 and extended Halasz's offer, which she declined, demanding $125 and the opportunity to sing Amneris. Halasz refused these terms and Rudel so advised Kreste, but she was unwilling to accept less.

Therefore, on May 12, Halasz began negotiations with artists' representative Ludwig Lustig for the services of his client, mezzo-soprano Margery Mayer, who had appeared with the company intermittently over the years. Mayer sang all of the larger roles in Kreste's repertoire—at least in those operas that were currently being planned—and the roles remaining could easily be filled by choristers just as Kreste herself had done. On June 22, the terms of Mayer's contract were set. The only role that might produce any casting difficulties was Marcellina in *The Marriage of Figaro*, as Mayer was not an outstanding comedienne, but this gap could be easily filled by Eunice Alberts, who had just sung a highly satisfactory audition on June 20. Thus, when Mary Kreste contacted Rudel on July 9 to say that she had reconsidered Halasz's offer, there was no longer any need for her services. Nonetheless, she requested a meeting with Halasz, which took place on July 16.

He explained that the needs in the mezzo department were filled, but for the sake of backup coverage and a certain amount of variety in casting, he was willing to offer her $100 per week, for which she could be called upon three times, and if this figure were ever exceeded, she would be compensated on a pro-rata basis. Kreste answered that $100 was in-sufficient, but she would now agree to the $118 he had originally offered. This was unacceptable to him, however, as that offer was extended when her services were a need rather than a luxury. He pointed out the com-pany's financial straits, but approved her request to go directly to Morton Baum for authorization for the higher amount. The only problem, he warned her, was one of time. This was Monday; on Wednesday, just two days later, he had to leave for the Midwest to arrange the fall tour, and the season's brochure had to go to the printer. He needed a definite answer by the eighteenth or it would be too late.

Kreste lost no time in seeing Baum—she saw him that afternoon, in fact. His position was noncommital. He would be willing to go along with the request for $118, and he agreed that the amount was not excessive, but he refused to make the ultimate decision.

He advised her to contact Halasz again. She did so by letter, rather than in person, and one would expect that she would have written im-mediately and hand-delivered the letter in view of the urgency. However, inexplicably, she delayed writing until the eighteenth, and when the letter arrived at Halasz's office, he had already left on his trip and Alberts's contract had been finalized. Furthermore, Kreste apparently had another change of heart, as she again requested $125.

The full text of her letter was:

My dear Mr. Halasz:

In reference to our talk of July 16, 1951, I am writing you and sending copy of same to Mr. Morton Baum in order to bring into sharper focus my work, years and remuneration at the City Center.

As you know I have been with the company from the first as a chorister for a weekly fee of $55.25. Later some major and minor roles were assigned to me for $57.50 weekly including extra choral fees for *Carmen* and *Butterfly*. In 1946 the weekly rate of $78.00 for solo-work, but still singing *Carmen* chorus. In 1949—no more chorus—now a full-fledged soloist at $90.00 per week. One season's absence—Spring 1949 because of ill health resulting from a premature return to work in 1948 only three weeks after a major operation. In 1949 Spring—per performance fees, sum total of which was $560.00. In 1950 Fall and Spring weekly fee of $100.00. In 1951 Fall and Spring weekly fee of $110.00.

The following is a list of performed operas at City Center: *Aïda, Salome, Meistersinger, Butterfly, Pelléas, Onegin, Cav. Rusticana, Traviata, Bartered Bride, Gypsy Baron, Faust, Barber of Seville, Flying Dutchman, Old Maid and Thief, Andrea Chenier, Marriage of Figaro, Love for Three Oranges, Pirates of Pen.* Sometimes two roles in these operas.

I would like to point out that I sang quite a few performances for indisposed artists, some at a moment's notice. My own scheduled performances and rehearsals were never missed in all the years at the Center. The Chicago season of 1948 a perfect example of my undaunting spirited effort in behalf of the company, with a list of 17 out of 21 performances after a heavy season in New York.

My request is from the present $110.00 to $125.00 per week. Surely with the enormously high cost of living the request is a modest one.

Please consider all the aspects of my letter carefully and kindly grant me another interview soon. Thank you.

This was forwarded to Halasz in Chicago, arriving on July 25, but it was too late.

Halasz returned to New York on August 6, and on August 9 he received a call from Baum, who said that Kreste was complaining about being fired because she had gone over Halasz's head (it should be kept in mind that she was certainly not dismissed as there was no contract in force; she simply was not reengaged, which is a very different matter). Baum thereupon accused Halasz of unethical practices. Halasz stewed over this a bit, gathered his data, and on August 15 he wrote a very bitter letter to Baum explaining the entire situation, stating:

That Miss Kreste is the victim of her own decisions, I cannot help. Why at this time this matter had to come up and in the form it has with the reaction you have had is beyond my comprehension. It is utterly unfair and the fact that you listen to outside gossip and make up your mind instead of requesting and listening to some of the facts from this side is degrading to your integrity as well as my own.

The Halasz-Baum relationship, strained in January by the mass resignation, was in no way improved by this letter.

On August 20, Kreste wrote to the American Guild of Musical Artists (AGMA), relating the incident, but significantly omitting any conversations prior to July 16.

Gentlemen:

On July 16, 1951, I was called to see Mr. Halasz in his office at City Center in order to negotiate a new contract. In the course of our talk I asked for a raise of $15.00 which would bring my present salary of $110.00 to $125.00 per week. Mr. Halasz rejected this request basing his rejection on budgetary difficulties which could not bear the slightest increase in salaries. He told me to contact Mr. Baum who apportions the available money, and see whether any fund could be made available for me.

I contacted Mr. Baum the same afternoon. He thought my request was not immoderate and advised me to write a letter to Mr. Halasz. I wrote this letter on July 18, 1951 reiterating my request for a raise in salary, gave a complete account of my work, time spent with the company, and salaries received, and asked for another interview. I sent a copy of that letter to Mr. Baum. (Please see attached letter.) Since then I have not heard from either of the gentlemen, and no doubt have been dropped from the company.

Word has reached me that my action in appealing to Mr. Baum has been interpreted at the opera office as "unethical" and I may therefore assume that this has been the reason for my dismissal.

I would appreciate your investigation of this case. It is indeed strange, to say the least, that the manager of the City Center Opera Company advises me to get in touch with a director of the Board and after I have done so, dismisses me as a punishment for having followed his advice. Is this a conspiracy on the part of these men to double deal with an artist and use it as an excuse to discharge her?

AGMA, like Kreste, delayed in answering. On September 4, the Guild's executive secretary, Hyman R. Faine, wrote a very militant letter to Newbold Morris which said, in part: "These instances tend to create the feeling in the members of the Company of a lack of confidence in the management of the Company and unless this injustice is remedied, I will not be able to be responsible for the actions of the other AGMA members."

On September 25, the following letter was sent to Halasz, with copies to Baum, Morris, and Faine:

Dear Mr. Halasz:

At a meeting held on September 24th of the special committee appointed by the Board of Directors of the City Center of Music and Drama, Inc., to investigate and take positive action on the claim of Miss Mary Kreste, the following motion was introduced and unanimously adopted:—

That the committee, having heard full evidence, decided to reinstate Miss Mary Kreste at her former salary of $110.00 per week for the two seasons, fall of 1951 and spring of 1952, and that she be assigned roles comparable to those which she sang in the past two seasons.

Faithfully yours,

(signed)
Macklin Marrow
Chairman, Special Committee

Clearly Halasz had lost the support of the board. But there were far greater repercussions, which will soon become apparent. To complete the

Kreste saga, however, she was reengaged at $110 per week for the seven-week season, and sang nine times. Margery Mayer sang seventeen performances and Eunice Alberts five. Of Kreste's nine performances, five had been previously assigned to choristers Ethel Greene and Carroll Taussig. Ironically, Halasz was later accused of improper conduct in making these promises and then not keeping them.

With the approach of the fall season, the City Center Opera Company was an armed camp.

11

The Dybbuk and the Devil to Pay

CITY OPERA OFFERS *DYBBUK* PREMIERE

The New York City Opera Company gave last night in the City Center of Music and Drama the premiere of David Tamkin's opera *The Dybbuk*, after the famous play of S. Ansky.

The production of a very difficult and individual work, which asks the utmost—musically and dramatically—of its interpreters, was one of the most brilliant and revealing that this enterprising company has given of any of its novelties. The opera itself is in some respects the most original and important of the five American works that have figured in its repertory.—

Olin Downes, *New York Times*, October 6, 1951

Downes's enthusiasm was, if anything, surpassed by that of Robert Coleman, the drama critic of the *Daily Mirror*. After witnessing the second performance, on October 10, he wrote:

DYBBUK MODERN MUSIC DRAMA AT ITS BEST

The venturesome New York City Opera Company has scored another resounding hit with the Tamkin brothers' musical version of S. Ansky's folk play, *The Dybbuk*. We have seen many productions of this classic in our time, but this is by all odds the most exciting. Here is modern music drama at its best.

. . . Laszlo Halasz, guiding genius of the New York City Opera Company, is entitled to several bows for his courage in presenting *The Dybbuk*. Operating on a limited budget, he has built an organization of which New York should be proud. He has produced works that even the august Metropolitan, with all its resources, would not attempt. And they have almost invariably been successes.

Every ticket for the scheduled performances of *The Dybbuk* has been sold, including an extra matinee. There are lines daily at the City Center box-office, but there are no tickets. So, we think the Board of Directors of the City Center of Music and Drama should consider extending the current opera season. *The Dybbuk*, in our opinion, could pack the Center for several weeks.

In the event that the Board should act favorably on our suggestion, we earnestly urge you to see and hear *The Dybbuk*, for it is extraordinary, magnificent music-theatre.

Halasz's confidence in the opera was rewarded by press and public alike. Coleman referred to an extra matinee, but before the season's end, a second unscheduled performance was added bringing the total to five. The success was due, in large part, to the work itself, a superb blend of text and music. Much of the credit, however, falls to the cast. Robert Rounseville was ideal as Channon, the tormented soul whose spirit takes over the body of his beloved; Leah, the victim of this supernatural possession was Patricia Neway, one of the finest dramatic sopranos of the day, making her company debut; and Joseph Rosenstock on the conductor's podium kept the entire performance at a feverish pitch of tension.

The success of *The Dybbuk* in no way improved Halasz's relationship with his board of directors. If anything, there was a further deterioration, because in addition to the previous difficulties, there was now an added sense of embarrassment.

The season had opened on September 27 with the fourth performance of *Manon*. James Pease replaced Ralph Herbert as Lescaut, but the cast was otherwise identical to that of the premiere, and the critical enthusiasm remained undiminished. Apart from *The Dybbuk*, the major event of fall 1951 was the first American performance of Wolf-Ferrari's *I Quattro Rusteghi*, a thoroughly enchanting work that deserves far greater public exposure than it has had until now. Again the company put its best foot forward in terms of casting, and the audience enjoyed the antics of Dorothy MacNeil, Ellen Faull, Frances Yeend, Margery Mayer, Gean Greenwell, and Richard Wentworth in the leading roles. Halasz conducted, the stage director was the brilliant Otto Erhardt, and the delightful English translation of Edward J. Dent was used.

Everything about *The Four Ruffians*, to give it its English title, was charming, and the cast was perfect. Yeend's last-act outburst against the tyranny of the four pigheaded boors of the title was a vocal tour de force, but the real star was baritone Emile Renan, who managed to transform the relatively small part of Cancian into the opera's most outstanding character.

Olin Downes expressed enthusiasm for the work, and on October 19, his *New York Times* review read, in part:

The piece is a delectable little bon-bon of a comic opera, or "opera buffa" essentially after the Italian tradition. It is a work in a special genre, delightfully contrived by librettist and composer; artistically and most amusingly set forth by Laszlo Halasz, who conducted, and his cast of artists; by Otto Erhardt, whose stage direction was a triumph of wit and sensitiveness to the text and music; by Charles Weidmann's original and imaginative choreography in the comedy spirit; and by Mstislav Dobujinsky, whose curtains and stage sets were not the least important and original feature of the production.

One could continue in this vein, in praise of Ruth Morley's masks and costumes, and indeed of every factor that enters into a brilliant operatic production. And the charming little opera amply deserves the interpretation it received.

The season proceeded very well until October 23, when tragedy struck. During the first act of *Die Meistersinger*, New Zealand basso Oscar Natzka, who was singing the part of Veit Pogner, suffered a heart attack. He staggered into the wings, unnoticed by the audience because of the usual commotion onstage at that time, and only one intimately familiar with the music would have missed his lines in the closing ensemble. During the intermission, Norman Scott hurriedly got into costume, and the performance continued without delay, the audience unaware of what had occurred. Natzka was rushed to the hospital and lingered for almost two weeks, but finally succumbed on November 5.

The New York season concluded on November 11, and the company headed West, for performances in Chicago, Detroit, East Lansing, and Milwaukee. Since neither *The Dybbuk* nor *The Four Ruffians* was included, the tour was unspectacular, although consistently at a high level. In retrospect, although no one could realize it at the time, one of the most important features of that season was the engagement of Thomas Schippers— not quite twenty-one—as an assistant conductor and music coach. Already hailed on the podium and championed by Gian Carlo Menotti, Schippers would, within the next few years, come to be regarded as an outstanding *wunderkind*. For now, however, he was considered no more than a competent conductor and an extremely capable coach.

When the tour ended on December 9, Halasz was deservedly jubilant. His two premieres had both been acclaimed, the overall level of the season was high, and, for the first time, the company showed a significant profit. The *Gypsy Baron* tour back in spring 1945 had yielded a gain of

$16,119.76,[1] but the local season had lost $17,842.34, for a net loss of $1,722.58; fall 1948 had a loss, at home, of about $14,000, but combined with the tour profits, the company was in the black to the extent of $665.19. Every other season had resulted in a loss, ranging from a low of $6,387.89 (spring 1950) to a high of $35,222.18 (fall 1946). This current season there was an incredible profit of $29,085.71 ($30,252.26 loss at home; $59,337.97 profit on tour). Halasz had good reason to be excited. He had achieved the near impossible—finally making opera profitable, without sacrificing quality.

He returned to New York on December 16, and two days later received a call from Newbold Morris. It seems that some company members had lodged very serious complaints, and Halasz was asked to appear before the board of directors on December 21. Morris refused to reveal the exact charges, or the sources, but in general, Halasz was accused of rudeness, foul and abusive language, and destroying company morale by his autocratic manner and unfair methods of casting. Since the company was between seasons, many of its staff were away, but during the next day and a half, Halasz contacted as many members as he could possibly reach, asking for a vote of confidence. He arrived at the board meeting armed with forty-five letters, which did not necessarily refute the specific charges; after all, he had not been told what the actual charges were. However, the testimonials clearly indicated that a large segment of the company stood behind him.

One of the most eloquent of these letters came from Carroll Taussig, a chorister who occasionally appeared in small roles, but who assumed a far greater importance as a member of the governing board of AGMA and one of the people designated to act as liaison between the union and the company. Ms. Taussig's letter was as follows:

Dear Mr. Morris:

I am a member of the New York City Opera chorus and comprimaria group. I have worked with the company since its beginning, in the year 1944, [and] therefore, I feel that I know something about the company and the way in which it has been run.

I am also a member of the board of governors of A.G.M.A.

Last Tuesday, December 18, during the A.G.M.A. board meeting, complaints against Mr. Halasz were brought to our attention. Certain members of the company had stated that they were unable to work with Mr. Halasz for various reasons, and would resign unless prevailing conditions were changed. It seems that your board of governors is seriously considering two measures:

1. All figures taken from the City Center's financial statements.

(1) The immediate dismissal of Mr. Halasz
(2) The appointment of someone with authority over him to deal with personnel matters until Mr. Halasz's contract terminated.

On the basis of the one-sided discussion that followed, I checked with Miss Colfer at the New York City Opera office for further information. I found out that a group of people wrote letters to your board of governors and to the union indicting Mr. Halasz on the following counts:

(1) An autocratic way of running the company
(2) Bad manners—violent actions—foul language
(3) Unjust methods of casting

I consider these charges unfair—naturally I can give my reasons only from my personal experience in working for Mr. Halasz—I hope, however, that in my small way to right an injustice.

Let us consider count No. 1—Mr. Halasz's autocratic way of running the company:

Is a man who is available at all times to the "least" of his employees, autocratic?

Is an opera manager who never refuses a member of the company an audition when requested, autocratic?

Is an opera manager who welcomes chorus members to come into solo rehearsals to study roles, autocratic?

Is an opera manager who allows chorus members to work themselves up from the ranks to a solo capacity, autocratic?

Since I have been with Mr. Halasz, he has always been ready to see me when I had a problem; he has always given me auditions when I requested them; has always allowed me to attend the soloists rehearsals; and has certainly allowed me to work up to the rank of soloist (I am now in the category of comprimaria on the roster).

With these questions in mind, compare him with other impresarios in the field!

Count No. 2—Foul language—violent actions—rude manners—inconsiderateness.

During the whole time that I have been at the City Center I have never heard Mr. Halasz use foul language. During his bursts of anger he becomes sarcastic—but that is as far as he ever goes. In my experience he has never become disagreeable without ample cause! As a Union delegate I have never found it necessary to lodge a complaint against him for—bad language—violent actions—inconsiderate treatment—or, for that matter, anything else. As for his "bad manners"—I have found him to be unfailingly civil—extremely courteous—and extremely considerate of people working with him. He drives people hard, but he never asks things of them that he would not do himself. When provoked to anger, he's pretty alarming—but never without just cause— and, never beyond the line of complete decency.

Count No. 3—Unjust methods of casting.

As I understood it, complaints have been made on the method of assigning and rehearsing roles—the process of assigning two people to the same role— then of observing them at rehearsals—finally selecting the one best suited to the needs of the production for the first performance. This is called by those who don't like it "a method of pitting people against one another—unfair competition leading to destruction of morale." What's unfair about it? Two people are selected as possibilities for a role and compete for it—this happens all the time in other companies—in all of the performing fields. Now I speak from the "loser's standpoint"—Many's the time I've lost out in the competition after having been one of the two people selected for a small role—so what! The other person was more suitable! Naturally I was disappointed, but I didn't rush madly around screaming "unfair competition! You promised that role to ME!"

In conclusion, I want to say that I believe that Mr. Halasz has done a great service for opera in New York City and throughout the country. For one thing he has broken the monopoly of the Metropolitan Opera in this town by producing in the short space of seven years, on a stringent budget, first class opera-theatre. His judgment of native talent has been so fine, that time and again the Metropolitan Opera Company have taken his soloists to be permanent members of their organization. I have worked for opera companies all over the country—and—nowhere else have I found such an excellent opportunity for concentrated study of opera, from the ground up! Nowhere else have I had a chance to rise and better myself steadily, quietly, without recourse to influence—politics—or "cash on the side"; and, for this great benefit I heartily thank and admire Mr. Halasz!

Most sincerely,

Carroll Wright Taussig

Armed with this type of support, and a triumphant season behind him, Halasz expected nothing more severe than a possible tongue-lashing. The most objective and impersonal way of commenting on the board meeting is by quoting from the actual minutes as prepared by the secretary, Claire M. Reis.

MEETING OF THE BOARD OF DIRECTORS OF THE
CITY CENTER OF MUSIC AND DRAMA, INC.
HELD IN THE EXECUTIVE OFFICES ON
FRIDAY, DECEMBER 21, 1951, AT 2:30 P.M.

THERE WERE PRESENT: Mesdames Hull, Pratt, Reis and Tibbett; Messrs. Baum, Delany, Feinberg, Mack, Marrow, Morgenthau, Morris, Suber, Umhey, Warburg and Warner of the Board; also Messrs. Falcone and Ketcham. Chairman Morris presided.

Tchaikovsky's *Golden Slippers* is known by a variety of names —*Cherevichki, Vakula the Smith, The Caprices of Oxane,* etc. Whatever the title, it is a charming work, although the critics agreed unanimously that it was under-rehearsed. Here, Donald Gramm, as the Devil, is attempting to make love to Solocha (Margery Mayer). (IMPACT/NEW YORK CITY OPERA ARCHIVES)

The Bartered Bride had been a great success under Halasz, and was now revived by Rosenstock. Jack Harrold is defying gravity, assisted by Maria Teresa Carillo and observed by Thomas Powell. (IMPACT/NEW YORK CITY OPERA ARCHIVES)

Beverly Sills made her company debut as Rosalinda in *Die Fledermaus* on October 29, 1955. Alfred, her would-be lover, was sung by Lloyd Thomas Leech. This photograph is from a later performance in which Jon Crain played the tenor with the seductive high Cs. (FRED FEHL)

Rosenstock's final new offering was a double bill of Rolf Liebermann's *School for Wives* and Mozart's *The Impresario*. Neither work pleased the critics. The leading roles in Liebermann's Molière-inspired comedy were taken by Joshua Hecht, Margery MacKay, William Pickett, Peggy Bonini, and John Reardon. (IMPACT/NEW YORK CITY OPERA ARCHIVES)

Frank Martin's *The Tempest* displeased both critics and public. The performance, however, surpassed the work. Outstanding among the cast was dancer Raimonda Orselli, who played the part of Ariel. (FRIEDMAN-ABELES/NEW YORK CITY OPERA ARCHIVES)

Julius Rudel's opening production as company director (Fall 1957) was a revival of *Turandot*. Here, stage director Vladimir Rosing inspects the supers. (NEW YORK CITY OPERA ARCHIVES)

Leonard Bernstein—pianist, conductor, composer, and lecturer—surely one of the greatest musicians America has produced. Early in his career he was greatly helped by Morton Baum, and the moving eulogy that he delivered at Baum's funeral appears at the beginning of this book. (NEW YORK CITY OPERA ARCHIVES)

516

Dinah and Sam in *Trouble in Tahiti* are a couple whose marriage is afflicted by boredom. Beverly Wolff and David Atkinson (foreground) played the roles; on the giant TV screen, the trio consists of Stanley Kolk, Naomi Collier, and William Metcalf. (THE NEW YORK TIMES/NEW YORK CITY OPERA ARCHIVES)

Kurt Weill's *Lost in the Stars* enjoyed a two-week run at the end of the regular season. Pictured above are Olga James as Linda and a young mezzo-soprano, Shirley Carter, making her professional debut in opera as Irina. Miss Carter subsequently became world-famous under the name of Shirley Verrett. (CHARLES ROSSI/NEW YORK CITY OPERA ARCHIVES)

The Taming of the Shrew was by Vittorio Giannini, brother of Dusolina, who starred in the very first City Opera performance. Petruchio and Katharina were sung by Walter Cassel and Phyllis Curtin. (CHARLES ROSSI/NEW YORK CITY OPERA ARCHIVES)

One of the most important works to emerge from the American opera seasons was *The Good Soldier Schweik* by Robert Kurka. Tragically, the thirty-five-year-old composer had died of leukemia on December 12, 1957, only a few months before the premiere. Above, an extremely arrogant army doctor (Emile Renan) points an accusing finger at Schweik (Norman Kelley), whom he suspects of malingering. Listening intently are Chester Ludgin (another doctor) and David Atkinson (Lt. Lukash, seated). (FRED FEHL)

After the success of *Susannah,* it was natural enough to introduce other operas by Floyd. The first was *Wuthering Heights,* a beautiful work. However, it does not have the immediacy of *Susannah,* and was not a box-office success at City Opera. In this photograph, Jon Crain and Frank Porretta are Hindler and Edgar, John Reardon is Heathcliff, and Phyllis Curtin and Jacquelynne Moody are Cathy and Isabella. (FRED FEHL)

Carmina Burana provided a good blend of song and dance. The vocalists were John Reardon, John Alexander, and, making her company debut, Reri Grist. The solo dancers, from left to right, are Glen Tetley, Carmen de Lavallade, Scott Douglas, and Veronika Mlakar. (CHARLES ROSSI/NEW YORK CITY OPERA ARCHIVES)

The City Opera's performance of Mozart's *Così Fan Tutte* could hold its own against any competition. The trio of Frances Bible, Judith Raskin, and Phyllis Curtin (as Dorabella, Despina, and Fiordiligi) left nothing to be desired, and the male contingent was equally strong, with John Reardon and John Alexander as Guglielmo and Ferrando and James Pease pulling all the strings as Don Alfonso. (CHARLES ROSSI/NEW YORK CITY OPERA ARCHIVES)

Marc Blitzstein's *The Cradle Will Rock* introduced Broadway's Tammy Grimes (foreground) to City Opera in the role of Moll. Behind her are Craig Timberlake (Mr. Mister), Ruth Kobart (Mrs. Mister), David Atkinson (Larry Foreman), and the composer. (CHARLES ROSSI/ NEW YORK CITY OPERA ARCHIVES)

Patricia Neway, as Magda Sorel, reaches the end of her patience in Menotti's *The Consul*. The implacable secretary is Regina Sarfaty. Other victims of the consulate's bureaucracy are Maria di Gerlando (Anna Gomez), Ruth Kobart (Mrs. Boronel), and Arnold Voketaitis (Mr. Kofner). (FRED FEHL)

Gérard Souzay was France's leading baritone when he came to City Opera
to sing the title role in Monteverdi's *Orfeo*. His Euridice, seated beside him,
was Judith Raskin. (FRED FEHL)

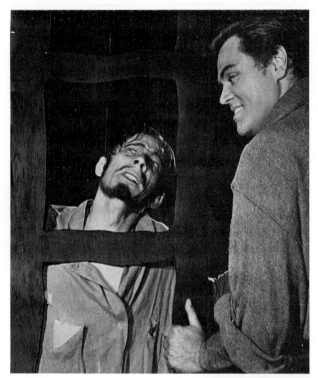

Norman Treigle was the anguished prisoner, Richard Cassilly his sadistic tormentor in Dallapiccola's *The Prisoner*. Offstage, the two were the closest of friends. (NEW YORK CITY OPERA ARCHIVES)

The Pirates of Penzance cast Frank Porretta and Ruth Kobart in the principal parts of Frederic and Ruth. (FRIEDMAN-ABELES/ NEW YORK CITY OPERA ARCHIVES)

Britten's *Turn of the Screw* was the second opera based on Henry James's work to enter the repertoire in less than six months (the first was *The Wings of the Dove*). The two demonic children were sung by Bruce Zahariades and Michele Farr. Mrs. Grose was Janis Martin, and the governess, Patricia Neway. (FRED FEHL)

Porgy and Bess made a belated appearance in 1962. This is Lawrence Winters (Porgy), surrounded by the residents of "Catfish Row." (FRED FEHL)

One of the many world premieres produced by City Opera was Carlisle Floyd's *Passion of Jonathan Wade,* a powerful drama set in the South immediately after the Civil War. In the scene shown here, Miriam Burton is Nicey, Frank Porretta is Lucas, Theodor Uppman sings Jonathan Wade, and Phyllis Curtin is Celia. (FRIEDMAN-ABELES/NEW YORK CITY OPERA ARCHIVES)

The Love for Three Oranges, absent from the repertoire since 1955, was revived in Spring 1963. Richard Wentworth (above right) was again the cook who falls in love with a ribbon; the reluctant donor of the ribbon, Truffaldino, was sung by Luigi Vellucci. (FRED FEHL)

In this rehearsal scene from *The Medium,* a perennial favorite, composer Gian Carlo Menotti is directing dancer Nikiforos Naneris, who played the mute, Toby, and Lili Chookasian, who portrayed the medium, Mme. Flora. (FRED FEHL)

Gentlemen, Be Seated! is an opera in the form of a minstrel show. Among the characters are Mr. Interlocutor, Mr. Bones, and Mr. Tambo. The setting is the Civil War, and the plot is reasonably accurate. Above, Dick Shawn (Mr. Interlocutor) explains why Matthew Brady never recorded any Civil War battle scenes. (FRED FEHL)

Norman Treigle, a particularly dapper Don Giovanni, is confronted by John McCollum, Arlene Saunders, Beverly Bower, and Judith Raskin (Ottavio, Elvira, Anna, and Zerlina) in a production staged by William Ball. (FRED FEHL)

Mr. Morris related the difficulties of last spring when Mr. Halasz, two weeks before the opening of the opera season, had tendered his resignation. At that time he had pleaded with him to hold the season together, and Mr. Baum, after several meetings with the opera staff, had arranged for the season to go on under Mr. Halasz's direction, with the thought that everything, including personality difficulties, might then be cleared up. However, more complaints had come to the attention of the board, and at a meeting of the directors held on September 6, 1951, a committee was appointed to investigate these compliants. . . . Mr. Marrow told the board that his committee had come into being because one singer had been dropped from the company without explanation or satisfaction to her or to her union. That was the first point. The committee heard her, Mr. Halasz and everyone else involved in the dispute, and it was determined that she be returned to the company. Then many letters had come in from members of the company asking to speak before this committee and many extraordinary things were brought out. Mr. Halasz was accused of destroying the morale of the company, of doing things which were not necessarily legal breaches of contract but were a question of ethics, of pitting one singer against another and destroying morale. After three or four sessions of seven or eight hours each, the committee felt that it would not be possible to continue the opera company with Mr. Halasz as director. . . . Mr. Marrow stated that after the first two or three days of hearings the pattern of testimony was the same from singers, musicians, stage crew, etc., and it was apparent that the organization had a serious situation on its hands with a person who was most thoroughly hated in the music world. . . . It was the unanimous recommendation of the committee that it was advisable to have Mr. Halasz withdraw or else terminate his services as director of the opera company.

Mr. Morgenthau, a member of the committee, reiterated the fact that the committee's decision was unanimous, after hearing people from all branches of the company, members of every union that dealt with the opera company, people who were now connected with the company and those no longer here. All of the testimony had proved the same thing. He pointed out that it was a good company, but a good deal more important than the opera was the relationship of one human being toward another. One member of the company had said: "Mr. Halasz is a person who has complete contempt for every human being. His treatment of people, his use of power has been so distorted and so perverted that the result is an outrage, and if this board continues to employ somebody of this calibre it will have to hold itself responsible."

Mr. Marrow stated it was pointed out frequently during the hearings that under Mr. Halasz's leadership the company had achieved great prestige but it was "in spite of" not "because of" him. . . . Letters of resignation had been received by the chairman from Julius Rudel, John White, and James Pease of the opera company, and word had come to him that other members of the conductorial staff were resigning at the end of the tour.

Mr. Baum told the board that it had the responsibility for the life of the organization and for its best interests. He pointed out that he personally had worked longer and closer with this situation than anyone, and he felt ashamed and sorry that this condition had not been met a year or two ago because the stench had come to his ears [sic] a long time ago. He pointed out that the lives and careers of some two hundred people were involved in the opera company and if the board closed its eyes and let the unions fight out the dispute with Mr. Halasz, the members of the company would have every right to feel that the board was blind to their claims. He felt that any action taken by the board would be in the sincere interests of the institution. He pointed out that Mr. Halasz had timed his resignation last spring so that the board could not put on the opera season without him, although Mr. Baum had told him he would do so, and Mr. Halasz had then changed his mind about resigning. Mr. Baum pointed out the efforts he had made to keep harmonious relations with the unions and with the Chicago and Detroit people despite Mr. Halasz's actions. With the spring opera season scheduled to begin on March 15 action must be taken on a new director immediately; otherwise the public would think that without Mr. Halasz there could be no City Center opera season. Mr. Baum asked that action be taken at this meeting and the decision on the new director reached so that the subject be closed as far as the public was concerned. . . .

Mrs. Hull felt there was nothing to gain by hearing Mr. Halasz at this time. Mrs. Tibbett concurred, stating that the Board must run the institution within its own discretion. Mrs. Reis felt that the board need not worry about the critics but should make a decision on the matter quickly. Mr. Morgenthau was in favor of Mr. Halasz being heard. Mr. Umhey stated that his dealings with Mr. Halasz in the past had always been satisfactory and the formation of the committee headed by Mr. Marrow was a surprise to him. On checking the minutes it was found that Mr. Umhey was not present at the board meeting when the committee was appointed. It was his feeling that Mr. Halasz should be heard by the board. . . .

Mr. Marrow felt that granting Mr. Halasz a hearing at this time would only delay a decision until it was too late to put on a spring opera season.

Mrs. Pratt pointed out that the board was not making charges against Mr. Halasz but that as an employer it had the right to dismiss, without a hearing, any employee who was not doing a satisfactory job.

Mr. Baum moved that this board make its decision without hearing Mr. Halasz at this meeting. Motion was seconded by Mrs. Hull. The vote being five in favor and seven opposed to the motion, it was agreed that only the chairman would question Mr. Halasz, who then entered the meeting.

Mr. Morris told him of events leading up to this meeting and of complaints that had been brought to the attention of the board over a period of years, adding that for several years the board had ignored them or accepted them as an inevitable part of the problems of an opera company. He recounted

Mr. Baum's efforts in bringing the opera staff together when Mr. Halasz had resigned last spring and of Mr. Halasz's decision then to return. At that time he said there had been considerable sentiment on the part of some board members to accept the resignation, but he had felt that having weathered this crisis Mr. Halasz might adopt a different attitude in the future. Complaints had continued to come in, however, and in the fall of this year he had appointed a special committee to hear grievances from members of the opera company. Mr. Morris emphasized that the board was not bringing charges against Mr. Halasz and that the committee headed by Mr. Marrow was not bringing charges. This meeting was called because the committee had reported back to the board, and the matter of Mr. Halasz continuing with the opera company was to be decided. Before any decision was reached some members of the board had wanted Mr. Halasz to be heard before them. He then turned the floor over to Mr. Halasz.

Mr. Halasz told the meeting that it was almost eight years to the day since he had presented a long view plan visualizing the formation of a great opera company in New York which would not only bring credit to all involved but one that could function without extensive financial outlays which made other opera companies impossible. He had returned four days ago at the end of the fall tour and felt he had achieved this goal with a most successful season behind him. During those eight years he felt he had made a lot of friends and lots of enemies, too, but knew of no opera director without enemies. He did not know what the complaints were in detail that had been brought to the board's attention this season. In one day since his return he had talked to the bulk of the company who were in New York and he was in a position to refute the idea of dissatisfaction in the company. He presented about thirty-five letters from members of the opera company, and said his relationships with its members were subject to a closer study than had been made. He asked for an opportunity to go into the statements made before the committee because there might be some truth to them.

He acknowledged that he was not as perfect as he might wish to be but felt that as far as his duties toward the institution and the board were concerned he had always fulfilled them to the letter. He said the charges presented were a serious matter for him since they involved his professional reputation and the institution he had built up with a lot of hard work, and he felt he had the right to defend them. He asked for more time to go into the matter.

Mr. Morris reminded Mr. Halasz of his dissatisfaction with the institution last spring when he had resigned. Mr. Halasz stated that he had done so for reasons he had given them, and when those reasons were removed he had withdrawn his resignation. Now he apologized to the board for that hasty action and wished to carry through with his artistic plans. He did not doubt for a moment that it was the board's privilege to wish to sever connections with anyone, but he did not believe that wish could be based without reason. Mr. Halasz then left the meeting, stating that he had nothing further to add. . . .

Mr. Mack asked if any member of the committee had changed his opinion since hearing Mr. Halasz. None having done so, he moved that the committee's report be accepted and acted upon. Mr. Warburg moved that the committee reexamine its findings in the light of hearing people who were in favor of Mr. Halasz, which was seconded by Mr. Warner.

Mr. Mack's motion was carried with twelve in favor and three opposed.

Mr. Feinberg moved that the chairman of the board, the officers and the chairman of the executive committee be authorized to take the matter up with Mr. Halasz, giving him the opportunity to resign, and arrange any necessary financial settlement. Motion carried.

Mr. Morris stated that an announcement would be made to the press and asked that all members abide by that statement. It was understood that Mr. Morris would be the spokesman for the board in this matter. . . .

It was moved that the chairman be authorized to appoint Dr. Rosenstock as director of the opera company on a pro tem basis for the spring season. Motion carried without a dissenting vote.

There being no further business the meeting was adjourned at 5:45 P.M.

The various board members then left, except for Morris and Baum, who stayed behind to speak to Halasz as authorized. Edna Bauman, who was taking notes for the board, also remained.

Morris then told Halasz of the decision to replace him, and suggested that he tender his resignation. The board, he explained, was fully prepared to pay him the $12,000 that was guaranteed to him under his contract, which still had one year to run.

Halasz refused, stating that he would not "sell the truth for $12,000 or any other amount," and threatened to bring suit against the company for breach of contract. Baum, a trained attorney, advised him against this decision, stating that if the matter came to court, the board would demonstrate that it had just cause to terminate Halasz's employment, and he would then receive absolutely nothing. Nonetheless, Halasz chose to fight.

The next day, the press, poorly informed because neither Morris nor Baum was available for comment, expressed surprise over the board's action and indignation over the secrecy. The newspapers were unanimous in their outspoken demands for candor and fair play.

12

Supreme Court KOs
Kangaroo Court

THE CASE of "Laszlo Halasz, Plaintiff, against City Center of Music and Drama, Inc., Defendant" came before the New York Supreme Court on May 15, 1952. Halasz's attorney was Milton Pollock; the defense counsel was Francis J. Bloustein; Justice Carroll G. Walter presided.

Halasz contended that the board of directors had acted without sufficient cause, and he sued for salary that would normally have been forthcoming in 1952 under the terms of his contract, as well as for various back payments still due. The total amount of his claim was $35,150.35.

During the trial many interesting conflicts came to light. The one item that most offended the sensibilities of the press was the board's creation of an investigating subcommittee whose hearings had been held in secret over the course of the past several months. There had been three hearings that occurred between September 14 and October 3. On September 14, John S. White, a member of Halasz's staff, testified before the full committee (Macklin Marrow, William Feinberg, Clarence Derwent, Hubert Delany, and Henry Morgenthau III); on September 24 (when Judge Delany was absent), they heard Pete Drambour (company carpenter), Jean Rosenthal (lighting designer), and singers Ann Ayars, James Pease, and Edwin Dunning; and on October 3 (when Mr. Morgenthau was absent), statements were given by former stage director John Primm, chorus union delegates Charles Kuestner and Madeleine Gari, and conductor Thomas Martin. The entire testimony was transcribed by a court stenographer and amounts to 179 typewritten pages.

In addition, other complaints against Halasz took the form of an AGMA resolution refusing to deal with him on contractual matters; the entire Kreste affair; letters of resignation from Julius Rudel, John S. White, and James Pease; and several bitter letters from Joseph Rosenstock, José Ruben, John Primm, Mstislav Dobujinsky, and James Pease. In all, then, there were seventeen complainants, of whom a dozen were current members of the company.

The testimony that emerged from these clandestine hearings suggest dislike of Halasz on the part of all those questioned, which was to be anticipated, since the committee was established to hear complaints. Many of the statements made, however, were only half-truths, as will be shown.

Here, for example, is a verbatim extract of Ann Ayars's statement as copied by the court stenographer:

MISS AYARS: Now, to start right at the beginning, my very first understanding, so far as my personal representation was concerned with Mr. Halasz: You see, I signed a two-year contract, to begin with, which I didn't care to do but I wasn't in a position not to.

THE CHAIRMAN: May I ask the question: So far as the two-year contract, was that a strict two-year contract or was it a contract for a year and an option for a year?

MISS AYARS: No, it was a contract, I believe, if I remember correctly, for one season, with options entirely on the side of management, of course.

THE CHAIRMAN: Yes.

MISS AYARS: Now, I was told at that time, or I think my agent said something about the fees being very low, and wouldn't there be any chance of an increase as the options were taken up, and Mr. Halasz said no, there would not, that rather than increased fees, that they simply tried to give their artists more performances in order to make the engagement of more value to them.

I believe that I started out with three performances, which was all right. And the second season, which was the fall season, I believe there were seven, or something like that. And then from there on it dropped down to three again, in the spring. And when I went to the office to ask what had happened or if there was some reason why I was given so few—I believe always they were all the last performances of the season, and I had been given premieres and I had success in all of them—I was told not to complain.

THE CHAIRMAN: Who told you that?

MISS AYARS: I talked to Mr. Jaretzky at that time. Mr. Halasz was unavailable.

MR. MORGENTHAU: He was Mr. Halasz's assistant at that time?

MISS AYARS: Yes, and I was told just very plainly that when I was in a position to bargain I could come up and complain about those things, and, apparently, not even an explanation was forthcoming. I really didn't go up there to complain.

This testimony, when scrutinized, reveals some intriguing points. Ms. Ayars made her company debut on April 6, 1947, as Naiad in *Ariadne auf Naxos*, a role she repeated on April 23; she also sang the first *Traviata* of the season on April 11 and a repeat on April 27; and Micaëla in *Carmen* on April 26. In all, she sang five times that season, including *two season premieres and opening night*. During her second season, she sang seven times—two performances of *La Bohème* (Mimi), four *Traviatas*, and one *Ariadne*. She was in the seasonal premiere of two of these operas (she had also been scheduled for the first *Ariadne*, but was indisposed). During her third season, she did indeed drop down to three performances, as she had indicated—the season's first *La Bohème*, and subsequent performances of *La Traviata* and *Pagliacci*. What she did not mention was that during the next six seasons, all of which preceded her appearance before the committee, she sang an average of *seven* performances per season with a total of *twelve seasonal firsts, one opening night, and two company premieres* (*Tales of Hoffmann* and *Manon*). Thus, her testimony, though not untrue (except for some understandable errors in detail), was completely misleading.

Furthermore, her dissatisfaction with her fees is not uncommon, particularly in a company dealing with a limited budget. She agreed to the contract because it was in her own best interests to do so. It should also be pointed out that this contract, which she considered so objectionable, was signed by Paul Moss as managing director, not by Halasz. In fact, *all* of her contracts were signed by either Moss or Morton Baum.

Continuing with Miss Ayars's testimony:

MISS AYARS: But that has been the constant thing all the way through my experience there, where I have had authorizations from Mr. Halasz personally on costumes. I would say, "Will you really say that you wish me to go out and rent costumes for such and such performances, there are not any available in the house?" And he would say, "Yes, by all means, go ahead and we will take care of it." When the time would come, there would be no memory whatever of the conversation, just none at all.

MR. MORGENTHAU: For example, your *Traviata* costumes were your own, weren't they?

MISS AYARS: One or two of them would be my own, but most of the time we had to rent them. There was nothing in the house. And then later, three or four seasons ago he had one gown made for *Traviata* and I have since used that. But then all the rest were still either my own or something that I rented.

MR. MORGENTHAU: In other words, he misled you into making commitments for costumes?

MISS AYARS: Well, I am still doing it, actually. Just to give you an example, I have in my purse a bill for $84 for rentals for *Manon* costumes.

Now Miss Morley, who is in charge of costumes, came with me. We went to Brooks. We rented one costume that we used last year and which seemed very satisfactory and was still in fairly good condition. So, we will use that.

We went through all the stock. Miss Morley knows it very well because she worked at Brooks herself. Since then we decided that we would have to go to Eaves to get the costume, and so we have gone to Eaves to get costumes. And they refused to deal with City Center at all and said if I would be personally responsible—because I have been going in there for years—that [if] I would pay for it in advance, which I have—I have the receipt—then I would do my best to get some sort of reimbursement.

THE CHAIRMAN: How long ago is this?

MISS AYARS: Well, this I just did today. But last year's costumes have not been paid for either.

THE CHAIRMAN: You have not been reimbursed for those costumes?

MISS AYARS: Well, actually, there has been a delay on this particular season because I had to leave before I could get in touch with the woman who was responsible for it.

THE CHAIRMAN: Actually, you haven't been paid for it?

MISS AYARS: Yes.

Apart from the obvious fact that Miss Ayars had not been reimbursed because she had not yet submitted any bills, there is a letter in the company files written to Paul Jaretzky by Sylvia Hahlo, Miss Ayars's manager at the time. The letter is dated August 25, 1948—just a few months after her debut—and the second paragraph reads: "I am writing her by airmail today saying that you feel this might all be adjusted satisfactorily[1]—but that it is not feasible to pay any part of her costume expenses—that you are acquiring more and more and that perhaps she might find some that would be suitable and avoid any additional expense to her."

The situation involving lighting designer Jean Rosenthal was considerably more complex. Although Halasz and Rosenthal each complained about the behavior of the other, the correspondence between them makes it perfectly clear that there was mutual guilt, as each was trying to take undue advantage of a situation at hand. Miss Rosenthal, who had been employed by the New York City Ballet Company for several years, was

---

1. This refers to role assignments.

engaged by the opera company in the spring of 1950. There were twelve operas in repertoire that season—eleven repeats and one new work (*Turandot*). Hans Sondheimer, the previous lighting designer, had quarreled with Halasz over a requested raise, and left the company. Suddenly, the company found that it had no workable lighting plans for its repertory operas, only rough sketches. Miss Rosenthal was engaged to reconstruct the lighting plans, for the old repertoire only, for a fee of $1,000. Her contract clearly precluded work on new productions. There was a delay in finalizing the terms, because she had arbitrarily inserted into the standard contract the following clause: "The Manager agrees to extend to the Designer full authority to . . . make purchases or arrange rentals, whenever the Designer deems necessary."

Since, in addition to functioning as a designer, Miss Rosenthal was the owner of a lighting company, this seemed to be a very dangerous clause. It had to be deleted before Halasz would sign, but since Mr. Sondheimer's departure—and, therefore, Miss Rosenthal's engagement—came within days of opening night, speed was imperative. Verbal agreement was reached (excluding the offensive clause). Miss Rosenthal's fee was paid to her, and she began to reconstruct the lighting before the contract was finally corrected and signed.

Meanwhile, Halasz asked her to assist in lighting *Turandot,* for which the lighting director was H. A. Condell. Clearly, this was not within the scope of the contract, which specifically excluded any new productions, and extra payment was in order. On the other hand, the fee that Miss Rosenthal requested was $425, which was the standard fee for designing the lighting of a new show, not for assisting. The following exchange of documents is interesting.

First is the rider added by Jean Rosenthal to the standard contract, which called for "lighting supervision of present repertory (no new shows)." The contract and rider are dated March 30, 1950 (the spring season had opened on March 26).

AMENDMENT TO STANDARD SCENIC ARTISTS CONTRACT FOR SCENIC DESIGNERS

The Designer agrees to provide lighting supervision for all Operas in the present repertory. These services to include only the following:

Attend lighting rehearsals.

Provide basic blueprint ground plan, of present lighting lay-out.

Cue sheets for all Operas supervised.

Hook up sheets for general repertory.

The Manager agrees to pay the sum of $1000.00, as fee for these services.

The Manager acknowledges that this fee does not cover a specific number of weeks work, although the total is based on the standard Art Director's weekly fee of $250.00 per week.

The Manager agrees to extend to the Designer full authority to:
Make crew calls whenever necessary.
Make purchases or arrange rentals, whenever the Designer deems necessary.

NOTE: It is understood that wherever possible, the Designer will procure a double bid in line with City Center purchasing policy.

The Manager agrees not to use names of Designer in conjunction with any advertising, printing, programs, or public statements.

WITNESS the hands and seals of the parties hereto in triplicate the day and year first above written. In the presence of:

WITNESS _____NAME _____

ADDRESS _____

WITNESS _____NAME _____

ADDRESS _____

APPROVED BY
UNITED SCENIC ARTISTS

Per _____

The rider was amended by Halasz. The line "attend lighting rehearsals" was changed to "attend all lighting rehearsals." The paragraph starting "The Manager agrees to extend . . ." and running through the NOTE was deleted. To the sentence, "The Manager agrees not to use names of the Designer in conjunction with any advertising, printing, programs, or public statements," Halasz added the phrase "except already printed." He then signed both contract and rider (acting for Morton Baum) and returned them to Miss Rosenthal.

On April 2, Halasz wrote to Rosenthal:

Dear Miss Rosenthal:
In view of your attitude toward the opera department of this institution we hereby give you the right to decide what falls within your contract, when and how long and if at all you wish to continue to work under your contract. Since you are fully paid for all your services, done or undone, I think you will agree with me that no institution in existence can do more.
Just for the sake of order we wish to inform you that our copy of your

contract has not been received by us which is rather strange considering the circumstances under which you insisted on an immediate delivery.

Yours very truly,

Laszlo Halasz
Artistic and Music Director
New York City Opera Company

On April 5, she responded:

Dear Mr. Halasz:

Replying to your letter of April second, I don't think even you would question my genuine interest in the City Center and the stimulating experience that it affords me in participating in the magnificent job it is doing. I am sure that you must share this feeling, so let's not take the position that I am trying to take advantage of you, or you of me. We have the common goal of the best possible production at the lowest cost within the union framework.

The contracts have been signed and sent to the union. In signing the contracts, I assumed that inserting the word "all" in respect to rehearsal, you did not mean to include operas not previously part of the repertory, as the union has specifically advised you from the inception of our negotiations that such operas come under a different classification.

Yours very truly,

Jean Rosenthal

Halasz then replied, on April 7:

Dear Miss Rosenthal:

Answering your letter of April 5, I would like to state that the fact that you signed your contract (after a delay of one week) which stipulates that you are obliged to come to all lighting rehearsals should not worry you at all. In my previous letter to you I gave you the right to decide what you wished to do for the thousand dollars you received. What I will not concede, however, is your attempt to blame the union for your failure to help us with the *Turandot* production. Mr. Karnolt informed me to the contrary—especially in view of the fact that the designer of the opera, Mr. Condell, a member of the union you yourself belong to, was in general charge of the lighting of the production.

During the short period I have had an opportunity to work with you I could not with good conscience say that you put forth your best efforts "for the best possible production at the lowest cost within the union framework." On March 30, between one and two p.m. you held up a lighting rehearsal for a full hour because your contract (into which you had inserted some arbitrary clauses) was not signed by us altho[ugh] payment for the whole amount of your contract was already in your hands.

In connection with *Turandot* you kept the only copies of the files and instructions covering this opera, which were given you by Messrs. Rosing and Condell, until the late afternoon of April 6, thereby preventing the possibility of any preliminary work on Monday night when the whole crew was sitting idle—which resulted in a disrupted rehearsal on Tuesday night because none of us had an opportunitoy to become familiarized with the contents of the files in your possession.

The basis of payment for your thousand-dollar fee was the union scale of $250.00 a week for a four-week period. Your attempt to get an additional $425.00 for the two days embodying the technical assistance needed by us for the lighting of *Turandot* was not a fair action on your part. And needless to say, the withholding of material until the last minute is completely outside the span of what is acceptable. To brand this sort of thing as in the interest of "the best possible production at the lowest cost" might well be termed "eyewash."

Had I been in your place I would have done the work first and argued afterward for additional payment. A person who is part of the theatre does not walk out on a job due to misinterpretation of terms, regardless of who in the situation is ultimately right, but finishes the work and argues later. It is here that I have to question your ethics or your attitude toward the whole institution of which the opera department is a part.

Copies of all these letters were sent to Morton Baum, and to Mr. Rudy Karnolt of the Scenic Designers' Union.

By the time Miss Rosenthal's testimony came to the complaint committee, the story had changed very slightly and quite subtly, but enough to make her a completely innocent victim. She made no mention of the difficulty brought about by her contract rider, no mention of the fact that she had been paid in full long before her obligations were fulfilled and no mention of retaining Condell's *Turandot* files until the day of the premiere (April 6). An extended extract from her testimony follows:

MISS ROSENTHAL: You see, the reason I went with the opera was because their stage manager and Mr. Halasz did not get along very well. . . .

He [Halasz] made a verbal contract with me, which I accepted quite simply because I worked for the ballet and I did five operas. And one day I thought, "Heavens, my contract isn't on the scenic arts," and quite frankly I wanted to check. So I called the union and asked for a check of that contract; and they said, "Well, your contract has not come in." So I said, "Call Mr. Halasz," and I said, "Is there some problem about my contract?" I said, "It should be at the office. I can't work without it."

Well, I went to see Mr. Halasz, and at this point he said I wanted too much money.

THE CHAIRMAN: But hadn't you come to terms previously?

MISS ROSENTHAL: We had already come to terms and since this had all occurred two or three days during the time the shows had started—it is quite a chore to piece it together—it wasn't as if every single record had disappeared, but this boy John Primm, who had taken over the stage, and I had taken over the lighting, would try to fill it out and put it together. And it was a situation that obviously required a great deal of good will and cooperation and understanding. And I must say that the staff there couldn't have been more generous in understanding the problem, trying to do the best they could, and being stuck with the fact that they never had any records.

So it came as quite a surprise, after the fifth opera had been put on and we were scrounging through this stuff, to find that he would not accept the terms. He refuted the entire deal and behaved as if I were the one who was making a very unfortunate request.

So we had quite an argument and in the end I said, "Well, Mr. Halasz, there is no point in my being here. I will just go." And I left. I thought, well, that's the way that will end. . . .

Then I was informed that there was a call at the theatre—you know how these things get—the union starts to call you and you call the union and you never deal directly. So, I went to the theatre and he put me, I thought, in a very miserable position because I have a reputation in the theatre; I work regularly commercially. And it is neither a happy position [n]or the way to work, to be put in a stalemate where the union says you can't work, and it becomes sort of a pressure thing, which has nothing to do with the work. . . .

I stayed there and finished their season. And then the next season I had another quite tough time with him, because I found that he was talking all over town. He was saying that I stood him up, that I had promised to do something and refused to do something—an overture the union would not let me light. [It] had a different classification from simply chasing out these old records and trying to piece [them] together, and they insisted on a new contract. Halasz refused to sign that contract and it was foolish, because in plain dollars and cents the union asked that I be paid the minimum which is $425. Instead of paying this—which was a simple labor requirement, not with me as an individual—instead of doing this, he decides that he will light the *Turandot*. Mr. Halasz and the designer, who is a very nice person but not very strong, and two or three other people, the director and everybody else, get out there and they spend sixteen hours doing what should normally be accomplished in seven or eight. Now, anybody can multiply eight hours and find the difference. And you see, this just doesn't make sense. It is just wrong-thinking and you find it over and over again.

Well, I stayed there and the next year Halasz asked me to stay. I had completed all the records and did *Meistersinger* and checked through the rest of the shows. I believe that was the only new one I did then.

MR. MORGENTHAU: Excuse me. First you had a verbal contract?

MISS ROSENTHAL: Yes.

MR. MORGENTHAU: And then he didn't live up to that, and offered a contract at a lower rate. Did you accept that then?

MISS ROSENTHAL: Oh, no. He finally went back to the proper settlement, but it was only after the union had ordered me not to work, which is bad. . . . I had to make the decision, was I going to allow City Center to waste crew hours because my union ordered me not to work on the one hand, and seemingly, I was the villain in the picture. I would be wasting the money; I was holding the works up.

Well, actually, Mr. Halasz arrived on the stage and he said to me—I was sitting there and waiting for the contract, and he said, "Who is paying for this time?" And I said, "Well, you are, Mr. Halasz." And then he said, "Well, this is a perfectly ridiculous situation," and proceeds, instead of turning on me. . . . the logical person, he proceeds to tear into the carpenter, which precipitates another argument. This sounds like a disjointed story because it goes on and on and it is always the same thing. It is a personal battle all the time.

Pete Drambour's testimony dealt entirely with personal difficulties in working with Halasz. Apparently this was a serious personality clash, as the following memoranda show:

Date: October 10, 1949

To: Mr. Halasz   From: Commissioner Moss

I just received the following note from Pete Drambour:

"The stage is getting so crowded with scenery that I will not be responsible for forcing the cyclorama downstage, especially during the performance of *Aida*."

This, to me, represents a very serious situation. If the cyc is forced downstage by reason of having too much scenery in back of it, it may cause either the cracking of the cyc or it may loosen the supports in the gridiron.

Either one of these would be a very serious situation in the theatre, especially if it happened during a performance.

Will you please see to it that something is done to correct this situation as the responsibility rests entirely with you.

                                            Date: October 11, 1949
To: Mr. Paul Moss   From: Laszlo Halasz

In connection with your memo from Mr. Drambour I wish to state that the responsibility for his work and department cannot and never will rest with me and I have to reject such responsibility in no uncertain terms.

I will gladly consult with Mr. Drambour and Mr. Sondheimer about the situation, but this is all I can do.

What this means in short is that if Mr. Drambour wants it we will have to move in and out operas for their subsequent repeats as the Met does—and which costs them $1000 per performance (and in this very way wrecks their budget). So the decision for this additional expense rests solely with Mr. Drambour, and it is up to him to save us this additional stagehands and trucking charge.

                                            Date: October 13, 1949
To: Mr. Ben Ketcham   From: Laszlo Halasz

I asked Mr. Hansen to do some work on the proscenium for *The Oranges*—I was informed that Mr. Drambour would give me the bid soon.

Today the news came through that Mr. Drambour is not going to give me a bid and will not let Mr. Hansen do the job either.

It is needless to say that it is becoming untenable for me to work my department with an uncooperative head of the carpenter department.

                                            Date: March 31, 1950
To: Mr. Ben Ketcham   From: Laszlo Halasz

Amidst the filthiest, dirtiest language I ever heard in my life, not only in any theatre but in any place in the world including the port cities of Africa, Mr. Peter Drambour stated the following:

1. That he wishes to resign and not to work for me any more.
2. That he is not taking any orders from me but only from you. The occasion which resulted in this situation was my request to get the best people available to correct the faulty operation of our curtains.

As far as I am concerned I hereby accept Mr. Drambour's resignation which of course, will eliminate the necessity of raising the issue as to whether or not I have the right to give orders to him during the opera season or the privilege of asking for correction of very obvious and amateurish shortcomings in our performances.

It would be greatly appreciated by the opera department if we might be consulted in the selection of his successor.

Date: April 10, 1950

To: Mr. Ketcham   From: Mr. Halasz

During last night's performance of *Don Giovanni* one of the arches in front of the cyclorama collapsed and also a column on stage left; both had not been nailed sufficiently.

At the end of the performance, the house curtain did not close completely.

It is with great regret that I must repeat that under these circumstances I must decline any responsibility for such or any similar occurrences on stage.

Mr. Drambour's opening statements seem to imply not that he came to the committee to register objections but that he was *asked* to come to submit complaints:

THE CHAIRMAN: I was told that you had some interesting things to tell us about the general operation, your experience.

MR. DRAMBOUR: Well, I don't know just what you mean, but I sort of surmise why I am here.

The most severe criticism of Halasz came from bass-baritone James Pease, who had, for about a year, borne a serious grudge against Halasz. This first manifested itself in a letter (February 26, 1951) that was so unpleasant it produced the following response from Jessica Colfer, Halasz's assistant:

I hope this letter clears up a few matters. You sounded so belligerent I could not believe it was you. We are really working hard here and certainly have your best interests at heart. I think you will understand that many of our plans were upset this year by the cancellation of first one and then another opera . . . and I hope to some extent you will bear with us.

Pease's position is made clear in two letters to Morton Baum. The first, dated October 22, 1951, reads:

Dear Mr. Baum,

I don't want to bother you with my difficulties with the "Maestro" this fall—they are mounting up; but I thought perhaps you would find a copy of my own current billet-doux of some interest. I await his next move with little interest; and I fear I must remain part of his "loyal-opposition" no matter what.

With best wishes,

Jim Pease

The second note, written on December 4, 1951, was extremely indiscreet:

Dear Mr. Baum,

Here is a copy of the letter I mentioned I was going to write. I tried to avoid little petty bickering in it, but I'm not sure I was very successful. That guy brings out the worst in one. I can truthfully say he is the only human being I have really disliked.

I have contact with White and have high hopes that the consummation devoutly to be wished is in the making. It will disappoint a lot of people if it fails.

All best wishes for a successful coup if that's the word I want. Incidentally, did the board of directors vote $200 to Mrs. Natzka, and was it sent directly to her? I had heard rumors to that effect . . . in fact Louslo [sic] told her in my presence that he had persuaded the board to appropriate it. She has never mentioned anything of it, and since nearly everything went through me, I've been curious.

                              Very sincerely,

                              Jim Pease

Pease's rancor was based on several incidents, but particularly on Halasz's occasional use of foreign artists. His entire correspondence file is spiked with letters making negative references to "Halasz's European fiascoes." In retrospect, there is a great paradox in this attitude, since between 1953 and his death in 1967, Pease's career was almost exclusively European: in Hamburg, London, and Zurich where *he* was a foreign artist.

By now it should be perfectly apparent, from the testimony solicited and accepted with no attempt at verification, that the committee was not created to *investigate* the situation, but rather to find a basis that could be used to dismiss Halasz. Taken in this light, part of John White's testimony to the committee is the height of irony:

MR. WHITE: I wanted to say we all love the City Center and we do not necessarily connect the actions of the present manager with the house. But would you believe it that a staff member like Mr. Martin was once asked by Mr. Halasz to go through a part with another singer, Miss Bryner, and find, purposely, faults with her delivery in order to get her out of the contract?

These, then, were the principal complaints against Halasz. As for the real reasons for the dismissal, it all goes back to the *Dybbuk* incident, as will soon be seen.

13

A House Divided

A S the previous chapter makes clear, Halasz was the victim of a campaign to oust him. Lacking genuine cause to do so, the board of directors solicited complaints that could be used for this purpose. There is no denying that Halasz was a difficult person with whom to work. Faced with a very limited budget, he was constantly searching for ways to save a little money here and there, and as a result, many company members felt that they were unfairly exploited.

The following letter from Hy Faine of the American Guild of Musical Artists may be amusing in retrospect, but it highlights some of the difficulties of those early years:

April 11th, 1951

Mr. Laszlo Halasz
City Center of Music & Drama, Inc.
130 West 56th Street
New York 19, New York

Dear Mr. Halasz:

I am writing to you about the claim for the four ballet dancers who appear as "supers" in the *Manon* production which has been under discussion with you for some time.

When this matter was brought to my attention I discussed it with Mr. Rudel, your assistant. He agreed with me that these dancers should be paid the fee called for in the basic agreement since they were "supers" and since in the same bit there were four dancers and two actual "supers." Having received confirmation from him of the correctness of our position, I so advised the delegate. Subsequently, he called me to say that you had over-ruled him. In an effort to avoid having the whole company be made aware of the ambiguous and humiliating position you have placed your assistant in, and the lack of authority he has, as well as to avoid dispute, you and I discussed it. You denied that this was "super" work and offered to have me see the performance as your guest and for me to decide whether or not it was. I made arrangements to see the performance tonight with that understanding.

Yesterday afternoon I was informed that prior to my seeing it, you called in Mr. Muradoff and had that whole bit rechoreographed, eliminating the two supers and using six dancers. Therefore, obviously, when I would see the performance tonight, it would be clearly choreography and dancing and I would so advise you.

This action on your part really hits a new low, both to me personally and to AGMA. It is particularly inconceivable that to save $30 or $40 you would so change the bit so that your claim would be substantiated. The whole incident has so aroused the ballet company, both initially when you refused to pay, and this last thing, that I cannot understand how you can expect any sympathetic understanding of yourself and the City Center's problems at a time when we are negotiating a new basic agreement and at a time when you are asking the company and AGMA to forego improvements in the contract which are clearly in order so that the City Center may continue next year.

In addition, to place me in this position and deceive me when such a pittance is involved seems to me to be the height of stupidity.

I shall certainly not attend this performance as your guest and while I see it I shall pay for my tickets.

I am repeating my claim for the payments to the dancers "who supered" in the performance heretofore.

> Very truly yours,
>
> AMERICAN GUILD OF MUSICAL
> ARTISTS, INC.
>
> (Signed)
> Hyman R. Faine
> Executive Secretary

There are other such letters in the file, all pointing to a dissatisfaction which, if not universal in the company, was at least sufficiently widespread to make the directors take notice. In addition, Halasz was often sarcastic in dealing with people, which did not increase his popularity.

"I want an E-flat, not a flat E" was not the type of statement destined to create friends. There were run-ins with soloists, choristers, directors, and conductors. Principally, however, he had offended the board with his letter of resignation at the time the *Dybbuk* production was cancelled, and their attitude toward him was summed up in a press release issued by Frederick Umhey, when he resigned in protest to the actions taken by the board:

Charging that the dismissal of Laszlo Halasz as director of the New York City Opera Co. was undemocratic and "in violation of the elementary concepts of our system of justice and fair dealing," Frederick F. Umhey today announced his resignation as charter member of the Board of Directors of the City Center of Music and Drama, which had discharged Mr. Halasz.

Mr. Umhey announced his action in a letter to Newbold Morris, chairman of the Board of Directors. The full text of the letter follows:

Mr. Newbold Morris
Chairman, Board of Directors
City Center of Music and Drama, Inc.
130 West 56th Street
New York 19, N. Y.

Dear Mr. Morris:

Having been one of the charter members of the City Center of Music and Drama and a member of its board of directors since its founding, it is naturally with very deep regret that I now find myself compelled to resign from that board.

In the many years that I have served, I have gone along with many decisions with which I was not in full accord. However, the decision which the board reached in dismissing Laszlo Halasz as director of the New York City Opera Co. involves ethical concepts that transcend the mere question of regularity and and which I cannot accept in clear conscience.

Mr. Halasz has a contract which still has a year to run. It contains a clause obligating the City Center not to produce any opera in the 1951 repertory during the years 1952 or 1953 if they were not under his auspices.

To me, a contract is a solemn obligation which should not be broken or disavowed by either party without good and substantial reasons for so doing. It is my firm belief that such reasons do not exist in the Halasz case.

The principal reasons which caused a majority of the board to vote for Mr. Halasz's ouster was his conduct in connection with *The Dybbuk* incident over a year ago. Even though the resignation which he then tendered had been withdrawn and he had resumed his direction of the opera company before the resignation was presented to the board, some members have never forgiven Mr. Halasz for that incident.

I vividly recall the hours of discussion we had as to how his resignation could be held over his head to be accepted at some time in the future. Evidently those antagonistic to Mr. Halasz did not then consider it wise to resort to that device. Instead, they seized upon a moment when other organizations, represented on the board, had aired some grievances against him, and brought about the appointment of a special committee to investigate all complaints.

This special committee held its hearings at secret times and places, made known only to those who had alleged grievances against Mr. Halasz. The latter was given no opportunity to confront or question his accusers; nor was he ever apprised of their complaints and given an opportunity to answer them.

This procedure was first known to the board at its meeting on December 21. I immediately protested against the undemocratic and un-American manner in which the committee had acted. It violated, in my opinion, the elementary concepts of our system of justice and fair dealing. When I suggested that the report be referred back to the committee to correct this flagrant omission of decency, I was met with the answer that there isn't time; that the spring opera season was upon us and that we cannot wait. Nevertheless, from the sub-committee chairman's own admission at yesterday's meeting, the sub-committee had fully agreed upon its recommendation to discharge Mr. Halasz at its meeting of October 3, 1951. Therefore, if this report had been made to the board promptly, instead of holding it for two and a half months, there would have been no basis for stampeding us into an immediate decision.

The answer of some of the board's members that the City Center, as an employer, owed no obligation to Mr. Halasz to hold hearings or to grant him the right to defend himself, would be true only if the City Center were a privately operated institution and did not have the public aspects of a civic venture which are attributable to the City Center. The City Center has no membership which might correct the misdeeds of its own self-perpetuating board. It is, however, answerable to the people of the City of New York who constitute its past supporters and its potential audience.

Moreover, mere decency required that a man to whom we owe so much and who, more than any other individual, was responsible for the remarkable success and outstanding prestige to which the City Center has risen, should receive different treatment than that accorded a mere hired hand.

Furthermore, most of the specifications enumerated by the special committee in its attempt to justify its report were, in my opinion, all matters which resulted from Mr. Halasz's effort to run the opera company as economically as possible and in the best interest of the City Center. He ran into difficulty principally because he was obliged to deal with individuals and organizations who had their own stake in his decisions, and he thereby had many occasions for creating enemies. All of them have now ganged up on him.

The decision which I am communicating to you is one which it has been difficult to make since I have been at all times concerned with the welfare and success of the City Center. My primary purpose in serving has been to help bring to the people of this city music, drama and the arts at a high level at a price which they could afford to pay. The dismissal of Mr. Halasz, in my opinion, will not further that purpose. I nonetheless wish the City Center a long period of future successes.

The press was very much in Halasz's favor, and a few days after the dismissal occurred the suggestion was made that the board had acted precipitately, and that Halasz's reengagement be seriously considered. This was put to a vote, and the majority of the board wished the dismissal to stand. It was then that Halasz brought suit, and revealed his side of the story in a press release dated December 24, 1951:

It was eight years ago, almost to the day, that I met Mr. Newbold Morris. At that time I outlined my vision of a great new opera company, based on radically progressive ideas, especially in comparison to the operatic standards of those days, and I prophesized to him that within a decade such an institution could be built and run practically on a break-even basis. The consensus of opinion was that this was impossible, especially since this meeting followed the reported quarter-million-dollar seasonal loss of the New Opera Company just about that time.

Now, eight years later, we have finished our most successful and most extensive fall operations. The artistic success of the past season is a matter of record. The financial picture is just now beginning to crystalize in the City Center's offices—and even to my own surprise—it shows a break-even or near break-even, after absorbing the total cost of two new productions, *The Dybbuk* and *The Four Ruffians*. This does not take into consideration the present 20% tax relief which, I understand, the City Center has not yet received officially. But when this happens, the opera company will have an additional $35,000. I feel that at this time the opera company is in its strongest position ever—at its best, artistically and financially. And only the company's fine spirit, morale and performing ability could produce such results, in my opinion.

I arrived in New York only on Sunday, December 16, after having visited, following our Chicago closing date on December 9, several midwestern cities, with the result that engagement offers for the fall of 1952 were received, totaling a guaranty of at least $100,000. I received a call to appear before Mr. Morris on Wednesday, December 19, at which time he informed me that for several months investigation of complaints of twelve to fifteen people were made by a committee of five, and that the charges were very serious and alarming to the board. He named nine complainants, three of whom were no longer members of the company. Mr. Morris informed me that the charges crystallized as follows: autocratic running of the company; the use of foul language; rude manners; insecurity of the artists in conjunction with premieres. He also mentioned some complaints on the part of the American Guild of Musical Artists (AGMA). He indicated that these charges alarmed him so much that he felt that if I stayed, I would have to do the conducting, and he would have to do the singing, because nobody else would be with me.

As to the personal complaints, I replied that I could not comment on the results of testimony, *the taking of which took several months*, without knowing them in great detail, but I offered to answer all of them, asking only for *sufficient time to learn the actual and detailed contents* of these complaints and a fair time for preparing defense. Mr. Morris countered with the suggestion that I resign and hinted that the board wished to live up to the terms of its contract with me specifically as to its financial obligations. . . .

Mr. Morris told me that he was for the complete airing of the truth and assured me that it would be done. He suggested that I remain available for a board meeting which was scheduled for Friday, December 21, at 2:30 PM, *leaving only one full day between the two meetings.*

After this first meeting with Mr. Morris I started to think about these complaints and, knowing that I cannot be as perfect as I would like to be, I tried to find the justification for the charges. But with the very best will in the world I did not succeed. Of all the charges, the last one worried me—that the company does not want to perform with me. This was the most alarming to me, because it was so contradictory to their spirit and the superior performances of the past season.

Therefore I spent the one day given to me for "preparing my defense" and investigating my faults by reaching every member of the company now in New York City, repeating to them the charges and asking for their reactions. To my great satisfaction and admiration of my company, even in this difficult situation where human cautiousness would have been permissable, 98% of those available volunteered to come through with statements completely refuting all charges. The result, in a matter of hours, was letters and telegrams representing forty-five members of the company—statements they understood would be, and which they requested to be, presented to the board. In fact, some of them were addressed and sent directly to Mr. Morris. These letters greatly outnumbered the complaints. The members involved represented staff, the bulk of my leading singers, leading choristers and comprimarios, ballet dancers, choreographers, composers and directors—and, regardless of what has happened, their expressions are still my guiding spirit and the basis for belief in my company.

At Friday's fateful meeting, to my great surprise, the chairman informed me that, just as *I* had resigned in the early months of the year, *they* wished to make a change now. He explained that such situations arise between employers and employees, and that this decision was not based on any charges. He felt that my previous resignation showed that my interest in the company must have diminished—so why not resign now? I can't "resign" under fire—of "charges". I could not discard the matter of charges, so strong represented a day and a half before, and I reiterated my request to have a fair investigation where my side of the story would be listened to. Also I was ready to refute that "I would have to conduct and Mr. Morris would have to sing" through the bundle of letters which I left on the table to be read. I explained at my first meeting with Mr. Morris, and again on Friday, that my resignation in the spring was due only to my dissatisfaction with the method of first authorizing me two new productions during December 1950. *The Dybbuk* and *Falstaff* and then, after I made promises and commitments, both were cut out, putting me in a position where I could not fulfill my word. The financial reasons given were not made known to me at that time, and it was only weeks later that I learned that the precarious financial position of the City Center was due to the $50,000 loss the ballet company suffered in England. Since this was not in my department, I did not know it at the time. Also, when I withdrew my resignation, I was assured that promises of two new productions, one of which would be *The Dybbuk*, would be made good, enabling me to keep my word with composer, stage director, artists, etc., only a few of whom received full payment for the spring cancellation of *The Dybbuk*. I explained that the reasons were removed, and therefore I withdrew my resignation at the request of the chairman of the board.

As to the charges, I repeated that, not knowing them in detail and all of the complainants against me, I would not answer, but I pleaded for reasonable time to learn their contents and a chance to meet them. I left, and the board deliberated. I was called back, with Mr. Morris, Mr. Morton Baum, and Miss Edna Bauman present. Mr. Morris put before me the intended official statement that they were terminating their association with me, explaining that he was authorized to pay me $12,000 toward the monetary part of their contractual obligations, and to change the first sentence to "resignation" if I accepted. My contract covers operations of the opera company for 1952 and 1953.

I reiterated again that I did not wish to sell the truth for $12,000 or any other sum of money. Mr. Baum informed me "as a lawyer" that if I did not accept now, I would have to sue for payment, in which case I might get nothing, because the board would try to prove that they were entitled to dismiss me because of my breaking the morale of the company, which, by the way, would hurt my future in the music world. This, with letters from forty-five of the company on the table and presumably read! . . . I also mentioned that I did not wish to resign because *I* did not wish to break my contract. If I had been guilty of these shadowy, unnamed charges, I might have run for cover and taken refuge in a resignation. This I did not feel and do not wish to do. I do wish to bring the whole procedure into the open. My actions are an open book—*I WISH TO HAVE THEM EXAMINED*, but I ask for the same privilege accorded to the twelve to fifteen dissident members of this large company. I left the room saying that I held no rancor or ill-feeling for Mr. Morris, Mr. Baum, or the members of the board. . . .

As to AGMA's part in this complaint, some very strange actions were brought to my attention only a few hours ago. They explain why none of the members of AGMA who wrote in my behalf knew anything about the mysterious resolution of their union to which the papers referred. Among the signatories of these letters to the City Center board or to me are two vice-presidents of AGMA, three board members, including two delegates. *May I ask AGMA how it is possible that the majority of the members of the New York City Opera Company did not know about a resolution taken by the board of governors of their union—an action seriously affecting their interests?* These loyal company members uniformly tied the institution's existence to my efforts and were unanimous in saying so. Seemingly the membership of the City Opera company was not consulted about this resolution but are learning about it just now. . . .

I would not have believed that "it could happen here," and I will fight it to the last, not only to have justice in my own case, but to prevent its happening to anyone else—in any profession—in any part of this country. I would like to add—in any part of the world.

The trial lasted for two weeks, running from May 15 through May 28, 1952. The court ruled in Halasz's favor and decided that the City Center had acted without sufficient cause. In principle, he had been vindicated. As to the financial settlement, the jury chipped away large segments of his claim, and in the end he was awarded $15,324.80. Nonetheless, he considered himself the victor.

Several years later, when Lincoln Kirstein resigned his position of managing director of the City Center, Olin Downes reopened the Halasz issue by writing to Newbold Morris, and asking for specific answers to the points stated in Umhey's press release. Downes made these answers available to Halasz, who succeeded in tearing them apart, assisted in some instances by publicist Richard Pleasants. Morris's explanations were really quite feeble, particularly in view of his legal training, as the following example will demonstrate.

Referring to the third paragraph of the Umhey letter, ". . . it contains a clause obligating the City Center not to produce any opera in the 1951 repertoire, during the years 1952 and 1953 if they were not under his auspices," Morris responded:

As to the first question he raised with regard to a clause in Mr. Halasz's contract, it did contain an agreement on the part of the City Center not to produce any opera put on under Mr. Halasz's direction in the years 1952 or 1953. This clause never should have been in the contract, but it was included at his insistence. Obviously there is nothing unique in operas such as *Bohème*, *Tosca*, etc. All of the works in the City Center repertory were in the public domain and such a clause is against public policy. In any event, Halasz never moved for an injunction, and certainly he had very competent counsel, who, if he thought such a clause could have been enforceable, would certainly have included it among the various causes of action.

Halasz's reaction to Morris's answer was:

The clause referred to in my last contract with the New York City Center of Music and Drama reads as follows:

"It is agreed that none of the *productions* of opera which will be in the repertory during the seasons of 1951 or 1952 will be given under our or any other auspices in or outside of New York without engaging you as Artistic and Music Director. This condition will continue only up to December 31, 1953."

This clause (except for a change of dates) was in all my contracts. The intent was to prevent the possible use of my *productions* which incorporate ideas and interpretations not present in other opera productions, under conditions beyond my artistic control. Such a protection clause is not unusual for producer-directors and certainly would not prevent the City Center's presenting different productions of the same operas. The contract was signed by Morton Baum, a lawyer, who surely knew what it meant.

After the Supreme Court had adjudged my dismissal illegal and unfounded and I had been cleared of the dubious charges made against me neither my attorney nor I saw any reason to continue action against the City Center—especially through an injunction which might hamper the then forthcoming opera season. The fact remains, however, that the New York City Center of Music and Drama completely ignored its obligations under this paragraph of the contract and made no attempt to resolve the issue in any way.

Mr. Pleasants went a step further by attacking Morris personally, and in a somewhat disjointed statement said:

And though the board was not unanimous and resignations followed, assuming to represent the board, broke a contract which earlier, assuming to represent the board, he had made (with the aid of Morton Baum) with the full technical knowledge of an attorney at law, and renewed, each time with a man of no legal training but representing the board in his unselfish way, he had not been wise or, therefore, efficient. (The contract originally made was not good "public policy.") "The contract should never have been made"—or, perhaps renewed? CONCLUSION (inevitable—but he dodges it): He is not a wise or good representative of the public's interest.

Halasz, in his letter to Downes, pointed out some irregularities concerning dates. The committee of the board that conducted the secret hearings had been officially formed on September 6, 1951. But there was a letter from John White to Morton Baum, dated April 3, 1951, which said, "I am ready to meet any time with the committee of the board of directors to hear the facts in the case." A copy of this letter was also included in the material sent to Downes.

In summary, Halasz speculated on what had actually happened, as follows:

Mr. Morris states that "everything was done with fairness, restraint and deliberation." It would seem to me that Mr. Morris's very profession precludes his crying "fairness" in the face of a one-sided trial. To have reached this point in Mr. Morris's letter without having been lulled by its blandishments is something of an accomplishment. Personally, I credit him with a masterpiece of persuasion. Even I am almost cajoled into believing that there was much ado about nothing—I should have philosophically acceded to the charges, foregone the court proceedings, slapped an injunction on the City Center, thanked the committee for its diligent research and credited the complainants with constructive criticism. However, Mr. Morris read the testimony, had opportunity to reflect on the whole situation, asked me to defend myself against unidentified accusations, and then sat back and "let the chips fall."

It is quite possible that he may not have been the motivating force behind this business of my dismissal, but I don't think he can claim to have been innocent. His strategy is not without guile—and his smoothness discloses knowledge. Let us assume, for the moment, that Mr. Baum because of the *Dybbuk* rumpus resolved to get rid of me; that the idea of the committee was formed sometime prior to April 3, 1951 and that John White acted as Mr. Baum's deputy by finding members of the company who were willing to cooperate (I have learned—but through hearsay—that such a campaign was in existence). This would account for a few copy-to-Mr. Baum letters that came in during the fall of 1951. The Kreste case was twisted to serve as a basis for the formation of the committee and the complaints were utilized as material for its continuation. This could have been the situation—and it is what I see in retrospect—but even so it must have been done with Mr. Morris's knowledge for he is no fool—and the testimony is self evident. Mr. Morris may be very thankful to Macklin Marrow and his four colleagues who "spent so many hours during those hot summer months" serving a purpose for which they were selected. However, in the Supreme Court, after both sides were heard, the dismissal based on the committee's findings were termed *unfounded* and *illegal*.

It is not the purpose of this book to pass moral judgments, but simply to report, in as objective a manner as possible, what actually occurred. Whether or not the end justifies the means is a question of ethics that will probably be debated for all time to come. In all fairness to Newbold Morris, it should be pointed out that he sincerely felt that it was absolutely necessary to get rid of Halasz. There was an undated handwritten note in Morton Baum's files saying: "Are we better off with an opera company without Halasz or with Halasz but no company?" It is signed "Newbold." Clearly this note was intended for Baum's eyes only, and so it was not written to create any special effect. Rather, it is an expression of genuine concern.

That Newbold's fears were legitimate seems highly unlikely, in retrospect. It is true that a few notes of resignation were received, but certainly the company could have continued functioning without these people for the one year that still remained under Halasz's contract. It is also noteworthy that all of the resignations are dated November 1951—after the subcommittee had agreed to recommend Halasz's termination, but before the matter was presented to the board. In any case, whether the resignations were genuine or simply more fuel for the fire, the company does not seem to have been on the verge of collapse.

And so ended Laszlo Halasz's regime after seventeen seasons (eight years). The board now had to pick up a lot of broken pieces very quickly, for a new season was almost at hand.

14

Rosenstock Steps In

W I T H Halasz now gone and the spring 1952 season only three months off, a new general director had to be appointed immediately. First choice of the executive committee of the board of directors was Jean Paul Morel,[1] who was not only a brilliant conductor but also a man of great personal charm and flair. Morel declined, however, stating that he had "neither the vices nor the talent necessary to run the company." He also went one step further. In protest against the board's methods in dealing with Halasz, he submitted his resignation as conductor, which the board refused to accept, pointing out that he was contractually bound for another year.

The board of directors next turned to Dr. Joseph Rosenstock, who accepted the position, whereupon Morel again attempted to withdraw and again met with refusal. Morel then pointed to a clause in his contract stating that no member of the musical staff, with the exception of Mr. Halasz, would enjoy a position of preeminence over Mr. Morel. When he threatened to bring suit for breach of contract, his resignation was accepted.

Joseph Rosenstock had begun his City Opera career on October 14, 1948, leading the company's first performance of Mozart's *Marriage of Figaro*, to this day one of the most popular operas in its repertoire. He was a highly esteemed conductor with impressive credentials and a strong tendency toward the avant-garde. What he lacked, however, was Halasz's

---

1. Since the minutes of the December 21, 1951, board of directors' meeting specifically authorized the choice of Rosenstock, it seems inexplicable that they would first approach Morel. Apparently, despite the decision of the board, the executive committee was taking matters into its own hands.

showmanship. His wartime difficulties, detailed in the following pages, could have made him a very glamorous figure, but they went almost entirely unnoticed except in musical circles.

Born in Cracow[2] on January 27, 1895, he attended the Vienna Conservatory, then studied privately with composer Franz Schreker, whose *Der Ferne Klang* had been denounced for its modern style. Another Schreker opera, the atonal *Das Spielwerk und die Prinzessin*, created such a scandal at its premiere (Vienna, 1913) that it had to be withdrawn.

A child prodigy, Rosenstock was, before reaching his teens, the toast of Berlin and Vienna for his pianistic talents. During the First World War, as a member of the Austrian army, his left hand suffered severe injuries, and his musical career was forced into new directions. He was appointed to the Berlin Academy of Music, where he taught composition and score reading, the youngest professor in the history of that famed institution. Then, in 1919, he became conductor of the Vienna Philharmonic Choir, and almost immediately was persuaded by Fritz Busch to come to Stuttgart as assistant conductor at the Landestheater—his initiation into the world of opera. Less than one month later, Busch fell ill and Rosenstock made an unscheduled debut conducting *The Bartered Bride*—without a single rehearsal!

The following year, he was called to Darmstadt to succeed George Szell as chief conductor of that company, and within three years became its general music director; subsequently, he filled a similar post at Wiesbaden, replacing Otto Klemperer. There his interest in modern music became manifest through productions of works by Krenek and Schönberg.

Rosenstock joined the staff of the Metropolitan Opera in 1929, conducting *Die Meistersinger, Der Rosenkavalier,* and *Die Walküre,* but returned to Germany in 1930 to head the Mannheim Opera, following in the footsteps of Felix Weingartner, Wilhelm Furtwängler, and Erich Kleiber. Here he continued his championing of Krenek, and also produced works of Janáček, Stravinsky, Hindemith, Pfitzner, Berg, and other contemporary composers.

Hitler's rise to power in 1933 drastically changed the artistic life of Germany. As a Jew, Rosenstock was removed from his Mannheim directorship. The persecution had not yet become unbridled—it would be several years before its nightmare proportions were fully reached. At the beginning of Hitler's reign, however, Jews in Germany were barred from attending "Aryan" performances, and Rosenstock was one of the founders

2. Standard reference works alternately list Rosenstock as Polish and Austrian. Cracow, now in Poland, was part of the Austrian Empire until the end of World War I, so that when Rosenstock was born it was as an Austrian subject.

of the Jüdisches Kulturbund in Berlin, an organization that, in response to this imposed loss, presented cultural attractions for the large Jewish population.

Rosenstock's fame was international, and during this period, while he tried desperately to get out of Germany, his services were being actively solicited by the Nippon Philharmonic Orchestra. Thus, when he finally succeeded in obtaining an exit permit in 1936, he went to Tokyo, which was still perfectly safe, and became head of Japan's leading orchestra. The musical environment in Japan was extremely rewarding: receptive audiences, dedicated musicians, and—a real rarity in the musical field— adequate rehearsal time. He endeared himself to the orchestra through his thorough musicianship, but even more because of his personal stoicism. During a rehearsal of the Brandenberg concerti one day, the tremors of an earthquake were felt. The hall began to shake, and finally the podium began to slide from side to side. He realized that the musicians were studying him, looking for signs of fear and weakness, and so, gritting his teeth, he simply said, "Gentlemen, there is too much vibrato in the strings"— and continued the rehearsal. Every man in the orchestra was won over.

In 1939, Rosenstock applied for a visa to the United States and was told that he could pick it up at the embassy at any time; but, since there seemed to be no urgency, he did nothing about it. Finally, in July 1941, the embassy called him and advised him to leave as soon as possible. Scheduled concerts, however, prevented his following this advice for a few weeks. When he finally did appear at the embassy, it was too late. Only two days earlier, all records had been recalled by the State Department in Washington, and all visas were revoked. Rosenstock was now caught in Japan, where he would have to wait for the duration of the war.

On December 6, 1941, a concert was scheduled that was to be attended by U.S. Ambassador Joseph Clark Grew and his wife. Through some clerical error, the ambassador's tickets were sold—along with every other seat in the hall. Several telephone conversation took place between Rosenstock and the embassy in an attempt to make arrangements for the ambassador's attendance. The Japanese secret police, having tapped the embassy's phones, assumed that these were messages in code. Rosenstock immediately became suspected of being a spy. During a rehearsal the following day, December 7, the news of Pearl Harbor was received. Foreign aliens were immediately expelled from the principal cities, and with about two hundred other displaced persons Rosenstock was sent by the police to Karuizawa, a small town two hundred miles north of Tokyo.[3]

3. Although the Japanese did not generally regard German subjects as foreign aliens, they did in Rosenstock's case because he was Jewish.

Karuizawa was a beautiful spot nestled in the mountains, a resort in summer, but bitterly cold during winter. The parents of one of Rosenstock's private pupils owned a small, primitive cabin there, and they turned this over to the maestro. Since the cabin was normally used only during the summer, it lacked heating facilities, and Rosenstock frequently went to sleep in subfreezing temperatures, wearing two sets of underclothes, a fur coat, ski hat, and gloves. With time, the clothing supply diminished as items were bartered with the local farmers for supplies of rice and potatoes.

This was home for four years. When he was not gathering firewood in the nearby forest, Rosenstock passed the time composing; his symphonic "Variations on an Original Theme" was successfully presented in both Europe and Japan after the war.

Finally, in 1945, the ordeal came to an end. A Swiss Red Cross truck rolled into Karuizawa, and Rosenstock was liberated.

General Charles A. Willoughby requested that he reorganize Japanese musical life and present several concerts for the American occupation troops. At the end of that year, Rosenstock returned to the United States.

Except for continued attacks by the press, which received added stimulus from Halasz's forthcoming law suit, matters returned to normal at the City Opera. Preparations for the new season got under way, as always, at a breakneck pace. Halasz's contractual guarantee—that productions given under his last year of leadership could not be offered by the company for a two-year period—was completely ignored. In fact, ten of the fifteen operas selected by Rosenstock for his first season fell into this category, including, as salt in an open wound, *The Dybbuk*. Of the remaining five, two were new to the repertoire: Menotti's *Amahl and the Night Visitors*, a tremendous success on television and now being given its stage premiere, and Alban Berg's *Wozzeck*, one of the most controversial of contemporary operas. Also planned for that season was Kurt Weill's *Three Penny Opera* in the arrangement by Marc Blitzstein, but this was dropped due to the ever-present financial crisis.

Rosenstock experienced a very difficult tenure. He began with an unfriendly press agitating for reinstatement of Halasz. Much of the journalistic hostility, it seemed, took the form of undeservedly negative reviews. Of course, this is a purely subjective matter; one can not state unequivocally that any particular critic was biased. Nonetheless, anyone having followed both performances and reviews since the company's inauguration, and having been in basic agreement with most of the critics for Halasz's eight years, might suddenly have found a drastic lack of correspondence between performance and review.

Susannah had established Treigle as a star of the first magnitude; *Boris Godunov,* which opened the Fall 1964 season, confirmed the impression. The sly, insinuating Prince Shuisky in this photograph is Norman Kelley. The production also boasted another young, unknown performer destined for major stardom—Tatiana Troyanos, who was heard as Marina. (FRED FEHL)

Eileen Schauler made her City Opera debut on March 4, 1965 as the
totally wanton Katerina Ismailova. Her impassioned lover, Sergei, was
Richard Cassilly. (FRED FEHL)

When the company decided to do Kurt Weill's *Three Penny Opera* (or,
more properly, *Die Dreigroschenoper,* since it was performed in German),
it turned quite properly to the world of theater and cabaret. Kurt Kasznar
and Martha Schlamme were engaged for the pivotal roles of Macheath and
Jenny. Here they are in Jenny's bordello. (FRED FEHL)

The choice of Ginastera's *Don Rodrigo* for the inauguration of the new house at Lincoln Center was as brilliant a move as it was bold. An unfamiliar, atonal work—the first opera of an obscure composer with unknown leading singers—would not seem an auspicious beginning. However, Ginastera's score was powerful and compelling, Capobianco's direction and Rudel's conducting superb, and the star of the performance, although he had not yet established a following or even a reputation, was twenty-four-year-old Placido Domingo. It was a tremendous success, and achieved a total of seventeen local performances—no mean feat for a contemporary opera. Domingo (above) soon found himself a major operatic celebrity. (FRED FEHL)

Moore's *Ballad of Baby Doe* had become a well-established favorite by the time the company moved to Lincoln Center. In its first production in the new house, Beverly Sills and Walter Cassel re-created the roles they had sung during the first American season. (FRED FEHL)

Apart from *Don Rodrigo,* two new operas were introduced during the Spring 1966 season. Coincidentally, both operas are historical and set during the French Revolution. The first of these was Poulenc's *Dialogues of the Carmelites,* performed in an English translation by Joseph Machlis. In this scene, the Mother Superior (Claramae Turner) comforts Blanche de la Force (Donna Jeffrey). (FRED FEHL)

On September 27, 1966, Leontyne Price sang the role of Cleopatra in
Samuel Barber's 11-day-old opera *Antony and Cleopatra*. That same
evening, across the Lincoln Center Plaza, Beverly Sills sang Cleopatra in
Handel's 242-year-old *Julius Caesar*. This proved to be the turning point
in Sills's career, catapulting her to international fame. Here she is joined by
Norman Treigle (Caesar). Behind Treigle is Spiro Malas as Tolomeo.
(FRED FEHL)

The critics described *Tosca,* in Tito Capobianco's new staging, as the most dramatic in recent memory. In this scene from Act II, Scarpia (Sherrill Milnes) has just thrown Tosca (Jeannine Crader) to the floor. (FRED FEHL)

The Tamino in the Beni Montresor production of Mozart's *The Magic Flute* was Michele Molese, who charmed the audience as he did the wild animals. (FRED FEHL)

The new production of *La Traviata* featured Patricia Brooks and Placido Domingo as Violetta and Alfredo. Here is designer Patton Campbell's sketch for Flora's Act I costume. (NEW YORK CITY OPERA ARCHIVES)

Puccini's *Trittico* returned to the repertoire after a two-year absence. Here we see Norman Treigle as Gianni Schicchi, surrounded by Buoso's greedy relatives. (FRED FEHL)

Madama Butterfly had a new production in Spring 1967. Francesca Roberto was a sensitive, moving Butterfly, Placido Domingo a suitably callous Pinkerton, the role of his City Opera debut. (FRED FEHL)

Successes in *Don Giovanni, The Tales of Hoffmann,* and *Julius Caesar* led to another Sills-Treigle-Rudel collaboration. This time it was Rimsky-Korsakov's *Le Coq d'Or.* Here we see Treigle as the addlepated King Dodon, and Sills as the wily Queen of Shemakha. (FRED FEHL)

One of the highlights of Fall 1967 was the new production of *Cavalleria* and *Pagliacci*. From the latter opera we see the tender Nedda-Silvio love scene (Patricia Brooks and Dominic Cossa), and a jealousy-crazed Canio (Placido Domingo) being goaded by Tonio (Sherrill Milnes). (FRED FEHL)

Borodin's *Prince Igor* had not been heard in New York since the Metropolitan Opera performance on December 15, 1917, so its revival a half
century later was very welcome. Making his company debut was Edward
Villella, one of the leading dancers of the New York City Ballet. As he
leaps into the air during the Polovtsian dances, he is watched intently by
Kontchakovna (Joy Davidson). (FRED FEHL)

Boito's *Mefistofele* proved to be one of the company's most successful productions. Here is a dressing-room photograph of Norman Treigle in the title role showing his spectacular makeup. (FRED FEHL)

After Treigle's death, there were few performances of *Mefistofele* until Samuel Ramey assumed the role in 1977. We see him here in the Classical Sabbath scene with Johanna Meier as Helen of Troy. Note the details of his makeup in the inset. (FRED FEHL)

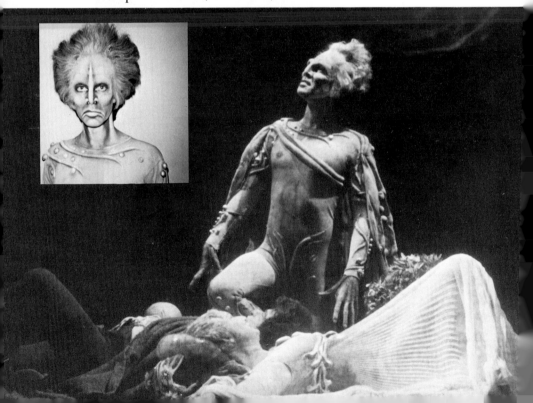

Ravel's delightful *L'Heure Espagnole* had been introduced by Rosenstock as part of a double bill with Bartók's *Bluebeard's Castle*. Rudel brought back the Ravel work in Fall 1969, starring Nico Castel (Torquemada), Richard Fredricks (Ramiro), and Karan Armstrong (Concepción). (FRED FEHL)

The companion piece to *L'Heure Espagnole* was Orff's *Catulli Carmina*. The music was beautifully sung by Patricia Wise and William DuPree, and spectacularly danced by Robert Powell and Carmen de Lavallade as Catullus and Lesbia. (FRED FEHL)

Donizetti's *Roberto Devereux* was one of the company's most unforgettable productions. Beverly Sills is seen as Queen Elizabeth, with Placido Domingo in the title role. This was the first of the so-called Tudor trilogy —three Donizetti operas based upon English royalty. (FRED FEHL)

Maralin Niska was awarded her own production during Fall of 1970—
Janáček's *The Makropoulos Affair*. Niska played a 316-year-old woman
whose father, a physician, had discovered a formula to add 300 years to
one's life span. She is now known as Emilia Marty, although at other times
she has had other identities—Elena Makropoulos, Ellian McGregor, Elsa
Mueller, and Eugenia Montez. We see her here with Hauk-Sendorf (Nico
Castel), a former love. (FRED FEHL)

The Most Important Man was the ninth Menotti opera to be produced by
the company. This photograph from the world-premiere performance is
of Beverly Wolff and Harry Theyard as Leona and Dr. Otto Arnek. (FRED
FEHL)

Susannah, Carlisle Floyd's opera of life in Tennessee, was revived in a new production starring Maralin Niska and Norman Treigle (Susannah and Olin Blitch). The square dance shown above occurs during the first scene. (FRED FEHL)

While preparations for this season were under way, Newbold Morris received an urgent request from Attorney General J. Howard McGrath to begin an investigation of corruption in the federal government. Morris asked Baum to assist him, and Baum, because of the gravity of the assignment, agreed. They went to Washington, leaving Rosenstock to fend for himself at this critical moment—a true "baptism by fire."

Despite the frequently poor reviews, attendance remained at a comfortable level—72 percent of capacity throughout the season.[4] The two scheduled performances of *Wozzeck* had houses of 94 percent and 97 percent, which led to an extra, unscheduled performance on April 22. The double bill of *Amahl* and *The Old Maid and the Thief* also drew large audiences averaging 84 percent for the three performances. *The Dybbuk,* however, was a great disappointment, dropping from an average paid attendance of 95 percent[5] in fall 1951 to 59 percent in spring 1952. Other operas that fared particularly badly were *Manon* (58 percent), *The Marriage of Figaro* (60 percent), *Love for Three Oranges* (61 percent), and *Andrea Chénier* (62 percent), while *Don Giovanni, Der Rosenkavalier, Madama Butterfly,* and *La Bohème* had above-average attendance. All in all, Rosenstock's first season was considerably more successful, both artistically and financially, than anyone had the right to expect under the circumstances.

Just before the season started, however, when contracts for the performers were renegotiated, the various unions involved demanded not only higher wage scales but unemployment insurance as well, and so the season ran a deficit of almost $42,000.

The City Center Ballet Company, under the direction of Lincoln Kirstein, had been having problems of its own. While the opera company had to establish itself despite tremendous competition from the Met, there was, at least, an existing audience for opera as an art form. This was not yet true of the ballet, and so its early seasons fared very poorly. It probably

4. Paid attendance during the Halasz regime ranged from a low of 61 percent (fall 1945) to a high of 90 percent (spring 1946), for an overall average of 79 percent during the course of his seventeen seasons.

5. It has previously been indicated that *The Dybbuk* performances in 1951 were sold out. The 95 percent figure given here does not conflict with the earlier statement. For all operas, a certain number of tickets are set aside for the press, the composer and librettist (if living), etc. Generally, a larger block is held in reserve for new works, where critical interest is higher. Thus, a sold-out house means that no further tickets are available for purchase. However, the number of tickets sold will be several percentage points below the house capacity. Of the five *Dybbuk* performances given under Halasz, only the last was not completely sold out. The paid attendances for the five performances were 94 percent, 98 percent, 98 percent, 98 percent, and 90 percent, for a seasonal average of 95.6 percent.

could not have endured at all, in fact, without extensive subsidy from Kirstein himself. A further detrimental factor was that it had been created as an avant-garde company, and in order to retain its limited audience it had either to keep producing novelty after novelty—an exceedingly expensive proposition—or to limit severely the length of its seasons; and this would make it impossible for the dancers to survive economically. Thus, when the famed impresario Leon Leonidoff offered the company an extended European tour, it was like manna from heaven. The only drawback was that Leonidoff insisted on including Spain in the tour. Because of political and public sentiment against the fascist Franco government, Baum and Kirstein tried their utmost to dissuade Leonidoff, but he was adamant—no Spain, no tour. Finally, they agreed. Jacob Potofsky, one of the most active members of the board since the company's formation, already enraged over the Halasz incident, now resigned. The City Center was therefore facing internal problems, as well as box-office deficits.

Meanwhile, Morris, in his role as federal investigator, plunged himself into the job with zeal and energy. Much to the surprise of McGrath, his employer, Morris began his investigation with the attorney general's office. He prepared a questionnaire to be completed by all federal employees—including McGrath—which called for the supplying of financial information and tax returns. McGrath bristled and adamantly refused to provide this material, whereupon Morris requested that Congress grant him the power of subpoena. This was denied, the newspapers of the time suggesting that the legislature was no more anxious than McGrath to be subjected to close scrutiny. On April 3, 1952, McGrath sent the following note to Morris: "Sir: Please be informed that your appointment as a Special Assistant to the Attorney General is hereby terminated and your services as an employee of the Department of Justice shall cease at the close of business today."

Immediately after sending this note, McGrath telephoned President Truman and tendered his resignation, which was accepted.

Later that evening, some members of the press visited Morris to get his comments. In his typewriter was the following response to McGrath's terse note: "Dear Howard: I am not mad at you. I'm only sorry that you do not really want to clean house. Keep your shirt on! Private life is not so bad."

Morris and Baum returned to New York to find large deficits awaiting them at City Center. The company had no real collateral on which to secure loans, and so Morris contacted all of the guarantors and directors, and raised $15,000, including an anonymous gift of $5,000 from John D. Rockefeller, Jr. This was not nearly enough, however, and Ralph Falcone, the comptroller, asked all tenants of the building if they would pay a year's rent in advance. Surprisingly, all complied, and this produced another $35,000. In addition, the company obtained a loan of $10,000 from Kirstein's School of American Ballet, and one of $3,000 from John S. White. The immediate problem of having cash on hand was solved, but, with loans to be repaid and no rent forthcoming for a year, the situation was so desperate that Falcone went so far as to ask Baum for instructions on liquidating the company.

The heads of the various performing units—opera, ballet, and drama—were all told to tighten up their belts. New productions were reduced to a minimum and other economies were to be put into effect, but the board realized that this was not enough. They needed one man to serve as a full-time employee, coordinating the efforts of all departments, contacting foundations and associations for aid, and empowered to make decisions without constant board approval.

The ballet company, for the five years since its formation, had been under the directorship of Lincoln Kirstein and the artistic direction of George Balanchine. Both men had served without remuneration, a situation that proved no hardship for Kirstein, but was becoming increasingly difficult for Balanchine. Because Kirstein had long been involved with artistic presentations and had many affluent associates with an interest in the arts, he seemed the ideal person for the newly designated function of coordinator. On October 1, 1952, he officially became managing director of the City Center, a post he filled without compensation.

The fall opera season opened on September 18. Many staples of the repertoire were held over from the previous season, along with both *Wozzeck* and *Amahl*, which turned out to be the two works most poorly attended—58 percent and 44 percent of capacity, respectively. Even more disappointing—and surprising—was that neither of the *new* productions sold well. Menotti's *Consul*, which had enjoyed considerable success during its previous Broadway run, played to only 63 percent of capacity, despite the presence of Patricia Neway, who was overwhelming in the role of Magda Sorel. The double bill of Béla Bartók's *Bluebeard's Castle* and Ravel's *L'Heure Espagnole* attracted somewhat larger audiences, with an average attendance of 77 percent. But it was the standard repertoire that saved the season from disaster, with *Carmen, Faust, Tosca, La Bohème,* and *Madama Butterfly* leading the box-office lists. When figures were tallied at the season's end, it was learned that the average attendance was 72 percent, and the deficit was $48,590.76. The fall tour, however, was profitable as always, and this reduced the season's loss to $15,485.32—a manageable figure.

The coup of the season was the acquisition of Tullio Serafin as a member of the conducting staff. Serafin, considered the dean of Italian operatic conductors, had enjoyed a prestigious career at both the Met and La Scala. There were rumors that Rudolf Bing, the Met's manager, had tried to persuade Serafin to reject the City Opera engagement, but, whatever Serafin's own reasons may have been, he accepted, and his reputation brought a new glamour to the company.

One other outstanding attraction of the season was a visit by the Fujiwara Opera Company of Tokyo. Rosenstock, because of his revered position in Japan, was able to negotiate successfully for the appearance of the company in two performances of *Madama Butterfly*. They would furnish all scenery, costumes, and props, providing a hitherto unachieved level of authenticity; all of the Japanese roles would be sung by members of the company (in Japanese), while the three American parts would be portrayed by Americans (in Italian). When the performances took place, they were staged without the Japanese scenery, which was not fireproof and could therefore not be used. Nonetheless, the costumes—and particularly the stage motions and gestures—added a dimension that had never before been witnessed by American audiences. Both performances were completely sold out, and the public was wildly demonstrative in its appreciation.

One of the most significant chapters in the City Center's brief history began to unfold at this time. From the very outset, the company had been led to believe that they would have the use of the theater at the rental rate of $1 a year. As soon as the various principals involved were too deeply committed to withdraw, however, the city had altered its position. Now, less than ten years later, the company had already paid more than $120,000 in rent to the city; another $60,000 in back rental was owed; and an additional $23,000 would accrue during the coming year. The situation had become completely untenable. Suddenly, and without warning, auditors from the city comptroller's office appeared to examine the company's books, to determine the exact amount of rent past due.[6] In the face of all the other financial burdens, this was the breaking point. Whenever the directors had approached the city for aid, the answer had been the same. The city was very sympathetic to the problems, but was legally powerless to assist in any way.

6. The rental finally decided upon was 1½ percent of the company's gross box-office receipts. Thus, an audit was necessary for an accurate determination.

It now became obvious to both Baum and Morris that City Center's only chance of survival rested with new legislation. The major problem was one of timing. The state legislature was scheduled to adjourn very shortly, and it seemed virtually impossible to push any new measures through in the few days remaining. Nonetheless, both men had extensive experience in municipal government and many friends holding high political offices. If anyone could succeed in a quest of this type, it was this team.

Fortunately, there was some sort of precedent. An enabling act was already in existence with regard to the Brooklyn Academy of Music, allowing the city to charge a rental of $1 annually. The BAM situation, however, was quite different in that the building had been owned by the Institute of Arts and Sciences and then donated to the city, a gift evaluated at $1 million. City Center was, however, a municipally owned structure on which a large back rental was due. Nonetheless, there was no viable alternative. Racing against the clock, Baum drafted an enabling act over-night, using the Brooklyn Academy act as a model, but adding one very important sentence: "Upon the making of such lease, the board of estimate may annually, at its discretion, appropriate such sum or sums as it may determine for the care, maintenance, and support of the said land and buildings and the activities of the said City Center in connection there-with." This was obviously a crucial addition because, if the bill could be enacted into law, the city would not only be permitted to charge the nominal rental, but could render other fiscal aid as well.

Baum called his friend, Senator McNeil Mitchell, chairman of the State Senate Committee on Affairs of the City of New York. Mitchell agreed to propose the bill in the senate and arranged to have Assemblyman John Brook present it in the assembly at the same time. This was one day before the deadline for introducing new bills into the legislative hopper!

Due to the intricacies of the legal system, this act could not be passed by the legislature until a legal home rule message was obtained from the mayor and the city council. However, Mayor Vincent Impellitteri was in the midst of a financial feud with Governor Thomas E. Dewey over a request for greater state aid for the city. It would have been extremely awkward for the mayor, on the one hand, to say that the city was in desperate need of funds, and, on the other, to willingly relinquish a $20,000 source of annual income. Faced with this apparent impasse, Baum met with Stanley Isaacs, the minority leader of the city council. Isaacs indicated that a two-thirds vote of the council would suffice, even without the mayor's message. On March 10, Baum appeared before a meeting of the finance committee of the council, but action on the resolution was postponed. The next council meeting was scheduled for

March 17, but that would be too late, as the legislature was scheduled to adjourn on March 19,[7] leaving insufficient time for passage of the act.

Now Morris swung into action. Baum had already secured the cooperation of Joseph Sharkey, majority leader of the city council, and Morris, having served as president of the council for many years, had both the friendship and respect of a large segment of its membership. After a few well-placed telephone calls, a special meeting of the council was called, and the home rule request to the legislature was passed unanimously. The resolution was immediately sent to Albany, where it was awaited by Reuben Lazarus, Morris's former chief assistant. Lazarus, who was now the legislative advisor to Oswald Heck, speaker of the assembly, had been alerted to watch for the bill, and he was prepared to do everything in his power to assist in its passage.

Morton Baum captured the feeling of urgency surrounding this episode in the following extract from a history of the City Center he had started to write before his death:

Here was the situation. . . . I was on the phone with Senator Mitchell's office, who was waiting for the city council's message in the senate; Mr. Morris was on the phone with Reuben Lazarus, who was awaiting word in the assembly. Friday morning the message of necessity was received, and the enabling act immediately passed the senate under Senator Mitchell's skillful guidance. Reuben Lazarus was waiting in the senate, and he raced with the bill over to the assembly. On Saturday, just a few hours before the legislature adjourned, the bill passed the assembly.

It was a magnificent job done by experienced veterans.

Although this was a major breakthrough, the company was not yet out of the woods. The bill still had to be signed within thirty days by Governor Dewey. Baum prepared a detailed memorandum in support of the measure, which he sent to the governor. Dewey's counsel replied, however, that there was a defect in the bill. In his haste, Baum had failed to proofread the draft closely enough to notice that a line had inadvertently been omitted from the typescript. As a result, the property's boundaries were inaccurately defined. This was only a minor point; the intent was perfectly clear. What was serious, however, was that the governor refused to sign it without a specific request from Mayor Impellitteri, even though this was not a legal requirement.

Getting such a request was a ticklish situation because of the city's

7. The adjournment, it later developed, was postponed two days until March 21, 1953.

quest for additional state aid. As it happened, both the mayor's wife and Thomas Todarelli, one of his closest friends, were members of the City Center board, and they were successful in impressing upon him the urgency of the situation. Just as the thirty-day signing period was about to expire, Impellitteri drafted the necessary statement, and Dewey signed the bill into law.

Apart from the actual formation of the company, this was the single most important event in its ten-year history. No longer could the city say, "We would like to help, but. . . ."

15
Failing Box Office

A L T H O U G H the rent situation was now well in hand, the City Center was facing a severe crisis. The drama company, which could normally be counted on to turn a handsome profit, suddenly began to lose money. Although reviews were good, the choice of plays—*Love's Labour's Lost, The Misalliance,* and *The Merchant of Venice*—apparently did not appeal to the public, and instead of producing a surplus, the result was a $50,000 loss. The new opera season (spring 1953) was about to start and funds were desperately needed. In the past, contributions had been solicited privately and quietly. Now, however, the situation was too grave for so discreet an approach, and for the first time a public appeal was made. David Hayman, president of the New York Foundation, contributed $25,000, while patrons donated what they could, ranging from 15¢ up. Within three months, Morris, who headed the fund-raising drive, managed to secure $100,000, and by summer an additional $40,000 had poured in. Clearly, the City Center had many friends.

While the immediate problem of survival had been solved, austerity measures were necessary throughout the institution. The opera company would normally have curtailed the length of its season, but a recent contract with the American Guild of Musical Artists, which guaranteed the performers fourteen weeks of employment in New York each year, prevented this. There were, however, two works that could be brought into the repertoire with only minimal expense. They were Marc Blitzstein's *Regina,* which had enjoyed a Broadway run in 1949, and Johann Strauss's *Die Fledermaus,* which had toured under Hurok a year earlier. The costumes and scenery for both of these were available at a low rental, and so both operas were announced for the forthcoming season.

Lincoln Kirstein had seen Rossini's *La Cenerentola* at Glyndebourne, during the previous summer and found it a completely captivating work. So strongly did he advocate performing it in New York that, financial difficulties notwithstanding, the board went along with his plea. It was an expensive production, but turned out to be one of the company's great successes.

Cenerentola and *Regina* scored the largest box-office receipts of the season, but *Fledermaus* made a very poor showing, perhaps because it was also in the Metropolitan repertoire. All in all, despite the success of *Cenerentola*, the average attendance for the forty-six performances was only 56 percent of capacity—the poorest showing since the company's formation ten years earlier. The deficit was an unprecedented $70,000!

The two most important events that season went virtually unnoticed. One was a minor debut—a young bass who, on March 28, appeared in the unspectacular role of Colline in *La Bohème*. Three and a half years later, after he portrayed Olin Blitch in Floyd's *Susannah*, the entire operatic world knew of Norman Treigle.

The other major event that season was an administrative change. John S. White was promoted from artistic secretary to assistant general director, with far-flung consequences, as will be seen.

Kirstein had long been a close friend of both Nelson Rockefeller and John Marshall, who headed the Division of Arts and Humanities of the Rockefeller Foundation. This seemed to be a potential source of income, and a meeting was arranged among Baum, Kirstein, and Marshall. The meeting's results were encouraging but essentially noncommittal. Marshall explained that funds might become available if the proper approach could be devised. The foundation did not engage in deficit financing, but might be willing to sponsor some new project.

Although Baum and Morris searched for some plan that would be acceptable to the Rockefeller Foundation and would assist the City Center, none could be found. Nevertheless, Morris submitted a formal request on the theory that there was nothing to be lost. Surprisingly, his efforts were rewarded, and in addition to the successful fund-raising drive and the reduced rental, the Rockefeller Foundation bestowed $200,000 upon the company. Almost overnight, it had gone from near catastrophe to financial security.

As if some divine force were at work, other unanticipated rewards began to pour in. José Ferrer, at Jean Dalrymple's request, agreed to return to the company to produce, direct, and star in four plays, *Cyrano de*

Bergerac, *The Shrike*, *Richard III*, and *Charley's Aunt*. He accepted the minimum fee permissible under union regulations, then returned it to the company in the form of a donation. *Misalliance*, which had been running at a Broadway theater under City Center sponsorship and losing money week after week, suddenly began to draw crowds, so that by the time the engagement was completed, it actually produced a gain in revenue. And finally, Rodgers and Hammerstein agreed to permit the Center to produce *Oklahoma!* for a very lucrative five-week run.

Troubles soon began to develop in another area, however. Lincoln Kirstein, in his position as managing director, assumed a greater responsibility (and authority) than the board had ever intended. The first serious problem involved Ferrer. Kirstein felt that Ferrer's engagement was in the nature of a "showcase" or a booking, and, as such, was of negligible value. What the City Center needed, he felt, was its own permanent dramatic production company, organized along the same lines as opera and ballet. Unfortunately these opinions found their way into the press. It took a great deal of diplomacy from both Baum and Dalrymple to persuade Ferrer to remain. The board told Kirstein to keep such feelings to himself, and, although immediate antagonisms passed, a scar remained.

The second serious problem involved Rosenstock and the Rockefeller grant. At the time the grant was made, there were stringent terms attached. The $200,000 was to be used over a three-year period: $100,000 in the first year; $60,000 in the second; and $40,000 in the third. The money was to be divided equally between opera and ballet, and could be used only to commission and design new productions. Not surprisingly, Kirstein was named trustee of the fund, partly because he was managing director, partly because of his own artistic successes in ballet, and, not least, because of his relationship with Rockefeller and Marshall. The allocation of money to the ballet posed no problem, since Kirstein was himself head of that unit. Friction did develop between Kirstein and Rosenstock, however. Rosenstock felt that as director of the opera company, he should have the option of using the money allocated to opera as needed, provided, of course, that the terms of the grant be respected. Kirstein felt that since he was administering the grant, he should oversee its use—particularly since as managing director, he felt that he had the ultimate responsibility for all producing units.

Here was a situation where both men acted with integrity and out of a sense of dedication to the company, but they were in a stalemate. Kirstein won out, as one would expect, since he had the support of the foundation whose money was in dispute. But the rift between Kirstein and Rosenstock was very deep and, in fact, worsened with time.

Kirstein managed to antagonize the opera company's director on other occasions. He commissioned Gian Carlo Menotti to compose a new opera, *The Saint of Bleecker Street*, without consulting Rosenstock. A $6,000 grant was given to Menotti as part of the commission. Kirstein also requested a new opera of the Mexican composer Carlos Chávez. This was to be *The Tuscan Players*,[1] and $7,000 of the opera company's money was given to Chávez. Thus, more than 25 percent of the first year's available funds was spent by Kirstein, without Rosenstock's prior knowledge or approval. It is easy to see why tempers reached the boiling point.

Another $37,000 remained available to the opera company during the 1953–54 season. This was used for four new productions, two in fall 1953, two in spring 1954.

The fall of 1953 saw the introduction of Gottfried von Einem's *The Trial*, an expensive production that was noteworthy only for the debut of Phyllis Curtin in the triple roles of Fräulein Burstner, the wife of the court attendant, and Leni. The work failed to please the public, and vanished after two performances. The other new opera that fall was *Hansel and Gretel*. It did moderately well—enough to be retained in the repertoire for three consecutive seasons. On the other hand, because of the poor *Fledermaus* attendance during the previous season, only two performances of that production were on the current schedule. As it happened, they averaged 88 percent attendance, the highest percentage of the season.

Overall ticket sales increased dramatically, from 56 percent to 69 percent of capacity, due primarily to seasonal fluctuation (the four fall seasons beginning with 1952 averaged 66 percent attendance; the following spring seasons, only 56 percent). It seems reasonable to assume that after the summer hiatus, opera lovers were eager to return to the theater. By the time the spring season came around, New Yorkers had already been exposed to about six months of opera, so that appetites—and probably available budgets—were diminished.

Shortly before the next season (spring 1954) another Kirstein-Rosenstock confrontation took place. Each of the operating units—opera, ballet, light opera, and drama—theoretically functioned independently. When Kirstein assumed the position of managing director, he felt that certain functions could be combined, thereby effecting a more efficient and economical operation. Phillip Bloom had been successfully handling publicity for the ballet company for several years, and Jean Rosenthal had

1. Although the company had a substantial investment in *The Tuscan Players*, production costs prevented the performances from materializing. Under a different title, *Panfilo and Lauretta*, Chávez's opera was later presented by Columbia University in New York City on May 9, 1957.

been its main lighting designer. Kirstein prevailed upon Rosenstock to engage both of them, along with choreographer John Butler, to serve the opera company in addition to the ballet company. Rosenstock was by no means bound to follow Kirstein's suggestion, but in the interest of harmony, he did so.

Suddenly, in early spring of 1954, when Kirstein was out of the country, Rosenstock dismissed all three, stating that their work was not up to par. Kirstein learned of this when he read it in *Variety*, and took Rosenstock's act as a personal affront.

At a rehearsal some weeks later, Kirstein criticized the lighting, and tempers flared up again, with both Rosenstock and Kirstein claiming ultimate responsibility for the overall production quality. Of course, each man was right in his own way. The fault lay squarely with the board of directors for creating a structure of this sort. Had Kirstein been a weaker person who would content himself with merely being a figurehead, there would have been no problem. However, with many years of solid theatrical achievement behind him, he could hardly step aside and approve ideas in conflict with his own artistic integrity.

Spring 1954 got off to an exciting start—the return of Strauss's *Salome* to the repertoire after an absence of ten seasons. Phyllis Curtin, who had made her debut in the ill-fated *Trial*, appeared as the depraved princess, with Walter Cassel as the object of her lust. The English comedienne Anna Russell, as the witch in *Hansel and Gretel*, also made a brilliant debut that season. Three new works were added to the growing list—Aaron Copland's *The Tender Land* (world premiere), Jerome Kern's *Show Boat*, and Verdi's *Falstaff* in an English translation by Chester Kallman. *Show Boat* did a good box-office business (76 percent attendance), but the season's average was a scant 60 percent. Except for *La Bohème*, which inexplicably filled 87 percent of the house, standard repertoire attendance was pitifully low—44 percent for *Traviata*, 45 percent each for *Rigoletto* and *The Marriage of Figaro*, 47 percent for *Don Giovanni*. The major new productions, the lifeblood of the company, achieved only a 65 percent sale. Evidently, the public was losing interest in the company.

Ironically, *Show Boat*, one of the major successes of the season, was treated very harshly by the press, which felt that it had no place in an operatic repertoire. Rosenstock was taken to task for its inclusion, but, as it happened, he too felt that it was out of place. His decision to include it was a concession for the overall welfare of City Center. Morton Baum had very much wanted to have the light opera company produce it, but Oscar Hammerstein II, who wrote the lyrics, gave his approval for this only if it entered by way of the opera company. He never gave his reasons for this decision, but presumably he felt that greater prestige would result. *Tender Land* was dropped after two performances, while *Show Boat* and *Falstaff* each managed to achieve a second season.

The fall 1954 season was to have been a very exciting one. Scheduled for production were Menotti's new work, *The Saint of Bleecker Street*, and the American premiere of Richard Strauss's *Die Frau ohne Schatten*, anticipating the Metropolitan Opera production by a dozen years. Large sums of money had already been spent on both works—$7,000 on *The Saint* and $3,000 for designing the decor for *Frau*. Poor attendance during the previous season had, however, produced a loss of $100,000, and the board decided that the coming season must have no new productions. It should be pointed out that the Rockefeller grant money could be used only for the *theoretical* creation of new works—that is, commission fees to composers and/or librettists, and the cost of designing (but not manufacturing) scenery, costumes, and props. Thus, although the grant money existed, adding any new works to the repertoire would still have been extremely costly. Accordingly, the fall season was billed as "all-request," and consisted of repeats only. The predictable result was an apathetic and dwindling audience—only 62 percent of capacity, which would have been acceptable for a spring season, but was a very poor fall showing. Despite the fact that it was an inexpensive season to produce, the loss was $50,000.

Several major crises occurred that year. The first involved *The Saint of Bleecker Street*. City Opera was to have performed the premiere, and Menotti had already signed a contract with Italy's La Scala permitting it to do the work the following spring. With the board's decision to exclude *The Saint* from the fall '54 repertoire, there were no scheduled performances prior to the Italian production, and Menotti was extremely anxious to have the premiere take place in America. In addition, Kirstein had given Menotti his promise of a fall '54 production—a promise he was now unable to keep. Accordingly, he released Menotti from any City Opera obligations and helped to organize a group of private sponsors to underwrite a Broadway run. This meant that the money already expended was wasted, as far as City Opera was concerned, and Rosenstock felt that Kirstein had betrayed the company.

Shortly after the season ended, Baum went on a European trip and saw *Die Frau ohne Schatten*. Magnificent as the music was, he felt that the libretto was atrocious, and that the vocal and orchestral requirements were beyond the scope of the company. The result was that plans for *Frau* were dropped and its $3,000 investment was also wasted. Chávez's *Tuscan*

Players failed to meet company standards, and this, too, was dropped. All in all, $16,000 of the $50,000 allocated for that first year went down the drain.

To add to the company's woes, the annual Chicago tour, which had always produced a handsome profit, was now canceled because the Chicago Opera was resuming operations after a lapse of eight years.

Arranging the tour schedule was part of John White's job, a difficult task at best. The loss of Chicago greatly increased those difficulties. White succeeded in arranging a four-and-a-half-week itinerary to Worcester, Boston, Philadelphia, Hershey, Pittsburgh, Cleveland, Detroit, East Lansing, Grand Rapids, Kalamazoo, Buffalo, and Rochester—thirty-three performances in all. But, despite guarantees in most of the cities, the tour showed a net loss. Chicago was irreplaceable. Dark clouds hung over the New York City Opera.

When Rosenstock was engaged as general director in spring 1952, he was granted a three-year contract. Since he had just completed his sixth season, the question of renewal or replacement would soon arise. Kirstein was strongly opposed to extending the contract, and he spoke privately to many members of the board, urging that the position now be filled by Gian Carlo Menotti. Baum and Morris felt that Kirstein's motivation was purely personal, and they were opposed to the idea of his private feuds governing company policy. Once again a very tense situation developed, probably the most difficult period since Halasz's ouster. Kirstein was not able to muster quite as much support as his opponents, and when the matter was presented to the board the vote was thirteen to twelve in favor of retaining Rosenstock. Having determined that he would remain, Morris then made a plea for solidarity in backing him. He asked for a second vote, requesting that each director endorse Rosenstock. All complied except Kirstein, and the press was advised that Rosenstock's contract was extended for two years by a vote of twenty-four to one.

Kirstein, feeling that his position was completely undermined, resigned from both the board and the managing directorship. When word of this reached the press, Kirstein was beseiged with interviews, and was quite outspoken in his condemnation of City Center. Since Rosenstock had always been unpopular with the press, they now took up Kirstein's cause, and, as in the days following the Halasz incident, the board came under heavy attack.

Spring '55 featured two new productions, Donizetti's sparkling *Don Pasquale* and Nicolai's *Merry Wives of Windsor*, which had last been seen at the Met in 1900. The Donizetti opera achieved only 35 percent sales, the poorest showing of the season, and *Merry Wives* (56 percent) just barely exceeded the overall season average of 54 percent.

It's a pity that *Pasquale* fared so badly, as it was done with a great deal of charm. Its inclusion in the repertoire at this time demonstrated, however, poor planning. Although almost ten years had elapsed since its last Met performance, it was scheduled for a revival the following fall, starring Roberta Peters, Cesare Valletti, and Fernando Corena—a stellar cast and overwhelming competition for City Opera.

Fall 1955 arrived, and with it, too, came two new productions, a revival of *The Bartered Bride* after seventeen seasons, and several important debuts. The new works were Sir William Walton's *Troilus and Cressida* and Tchaikovsky's *The Golden Slippers* (also known as *Cherevichki, Vakula the Smith,* and *The Caprices of Oxane*). *Troilus and Cressida,* with Jon Crain and Phyllis Curtin in the title roles, was the hit of the season, averaging 79 percent attendance. *The Bartered Bride* attained only 64 percent, however, and *Golden Slippers* a pitiful 44 percent. Richard Cassilly,who later went on to many heroic roles at Covent Garden, Berlin, Vienna, La Scala, and the Metropolitan, made his debut on October 9 as Turiddu in *Cavalleria Rusticana*; Louis Quilico, who had a major career, bowed as Germont in *La Traviata* in a matinee performance the same day. The most important debut of the season, however, was on October 29, when *Fledermaus* was enriched by the Rosalinda of Beverly Sills. However exciting the season may appear in retrospect, it was nevertheless received indifferently at the time, with only 59 percent of all tickets sold.

The poor box office was creating dire financial problems, but that was not all. After singing to half-empty houses night after night, the singers began to show serious signs of low morale. The public's reduced attendance was at least in part due to City Opera's press. Rosenstock had been unpopular with the press because he was Halasz's replacement, but he was attacked more bitterly than ever after the Kirstein altercation. Unfortunately, critics have a profound effect upon the theater-going public, and the fraternity, almost to a man, was destroying the City Opera.

Rosenstock met with Baum to discuss the situation, and both men agreed that perhaps the best course would be for Rosenstock to resign. Accordingly, although there was still another season to run, he withdrew at the end of the spring 1956 season. It was with great sorrow that the board accepted his resignation, although they knew there was no real alternative.

Rosenstock's final season began on March 28, 1956, with the previous year's big success, *Troilus and Cressida*. Making her debut in a relatively small role was Mignon Dunn, currently a well-known mezzo-soprano at the Metropolitan. Other important debuts included those of Beverly Bower, a fine artist with an engaging personality, and two imports from Italy, tenor Piero Miranda Ferraro and baritone Aldo Protti. New productions featured a double bill of Rolf Liebermann's *School for Wives* and Mozart's *The Impresario,* as well as the company's fifth Verdi opera, *Il Trovatore.* *Troilus* dropped from 79 percent to 41 percent attendance, and *Trovatore* achieved a scant 46 percent, while the double bill was the most poorly attended production of the season, with only 36 percent of the seats sold.

Once again, the seasonal average was a house only slightly over half full, and with the *Trovatore* performance of April 15, Rosenstock's reign as general director came to an end. During his nine seasons, he produced forty-two operas, twenty of them new to the company's repertoire. There were 318 performances in New York, and many major debuts, including those of Tulio Serafin, Beverly Sills, Norman Treigle, and Phyllis Curtin. Poor press notwithstanding, it was a record of which he could be justifiably proud.

16

Leinsdorf and
Near Disaster

W H E N City Center had first been organized in 1943, one of the people asked to be an initial incorporator was Erich Leinsdorf. He was a conductor of international prestige, even though he was barely past his twenties at the time.

Leinsdorf was born in Vienna on February 4, 1912. His father was an avid amateur pianist. Because Erich had been an infant when his father died, he had felt no direct paternal influence. His house was nevertheless filled with bound volumes of music. At the age of seven Erich began to take piano lessons as a matter of course; he was not particularly interested, but some three years later music suddenly became very meaningful to him. At this point he began to explore the treasures his father had left, and his skills developed quickly. He continued studying piano until age seventeen, when he realized that his ambition was to conduct. He felt very strongly that every conductor should have a solid background in piano, but he also recognized that the techniques necessary for a conductor were very different from those required by a virtuoso. Accordingly, he resumed his studies, but this time with a conductorial career in view. His new teacher was Hedwig Kanner-Rosenthal, the wife of the famed pianist Moritz Rosenthal.

The following year, he entered the University of Vienna as a music student. He found, however, that his classmates were primarily dilettantes, and that he would need more serious training if music were to become a solid profession for him. He transferred to the State Academy of Music. Here he was inundated with composition, theory, piano, and cello.

In 1934 he went to Salzburg to try to secure a position with Bruno Walter, who was conducting *Don Giovanni* that year. During a rehearsal, Leinsdorf slipped unobserved into the opera house. Once, as Walter left his piano to walk across stage and speak to one of the artists, Leinsdorf, lying in wait, quickly took Walter's seat and continued playing where Walter had left off—from memory. The older conductor was decidedly impressed, and Leinsdorf was immediately engaged as a preseason coach.

The *Don Giovanni* cast consisted of both Italians and Germans, which created problems because the two countries had different prompting traditions. In Germany and Austria, the prompter was usually a retired actor who spoke the next words. In Italy, however, the prompter sang the cues. Since the Salzburg prompter was an actor with no musical training, he could not possibly sing cues, much to the consternation of the Latin performers. The *Don Giovanni* title role was played that year by Ezio Pinza, and he was trying desperately to explain all of this to the prompter—with no success, as Pinza spoke no German and the prompter did not know a word of Italian. Leinsdorf, who spoke both languages, stepped in to assist and demonstrated Pinza's request by singing a few of the cues. Pinza was delighted at having been understood, and requested that the Salzburg management engage Leinsdorf to prompt. Thus, Leinsdorf's first professional operatic engagement was in an essentially nonmusical capacity. Recalling the location of the prompter's box, Leinsdorf later quipped, "I really learned the opera business from the bottom up."

Although his engagement as prompter was, to a certain extent, a stroke of luck, it reflected Leinsdorf's determination. All operas in the Austria of that period were performed in German translation, and Leinsdorf's knowledge of Italian was therefore rather surprising. He had merely felt that anyone with a really serious interest in opera should know Italian, and so he had studied it at the conservatory.

Returning to Vienna, he learned that Toscanini was looking for a pianist to assist in rehearsals of Kodály's *Psalmus Hungaricus*. Leinsdorf auditioned for the job and was accepted. He subsequently applied for the position of assistant conductor at Salzburg, where Toscanini would be performing the following year. Toscanini agreed, and Leinsdorf found himself back at Salzburg, working for both Toscanini and Walter, but this time as assistant conductor. He remained at Salzburg for three seasons, preparing the soloists for *Falstaff*, *Fidelio*, *Meistersinger*, *Magic Flute*, Beethoven's Ninth Symphony, and the requiems of Verdi and Brahms.

As Hitler's rise to power began to curtail musical life in Austria, Leinsdorf spent more and more time in Italy, where he conducted at

Bologna, Trieste, and San Remo. He continued to spend summers at Salzburg until 1937, when Walter and Toscanini also left the festival.

That year, Edward Johnson, general manager of the Metropolitan Opera, was looking for an assistant for his overworked German-wing conductor, Artur Bodanzky. Toscanini recommended Leinsdorf, who was hired sight unseen.

During rehearsals, Leinsdorf so impressed the Met management, that he was permitted to conduct the *Walküre* performance of January 21, 1938, drawing rave reviews from the critics. Later that season he conducted performances of *Die Walküre,* along with *Parsifal* and *Elektra.* He was also offered the chance to conduct in San Francisco that year; his October 19 debut there was in his favorite opera, Débussy's *Pelléas and Mélisande.*

The next season, his Metropolitan repertoire was augmented by *Rheingold, Siegfried, Lohengrin, Tannhäuser,* and *Amelia Goes to the Ball.*

In November 1939 Bodanzky died, and during the 1939–40 Met season Leinsdorf conducted *every* German-language performance, in addition to Gluck's *Orpheus and Eurydice* and *Pelléas and Mélisande*—almost 40 percent of the performances, although there were seven other conductors on the roster.

This was certainly an enviable position for someone just turned twenty-eight, but such fortune had its disturbing side as well. Leinsdorf disliked being characterized as a Wagner specialist. He longed to explore the world of symphonic music. He remained with the Met for another three seasons, but in 1942, when Artur Rodzinski decided to leave the Cleveland Symphony Orchestra to assume leadership of the New York Philharmonic, Leinsdorf was nominated as his replacement. Two other conductors, Vladimir Golschmann and George Szell, were also contenders for the position. The Cleveland board of directors was divided, with none of the three candidates winning a majority vote, but Leinsdorf's supporters constituted a plurality, and he was signed to a three-year contract.

His first concert was on October 14, 1943; the very next morning he received the familiar "the President of the United States sends his greetings. . . ." Leinsdorf had been drafted into the army.

He entered military service in December 1943, but was discharged six months later because of curvature of the spine. His Cleveland post had already been filled by guest conductors, and although the law stipulated that returning servicemen were guaranteed their pre-military jobs, Leinsdorf chose not to press the point, and found himself with no engagements to speak of for the 1944–45 season. As it happened,

Cleveland did have two concerts earmarked for him, hoping that he might be able to conduct them during a furlough. And then, unexpectedly, the Metropolitan Opera, by juggling schedules, was able to offer him thirteen performances in New York and seven on tour. All in all he conducted a light schedule, but the season was not nearly as catastrophic for him as it originally seemed destined to be.

The following year, when plans were being made for the 1945–46 season (the last under Leinsdorf's original contract), the Cleveland board decided to split assignments—recordings as well as concerts—equally among Leinsdorf, Szell, and Golschmann. Piqued, Leinsdorf submitted his resignation, and Szell was named to the post.

By this time, the war had ended, and Leinsdorf began a whirlwind tour that embraced Havana, St. Louis, Chicago, Minneapolis, Great Britain, Vienna, and Amsterdam. Returning to the United States, he was engaged for five weeks of guest appearances with the Rochester Philharmonic. There was also a strong possibility of a permanent assignment with them, as they had been without a resident conductor since 1945, when José Iturbi resigned. Leinsdorf went to Rochester to fulfill his five-week engagement, and stayed for almost nine years, until the end of 1955.

It was in October of 1955 that Rosenstock and Baum decided that a replacement was needed at City Opera. This had not yet been made public, but somehow or other news of this sort leaks out. Word reached Leinsdorf, who was then in San Francisco conducting the American premiere of *Troilus and Cressida*. He made it known to Baum that he would be available for the post if asked, and in view of his credentials, very little consideration was necessary.

Leinsdorf came to City Opera like the proverbial house on fire. He felt that interest in the company had waned to the point where radical surgery was needed, and he brought with him a whirlwind of ideas.

He planned to do fewer repertoire works but with more performances of each and with no cast changes for any opera during a given season. In this way, he felt, a higher quality of performance would emerge. He also felt that the way to attract new audiences was through a contemporary repertoire, music in the idiom of the day. Later on, appreciation of nineteenth- and eighteenth-century literature could be cultivated. He was very much aware of the shortcomings in dramatic technique frequently exhibited by opera singers, and wished to engage the well-known dramatic coach, Ludwig Donath, for several weekly acting classes; he hoped to create an opera workshop for promising newcomers in conjunction with Columbia University but wanted only experienced performers to participate in City Opera productions; he planned to install a subscription system so that ticket sales would not be on a day-to-day basis and funds could be better allocated; he initiated negotiations with NBC for televised operatic performances; he wanted to bring in a few major European artists to add a sense of luster and excitement—singers such as Franco Corelli, Ebe Stigniani, Ferruccio Tagliavini, Giangiacomo Guelfi, and Gabriella Sciutti.

Leinsdorf had no shortage of ideas, and if only a few of them had come to pass, the company might have been well on its way to a revitalized existence.

One of his more radical ideas involved stage design. He wanted a basic set with a revolving stage that would be used for all productions. Stage sets would be minimal, and the different frameworks required for each opera would be controlled principally through lighting. In this way, new productions would be very inexpensive to install, although the initial cost of the basic set would be quite high.

To achieve this, he engaged Leo Kerz, a former CBS-TV designer and art director. Unfortunately, the experiment failed. Initial costs were much higher than the amounts budgeted, the turntable was noisy and distracting, and audiences were unhappy about the relative sameness of the sets from one opera to the next.

In addition, the company could not afford to mount every opera in the repertoire as a new production, even at the low per-opera cost, so Leinsdorf decided to adapt the existing scenery for those five planned operas that were already in repertoire—*Carmen, Bohème, Rigoletto, Traviata*, and *Fledermaus*. The old scenery was too large for the new framework, however, and had to be cut down. When the unit set was abandoned, the scenery for these five operas no longer fit the stage, and was scrapped. In the end, Leinsdorf's staging innovations became an extravagantly costly venture.

Thirty-nine performances were scheduled for the fall 1956 season—two *Rigoletto*s, three *Bohème*s, four *Carmen*s, four *Traviata*s, three *Fledermaus*es, two of Carl Orff's *The Moon* double-billed with Stravinsky's *L'Histoire du Soldat*, three of a new American opera, *Susannah* by Carlisle Floyd, two of *The Tempest* by Frank Martin, and three of Thomas's *Mignon*. Six dates were listed as "to be announced," in order to provide those works for which the public response was greatest. Leinsdorf pinned all of his hopes that season on Offenbach's *Orpheus in the Underworld*, new to the repertoire, which was scheduled for seven performances. The *Orpheus* was done in a new English version by Eric Bentley—and unfortunately it failed. The humor was deemed heavy-handed, the rhyming couplets annoying, and the bawdy text, which many felt went beyond the dictates of good taste, shocked and embarrassed the audience. Although public interest was quite high at the outset, it quickly waned. Attendance was poor except for a few scattered performances, and eight of the scheduled thirty-nine presentations were canceled. The season's overall attendance was 57 percent, somewhat lover than attendance during Rosenstock's[1] tenure, and production costs were very much higher due to the installation of the revolving stage. The season lost $157,359 despite a Rockefeller grant of almost $34,000. Leinsdorf's loss was between three and four times the expected loss for a season, and the scenery for five standard operas had been rendered useless.

Leo Kerz bore the brunt of the criticism, but, as he pointed out, he had discussed his plans for the revolving stage with the board of directors every step of the way. Leinsdorf got approval for his innovative ideas, but when they failed, the board was very quick to point an accusing finger. It must be noted that the one board member who had dissented, taking exception to Kerz's plan was Morton Baum. He had been voted down, however. This was one of the very rare instances when his opinion had not prevailed, and it proved a very costly error.

Ralph Falcone had sent two prior warnings to Morris, on May 14 and on August 13. In the earlier of these, he advised:

The program he [Leinsdorf] is contemplating staging may bring disaster upon City Center before it starts. After twelve years of association with Mr. Baum, and I have closely scrutinized his activities in programming the opera, I believe that Mr. Baum is qualified to know whether this type of program is the proper thing for us to undertake.

. . . I am taking the trouble of writing to you so that you will understand the problem we are facing and will fight the battle with us. I know that many members of the board will be favorable to Mr. Leinsdorf and may vote for his program to go into effect without consideration of the consequences of the possible deficit that he may create which may be the end of all things since our cash is nil.

By the time August came around, it was too late to change plans. Nevertheless, Falcone felt duty-bound to comment:

In the May meeting, when Mr. Leinsdorf presented his budget, Mr. Baum very strenuously objected to the entire program but since Mr. Leinsdorf has so many friends on the board, they have voted to inaugurate his plans. I have noted that of the entire membership of the board only seven responded to financial aid but most of them voted for Mr. Leinsdorf's program.

1. The lowest seasonal average under Rosenstock was 52 percent (spring 1956); the highest, 74 percent (fall 1952); the overall average for the nine seasons, 61 percent.

I do not wish to appear critical of the way things are handled but I must call a spade a spade. Although I am called a pessimist, an alienist and a worrier, let me assure you that is why City Center has existed twelve years.

On April 7, long before the fall season had been announced, Baum, as chairman of the finance committee, realized that the company's economic position would not support the next two opera seasons, and that one of them would have to be canceled. Since fall always sold much better than spring, he decided to cancel the spring '57 season. Leinsdorf was immediately informed, but he convinced the board to withhold any announcement until after the fall season. In a letter written to Newbold Morris on April 7, he stated: "Any public display of crisis will not help the immediate financial problem but on the contrary severely prejudice our efforts. I have reason to hope and believe that we may be in a better position seven or eight months from now, as long as we do not jeopardize this great intangible element of optimism, hope and expectancy which accompanies a change of administration."

When the announcement of spring cancellation did finally come upon the heels of Leinsdorf's debacle, he was, of course, blamed for that too.

So desperate had the company's position become that there was talk of the Metropolitan's taking it over and converting it into a sort of Opéra-Comique, a second house where they would perform small-scale works. These plans had progressed far enough for the Met to begin examining the company's rather meager assets in preparation for the takeover. Baum, however, persuaded the board to redouble efforts to raise funds, and not to let the company slip through its fingers. He succeeded at the eleventh hour, but the future was far from bright.

On the artistic side of the Leinsdorf season, the major event was the premiere of *Susannah*, considered by many to be the finest American opera to date. Subsequent seasons would involve two other Floyd operas, *Wuthering Heights* and *The Passion of Jonathan Wade*, neither of which had the impact of *Susannah*. Norman Treigle became a superstar overnight through his compelling portrayal of the itinerant preacher Olin Blitch, and Phyllis Curtin, who had established herself as a major artist in *Salome*, reinforced her status in the title role.

Mignon was another highlight, marked by the beautiful, velvety performance of Frances Bible as the forlorn waif, and some incredible coloratura singing by Beverly Sills as Philine. Unfortunately, the production itself was a dreary affair, but the musical forces under the direction of Jean Paul Morel—who had agreed to rejoin the company after Rosenstock's departure—were first-rate.

An ugly situation regarding Leinsdorf's status now developed. Verbal agreement on terms had been reached in November 1955, and on January 9, 1956, the company drafted a contract and forwarded it to his attorney, Charles B. Seton. The period of employment, officially, was to be September 1, 1956, through August 31, 1957, with an option for an additional year, and Leindorf's fee was to be $15,000 in salary and $2,500 in expenses.

The fall season ran from September 20 through November 3, and although Leinsdorf did not technically begin his job until September 1, in point of fact he started the previous March, in order to adequately prepare the season. His salary was to be paid in five installments of $3,000 each on October 1, November 1, December 1, April 1, and May 1, and expenses paid as they accrued. Due to some oversight, Leinsdorf never signed the contract, and the subject never arose. October, November, and December passed without his receiving any payment, but Morris informed him that the company simply had no funds, and that he would be paid when money became available.

After the failure of the fall season, the board, now thoroughly disenchanted, decided to ignore its obligations, and on December 18, Baum wrote to Seton: "On January 9, 1956, I sent you copies of a contract to be entered into between the City Center of Music & Drama, Inc., and Erich Leinsdorf. I have not heard from you since and have never received any signed agreement. Please consider our offer to Mr. Leinsdorf now canceled and revoked."

On December 24, Seton met with Morris, who gave his assurance that Leinsdorf would be paid when funds became available. By April, Leinsdorf's patience, justifiably, came to an end, and on April 25, Seton wrote to Morris demanding payment. If the cavalier attitude about debts had angered Leinsdorf, Morris's reply enraged him. On April 30, Morris wrote to Seton:

I am surprised that Erich is concerned about being paid for his services, because I thought he had the same attitude toward the organization that Leopold Stokowski demonstrated (when he conducted the City Center orchestra for two years, not only without salary, but made a contribution of $10,000 to help finance the production of the Bach *Christmas Oratorio*), Helen Hayes, José Ferrer and Maurice Evans. . . . The reason all these people have made these contributions is because they have believed in the City Center. . . . I have always thought of Erich as a friend, and I regret that he would have to turn to his attorney to give the chairman of the board notice that "Mr. Leinsdorf considers that he has waited long enough." I will bring your letter to the attention of the finance committee of the City Center, and

I hope we do not find ourselves in litigation, with all the asperity which seems to be inevitable in a courtroom with one side claiming an amount due and the other side introducing evidence to show that services were not properly performed.

On May 17, Leinsdorf wrote to all members of the board, enclosing copies of Seton's letter of April 25 and Morris's response. Leinsdorf briefly recounted the situation and added:

Since your chairman has expressed "regret" at my being concerned that I should start to receive payment in the middle of 1957 for moneys which your organization agreed to pay me in 1956, I wish to have the opportunity to state to you some of my regrets about your chairman's letter.

. . . I regret your chairman's insinuation that by making request for moneys due to me, I do not believe in the City Center.

I regret much more your chairman's statement that he assumed that when an agreement was reached that I was to render services and be paid $17,500, that this was my way of making a contribution. As an original incorporator of the City Center, I consider that your chairman's letter is shocking.

. . . Dear friends, it is not I, but your chairman who has referred to "litigation" and "asperity." It is still quite difficult for me to believe that your chairman would write the letter of April 30th.

Since Mr. Seton's letter was addressed to Mr. Morris as your chairman, and your chairman's reply is set forth in the letter of April 30th, I send these to you without asperity, but with deep disappointment and hurt, and with the faith and hope that your board will see to it that I am dealt with fairly.

Unfortunately, he was not dealt with fairly. He never received payment, but declined to make a legal issue of it, and stoically accepted the loss.

The following year, he made a contribution to the Musicians' Emergency Fund, which was headed by Mrs. Lytle Hull, who was also a member of the City Center board. In response to her acknowledgment of the donation, he wrote: "It was courteous of you to acknowledge my contribution to the Musicians' Emergency Fund. This I consider a pledge which I made several years ago and as I have grown up since my childhood to honor all my promises and commitments I do not deserve any special commendation."

Thus, the New York City Opera had gone through three general directors in thirteen years. The future was uncertain and perilous, but miraculously the company still existed.

17

John S. White—
The Man Behind the
Scenes

I M M E D I A T E L Y after the fall 1956 season, the future of the company appeared almost hopeless. It was without a general director, finances were at an all-time low, the most lucrative city in their annual tour had been lost, public confidence and interest had dwindled, and for the first time in their thirteen years of existence it became necessary to cancel a season. It says much for Morton Baum's determination that the opera company survived at all.

John S. White had entered the company in the modest capacity of language coach during the spring 1946 season.[1] Born Hans Schwarzkopf[2] in Vienna on March 4, 1910, he is the reincarnation of the "Renaissance man," with strong interests and a deep knowledge of a wide variety of subjects. His academic training at the University of Vienna and the Sorbonne included a concentration in Romance languages, art history, and philosophy, and he studied piano privately. Opera was a strong love from early childhood, and he attended countless performances at the Vienna State Opera. To this day, he is regarded as a leading authority on the career of Alfred Piccaver, Vienna's outstanding tenor of the 1920s and 1930s.

1. The advertising brochure sent out in advance of each season listed all staff members. White's first contract is dated April 2, 1946, *after* the spring brochure went to the printer, and so he was not listed until the following fall season.

2. White's change of name demonstrates the more whimsical side of his nature. *Schwarz* is the German word for black, *Kopf* for head. In going from Schwarzkopf ("Blackhead") to White, he first dropped the second part of his name because, as he explains it, the entire world was losing its head, and therefore he lost his. The rest of the change was because "the past was all black, the future all white."

While a student at the University of Vienna, White was awarded the first prize of the Italian Cultural Institute for his book *Il Cortigiano del Castiglione*, which resulted in further study at the University of Perugia. Returning to Vienna, he joined the faculty of the Schotten Realschule, where he taught French and German literature. At about this time, in 1937, he was offered a professorship in Italy, which, considering the holocaust to come, he was wise to decline. Instead, he came to the United States, arriving the following year. Like most of his fellow immigrants, he was unable to find employment befitting his education, and his first job here was carrying carrots in the open-air markets, at a salary of $6 per week. He was soon employed, however, by the New School for Social Research, where he taught German, and by the Lycée Française, where he instructed French-speaking refugees in Shakespeare.

The New School is unique among American institutions of higher learning. It was formed in 1919 as a small, informal center for discussion between adults anxious to increase their knowledge in diverse fields. It is the only accredited university to have evolved in such a manner. During the 1930s, it created the University in Exile, a group of distinguished European refugee scholars who subsequently became the Graduate Faculty of Political and Social Science.[3]

After teaching at the New School for several years, White was drafted into the army in 1942. Under legislation then in effect, he could have become a citizen within three months, but he came under suspicion as a possible German sympathizer because one of his cousins, an inventor-industrialist named Paul R. Schwarzkopf, was associated with the munitions magnate and war lord, Alfred Krupp. For months, White was harassed, followed by F.B.I. investigators when he went on leave, questioned by his superior officers, his locker thrown open to periodic searches. In the library one day he met Lieutenant Prendergast, an assistant to Attorney General Francis Biddle. The lieutenant was engaged in certain research on armored tanks, and White offered to help. During the ensuing conversation, Prendergast mentioned the part he had played in a roundup of enemy aliens, which included Paul Schwarzkopf. White thereupon commended Prendergast for doing his job so thoroughly and added that this efficiency was the cause of all of White's problems. At Prendergast's request he explained himself further and within two weeks was granted his citizenship papers.

Returning to civilian life in 1945, he resumed his teaching career. Prior to entering the military, however, one of his private language stu-

3. By a happy coincidence, the author of this volume has also been a member of the New School faculty since February 1974.

dents had been Morton Baum, with whom he now renewed contact. Baum had long been impressed by White's multifaceted talents and, in fact, the position of prompter at the Radio City Opera Company, which Baum had tried to launch in 1940, had been allocated to White. Baum now spoke to Halasz, requesting that the director attempt to find a staff position for his protégé, and on April 2, 1946, John White was officially engaged as a language teacher, at a weekly salary of $40. Throughout the Halasz regime, White's title was assistant stage director. He functioned as a full-fledged stage director, however, with productions of *Cavalleria Rusticana, Pagliacci, Aïda, Don Giovanni,* and *Madama Butterfly* entrusted to him. He also served as head of the wardrobe department and as a jack-of-all-trades.

During Rosenstock's first season, White was designated artistic secretary and, one year later, assistant general director. Because Rosenstock concerned himself principally with artistic matters, and only peripherally with administrative problems, the actual running of the company fell largely to White, assisted by Julius Rudel, who had been named assistant to the director in fall 1950, music secretary in spring 1952, and music administrator in spring 1953.

White enjoyed Baum's friendship as well as his respect, and consequently was in a stronger position than was immediately apparent to the casual observer. It was not a case of Baum's letting White have his way because they were friends, but rather that White was in a better position than most to present his ideas and expand upon them at the most opportune times. Despite this, he always kept a low profile, being a firm believer in Lord Cromer's theory of power. Cromer (né Evelyn Baring, 1841–1917) was the English consul-general to Egypt, and his philosophy is summed up in Hannah Arendt's *The Origins of Totalitarianism* (New York; Harcourt, Brace and Company, 1951):

Cromer started by recognizing that "personal influence" without a legal or written political treaty could be enough for "sufficiently effective supervision over public affairs" in foreign countries. This kind of informal influence was preferable to a well-defined policy because it could be altered at a moment's notice and did not necessarily involve the home government in case of difficulties. It required a highly trained, highly reliable staff whose loyalty and patriotism were not connected with personal ambition or vanity and who would even be required to renounce the human aspiration of having their names connected with their achievements. Their greatest passion would have to be for secrecy ("The less British officials are talked about the better"), for a role behind the scenes; their greatest contempt would be directed at publicity and people who love it.

Cromer himself possessed all these qualities to a very high degree; his wrath was never more strongly aroused than when he was "brought out of [his] hiding place," when the "reality which before was only known to a few behind the scenes [became] patent to all the world." His pride was indeed to "remain more or less hidden [and] to pull the strings." In exchange, and in order to make his work possible at all, the bureaucrat has to feel safe from control—the praise as well as the blame, that is—of all public institutions, either Parliament, the "English Departments," or the press. Every growth of democracy or even the simple functioning of existing democratic institutions can be a danger, for it is impossible to govern "a people by a people—the people of India by the people of England." Bureaucracy is always a government of experts, of an "experienced minority" which has to resist as well as it knows how the constant pressure from the "inexperienced majority." Each people is fundamentally an inexperienced majority and can therefore not be trusted with such a highly specialized matter as politics and public affairs.

John White has patterned his entire career at City Opera according to Cromer's theories. In a position of very high responsibility for more than twenty-five years, his name is barely known even to frequent opera-goers.

When the public apathy of 1955 forced the board to seek a new general director, it was White who first suggested his old friend Eric Leinsdorf for the position.[4] When Leinsdorf's successor had to be found, White nominated Rudel for the directorship, pointing out that he and Rudel had considerable experience in running the company, in fact if not in name. Baum concurred with the choice, but since White's credibility had suffered considerably over the Leinsdorf fiasco, he thought it might be difficult to persuade the board to go along with another White recommendation. He felt that the best approach would be to muster artistic support behind Rudel. This was not difficult to do. Rudel had been a member of the company since its very outset, and he was well liked and respected by the singers.

On January 10, 1957, a general meeting of all City Opera performers and staff members was held. The company was solidly behind Rudel, and three of the singers—Phyllis Curtin, Michael Pollock, and Cornell Mac-Neill—were elected as a committee to convey this information to the board. They drafted a letter to Newbold Morris, which was presented to the board on January 17. The letter said, in part: "His experience with the unique and specialized problems of the City Center over the past

4. Others considered for the post were Maurice Abravanel, Giuseppe Antonicelli, Giuseppe Bamboschek, Paul Breisach, Fausto Cleva, Emil Cooper, Antal Dorati, Massimo Freccia, Vladimir Golschmann, Walter Hendl, Thor Johnson, Rafael Kubelik, Edwin D. McArthur, Jean Paul Morel, Wilfred Pelletier, Nicholas Rescigno, Hans Schweizer, Fabien Sevitzky, Alexander Smallens, William Steinberg, George Szell, and Frieder Weissman.

thirteen years has qualified him for the job of general director. There is not a single aspect of the management of the company with which he is not acquainted."

With Baum's own endorsement added to this, the board was happy to award the position to Rudel.

John White remained administrative director until the fall of 1960, when his designation was changed to associate director; in spring 1970 he was named managing director, the title he retained during the remainder of the Rudel regime.

Except for his early years as a stage director, White's official duties have always been in the administrative and business end of running the company, while Rudel's were on the artistic side. White's knowledge of music in general and opera in particular, combined with an overall sense of art and aesthetics, has freed him from strict adherence to stipulated duties. He has assisted in repertoire planning and casting, just as Rudel contributed to the making of purely business decisions.

Apart from art, philosophy and music, John White has two great loves. One is his godchild, Cristina Gegenschatz; the other, dating from childhood, is horses. His grandfather, Jakob Pollack, had been administrator to the last master of horse equerry under Emperor Franz Josef. White grew up surrounded by horsemanship of the highest level. An avid rider himself, his home is filled with equestrian photographs, sketches, paintings, and figurines.

A person's library is the key to his personality, and White's office is filled with floor-to-ceiling bookcases overflowing with classical literature and reference works on every subject imaginable; prominently displayed are photos of Morton Baum, Alfred Piccaver, Cristina Gegenschatz, Beverly Sills, and Gert von Gontard, about whom we will read later.

Cromer's belief in anonymity combined with John White's own natural reticence and shyness have made White an unseen force—"the man behind the scenes."

Julius Rudel and the
Broken Pieces

I T   W A S on January 17, 1957, that the City Center board of directors agreed to appoint Julius Rudel the fourth general director of the opera company, and on February 4 that the contract went into effect. His background with the City Opera went back as far as the auditions he accompanied for Halasz's initial season. In addition to serving as rehearsal coach and *répétiteur*, he had conducted many performances since his podium debut on November 25, 1944.

Rudel, like his predecessor, was born in Vienna (March 6, 1921). His family was prosperous, comprised of lawyers and insurance company executives. Vienna was one of the most musical of cities, and this made its impression upon Rudel at a very early age. He grew up with a keen love of music, and began to study both violin and piano when he was three. It was opera, however, that really attracted him, and at an age when most children are put to bed by nightfall, Rudel stood night after night through performances at the Staatsoper. He was particularly fascinated by stagecraft, and his favorite toys were shoe boxes that he converted to miniature theaters—some of them sophisticated enough to include revolving stages. This early interest in the theatrical side of opera, as opposed to the purely musical side, was almost prophetic. One of the characteristics that sets Rudel apart from the majority of operatic conductors is his devotion to the proper fusion of music and drama. In far too many cases, a conductor is deeply concerned about what is heard but indifferent to the visual and dramatic aspects of his production. There are, of course, some notable exceptions, such as Herbert von Karajan and Sarah Caldwell, but these are rare.

In addition to his private piano and violin lessons, Rudel attended the Vienna Academy of Music, where he studied composition. While still in his teens he composed to his own texts two one-act operas, *König Ferdinand* and *Die Bauern*. Neither of these was ever produced, although he had entered *Die Bauern* in a competition for works by young composers. It was disqualified because, at the time of the contest, he had already reached sixteen, the cut-off age.

Suddenly the peaceful flow of life stopped. In 1938 his father died, leaving him the head of the family, which consisted of his mother and a younger brother. Immediately thereafter Austria was annexed by Germany, and the Rudels, who were Jewish, fled, arriving in New York that summer. To provide an education for himself and his brother, as well as sustenance for the family, he worked at a series of odd jobs—in a button factory, as a delivery boy, a stock clerk, and a switchboard operator. During this time he attended the Greenwich Street Music Settlement, where he studied diligently, his only distraction being a pretty classmate named Rita Gillis.

Upon completion of his studies at Greenwich Street, he won a scholarship to the David Mannes School of Music, where he earned a degree in conducting. His formal studies concluded, he gave up his job at the switchboard, married Rita, and decided firmly upon a conducting career.

In an attempt to gain practical experience, he began to conduct small groups, in diverse areas of music—an amateur orchestra known as the Parkchester Symphony, a choral group that performed at the Brooklyn Academy of Music, and the La Puma Opera Company, where he used the pseudonym Rudolfo di Giulio.

It was immediately after this that City Center was organized. Rudel had heard vague rumors of city-sponsored musical events about to take place. One day, as preparations were getting under way for the initial season, he happened to be passing the theater. On a whim, he wandered in off the street, requesting any job at any pay, just to be part of the venture. Auditions were in progress at that moment, and Halasz immediately put him to work accompanying the hopeful young singers. It was during the company's third season that he got the chance he was waiting for, conducting the company's fourth performance of Johann Strauss's *Gypsy Baron*. Successive seasons brought further conducting assignments, and by the end of Halasz's tenure, Rudel had been entrusted with many orchestrally complex scores, such as *Turandot* and *The Love for Three Oranges*.

Conducting was only one part of Rudel's job, which ranged from

L'Incoronazione di Poppea was the company's second Monteverdi production. Carol Neblett was a beautiful Poppea, Alan Titus an attentive Nero. (FRED FEHL)

Beatrix Cenci was the third opera of Alberto Ginastera to be produced at City Opera. Arlene Saunders is the tortured heroine, Justino Diaz her repulsive father. (FRED FEHL)

(RIGHT) Having sung four Donizetti roles in the past four years, Sills turned to Bellini. As Elvira in *I Puritani,* she was supported by Enrico Di Giuseppe as Lord Arthur Talbot, a role remarkable for its extreme vocal requirements. (FRED FEHL)

General Director Julius Rudel and stage director Sarah Caldwell watch as Sir Rudolf Bing signs his contract to appear in Henze's *The Young Lord*. He was cast as Sir Edgar, a silent but dramatically important part. (FRED FEHL)

Manon Lescaut (Puccini) had last been performed by the company in Spring 1948. It was revived in 1974 for Maralin Niska, staged by Frank Corsaro. This sketch, by Corsaro, shows his conception of Manon. (COURTESY OF FRANK COSARO)

Puccini's *Turandot,* which initiated Julius Rudel's directorship in 1957, was dropped from the repertoire in 1959. It reappeared on February 21, 1975, with soprano Catherine Malfitano, an exquisitely touching Liu. (FRED FEHL)

Dominic Cossa as Fritz (right) sang the haunting Pierrot-Ballad to his companions when Korngold's *Die Tote Stadt* entered the repertoire in Spring 1975. (FRED FEHL)

John S. White, whose duties at City Opera over the years have included stage direction, wardrobe, language coaching, and administration is seen here with his lovely godchild, Cristina Gegenschatz, a talented young dancer and devotée of folk singers Peter, Paul, and Mary. (COURTESY JOHN S. WHITE)

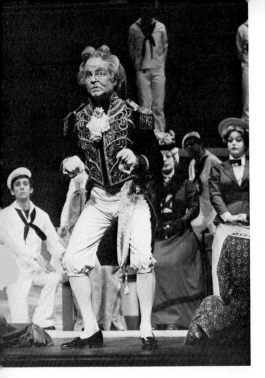

(RIGHT) Beverly Sills's spectacular success in Donizetti's Tudor trilogy (*Anna Bolena, Maria Stuarda,* and *Roberto Devereux*), *Lucia di Lammermoor,* and *Daughter of the Regiment* was followed by her assumption of the title role of his *Lucrezia Borgia,* a very beautiful work, which nevertheless achieved only a single hearing at the Metropolitan, on December 5, 1904. (FRED FEHL)

James Billings has never failed to delight audiences with his superb characterizations, which range from Beckmesser in Wagner's *Die Meistersinger* to Sir Joseph Porter, K.C.B. (left) in Gilbert and Sullivan's *H.M.S. Pinafore.* (FRED FEHL)

Frederica Von Stade, a superlative mezzo-soprano, made her company debut in the first City Opera performance of Claudio Monteverdi's *Il Ritorno d'Ulisse in Patria* on February 29, 1976. We see her here as Penelope, joined by baritone Richard Stilwell (Ulisse). (FRED FEHL)

For the April 22, 1976 revival of Jack Beeson's *Lizzie Borden,* Eileen
Schauler (left) sang the title role. Her stepmother was Ellen Faull,
re-creating the part she had sung in the world premiere on March 25, 1965.
(FRED FEHL)

Sarah Caldwell's production of Rossini's *The Barber of Seville* was introduced on October 24, 1976. From that production we see Donald Gramm
as Dr. Bartolo and Samuel Ramey as Don Basilio. (FRED FEHL)

Leon Kirchner's *Lily* was based on Saul Bellow's *Henderson, the Rain Maker*. The opera failed to please critics or public, but visually it was spectacular. Pictured above are five of the principals of the world premiere (April 14, 1977): George Shirley (Romilayu), Ara Berberian (Gene Henderson), Joy Blackett (Queen Willatale), Benjamin Matthews (Prince Itelo), and Geanie Faulkner (Princess Mtalba). (FRED FEHL)

Poulenc's *La Voix Humaine* is a tour de force for the soprano, the only character in an opera of approximately forty-five minutes' duration. It was first produced with Maralin Niska on April 22, 1977, as part of a triple bill. (FRED FEHL)

Puccini's *La Fanciulla del West* was first produced on October 16, 1977,
with Maralin Niska, Ermanno Mauro, and Charles Long. When the opera
had its world premiere in 1910, the three principals (Emmy Destinn,
Enrico Caruso, and Pasquale Amato) were photographed in a scene
strikingly similar to the above. (FRED FEHL)

La Fanciulla was the third opera broadcast from the stage of
the New York State Theater, but the first in a regularly
scheduled radio series. The producer of the broadcasts was the
author of this book (right) and the host-commentator was the
well-known television personality and author, Edwin Newman.
The photograph above was taken in the broadcast booth.
(MICHAEL EDELSON)

When difficulties arose with the pianist who was to portray Flando
Fiorinelli in *Andrea Chénier,* Julius Rudel, undaunted, donned Fiorinelli's
costume and performed the role himself. (COURTESY JULIUS RUDEL)

Mariana Niculescu (right) was a most appealing Marguerite in Gounod's
Faust when, in Spring 1979, the opera returned to the repertoire after an
absence of seven seasons. With her are Luis Lima as Faust and Jane
Shaulis as Marthe. (FRED FEHL)

For the 1979 revival of *Lucia,* the title role, originally sung by Beverly Sills, was assumed by Gianna Rolandi. This photograph is of the Mad Scene. Lucia has just stabbed her husband, Arturo, to death. (FRED FEHL)

The role of Aurelia Havisham in Dominick Argento's *Miss Havisham's Fire* is so grueling that two sopranos were used to portray her. Gianna Rolandi was the young Aurelia, while Rita Shane (above) played the same character some twenty years later. Her mad scene during the finale resulted in a thunderous and well-deserved ovation. The opera was premiered on March 22, 1979. (FRED FEHL)

On April 1, 1979, soprano Ashley Putnam (right) assumed the role of Marie in Donizetti's *The Daughter of the Regiment*. She and Gianna Rolandi shared the part, which had first been sung at City Opera by Beverly Sills on September 7, 1975. (FRED FEHL)

Although several works performed by City Opera are not generally classified as operas (*El Amor Brujo, l'Histoire du Soldat, Carmina Burana, Catulli Carmina*), Richard Strauss's ballet *Le Bourgeois Gentil-homme* (April 8, 1979) was the first work performed by the company that made no use whatever of the human voice. It brought together five of the outstanding talents in the world of Dance: Jean-Pierre Bonnefous (Monsieur Jourdain), Rudolf Nureyev (Cléonte), Patricia McBride (Lucile), and choreographers George Balanchine and Jerome Robbins. (FRED FEHL)

The New York City Opera has performed more operas by Gian Carlo
Menotti (ten) than by any other composer. Runners-up are Puccini
(nine), and Mozart and Verdi (eight each). The tenth Menotti opera
produced was *La Loca*. It had been composed as a vehicle for Beverly
Sills, and it was the last complete opera that she sang at the New York
State Theater (November 1, 1979). Here she is as Juana, the mad queen
of Spain. At the end of the performance, responding to the continuing
applause, she thanked the audience and promised "the best is yet to come"
—a vow that seems well on its way to fruition. (FRED FEHL)

In her new role as general director, Beverly Sills attends an audition.
Seated behind her is John S. White, then the company's managing
director. (HENRY GROSSMAN)

Kurt Weill's *Silverlake,* which
entered the company's repertoire on
March 20, 1980, featured the debut
of Joel Grey, one of Broadway's
most exciting personalities. He is
seen here as Officer Olim (left),
with William Neill as Severin.
(FRED FEHL)

It had been more than sixty years
since Bizet's *The Pearl Fishers* was
last heard at the Metropolitan, when
City Opera revived it on September
25, 1980. In the Act I Prayer are
Diana Soviero (Leila), John Seabury (Nourabad), and Dominic
Cossa (Zurga). (FRED FEHL)

running errands to cueing singers, and occasionally singing a line that was missed. On one occasion, the guide who was to escort Micaëla onstage in Act III of *Carmen* failed to appear. Rudel tore off his shirt, draped a blanket around his shoulders, and filled the gap.

A few years after joining the company, Rudel was assigned to one of the most unpleasant but most necessary tasks in any performing organization—the preparation of rehearsal schedules. Trying to juggle the availabilities of a group of singers, the musical needs of the work in question, and the limited rehearsal space is a mammoth undertaking. It was, however, good training in dealing with performers on a basis other than a purely musical one.

With the arrival of Rosenstock, Rudel assumed more administrative functions along with John White. He knew the company inside out, for he had grown up with it.

In 1956 an incident occurred that came close to radically altering the entire future of the company. Rudel was offered the directorship of the Houston Opera, and he flew down to Texas to meet with the board of directors. The offer was very tempting, of course, since at that time he had no inkling that City Opera would soon be his. It took him only a few days of thought to realize that, after Vienna and New York, he would not be happy living in Texas, and he declined the offer. During that brief time, though, reports reached Leinsdorf that Rudel was about to leave. Without waiting for confirmation, Leinsdorf made his preseason plans excluding Rudel, and, upon returning, Rudel found that he was out of the company. It was due to Baum's intervention that he was reengaged, but his only conducting assignment was two performances of *Rigoletto* during the final three days of the season.

Having come so close to dismissal from the company, Rudel enjoyed a double victory when only a few months later he replaced Leinsdorf. At the time, one member of the board was quoted as saying, "We were terribly tired of prima-donna conductors, and Rudel was the only man in the place who knew where all the scenery was buried."

Julius and Rita Rudel had theater tickets for the evening of January 17, 1957. Shortly before leaving their apartment, the telephone rang. It was Newbold Morris, who asked Rudel what he was doing that evening. "I'm going to *Inherit the Wind*," Julius replied, to which Morris responded, "You just have!"

With a popular and respected director at its head, the company felt its morale soar instantly. There were still many budgetary problems, to be sure, but the prognosis was good for the first time in years.

19

American Opera and the
Ford Foundation

JULIUS RUDEL'S administration began with high hopes on the part of the public, the press, and the company members. Projected for the fall 1957 season were the company's first performances of Verdi's *Macbeth*, Lehár's *The Merry Widow*, Mozart's delightful *Abduction from the Seraglio*, and a double bill of de Falla's *La Vida Breve* and *El Amor Brujo*. For his inaugural performance on October 9, 1957, Rudel chose Puccini's *Turandot*, not done by the company since fall 1950 and last heard at the Met twenty years before that. His experience conducting the score had been limited to a single appearance (April 25, 1950), and, since it is an exceedingly complex work, this was a very daring move. He was more than equal to the task, however, and received superb notices in the press. Howard Taubman, whose review was typical, wrote in the *New York Times* (October 10):

> The New York City Opera Company began its new season at the City Center last night with a remarkably fine *Turandot*. Puccini's last opera is a challenge to the greatest opera houses, and one shuddered in advance at this company's temerity. But under the guidance of its new general director, Julius Rudel, the City Center troupe carried it off with high honors.
>
> The feat was all the more notable because the company was rising from the ashes of grave artistic and economic troubles, which caused the cancellation of the last spring season. If this *Turandot* is any indication, morale has been re-established and the new season will be lively.
>
> . . . The City Center's *Turandot* managed to capture the effect of a fairytale told with excitement and warmth. Mr. Rudel's leadership as conductor had most to do with this achievement. Throughout, this was a well-knit ensemble.

148

There were individual performances of excellence, but they were never out of the frame of a unified conception.

Only the delight and eagerness of the audience led to occasional disruption of the mood of the performance. This gathering was so determined to show its approval that its applause and shouts broke the musical continuity time and again. Mr. Rudel continued to conduct determinedly.

. . . Mr. Rudel has waved his wand and decreed a community of effort. Let us hope that this cohesive and glowing *Turandot* is but the first proof of his magic.

Floyd's *Susannah* followed with increased attendance over the previous year's scant 38 percent, but despite the critical accolades, its seasonal average was only 55 percent. The remainder of the first week consisted of standard repertoire, with larger audiences than the house had experienced in many years. Several important debuts highlighted the week's activities. The opening-night Calaf was a young Italian tenor named Giuseppe Gismondo, the possessor of a beautiful voice and a good sense of style. Unfortunately, he remained with the company for only two seasons, thereafter singing almost exclusively in Italy. *La Traviata*, on October 11, featured three very important debuts: tenor John Alexander and baritone Louis Quilico as Alfredo and Giorgio Germont, and, on the podium, Arturo Basile, who had already established an enviable career in Italy.[1] Further excitement was provided by the first City Opera Violetta of soprano Beverly Sills.

One of the most eagerly anticipated events of the season took place a few evenings later: the New York City Opera debut of world-famed pianist José Iturbi. His association with City Center extended back to the company's first-anniversary concert in 1944, but that was in his accustomed role at the piano; he was now appearing with the company for the first time as conductor, leading the initial performances of Manuel de Falla's *La Vida Breve* and *El Amor Brujo*. The official premiere took place on October 17, but on the previous evening there was a public performance listed as a preview, for the benefit of the Soldiers', Sailors', and Airmen's Club. The stage director was Jean Dalrymple, who had made the necessary arrangements for Iturbi's appearance. The production brought critical acclaim, although at very great cost, due to extravagant planning and budgets. It also brought about a considerable amount of internal strife, a result of "pressure politics."

Shortly after Rudel's appointment as general director, Dalrymple had

1. Basile was well known to record collectors as the conductor of Maria Callas's first three records and a fairly long list of complete operas for Cetra, including *Andrea Chénier* with Renata Tebaldi.

suggested to him a Spanish evening to consist of *La Vida Breve* double-billed with Ravel's *L'Heure Espagnole*, which had been done by the company five years earlier (October 2, 1952). Iturbi was to conduct both works. Several meetings between Rudel, Iturbi, and Dalrymple took place, but no agreement was reached because Iturbi was not yet certain of his availability. Meanwhile, Rudel had to ready his plans for the fall season, so that first steps could be taken. His budget and proposed repertoire naturally excluded the double bill.

On the day that Rudel was to meet with the board to submit his plans for their approval, Dalrymple told him, "I spoke to Iturbi and he can do it." Of course, at that point, it was too late for Rudel to incorporate this into his proposal. At the board meeting, Dalrymple (who was by then a member of the board) made no reference to this event, and Rudel's plans were approved. When Iturbi was next in New York, the three protagonists met again. Iturbi suggested that *El Retablo de Maese Pedro* be substituted for *L'Heure Espagnole*, thereby providing an all de Falla evening. Rudel felt that this would be too short an evening, and eventually *El Amor Brujo* was settled upon. Rudel could not give his approval for this, however, as his plans had already been presented to the board. Furthermore, he was afraid that it would be a very costly production. He suggested that if board approval could be obtained, they should consider doing it in concert form to eliminate the cost of scenery and costumes, but Iturbi refused to do it as anything less than a full-scale production. Again the meeting ended with no agreement reached. Dalrymple then informed Newbold Morris that the Spanish press was upset, and embarrassment and outraged feelings were rampant. On May 14, 1957, Morris wrote to Dalrymple stating, "I think you know how I feel about you, and I hope that this won't cause you to stop your wonderful work with the City Center. That would break my heart and one thousand others."

Referring to Rudel, Morris continued: "As you know, he alone is responsible for the opera season and I think we ought to back him up, just as we back you up in the direction of the Theatre Company and the Light Opera Company.[2] If we don't have responsibility centered on one person for the excellence of each operating unit, the result is chaotic."

Dalrymple remained, and a special meeting of the board was called to consider the feasibility of adding these works to the repertoire. Addi-

---

2. Dalrymple had been named director of the Theatre Company in 1953 and of the Light Opera Company in 1956.

tional funds were allocated to the opera company, and, on June 7, Rudel wrote a very gracious letter to Iturbi, which began:

As you have probably heard from Jean Dalrymple, the board has agreed to provide the additional funds to make it possible for us to do full scenic productions of *Amor Brujo* and *Vida Breve*. Jean's not inconsiderable powers of persuasion had much to do, you can be sure, with their agreement to go ahead with this. I am delighted that it has worked out this way and that we will have you as our guest.

In her book *From the Last Row* (James T. White & Co., 1975), Dalrymple wrote:

I induced José Iturbi to conduct and supervise a Spanish program of de Falla's *La Vida Breve* and *El Amor Brujo*, which I produced and staged at Iturbi's request. There were four performances of these lovely works, sung in Spanish, and all of them sold out, to Morton's amazement. He and Rudel had wanted them done in a "concert version," to save money, but Iturbi wouldn't do them that way, and I had been able to present a good-looking production without spending very much by borrowing the sets from the Barcelona Opera Company in Spain, where the City Opera Company's founder, Laszlo Halasz, was then general director.

Implications of an inexpensive presentation notwithstanding, the production was catastrophic from a purely financial point of view. After the season's end, Rudel wrote a memo to Morris, Baum, and Falcone, pointing up some of the problems:

The expenses over and above expenses for any other performance we would have had in place of the de Falla evening (such as *Cenerentola*) are roughly $22,500. To give you a few examples of how this total was run up:

Rental of costumes for this one production amounted to $2,800; whereas rental of costumes for the rest of the repertoire for the entire season, including the tour, amounts to $4,000.

The cost for Miss Peggy Clark and her special assistant to light the production (without particular distinction) was $1,312 against the fee for our technical and lighting director, Mr. Hans Sondheimer, for our entire season, $1,520.

Cost of the special ballet was $3,800 exclusive of choreographers' fees, against the total cost of the regular ballet for the entire season, $4,300.

. . . For the sake of harmony and in view of the contributions Miss Dalrymple had promised to help this production, I have OKed all these bills, though I had never been consulted about them. Incidentally, I am still getting bills that are sent from Miss D's department. Also, Mr. Falcone informs me that the contributions amount to $13,500, not $20,000 as was promised. Frankly, I find it very difficult to control my department under such circumstances and I should not like to go through a similar experience again. I bring this up at this moment because Miss Dalrymple has already started making suggestions about a similar cooperation in the next fall season.

There had been serious doubts in the minds of many opera-goers about the wisdom of having Iturbi conduct. His piano recording of the "Ritual Fire Dance" from *El Amor Brujo* was a best seller on RCA Victor, and there was widespread feeling that his engagement was a "gimmick," exploiting his name and reputation. Happily, doubts were dispelled after the premiere. His conducting was superb. Harriet Johnson reported in the *New York Post* (October 18, 1957): "Iturbi conducted both works with a sensitive musicianship and with a feeling for the special coloring necessary to bring out the music's sensuousness. The symphonic scene, which, in bridging to the second act, suffuses the ear with a tone picture of Granada, came through with vibrancy."

In addition to Iturbi, two other "name" artists appeared with the company for the first time. They were soprano Consuelo Rubio and baritone Hernán Pelayo, both of whom had already established significant recording careers.

Attendance remained good throughout the second week—in fact, it increased from 72 percent to 75 percent.

The third week opened with Verdi's *Macbeth*. Sixteen months later the opera would have its first Metropolitan production, conducted by former City Opera general director Erich Leinsdorf.[3] Making her company debut in the fierce role of the Scottish queen was Irene Jordan, a spectacular singer who had made the transition from mezzo-soprano to soprano in grand fashion. Between 1946 and 1948 she had appeared at the Met as Mallika in *Lakmé* and in a variety of small roles, such as Kate Pinkerton in *Madama Butterfly*, a page in *Rigoletto*, etc. In 1957 she returned as the Queen of the Night in *The Magic Flute*, high F's and all. At City Opera she handled the role of Lady Macbeth brilliantly, and was ably partnered by William Chapman, another newcomer to the company. The added

3. During the season after the Met's initial *Macbeth*, *Turandot* was brought back after an absence of more than thirty years. The critical acclaim that these works received at the City Opera was presumably a strong factor. More recently, Met revivals of Puccini's *Trittico* and Bellini's *I Puritani* followed on the heels of triumphant City Opera productions.

presence of Norman Treigle as Banquo, Giuseppe Gismondo as Macduff, Margaret Webster as stage director, and Arturo Basile in the pit made this a truly memorable occasion. Oddly enough, it did not draw well, its three performances averaging only 66 percent paid attendance.

The last new work of the season was Mozart's *Abduction from the Seraglio*. Immensely popular throughout the German-speaking world, it had achieved only a handful of performances in the United States prior to its Metropolitan Opera premiere (November 29, 1946). When it did finally reach the Met, the production was lackluster, and after only four performances it vanished from the repertoire. At City Opera, however, it was treated with great love and care, and soon became a favorite with the audience. Phyllis Curtin as Constanza revealed a superb coloratura technique, and demonstrated that she was as much at home in eighteenth-century repertoire as in twentieth. Her supporting cast was excellent, and the highly respected conductor Peter Herman Adler was featured in his company debut. The production itself, which was utterly charming, was made available without charge by Lincoln Kirstein. Considering his earlier difficulties with the board of City Center, his spirit of cooperation with the new operatic administration revealed that he was a person of the highest artistic integrity. On January 28, 1957, almost immediately after Rudel's appointment, Kirstein wrote to him:

Thank you for your cordial note. As you know, I should like to help the New York City Opera Company in any way I can; in spite of what you may have heard, I had no real ambition to run it; I never could have; I don't know anything about it; my interest was purely selfish: to avoid a deficit which would, in turn, cripple my own operations in the ballet. I have every assurance that you will conduct an admirable operation and I want to put myself on record in offering you the following suggestions and properties, which would only involve myself up to the point of whatever use you could make of me.

1. *The Abduction from the Seraglio*: the production presented at Stratford, conducted by Leinsdorf, with excellent decor by Fletcher and costumes by Karinska.

. . . Should you wish the active participation of Balanchine and myself, in relation to the dance services of the house, we could give you the best we have to offer. It is likely that the ballet company will not be working during the opera-season. We could provide you with our soloists and other dancers if you should desire them.

In any case, I hope you will believe that I am at your disposal only if you wish to use me; that I have no thought of intruding on your own necessary authority, and that everything in this letter is by way of being a tentative suggestion.

Other suggestions and productions offered by Kirstein included Chávez's *The Tuscan Players* (by now renamed *Panfilo and Lauretta*), Copland's *The Tender Land* in its revised version, *The Saint of Bleecker Street*, and Stravinsky's *The Rake's Progress*. Eventually (on March 18, 1965) *The Saint* did enter the City Opera repertoire, but the other works, as well as the assistance of Balanchine, were declined.

By the end of the fourth week, the season had been going so well (74 percent average attendance) that seven extra performances were scheduled for the week of November 13 through 17. This proved to be a miscalculation, however. Apparently the last-minute addition did not give audiences sufficient time for planning. The fifth week, which was part of the original announcement, showed a rise in attendance to 81 percent, but the additional seven performances averaged only 54 percent, bringing the total for the entire season to 72 percent. Nevertheless, this was a significant improvement over recent years, and it was encouraging that the audiences increased weekly during the originally scheduled period (72 percent, 75 percent, 75 percent, 75 percent, 81 percent), despite the fact that halfway through, on October 28, the Metropolitan started its new season.

For the first time since Halasz's departure six years earlier, the company was received enthusiastically by press and public. It was now just a matter of time until it would resume its place among the world's major companies.

During its twenty-eight seasons of activity, the City Opera had presented sixty-eight different works, of which twenty-nine had never been performed by the Met, and an additional thirteen had been out of the Met repertoire for ten years or more. Little wonder, therefore, that the company had achieved a reputation for novelty. Now with the spring 1958 season approaching, they embarked on an experiment that was without parallel in the history of opera.

One year earlier, in March 1957, the Ford Foundation created its Program in Humanities and the Arts, and appointed W. McNeil Lowry as its director. This was at a time when City Center finances were so poor that it became necessary, for the first time, to cancel a season. It was natural—almost inevitable—that Morton Baum would turn to Lowry for help.

Ford Foundation grants, like those of the Rockefeller Foundation, were awarded only on the basis of specific projects; deficits incurred by normal day-to-day operations were not covered. A series of meetings took place between Lowry, Baum, and Rudel in search of a suitable and worthwhile project. Eventually, out of these meetings, emerged an exciting concept—a season devoted entirely to American opera.

Contrary to popular opinion, it had not been particularly difficult for American composers to get their operas produced. The widespread publicity attached to a world premiere was such that many performing organizations were willing to introduce new works. However, once the initial series of performances took place, companies were generally loath to keep the works in repertoire, and consequently they were never given a fair chance to establish their popularity.[4]

The plan devised, therefore, was to do a season of American works that had been previously presented, either at City Opera or elsewhere. To generate additional excitement, however, Baum felt that there should be one world premiere. Rudel was initially skeptical of an all-American season, but Baum was determined, and his will prevailed.

Opening night was April 3, 1958, the company's first performance of *The Ballad of Baby Doe*. Douglas Moore's opera about silver mining in Colorado had been commissioned by the Central City Opera Festival and received its first performance there on July 7, 1956 (Max Di Julio's *Baby Doe* had its premiere in Loretto, Colorado, just forty-four days earlier), with Dolores Wilson in the title role, Walter Cassel as Horace Tabor, Martha Lipton as his first wife, Augusta, and Lawrence Davidson as William Jennings Bryan; in the alternate cast, these roles were filled by Leyna Gabriele, Clifford Harvuot, Frances Bible, and Norman Treigle. All performances were conducted by Emerson Buckley. *Baby Doe* was a tremendous success in Central City. Because the sixteen planned performances were sold out, several additional showings were scheduled, and these, too, filled the house. Negotiations were under way to have it open on Broadway in fall of 1956, but before this could take place, the backers withdrew, fearful that an opera could not enjoy a popular success. True, several works of Menotti had been profitable in extended runs, but these had been billed as "musical dramas"; *The Ballad of Baby Doe* already had the stigma of opera attached to it. Broadway's loss was City Opera's gain, and by the end of Julius Rudel's directorship in 1979, it had achieved thirty-five performances in eleven seasons. The four performances during that initial season averaged 67 percent attendance, a completely acceptable figure for a contemporary American work.

Lipton and Cassel repeated the roles they had created, and Beverly Sills assumed the title part. In her autobiography, *Bubbles* (Bobbs-

4. By the end of the 1956–57 season, the Metropolitan had produced 212 different operas—20 American and 192 foreign. Of these, 8 of the American works (40 percent) reached a second season, while 131 of the foreign, or 62 percent, survived beyond the initial season. At City Center, 11 of the 66 operas produced by then were American. Nine of these, or 81 percent, appeared in two or more seasons, while 38 percent of the foreign, (69 percent) were repeated.

Merrill, 1976), Miss Sills speaks of the circumstances under which she was
cast as Baby Doe. She was living in Cleveland at the time and had heard
rumors that Moore considered her too tall for the role. Therefore, when
Rudel called to ask her to audition for it, she refused, since she felt it was
pointless to come to New York only to be rejected. Rudel, with Emerson
Buckley's help, finally convinced her to try. In defiance, she wore the
highest-heeled boots she could find, and a white mink hat that made her
appear substantially taller than she really is. Addressing the composer, she
said, "Mr. Moore, this is how tall I am before I begin to sing for you and
I'm going to be just as tall when I'm finished." Chivalrously, he responded,
"Why, Miss Sills, you look just perfect to me." After she sang "The
Willow Song," he stated, "Miss Sills, you *are* Baby Doe." It turned out
to be one of the finest portrayals in her repertoire.

Four of the ten operas performed that season were repeats from past
years—*Susannah*, *Regina*, and a Menotti double bill consisting of *The Old
Maid and the Thief* and *The Medium*. The reception for these was lukewarm, averaging a shade over 50 percent. Of the new productions, only
Kurt Weill's *Lost in the Stars* was successful at the box office, with the
six scheduled performances averaging ticket sales of 66 percent. A week-
long run of the work was hastily added but, as had happened during the
previous season, the additional week was catastrophic financially, the
eight performances averaging only 25 percent attendance. Lawrence
Winters sang the role of Stephen Kumalo, the part created by Todd
Duncan at the Broadway premiere on October 30, 1949; Irina, originally
entrusted to Inez Matthews, was sung in this revival by a beautiful young
mezzo-soprano named Shirley Carter, who some years later, under her
maiden name of Shirley Verrett, would become a major international
celebrity.

It is instructive but disheartening to witness the drop in attendance
when the label "opera" becomes associated with a work. Fourteen performances of *Lost in the Stars* averaged only 43 percent overall attendance
at City Opera, despite superb reviews; yet, on Broadway, it ran successfully for about nine months (273 performances).

One of the season's highlights was a guest appearance by Leonard
Bernstein conducting his *Trouble in Tahiti* on April 6. Beverly Wolff, in
her company debut, recreated the part of Dinah, which she had sung at
the world premiere on June 12, 1952 (at Brandeis University in Massachusetts). Bernstein's presence in the pit resulted in 86 percent attendance,
but the remaining performances that season averaged only 53 percent,
after Bernstein had been replaced by Seymour Lipkin (who had been in
charge of the premiere, and who performed superbly).

Trouble in Tahiti was double-billed with another opera that had first been performed in Massachusetts—Mark Bucci's *Tale for a Deaf Ear* (premiere at Tanglewood, August 5, 1957). The conductor of the first performance was James Billings, who years later became one of City Opera's finest comic baritones, and whose appearances in Gilbert and Sullivan, *Die Meistersinger*, *La Belle Hélène*, and *The Turk in Italy* consistently resulted in ovations. At City Opera, Bucci's work was conducted by Arnold Gamson, the artistic head of the now defunct American Opera Society. The leading roles were brilliantly sung by Patricia Neway and William Chapman, with cameo appearances by Lee Venora, Beverly Bower, and Richard Cassilly. Both operas were imaginatively staged by Michael Pollock, who having achieved a career as a first-rate character tenor was now proving himself equally talented as a director.

The City Opera's very first performance, fourteen years earlier, had starred soprano Dusolina Giannini. Now the company turned to her brother, composer Vittorio Giannini, whose *Taming of the Shrew* was produced with loving care on April 13. Margaret Webster directed, and *Opera* magazine reported that "Phyllis Curtin, as Katherina, managed the almost impossible task of singing musically and sounding shrewish at the same time." Others in the cast included Walter Cassel, Chester Watson, John Alexander, and Paul Ukena in his company debut. The small audience present (34 percent of capacity) responded enthusiastically, but for some reason the public stayed away, making this the most poorly attended opera.

The single world premiere of the season, *The Good Soldier Schweik*, occurred on April 23. There was a cloud of gloom over the production due to the tragic and untimely death of the composer, Robert Kurka, only four months earlier. Kurka, at the age of thirty-five, had succumbed to leukemia, leaving the orchestration to be completed by his friend Hershy Kay. Most of the audience was aware of the circumstances, as there was a note included in the program. One person, however, had apparently failed to read it, and at the end of the performance he clamored for a curtain call by Kurka, casting a pall throughout the theater.

Schweik has prospered, however, and has now had close to one hundred different productions throughout the world, in more than a dozen languages. Norman Kelley had a personal triumph in the title role (which was written with his voice in mind), and artistically, the emergence of *Schweik* alone would have justified the entire season—if, indeed, any justification was required. It, too, fared poorly at the box office, however, achieving only a 45 percent ticket sale.

And so the first American season came to a close. There were thirty-five performances of ten operas, including one world premiere and six works new to City Opera. Among the other operas seriously considered that season were the three American works that had previously been premiered by the company (*The Dybbuk, The Tender Land,* and *Troubled Island*) and seven others (*The Consul, The Devil and Daniel Webster, The Cradle Will Rock, The Ruby, Down in the Valley, The Trial at Rouen,* and *Venus in Africa*), four of which were ultimately added to the repertoire.

The deficit for the season ran to $139,234.21, but the Ford Foundation provided $100,000, so that the loss was not excessive. In addition, the Foundation supplied another $5,000 to enable the company to bring promising young composers from all parts of the country to New York, so that they could witness rehearsals and learn, at first hand, some of the problems and pitfalls to be avoided.

All in all, the season was deemed a major success, and did more for the cause of American opera than anything that had come before.

It has been an exhausting season for all concerned. Adding that many new works in so short a period of time required endless rehearsal. The next fall season, despite two company premieres, was substantially less harried.

The season started on October 7, 1958, with the first performance in America of Richard Strauss's *Die Schweigsame Frau* (performed in English as *The Silent Woman*). Joan Carroll, John Alexander, Paul Ukena, and Herbert Beattie sang the principal parts, with conductor Peter Herman Adler and director Margaret Webster at the helm. Audiences, however, were not adventurous, and the four performances achieved only 52 percent attendance (as against 81 percent for *Carmen*). The season's other new work, Benjamin Britten's *Rape of Lucretia,* filled only 30 percent of the house, and both operas were dropped after a single season. The average attendance for fall 1958 was only 62 percent, and this time there was no Ford Foundation to make up the deficit.

One of the principal purposes of producing an all-American season was to determine whether there was a body of contemporary American operas that could be successfully sustained in a repertory company. However, at the season's end, this question remained unanswered. Attendance had been somewhat higher than anticipated, an encouraging sign. Nevertheless, that short an experiment was insufficient, as there was no way of judging how many people came out of curiosity or, perhaps, even a vague sense of duty. That portion of the audience could be discounted. The important statistics were the number of opera-goers who attended in search of excellent musical theater and, more importantly, how many were satisfied. To find the answers to these questions, a continuity was needed so that the works could be judged on merit rather than on novelty appeal. The Foundation therefore agreed to extend the experiment.

After demonstrating his reluctance prior to the first American season, Rudel now enthusiastically embraced the continuation of the plan. Baum had wanted to present a second season of ten productions, all works new to the company's repertoire, but Rudel felt that this would not achieve the stated purpose, since the appeal would again be based on novelty rather than established quality. Furthermore, the effort involved in preparation would tax company members almost beyond endurance. Morris concurred, and the plan eventually adopted for spring 1959 was to present ten different offerings (actually, twelve operas since there were two double bills), which would include one world premiere, four of the most successful works previously done, and seven other operas new to the company. The four repeats, predictably, were *Susannah*, *The Medium*, *Baby Doe*, and *Regina*, all of which seemed to be on their way to becoming standard City Opera fare; the company was starting to develop an identity. The City Opera's fifth world premiere was Hugo Weisgall's *Six Characters in Search of an Author* (April 26), with a superb libretto by Denis Johnston. The press was consistent in its praise of the dramatic aspects, but the music failed to please either critics or public. Douglas Watt's review in the *Daily News* carried the headline "Six Characters in Need of a Composer," a sentiment echoed by most of his colleagues.

The relative success, one year earlier, of *Lost in the Stars* led to the presentation of another Kurt Weill opera, *Street Scene* (first performed in Philadelphia on December 1, 1946). It was orginally scheduled for more performances than any other work that season, but public response resulted in two additional showings. Everything about *Street Scene* elicited critical praise, from the work itself through the staging, conducting, and individual performances, particularly those of soprano Elizabeth Carron and dancer Sondra Lee.

The season had opened with Menotti's *Maria Golovin*, poorly attended because it had just completed a run at Broadway's Martin Beck Theater. After two performances it vanished from the company's repertoire.

Floyd's *Wuthering Heights* had been successfully premiered at Santa Fé on July 16, 1958. Now at its introduction to New York it was superbly cast with Phyllis Curtin, John Reardon, and Patricia Neway, while the smaller roles were entrusted to other company favorites, Jacquelynne Moody, Frank Porretta, and Jon Crain. After the success of *Susannah*, management had good reason to expect a flurry of excitement at the box office, but audiences are unpredictable, and only 40 percent of the house was filled for the three performances. Like *Maria Golovin*, it lasted for only a single season.

Robert Ward's *He Who Gets Slapped* had the poorest attendance, a great pity, as it is a work of substance and beauty. Only 22 percent of the tickets were sold for the first performance, and despite excellent reviews, the sale dropped to 16 percent for the second hearing. Louis Biancolli of the *New York World-Telegram and Sun* wrote:

> To begin with, Michael Pollock has given the production real theatrical force. Nothing has been overlooked in the staging to create the combined illusion of valid drama and plausible life.
>
> The orchestra commentary is always alive and helpful in the general momentum, and Mr. Ward and his librettist, Bernard Stambler, know how to face dramatic crisis without flinching. This opera has guts.

In the *New Yorker*, Winthrop Sargeant stated:

> I should unhesitatingly list "He Who Gets Slapped" as one of the half-dozen finest operas to emerge from the contemporary ferment among American opera composers—and that is saying a great deal.

The opera had first been performed by the Columbia University Opera Workshop at the Juilliard School of Music on May 17, 1956, under the title *Pantaloon*. For the City Opera production, composer and librettist reverted to the title of the Andreyev play upon which the opera is based. Brenda Lewis had been cast in the pivotal role of Zinida, the lion tamer, but was indisposed; the part was assumed by Regina Sarfaty, who had created it at the premiere. She turned in a spectacular performance, as did Lee Venora as Consuelo, Norman Kelley as Count Mancini, and David Atkinson as Pantaloon. Along with Kurka's *Schweik*, this is an outstanding American work, and one can only hope that it will someday establish itself.

On April 8, 1956, there had been a television production, on NBC, of *The Trial at Rouen* by Norman Dello Joio, starring Elaine Malbin and Hugh Thompson. This was the world premiere of the revised (two-act) version of the work; the original version, in three acts, had first been performed at Sarah Lawrence College on May 9, 1950, under the title *The Triumph of Joan*. After the TV production, Dello Joio again revised the opera, cutting it down to one act and retitling it *The Triumph of St. Joan*. In this latest form it was premiered at City Opera on April 16, double-billed with the perennial *The Medium*. Lee Venora as the tormented Maid of Orleans sang exquisitely and acted the part to perfection. Of the work itself, Harriet Johnson reported in the *New York Post*:

More than a single triumph emerged last night on the City Center stage, from Norman Dello Joio's *The Triumph of St. Joan.*

The New York City Opera's production of the work, in its premiere by the company, proved to be a masterpiece of dramatic and musical integration.

Ticket sales averaged only 32 percent, and one more work seemed doomed to obscurity.

The final offering of the season was the double bill of *The Scarf* by Lee Hoiby and Douglas Moore's *The Devil and Daniel Webster.* Hoiby's work, receiving its American premiere, had been composed for the Spoleto Festival, whose artistic director, Gian Carlo Menotti, was one of Hoiby's teachers (the other was Darius Milhaud). The Spoleto premiere, on June 20, 1958, created an excellent impression, and Patricia Neway as the sorceress Miriam drew the following commentary in *Opera* magazine (September, 1958):

There are three characters, one of whom is a witch; she lures and bewitches her lovers in her old husband's despite by means of a long red scarf [sic]. Patricia Neway made her quite unforgettable, drawing on a formidable gamut of sounds which ranged from shimmering legato phrases to eerie animal howls.

Miss Neway repeated her spectacular portrayal at City Opera, as did baritone Richard Cross, the postman (Miriam's lover) of the original production. John Druary impersonated her husband, Reuel, sung originally by tenor John McCollum.

The Scarf drew critical accolades at City Opera. Taubman reported in the *New York Times*:

Mr. Hoiby has planned his musical design with an assurance to be expected of a composer who has had extensive experience in the theater. The brief prelude postulates some of the thematic material that is to be important in the opera. The writing for the voices is always ingratiating, and the handling of the orchestra has dramatic cogency.

The style is in the romantic tradition. Mr. Hoiby can write a long, arching melody, and he does not hesitate to give his characters old-fashioned arias. But he does not stop the action for a vocal showpiece. The story has insistent forward momentum, and the opera builds to a powerful climax. It is an achievement when a young American can turn out an opera that has so much craft and holds the audience so effectively.

The Devil and Daniel Webster, with which *The Scarf* was coupled, was a very different type of work. It was a slick score, as American as the proverbial apple pie, with an instant appeal and easy accessibility. It had first been performed on Broadway on May 18, 1939, then made the rounds of virtually every opera workshop and small company in the country. Although the New York City Opera production marked its major-league debut, it was described in H. Earle Johnson's *Operas on American Subjects* (Coleman-Ross Company, Inc., 1964) as "the most frequently performed opera on an American subject by a native composer."[5]

It was almost a foregone conclusion that the opera would be well received, but once again the company put its best foot forward in casting, and the result was superb. Norman Kelley and Walter Cassell in the title roles romped through their parts. Joshua Hecht, who portrayed Jabez Stone, was dramatically moving and sonorous of voice, while Adelaide Bishop (a last-minute replacement for Marguerite Willauer) demonstrated a beauty of tone and superb musicianship—phrasing that revealed every nuance of her role. Another artistic triumph—and another box-office failure—27 percent attendance for the three performances. When the results were tallied, it was learned that the seasonal attendance was only 41 percent of capacity—the first time in the company's history that the audience fell below the halfway mark. So far, the Rudel regime, now four seasons old, had elicited approximately the same audience response as those of his predecessors. In his favor, however, was the fact that half of the seasons were expected to produce severe deficits; the world was simply not ready for an American operatic repertoire. It was a noble experiment and, in the long run, very helpful in establishing a national operatic form, but not subject to determination of success or failure by the usual standards.

The second American season was generally considered more successful artistically and more important than the first. Lester Trimble of *The Nation* commented:

I shall be surprised if musical history does not record that American opera, as a movement, had its beginnings at the New York City Center in the spring seasons of 1958 and 1959. For more years than one likes to consider, American composers have been writing for the lyric stage, but in hope rather than expectation. A few works have been produced by professional companies. University and conservatory workshops have, in recent times, provided possibilities for small-scale productions. Even the Metropolitan Opera, which is oriented toward music of the eighteenth and nineteenth centuries, has paid occasional attention to the homegrown, twentieth-century product.

5. Fifteen years later, at the time of writing this book, *The Devil and Daniel Webster* had been ousted from its position of preeminence by Moore's *Ballad of Baby Doe*, Floyd's *Susannah*, and Bernstein's *Trouble in Tahiti*. Several works of both Menotti and Weill are more frequently performed, but the statistic referred to native (American) composers. Menotti was born in Cadegliano, Italy, and Weill in Dessau, Germany.

But a scattering of performances does not create a dynamic or a movement —nor do semi-amateur or student undertakings. For this, a certain concentration of force must be achieved, and a continuity then established. The enthusiasm of the public must be drawn into the venture, too, for without it the lyric theater cannot exist. These things can happen only in a professional opera house; one unhampered either by innate traditionalism or by an audience preconditioned to enjoy only established repertory. In America, they could happen only at a place like the City Center, and under the stimulus of a lively-minded director like Julius Rudel.

The fall season again featured more traditional fare. *Street Scene* was retained from the previous spring, but without box-office success (26 percent). The new productions presented an interesting variety—Mozart's *Così fan Tutte* as a follow-up to the successful *Seraglio* production, Gilbert and Sullivan's *Mikado*, and a double bill of Stravinsky's *Oedipus Rex* and Carl Orff's *Carmina Burana*. The works were well chosen and well prepared, leading to an enthusiastic press and excellent box-office sales.

The opening-night performance was given over to the double bill, and featured world-famous Leopold Stokowski as conductor. The soprano soloist in *Carmina Burana* was Reri Grist, who was unknown at the time, but subsequently achieved a major European career. Others in the cast included stalwarts Richard Cassilly, Joshua Hecht, John Macurdy, Claramae Turner, John Alexander, and John Reardon. The opening-night performance was billed as a benefit, with ticket prices at approximately two and a half times the normal rate. As expected, the turnout was far from overwhelming at the inflated price scale; nonetheless, the company did manage to sell 47 percent of its tickets, even at premium prices. The other three scheduled performances averaged 93 percent attendance, and consequently the *Street Scene* of October 14 and *La Traviata* of November 1 were both replaced by additional showings of the *Oedipus/Carmina*. It is particularly interesting to note the success of *Carmina* after the dismal failure of *The Moon* five seasons earlier—especially since the two works are stylistically so similar that they are almost indistinguishable.

The Mikado was a happy romp, the company's first excursion into Gilbert and Sullivan since the fall season of 1946. Here, too, audience response brought two additional performances beyond the five originally scheduled. Wisely, more than half of the presentations were matinees, thereby encouraging a juvenile audience. Robert Coleman (*New York Mirror*, October 18, 1959) offered the ultimate praise when he wrote: "None of the fabulous D'Oyly Carte, nor Sam Chartok productions has ever offered better all-around singing and acting. And none has surpassed current manifestation for diction." Frank Porretta (Nanki-Poo), Herbert

Beattie (Pooh-Bah), and Claramae Turner (Katisha) were particularly singled out for praise.

If both of these new productions added luster to the company's image, the real brilliance emerged with *Così fan Tutte*.

The new *Così fan Tutte* is the happiest production ever put on by the New York City Opera Company. If the town offers a better musical buy than this Mozart revival, which opened at the City Center last night, this deponent knoweth not where it may be found.—Howard Taubman, *New York Times*.

Mozart's *Così fan Tutte* was altogether superb. As a whole, the New York City Opera's *Così fan Tutte* was not only one of the most admirable productions in the company's career but also, perhaps, the most memorable one I have encountered in a long list of *Così fan Tutte*s, stretching back to the famous Redoutensaal performances in Vienna in the early nineteen-twenties.
                          —Winthrop Sargeant, *The New Yorker*.

And so they went—unanimously. Probably no opera house in the world could have matched that *Così* production. Phyllis Curtin and Frances Bible as the flighty sisters, John Alexander and John Reardon as their soon-to-be-disillusioned lovers, James Pease as the cynical Don Alfonso, and Judith Raskin in her company debut as a saucy Despina. Julius Rudel's conducting, William Ball's direction, and the excellent English translation of Ruth and Thomas Martin all added to the general festivities.

Surely this was one of the high-water marks of the company's existence. Unfortunately overall attendance remained relatively low, 63 percent. Obviously some radical move was needed to stir potential opera-goers out of their lethargy. But what?

With the approach of spring 1960, the company witnessed the last American season under the Ford Foundation grant. It was of short duration—only eleven days, because the original grant terms called for an extended tour through the eastern half of the United States. The foundation had given $300,000 for the spring 1959 and spring 1960 seasons, and an additional $10,000 to continue the program of providing on-the-spot education to talented young composers.

Initially, spring 1960 was to consist only of a tour, with no performances at home. Five of the most successful works of the previous American seasons would be presented in nineteen cities east of the Mississippi. Ultimately the terms changed slightly. It was felt that unless each opera were presented at least once on a familiar stage before entering new theaters, the results would be chaotic. Once agreement was reached on a New York season—even a short one—it was deemed necessary to have a new production to provide excitement, and Marc Blitzstein's *The Cradle Will Rock* was chosen. For the role of Moll, Broadway's Tammy Grimes joined the company, supported by Craig Timberlake, David Atkinson, and Ruth Kobart. Three performances of *Cradle* had been scheduled, and a fourth added (replacing *Susannah*). It was the best-attended opera of the season, averaging 63 percent.

In addition, Menotti's *The Consul*, last heard during the Rosenstock regime, returned for two performances starring Patricia Neway, Evelyn Sachs, Chester Ludgin, Regina Sarfaty, and Jack Harrold.

Because of the expense of adding *Cradle* to the repertoire, the Ford Foundation agreed to the company's touring four operas rather than five, and the works chosen were *Baby Doe, Six Characters, Susannah*, and *Street Scene*.

There would be further collaborations between City Opera and the Ford Foundation, involving both American opera and contemporary opera of other nations, but with the close of the spring 1960 season the first great experiment came to an end. Now, approximately twenty years later, it has already had a profound effect. American operas no longer elicit an indulgent raised eyebrow in the opera houses of the world, and every year we are witness to international productions of operas by Floyd, Moore, Gershwin, Kurka, Menotti, Weill, Blitzstein, and many others.

Since 1958, it would not be amiss to think of the New York City Opera as America's opera company, which happens, coincidentally, to be situated in New York.

During the spring of 1961, the University of Vermont conferred an honorary degree upon Rudel. This was one of many awards that came about as a direct result of his service to the cause of American opera, and it prompted the following note to Morton Baum:

Dear Mr. Baum:

While sitting (for three hours) on the platform during the commencement exercises of the University of Vermont, I couldn't help but have a few nostalgic moments in retrospect. No matter where my thoughts wandered, they came back to one point of focus: how much of all that has happened is due to you. It was you who first encouraged me to stick out some of the bad days and then went ahead to protect me during them. Finally, it was you who had the confidence to entrust me with a formidable task and then your guidance that saw us through some of the tribulations to the triumphs—per aspera ad astra.

So, if I am to be known as a Doctor of Music, it must surely be said that you are the Doctor of the Doctor of Music.

20

On to Lincoln Center

THE WESTWARD VIEW from Broadway and Sixty-fourth Street embraces the greatest consolidation of culture in the world. To the left is the New York State Theater, home of the City Opera and New York City Ballet. To the right is Avery Fisher (formerly Philharmonic) Hall, where some of the nation's most exciting concerts take place. Straight ahead, only slightly obscured by the beautiful fountain, is the Metropolitan Opera with its stunning Chagall murals. West of Avery Fisher Hall is a pleasant reflecting pool containing Henry Moore's impressive sculpture, *Reclining Figure*. This pond with its tree-lined lanes is probably the most idyllic part of the complex. Behind it is the Vivian Beaumont Theater, a small house that has been witness to many superb dramatic productions, and nestled between it and the Metropolitan Opera is the Library and Museum of the Performing Arts—a collection of books, prints, memorabilia, and recordings that cover all aspects of music, drama, and dance. On the other side of the Met is Damrosch Park, a charming wooded area with a bandshell for outdoor concerts. To complete the Lincoln Center panorama, there is the Juilliard School, once devoted entirely to music, but now including drama as an intergral part of its curriculum.

To the casual observer, Lincoln Center represents the epitome of artistic grace and beauty. It is therefore extremely jarring to consider the ugly politics and power plays that went into its creation.

It is impossible to say when the idea was first born. Plans of this scope develop gradually from lesser ideas; bit by bit they change, until eventually the original ideas may be completely lost. Perhaps Mayor William J. Gaynor's 1912 attempt at an arts center (see page 2) was the forerunner of Lincoln Center; perhaps it took its impetus from City Center—an idea less far-fetched than one might imagine, since City Center was virtually unique in that it was an amalgamation of various performing arts. In any event, and whatever the causes, New York was ready for Lincoln Center (or, as it was originally termed, The Lincoln Square Project).

Charles M. Spofford is frequently regarded as the original moving force (see *Lincoln Center for the Performing Arts* by Ralph G. Martin, Prentice-Hall, Inc., page 10). The initial exploratory meeting took place on October 25, 1955, and the formal incorporation, with John D. Rockefeller III elected president, dates from June 22, 1956. In light of these dates, a memorandum written by Lincoln Kirstein on December 28, 1953, to both Morris and Baum is particularly interesting. It says, in part:

The City Center needs a new building . . . the ideal site would be central; a block, or indeed two blocks . . . attached to the heart of the Rockefeller Center complex. . . . The ideal City Center would include: a large auditorium (4,500 seats), for opera and ballet; a smaller auditorium for theatre (2,000 seats), a smaller concert hall, with orchestra-pit for Mozart-type opera. Also included would be the School of American Ballet, which would pay annual rent; possibly the Julliard School on a similar basis, and a theatre-school. . . . Having obtained parcels of land to complete a suitable site, there would be the possibility that the municipal government, the state of New York, and the Federal government . . . could be involved. . . . It is no secret that other organizations of power and an honorable history in New York are seeking new homes, chiefly the Philharmonic and the Metropolitan Opera. It would be extremely unwise to involve the City Center in dragging negotiations with any groups, which by manifest action due to past history and social background would only tend to nullify any real development on the part of City Center. . . . Such a plan fulfills an inevitable necessity in New York City today. The cultural capital of the world, the port of New York as never before deserves a monumental focus as criterion of free world music, art, theatre and dance. The United Nations is seeking a frame for visiting national groups (La Scala Opera, the Staatsoper from Berlin and Vienna, The French National Ballet; the Old Vic and Stratford dramatic companies; the Comedie Française, etc; etc). Certain portions of every season could be reserved at one of the three theatres for the distinguished visitors, so that New York could, for the first time in its three hundred years, play the role of host to the world in a manner which is fitting and demanded.

Nothing came of Kirstein's suggestions, but many of the ideas he expressed were incorporated into Lincoln Center, and some of the pitfalls he warned of eventually proved to be very real problems.

The situation regarding the City Center's participation in the Lincoln

Center project was a particularly frustrating and perplexing one. To begin with, Lincoln Center did not want City Center as a constituent.[1] To continue, City Center did not want to be a constituent. Ballet could take care of itself—that was no problem. However, it was considered risky to have the opera company in such close proximity to the Met. Because of the relative budgets, City Opera could never hope to get stars of the same stature (or at least of the same reputation) as the Met,[2] and as neighbors, comparisons would be inevitable.

There were other dangers inherent in the move. For one thing, the State Theater (originally called Theater for the Dance and Operetta) was significantly smaller than City Center, thereby limiting possible income. Secondly it was feared (and in retrospect, the fear has been realized) that whenever some group at the Metropolitan—chorus, orchestra, stage hands, etc.—might win a salary increase, the corresponding group at City Opera would make the same demands the next time contracts came up for negotiation. On the face of it, this may seem entirely fair. However, the Metropolitan has approximately ten times the New York City Opera's budget, a theater with 1,300 additional seats, and a price scale about two and a half times as high as City Opera's.[3] Certainly, the Met also has its financial problems, but what becomes exceedingly difficult for the Met becomes virtually impossible for City Opera. Several seasons ago (fall 1976) the company nearly went the way of the *New York Herald Tribune* and other newspapers driven out of existence by excessive union demands. The company was saved by minutes—literally—just before an announcement to the press cancelling the remainder of that season and all of the next.

These, then, were some of the problems facing the New York City Opera if it was to move to Lincoln Center. The most severe problem of all, however, was that the Met demanded control over the City Opera's artistic

1. They did want the New York City Ballet, by then recognized as the finest in the country. However, the opera, drama, and light opera companies were in direct competition with Lincoln Center's projected groups in these areas, and at a fraction of the cost.

2. Actually, if one goes through the City Opera rosters, one finds performers such as John Alexander, José Carreras, Phyllis Curtin, Placido Domingo, Mignon Dunn, Reri Grist, Laurel Hurley, Dorothy Kirsten, Brenda Lewis, Cornell MacNeill, John Macurdy, Sherrill Milnes, Barry Morrell, Carol Neblett, Judith Raskin, John Reardon, Regina Resnik, Beverly Sills, Tatiana Troyanos, Theodor Uppman, Giuseppe Valdengo, Shirley Verrett, Ramon Vinay . . . etc. The list is almost endless. However, for the most part, these artists were not yet established stars when they were at City Opera. The quality of performance was present, but the mystique was still to come.

3. At the time of writing this book, City Opera seats ranged from $3.50 to $25; Met seats from $10 to $60.

policies. According to the contract draft of January 15, 1959, drawn up by Lincoln Center:

> It would be mutually understood that Lincoln Center recognizes the Metropolitan Opera as its primary constituent in the field of opera. City Center would refrain from producing grand opera of the production magnitude characterized by *Aïda, Faust, Macbeth, Turandot* and the Wagnerian operas. It would be recognized that City Center's opera repertoire will require the inclusion of several of the highly popular Italian operas of modest production requirements such as *Traviata, Bohème, Butterfly, Tosca* and the smaller Mozart operas. It is recognized that these are traditionally part of the repertoire of the Metropolitan and therefore, in scheduling any such operas, the Metropolitan will have the priority and City Center will in any given week avoid scheduling the same operas as may be scheduled by the Metropolitan.
>
> It is recognized that City Center would include in its repertoire contemporary opera in English. However, insofar as such operas may in any given season be included in the Metropolitan's repertoire, those particular operas will be omitted for that season from City Center.

Finally, there was the matter of rent. After years of blood, sweat, and tears the City Center managed to acquire a $1-per-year rental. Lincoln Center, on the other hand, wanted City Center to pay a significant fee for the theater itself in addition to "it's proportionate share as a constituent unit of Lincoln Center for the overhead, administrative and operating costs of Lincoln Center."

This was hardly red-carpet treatment, and it is little wonder that City Center was not particularly enthusiastic. Yet there was an even more serious problem in not making the move to Lincoln Center. The principal control of the entire complex was in the hands of the Metropolitan Opera, and there was a beautiful theater that obviously would not sit idle. Therefore, unless City Opera joined Lincoln Center, it seemed obvious that the Met would create its own subsidiary company—an *opéra-comique* of sorts —to fill the house. A company of this genre would probably duplicate City Opera repertoire to a large extent, and would have the added advantage of Met soloists to fill the roster. Could City Opera survive against this sort of competition? Of course, it is impossible to say yes or no with certainty, but the feeling at the time was that it could not take the risk. It therefore became essential, if undesirable, for City Opera to join Lincoln Center.

On the other side of the coin, Lincoln Center was not particularly anxious to incorporate City Center into its activities (always excluding the

New York City Ballet). However, it became a virtual necessity to do so for economic reasons. The Theater for the Dance and Operetta was purchased by New York State as its display case for the 1964 World's Fair. Upon the fair's completion two years later, the building was to be turned over to the city, for the use of City Center. Only in this way could public funds be allocated, since we would otherwise be dealing with a strictly private enterprise. Even under these conditions, a great deal of political mudslinging evolved. The amounts involved were by no means insignificant —$15,000,000 for the theater, and $300,00 annually toward expenses.

And so, here was a totally absurd set of circumstances in which both parties were being forced into an association that neither wanted, simply as a matter of expedience.

Various tactics were attempted by Lincoln Center as a means of minimizing City Center's impact on the overall project. The first was to invite the New York City Ballet to participate to the exclusion of the other performing units. Had this succeeded, perhaps the powers in force could have persuaded the city and the state legislature that their requirements were being fulfilled. In any case, they did not reckon with Lincoln Kirstein. Volatile, impulsive, occasionally less than diplomatic, he never lost his artistic integrity or sense of honor; he was the last person who would sell City Center short in order to glorify his own ballet unit. Other tactics tried by Lincoln Center included the attempt to have the city lease the State Theater to Lincoln Center, which in turn would sublease it to City Center (at a much inflated rate) for only specified periods of time throughout the year. This would then put City Center scheduling at the mercy of Lincoln Center planning.

The battle for control of the State Theater was waged on many fronts. Baum and Morris fought discreetly at first—small gatherings over dinner or drinks, an occasional telephone call, etc. Eventually this technique failed, and the fight was taken to the press. The ultimate success of City Center against Lincoln Center—David against Goliath—was the result of public pressure and an informed citizenry.

Early in the fight, Kirstein used more direct tactics. Three of his letters are worth quoting, in part at least. The first, dated March 27, 1961, was addressed to Newbold Morris:

The present situation obtaining in the Lincoln Center–City Center situation prompts some observations. As you know, I was in at the start of the organization of Lincoln Center and only resigned from the Board of Directors when I realized that Messrs. Bliss and Spofford were dedicated to the destruction of the City Center as the only possible competitor for the Met at such a time as rising costs would mark the distinction between the rich man's house and the poor man's house impossible for the ultimate control of the Met.

I am not naive enough to think that Bliss and Spofford care anything about the City Center as a purveyor of art or culture; they know little of those commodities; but they well understand the control of trusteeships: witness the interlock of control in the Juillard-Philharmonic-Met cartel. It is probable that as trusteees, Bliss and Spofford would be no worse than the generality of trustees, but the principle of over-all control of all performing-arts services in New York City under the hegemony of the Met is not, as I think you agree, a good principle for the City Center which has a different public and a different attitude to serve.

The Philharmonic and the Juilliard are of no real importance in the picture; the first is not a true constituent and is merely manipulated by the Met which could not raise funds for the new building alone; the Juilliard merely guarantees tax-relief as an Educational Institution attached to the other holding companies. The Met is of necessity a conservative organization which purveys luxury-repertory at luxury-prices. This necessitates control of all contracts of any singer useful or inimical to the Met's convenience. It is not exactly malign; but the by-products of its compulsion toward absolute control is.

Three days later, he wrote to Nelson Rockefeller:

It is perhaps premature and unnecessary for me to make some further remarks about the Lincoln Center vs City Center situation at this time, but I was distressed that a great confusion exists in the mind of the general public about the true character of Lincoln Center, which was reflected partially in the image of this development which permitted Mr. Sharkey to make the remarks that he did.

As you know, I was an original board-member and served in several capacities which were historically useful over four years. I resigned from the board when I realized that there was neither philosophy nor patronage in the situation, that the project was a real-estate development handled by able bankers, lawyers and insurance agents, in which art would only receive a more hygienic facility. In the small view it is a fight between the powerful board of the Metropolitan Opera Association and the weak board of Lincoln Center for control of time and services in the various auditoria. For all clear purposes, the Met has won. As for the so-called "constituents" the Philharmonic is merely one attraction that rents space at a basic fee for what nights it requires.

The compulsion towards over-all control on the part of the Met is nothing to you; the last previous attempt almost wrecked the building of the theaters in Rockefeller Center in 1930. The Met has long been dedicated to the destruction of the City Center since it cannot tolerate the discrepancy of a low-price house with a dynamic philosophy next to a conservative luxury theatre; it must control all artists' contracts and all time of playing.

If the state of New York builds the ballet-operetta house and deeds the lease to Lincoln Center for the Performing Arts, Inc., a private corporation, it means effectively the Met will have won the fight for total control. The interlocking directorate of the Met, the Philharmonic and the Juilliard insure this. Naturally, this is not generally known, but it is no secret. It is not now the moment to arouse any public indignation since the ultimate disposition of the theatre is obscure, but the essential situation is explosive. The City Center has the most vocative, passionately loyal and intelligent audience in the greatest city in the world. Its list of 125,000 repeating customers over the last twenty years insures a certain security.

. . . In the event that the state of New York makes a direct lease to Lincoln Center, so that, in effect, Messers Bliss and Spofford contract the costs, playing-time, scheduling and policy of the City Center, the name and properties of the New York City Ballet may well be transferred to Lincoln Center, but Balanchine and I will withdraw those dancers who wish to stay with us and find funds to operate elsewhere. We are not in particular need; Lincoln Center has smothered, for the moment, any possibility of independent appeal either to the public or private patrons, but I have no doubt that a "Save the City Center" movement would have as much chance to succeed as "Save Carnegie Hall."

. . . I have had a very good view of the spectacle it has afforded from the inside and from the outside. It is not a pretty picture.

And finally, in 1964, Kirstein wrote the following to Charles M. Spofford, who was vice-chairman of the board of Lincoln Center:

It is important that the Directors of Lincoln Center should be aware of the position taken by George Balanchine and myself, relative to the control of the New York State Theater. Ethical and legal aspects of the fight are in balance, but certain historical precedents illuminate the problem.

The City Center of Music and Drama was founded by Fiorello La Guardia in 1943, at the suggestion of Newbold Morris, as a popular-priced cultural center, affording citizens of New York with the best in opera, drama, dance and musical-comedy, while also providing a chance for young performing artists. The City Center was a Center for the performing arts long before Lincoln Center was imagined. Without its precedent, it would not have been so easy or logical to promulgate an idea of a coherent performing arts center. Naturally, both the general public, enlightened patrons and the progressive foundations were enthusiastic in supporting a richer plan, which was to provide absolute standards of artistic efficiency, released from the need of constricting conditions.

From the earliest discussions of Lincoln Center, the presence of City Center was presupposed, not alone as a convenience in order to attract State and City monies, but as a come-on for wide popular support which could not be ex-

pected to back such exclusive institutions as the Metropolitan or the Philharmonic. As a director of Lincoln Center from its inception, I was privy to
these considerations; I resigned when I realized that there was little interest on
the part of the board in anything but problems affecting their chosen institutions; that they neither understood, nor were responsible for the general nature of
culture for the whole community.

. . . It is for this reason that we are engaged in this bitter fight, and we will
use every argument and device of which we are capable, to resist the usurpation
of the Enabling Act, a copy of which you are sent herewith.

Of course, City Center ultimately won its fight on all points—the lease
did not go through Lincoln Center, it was able to establish its own artistic
policies, etc. At best, however, it was a Pyrrhic victory, as reduced seating
and spiraling costs have sent the top price from $5.50 to $25 in only
fifteen years.

While the City Center–Lincoln Center battle was raging—generally
behind closed doors, but with occasional hints in the press, the opera
company continued its operations at Fifty-fifth Street.

The three American seasons had ended, but rather than closing a door,
two others were opened. The first of these was a series of commissions for
new American works, underwritten by the Ford Foundation. Eventually
eleven new operas saw the light of day under that aspect of the program.
Four of these were by composers whose works had not been previously
performed by the company—Jack Beeson, Abraham Ellstein, Jerome
Moross, and Ned Rorem; the others were by Floyd, Giannini, Hoiby,
Menotti, Moore, Ward, and Weisgall.

The second new project initiated by the American seasons was to see
how these works would stand up against the international repertoire, and
so two contemporary seasons were planned which would enable the public
to judge American achievement in a broader scope.

Apart from these special seasons, the company ran a predictable
course. There were always new works being introduced, but most of these
failed to make any lasting impression. Among the more noteworthy events
were the return engagement of Leopold Stokowski conducting a double bill
of Monteverdi's *Orfeo* and Dallapiccola's *The Prisoner*, a revival of Puccini's trilogy, not heard as a unit in New York in over forty years, and
several world premieres commissioned under Ford auspicies. Of these,
Ward's *The Crucible* has had some lasting success and a smattering of
European productions. Ellstein's *The Golem* was most noteworthy for the
terrifying creation of baritone Chester Ludgin in the title role. Neither
Moore's *Wings of the Dove* nor Floyd's *Passion of Jonathan Wade* made

much of an impression upon the audiences, nor did Jerome Moross's *Gentlemen, Be Seated!*, an opera in the form of a minstrel show, by the composer of *The Golden Apple*.[4]

The fall 1964 season was marked by two very important events. The first of these was the introduction into the repertoire of Mussorgsky's *Boris Godunov* in English with Norman Treigle in the title role (an as yet unknown Tatiana Troyanos was the Marina). On the face of it, this does not appear extremely unusual. *Boris* had been in and out of the Met repertoire with great regularity for about twenty-five years. And this is precisely the point. Unlike *Bohème*, *Carmen*, or *Traviata*, *Boris* has never been so popular a work that it merited a place in the repertoire of both companies. Recent Met performances had featured Cesare Siepi, George London, Jerome Hines, and Giorgio Tozzi in the title role. It therefore seemed the height of foolhardiness for City Opera to schedule it.

The company had always referred to itself as an ensemble group and decried the "star system." This seems a bit foolish. It is the audience rather than management that makes stars, and there is no way that a Treigle, Sills, Curtin, Neway, or Domingo could have been held back.[5] In scheduling *Boris* for Norman Treigle, the company was taking that first step and publicly admitting, "Yes, we are a star company . . . when we have suitable stars." When Norman Treigle as the cardiac-stricken Boris fell down the long flight of stairs upon which his throne was perched, the audience gasped—one or two spectators even screamed. A few months later in a letter to Rudel, Treigle said that he considered himself the world's finest Boris. This is the type of statement that immediately produces a bristling reaction, but on sober consideration, he may have been right.

The other major event that season was the institution of a subscription series. This is important for several reasons. First of all, it enables the company to predict more accurately its seasonal income and therefore budget more efficiently. Secondly, the company receives the money before the season's start, when it is most needed for scenery, costumes, and rehearsal expense, thereby easing the cash-flow problem. With the advent of subscription sales, attendance figures become less meaningful, since they now represent the composite appeal of a group of works, rather than the popularity of any one work.

4. Personally, I was extremely partial to both *Gentlemen, Be Seated!* and *The Golden Apple*. Neither is a profound or complex work, but both are utterly charming, melodious, occasionally moving, and well worth reviving.

5. There were, of course, scores of others. This short list is illustrative, rather than comprehensive.

One week after *Boris,* there was another world premiere, the company's eleventh. This was *Natalia Petrovna* by Lee Hoiby, pleasant but unremarkable.

Spring 1965 was the first of the two seasons in which American repertoire was to be tested against international. Menotti's *Saint of Bleecker Street* finally entered the repertoire almost ten years after it was commissioned, Jack Beeson's *Lizzie Borden* was premiered with greater success than most, Shostakovich's *Katerina Ismailova* and Weill's *Three Penny Opera* were added, and there were many repeats from past seasons—the Puccini *Trittico, Baby Doe, Susannah, Oedipus Rex* and *Carmina Burana, Porgy and Bess,* and Benjamin Britten's *A Midsummer Night's Dream.*

The American works held up very well, but the audiences were equally enthusiastic about the *Three Penny Opera,* and particularly the interpretations of Martha Schlamme as Jenny and Kurt Kasznar as Macheath.

Fall 1965 was billed as a more traditional season—*Traviata, Bohème, Fledermaus, Carmen,* etc. However, it introduced three new works, all products of the twentieth century—an exciting *Flaming Angel* of Prokofiev, a stunning production of Richard Strauss's *Capriccio,* and another world premiere, Ned Rorem's *Miss Julie.*

More and more I began to overhear intermission conversations complaining about the company's repertoire. Of the 116 operas done so far, one was by Donizetti, two by Rossini, eight by Menotti, and three each by Britten, Weill, and Stravinsky. The choice was not destined to make many new converts to opera, nor particularly to satisfy the established fans.

The second contemporary season, spring 1966, was also the company's introduction into the new theater. It had opened in 1964 as part of the World's Fair festivities, but now, after all the bitter fighting was over, it was the new home of the City Center. Its capacity was only 2,735—approximately 500 fewer seats than the Fifty-fifth Street theater. The sight lines were excellent from all parts of the house, the acoustics variable. Like the old theater, there was no prompter's box, placing an additional demand on the singers. The architecture was handled by the firm of Philip Johnson Associates, and unlike the old Mecca Temple, the new theater was quite beautiful. The Grand Foyer with its encircling promenade is a favorite intermission spot, and there is a perpetually festive atmosphere. Of course, such items as stage equipment and lighting facilities are vastly improved over the old house.

On February 22, 1966, at 7:45 P.M., the curtain went up on Alberto Ginastera's *Don Rodrigo.* John Ardoin, writing in *Opera* (April 1966) stated:

To inaugurate its new quarters, the company's general manager, Julius Rudel, offered the North American premiere of Alberto Ginastera's *Don Rodrigo* on February 22. It was for all concerned a brilliant triumph. The most costly production in the company's history was lavished on one of the most stageworthy new operas to be heard in New York in many a season.

. . . There were superb, economical yet telling sets by Ming Cho Lee; dazzling costumes by Theoni V. Aldredge, which perfectly completed Mr. Lee's *decor*, and alive, vital staging by Tito Capobianco. In the pit, under Mr. Rudel, the orchestra played with a virtuosity, awareness and exactitude any opera house might envy. In the main parts of Florinda and Don Rodrigo, the soprano Jeannine Crader and tenor Placido Domingo proved to have dramatic instincts as sure and distinctive as their fine voices. Lesser parts were expertly filled by David Clatworthy (Don Julian) and Spiro Malas (Teudiselo).

Other new works that season were two operas dealing with the French revolution, Poulenc's brilliant *Dialogues of the Carmelites* and von Einen's austere *Danton's Death*, both performed in English. Neither opera enjoyed much success with either critics or audience, but John Reardon as Danton turned in one of the finest characterizations of his career.

As the first Lincoln Center season ended, there was great cause for jubilation—but not for long. Three days later, on March 30, 1966, Newbold Morris died in his sixty-fourth year. Morris had been a dedicated servant of City Center for a third of his life, and his passing was deeply mourned. It was Morton Baum who had actually run the company over the years, but it was the revered Morris name that provided respectability, contacts, and dollars.

Baum wrote a touching tribute that appeared in the program:

The City Center of Music and Drama has survived many grievous blows. It will be difficult to support the disappearance of Newbold Morris. More than any single person, he was responsible for the uses of the auditorium on 55th Street, which must always be associated with his name. He loved to tell of entering the abandoned Mecca Temple, then a mere item on the tax rolls of bankruptcy. There with a caretaker's flashlight he would throw a thin beam on the weird and wonderful decoration of past glory. That flashlight was prophetic of spotlights and footlights which were to illuminate much that was best in the performing arts in the city for the next two decades. What will appear there in decades to come is his most vivid memorial. With the aid and interest of Fiorello La Guardia, Mrs. Lytle Hull, Ruth Pratt and so many others, champions, patrons, friends,—Morris called into being an institution of whose rugged annals he was both author and hero.

If there is an aristocracy in the United States, it is one of responsibility assumed and service performed. Newbold was bred into an historic line which has contributed to the dreams of American possibility since the founding of these States. While he could, and did, touch the resources of his class and tradition both morally and materially, he was in the best sense a democratic citizen. He was too secure socially ever to worry about class structure. He chose to apply himself with the birth of a new sort of cultural service, a people's theater, while at the same time aiding, as was the habit of his family and friends, the more ancient organizations. Newbold was at home everywhere; when he stopped a singer, a dancer, an actor or a stagehand to ask how it was going, it was no idle question. While he never interfered in an artistic sense, he partook of the experience of preparation and performance to the highest degree.

Newbold loved public service. He would have glorified the highest elective office. But there was at his core a benevolence, a sweetness which could have been mistaken for softness. His nature was not suited to the ferocity of the biggest arena. So he chose as his theater of service, a more intimate stage with a far more discriminating audience, a public that cares less for political power than for powerful performances by the most skilled practitioners of dance, music and drama. There is slight space here to honor his great political services; these will be covered in many other columns. Here, the family of the City Center,—on 55th Street and at the State Theater in Lincoln Center, which he manfully supported, take a long farewell of founder and friend.

Baum was immediately named chairman of the board, a position he had filled until now in all but name. Morris was missed as a friend, but the functioning of the company was not impaired by his loss.

Opening night of the fall 1966 season was another of those magical events. If *Boris Godunov* had made Norman Treigle a star, Handel's *Julius Caesar* did the same for Beverly Sills. She had attracted a certain amount of attention in the past for her Philine in *Mignon, Traviata, Baby Doe,* and Donna Anna in *Don Giovanni,* but it was Cleopatra that turned success into stardom. A long and taxing role, extremely florid yet dramatic, makes the part almost impossible to sing properly. Miss Sills's voice rippled and shimmered; one was reminded of moonbeams at play. Hubert Saal wrote in *Newsweek* that "her coloratura is unmatched by anyone's. Not only is it remarkably flexible, incredibly quick and perfectly true, but the florid notes are crystal-clear, variable in color even at such altitudes and speeds, and full-bodied, taking part in the drama of the opera rather, than being mere exhibitions of agility."

Nor was Norman Treigle in the title role any less spectacular. Of the production itself, Winthrop Sargeant wrote in the *New Yorker*: "The total effect constituted the finest staging of its sort that I have ever witnessed in any opera house, and it caught the majestic formal spirit of Handel's opera with uncanny rightness."

By a quirk of fate, it almost failed to happen. Phyllis Curtin had been gone from the company for about a year, and Rudel had planned the *Julius Caesar* as the vehicle for her return. However, her schedule left her available for only two of the four projected performances, which was unsatisfactory to Rudel. Sills was very anxious for the part, and with John White's prodding made a very strong demand for the role. So strong, in fact, that she threatened to leave the company if she did not get the part. Although she was not so solidly established that the company could not afford to lose her, she was reliable, well liked, and a strong asset. She won—and so did the company and the audiences. After a decade with City Opera, she was discovered overnight.

That season also saw the City Opera's first *Magic Flute*. The decor by Beni Montresor was enchanting, fair competition for the Met's Marc Chagall production. Sills negotiated the Queen of the Night with little involvement (along with Mimi in *La Bohème*, this is her least favorite role), Veronica Tyler and Michele Molese were sympathetic as the young lovers, but only John Reardon as Papageno really stood out. Considering the company's overwhelming success with *Don Giovanni, The Marriage of Figaro, Così,* and *Seraglio,* the *Magic Flute* was a definite disappointment.

Another Ford Foundation world premiere was the outstanding feature of the next season. This was Vittorio Giannini's *The Servant of Two Masters,* based on a Goldoni comedy. Less substantial than his *Taming of the Shrew,* it disappeared after that season.

Another Sills-Treigle collaboration was the feature of the fall 1967 season. This was Rimsky-Korsakov's *Coq d'Or,* spectacular because of its two leads, and even more so for the Astrologer of Enrico di Giuseppe.

Less than two years after Morris's death, Morton Baum, not yet sixty-three, was also fatally stricken. He was, of course, missed to a much greater extent, having played an active part in every significant decision since the founding of City Center. There were many testimonials, and the sense of loss was keenly captured by Julius Rudel's:

Morton Baum is dead. I have read it, written it, said it, and heard it, but these four words still fail to elicit a sense of reality. I am not ready to face the void, for I feel that I have been orphaned. The man who fathered the idea which shaped so much of my life had, in the course of time, become a father to me.

Here was no indifferent progenitor, for with that germinal act, there arose a sense of responsibility, of pride, and of destiny that hard facts and harsher reality ever failed to shake. This was no comradely father, no contemporary pal but a pre-Freudian, biblical patriarch who moved heaven and earth and parted seas, courted friends and made great enemies that his offspring might survive. He was stern, always demanding and although one would cry out "it's impossible," he always evoked more from us then we thought we had it in us to give. He shaped a dream, that benevolent tyrant, but he earned our love and deep respect by letting us glimpse through his eyes his limitless horizons.

It was almost twenty-five years ago that I first met him. I had only five years before fled a maddened Europe and was just beginning to find myself in the musical world. Incredibly, my luck had taken me headlong into a grand plan to bring the best in culture to the people. There was no cynicism in this, no "bread and circuses" for the masses. It was a revelation to see dedicated practical men wanting, without political motivation, to do something for that mysterious entity known as the people. Nor was there condescension in this, for Morton Baum had the deep conviction that poor people had all the capacity of the rich, if not the money, to enjoy the better things of life. He set out to prove this and in doing so provided us with the finest audience I have ever known or could have wished. Two theaters filled with people every night are his living monument. What temple ever built, what pyramid ordered into being by a powerful pharaoh can equal the living monument Morton Baum created, but for which he gave his life.

There are many men with artistic convictions, there are many builders of monuments, but few of them are artists themselves. Morton Baum was an artist. It is not only that he could read a score, play the piano, or sing operatic roles; he had the discerning eye, discriminating ear, and the unfettered soul of the artist. He was a thorough realist, but in an uncanny way Morton Baum's reality was vaster than anyone else's. He did not "play it safe" for himself, but never risked our existence. He could see what was beyond the vision of others and then take the most practical steps, make the most mundane gestures to grasp what had only a short time before appeared to be beyond reach. There is no truer artist than the man who can make real or tangible what others have never fully envisioned. It was with this gift and not with his financial wizardry that he created the most unique climate for other artists. It was a climate churning with creative challenge, not one tempered by affluence.

These years we spent together, Morton Baum, John White, and I, were rich ones, filled with terrors and hopes, anxieties and laughter, nadirs and crests. The three of us were riding a crest on February 6th, but until the moment he left us, Morton Baum was searching, from that lovely vantage point, for the next peak to conquer. He never let up, not out of need for personal accomplishment, but because there was so much to do, more than most of us could even imagine. Without him, that soaring crest had ebbed for John and me.

Like the austere father he was, Morton Baum was sparing in his praise, but John and I knew how he exulted in the cheers of the crowds, in the mounting success, in the increasing recognition we achieved. We didn't need to hear praise or words of affection from his lips. We read it in the way he always referred to us as "the boys" when he spoke of us to others. Just recently I heard it in his voice when, looking at me, he remarked to John, "The boy is becoming so gray." He acknowledged the passage of the years, my graying hair, my growing children, but to him I could never grow old. And to me he can never be dead.

On a slightly less emotional and more detached level, Harold C. Schonberg wrote in the *New York Times* (February 18, 1968):

The New York City Opera will open its winter season on Thursday at the State Theater, but what normally would be a gay occasion, will be haunted by a spectre. Morton Baum died on Feb. 7—died unexpectedly at the age of 62, and with him died a part of the New York City Center of Music and Drama.

They say there is no such thing as an indispensable man. Wrong. When it came to the City Center, Morton Baum was irreplaceable, and his death is going to leave the organization with some formidable problems. He was its leader in fact and deed, its guiding force, its shaper, its counselor, its knight in shining armor. This is not written as a conventional tribute to one who has left us. Every word is meant. Without Baum, the City Center operation seems almost inconceivable, and no one man is ever going to do half the job he did.

Baum, a lawyer and a man well versed in New York politics, had been instrumental in founding the City Center of Music and Drama in 1943. He was that rare combination of man of action and man of culture. He was a skillful pianist, a good score reader, a better than average chess player, a man who read everything that came his way, the possessor of a fine critical mind. Coupled to that was a love for battle, a magnificent ability to manipulate and operate, a tough and even ruthless attitude, and an enormous competitive sense. Not many have this combination; and Baum, who was competent and confident, who did not mind how many toes he trampled on (that sometimes included the sensitive toes of the press as well as the well-manicured toes of Wall Street bigwigs and society lords and ladies), was not the most popular man who ever jostled his way through the mob.

Something of a grey eminence, Baum shunned publicity and preferred to work behind the scenes.

But he was never bashful, and when he had to, as during the dispute with Lincoln Center over the State Theater building, he could yell very very loud. On the whole he worked away from the public eye, and his gratification came with the results achieved by the City Center. He was the catalyst. All heads of the City Center—Julius Rudel at the opera, Jean Dalrymple in the drama section, George Balanchine in ballet—all say that Baum never dictated to them, never imposed his own tastes, never interfered with the operation of the various constituents.

What he did was supply ideas. "He gave everybody impetus to think not only more freely but even widely. He thought big," says Rudel. "He had imagination." Thus when Baum became interested in the Joffrey Ballet, it was only natural that he extend to that struggling company the hospitality of the City Center. Basically he had the final say in its over-all operations. He took care of the bookings, the budgets, the financing, balancing everything delicately, working with the city administration. "Morton always was the one to go down City Hall and have a big fight, which he loved," says Dalrymple. For none of this did he accept any money.

It was during the State Theater fight that Baum rose to his greatest height. Lincoln Center wanted the building. Baum insisted that it originally had been conceived as a home for the City Center. He went tearing in like a hellcat. At the beginning the general feeling was that it was a David and Goliath affair. Here was the weak, impoverished City Center fighting those Lincoln Center capitalists—all those infighters, those bankers and politicians, all that power and money. But some on the sidelines almost from the beginning took a different point of view. Don't kid yourself, they kept saying. You will find that Baum is the Goliath, and this is one Goliath who is not going to be knocked down. They were right, of course. Poor Lincoln Center never had a chance.

Baum threw the book at Lincoln Center and showed them legalistic tricks they did not even know existed. When it came to infighting, Baum was in a class by himself. Anybody who had anything to do with him those days remembers the sheer joy and relish with which he blocked, countered, pressed the attack. How that man loved a scrap! And once the City Center moved into the State Theater, he jealously guarded their rights. Nobody could push him around. There is talk of his demand that all books be examined to show operating inefficiences on the part of some other constituents of the Lincoln Center operation. It is in this area that Baum will be irreplaceable.

The City Center people are still in a state of shock, but the current feeling is that although the bottom has dropped out, there are no major operating problems that cannot be handled. The feeling also is that there will be hitches here and there along the line. Baum never could delegate authority. He did everything himself, down to the tinest details, and never trained anybody to take his place. He knew more about the financial structure of the City Center than anybody else, and he also knew more about the ins and outs of negotiations with the city and with labor unions than anybody else. Thus the apparatus he created will creak without him at the wheel.

But the City Center will manage. Where they may not manage so well is in finding somebody so ferociously capable of protecting City Center rights. It may be that the City Center is a little defensive about its relation to the other Lincoln Center constituents, and is apt to see ghosts where there really are not even shadows. Baum, always a realist, always confident, never fell into this trap. But when he decided that a real issue was at hand, that the City Center was getting short-changed, there were seismic upheavals. He was an amazing, complicated man; a brilliant one; sometimes a savage one; always a dedicated one. And there was a soft side to him that made everybody at the City Center love him. He was father figure, brother figure, and of authentic stature—the most practical visionary, perhaps, of his time.

Although both Morris and Baum were gone, life continued at the City Opera. Another Ginastera opera was introduced in March 1968. This was *Bomarzo*, less overwhelming than *Don Rodrigo*, but still powerful and gripping. The title role was sung by an excellent Mexican tenor, Salvador Novoa, and Julius Rudel conducted. Douglas Moore's *Carry Nation* also entered the repertoire, the fourth of his operas to be performed by City Opera. Beverly Wolff as the axe-wielding arch-enemy of alcohol was superb, but the work itself, despite some marvelous moments, was not especially noteworthy.

Massenet's *Manon* had not been given by the company since 1952. It was now revived for Sills, who drew the most lavish praise imaginable from the press. According to Herbert Weinstock (*Opera*, June 1968):

Manon (March 21) was a triumph of taste and ability for everyone concerned. The star was Beverly Sills in the title-role, giving probably the outstanding operatic characterization of the past several seasons in New York. Vocally, visually, dramatically, humanly, she *was* Manon, a complex girl whose evolution from Act 1 through to Act 4 was a masterly accomplishment.

Hugo Weisgall's *Nine Rivers from Jordan* had its premiere the following season—another Ford Foundation work. It can best be termed a total fiasco. *Opera* (January 1969) described the event as "a disaster," and went on to say:

A very large cast, headed by Julian Patrick as Lance Corporal Don Hanwell, could be seen and heard to struggle with thoroughly thankless assignments. Audience departures from the house during the two intervals were numerous. Proof has been offered one wearying time more that viable opera cannot be created by *fiat* or by foundation grants.

Faust returned that season after a three-year absence. The brilliant staging of Frank Corsaro turned the old war-horse into a genuinely dramatic experience, and the team of Sills and Treigle as Marguerite and Méphistophélès provided reinforcement. Molese's Faust, Frances Bible's Siébel, Dominic Cossa's Valentin, and Muriel Greenspon's Marthe completed the cast to perfection. Weinstock, who so thoroughly disliked the Weisgall opera, reported, "I should not like to give the impression that, with Julius Rudel's rightly *operatic* conducting, this was anything less than the most convincing production of *Faust* in my experience."

Borodin's *Prince Igor* is a superb opera—colorful, exciting, melodious, and exotic. In addition, there is enough of a déjà vu feeling about the music from *Kismet* to provide audiences with the sense of satisfaction that comes with recognition. It had last been done in New York in 1917. City Opera conceived of it as a vehicle for Treigle, and the spectacular solo dancing, with the incredible leaps, was entrusted to Edward Villella. For whatever reason, Treigle refused the part, and it was assumed by Julian Patrick. Maralin Niska as Jaroslavna and Joy Davidson as Kontchakovna were both excellent, as were the Prince Galitsky of Roy Samuelsen and the Khan Kontchak of William Chapman. Rudel's conducting was first-rate and was matched by Corsaro's staging: but the star was Villella. *Igor* remained in the repertoire for two seasons. The eleven performances were enthusiastically attended, and a revival of it would be very welcome.

Treigle was becoming as much of a star personality as Sills, and he now wrote to Rudel with some repertoire demands, which he insisted must be met if the company wanted him to remain on the roster. He sent a list of four operas that he wanted to sing, and demanded that the company do at least two of them with him in the leading bass/baritone role. The operas were Boito's *Mefistofele*, Massenet's *Don Quichotte*, and *Attila* and *Don Carlo*, both by Verdi.

Don Carlo was immediately dismissed. It is an expensive production, making extreme vocal demands on the entire cast, and it was current in the Met repertoire. *Don Quichotte* and *Attila* were taken under consideration (both are magnificent works), and *Mefistofele* was immediately approved. In fact, it became one of the company's greatest successes, critically and financially.

September 21, 1969, was the premiere date of the *Mefistofele*. With Carol Neblett in the dual role of Margherita and Helen of Troy, Rudel in the pit, and Tito Capobianco staging it, the opera was in excellent hands. Only tenor Robert Nagy was weak, but it hardly mattered. The show was Treigle's.

Sills got her own revival that season, the company's first *Lucia di Lammermoor*. The production was uncut, and *Opera* reported that she was the most convincing Lucia since Callas.

Another Orff work reached the boards. This was *Catulli Carmina*, the second part of the trilogy of which *Carmina Burana* is the first part. Neither *Catulli* nor the final work in the group, *The Triumph of Aphrodite* has the instant appeal of *Burana*, and *Catulli* (which was double-billed with Ravel's *L'Heure Espagnole*) was performed only four times.

Spring 1970 brought back Débussy's *Pelléas et Mélisande*, which had been previously performed by the company in its very early days, starring Maggie Teyte and as an yet unknown Theodor Uppman. This revival featured Patricia Brooks, a sensitive, moving Mélisande, and André Jobin as Pelléas (his father, Raoul Jobin, had sung the same role at the Met in 1940). The principal stars of the production, however, were conductor Julius Rudel and stage director Frank Corsaro, both of whom succeeded in capturing the diaphanous, otherworldly quality that makes Débussy's masterpiece unique.

Both *Mefistofele* and *Lucia* had been underwritten by the Corbett Foundation, which continued its generosity by funding Donizetti's *Roberto Devereux*, an exceedingly beautiful opera unduly neglected for about a century. It was a triumph for all involved—Sills, Domingo, Capobianco, Donizetti—but mostly for Sills. Critic Herbert Weinstock reported in *Opera* (December 1970):

As Queen Elizabeth I, Beverly Sills again proved that she is not a second-flight Callas or Sutherland, but, and dazzlingly, a first-flight Beverly Sills. . . . She deserved the standing applause that she received at the end of the powerful scene in the Great Hall of Westminster. . . . Under the rightly dominating baton of Julius Rudel, the opera swept violently to its violent conclusion—and won its audience completely.

The success of *Roberto Devereux* led to future productions of other Donizetti operas dealing with British royalty, *Maria Stuarda* in spring 1972 and *Anna Bolena* in fall 1973. Both of these starred Miss Sills, and the title role of *Maria Stuarda* joined the ranks of her foremost creations—Cleopatra, Baby Doe, and Manon.

The period between 1970 and 1973 was also witness to a number of contemporary operas new to the repertoire—Janáček's *The Makropoulos Affair* with a stunning performance by Maralin Niska, the world premiere of Menotti's *The Most Important Man* composed under a Ford Foundation grant, Ginastera's new *Beatrix Cenci*, *Albert Herring* of Britten, Hoiby's *Summer and Smoke*, and Hans Werner Henze's *The Young Lord*. This last work was notable on two accounts. First, the role of Sir Edgar—silent, but critical to the drama— was assumed by Sir Rudolf Bing, the former general manager of the Metropolitan Opera; second, the production was the first gift to the company of Dr. Gert von Gontard, a remarkable man with a strong theatrical background, which included assisting the immortal Max Reinhardt. Gontard became one of the most active members of the board of directors, and an extremely generous patron who had donated some of the company's most beautiful productions.

Sills's success with the Donizetti heroines led naturally into Bellini, and on February 21, 1974, the company offered its first New York performance of *I Puritani*. Technically, the work had entered the company repertoire some months earlier, on November 28, as part of the annual Los Angeles tour.

It was after a rehearsal of *Puritani* one night that Sills and Rudel had their first conversation on a topic of monumental importance. She had begun to express an interest in operatic management, seeking new worlds to conquer. He wanted to devote more of his time and energy to conducting, and less to adminstration.

Perhaps there was some mutually beneficial plan to be worked out. . . .

21

The Best Is Yet
to Come

FALL OF 1973 had been a difficult season; in fact, it very nearly signaled the end of the company's existence. Almost immediately after opening night, the orchestra went on strike, and it was four weeks before terms suitable to both sides were agreed upon. All performances during that period were canceled, but most of the company's running expenses remained the same. There was therefore a tremendous loss of revenue, which was exceedingly difficult to absorb, since even under the best of circumstances the company was unable to make ends meet.

More serious than the financial loss was the uncertainty about the future. In a field where artists are frequently engaged several years ahead of time, the inability to enter into contract negotiations on schedule can have long-term repercussions. It was literally the eleventh hour when the strike was finally settled—immediately prior to canceling the remainder of the season and all of the next year.

With a new orchestral contract reached, the company was safe for another three years, and the spring 1974 season added two operas to the growing repertoire. Bellini's *I Puritani*, which had not been staged in New York since the Metropolitan's 1917–18 season, was brought back for Beverly Sills, who created a sensation as Elvira. The extremely difficult role of Arturo, originally composed for the great Rubini, was capably sung by Enrico Di Giuseppe. With Bellini added to the list of unusual Donizetti operas that had been performed in recent years, the company seemed to be taking on a new direction—the vast field of "bel canto," neglected by most opera companies throughout the world for many years.

While Sills was firmly established in the public's affection, another soprano, Maralin Niska, was generating an ever-increasing public and the spring season witnessed a major production for her as well. Cherubini's *Medea* had never been professionaly produced in New York (although there had been a concert performance some seven years earlier) and was known to local audiences only through recordings. The woman who murders her children in order to torture their father has inspired loathing in dramatists and composers for centuries, and Niska dominated the work with her intense acting, as well as her superb singing.

Fall 1974 offered no new operas, a consequence of the strike one year earlier. Puccini's *Manon Lescaut,* which had been done by the company almost thirty years earlier, was brought back in a new production, but since this had been in and out of the Metropolitan repertoire for quite a few years, no great enthusiasm was in evidence.

Two new operas appeared the following spring. The first of these was Mozart's *Idomeneo* on March 16. The sublime music was not enough to overcome the static action, and it was dropped after three performances. The other new work, however, took the public by storm. Korngold's *Die Tote Stadt*, with Carol Neblett, John Alexander, and Dominic Cossa in the leading roles, played to full houses, and it looked like the company had another major success, like Boito's *Mefistofele*. The production was visually magnificent, with superb projections in lieu of conventional scenery, and the inspired stage direction of Frank Corsaro and incisive conducting of Imre Pallo evoked brilliant performances from all of the soloists. The first complete recording of the opera, with Neblett in the dual role of Marietta and Marie, was announced by RCA Victor, and this added to the general aura of excitement. During subsequent seasons, interest waned a bit, but remained at a sufficiently high level to warrant several revivals. The production was a gift of Gert von Gontard, his third to the company (Henze's *The Young Lord* and Strauss's *Ariadne auf Naxos* were the first two).

Fall 1975 produced another Donizetti revival, *The Daughter of the Regiment*, with Sills and Di Giuseppe again sharing vocal honors. The production had a certain amount of charm, but the edge had been taken off the excitement by the recent Met performances (January 1973) with Sutherland and Pavarotti. Wagner's *Die Meistersinger*, last performed under Halasz's aegis, returned to the repertoire in a handsome new production, which many considered Rudel's finest achievement.

Perhaps the most significant event of the season was the company's first radio broadcast from the New York State Theater. During the ill-fated Leinsdorf season (Fall 1956), there had been three broadcasts over station

WNYC—a double bill of *The Moon* by Orff and *L'Histoire du Soldat* of Stravinsky; Verdi's *La Traviata* and Bizet's *Carmen*. Apart from these and a closed-circuit TV screening of Rimsky-Korsakov's *Le Coq d'Or,* New York City Opera audiences had been limited to those actually in the house. However, during fall 1975 arrangements were made with the newly reorganized WNCN for a full weekend of broadcast time. The station made twenty-four hours available, noon to midnight on November 8th and 9th, and the time was used for company promotion which took the form, primarily, of a subscription drive. There were interviews and special features, culminating in a live broadcast from the stage of *I Puritani.* A tremendous effort went into the organization and preparation of the weekend, all under the supervision of City Opera Guild member Jeffrey Laikind, whose original conception it was, and who was subsequently elected to the board of directors. The author of this volume was privileged to be the host-commentator for *I Puritani,* and to produce an additional five hours for the festivities, which came to be known as the "Operathon."

By now, the earlier conversations between Sills and Rudel regarding company management were beginning to reach the public. There were persistent rumors that she would soon assume the position of co-director—rumors that were strengthened by a weakening of Rudel's position in the press. Remarks in the gossip columns indicated a dissatisfaction by the board of directors due in part to a waning aura of excitement about the company in the minds of the public, and in part to his prolonged absences from New York while conducting elsewhere.

One of the problems with the Rudel years, as indicated by both press and public, was the heavy concentration on twentieth-century repertoire. The feeling that an opera house is not a museum and that, in order to remain vital and alive, new works must be presented, is a point well taken. However, the extreme concentration on the contemporary scene did a great deal to turn the public away. Even excluding the three seasons of American opera, approximately 60 percent of the works introduced by Rudel were composed after 1900; if the American seasons are included, the ratio increases to 75 percent. This makes for impressive statistics in terms of premieres, but does little toward building a large and enthusiastic audience. By the end of fall 1975, Rudel had introduced eighty-five works to the company repertoire, of which forty-two had vanished after a single season.

On the other side of the coin, before Rudel, it had been all but impossible for a contemporary operatic composer to see his works produced. Naturally, many extremely talented artists turned away from opera and devoted themselves to the instrumental field. Rudel injected new life into the medium, and transformed a dying art into a living one. His contribution in this area must not be overlooked. But to the board of directors who examined profit and loss statements, as well as artistic achievement—and the much less tangible quality of vitalization—it was a very costly way of running the company, even with foundation grants and private funding.

Three new works were introduced in spring 1976. Monteverdi's *Il Ritorno d'Ulisse in Patria* took its place alongside the previous productions of his *Orfeo* and *L'Incoronazione di Poppea*. The first giant among composers for the stage was well served by the New York City Opera, and the performance itself was distinguished by the company debut of Frederica von Stade, who sang superbly. She was ably joined by Richard Stilwell, but the success of both of these artists was anticipated. The surprise of the occasion was the exquisite vocalism of two relative unknowns in the cast, mezzo-soprano Hilda Harris and tenor Henry Price, who was almost immediately established as a star of the first magnitude.

The company also introduced its seventh Donizetti opera, his *Lucrezia Borgia*, which had previously achieved a single performance at the Met (December 5, 1904). During Donizetti's day, this was considered one of his most important works, rivaling *Lucia di Lammermoor* in popularity. Unfortunately, the physical production, borrowed from the Dallas Civic Opera, was a dreary affair, and it vanished after only a season.

The third new offering was *Ashmedai* by Joseph Tal. Despite splendid performances by John Lankston in the title role, Paul Ukena as the king, and exciting direction by Hal Prince, the audience was offended by the cacophony, and approximately half of those present at the premiere left during the first intermission. Many who remained were indignant. I cannot recall such a strong negative reaction since Hugo Weisgall's *Nine Rivers from Jordan* about eight years earlier.

When the next fall season began, the orchestra's contract was due for renewal and a repeat of the 1973 difficulties was encountered. Another strike of several weeks' duration again threatened the company's existence, and, as before, several weeks' performances were lost. Once again, the contract was settled just hours before cancellation of the remainder of the season. Offenbach's *La Belle Hélène*, another gift of Gert von Gontard, received its premiere, with gorgeous scenery and costumes and an outstanding performance by James Billings as Menelaeus. The dialogue, however, was both old-fashioned and heavy-handed, and consequently the work fell short of its potential. For subsequent performances, it was tightened up and played to enthusiastic audiences and a somewhat less delighted press.

Leon Kirchner's *Lily*, based upon Saul Bellow's *Henderson the Rain*

King and commissioned by Rudel, had its world premiere on April 14, 1977. The handsome production was nothing short of a fiasco, and members of the audience began to leave after about twenty minutes. If most listeners were offended by *Ashmedai*, they were simply bored by *Lily*. First-rate performances were given by George Shirley as Romilayu and Susan Belling in the title role, but it was an exercise in futility.

The other principal novelty of the season was a triple bill consisting of Mozart's *The Impresario*, Poulenc's *La Voix Humaine*, and Stravinsky's *L'Histoire du Soldat*. The works were staged by Frank Corsaro, whose unconventional approach frequently resulted in masterpieces and occasionally in catastrophe—rarely anything between. The Mozart opera was charming, and Nico Castel, who played his part as a traditional "dirty old man," stated in an interview that he patterned the role after John White. It was done good-naturedly, of course, but many of White's mannerisms were apparent, providing an excellent private joke for company members (and for White as well). Niska was nothing short of miraculous in the Poulenc opus, an outstanding tour de force for the sole character, who must sing and act with intensity for approximately forty minutes. There is no let-up from start to finish, and she received the type of ovation performers dream about. The third part of the trilogy, the Stravinsky opera-ballet-play, was one of the Corsaro catastrophes mentioned above, and produced a fair amount of booing and hissing. When the triple bill was carried over to the following season, Ravel's *L'Heure Espagnole* replaced *L'Histoire du Soldat*.

Rumors of conflict between the board and Rudel continued to reach the press and, in fact, became a frequent topic of intermission conversation.

Two new works were introduced during fall 1977. One was Thea Musgrave's *The Voice of Ariadne*, the company's first opera composed by a woman. It had many beautiful and exciting moments, and although some spots might have benefited from tightening up, the overall reaction was definitely positive. Cynthia Clarey had a very promising debut, taking over at short notice Diana Soviero's role of the countess.

The initial "Operathon" broadcast of 1975 had led to a close association between City Opera and WNCN, and by fall 1977 this had ripened into a regularly scheduled broadcast series, sponsored by Pioneer High Fidelity. I was invited to produce the series, which I did with the greatest of pleasure.

The initial broadcast was the season's other new production, Puccini's *La Fanciulla del West*. This had appeared an unlikely work to bring into the repertoire, since it had never succeeded in establishing itself at the Met. However, with Maralin Niska, Ermanno Mauro, and Charles Long in the leading roles, it was an instant hit, greatly abetted by Corsaro's direction and Sergiu Comissiona's conducting. The host for the first broadcast was Edwin Newman, a longtime opera fan whose knowledge was matched by his articulate expression. Other hosts for the season were Kevin McCarthy (Monteverdi's *L'Incoronazione di Poppea*), Victor Borge (*The Marriage of Figaro*), opera guild president Martha Sykes (*The Magic Flute*), and Nico Castel (*Cavalleria* and *Pagliacci*).

No new works appeared during the spring 1978 season, although *The Merry Widow* was revived after a thirteen-year absence. Sills was an exuberant Anna Glawari, and this was one of the five operas broadcast that season. The others were *Mefistofele, Tosca, La Traviata,* and *The Barber of Seville*. By now, the company had dispensed with multiple hosts, and George Movshon was the commentator for all five broadcasts.

Other highlights of the season were the Violetta of Rumanian soprano Mariana Niculescu (broadcast February 26th), and the *Fanciulla* of Marilyn Zschau, an American soprano now residing in Zurich.

Fall 1978 opened in novel fashion, with a two-week run of Victor Herbert's *Naughty Marietta*. The production had fallen apart during rehearsals and had to be entirely restaged. This was at a time when Rudel was away, and his absence at so crucial a moment caused great antagonism to the board.

Kurt Weill's *Street Scene* and Giordano's *Andrea Chénier* reappeared after many years, the latter a revival for Zschau and Mauro. The season's major excitement was generated by the company's first *Turk in Italy* by Rossini, featuring Sills, Donald Gramm, Alan Titus, and Billings. Another von Gontard gift, it was conducted brilliantly by Rudel and superbly showed Sills's talent as a comedienne. Andrew Porter, who did the excellent English translation, also came in for his share of accolades. The work itself, however, although a spectacular showpiece for the soprano, is relatively minor Rossini and was unable to sustain itself for long.

On the evening of December 12, TV viewers watching the late news heard an unconfirmed report that Julius Rudel had been asked to step down from his post as company director. At a press conference the following day, he announced that he was, indeed, relinquishing the position to Ms. Sills as of July 1, 1979. When one of the members of the press asked board chariman John Samuels III if this was a voluntary move on Rudel's part, Samuels declined to answer and abruptly announced that the press conference was ended.

Rudel's final season introduced two new productions. The first was Dominick Argento's *Miss Havisham's Fire* (March 22, 1979) based on an incident in Dickens's *Great Expectations*. The opera spans the period from Aurelia Havisham's wedding day to her death in flames a score of years later. Several of the roles must be performed by two singers, one portraying a youthful character, the other playing the same character some twenty years later. Both parts of the title role were conceived for Sills, but suddenly faced with the task of assuming the company's leadership, she was forced to drop out. The young Miss Havisham was then assigned to Gianna Rolandi, and her older counterpart to Rita Shane. The "mad scene" that ends the work is incredibly difficult, and Shane turned in one of the finest performances of her career, winning a standing ovation and vociferous approval.

Also new that season was a double bill of Purcell's *Dido and Aeneas* and Strauss's ballet *Le Bourgeois Gentilhomme*. This was von Gontard's sixth gift to the company! A production of Kurt Weill's *Der Silbersee* (to be done in English as *Silverlake*) had already been donated, although not yet publicly announced, when von Gontard died, suddenly, on September 28, 1979, in Zurich. *Dido,* although well performed, was generally considered dull. The ballet, on the other hand, sparkled. Choreographed by George Balanchine, it featured Patricia McBride, Rudolph Nureyev, and Jean-Pierre Bonnefous—all titans in the field. Balanchine had previously done some choreography for the company, during its earliest period when Halasz was in charge, but this was on a much less formal basis. With the opera company and the then newly formed ballet company struggling for their daily existence, Balanchine had offered to "help out."

The spring 1979 season ended on April 29th with a performance of *Havisham* conducted by Rudel, concluding his twenty-two years as the company director. During that period, he introduced ninety-seven new works to the company repertoire, and was responsible for almost 2,500 performances in New York (plus several hundred on tour). Many former company members had been invited to the final performance and, when the curtain descended, they all streamed onto the stage to join in singing "For He's a Jolly Good Fellow" and offering a champagne toast to his future success.

When the fall 1979 season opened, Sills was heading the company, and Rudel occupied the newly created post of principal conductor. The repertoire, however, did not reflect her choice as this had been planned far in advance; in fact, the first season that can truly be considered hers was spring 1981.

Verdi's *Falstaff* was revived with Gramm interpreting the portly knight. Mozart's *La Clemenza di Tito* entered the repertoire for the first time, along with Rossini's *Le Comte Ory*. This last work was generally regarded as a vehicle for relative newcomer Ashley Putnam, who had previously created a sensation as Violetta and who appears to be headed for a stellar career. It was also the debut vehicle for tenor Rockwell Blake. Samuel Ramey, who has successfully filled the gap created by Norman Treigle's death, appeared as the tutor. The principal excitement of the season, however, was created by Gian Carlo Menotti's *La Loca*, written expressly for Miss Sills. Commissioned by Lawrence E. Deutsch, it was intended as a fiftieth-birthday present to Beverly. Deutsch was on the board of directors of the company and a generous donor who, in addition to making outright gifts, underwrote the annual Los Angeles tour.

During the course of the season, some of Sills's plans were made public —new productions of several Verdi operas including *Nabucco, I Lombardi,* and *Attila*; Janáček's *Cunning Little Vixen*; Puccini's *La Rondine*; Bizet's *Pearl Fishers*, and others.

Among the most eagerly anticipated events of the season were the scheduled appearances of Victoria de los Angeles in both *Carmen* and *The Marriage of Figaro*. Unfortunately, she was not in good form and after her initial *Carmen*, she canceled the remainder of her season's commitments.

Like clockwork, the orchestra again went on strike, three years having elapsed since the previous one. These were certainly difficult circumstances for Sills's first season, but like the previous two strikes, a last-minute settlement was reached after causing similar devastation of company resources.

In order to head the company, Sills had announced her intention to retire as a performer. She canceled those engagements that she could, but some companies held her to previously signed contracts. Her final New York operatic appearance was scheduled for October 4th, but this was one of the dates canceled by the strike. Therefore, when it was settled, an extra *La Loca* was slated in place of a previously scheduled *Clemenza di Tito.*

On November 1, her final performance as the mad queen of Spain took place. It was an inspired portrayal and obviously a highly emotional event. Although long ovations were generally the rule at Sills's performances, this one lasted an unprecedented twenty minutes, and flowers rained onto the stage from all parts of the house. The audience was not going to relinquish its favorite diva without giving her a proper send-off. Finally, Miss Sills made a brief curtain speech—optimistic and to the point: "I just want to thank you for a wonderful love affair, and the best is yet to come."

22

Transition

W H E N Beverly Sills sang her eighth audition for the New York City Opera during the spring of 1955, no one expected that twenty-five years later she would become the company's fifth general director. When she did finally assume that post, she was just over fifty and, incredibly, she came with almost fifty years of public performing experience.

At the age of three, Sills sang before an audience for the first time—a song entitled "The Wedding of Jack and Jill." The occasion was a beauty contest—an attempt to find the most beautiful baby of 1932. Sills won the main award as well as the prize for talent, the start of an overwhelmingly successful career.

She was fortunate to have been born into a family that had phonograph records—twenty-two selections by Amelita Galli-Curci, all of which Sills[1] had committed to memory before her seventh birthday. Various radio appearances were part of her early childhood, beginning with her debut, at the advanced age of four, on "Uncle Bob's Rainbow Hour" over station WOR. Three years later she made a film, *Uncle Sol Solves It*. At just about that time she auditioned for Estelle Liebling, a well-known voice teacher who had also instructed Freda Hempel, Maria Jeritza, Amelita Galli-Curci, and Titta Ruffo. Liebling was impressed and although she did not normally work with children—she claimed that she did not even know any children —she accepted Sills as a pupil. When Estelle Liebling died in 1970 at the age of ninety-two, she had been the only voice teacher ever to instruct Beverly Sills.

1. She became Beverly Sills at age seven; before that she was Belle Silverman. We have used Sills throughout to avoid confusion.

Sills studied, in addition to voice, the other skills necessary for a successful operatic career. Musicianship was learned through piano study with Paolo Gallico (father of the writer, Paul Gallico), and by age ten she was proficient in French and Italian.

Liebling had been a friend of Major Bowes, who produced a popular radio series, "Major Bowes's Amateur Hour." An audition was arranged for Sills, who was accepted. Her rendition of "Caro Nome" won the amateur contest, and thereafter she was heard coast-to-coast weekly on "Major Bowes's Capitol Family Hour." Soon after, she signed a contract for thirty-six installments of a radio soap opera, "Our Gal Sunday," earning $67.50 per broadcast. By the age of twelve, she was a professional entertainer! There were other radio appearances, including "The Cresta Blanca Carnival," in which she appeared opposite Robert Merrill (who was still named Merill Miller), and a catchy little Rinso White commercial, as well as an early TV appearance on NBC's "Stars of the Future," a prophetic title.

At twelve, Sills left the public eye temporarily to concentrate on schoolwork, but she continued voice and piano lessons without interruption.

She returned to public sight in 1945, now sixteen years old, in a Gilbert and Sullivan tour arranged by J. J. Shubert. She appeared in seven of the Savoy operettas, at a weekly salary of $100. The following year, Shubert presented her in another tour, this time of *The Merry Widow* and *Countess Maritza*.

When she was nineteen she made her operatic debut, singing Frasquita in *Carmen* with the Philadelphia Opera Company. Various concerts and club dates followed, and finally, in 1951, her operatic career began in earnest. She was engaged by the Charles Wagner touring company to sing Violetta in *La Traviata* (opposite John Alexander). The tour lasted sixty-three days, and Sills sang Verdi's consumptive heroine more than forty times; the following year she sang sixty-three Micaëlas with Wagner.

Her next important engagement was with Rosa Ponselle's newly formed Baltimore Opera Company as Massenet's Manon, which was to become one of her truly great roles. And then, an important breakthrough: She entered the major leagues with her San Francisco Opera debut in the unlikely role of Helen of Troy in Boito's *Mefistofele*, a part generally assumed by a dramatic soprano. Others in the cast were Nicola Rossi-Lemeni, Licia Albanese, and Jan Peerce. She also sang Donna Elvira to Rossi-Lemeni's Don Giovanni, and small roles in *Die Walküre* (Gerhilde) and *Elektra* (the fifth handmaiden). The following year, 1954, saw another atypical role—Aïda, in Salt Lake City.

In 1955, Sills auditioned for City Opera, then headed by Joseph Rosenstock. Her debut as Rosalinda in *Die Fledermaus* was on October 29 of that year. Stardom came a year later when she sang Philine in *Mignon* during Leinsdorf's only season. *The Gramophone* magazine (August 1975) quotes her as stating that this was her "first coloratura role, first rave review, and first screaming ovation from a New York audience."

Rudel assumed the company directorship in 1957 and during his first American season, spring 1958, Sills sang another role that was to become her own: Baby Doe in Douglas Moore's melodic saga of Colorado. There were other important successes: *Louise,* Donna Anna in *Don Giovanni,* Constanza in Mozart's *Abduction,* and all the heroines in *The Tales of Hoffmann.* Major stardom, however, came with the role of Cleopatra in Handel's *Julius Caesar.* Ironically, the opera entered the repertoire not for Sills but for Phyllis Curtin, who was by then a member of the Metropolitan Opera. Sills threatened to leave the company unless she got the part, claiming that if Rudel had to go beyond the company roster to cast the role, it was tantamount to admitting that no company member could sing it. It was a calculated risk, but she won and the rest is well-known. Winthrop Sargeant wrote in the *New Yorker,* "If I were recommending the wonders of New York City to a tourist, I should place Beverly Sills at the top of the list—way ahead of such things as the Statue of Liberty and the Empire State Building."

After *Julius Caesar,* Sills starred in a number of neglected masterpieces by Donizetti, Bellini, and Rossini: the so-called Tudor Trilogy consisting of *Anna Bolena, Maria Stuarda,* and *Roberto Devereux; Lucrezia Borgia; The Daughter of the Regiment; I Puritani; The Turk in Italy;* and, along more standard lines, *The Barber of Seville* and *Lucia di Lammermoor.* These were followed by appearances with the world's leading opera houses —La Scala, Covent Garden, the Metropolitan, the Vienna Staatsoper, the Teatro San Carlo in Naples, the Berlin Opera, and the Teatro Colon.

Unlike many of her colleagues, Sills never left the City Opera after successes with other companies, and, if one were to assess her principal contribution to her artistic home, it would probably be this constancy. By remaining with City Opera after attaining international superstardom, she bestowed a status on the company that it had hitherto lacked.

When, on November 1, 1979, she promised, "The best is yet to come," she set an incredibly high goal—the past had been pretty spectacular.

It is still too early to evaluate her success as the company's general director, but her start is certainly promising. In appointing her to the directorship, a long-standing tradition was broken. For the first time in thirty-five years, the company leadership was not in the hands of a conductor. More to the point, it was not entrusted to an active participant in its performances, since she immediately ended her career as a singer. There is much to be said for this. All too frequently, performer-managers have been caught in the trap of divided interests, the manager half introducing repertoire that the participant half wishes to perform. There was, however, one question that worried many of the company members: Would she be overly critical of other sopranos? Could a person, after so many years in a highly competitive field, suddenly shift gears and begin to promote artists who until very recently had been professional rivals? All doubts were immediately dispelled. In the four seasons that Sills has been at the company's helm, several of the operas most closely associated with her have either been revived or announced for revival; they include *Julius Caesar, I Puritani, Anna Bolena, Maria Stuarda, The Tales of Hoffmann, Lucia di Lammermoor, Manon,* and *The Daughter of the Regiment.* Not only have other sopranos not suffered under the new management, they've been given greater opportunities than ever before.

There have been significant changes in the company's organization, the most important being the retirement of John White as Managing Director, Hans Sondheimer as Technical Director, J. Edgar Joseph as Costumer, Felix Popper as Music Administrator, Thomas Martin as head of Musical Research, and Julius Rudel as Principal Conductor. However, the first four have remained as consultants and have been replaced, respectively, by Daniel R. Rule, Gilbert V. Hemsley, Jr., Joseph A. Citarella and Donald Hassard. Nor were the changes restricted to members of the New York City Opera staff. Toward the end of the spring 1981 season, John S. Samuels, III, resigned his position as Chairman of the Board; Robert W. Wilson was appointed his successor.

During spring 1981, the first season over which Sills had full control (because artists must be contracted and repertoire set well in advance), Verdi's *Attila,* Janáček's *Cunning Little Vixen,* and Musgrave's *Mary, Queen of Scots* all entered the repertoire for the first time—a very exciting beginning. Perhaps the best *is* yet to come. . . .

Appendices

TABLE I

Original Sponsors of New York City Center of Music and Drama, Inc.

1. Pledged Loans

Marshall Field	$	5,000
Walter S. Mack, Jr.		5,000
Mrs. David Levy		5,000
National Broadcasting Company		5,000
International Ladies Garment Workers Union		5,000
Amalgamated Clothing Workers of New York		5,000
Congress of Industrial Organizations		5,000
American Federation of Musicians, Local 802		5,000
Workmen's Circle		2,500
Edmond A. Guggenheim		2,500
Mrs. John T. Pratt		2,500
Samuel Wechsler		2,500
Mrs. Myron Taylor		1,750
Howard S. Cullman		1,000
Morton Baum		1,000
Maurice Wertheim		1,000
Gerald F. Warburg		1,000
Mrs. Lytle Hull	$	1,000
J. Robert Rubin		1,000
Playwrights' Producing Company		1,000
George V. McLaughlin		1,000
Walter W. Naumburg		1,000
John Golden		500
Mrs. Arthur M. Reis		500
Erich Leinsdorf		250
Clarke G. Dailey		250
TOTAL:	$	62,250

2. Outright Gifts

John D. Rockefeller, Jr.	$	5,000
Altman Foundation		5,000
Warren Bloom		500
George A. Sloan		100
TOTAL:	$	10,600

TOTAL WORKING CAPITAL:	$	72,850

TABLE II

Original Incorporators of New York City Center of Music and Drama, Inc.

Luigi Antonini	*President, Italian Dress and Waist Makers' Union*
Morton Baum	*Former tax counsel, City of New York; a director of Metropolitan Opera Association*
John S. Burke	*President, Friedsam Foundation*
Frank R. Crosswaith	*Chairman, Negro Labor Committee*
Howard S. Cullman	*Vice-president, Port of New York Authority*
Joseph Curran	*President, National Maritime Union*
Clarke G. Dailey	*Former president, Real Estate Board*
Hubert T. Delany	*Justice, Domestic Relations Court*
David Dubinsky	*President, ILGWU*
William Feinberg	*Secretary, American Federation of Musicians, Local 802*
Marshall Field	*Chairman of the board, Philharmonic Symphony Society*
Lillian Gish	*Actress*
John Golden	*Theatrical producer*
Edmond A. Guggenheim	*President, Guggenheim Foundation*
John Hammond	*Authority on American dance music*
Adolph Held	*Chairman, Jewish Labor Committee*
Ira A. Hirschmann	*New York City Board of Higher Education*
Mrs. Lytle Hull	*President, New Opera Company*
Robert Edmond Jones	*Scenic designer*
Fiorello H. La Guardia	*Mayor, City of New York*
Richard W. Lawrence	*President, YMCA*
Erich Leinsdorf	*Conductor, Cleveland Symphony Orchestra*
Mrs. David Levy	*Trustee, Rosenwald Foundation*
Bert Lytell	*President, Actors' Equity*
Walter S. Mack, Jr.	*President, Pepsi-Cola Company*

Macklin Marrow	*Composer and conductor*
Joseph D. McGoldrick	*Comptroller of the City of New York*
George V. McLaughlin	*Former police commissioner, City of New York*
Saul Mills	*Secretary-Treasurer, Greater New York Industrial Union*
Newbold Morris	*President, New York City Council*
Walter W. Naumburg	*Board of directors, Town Hall; founder of Naumburg Concerts*
Jaocb S. Potofsky	*Secretary-Treasurer, Amalgamated Clothing Workers of New York*
Mrs. Ruth Pratt	*Former congresswoman; a director of Philharmonic Symphony Society*
Mrs. Arthur M. Reis	*Chairwoman, Executive Board of League of Composers*
Elmer Rice	*Playwright, president of Dramatists' Guild*
Paul Robeson	*Actor and singer*
Alex Rose	*Secretary-Treasurer, Millinery Workers of America*
Jacob Rosenberg	*President, American Federation of Musicians, Local 802*
J. Robert Rubin	*Vice-president and general counsel, Loews, Inc.*
Deems Taylor	*Composer, critic, commentator; president, ASCAP*
Mrs. Myron Taylor	*League of Composers*
Lawrence Tibbett	*Metropolitan Opera baritone; president, AGMA*
Frederick F. Umhey	*Executive secretary, ILGWU*
Gerald F. Warburg	*Cellist, conductor, and composer*
Maurice Wertheim	*Founder of Theatre Guild, Inc.*
Blanche Witherspoon	*Executive secretary, AGMA*

TABLE III

Broadcasts, Television, Recordings, and Films

This table details all radio, television, recorded, and filmed performances of the New York City Opera—in short, all public exposure outside
the theater itself.

A. Radio

The dates given are the dates of performance, which are not necessarily
the same as broadcast dates. In many cases, a performance was broadcast some
time after it had been recorded. For casting details, see the Annals section.

Broadcast

1.	October 4, 1951	*The Dybbuk.* The world premiere perfor- mance was recorded by the Voice of America for overseas broadcast only. It was subse- quently issued as a two-record album by a group known as the Dybbuk Sponsoring Committee. They secured domestic broad- cast clearance from the unions involved, and the performance was finally aired in the U.S. some twenty-five years after it took place. For further information, see Section C of this table (Recordings).
2.	September 29, 1956 matinee	*La Traviata*
3.	October 6, 1956 matinee	*Carmen*
4.	October 20, 1956 matinee	*The Moon* and *L'Histoire du Soldat*
5.	November 8 & 9, 1975	Operathon I. Radio station WNCN–FM in

New York made thirty-two hours of air time available to City Opera for fund-raising and a subscription drive. There were numerous interviews, reminiscences, recordings of City Opera artists, etc. There was also a segment consisting of current artists performing rarely heard selections, with piano accompaniment provided by Assistant Conductor Martha Gerhart. The selections consisted of:

Don Procopio (Bizet):
"Sulle piume" .... Glenys Fowles,
John Sandor
Linda di Chamounix (Donizetti):
"Per sua madre" .... Hilda Harris
Moses (Rossini):
"Prayer" .... Eleanor Bergquist,
Diane Curry, Jerold Siena and
Samuel Ramey
Barber of Seville (Paisiello):
"Saper bramate" .... Henry Price
(mandolin by Joseph Diamante)
Barber of Seville (Paisiello):
"Ma dov' eri tu" .... Richard McKee,
Alan Baker, James Billings
Iris (Mascagni):
"Un dì, ero piccina" .. Sung Sook Lee
Le Pre-aux-Clercs (Herold):
"Les rendez-vous" .. Gianna Rolandi,
Robert Hale

The Operathon concluded with the first radio broadcast from the stage of the New York State Theater. It was:

5-A.	November 9, 1975	*I Puritani*
6.	November 6 & 7, 1976	Operathon II, which followed the same format as Operathon I. The live musical portion consisted of scenes from the Ricci brothers' *Crispino e la Comare* with the following cast:

Annetta .... Maria Spacagna
La Comare .... Eunice Hill
Crispino .... Richard McKee
Contino del Fiore .... Alan Kays
Dr. Fabrizio .... Thomas Jamerson
Dr. Mirabolano .... James Billings
Don Asdrubale .... Don Yule

Musical Director and
Accompanist .... Brian Salesky

There was also a section on operatic drinking songs, including:

"The Merry Wives of Windsor"
(Nicolai)—Richard McKee

"La Jolie Fille de Perth"
   (Bizet)—Samuel Ramey
"Ione" (Petrella)—Kenneth Collins
"Hamlet" (Thomas)—Pablo Elvira

The accompanist for this section was Assistant Conductor Leann Hilmer. Operathon II concluded with:

6-A.	November 7, 1976	*Die Fledermaus*
7.	October 16, 1977	*La Fanciulla del West*
8.	October 23, 1977	*L'Incoronazione di Poppea*
9.	October 30, 1977	*The Marriage of Figaro*
10.	November 3, 1977	*Cavalleria Rusticana* and *Pagliacci*
11.	November 13, 1977	*The Magic Flute*
12.	February 26, 1978	*La Traviata*
13.	March 12, 1978	*Tosca*
14.	April 2, 1978	*The Merry Widow*
15.	April 9, 1978	*Mefistofele*
16.	April 15 & 16, 1978	Operathon III. Same format as Operathon I ending with:
16-A.	April 16, 1978	*The Barber of Seville*
17.	September 3, 1978	*Naughty Marietta*
18.	September 17, 1978	*Andrea Chénier*
19.	October 1, 1978	*The Turk in Italy*
20.	October 15, 1978 matinee	*Le Coq d'Or*
21.	November 5, 1978	*Street Scene*
22.	March 4, 1979	*Rigoletto*
23.	March 18, 1979 matinee	*Faust*
24.	April 1, 1979 matinee	*Daughter of the Regiment*
25.	April 22, 1979	*Manon*
26.	April 29, 1979	*Miss Havisham's Fire*
27.	September 16, 1979	*La Loca*
28.	September 23, 1979	*Count Ory*
	October 7, 1979 matinee	*Falstaff*, originally scheduled for broadcast, but changed to:
29.	October 14, 1979 matinee	*Falstaff*
	October 14, 1979	*Carmen*, originally scheduled for broadcast, but changed to:
30.	October 21, 1979 matinee	*Carmen*
31.	November 4, 1979 matinee	*La Clemenza di Tito*
32.	February 24, 1980	*Die Fledermaus*
33.	March 22, 1980	*Don Giovanni*

34.	April 6, 1980 matinee	*The Love for Three Oranges*
35.	April 13, 1980 matinee	*La Cenerentola*
36.	April 20, 1980	*Les Contes d'Hoffmann*
	September 14, 1980	*Anna Bolena*
	September 28, 1980	*Les Pêcheurs de Perles*
	October 12, 1980	*An American Trilogy*
	October 19, 1980	*La Bohème*
	November 2, 1980	*Giulio Cesare*

Scheduled, but broadcast season canceled. (bracketing the last five entries)

Note: Between November 13, 1980 and April 23, 1981, National Public Radio taped twenty-three performances of thirteen operas for broadcast during the summer of 1981. Ten of the operas were taped in two performances each, and at the time of this book's going to press, no decision has been made as to which of the two performances will actually be broadcast. We are therefore providing details on both performances of each of the ten. The first eight operas —those that took place in 1980—were taped in Los Angeles while the company was on tour. Since tour casts are not provided in the Annals section, this information will be found at the end of the broadcast list. The five operas taped in New York (two performances each), which took place in March and April 1981, will be found in the Annals.

37.	November 13 or 16, 1980	*Anna Bolena*
38.	November 14, 1980	*La Bohème*
39.	November 15, 1980	*Don Giovanni*
40.	November 18 or 21, 1980	*Die Fledermaus*
41.	November 20 or 23, 1980 matinee	*Les Pêcheurs de Perles*
42.	November 22, 1980	*Les Contes d'Hoffmann*
43.	November 25 or 28, 1980	*Giulio Cesare*
44.	December 2 or 6, 1980	*The Merry Wives of Windsor*
45.	March 3 or 7, 1981	*Mary, Queen of Scots*
46.	March 13 or 17, 1981	*Attila*
47.	March 14 or 18, 1981	*Madama Butterfly*
48.	April 18 or 21, 1981	*The Love for Three Oranges*
49.	April 19 or 23, 1981	*The Makropoulos Affair*

Broadcast 1 was produced by the Voice of America; broadcasts 2 through 4 by station WNYC in New York; 5 through 36 by WNCN–FM in New York; and 37 through 49 by National Public Radio in Washington, D.C.

It can be seen from the above that WNCN–FM has championed the City Opera. By a curious coincidence, 104.3 (the frequency of WNCN) was formerly assigned to station WFDR–FM, so named in memory of Franklin Delano Roosevelt. The inaugural broadcast of WFDR–FM was on June 16, 1949, and featured the New York City Opera orchestra, conducted by Laszlo Halasz. There were various musical selections, speeches in honor of Roosevelt, and a section entitled "Salute from Hollywood," featuring Eddie Cantor, Gene Kelly, Milton Berle, Anna Roosevelt, and Ronald Reagan.

Casts of Los Angeles Broadcast Performances

ANNA BOLENA (Broadcast 37)

Anna Bolena .... Olivia Stapp
Giovanna Seymour .. Susanne Marsee
Smeton .... Mimi Lerner
Percy .... Rockwell Blake
Enrico VIII .... Samuel Ramey
Lord Rochefort ...... Ralph Bassett
Sir Hervey .... James Clark
Conductor ..... Charles Wendelken-
Wilson

LA BOHÈME (Broadcast 38)

Mimi .... Diana Soviero
Musetta .... Stephanie Sundine
Rodolfo .... Riccardo Calleo
Marcello ...... Frederick Burchinal
Schaunard ...... Robert McFarland
Colline .... Robert Hale
Benoit .... Don Yule
Alcindoro .... Don Yule
Parpignol .... James Clark
Conductor .... John Mauceri

DON GIOVANNI (Broadcast 39)

Donna Anna .... Carol Vaness
Donna Elvira .... June Anderson
Zerlina .... Faith Esham
Don Ottavio .... Alan Kays
Don Giovanni .... Justino Diaz
Leporello .... Samuel Ramey
Masetto .... Harlan Foss
The Commendatore .. Ralph Bassett
Conductor .... John Mauceri

DIE FLEDERMAUS (Broadcast 40)

Rosalinda .... Maralin Niska
Adele .... Inga Nielsen
Sally .... Nadia Pelle
Alfred .... Gerald Grahame
Eisenstein .... Alan Titus
Dr. Falke .... Robert McFarland
Orlofsky .... James Billings
Ivan .... Gary Dietrich
Frank .... Harlan Foss
Frosch .... Jack Harrold
Dr. Blind .... Norman Large
Conductor .... Brian Salesky

LES PÊCHEURS DE PERLES
(Broadcast 41)

Leila .... Diana Soviero
Nadir .... Barry McCauley

Zurga .... Dominic Cossa
Norabad .... John Seabury
Conductor .... Calvin Simmons

LES CONTES D'HOFFMANN
(Broadcast 42)

Olympia .... Barbara Carter
Giulietta .... Joanna Simon
Antonia .... Carol Vaness
Nicklause .... Nadia Pelle
Hoffmann .... Riccardo Calleo
Lindorf ....
Coppelius .... } Justino Diaz
Dappertutto ....
Dr. Miracle ....
Andres ....
Cochenille .... } Douglas Perry
Pitichinaccio ....
Franz ....
Hermann .... Thomas Jamerson
Nathaniel .... Norman Large
Luther .... Don Yule
Spalanzani .... James Billings
Schlemil .... James Sergi
Crespel .... Maurice Brown
Antonia's mother ...... Jane Shaulis
Conductor .... David Effron

GIULIO CESARE (Broadcast 43)

Cleopatra .... Gianna Rolandi
Sesto .... Delia Wallis
Cornelia .... Diane Curry
Giulio Cesare .... Robert Hale
Achilla .... Dominic Cossa
Tolomeo .... Donnie Ray Albert
Nireno .... Harlan Foss,
(s, Steven Alexus Williams)
Curio .... William Ledbetter
Conductor .... Ralf Weikert

THE MERRY WIVES OF WINDSOR
(Broadcast 44)

Mistress Ford .... Carol Vaness
Mistress Page .... RoseMarie Freni
Anne .... Janice Hall
Falstaff .... William Wildermann
Fenton .... Vinson Cole
Ford .... Stephen Dickson
Slender .... Norman Large
Dr. Caius .... Harlan Foss
Conductor .... Julius Rudel

B. Television*

1. November 9, 1971   *Le Coq d'Or* (televised on closed-circuit cable TV)
2. April 21, 1976   *The Ballad of Baby Doe*
3. November 3, 1976   *The Barber of Seville*
4. October 18, 1977   *Manon*
5. April 19, 1978   *The Saint of Bleecker Street*
6. October 4, 1978   *The Turk in Italy*
    March 21, 1979   *Lucia di Lammermoor*, scheduled, but telecast canceled
7. October 27, 1979   *Street Scene*
8. October 27, 1980   *Beverly Sills's Farewell*
9. November 6, 1980   *La Cenerentola*

As in the case of radio broadcasts, the dates above are performance dates and are not necessarily the same as telecast dates.

C. Recordings

Many New York City Opera artists made recordings, especially those who achieved major international stardom (Giannini, Kirsten, Sills, Tourel, Verrett, Domingo, Carreras, Milnes, etc.), but the subject of this section is recordings made by City Opera as a company, making use only of their artists, chorus, and orchestra. Thus, although virtually all of the artists were with City Opera, a recording such as Columbia's *The Tender Land* is excluded because the orchestra employed was the New York Philharmonic, and the album was not made under the auspices of City Opera. Also excluded from this list are so-called pirate recordings—live performances issued on records without official sanction.

1. LA BOHÈME   "Mi chiamano Mimi"—Irma Gonzales, with the City Opera Orchestra conducted by Laszlo Halasz. V-Disc 52-A, recorded 1944.
2. I PAGLIACCI   "Vesti la giubba"—Norbert Ardelli, with the City Opera Orchestra conducted by Laszlo Halasz. V-Disc 52-B, recorded 1944.

Note: During World War II, James C. Petrillo, president of the American Federation of Musicians, Local 802, imposed a ban on all recording activities. Exempt from the ban were records that were produced for use in military recreational halls and U.S.O. lounges. Artists contributed their services, and the records, which were known as V-Discs, were never placed on sale com-

* See Annals for cast details.

mercially. The technical jobs of mastering and pressing (on 78 rpm) were handled by R.C.A. Victor and Columbia records. The two selections listed above were pressed back-to-back, and were recorded by R.C.A.

3. Gounod:
    FAUST (highlights)

    Marguerite .... Frances Yeend
    Siebel .... Frances Bible
    Faust .... Rudolph Petrak
    Valentin .... Walter Cassel
    Mephistopheles .... Norman Scott

    Conductor .... Laszlo Halasz

The excerpts issued consisted of:

    "Avant de quitter ces lieux" .... Cassel
    "Le veau d'or" .... Scott
    "Faites-lui mes aveux" .... Bible
    "Salut demeure" .... Petrak
    "Jewel Song" .... Yeend
    Love duet .... Yeend and Petrak
    "Vous qui faites l'endormie" .... Scott
    Prison scene ..... Yeend, Petrak, and Scott

The record was issued as a 10-inch LP by MGM, No. E-553. It subsequently came out as a 45-rpm album, No. K-80 ultimately, portions of it appeared as one side of a 12-inch LP, coupled with portions of the abridged *Aida* recording (No. 4, below). The record number of this final version was E-3023. The album was recorded in 1950.

4. Verdi:
    AIDA (highlights)

    Aida .... Camilla Williams
    Amneris .... Lydia Ibarrondo
    Radames .... Giulio Gari
    Amonasro .... Lawrence Winters

    Conductor .... Laszlo Halasz

The excerpts issued consisted of:

    "Celeste Aida" .... Gari
    "Ritorna vincitor" .... Williams
    "Fu la sorte" ..... Williams and Ibarrondo
    "Triumphal march" .... Orchestra
    "Ciel, mio padre" ... Williams and Winters
    "Rivedrai le foreste".. Williams and Winters
    "Già i sacerdoti adunansi" ..... Ibarrondo
                                     and Gari
    "O terra addio" .... Williams and Gari

The record was issued as a 10-inch LP by MGM, record No. E-554, then as a 45-rpm album, No. K-81, and finally, excerpted, as one side of a 12-inch LP, No. E-3023, coupled with selections from *Faust*. Recorded in 1950.

5. Tamkin:
    THE DYBBUK

The world premiere performance had been recorded by Voice of America for overseas broadcast. Years later, a group known as the Dybbuk Restoration Committee negotiated

with the unions involved and obtained per-
mission to bring the performance out on
records. It was not sold, but was given as a
premium to supporters of the committee.
The album consists of two records, and bears
the number Phoenix IX. For cast information, see the performance of October 4, 1951,
in the Annals section.

6.   Blitzstein:
     REGINA (complete)

Regina Giddens .... Brenda Lewis
Alexandra Giddens .... Helen Strine
Birdie Hubbard .... Elisabeth Carron
Addie .... Carol Brice
Horace Giddens .... Joshua Hecht
Benjamin Hubbard .... George Irving
Oscar Hubbard .... Emile Renan
Leo Hubbard .... Loren Driscoll
Cal .... Andrew Frierson
William Marshall ...... Ernest McChesney

Conductor .... Samuel Krachmalnick

Issued by Columbia as a 3-record LP album, No. 03S-202, subsequently
re-issued as album No. Y3-35236. Recorded on April 28, 1958.

7.   Moore:
     THE BALLAD OF BABY DOE

An old miner .... Grant Williams
A bartender .... Chester Ludgin
Horace Tabor .... Walter Cassel
Sam .... Jack DeLon
Bushy .... Keith Kaldenberg
Barney .... George Del Monte
Jacob .... Arthur Newman
Augusta Tabor .... Frances Bible
Baby Doe .... Beverly Sills
Kate .... Greta Wolff
Mag .... Helen Baisley
Samantha .... Lynda Jordan
Hotel clerk .... Keith Kaldenberg
Albert, a bellboy .... Robert Atherton
Sarah .... Mary LeSawyer
Mary .... Jennie Andrea
Emily .... Lou Rodgers
Effie .... Dorothy White
Mama McCourt .... Beatrice Krebs
Four dandies .... Edson Hoel, Dan Marek,
                      Peter Sliker, John Dennison
McCourt
  family ..... Greta Wolff, Helen Baisley,
                  Donald Arthur, William Saxon
Father Chappelle .... Grant Williams
A footman .... Arthur Newman
Chester A. Arthur .... Jack DeLon
Elizabeth .... Lynn Taussig

Mayor of Leadville .... William Saxon
William Jennings Bryan .... Joshua Hecht
Stage doorman .... Grant Williams
Denver politician .... Chester Ludgin
Silver Dollar (grown-up) ... Helen Baisley

Conductor .... Emerson Buckley

Issues by MGM as a 3-record LP album, No. 3GC1; later re-issued by Deutsche Grammophon, album No. 2709061. Recorded in 1959.

8.   Ward:
     THE CRUCIBLE (complete)   Betty Parris .... Joyce Ebert
                                 Rev. Samuel Parris ...... Norman Kelley
                                 Tituba .... Gloria Wynder
                                 Abigail Williams .... Patricia Brooks
                                 Ann Putnam .... Naomi Farr
                                 Thomas Putnam .... Paul Ukena
                                 Rebecca Nurse .... Eunice Alberts
                                 Francis Nurse .... Spiro Malas
                                 Giles Corey .... Maurice Stern
                                 John Proctor .... Chester Ludgin
                                 Rev. John Hale .... John Macurdy
                                 Elizabeth Proctor .... Frances Bible
                                 Mary Warren .... Nancy Foster
                                 Ezekiel Cheever .... Richard Krause
                                 Judge Danforth .... Jack DeLon
                                 Sarah Good .... Naomi Farr
                                 Ruth Putnam .... Lorna Ceniceros
                                 Susanna Walcott .... Helen Guile
                                 Martha Sheldon .... Marija Kova
                                 Mercy Lewis .... Elizabeth Schwering
                                 Bridget Booth .... Beverly Evans

                                 Conductor .... Emerson Buckley

Issued by CRI Records as a 2-disk LP album, No. 168. Recorded March 25, 1962.

9.   Beeson:
     LIZZIE BORDEN (complete)   Andrew Borden .... Herbert Beatty
                                 Abigail Borden .... Ellen Faull
                                 Elizabeth Borden .... Brenda Lewis
                                 Margret Borden .... Ann Elgar
                                 Rev. Harrington .... Richard Krause
                                 Capt. Jason MacFarlane. . Richard Fredricks

                                 Conductor .... Anton Coppola

Issued as a 3-record LP album by Desto, album No. D-455/56/57 (monaural) or DST-6455/56/57 (stereo). Recorded early in 1966.

10.   Handel:
     GIULIO CESARE (complete)   Julius Caesar .... Norman Treigle
                                 Cleopatra .... Beverly Sills
                                 Cornelia .... Maureen Forrester
                                 Sextus .... Beverly Wolff

Ptolemy .... Spiro Malas
Achillas .... Dominic Cossa
Nirenus .... Michael Devlin
Curio .... William Beck

Conductor .... Julius Rudel

Issued as a 3-record LP album by R.C.A. Victor, album No. LSC-6182.
Recorded April 28–May 2, 1967.

11.   Moore:
        CARRY NATION (complete)   Carry Nation .... Beverly Wolff
                                  Her father .... Arnold Voketaitis
                                  Her mother .... Ellen Faull
                                  Charles .... Julian Patrick
                                  Two men in saloon .... Dan Kingman,
                                                                    Don Carlo
                                  City marshal .... Don Yule
                                  Ben .... Kellis Miller
                                  Preacher .... Edward Pierson
                                  Men at hoedown .... Ronald Bentley,
                                                                   John Stewart
                                  Girl at hoedown .... Arlene Adler
                                  Toaster at hoedown .... Jack Bittner
                                  A boy .... Michael Ahearn
                                  A girl .... Colette Martin
                                  Four ladies of
                                    Auxiliary .... Joan August, Maria West,
                                                         Lila Herbert, Donna Owen
                                  Caretaker .... Jack Bittner

                                  Conductor .... Samuel Krachmalnick

Issued by Desto as a 3-record LP album, No. DC-6463/65. Recorded in
1968.

12.   Lehár:
        THE MERRY WIDOW
          (highlights)   Anna Glawari .... Beverly Sills
                                  Count Danilo .... Alan Titus
                                  Baron Mirko Zeta ...... David Rae Smith
                                  Valencienne .... Glenys Fowles
                                  Camille de Rosillon .... Henry Price
                                  Njegus .... James Billings
                                  Vicomte Cascada ...... Thomas Jamerson
                                  Raoul St. Brioche .... Alan Kays
                                  Bogdanovitch .... Vincent Angeli
                                  Kromov .... Harlan Foss
                                  Pritchitch .... James Billings

                                  Conductor .... Julius Rudel

The selections included are: Anna's entrance (No. 3)
                                "Oh, Fatherland" (Maxim's) (No. 4)
                                "Do Listen, Please" (No. 2)
                                Act I finale (No. 6)

Dances & Vilia (No. 7)
"Heia! See the Horseman Come" (No. 8)
"Ev'ry Woman" (No. 9)
"Just as a Rosebud Blossoms" (No. 11)
Act II finale (No. 12)
"Grisette Song" (No. 14) & "Très parisien"
"Strings Are Sighing" (waltz) and
Act III finale (Nos. 15 & 16)

Issued as a one-record LP album by Angel, No. S-37500.
Recorded February 1–February 3, 1978.

13.   Weill:
      SILVERLAKE
      (complete musically;
      dialogue cut)

Olim .... Joel Grey
Severin .... William Neill
Frau von Luber .... Elaine Bonazzi
Baron Laur ....⎫
A lottery agent ....⎬ Jack Harrold
Fennimore .... Elizabeth Hynes
Salesgirls ...... Penny Orloff, Jane Shaulis
Johann .... Harlan Foss
Dietrich .... Robert McFarland
Klaus .... James Clark
Hans .... Norman Large
Handke .... David Rae Smith

Conductor .... Julius Rudel

Issued as a 2-record LP album by Nonesuch, No. DB-79003. Recorded
March 24 through March 27, 1980.

D. Films

The Paramount film *Foul Play* included a sequence consisting of the New
York City Opera Company in scenes from *The Mikado*. Soloists, chorus, and
orchestra were taped in New York (audio), and when the company was later
on tour in Los Angeles, the sequences were filmed, using the San Francisco
Opera's sets of *Madama Butterfly*. The artists involved were:

Yum-Yum .... Glenys Fowles
Pitti-Sing .... Kathleen Hegierski
Peep-Bo .... Sandra Walker (audio),
                      Diana Kehrig (film)
Nanki-Poo .... Enrico di Giuseppe
Katisha .... Jane Shaulis
Pish-Tush .... Thomas Jamerson
Pooh-Bah .... Richard McKee

Conductor .... Julius Rudel

Note: No scenes involving Ko-Ko or the Mikado were included.

Annals of
THE NEW YORK
CITY OPERA

1944-1981

COMPILED BY **George Louis Mayer**

(THROUGH 1979)

AND **Martin L. Sokol**

(1980 AND 1981)

Introduction

In compiling these annals of the performances given by the New York City Opera in New York, every attempt has been made to track down correct casting information. No complete set of programs or records exists anywhere. The "official" set of programs maintained by the company is substantially complete, as is the set on deposit in the Music Division of the Performing Arts Research Center of the Library and Museum of the Performing Arts at Lincoln Center. An additional set, far from complete, was brought together by the Archives Committee of the New York City Opera Guild. Casting and cast-change information has been culled from all three sets. In a very few instances, cast listings have had to be partially reconstructed from announcements and reviews. No programs with cast information have been located for a few student performances given by the company.

The difficulties of verifying that the performers listed on the programs actually appeared in the performances have been formidable. Company records for the seasons since the organization moved into the New York State Theater at Lincoln Center for the spring 1966 season have been made available to me, and unequivocal answers to most questions have been found. Records for the earlier seasons at the City Center are incomplete and often inconclusive. Questions that have arisen about cast changes for these earlier seasons have been more difficult to answer. Fortunately, New York City had more newspapers and musical periodicals for the period 1944 to 1965 than it has now, and coverage of the company's activities was extensive. The *New York Times, New York Herald Tribune, Musical America,* and *Musical Courier* have all been searched for information on every performance given by the company for this period. Other newspapers and periodicals have been checked selectively, and, in some cases, exhaustively. Unfortunately, extensive checking of this kind can both raise and answer questions. Frequent discrepancies between program cast listings and review cast listings were discovered. Substitutions (especially for singers appearing in small roles) were not always specified as such in reviews. Two different performers have, on occasion, been reviewed by different critics as having sung a given performance. Many performances (especially those presented during the end of a season) have not been reviewed at all. In some cases, reviewers have probably headed their reviews with cast listings from press releases or other advance information rather than from the final printed program. Others may have been on hand to catch announced substitutions that were missed by critics who arrived somewhat later. It has not always been possible to reconcile conflicting information.

The attempt to bring consistency to performers' names has presented problems. The names of some singers and conductors have appeared on the programs in an amazing variety of forms and spellings. George Jongeyans changed his name to Jon Geyans and later to George Gaynes. Shirley Verrett first appeared with the company as Shirley Carter. Dragica and Carla Martinis are the same soprano. David Smith became David Rae Smith and Charles Wilson became Charles Wendelken-Wilson. Other singers have been slow to decide upon the best form for their names and have experimented with such variants as Eleanor, Leonore, Leonora, Eleanore, etc., before making a final choice—if they ever did. When a final decision has been reached, this form has been adopted in the annals, and earlier entries changed to conform. In other cases, where no consistency could be found or logically created (as in the cases of some singers whose later name forms were made upon marriage), both forms of the names have been used. During certain periods, some singers were permitted to sing small roles under assumed names. It has not been possible to single out these dual identities. In cases where names can be spelled in a variety of ways, it is most likely that they have been. Whim and the probable lack of a consistent editorial policy in the preparation of brochures and programs from season to season must both account for the mixtures of Allen, Allan, Alan, and other such, which have appeared for some performers. Also Bills and Jacks have been changed to Williams and Johns and vice versa. Some arbitrary decisions have had to be made when no definitive, correct information could be found. I can only make my apologies to those to whom my choices are displeasing, and hope that they will understand my dilemmas.

Titles of operas have usually been given to indicate the language of the performances. Complete consistency, however, has not been possible since some operas (Rossini's *La Cenerentola* for one) have been performed by the company in both the original language and in English at different times. Common usage and personal preference have dictated some choices in deciding upon title entries. When operas have been performed in English, this has been noted in the first entries of the season for these titles, and translators' names have been given whenever possible.

Making decisions about the forms of characters' names has also presented difficulties. For space reasons, they have been made as brief as possible. Common contemporary usage and New York City Opera policies have guided the decisions. While some entries match current company listings, others do not, but forms of names have been made fairly consistent throughout the annals. Thus, *Don Giovanni* entries list the Commendatore even though the company earlier identified this character as The Commandant or as Don Pedro. Foreign language accents have been used with some inconsistencies and with regard for personal choices, but generally follow current usage. Research into the use of accents for character names in some French operas, such as *Carmen* and *Les Contes d'Hoffmann,* has revealed great inconsistency of usage from the time of the earliest published scores and libretti right up to the present day.

Currently, opera directors are given credit for directing or staging operas, and the term "stage director" is used to denote a member of the staging staff who has responsibility for maintaining the original director's production in subsequent seasons. In the early years, terminology was less specific. I have, therefore, for these early seasons, maintained the program designations in all their variety, since it has not always been possible to interpret exactly how these terms were used.

These annals, being limited to the performances given by the New York City Opera in their home city, only chronicle part of the company's history. The full story will have to await another time and another place.

Using the Annals

Format

The basic format used for these annals is the one established by William H. Seltsam for his original work on the *Metropolitan Opera Annals,* and used by many other compilers of operatic annals since then. Full cast information is given for the first performance of each opera during a season with subsequent performances listed as being the same as this original listing except for noted changes. Since I do not believe that any opera annals should be completely singer oriented (as many have been), I have added complete production information about directors, designers, choreographers, etc. It seems just as important to document contributions to an opera company of a Frank Corsaro, a Theoni V. Aldredge, and a George Balanchine as that of the singers. In order to save space, however, full production information is only given on the occasion of a new production. In subsequent seasons, only the changes from the original production are noted. Thus, for the first performance of an opera during a season after the season of the premiere, a new choreographer, a stage director, etc., is indicated only when different from that of the original production team. This format worked throughout these annals in all categories until very recent seasons when, in a few instances, a director returned to re-direct his production. To omit this information would be to imply that the directing responsibilities were still in the hands of the last noted stage director. Since this would not be so, the following kind of entry has been made:

> (Assistant to Mr. Corsaro: Bentley) March 4, 1978
> RIGOLETTO.

Normally, assistants have been omitted from these annals, so these entries do not conflict with any others to cause confusion. All such entries document the return of the original director with a new assistant, who will prob-

221

ably take over the responsibility for the production in subsequent seasons. Since stage directors have only been given debut credit when taking on major responsibilities for productions, stage directors noted in this fashion as assistants have in a few instances been given debut symbols in these annals at a later date.

Roster Listings

At the beginning of each season, the major artists who have appeared with the company during the season are listed by category as follows:

Female artists: includes all singers, actresses, children, and other stage performers listed on the programs during the season.
Male artists: includes all singers, actors, children, acrobats, and other stage performers listed on the programs during the season.
Conductors: includes only those members of the musical staff who actually conducted performances during the season. The frequent omission of members of the musical staff who only occasionally were scheduled to conduct does not necessarily indicate that they were not members of the company during those seasons.
Chorus masters: included when possible. No such listings appeared in programs prior to the fall 1956 season, and listings have been inconsistent since then.
Choreographers: includes all choreographers whose works have been performed during the season, whether new or in revival.
Directors: includes all directors whose works have been performed during the season, and those members of the staging staff who have been given program credit as stage directors for revivals. Assistants have been omitted except as noted on page 221.
Designers: includes set and costume designers, and others given credit for design elements of productions (film, projections, etc.) whose works have been performed during the season.

Performance Listings

SUBSTITUTIONS

Cast-change information has been given to indicate both the artist scheduled on the program and the substitute performers. This should eliminate any confusion between these annals and other sources. So many of these changes have been difficult to verify that it seems important to document them as specifically as possible.

Substitute listings appear as follows:

Schaunard .. Renan, (s, Rael)

Eduardo Rael was scheduled on the program to sing the role of Schaunard, but was replaced by Emile Renan.

The use of "(for . . .)" does not indicate a substitution. Listings in this form have been limited to scheduled changes of cast among large, grouped cast members (servants, apprentices, etc.) for performances when the casting has been different from the first performance of the season. The March 6, 1968 performance of *Carmina Burana* lists:

Solo dancers ..... Sandonato,
(for Mlakar)

indicating that all of the performers scheduled as apprentices for this performance are the same as those scheduled for the season's first performance of the work on February 22, except for this one casting difference.

DEBUTS

Debuts have been indicated on the rosters by an asterisk (*), and in the annals by the symbol (d). These notations are for debuts with the company in New York. Some performers have made their first appearances with the company prior to this but in other cities. Debuts have always been indicated for singers of major roles. Before the spring 1952 season, all singers have been credited with debut designations. After this, debuts have not been indicated for singers in small roles who have been listed as being members of the chorus in the chorus rosters published in the programs. In some cases, singers have left the chorus and moved on to more important solo assignments, but the lack of a debut symbol indicates that they were members of the chorus at the time of their first appearance in these annals.

Dancers appearing as soloists have all been given debut symbols. In some cases dancers may have appeared with the company as members of the corps de ballet prior to these debut listings. It was not possible to note such specific distinctions between dancers as soloists and as members of the corps, as it was between solo singers and chorus members.

Some artists have made more than one debut with the company. Placido Domingo has appeared as both tenor and conductor. Julius Rudel has directed operas, as have some choreographers. Second debut indications have been made in these cases.

PROGRAM ADDITIONS WITHIN A SEASON

If programs for any opera within a season have expanded on the cast listing as given for the first performance or performances of a season, an "added to program" note has been made. In most cases, these additions have been made on the programs for all subsequent performances of the season. Should a debut be indicated in one of these notes, it has been impossible to establish the actual date of the performer's debut. The performer may have done all of the performances prior to this first listing (while agitating to get a printer's oversight corrected), or the earlier performances may have been done by other performers. In recent seasons, program variations of this type have not been noted in the annals when it has been possible to verify full casting information from company records and to make the entries complete here even though program omissions have occurred.

LIGHTING DESIGNERS, MAKE-UP ARTISTS, COSTUMERS

Roster credit has not been given for artists in these categories, since program credits have been so inconsistent over the years. Lighting designers have been listed in the production credits for new productions when the information has been available. Hans Sondheimer, who was responsible for the lighting for many years, first received credit during the spring 1948 season. Other designers received their first credits as follows: Jean Rosenthal (fall 1950), Lee Watson (spring 1958), Donald Oenslager (fall 1959), Jules Fisher (spring 1963), Will Steven Armstrong (spring 1965), Charles Elson (spring 1966), Nananna Porcher (spring 1975), Ken Billington (spring 1976), Richard Nelson (spring 1977), and Gilbert V. Hemsley, Jr. (fall 1978).

Not noted in these annals are those make-up artists listed on brochures and programs over the years. These artists were first listed by the company as follows: Joseph Madzison (spring 1944), Michael Arshansky (fall 1951), Charles Mullen (fall 1964), and Ted Marcinkowski (fall 1965). Staff costumers have also been omitted, but have been listed on some rosters in the programs: Ruth Morley (in the 1950s) and J. Edgar Joseph (beginning with the spring 1965 season).

A FINAL NOTE

Had these annals been compiled by a veteran insider of the company, certain mistakes or omissions I have undoubtedly made might have been avoided. Certainly, there are entries here that will need correction, and information needed to make such corrections will be welcome.

Acknowledgments

I would like to acknowledge the great help I have received from Henry Wisneski in every phase of the compilation of these annals. Ruth M. Hider, director of operations for the New York City Opera, was always willing to help me with my problems and solved a great many. Bob Nash, active for many years with the Opera Guild's Archives Committee, has been a constant source of support. Kris Shuman, Steve Maguire, Emma Nordsick, and Harold McKenna also offered assistance. Caroline Newhouse provided a grant that made the compilation possible. I am grateful to them all.

GEORGE LOUIS MAYER

Winter 1944 (FEBRUARY 21 – 27)

Female artists
Benfield, Dorothy
Briney, Mary Martha
Colt, Ethel Barrymore
Giannini, Dusolina
Lipton, Martha
Nadell, Rosalind
Resnik, Regina
Sten, Suzanne
Tourel, Jennie

Male artists
Ardelli, Norbert
Belarsky, Sidor
Berini, Mario
Brink, Robert
Carlson, Stanley
Cordy, Henry
Czaplicki, George
Kane, Edward
Kazaras, Emanuel
Leonard, Ralph
Lorber, Alexander
Norville, Hubert
Renan, Emile
Rogatchewsky, Joseph
Thompson, Hugh

Conductors
Halasz, Laszlo
Sample, James

Solo dancers
Gomez, Pilar
Rozzino, Giovanni

Director
Wolmut, Hans

Designer
Rychtarik, Richard

February 21
TOSCA (Puccini)

Stage director ... Wolmut (d)
Designer ..... Rychtarik (d)
Conductor .... Halasz (d)

Tosca .... Giannini (d)
Cavaradossi ...... Berini (d)
Scarpia .... Czaplicki (d)

Angelotti ...... Belarsky (d)
Spoletta .... Norville (d)
Sacristan .... Renan (d)
Sciarrone .... Kazaras (d)
Jailer .... Lorber (d)

February 22
MARTHA (Von Flotow)
(Adapted for the American stage by Vicki Baum and Ann Ronell)

Stage director ...... Wolmut
Designer .... Rychtarik
Conductor .... Halasz

Lady Harriet .... Colt (d)
Nancy .... Sten (d)
Lord Tristram ... Carlson (d)
Plunkett .... Brink (d)
Lionel .... Kane (d)
Sheriff .... Leonard (d)

February 23
TOSCA
Same cast as February 21 except:
Cavaradossi ..... Ardelli (d)
Sacristan .... Carlson

February 24
CARMEN (Bizet)

Stage director ...... Wolmut
Designer .... Rychtarik
Conductor .... Halasz

Carmen .... Tourel (d)
Don José .... Berini
Escamillo .... Czaplicki
Micaëla .... Briney (d)
Zuniga .... Belarsky
Frasquita .... Resnik (d)
Mercédès .... Nadell (d)
Remendado ...... Cordy (d)
Dancairo .... Renan
Morales .... Thompson (d)
Solo dancers .... Gomez (d),
Rozzino (d)

February 25
MARTHA
Same cast as February 22 except:
Conductor ...... Sample (d)
Lady Harriet .... Briney
Nancy .... Lipton (d)
Lord Tristram .... Renan
Plunkett .... Thompson

February 26 (m)
CARMEN
Same cast as February 24 except:
Don José ..Rogatchewsky (d),
(s, Berini)

February 26
MARTHA
Same cast as February 22 except:
Conductor .... Sample

February 27 (m)
MARTHA
Same cast as February 22 except:
Conductor .... Sample
Nancy .... Lipton

February 27
CARMEN
Same cast as February 24 except:
Don José ..... Rogatchewsky
Escamillo .... Thompson
Micaëla .... Resnik
Frasquita ...... Benfield (d)
Remendado .... Norville
Dancairo .... Leonard
Morales .... Renan

Spring 1944 (M A Y I - I 4)

Female artists
Abbot, Adelaide*
Aronovich, Sura*
Benfield, Dorothy
Bodanya, Natalie*
Briney, Mary Martha
Giannini, Dusolina
Gonzalez, Irma*
Greco, Norina*
Howland, Alice*
King, Marjorie*
Kirsten,' Dorothy*
Piazza, Marguerite*
Resnik, Regina
Sanya, Nina*
Sten, Suzanne
Szendy, Ilona*
Taussig, Carroll*

Male artists
Ardelli, Norbert
Belarsky, Sidor
Benz, Hamilton*
Berini, Mario
Cordy, Henry
Czaplicki, George
DeSurra, John*
Hamill, John*
Harrell, Mack*
Kane, Edward
Kazaras, Emanuel
Leonard, Ralph
Lorber, Alexander
Murray, Frank*
Norville, Hubert
Rael, Eduardo*
Renan, Emile
Row, Francis*
Romani, Bila*
Visca, Edward*
Yearsley, Charles*

Solo dancers
Gomez, Pilar
Rozzino, Giovanni

Conductors
Halasz, Laszlo
Martin, Wolfgang*
Sample, James
Schwieger, Hans*

Directors
Ruben, José*
Wolmut, Hans

Designers
Condell, H. A.*
Rychtarik, Richard

* New artist

May 1

CARMEN (Bizet)

Conductor .... Halasz

Carmen .... Giannini
Don José .... Berini
Escamillo .... Czaplicki
Micaëla .... Briney

Zuniga .... Belarsky
Frasquita .... Resnik
Mercédès ..... Howland (d)
Remendado .... Cordy
Dancairo .... Renan
Morales .... Rael (d)

May 3

TOSCA (Puccini)

Conductor .... Halasz

Tosca .... Giannini
Cavaradossi .... Ardelli
Scarpia .... Czaplicki
Angelotti .... Belarsky
Spoletta .... Norville
Sacristan .... Renan
Sciarrone .... Kazaras
Jailer .... Lorber

May 4

LA BOHÈME (Puccini)
First performance by The New
York City Opera Company

Stage director .... Ruben (d)
Designer .... Condell (d)
Conductor .... Halasz

Mimi .... Gonzalez (d)
Musetta .... Bodanya (d)
Rodolfo .... Berini
Marcello ..... DeSurra (d)
Schaunard .... Renan
                  (s, Rael)
Colline .... Leonard
Benoit, Alcindoro .. Benz (d)

May 5

CAVALLERIA RUSTICANA
(Mascagni)
First performance by The New
York City Opera Company

Stage director ..... Wolmut
Designer .... Rychtarik
Conductor .... Schwieger (d)

Santuzza .... Giannini
Turiddu .... Kane
Alfio .... Row (d)
Lola .... Howland
Mamma
Lucia ..... Aronovich (d)

Followed by:

I PAGLIACCI (Leoncavallo)
First performance by The New
York City Opera Company

Stage director ..... Wolmut
Designer .... Rychtarik
Conductor .... Halasz

Nedda .... Greco (d)
Canio .... Ardelli
Tonio .... DeSurra
Silvio .... Rael
Beppe .... Cordy

May 6

LA BOHÈME

Same cast as May 4

May 7 (m)

MARTHA (Von Flotow)

Conductor .... Sample

Lady Harriet ..... Abbot (d)
Nancy .... Sten
Lionel .... Kane
Plunkett .... Renan
Lord Tristram .... Benz
Sheriff .... Kazaras

May 7

CAVALLERIA RUSTICANA

Same cast as May 5 except:

Santuzza .... Resnik
Mamma Lucia .. Taussig (d)

Followed by:

I PAGLIACCI

Same cast as May 5

May 8

LA TRAVIATA (Verdi)
First performance by The New
York City Opera Company

Stage director .... Ruben
Designer .... Rychtarik
Conductor ..... Martin (d)

Violetta ...... Kirsten (d)
Alfredo .... Hamill (d)
Germont .... Harrell (d)
Flora .... King (d)
Annina .... Sanya (d)
Gaston .... Cordy
Douphol .... Benz
D'Obigny .... Visca (d)
Dr. Grenvil .... Leonard
Solo dancers .... Gomez,
                    Rozzino

May 9

CARMEN

Same cast as May 1 except:

Micaëla .... Resnik
Zuniga .... Leonard
Frasquita .... Benfield
Remendado .... Norville

May 10

LA TRAVIATA

Same cast as May 8 except:

Dr. Grenvil .... Lorber

May 11

LA BOHÈME

Same cast as May 4 except:

Colline .... Belarsky
Schaunard .... Rael

May 12

CARMEN

Same cast as May 1 except:

Don José .... Ardelli
Micaëla .... Gonzalez
Frasquita .... Benfield
Remendado .... Norville

May 13 (m)

MARTHA

Same cast as May 7 (m)
except:

Lady Harriet .... Briney
Nancy .... Howland
Plunkett ...... Yearsley (d)

Lord Tristram .... Renan
Sheriff .... Benz
                (s, Kazaras)

May 13

LA TRAVIATA

Same cast as May 8 except:

Flora .... Szendy (d)
Gaston .... Murray (d)
Dr. Grenvil .... Lorber

May 14 (m)

CAVALLERIA RUSTICANA

Same cast as May 5 except:

Santuzza .... Resnik

Followed by:

I PAGLIACCI

Same cast as May 5 except:

Conductor .... Martin
                (s, Halasz)
Nedda .... Piazza (d)
                (s, Gonzales)
Canio .... Rowton (d)
Beppe .... Murray

May 14

TOSCA

Same cast as May 3 except:

Cavaradossi .... Berini
Angelotti .... Leonard

Fall 1944 (NOVEMBER 9–DECEMBER 10)

Female artists
Archambault, Blanche*
Bodanya, Natalie
Cassard, Frances*
Gonzalez, Irma
Greene, Harriet*
Howland, Alice
King, Marjorie
Kirsten, Dorothy
Kreste, Mary*
LeClaire, Helen*
Lushanya, Mobley*
Piazza, Marguerite
Sten, Suzanne
Stoska, Polyna*
Taussig, Carroll
Wysor, Elizabeth*

Male artists
Ardelli, Norbert
Berini, Mario
Carlson, Stanley
Czaplicki, George
Dennis, Paul*
De Spirito, Romolo*
DeSurra, John
Gauld, Carlton*
Hayward, Thomas*
Horne, William*
Kazaras, Emanuel
Lorber, Alexander
Rael, Eduardo
Renan, Emile
Row, Francis
Rowton, Eric
Telasko, Ralph*
Trautman, Rudy*
Ulisse, Arthur*
Visca, Edward
Walters, Jess*

Conductors
Halasz, Laszlo
Martin, Thomas P.*
Morel, Jean*
Rudel, Julius*

Solo dancers
Dysart, Alice*
Gomez, Pilar

* New artist

Harris, Ruth*
Kantro, Leila*
Tashamira*

Rozzino, Giovanni

Choreographer
Platova, Helene*

Directors
Ruben, José
Wymetal, William*

Dialogue director
Landis, Jessie Royce*

Designers
Condell, H. A.
Rychtarik, Richard

* New artist

November 9

MANON LESCAUT (Puccini)
First performance by The New
    York City Opera Company

Stage director .... Ruben
Designer .... Rychtarik
Conductor .... Halasz

Manon .... Kirsten
Lescaut .... DeSurra
Des Grieux ...... Horne (d)
Geronte .... Telasko (d)
Edmondo ...... Hayward (d)
Innkeeper .... Trautman (d)
Singer .... LeClaire (d)
Dancing Master .. Ulisse (d)
Lamplighter .... Visca
Captain in the Navy .. Kazaras
Solo dancers ... Dysart (d),
                Kantro (d)

November 10

LA BOHÈME

Conductor .... Halasz

Mimi .... Gonzalez
Musetta .... Piazza
Rodolfo .... Berini

Marcello .... DeSurra
Schaunard .... Renan
Colline .... Gauld (d)
Benoit,
    Alcindoro .... Dennis (d)

November 11

CAVALLERIA RUSTICANA
        (Mascagni)

Stage director .. Wymetal (d)
Conductor ...... Morel (d)

Santuzza ...... Lushanya (d)
Turiddu .... Rowton
Alfio .... Row
Lola .... Howland
Mamma Lucia ...... Taussig

Followed by:

I PAGLIACCI (Leoncavallo)

Stage director .. Wymetal (d)
Conductor ...... Morel (d)

Nedda .... Bodanya
Canio .... Ardelli
Tonio .... Walters (d)
Silvio .... Rael
Beppe .... Ulisse
                (s, De Spirito)

November 12

LA TRAVIATA (Verdi)

Choreographer .. Platova (d)
Conductor .... Morel

Violetta .... Kirsten
Alfredo .... Berini
Germont .... Czaplicki
Flora .... King
Annina .... Greene (d)
Gaston .... Ulisse
Douphol .... Kazaras
D'Obigny .... Visca
Dr. Grenvil .... Dennis
Solo dancers .... Gomez,
                Rozzino

November 14

THE GYPSY BARON (J. Strauss)
First performance by The New
York City Opera Company
(Libretto revised and adapted
into English by George Mead)

Stage director ..... Wymetal
Dialogue
director .... Landis (d)
Designer .... Condell
Choreographer ..... Platova
Conductor .... Halasz

Barinkay .... Horne
Saffi .... Stoska (d)
Czipra .... Howland
Arsena .... Piazza
Zsupan .... Carlson
Ottokar .... Hayward
Carnero .... Dennis
Count Homonnay .... Gauld
Solo dancers .... Harris (d),
                   Tashamira (d)

November 15

TOSCA (Puccini)

Stage director ..... Wymetal
Scenic designer ..... Condell
Conductor .... Halasz

Tosca .... Cassard (d)
Cavaradossi .... Berini
Scarpia .... Czaplicki
Angelotti .... Telasko
Spoletta .... Dennis
Sacristan .... Carlson
Sciarrone .... Kazaras
Jailer .... Lorber

November 16

MANON LESCAUT

Same cast as November 9
except:

Des Grieux .... Ardelli
Dancing Master .... Rael

November 17

LA BOHÈME

Same cast as November 10
except:

Musetta .... Bodanya
Colline .... Telasko

November 18 (m)

THE GYPSY BARON

Same cast as November 14
except:

Conductor ...... Martin (d)

Czipra .... Wysor (d)
Carnero .... Renan

November 18

LA TRAVIATA

Same cast as November 12
except:

Germont .... Walters
Annina .... Greene
                (s, Archambault)
Dr. Grenvil .... Lorber

November 19 (m)

CAVALLERIA RUSTICANA

Same cast as November 11
except:

Turiddu .... Hayward

Followed by:

I PAGLIACCI

Same cast as November 11
except:

Nedda .... Gonzalez
Canio .... Rowton
Tonio .... DeSurra

November 19

TOSCA

Same cast as November 15
except:

Sacristan .... Renan

November 21

LA BOHÈME

Same cast as November 10

November 22

THE GYPSY BARON

Same cast as November 14
except:

Conductor .... Martin

Czipra .... Wysor
Carnero .... Renan

November 23

LA TRAVIATA

Same cast as November 12
except:

Alfredo ...... De Spirito (d)
                   (s, Berini)
Annina .... Archambault (d)
Dr. Grenvil .... Lorber

November 24

LA BOHÈME

Same cast as November 10
except:

Mimi .... Kirsten
Musetta .... Bodanya
Rodolfo .... Ardelli
                   (s, Horne)
Schaunard .... Rael
Colline .... Telasko

November 25 (m)

CAVALLERIA RUSTICANA

Same cast as November 11
except:

Santuzza .... Sten
                (s, Lushanya)
Turiddu .... Hayward
                (s, Rowton)
Mamma Lucia ... Kreste (d)

Followed by:

I PAGLIACCI

Same cast as November 11
except:

Canio .... Rowton
                   (s, Ardelli)

November 25

THE GYPSY BARON

Same cast as November 14
except:

Conductor .... Rudel (d)

Saffi .... Piazza
Czipra .... Wysor
Arsena .... King
Zsupan .... Renan

November 26 (m)

TOSCA

Same cast as November 15
except:

Conductor .... Martin

November 28

THE GYPSY BARON

Same cast as November 14
except:

Carnero .... Renan
Solo dancer .... Harris

(Note: In this performance,
as well as all remaining *Gypsy
Baron* performances this
season, only one solo dancer,
Ruth Harris, was listed in
the program.)

November 29

THE GYPSY BARON

Same cast as November 14
except:

Conductor .... Martin
Carnero .... Renan

November 30

THE GYPSY BARON

Same cast as November 14
except:

Conductor .... Rudel
Carnero .... Renan

December 1

THE GYPSY BARON

Same cast as November 14
except:

Conductor .... Martin
Carnero .... Renan

December 2(m)

THE GYPSY BARON

Same cast as November 14
except:

Conductor .... Martin
Saffi .... Piazza
Czipra .... Wysor

Arsena .... King
Zsupan .... Renan
Ottokar .... Ulisse

December 2

THE GYPSY BARON

Same cast as November 14
except:

Conductor .... Rudel
Carnero .... Renan

December 3(m)

THE GYPSY BARON

Same cast as November 14
except:

Conductor .... Rudel
Saffi .... Piazza
Czipra .... Wysor
Arsena .... King
Zsupan .... Renan
Ottokar .... Ulisse

December 3

THE GYPSY BARON

Same cast as November 14
except:

Conductor .... Martin
Carnero .... Renan

December 5

THE GYPSY BARON

Same cast as November 14
except:

Conductor .... Rudel
Carnero .... Renan

December 6

THE GYPSY BARON

Same cast as November 14
except:

Conductor .... Martin
Carnero .... Renan

December 7

THE GYPSY BARON

Same cast as November 14
except:

Conductor .... Rudel
Carnero .... Renan

December 8

THE GYPSY BARON

Same cast as November 14
except:

Conductor .... Martin
Carnero .... Renan

December 9(m)

THE GYPSY BARON

Same cast as November 14
except:

Conductor .... Rudel
Saffi .... Piazza
Czipra .... Wysor

December 9

THE GYPSY BARON

Same cast as November 14
except:

Conductor .... Martin
Carnero .... Renan

December 10(m)

THE GYPSY BARON

Same cast as November 14
except:

Conductor .... Martin
Saffi .... Piazza
Czipra .... Wysor
Arsena .... King
Zsupan .... Renan
Ottokar .... Ulisse

December 10

THE GYPSY BARON

Same cast as November 14
except:

Conductor .... Rudel
Carnero .... Renan

Arsena .... King
Zsupan .... Renan
Ottokar .... Ulisse

Spring 1945 (APRIL 12–29)

Female artists
Archambault, Blanche
Aronovich, Sura
Doree, Doris*
George, Helen*
Gonzalez, Irma
Greene, Harriet
Griska, Susan*
Howland, Alice
Kirsten, Dorothy
Kreste, Mary
Kuzak, Andzia*
Lewis, Brenda*
MacDonald, Eloise*
Parker, Lenore*
Reggani, Hilde*
Stoska, Polyna
Szantho, Enid*
Taussig, Carroll

Male artists
Belarsky, Sidor
Benz, Hamilton
Conley, Eugene*
Cordy, Henry
Davenport, Morton*
Destal, Frederick*
DeSurra, John

* New artist

Doubrovsky, George*
Dudley, John*
Duno, Daniel*
Ferrara, Pasquale*
Gari, Giulio*
Garnell, Grant*
Hamill, John
Hayward, Thomas
Horne, William
Laderoute, Joseph*
Leonetti, Mario*
Newman, Arthur*
Norville, Hubert
Orda, Alfred*
Rivers, Richard*
Row, Francis
Rowton, Eric
Silva, Roberto*
Sprinzena, Nathaniel*
Telasko, Ralph
Trautman, Rudy
Visca, Edward

Conductors
Halasz, Laszlo
Martin, Thomas P.
Morel, Jean
Rudel, Julius

* New artist

Solo dancers
Abilena, Mia*
Dysart, Alice
Kantro, Leila
Kiser, Jane*
Leporska, Zoya*

Choreographer
Sartorio, Angiola*

Directors
Newfield, John*
Ruben, José
Stubblefield, Sally*

Designers
Condell, H. A.
Rychtarik, Richard

* New artist

April 12

DER FLIEGENDE HOLLÄNDER
(Wagner)

First performance by The New
York City Opera Company

Stage director .... Ruben
Designer .... Rychtarik
Conductor .... Halasz

Daland .... Belarsky
Dutchman .... Destal (d)
Steersman .... Gari (d)
Erik .... Horne
Senta .... Doree (d)
Mary .... Szantho (d)

April 13

LA TRAVIATA (Verdi)

Choreographer .. Sartorio (d)
Conductor .... Morel

Violetta .... Reggiani (d),
                 (s, Kirsten)
Alfredo .... Hamill
Germont .... DeSurra
Flora .... Griska (d)
Annina .... Greene
Gaston .... Cordy
Douphol .... Benz
D'Obigny .... Visca
Dr. Grenvil .... Newman (d)

April 14

LA BOHÈME (Puccini)

Conductor .... Halasz

Mimi .... Gonzalez
Musetta .... Kuzak (d)
Rodolfo .... Conley (d)
Marcello .... DeSurra
Schaunard .... Newman
Colline .... Telasko
Benoit .... Benz
Alcindoro .... Norville
Parpignol ...... Leonetti (d)

April 15 (m)

THE GYPSY BARON (J. Strauss)

Stage director .. Newfield (d)
Choreographer ..... Sartorio
Conductor .... Rudel

Barinkay .... Hayward
Czipra .... Howland
Saffi .... Stoska
Zsupan .... Norville
Arsena .... George (d)
Ottokar .... Leonetti
Carnero .... Benz
Count
  Homonnay .... Garnell (d)
Solo dancers .... Abilena (d),
                 Kiser (d),
                 Leproska (d)

April 15

MANON LESCAUT (Puccini)

Conductor .... Halasz

Manon .... Kirsten
Lescaut .... DeSurra
Des Grieux .... Horne
Geronte .... Telasko
Edmondo .... Hayward
Innkeeper .... Trautman
Singer .... Taussig
Dancing Master .... Norville
Lamplighter .... Visca

Captain .... Garnell
Sergeant .... Newman
Solo dancers .... Dysart,
                 Kantro

April 16

FAUST (Gounod)
Benefit preview
First performance by The New
York City Opera Company

Stage director .... Ruben
Designer .... Condell
Conductor .... Morel

Faust .... Laderoute (d)
Méphistophélès .... Silva (d)
Valentin .... Duno
Wagner .... Rivers (d)
Marguerite .... Kirsten
Siébel .... Cordy
Marthe .... Szantho

April 17

CAVALLERIA RUSTICANA
(Mascagni)

Stage director ...... Newfield
Conductor .... Halasz

Santuzza .... Lewis (d)
Turiddu .... Hayward
Alfio .... Row
Lola .... Howland
Mamma Lucia .... Kreste

Followed by:

I PAGLIACCI (Leoncavallo)

Stage director ...... Newfield
Conductor .... Martin

Canio .... Rowton
Nedda .... Gonzalez
Tonio .... Duno (d)
Beppe .... Cordy
Silvio .... Orda (d)

April 18

FAUST

Same cast as April 16 except:
Siébel .... Howland,
                 (s, Cordy)

April 19

LA BOHÈME

Same cast as April 14 except:
Conductor .... Martin,
                 (s, Halasz)
Colline .... Silva
Benoit .... Norville
Alcindoro,
  Parpignol ... Sprinzena (d)

April 20

MANON LESCAUT

Same cast as April 15

April 21 (m)

THE GYPSY BARON

Same cast as April 15 (m)
except:

Conductor .... Martin

Barinkay .... Dudley (d)
Czipra .... Szantho
Saffi .... Lewis
Ottokar .... Hayward

April 21

DER FLIEGENDE HOLLÄNDER

Same cast as April 12

April 22 (m)

LA TRAVIATA

Same cast as April 13 except:

Violetta .... Kirsten
Flora .... Parker (d)
Annina .... Archambault
Gaston .... Visca
D'Obigny .... Rivers

April 22

CAVALLERIA RUSTICANA

Same cast as April 17

Followed by:

I PAGLIACCI

Same cast as April 17 except:

Canio .... Ferrara (d),
                 (s, Rowton)

April 24

MANON LESCAUT

Same cast as April 15 except:

Lescaut .... Telasko
Geronte .... Newman
Singer .... Greene
Sergeant ..... Davenport (d)

April 25

THE GYPSY BARON

Same cast as April 15 (m)
except:

Conductor .... Martin

Barinkay .... Dudley
Czipra .... Szantho
Saffi .... Lewis
Zsupan .... Telasko
Ottokar .... Hayward

April 26

FAUST

Same cast as April 16 except:

Faust .... Hamill
Wagner .... Davenport
Marguerite .... Gonzalez

Siébel .... Howland
Marthe .... Kreste

April 27
DER FLIEGENDE HOLLÄNDER

Same cast as April 12 except:
Senta .... Doree,
(s, Stoska)

April 28 (m)
LA BOHÈME

Same cast as April 14 except:
Conductor .... Martin
Rodolfo .... Gari
Marcello .... Duno,
(s, DeSurra)
Parpignol .... Sprinzena

April 28
THE GYPSY BARON

Same cast as April 15 (m) except:
Barinkay .... Horne
Arsena ..... MacDonald (d)
Ottokar .... Hayward

April 29 (m)
CAVALLERIA RUSTICANA

Same cast as April 17 except:
Stage director ... Stubblefield (d)
Conductor .... Rudel
Santuzza .... Doree
Turiddu .... Gari
Mamma Lucia .... Aronovich

Followed by:
I PAGLIACCI

Same cast as April 17 except:
Stage director ... Stubblefield (d)
Nedda .... George
Beppe .... Sprinzena

April 29
FAUST

Same cast as April 16 except:
Faust .... Hamill
Méphistophélès .. Doubrovsky
(d)
Valentin .... Garnell
Wagner .... Davenport
Marguerite .... Gonzalez
Siébel .... Howland

Fall 1945 (SEPTEMBER 27– DECEMBER 23)

Female artists
Archambault, Blanche
Bernhardt, Louise*
Bodanya, Natalie
Brancato, Rosemarie*
Doree, Doris
Fawcett, Lillian*
George, Helen
Griska, Susan
Heidt, Winifred*
Kreste, Mary
Lewis, Brenda
Manners, Lucille*
Parker, Lenore
Ray, Nadine*
Rozner, Elsa*
Sarnoff, Dorothy*
Stoska, Polyna
Szantho, Enid
Taussig, Carroll
Zieher, Gladys*

Male artists
Belarsky, Sidor
Bowe, Morton*
Conley, Eugene
Cosman, Ian*
Davenport, Morton
Destal, Frederick
Dillon, Irwin*
Dilworth, Gordon*
Doubrovsky, George
Dudley, John
Duncan, Todd*
Duno, Daniel
Gallagher, Gil*
Gari, Giulio
Garnell, Grant
Gauld, Carlton
Greenwell, Gean*
Harrold, Jack*

* New artist

LeGares, Rafael*†
Lipton, George*
Newman, Arthur
Norville, Hubert
Sprinzena, Nathaniel
Vinay, Ramon*
Winston, Alan*

Conductors
Halasz, Laszlo
Martin, Thomas P.
Morel, Jean
Rudel, Julius

Solo dancers
Kiser, Jane
Leporska, Zoya
Werbitsky, Anthony*

Choreographer
Randall, Carl*

Directors
Bryden, Eugene S.*
Sachse, Leopold*
Stanfield, Sally*

Designers
Condell, H. A.
Rychtarik, Richard

* New artist
† His European career was under the name of Lagares. Since he is best known in that form, we have consistently shown him that way although, at the New York City Opera, he used the name LeGares.

September 27
TOSCA (Puccini)

Stage director .... Sachse (d)
Conductor .... Halasz
Tosca .... Sarnoff (d)

Cavaradossi .... Conley
Scarpia .... Doubrovsky
Angelotti .... Garnell
Spoletta .... Norville
Sacristan .... Lipton (d)
Sciarrone .... Newman
Jailer .... Winston (d)
Shepherd .... Rozner (d)

September 28
CAVALLERIA RUSTICANA (Mascagni)

Stage director ... Bryden (d)
Conductor .... Halasz
Santuzza .... Doree
Turiddu .... Gari
Alfio .... Garnell
Lola .... Bernhardt (d)
Mamma Lucia .... Kreste

Followed by:
I PAGLIACCI (Leoncavallo)

Stage director ... Bryden (d)
Conductor .... Halasz
Canio .... Dudley
Nedda .... George
Tonio .... Duncan (d)
Beppe .... Sprinzena
Silvio .... Dilworth (d)

September 29
LA BOHÈME (Puccini)

Stage director ..... Stanfield
Conductor .... Martin
Mimi .... Manners (d),
(s, Gonzalez)
Musetta .... Fawcett (d)
Rodolfo .... Gari

Marcello .... Duno,
(s, DeSurra)
Schaunard .... Newman
Colline .... Gauld
Benoit .... Lipton
Alcindoro .... Norville
Parpignol .... Sprinzena

(Note: Irma Gonzalez and John DeSurra were not to appear with the company this season.)

September 30 (m)

LA TRAVIATA (Verdi)

Stage director ...... Stanfield
Choreographer .. Randall (d)
Conductor .... Morel

Violetta .... Brancato (d)
Alfredo .... Conley
Germont .... Dilworth
Flora .... Griska
Annina .... Archambault
Gaston .... Sprinzena
Douphol .... Garnell
D'Obigny ..... Gallagher (d)
Dr. Grenvil .... Newman

September 30

CARMEN (Bizet)

Stage director .... Sachse
Choreographer ...... Randall
Conductor .... Morel

Carmen .... Heidt (d)
Don José .... Vinay (d)
Escamillo .... Duncan
Micaëla .... George
Zuniga .... Greenwell (d)
Frasquita .... Parker
Mercédès .... Guinta
Remendado .... Sprinzena
Dancairo .... Norville
Morales .... Newman
Solo dancers ...... Leporska,
Werbitsky (d),
Kiser

October 3

THE BARTERED BRIDE
(Smetana)
First performance by The New York City Opera Company
(English version by Joan Cross and Eric Crozier, after the translation by Rosa Newmarch)

Stage director ...... Bryden
Designer .... Rychtarik
Choreographer ...... Randall
Conductor .... Halasz

Marenka .... Stoska
Jenik .... Bowe (d)
Kecal .... Gauld
Krushina .... Garnell
Ludmilla .... Szantho
Vashek .... Norville
Tobias Micha ...... Newman
Hata .... Kreste
Principal .... Gallagher

Esmeralda .... Fawcett
Indian .... Winston

(Note: Performed with spoken recitatives)

October 4

CAVALLERIA RUSTICANA
Same cast as September 28
Followed by:

I PAGLIACCI
Same cast as September 28

October 5

FAUST (Gounod)

Stage director ...... Stanfield
Choreographer ...... Randall
Conductor .... Morel

Marguerite .... Lewis,
(s, Sarnoff)
Faust .... Conley
Méphistophélès .. Doubrovsky
Valentin .... Duno
Wagner .... Newman
Siébel .... Bernhardt
Marthe .... Szantho

October 6 (m)

CARMEN
Same cast as September 30

October 6

THE GYPSY BARON
(J. Strauss)

Stage director .... Sachse
Choreographer ...... Randall
Conductor .... Rudel

Barinkay .... Dilworth
Czipra .... Szantho
Saffi .... Lewis
Zsupan .... Lipton
Arsena .... George
Ottokar .... Sprinzena
Carnero .... Norville
Count Homonnay ... Garnell

October 7 (m)

LA BOHÈME
Same cast as September 29

October 7

TOSCA
Same cast as September 27 except:

Tosca .... Doree,
(s, Sarnoff)

October 10

DER FLIEGENDE HOLLÄNDER
(Wagner)

Stage director ...... Stanfield
Conductor .... Halasz

Daland .... Greenwell
Dutchman .... Destal

Steersman .... Dillon (d)
Erik .... Gari
Senta .... Stoska
Mary .... Szantho

October 11

CARMEN
Same cast as September 30 except:

Micaëla .... Ray (d)

October 12

THE GYPSY BARON
Same cast as October 6

October 13 (m)

FAUST
Same cast as October 5 except:

Marguerite .... Manners,
(s, Sarnoff)
Méphistophélès .... Gauld

October 13

LA TRAVIATA
Same cast as September 30 (m) except:

Conductor .... Martin
Alfredo .... Dudley
Germont .... Duno
Annina .... Rozner

October 14 (m)

CAVALLERIA RUSTICANA
Same cast as September 28 except:

Conductor .... Rudel
Turiddu .... Cosman (d)
Followed by:

I PAGLIACCI
Same cast as September 28

October 14

THE BARTERED BRIDE
Same cast as October 3

October 17

LA BOHÈME
Same cast as September 29 except:

Musetta .... Ray
Rodolfo .... Conley
Colline .... Greenwell

October 18

DER FLIEGENDE HOLLÄNDER
Same cast as October 10 except:

Daland .... Belarsky
Senta .... Doree

October 19
CARMEN
Same cast as September 30
except:
Don José .... Dudley
Micaëla .... Ray

October 20 (m)
THE BARTERED BRIDE
Same cast as October 3 except:
Conductor .... Martin
Kecal .... Greenwell
Vashek .... Harrold (d)

October 20
TOSCA
Same cast as September 27
except:
Tosca .... Doree

October 21 (m)
FAUST
Same cast as October 5 except:
Faust .... Gari
Méphistophélès ...... Gauld

October 21
CAVALLERIA RUSTICANA
Same cast as September 28
except:
Conductor .... Rudel
Turiddu .... Cosman
Lola .... Zieher (d)
Mamma Lucia ...... Taussig
Followed by:
I PAGLIACCI
Same cast as September 28
except:
Conductor .... Rudel
Canio .... Lagares (d)

October 24
CARMEN
Same cast as September 30

October 25
LA TRAVIATA
Same cast as September 30
(m) except:
Alfredo .... Dudley
Germont .... Duno
Annina .... Rozner
D'Obigny .... Davenport

October 26
THE BARTERED BRIDE
Same cast as October 3 except:
Conductor .... Martin
Marenka .... Lewis
Jenik .... Dudley
Kecal .... Greenwell

October 27 (m)
LA BOHÈME
Same cast as September 29
except:
Musetta .... Bodanya
Colline .... Greenwell

October 27
(Change of opera; Originally
DER FLIEGENDE HOLLÄNDER)
CAVALLERIA RUSTICANA
Same cast as September 28
except:
Santuzza .... Lewis
Turiddu .... Cosman
Followed by:
I PAGLIACCI
Same cast as September 28
except
Silvio .... Garnell

October 28 (m)
TOSCA
Same cast as September 27
except:
Tosca .... Doree

October 28
THE GYPSY BARON
Same cast as October 6 except:
Ottokar .... Harrold

November 1
CARMEN
Same cast as September 30

November 2
LA BOHÈME
Same cast as September 29
except:
Colline .... Greenwell

November 3
THE BARTERED BRIDE
Same cast as October 3 except:
Marenka .... Lewis
Kecal .... Greenwell
Vashek .... Harrold

November 4 (m)
CARMEN
Same cast as September 30
except:
Don José .... Dudley
Micaëla .... Manners

November 4
TOSCA
Same cast as September 27
except:
Tosca .... Doree

November 8
LA TRAVIATA
Same cast as September
30 (m) except:
Alfredo .... Lagares
Germont .... Duno
Gaston .... Harrold
D'Obigny .... Davenport

November 9
CARMEN
Same cast as September 30
except:
Escamillo ...... Doubrovsky
Micaëla .... Manners
Zuniga .... Lipton

November 10
THE GYPSY BARON
Same cast as October 6

November 11 (m)
THE BARTERED BRIDE
Same cast as October 3 except:
Marenka .... Lewis
Jenik .... Dudley

November 11
FAUST
Same cast as October 5 except:
Marguerite .... Manners
Faust .... Gari
Valentin .... Garnell
Siébel .... Parker
Marthe .... Kreste

December 6
THE BARTERED BRIDE
Same cast as October 3 except:
Marenka .... Lewis
Kecal .... Greenwell
Vashek .... Harrold

December 7
THE BARTERED BRIDE
Same cast as October 3 except:
Conductor .... Martin
Vashek .... Harrold

December 8
THE BARTERED BRIDE
Same cast as October 3 except:
Conductor .... Martin
Kecal .... Greenwell

December 9(m)
THE BARTERED BRIDE
Same cast as October 3 except:
Conductor .... Martin
Marenka .... Lewis
Jenik .... Dudley

December 9

THE BARTERED BRIDE
Same cast as October 3

December 13

THE BARTERED BRIDE
Same cast as October 3 except:

Conductor .... Rudel
Marenka .... Lewis
Kecal .... Greenwell

December 14

THE BARTERED BRIDE
Same cast as October 3

December 15

THE BARTERED BRIDE
Same cast as October 3 except:

Conductor .... Rudel
Jenik .... Dudley
Kecal .... Greenwell

December 16(m)

THE BARTERED BRIDE
Same cast as October 3 except:

Conductor .... Rudel
Marenka .... Lewis
Jenik .... Dudley

December 16

THE BARTERED BRIDE
Same cast as October 3 except:

Kecal .... Greenwell

December 20

THE BARTERED BRIDE
Same cast as October 3 except:

Conductor .... Rudel
Marenka .... Lewis
Kecal .... Greenwell

December 21

THE BARTERED BRIDE
Same cast as October 3

December 22

THE BARTERED BRIDE
Same cast as October 3 except:

Conductor .... Rudel
Jenik .... Dudley
Kecal .... Greenwell

December 23(m)

THE BARTERED BRIDE
Same cast as October 3 except:

Conductor .... Rudel
Marenka .... Lewis

December 23

THE BARTERED BRIDE
Same cast as October 3 except:

Kecal .... Greenwell

Spring 1946 (M A Y 9 – J U N E I)

Female artists
Anderson, Frances*
Brancato, Rosemarie
Fawcett, Lillian
Freyhan, Irene*
George, Helen
Gonzalez, Enya*
Griska, Susan
Heidt, Winifred
Judith, Catherine*
Kirsten, Dorothy
Kreste, Mary
MacWatters, Virginia*
Manners, Lucille
Mayer, Margery*
Nadell, Rosalind
Parker, Lenore
Polynack, Mary*
Ribeiro, Alice*
Szantho, Enid
Williams, Camilla*

Male artists
Bowe, Morton
Conley, Eugene
Dudley, John
Gari, Giulio
Garnell, Grant
Greenwell, Gean
Hamill, John
Mascherini, Enzo*
Newman, Arthur
Norville, Hubert
Pease, James*
Petroff, Ivan*
Renan, Emile
Sprinzena, Nathaniel
Vinay, Ramon
Winston, Alan

* New artist

Conductors
Halasz, Laszlo
Martin, Thomas P.
Morel, Jean
Rudel, Julius

Solo dancers
Kiser, Jane
Leporska, Zoya
O'Brien, Olaine*

Choreographer
Schwezoff, Igor*

Directors
Bryden, Eugene S.
Sachse, Leopold

Designers
Condell, H. A.
Rychtarik, Richard

* New artist

May 9

RIGOLETTO (Verdi)

First performance by The New
York City Opera Company

Stage director .... Sachse
Scenic designer ... Rychtarik
Choreographer ... Schwezoff
(d)
Conductor .... Halasz

Duke .... Conley
Rigoletto .... Petroff (d)
Sparafucile ...... Pease (d)
Monterone .... Garnell
Ceprano .... Renan
Marullo .... Newman
Borsa .... Sprinzena

Gilda .... Brancato
Maddalena .... Nadell
Giovanna .... Kreste
Countess Ceprano .... Griska
Page .... Parker

May 10

LA BOHÈME (Puccini)

Stage director .... Sachse
Conductor .... Martin

Mimi .... Ribeiro (d)
Musetta .... George
Rodolfo .... Gari
Marcello .... Mascherini (d)
Schaunard .... Newman
Colline .... Pease
Benoit .... Renan
Alcindoro .... Norville
Parpignol .... Sprinzena

May 11

THE BARTERED BRIDE
(Smetana)

Choreographer .... Schwezoff
Conductor .... Martin

Marenka .... Manners
Jenik .... Bowe
Kecal .... Greenwell
Krushina .... Garnell
Ludmilla .... Szantho
Vashek .... Norville
Micha .... Newman
Hata .... Kreste
Principal .... Renan
Esmeralda .... Fawcett
Indian .... Winston

May 12 (m)

THE PIRATES OF PENZANCE
(Sullivan)
First performance by The New
York City Opera Company

Stage director .... Bryden
Scenic designer ...... Condell
Choreographer .... Schwezoff
Conductor .... Rudel

Pirate King .... Greenwell
Samuel .... Norville
Frederic .... Hamill
Ruth .... Judah (d)
Major-General
  Stanley .... Dudley
Mabel ...... MacWatters (d)
Edith .... Griska
Kate .... Parker
Isabel .... Polynack (d)
Police Sergeant .... Renan

(Note: Preview performance
for student subscribers)

May 12

CARMEN (Bizet)

Stage director .... Sachse
Choreographer .... Schwezoff
Conductor .... Morel

Carmen .... Heidt
Don José .... Vinay
Escamillo .... Pease
Micaëla .... George
Zuniga .... Greenwell
Frasquita .... Parker
Mercédès .... Griska
Remendado .... Sprinzena
Dancairo .... Norville
Morales .... Newman
Solo dancers .... Kiser,
  Leporska, O'Brien (d)

May 15

MADAMA BUTTERFLY (Puccini)
First performance by The New
York City Opera Company

Stage director .... Bryden
Scenic designer ..... Condell
Conductor .... Halasz

Butterfly ...... Williams (d)
Suzuki .... Mayer (d)
Pinkerton .... Conley
Sharpless .... Petroff
Goro .... Norville
Yamadori .... Renan
The Bonze .... Greenwell
Imperial
  Commissioner .... Newman

(Note: *Kate Pinkerton* added
to program May 23)

May 16

THE PIRATES OF PENZANCE
Same cast as May 12 (m)

May 17

RIGOLETTO
Same cast as May 9 except:

Sparafucile .... Greenwell

May 18

CARMEN
Same cast as May 12 except:

Micaëla .... Ribeiro

May 19 (m)

MADAMA BUTTERFLY
Same cast as May 15 except:

Pinkerton .... Gari
The Bonze .... Garnell

May 19

LA TRAVIATA (Verdi)

Stage director .... Sachse
Choreographer .... Schwezoff
Conductor .... Morel

Violetta .... Brancato
Alfredo .... Conley
Germont .... Mascherini
Flora .... Griska
Annina .... Kreste
Gaston .... Sprinzena
Douphol .... Garnell
D'Obigny .... Norville
Dr. Grenvil .... Newman

May 22

THE PIRATES OF PENZANCE
Same cast as May 12 (m)
except:

Pirate King .... Pease

May 23

MADAMA BUTTERFLY
Same cast as May 15 except:

Butterfly ...... Gonzalez (d)
Suzuki .... Nadell
Pinkerton .... Gari
The Bonze .... Garnell
Added to this program:
Kate Pinkerton ..... Freyhan
                              (d)

May 24

THE BARTERED BRIDE
Same as May 11 except:

Kecal .... Pease

May 25 (m)

CARMEN
Same cast as May 12

May 25

LA TRAVIATA
Same cast as May 19 except:

Flora .... Parker

May 26 (m)

RIGOLETTO
Same cast as May 9 except:

Duke .... Gari
Gilda .... MacWatters
Maddalena .... Mayer
Page .... Freyhan

May 26

LA BOHÈME
Same cast as May 10 except:

Mimi .... Manners
Musetta .... Fawcett
Rodolfo .... Conley
Colline .... Greenwell

May 29

LA TRAVIATA
Same cast as May 19 except:

Violetta .... Kirsten,
                 (s, Brancato)
Flora .... Parker

May 30

MADAMA BUTTERFLY
Same cast as May 15 except:

Kate Pinkerton ...... Griska
Pinkerton .... Gari
The Bonze .... Garnell

May 31

THE PIRATES OF PENZANCE
Same cast as May 12 (m)
except:

Pirate King .... Pease
Ruth .... Kreste

June 1

CARMEN
Same cast as May 12 except:

Micaëla ...... Anderson (d)
Zuniga .... Garnell

Fall 1946 (SEPTEMBER 19– NOVEMBER 30)

Female artists
Anderson, Frances
Brancato, Rosemarie
Bryner, Vera*
Doree, Doris
Edwards, Lydia*
Evangelista, Lucia*
Fawcett, Lillian
Flesch, Ella*
Griska, Susan
Heidt, Winifred
Jorjorian, Neure*
Kreste, Mary
Lane, Beverley*
LeSawyer, Mary*
MacWatters, Virginia
Manners, Lucille
Marino, Herva*
Mayer, Margery
Miller, Brenda*
Nadell, Rosalind
Portnoy, Lenore*
Reggiani, Hilde
Sarnoff, Dorothy
Shelley, Camille*
Sprinzena, Donna*
Stoska, Polyna
Williams, Camilla

Male artists
Argyris, Vasso*
Brancato, Peter*
Conley, Eugene
Dennis, Paul
Dillon, Irwin
Doubrovsky, George
Dudley, John
Fratesi, Gino*
Gari, Giulio
Garnell, Grant
Greenwell, Gean
Hamill, John
Harwood, Lawrence*
Herbert, Ralph*
Horne, William
Kennedy, Steven*
Mascherini, Enzo
Newman, Arthur
Norville, Hubert
Pease, James
Petroff, Ivan
Renan, Emile
Sprinzena, Nathaniel
Stewart, Allen*
Valdengo, Giuseppe*
Vinay, Ramon
Winston, Alan
Young, Norman*

Conductors
Halasz, Laszlo
Martin, Thomas P.
Morel, Jean
Rudel, Julius

Solo dancers
Horvath, Julia*
Kiser, Jane
Leith, Patricia*

* New artist

Dantiere, Victor*
Dragon, Edward*

Choreographer
Schwezoff, Igor

Directors
Bryden, Eugene S.
Komisarjevsky, Theodore*
Sachse, Leopold

Designers
Condell, H. A.
Rychtarik, Richard

* New artist

September 19

MADAMA BUTTERFLY (Puccini)

Conductor .... Halasz

Butterfly .... Williams
Suzuki .... Mayer
Kate Pinkerton .... Edwards (d)
Pinkerton .... Gari
Sharpless ..... Valdengo (d)
Goro .... Norville
Trouble ..... P. Brancato (d)
Yamadori .... Renan
The Bonze .... Greenwell
*Imperial
Commissioner* .... Newman

September 20

THE PIRATES OF PENZANCE (Sullivan)

Conductor .... Rudel

Pirate King .... Pease
Samuel .... Norville
Frederic .... Hamill
Ruth .... Kreste
*Major-General
Stanley* .... Dudley
Mabel .... MacWatters
Edith .... Portnoy (d)
Kate .... Edwards
Isabel .... LeSawyer (d)
Police Sergeant .... Renan

September 21

CAVALLERIA RUSTICANA (Mascagni)

Conductor .... Rudel

Santuzza .... Doree
Turiddu .... Gari
Alfio .... Garnell
Lola .... Nadell
Mamma Lucia .... Kreste

Followed by:

I PAGLIACCI (Leoncavallo)

Conductor .... Halasz

Nedda .... Williams
Canio .... Argyris (d)

Tonio .... Valdengo
Silvio .... Young (d)
Beppe .... N. Sprinzena

September 22 (m)

CARMEN (Bizet)

Conductor .... Morel

Carmen .... Heidt
Don José .... Vinay
Escamillo .... Pease
Micaëla .... Manners
Zuniga .... Greenwell
Frasquita .... Portnoy
Mercédès .... Edwards
Remendado .... N. Sprinzena
Dancairo .... Norville
Morales .... Newman
Solo dancers ... Dantiere (d),
Leith (d), Kiser

September 22

LA TRAVIATA (Verdi)

Conductor .... Martin

Violetta ..... Evangelista (d)
Alfredo .... Fratesi (d)
Germont .... Mascherini
Flora .... Portnoy
Annina .... Kreste
Gaston .... N. Sprinzena
Douphol .... Garnell
D'Obigny .... Newill
Dr. Grenvil .... Newman

(Note: Solo dancer added to program October 4)

September 26

FAUST (Gounod)

Stage director .... Sachse
Choreographer .... Schwezoff
Conductor .... Morel

Marguerite .... Sarnoff, (s, Reggiani)
Faust .... Conley
Méphistophélès .... Pease
Valentin .... Valdengo
Siébel .... Nadell
Marthe .... Kreste
Wagner .... Newman

September 27

CAVALLERIA RUSTICANA

Same cast as September 21

Followed by:

I PAGLIACCI

Same cast as September 21 except:

Tonio .... Herbert (d) (s, Mascherini)

Silvio .... Mascherini
                    (s, Young)

(Note: Mascherini, in the role
of *Silvio*, also sang the
prologue.)

September 28

LA BOHÈME (Puccini)

Conductor .... Morel

Mimi .... Sarnoff
Musetta .... MacWatters
Rodolfo .... Conley
Marcello .... Mascherini
Schaunard .... Newman
Colline .... Pease
Benoit .... Renan
Alcindoro .... Norville
Parpignol ...... N. Sprinzena

September 29 (m)

MADAMA BUTTERFLY

Same cast as September 19

September 29

THE BARTERED BRIDE
(Smetana)

Conductor .... Martin

Marenka .... Manners
Jenik .... Dudley
Kecal .... Greenwell
Krushina .... Garnell
Ludmilla .... Kreste
Vashek .... Norville
Micha .... Newman
Hata .... Edwards
Principal .... Renan
Esmeralda .... Fawcett
Indian .... Winston
Solo dancer .... Horvath (d)

October 3

TOSCA (Puccini)

Conductor .... Halasz

Tosca .... Flesch (d)
Cavaradossi .... Fratesi,
                    (s, Gari)
Scarpia .... Doubrovsky
Angelotti .... Garnell
Spoletta .... Norville
Sacristan .... Dennis
Sciarrone .... Newman
Shepherd .... Edwards

(Note: *Jailer* added to
program October 19)

October 4

LA TRAVIATA

Same cast as September 22
except:

Violetta .... Reggiani
Alfredo .... Conley
Gaston .... Stewart (d)
D'Obigny ..... Harwood (d)

Added to program:
Solo dancer .... Horvath

October 5

CARMEN

Same cast as September 22
(m) except:

Carmen .... Mayer
Don José .... Argyris
Micaëla .... Evangelista
Solo dancers .... Dragon (d),
                    (for Dantiere)

October 6 (m)

LA BOHÈME

Same cast as September 28
except:

Mimi .... Manners
Musetta .... Fawcett
Rodolfo .... Fratesi
Colline .... Greenwell
Benoit .... Dennis

October 6

FAUST

Same cast as September 26
except:

Marguerite .... Reggiani
Méphistophélès .. Doubrovsky
Valentin .... Garnell

October 10

ARIADNE AUF NAXOS (Strauss)
First performance by The New
York City Opera Company
(English translation of the
prologue by Lewis Sydenham)

Stage director .... Sachse
Scenic designer ..... Condell
Conductor .... Halasz

Major-Domo .... Greenwell
Music Master .... Pease
Composer .... Stoska
Tenor, Bacchus .... Argyris
An Officer .... Harwood
Dancing Master ..... Stewart
Wigmaker .... Garnell
Lackey .... Newman
Zerbinetta ...... MacWatters
Prima Donna,
Ariadne .... Flesch
Harlequin .... Herbert
Scaramuccio .... Norville
Truffaldin .... Dennis
Brighella ...... N. Sprinzena
Najade .... Fawcett
Dryade .... Nadell
Echo .... Portnoy

October 11

MADAMA BUTTERFLY

Same cast as September 19
except:

Conductor .... Martin

Suzuki .... Nadell
Trouble .... D. Sprinzena (d)
Yamadori .... Dennis
Imperial
Commissioner ... Harwood

October 12 (m)

CARMEN

Same cast as September 22
(m) except:

Carmen .... Mayer
Don José .... Argyris
Micaëla .... Anderson
Solo dancers .... Dragon,
                    (for Dantiere)

October 12

THE PIRATES OF PENZANCE

Same cast as September 20
except:

Pirate King ...... Greenwell
Police Sergeant ...... Dennis

October 13 (m)

CAVALLERIA RUSTICANA

Same cast as September 21
except:

Santuzza .... Heidt

Followed by:

I PAGLIACCI

Conductor .... Rudel

Canio .... Dudley

October 13

RIGOLETTO

Conductor .... Martin,
                    (s, Halasz)

Duke .... Conley
Rigoletto .... Mascherini
Sparafucile .... Pease
Monterone .... Garnell
Ceprano .... Dennis
Marullo .... Newman
Borsa .... N. Sprinzena
Gilda .... Reggiani
Maddalena .... Nadell
Giovanna .... Kreste
Countess Ceprano ... Griska,
                    (s, Edwards)
Page .... Portnoy

October 16

MADAMA BUTTERFLY

Same cast as September 19
except:

Goro .... N. Sprinzena
Trouble .... unlisted
Yamadori .... Dennis

October 17

LA BOHÈME

Same cast as September 28
except:

Mimi .... Reggiani
Musetta .... Fawcett

Rodolfo .... Gari
Benoit, Alcindoro .... Dennis

(Note: Arthur Newman as *Schaunard* fell and fractured his arm during the last act. Newspaper reports differ as to whether he returned to the stage to finish the final scene or was replaced by an unidentified colleague.)

October 18

THE BARTERED BRIDE

Same cast as September 29 except:

Marenka .... Stoska
Vashek .... Stewart
Micha .... Harwood,
                    (s, Newman)
Principal .... Dennis

October 19

TOSCA

Same cast as October 3 except:

Cavaradossi .... Conley
Scarpia .... Herbert
Spoletta .... Stewart

Added to program:
Jailer .... Winston

October 20 (m)

LA TRAVIATA

Same cast as September 22 except:

Violetta .... R. Brancato
Alfredo .... Gari
D'Obigny .... Harwood

October 20

CARMEN

Same cast as September 22 (m) except:

Don José .... Argyris
Micaëla .... Anderson
Solo dancers .... Dragon
                    (for Dantiere)

October 24

RIGOLETTO

Same cast as October 13 except:

Countess Ceprano .. Edwards

October 25

ARIADNE AUF NAXOS

Same cast as October 10

October 26

MADAMA BUTTERFLY

Same cast as September 19 except:

Kate Pinkerton ..... Portnoy
Sharpless ...... Kennedy (d)
Goro .... N. Sprinzena

Trouble .... D. Sprinzena
Yamadori .... Dennis

October 27 (m)

FAUST

Same cast as September 26 except:

Marguerite .... Manners
Valentin .... Young
Siébel .... Edwards

October 27

THE PIRATES OF PENZANCE

Same cast as September 20 except:

Pirate King ...... Greenwell
Samuel .... N. Sprinzena
Police Sergeant .... Newman

October 30

ARIADNE AUF NAXOS

Same cast as October 10 except:

Tenor, Bacchus ...... Dillon

October 31

CARMEN

Same cast as September 22 (m) except:

Don José .... Argyris
Micaëla .... Lane (d)
Dancairo .... Stewart
Morales .... Garnell
Solo dancers .... Dragon,
                    (for Dantiere)

November 1

MADAMA BUTTERFLY

Same cast as September 19 except:

Butterfly .... Evangelista
Kate Pinkerton ...... Portnoy
Pinkerton .... Conley
Sharpless .... Petroff
Goro .... N. Sprinzena
Trouble .... D. Sprinzena
The Bonze .... Garnell
*Imperial
  Commissioner* ..... Dennis

November 2

LA TRAVIATA

Same cast as September 22 except:

Violetta .... Reggiani
Alfredo .... Conley
D'Obigny .... Renan
Dr. Grenvil .... Dennis

November 3 (m)

LA BOHÈME

Same cast as September 28 except:

Mimi .... Manners
Musetta .... Anderson

Rodolfo .... Fratesi
Schaunard .... Renan
Benoit, Alcindoro .... Dennis

November 3

CAVALLERIA RUSTICANA

Same cast as September 21 except:

Santuzza .... Marino (d)
Alfio .... Herbert

Followed by:

I PAGLIACCI

Same cast as September 21 except:

Conductor .... Rudel

Nedda .... Evangelista
Tonio .... Herbert
Silvio .... Valdengo

November 7

ARIADNE AUF NAXOS

Same cast as October 10 except:

Tenor, Bacchus ...... Dillon
Scaramuccio .... Stewart

November 8

FAUST

Same cast as September 26 except:

Valentin .... Young
Siébel .... Edwards

November 9

RIGOLETTO

Same cast as October 13 except:

Duke .... Fratesi
Ceprano .... Renan
Gilda .... R. Brancato
Countess Ceprano .. Edwards

November 10 (m)

MADAMA BUTTERFLY

Same cast as September 19 except:

Conductor .... Rudel

Butterfly ...... Jorjorian (d)
Kate Pinkerton ..... Portnoy
Sharpless .... Petroff
Goro .... N. Sprinzena
Trouble .... D. Sprinzena
The Bonze .... Garnell
*Imperial
  Commissioner* ..... Dennis

November 10

TOSCA

Same cast as October 3 except:

Cavaradossi .... Conley
Scarpia .... Herbert
Sacristan .... Renan
Spoletta .... Dennis

November 14

EUGENE ONEGIN
(Tchaikovsky)
First performance by The New
York City Opera Company

Stage director..Komisarjevsky
(d)
Scenic designer ..... Condell
Conductor .... Halasz

Larina .... Edwards
Tatjana .... Miller (d)
Olga .... Mayer
Filipjevna .... Kreste
Onegin .... Petroff
Lenski .... Horne
Gremin .... Greenwell,
(s, Doubrovsky)
Captain .... Garnell
Saretzki .... Newman
Triquet .... N. Sprinzena

(Note: Solo dancer added to
program November 24)

November 15

ARIADNE AUF NAXOS

Same cast as October 10
except:

Tenor, Bacchus ...... Dillon
Scaramuccio .... Stewart

November 16

CARMEN

Same cast as September 22
(m) except:

Don José .... Argyris
Micaëla .... Portnoy

Frasquita .... Shelley (d)
Dancairo .... Stewart
Dancers .... Dragon,
(for Dantiere)

November 17 (m)

CAVALLERIA RUSTICANA

Same cast as September 21
except:

Santuzza .... Marino
Turidda .... Fratesi

Followed by:

I PAGLIACCI

Same cast as September 21
except:

Conductor .... Rudel
Nedda .... Evangelista

November 17

EUGENE ONEGIN

Same cast as November 14
except:

Tatjana .... Bryner (d)
Gremin .... Doubrovsky

November 22

MADAMA BUTTERFLY

Same cast as September 19
except:

Kate Pinkerton ...... Portnoy
Pinkerton .... Fratesi
Goro .... N. Sprinzena
Trouble .... D. Sprinzena
Yamadori .... Dennis

November 23

LA TRAVIATA

Same cast as September 22
except:

Violetta .... Reggiani
Alfredo .... Dudley
D'Obigny .... Dennis

November 24

EUGENE ONEGIN

Same cast as November 14
except:

Tatjana .... Bryner
Gremin .... Doubrovsky

Added to program:
Solo dancer .... Horvath

November 29

ARIADNE AUF NAXOS

Same cast as October 10
except:

Tenor, Bacchus .... Dillon
Scaramuccio .... Stewart
Dryade .... Mayer

November 30

RIGOLETTO

Same cast as October 13
except:

Rigoletto .... Valdengo
Maddalena .... Mayer
Countess Ceprano ... Portnoy

Spring 1947 (APRIL 6 – 27)

Female artists
Ayars, Ann*
Bokor, Margit*
della Chiesa, Vivian*
Edwards, Lydia
Fischelli, Camille*
Flesch, Ella
George, Helen
Gerson, Teresa*
Haskins, Virginia*
Heidt, Winifred
Kreste, Mary
LeSawyer, Mary
Lewis, Brenda
Nadell, Rosalind
Parker, Lenore
Petina, Irra*
Portnoy, Lenore
Ribla, Gertrude*
Rivera, Graciela*
Sarnoff, Dorothy
Sprinzena, Donna
Stewart, Willa*
Watkins, Frances*
Williams, Camilla

* New artist

Male artists
Alexander, Carlos*
Argyris, Vasso
Conley, Eugene
Dennis, Paul
Dillon, Irwin
Dunning, Edwin*
Duno, Daniel
Gari, Giulio
Garnell, Grant
Greenwell, Gean
Harwood, Lawrence
Hecht, Manfred*
Herbert, Ralph
Horne, William
Infantino, Luigi*
Jagel, Frederick*
Ligeti, Desire*
Mandile, Frank*
Mascherini, Enzo
Murray, Frank
Newman, Arthur
Pease, James
Richards, Donald*
Sprinzena, Nathaniel

* New artist

Stewart, Allen
Valdengo, Giuseppe
Young, Norman

Conductors
Halasz, Laszlo
Martin, Thomas P.
Morel, Jean
Rudel, Julius

Solo dancers
Kiser, Jane
Leporska, Zoya

Dragon, Edward

Choreographer
Dollar, William*

Directors
Ambros, Edwin*
Komisarjevsky, Theodore

* New artist

Sachse, Leopold
White, John S.*

Designers
Condell, H. A.
Rychtarik, Richard

* New artist

April 6

ARIADNE AUF NAXOS
(R. Strauss)

(English translation of the
prologue by Lewis Sydenham)

Conductor	Halasz
Major-Domo	Greenwell
Music Master	Pease
Composer	Bokor (d)
Tenor, Bacchus	Dillon
Officer	Harwood
Dancing Master	A. Stewart
Wigmaker	Garnell
Lackey	Newman
Zerbinetta	Haskins (d)
Prima Donna, Ariadne	Flesch
Harlequin	Herbert
Scaramuccio	Murray
Truffaldin	Dennis
Brighella	N. Sprinzena
Najade	Ayars (d)
Dryade	Nadell
Echo	Portnoy

April 9

ANDREA CHÉNIER (Giordano)

First performance by The New
York City Opera Company

Stage director	Komisarjevsky
Scenic designer	Condell
Choreographer	Dollar (d)
Conductor	Halasz
Chénier	Argyris, (s, Dillon)
Gérard	Mascherini
Maddalena	della Chiesa (d)
Bersi	Nadell
Contessa di Coigny	Edwards
Madelon	Kreste, (s, Gerson)
Mathieu	Ligeti
Roucher	Garnell
Fléville	Newman
L'Abate	A. Stewart
Incredibile	N. Sprinzena
Schmidt	Dennis
Dumas	Newman
Fouquier-Tinville	Dunning (d)

April 10

CARMEN (Bizet)

Choreographer	Dollar
Conductor	Morel
Carmen	Petina (d)
Don José	Argyris

Escamillo	Valdengo
Micaëla	George, (s, Portnoy)
Zuniga	Ligeti
Frasquita	Fischelli (d)
Mercédès	Edwards
Remendado	N. Sprinzena
Dancairo	Dunning
Morales	Newman
Dancers	Kiser, Leporska, Dragon

April 11

LA TRAVIATA (Verdi)

Stage director	Ambros (d)
Choreographer	Dollar
Conductor	Morel
Violetta	Ayars
Alfredo	Infantino (d)
Germont	Mascherini
Flora	Edwards, (s, Portnoy)
Annina	Kreste
Gaston	A. Stewart
Douphol	Garnell
D'Obigny	Dunning
Dr. Grenvil	Newman
Dancers	Kiser, Leporska

(Note: A third solo dancer
added to program April 17)

April 12

CAVALLERIA RUSTICANA
(Mascagni)

Stage director	White (d)
Conductor	Rudel
Santuzza	W. Stewart (d)
Turiddu	Horne
(?)	Garnell
Lola	Portnoy
Mamma Lucia	Kreste

Followed by:

I PAGLIACCI (Leoncavallo)

Stage director	White (d)
Conductor	Rudel
Nedda	Sarnoff
Canio	Argyris
Tonio	Duno
Silvio	Young
Beppe	N. Sprinzena

April 13 (m)

MADAMA BUTTERFLY (Puccini)

Stage director	White
Conductor	Martin
Butterfly	Williams
Suzuki	Nadell
Kate Pinkerton	Portnoy
Pinkerton	Gari
Sharpless	Herbert
Goro	N. Sprinzena
Yamadori	Dunning
The Bonze	Garnell
Imperial Commissioner	Dennis
Trouble	D. Sprinzena

April 13

RIGOLETTO (Verdi)

Choreographer	Dollar
Conductor	Martin
Duke	Infantino
Rigoletto	Valdengo
Sparafucile	Ligeti
Monterone	Hecht (d)
Ceprano	Dunning
Marullo	Newman
Borsa	N. Sprinzena
Gilda	Watkins (d)
Maddalena	Nadell
Giovanna	Kreste
Countess Ceprano	Portnoy
Page	Parker

April 16

SALOME (R. Strauss)
First performance by The New
York City Opera Company

Stage director	Sachse
Designer	Condell
Conductor	Halasz
Herodes	Jagel (d)
Herodias	Gerson (d)
Salome	Lewis
Jochanaan	Herbert
Narraboth	Horne
Page	Nadell
1st Jew	N. Sprinzena
2nd Jew	Murray
3rd Jew	Garnell
4th Jew	A. Stewart
5th Jew	Dennis
Cappadocian	Dunning
Slave	Mandile (d)
1st Nazarene	Ligeti
2nd Nazarene	Harwood
1st Soldier	Hecht
2nd Soldier	Newman

April 17

LA TRAVIATA

Same cast as April 11 except:

Violetta	Bokor
Alfredo	Conley
Flora	Portnoy
Dancers	Dragon (in addition to Kiser and Leporska)

April 18

ANDREA CHÉNIER

Same cast as April 9 except:

Chénier	Dillon

April 19

RIGOLETTO

Same cast as April 13 except:

Monterone	Garnell
Gilda	Rivera (d)

April 20 (m)

CAVALLERIA RUSTICANA

Same cast as April 12 except:

Santuzza .... Ribla (d)
Turiddu .... Gari
Lola .... Nadell,
           (s, Portnoy)

Followed by:

I PAGLIACCI

Same cast as April 12 except:

Nedda .... Bokor
Silvio .... Richards (d)

April 20

SALOME

Same cast as April 16 except:

Page .... Edwards

April 23

ARIADNE AUF NAXOS

Same cast as April 6 except:

Composer .... Lewis,
           (s, Bokor)

Major-Domo .. Alexander (d)
Echo .... LeSawyer,
           (s, Portnoy)

April 24

MADAMA BUTTERFLY

Same cast as April 13 (m)
except:

Suzuki .... Edwards
Pinkerton .... Infantino
Sharpless .... Valdengo
The Bonze .... Ligeti

April 25

SALOME

Same cast as April 16 except:

Herodias .... Kreste
Jochanaan .... Alexander

April 26

CARMEN

Same cast as April 10 except:

Carmen .... Heidt
Don José .... Dillon

Escamillo .... Herbert
Micaëla .... Ayars
Frasquita .... Portnoy

April 27 (m)

LA TRAVIATA

Same cast as April 11 except:

Alfredo .... Conley
Germont .... Young
Flora .... Portnoy
Gaston .... N. Sprinzena
Dancers .... Dragon
        (in addition to
        Kiser and Leporska)

April 27

ANDREA CHÉNIER

Same cast as April 9 except:

Maddalena ...... W. Stewart
Bersi .... Portnoy
Madelon .... Gerson
L'Abate .... Murray

Fall 1947 (SEPTEMBER 25 – NOVEMBER 16)

Female artists
Aldaba, Dalisay*
Ayars, Ann
Edwards, Lydia
Faull, Ellen*
Forgues, Marie-José*
Genia, Panna*
Gerson, Teresa
Haskins, Virginia
Heidt, Winifred
Keller, Evelyn*
Kreste, Mary
Lewis, Brenda
MacWatters, Virginia
Miller, Brenda
Morris, Suzy*
Nadell, Rosalind
Parker, Lenore
Portnoy, Lenore
Ribla, Gertrude
Sarnoff, Dorothy
Silvain, Graciela*
Spence, Wilma*
Sprinzena, Donna
White, Joyce*
Williams, Camilla

Male artists
Anderson, Roy*
Argyris, Vasso
Bailey, John*
Conley, Eugene
Cordon, Norman*
Dennis, Paul
Dillon, Irwin

    * New artist

Dunning, Edwin
Gari, Giulio
Greenwell, Gean
Guarrera, Frank*
Harwood, Lawrence
Herbert, Ralph
Horne, William
Infantino, Luigi
Jagel, Frederick
Mandile, Frank
Mascherini, Enzo
Molitore, Edward*
Murray, Frank
Newman, Arthur
Pease, James
Randolph, Jess*
Rhodes, Michael*
Richards, Donald
Scott, Norman*
Sprinzena, Nathaniel
Tamarin, Ilia*
Valdengo, Giuseppe
Vincent, George*
Wentworth, Richard*
Young, Norman

Conductors
Halasz, Laszlo
Martin, Thomas P.
Morel, Jean
Rudel, Julius

Dancers
Gevurtz, Mattlyn*
Kiser, Jane

    * New artist

LeClercq, Tanaquil*
Leporska, Zoya
McBride, Pat*
Milton, Eloise*
Sandré, Irma*

Dragon, Edward

Choreographer
Dollar, William

Directors
Komisarjevsky, Theodore
Nagy, Elemer*
Sachse, Leopold
White, John S.

Designers
Condell, H. A.
Rychtarik, Richard

    * New artist

September 25

SALOME (R. Strauss)

Conductor .... Halasz

Herodes .... Jagel
Herodias .... Gerson
Salome .... Lewis
Jochanaan .... Herbert
Narraboth .... Horne
Page .... Nadell
1st Jew .... N. Sprinzena
2nd Jew .... Murray
3rd Jew .... Dunning
4th Jew .... Vincent (d)
5th Jew ..... Wentworth (d)

September 26

LA BOHÈME (Puccini)

Conductor .... Martin

Mimi .... Ayars
Musetta .... Haskins
Rodolfo .... Infantino,
                (s, Conley)
Marcello .... Young,
                (s, Mascherini)
Schaunard .... Dunning
Colline .... Pease
Benoit,
  Alcindoro .... Wentworth
Parpignol .... Murray

September 27

CARMEN (Bizet)

Conductor .... Morel

Carmen .... Heidt
Don José .... Dillon
Escamillo .... Pease
Micaëla .... Portnoy
Zuniga .... Greenwell
Frasquita .... Genia (d)
Mercédès .... Edwards
Remendado .... N. Sprinzena
Dancairo .... Dunning
Morales .... Newman
Dancers .... Kiser,
          Leporska, Dragon

September 28 (m)

RIGOLETTO (Verdi)

Conductor .... Martin

Duke .... Infantino
Rigoletto .... Valdengo,
               (s, Mascherini)
Sparafucile .... Pease
Monterone .... Scott
Ceprano .... Dunning
Marullo .... Newman
Borsa .... N. Sprinzena
Gilda .... MacWatters
Maddalena .... Nadell
Giovanna .... Kreste
Countess Ceprano ... Portnoy
Page .... Parker

September 28

EUGENE ONEGIN
(Tchaikovsky)

Conductor .... Halasz

Larina .... Edwards
Tatjana .... Keller (d)
Olga .... Nadell
Filipjevna .... Kreste
Onegin .... Herbert
Lenski .... Horne
Gremin .... Greenwell
Captain .... Dunning
Saretzki .... Newman
Triquet .... N. Sprinzena

October 2

WERTHER (Massenet)
First performance by The New
York City Opera Company

Stage director .... Sachse
Designer .... Condell
Conductor .... Morel

Werther .... Conley
Charlotte .... Heidt
Sophie .... Haskins
Albert .... Young
The Bailiff .... Greenwell
Schmidt .... N. Sprinzena
Johann .... Newman
Bruehlmann .... Bailey
Kaetchen .... Portnoy

October 3

SALOME
Same cast as September 25

October 4

LA TRAVIATA (Verdi)

Stage director ..... Nagy (d)
Conductor .... Morel

Violetta .... Ayars
Alfredo .... Infantino
Germont .... Mascherini
Flora .... Portnoy
Annina .... Kreste
Gaston .... N. Sprinzena
Douphol .... Wentworth
D'Obigny .... Dunning
Dr. Grenvil .... Newman

(Note: *Dancers* added to
program October 19.)

October 5 (m)

MADAMA BUTTERFLY (Puccini)

Conductor .... Martin

Butterfly .... Williams
Suzuki .... Kreste
Kate Pinkerton ..... Portnoy
Pinkerton .... Conley,
                (s, Gari)
Sharpless .... Valdengo
Goro .... N. Sprinzena
Yamadori .... Newman
The Bonze .... Greenwell
Imperial
  Commissioner .... Dunning
Trouble .... D. Sprinzena

October 5

IL BARBIERE DI SIVIGLIA
(Rossini)
First performance by the New
York City Opera Company

Stage director .... Nagy
Designer .... Condell
Conductor .... Halasz

Figaro .... Mascherini
Almaviva .... Infantino
Rosina .... Haskins
Bartolo .... Wentworth
Basilio .... Greenwell
Berta .... Gerson

Fiorello .... Newman
Officer .... N. Sprinzena

(Note on program: "Miss
Haskins will sing 'L'inutile
precauzione' by Pietro Cimara
in the Lesson Scene.")

October 9

ARIADNE AUF NAXOS
(R. Strauss)

Conductor .... Halasz

Major-Domo ..... Greenwell
Music Master .... Pease
Composer .... Spence (d)
Tenor, Bacchus ..... Dillon
An Officer .... Harwood
Dancing Master ..... Vincent
Wigmaker .... Dunning
Lackey .... Newman
Zerbinetta ...... MacWatters
Prima Donna,
  Ariadne .... Morris (d)
Harlequin .... Herbert
Scaramuccio .... Murray
Truffaldin .... Dennis,
              (s, Wentworth)
Brighella ...... N. Sprinzena
Najade .... White (d),
                (s, Ayars)
Dryade .... Nadell
Echo .... Portnoy

October 10

WERTHER
Same cast as October 2

October 11

EUGENE ONEGIN

Same cast as September 28
except:

Tatjana .... Miller

October 12 (m)

LA BOHÈME

Same cast as September 26
except:

Schaunard .... Newman
Colline .... Greenwell

October 12

CAVALLERIA RUSTICANA
(Mascagni)

Conductor .... Rudel

Santuzza .... Ribla
Turiddu .... Argyris,
                (s, Gari)
Alfio .... Dunning,
                (s, Herbert)
Lola .... Nadell
Mamma Lucia .... Kreste

Followed by:

I PAGLIACCI (Leoncavallo)

Conductor .... Rudel

Nedda .... Sarnoff
Canio .... Jagel

October 2

Cappadocian ..... Bailey (d)
Slave .... Mandile
1st Nazarene ..... Greenwell
2nd Nazarene ...... Harwood
1st Soldier .... Scott (d)
2nd Soldier .... Newman

Tonio .... Valdengo
Silvio .... Young,
                      (s, Herbert)
Beppe .... N. Sprinzena

October 16

MADAMA BUTTERFLY

Same cast as October 5 (m)
except:

Pinkerton .... Gari
Suzuki .... Nadell

October 17

SALOME

Same cast as September 25
except:

Herodias .... Kreste
Jochanaan ..... Rhodes (d),
                      (s, Herbert)
Slave .... Anderson (d)
1st Nazarene .... Pease

October 18

RIGOLETTO

Same cast as September 28
(m) except:

Duke .... Conley
Sparafucile .... Greenwell
Monterone ...... Wentworth

October 19 (m)

CARMEN

Same cast as September 27
except:

Don José .... Argyris
Micaëla .... Sarnoff
Frasquita .... Portnoy
Dancer .... Gevurtz (d),
                      (for Leporska)

October 19

LA TRAVIATA

Same cast as October 4 except:

Germont .... Valdengo

Added to program:

Dancers .... Dragon,
                 Gevurtz, Kiser,
                     LeClercq (d),
                      McBride (d),
                 Milton, Sandré (d)

October 23

DON GIOVANNI (Mozart)
First performance by The New
York City Opera Company

Stage director..Komisarjevsky
Designer .... Condell
Choreographer .... Dollar
Conductor .... Halasz

Don Giovanni .... Pease
Leporello .... Cordon (d)
Donna Elvira .... Lewis
Commendatore .... Greenwell

Donna Anna ...... Faull (d)
Don Ottavio .... Conley
Masetto .... Dunning
Zerlina .... Haskins

October 24

ARIADNE AUF NAXOS

Same cast as October 9 except:

Prima Donna,
Ariadne .... Ribla
Nyade .... Ayars

October 25

CAVALLERIA RUSTICANA

Same cast as October 12
except:

Santuzza .... Lewis
Turiddu .... Dillon
Alfio .... Herbert

Followed by:

I PAGLIACCI

Same cast as October 12
except:

Canio .... Argyris
Tonio .... Mascherini,
                      (s, Young)
Silvio .... Guarrera (d)

October 26 (m)

IL BARBIERE DI SIVIGLIA

Same cast as October 5 except:

Conductor .... Rudel
Rosina .... MacWatters
Berta .... Kreste
Officer .... Dunning

(Note on program: "Miss
MacWatters will sing the
'Shadow Dance' from Meyer-
beer's *Dinorah* in the Lesson
Scene.")

October 26

LA BOHÈME

Same cast as September 26
except:

Mimi .... Williams
Musetta .... Portnoy
Rodolfo .... Horne,
                      (s, Gari)
Marcello .... Mascherini
                      (s, Young)
Schaunard .... Newman

October 30

SALOME

Same cast as September 25
except:

Herodes .... Molitore (d)
1st Nazarene .... Pease
2nd Nazarene...Randolph (d)

October 31

DON GIOVANNI

Same cast as October 23
except:

Donna Elvira .... Keller
Don Ottavio .... Conley,
                      (s, Infantino)

November 1

MADAMA BUTTERFLY

Same cast as October 5 (m)
except:

Sharpless .... Herbert
Trouble .... unlisted

November 2 (m)

LA TRAVIATA

Same cast as October 4

November 2

CARMEN

Same cast as September 27
except:

Micaëla .... Forgues (d)
Frasquita .... Portnoy
Dancers .... Gevurtz,
                      (for Leporska)

November 5

DON GIOVANNI

Same cast as October 23
except:

Don Ottavio ...... Infantino

November 6

IL BARBIERE DI SIVIGLIA

Same cast as October 5 except:

Conductor .... Rudel
Berta .... Kreste
Officer .... Dunning

November 7

EUGENE ONEGIN

Same cast as September 28
except:

Lenski .... Tamarin (d)
Gremin .... Scott

November 8

LA BOHÈME

Same cast as September 26
except:

Mimi .... Williams
Musetta .... Portnoy
Rodolfo .... Horne
Schaunard .... Newman

November 9 (m)

CAVALLERIA RUSTICANA

Same cast as October 12 except:

Turiddu .... Dillon
Alfio .... Herbert,
(s, Young)

Followed by:

I PAGLIACCI

Same cast as October 12 except:

Canio .... Argyris
Silvio .... Richards

November 9

SALOME

Same cast as September 25 except:

Herodias .... Kreste
Slave .... Anderson
1st Nazarene .... Pease
2nd Nazarene ..... Randolph

November 13

DON GIOVANNI

Same cast as October 23 except:

Donna Elvira .... Keller
Commendatore .... Scott
Donna Anna .... Faull,
(s, Ribla)

November 14

LA TRAVIATA

Same cast as October 4 except:

Germont .... Young

November 15

RIGOLETTO

Same cast as September 28 (m) except:

Rigoletto .... Mascherini
Sparafucile .... Scott

Monterone ...... Wentworth
Gilda .... Silvain (d)

November 16 (m)

CARMEN

Same cast as September 27 except:

Don José .... Argyris
Escamillo .... Valdengo
Micaëla .... Sarnoff
Frasquita .... Portnoy
Dancer .... Gevurtz,
(for Leporska)

November 16

MADAMA BUTTERFLY

Same cast as October 5 (m) except:

Butterfly .... Aldaba (d)
Suzuki .... Nadell
Sharpless .... Herbert
The Bonze .... Wentworth
Trouble .... unlisted

Spring 1948 (MARCH 19–APRIL 25)

Female artists
Aldaba, Dalisay
Ayars, Ann
Bishop, Adelaide*
Canario, Rosa*
Carmen, Arlene*
Dubro, Bette*
Faull, Ellen
Forgues, Marie-José
Greene, Harriet
Haskins, Virginia
Heidt, Winifred
Keller, Evelyn
Kreste, Mary
LeSawyer, Mary
Lewis, Brenda
MacWatters, Virginia
Marrone, Rose*
Morris, Suzy
O'Hara, Carole*
Parker, Lenore
Piazza, Marguerite
Portnoy, Lenore
Powers, Marie*
Shor, Ruth*
Silvain, Graciela
Spence, Wilma
Taussig, Carroll
Teyte, Maggie*
White, Joyce
Williams, Camilla
Yeend, Frances*

Male artists
Annaloro, Antonio*
Binci, Mario*
Carlson, Stanley
Cassel, Walter*
Cordon, Norman

* New artist

Dillon, Irwin
Dunning, Edwin
Gainey, Andrew*
Gauld, Carlton
Greenwell, Gean
Gutman, Julius*
Harrell, Mack
Herbert, Ralph
Horne, William
Jagel, Frederick
Laderoute, Joseph
Martel, Fernand*
Murray, Frank
Natzka, Oscar*
Newman, Arthur
Pease, James
Petrak, Rudolf*
Randolph, Jess
Rhodes, Michael
Scott, Norman
Sprinzena, Nathaniel
Uppman, Theodor*
Valdengo, Giuseppe
Vincent, George
Weede, Robert*
Young, Norman

Conductors
Halasz, Laszlo
Martin, Thomas P.
Morel, Jean
Rudel, Julius

Dancers
Damon, Cathryn*
Kiser, Jane
Leporska, Zoya
Logne, Betty Ann*
Nadell, Estelle*

* New artist

Stewart, Harry*

Choreographer
Mahoney, Arthur*

Directors
Komisarjevsky, Theodore
Menotti, Gian Carlo*
Sachse, Leopold
White, John S.

Designers
Condell, H. A.
Rychtarik, Richard

* New artist

March 19

DON GIOVANNI (Mozart)

Choreographer .... Mahoney
(d)
Conductor .... Halasz

Don Giovanni .... Pease
Leporello .... Cordon
Donna Elvira .... Lewis
Commendatore .... Scott
Donna Anna .... Faull
Don Ottavio ...... Laderoute
Masetto .... Dunning
Zerlina .... Haskins

March 20

LA TRAVIATA (Verdi)

Stage director .... Sachse
Choreographer ..... Mahoney
Conductor .... Morel

Violetta .... Yeend (d)
Alfredo .... Horne

Germont .... Young
Flora .... LeSawyer
Annina .... Kreste
Gaston .... Sprinzena
Douphol .... Newman
D'Obigny .... Dunning
Dr. Grenvil .... Scott
Dancers .... Leporska,
  Damon (d), Kiser,
  Logne (d), Nadell (d)

March 21 (m)

CARMEN (Bizet)

Choreographer ..... Mahoney
Conductor .... Morel

Carmen .... Heidt
Don José .... Dillon
Escamillo .... Cassel (d)
Micaëla .... Portnoy,
  (s, Forgues)
Zuniga .... Greenwell
Frasquita .... White,
  (s, Portnoy)
Mercédès .... O'Hara (d)
Remendado .... Sprinzena
Dancairo .... Dunning
Morales .... Newman
Dancers .... Leporska,
  Nadell, Stewart (d)

March 21

LA BOHÈME (Puccini)

Conductor .... Halasz

Mimi .... Ayars
Musetta .... Portnoy
Rodolfo .... Petrak (d)
Marcello .... Herbert
Schaunard .... Newman
Colline .... Scott
Benoit .... Gutman (d)
Alcindoro .... Dunning
Parpignol .... Murray

March 25

PELLÉAS ET MÉLISANDE
(Débussy)

First performance by The New
  York City Opera Company
  (Production designed and
  directed by Komisarjevsky)

Costume designer ... Condell
Conductor .... Morel

Arkel .... Scott
Geneviève .... Kreste
Golaud .... Gauld
Pelléas .... Martel (d),
  (s, Uppman)
Mélisande .... Teyte (d)
Yniold .... Haskins
Physician .... Newman

(Note: Theodor Uppman was
originally to have replaced
French tenor Jacques Jansen,
who was also indisposed.)

March 26

MADAMA BUTTERFLY (Puccini)

Conductor .... Martin

Butterfly .... Williams
Suzuki .... Kreste
Kate Pinkerton ..... Portnoy
Pinkerton .... Dillon
Sharpless .... Valdengo
Goro .... Sprinzena
Yamadori .... Newman
The Bonze .... Greenwell
Imperial
  Commissioner .... Dunning

March 27

CAVALLERIA RUSTICANA
(Mascagni)

Conductor .... Rudel

Santuzza .... Morris
Turiddu ...... Annaloro (d)
Alfio .... Herbert
Lola .... Dubro (d)
Mamma Lucia .... Kreste

Followed by:

I PAGLIACCI (Leoncavallo)

Conductor .... Rudel

Nedda .... Keller
Canio .... Jagel
Tonio .... Valdengo
Silvio .... Young
Beppe .... Sprinzena

March 28 (m)

PELLÉAS ET MÉLISANDE

Same cast as March 25 except.

Pelléas .... Martel,
  (s, Uppman)
Yniold .... Forgues

March 28

DON GIOVANNI

Same cast as March 19

April 1

TOSCA (Puccini)

Conductor .... Halasz

Tosca .... Spence
Cavaradossi .... Petrak
Scarpia .... Cassel
Angelotti .... Scott
Spoletta .... Dunning
Sacristan .... Carlson
Jailer .... Randolph
Shepherd .... Greene

April 2

PELLÉAS ET MÉLISANDE

Same cast as March 25 except:

Pelléas .... Uppman (d)

April 3

LA TRAVIATA

Same cast as March 20 except:

Violetta .... Ayars
Alfredo .... Annaloro,
  (s, Binci)
Germont .... Valdengo
Flora .... Portnoy

(Note: Norman Scott, after
performing in Beethoven's
Ninth Symphony under
Toscanini, went to the City
Center and sang the role of
Dr. Grenvil.)

April 4 (m)

LA BOHÈME

Same cast as March 21 except:

Mimi .... Williams
Marcello .... Young

April 4

CARMEN

Same cast as March 21 (m)
except:

Don José .... Annaloro
Escamillo .... Valdengo
Micaëla .... Forgues
Frasquita .... Portnoy

April 7

DON GIOVANNI

Same cast as March 19 except:

Don Ottavio .... Horne

April 8

THE OLD MAID AND THE THIEF
(Menotti)
First performance by The New
  York City Opera Company

Stage director ... Menotti (d)
Designer .... Condell
Lighting .... Sondheimer
Conductor .... Martin

Laetitia .... MacWatters
Miss Todd ...... Powers (d)
Miss Pinkerton .... Faull
Bob .... Young

Followed by:

AMELIA GOES TO THE BALL
(Menotti)
First performance by The New
  York City Opera Company
  (English translation by
  George Mead)

Stage director ... Menotti (d)
Designer .... Condell
Lighting .... Sondheimer
Conductor .... Halasz

Amelia .... Yeend
Husband .... Cassel

Lover .... Horne
Police
   Commissioner .. Greenwell
Friend .... Dubro
1st Maid .... Portnoy
2nd Maid .... Shor (d)

April 9

RIGOLETTO (Verdi)

Choreographer .... Mahoney
Conductor .... Martin

Duke .... Binci (d)
Rigoletto .... Weede (d)
Sparafucile ...... Natzka (d)
Monterone .... Scott
Ceprano .... Dunning
Marullo .... Newman
Borsa .... Vincent
Gilda .... Silvain
Maddalena .... Dubro
Giovanna .... Kreste
Countess
   Ceprano .... LeSawyer,
              (s, Portnoy)
Page .... Parker

April 10

TOSCA

Same cast as April 1 except:

Scarpia .... Cassel,
             (s, Bardelli)
Shepherd .... Shor

(Note: Cesare Bardelli,
scheduled to debut at this
performance, was not to make
his first appearance with the
company until March 25,
1950.)

April 11 (m)

CAVALLERIA RUSTICANA

Same cast as March 27 except:

Turiddu .... Dillon

Followed by:

I PAGLIACCI

Same cast as March 27 except:

Canio .... Annaloro
Tonio .... Weede

April 11

MADAMA BUTTERFLY

Same cast as March 26 except:

Butterfly .... Aldaba
Suzuki .... Dubro
Pinkerton .... Binci

April 14

PELLÉAS ET MÉLISANDE

Same cast as March 25 except:

Golaud .... Harrell

April 15

LA TRAVIATA

Same cast as March 20 except:

Germont .... Valdengo
Flora .... Portnoy
D'Obigny .... Randolph

April 16

CARMEN

Same cast as March 21 (m)
except:

Don José .... Annaloro
Escamillo .... Herbert
Micaëla .... Canario (d)
Frasquita .... Portnoy

April 17

LA BOHÈME

Same cast as March 21 except:

Mimi .... Keller
Musetta .... Piazza
Rodolfo .... Binci
Colline .... Greenwell

April 18 (m)

RIGOLETTO

Same cast as April 9 except:

Duke .... Petrak
Gilda .... Bishop (d)
Giovanna .... Taussig
Countess Ceprano ... Portnoy

April 18

THE OLD MAID AND THE THIEF

Same cast as April 8

Followed by:

AMELIA GOES TO THE BALL

Same cast as April 8

April 21

PELLÉAS ET MÉLISANDE

Same cast as March 25 except:

Golaud .... Harrell
Pelléas .... Uppman

April 22

DON GIOVANNI

Same cast as March 19 except:

Donna Elvira .... Piazza
Commendatore .... Greenwell
Don Ottavio .... Horne

April 23

CAVALLERIA RUSTICANA

Same cast as March 27 except:

Turiddu .... Dillon
Alfio .... Rhodes
Lola .... Carmen (d)

Followed by:

I PAGLIACCI

Same cast as March 27 except:

Nedda .... Ayars
Canio .... Annaloro
Tonio .... Young,
            (s, Bardelli)
Silvio .... Herbert
Beppe .... Vincent

April 24

THE OLD MAID AND THE THIEF

Same cast as April 8 except:

Miss Todd .... Kreste
Bob .... Gainey (d)

Followed by:

AMELIA GOES TO THE BALL

Same cast as April 8 except:

Conductor .... Rudel
Amelia .... Piazza
Lover .... Dillon
2nd Maid .... Greene

April 25 (m)

MADAMA BUTTERFLY

Same cast as March 26 except:

Pinkerton .... Petrak
Sharpless .... Herbert

April 25

TOSCA

Same cast as April 1 except:

Tosca .... Morris
Cavaradossi .... Binci
Scarpia .... Cassel,
             (s, Bardelli)
Shepherd ...... Marrone (d)
Jailer .... Randolph

Fall 1948 (OCTOBER 7 – NOVEMBER 28)

Female artists
Ayars, Ann
Bible, Frances*
Bishop, Adelaide
Canario, Rosa
Edwards, Lydia
Faull, Ellen
Greene, Harriet
Haskins, Virginia
Heidt, Winifred
Keller, Evelyn
Kreste, Mary
LeSawyer, Mary
Lewis, Brenda
MacNeil, Dorothy*
MacWatters, Virginia
Marrone, Rose
Masiello, Alberta*
Morris, Suzy
Nadell, Rosalind
O'Malley, Muriel*
Piazza, Marguerite
Powers, Marie
Scheunemann, Leona*
Shelby, Lillian*
Shor, Ruth
Spence, Wilma
Taussig, Carroll
Teyte, Maggie
White, Joyce
Williams, Camilla
Yeend, Frances

Male artists
Bailey, John
Binci, Mario
Bonelli, Richard*
Brandin, Walter*
Cassel, Walter
Czaplicki, George†
Conley, Eugene
Cordon, Norman
Dillon, Irwin
Dunning, Edwin
Gainey, Andrew
Gauld, Carlton
Herbert, Ralph
Horne, William
Jagel, Frederick
Mandile, Frank
Martel, Fernand
Natzka, Oscar
Newman, Arthur
Pease, James
Petrak, Rudolf
Rothmueller, Marko*
Rounseville, Robert*
Scott, Norman
Sprinzena, Nathaniel
Stanz, William*
Szemere, László*

* New artist
† George Czaplicki, who appeared in the opening night performance, Anglicized the spelling of his name. For consistency, we have continued to list him as Czaplicki.

Tyers, John*
Vellucci, Luigi*
Vinay, Ramon
Vincent, George
Wentworth, Richard
Winters, Lawrence*
Young, Norman

Conductors
Halasz, Laszlo
Martin, Thomas P.
Morel, Jean
Rosenstock, Joseph*
Rudel, Julius

Solo dancers
LeClercq, Tanaquil
McBride, Pat
Marie-Jeanne*
Tallchief, Maria*

Bliss, Herbert*
Magallanes, Nicholas*
Moncion, Francisco*

Choreographer
Balanchine, George*

Directors
Komisarjevsky, Theodore
Menotti, Gian Carlo
Sachse, Leopold
White, John S.

Designers
Condell, H. A.
Rychtarik, Richard

* New artist

October 7

TOSCA (Puccini)

Conductor	Halasz
Tosca	Morris
Cavaradossi	Binci
Scarpia	Cassel
Angelotti	Scott
Spoletta	Dunning
Sacristan	Wentworth
Sciarrone	Newman
Shepherd	Bible (d)
Jailer	Brandin (d)

October 8

PELLÉAS ET MÉLISANDE
(Debussy)

Conductor	Morel
Arkel	Scott
Geneviève	Kreste
Golaud	Gauld
Pelléas	Martel
Mélisande	Teyte
Yniold	Haskins
Physician	Newman

October 9

AMELIA GOES TO THE BALL
(Menotti)
(English translation by
George Mead)

Conductor	Rudel
Amelia	Yeend
Husband	Cassel
Lover	Horne
Police Commissioner	Pease
Friend	Nadell
1st Maid	MacNeil (d)
2nd Maid	Greene

Followed by:

THE OLD MAID AND THE THIEF
(Menotti)

Conductor	Martin
Laetitia	MacWatters
Miss Todd	O'Malley (d)
Miss Pinkerton	Faull
Bob	Young

October 10 (m)

MADAMA BUTTERFLY (Puccini)

Conductor	Martin
Butterfly	Williams
Suzuki	Kreste
Kate Pinkerton	MacNeil
Pinkerton	Petrak
Sharpless	Herbert
Goro	Sprinzena
Yamadori	Newman
The Bonze	Wentworth
Imperial Commissioner	Dunning

October 10

CARMEN (Bizet)

Choreographer	Balanchine (d)
Conductor	Morel
Carmen	Masiello (d)
Don José	Dillon
Escamillo	Pease
Micaëla	Ayars
Zuniga	Scott
Frasquita	MacNeil
Mercédès	Bible
Remendado	Sprinzena
Dancairo	Dunning
Morales	Newman
Dancers	LeClercq, McBride, Moncion (d), Tallchief (d)

October 14

THE MARRIAGE OF FIGARO
(Mozart)
First performance of The New
York City Opera Company
(English version by
Ruth and Thomas Martin)

Staged by .... Sachse
Designer .... Condell
Choreographer ... Balanchine
Conductor ... Rosenstock (d)

Almaviva .... Cassel
Countess .... Yeend
Figaro .... Pease
Susanna .... MacWatters
Cherubino .... Bible,
  (s, Nadell)
Bartolo .... Wentworth
Marcellina .... Kreste
Basilio .... Vellucci (d)
Curzio .... Vincent,
  (s, Sprinzena)
Antonio .... Newman
Barbarina .... MacNeill
Peasant girls .. White, Greene

October 15

LA BOHÈME (Puccini)

Conductor ...... Rosenstock

Mimi .... Ayars
Musetta .... MacNeil
Rodolfo .... Conley
Marcello .... Herbert
Schaunard .... Newman
Colline .... Scott
Benoit .... Wentworth
Alcindoro .... Dunning
Parpignol .... Vellucci

October 16

CAVALLERIA RUSTICANA
(Mascagni)

Conductor .... Rudel

Santuzza .... Canario
Turiddu .... Binci
Alfio .... Herbert
Lola .... Nadell
Mamma Lucia .... Kreste

Followed by:

I PAGLIACCI (Leoncavallo)

Conductor .... Martin

Nedda .... Keller
Canio .... Szemere (d)
Tonio .... Young
Silvio .... Tyers (d)
Beppe .... Sprinzena

October 17 (m)

LA TRAVIATA (Verdi)

Choreographer ... Balanchine
Conductor .... Morel

Violetta .... Ayars
Alfredo .... Petrak

Germont .... Bonelli (d)
Flora .... MacNeil
Annina .... Kreste
Gaston .... Sprinzena
Douphol .... Wentworth
D'Obigny .... Dunning
Dr. Grenvil .... Newman
Dancers .... Bliss (d),
  Marie-Jeanne (d)

October 17

SALOME (R. Strauss)

Conductor .... Halasz

Salome .... Lewis
Herodes .... Jagel
Herodias .... Masiello
Jochanaan .... Cassel
Narraboth .... Petrak
Page .... Nadell
1st Jew .... Sprinzena
2nd Jew .... Vallucci
3rd Jew .... Dunning
4th Jew .... Vincent
5th Jew .... Wentworth
Cappadocian .... Bailey
Slave .... Stanz (d)
1st Nazarene .... Natzka
2nd Nazarene ..... Brandin
1st Soldier .... Scott
2nd Soldier .... Newman

October 21

DON GIOVANNI (Mozart)

Choreographer ... Balanchine
Conductor .... Halasz

Don Giovanni .... Pease
Leporello .... Cordon
Donna Elvira .... Piazza
Commendatore .... Scott
Donna Anna .... Faull
Don Ottavio .... Petrak
Masetto .... Dunning
Zerlina .... Haskins

October 22

AMELIA GOES TO THE BALL

Same cast as October 9

Followed by:

THE OLD MAID AND THE THIEF

Same cast as October 9 except:

Miss Todd .... Kreste

October 23

MADAMA BUTTERFLY

Same cast as October 10 (m)
except:

Pinkerton .... Petrak,
  (s, Binci)
Goro .... Vellucci

October 24 (m)

CARMEN

Same cast as October 10
except:

Escamillo .... Herbert
Micaëla .... Yeend

October 24

THE MARRIAGE OF FIGARO

Same cast as October 14
except:

Countess .... Faull
Cherubino .... Nadell
Curzio .... Sprinzena

October 28

AIDA (Verdi)

First performance by The New
York City Opera Company

Staged by .... Komisarjevsky
Designer .... Condell
Choreographer ... Balanchine
Conductor .... Halasz

King .... Pease
Amneris .... Morris
Aida .... Williams
Radames .... Vinay
Ramfis .... Natzka
Amonasro ...... Winters (d)
Messenger .... Dunning
Priestess .... Bible
Solo dancers ...... Tallchief,
  Magallanes (d),
  LeClercq

October 29

PELLÉAS ET MÉLISANDE

Same cast as October 8 except:

Geneviève .... O'Malley

October 30

LA TRAVIATA

Same cast as October 17 (m)
except:

Violetta .... Yeend
Alfredo .... Petrak,
  (s, Binci)
Germont .... Young
Gaston .... Vellucci

October 31 (m)

TOSCA

Same cast as October 7 except:

Conductor .... Martin

Tosca .... Spence
Cavaradossi .... Conley
Angelotti .... Pease
Shepherd .... Marrone

October 31

CAVALLERIA RUSTICANA

Same cast as October 16 except:

Alfio .... Gainey
Lola .... Bible

Followed by:

I PAGLIACCI

Same cast as October 16 except:

Nedda .... Ayars
Tonio .... Winters
Silvio .... Young

November 4

DON GIOVANNI

Same cast as October 21 except:

Commendatore ...... Natzka

November 5

AIDA

Same cast as October 28 except:

Amneris .... Heidt,
                (s, Masiello)
Radames .... Szemere

November 6

LA BOHÈME

Same cast as October 15 except:

Rodolfo .... Petrak

November 7 (m)

CARMEN

Same cast as October 10 except:

Carmen .... Heidt
Micaëla .... MacNeil
Frasquita .... LeSawyer

November 7

EUGENE ONEGIN
(Tchaikovsky)

Choreographer ... Balanchine
Conductor .... Halasz

Larina .... Edwards
Tatjana .... Lewis
Olga .... Nadell
Filipjevna .... Kreste
Eugene Onegin .... Czaplicki
Lenski .... Horne
Gremin .... Natzka
Captain .... Dunning
Saretzki .... Newman
Triquet .... Sprinzena

November 11

THE MARRIAGE OF FIGARO

Same cast as October 14 except:

Almaviva .... Young
Countess .. Scheunemann (d)
Susanna .... Bishop

November 12

LA TRAVIATA

Same cast as October 17 (m) except:

Alfredo .... Binci
Germont .... Cassel
Gaston .... Vellucci

November 13

SALOME

Same cast as October 17 except:

Herodes .... Szemere
Herodias .... Kreste
Page .... Bible

November 14 (m)

AIDA

Same cast as October 28 except:

Amneris .... Heidt
Aida .... Canario
Ramfis .... Scott
Amonasro .. Rothmueller (d)

November 14

AMELIA GOES TO THE BALL

Same cast as October 9 except:

Amelia .... Piazza
Police
  Commissioner .... Natzka
Friend .... Bible
2nd Maid .... Shor

Followed by:

THE OLD MAID AND THE THIEF

Same cast as October 9 except:

Laetitia .... Bishop
Miss Todd .... Powers
Bob .... Gainey

November 18

CARMEN

Same cast as October 10 except:

Conductor ...... Rosenstock

Carmen .... Heidt
Escamillo .... Bonelli
Micaëla .... MacNeil
Zuniga .... Wentworth

Frasquita .... LeSawyer
Remendado .... Vellucci

November 19

TOSCA

Same cast as October 7 except:

Cavaradossi .... Petrak
Scarpia .... Rothmueller,
                (s, Czaplicki)
Angelotti .... Pease

November 20

EUGENE ONEGIN

Same cast as November 7 except:

Larina .... Bible
Tatjana .... Keller
Olga .... Masiello
Eugene Onegin ...... Herbert
Gremin .... Scott

November 21 (m)

CAVALLERIA RUSTICANA

Same cast as October 16 except:

Santuzza .... Lewis
Alfio .... Gainey
Mamma Lucia ...... Taussig

Followed by:

I PAGLIACCI

Same cast as October 16 except:

Nedda .... Shelby (d)
Tonio .... Winters
Silvio .... Young

November 21

DON GIOVANNI

Same cast as October 21 except:

Donna Elvira .... Spence
Commendatore ...... Natzka
Donna Anna .... Canario
Don Ottavio .... Horne
Masetto .... Newman
Zerlina .... Ayars

November 24

THE MARRIAGE OF FIGARO

Same cast as October 14 except:

Almaviva .... Young
Countess .... Faull
Figaro .... Tyers
Cherubino .... Nadell
Curzio .... Sprinzena
Peasant girls..LeSawyer, Shor

November 25

PELLÉAS ET MÉLISANDE

Same cast as October 8 except:
Arkel .... Natzka
Pelléas ...... Rounseville (d)

November 26

AIDA

Same cast as October 28 except:
Amneris .... Masiello
Aida .... Scheunemann
Radames .... Szemere
Ramfis .... Scott

November 27

LA BOHÈME

Same cast as October 15 except:
Rodolfo .... Horne
Marcello .... Rothmueller

November 28 (m)

MADAMA BUTTERFLY

Same cast as October 10 (m) except:
Suzuki .... Nadell
Pinkerton .... Binci

Sharpless .... Tyers
The Bonze .... Scott

November 28

SALOME

Same cast as October 17 except:
Herodes .... Szemere
Herodias .... Kreste,
                (s, Masiello)
Jochanaan .... Herbert
Page .... Bible
4th Jew .... Stanz
Slave .... Mandile
1st Soldier .... Pease

Spring 1949 (MARCH 24 – MAY 1)

Female artists
Ayars, Ann
Bible, Frances
Bishop, Adelaide
Bliss, Helena*
Canario, Rosa
Faull, Ellen
Gonzalez, Irma
Haskins, Virginia
Heidt, Winifred
Keller, Evelyn
LeSawyer, Mary
Lewis, Brenda
MacNeil, Dorothy
MacWatters, Virginia
Masiello, Alberta
Mayer, Margery
Morris, Suzy
Nadell, Rosalind
O'Malley, Muriel
Piazza, Marguerite
Powers, Marie
Scheunemann, Leona
Shor, Ruth
Spence, Wilma
Stewart, Ruth
White, Joyce
Williams, Camilla
Yeend, Frances
Zambrana, Margarita*

Male artists
Bernauer, Robert*
Binci, Mario
Brandin, Walter
Cassel, Walter
Charles, Richard*
Cordon, Norman
Dunning, Edwin
Gainey, Andrew
Garen, David*
Gari, Giulio
Gauld, Carlton
Herbert, Ralph
Leech, Lloyd Thomas*
McFerrin, Robert*
Natzka, Oscar
Newman, Arthur
Pease, James
Petrak, Rudolf

* New artist

Powell, Thomas*
Rothmueller, Marko
Rounseville, Robert
Scott, Norman
Sprinzena, Nathaniel
Stanz, William
Tyers, John
Vellucci, Luigi
Vroons, Frans*
Weede, Robert
Wentworth, Richard
Winters, Lawrence
Young, Norman

Conductors
Halasz, Laszlo
Martin, Thomas P.
Morel, Jean
Rosenstock, Joseph
Rudel, Julius
Shaynen, Lee*

Solo dancers
LeClercq, Tanaquil

Bliss, Herbert
Coleman, Leo*

Choreographers
Balanchine, George
Destiné, Jean-Léon*

Directors
Bryden, Eugene S.
Komisarjevsky, Theodore
Menotti, Gian Carlo
Sachse, Leopold
White, John S.

Designers
Brodkin, Herbert*
Condell, H. A.
Rychtarik, Richard

    * New artist

March 24

AIDA (Verdi)

Conductor .... Halasz

King .... Scott
Amneris .... Mayer
Aida .... Williams
Radames .... Petrak

Ramfis .... Natzka
Amonasro .... Winters
Messenger .... Dunning
Priestess .... Bible
Solo dancers .. LeClercq, Bliss

March 25

LA TRAVIATA (Verdi)

Conductor .... Morel

Violetta .... Yeend
Alfredo .... Binci
Germont .... Young
Flora .... MacNeil
Annina .... O'Malley
Gaston .... Vellucci
Douphol .... Wentworth
D'Obigny .... Dunning
Dr. Grenvil .... Newman
Solo dancers .. LeClercq, Bliss

March 26

TOSCA (Puccini)

Conductor .... Martin

Tosca .... Spence
Cavaradossi .... Petrak
Scarpia .... Cassel
Angelotti .... Scott
Spoletta .... Dunning
Sacristan .... Newman
                (s, Wentworth)
Sciarrone .... Newman
Shepherd .... Bible
Jailer .... Brandin

March 27 (m)

MADAMA BUTTERFLY (Puccini)

Conductor .... Martin

Butterfly .... Gonzalez
Suzuki .... Nadell
Kate Pinkerton .... MacNeil
Pinkerton .... Binci
Sharpless .... Tyers
Goro .... Sprinzena
Yamadori .... Newman
The Bonze .... Scott
Imperial
Commissioner .... Dunning

March 27

THE MARRIAGE OF FIGARO
(Mozart)
(English version by
Ruth and Thomas P. Martin)

Conductor ...... Rosenstock

Almaviva .... Cassel
Countess .... Yeend
Figaro .... Pease
Susanna .... Haskins
Cherubino .... Bible
Bartolo .... Wentworth
Marcellina .... O'Malley
Basilio .... Vellucci
Curzio .... Sprinzena
Antonio .... Newman
Barbarina .... MacNeill
Peasant girls .... White, Shor

March 31

TROUBLED ISLAND (Still)
World premiere

Staged by .... Bryden
Designer .... Condell
Choreographer ... Balanchine
Special Haitian dances choreo-
graphed by .... Destiné (d)

Conductor .... Halasz

Celeste .... O'Malley
Popo .... Sprinzena
Azelia .... Powers
Dessalines .... Weede
Martel .... Natzka
Vuval .... Charles (d)
Stenio .... Newman
Popaloi ...... McFerrin (d)
Mamaloi .... Stewart (d)
Claire .... Bliss (d)
1st Servant .... MacNeil
2nd Servant .... Bible
3rd Servant .... Nadell
The Steward .... Dunning
The Chamberlain ..Wentworth
Messenger .... Stanz
Fisherman .... Dunning
Mango vendor .... Bible
Melon vendor .... LeSawyer

April 1

LA BOHÈME (Puccini)

Conductor ...... Rosenstock

Mimi .... Gonzalez
Musetta .... MacNeil
Rodolfo .... Petrak
Marcello .... Rothmueller
Schaunard .... Dunning
Colline .... Scott
Benoit .... Wentworth
Alcindoro .... Newman
Parpignol .... Vellucci

April 2

CAVALLERIA RUSTICANA
(Mascagni)

Conductor .... Rudel

Santuzza ...... Zambrana (d)
Turiddu .... Binci
Alfio .... Herbert

Lola .... Nadell
Mamma Lucia ..... O'Malley

Followed by:

I PAGLIACCI (Leoncavallo)

Stage director .... Bryden
Conductor .... Rosenstock

Nedda .... Bliss
Canio .... Gari
Tonio .... Herbert
Silvio .... Young
Beppe .... Sprinzena

(Note: Norman Young, who
sang the part of Silvio, also
sang the "Prologue.")

April 3 (m)

AIDA

Same cast as March 24 except:

Conductor ...... Rosenstock,
(s, Halasz)

Amneris .... Masiello
Radames .... Leech (d)

April 3

DON GIOVANNI

Conductor .... Halasz

Don Giovanni .... Pease
Leporello .... Cordon
Donna Elvira .... Spence
Commendatore .... Scott
Donna Anna .... Faull
Don Ottavio .... Petrak
Masetto .... Dunning
Zerlina .... Haskins

April 6

LES CONTES D'HOFFMANN
(Offenbach)
First performance by The New
York City Opera Company

Staged by .... Sachse
Scenic Designer..Brodkin (d)
Choreographer ... Balanchine
Conductor .... Morel

Hoffmann .... Rounseville
Nicklausse .... Nadell
Lindorff .... Gauld
Luther .... Wentworth
Nathanaël .... Stanz
Hermann .... Newman
Andrès .... Vellucci
Olympia ...... MacWatters
Coppélius .... Gauld
Spalanzani .... Dunning
Cochenille .... Vellucci
Giulietta .... Spence
Dappertutto .... Cassel
Schlémil .... Dunning
Pittichinaccio ...... Vellucci
Antonia .... Ayars
Dr. Miracle .... Gauld
Crespel .... Scott
Mother .... Bible
Frantz .... Vellucci

April 7

THE OLD MAID AND THE THIEF
(Menotti)

Conductor .... Martin

Laetitia .... MacWatters
Miss Todd .... Powers
Miss Pinkerton .... Faull
Bob .... Young

Followed by:

THE MEDIUM (Menotti)
First performance by The New
York City Opera Company

Staged by .... Menotti
Conductor ...... Rosenstock

Monica .... Keller
Toby .... Coleman (d)
Madame Flora ...... Powers
Mrs. Gobineau..Scheunemann
Mr. Gobineau ..... Dunning
Mrs. Nolan .... Bible

April 8

CARMEN (Bizet)

Conductor .... Morel

Carmen .... Heidt
Don José .... Vroons (d)
Escamillo ...... Rothmueller
Micaëla .... Gonzalez
Zuniga .... Scott
Frasquita .... MacNeil
Mercédès .... Bible
Remendado .... Vellucci
Dancairo .... Dunning
Morales .... Newman
Solo dancers .. LeClercq, Bliss

April 9

MADAMA BUTTERFLY

Same cast as March 27 (m)
except:

Butterfly .... Williams

April 10 (m)

LA TRAVIATA

Same cast as March 25 except:

Alfredo .... Petrak

April 10

TROUBLED ISLAND

Same cast as March 31 except:

Dessalines .... Winters
Melon vendor ...... MacNeil

April 14

AIDA

Same cast as March 24 except:

Amneris .... Heidt
Aida .... Scheunemann
Radames .... Leech,
(s, Petrak)
Amonasro ...... Rothmueller

April 15

THE MARRIAGE OF FIGARO

Same cast as March 27 except:

Countess .... Faull
Figaro .... Herbert

April 16

LA BOHÈME

Same cast as April 1 except:

Mimi .... Ayars
Musetta .... Bliss
Schaunard .... Newman
Alcindoro .... Dunning

April 17 (m)

CARMEN

Same cast as April 8 except:

Don José .... Rounseville
Escamillo .... Pease
Micaëla .... Yeend

April 17

THE OLD MAID AND THE THIEF

Same cast as April 7 except:

Bob .... Tyers

Followed by:

THE MEDIUM

Same cast as April 7

April 20

LES CONTES D'HOFFMANN

Same cast as April 6 except:

Hoffmann .... Vroons
Nicklausse .... Bible
Lindorff .... Herbert
Coppélius .... Herbert
Giulietta .... Lewis,
                            (s, Spence)
Antonia .... Yeend
Dr. Miracle .... Herbert
Crespel .... Pease
Mother .... Nadell

April 21

MADAMA BUTTERFLY

Same cast as March 27 (m)
except:

Butterfly .... Williams
Suzuki .... O'Malley,
                            (s, Nadell)

April 22

TOSCA

Same cast as March 26 except:

Tosca .... Morris
Cavaradossi .... Binci
Scarpia .... Rothmueller
Sacristan .... Wentworth

April 23

DON GIOVANNI

Same cast as April 3 except:

Donna Elvira .... Lewis

April 24 (m)

CAVALLERIA RUSTICANA

Same cast as April 2 except:

Santuzza .... Canario
Turiddu .... Garen (d)
Alfio .... Gainey
Lola .... Bible

Followed by:

I PAGLIACCI

Same cast as April 2 except:
Nedda .... Keller
Tonio .... Young
Silvio .... Tyers

April 24

LA TRAVIATA

Same cast as March 25 except:

Conductor ..... Shaynen (d)

Violetta .... Ayars
Alfredo .... Petrak
Germont .... Cassel

April 27

THE MARRIAGE OF FIGARO

Same cast as March 27 except:

Countess ...... Scheunemann
Susanna .... MacWatters
Cherubino .... Nadell

Pinkerton .... Gari
Sharpless .... Herbert
Goro .... Vellucci
The Bonze .... Wentworth

Marcellina .... Bible
1st Peasant girl .... LeSawyer

April 28

LES CONTES D'HOFFMANN

Same cast as April 6 except:

Hoffmann ...... Rounseville
                            (Act I); Vroons
                            (Acts II-IV)
Olympia .... Haskins
Giulietta .... Lewis
Dappertutto .... Rothmueller

April 29

CARMEN

Same cast as April 8 except:

Carmen .... Masiello
Micaëla .... Ayars
Remendado .... Sprinzena

April 30

THE OLD MAID AND THE THIEF

Same cast as April 7 except:

Laetitia .... Bishop

Followed by:

THE MEDIUM

Same cast as April 7 except:

Monica .... MacNeil

May 1 (m)

AIDA

Same cast as March 24 except:

Conductor ...... Rosenstock

King .... Pease
Aida .... Canario
Radames ...... Bernauer (d)
Ramfis .... Scott

May 1

TROUBLED ISLAND

Same cast as March 31 except:

Conductor .... Rudel

Martel .... Wentworth
Stenio .... Powell (d)
Claire .... Piazza
2nd Servant .... Shor
Chamberlain .... Brandin

Fall 1949 (SEPTEMBER 29– NOVEMBER 20)

Female artists
Ayars, Ann
Bible, Frances
Bishop, Adelaide
Canario, Rosa
Carroll, Christina*
Cummings, Lucille*
Farnsworth, Lorraine*
Faull, Ellen
Gaston, Conchita*
Greene, Ethel*
Hammond, Joan*
Haskins, Virginia
Heidt, Winifred
Jessner, Irene*
Kreste, Mary
Lager, Frances*
Landia, Basil*
LeSawyer, Mary
Likova, Eva*
MacNeil, Dorothy
MacWatters, Virginia
Manners, Lucille
Mayer, Margery
Morris, Suzy
Nadell, Rosalind
Patton, Barbara*
Piazza, Marguerite
Powers, Marie
Reining, Maria*
Scheunemann, Leona
Shawn, Dorothy*
Warren, Louise*
White, Joyce
Williams, Camilla
Yeend, Frances
Zambrana, Margarita

Male artists
Alvary, Lorenzo*
Berini, Mario
Bonelli, Richard
Brandin, Walter
Cassel, Walter
Conley, Eugene
Dennis, Paul
Ducree, Leonard*
Dunning, Edwin
Farruggio, Matthew*
Gainey, Andrew
Gamboni, Frank*
Garen, David
Gari, Giulio
Gauld, Carlton
Greenwell, Gean
Jagel, Frederick
Johnston, Donald*
Jongeyans, George*
Leech, Lloyd Thomas
Natzka, Oscar
Newman, Arthur
Norville, Hubert
Pease, James
Petrak, Rudolf
Pollock, Michael*
Powell, Thomas
Primm, John*

* New artist

Rothmueller, Marko
Rounseville, Robert
Sprinzena, Nathaniel
Tyers, John
Vellucci, Luigi
Wentworth, Richard
Winston, Alan
Winters, Lawrence
Wright, Richard*
Young, Norman

Conductors
Halasz, Laszlo
Martin, Thomas P.
Morel, Jean
Rosenstock, Joseph
Rudel, Julius
Shaynen, Lee

Solo dancers
Bowers, Jamie*
Conde, Felisa*

Coleman, Leo
Vanoff, Nick*

Choreographer
Weidman, Charles*

Directors
Bryden, Eugene S.
Komisarjevsky, Theodore
Menotti, Gian Carlo
Rosing, Vladimir*
Sachse, Leopold
White, John S.

Designers
Brodkin, Herbert
Condell, H. A.
Dobujinsky, Mstislav*
Rychtarik, Richard

* New artist

September 29

ARIADNE AUF NAXOS
(R. Strauss)
(English Translation of the
prologue by Lewis Sydenham)

Conductor .... Halasz

Major-Domo ..... Greenwell
Music Master .... Pease
Composer .... Patton (d)
Tenor, Bacchus ..... Petrak
An Officer .... Farruggio (d)
Dancing Master .. Rounseville
Wigmaker .... Dunning
Lackey .... Newman
Zerbinetta ...... MacWatters
Prima Donna,
    Ariadne ...... Reining (d)
Harlequin .... Tyers
Scaramuccio .... Vellucci

Truffaldino .... Dennis
Brighella .... Sprinzena
Najade .... Ayars
Dryade .... Nadell
Echo .... MacNeil

(Note: Only the opera seria
portions were sung in German.
Lewis Sydenham provided the
English translation for the
"Prologue" and the harle-
quinade passages of the
opera proper.)

September 30

LES CONTES D'HOFFMANN
(Offenbach)

Choreographer .... Weidman
                          (d)
Conductor .... Morel

Hoffmann .... Rounseville
Nicklausse .... Nadell
Lindorff .... Gauld
Luther .... Wentworth
Nathanaël .... Sprinzena
Hermann .... Newman
Andrès .... Vellucci
Olympia .... MacWatters
Coppélius .... Gauld
Spalanzani .... Dunning
Cochenille .... Vellucci
Giulietta .... Morris
Dappertutto .... Cassel
Schlémil .... Dunning
Pittichinaccio ...... Vellucci
Antonia .... Yeend
Dr. Miracle .... Gauld
Crespel .... Pease
Mother .... Bible
Frantz .... Vellucci

October 1

MADAMA BUTTERFLY (Puccini)

Conductor .... Martin

Butterfly .... Williams
Suzuki .... Nadell
Kate Pinkerton ..... MacNeil
Pinkerton .... Gari
Sharpless .... Tyers
Goro .... Sprinzena
Yamadori .... Newman
The Bonze .... Jongeyans (d)
Imperial
    Commissioner .... Dunning

October 2 (m)

AIDA (Verdi)

Choreographer .... Weidman
Conductor .... Halasz

King .... Greenwell
Amneris .... Mayer
Aida .... Scheunemann
Radames .... Petrak

Ramfis .... Natzka
Amonasro .... Winters
Messenger .... Dunning
Priestess .... Bible
Dancers .... Bowers (d),
    Conde (d), Vanoff (d)

October 2

THE MARRIAGE OF FIGARO
(Mozart)
(English version by
Ruth and Thomas Martin)

Choreographer .... Weidman
Conductor ...... Rosenstock

Almaviva .... Cassel
Countess .... Yeend
Figaro .... Pease
Susanna .... Haskins
Cherubino .... Bible
Bartolo .... Wentworth
Marcellina .... Kreste
Basilio .... Vellucci
Curzio .... Vellucci
Antonio .... Newman
Barbarina .... MacNeil
Peasant girls .... White,
    Shawn (d)

October 6

DER ROSENKAVALIER
(R. Strauss)
First performance by The New
York City Opera Company

Staged by .... Sachse
Scenic designer ...... Condell
Conductor ...... Rosenstock

Marschallin .... Reining
Baron Ochs ...... Alvary (d)
Octavian .... Bible
Faninal .... Wentworth
Sophie .... Haskins
Marianne ..... Scheunemann
Annina .... Nadell
Valzacchi .... Vellucci
Police
   Commissioner .... Newman
Singer .... Petrak
Innkeeper .... Sprinzena
Major-Domo of
  the Marschallin .... Powell
Major-Domo of
  Faninal .... Wright (d)
Attorney .... Newman
1st Orphan ...... Landia (d)
2nd Orphan .... LeSawyer
3rd Orphan .. Farnsworth (d)
Animal vendor .. Pollock (d)
Milliner .... MacNeil
Leopold .... Winston

(Note: *Mohamet* added to
program November 15)

October 7

LA TRAVIATA (Verdi)

Choreographer .... Weidman
Conductor .... Shaynen

Violetta .... Likova (d)
Alfredo .... Conley
Germont .... Young
Flora .... MacNeil
Annina .... Kreste
Gaston .... Sprinzena
Douphol .... Wentworth
D'Obigny .... Dunning
Dr. Grenvil .... Newman
Dancers ..... Bowers, Conde,
    Vanoff

October 8

TOSCA (Puccini)

Conductor .... Morel

Tosca .... Morris
Cavaradossi .... Conley
Scarpia .... Cassel
Angelotti .... Pease
Spoletta .... Dunning
Sacristan .... Wentworth
Sciarrone .... Newman
Shepherd .... Bible
Jailer .... Brandin

October 9 (m)

CARMEN (Bizet)

Choreographer .... Weidman
Conductor .... Morel

Carmen .... Heidt
Don José .... Rounseville
Escamillo .... Pease
Micaëla .... Yeend
Zuniga .... Jongeyans
Frasquita .... MacNeil
Mercédès .... Bible
Remendado .... Sprinzena
Dancairo .... Dunning
Morales ..... Gamboni (d)
Dancers ...... Bowers, Conde,
    Vanoff

October 9

LA BOHÈME (Puccini)

Conductor .... Martin

Mimi .... Ayars
Musetta .... MacNeil
Rodolfo .... Petrak
Marcello .... Young
Schaunard .... Newman
Colline .... Natzka
Benoit .... Wentworth
Alcindoro .... Dunning
Parpignol .... Vellucci

October 13

DON GIOVANNI (Mozart)

Choreographer .... Weidman
Conductor .... Halasz

Don Giovanni .... Pease
Leporello .... Jongeyans
Donna Elvira ...... Piazza
Commendatore .... Greenwell
Donna Anna .... Faull
Don Ottavio .... Petrak
Masetto .... Dunning
Zerlina .... Haskins

October 14

DER ROSENKAVALIER

Same cast as October 6 except:

Marschallin ..... Jessner (d),
    (s, Reining)

October 15

THE OLD MAID AND THE THIEF
(Menotti)

Conductor .... Martin

Laetitia .... MacWatters
Miss Todd .... Powers
Miss Pinkerton .... Faull
Bob .... Young

Followed by:

THE MEDIUM (Menotti)

Conductor ...... Rosenstock

Monica .... MacNeil
Toby .... Coleman
Madame Flora ..... Powers
Mrs. Gobineau .. Scheunemann
Mr. Gobineau ...... Dunning
Mrs. Nolan .... Bible

October 16 (m)

CAVALLERIA RUSTICANA
(Mascagni)

Conductor .... Rudel

Santuzza .... Zambrana
Turiddu .... Gari
Alfio .... Gainey
Lola .... Nadell
Mamma Lucia .... Kreste

Followed by:

I PAGLIACCI (Leoncavallo)

Conductor ...... Rosenstock

Nedda .... Ayars
Canio .... Jagel
Tonio .... Winters
Silvio .... Young
Beppe .... Sprinzena

October 16

MADAMA BUTTERFLY

Same cast as October 1 except:

Butterfly ..... Hammond (d)
Suzuki .... Kreste
Pinkerton .... Conley
Goro .... Norville

October 19

LES CONTES D'HOFFMANN

Same cast as September 30
except:

Hoffmann .... Berini
Lindorff .... Winters
Coppélius .... Winters
Dappertutto .... Winters
Antonia .... Ayars
Dr Miracle .... Winters
Crespel .... Jongeyans

October 20

AIDA

Same cast as October 2 (m)
except:

Conductor ...... Rosenstock
Aida .... Hammond
Radames .... Leech

[Note: Additional dancer
added to program. . Keene (d)]

October 21

ARIADNE AUF NAXOS

Same cast as September 29
except:

Composer .... Manners
Prima Donna,
* Ariadne* .... Morris

October 22

THE MARRIAGE OF FIGARO

Same cast as October 2 except:

Countess .... Faull
Cherubino .... Nadell,
                    (s, Bible)
Curzio .... Sprinzena

October 23 (m)

LA TRAVIATA

Same cast as October 7 except:

Violetta .... Yeend

October 23

CARMEN

Same cast as October 9 (m)
except:

Carmen .... Gaston (d)
Don José .... Berini
Escamillo .... Pease,
                 (s, Rothmueller)
Micaëla .... Ayars
Mercédès .... Nadell,
                    (s, Bible)

(October 27—*The Love for
Three Oranges*—performance
postponed)

October 28

TOSCA

Same cast as October 8 except:

Tosca .... Hammond
Angelotti .... Jongeyans

October 29

DON GIOVANNI

Same cast as October 13
except:

Donna Elvira .... Likova
Zerlina .... Ayars

October 30 (m)

LA BOHÈME

Same cast as October 9 except:

Mimi .... Yeend
Musetta .... Bishop
Rodolfo .... Conley

October 30

DER ROSENKAVALIER

Same cast as October 6 except:

Marschallin ... Scheunemann,
                    (s, Reining)
Faninal .... Rothmueller
Sophie .... Carroll (d)
Marianne .... Faull,
                (s, Scheunemann)
Singer .... Gari
1st Orphan .... White

November 1

THE LOVE FOR THREE ORANGES
(Prokofiev)
First performance by The New
York City Opera Company
(English translation by Victor
Seroff; spoken prologue by
Komisarjevsky after
Carlo Gozzi)
Production devised by
Komisarjevsky

Staged by .... Rosing (d)
Designer .... Dobujinsky (d)
Masks executed by Yugi Ito
and Michael Arshansky
Choreographer .... Weidman
Conductor .... Halasz

King .... Greenwell
Prince .... Rounseville
Princess Clarissa ..... Mayer
Leandro .... Gauld
Pantalone .... Tyers
Truffaldino .... Vellucci
Celio .... Winters
Fata Morgana .... Faull
Princess Linetta ... Lager (d)
Princess Nicoletta .... Shawn
Princess Ninetta .... Haskins
Cook .... Wentworth
Farfarello .... Vanoff
Smeraldina .... Nadell
Prologue .... Primm (d)

(Note: Vladimir Rosing took
over the stage direction when
Theodore Komisarjevsky
became ill two weeks before
the first performance, orginally
scheduled for October 27,
1949. Many of the costumes
used for the original 1921
Chicago production were
discovered in a warehouse. The
New York City Opera used
many of them for lesser
characters in this 1949
production.)

November 2

THE LOVE FOR THREE ORANGES

Same cast as November 1

November 3

DER ROSENKAVALIER

Same cast as October 6 except:

Marschallin ... Scheunemann,
                    (s, Reining)
Faninal .... Rothmueller
Sophie .... Bishop
Singer .... Gari
Marianne .... Faull,
                (s, Scheunemann)
1st Orphan .... White
2nd Orphan .... Shawn

November 4

LA TRAVIATA

Same cast as October 7 except:

Alfredo .... Petrak
Germont .... Bonelli
Annina .... Shawn
Gaston .... Vellucci

November 5

THE OLD MAID AND THE THIEF

Same cast as October 15
except:

Laetitia .... Bishop
Bob .... Tyers

Followed by:

THE MEDIUM

Same cast as October 15
except:

Monica .... Ayars

November 6 (m)

MADAMA BUTTERFLY

Same cast as October 1 except:

Suzuki .... Kreste
Pinkerton .... Conley
Sharpless ..... Johnston (d),
                    (s, Young)

November 6

CAVALLERIA RUSTICANA

Same cast as October 16 (m)
except:

Santuzza .... Canario
Turiddu .... Garen
Alfio .... Rothmueller

Followed by:

I PAGLIACCI

Same cast as October 16 (m)
except:

Nedda .... Landia
Canio .... Gari
Tonio .... Bonelli
Silvio .... Gamboni

November 9

DER ROSENKAVALIER

Same cast as October 6 except:

Marschallin ... Scheunemann,
                    (s, Reining)
Baron Ochs .... Pease

Marianne .... Faull	**November 13**	*Commendatore* ...... Natzka
Annina .... Gaston	Tosca	*Donna Anna* .... Canario
1st Orphan .... White		*Don Ottavio* .... Conley
2nd Orphan .... Shawn	Same cast as October 8 except:	

November 10

CARMEN

Same cast as October 9 (m)
except:

Carmen .... Nadell,
(s, Heidt)
Don José .... Gari
Escamillo .... Winters
Micaëla .... MacNeil
Frasquita .... White
Remendado .... Vellucci
Morales .... Newman

November 11

AIDA

Same cast as October 2 (m)
except:

Conductor .... Martin

Amneris ..... Cummings (d)
Aida .... Canario
Ramfis .... Jongeyans
Amonasro ...... Rothmueller

November 12

LA BOHÈME

Same cast as October 9 except:

Mimi .... Williams
Rodolfo .... Gari
Marcello .... Rothmueller
Parpignol .... Sprinzena

November 13 (m)

THE MARRIAGE OF FIGARO

Same cast as October 2 except:

Almaviva .... Young
Countess ...... Scheunemann
Susanna .... MacWatters
Cherubino .... Nadell
Marcellina ..... Warren (d)
Curzio .... Sprinzena

Cavaradossi .... Petrak
Scarpia .... Bonelli
Angelotti .... Jongeyans

November 15

DER ROSENKAVALIER

Same cast as October 6 except:

Singer .... Gari
1st Orphan .... White
2nd Orphan .... Shawn
3rd Orphan ..... Greene (d)

Added to this program:
Mohamet .... Ducree (d)

November 16

LES CONTES D'HOFFMANN

Same cast as September 30
except:

Olympia .... Bishop
Giulietta .... Likova
Dappertutto .... Young
Antonia .... Ayars
Crespel .... Jongeyans

November 17

THE LOVE FOR THREE ORANGES

Same cast as November 1
except:

Princess Clarissa .... Bible
Pantalone .... Dunning
Celio .... Pease
Fata Morgana ..Scheunemann

November 18

DON GIOVANNI

Same cast as October 13
except:

Leporello .... Wentworth
Donna Elvira .... Likova,
(s, Piazza)

November 19 (m)

THE LOVE FOR THREE ORANGES

Same cast as November 1
except:

Princess Clarissa ..... Bible
Leandro .... Jongeyans
Celio .... Pease

November 19

LA TRAVIATA

Same cast as October 7 except:

Violetta .... Ayars
Alfredo .... Petrak
Germont .... Bonelli

November 20 (m)

CARMEN

Same cast as October 9 (m)
except:

Carmen .... Gaston,
(s, Heidt)
Don José .... Gari
Escamillo .... Cassel
Micaëla .... MacNeil
Frasquita .... White
Dancairo .... Wentworth
Morales .... Newman

November 20

MADAMA BUTTERFLY

Same cast as October 1 except:

Conductor .... Rudel

Butterfly .... Zambrana
Pinkerton .... Petrak
Sharpless .... Dunning
Goro .... Vellucci
*Imperial
Commissioner* .... Newman

Spring 1950 (MARCH 24–APRIL 30)

Female artists	LeSawyer, Mary	White, Joyce
Aldaba, Dalisay	Likova, Eva	Williams, Camilla
Ayars, Ann	MacNeil, Dorothy	Yeend, Frances
Bible, Frances	MacWatters, Virginia	
Bishop, Adelaide	Martinis, Carla*	**Male artists**
Canario, Rosa	Mayer, Margery	Alvary, Lorenzo
Farnsworth, Lorraine	Morris, Suzy	Bardelli, Cesare*
Faull, Ellen	Nadell, Rosalind	Brandin, Walter
Gari, Madeleine*	Petina, Irra	Cassel, Walter
Greene, Ethel	Scheunemann, Leona	Conley, Eugene
Haskins, Virginia	Shawn, Dorothy	Drake, Martin*
Heidt, Winifred	Spence, Wilma	Ducree, Leonard
Kreste, Mary	Turcano, Lucia*	Dunning, Edwin
Lager, Frances	Warren, Louise	Fredericks, Walter*
		Gainey, Andrew

* New artist	* New artist	* New artist

Garen, David
Gari, Giulio
Gauld, Carlton
Greenwell, Gean
Herbert, Ralph
Jongeyans, George
Leech, Lloyd Thomas
Ligeti, Desire
Newman, Arthur
Pease, James
Petrak, Rudolf
Pollock, Michael
Powell, Thomas
Primm, John
Rogers, Emmett*
Rounseville, Robert
Sprinzena, Nathaniel
Stanz, William
Tyers, John
Vellucci, Luigi
Vroons, Frans
Wentworth, Richard
Winston, Alan
Winters, Lawrence
Wright, Richard

Conductors
Halasz, Laszlo
Martin, Thomas P.
Morel, Jean
Rosenstock, Joseph
Rudel, Julius
Shaynen, Lee

Dancer
Vanoff, Nick

Choreographer
Weidman, Charles

Directors
Bryden, Eugene S.
Rosing, Vladimir
Sachse, Leopold
White, John S.

Designers
Brodkin, Herbert
Condell, H. A.
Dobujinsky, Mstislav
Rychtarik, Richard

* New artist

March 24

THE LOVE FOR THREE ORANGES
(Prokofiev)
(English translation by Victor
Seroff; spoken prologue by
John Primm after Carlo Gozzi)

Conductor .... Halasz

King .... Greenwell
Prince .... Rounseville
Princess Clarissa ...... Mayer
Leandro .... Gauld
Pantalone .... Tyers
Truffaldino .... Vellucci
Celio .... Winters
Fata Morgana ..Scheunemann
Princess Linetta ...... Lager
Princess Nicoletta .... Shawn
Princess Ninetta .... Haskins
Cook .... Wentworth
Farfarello .... Vanoff

Smeraldina .... Nadell
Prologue .... Primm

March 25

LA BOHÈME (Puccini)

Conductor .... Martin

Mimi .... Yeend
Musetta .... MacNeil
Rodolfo .... G. Gari
Marcello .... Bardelli (d)
Schaunard .... Newman
Colline .... Jongeyans
Benoit .... Wentworth
Alcindoro .... Dunning
Parpignol .... Sprinzena

March 26 (m)

THE MARRIAGE OF FIGARO
(Mozart)
(English version by
Ruth and Thomas Martin)

Conductor ...... Rosenstock

Almaviva .... Gainey
Countess .... Faull
Figaro .... Pease
Susanna .... Haskins
Cherubino .... Bible
Bartolo .... Wentworth
Marcellina .... Kreste
Basilio .... Vellucci
Curzio .... Sprinzena
Antonio .... Newman
Barbarina .... MacNeil
Peasant
girls .... LeSawyer, Shawn

March 26

LA TRAVIATA (Verdi)

Staged by .... Rosing
Conductor .... Shaynen

Violetta .... Ayars
Alfredo .... Petrak
Germont .... Cassel
Flora .... MacNeil
Annina .... Kreste
Gaston .... Vellucci
Douphol .... Wentworth
D'Obigny .... Dunning
Dr. Grenvil .... Newman

(Note: The sets for the final
three acts were acquired for
this 1950 spring season through
an exchange of scenery with
the American Opera Company
of Philadelphia. The first act
set employed a backdrop from
the New York City Opera
production of Eugene Onegin.)

March 30

LES CONTES D'HOFFMANN
(Offenbach)

Conductor .... Morel

Hoffmann .... Rounseville
Nicklausse .... Nadell
Lindorff .... Gauld

Luther .... Wentworth
Nathanaël .... Stanz
Hermann .... Newman
Andrès .... Vellucci
Olympia .... MacWatters
Coppélius .... Gauld
Spalanzani .... Dunning
Cochenille .... Vellucci
Giulietta .... Likova
Dappertutto .... Cassel
Schlémil .... Dunning
Pittichinaccio ...... Vellucci
Antonia .... Yeend
Dr. Miracle .... Gauld
Crespel .... Jongeyans
Mother .... Bible
Frantz .... Vellucci

March 31

MADAMA BUTTERFLY (Puccini)

Conductor .... Martin

Butterfly .... Aldaba,
(s, Williams)
Suzuki .... Kreste
Kate Pinkerton ..... MacNeil
Pinkerton .... G. Gari
Sharpless .... Tyers
Goro .... Sprinzena
Yamadori .... Newman
The Bonze .... Jongeyans
Imperial
Commissioner .... Dunning

(Both Camilla Williams and
her "cover," Margarita
Zambrana, were indisposed.
Dalisay Aldaba, who had sung
the role of Butterfly the night
before in Philadelphia,
happened to be in New York
and agreed to take over the
title role.)

April 1

TOSCA (Puccini)

Conductor .... Morel

Tosca .... Spence
Cavaradossi .... Conley
Scarpia .... Cassel
Angelotti .... Jongeyans
Spoletta .... Dunning
Sacristan .... Wentworth
Sciarrone .... Newman
Shepherd .... Bible
Jailer .... Brandin

April 2 (m)

CAVALLERIA RUSTICANA
(Mascagni)

Conductor .... Rudel

Santuzza .... Canario,
(s, Zambrana)
Turiddu .... Garen
Alfio .... Gainey
Lola .... Nadell
Mamma Lucia .... Kreste

Followed by:

I PAGLIACCI (Leoncavallo)

Stage director .... White
Conductor ...... Rosenstock

Nedda .... Likova
Canio .... Fredericks (d),
(s, G. Gari)
Tonio .... Winters
Silvio .... Tyers
Beppe .... Sprinzena

April 2

THE LOVE FOR THREE ORANGES

Same cast as March 24 except:

Prince .... Leech,
(s, Rounseville)
Pantalone .... Dunning
Celio .... Pease
Fata Morgana .... Faull

April 6

TURANDOT (Puccini)
First performance by The New
York City Opera Company

Staged by .... Rosing
Designer .... Condell
Masks by .... Arshansky
Choreographer .... Weidman
Conductor .... Halasz

Turandot ...... Martinis (d)
Liù .... MacNeil
Timur .... Wentworth
Calaf .... G. Gari
Ping .... Winters
Pang .... Vellucci
Pong .... Sprinzena
Emperor .... Dunning
Mandarin .... Newman

April 7

DER ROSENKAVALIER
(R. Strauss)

Conductor ...... Rosenstock

Marschallin ... Scheunemann
Baron Ochs .... Alvary
Octavian .... Bible
Faninal .... Wentworth
Sophie .... Bishop
Marianne .... Faull
Valzacchi .... Vellucci
Annina .... Nadell
Police
Commissioner .... Newman
Singer .... Garen,
(s, G. Gari)
Innkeeper .... Sprinzena
Major-domo of
the Marschallin ..... Stanz
Major-domo of
Faninal .... Wright
Attorney .... Newman
1st Orphan .... White
2nd Orphan .... LeSawyer
3rd Orphan .... Farnsworth
Animal vendor ...... Pollock
Milliner .... MacNeil
Leopold .... Winston

(Note: *Mohamet* added to
program April 16)

April 8

LA TRAVIATA

Same cast as March 26 except:

Violetta .... Yeend
Alfredo .... Drake (d)
Germont .... Bardelli

April 9 (m)

CARMEN (Bizet)

Conductor .... Morel

Carmen .... Heidt
Don José .... Vroons
Escamillo .... Bardelli
Micaëla .... MacNeil
Zuniga .... Greenwell
Frasquita .... White
Mercédès ...... M. Gari (d),
(s, Bible)
Remendado .... Sprinzena
Dancairo .... Dunning
Morales .... Gainey

April 9

DON GIOVANNI (Mozart)

Stage director .... White
Conductor .... Halasz

Don Giovanni ...... Cassel
Leporello .... Jongeyans
Donna Elvira .... Likova
Commendatore .... Ligeti
Donna Anna .... Faull
Don Ottavio .... Petrak
Masetto .... Dunning
Zerlina .... Haskins

April 12

TURANDOT

Same cast as April 6 except:

Turandot ...... Turcano (d)
Timur .... Ligeti

April 13

THE MARRIAGE OF FIGARO

Same cast as March 26 (m)
except:

Almaviva .... Cassel
Susanna .... MacWatters

April 14

LA BOHÈME

Same cast as March 25 except:

Mimi .... Ayars
Rodolfo .... Conley
Marcello .... Tyers

April 15 (m)

THE LOVE FOR THREE ORANGES

Same cast as March 24 except:

Conductor .... Rudel

Princess Clarissa ...... Bible
Leandro .... Jongeyans

Pantalone .... Dunning
Celio .... Pease

April 15

TOSCA

Same cast as April 1 except:

Tosca .... Morris
Cavaradossi .... Petrak
Scarpia .... Bardelli
Shepherd .... Shawn

April 16 (m)

MADAMA BUTTERFLY

Same cast as March 31 except:

Butterfly .... Williams,
(s, Zambrana)
Suzuki .... Nadell
Pinkerton .... Conley
Imperial
Commissioner .... Newman

April 16

DER ROSENKAVALIER

Same cast as April 7 except:

Marschallin .... Faull
Baron Ochs .... Pease
Marianne ..... Scheunemann
Singer .... Petrak

Added to this program:

Mohamet .... Ducree

April 18

TURANDOT

Same cast as April 6 except:

Liù .... Likova
Timur .... Ligeti

April 19

THE LOVE FOR THREE ORANGES

Same cast as March 24 except:

Prince .... Leech
Princess Clarissa ...... Bible
Leandro .... Jongeyans
Fata Morgana .... Faull

April 20

TURANDOT

Same cast as April 6 except:

Turandot .... Turcano
Calaf .... Fredericks

April 21

CARMEN

Same cast as April 9 (m)
except:

Conductor ...... Rosenstock

Escamillo .... Pease
Micaëla .... Likova
Zuniga .... Jongeyans

Frasquita .... MacNeil
Mercédès .... Bible
Morales .... Newman

April 22 (m)

THE LOVE FOR THREE ORANGES

Same cast as March 24 except:

Conductor .... Rudel
Prince .... Leech
Princess Clarissa ...... Bible,
(s, Mayer)
Leandro .... Jongeyans,
(s, Gauld)
Pantalone .... Dunning
Celio .... Pease
Fata Morgana .... Faull
Prologue .... Rogers (d),
(s, Primm)

April 22

CAVALLERIA RUSTICANA

Same cast as April 2 (m)
except:

Santuzza .... Turcano
Turiddu .... G. Gari
Alfio .... Herbert,
(s, Gainey)

Followed by:

I PAGLIACCI

Same cast as April 2 (m)
except:

Nedda .... Ayars
Silvio .... Tyers,
(s, Gainey)

April 23 (m)

LA TRAVIATA

Same cast as March 26 except:

Violetta .... Likova

April 23

LES CONTES D'HOFFMANN

Same cast as March 30 except:

Hoffmann .... Vroons
Lindorff .... Winters
Olympia .... Bishop
Coppélius .... Winters
Giulietta .... Spence
Dr. Miracle .... Winters

April 25

TURANDOT

Same cast as April 6 except:

Conductor .... Rudel
Ping .... Dunning
Emperor .... Powell

April 26

DER ROSENKAVALIER

Same cast as April 7 except:

Baron Ochs ...... Greenwell
Sophie .... Haskins
Singer .... Petrak
3rd Orphan .... Greene

April 27

DON GIOVANNI

Same cast as April 9 except:

Don Giovanni .... Pease
Don Ottavio .... Conley
Zerlina .... Haskins,
(s, MacNeil)

April 28

MADAMA BUTTERFLY

Same cast as March 31 except:

Butterfly .... Williams
Sharpless .... Dunning
Imperial
Commissoner .... Newman

April 29 (m)

THE LOVE FOR THREE ORANGES
(Spoken prologue written by
David Thornton)

Same cast as March 24 except:

Conductor .... Rudel
Prince .... Leech
Pantalone .... Dunning
Celio .... Pease
Prologue .... Rogers

April 29

LA BOHÈME

Same cast as March 25 except:

Mimi .... Ayars
Musetta .... Likova
Rodolfo .... Petrak
Marcello .... Dunning
Colline .... Ligeti
Alcindoro .... Wentworth

April 30 (m)

CARMEN

Same cast as April 9 (m)
except:

Carmen .... Petina
Don José .... Rounseville
Escamillo .... Pease
Mercédès .... Bible
Morales .... Newman

April 30

THE MARRIAGE OF FIGARO

Same cast as March 26 (m)
except:

Almaviva .... Cassel
Countess .... Yeend
Figaro .... Jongeyans
Susanna .... MacWatters
Cherubino .... Nadell
Marcellina .... Warren
2nd Peasant girl ..... Greene

Fall 1950 (SEPTEMBER 21– NOVEMBER 12)

Female artists
Aldaba, Dalisay
Ayars, Ann
Bampton, Rose*
Bible, Frances
Bishop, Adelaide
Doree, Doris
Evans, Edith*
Falcon, Bruni*
Farnsworth, Lorraine
Faull, Ellen
Greene, Ethel
Kreste, Mary
Lager, Frances

* New artist

LeSawyer, Mary
Likova, Eva
MacNeil, Dorothy
MacWatters, Virginia
Malbin, Elaine*
Martinis, Carla
Mayer, Margery
Nadell, Rosalind
Petina, Irra
Resnik, Regina
Scheunemann, Leona
Shawn, Dorothy
Spector, Gladys*
Spence, Wilma

* New artist

Taussig, Carroll
Turcano, Lucia
Wermine, Bette*
White, Joyce
Williams, Camilla
Yeend, Frances
Zambrana, Margarita

Male artists
Argyris, Vasso
Arié, Raffaele*
Bandera, Fernando*
Bardelli, Cesare

* New artist

Beirer, Hans*
Cassel, Walter
Cosman, Ian
Crockett, Sumner*
De Decker, Edward*
Dill, John*
Druary, John*
Ducree, Leonard
Dunning, Edwin
Gari, Giulio
Gauld, Carlton
Jongeyans, George
Laderoute, Joseph
Leech, Lloyd Thomas
Lloyd, David*
Luciano, Nino*
Miller, Niels*
Morris, Robert*
Natzka, Oscar
Newman, Arthur
Pease, James
Petrak, Rudolf
Pichardo, Luis*
Pollock, Michael
Powell, Thomas
Renan, Emile
Rounseville, Robert
Scarfeo, Russel*
Schon, Kenneth*
Scott, Norman
Sprinzena, Nathaniel
Stanz, William
Torres, Raimundo*
Tyers, John
Vellucci, Luigi
Wentworth, Richard
Winters, Lawrence
Wright, Richard

Conductors
Halasz, Laszlo
Martin, Thomas P.
Morel, Jean
Rosenstock, Joseph
Rudel, Julius
Shaynen, Lee

Dancers
Bowers, Jamie
Caputo, Paula*
Conde, Felisa
Gerard, Saida*
Lee, Betts*

Decker, Jerry*
Lemmon, Frank*
Murray, Lee
Smith, James*

Choreographer
Weidman, Charles

Directors
Bryden, Eugene S.
Erhardt, Otto*
Rosing, Vladimir
Sachse, Leopold
White, John S.

**Artistic counsellor—
German wing**
Schorr, Friedrich*

Designers
Brodkin, Herbert
Condell, H. A.
Dobujinsky, Mstislav
Rychtarik, Richard

    * New artist

September 21

TURANDOT (Puccini)

Lighting .... Rosenthal
Conductor .... Halasz

Turandot .... Martinis
Liù .... MacNeil
Timur .... Arié (d)
Calaf .... Gari
Ping .... Winters
Pang .... Vellucci
Pong .... Sprinzena
Emperor .... Dunning
Mandarin .... Newman

September 22

MADAMA BUTTERFLY (Puccini)

Conductor .... Martin

Butterfly .... Williams
Suzuki .... Kreste
Kate Pinkerton ..... MacNeil
Pinkerton .... Petrak
Sharpless .... Tyers
Goro .... Sprinzena
Yamadori .... Renan
The Bonze ..... Wentworth
Imperial
  Commissioner .... Dunning

September 23

DER ROSENKAVALIER
(R. Strauss)

Conductor ...... Rosenstock

Marschallin .... Bampton (d)
Baron Ochs .... Pease
Octavian .... Bible
Faninal .... Wentworth
Sophie .... Bishop
Marianne ..... Scheunemann
Valzacchi .... Vellucci
Annina .... Nadell
Police
  Commissioner .... Newman
Singer .... Petrak
Innkeeper .... Sprinzena
Major-Domo of
  the Marschallin ..... Stanz
Major-Domo of
  Faninal .... Wright
Attorney .... Newman
1st Orphan .... White
2nd Orphan ...... LeSawyer
3rd Orphan .... Taussig
Animal vendor ...... Pollock
Milliner .... MacNeil
Mohamet .... Ducree

September 24 (m)

LA TRAVIATA (Verdi)

Conductor .... Shaynen

Violetta .... Likova
Alfredo .... Bandera (d)
Germont .... Torres (d)
Flora .... MacNeil
Annina .... Kreste
Gaston .... Sprinzena
Douphol .... Wentworth
D'Obigny .... Renan
Dr. Grenvil .... Newman

September 24

LES CONTES D'HOFFMANN
(Offenbach)

Conductor .... Morel

Hoffmann .... Rounseville
Nicklausse .... Nadell
Lindorff .... Gauld
Luther .... Wentworth
Nathanaël .... Stanz
Hermann .... Newman
Andrès .... Vellucci
Olympia .... MacWatters
Coppélius .... Gauld
Spalanzani .... Dunning
Cochenille .... Vellucci
Giulietta .... Spence
Dappertutto .... Cassel
Schlémil .... Dunning
Pittichinaccio ...... Vellucci
Antonia .... Yeend
Dr. Miracle .... Gauld
Crespel .... Scott
Mother .... Bible
Frantz .... Vellucci

September 28

THE LOVE FOR THREE ORANGES
(Prokofiev)
(English translation by
Victor Seroff; spoken prologue
by David Thornton)

Conductor .... Halasz

King .... Pease
Prince .... Rounseville
Princess Clarissa ...... Bible
Leandro .... Gauld
Pantalone .... Tyers
Truffaldino .... Vellucci
Celio .... Winters
Fata Morgana .... Faull
Princess Linetta ..... Lager
Princess Nicoletta .... Shawn
Princess Ninetta ..Malbin (d)
Cook .... Wentworth
Smeraldina .... Nadell
Prologue .... Miller (d)

September 29

FAUST (Gounod)
New production

Staged by .... Rosing
Designer .... Condell
Choreographer .... Weidman
Conductor .... Morel

Marguerite .... Yeend
Old Faust .... Gari
Young Faust .... Petrak
Méphistophélès .... Arié
Valentin .... Cassel
Siébel .... Bible
Marthe .... Kreste
Wagner .... Newman

(Note: Vladimir Rosing
introduced double casting for
the title role, i.e., one tenor for
the "Prologue" and another for
the balance of the opera. In
this revival Gounod's opera
was performed without the
standard cuts.)

September 30

CAVALLERIA RUSTICANA
(Mascagni)

Conductor .... Rudel

Santuzza .... Zambrana
Turiddu .... Luciano (d)
Alfio .... Wentworth
Lola .... Nadell
Mamma Lucia .... Kreste

Followed by:

I PAGLIACCI (Leoncavallo)

Conductor ...... Rosenstock

Nedda .... Ayars
Canio .... Gari
Tonio .... Winters
Silvio .... Tyers
Beppe .... Sprinzena

October 1 (m)

CARMEN (Bizet)

Conductor .... Morel

Carmen .... Resnik,
                (s, Heidt)
Don José .... Rounseville
Escamillo .... Torres
Micaëla .... MacNeil
Zuniga .... Scott
Frasquita .... Malbin
Mercédès .... Evans (d)
Remendado .... Sprinzena
Dancairo .... Renan
Morales .... Dunning

October 1

THE MARRIAGE OF FIGARO
(Mozart)
(English version by
Ruth and Thomas Martin)

Conductor ...... Rosenstock

Almaviva .... Cassel
Countess .... Yeend
Figaro .... Pease
Susanna .... Bishop
Cherubino .... Bible
Bartolo .... Wentworth
Marcellina .... Kreste
Basilio .... Vellucci
Curzio .... Sprinzena
Antonio .... Newman
Barbarina .... MacNeil

October 4

DON GIOVANNI (Mozart)

Conductor .... Halasz

Don Giovanni .... Torres
Leporello .... Jongeyans
Donna Elvira .... Likova
Commendatore .... Scott
Donna Anna .... Faull
Don Ottavio .... Petrak
Masetto .... Dunning
Zerlina .... Malbin

October 5

DER ROSENKAVALIER

Same cast as September 23
except:

Annina .... Evans
Police
Commissioner ..... Powell
Singer .... Gari
1st Orphan .... Malbin
2nd Orphan .... Shawn
3rd Orphan .... Greene

October 6

LA BOHÈME (Puccini)

Conductor .... Martin

Mimi .... Ayars
Musetta .... Likova
Rodolfo .... Bandera,
                (s, Petrak)
Marcello .... Torres
Schaunard .... Newman
Colline .... Scott
Benoit .... Wentworth
Alcindoro .... Dunning
Parpignol .... Vellucci

October 7

TURANDOT

Same cast as September 21
except:

Timur .... Wentworth
Calaf .... Druary (d),
                (s, Gari)

October 8 (m)

MADAMA BUTTERFLY

Same cast as September 22
except:

Suzuki .... Nadell
Kate Pinkerton .... White
Pinkerton .... Bandera

October 8

FAUST

Same cast as September 29
except:

Young Faust .... Gari,
                (s, Petrak)
Méphistophélès
Acts I - II..De Decker (d),
                (s, Arié)
Acts III - V .... Scott,
                (s, Arié)

(Note: Gari sang both Young
and Old Faust.)

October 13

DIE MEISTERSINGER (Wagner)
First performance by The New
York City Opera Company

Staged by ...... Erhardt (d)
Artistic
counsellor ..... Schorr (d)
Scenic designer ...... Condell

Lighting .... Rosenthal
Choreographer .... Weidman
Conductor ...... Rosenstock

Hans Sachs .... Pease
Pogner .... Natzka
Vogelgesang .... Luciano
Nachtigall .... Newman
Beckmesser .... Renan
Kothner .... Wentworth
Zorn .... Crockett (d)
Eisslinger .... Vellucci
Moser .... Sprinzena
Ortel .... Powell
Schwarz .... Pichardo (d)
Foltz .... Jongeyans
Walther .... Beirer (d)
David .... Lloyd (d)
Eva .... Yeend
Magdalene .... Mayer
Night
Watchman .... Winters

(Note: The costumes, designed
for a 1938 Chicago production
of *Die Meistersinger*, were
loaned by the Chicago Civic
Opera. James Pease's costumes,
however, were loaned by
Friedrich Schorr.)

October 14 (m)

THE LOVE FOR THREE ORANGES

Same cast as September 28
except:

Conductor .... Rudel,
                (s, Halasz)
King .... Scott,
                (s, Pease)
Leandro .... Jongeyans
Pantalone .... Dunning

October 14

CARMEN

Same cast as October 1 (m)
except:

Carmen .... Petina
Don José .... Gari
Escamillo .... Bardelli
Frasquita .... White

October 15 (m)

THE MARRIAGE OF FIGARO

Same cast as October 1 except:

Countess ...... Scheunemann
Susanna .... MacWatters
Barbarina .... Malbin

October 15

LA TRAVIATA

Same cast as September 24
(m) except:

Violetta .... Yeend
Gaston .... Vellucci
D'Obigny .... Dunning

October 17

DIE MEISTERSINGER

Same cast as October 13
except:

Eva .... Faull

October 18

TURANDOT

Same cast as September 21
except:

Turandot .... Turcano
Liù .... Likova,
          (s, MacNeil)
Calaf .... Druary
Ping .... Dunning
Emperor .... Powell

October 19

AIDA (Verdi)

Stage director .... White
Conductor .... Halasz

King .... Pease
Amneris .... Wermine (d)
Aida .... Martinis
Radames .... Beirer
Ramfis .... Natzka
Amonasro .... Winters
Messenger .... Dunning
Priestess .... Spector (d)
Dancers .... Bowers, Caputo
          (d), Conde, Gerard (d),
          Lee (d); Decker (d),
          Lemmon (d), Murray,
                    Smith (d)

October 20

LES CONTES D'HOFFMANN

Same cast as September 24
except:

Antonia .... Ayars

October 21 (m)

FAUST

Same cast as September 29
except:

Marguerite .... Likova
Méphistophélès .... Scott
Valentin .... Torres
Siébel .... Nadell

October 21

LA BOHÈME

Same cast as October 6 except:

Mimi .... Yeend
Musetta .... MacNeil
Marcello .... Bardelli
Colline .... Arié
Parpignol .... Sprinzena

October 22 (m)

CAVALLERIA RUSTICANA

Same cast as September 30
except:

Turiddu .... Druary

Followed by:

I PAGLIACCI

Same cast as September 30
except:

Silvio .... Cassel

(Note: Walter Cassel also
sang the "Prologue" at this
performance.)

October 22

DON GIOVANNI

Same cast as October 4 except:

Don Giovanni .... Pease
Leporello .... Arié
Don Ottavio ...... Laderoute

October 24

DIE MEISTERSINGER

Same cast as October 13
except:

Hans Sachs ...... Schon (d)
Pogner .... Scott
Beckmesser .... Dunning
Eva .... Faull,
          (s, Yeend)
Magdalene .... Kreste

October 25

THE LOVE FOR THREE ORANGES

Same cast as September 28
except:

Princess Clarissa ..... Mayer,
          (s, Bible)
Pantalone .... Dunning
Fata Morgana .. Scheunemann
Smeraldina .... Bible,
          (s, Nadell)

October 26

CARMEN

Same cast as October 1 (m)
except:

Carmen .... Petina
Don José .... Gari
Zuniga .... Jongeyans
Mercédès .... Bible
Morales .... Newman

October 27

LA TRAVIATA

Same cast as September 24
(m) except:

Violetta .... Ayars
Alfredo .... Petrak
Germont .... Bardelli
Flora .... LeSawyer
Gaston .... Vellucci
D'Obigny .... Dunning

October 28 (m)

MADAMA BUTTERFLY

Same cast as September 22
except:

Butterfly .... Aldaba,
          (s, Zambrana)
Suzuki .... Kreste,
          (s, Nadell)
Pinkerton .... Bandera
Sharpless .... Dunning
Imperial
   Commissioner .... Newman

October 28

THE MARRIAGE OF FIGARO

Same cast as October 1

October 29 (m)

AIDA

Same cast as October 19
except:

Conductor .... Martin

King .... Jongeyans
Amneris .... Mayer
Radames .... Beirer,
          (s, Gari)
Ramfis .... Arié
Messenger .... Cosman
Priestess .... Taussig

October 29

FAUST

Same cast as September 29
except:

Old Faust .... Petrak,
          (s, Gari)
Marguerite .... Likova
Méphistophélès ... De Decker
Valentin .... Torres
Siébel .... Nadell

(Note: Petrak sang both
Young and Old Faust.)

October 31

TURANDOT

Same cast as September 21
except:

Liù .... Malbin
Timur .... Scott
Ping .... Dunning
Emperor .... Powell

November 1

DER ROSENKAVALIER

Same cast as September 23
except:

Baron Ochs ...... De Decker
Sophie .... MacNeil
3rd Orphan ..... Farnsworth
Milliner .... Malbin
Mohamet .... Dill (d)

November 2

LA BOHÈME

Same cast as October 6 except:

Conductor .... Rudel,
(s, Halasz)
Rodolfo .... Petrak
Parpignol .... Sprinzena

November 3

CAVALLERIA RUSTICANA

Same cast as September 30 except:

Santuzza .... Doree,
(s, Turcano)
Turiddu .... Gari

Followed by:

I PAGLIACCI

Same cast as September 30 except:

Nedda .... Falcon (d)
Canio .... Argyris,
(s, Beirer)
Tonio .... Bardelli
Silvio .... Scarfeo (d)

November 4 (m)

THE LOVE FOR THREE ORANGES

Same cast as September 28 except:

Prince .... Lloyd
Pantalone .... Renan
Celio .... Newman
Fata Morgana ..Scheunemann

November 4

LES CONTES D'HOFFMANN

Same cast as September 24 except:

Lindorff .... Winters
Luther .... Powell
Coppélius .... Winters
Antonia .... Likova
Dr. Miracle .... Winters

November 5 (m)

MADAMA BUTTERFLY

Same cast as September 22 except:

Conductor .... Rudel
Pinkerton .... Bandera

November 5

DON GIOVANNI

Same cast as October 4 except:

Don Giovanni .... Pease

November 7

FAUST

Same cast as September 29 except:

Marguerite .... Ayars
Valentin .... Torres
Siébel .... Nadell

November 8

DIE MEISTERSINGER

Same cast as October 13 except:

Hans Sachs .... Pease,
(s, De Decker)
Hans Foltz ...... Morris (d)
Eva .... Spence
Magdalene .... Kreste

November 9

THE LOVE FOR THREE ORANGES

Same cast as September 28 except:

Celio .... Newman
Fata Morgana ..Scheunemann

November 10

AIDA

Same cast as October 19 except:

King .... Newman
Amneris .... Bible

Radames .... Leech,
(s, Gari)
Ramfis .... Scott

November 11 (m)

THE LOVE FOR THREE ORANGES

Same cast as September 28 except:

Conductor .... Rudel
Prince .... Lloyd
Princess Clarissa ..... Kreste
Pantalone .... Dunning
Celio .... Newman

November 11

LA TRAVIATA

Same cast as September 24 (m) except:

Germont .... Bardelli
Flora .... LeSawyer
Gaston .... Vellucci
D'Obigny .... Dunning

November 12 (m)

CARMEN

Same cast as October 1 (m) except:

Carmen .... Mayer,
(s, Resnik)
Don José .... Gari
Micaëla .... Malbin
Frasquita .... White
Morales .... Dunning

November 12

LA BOHÈME

Same cast as October 6 except:

Conductor .... Rudel
Musetta .... MacNeil
Rodolfo .... Petrak
Marcello .... Tyers
Colline .... Arié
Parpignol .... Sprinzena

Spring 1951 (MARCH 14–APRIL 22)

Female artists
Aldaba, Dalisay
Ayars, Ann
Bible, Frances
Bishop, Adelaide
Evans, Edith
Faull, Ellen
Giannini, Dusolina
Haskins, Virginia
Ibarrondo, Lydia*
Kreste, Mary
Lager, Frances
LeSawyer, Mary

Likova, Eva
MacNeil, Dorothy
MacWatters, Virginia
Malbin, Elaine
Mayer, Margery
Menzel, Greta*
Nadell, Rosalind
Nelli, Herva*
Russell, Shirley*
Shawn, Dorothy
Spence, Wilma
Sydney, Lorna*
Taussig, Carroll

White, Joyce
Williams, Camilla
Yeend, Frances

Male artists
Bandera, Fernando
Bardelli, Cesare
Bonelli, Richard
Cassel, Walter
Crockett, Alan Sumner
Druary, John
Fredericks, Walter
Gari, Giulio

* New artist

* New artist

* New artist

Gauld, Carlton
Herbert, Ralph
Jongeyans, George
Kaldenberg, Keith*
Kuestner, Charles*
Laderoute, Joseph
Leech, Lloyd Thomas
Lloyd, David
Luciano, Nino
Morris, Robert
Natzka, Oscar
Newman, Arthur
Norville, Hubert
Pease, James
Petrak, Rudolf
Pichardo, Luis
Poleri, David*
Pollock, Michael
Powell, Thomas
Primm, John
Renan, Emile
Richards, Donald
Rounseville, Robert
Scott, Norman
Sprinzena, Nathaniel
Stanz, William
Tyers, John
Vellucci, Luigi
Wentworth, Richard
Winters, Lawrence

Conductors
Halasz, Laszlo
Martin, Thomas P.
Morel, Jean
Rosenstock, Joseph
Rudel, Julius
Shaynen, Lee

Solo dancers†
Svetlova, Marina*

Muradoff, Grant*
Smith, James

Choreographers
Muradoff, Grant*
Weidman, Charles

Directors
Erhardt, Otto
Komisarjevsky, Theodore
Rosing, Vladimir
Ruben, José
Sachse, Leopold
White, John S.

**Artistic counsellor—
German wing**
Schorr, Friedrich

Designers
Brodkin, Herbert
Condell, H. A.
Dobujinsky, Mstislav
Morley, Ruth*

* New artist
† No other dancers listed on
programs for this season

March 14

DIE MEISTERSINGER (Wagner)

Conductor ...... Rosenstock

Hans Sachs .... Pease
Pogner .... Natzka

Vogelgesang .... Luciano
Nachtigall .... Newman
Beckmesser .... Renan
Kothner .... Wentworth
Zorn .... Crockett
Eisslinger .... Vellucci
Moser .... Sprinzena
Ortel .... Powell
Schwarz .... Pichardo
Foltz .... Jongeyans
Walther .... Petrak
David .... Lloyd
Eva .... Yeend
Magdalene .... Mayer
Night Watchman .... Winters

March 15

MADAMA BUTTERFLY (Puccini)

Conductor .... Martin

Butterfly .... Williams
Suzuki .... Kreste
Kate Pinkerton ..... MacNeil
Pinkerton .... Gari
Sharpless .... Tyers
Goro .... Norville
Yamadori .... Renan
The Bonze .... Wentworth
*Imperial
  Commissioner* .... Newman

March 16

LA TRAVIATA (Verdi)

Conductor .... Shaynen

Violetta .... Ayars
Alfredo .... Poleri (d)
Germont .... Bonelli
Flora .... MacNeil
Annina .... Kreste
Gaston .... Vellucci
Douphol .... Wentworth
D'Obigny .... Renan
Dr. Grenvil .... Newman

March 17 (m)

THE LOVE FOR THREE ORANGES
(Prokofiev)
(English translation by
Victor Seroff; spoken
prologue written by
Theodore Komisarjevsky)

Conductor .... Rudel

King .... Pease
Prince .... Lloyd
Princess Clarissa ..... Kreste
Leandro .... Gauld
Pantalone .... Renan
Truffaldino .... Vellucci
Celio .... Winters
Fata Morgana .... Faull
Princess Linetta ...... Evans
Princess Nicoletta ... Shawn
Princess Ninetta .... MacNeil
Cook .... Wentworth
Smeraldina .... Bible
Prologue .... Primm

(Note: *Farfarello* added to
program April 21 [m])

March 17

LA BOHÈME (Puccini)

Conductor .... Martin

Mimi .... Menzel (d)
Musetta .... Likova
Rodolfo .... Bandera
Marcello .... Herbert
Schaunard .... Newman
Colline .... Pichardo,
                 (s, Scott)
Benoit .... Wentworth
Alcindoro .... Renan
Parpignol .... Vellucci

March 18 (m)

CARMEN (Bizet)

Conductor .... Morel

Carmen ...... Ibarrondo (d)
Don José .... Rounseville
Escamillo .... Cassel
Micaëla .... Ayars
                (s, White)
Zuniga .... Jongeyans,
                (s, Scott)
Frasquita .... White,
                (s, MacNeil)
Mercédès .... Evans
Remendado .... Sprinzena
Dancairo .... Renan
Morales .... Newman

March 18

DON GIOVANNI (Mozart)

Choreographer..Muradoff (d)
Conductor .... Halasz

Don Giovanni .... Pease
Leporello .... Jongeyans
Donna Elvira .... Likova
Commendatore ...... Natzka
Donna Anna .... Faull
Don Ottavio .... Petrak
Masetto .... Renan
Zerlina .... Haskins
A Devil ...... Muradoff (d)

March 22

MANON (Massenet)
First performance by The New
York City Opera Company

Staged by .... Ruben
Scenic designer ...... Condell
*Costume
  designer* ...... Morley (d)
Choreographer .... Muradoff
Conductor .... Morel

Des Grieux .... Poleri
Count des Grieux ..... Gauld
Lescaut .... Herbert
Manon .... Ayars
Guillot .... Pollock
Pousette .... MacNeil
De Brétigny ...... Jongeyans
Rosette .... Evans
Javotte .... LeSawyer
Innkeeper .... Wentworth
Solo dancers ... Svetlova (d);
                 Muradoff

March 23

DIE MEISTERSINGER

Same cast as March 14 except:

Eisslinger ... Kaldenberg (d)
Foltz .... Morris
Walther .... Druary,
                    (s, Gari)
David .... Vellucci
Eva .... Faull
Magdalene .... Bible

March 24

FAUST (Gounod)

Conductor .... Morel

Marguerite .... Likova
Old Faust .... Bandera
Young Faust .... Petrak
Méphistophélès .... Scott
Valentin .... Cassel
Siébel .... Bible
Marthe .... Kreste
Wagner .... Newman

March 25 (m)

CAVALLERIA RUSTICANA
(Mascagni)

Conductor .... Rudel

Santuzza .... Ibarrondo
Turiddu .... Gari
Alfio .... Wentworth
Lola .... Evans
Mamma Lucia .... Kreste

Followed by:

I PAGLIACCI (Leoncavallo)

Conductor ...... Rosenstock

Nedda .... Ayars
Canio .... Gari,
                (s, Mazzieri)
Tonio .... Winters
Silvio .... Tyers
Beppe .... Sprinzena

(Note: Because of delays
involving the obtaining of a
visa, Italian tenor Giovanni
Mazzieri was not to debut
with the company.)

March 25

THE MARRIAGE OF FIGARO
(Mozart)
(English version by
Ruth and Thomas Martin)

Conductor ...... Rosenstock

Almaviva .... Cassel
Countess .... Faull
Figaro .... Pease
Susanna .... Haskins
Cherubino .... Bible
Bartolo .... Wentworth
Marcellina .... Kreste
Basilio .... Vellucci
Curzio .... Sprinzena
Antonio .... Newman
Barbarina .... MacNeil

March 28

MANON

Same cast as March 22 except:

Des Grieux .... Petrak
Lescaut .... Herbert,
                  (s, Pease)
Manon .... Likova
De Brétigny .... Tyers
Javotte .... Malbin

March 29

LES CONTES D'HOFFMANN
(Offenbach)

Conductor .... Morel

Hoffmann .... Rounseville
Nicklausse .... Bible
Lindorff .... Gauld
Luther .... Wentworth
Nathaniël .... Stanz
Hermann .... Newman
Andrès .... Vellucci
Olympia .... MacWatters
Coppélius .... Gauld
Spalanzani .... Norville
Cochenille .... Vellucci
Giulietta .... Spence
Dappertutto .... Cassel
Schlémil .... Renan
Pittichinaccio .... Vellucci
Antonia .... Ayars
Dr. Miracle .... Gauld
Crespel .... Scott
Mother .... Evans
Frantz .... Vellucci

March 30

DON GIOVANNI

Same cast as March 18 except:

Don Giovanni .... Cassel
Commendatore .... Scott
Don Ottavio ..... Laderoute
Zerlina .... Malbin

March 31 (m)

DIE MEISTERSINGER

Same cast as March 14 except:

Pogner .... Scott
Zorn .... Stanz
Foltz .... Morris
Eva .... Spence
Magdalene .... Bible

March 31

LA TRAVIATA

Same cast as March 16 except:

Violetta .... Bishop
Alfredo .... Bandera
Germont .... Bardelli
Flora .... Evans
Gaston .... Sprinzena

April 1 (m)

MADAMA BUTTERFLY

Same cast as March 15 except:

Sharpless .... Bonelli
Goro .... Sprinzena
The Bonze .... Winters

April 1

THE LOVE FOR THREE ORANGES

Same cast as March 17 (m)
except:

Conductor .... Halasz

Prince .... Rounseville
Princess Clarissa ...... Bible
Leandro .... Jongeyans
Pantalone .... Renan,
                  (s, Tyers)
Truffaldino .... Lloyd
Fata Morgana ... Sydney (d)
Princess Linetta ...... Lager
Princess Ninetta ..... Malbin
Smeraldina .... Evans

April 4

DIE MEISTERSINGER

Same cast as March 14 except:

Pogner .... Scott
Beckmesser .... Herbert
Zorn .... Stanz
Moser .... Kuestner (d)
Foltz .... Morris
David .... Sprinzena
Eva .... Spence
Magdalene .... Bible

April 6

AIDA (Verdi)

Choreographer .... Muradoff
Conductor .... Halasz

King .... Scott
Amneris .... Giannini
                 (Acts I - III);
                Ibarrondo (Act IV)
Aida .... Williams
Radames .... Gari
Ramfis .... Natzka
Amonasro .... Winters
Messenger .... Luciano
Priestess .... Bible,
                   (s, Evans)
Solo dancers ...... Svetlova;
                    Muradoff

April 7 (m)

CARMEN

Same cast as March 18 (m)
except:

Don José .... Poleri
Escamillo .... Bardelli
Micaëla .... Malbin

April 7

THE MARRIAGE OF FIGARO

Same cast as March 25 except:

Susanna .... Russell (d)

April 8 (m)

LA BOHÈME

Same cast as March 17 except:

Mimi .... Ayars
Musetta .... Malbin
Marcello .... Tyers

April 8

FAUST

Same cast as March 24 except:

Marguerite .... Yeend
Old Faust .... Gari

April 11

MANON

Same cast as March 22 except:

Count des Grieux ...... Scott
Lescaut .... Pease
De Brétigny ...... Jongeyans,
(s, Tyers)
Javotte .... Malbin

April 12

THE LOVE FOR THREE ORANGES

Same cast as March 17 (m) except:

King .... Scott
Prince .... Rounseville
Princess Clarissa ...... Bible
Fata Morgana .... Sydney
Princess Linetta ...... Lager
Princess Ninetta ..... Malbin
Smeraldina .... Evans

April 13

CAVALLERIA RUSTICANA

Same cast as March 25 (m) except:

Santuzza .... Nelli (d),
(s, Ibarrondo)

Followed by:

I PAGLIACCI

Same cast as March 25 (m) except:

Nedda .... Yeend
Canio .... Fredericks,
(s, Mazzieri)
Tonio .... Bardelli
Silvio .... Richards

April 14 (m)

MADAMA BUTTERFLY

Same cast as March 15 except:

Butterfly .... Aldaba
Suzuki .... Nadell,
(s, Kreste)

Kate Pinkerton .... Evans
Pinkerton .... Druary
Goro .... Vellucci
The Bonze .... Winters

April 14

DON GIOVANNI

Same cast as March 18 except:

Leporello .... Wentworth
Masetto .... Newman

April 15 (m)

AIDA

Same cast as April 6 except:

Conductor .... Rudel
Aida .... Nelli,
(s, Williams)
King .... Pichardo
Amneris .... Bible,
(s, Ibarrondo)
Radames .... Leech,
(s, Mazzieri)
Ramfis .... Scott
Messenger .... Sprinzena
Priestess .... Taussig

April 15

CARMEN

Same cast as March 18 (m) except:

Carmen .... Ibarrondo,
(s, Giannini)
Don José .... Gari
Escamillo .... Pease
Micaëla .... MacNeil
Frasquita .... Malbin

April 18

LES CONTES D'HOFFMANN

Same cast as March 29 except:

Lindorff .... Herbert
Nathaniël .... Sprinzena
Coppélius .... Herbert
Dr. Miracle .... Herbert

April 19

THE MARRIAGE OF FIGARO

Same cast as March 25 except:

Almaviva .... Tyers
Countess .... Yeend
Susanna .... Bishop

Cherubino .... Evans
Basilio .... Vellucci,
(s, Norville)
Barbarina .... Malbin

April 20

LA BOHÈME

Same cast as March 17 except:

Mimi .... Ayars
Musetta .... MacNeil
Colline .... Scott

April 21 (m)

THE LOVE FOR THREE ORANGES

Same cast as March 17 (m) except:

Prince .... Rounseville
Celio .... Newman
Princess Ninetta ..... Malbin

Added to this program:

Farfarello .... Smith

April 21

FAUST

Same cast as March 24 except:

Old Faust .... Petrak
Young Faust .... Gari
Valentin .... Cassel,
(s, Bardelli)

April 22 (m)

LA TRAVIATA

Same cast as March 16 except:

Violetta .... Yeend
Alfredo .... Petrak
Germont .... Cassel
Flora .... Evans

April 22

AIDA

Same cast as April 6 except:

King .... Pichardo
Amneris .... Sydney
Aida .... Nelli
Radames .... Leech
Ramfis .... Scott
Amonasro .... Herbert,
(s, Bardelli)
Messenger .... Sprinzena
Priestess .... Evans

Fall 1951 (SEPTEMBER 27 – NOVEMBER 11)

Female artists
Alberts, Eunice*
Ayars, Ann
Bible, Frances
Bishop, Adelaide

Evangelista, Lucia
Evans, Edith
Faull, Ellen
Greene, Ethel
Ibarrondo, Lydia

Kreste, Mary
Lager, Frances
LeSawyer, Mary
Likova, Eva
MacNeil, Dorothy

* New artist
* New artist
* New artist

Malbin, Elaine
Mayer, Margery
Nelli, Herva
Neway, Patricia*
Richmond, Alice*
Rivera, Graciela
Russell, Shirley
Santo, Tuso*
Spence, Wilma
Sydney, Lorna
Taussig, Carroll
Underwood, Willabelle*
Williams, Camilla
Yeend, Frances

Male artists
Arié, Raffaele
Baylé, Theo*
Bondon, Michael*
Bonelli, Richard
Boyle, Raymond*
Cassel, Walter
Dalton, Wesley*
Gari, Giulio
Gauld, Carlton
Greenwell, Gean
Harkless, Armand*
Harrell, Mack
Heide, Rolf*
Jongeyans, George
Kaldenberg, Keith
Lalli, Mario*
Lloyd, David
Luciano, Nino
Morgan, Mack*
Natzka, Oscar
Newman, Arthur
Pease, James
Petrak, Rudolf
Pichardo, Luis
Poleri, David
Pollock, Michael
Powell, Thomas
Renan, Emile
Rounseville, Robert
Scott, Norman
Singher, Martial*
Sprinzena, Nathaniel
Torigi, Richard*
Vellucci, Luigi
Vroons, Frans
Wentworth, Richard
Winters, Lawrence

Conductors
Halasz, Laszlo
Martin, Thomas P.
Morel, Jean
Rosenstock, Joseph
Rudel, Julius
Shaynen, Lee

Solo dancers
Danela, Oriana*
Marie-Jeanne
Svetlova, Marina

Ziegler, Elfriede*
Fealy, John*
Gifford, Joseph*
James, Earl*
McKayle, Donald*

* New artist

Muradoff, Grant
Smith, James

Choreographers
Maslow, Sophie*
Muradoff, Grant
Weidman, Charles

Directors
Erhardt, Otto
Pichel, Irving*
Rosing, Vladimir
Ruben, José
Sachse, Leopold
White, John S.

**Artistic counsellor—
German wing**
Schorr, Friedrich

Designers
Brodkin, Herbert
Condell, H. A.
Dobujinsky, Mstislav
Morley, Ruth
Rychtarik, Richard

* New artist

September 27

MANON (Massenet)

Conductor .... Morel

Des Grieux .... Poleri
Count des Grieux ..... Gauld
Lescaut .... Pease
Manon .... Ayars
Guillot .... Pollock
De Brétigny ...... Jongeyans
Pousette .... MacNeil
Rosette .... Evans
Javotte .... LeSawyer
Innkeeper .... Wentworth
Solo dancers .... Svetlova;
Muradoff

September 28

THE MARRIAGE OF FIGARO
(Mozart)
(English version by
Ruth and Thomas Martin)

Conductor ...... Rosenstock

Almaviva .... Cassel
Countess .... Yeend
Figaro .... Pease
Susanna .... Bishop
Cherubino .... Bible
Bartolo .... Wentworth
Marcellina .... Mayer
Basilio .... Vellucci
Curzio .... Sprinzena
Antonio .... Newman
Barbarina .... Russell

September 29 (m)

MADAMA BUTTERFLY (Puccini)

Conductor .... Halasz

Butterfly .... Williams
Suzuki .... Mayer

Kate Pinkerton .... Evans
Pinkerton .... Gari
Sharpless .... Bonelli
Goro .... Vellucci,
(s, Sprinzena)
Yamadori .... Renan
The Bonze .... Winters
Imperial
Commissioner ...... Powell

September 29

FAUST (Gounod)

Conductor .... Morel

Marguerite .... Likova
Old Faust .... Gari
Young Faust .... Petrak
Méphistophélès .... Scott
Valentin .... Cassel
Siébel .... Bible
Marthe .... Kreste
Wagner .... Newman

September 30 (m)

CARMEN (Bizet)

Staged by .... Ruben
Choreographer .... Muradoff
Conductor .... Morel

Carmen .... Ibarrondo
Don José .... Vroons
Escamillo .... Baylé (d)
Micaëla .... MacNeil
Zuniga .... Jongeyans
Frasquita .... Russell
Mercédès .... Evans
Remendado .... Vellucci,
(s, Sprinzena)
Dancairo .... Pollock
Morales .... Newman
1st Solo dancer .. Danela (d)
2nd Solo dancer ... Muradoff

September 30

LA BOHÈME (Puccini)

Conductor .... Halasz

Mimi .... Ayars
Musetta .... Likova
Rodolfo .... Poleri
Marcello .... Bonelli
Schaunard .... Newman
Colline .... Arié
Benoit .... Wentworth
Alcindoro .... Renan
Parpignol .... Vellucci

October 4

THE DYBBUK (Tamkin)
World stage premiere

Staged by .... Pichel (d)
Scenic designer .. Dobujinsky
Costume designer .... Morley
Choreographer .. Maslow (d)
Conductor ...... Rosenstock

Channon .... Rounseville
Leah .... Neway (d)
The Messenger ...... Winters
Rabbi Azrael .... Harrell
Meyer .... Renan
Sender .... Gauld
Chennoch .... Newman

Frade .... Bible
Elderly woman .. Alberts (d)
Gittel .... Russell
Bassia .... Evans
1st Batlon .... Sprinzena
2nd Batlon ...... Wentworth
3rd Batlon .... Pollock
Menashe ...... Harkless (d)
Rabbi Mendel ..... Vellucci
Asher .... Kaldenberg
Rabbi Schmelke .. Gifford (d)
Poor man .... Fealy (d)
Rich man ..... McKayle (d)
Michoel .... Newman
1st Chassid ...... Sprinzena
2nd Chassid .... Vellucci
3rd Chassid .... Renan
Wedding guest ...... Pollock
Old woman .... Taussig
Nachmon .... James (d)

October 5

LES CONTES D'HOFFMANN
(Offenbach)

Conductor .... Morel

Hoffmann .... Vroons
Nicklause .... Bible
Lindorff .... Gauld
Luther .... Wentworth
Nathaniël .... Sprinzena
Hermann .... Newman
Andrès .... Vellucci
Olympia .... Rivera
Coppélius .... Gauld
Spalanzani .... Pollock
Cochenille .... Vellucci
Giulietta .... Spence
Dappertutto .... Baylé
Schlémil .... Newman,
                       (s, Renan)
Pittichinaccio .... Vellucci
Antonia .... Yeend
Dr. Miracle .... Gauld
Crespel .... Scott
Mother .... Mayer
Frantz .... Vellucci

October 6 (m)

THE LOVE FOR THREE ORANGES
(Prokofiev)
(English translation by
Victor Seroff; spoken prologue
by David Thornton)

Conductor .... Rudel

King .... Greenwell
Prince .... Lloyd
Princess Clarissa ..... Mayer
Leandro .... Jongeyans
Pantalone .... Renan
Truffaldino .... Vellucci
Celio .... Winters
Fata Morgana .... Sydney
Princess Linetta .... Lager
Princess Nicoletta .. MacNeil
Princess Ninetta ..... Malbin
Cook .... Wentworth
Smeraldina .... Evans
Farfarello .... Smith

(Note: "Prologue" added to
program October 21)

October 6

DON GIOVANNI (Mozart)

Conductor .... Halasz

Don Giovanni .... Cassel
Leporello .... Arié
Donna Elvira .... Likova
Commendatore .... Scott
Donna Anna .... Faull
Don Ottavio .... Petrak
Masetto .... Renan
Zerlina .... MacNeil

October 7 (m)

LA TRAVIATA (Verdi)

Staged by .... Ruben
Conductor .... Shaynen

Violetta .... Evangelista
Alfredo .... Poleri
Germont .... Bonelli
Flora .... Evans
Annina .... Kreste
Gaston .... Vellucci
Douphol .... Wentworth
D'Obigny .... Powell
Dr. Grenvil .... Newman

October 7

DIE MEISTERSINGER (Wagner)

Conductor ...... Rosenstock

Hans Sachs .... Pease
Pogner .... Natzka
Vogelgesang .... Luciano
Nachtigall .... Newman
Beckmesser .... Renan
Kothner .... Wentworth
Zorn .... Harkless
Eisslinger .... Vellucci
Moser .... Sprinzena
Ortel .... Powell
Schwarz .... Pichardo
Foltz .... Jongeyans
Walther .... Gari
David .... Lloyd
Eva .... Yeend
Magdalene .... Mayer
Night Watchman .... Winters

October 10

THE DYBBUK

Same cast as October 4

October 11

MADAMA BUTTERFLY

Same cast as September 29
(m) except:

Suzuki .... Bible
Pinkerton .... Petrak
Goro .... Harkless

Imperial
  Commissioner .... Newman

October 12

RIGOLETTO (Verdi)

Staged by .... Ruben
Choreographer .... Muradoff
Conductor .... Morel

Duke .... Poleri
Rigoletto .... Winters,
                    (s, Baylé)
Gilda .... Rivera
Sparafucile .... Natzka
Maddalena .... Mayer
Giovanna .... Kreste
Monterone ...... Wentworth
Marullo .... Newman
Borsa .... Sprinzena
Ceprano .... Renan
Countess Ceprano .. LeSawyer
Page .... Greene

October 13 (m)

DIE MEISTERSINGER

Same cast as October 7 except:

Hans Sachs .... Pease,
                     (s, Harrell)
Eva .... Faull

October 13

MANON

Same cast as September 27
except:

Des Grieux .... Vroons
Lescaut .... Singher (d),
                    (s, Pease)
Manon .... Likova

October 14 (m)

CAVALLERIA RUSTICANA
(Mascagni)

Conductor .... Rudel

Santuzza .... Neway
Turiddu .... Poleri
Alfio .... Wentworth
Lola .... Evans
Mamma Lucia .... Kreste

Followed by:

I PAGLIACCI (Leoncavallo)

Conductor ...... Rosenstock

Nedda .... Yeend
Canio .... Gari
Tonio .... Winters
Silvio .... Torigi (d)
Beppe .... Sprinzena

October 14

CARMEN

Same cast as September 30
(m) except:

Don José .... Rounsevill

October 18

THE FOUR RUFFIANS
(Wolf-Ferrari)
United States premiere
(*I Quattro Rusteghi*; the
translation used was a
modification of Edward Dent's
adaptation for the Sadler's
Wells Theatre in London,
where the work was
staged under the title
School for Fathers.)

Staged by	Erhardt
Scenic designer	Dobujinsky
Costume designer	Morley
Choreographer	Weidman
Conductor	Halasz

Lucieta	MacNeil
Margarita	Mayer
Lunardo	Greenwell
Maurizio	Wentworth
Marina	Faull
Maid to Marina	Evans
Filipeto	Lloyd
Simon	Jongeyans
Felice	Yeend
Cancian	Renan
Count	
Riccardo Arcolai	Harkless

October 19

LA BOHÈME

Same cast as September 30
except:

Conductor .... Rudel

Mimi	Santo (d)
Rodolfo	Petrak
Marcello	Baylé
Parpignol	Sprinzena

October 20 (m)

LA TRAVIATA

Same cast as October 7 (m)
except:

Violetta	Yeend
Germont	Harrell
Annina	Taussig
D'Obigny	Renan

October 20

THE MARRIAGE OF FIGARO

Same cast as September 28
except:

Almaviva	Bondon (d)
Countess	Faull
Susanna	Russell
Marcellina	Alberts
Barbarina	LeSawyer, (s, MacNeil)

October 21 (m)

RIGOLETTO

Same cast as October 12
except:

Rigoletto	Baylé
Sparafucile	Scott

Maddalena	Evans
Giovanna	Taussig

October 21

THE LOVE FOR THREE ORANGES

Same cast as October 6 (m)
except:

Conductor .... Rudel,
(s, Halasz)

King	Pease
Prince Tartaglia	Rounseville
Pantalone	Morgan (d)
Truffaldino	Lloyd
Princess Linetta	Evans
Princess Ninetta	Russell
Smeraldina	Bible

Added to this program:

Prologue .... Boyle (d)

October 23

DIE MEISTERSINGER

Same cast as October 7 except:

Hans Sachs	Harrell
Pogner	Natzka (Act I); Scott (Acts II and III)
Beckmesser	Heide (d)
Walther	Petrak

October 24

LES CONTES D'HOFFMANN

Same cast as October 5 except:

Hoffmann	Rounseville
Lindorff	Baylé
Coppélius	Baylé
Schlémil	Renan
Antonia	Ayars
Dr. Miracle	Baylé
Mother	Alberts

October 25

AIDA (Verdi)

Conductor	Halasz

King	Scott
Amneris	Ibarrondo
Aida	Nelli
Radames	Gari
Ramfis	Arié
Amonasro	Winters
Messenger	Sprinzena
Priestess	Evans
1st Solo dancer	Marie-Jeanne
2nd Solo dancer	Muradoff

October 26

DON GIOVANNI

Same cast as October 6 except:

Don Giovanni	Pease
Leporello	Jongeyans
Zerlina	Malbin

October 27 (m)

CARMEN

Same cast as September 30
(m) except:

Carmen	Mayer
Escamillo	Bondon
Remendado	Sprinzena

October 27

FAUST

Same cast as September 29
except:

Marguerite	Yeend
Old Faust	Petrak
Méphistophélès	Arié
Valentin	Bonelli
Marthe	Alberts

(Note: Petrak sang both Old
and Young Faust.)

October 28 (m)

MADAMA BUTTERFLY

Same cast as September 29
(m) except:

Conductor	Shaynen

Suzuki	Kreste
Pinkerton	Dalton (d)
Sharpless	Bonelli, (s, Morgan)
Goro	Sprinzena
The Bonze	Wentworth

October 28

THE DYBBUK

Same cast as October 4 except:

Channon	Vroons
Sender	Scott
Elderly woman	Mayer

October 30

THE FOUR RUFFIANS

Same cast as October 18
except:

Lucieta	Russell
Lunardo	Pease
Maid to Marina	Greene
Simon	Scott
Cancian	Newman

October 31

THE LOVE FOR THREE ORANGES

Same cast as October 6 (m)
except:

Conductor	Halasz

King	Pease
Prince	Rounseville
Fata Morgana	Faull

Princess Linetta ...... Evans
Princess Nicoletta .... Russell
Princess Ninetta .... MacNeil
Smeraldina .... Bible

November 1

RIGOLETTO

Same cast as October 12
except:

Rigoletto .... Winters,
(s, Bonelli)
Sparafucile .... Scott
Maddalena .... Evans

November 2

CAVALLERIA RUSTICANA

Same cast as October 14 (m)
except:

Lola .... MacNeil

Followed by:

I PAGLIACCI

Same cast as October 14 (m)
except:

Nedda .... Richmond (d)
Tonio .... Winters,
(s, Baylé)
Silvio .... Morgan
Beppe .... Lalli (d)

November 3 (m)

THE DYBBUK

Same cast as October 4 except:

The Messenger .... Pease,
(s, Winters)
Sender .... Scott
Elderly woman ...... Mayer

November 3

LA TRAVIATA

Same cast as October 7 (m)
except:

Violetta .... Ayars
Alfredo .... Petrak
Germont .... Harrell,
(s, Baylé)

Annina .... Greene
D'Obigny .... Renan

November 4 (m)

AIDA

Same cast as October 25
except:

King .... Pease
Ramfis .... Scott
1st Solo dancer ..... Svetlova

November 4

THE MARRIAGE OF FIGARO

Same cast as September 28
except:

Almaviva .... Bondon
Figaro .... Jongeyans
Susanna .... MacNeil
Marcellina .... Kreste
Basilio .... Pollock

November 5

THE DYBBUK

Same cast as October 4 except:

Leah .... Spence
Sender .... Gauld,
(s, Scott)
Elderly woman .... Mayer

November 7

MANON

Same cast as September 27
except:

Count des Grieux ...... Arié
Lescaut .... Baylé

November 8

CARMEN

Same cast as September 30
(m) except:

Escamillo .... Pease
Zuniga .... Scott
Dancairo .... Renan
1st Solo dancer ...... Ziegler

November 9

AIDA

Same cast as October 25
except:

King .... Jongeyans
Amneris .... Mayer
Ramfis .... Scott
1st Solo dancer ..... Svetlova

November 10 (m)

THE LOVE FOR THREE ORANGES

Same cast as October 6 (m)
except:

King .... Pease
Prince .... Rounseville
Princess Clarissa ...... Kreste
Princess Nicoletta .... Russell
Princess Ninetta .... MacNeil

November 10

MADAMA BUTTERFLY

Same cast as September 29 (m)
except:

Conductor .... Shaynen,
(s, Halasz)
Butterfly .... Faull
Suzuki .... Alberts
Pinkerton .... Poleri
Goro .... Lalli
The Bonze .... Jongeyans,
(s, Winters)

November 11 (m)

LA BOHÈME

Same cast as September 30
except:

Conductor .... Rudel
Musetta .... MacNeil
Rodolfo .... Dalton
Marcello .... Herbert
Parpignol .... Sprinzena

November 11

DON GIOVANNI

Same cast as October 6 except:

Don Giovanni .... Pease
Leporello .... Jongeyans
Donna Anna ..Underwood (d)
Zerlina .... Malbin

Spring 1952 (MARCH 20—APRIL 27)

Female artists
Ayars, Ann
Bible, Frances
Bishop, Adelaide
Evans, Edith
Faull, Ellen
Greene, Ethel
Haskins, Virginia
Ibarrondo, Lydia

Krebs, Beatrice*
Kreste, Mary
Kuhlmann, Rosemary*
LeSawyer, Mary
Lewis, Brenda
Likova, Eva
MacNeil, Dorothy

* New artist

Mayer, Margery
Moll, Mariquita*
Nelli, Herva
Neway, Patricia
Oram, Linda*
Richmond, Alice
Spence, Wilma

* New artist

Taussig, Carroll
Tynes, Margaret*
Underwood, Willabelle
Williams, Camilla
Yeend, Frances

Male artists
Allen, Chet*
Bondon, Michael
Bonelli, Richard
Cassel, Walter
Dalton, Wesley
Ducree, Leonard
Gainey, Andrew
Gari, Giulio
Gauld, Carlton
Gaynes, George (formerly
   Jongeyans, George)
Gbur, Jan*
Giddens, Marion*
Greenwell, Gean
Harkless, Armand
Harrell, Mack
Harrower, Rexford*
Hecht, Manfred
Herbert, Ralph
Kuestner, Charles
Lalli, Mario
Leech, Lloyd Thomas
Lloyd, David
Luciano, Nino
Mincer, Dick*
Newman, Arthur
Pease, James
Petrak, Rudolf
Pichardo, Luis
Poleri, David
Pollock, Michael
Powell, Thomas
Renan, Emile
Rothmueller, Marko
Rounseville, Robert
Sprinzena, Nathaniel
Starling, William*
Tipton, Thomas*
Torigi, Richard
Vandenburg, Howard*
Vellucci, Luigi
Wentworth, Richard
Williams, Lee*
Winters, Lawrence

Conductors
Breisach, Paul*
Martin, Thomas P.
Rosenstock, Joseph
Rudel, Julius
Schippers, Thomas*
Shaynen, Lee

Solo dancers
Hinkson, Mary*
Solskaya, Helene*
Waugh, Anne*

Breaux, Marc*
Fealy, John
McKayle, Donald
Muradoff, Grant
Smith, James

   * New artist

Tetley, Glen*
Weidman, Charles*

Choreographers
Butler, John*
Maslow, Sophie
Muradoff, Grant
Weidman, Charles

Directors
Harrower, Rexford*
Komisarjevsky, Theodore
Menotti, Gian Carlo
Pichel, Irving
Ruben, José
Sachse, Leopold
White, John S.

Designers
Berman, Eugene*
Condell, H. A.
Dobujinsky, Mstislav
Morley, Ruth

   * New artist

March 20

DER ROSENKAVALIER
(R. Strauss)

Costume designer .... Morley
Conductor ...... Rosenstock

Marschallin .... Moll (d)
Baron Ochs .... Pease
Octavian .... Bible
Faninal .... Wentworth
Sophie .... Haskins
Marianne .... Faull
Valzacchi .... Vellucci
Annina .... Evans
Police
   Commissioner .... Newman
Singer .... Petrak,
                  (s, Gari)
Innkeeper .... Sprinzena
Major-Domo of
   the Marschallin .... Powell
Major-Domo of
   Faninal .... Kuestner,
                (s, Pollock)
Attorney .... Newman
1st Orphan .... LeSawyer
2nd Orphan .... Taussig
3rd Orphan .... Greene
Animal vendor ..Giddens (d),
                (s, Pollock)
Milliner .... Richmond
Leopold ...... Weidman (d)
Mohamet .... Ducree

March 21

LA BOHÈME (Puccini)

Conductor ..... Breisach (d)

Mimi .... Ayars
Musetta .... MacNeil
Rodolfo .... Poleri
Marcello .... Torigi
Schaunard .... Newman

Colline .... Gaynes
Benoit .... Wentworth
Alcindoro .... Renan
Parpignol .... Vellucci

March 22

LA TRAVIATA (Verdi)

Conductor .... Martin

Violetta .... Likova
Alfredo .... Petrak
Germont .... Bonelli
Flora .... Evans
Annina .... Kreste
Gaston .... Vellucci
Douphol .... Wentworth
D'Obigny .... Renan
Dr. Grenvil .... Newman
Solo dancers .... Waugh (d);
                   Smith

March 23 (m)

MADAMA BUTTERFLY (Puccini)

Conductor .... Martin

Butterfly .... C. Williams
Suzuki .... Mayer
Kate Pinkerton .... Evans
Pinkerton .... Gari
Sharpless .... Herbert
Goro .... Sprinzena
Yamadori .... Renan
The Bonze .... Winters
Imperial
   Commissioner ...... Powell

March 23

THE MARRIAGE OF FIGARO
(Mozart)
(English version by
Ruth and Thomas Martin)

Conductor ...... Rosenstock

Almaviva .... Cassel
Countess .... Yeend
Figaro .... Pease
Susanna .... Bishop
Cherubino .... Bible
Bartolo .... Wentworth
Marcellina .... Kreste
Basilio .... Vellucci
Curzio .... Pollock
Antonio .... Newman
Barbarina .... MacNeil

March 27

THE DYBBUK (Tamkin)

Conductor ...... Rosenstock

Channon .... Leech
Leah .... Spence
Messenger .... Winters
Rabbi Azrael .... Harrell
Meyer .... Renan
Sender .... Gauld
Chennoch .... Newman
Frade .... Bible
Elderly woman .... Mayer
Gittel .... Richmond
Bassia .... Evans
1st Batlon .... Sprinzena
2nd Batlon ...... Wentworth

3rd Batlon .... Pollock
Menashe .... Harkless
Rabbi Mendel ...... Vellucci
Asher .... Kuestner
Rabbi Schmelke .... Gifford
Poor man .... Fealy
Rich man .... McKayle
Michoel .... Newman
1st Chassid .... Sprinzena
2nd Chassid .... Vellucci
3rd Chassid .... Renan
Wedding guest ...... Pollock
Old woman .... Taussig
Nachmon .... L. Williams (d)

March 28

CAVALLERIA RUSTICANA
(Mascagni)

Conductor .... Shaynen

Santuzza .... Ibarrondo
Turiddu .... Poleri
Alfio .... Wentworth
Lola .... Evans
Mamma Lucia .... Kreste

Followed by:

I PAGLIACCI (Leoncavallo)

Conductor .... Rudel

Nedda .... Likova
Canio .... Gari
Tonio .... Winters
Silvio .... Torigi
Beppe .... Lalli

March 29

DON GIOVANNI (Mozart)

Conductor .... Breisach

Don Giovanni .... Cassel
Leporello .... Gaynes
Donna Elvira .... Likova
Commendatore ...... Hecht
Donna Anna .... Faull
Don Ottavio .... Petrak
Masetto .... Renan
Zerlina .... Haskins
A Devil .... Muradoff

March 30 (m)

THE LOVE FOR THREE ORANGES
(Prokofiev)
(English translation by Victor
Seroff; spoken prologue by
Komisarjevsky after
Carlo Gozzi)

Stage director .. Harrower (d)
Conductor .... Rudel

King .... Greenwell
Prince .... Leech
Princess Clarissa ...... Mayer
Leandro .... Gaynes
Pantalone .... Renan
Truffaldino .... Vellucci
Celio .... Winters
Fata Morgana .... Tynes (d)
Princess Linetta ...... Evans
Princess Nicoletta ..Richmond

Princess Ninetta .... MacNeil
Cook .... Wentworth
Smeraldina .... Bible
Farfarello .... Smith
Prologue ..... Harrower (d)

March 30

MANON (Massenet)

Conductor .... Breisach

Des Grieux .... Poleri
Count des Grieux ..... Gauld
Lescaut .... Herbert
Manon .... Ayars
Guillot .... Pollock
De Brétigny .... Gaynes
Pousette .... MacNeil
Rosette .... Evans
Javotte .... LeSawyer
Innkeeper .... Wentworth
Solo dancers ... Solskaya (d);
Muradoff

April 3

WOZZECK (Berg)
First performance by The New
York City Opera Company
(English translation by Eric
Blackhall and Vida Harford)

Staged by .... Komisarjevsky
Designer .... Dobujinsky
Lighting .... Rosenthal
Conductor ...... Rosenstock

Captain .... Vellucci
Wozzeck .... Rothmueller
Marie .... Neway
Child .... Oram (d)
Doctor .... Herbert
Andrès .... Lloyd
Margaret .... Evans
Drum major ..Vandenburg (d)
1st Workman ..... Newman,
(s, Wentworth)
2nd Workman .... Harkless
The Idiot .... Pollock

(Children: courtesy of
Children's Opera Company
of New York)

April 4

MADAMA BUTTERFLY

Same cast as March 23 (m)
except:

Suzuki .... Ibarrondo
Kate Pinkerton .... LeSawyer
Pinkerton .... Petrak
Sharpless .... Torigi
Goro .... Vellucci
*Imperial
Commissioner* .... Newman

April 5

THE MARRIAGE OF FIGARO

Same cast as March 23 except:

Countess .... Faull
Figaro .... Gaynes

Susanna .... MacNeil
Cherubino .... Evans
Bartolo .... Renan,
(s, Wentworth)
Marcellina .... Mayer
Barbarina .... LeSawyer

April 6 (m)

LA TRAVIATA

Same cast as March 22 except:

Violetta .... Ayars
Alfredo .... Poleri
Douphol .... Powell,
(s, Wentworth)

April 6

DER ROSENKAVALIER

Same cast as March 20 except:

Marschallin .... Spence
Baron Ochs .... Hecht
Faninal .... Herbert
Sophie .... Bishop
Marianne .... Underwood
Singer .... Gari
Innkeeper .... Harkless,
(s, Sprinzena)
*Major-Domo of
Faninal* .... Pollock
Animal vendor ...... Pollock

April 9

THE OLD MAID AND THE THIEF
(Menotti)

Conductor .... Schippers (d)

Laetitia .... Bishop
Miss Todd .... Kreste
Miss Pinkerton .... Faull
Bob .... Gainey

Followed by:

AMAHL AND THE NIGHT
VISITORS (Menotti)
First performance by The New
York City Opera Company

Staged by .... Menotti
Designer .... Berman (d)
Choreographer ... Butler (d)
Conductor .... Schippers (d)

Amahl .... Allen (d)
His Mother .. Kuhlmann (d)
King Kaspar .... Pollock
King Melchior ...... Winter
King Balthazar .. Wentworth
Page .... Starling (d)
Shepherdess .... Hinkson (d)
Two Shepherds .. Breaux (d)
Tetley (d)

April 10

THE LOVE FOR THREE ORANGE

Same cast as March 30 (m)
except:

Prince .... Rounsevil
Fata Morgana .... Fau
Princess Nicoletta .. LeSawye
Cook .... Newma
(s, Wentworth

April 11

DON GIOVANNI

Same cast as March 29 except:

Donna Elvira ..... Richmond
Commendatore .... Gbur (d)
Don Ottavio .... Dalton,
                    (s, Petrak)
Zerlina .... MacNeil

April 12

LA BOHÈME

Same cast as March 21 except:

Mimi .... Yeend
Musetta .... Likova
Rodolfo .... Gari
Marcello .... Gainey
Schaunard .... Renan
Colline .... Bondon
Alcindoro .... Newman

April 13 (m)

CAVALLERIA RUSTICANA

Same cast as March 28

Followed by:

I PAGLIACCI

Same cast as March 28 except:

Nedda .... Ayars
Canio .... Vandenburg
Beppe .... Sprinzena

April 13

THE DYBBUK

Same cast as March 27 except:

Channon .... Luciano
Leah .... Neway
Rabbi Azrael .... Herbert
Elderly woman .... Kreste

April 16

ANDREA CHÉNIER (Giordano)

Choreographer .... Weidman
Conductor .... Rudel

Chénier .... Poleri
Gérard .... Cassel
Maddalena .... Nelli
Bersi .... Evans
Contessa di Coigny ... Mayer
Madelon .... Kreste
Mathieu .... Gaynes
Roucher .... Torigi
Fléville .... Newman
l'Abate .... Vellucci
Incredible .... Pollock,
                   (s, Sprinzena)
Schmidt .... Wentworth

Dumas .... Renan
Fouquier-Tinville ... Newman

April 17

THE OLD MAID AND THE THIEF

Same cast as April 9 except:

Miss Todd .... Krebs (d)

Followed by:

AMAHL AND THE
NIGHT VISITORS

Same cast as April 9

April 18

WOZZECK

Same cast as April 3 except:

Marie .... Lewis,
                   (s, Neway)
Doctor .... Renan
1st Workman .... Wentworth

April 19

MANON

Same cast as March 30 except:

Lescaut .... Pease

April 20 (m)

THE MARRIAGE OF FIGARO

Same cast as March 23 except:

Conductor .... Martin

Almaviva .... Bondon
Countess .... Faull
Figaro .... Gaynes
Susanna .... MacNeil
Barbarina .... Richmond

April 20

LA TRAVIATA

Same cast as March 22 except:

Conductor .... Shaynen

Violetta .... Yeend
Alfredo .... Dalton
Germont .... Cassel

April 22

WOZZECK

Same cast as April 3 except:

Wozzeck .... Pease
Marie .... Lewis
Doctor .... Renan
Andrès .... Sprinzena
Drum major .... Leech
1st Workman .... Wentworth
2nd Workman .... Powell

April 23

THE DYBBUK

Same cast as March 27 except:

Channon .... Rounseville
Sender .... Greenwell
Menashe .... Lalli

April 24

ANDREA CHÉNIER

Same cast as April 16 except:

Madelon .... Mayer
Mathieu .... Bondon
Incredible .... Sprinzena

April 25

DER ROSENKAVALIER

Same cast as March 20 except:

Conductor .... Breisach

Marianne .... Underwood
Annina .... Ibarrondo
Innkeeper .... Harkless
Major-Domo of
   Faninal .... Pollock
Animal vendor ...... Pollock

April 26

MADAMA BUTTERFLY

Same cast as March 23 (m)
except:

Conductor .... Shaynen

Butterfly .... Faull
Suzuki .... Kreste
Kate Pinkerton ...... Greene
Sharpless .... Torigi
Goro .... Vellucci

April 27 (m)

THE OLD MAID AND THE THIEF

Same cast as April 9 except:

Miss Pinkerton ... Richmond
Bob .... Tipton (d)

Followed by:

AMAHL AND THE
NIGHT VISITORS

Same cast as April 9 except:

Amahl .... Mincer (d)

April 27

LA BOHÈME

Same cast as March 21 except:

Conductor .... Martin

Mimi .... C. Williams
Rodolfo .... Petrak
Marcello .... Herbert
Colline .... Pichardo

Fall 1952 (SEPTEMBER 18 – NOVEMBER 2)

Female artists
Ayars, Ann
Bible, Frances
Bishop, Adelaide
Bollinger, Anne*
Evans, Edith
Faull, Ellen
Georgiou, Vilma*
Grant, Jeanne*
Greene, Ethel
Hurley, Laurel*
Krebs, Beatrice
Kreste, Mary
Kuhlmann, Rosemary
Lane, Gloria*
LeSawyer, Mary
Manners, Gail*
Marlo, Maria*
Mayer, Margery
McKnight, Anne*
Neway, Patricia
Oram, Linda
Palmer, Christine*
Richmond, Alice
Scheunemann, Leona
Spence, Wilma
Tynes, Margaret
Underwood, Willabelle
Williams, Camilla
Yeend, Frances

Male artists
Anderson, Robert*
Ballarini, Stephen*
Bonelli, Richard
Cassel, Walter
Crain, Jon*
Dalton, Wesley
Dillon, Irwin
Gari, Giulio
Gauld, Carlton
Gaynes, George
Gramm, Donald*
Kelley, Norman*
Kluge, George*
Kuestner, Charles
Leech, Lloyd Thomas
Lloyd, David
Medinets, Alfred*
Moss, Arnold*
Newman, Arthur
Pease, James
Petrak, Rudolf
Poleri, David
Pollock, Michael
Powell, Thomas
Renan, Emile
Sammarco, James*
Scott, Norman
Sprinzena, Nathaniel
Starling, William
Symonette, Randolph*
Tipton, Thomas
Torigi, Richard
Turrini, Roberto*
Vellucci, Luigi
Wentworth, Richard
Winters, Lawrence

* New artist

Members of the Fujiwara Opera Company of Tokyo
Ishizu, Kenichi*
Kawasaki, Shizuko*
Matsuchi, Kazuko*
Miyake, Harue*
Miyamoto, Ryohei*
Takagi, Kiyoshi*
Takehara, Shyozo*

Conductors
Bamberger, Carl*
Martin, Thomas
Rosenstock, Joseph
Rudel, Julius
Schippers, Thomas
Serafin, Tullio*
Shaynen, Lee

Dancers
Anthony, Mary*
Hinkson, Mary
Kai, Una*
Mounsey, Yvonne*
Savoia, Patricia*
Waugh, Anne
Widman, Annalise

Butler, John*
Gitlin, Murray*
Schulman, Alvin*
Smith, James
Tetley, Glen

Choreographers
Butler, John
Weidman, Charles

Directors
Butler, John*
Erhardt, Otto
Menotti, Gian Carlo
Ruben, José
Sachse, Leopold
Tavernia, Patrick*
White, John
Williams, Lee*

Designers
Armistead, Horace*
Berman, Eugene
Condell, H. A.
Dobujinsky, Mstislav
Ter-Arutunian, Rouben*

* New artist

September 18

TOSCA (Puccini)

Conductor ...... Serafin (d)

Tosca .... McKnight (d)
Cavaradossi .... Poleri
Scarpia .... Cassel
Angelotti .... Gaynes
Spoletta .... Vellucci
Sacristan .... Wentworth
Sciarrone .... Newman
Shepherd .... Greene,
             (s, Evans)
Jailer .... Powell

September 19

THE OLD MAID AND THE THIEF (Menotti)

Conductor .... Schippers

Laetitia .... Bishop
Miss Todd .... Kreste
Miss Pinkerton .... Faull
Bob .... Tipton

Followed by:

AMAHL AND THE NIGHT VISITORS (Menotti)

Conductor .... Schippers

Amahl .... Sammarco (d)
Mother .... Kuhlmann
King Kaspar .... Pollock
King Melchior ...... Winters
King Balthazar .. Wentworth
Page .... Starling
Shepherdess .... Hinkson
Two Shepherds .. Butler (d),
             Tetley

September 20

DON GIOVANNI (Mozart)

Choreographer .... Butler
Conductor ... Bamberger (d)

Don Giovanni .... Pease
Leporello .... Gaynes
Donna Elvira .. Scheunemann
Commendatore ... Symonette
             (d)
Donna Anna .... Faull
Don Ottavio .... Petrak
Masetto .... Renan
Zerlina .... Hurley (d)

September 21 (m)

MADAMA BUTTERFLY (Puccini)

Staged by .... Ruben
Conductor .... Martin

Butterfly .... Williams
Suzuki .... Bible
Kate Pinkerton .... LeSawyer
Pinkerton .... Gari
Sharpless .... Torigi
Goro .... Vellucci
Yamadori .... Renan
The Bonze .... Winters
Imperial Commissioner ..... Powell

September 21

LA TRAVIATA (Verdi)

Conductor .... Serafin

Violetta .... Yeend
Alfredo .... Poleri
Germont .... Cassel
Flora .... LeSawyer
             (s, Evans)

Annina .... Kreste
Gaston .... Vellucci
Douphol .... Wentworth
D'Obigny .... Renan
Dr. Grenvil .... Newman
Solo dancers .. Waugh; Smith

September 25

AIDA (Verdi)

Choreographer .... Butler
Conductor .... Serafin

King .... Gaynes
Amneris .... Mayer
Aida .... McKnight
Radames .... Turrini (d)
Ramfis .... Symonette
Amonasro .... Winters
Messenger .... Pollock
Priestess .... Richmond,
                (s, Evans)
Solo dancers. .Hinkson; Tetley

September 26

LA BOHÈME (Puccini)

Conductor .... Schippers

Mimi .... Ayars
Musetta .... Palmer (d)
Rodolfo .... Poleri
Marcello .... Torigi
Schaunard .... Newman
Colline .... Gramm (d)
Benoit .... Wentworth
Alcindoro .... Renan
Parpignol .... Pollock

September 27 (m)

THE OLD MAID AND THE THIEF

Same cast as September 19
except:

Laetitia .... Hurley
Miss Todd .... Krebs
Miss Pinkerton .... Richmond

Followed by:

AMAHL AND THE NIGHT VISITORS

Same cast as September 19
except:

Mother .... Mayer

September 27

THE MARRIAGE OF FIGARO (Mozart)
(English version by
Ruth and Thomas Martin)

Conductor ...... Rosenstock

Almaviva .... Cassel
Countess .... Faull
Figaro .... Pease
Susanna .... Bishop
Cherubino .... Bible
Bartolo .... Renan
Marcellina .... Kreste
Basilio .... Vellucci
Curzio .... Pollock
Antonio .... Newman
Barbarina .... Richmond

September 28 (m)

CAVALLERIA RUSTICANA (Mascagni)

Conductor .... Shaynen

Santuzza ...... Scheunemann,
                (s, Neway)
Turiddu .... Poleri
Alfio .... Wentworth
Lola .... Bible
Mamma Lucia .... Kreste

Followed by:

I PAGLIACCI (Leoncavallo)

Conductor .... Rudel

Nedda .... Richmond
Canio .... Gari
Tonio .... Winters
Silvio .... Torigi
Beppe .... Pollock

September 28

TOSCA

Same cast as September 18
except:

Cavaradossi .... Petrak
Sacristan .... Renan
Shepherd .... Greene,
                (s, Evans)

October 2

BLUEBEARD'S CASTLE (Bartók)
United States stage premiere
(English version by
Chester Kallman)

Staged by ...... Butler (d)
Designer .. Ter-Arutunian (d)
Choreographer .... Butler
Conductor ...... Rosenstock

Bluebeard .... Pease
Judith .... Ayars
Judith's Inner Self .. Hinkson
1st Door .... Gitlin (d)
2nd Door .... Smith
3rd Door ...... Anthony (d)
4th Door .... Widman;
                Schulman (d)
6th Door .... Tetley
7th Door .... Kai (d),
        Mounsey (d), Savoia (d)

Followed by:

L'HEURE ESPAGNOLE (Ravel)
First performance by The New
York City Opera Company
(Prologue written by
José Ruben)

Staged by .... Ruben
Designer .. Ter-Arutunian (d)
Conductor .... Serafin

Concepcion .... Manners (d)
Gonzalve .... Lloyd
Torquemada .... Vellucci
Ramiro .... Cassel
Don Inigo Gomez .... Gauld
Prologue .... Moss (d)

October 3

AIDA

Same cast as September 25
except:

Amneris .... Bible
Aida .... Williams
Priestess .... Evans

October 4 (m)

THE LOVE FOR THREE ORANGES (Prokofiev)
(English translation by Victor
Seroff; spoken prologue written
by David Thornton)

Stage director ... Williams (d)
Conductor .... Rudel

King .... Pease
Prince .... Leech
Princess Clarissa ...... Kreste
Leandro .... Gaynes
Pantalone .... Renan
Truffaldino .... Vellucci
Celio .... Winters
Fata Morgana .... Faull
Princess Linetta .... LeSawyer
Princess Nicoletta ..Richmond
Princess Ninetta ...... Hurley
Cook .... Wentworth
Smeraldina .... Evans
Farfarello .... Smith
Prologue .... Kluge (d)

October 4

FAUST (Gounod)

Staged by .... Ruben
Choreographer .... Butler
Conductor .... Martin

Marguerite .... Yeend
Faust .... Petrak
Méphistophélès .... Scott
Valentin .... Cassel
Siébel .... Bible
Marthe .... Kreste
Wagner .... Newman

October 5 (m)

LA TRAVIATA

Same cast as September 21
except:

Conductor .... Rudel

Violetta .... Ayars
Alfredo .... Crain (d)
Germont .... Bonelli
Flora .... Evans

October 5

DON GIOVANNI

Same cast as September 20
except:

Donna Elvira ..... Richmond
Donna Anna .... Underwood
Don Ottavio .... Dalton
Zerlina .... Palmer

October 8

THE CONSUL (Menotti)
First performance by The New
York City Opera Company

Staged by .... Menotti
Designer ..... Armistead (d)
Choreographer .... Butler
Conductor .... Schippers

John Sorel .... Torigi
Magda Sorel .... Neway
The Mother .... Kreste
Secret Police Agent ... Renan
1st Plainclothesman ..Kuestner
2nd Plainclothesman .. Powell
Secretary .... Lane (d)
Mr. Kofner .... Gaynes
The Foreign
   Woman .... Marlo (d)
Anna Gomez ... Georgiou (d)
Vera Boronel .... Evans
The Magician
   Magadoff ...... Kelley (d)
Assan .... Newman
Voice on the
   record ...... Mabel Mercer

October 9

MADAMA BUTTERFLY (Puccini)
With members of the
Fujiwara Opera Company of
Tokyo as guests

Conductor .... Rosenstock

Butterfly .... Miyake (d)
Suzuki .... Kawasaki (d)
Kate Pinkerton .... LeSawyer
Pinkerton .... Petrak
Sharpless .... Torigi
Goro .... Takagi (d)
Yamadori ..... Takehara (d)
The Bonze .... Ishizu (d)
Imperial
   Commissioner ... Miyamoto
                         (d)

(Note: The performance was
bilingual. The Cio-Cio-San
began in Italian but lapsed into
Japanese toward the end of the
first act. The Goro sang in
Japanese only. The Suzuki sang
in Italian for the scene with the
American characters and in
Japanese otherwise.)

October 10

CARMEN (Bizet)

Staged by .... Erhardt
Choreographer .... Butler
Conductor .... Rosenstock

Carmen .... Lane
Don José .... Gari
Escamillo .... Cassel
Micaëla .... Yeend
Zuniga .... Gaynes
Frasquita .... Richmond
Mercédès .... Evans
Dancairo .... Pollock
Remendado .... Renan
Morales .... Newman
Gypsy dancers ..... Hinkson;
                         Tetley

October 11 (m)

THE MARRIAGE OF FIGARO

Same cast as September 27
except:

Conductor .... Martin
Almaviva .... Gramm
Countess .... Underwood
Cherubino .... Evans
Bartolo .... Wentworth
Marcellina .... Krebs
Barbarina .... LeSawyer

October 11

LA BOHÈME

Same cast as September 26
except:

Mimi .... Williams
Rodolfo .... Petrak
Schaunard .... Renan
Colline .... Gaynes
Alcindoro .... Newman

October 12 (m)

AIDA

Same cast as September 25
except:

Radames .... Leech
Priestess .... Evans

October 12

CAVALLERIA RUSTICANA

Same cast as September 28
(m) except:

Turiddu .... Crain
Lola .... Evans

Followed by:

I PAGLIACCI

Same cast as September 28
(m) except:

Nedda .... Manners
Tonio .... Bonelli
Beppe .... Sprinzena

October 15

WOZZECK (Berg)
(English translation by Eric
Blackall and Vida Harford)

Stage director .. Tavernia (d)
Scenic arrangement
                    Ter-Arutunian
Conductor .... Rosenstock

Captain .... Vellucci
Wozzeck .... Pease
Marie .... Neway
Child .... Oram
Doctor .... Renan
Andrès .... Lloyd
Margaret .... Evans
Drum major .... Dillon
1st Workman .... Wentworth
2nd Workman .... Powell
The Idiot .... Pollock

October 16

BLUEBEARD'S CASTLE

Same cast as October 2

Followed by:

L'HEURE ESPAGNOLE

Same cast as October 2

October 17

TOSCA

Same cast as September 18
except:

Tosca .... Spence
Cavaradossi .... Crain
Shepherd .... Evans

October 18 (m)

MADAMA BUTTERFLY

Same cast as October 9 except:

Conductor .... Martin

Suzuki .... Matsuchi (d)
Kate Pinkerton ...... Greene
Sharpless .... Renan

October 18

LA TRAVIATA

Same cast as September 21
except:

Conductor .... Rudel
Violetta .... Bollinger (d)
Germont .... Torigi
Flora .... Evans
Annina .... Greene

October 19 (m)

THE OLD MAID AND THE THIEF

Same cast as September 19
except:

Laetitia .... Hurley
Miss Pinkerton .... Richmond

Followed by:

AMAHL AND THE
NIGHT VISITORS

Same cast as September 19

October 19

FAUST

Same cast as October 4 except:

Faust .... Gar

October 22

BLUEBEARD'S CASTLE

Same cast as October 2

Followed by:

L'HEURE ESPAGNOLE

Same cast as October 2 except:

Concepcion .... Manner
                    (s, Bollinger
Gonzalve .... Kelle
Don Inigo Gomez..Wentwort

October 23

THE CONSUL

Same cast as October 8 except:

Assan .... Starling

October 24

DON GIOVANNI

Same cast as September 20 except:

Donna Elvira ..... Richmond
Commendatore ..Anderson (d)
Zerlina .... Palmer

October 25 (m)

CARMEN

Same cast as October 10 except:

Carmen .... Mayer
Don José .... Poleri
Escamillo ...... Ballarini (d)
Micaëla .... Hurley
Frasquita .... LeSawyer
Dancairo ...... Medinets (d)
Remendado .... Vellucci

October 25

CAVALLERIA RUSTICANA

Same cast as September 28 (m) except:

Santuzza .... Neway
Turiddu .... Crain
Lola .... Evans

Followed by:

I PAGLIACCI

Same cast as September 28 (m) except:

Conductor .... Shaynen
Nedda .... Grant (d)

October 26 (m)

THE LOVE FOR THREE ORANGES

Same cast as October 4 (m) except:

Leandro .... Gauld
Celio .... Newman
Fata Morgana .... Tynes
Princess Linetta .... Evans
Smeraldina .... Bible

October 26

AIDA

Same cast as September 25 except:

Amneris .... Lane
Ramfis .... Pease

October 29

THE CONSUL

Same cast as October 8 except:

Magda Sorel ..... Kuhlmann

October 30

WOZZECK

Same cast as October 15 except:

Captain .... Pollock
Marie .... Grant,
                    (s, Neway)
The Idiot .... Kuestner

October 31

THE MARRIAGE OF FIGARO

Same cast as September 27 except:

Figaro .... Gaynes
Susanna .... Hurley

Bartolo .... Wentworth
Antonio .... Powell

November 1

MADAMA BUTTERFLY

Same cast as September 21 (m) except:

Conductor .... Shaynen

Suzuki .... Kreste
Kate Pinkerton ...... Greene
Pinkerton .... Lloyd
Goro .... Sprinzena
Imperial
Commissioner .... Newman

November 2 (m)

CARMEN

Same cast as September 10 except:

Conductor .... Rudel

Escamillo .... Tipton
Micaëla .... Bollinger
Frasquita .... LeSawyer
Dancairo .... Medinets
Remendado .... Pollock

November 2

LA BOHÈME

Same cast as September 26 except:

Conductor .... Bamberger

Mimi .... Yeend
Musetta .... Richmond
Rodolfo .... Petrak
Colline .... Pease

Spring 1953 (MARCH 19–MAY 3)

Female artists
Ayars, Ann
Beauvais, Jeanne*
Bible, Frances
Blum, Kathryna*
Evans, Edith
Faull, Ellen
Fenn, Jean*
Georgiou, Vilma
Gillette, Priscilla*
Grant, Jeanne
Greene, Ethel
Haskins, Virginia
Hurley, Laurel
Kreste, Mary
Kuhlmann, Rosemary
Lane, Gloria
LeSawyer, Mary
Lewis, Brenda

Likova, Eva
Malbin, Elaine
Manners, Gail
Mari, Dolores*
Marlo, Maria
Mayer, Margery
McKnight, Anne
Nadell, Rosalind
Neway, Patricia
Omeron, Guen*
Richmond, Alice
Scheunemann, Leona
Spence, Wilma
Taussig, Carroll
Turner, Claramae*
Tynes, Margaret
Underwood, Willabelle
West, Lucretia*
Williams, Camilla

Yeend, Frances
Zambrana, Margarita

Male artists
Aiken, David*
Allen, Chet
Anderson, Robert
Arshansky, Michael
Cassell, Walter
Chabay, Leslie*
Crain, Jon
Dalton, Wesley
Dillard, William*
Ducree, Leonard
Fredericks, Walter
Gauld, Carlton
Gaynes, George
Goodwin, Russell

* New artist   * New artist   * New artist

Gramm, Donald
Greenwell, Gean
Herbert, Ralph
Kelley, Norman
Kluge, George
Kuestner, Charles
Leech, Lloyd Thomas
Lishner, Leon*
Lloyd, David
MacNeil, Cornell*
Manning, Riccardo*
Medinets, Alfred
Newman, Arthur
Pease, James
Petrak, Rudolf
Poleri, David
Pollock, Michael
Powell, Thomas
Renan, Emile
Russell, Jack*
Sammarco, James
Sarracino, Ernest*
Shriner, William*
Sprinzena, Nathaniel
Starling, William
Tipton, Thomas
Torigi, Richard
Treigle, Norman*
Vellucci, Luigi
Vertecchi, Giuseppe*
Wentworth, Richard
White, Andrew*
Wilderman, William*
Winters, Lawrence

Conductors
Martin, Thomas P.
Rosenstock, Joseph
Rudel, Julius
Schippers, Thomas

Dancers
Anthony, Mary
Bauer, Jamie*
Beck, Eve*
Hinkson, Mary
Kai, Una
Savoia, Patricia
Widman, Annalise

Butler, John
Meade, Gardiner*
Schulman, Alvin
Smith, James
Tetley, Glen

Choreographer
Butler, John

Directors
Butler, John
Englander, Roger*
Erhardt, Otto
Lewis, Robert*
Menotti, Gian Carlo
Sachse, Leopold
Tavernia, Patrick
Westerfield, James*
Williams, Lee

Designers
Armistead, Horace
Berman, Eugene
Bernstein, Aline*
Condell, H. A.
Dobujinsky, Mstislav
Fletcher, Robert*
Ter-Arutunian, Rouben

* New artist

March 19

BLUEBEARD'S CASTLE (Bartók)

Conductor ...... Rosenstock

Bluebeard .... Winters
Judith .... Ayars
Judith's Inner Self .. Hinkson
1st Door .... Schulman
2nd Door .... Smith
3rd Door .... Anthony
4th Door .... Widman
6th Door .... Tetley
7th Door ..... Kai, Beck (d),
                                    Savoia

Followed by:

L'HEURE ESPAGNOLE (Ravel)

Stage director ...... Tavernia
Conductor .... Schippers

Concepcion .... Manners
Gonzalve .... Lloyd
Torquemada .... Vellucci
Ramiro .... Cassel
Don Inigo Gomez ..... Gauld

(Note: In *L'Heure Espagnole*,
the spoken prologue of the
previous season's production
was omitted.)

March 20

CARMEN (Bizet)

Conductor .... Rosenstock

Carmen .... Lane
Don José .... Fredericks
Escamillo .... White (d)
Micaëla .... Mari (d)
Zuniga .... Gramm
Frasquita .... Richmond
Mercédès .... Tynes
Remendado .... Pollock
Dancairo .... Medinets
Morales .... Newman
Gypsy dancers .... Bauer (d);
                                    Tetley

March 21 (m)

LA TRAVIATA (Verdi)

Stage director ...... Tavernia
Choreographer .... Butler
Conductor .... Martin

Violetta .... Yeend
Alfredo .... Petrak
Germont .... MacNeil (d)
Flora .... LeSawyer
Annina .... Kreste
Gaston .... Vellucci
Douphol .... Wentworth
D'Obigny .... Renan
Dr. Grenvil .... Newman
Solo dancers ... Bauer; Tetley

March 21

THE MARRIAGE OF FIGARO
(Mozart)
(English version by
Ruth and Thomas Martin)

Choreographer .... Butler
Conductor .... Rosenstock

Almaviva .... Cassel
Countess .... Underwood

Figaro .... Herbert
Susanna .... Haskins
Cherubino .... Bible
Bartolo .... Wentworth
Marcellina .... Kreste
Basilio .... Vellucci
Curzio .... Pollock
Antonio .... Newman
Barbarina .... Richmond

March 22 (m)

MADAMA BUTTERFLY (Puccini)

Stage director ...... Williams
Conductor .... Martin

Butterfly .... Williams
Suzuki .... Mayer
Kate Pinkerton ...... Greene
Pinkerton .... Dalton
Sharpless .... Torigi
Goro .... Vellucci
Yamadori .... Renan
The Bonze .... Winters
*Imperial
  Commissioner* .... Newman

March 22

THE MEDIUM (Menotti)

Stage director ..Englander (d)
Conductor .... Schippers

Monica .... Haskins
Toby .... Allen
Madame Flora ... Turner (d)
Mrs. Gobineau ... Georgiou
Mr. Gobineau ..... Newman
Mrs. Nolan .... Evans,
                                    (s, Bible)

Followed by:

AMAHL AND THE
NIGHT VISITORS (Menotti)

Conductor .... Schippers

Amahl .... Sammarco
Mother .... Kuhlmann
King Kaspar .... Pollock
King Melchior ...... Winters
King Balthazar ... Wentworth
Page .... Starling
Shepherdess .... Bauer
Two Shepherds..Butler, Tetley

March 26

LA CENERENTOLA (Rossini)
First performance by The New
York City Opera Company

Staged by .... Erhardt
Designer ...... Ter-Arutunian
Choreographer .... Butler
Conductor .... Rosenstock

Prince Ramiro .. Manning (d)
Dandini .... Gaynes
Don Magnifico ... Wentworth
Clorinda .... Hurley
Tisbe .... Evans
Angelina .... Bible
Alidoro .... Newman

March 27

TOSCA (Puccini)

Conductor .... Rudel

Tosca .... McKnight
Cavaradossi .... Crain
Scarpia .... Cassel
Angelotti .... White
Spoletta .... Vellucci
Sacristan .... Wentworth
Sciarrone .... Newman
Shepherd .... Evans
Jailer .... Powell

March 28 (m)

THE LOVE FOR THREE ORANGES
(Prokofiev)
(English translation by Victor
Seroff; spoken prologue written
by David Thornton)

Choreographer .... Butler
Conductor .... Rudel

King .... Greenwell
Prince .... Lloyd
Princess Clarissa ...... Kreste
Leandro .... Gauld
Pantalone .... Renan
Truffaldino .... Vellucci
Celio .... Winters
Fata Morgana .... Faull
Princess Linetta ... LeSawyer
Princess Nicoletta ..Richmond
Princess Ninetta ..... Hurley
Cook .... Wentworth
Smeraldina .... Evans
Farfarello .... Tetley
Punch .... Tetley
Judy .... Bauer
Prologue .... Kluge

March 28

LA BOHÈME (Puccini)

Conductor .... Martin

Mimi .... Yeend
Musetta .... Fenn (d)
Rodolfo .... Petrak
Marcello .... Torigi
Schaunard .... Newman
Colline .... Treigle (d)
Benoit .... Wentworth
Alcindoro .... Renan
Parpignol .... Pollock

March 29 (m)

AIDA (Verdi)

Stage director ...... Williams
Conductor .... Rosenstock

King .... Greenwell
Amneris .... Bible
Aida .... Scheunemann
Radames ..... Vertecchi (d)
Ramfis .... Anderson
Amonasro .... Winters
Messenger .... Pollock
Priestess .... Evans
Solo dancers ... Bauer; Tetley

March 29

DON GIOVANNI (Mozart)

Staged by .... Erhardt
Conductor .... Rosenstock

Don Giovanni .... Cassel
Leporello .... Gaynes
Donna Elvira ..... McKnight
Commendatore .... Anderson
Donna Anna .... Faull
Don Ottavio ..... Chabay (d)
Masetto .... Renan
Zerlina .... Haskins

April 2

REGINA (Blitzstein)
First performance by The New
York City Opera Company

Director ...... Lewis, R. (d)
Scenic designer ... Armistead
Costume
  designer ..... Bernstein (d)
Choreographer .... Butler
Conductor .... Rudel

Regina Giddens .... Lewis, B.
Horace
  Giddens ... Wilderman (d)
Alexandra
  Giddens ...... Gillette (d)
Ben Hubbard .... Lishner (d)
Oscar Hubbard .... Renan
Birdie Hubbard .... Faull
Leo Hubbard .... Pollock
Jazz .... Dillard (d)
Addie .... West (d)
Cal .... Winters
Marshall .... Leech
Belle .... Tynes
Bagtry .... Goodwin
Manders .... Kuestner

(Note: Sets and costumes were
from the original 1949
Broadway production.)

April 3

AIDA

Same cast as March 29 (m)
except:

King .... Treigle
Amneris .... Mayer
Aida .... Scheunemann,
              (s, McKnight)
Ramfis .... Wilderman

April 4 (m)

THE MEDIUM

Same cast as March 22

Followed by:

AMAHL AND THE
NIGHT VISITORS

Same cast as March 22 except:

Mother .... Neway

April 4

CAVALLERIA RUSTICANA
(Mascagni)

Stage director ...... Tavernia
Conductor .... Rudel

Santuzza .... Zambrana
Turiddu .... Crain
Alfio .... Wentworth
Lola .... Richmond,
               (s, Evans)
Mamma Lucia .... Kreste

Followed by:

I PAGLIACCI (Leoncavallo)

Stage director ...... Tavernia
Conductor .... Rudel

Nedda .... Fenn
Canio .... Vertecchi
Tonio .... MacNeil
Silvio .... Torigi
Beppe .... Sprinzena

April 5 (m)

CARMEN

Same cast as March 20 except:

Don José .... Poleri
Escamillo .... Winters
Micaëla .... Blum (d)
Zuniga .... Wilderman
Mercédès .... Evans
Remendado .... Vellucci
Dancairo .... Renan

April 5

LA CENERENTOLA

Same cast as March 26

April 8

DIE FLEDERMAUS (Strauss)
First performance by The New
York City Opera Company
(English book and lyrics by
Ruth and Thomas Martin)

Staged by .... Westerfield (d)
Costume
  supervisor .... Fletcher (d)
Choreographer .... Butler
Conductor .... Martin

Eisenstein .... Russell (d)
Rosalinda .... Hurley
Adele .... Malbin
Alfred .... Crain
Falke .... Shriner (d)
Frank .... Wentworth
Blind .... Vellucci
Prince Orlofsky ..... Gramm
Sally .... Beauvais (d)
Frosch .... Sarracino (d)
Ivan .... Arshansky
Solo dancers ... Bauer; Tetley

(Note: The sets and costumes
were borrowed from various
sources and productions,
including a Sol Hurok touring
production of Die Fledermaus
and the 1952 Broadway show
My Darlin' Aida.)

April 9

BLUEBEARD'S CASTLE

Same cast as March 19

Followed by:

L'HEURE ESPAGNOLE

Same cast as March 19 except:

Gonzalve .... Kelley
Don Inigo Gomez .... Gauld,
    (s, Wentworth)

April 10

LA TRAVIATA

Same cast as March 21 (m)
except:

Violetta .... Likova
Alfredo .... Poleri
Flora .... LeSawyer,
    (s, Evans)

April 11 (m)

MADAMA BUTTERFLY

Same cast as March 22 (m)
except:

Suzuki .... Kreste,
    (s, Evans)
Pinkerton .... Fredericks
Goro .... Pollock
Imperial
  Commissioner ...... Powell

April 11

DON GIOVANNI

Same cast as March 29 except:

Donna Elvira .. Scheunemann
Commendatore .... Treigle
Don Ottavio .... Petrak
Masetto .... Newman
Zerlina .... Hurley

April 12 (m)

LA BOHÈME

Same cast as March 28 except:

Mimi .... Ayars
Musetta .... Richmond
Rodolfo .... Poleri
Schaunard .... Renan
Colline .... Gramm
Alcindoro .... Newman

April 12

AIDA

Same cast as March 29 (m)
except:

King .... Treigle
Amneris .... Mayer
Aida .... McKnight
Priestess .... Richmond,
    (s, Evans)

April 15

DER ROSENKAVALIER
(R. Strauss)

Conductor .... Rosenstock

Marschallin ..... McKnight
Baron Ochs .... Pease
Octavian .... Bible
Faninal .... Wentworth
Sophie .... Haskins
Marianne ...... Underwood
Valzacchi .... Vellucci
Annina .... Evans
Police
  Commissioner .... Newman
Singer .... Petrak
Innkeeper .... Sprinzena
Major-Domo of
  the Marschallin .... Powell
Major-Domo of
  Faninal .... Pollock
Attorney .... Newman
1st Orphan .... LeSawyer
2nd Orphan .... Tynes
3rd Orphan .... Greene
Animal vendor ..... Pollock
Milliner .... Richmond
Leopold .... Sarracino
Mohamet .... Ducree

April 16

THE CONSUL (Menotti)

Conductor .... Schippers

John Sorel .... Torigi
Magda Sorel .... Neway
The Mother .... Kreste
Secret Police Agent .. Lishner
1st Plainclothesman .. Kuestner
2nd Plainclothesman .. Powell
Secretary .... Lane
Mr. Kofner .... Aiken (d)
The Foreign Woman .. Marlo
Anna Gomez ...... Georgiou
Vera Boronel .... Evans
The Magician
  Magadoff .... Kelley
Assan .... Newman
Voice on the
  record ...... Mabel Mercer

April 17

REGINA

Same cast as April 2

April 18 (m)

DIE FLEDERMAUS

Same cast as April 8 except:

Rosalinda ...... Omeron (d)
Alfred .... Leech
Prince Orlofsky ..... Pollock

April 18

THE MARRIAGE OF FIGARO

Same cast as March 21 except:

Almaviva .... Gramm
Countess .... Yeend

Susanna .... Hurley
Cherubino .... Evans
Antonio .... Powell
Barbarina .... LeSawyer

April 19 (m)

TOSCA

Same cast as March 27 except:

Tosca .... Spence
Cavaradossi .... Petrak
Angelotti .... Treigle
Shepherd .... Greene

April 19

CARMEN

Same cast as March 20 except:

Escamillo .... Tipton
Micaëla .... Hurley
Zuniga .... Gaynes
Mercédès .... Evans
Dancairo .... Renan
Morales .... Torigi

April 22

LA CENERENTOLA

Same cast as March 26

April 23

DER ROSENKAVALIER

Same cast as April 15 except:

Octavian .... Evans
Sophie .... Mari
Annina .... Nadell,
    (s, Lane)
Singer .... Crain
2nd Orphan .... Taussig
3rd Orphan .... Daniels

April 24

LA BOHÈME

Same cast as March 28 except:

Mimi .... Williams
Musetta .... Richmond
Marcello .... Tipton
Benoit .... Renan

April 25 (m)

THE LOVE FOR THREE ORANGES

Same cast as March 28 (m)
except:

King .... Pease
Prince .... Leech
Fata Morgana .... Tynes

April 25

THE CONSUL

Same cast as April 16 except:

Magda Sorel ..... Kuhlmann
Secret Police Agent ... Renan

April 26 (m)

CAVALLERIA RUSTICANA

Same cast as April 4 except:

Santuzza .... Neway
Alfio .... Newman
Lola .... Evans

Followed by:

I PAGLIACCI

Same cast as April 4 except:

Nedda .... Grant
Canio .... Fredericks
Tonio .... Winters
Silvio .... Tipton

April 26

TOSCA

Same cast as March 27 except:

Cavaradossi .... Petrak
Sacristan .... Renan

April 29

REGINA

Same cast as April 2

April 30

DIE FLEDERMAUS

Same cast as April 8 except:

Rosalinda .... Omeron
Prince Orlofsky ...... Pollock

May 1

LA CENERENTOLA

Same cast as March 26 except:

Angelina .... Kuhlman

May 2 (m)

CARMEN

Same cast as March 20 except:

Micaëla .... Richmond,
                     (s, Hurley)
Zuniga .... Treigle
Frasquita .... LeSawyer
Mercédès .... Evans

May 2

MADAMA BUTTERFLY

Same cast as March 22 (m) except:

Butterfly .... Faull
Suzuki .... Kreste
Kate Pinkerton .... LeSawyer
Pinkerton .... Crain
Sharpless .... Tipton
The Bonze .... Wentworth

May 3 (m)

DIE FLEDERMAUS

Same cast as April 8 except:

Rosalinda .... Omeron
Alfred .... Leech
Frank .... Newman,
                 (s, Wentworth)

May 3

LA CENERENTOLA

Same cast as March 26

Fall 1953 (OCTOBER 8 – NOVEMBER 8)

Female artists
Andrea, Jennie
Ayars, Ann
Bible, Frances
Bishop, Adelaide
Bunn, Catherine*
Caputo, Lila
Clayton, Helen*
Cundari, Emily*
Curtin, Phyllis*
Di Gerlando, Maria*
Evans, Edith
Fenn, Jean
Gannon, Teresa*
Georgiou, Vilma
Haskins, Virginia
Heckman, Winifred*
Hurley, Laurel
Kreste, Mary
Kuhlmann, Rosemary
Lane, Gloria
LeSawyer, Mary
Lewis, Brenda
Likova, Eva
MacNeil, Dorothy
McKnight, Anne
Mari, Dolores
Turner, Claramae
Tynes, Margaret
Underwood, Willabelle
West, Lucretia
Williams, Camilla

Male artists
Anderson, Robert

* New artist

Arshansky, Michael
Cassel, Walter
Crain, Jon
Dillard, William
Druary, John
Fredericks, Walter
Frigerio, Claudio*
Gaynes, George
Goodwin, Russell
Gramm, Donald
Hecht, Manfred
Herbert, Ralph
Iaia, Gianni*
Kuestner, Charles
Leech, Lloyd Thomas
Lishner, Leon
Lloyd, David
MacNeil, Cornell
Manning, Riccardo
Medinets, Alfred
Newman, Arthur
Petrak, Rudolf
Poleri, David
Pollock, Michael
Powell, Thomas
Redding, Earl*
Renan, Emile
Rubes, Jan*
Russell, Jack
Starling, William
Tipton, Thomas
Torigi, Richard
Treigle, Norman
Vellucci, Luigi
Wentworth, Richard

* New artist

Wilderman, William
Winters, Lawrence
Worth, Coley*

Members of the Fujiwara Opera Company of Tokyo
Kurimoto, Tadashi*
Matsuchi, Kazuko
Saito, Tatsuo*
Sunahara, Michiko*
Takagi, Kijoshi
Yamaguchi, Kazuko*

Conductors
Martin, Thomas P.
Rosenstock, Joseph
Rudel, Julius
Schippers, Thomas

Solo dancers
Conde, Felisa

Tetley, Glen

Choreographer
Butler, John

Directors
Ehrhardt, Otto
Geiger-Torel, Herman*
Jordan, Glenn*

* New artist

Lewis, Robert
Preminger, Otto*
Sachse, Leopold
Tavernia, Patrick
Williams, Lee

Designers
Armistead, Horace
Condell, H. A.
Ter-Arutunian, Rouben

* New artist

October 8

LA CENERENTOLA (Rossini)

Conductor .... Rosenstock

Prince Ramiro ..... Manning
Dandini .... Gaynes
Don Magnifico ... Wentworth
Clorinda .... Hurley
Tisbe .... Evans
Angelina .... Bible
Alidoro .... Newman
Solo dancers .. Conde; Tetley

October 9

REGINA (Blitzstein)

Conductor .... Rudel

Regina Giddens .... Lewis
Horace Giddens .. Wilderman
*Alexandra
  Giddens* ...... D. MacNeil
Ben Hubbard .... Lishner
Oscar Hubbard .... Renan
Birdie Hubbard .. Underwood
Leo Hubbard .... Pollock
Jazz .... Dillard
Addie .... West
Cal .... Winters
Marshall .... Leech
Belle .... Tynes
Bagtry .... Goodwin
Manders .... Kuestner

October 10 (m)

CARMEN (Bizet)

Conductor .... Rosenstock

Carmen .... Lane
Don José .... Fredericks
Escamillo .... Winters
Micaëla .... Clayton (d)
Zuniga .... Wilderman
Frasquita .... Hurley
Mercédès .... Evans
Remendado .... Pollock
Dancairo .... Medinets
Morales .... Torigi
Solo dancers ... Conde; Tetley

October 10

DIE FLEDERMAUS (Strauss)

Staged by .... Jordan (d)
Conductor .... Martin

Eisenstein .... Russell
Rosalinda .... Fenn
Adele .... Bishop
Alfred .... Leech

Falke .... Redding (d)
Frank .... Wentworth
Blind .... Vellucci
Prince Orlofsky .... Gramm
Sally .... Andrea
Frosch .... Worth (d)
Ivan .... Arshansky
Solo dancers .. Conde; Tetley

October 11 (m)

LA BOHÈME (Puccini)

Conductor .... Martin,
        (s, Schippers)

Mimi .... C. Williams
Musetta .... Hurley
Rodolfo .... Crain
Marcello .... Torigi
Schaunard .... Newman
Colline .... Rubes (d)
Benoit .... Wentworth
Alcindoro .... Renan
Parpignol .... Pollock

October 11

DON GIOVANNI (Mozart)

Stage director ...... Williams
Conductor .... Rosenstock

Don Giovanni .... Cassel
Leporello .... Gaynes
Donna Elvira .... McKnight
Commendatore ...... Treigle
Donna Anna ... Underwood
Don Ottavio .... Petrak
Masetto .... Renan
Zerlina .... Haskins

October 14

HANSEL AND GRETEL
(Humperdinck)
First performance by The New
York City Opera Company
(Sung in an English
translation)

Staged by ... Geiger-Torel (d)
Designer ...... Ter-Arutunian
Conductor .... Schippers

Father .... Wentworth
Mother .... Underwood
Hansel .... Bible
Gretel .... Hurley
Witch .... Turner
Sandman .... Gannon (d)
Dew Fairy ..... Cundari (d)

October 15

REGINA

Same cast as October 9

October 16

TOSCA (Puccini)

Conductor .... Rudel

Tosca .... McKnight
Cavaradossi .... Poleri
Scarpia .... Cassel
Angelotti .... Anderson
Spoletta .... Vellucci
Sacristan .... Wentworth

Sciarrone .... Newman
Shepherd .... Kreste
Jailer .... Powell

October 17 (m)

LA CENERENTOLA

Same cast as October 8 except:

Prince Ramiro .... Lloyd
Dandini .... Herbert
Angelina .... Kuhlmann,
        (s, Bible)

October 17

LA TRAVIATA (Verdi)

Conductor .... Martin

Violetta .... Fenn
Alfredo .... Manning
Germont .... C. MacNeil
Flora .... LeSawyer
Annina .... Kreste
Gaston .... Vellucci
Douphol .... Gramm
D'Obigny .... Renan
Dr. Grenvil .... Lishner
Solo dancers .. Conde; Tetley

October 18 (m)

CARMEN

Same cast as October 10 (m)
except:

Conductor .... Rudel,
        (s, Rosenstock)

Escamillo .... Tipton
Micaëla .... Mari
Frasquita ...... D. MacNeil
Mercédès ..... Heckman (d),
        (s, Evans)

October 18

THE MARRIAGE OF FIGARO
(Mozart)
(English version by
Ruth and Thomas Martin)

Conductor .... Rosenstock

Almaviva .... Cassel
Countess .... Ayars
Figaro .... Gaynes
Susanna .... Haskins
Cherubino .... Bible
Bartolo .... Wentworth
Marcellina .... Kreste
Basilio .... Vellucci
Curzio .... Pollock
Antonio .... Newman
Barbarina .... Georgiou

October 22

THE TRIAL (Von Einem)
American premiere
(*Der Prozess*; English version
by Ruth and Thomas Martin)

Directed by ... Preminger (d)
Designer ...... Ter-Arutunian
Conductor .... Rosenstock

Joseph K. .... Druary
Franz .... Treigle

Willem .... Renan
Inspector .... Winters
Frau Grubach .... Evans
Fräulein Burstner ..Curtin (d)
A passerby .... Winters
Janitor's son .... Kuestner
A young lad .... Vellucci,
                    (s, Kuestner)
Investigating
  magistrate ..... Wilderman
Wife of the
  court attendant ..Curtin (d)
Student .... Pollock
Court attendant ...... Renan
The whipper .... Wilderman
Albert K. .... Lishner
Leni .... Curtin (d)
The lawyer .... Herbert
Court recorder ...... Starling
Manufacturer .... Winters
Three businessmen .. Vellucci,
                  Torigi, Newman
Assistant manager .... Pollock
A hunchback girl ... Gannon
Titorelli .... Crain
Priest .... Winters
Two gentlemen in
  black .... Powell, Goodwin

October 23

DON GIOVANNI

Same cast as October 11
except:

Don Giovanni ... Wildermann
Leporello .... Wentworth
Donna Elvira ..... Bunn (d)
Commendatore .... Anderson
Donna Anna .... Likova
Zerlina .... D. MacNeil

October 24 (m)

HANSEL AND GRETEL

Same cast as October 14
except:

Father .... Hecht
Mother .... Kreste
Dew Fairy .... LeSawyer

October 24

LA BOHÈME

Same cast as October 11 (m)
except:

Mimi .... Ayars
Musetta .... D. MacNeil
Rodolfo .... Petrak
Colline .... Treigle

October 25 (m)

LA TRAVIATA

Same cast as October 17
except:

Violetta .... Di Gerlando (d)
Alfredo .... Crain
Germont .... Frigerio (d)

October 25

LA CENERENTOLA

Same cast as October 8 except:

Angelina .... Kuhlmann

October 27

MADAMA BUTTERFLY (Puccini)

Staged by .... Sachse
Conductor .... Martin

Butterfly .... Sunahara (d)
Suzuki .... Matsuchi
Kate Pinkerton .... LeSawyer
Pinkerton .... Lloyd
Sharpless .... Torigi
Goro .... Takagi
Yamadori ..... Kurimoto (d)
The Bonze .... Kurimoto (d)
Imperial
  Commissioner ... Saito (d)

(Note: The performance was
bilingual, Japanese and Italian.
The Japanese costumes were
loaned by the Fujiwara Opera
Company of Tokyo.)

October 28

MADAMA BUTTERFLY

Same cast as October 27
except:

Pinkerton .... Petrak
Sharpless .... Tipton
The Bonze .. Yamaguchi (d),
               (s, Kurimoto)

October 29

LA CENERENTOLA

Same cast as October 8 except:

Dandini .... Herbert
Don Magnifico ..... Lishner,
               (s, Wentworth)
Angelina .... Kuhlmann

October 30

RIGOLETTO (Verdi)

Staged by .... Sachse
Choreographer .... Butler
Conductor .... Rudel

Duke .... Fredericks
Rigoletto .... Cassel
Gilda .... Likova
Sparafucile .... Treigle
Maddalena .... Evans,
               (s, Heckman)
Giovanna .... Kreste
Monterone .... Wentworth
Marullo .... Newman
Borsa .... Pollock
Ceprano .... Lishner
Countess Ceprano .. LeSawyer
Page .... Caputo
Solo dancers .. Conde; Tetley

October 31 (m)

MADAMA BUTTERFLY

Same cast as October 27
except:

Pinkerton .... Crain

October 31

THE MARRIAGE OF FIGARO

Same cast as October 18
except:

Countess .... McKnight
Figaro .... Herbert
Barbarina .... LeSawyer

November 1 (m)

HANSEL AND GRETEL

Same cast as October 14
except:

Father .... Hecht
Mother .... Kreste
Gretel .... Bishop
Dew Fairy .... LeSawyer

November 1

THE TRIAL

Same cast as October 22
except:

Janitor's son .... Vellucci

(Note: Role of A Young Lad
does not appear on this
program.)

November 5

RIGOLETTO

Same cast as October 30
except:

Duke .... Iaia (d)
Gilda .... Mari
Sparafucile ...... Wilderman
Maddalena .... Heckman

November 6

CARMEN

Same cast as October 10 (m)
except:

Carmen .... Kuhlmann
Escamillo .... Torigi
Micaëla .... D. MacNeil
Zuniga .... Gramm
Frasquita .... LeSawyer
Morales .... Newman

November 7 (m)

DIE FLEDERMAUS

Same cast as October 10
except:

Prince Orlofsky ..... Pollock

November 7

TOSCA

Same cast as October 16
except:

Cavaradossi .... Petrak
Scarpia .... Winters
Angelotti .... Treigle

November 8 (m)

LA TRAVIATA

Same cast as October 17
except:

Violetta .... Ayars
Alfredo .... Lloyd
Douphol .... Newman

November 8

LA BOHÈME

Same cast as October 11 (m)
except:

Musetta .... D. MacNeil
Colline .... Treigle

Spring 1954 (MARCH 25 – MAY 2)

Female artists
Andrea, Jennie
Bible, Frances
Bishop, Adelaide
Bliss, Helena
Bonini, Peggy*
Bunn, Catherine
Carlos, Rosemary*
Chambers, Madelaine*
Cundari, Emily
Curtin, Phyllis
Curtis, Mary*
Drake, Diana*
Faull, Ellen
Floyd, Sarah*
Gannon, Teresa
Gateson, Marjorie*
Handzlik, Jean*
Hurley, Laurel
Kreste, Mary
Kuhlmann, Rosemary
Lane, Gloria
LeSawyer, Mary
Likova, Eva
Lind, Gloria*
Mari, Dolores
Mayer, Margery
Nadell, Rosalind
Newton, Adele*
Phillips, Helen
Resnik, Regina
Russell, Anna*
Smith, Carol*
Sullivan, Jo*
Underwood, Willabelle
West, Lucretia
Williams, Camilla
Wynder, Gloria*
Yeend, Frances

Male artists
Albertson, Jack*
Anderson, Robert
Arshansky, Michael
Brown, Walter*
Carlson, Stanley
Cassel, Walter
Crain, Jon
Druary, John
Eckart, Frank*
Emanuel, Dawin
Fredericks, Walter
Gainey, Andrew
Gallagher, Robert*
Gaynes, George
Gramm, Donald
Harper, Fred*
Hawthorne, Jim*

Herbert, Ralph
Ives, Burl*
Kuestner, Charles
Leech, Lloyd Thomas
Lishner, Leon
Lloyd, David
Lyon. Milton*
MacNeil, Cornell
McChesney, Ernest*
McIver, William*
Medinets, Alfred
Nekolny, Miles*
Newman, Arthur
Petrak, Rudolf
Plotkin, Benjamin
Pollock, Michael
Powell, Thomas
Renan, Emile
Rounseville, Robert
Russell, Jack
Scott, Norman
Smith, Bill*
Sprinzena, Nathaniel
Starling, William
Stewart, Thomas*
Torigi, Richard
Treigle, Norman
Vellucci, Luigi
Vinay, Ramon
Wentworth, Richard
Wilderman, William
Winters, Lawrence

Conductors
Martin, Thomas P.
Rosenstock, Joseph
Rudel, Julius
Schippers, Thomas

Solo dancers
Conde, Felisa

Butler, John
Driver, Donn*
Tetley, Glen

Choreographer
Butler, John

Directors
Butler, Bill*
Erhardt, Otto
Geiger-Torel, Herman
Hammerstein, William*
Jordan, Glenn

* New artist

Menotti, Gian Carlo
Robbins, Jerome*
Sachse, Leopold

Designers
Bay, Howard*
Berman, Eugene
Boyt, John*
Condell, H. A.
Smith, Oliver*
Ter-Arutunian, Rouben

* New artist

March 25

SALOME (R. Strauss)

Costume designer ... Boyt (d)
Conductor .... Rosenstock

Herodes ..... McChesney (d)
Herodias .... Kreste
Salome .... Curtin
Jochanaan .... Cassel
Narraboth .... Crain
Page .... Bible
1st Jew .... Sprinzena
2nd Jew .... Vellucci
3rd Jew .... Medinets
4th Jew .... Pollock
5th Jew .... Wentworth
Cappadocian .... Powell
Slave .... Kuestner
1st Nazarene ..... Wilderman
2nd Nazarene ...... Emanuel
1st Soldier .... Treigle
2nd Soldier .... Newman

March 26

RIGOLETTO (Verdi)

Conductor .... Rudel

Duke .... Petrak
Rigoletto .... Cassel
Gilda .... Likova
Sparafucile .... Treigle
Maddalena .... West
Giovanna .... Kreste
Monterone .... Wentworth
Marullo .... Newman
Borsa .... Pollock
Ceprano .... Lishner
Countess Ceprano .. LeSawyer
Page .... Caputo
Solo dancers .. Conde; Tetley

March 27 (m)

CARMEN (Bizet)

Conductor .... Rosenstock

Carmen .... Kuhlmann
Don José .... Rounseville
Escamillo .... MacNeil
Micaëla ...... Chambers (d)
Zuniga .... Treigle
Frasquita .... Bonini (d)
Mercédès .... West
Remendado .... Pollock
Dancairo .... Renan
Morales .... Torigi
Gypsy dancers. .Conde; Tetley

March 27

DIE FLEDERMAUS (J. Strauss)
(English book and lyrics by
Ruth and Thomas Martin)

Conductor .... Martin

Eisenstein .... J. Russell
Rosalinda .... Lind (d)
Adele .... Hurley
Alfred .... Leech
Falke .... Wilderman
Frank .... Wentworth
Blind .... Vellucci
Prince Orlofsky ..... Gramm
Sally .... Andrea
Frosch .... Harper (d)
Ivan .... Arshansky
Guests at Prince
 Orlofsky's party .... Resnik,
 Scott, Vinay

(Note: A gala performance
celebrating the tenth anni-
versary of The New York City
Opera's first performance,
February 21, 1944. Norman
Scott was heard in "La
Calunnia" from The Barber of
Seville, Regina Resnik sang
Strauss's "Tales from the
Vienna Woods," and Ramon
Vinay sang Joaquin Nin's song
"El vito." After singing "La
Calunnia," Norman Scott went
to the Metropolitan Opera,
where he was to sing in a gala
performance at that house.)

March 28 (m)

LA TRAVIATA (Verdi)

Staged by .... Jordan
Conductor .... Martin

Violetta .... Yeend
Alfredo .... Crain
Germont .... Cassel
Flora .... LeSawyer
Annina .... Kreste
Gaston .... Vellucci
Douphol .... Newman
D'Obigny .... Renan
Dr. Grenvil .... Lishner
Solo dancers ... Conde; Tetley

March 28

DON GIOVANNI (Mozart)

Staged by .... Erhardt
Conductor ...... Rosenstock

Don Giovanni .... Wilderman
Leporello .... Wentworth
Donna Elvira .... Likova
Commendatore .... Anderson
Donna Anna ...... Curtis (d)
Ottavio .... Petrak,
 (s, Manton)
Masetto .... Renan
Zerlina .... Chambers

(Note: Raymond Manton was
not to appear with The New
York City Opera Company.)

April 1

THE TENDER LAND (Copland)
World premiere

Staged by ...... Robbins (d)
Scenic designer .... Smith (d)
Costume designer ...... Boyt
Choreographer .... Butler
Conductor .... Schippers

Beth .... Newton (d)
Ma Moss ...... Handzlik (d)
Mr. Splinters .... Pollock
Laurie Moss ..... Carlos (d)
Top .... Gainey
Martin .... Crain
Grandpa Moss .... Treigle
Mr. Jenks .... Powell
Mrs. Splinters .... Kreste
Mrs. Jenks .... Gannon

Followed by:

AMAHL AND THE
NIGHT VISITORS (Menotti)

Stage director .. B. Butler (d)
Conductor .... Schippers

Amahl .... McIver (d)
Mother .... Kuhlmann
King Kaspar .... Pollock
King Melchiòr ...... Winters
King Balthazar ... Wentworth
Page .... Starling
Shepherdess .... Conde
Two
 Shepherds ... Butler, Tetley

April 2

THE MARRIAGE OF FIGARO
(Mozart)
(English version by
Ruth and Thomas Martin)

Conductor ...... Rosenstock

Almaviva .... Winters
Countess .... Faull
Figaro .... Herbert
Susanna .... Hurley
Cherubino .... Bible
Bartolo .... Renan,
 (s, Wentworth)
Marcellina .... Kreste
Basilio .... Vellucci

Curzio .... Pollock
Antonio .... Newman
Barbarina .... Bonini

April 3 (m)

HANSEL AND GRETEL
(Humperdinck)
(Sung in an
English translation)

Conductor .... Schippers

Father .... Newman,
 (s, Wentworth)
Mother .... Kreste
Hansel .... Nadell
Gretel .... Bishop
Witch .... A. Russell (d)
Sandman .... Cundari
Dew Fairy .... LeSawyer

April 3

LA CENERENTOLA (Rossini)

Conductor ...... Rosenstock

Prince Ramiro ...... Druary
Dandini .... Gramm
Don Magnifico ...... Lishner
Clorinda .... Hurley
Tisbe .... Nadell
Angelina .... Bible
Alidoro .... Newman
Solo dancers .. Conde; Tetley

April 4 (m)

LA CENERENTOLA

Same cast as April 3 except:

Prince Ramiro .... Lloyd
Dandini .... Gaynes
Don Magnifico ... Wentworth
Angelina .... Kuhlmann

April 4

TOSCA (Puccini)

Conductor .... Rudel

Tosca .... Curtis
Cavaradossi .... Crain
Scarpia .... Cassel
Angelotti .... Treigle
Spoletta .... Vellucci
Sacristan .... Renan
Sciarrone .... Newman
Shepherd .... Gannon
Jailer .... Powell

April 8

SHOW BOAT (Kern)
First performance by The New
York City Opera Company

Staged by .. Hammerstein (d)
Scenic designer ..... Bay (d)
Costume designer ...... Boyt
Choreographer .... Butler
Conductor .... Rudel

Captain Andy .... Carlson
Parthy Ann
 Hawks ...... Gateson (d)
Magnolia .... Hurley
Gaylord Ravenal ..Rounseville

Julie .... Bliss
Steve .... Gallagher (d)
Queenie .... West
Joe .... B. Smith (d)
Frank .... Albertson (d)
Ellie .... Drake (d)
Jim .... Pollock
McLain .... Newman
Guitar player ...... Kuestner
Piano player ...... Lyon (d)
Landlady .... Floyd (d)
Pete .... Pollock
Sheriff Vallon .... Lishner
Doorman .... Brown (d)
Old Lady .... Floyd (d)
Ethel .... Wynder (d)
Kim .... Newton
Two
 Backwoodsmen .. Newman,
                    Plotkin

April 9

DON GIOVANNI

Same cast as March 28 except:

Donna Elvira .... Bunn
Commendatore .. Stewart (d)
Masetto .... Lishner

April 10 (m)

MADAMA BUTTERFLY (Puccini)

Staged by .... Jordan
Conductor .... Martin

Butterfly .... C. Williams
Suzuki .... Bible
Kate Pinkerton .... LeSawyer
Pinkerton .... Lloyd
Sharpless .... Herbert
Goro .... Vellucci
Yamadori .... Renan
The Bonze .... Lishner
Imperial
 Commissioner .... Powell,
                    (s, Newman)

April 10

LA BOHÈME (Puccini)

Conductor .... Schippers,
                    (s, Martin)

Mimi .... Mari
Musetta .... Bonini
Rodolfo .... Crain
Marcello .... Torigi
Schaunard .... Newman
Colline .... Treigle
Benoit .... Wentworth
Alcindoro .... Renan
Parpignol .... Pollock

April 11 (m)

RIGOLETTO

Same cast as March 26 except:

Duke .... Fredericks
Rigoletto .... MacNeil
Sparafucile ...... Wilderman
Maddalena .... Lane
Monterone .... Treigle

April 11

SALOME

Same cast as March 25 except:

Narraboth ... Hawthorne (d)

April 15

FALSTAFF (Verdi)
First performance by The New
York City Opera Company
(English translation by
Chester Kallman)

Staged by .... Erhardt
Designer .... Boyt
Conductor ...... Rosenstock

Sir John Falstaff .. Wentworth
Fenton .... Crain
Ford .... Cassel
Dr. Caius .... Pollock
Bardolph .... Vellucci
Pistol .... Treigle
Alice Ford .... Curtin
Nannetta .... Chambers
Meg Page .... Kuhlmann
Dame Quickly .... Mayer

April 16

CARMEN

Same cast as March 27 (m)
except:

Carmen .... Lane
Don José .... Fredericks
Micaëla .... Mari
Mercédès .... Nadell
Remendado .... Vellucci

April 17 (m)

SHOW BOAT

Same cast as April 8 except:

Magnolia .... Sullivan (d)

April 17

LA TRAVIATA

Same cast as March 28 (m)
except:

Violetta .... Likova
Alfredo .... Druary
Germont .... MacNeil

April 18 (m)

HANSEL AND GRETEL

Same cast as April 3 (m)
except:

Hansel .... Bible
Gretel .... Hurley

April 18

THE MARRIAGE OF FIGARO

Same cast as April 2 except:

Almaviva .... Cassel
Countess .... Underwood

Figaro .... Treigle
Susanna .... Bishop,
                    (s, Bonini)
Cherubino .... Nadell
Bartolo .... Wentworth
Curzio .... Kuestner
Barbarina .... LeSawyer

April 21

SALOME

Same cast as March 25 except:

Jochanaan .... Herbert
Narraboth .... Hawthorne
1st Soldier .... Stewart,
                    (s, Treigle)

April 22

THE TENDER LAND

Same cast as April 1

Followed by:

AMAHL AND THE
NIGHT VISITORS

Same cast as April 1 except:

Mother .... Lane
King Kaspar .... Vellucci
King Melchior .. Nekolny (d)
King Balthazar ...... Lishner

April 23

LA BOHÈME

Same cast as April 10 except:

Mimi .... Yeend
Rodolfo .... Crain,
                    (s, Petrak)
Colline .... Wilderman

April 24 (m)

LA CENERENTOLA

Same cast as April 3 except:

Dandini .... Herbert
Don Magnifico ... Wentworth

April 24

MADAMA BUTTERFLY

Same cast as April 10 (m)
except:

Butterfly .... Faull
Suzuki .... Kreste
Pinkerton .... Petrak
Sharpless .... Torigi
The Bonze .... Treigle
Imperial
 Commissioner .... Newman

April 25 (m)

DIE FLEDERMAUS

Same cast as March 27 except:

Frank .... Newman
Prince Orlofsky ..... Pollock
Sally .... Bonini

April 25

FALSTAFF

Same cast as April 15 except:

Fenton .... Hawthorne
Dame Quickly ..C. Smith (d)

April 30

FALSTAFF

Same cast as April 15 except:

Sir John Falstaff .. Wilderman
Fenton .... Hawthorne
Dame Quickly ..... C. Smith

May 1 (m)

DIE FLEDERMAUS

Same cast as March 27 except:

Adele .... Sullivan
Frank .... Newman
Sally .... Bonini

May 1

CARMEN

Same cast as March 27 (m)
except:

Don José .... Fredericks
Micaëla .... Mari
Mercédès .... Nadell

May 2 (m)

TOSCA

Same cast as April 4 except:

Cavaradossi ...... Eckart (d)
Shepherd .... Kreste

May 2

SHOW BOAT

Same cast as April 8 except:

Captain Andy ...... Ives (d)
Gaylord Ravenal .. Hawthorne
Queenie .... Phillips
Joe .... Winters
Frank .... Driver (d)

Fall 1954 (SEPTEMBER 29– OCTOBER 31)

Female artists
Allen, Betty*
Andrea, Jennie
Bible, Frances
Bliss, Helena
Bonini, Peggy
Bunn, Catherine
Chambers, Madelaine
Cundari, Emily
Curtin, Phyllis
Evans, Edith
Faull, Ellen
Fleming, Sarah*
Floyd, Sarah
Gannon, Teresa
Handzlik, Jean
Hurley, Laurel
Jager, Susan*
Kuhlmann, Rosemary
Lane, Gloria
LeSawyer, Mary
Likova, Eva
Mari, Dolores
Mayer, Margery
Newton, Adele
Niles, Marian*
Ribla, Gertrude
Russell, Anna
Spence, Wilma
Underwood, Willabelle
Virga, Rose
West, Lucretia
Willauer, Marguerite*
Williams, Mary
Wynder, Gloria
Yeend, Frances

Male artists
Brown, Walter
Cassel, Walter
Cocolios-Bardi, Giorgio*
Cooper, William
Crain, Jon

* New artist

Cunningham, Davis*
Druary, John
Eckart, Frank
Emanuel, Dawin
Fredericks, Walter
Gallagher, Robert
Gauld, Carlton
Gramm, Donald
Grinnage, Leonard*
Hecht, Manfred
Kluge, George
Kuestner, Charles
Leech, Lloyd Thomas
Lishner, Leon
Lyon, Milton
MacNeil, Cornell
McChesney, Ernest
Newman, Arthur
Petrak, Rudolf
Pollock, Michael
Powell, Thomas
Reardon, John*
Renan, Emile
Rounseville, Robert
Thompson, Hugh
Torigi, Richard
Treigle, Norman
Urhausen, Roy*
Vellucci, Luigi
Wentworth, Richard
Wilderman, William
Winters, Lawrence
Worth, Coley

Conductors
Martin, Thomas P.
Rosenstock, Joseph
Rudel, Julius
Schippers, Thomas

Solo dancers
Lewis, Lila*
Seckler, Beatrice*
Winter, Ethel*

* New artist

Blair, Jack*
Jackwith, Gerald*
McKayle, Donald
Schulman, Alvin

Choreographers
Maslow, Sophie
Weidman, Charles

Directors
Erhardt, Otto
Geiger-Torel, Herman
Hammerstein, William
Jordan, Glenn
Rosing, Vladimir
Sachse, Leopold
Williams, Lee

Designers
Bay, Howard
Boyt, John
Condell, H. A.
Ter-Arutunian, Rouben

* New artist

September 29

AIDA (Verdi)

Staged by .... Jordan
Choreographer ...... Maslow
Conductor ...... Rosenstock

King .... Treigle
Amneris .... Lane
Aida .... Yeend
Radames .. Cocolios-Bardi (d)
Ramfis .... Wilderman
Amonasro .... Winters
Messenger .... Pollock
Priestess .... Evans,
(s, Bonini)
Solo dancers .... Seckler (d);
McKayle

September 30

LA CENERENTOLA (Rossini)

Choreographer ..... Weidman
Conductor ...... Rosenstock

Ramiro .... Druary
Dandini .... Gramm
Don Magnifico ... Wentworth
Clorinda .... Hurley
Tisbe .... Evans
Angelina .... Kuhlmann,
(s, Bible)
Alidoro .... Newman

(Note: According to Francis
Perkins, who reviewed the
performance for the *New York
Herald Tribune*, Rossini's
overture to *Il Signor Bruschino*
was used for the ballet music.)

October 1

THE MARRIAGE OF FIGARO
(English version by
Ruth and Thomas Martin)

Choreographer ..... Weidman
Conductor ...... Rosenstock

Almaviva .... Cassel
Countess .... Willauer (d)
Figaro .... Treigle
Susanna .... Hurley
Cherubino .... Evans,
(s, Bible)
Bartolo .... Wentworth
Marcellina .... Handzlik
Basilio .... Vellucci
Curzio .... Pollock
Antonio .... Newman
Barbarina .... Bonini

October 2 (m)

CARMEN (Bizet)

Choreographer ...... Maslow
Conductor .... Rudel

Carmen .... Kuhlmann
Don José .... Eckart
Escamillo .... Winters
Micaëla .... Fleming (d)
Zuniga .... Wilderman
Frasquita .... Bonini
Mercédès .... West
Remendado .... Pollock
Dancairo .... Renan
Morales .... Torigi
Solo dancers .... Winter (d);
McKayle, Schulman

October 2

MADAMA BUTTERFLY (Puccini)

Conductor .... Martin

Butterfly .... Faull
Suzuki .... Evans
Kate Pinkerton .... LeSawyer
Pinkerton .... Petrak
Sharpless .... MacNeil
Goro .... Vellucci
Yamadori .... Renan

The Bonze .... Lishner
Imperial
Commissioner .... Newman

October 3 (m)

LA BOHÈME (Puccini)

Conductor .... Schippers

Mimi .... Mari
Musetta .... Bonini
Rodolfo .... Crain
Marcello .... Torigi
Schaunard .... Newman
Colline .... Wilderman,
(s, Treigle)
Benoit .... Wentworth
Alcindoro .... Renan
Parpignol .... Pollock

October 3

DIE FLEDERMAUS (J. Strauss)
(English book and lyrics by
Ruth and Thomas Martin)

Choreographer ...... Maslow
Conductor .... Martin

Eisenstein .... McChesney
Rosalinda .... Jager (d)
Adele .... Hurley
Alfred .... Leech
Falke .... Wilderman
Frank .... Wentworth
Blind .... Vellucci
Prince Orlofsky ..... Gramm
Sally .... Bonini
Frosch .... Worth
Ivan .... Powell
Solo dancers .... Winter,
McKayle, Schulman

October 7

FALSTAFF (Verdi)
(English translation by
Chester Kallman)

Stage director ...... Williams
Choreographer ..... Maslow
Conductor ...... Rosenstock

Sir John Falstaff .. Wilderman
Fenton .... Crain
Ford .... Cassel
Dr. Caius .... Pollock
Bardolph .... Vellucci
Pistol .... Lishner,
(s, Treigle)
Alice Ford .... Curtin
Nannetta .... Chambers
Meg Page .... Kuhlmann
Dame Quickly .... Mayer

October 8

FAUST (Gounod)

Restaged by .... Rosing
Choreographer ..... Weidman
Conductor .... Martin

Marguerite .... Yeend
Faust .... Petrak
Méphistophélès ...... Treigle
Valentin .... Cassel
Siébel .... Bible
Marthe .... Handzlik
Wagner .... Newman

October 9 (m)

LA CENERENTOLA

Same cast as September 30
except:

Angelina .... Bible

October 9

TOSCA (Puccini)

Conductor .... Rudel

Tosca .... Spence
Cavaradossi .... Crain
Scarpia .... Cassel
Angelotti .... Lishner
Spoletta .... Vellucci
Sacristan .... Wentworth
Sciarrone .... Newman
Shepherd .... Handzlik
Jailer .... Powell

October 10 (m)

LA TRAVIATA (Verdi)

Choreographer .... Weidman
Conductor .... Martin

Violetta .... Hurley
Alfredo .... Druary
Germont .... MacNeil
Flora .... LeSawyer
Annina .... Gannon
Gaston .... Vellucci
Douphol .... Newman
D'Obigny .... Renan
Dr. Grenvil .... Lishner
Solo dancers .... Lewis (d);
Jackwith (d)

October 10

AIDA

Same cast as September 29
except:

King .... Lishner
Priestess .... Bonini

October 12

AIDA

Same cast as September 29
except:

Amneris .... Bible
Aida .... Ribla
Priestess .... Bonini

October 13

THE LOVE FOR THREE ORANGES
(Prokofiev)
(English translation by Victor
Seroff; spoken prologue by
David Thornton)

Choreographer .... Weidman
Conductor .... Rudel

King .... Wilderman
Prince .... Leech
Princess Clarissa ..... Mayer
Leandro .... Gauld
Pantalone .... Renan

Truffaldino .... Vellucci
Celio .... Winters
Fata Morgana .... Faull
Princess Linetta ..... Cundari
Princess Nicoletta ..... Virga
Princess Ninetta ...... Bonini
Cook .... Wentworth
Smeraldina .... Evans
Farfarello .... Jackwith
Prologue .... Kluge

October 14

FALSTAFF

Same cast as October 7 except:

Sir John Falstaff .. Wentworth
Pistol .... Treigle

October 15

LES CONTES D'HOFFMANN
(Offenbach)

Restaged by .... Sachse
Scenic designer .... Boyt
Conductor .... Schippers

Hoffmann .. Cunningham (d)
Nicklausse .... Bible
Lindorff .... Gauld
Luther .... Powell
Nathanaël .... Kuestner
Hermann .... Newman
Olympia .... Hurley
Coppélius .... Gauld
Spalanzani .... Pollock
Cochenille .... Vellucci
Giulietta .... Likova
Dappertutto .... Cassel
Schlémil .... Renan
Pittichinaccio .... Vellucci
Antonia .... Curtin
Dr. Miracle .... Gauld
Crespel .... Lishner
Mother .... Lane
Frantz .... Vellucci

(Note: Scenic designer John
Boyt adapted to the full stage
the sets that had previously
served as a stage within the
stage.)

October 16 (m)

MADAMA BUTTERFLY

Same cast as October 2 except:

Butterfly .... Mari
Sharpless .... Torigi
Goro .... Pollock
Imperial
  Commissioner ...... Powell

October 16

DIE FLEDERMAUS

Same cast as October 3 except:

Rosalinda .... Curtin
Alfred .... Crain
Falke .... Reardon (d)
Sally .... Andrea

October 17 (m)

CARMEN

Same cast as October 2 (m)
except:

Carmen .... Lane
Escamillo .... Thompson
Micaëla .... Chambers
Mercédès .... Evans
Dancairo .... Newman

October 17

TOSCA

Same cast as October 9 except:

Conductor ...... Rosenstock

Tosca .... Jager
Cavaradossi ...... Fredericks
Scarpia .... Winters
Angelotti .... Treigle

October 20

DER ROSENKAVALIER
(R. Strauss)

Conductor ...... Rosenstock

Marschallin .... Spence
Baron Ochs ...... Wilderman
Octavian .... Bible
Faninal .... Thompson
Sophie .... Hurley
Marianne .... Gannon
Valzacchi .... Vellucci
Annina .... Evans
Police
  Commissioner .... Newman
Singer .... Petrak
Innkeeper .... Cooper
Major-Domo of
  the Marschallin .... Powell
Major-Domo of
  Faninal .... Pollock
Attorney .... Newman
1st Orphan .... LeSawyer
2nd Orphan .... Gannon
3rd Orphan .... M. Williams
Animal vendor ...... Pollock
Milliner .... Bonini
Leopold ...... Urhausen (d)
Mohamet ...... Grinnage (d)

October 21

LES CONTES D'HOFFMANN

Same cast as October 15
except:

Hoffmann .... Rounseville
Nicklausse .... Kuhlmann
Olympia .... Yeend
Giulietta .... Yeend
Antonia .... Yeend

October 22

FAUST

Same cast as October 8 except:

Marguerite .... Likova
Siébel .... Evans

October 23 (m)

THE LOVE FOR THREE ORANGES

Same cast as October 13
except:

Prince .... Rounseville
Princess Clarissa .... Handzlik
Leandro .... Treigle

October 23

LA TRAVIATA

Same cast as October 10 (m)
except:

Violetta .... Likova
Alfredo .... Crain
Germont .... Torigi
D'Obigny .... Powell

October 24 (m)

HANSEL AND GRETEL
(Humperdinck)
(Sung in English)

Choreographer ...... Maslow
Conductor .... Schippers

Father .... Hecht
Mother .... Bunn
Hansel .... Bible
Gretel .... Bonini
Witch .... Russell
Sandman .... Cundari
Dew Fairy .... LeSawyer

October 24

LA BOHÈME

Same cast as October 3 (m)
except:

Mimi .... Faull
Musetta .... Likova
Rodolfo .... Cunningham
                (Act I); Crain
               (Acts II, III, IV)
Colline .... Treigle
Benoit .... Lishner

October 26

DER ROSENKAVALIER

Same cast as October 20
except:

Baron Ochs .... Hecht
Faninal .... Wentworth
Marianne .... Underwood
Annina .... Lane
Singer .... Crain
Innkeeper .... Pollock

October 27

LES CONTES D'HOFFMANN

Same cast as October 15
except:

Hoffmann ...... Rounseville,
            (s, Cunningham)
Nicklausse .... Evans

Hermann .... Emanuel	Pete .... Pollock
Olympia .... Hurley,	Sheriff Vallon ..... Urhausen
(s, Likova)	Doorman .... Brown
Giulietta .... Willauer	Old lady .... Floyd
Dappertutto .... MacNeil	Ethel .... Wynder
Schlémil .... Newman	Kim .... Newton
Mother .... Bible	Two
	Backwoodsmen ..Urhausen;
	Newman

October 28

SHOW BOAT (Kern)

Conductor .... Rudel

Captain Andy .... Wentworth
Parthy Ann Hawks ..Handzlik
Magnolia .... Hurley
Gaylord Ravenal ..Rounseville
Julie .... Bliss
Steve .... Gallagher
Queenie .... Allen (d)
Joe .... Winters
Frank .... Blair (d)
Ellie .... Niles (d)
Jim .... Pollock
McLain .... Newman
Guitar player ...... Kuestner
Piano player .... Lyon
Landlady .... Floyd

October 29

THE MARRIAGE OF FIGARO

Same cast as October 1 except:

Countess .... Curtin
Susanna .... Bonini
Cherubino .... Bible
Barbarina .... LeSawyer

October 30 (m)

HANSEL AND GRETEL

Same cast as October 24 (m)
except:

Father .... Newman
Hansel .... Evans
Gretel .... Hurley

October 30

CARMEN

Same cast as October 2 (m)
except:

Conductor ...... Rosenstock

Carmen .... Lane
Don José .... Fredericks
Escamillo .... MacNeil
Micaëla .... Chambers
Zuniga .... Treigle
Frasquita .... LeSawyer
Remendado .... Vellucci

October 31 (m)

SHOW BOAT

Same cast as October 28

October 31

THE LOVE FOR THREE ORANGES
(Spoken prologue by
Theodore Komisarjevsky)

Same cast as October 13
except:

Princess Clarissa ... Handzlik
Leandro .... Treigle

Spring 1955 (MARCH 17–APRIL 17)

Female artists
Addison, Adele*
Andrea, Jennie
Asaro, Josephine*
Baisley, Helen
Bible, Frances
Bishop, Adelaide
Bonini, Peggy
Chambers, Madelaine
Cundari, Emily
Curtin, Phyllis
Evans, Edith
Faull, Ellen
Gannon, Teresa
Gordon, Marjorie*
Handzlik, Jean
Kuhlmann, Rosemary
Lane, Gloria
LeSawyer, Mary
Likova, Eva
Lind, Gloria
MacKay, Margery*
Mari, Dolores
Moll, Mariquita
Novic, Mija*
Savoia, Rosa*
Spence, Wilma
Williams, Mary
Witkowska, Nadja*
Yeend, Frances

Male artists
Aiken, David
Bond, Philip*
Crain, Jon
Cunningham, Davis
Druary, John
Eckart, Frank

Fredericks, Walter
Gauld, Carlton
Gero, Constanzo*
Gramm, Donald
Green, Bernard*
Grinnage, Leonard
Hauptman, Lee*
Hecht, Joshua*
Herbert, Ralph
Kuestner, Charles
Leech, Lloyd Thomas
Lishner, Leon
Lloyd, David
MacNeil, Cornell
McChesney, Ernest
Markow, Emile*
Meredith, Morley*
Morell, Barry*
Newman, Arthur
Petrak, Rudolf
Pollock, Michael
Powell, Thomas
Reardon, John
Rounseville, Robert
Russell, Gilbert*
Shriner, William
Torigi, Richard
Treigle, Norman
Vellucci, Luigi
Wentworth, Richard
Wilderman, William
Winters, Lawrence
Worth, Coley

Conductors
Buckley, Emerson*
Lee, Everett*
Martin, Thomas P.

Rosenstock, Joseph
Rudel, Julius

Solo dancers
Hinkson, Mary
Tetley, Glen

Choreographer
Butler, John

Directors
Erhardt, Otto
Jordan, Glenn
Rosing, Vladimir
Sachse, Leopold

**Artistic adviser for
Don Pasquale**
Baccaloni, Salvatore*

Designers
Boyt, John
Condell, H. A.
Ter-Arutunian, Rouben

* New artist

March 17

DER ROSENKAVALIER
(R. Strauss)

Conductor ...... Rosenstock

Baron Ochs ...... Wilderman
Octavian .... Bible
Faninal .... Wentworth
Sophie .... Mari
Marianne .... Novic (d)
Valzacchi .... Vellucci
Annina .... Evans

Police
Commissioner .... Newman
Singer .... Fredericks
Innkeeper .... Pollock
Major-Domo of
the Marschallin .... Powell
Major-Domo of
Faninal .... Pollock
Attorney .... Newman
1st Orphan .... LeSawyer
2nd Orphan .... Gannon
3rd Orphan .... Williams
Animal vendor .... Kuestner
Milliner .... Bonini
Leopold .... Hauptman
Mohamet .... Grinnage

March 18

RIGOLETTO (Verdi)

Conductor ...... Buckley (d)

Duke .... Crain
Rigoletto .... MacNeil
Gilda .... Likova
Sparafucile .... Treigle
Maddalena .... Evans
Giovanna .... Handzlik
Monterone .... Wentworth
Marullo .... Newman
Borsa .... Pollock
Ceprano .... Lishner
Countess Ceprano .. LeSawyer
Page .... Baisley

March 19 (m)

DIE FLEDERMAUS (J. Strauss)
(English book and lyrics by
Ruth and Thomas Martin)

Choreographer .... Butler
Conductor .... Martin

Eisenstein .... McChesney
Rosalinda .... Lind
Adele .... Bishop
Alfred .... Leech
Falke .... Wilderman
Frank .... Wentworth
Blind .... Vellucci
Prince Orlofsky ..... Gramm
Sally .... Bonini
Frosch .... Worth
Ivan .... Powell
Solo dancers ..Hinkson; Tetley

March 19

LA TRAVIATA (Verdi)

Choreographer .... Butler
Conductor .... Rudel

Violetta .... Yeend
Alfredo .... Cunningham
Germont .... Winters
Flora .... LeSawyer
Annina .... Gannon
Gaston .... Pollock
Douphol .... Newman
D'Obigny .... Reardon
Dr. Grenvil .... Lishner
Solo dancers ..Hinkson; Tetley

March 20 (m)

FAUST (Gounod)

Choreographer .... Butler
Conductor .... Martin

Marguerite .... Likova
Faust .... Crain
Méphistophélès ...... Treigle
Valentin .... MacNeil
Siébel .... Kuhlmann
Marthe .... Handzlik
Wagner .... Newman

March 20

LA CENERENTOLA (Rossini)
(English translation by
Martha W. England and
James Durbin, Jr.)

Choreographer .... Butler
Conductor ...... Rosenstock

Prince Ramiro .... Lloyd
Dandini .... Gramm
Don Magnifico ... Wentworth
Clorinda .... Bonini
Tisbe .... Evans
Angelina .... Bible
Alidoro .... Newman

March 24

DON PASQUALE (Donizetti)
First performance by The New
York City Opera Company

Staged by .... Sachse
Designer .... Boyt
Artistic
adviser .... Baccaloni (d)
Conductor .... Rosenstock

Don Pasquale .... Wentworth
Malatesta .... Torigi
Ernesto .... Cunningham
Norina .... Bishop
Notary .... Newman

(Note: Possible substitution
of Pollock for Newman as
Notary.)

March 25

CAVALLERIA RUSTICANA
(Mascagni)

Staged by .... Jordan
Conductor .... Buckley

Santuzza .... Savoia (d)
Turiddu .... Fredericks
Alfio .... Winters
Lola .... Evans
Mamma Lucia .... Handzlik

Followed by:

I PAGLIACCI (Leoncavallo)

Staged by .... Rosing
Choreographer .... Butler
Conductor .... Buckley

Nedda .... Mari
Canio .... Eckart
Tonio .... MacNeil
Silvio .... Torigi
Beppe .... Pollock

March 26 (m)

MADAMA BUTTERFLY (Puccini)

Conductor .... Martin

Butterfly .... Mari
Suzuki .... Evans
Kate Pinkerton .... LeSawyer
Pinkerton .... Morell (d)
Sharpless .... Torigi
Goro .... Vellucci
Yamadori .... Newman
The Bonze .... Lishner
Imperial
Commissioner ...... Powell

March 26

CARMEN (Bizet)

Staged by .... Rosing
Choreographer .... Butler
Conductor .... Rudel

Carmen .... Lane
Don José .... Fredericks
Escamillo ..... Meredith (d)
Micaëla .... Chambers
Zuniga .... Treigle
Frasquita .... Bonini
Mercédès ..... MacKay (d)
Remendado .... Pollock
Dancairo .... Reardon
Morales .... Newman
Solo dancers ..Hinkson; Tetley

March 27 (m)

LA BOHÈME (Puccini)

Conductor ...... Rosenstock

Mimi .... Addison (d)
Musetta .... Bonini
Rodolfo .... Petrak
Marcello .... Torigi
Schaunard .... Newman
Colline .... Wilderman
Benoit .... Wentworth
Alcindoro .... Lishner
Parpignol .... Pollock

March 27

FAUST

Same cast as March 20 (m)
except:

Marguerite .... Faull
Valentin .... Winters
Siébel .... Bible

March 31

THE MERRY WIVES OF WINDSOR
(Nicolai)
First performance by The New
York City Opera Company
(Die lustigen Weiber von
Windsor; English version by
Josef Blatt)

Staged by .... Rosing
Designer .... Boyt
Choreographer .... Butler
Conductor ...... Rosenstock

Falstaff .... Wilderman
Mr. Ford .... Shriner
Mr. Page .... Lishner

Fenton .... Crain
Slender .... Pollock
Dr. Caius .... Reardon
Mistress Ford .... Curtin
Mistress Page .... Evans
Anne Page .... Bonini
Host .... Powell
Citizen .... Kuestner

(Note: John Boyt's sets and
costumes for his 1954
production of *Falstaff* were
utilized.)

April 1

LA TRAVIATA

Same cast as March 19 except:

Alfredo .... Crain
Germont .... Green (d)

April 2 (m)

LA CENERENTOLA

Same cast as March 20 except:

Prince Ramiro ...... Druary

April 2

MADAMA BUTTERFLY

Same cast as March 26 (m)
except:

Butterfly .... Faull
Suzuki .... MacKay

April 3 (m)

RIGOLETTO

Same cast as March 18 except:

Gilda .... Witkowska (d)
Sparafucile .... Bond (d)
Maddalena .... Lane,
                (s, Evans)
Monterone .... Hecht (d)

April 3

DER ROSENKAVALIER

Same cast as March 17 except:

Marschallin .... Moll
Octavian .... Evans,
                (s, Bible)
Annina .... Lane,
                (s, Evans)

April 5

DER ROSENKAVALIER

Same cast as March 17 except:

Baron Ochs .... Herbert
Octavian .... Evans
Faninal .... Aiken
Annina .... Lane
Singer .... Petrak

April 6

DON PASQUALE

Same cast as March 24 except:

Ernesto .... Gero (d),
                (s, Cunningham)
Norina .... Bonini

April 7

LES CONTES D'HOFFMANN
(Offenbach)

Choreographer .... Butler
Conductor .... Rudel

Hoffmann .... Rounseville
Nicklausse .... Evans
Lindorff .... Gauld
Luther .... Powell
Nathanaël .... Kuestner
Hermann .... Reardon
Andrès .... Vellucci
Olympia .... Witkowska
Coppélius .... Gauld
Spalanzani .... Pollock
Cochenille .... Vellucci
Giulietta .... Curtin
Dappertutto .... MacNeil
Schlémil .... Newman
Pittichinaccio .... Vellucci
Antonia .... Yeend
Dr. Miracle .... Gauld
Crespel .... Lishner
Mother .... Kuhlmann
Frantz .... Vellucci

April 8

LA BOHÈME

Same cast as March 27 (m)
except:

Mimi .... Yeend
Rodolfo .... Crain

April 9 (m)

CARMEN

Same cast as March 26 except:

Carmen .... Kuhlmann
Don José .... Rounseville
Escamillo .... Winters
Micaëla .... Asaro (d)
Zuniga .... Markow (d)
Frasquita .... LeSawyer

April 9

DIE FLEDERMAUS

Same cast as March 19 (m)
except:

Rosalinda .... Curtin
Adele .... Bonini
Prince Orlofsky ...... Pollock
Sally .... Andrea

April 10 (m)

CAVALLERIA RUSTICANA

Same cast as March 25 except:

Turiddu .... Morell
Alfio .... Newman

Followed by:

I PAGLIACCI

Same cast as March 25 except:

Nedda .... Lind
Tonio .... Winters
Silvio .... Reardon,
                (s, Torigi)

April 10

THE MERRY WIVES OF WINDSOR

Same cast as March 31

April 12

DON PASQUALE

Same cast as March 24 except:

Don Pasquale .... Lishner
Malatesta .... Aiken,
                (s, Torigi)
Ernesto .... Russell (d)
Norina .... Bonini

April 13

THE MERRY WIVES OF WINDSOR

Same cast as March 31 except:

Fenton .... Russell
Anne Page .... Chambers

April 14

CARMEN

Same cast as March 26 except:

Don José .... Eckart
Escamillo .... Winters
Zuniga .... Wilderman

April 15

MADAMA BUTTERFLY

Same cast as March 26 (m)
except:

Butterfly .... Faull
Pinkerton .... Morell,
                (s, Rounseville)

April 16 (m)

LES CONTES D'HOFFMANN

Same cast as April 7 except:

Hoffmann ...... Cunningham
Lindorff .... Winters
Olympia .... Gordon (d)
Coppélius .... Winters
Dappertutto .... Winters
Antonia .... Yeend,
                (s, Fleming)
Dr. Miracle .... Winters
Crespel .... Markow,
                (s, Lishner)

April 16

CAVALLERIA RUSTICANA

Same cast as March 25 except:

Alfio .... Meredith

Followed by:

I PAGLIACCI

Same cast as March 25 except:

Nedda .... Lind
Canio .... McChesney
Silvio .... Reardon

April 17 (m)

LA TRAVIATA

Same cast as March 19 except:

Conductor .... Lee (d)

Violetta .... Likova
Alfredo .... Petrak

Germont .... MacNeil
Gaston .... Vellucci

April 17

LA BOHÈME

Same cast as March 27 (m) except:

Mimi .... Yeend

Rodolfo ... Petrak (Acts I, II, III); Crain (Act IV)
Benoit .... Lishner
Alcindoro .... Reardon

(Note: Rudolf Petrak substituted for Jon Crain but then became indisposed during the performance. Crain agreed to finish the opera.)

Fall 1955 (OCTOBER 5 – NOVEMBER 6)

Female artists
Addison, Adele
Andrea, Jennie
Baisley, Helen
Bonini, Peggy
Carrillo, Maria Teresa*
Chambers, Madelaine
Collier, Naomi
Cundari, Emily
Curtin, Phyllis
Evans, Edith
Faull, Ellen
Fenn, Jean
Gordon, Marjorie
Hurley, Laurel
Kramarich, Irene*
Kuhlmann, Rosemary
Lane, Gloria
LeSawyer, Mary
Likova, Eva
MacKay, Margery
Mari, Dolores
Mayer, Margery
Moody, Jacquelynne*
Novic, Mija
Savoia, Rosa
Sills, Beverly*
Tynes, Margaret
Yeend, Frances

Male artists
Cassilly, Richard*
Crain, Jon
Cunningham, Davis
Druary, John
Elyn, Mark*
Gari, Giulio
Gauld, Carlton
Gramm, Donald
Green, Bernard
Greenwell, Gean
Harris, Lloyd*
Harrold, Jack
Hecht, Joshua
Jordan, James*
Kelley, Norman
Kemalyan, Stephen*
Leech, Lloyd Thomas
McChesney, Ernest
Marcella, Luigi
Morell, Barry

Newman, Arthur
Petrak, Rudolf
Pollock, Michael
Powell, Thomas
Quilico, Louis*
Reardon, John
Rubes, Jan
Rue, Robert*
Russell, Jack
Shriner, William
Sze, Yi-Kwei*
Tibbs, DeLloyd
Torigi, Richard
Vellucci, Luigi
Wentworth, Richard
Wilderman, William
Winters, Lawrence
Worth, Coley

Conductors
Buckley, Emerson
Grossman, Herbert*
Lee, Everett
Rosenstock, Joseph
Rudel, Julius

Dancers
No solo dancers listed this season.

Choreographer
Harrison, Ray*

Directors
Donath, Ludwig*
Erhardt, Otto
Jordan, Glenn
Mahan, Chris*
Rosing, Vladimir
Webster, Margaret*

Designers
Boyt, John
Condell, H. A.
Dobujinsky, Mstislav
Remisoff, Nicolai*
Ter-Arutunian, Rouben

October 5

THE MERRY WIVES OF WINDSOR (Nicolai)
(English version by Josef Blatt)

Choreographer ..Harrison (d)
Conductor .... Rosenstock

Falstaff .... Wentworth
Mr. Ford .... Shriner
Mr. Page .... Newman
Fenton .... Crain
Slender .... Pollock
Dr. Caius .... Reardon
Mistress Ford .... Curtin
Mistress Page .... Evans
Anne Page .... Bonini
Host .... Powell
Citizen .... Tibbs

October 6

MADAMA BUTTERFLY (Puccini)

Conductor .... Buckley

Butterfly .... Mari
Suzuki .... Evans
Kate Pinkerton .... LeSawyer
Pinkerton .... Morell
Sharpless .... Torigi
Goro .... Vellucci
Yamadori .... Harris (d), (s, Newman)
The Bonze .... Harris (d)
Imperial Commissioner ...... Powell

(Note: *Trouble* added to program November 6)

October 7

LA BOHÈME (Puccini)

Stage director .... Mahan (d)
Conductor .... Lee

Mimi .... Addison
Musetta .... Bonini
Rodolfo .... Crain
Marcello .... Torigi
Schaunard .... Reardon, (s, Newman)
Colline .... Hecht
Benoit .... Wentworth

Alcindoro .... Harris
Parpignol .... Pollock

October 8 (m)

DIE FLEDERMAUS (J. Strauss)
(English book and lyrics by
Ruth and Thomas Martin)

Choreographer ..... Harrison
Conductor ...... Rosenstock

Eisenstein .... Russell
Rosalinda .... Curtin
Adele .... Bonini
Alfred .... Leech
Falke .... Reardon
Frank .... Wentworth
Blind .... Vellucci
Prince Orlofsky ..... Pollock
Sally .... Andrea
Frosch .... Worth
Ivan .... Powell

October 8

CARMEN (Bizet)

Choreographer ..... Harrison
Conductor .... Rudel

Carmen .... Lane
Don José .... Gari,
                    (s, Petrak)
Escamillo .... Winters
Micaëla .... Chambers
Zuniga .... Hecht
Frasquita .... Gordon
Mercédès .... MacKay
Remendado .... Pollock
Dancairo .... Reardon
Morales .... Torigi,
                    (s, Newman)

October 9 (m)

LA TRAVIATA (Verdi)

Choreographer .... Harrison
Conductor .... Lee

Violetta .... Likova
Alfredo .... Morell
Germont .... Quilico (d)
Flora .... LeSawyer
Annina .... MacKay
Gaston .... Vellucci
Douphol .... Wentworth,
                    (s, Newman)
D'Obigny .... Reardon
Dr. Grenvil .... Harris

October 9

CAVALLERIA RUSTICANA
(Mascagni)

Staged by .... Jordan
Conductor .... Buckley

Santuzza .... Savoia
Turiddu .... Crain
Alfio .... Kemalyan (d)
Lola .... MacKay,
                    (s, Evans)
Mamma Lucia ... Kramarich
                    (d)

Followed by:

I PAGLIACCI (Leoncavallo)

Staged by .... Rosing
Conductor .... Buckley
Nedda .... Mari
Canio .... Leech
Tonio .... Winters
Silvio .... Torigi
Beppe .... Pollock

October 13

THE GOLDEN SLIPPERS
(Tchaikovsky)
First performance by The New
York City Opera Company
(*Tcherevichky*; also known in
western Europe as *Oxana's
Caprices*; English version by
Ruth and Thomas Martin)

Staged by .... Rosing
Designer .... Remisoff (d)
Choreographer .... Harrison
Conductor ...... Rosenstock

Vakula .... Cassilly (d)
Tschub .... Wentworth
Oxana .... Fenn
Devil .... Gramm
Solocha .... Mayer
Village mayor ...... Harris,
                    (s, Newman)
Schoolmaster .... Pollock
Majordomo .... Reardon
Czarina .... Kuhlmann
Wood demon .... Hecht
Kosak .... Powell

October 14

THE MARRIAGE OF FIGARO
(Mozart)
(English version by
Ruth and Thomas Martin)

Staged by .... Donath (d)
Choreographer .... Harrison
Conductor ...... Rosenstock
Almaviva .... Shriner
Countess .... Faull
Figaro .... Gramm
Susanna .... Moody (d)
Cherubino .... Bonini
Bartolo .... Wentworth
Marcellina .... MacKay
Basilio .... Vellucci
Curzio .... Pollock
Antonio .... Powell,
                    (s, Newman)
Barbarina .... Cundari

October 15 (m)

THE MERRY WIVES OF WINDSOR

Same cast as October 5 except:

Anne Page .... Chambers

October 15

LA BOHÈME

Same cast as October 7 except:

Conductor .... Rudel
Mimi .... Yeend
Musetta .... Likova

Rodolfo .... Morell
Schaunard .... Newman
Colline .... Wilderman
Benoit .... Harris
Parpignol .... Marcella

October 16 (m)

LA CENERENTOLA (Rossini)
(English translation by
Martha W. England and
James Durbin, Jr.)

Choreographer .... Harrison
Conductor .... Rosenstock

Prince Ramiro .... Druary
Dandini .... Gramm
Don Magnifico ... Wentworth
Clorinda .... Bonini
Tisbe .... Evans
Angelina .... Kuhlmann
Alidoro .... Newman

October 16

DIE FLEDERMAUS

Same cast as October 8 (m)
except:

Conductor .... Rudel

Eisenstein .... McChesney
Adele .... Moody
Falke .... Wilderman
Frank .... Wentworth,
                    (s, Newman)

October 20

THE LOVE FOR THREE ORANGES
(Prokofiev)
(English translation by
Victor Seroff; spoken dialogue
written by David Thornton)

Choreographer ..... Harrison
Conductor .... Rudel

King .... Greenwell
Prince .... Leech
Princess Clarissa .... Mayer
Leandro .... Gauld,
                    (s, Kemalyan)
Pantalone .... Reardon
Truffaldino .... Vellucci
Celio .... Winters
Fata Morgana .... Novic
Princess Linetta ..... Baisley,
                    (s, Cundari)
Princess Nicoletta .... Gordon
Princess Ninetta .... Hurley,
                    (s, Bonini)
Cook .... Wentworth
Smeraldina .... MacKay
Prologue .... Pollock

October 21

TROILUS AND CRESSIDA
(Walton)
First performance by The New
York City Opera Company

Staged by ...... Webster (d)
Designer .... Boyt
Conductor ...... Rosenstock

Calkas .... Sze (d)
Antenor .... Torigi

Troilus .... Crain
Pandarus .... Kelley
Cressida .... Curtin
Evadne .... Lane
Horaste .... Reardon
Diomede .... Winters
1st Lady .... LeSawyer,
(s, Chambers)
2nd Lady .... MacKay
3rd Lady .... Bonini
4th Lady .... Evans

October 22 (m)

CARMEN

Same cast as October 8 except:

Conductor .... Grossman (d)

Don José .... Petrak
Escamillo .... Kemalyan
Micaëla .... Mari
Frasquita .... LeSawyer,
(s, Bonini)
Morales .... Newman

October 22

LA TRAVIATA

Same cast as October 9 (m)
except:

Gaston .... Pollock

October 23 (m)

MADAMA BUTTERFLY

Same cast as October 6 except:

Suzuki .... MacKay
Pinkerton .... Crain
Yamadori .... Newman
The Bonze .... Hecht

October 23

THE MARRIAGE OF FIGARO

Same cast as October 14
except:

Countess .... Yeend
Antonio .... Newman
Barbarina .... LeSawyer

October 26

THE BARTERED BRIDE
(Smetana)
(English version by Joan Cross
and Eric Crozier, after a translation by Rosa Newmarch)

Stage director ..... G. Jordan
Choreographer .... Harrison
Conductor .... Rudel

Marenka .... Bonini
Jenik .... Cunningham
Kecal .... Rubes

Krushina .... Torigi
Ludmilla .... Novich
Vashek .... Harrold
Tobias Micha ...... Newman
Hata .... MacKay
Ringmaster .... Pollock
Esmeralda ..... Carrillo (d)
Clown .... Powell

October 27

THE GOLDEN SLIPPERS

Same cast as October 13

October 28

THE MERRY WIVES OF WINDSOR

Same cast as October 5 except:

Fenton .... Druary

October 29 (m)

LA CENERENTOLA

Same cast as October 16 (m)
except:

Prince Ramiro .. Cunningham

October 29

DIE FLEDERMAUS

Same cast as October 8 (m)
except:

Conductor .... Rudel

Eisenstein .... McChesney
Rosalinda .... Sills (d)
Adele .... Moody
Frank .... Newman
Sally .... Collier

October 30 (m)

LA BOHÈME

Same cast as October 7 except:

Conductor .... Rudel

Rodolfo .... Morell
Schaunard .... Newman
Benoit .... Harris
Parpignol .... Marcella

October 30

TROILUS AND CRESSIDA

Same cast as October 21

November 1

TROILUS AND CRESSIDA

Same cast as October 21

November 2

THE GOLDEN SLIPPERS

Same cast as October 13
except:

Oxana .... Sills
Solocha .... MacKay
Village major ...... Newman
Czarina .... Evans

November 3

THE BARTERED BRIDE

Same cast as October 26
except:

Kecal .... Wentworth

November 4

LA TRAVIATA

Same cast as October 9 (m)
except:

Violetta .... Fenn
Germont .... Winters
Dr. Grenvil .... Elyn (d)

November 5 (m)

THE LOVE FOR THREE ORANGES

Same cast as October 20
except:

Princess Clarissa .. Kramarich
Leandro .... Kemalyan
Celio .... Newman
Fata Morgana .... Tynes
Princess Ninetta ...... Bonini

November 6 (m)

CARMEN

Same cast as October 8 except:

Don José .... Cassilly
Escamillo .... Kemalyan
Micaëla .... Mari
Frasquita .... LeSawyer
Morales .... Rue (d)

November 6

MADAMA BUTTERFLY

Same cast as October 6 except:

Butterfly .... Faull
Sharpless .... Green
Yamadori .... Newman
The Bonze .... Hecht

Added to this program:

Trouble .... J. Jordan

Spring 1956 (MARCH 28 – APRIL 15)

Female artists
Addison, Adele
Andrea, Jennie
Asaro, Josephine
Baisley, Helen
Bible, Frances
Bonini, Peggy
Bower, Beverly*
Collier, Naomi
Curtin, Phyllis
Dunn, Mignon*
Faull, Ellen
Jacobs, Dorothy
Kramarich, Irene
LeSawyer, Mary
Likova, Eva
Lind, Gloria
MacKay, Margery
Mari, Dolores
Moody, Jacquelynne
Sills, Beverly
Yeend, Frances

Male artists
Cassilly, Richard
Crain, Jon
Donath, Ludwig*
Farrar, James*
Ferraro, Piero Miranda*
Fredericks, Walter
Fried, Howard*
Hecht, Joshua
Kelley, Norman
Leech, Lloyd Thomas
McChesney, Ernest
MacNeil, Cornell
Marcella, Luigi
Morell, Barry
Nahr, William
Newman, Arthur
Pickett, William*
Pollock, Michael
Powell, Thomas
Protti, Aldo*
Quilico, Louis
Quinn, Michael*
Reardon, John
Russell, Jack
Tibbs, DeLloyd
Treigle, Norman
Wentworth, Richard
Winters, Lawrence
Worth, Coley

Conductors
Bomhard, Moritz*
Buckley, Emerson
Grossman, Herbert
Martin, Thomas P.
Rosenstock, Joseph
Rudel, Julius

Solo dancer
Revene, Nadine

* New artist

Choreographer
Harrison, Ray

Directors
Bomhard, Moritz*
Erhardt, Otto
Field, Bill*
Jordan, Glenn
Rosing, Vladimir
Webster, Margaret

Designers
Boyt, John
Condell, H. A.
Polakov, Lester*
Roth, Wolfgang*

* New artist

March 28

TROILUS AND CRESSIDA
(Walton)

Stage director ..... Field (d)
Conductor ...... Rosenstock

Calkas .... Treigle
Antenor .... Farrar (d)
Troilus .... Crain
Pandarus .... Kelley
Cressida .... Curtin
Evadne .... Bible
Horaste .... Reardon
Diomede .... Winters
1st Lady .... LeSawyer
2nd Lady .... MacKay
3rd Lady .... Bonini
4th Lady .... Dunn (d)

March 29

RIGOLETTO (Verdi)

Choreographer .... Harrison
Conductor .... Buckley

Duke .... Fredericks
Rigoletto .... Protti (d)
Gilda .... Likova
Sparafucile .... Treigle
Maddalena .... MacKay
Giovanna .... Jacobs
Monterone ...... Wentworth
Marullo .... Newman
Borsa .... Pollock
Ceprano .... Reardon
Countess Ceprano .. LeSawyer
Page .... Baisley

(Note: No director credit
given this season, but Erhardt
listed for *Rigoletto* on
announcements)

March 30

LA BOHÈME (Puccini)

Stage director .... Jordan
Conductor .... Martin

Mimi .... Mari
Musetta .... Bonini
Rodolfo .... Morell
Marcello .... Quilico
Schaunard .... Reardon
Colline .... Hecht
Benoit .... Wentworth
Alcindoro .... Newman
Parpignol .... Pollock

March 31 (m)

DIE FLEDERMAUS (J. Strauss)
(English book and lyrics by
Ruth and Thomas Martin)

Conductor ...... Rosenstock

Eisenstein .... McChesney
Rosalinda .... Sills
Adele .... Moody
Alfred .... Crain
Falke .... Reardon
Frank .... Wentworth
Blind .... Fried (d)
Prince Orlofsky .... Pollock
Sally .... Andrea
Frosch .... Worth
Ivan .... Powell

March 31

CARMEN (Bizet)

Conductor .... Rudel

Carmen .... Dunn
Don José .... Cassilly
Escamillo .... Treigle
Micaëla .... Mari
Zuniga .... Hecht
Frasquita .... Bonini
Mercédès .... MacKay
Remendado .... Pollock
Dancairo .... Reardon
Morales .... Newman

April 1 (m)

MADAMA BUTTERFLY (Puccini)

Conductor .... Buckley

Butterfly .... Faull
Suzuki .... MacKay
Kate Pinkerton .... LeSawyer
Pinkerton .... Morell
Sharpless .... MacNeil
Goro .... Pollock
Yamadori .... Newman
The Bonze .... Hecht
Imperial
    Commissioner ..... Powell

April 1

TOSCA (Puccini)

Restaged by .... Rosing
Conductor ...... Rosenstock

Tosca .... Yeend
Cavaradossi ..... Ferraro (d)
Scarpia .... Protti
Angelotti .... Hecht
Spoletta .... Pollock
Sacristan .... Wentworth
Sciarrone .... Newman
Shepherd .... Baisley
Jailer .... Powell

April 4

IL TROVATORE (Verdi)
First performance by The New
York City Opera Company

Staged by .... Erhardt
Scenic designer .. Polakov (d)
Conductor .... Rudel

Di Luna .... Protti
Leonora .... Faull
Azucena .... Kramarich
Manrico .... Ferraro
Ferrando .... Treigle
Ines .... MacKay
Ruiz .... Pollock
Gypsy .... Powell
Messenger .... Tibbs

April 5

TROILUS AND CRESSIDA

Same cast as March 28

April 6

RIGOLETTO

Same cast as March 29 except:

Duke .... Ferraro
Sparafucile .... Hecht
Marullo .... Powell
Borsa .... Nahr
Countess Ceprano .... Collier

April 7 (m)

LA TRAVIATA (Verdi)

Conductor .... Martin

Violetta .... Yeend
Alfredo .... Morell
Germont .... MacNeil
Flora .... LeSawyer
Annina .... MacKay
Gaston .... Pollock
Douphol .... Newman
D'Obigny .... Reardon
Dr. Grenvil .... Hecht

April 7

DIE FLEDERMAUS

Same cast as March 31 except:
Eisenstein .... Russell
Rosalinda .... Sills,
                (s, Bower)
Alfred .... Leech
Sally .... Collier

April 8 (m)

LA BOHÈME

Same cast as March 30 except:
Mimi .... Addison
Schaunard .... Newman
Alcindoro .... Reardon
Parpignol .... Marcella

April 8

IL TROVATORE

Same cast as April 4 except:
Ferrando .... Hecht

April 11

SCHOOL FOR WIVES
(Liebermann)
First performance by The New
York City Opera Company
(Original English version by
Elizabeth Montagu)

Staged by ..... Bomhard (d)
Designer .... Roth (d)
Conductor ...... Rosenstock

Poquelin
  (Alain, Henry) ... Reardon
Arnolphe .... Pickett (d)
Agnes .... Bonini
Horace .... Crain
Georgette .... Dunn
Oronte .... Hecht

Followed by:

THE IMPRESARIO (Mozart)
First performance by The New
York City Opera Company
(Der Schauspieldirektor;
English adaptation by
Giovanni Cardelli)

Staged by .... Rosing
Conductor ...... Rosenstock

Mr. Scruples .... Donath (d)
Mr. Bluff .... Russell
Mr. Angel .... Pollock
Madame Goldentrill ..... Sills
Miss Silverpeal ...... Moody
Music director .... Tibbs
Stage director .... Powell
Prima ballerina ...... Revene

(Note: John Boyt's scenery
for act I, scene 1 of Don
Pasquale was utilized for
The Impresario.)

April 12

TOSCA

Same cast as April 1 except:

Conductor .... Martin

Tosca .... Lind
Cavaradossi .... Morell
Sacristan .... Quinn (d)
Shepherd .... MacKay

April 13

MADAMA BUTTERFLY

Same cast as April 1 (m)
except:

Butterfly .... Asaro,
              (s, Savoia)
Suzuki .... Bible
Kate Pinkerton ...... Baisley
Pinkerton .... Ferraro
Sharpless .... Winters

April 14 (m)

CARMEN

Same cast as March 31 except:

Escamillo .... Winters
Micaëla .... Asaro

April 14

LA TRAVIATA

Same cast as April 7 (m)
except:

Conductor .... Grossman

Violetta .... Bower (d)
Annina .... Jacobs

April 15 (m)

SCHOOL FOR WIVES

Same cast as April 11 except:

Conductor .... Bomhard (d)

Followed by:

THE IMPRESARIO

Same cast as April 11 except:

Conductor .... Bomhard (d)

April 15

IL TROVATORE

Same cast as April 4 except:

Di Luna .... MacNeil
Ferrando .... Hecht

Fall 1956 (SEPTEMBER 20–NOVEMBER 3)

Female artists
Addison, Adele
Baisley, Helen
Bible, Frances
Bonelli, Olivia*
Bower, Beverly
Casselle, Jola*
Charney, Eudice*
Collier, Naomi
Curtin, Phyllis
Dunn, Mignon
Fleming, Sarah
Fry, Cleo
Gillette, Priscilla
Jacobs, Dorothy
Kramarich, Irene
Lane, Gloria
Laurence, Paula*
LeSawyer, Mary
MacDonald, Pat
Moll, Mariquita
Moody, Jacquelynne
Sills, Beverly
Stahlman, Sylvia*
Winston, Shirley*
Yeend, Frances

Male artists
Atherton, Robert
Cassilly, Richard
Crain, Jon
Del Monte, George
Druary, John
Elyn, Mark
Gramm, Donald
Green, Bernard
Hatfield, Hurd*
Hecht, Joshua
Hoel, Edson
Humphrey, Richard*
Kelley, Norman
Lick, John
McChesney, Ernest
MacNeil, Cornell
Markow, Emile
Millar, Gregory*
Modenos, John*
Morell, Barry
Nahr, William
Newman, Arthur
O'Leary, William
Person, John
Petrak, Rudolf
Plank, Tom
Plummer, Christopher*
Pollock, Michael
Porretta, Frank*
Powell, Thomas
Ruddy, Robert
Sherman, Hiram*
Shriner, William
Smith, Kenneth*
Thomas, Eb*
Tibbs, DeLloyd
Treigle, Norman
Verreau, Richard*

* New artist

Wayne, Don
Wentworth, Richard
Wilderman, William
Worth, Coley

Conductors
Leinsdorf, Erich*
Morel, Jean
Rosenstock, Joseph
Rudel, Julius

Choral director
Hillis, Margaret

Solo dancers
Coy, Judith*
Orselli, Raimonda*

Mitchell, James*
Moore, Jack*

Choreographer
Sokolow, Anna*

All productions new this
season; all were designed or
designed and directed by Leo
Kerz with the following:

Directors
Cisney, Marcella*
Kerz, Leo*
Pollock, Michael*
Pressman, David*
Sokolow, Anna*

Designers
Kerz, Leo*
Van Witsen, Leo*

* New artist

September 20

ORPHEUS IN THE UNDERWORLD
(Offenbach)
First performance by The New
York City Opera Company
(*Orphée aux enfers*; English
version by Eric Bentley)

Staged and
  designed by ..... Kerz (d)
Costume
  designer ... Van Witsen (d)
Choreographer .. Sokolow (d)
Conductor .... Leinsdorf (d)

Eurydice ...... Stahlman (d)
Orpheus .... Crain
Pluto .... Kelley
Miss
  P. Opinion .. Laurence (d)
Cupid .... Moody
Mars .... Hecht
Venus .... Moll
Jupiter .... Sherman (d)

Diana .... Bower
Juno .... Kramarich
Mercury .... Pollock
Minerva .... Dunn
John Styx .... Humphrey (d)

September 21

ORPHEUS IN THE UNDERWORLD
Same cast as September 20

September 22

LA TRAVIATA (Verdi)

Staged by ..... Pressman (d)
Designer .... Kerz
Choreographer .... Sokolow
Conductor ...... Rosenstock

Violetta .... Yeend
Alfredo .... Morell
Germont .... MacNeil
Flora .... Winston (d)
Annina .... Jacobs
Gaston .... Pollock
Douphol .... Newman
D'Obigny ..... Modenos (d)
Dr. Grenvil .... Elyn

September 25

MIGNON (Thomas)
First performance by The New
York City Opera Company

Staged by .... Cisney (d)
Designer .... Kerz
Costume
  designer ...... Van Witsen
Choreographer ..... Sokolow
Conductor .... Morel

Mignon .... Bible
Philine .... Sills
Frédérick ...... Porretta (d)
Wilhelm Meister . . Verreau (d)
Laërte .... Gramm
Lothario .... Markow
Jarno .... Wentworth
Antonio .... Elyn
Gypsy dancer ..... Orselli (d)

September 27

SUSANNAH (Floyd)
First performance by The New
York City Opera Company

Staged and
  designed by .... Kerz
Men's costume
  designer ...... Van Witsen
Choreographer ..... Sokolow
Conductor .... Leinsdorf

Susannah .... Curtin
Sam Polk .... Crain

Olin Blitch .... Treigle
Little
  Bat McLean .. Thomas (d)
Elder McLean ..... Newman
Elder Gleaton .... Millar (d)
Elder Hays .... Druary
Elder Ott .... Hecht
Mrs. McLean ... Kramarich
Mrs. Gleaton .... Fleming
Mrs. Hays .... Bonelli (d)
Mrs. Ott .... Dunn

Women's costumes courtesy of
the School of Music,
Florida State University

September 28

ORPHEUS IN THE UNDERWORLD

Same cast as September 20

September 29 (m)

LA TRAVIATA

Same cast as September 22

Broadcast Performance

September 29

DIE FLEDERMAUS
(J. Strauss)
(English book and lyrics by
Ruth and Thomas Martin)

Staged by .... Pressman
Designer .... Kerz
Choreographer ..... Sokolow
Conductor ...... Rosenstock

Rosalinda .... Sills
Eisenstein .... McChesney
Adele .... Moody
Sally .... Collier
Alfred .... Crain
Prince Orlofsky .... Bible
Falke .... Wilderman
Frank .... Wentworth
Frosch .... Worth
Blind .... Pollock

September 30

SUSANNAH

Same cast as September 27

October 2

ORPHEUS IN THE UNDERWORLD
Same cast as September 20
except:

John Styx ...... Wentworth,
             (s, Humphrey)

October 4

MIGNON

Same cast as September 25

October 5

LA TRAVIATA

Same cast as September 22

October 6 (m)

CARMEN (Bizet)

Staged and
  designed by .... Kerz
Costume
  designer ...... Van Witsen
Choreographer ..... Sokolow
Conductor .... Morel

Carmen .... Lane
Don José .... Cassilly
Escamillo .... Treigle
Micaëla .... Addison
Zuniga .... Hecht
Frasquita .... Casselle (d)
Mercédès .... Fleming
Remendado .... Pollock
Dancairo .... Newman
Morales .... Modenos

Broadcast Performance

October 6

MIGNON

Same cast as September 25

October 11

THE TEMPEST (Martin)
American premiere
(*Der Sturm*; readapted to the
original English text of
Shakespeare)

Produced and
  directed by ...... Kerz and
                Leinsdorf
Designer .... Kerz
Costume
  designer ...... Van Witsen
Choreographer ..... Sokolow
Conductor .... Leinsdorf

Alonso .... Hecht
Sebastian .... Wentworth
Prospero .... Smith (d)
Antonio .... Millar
Ferdinand .... Cassilly
Gonzalo .... Gramm
Adrian .... Petrak
Caliban .... Humphrey
Trinculo .... Pollock
Stephano .... MacNeil
Boatswain .... Druary
Master of a ship .... Newman
Miranda .... Gillette
Ariel .... Orselli
Ariel's voices .... Baisley,
  Charney, Dunn, Fleming,
    Fry, LeSawyer,
  MacDonald, Stahlman,
  Winston; Druary, Elyn,
  Hoel, Markow, O'Leary,
  Person, Plank, Porretta

October 12

DIE FLEDERMAUS

Same cast as September 29
except:

Adele .... Casselle
Falke .... Shriner

October 13

CARMEN

Same cast as October 6 (m)

October 14

LA BOHÈME (Puccini)

Staged by .... Pressman
Designer .... Kerz
Conductor .... Morel

Mimi .... Yeend,
            (s, Fleming)
Musetta .... Bower
Rodolfo .... Morell
Marcello .... MacNeil
Schaunard .... Green
Colline .... Hecht
Benoit .... Wentworth
Alcindoro .... Newman
Parpignol .... Nahr

October 16

L'HISTOIRE DU SOLDAT
(Stravinsky)
First performance by The New
York City Opera Company
(English version by Michael
Flanders and Kitty Black)

Directed by .... Cisney
Designer .... Kerz
Choreographer ..... Sokolow
Conductor .... Morel

Narrator ...... Plummer (d)
Soldier .... Mitchell (d)
Devil .... Hatfield (d)
Princess .... Coy (d)

Followed by:

THE MOON (Orff)
United States premiere
(*Der Mond*; English translation
by Maria Massey)

Staged and choreo-
  graphed by ...... Sokolow
Designer .... Kerz
Costume
  designer ...... Van Witsen
Conductor ...... Rosenstock

Narrator .... Kelley
1st Fellow .... Gramm
2nd Fellow ...... Wentworth
3rd Fellow .... Pollock
4th Fellow .... Hecht
Peasant .... Green
Mayor .... Millar
Innkeeper .... Powell
Mayor .... Moore (d)
Peasant .... Wayne
1st Card player ..... Atherton
2nd Card player .. Del Monte
3rd Card player ..... Wayne
1st Dice player ...... Powell
2nd Dice player ...... Tibbs
3rd Dice player ...... Ruddy
1st Bowler .... Lick
2nd Bowler .... Person
1st Drinker .... Hoel
2nd Drinker .... Nahr
3rd Drinker .... O'Leary

4th Drinker .... Plank
Girl .... LeSawyer
Boy .... Plank
St. Peter .... Treigle

October 17
THE TEMPEST
Same cast as October 11

October 19
SUSANNAH
Same cast as September 27

October 20 (m)
L'HISTOIRE DU SOLDAT
Same cast as October 16
Followed by:
THE MOON
Same cast as October 16
Broadcast Performance

October 20
LA BOHÈME
Same cast as October 14
except:
Mimi .... Fleming
Parpignol .... Miller

October 21
ORPHEUS IN THE UNDERWORLD
Same cast as September 20
except:
Minerva .... Winston

October 25
CARMEN
Same cast as October 6 (m)
except:
Frasquita .... LeSawyer,
              (s, Casselle)

October 26
LA BOHÈME
Same cast as October 14

October 27
ORPHEUS IN THE UNDERWORLD
Same cast as September 20
except:
Minerva .... Winston

October 31
L'HISTOIRE DU SOLDAT
Same cast as October 16

Followed by:
THE MOON
Same cast as October 16

November 1
RIGOLETTO (Verdi)

Staged by .... Pollock (d)
Designer .... Kerz
Conductor .... Rudel

Duke .... Morell
Rigoletto .... MacNeil
Gilda .... Stahlman
Sparafucile .... Humphrey
Maddalena .... Dunn
Giovanna .... Winston
Monterone .... Hecht
Marullo .... Newman
Borsa .... Porretta
Ceprano .... Elyn
Countess Ceprano .... Baisley

November 2
ORPHEUS IN THE UNDERWORLD
Same cast as September 20

November 3
RIGOLETTO
Same cast as November 1

Season of Spring 1957 canceled

Fall 1957 (OCTOBER 9 – NOVEMBER 17)

Female artists
Addison, Adele
Andrea, Jennie
Baisley, Helen
Bonelli, Olivia
Bonini, Peggy
Bower, Beverly
Carron, Elisabeth*
Collier, Naomi
Curtin, Phyllis
Dunn, Mignon
Frank, Phyllis*
Fry, Cleo
Greene, Ethel
Haskins, Virginia
Hensley, Mary*
Jordan, Irene*
Lane, Gloria
Leonard, Lu*
LeSawyer, Mary
Likova, Eva
Mari, Dolores
Moody, Jacquelynne
Polacco, Graziella*

Rubio, Consuelo*
Sanders, Jean*
Sarrand, Mathilde*
Savoia, Rosa
Sills, Beverly
Simmons, Georgia*
Yeend, Frances

Male artists
Alexander, John*
Beattie, Herbert*
Cassilly, Richard
Chapman, William*
Constantino, Antonio*
Del Monte, George
Driscoll, Loren*
Druary, John
Gauld, Carlton
Gismondo, Giuseppe*
Hecht, Joshua
Huddleston, Paul*
Humphrey, Richard
Lewis, William*
Lloyd, David

Ludgin, Chester*
McChesney, Ernest
Morell, Barry
Neagu, Aureliano*
Newman, Arthur
Olvis, William*
Pelayo, Hernán*
Person, John
Pollock, Michael
Quilico, Louis
Reardon, John
Rounseville, Robert
Sherman, Hiram
Thomas, Eb
Treigle, Norman
Wentworth, Richard
Williams, David*
Worth, Coley

Conductors
Adler, Peter Herman*
Allers, Franz*
Basile, Arturo*

* New artist   * New artist   * New artist

Iturbi, José*
Rudel, Julius

Choral director
Smart, Gino*

Dancers
Consoer, Dianne*
Goya, Carola*
Osta, Teresita*
Tompkins, Beatrice*
Vega, Rita*

Arpino, Gerald*
De Natale, Don*
Matteo*
Triana, Antonio*
Watts, Jonathan

Choreographers
Goya, Carola*
Joffrey, Robert*
Matteo*
Triana, Antonio*

Directors
Cisney, Marcella
Dalrymple, Jean*
Gauld, Carlton*
Jordan, Glenn
Pollock, Michael
Rosing, Vladimir
Webster, Margaret

Designers
Condell, H. A.
Fletcher, Robert
Jenkins, George*
Muntanola, Manuel*
Nomikos, Andreas*

* New artist

October 9

TURANDOT (Puccini)

Choreographer ... Joffrey (d)
Conductor .... Rudel

Turandot .... Yeend
Liù .... Addison
Timur .... Hecht
Calaf .... Gismondo (d)
Ping .... Reardon
Pang .... D. Williams (d)
Pong .... Huddleston (d)
Emperor .... Driscoll (d)
Mandarin .... Newman

October 10

SUSANNAH (Floyd)

Staged by .... Cisney
Scenic designer ..Nomikos (d)
Choreographer ...... Joffrey
Conductor .... Rudel

Susannah .... Curtin
Sam Polk .... Cassilly
Olin Blitch .... Treigle
Little Bat McLean ... Thomas
Elder McLean ...... Newman
Elder Gleaton ... D. Williams
Elder Hays .... Driscoll
Elder Ott .... Hecht
Mrs. McLean .... Sanders (d)
Mrs. Gleaton .... Moody
Mrs. Hays .... Bonelli
Mrs. Ott .... Dunn

October 11

LA TRAVIATA (Verdi)

Staged by .... Pollock
Choreographer .... Joffrey
Conductor .... Basile (d)

Violetta .... Sills
Alfredo ...... Alexander (d)
Germont .... Quilico
Flora .... Polacco (d)
Annina .... Baisley
Gaston .... Driscoll
Douphol .... Beattie (d)
D'Obigny .... Reardon
Dr. Grenvil .... Newman
Solo dancers ... Consoer (d),
                  Arpino (d)

October 12

LA BOHÈME (Puccini)

Staged by .... Gauld (d)
Designer .... Condell
Conductor .... Basile

Mimi .... Savoia
Musetta .... Bonini
Rodolfo .... Morell
Marcello .... Quilico
Schaunard .... Newman,
                 (s, Reardon)
Colline .... Treigle
Benoit .... Wentworth
Alcindoro .... Beattie
Parpignol .... D. Williams

October 13 (m)

DIE FLEDERMAUS (J. Strauss)
(English book and lyrics by
Ruth and Thomas Martin)

Staged by .... Pollock
Choreographer .... Joffrey
Conductor .... Allers (d)

Rosalinda .... Curtin
Eisenstein .... McChesney
Adele .... Moody
Sally .... Collier
Alfred .... Lloyd
Prince Orlofsky ..... Driscoll
Falke .... Ludgin (d),
               (s, Reardon)
Frank .... Wentworth

Frosch .... Worth
Blind .... D. Williams
Solo dancers ..Consoer; Watts

October 13

CARMEN (Bizet)

Staged by .... Pollock
Choreographer .... Joffrey
Conductor .... Rudel,
              (s, Bloomfield)

Carmen .... Lane
Don José .... Cassilly
Escamillo .... Treigle
Micaëla .... Bower
Zuniga .... Beattie
Frasquita .... Frank (d)
Mercédès .... Sanders
Remendado ..... D. Williams
Dancairo .... Newman
Morales .... Pelayo (d)
Solo dancers ..Consoer; Arpino

October 16 (benefit preview)

LA VIDA BREVE (Falla)
First performance by The New
York City Opera Company

Staged by .... Dalrymple (d)
Scenic
  designer ... Muntanola (d)
Choreographers ..Carola Goya
         (d) and Matteo (d)
Conductor .... Iturbi (d)

Grandmother .... Dunn
Salud .... Rubio (d)
Paco .... Cassilly
Uncle Sarvaor .... Wentworth
Singer .... Pelayo
Manuel .... Reardon
Carmela .... Moody
Worker .... Huddleston
1st Vendor .... Collier
2nd Vendor .... Baisley
3rd Vendor .... Fry
4th Vendor ..... D. Williams
Solo dancers ... Carola Goya
          (d); Matteo (d)

Followed by:

EL AMOR BRUJO (Falla)
First performance by The New
York City Opera Company

Staged by .... Dalrymple (d)
Scenic
  designer ... Muntanola (d)
Choreographer ... Triana (d)
Conductor .... Iturbi (d)

Carmelo .... Triana (d)
Candelas .... Vega (d)
Lucia .... Osta (d)
Spectre ...... De Natale (d)
Witch .... Simmons (d)
Singer .... Dunn,
              (s, Lane)

(Note: The scenery for both works was loaned by the Teatro Liceo, Barcelona, Spain.)

October 17

LA VIDA BREVE

Same cast as October 16

Followed by:

EL AMOR BRUJO

Same cast as October 16 except:

Singer .... Lane

October 18

FAUST (Gounod)

Choreographer .... Joffrey
Conductor .... Rudel

Marguerite .... Yeend
Faust .... Morell
Méphistophélès ...... Treigle
Valentin .... Quilico
Siébel .... Hensley (d)
Marthe .... Dunn
Wagner .... Newman

October 19 (m)

MADAMA BUTTERFLY (Puccini)

Staged by .... Rosing
Conductor .... Rudel,
(s, Basile)

Butterfly .... Carron (d)
Suzuki .... Sanders
Kate Pinkerton ...... Baisley
Pinkerton .... Gismondo
Sharpless .... Quilico
Goro .... D. Williams
Yamadori .... Newman
The Bonze .... Hecht
*Imperial
Commissioner* ... Newman,
(s, Del Monte)

October 19

DIE FLEDERMAUS

Same cast as October 13 (m) except:

Rosalinda .... Bower
Adele .... Bonini
Sally .... Andrea
Alfred .... Lewis (d)

October 20 (m)

LA TRAVIATA

Same cast as October 11

October 20

LA VIDA BREVE

Same cast as October 16

Followed by:

EL AMOR BRUJO

Same cast as October 16 except:

Singer .... Lane

October 24

MACBETH (Verdi)
First performance by The New York City Opera Company

Staged by .... Webster
Designer .... Nomikos
Choreographer ...... Joffrey
Conductor .... Basile

Macbeth ...... Chapman (d)
Banquo .... Treigle
Lady Macbeth ... Jordan (d)
Macduff .... Gismondo
Malcolm .... McChesney
Lady-in-Waiting ...... Baisley
Doctor .... Newman
*Macbeth's
Aide-de-Camp* ..... Beattie
Hecate .... Tompkins (d)

October 25

LA BOHÈME

Same cast as October 12 except:

Schaunard .... Reardon
Colline .... Hecht
Parpignol .... Person

October 26 (m)

EL AMOR BRUJO

Same cast as October 16

Followed by:

LA VIDA BREVE

Same cast as October 16 except:

Paco .... McChesney
Singer .... Reardon
Manuel .... Newman

October 26

CARMEN

Same cast as October 13 except:

Conductor .... Rudel,
(s, Bloomfield)

(Note: Theodore Bloomfield was not to debut with the New York City Opera Company.)

October 27 (m)

MADAMA BUTTERFLY

Same cast as October 19 (m) except:

Conductor .... Basile

*Imperial
Commissioner* .. Del Monte

October 27

THE MERRY WIDOW (Lehár)
First performance by The New York City Opera Company
(Words by Adrian Ross)

Staged by .... Jordan
Scenic designer .. Jenkins (d)
Choreographer .... Joffrey
Conductor .... Allers

Sonia .... Sills
Prince Danilo ... Rounseville
Baron Popoff ...... Sherman
Natalie .... Bonini
De Jolidon .... Lewis
Marquis de Cascada .. Beattie
St. Brioche .... Reardon
Admiral Khadja ... Newman
Mme. Khadja .... Baisley
*General
Novikovich* .... Wentworth
*Mme.
Novikovich* .. Leonard (d)
Nish .... Worth
King .... Del Monte
Lo-Lo .... Collier
Solo dancers ...... Consoer,
Tompkins, Arpino

October 30

THE ABDUCTION FROM THE SERAGLIO (Mozart)
First performance by The New York City Opera Company
(*Die Entführung aus dem Serail;* English translation by John Bloch)

Staged by .... Pollock
Designer .... Fletcher
Conductor .... Adler (d)

Constanza .... Curtin
Blonde .... Haskins
Belmonte .... Rounseville
Pedrillo .... Lloyd
Osmin .... Humphrey
Pasha Selim .... Gaule

(Note: The sets and costumes were borrowed from the Stratford, Connecticut, Shakespeare Festival, where the opera had been given the previous year.)

October 31

TURANDOT

Same cast as October 9

November 1

THE MERRY WIDOW

Same cast as October 27
except:

Mme. Novikovich .... Greene

November 2 (m)

FAUST

Same cast as October 18
except:

Valentin .... Reardon

November 2

LA TRAVIATA

Same cast as October 11
except:

Violetta .... Likova
Alfredo .... Alexander,
                      (s, Lloyd)
Flora .... Bonelli
Annina .... Fry

November 3 (m)

THE ABDUCTION FROM
THE SERAGLIO

Same cast as October 30
except:

Constanza .... Bower
Osmin .... Beattie,
                    (s, Humphrey)

(Note: Hecht, the "cover" for
Osmin, was also ill. Beattie,
who had only sung the role in
German, sang partly in English
and partly in German.)

November 3

MACBETH

Same cast as October 24

November 5

MACBETH

Same cast as October 24
except:

Macbeth .... Neagu (d)
Banquo .... Hecht
Macduff .... Druary

November 6

TURANDOT

Same cast as October 9 except:

Liù .... Bonini
Timur .... Wentworth
Ping .... Ludgin

November 7

THE ABDUCTION FROM
THE SERAGLIO

Same cast as October 30
except:

Constanza .... Bower
Pedrillo .... Pollock

November 8

SUSANNAH

Same cast as October 10

November 9 (m)

CARMEN

Same cast as October 13
except:

Carmen .... Dunn
Escamillo .... Quilico
Micaëla .... Sarrand (d)
Frasquita .... Bonelli
Mercédès .... Baisley

November 9

MADAMA BUTTERFLY

Same cast as October 19 (m)
except:

Conductor .... Basile
Butterfly .... Mari
Suzuki .... Hensley
Kate Pinkerton .... LeSawyer
Pinkerton .... Druary
Sharpless .... Chapman
*Imperial
   Commissioner* .. Del Monte

November 10 (m)

THE MERRY WIDOW

Same cast as October 27
except:

De Jolidon .... Olvis (d)
St. Brioche .... Ludgin
General Novikovich ... Hecht
Mme. Novikovich .... Greene

November 10

LA BOHÈME

Same cast as October 12
except:

Mimi .... Addison
Musetta .... Moody
Rodolfo .... Gismondo
Colline .... Hecht
Benoit .... Beattie

November 13

SUSANNAH

Same cast as October 10

November 14

TURANDOT

Same cast as October 9 except:

Ping .... Ludgin

November 15

MADAMA BUTTERFLY

Same cast as October 19 (m)
except:

Conductor .... Basile
Kate Pinkerton .... Collier
Pinkerton .... Morell
Goro .... Huddleston
*Imperial
   Commissioner* .. Del Monte

November 16 (m)

THE ABDUCTION FROM
THE SERAGLIO

Same cast as October 30
except:

Blonde .... Moody
Osmin .... Beattie

November 16

LA TRAVIATA

Same cast as October 11
except:

Alfredo ..... Constantino (d)
Annina .... Fry

November 17 (m)

LA BOHÈME

Same cast as October 12
except:

Mimi .... Addison
Musetta .... Moody
Rodolfo .... Gismondo
Schaunard .... Reardon

November 17

DIE FLEDERMAUS

Same cast as October 13 (m)
except:

Rosalinda .... Bower
Adele .... Bonini
Sally .... Andrea
Falke .... Reardon

Spring 1958 (APRIL 3 – MAY 11)

Female artists
Alpert, Anita
Andrea, Jennie
Austin, Patti*
Baisley, Helen
Becker, Barbara*
Bower, Beverly
Brice, Carol*
Carroll, Joan*
Carron, Elisabeth
Carter, Shirley*†
Collier, Naomi
Curtin, Phyllis
Fabray, Claretta
Ferguson, Helen*
Haynes, Hilda*
James, Olga*
Jessye, Eva*
Kobart, Ruth*
Kolasz, Rita*
Krebs, Beatrice
Le Noire, Rosetta*
LeSawyer, Mary
Lewis, Brenda
Lipton, Martha
Lockard, Barbara
Louise, Mary
Manners, Gail
Mari, Dolores
Moody, Jacquelynne
Neway, Patricia
Parker, Louise*
Rodgers, Lou
Sanders, Jean
Sills, Beverly
Stolin, Sonia*
Strine, Helen*
Taussig, Lynn*
Turner, Claramae
Venora, Lee*
Webb, Alyce
Wolff, Beverly*

Male artists
Alexander, John
Atherton, Robert
Atkinson, David*
Bain, Conrad*
Barbusci, Nicola
Bates, Lawson*
Boatwright, McHenry*
Bowler, Richard*
Cambridge, Godfrey*
Cassel, Walter
Cassilly, Richard
Cathrey, George*
Chapman, William
Charles, Lee*
Code, Grant*
Crowley, Edward*
De Lon, Jack*
Del Monte, George
Dennison, John
Driscoll, Loren
Edmonson, William*
Elliott, William

* New artist
† Later Shirley Verrett

Farrell, Walter*
Fitzgerald, Neil*
Fried, Howard
Frierson, Andrew*
Ghazal, Edward
Gillaspy, John*
Gossett, Louis*
Hecht, Joshua
Hoel, Edson
Irving, George S.*
Irving, John*
Joy, Nicholas*
Kaldenberg, Keith
Kelley, Norman
Kolk, Stanley*
Ludgin, Chester
Malone, Pat*
McChesney, Ernest
Metcalf, William*
Moulson, Robert*
Newman, Arthur
O'Neil, Frederick*
Perkins, Garwood*
Porretta, Frank
Reardon, John
Renan, Emile
Richardson, Emery*
Riley, Jr., Frank*
Ruddy, Robert
Sliker, Peter
Snell, Chris*
Turner, Douglas*
Ukena, Paul*
Watson, Chester*
Watson, Laurence*
Wheeler, John
Williams, Grant*
Winters, Lawrence
Yancy, Jr., Alexander
Zakariasen, William

Conductors
Adler, Peter Herman
Bernstein, Leonard*
Buckley, Emerson
Gamson, Arnold*
Krachmalnick, Samuel*
Lipkin, Seymour*
Rudel, Julius
Smart, Gino*
Whallon, Evan*

Chorus master
Smart, Gino

Solo dancers
Scott, Mare*

Choreographer
Joffrey, Robert

Stage directors
Butler, Bill
Capalbo, Carmen*

* New artist

Corsaro, Frank*
Pollock, Michael
Quintero, José*
Rosing, Vladimir
Shumlin, Herman*
Webster, Margaret

Designers
Armistead, Horace
Barratt, Watson*
Bay, Howard
Bernstein, Aline
Condell, H. A.
Morley, Ruth
Nomikos, Andreas
Oenslager, Donald*
Sylbert, Paul*

* New artist

April 3

THE BALLAD OF BABY DOE
(Moore)
First performance by The New
York City Opera Company

Staged by .... Rosing
Designer ...... Oenslager (d)
Conductor .... Buckley

An old silver miner .... Fried
Saloon bartender ..... Ludgin
Horace Tabor .... Cassel
Sam .... Kaldenberg
Bushy .... De Lon (d)
Barney .... Del Monte
Jacob .... Newman
Augusta .... Lipton
Baby Doe .... Sills
Kate .... Collier
Mag .... Baisley
Samantha .... Rodgers
Hotel clerk ...... Kaldenberg
Albert .... Atherton
Sarah .... LeSawyer
Mary .... Andrea
Emily .... Alpert
Effie .... Lockard
McCourt family ..... Baisley,
Collier, Barbusci,
Zakariasen
Mama McCourt ..... Krebs
1st Washington
dandy .... Wheeler
2nd Washington
dandy .... Elliott
3rd Washington
dandy .... Sliker
4th Washington
dandy .... Dennison
Father Chapelle .... Fried
Hotel footman ..... Newman
Chester A. Arthur ... De Lon
(d
Elizabeth and
Silver Dollar .. Taussig (d)
Becker (d
Mayor of Leadville ... Rudd

William
   Jennings Bryan ..... Hecht
Stage doorman .... Fried
Denver politician ..... Ludgin
Silver Dollar
   (grown up) .... Baisley

(Note: Possible substitution of
Newman for Atherton as
Albert and Hoel for Wheeler
as 1st Washington dandy.)

April 5

THE BALLAD OF BABY DOE

Same cast as April 3

April 6

TALE FOR A DEAF EAR (Bucci)
First performance by The New
   York City Opera Company

Staged by .... Pollock
Designer .... Sylbert (d)
Conductor ..... Gamson (d)

Laura Gates .... Neway
Tracy Gates ...... Chapman
The Woman .... Bower
The Girl .... Venora (d)
The Soldier .... Cassilly
The Doctor .... Newman

Followed by:

TROUBLE IN TAHITI (Bernstein)
First performance by The New
   York City Opera Company

Staged by .... Pollock
Designer .... Nomikos
Conductor .... Bernstein (d)

Dinah .... Wolff (d)
Sam .... Atkinson (d)
Trio .... Collier,
    Metcalf (d), Kolk (d)

April 9 (preview)

LOST IN THE STARS (Weill)
First performance by The New
   York City Opera Company

Staged by ...... Quintero (d)
Designer .... Nomikos
Lighting .... Watson
Conductor .... Rudel

Leader .... Charles (d)
Answerer .... Atherton
Nita .... Austin (d)
Grace Kumalo ..Le Noire (d)
Stephen Kumalo .... Winters
Station master .... Ruddy
The Young Man ...... Yancy
The Young Woman ... Louise
James Jarvis .... Joy (d)
Edward Jarvis ..... Snell (d)
Arthur Jarvis ... J. Irving (d)
John Kumalo .... O'Neill (d)
Paulus ...... Richardson (d)
William .... Bates
Alex .... Riley (d)
Foreman .... Dennison

Mrs. Mkize ...... Jessye (d)
Hlabeni .... Perkins
Eland .... Bain (d)
Linda .... James (d)
Johannes
   Pafuri ..... Cambridge (d)
Matthew
   Kumalo .... D. Turner (d)
Absalom
   Kumalo .... Gossett (d)
Rose .... Webb
The Other Girl ...... Fabray
Irina .... Carter (d)
Servant ...... L. Watson (d)
Policeman .... Zakariasen
White woman .... Collier
White Man .... Dennison
Burton .... Bowler (d)
The Judge .... Fitzgerald (d)

April 10

LOST IN THE STARS

Same cast as April 9

April 11

THE BALLAD OF BABY DOE

Same cast as April 3 except:

Augusta .... Kobart (d)

April 12

TALE FOR A DEAF EAR

Same cast as April 6

Followed by:

TROUBLE IN TAHITI

Same cast as April 6 except:

Conductor .... Lipkin (d)

Dinah .... Sanders,
    (s, Wolff)

April 13

THE TAMING OF THE SHREW
   (Giannini)
First performance by The New
   York City Opera Company

Staged by .... Webster
Scenic designer .. Barratt (d)
Conductor .... Adler

Lucentio .... Alexander
Tranio .... Ukena (d)
Baptista .... C. Watson (d)
Katharina .... Curtin
Bianca .... Stolin (d)
Gremio .... Williams (d)
Hortensio .... Farrell (d)
Biondello ...... Gillaspy (d)
Petruchio .... Cassel
Grumio .... Kaldenberg
Curtis .... Del Monte
A Tailor .... Wheeler
Vincentio .... Newman
A Pedant .... De Lon

April 17

REGINA (Blitzstein)

Staged by ...... Shumlin (d)
Scenic designer .... Bay
Costume designer .. Bernstein
Choreographer .... Joffrey
Conductor..Krachmalnick (d)

Addie .... Brice (d)
Cal .... Frierson (d)
Alexandra Giddens..Strine (d)
Birdie Hubbard ...... Carron
Oscar Hubbard .... Renan
Leo Hubbard .... Driscoll
Regina Giddens .... Lewis
Marshall .... McChesney
Ben Hubbard ... G. S. Irving
    (d)
Horace Giddens ...... Hecht
Manders .... Ruddy

(Note: *Dancers* added to
program April 27)

April 18

TALE FOR A DEAF EAR

Same cast as April 6 except:

The Woman ..... Kolacz (d)
The Soldier .... Moulson (d)

Followed by:

TROUBLE IN TAHITI

Same cast as April 6 except:

Conductor .... Lipkin
Dinah .... Sanders

April 19

THE TAMING OF THE SHREW

Same cast as April 13

April 20 (m)

LOST IN THE STARS

Same cast as April 9 except:

Burton .... Malone (d)

April 20

THE OLD MAID AND THE THIEF
   (Menotti)

Staged by .... Butler
Conductor ..... Whallon (d)

Laetitia .... Moody
Miss Todd .... Kobart
Miss Pinkerton .... Bower
Bob .... Reardon

Followed by:

THE MEDIUM (Menotti)

Staged by .... Butler
Scenic designer ... Armistead
Conductor ..... Whallon (d)

Monica .... Carroll (d)
Toby .... Scott (d)
Madame Flora .... C. Turner

Mrs. Gobineau .... LeSawyer
Mr. Gobineau ...... Newman
Mrs. Nolan .... Sanders

April 23

THE GOOD SOLDIER SCHWEIK
(Kurka)
World premiere

Staged by ...... Capalbo (d)
Scenic designer .... Nomikos
Costume designer .... Morley
Choreographer .... Joffrey
Lighting .... Watson
Conductor .... Rudel

Gentleman of
 Bohemia ...... G. S. Irving
Joseph Schweik ...... Kelley
Mrs. Muller ...... LeSawyer
Palivec .... C. Watson
Bretschneider .... De Lon
Police officer ...... Newman
Guard .... Kaldenberg
1st Prisoner .... Ruddy
2nd Prisoner ..... Zakariasen
3rd Prisoner .... Atherton
4th Prisoner ...... Del Monte
5th Prisoner .... Ghazal
1st Psychiatrist .... Fried
2nd Psychiatrist ..... Ludgin
3rd Psychiatrist .... Hecht
1st Doctor .... Ludgin
2nd Doctor .... Ruddy
Consumptive .... Sliker
1st Malingerer .... Elliott
2nd Malingerer .... Hoel
3rd Malingerer .... Dennison
4th Malingerer ...... Ghazal
Sergeant .... Newman
Army doctor .... Renan
Baroness
 von Botzenheim ... Kobart
Army chaplain ...... De Lon
Lieutenant
 Henry Lukash .... Atkinson
Fox, a dog .... Renan
Katy Wendler .... Baisley
Colonel
 von Zillergut .. G. S. Irving
Mr. Wendler .... Kaldenberg
General von
 Schwartzburg .. C. Watson
Voditchka .... Ludgin
Mr. Kakonyi ...... Renan
Madame Kakonyi .... Collier
Sergeant Vanek .... Fried

April 24

LOST IN THE STARS

Same cast as April 9 except:

Burton .... Malone

April 25

LOST IN THE STARS

Same cast as April 9 except:

Burton .... Malone

April 26 (m)

THE BALLAD OF BABY DOE

Same cast as April 3 except:

Baby Doe .... Moody

April 26

THE OLD MAID AND THE THIEF

Same cast as April 20 except:

Laetitia .... Venora

Followed by:

THE MEDIUM

Same cast as April 20

April 27 (m)

THE TAMING OF THE SHREW

Same cast as April 13 except:

Lucentio .... Porretta
Katharina .... Manners
Bianca .... Mari

April 27

REGINA

Same cast as April 17

April 29

THE GOOD SOLDIER SCHWEIK

Same cast as April 23 except:

2nd Malingerer ... Zakariasen

April 30

SUSANNAH (Floyd)

Staged by ...... Corsaro (d)
Set designer .... Sylbert
Choreographer .... Joffrey
Conductor .... Rudel

Susannah .... Curtin
Sam Polk .... Cassilly
Olin Blitch .... Chapman
Little Bat
 McLean .... Kaldenberg
Elder McLean ...... Newman
Elder Gleaton .... De Lon
Elder Hays .... Driscoll
Elder Ott .... Hecht
Mrs. McLean .... Sanders

Mrs. Gleaton ...... LeSawyer
Mrs. Hays .... Moody
Mrs. Ott .... Kobart

May 1

THE OLD MAID AND THE THIEF

Same cast as April 20 except:

Miss Todd .... Krebs
Miss Pinkerton ...... Carron
Bob .... Metcalf

Followed by:

THE MEDIUM

Same cast as April 20 except:

Monica .... Venora
Madame Flora .... Neway
Mrs. Nolan .... Baisley

May 2

REGINA

Same cast as April 17 except:

Addie .... Parker (d)

May 3

LOST IN THE STARS

Same cast as April 9 except:

Conductor .... Smart (d)

Grace Kumalo ... Haynes (d)
John Kumalo ..Edmonson (d)
Linda .... Ferguson (d)
The Judge ...... Cathrey (d)

May 4

SUSANNAH

Same cast as April 30 except:

Sam Polk .... Moulson

May 6–9, 10 (matinee and evening), 11 (matinee and evening)

LOST IN THE STARS

Same cast as April 9 except:

Conductor .... Smart

Grace Kumalo ...... Haynes
Stephen
 Kumalo ... Boatwright (d)
    (May 11 mat.)
James Jarvis ...... Code (d)
John Kumalo ..... Edmonson
Eland .... Crowley (d)
Linda .... Ferguson
Burton .... Malone

Fall 1958 (OCTOBER 7 – NOVEMBER 16)

Female artists
Addison, Adele
Amundsen, Monte*
Andrea, Jennie
Baisley, Helen
Becker, Barbara
Bible, Frances
Bower, Beverly
Brown, Debria*
Candida, Maria*
Carroll, Joan
Carron, Elisabeth
Curtin, Phyllis
Galli, Gianna*
Kobart, Ruth
Krebs, Beatrice
LeSawyer, Mary
Lewis, Brenda
Lockard, Barbara
Mari, Dolores
Moody, Jacquelynne
Packard, Florence*
Pascale, Betty
Resnik, Regina
Ribla, Gertrude
Rodgers, Lou
Sanders, Jean
Sarfaty, Regina*
Scott, Helena*
Sena, Joan*
Sills, Beverly
Taussig, Lynn
Venora, Lee
Wolff, Greta
Yeend, Frances

Male artists
Alexander, John
Atherton, Robert
Baratti, Giuseppe*
Barbusci, Nicola
Beattie, Herbert
Cassel, Walter
Cassilly, Richard
Chapman, William
Christopher, Russell*
Cooper, Michael*
Crain, Jon
Del Monte, George
Dennison, John
Driscoll, Loren
Gauld, Carlton
Gismondo, Giuseppe
Harrold, Jack
Hecht, Joshua
Herbert, Ralph
Hoel, Edson
Kaldenberg, Keith
Lazarus, Roy*
Lishner, Leon
Lloyd, David
Ludgin, Chester
Maero, Philip*
Maran, George*
Marek, Dan
McChesney, Ernest
Newman, Arthur
Poleri, David

* New artist

Porretta, Frank
Reardon, John
Renan, Emile
Sliker, Peter
Treigle, Norman
Ukena, Paul
Voketaitis, Arnold*
Williams, Grant
Worth, Coley
Zakariasen, William

Conductors
Adler, Peter Herman
Basile, Arturo
Buckley, Emerson
Callinicos, Constantine*
Lipkin, Seymour
Rudel, Julius
Smart, Gino

Chorus master
Smart, Gino

Dancers
Consoer, Dianne
Dynowska, Oldyna*
Martinet, Françoise
Paquet, Marie
Ruiz, Brunilda
Tompkins, Beatrice
Zide, Rochelle*

Arpino, Gerald
Jorgensen, Nels
Nebreda, Vicente
Sutherland, Paul*
Watts, Jonathan

Choreographer
Joffrey, Robert

Directors
Corsaro, Frank
Field, Bill
Gauld, Carlton
Howell, John Daggett*
Owens, Barbara*
Pollock, Michael
Rosing, Vladimir
Webster, Margaret

Designers
Condell, H. A.
Fletcher, Robert
Jenkins, George
Nomikos, Andreas
Oenslager, Donald
Sylbert, Paul
Ter-Arutunian, Rouben

* New artist

October 7

THE SILENT WOMAN
(R. Strauss)
United States premiere
(*Die schweigsame Frau*;
English translation by
Herbert Bedford)

Staged by .... Webster
Designer .... Nomikos
Conductor .... Adler

Housekeeper .... Kobart
Cutbeard .... Ukena
Sir Morosus Blunt .... Beattie
Henry .... Alexander
A company of singers:
Vanuzzi ...... Voketaitis (d)
Morbio .... Newman
Farfallo .... Hecht
Isotta .... Moody
Carlotta .... Sarfaty (d)
Aminta .... Carroll

October 9

THE BALLAD OF BABY DOE
(Moore)

Conductor .... Buckley

An old silver miner .. Williams
Saloon bartender ..... Ludgin
Horace Tabor .... Cassel
Sam .... Kaldenberg
Bushy .... Harrold
Barney .... Del Monte
Jacob .... Newman
Augusta .... Bible
Baby Doe .... Sills
Kate .... Wolff
Mag .... Baisley
Samantha .... Pascale
Hotel clerk ...... Kaldenberg
Albert .... Atherton
Sarah .... LeSawyer
Mary .... Andrea
Emily .... Rodgers
Effie .... Lockard
McCourt family ..... Baisley,
Wolff, Barbusci,
Zakariasen
Mama McCourt .... Krebs
Four Washington
dandies .. Hoel, Marek (d),
Sliker, Dennison
Father Chapelle .... Williams
Hotel footman ..... Newman
Chester A. Arthur ... Harrold
Elizabeth and Silver
Dollar ..... Taussig, Becker
Mayor of
Leadville ...... Zakariasen
William
Jennings Bryan ..... Hecht
Stage doorman ..... Williams
Denver politician .... Ludgin
Silver Dollar
(grown up) .... Baisley

October 10

TURANDOT (Puccini)

Conductor .... Rudel

Turandot .... Yeend
Liù .... Addison
Timur .... Hecht
Calaf .... Gismondo
Ping .... Reardon
Pang .... Williams

Pong .... Kaldenberg
Emperor .... Christopher (d)
Mandarin .... Newman

October 11

MADAMA BUTTERFLY (Puccini)

Stage director .... Field
Conductor .... Basile

Butterfly .... Carron
Suzuki .... Sanders
Kate Pinkerton ...... Baisley
Pinkerton .... Poleri
Sharpless .... Maero (d),
(s, Chapman)
Goro .... Cooper (d)
Yamadori .... Newman
The Bonze .... Voketaitis
Imperial
Commissioner .. Del Monte

October 12 (m)

LA TRAVIATA (Verdi)

Conductor .... Basile

Violetta .... Sills
Alfredo .... Alexander
Germont .... Cassel
Flora .... LeSawyer
Annina .... Baisley
Gaston .... Driscoll
Douphol .... Newman
D'Obigny .... Christopher
Dr. Grenvil .... Voketaitis
Solo
dancers .. Martinet; Arpino

October 12

THE ABDUCTION FROM
THE SERAGLIO (Mozart)
(English translation by
John Bloch)

Conductor .... Adler

Constanza .... Curtin
Blonde .... Moody
Belmonte .. Maran (d) (Act I
beginning); Porretta
(Act I conclusion,
Acts II & III)
Pedrillo .... Lloyd
Osmin .... Lishner
Pasha Selim .... Gauld

October 15

THE SILENT WOMAN

Same cast as October 7

October 16

CARMEN (Bizet)

Staged by .... Gauld
Conductor .... Buckley

Carmen .... Resnik
Don José .... Cassilly
Escamillo .... Chapman
Micaëla .... Venora
Zuniga .... Lazarus (d)

Frasquita .... LeSawyer
Mercédès .... Sarfaty
Remendado .... Williams
Dancairo .... Newman
Morales .... Ludgin
Solo
dancers .. Martinet; Arpino

October 17

THE BALLAD OF BABY DOE

Same cast as October 9 except:

Augusta .... Kobart

October 18

LA BOHÈME (Puccini)

Conductor .... Basile

Mimi .... Addison
Musetta .... Moody
Rodolfo .... Gismondo
Marcello .... Reardon
Schaunard .... Newman
Colline .... Hecht
Benoit .... Renan
Alcindoro .... Renan
Parpignol .... Williams

October 19 (m)

DIE FLEDERMAUS
(J. Strauss)
(English book and lyrics by
Ruth and Thomas Martin)

Stage director .... Owens (d)
Conductor .... Lipkin

Rosalinda .... Bower
Eisenstein ...... McChesney
Adele .... Amundsen (d)
Sally .... Andrea
Alfred .... Crain
Prince Orlofsky ..... Driscoll
Falke .... Ludgin
Frank .... Ukena
Frosch .... Worth
Blind .... Williams
Solo dancers .. Consoer; Watts

October 19

LA CENERENTOLA (Rossini)

Staged by .... Pollock
Choreographer .... Joffrey
Conductor .... Basile

Prince Ramiro ... Baratti (d)
Dandini .... Reardon
Don Magnifico ...... Herbert
Clorinda .... Moody
Tisbe .... Sarfaty
Angelina .... Bible
Alidoro .... Newman
Ballet of the Four Seasons:
Spring ..... Zide (d); Arpino
Summer ..... Ruiz; Nebreda
Autumn .... Paquet;
Sutherland (d)
Winter ... Martinet; Jorgensen

(Note: *Fairy godmother* added
to dancers November 1)

October 23

THE RAPE OF LUCRETIA
(Britten)
First performance by The New
York City Opera Company

Staged by .... Howell (d)
Designer .... Nomikos
Lighting .... Watson
Conductor .... Rudel

Male Chorus .... Lloyd
Female Chorus .... Lewis
Collatinus .... Hecht
Junius .... Renan
Tarquinius .... Chapman
Lucretia .... Bible
Bianca .... Kobart
Lucia .... Venora

October 24

MADAMA BUTTERFLY

Same cast as October 11
except:

Butterfly .... Mari
Suzuki .... Sarfaty
Pinkerton .... Cassilly
Goro .... Williams,
(s, Kaldenberg)

October 25 (m)

THE ABDUCTION FROM
THE SERAGLIO

Same cast as October 12
except:

Belmonte .... Maran

October 25

CARMEN

Same cast as October 16
except:

Carmen .... Sanders
Micaëla .... Packard (d)
Mercédès .... Baisley

October 26 (m)

THE BALLAD OF BABY DOE

Same cast as October 9 except:

Baby Doe .... Moody
William
Jennings Bryan .... Lazaru

October 26

THE SILENT WOMAN

Same cast as October 7 except

Sir Morosus .... Lishne

October 28

TURANDOT

Same cast as October 10

October 29

THE RAPE OF LUCRETIA

Same cast as October 23

October 30

THE ABDUCTION FROM
THE SERAGLIO

Same cast as October 12
except:

Constanza .... Bower
Blonde .... Carroll
Belmonte .... Porretta
Pedrillo .... Kaldenberg

October 31

THE MERRY WIDOW (Lehár)
(Words by Adrian Ross)

Staged by .... Pollock
Conductor .... Rudel
Sonia .... Sills
Prince Danilo ...... Reardon
Baron Popoff .... Harrold
Natalie .... Scott (d)
De Jolidon .... Alexander
Marquis
  de Cascada .... Voketaitis
St. Brioche .... Ludgin
Admiral Khadja .... Newman
Mme. Khadja .... Baisley
General
  Novikovich .... Kaldenberg
Mme. Novikovich ... Lockard
Nish .... Worth
Lo-Lo .... Baisley
Solo dancers .... Martinet,
               Tompkins; Arpino

November 1 (m)

LA CENERENTOLA

Same cast as October 19
except:

Added to this program:
Fairy
  godmother .. Dynowska (d)

November 1

DIE FLEDERMAUS

Same cast as October 19 (m)

November 2 (m)

LA BOHÈME

Same cast as October 18
except:

Mimi .... Galli (d)
Musetta .... Scott
Schaunard .... Newman,
         (s, Christopher)

November 2

SUSANNAH (Floyd)

Conductor .... Rudel

Susannah .... Curtin
Sam Polk .... Cassilly

Olin Blitch .... Treigle
Little
  Bat McLean ... Kaldenberg
Elder McLean ...... Ludgin
Elder Gleaton ...... Williams
Elder Hays .... Driscoll
Elder Ott .... Voketaitis
Mrs. McLean .... Kobart
Mrs. Gleaton ...... LeSawyer
Mrs. Hays .... Moody
Mrs. Ott .... Lockard

November 7

LA TRAVIATA

Same cast as October 12 (m)
except:

Violetta .... Curtin
Germont .... Maero
Flora .... Baisley
Annina .... Rodgers
Gaston .... Williams

November 8 (m)

CARMEN

Same cast as October 16
except:

Carmen .... Brown (d)
Don José .... Crain
Escamillo .... Treigle
Micaëla .... Sena (d)
Morales .... Reardon

November 8

THE MERRY WIDOW

Same cast as October 31
except:

Conductor .... Smart

Sonia .... Bower
Natalie .... Moody
St. Brioche .... Cooper
Mme. Khadja .... Wolff

November 9 (m)

MADAMA BUTTERFLY

Same cast as October 11
except:

Butterfly .... Mari
Suzuki .... Sarfaty
Kate Pinkerton .... LeSawyer
Pinkerton .... Gismondo
Goro .... Wililams

November 9

DIE FLEDERMAUS

Same cast as October 19 (m)
except:

Rosalinda .... Sills
Eisenstein .... Herbert
Adele .... Moody
Sally .... Baisley
Falke .... Reardon

November 12

TURANDOT

Same cast as October 10
except:

Turandot .... Ribla
Liù .... Carron
Ping .... Ludgin

November 13

THE SILENT WOMAN

Same cast as October 7 except:

Housekeeper .... Krebs

November 14

SUSANNAH

Same cast as November 2
except:

Susannah .... Venora
Olin Blicth .... Hecht
Mrs. Ott .... Lockard,
        (s, Sarfaty)

November 15 (m)

MADAMA BUTTERFLY

Same cast as October 11
except:

Conductor .... Callinicos (d)
Suzuki .... Sarfaty
Pinkerton .... Gismondo
Sharpless .... Reardon
Goro .... Williams

November 15

LA TRAVIATA

Same cast as October 12 (m)
except:

Violetta .... Curtin
Alfredo .... Baratti
Germont .... Maero
Gaston .... Williams

November 16 (m)

THE MERRY WIDOW

Same cast as October 31
except:

Conductor .... Smart

Sonia .... Bower
Prince Danilo ...... Reardon,
      (s, McChesney)
Natalie .... Scott,
        (s, Moody)
De Jolidon .... Porretta
Mme. Khadja .... Wolff

November 16

LA BOHÈME

Same cast as October 18
except:

Mimi .... Yeend
Musetta .... Candida (d)
Rodolfo .... Poleri
Marcello .... Ludgin
Schaunard ...... Christopher

Spring 1959 (MARCH 30 – MAY 3)

Female artists
Andrea, Jennie
Anglin, Florence*
Baisley, Helen
Becker, Barbara
Bible, Frances
Bishop, Adelaide
Brice, Carol
Carron, Elisabeth
Clements, Joy*
Curtin, Phyllis
Darian, Anita*
Dussault, Nancy*
Jordan, Lynda
Kobart, Ruth
Kombrink, Ilona*
Krebs, Beatrice
LeSawyer, Mary
Lewis, Brenda
Louise, Mary
Mannion, Elizabeth
Mari, Dolores
Metzger, Rita
Moody, Jacquelynne
Moser, Margot*
Neway, Patricia
Rodgers, Lou
Sarfaty, Regina
Scott, Helena
Scovotti, Jeanette*
Sills, Beverly
Spence, Wilma
Taussig, Lynn
Turner, Claramae
Venora, Lee
Viracola, Fiddle*
White, Dorothy
Willauer, Marguerite
Williams, Sharon*
Wolff, Greta

Male artists
Able, Will B.*
Arthur, Donald
Atherton, Robert
Atkinson, David
Balestrieri, Anthony
Bruns, Philip*
Cassel, Walter
Cassilly, Richard
Chapman, William
Clemence, Richard*
Crain, Jon
Cross, Richard*
De Lon, Jack
Del Monte, George
Dennison, John
Dooley, Paul*
Driscoll, Loren
Druary, John
Frank, David*
Fried, Howard
Frierson, Andrew
Harrell, Mack
Hecht, Joshua
Hoel, Edson
Huddleston, Paul
Irving, George S.
Kaldenberg, Keith

* New artist

Kelley, Norman
Lewis, Albert*
Ludgin, Chester
Macurdy, John*
McChesney, Ernest
Mann, Michael*
Marek, Dan
Merrill, Scott*
Merriman, Dan*
Nahr, William
Newman, Arthur
Poleri, David
Porretta, Frank
Reardon, John
Renan, Emile
Saxon, William†
Sechler, Craig*
Sliker, Peter
Storch, Arthur*
Sullivan, Marc*
Theyard, Harry*
Timberlake, Craig*
Trehy, Robert*
Ukena, Paul
Voketaitis, Arnold
Watson, Chester
Williams, Grant
Zakariasen, William

Conductors
Buckley, Emerson
Goberman, Max*
Grossman, Herbert
Krachmalnick, Samuel
Levin, Sylvan*
Rudel, Julius
Saffir, Kurt*
Smart, Gino
Stanger, Russell*
Torkanowsky, Werner*

Chorus master
Smart, Gino

Solo dancers
Lee, Sondra*

Perez, José*
Tone, Richard*

Choreographers
Joffrey, Robert
Machiz, Herbert*
Tone, Richard*

Directors
Ball, William*
Browning, Kirk*
Corsaro, Frank
Field, Bill
Houseman, John*

* New artist
† William Saxon was the stage
name sometimes used by William
Zakariesen, who is now one of
New York's most respected music
critics. For consistency in the
Annals, all occurrences of Saxon
have been changed to Zakariesen.

Machiz, Herbert*
Mann, Delbert*
Pollock, Michael
Quintero, José
Rosing, Vladimir
Shumlin, Herman

Designers
Armistead, Horace
Bay, Howard
Campbell, Patton*
Hays, David*
Morley, Ruth
Nomikos, Andreas
Oenslager, Donald
Polakov, Lester
Smith, Gary*
Sylbert, Paul
Ter-Arutunian, Rouben

* New artist

March 30

MARIA GOLOVIN (Menotti)
First performance by The New
York City Opera Company

Staged by ..... Browning (d)
Scenic designer .. Ter-Arutunian
Costume designer .... Morley
Conductor .... Grossman

Donato .... Cross (d)
Agata .... Sarfaty
Mother .... Neway
Dr. Zuckertanz ...... Ludgin
Maria Golovin .. Kombrink (d)
Trottolo .... Sechler (d)
Prisoner .... Ludgin

April 2

STREET SCENE (Weill)
First performance by The New
York City Opera Company

Staged by .... Machiz (d)
Designer .... Sylbert
Choreography by .. Tone (d)
                and Machiz (d)
Children's number
   supervised by ...... Joffrey
Conductor .... Krachmalnick

Abraham Kaplan ...... Fried
Greta Fiorentino .... Mari
Carl Olsen .... Voketaitis
Emma Jones .... Kobart
Olga Olsen .... Krebs
Shirley Kaplan ... Anglin (d)
Mrs. Davis .... Louise
Henry Davis .... Frierson
Willie Maurrant ... Mann (d)
Anna Maurrant ..... Carron
                (s, Spence)
Sam Kaplan .... Poleri
Daniel Buchanan .. Kaldenberg
Frank Maurrant ... Chapman
George Jones ..... Newman
Steve Sankey ..... Storch (d)

Lippo Fiorentino .... De Lon
Jennie
   Hildebrand .. Dussault (d)
2nd Graduate .. Viracola (d)
3rd Graduate .... Andrea
Mrs. Hildebrand ... Mannion
Charlie
   Hildebrand .. Clemence (d)
Mary Hildebrand .... Taussig
Grace Davis .. S. Williams (d)
Rose Maurrant .... Scott (d)
Harry Easter .... Merrill (d)
Mae Jones .... Lee (d)
Dick McGann ..... Tone (d)
Vincent Jones .. A. Lewis (d)
Dr. Wilson .... Macurdy (d)
Officer
   Murphy .... Merriman (d)
City Marshall .... Del Monte
Fred Cullen ...... Zakariasen
1st Nursemaid ..... LeSawyer
2nd Nursemaid .... Wolff

April 3

THE BALLAD OF BABY DOE
(Moore)

Directed by .... Field
Designer .... Oenslager
Conductor .... Buckley

An old silver
   miner .... G. Williams
Saloon bartender ..... Ludgin
Horace Tabor .... Cassel
Sam .... Kaldenberg
Bushy .... De Lon
Barney .... Del Monte
Jacob .... Newman
Augusta .... Bible
Baby Doe .... Sills
Kate .... Wolff
Mag .... Baisley
Samantha .... Jordan
Hotel clerk ...... Kaldenberg
Albert .... Atherton
Sarah .... LeSawyer
Mary .... Andrea
Emily .... Rodgers
Effie .... White
McCourt family ..... Baisley,
   Wolff, Arthur, Zakariasen
Mama McCourt ...... Krebs
Four Washington
   dandies ...... Hoel, Marek,
     Sliker, Dennison
Father Chapelle .. G. Williams
Hotel footman ..... Newman
Chester A. Arthur ... De Lon
Elizabeth and Silver
   Dollar .... Taussig, Becker
Mayor of
   Leadville ...... Zakariasen
William
   Jennings Bryan ..... Hecht
Stage doorman .. G. Williams
Denver politician .... Ludgin
Silver Dollar
   (grown up) .... Baisley

April 4

STREET SCENE

Same cast as April 2 except:

Anna Maurrant ..... Carron,
     (s, Spence)

April 5

THE SCARF (Hoiby)
United States premiere

Staged by .... Browning
Designer ..... Ter-Arutunian
Conductor ...... Stanger (d)

Miriam .... Neway
Reuel .... Druary
Postman .... Cross

Followed by:

THE DEVIL AND
DANIEL WEBSTER (Moore)
First performance by The New
York City Opera Company

Staged by .... Houseman (d)
Designer ...... Ter-Arutunian
Choreographer .... Joffrey
Conductor .... Goberman (d)

Jabez Stone .... Hecht
Mary Stone .... Bishop
Daniel Webster .... Cassel
Fiddler .... Kaldenberg
Mr. Scratch .... Kelley
Justice Hathorne ...... Renan
Clerk .... Newman
Voice of
   Miser Stevens .. G. Williams
The Jury of the Dead:
Walter Butler .... Ludgin
Blackbeard Teach .. Del Monte
King Philip ...... Voketaitis
Simon Girty .... G. Williams
Others .... De Lon, Fried,
   Frierson, Huddleston,
   Macurdy, Merriman,
   Nahr, Theyard (d)

(Note: *An old man* and *An
old woman* added to program
April 17)

April 9

WUTHERING HEIGHTS (Floyd)
First performance by The New
York City Opera Company

Staged by .... Mann (d)
Scenic designer ..... Polakov
Costume
   designer ..... Campbell (d)
Choreographer .... Joffrey
Conductor .... Rudel

Lockwood .... De Lon
Heathcliff .... Reardon
Joseph .... G. Williams
Isabella Linton ...... Moody
Catherine Earnshaw ... Curtin
Nelly .... Neway
Mr. Earnshaw .... Voketaitis
Hindley Earnshaw ..... Crain
Edgar Linton .... Porretta

April 10

STREET SCENE

Same cast as April 2 except:

Abraham Kaplan .. G. Williams
Anna Maurrant ..... Carron,
     (s, Spence)

April 11

STREET SCENE

Same cast as April 2 except:

Abraham Kaplan .. G. Williams
Anna Maurrant ..... Carron,
     (s, Spence)

April 12 (m)

THE BALLAD OF BABY DOE

Same cast as April 3 except:

Baby Doe .... Moody

April 12

HE WHO GETS SLAPPED
(Ward)
First performance by The New
York City Opera Company

Staged by .... Pollock
Designer .... Nomikos
Conductor .... Buckley

Tilly .... Bruns (d)
Polly .... Dooley (d)
Briquet .... Ludgin
Count Mancini .... Kelley
Zinida .... Sarfaty,
     (s, B. Lewis)
Pantaloon .... Atkinson
Consuelo .... Venora
Bezano .... Porretta
Baron Regnard .... Renan
Maestro .... Able (d)

April 16

THE TRIUMPH OF SAINT JOAN
(Dello Joio)
First performance by The New
York City Opera Company

Staged by .... Quintero
Scenic designer .... Hays (d)
Costume designer .... Morley
Conductor .... Grossman

Saint Joan .... Venora
Pierre Cauchon ...... Harrell
Friar Julien .... Watson
English sentry ...... Porretta
Jailer .... Ludgin
Inquisitors .... De Lon,
   G. Williams, Kaldenberg,
   Theyard, Merriman,
   Newman, Macurdy,
     Voketaitis
Joan's Voices .... Moody,
   Sarfaty, S. Williams

Followed by:

THE MEDIUM (Menotti)

Staged by .... Pollock
Costume designer .... Morley
Conductor .. Torkanowsky (d)

Monica .... Clements (d)
Toby .... Perez (d)
Madame Flora .... Turner
Mrs. Gobineau ..... LeSawyer
Mr. Gobineau ...... Newman
Mrs. Nolan .... Sarfaty

April 17

THE SCARF

Same cast as April 5

Followed by:

THE DEVIL AND
DANIEL WEBSTER

Same cast as April 5 except:

Mary Stone .... Willauer

Added to this program:

An old man .... Marek
An old woman .... White

April 18

SUSANNAH (Floyd)

Conductor .... Rudel

Susannah .... Curtin
Sam Polk .... Cassilly
Olin Blitch .... Hecht
Little
  Bat McLean ... Kaldenberg
Elder McLean .... Ludgin
Elder Gleaton .... De Lon
Elder Hays ...... G. Williams
Elder Ott .... Voketaitis
Mrs. McLean .... Kobart
Mrs. Gleaton ..... LeSawyer
Mrs. Hays .... Moody
Mrs. Ott .... Sarfaty

April 19 (m)

STREET SCENE

Same cast as April 2 except:

Conductor .... Smart

Olga Olsen .... Mannion
Anna Maurrant ..... Spence
Sam Kaplan .... Porretta
Mrs. Hildebrand .... Rodgers
Rose Maurrant .... Clements

April 19

REGINA (Blitzstein)

Conductor .... Krachmalnick

Addie .... Brice
Cal .... Frierson
Alexandra
  Giddens .... Moser (d)
Birdie Hubbard ...... Carron
Oscar Hubbard .... Renan
Leo Hubbard .... Driscoll
Regina Giddens ..... B. Lewis
Marshall .... McChesney
Ben Hubbard .... Irving
Horace Giddens ...... Hecht
Manders .... Hoel

April 22

STREET SCENE

Same cast as April 2 except:

Sam Kaplan .... Porretta

April 23

MARIA GOLOVIN

Same cast as March 30

April 24

THE TRIUMPH OF SAINT JOAN

Same cast as April 16 except:

English sentry ... Kaldenberg

Followed by:

THE MEDIUM

Same cast as April 16 except:

Monica .... Scovotti (d)
Mrs. Nolan .... Kobart

April 25

WUTHERING HEIGHTS

Same cast as April 9 except:

Lockwood ...... Kaldenberg,
                   (s, De Lon)
Nelly .... Sarfaty

April 26 (m)

THE SCARF

Same cast as April 5 except:

Reuel .... Fried
Postman .... Ludgin

Followed by:

THE DEVIL AND
DANIEL WEBSTER

Same cast as April 5 except:

Jabez Stone .... Macurdy
Mary Stone .... Willauer

(Note: At this performance
John Macurdy was not listed
among *Others*.)

April 26

SIX CHARACTERS IN SEARCH OF
AN AUTHOR (Weisgall)
World premiere

Staged by .... Ball (d)
Designer .... Smith (d)
Conductor .... Levin (d)

Director .... McChesney
Tenore buffo .... G. Williams
Accompanist ..Timberlake (d)
Basso cantante ..... Macurdy
Stage manager .... Voketaitis
Coloratura .... Sills
Prompter .... Darian (d)
Mezzo .... Sarfaty
Wardrobe mistress .. Mannion
Chorus, the Seven Deadly Sins:
Pride .... LeSawyer
Envy .... Andrea
Sloth .... Rodgers
Lust .... Metzger

Anger .... Zakariesen
Avarice .... Del Monte
Gluttony .... Sliker
Another Tenor .... Balestrieri
Characters:
Father .... Ukena
Son .... Trehy (d)
Stepdaughter .... Bishop
Mother .... Neway
Madame Pace .... Kobart
Boy .... Sullivan (d)
Child .... Becker

April 28

HE WHO GETS SLAPPED

Same cast as April 12

April 29

STREET SCENE

Same cast as April 2 except:

Conductor .... Smart

Greta Fiorentino ..... Moody
Sam Kaplan .... Porretta
Steve Sankey ..... Frank (d)
Rose Maurrant .... Clements

April 30

SIX CHARACTERS IN SEARCH OF
AN AUTHOR

Same cast as April 26

May 1

REGINA

Same cast as April 19

May 2

THE BALLAD OF BABY DOE

Same cast as April 3 except:

Augusta .... Kobart
Mama McCourt ..... Sarfaty
William
  Jennings Bryan ... Macurdy

May 3 (m)

SUSANNAH

Same cast as April 18 except:

Conductor .... Saffir (d)

Susannah .... Venora
Elder Ott .... Del Monte

May 3

WUTHERING HEIGHTS

Same cast as April 9 except:

Mr. Earnshaw ..... Macurdy
                    (s, Voketaitis
Hindley Earnshaw .... Druar

Fall 1959 (SEPTEMBER 24 – NOVEMBER 1)

Female artists
Andrea, Jennie
Anglin, Florence
Bible, Frances
Bower, Beverly
Carron, Elisabeth
Clements, Joy
Curtin, Phyllis
Darian, Anita
De Van, Sylvia*
Di Gerlando, Maria
Dussault, Nancy
Galli, Gianna
Grist, Reri*
Jordan, Lynda
Kailer, Lucille*
Kobart, Ruth
Krebs, Beatrice
Landia, Basil
Leigh, Adele*
LeSawyer, Mary
Louise, Mary
Mari, Dolores
Meister, Barbara*
Metzger, Rita
Moody, Jacquelynne
Raskin, Judith*
Ribla, Gertrude
Sanders, Jean
Sandlin, Dorothy*
Sarfaty, Regina
Scott, Helena
Starling, Lynn
Steffan, Sophia*
Taussig, Lynn
Turner, Claramae
White, Dorothy
Williams, Sharon
Yeend, Frances

Male artists
Addy, Wesley*
Alexander, John
Arshansky, Michael
Atkins, Norman*
Beattie, Herbert
Bruns, Philip
Cassilly, Richard
Chapman, William
Christopher, Russell
Clemence, Richard
Constantine, Spelios*
Crain, Jon
Deis, Jean*
Del Monte, George
Fredericks, Walter
Frierson, Andrew
Gaynes, George
Handt, Herbert*
Harrold, Jack
Hayward, Thomas
Hecht, Joshua
Kaldenberg, Keith
Kelley, Norman
Kerns, Robert*
Labò, Flaviano*

* New artist

Leech, Lloyd Thomas
Lewis, Albert
Ludgin, Chester
McChesney, Ernest
Macurdy, John
Mann, Michael
Maero, Philip
Merriman, Dan
Metcalf, William
Pease, James
Porretta, Frank
Reardon, John
Riggs, Seth*
Rounseville, Robert
Sprinzena, Nathaniel
Stern, Maurice*
Storch, Arthur
Stuart, Roy*
Torigi, Richard
Ukena, Paul
Verreau, Richard
Voketaitis, Arnold
Williams, Grant
Zakariesen, William
(as William Saxon)

Conductors
Annovazzi, Napoleone*
Buckley, Emerson
Irving, Robert*
Jonson, William*
Krachmalnick, Samuel
Rudel, Julius
Saffir, Kurt
Stokowski, Leopold*

Chorus master
Smart, Gino

Associate Chorus master
Jonson, William

Dancers
Consoer, Dianne
de Lavallade, Carmen*
Lee, Sondra*
Mlakar, Veronika*
Reed, Sara*

Brown, Kelly*
Douglas, Scott*
Nebreda, Vicente
Tetley, Glen
Tone, Richard
Watts, Jonathan

Choreographer
Joffrey, Robert

Directors
Ball, William
Butler, John
Gauld, Carlton
Machiz, Herbert
Pollock, Michael
Raedler, Dorothy*
Sylbert, Paul*

Designers
Campbell, Patton
Condell, H. A.

* New artist

Fletcher, Robert
Jenkins, George
Morley, Ruth
Oenslager, Donald
Sylbert, Paul

* New artist

September 24

OEDIPUS REX (Stravinsky)

First performance by The New York City Opera Company (English narration translated by e.e. cummings)

Directed by ..... Sylbert (d)
Designer .... Sylbert
Conductor .... Stokowski (d)

Narrator .... Addy (d),
(s, Robards, Jr.)
Oedipus .... Cassilly
Creon .... Voketaitis
Tiresias .... Hecht
Jocasta .... Turner
Messenger .... Macurdy
Shepherd .... G. Williams

Followed by:

CARMINA BURANA (Orff)

First performance by the New York City Opera Company

Directed and
choreographed by ... Butler
Scenic designer ...... Sylbert
Costume designer .... Morley
Conductor .... Stokowski (d)

Soprano .... Grist (d)
Tenor .... Alexander
Baritone .... Reardon
Solo
dancers .. de Lavallade (d),
Mlakar (d), Douglas (d),
Tetley

(Note: Jason Robards, Jr., was not to appear with the New York City Opera Company.)

September 25

OEDIPUS REX

Same cast as September 24 except:

Narrator .... Addy,
(s, Robards, Jr.)

Followed by:

CARMINA BURANA

Same cast as September 24

September 26 (m)

MADAMA BUTTERFLY (Puccini)

Staged by .... Pollock
Conductor .... Buckley

Butterfly .... Carron
Suzuki .... Sarfaty
Kate Pinkerton .... LeSawyer
Pinkerton .... Crain
Sharpless .... Maero
Goro .... G. Williams
Yamadori .... Frierson
The Bonze .... Voketaitis
Imperial
    Commissioner .... Macurdy

September 26

DIE FLEDERMAUS
(J. Strauss)
(English book and lyrics by
Ruth and Thomas Martin)

Staged by .... Pollock
Conductor .... Rudel

Rosalinda .... Bower
Eisenstein .... McChesney
Adele .... Moody
Sally .... Andrea
Alfred .... Hayward
Prince Orlofsky ..... Harrold
Falke .... Ludgin
Frank .... Ukena
Frosch .... Bruns
Blind .... G. Williams
Solo dancers...Consoer; Watts

(Note: *Ivan* added to program
October 11 [m])

September 27 (m)

STREET SCENE (Weill)

Conductor .... Krachmalnick

Abraham Kaplan..G. Williams
Greta Fiorentino .... Mari
Carl Olsen .... Voketaitis
Emma Jones .... Kobart
Olga Olsen .... Krebs
Shirley Kaplan .... Anglin
Mrs. Davis .... Louise
Henry Davis .... Frierson
Willie Maurrant ...... Mann
Anna Maurrant ...... Carron
Sam Kaplan .... Porretta
Daniel Buchanan ..Kaldenberg
Frank Maurrant .... Chapman
George Jones .... Ludgin
Steve Sankey .... Storch
Lippo Fiorentino ... Harrold
Jennie Hildebrand .. Dussault
2nd Graduate ... De Van (d)
3rd Graduate .... Andrea
Mrs. Hildebrand .. Steffan (d)
Charlie Hildebrand..Clemence
Mary Hildebrand .... Taussig
Grace Davis ..... S. Williams
Rose Maurrant .... Scott
Harry Easter ...... Riggs (d)
Mae Jones .... Lee (d)
Dick McGann .... Tone
Vincent Jones .... Lewis
Dr. Wilson .... Macurdy
Officer Murphy .... Merriman

City Marshall .... Del Monte
Fred Cullen ..... Zakariesen
1st Nursemaid ..... LeSawyer
2nd Nursemaid .... Metzger

September 27

STREET SCENE

Same cast as September 27 (m)

October 1

THE MIKADO (Sullivan)
First performance by The New
York City Opera Company

Staged by .... Raedler (d)
Scenic designer .... Oenslager
Costume designer .. Campbell
Lighting .... Oenslager
Conductor .... Irving (d)

Mikado .... Gaynes
Nanki-Poo .... Porretta
Ko-Ko .... Kelley
Pooh-Bah .... Beattie
Pish-Tush .... Kerns (d)
Yum-Yum .... Meister (d)
Pitti-Sing .... Dussault
Peep-Bo .... Steffan
Katisha .... Turner

October 2

LA BOHÈME (Puccini)

Conductor .... Annovazzi (d)

Mimi .... Galli
Musetta .... Kailer (d)
Rodolfo .... Alexander
Marcello .... Torigi
Schaunard ..... Christopher
Colline .... Hecht
Benoit ...... Constantine (d)
Alcindoro .... Voketaitis
Parpignol .... G. Williams

October 3 (m)

THE MIKADO

Same cast as October 1 except:

Yum-Yum .... Clements
Katisha .... Kobart

October 3

MADAMA BUTTERFLY

Same cast as September 26 (m)
except:

Butterfly .... Mari
Pinkerton .... Deis (d)
The Bonze .... Ludgin

October 4 (m)

CARMEN (Bizet)

Conductor .... Buckley

Carmen .... Turner
Don José .... Cassilly
Escamillo .... Chapman
Micaëla .... Meister
Zuniga .... Macurdy

Frasquita .... LeSawyer
Mercédès .... Steffan
Remendado .... G. Williams
Dancairo .... Metcalf
Morales .... Ludgin

(Note: *Solo dancers* added to
program October 9)

October 4

OEDIPUS REX

Same cast as September 24
except:

Oedipus .... McChesney
Creon .... Macurdy
Jocasta .... Sarfaty
Messenger .... Frierson

Followed by:

CARMINA BURANA

Same cast as September 24
except:

Tenor .... Porretta

October 7

OEDIPUS REX

Same cast as September 24
except:

Jocasta .... Sarfaty

Followed by:

CARMINA BURANA

Same cast as September 24
except:

Tenor .... Porretta
Baritone .... Maero

October 8

COSÌ FAN TUTTE (Mozart)
First performance by The New
York City Opera Company
(English version by
Ruth and Thomas Martin)

Staged by .... Ball
Designer .... Fletcher
Conductor .... Rudel

Fiordiligi .... Curtin
Dorabella .... Bible
Guglielmo .... Reardon
Ferrando .... Alexander
Despina .... Raskin (d)
Don Alfonso .... Pease

October 9

CARMEN

Same cast as October 4 (m)
except:

Mercédès .... Sarfaty

Added to this program:

Solo dancers ...... Reed (d)
                    Nebreda

October 10 (m)

THE MERRY WIDOW (Lehár)
(Words by Adrian Ross)

Conductor .... Rudel

Sonia .... Bower
Prince Danilo ...... Reardon
Nish .... Stuart (d)
Baron Popoff .... Harrold
Natalie .... Scott
De Jolidon .... Porretta
Marquis
  de Cascada ..... Voketaitis
St. Brioche .... Ludgin
Admiral Khadja ... Merriman
Mme. Khadja .... White
General
  Novikovich .... G. Williams
Mme. Novikovich .... Jordan
Lo-Lo .... Starling
Solo dancers .. Consoer; Watts

October 10

LA TRAVIATA (Verdi)

Conductor .... Annovazzi

Violetta .... Di Gerlando
Alfredo .... Handt (d)
Germont .... Maero
Flora .... Steffan
Annina .... Kobart
Gaston .... Stern (d)
Douphol .... Voketaitis
D'Obigny .... Kerns
Dr. Grenvil .... Macurdy
Solo dancers .. Consoer; Watts

October 11 (m)

DIE FLEDERMAUS

Same cast as September 26
except:

Rosalinda .... Curtin
Eisenstein .... Leech,
                (s, McChesney)
Alfred .... Crain

Added to this program:

Ivan .... Arshansky

October 11

LA BOHÈME

Same cast as October 2 except:

Musetta .... Landia
Marcello .... Ludgin
Colline .... Macurdy
Parpignol .... Zakariesen

October 14

OEDIPUS REX

Same cast as September 24
except:

Conductor .... Rudel
Jocasta .... Sarfaty

Followed by:

CARMINA BURANA

Same cast as September 24
except:

Conductor .... Rudel
Tenor .... Porretta

October 15

STREET SCENE

Same cast as September 27 (m)
except:

Conductor .... Jonson (d)

Abraham Kaplan .. Sprinzena
Greta Fiorentino..Di Gerlando
Anna Maurrant .. Sandlin (d)
Frank Maurrant .. Atkins (d)
Rose Maurrant ..... Clements
Dick McGann .... Brown (d)

October 16

THE MIKADO

Same cast as October 1 except:
Ko-Ko .... G. Williams
Katisha .... Kobart

October 17 (m)

COSÌ FAN TUTTE

Same cast as October 8

October 17

CARMEN

Same cast as October 4 (m)
except:

Carmen .... Sanders
Don José .... Fredericks
Micaëla .... Clements
Mercédès .... Sarfaty
Remendado .... Stern
Dancairo .... Christopher

October 18 (m)

THE MIKADO

Same cast as October 1 except:
Ko-Ko .... G. Williams

October 18

TURANDOT (Puccini)

Staged by .... Pollock
Conductor .... Rudel

Turandot .... Yeend
Liù .... Carron
Timur .... Hecht
Calaf .... Labò (d)
Ping .... Ludgin
Pang .... G. Williams
Pong .... Sprinzena
Emperor .... Christopher
Mandarin .... Frierson

October 22

LA BOHÈME

Same cast as October 2 except:

Musetta .... Landia
Rodolfo .... Labò
Marcello .... Ludgin
Parpignol .... Zakariesen

October 23

LA TRAVIATA

Same cast as October 10
except:

Germont .... Ludgin
Gaston .... G. Williams
D'Obigny .... Christopher

October 24 (m)

DIE FLEDERMAUS

Same cast as September 26
except:

Conductor .... Krachmalnick

Adele .... Kailer
Sally .... Steffan
Alfred .... Porretta
Frank .... Beattie

October 24

THE MERRY WIDOW

Same cast as October 10 (m)
except:

Sonia .... Leigh (d)
Natalie .... Darian
De Jolidon .... Alexander
St. Brioche .... Stern,
                (s, Ludgin)

October 25 (m)

THE MIKADO

Same cast as October 1 except:

Mikado .... Ukena
Nanki-Poo .... Handt
Yum-Yum .... Clements
Pitti-Sing .... Darian
Katisha .... Kobart

October 25

THE MIKADO

Same cast as October 1 except:

Conductor .... Saffir

Mikado .... Ukena
Nanki-Poo .... Handt
Yum-Yum .... Clements
Pitti-Sing .... Darian
Katisha .... Kobart

October 27

TURANDOT

Same cast as October 18
except:

Turandot .... Ribla
Timur .... Macurdy
Pong .... Kaldenberg

October 28

COSÌ FAN TUTTE

Same cast as October 8 except:

Dorabella .... Sarfaty
Despina .... Meister

October 29

TURANDOT

Same cast as October 18 except:

Emperor .... Stern
Pong .... Kaldenberg,
(s, Sprinzena)

October 30

MADAMA BUTTERFLY

Same cast as September 26 (m) except:

Butterfly .... Di Gerlando
Suzuki .... Steffan

Pinkerton .... Handt
Sharpless .... Chapman

October 31 (m)

CARMEN

Same cast as October 4 (m) except:

Don José .... Rounseville
Escamillo .... Atkins
Micaëla .... Clements
Zuniga .... Voketaitis
Morales .... Kerns

October 31

LA BOHÈME

Same cast as October 2 except:

Mimi .... Carron
Musetta .... Moody
Rodolfo .... Verreau
Marcello .... Ludgin
Benoit .... Del Monte
Parpignol .... Zakariesen

November 1 (m)

THE MIKADO

Same cast as October 1 except:

Conductor .... Saffir
Nanki-Poo .... Handt
Yum-Yum .... Clements
Pitti-Sing .... Dussault,
(s, Darian)

November 1

OEDIPUS REX

Same cast as September 24 except:

Conductor .... Rudel
Oedipus .... McChesney
Jocasta .... Sarfaty

Followed by:

CARMINA BURANA

Same cast as September 24 except:

Conductor .... Rudel
Soprano .... Di Gerlando

Spring 1960 (FEBRUARY 11–21)

Female artists
Andrea, Jennie
Becker, Barbara
Bedelia, Bonnie*
Bible, Frances
Bishop, Adelaide
Carron, Elisabeth
Clements, Joy
Curtin, Phyllis
Di Gerlando, Maria
Dussault, Nancy
Ginn, Sophie*
Grimes, Tammy*
Johnston, Jane*
Jordan, Lynda
Kobart, Ruth
Kraft, Jean*
Krebs, Beatrice
LeSawyer, Mary
Mari, Dolores
Marlo, Maria
Metzger, Rita
Neway, Patricia
Raskin, Judith
Reynolds, Stephanie
Rodgers, Lou
Sachs, Evelyn*
Sandlin, Dorothy*
Sarfaty, Regina
Scott, Helena
Sills, Beverly
Starling, Lynn
Taussig, Lynn
Viracola, Fiddle
White, Dorothy
Zambrana, Margarita

* New artist

Male artists
Atkins, Norman
Atkinson, David
Beattie, Herbert
Bruns, Philip
Cassel, Walter
Cassilly, Richard
Clemence, Richard
Cowles, Chandler*
Culkin, Terry*
Del Monte, George
De Lon, Jack
Dennison, John
Dowlen, Glenn*
DuPree, William*
Engel, Lehman*
Fried, Howard
Frierson, Andrew
Griffis, William*
Harrold, Jack
Hecht, Joshua
Hoel, Edson
Kaldenberg, Keith
Kerns, Robert
Kirkham, Sam
Lago, Woody*
Linton, William
Ludgin, Chester
Macurdy, John
Merriman, Dan
Porretta, Frank
Riggs, Seth
Sallade, David
Shaver, Bob*
Sherman, Ricky*
Smith, Kenneth

* New artist

Stern, Maurice
Timberlake, Craig
Trehy, Robert
Treigle, Norman
Ukena, Paul
Voketaitis, Arnold
Wager, Michael*
Williams, Grant
Yule, Don*
Zakariesen, William
(as William Saxon)

Conductors
Buckley, Emerson
Engel, Lehman*
Jonson, William
Rudel, Julius
Saffir, Kurt
Torkanowsky, Werner

Chorus master
Jonson, William

Solo dancers
Lee, Sondra
Tone, Richard

Choreographer
Parsons, Billy*

Directors
Ball, William
Corsaro, Frank
Da Silva, Howard*
Field, Bill
Keating, Fred*
Machiz, Herbert

* New artist

Menotti, Gian Carlo
Rosing, Vladimir

Designers
Armistead, Horace
Hays, David
Morley, Ruth
Oenslager, Donald
Smith, Gary
Sylbert, Paul

* New artist

February 11

THE CRADLE WILL ROCK
(Blitzstein)
First performance by The New
York City Opera Company

Staged by ...... Da Silva (d)
Scenic designer .... Hays
Costume designer .... Morley
Choreographer .. Parsons (d)
Conductor .... Engel (d)
Moll .... Grimes (d)
Gent .... Riggs
Dick .... Voketaitis
Cop .... Merriman
Reverend Salvation .... Smith
Editor Daily .... Harrold
Yasha .... Wager (d)
Dauber .... Cowles (d)
President Prexy .... Macurdy
Professor Trixie .... Bruns
Professor Mami ...... Stern
Professor Scoot ...... Fried
Dr. Specialist .... Hecht
Harry Druggist ... Griffis (d)
Clerk .... Engel (d)
Mr. Mister ...... Timberlake
Mrs. Mister ...... Kobart
Junior Mister .... Kaldenberg
Sister Mister .... Dussault
Steve .... Porretta
Bugs .... Del Monte
Sadie Polock ...... Ginn (d)
Gus Polock .... Kerns
Larry Foreman .... Atkinson
Ella Hammer ... Johnston (d)
Reporters .. Riggs, Zakariesen

February 12

SUSANNAH (Floyd)

Conductor .... Rudel

Susannah .... Curtin
Sam Polk .... Cassilly
Olin Blitch .... Treigle
Little
  Bat McLean ... Kaldenberg
Elder McLean .... Ludgin
Elder Gleaton .... Stern
Elder Hays .... Fried
Elder Ott .... Voketaitis
Mrs. McLean .... Kobart
Mrs. Gleaton ...... LeSawyer
Mrs. Hays .... Clements
Mrs. Ott .... Sarfaty

February 13 (m)

STREET SCENE (Weill)

Conductor .... Rudel
Abraham Kaplan ...... Fried
Greta Fiorentino .... Mari

Carl Olsen .... Voketaitis
Emma Jones .... Kobart
Olga Olsen .... Krebs
Shirley Kaplan ...... Sarfaty
Henry Davis .... Frierson
Willie Maurrant .. Culkin (d)
Anna Maurrant ..... Carron
Sam Kaplan .... Porretta
Daniel Buchanan ..Kaldenberg
Frank Maurrant ...... Atkins
George Jones .... Timberlake
Steve Sankey .... Stern
Lippo Fiorentino .... De Lon
Jennie Hildebrand .. Viracola
2nd Graduate ...... Reynolds
3rd Graduate .... Andrea
Mrs. Hildebrand .... Rodgers
Charlie Hildebrand..Clemence
Mary
  Hildebrand ... Bedelia (d),
              (s, Taussig)
Rose Maurrant ..... Clements
Harry Easter .... Riggs
Mae Jones .... Lee
Dick McGann .... Tone
Vincent Jones .... Ludgin
Dr. Wilson .... Macurdy
Officer Murphy ... Merriman
City Marshall ..... Macurdy
Fred Cullen ..... Zakariesen
1st Nursemaid ..... LeSawyer
2nd Nursemaid .... Metzger

February 13

STREET SCENE

Same cast as February 13 (m)

February 14 (m)

THE BALLAD OF BABY DOE
(Moore)

Conductor ....,, Buckley

An old silver miner .... Stern
Saloon bartender .. Voketaitis
Horace Tabor .... Cassel
Sam .... Kaldenberg
Bushy .... Harrold
Barney .... Timberlake
Jacob .... Macurdy
Augusta .... Bible
Baby Doe .... Sills
Kate .... Reynolds
Mag .... Starling
Samantha .... Jordan
Hotel clerk ..... Kaldenberg
Albert .... Dennison
Sarah .... LeSawyer
Mary .... Andrea
Emily .... Rodgers
Effie .... White
McCourt family ... Reynolds,
   Starling, Kirkham, Zakariesen
Mama McCourt .... Krebs
Four Washington
  dandies ...... Hoel, Linton,
        Dowlen (d), Dennison
Father Chapelle .... Stern
Hotel footman .... Lago
Chester A. Arthur ... Harrold
Elizabeth and Silver
  Dollar ..... Taussig, Becker
Mayor of
  Leadville ..... Zakariesen

William
  Jennings Bryan ..... Hecht
Stage doorman .... Stern
Denver politician .. Voketaitis
Silver Dollar
  (grown up) .... Starling

February 14

THE CONSUL (Menotti)

Magic sequences created
  and staged by .. Keating (d)
Conductor ..... Torkanowsky

John Sorel .... Ludgin
Magda Sorel .... Neway
The Mother ...... Sachs (d)
Secret Police Agent .... Hecht
1st plain-
  clothesman .... Zakariesen
2nd plainclothesman..Kirkham
Secretary .... Sarfaty
Mr. Kofner .... Voketaitis
The Foreign Woman .. Marlo
Anna Gomez .... Di Gerlando
Vera Boronel .... Kobart
The Magician
  Magadoff .... Harrold
Assan .... Merriman
Voice on
  the record .. Mabel Mercer

February 17

THE CRADLE WILL ROCK

Same cast as February 11

February 18 (m)

THE BALLAD OF BABY DOE

Same cast as February 14
(m)

Student matinee

February 18

SIX CHARACTERS IN SEARCH OF
AN AUTHOR (Weisgall)

Conductor .... Rudel

Director .... Fried
Tenor buffo .... Williams
Accompanist .... Timberlake
Basso cantante ..... Macurdy
Stage manager .... Voketaitis
Coloratura .... Sills
Prompter .... Clements
Mezzo .... Sarfaty
Wardrobe mistress .... Krebs
Chorus, the Seven Deadly Sins:
Pride .... LeSawyer
Envy .... Andrea
Sloth .... Rodgers
Lust .... Metzger
Anger .... Zakariesen
Avarice .... Dennison
Gluttony .... Yule (d)
Another Tenor ...... Sallade
Characters:
Father .... Ukena
Son .... Trehy
Stepdaughter .... Bishop
Mother .... Kraft (d)

Madame Pace .... Kobart
Boy .... Sherman (d)
Child .... Becker

February 19

STREET SCENE

Same cast as February 13 (m)
except:

Conductor .... Jonson

Anna Maurrant .. Sandlin (d)
Sam Kaplan .... DuPree (d)
Frank Maurrant ..... Beattie
Lippo Fiorentino .... Harrold
Rose Maurrant .... Scott

February 20 (m)

THE CRADLE WILL ROCK

Same cast as February 11

February 20

THE BALLAD OF BABY DOE

Same cast as February 14 (m)
except:

Conductor .... Saffir

Horace Tabor .... Ludgin
Jacob .... Del Monte
Augusta .... Kobart
Baby Doe .... Raskin

*William
Jennings Bryan* ... Macurdy

February 21 (m)

THE CONSUL

Same cast as February 14
except:

Magda Sorel ...... Zambrana

February 21

THE CRADLE WILL ROCK

Same cast as February 11
except:

Steve .... Shaver (d),
                     (s, Porretta)

Fall 1960 (S E P T E M B E R 2 9 –
N O V E M B E R 6)

Female artists
Andrea, Jennie
Bible, Frances
Bower, Beverly
Brooks, Patricia*
Carron, Elisabeth
Clements, Joy
DeCurtis, Giulia*
Delmonte, Diana*
Di Gerlando, Maria
Dussault, Nancy
Jung, Doris*
Kobart, Ruth
Krebs, Beatrice
Kroschell, Joan*
Lane, Gloria
Leigh, Adele
LeSawyer, Mary
Loraine, Karol*
McKnight, Anne
Mari, Dolores
Meister, Barbara
Messina, Lillian*
Metzger, Rita
Porter, Joan*
Raskin, Judith
Reynolds, Stephanie
Sachs, Evelyn
Sanders, Jean
Sarfaty, Regina
Stark, Paula
Steffan, Sophia
Ward, Cecilia*
Witkowska, Nadja
Yarick, Doris*

Male artists
Alexander, John
Allen, Raymond*
Beattie, Herbert
Broadhurst, Charles*
Carolan, Michael*
Cassilly, Richard
Chapman, William
Crain, Jon
Davis, Donald*
Dennison, John

* New artist

Dowlen, Glenn
Fredricks, Richard*
Frierson, Andrew
Gaynes, George
Hecht, Joshua
Herbert, Ralph
Herrick, Charles*
Kelley, Norman
Ludgin, Chester
McChesney, Ernest
Macurdy, John
Merriman, Dan
Metcalf, William
Morell, Barry
Pease, James
Poleri, David
Porretta, Frank
Quilico, Louis
Reardon, John
Souzay, Gérard*
Stern, Maurice
Treigle, Norman
Vellucci, Luigi
Verreau, Richard
Voketaitis, Arnold
Warner, Charles
Williams, Robert*
Yule, Don

Conductors
Buckley, Emerson
Egk, Werner*
Irving, Robert
Jonson, William
Krachmalnick, Samuel
Popper, Felix*
Rudel, Julius
Saffir, Kurt
Stokowski, Leopold

Chorus master
Jonson, William

Solo dancers
Borys, Carolyn*
de Lavallade, Carmen
Martinet, Françoise

* New artist

Mlakar, Veronika
Ruiz, Brunhilda

Arpino, Gerald
Taylor, Paul*
Watts, Jonathan

Choreographers
Butler, John
Joffrey, Robert

Directors
Ball, William
Butler, John
Felmar, Albert*
Fletcher, Allen*
Gauld, Carlton
Herbert, Ralph*
Raedler, Dorothy
Sylbert, Paul
West, Christopher*

Designers
Campbell, Patton
Condell, H. A.
Fletcher, Robert
Morley, Ruth
Oenslager, Donald
Sylbert, Paul
Weishar, Joseph*

* New artist

September 29

ORFEO (Monteverdi)
First performance by The New
York City Opera Company

Staged by .... West (d)
Designer .... Oenslager
Choreographer ...... Joffrey
Lighting .... Oenslager
Conductor .... Stokowski

La Musica .... Yarick (d)
Orfeo .... Souzay (d)
Euridice .... Raskin
Messaggera .... Sarfaty
Speranza .... Clements
Caronte .... Frierson

Proserpina .... Sachs
Plutone .... Hecht
Apollo .... Porretta
Ninfa .... LeSawyer
Shepherds ... Stern, Dennison
Pluto's chamberlain .... Stern
Solo dancers ..... Borys (d),
    Martinet, Ruiz; Watts

Followed by:

THE PRISONER (Dallapiccola)
First performance by The New
York City Opera Company
(Il prigioniero; English
translation by Harold Heiberg)

Staged by .... West (d)
Designer .... Oenslager
Lighting .... Oenslager
Conductor .... Stokowski

Mother .... McKnight
Prisoner .... Treigle
Jailer .... Cassilly
Two priests .. Macurdy; Stern
Inquisitor .... Cassilly

September 30

THE MIKADO (Sullivan)

Conductor .... Irving

Mikado .... Pease
Nanki-Poo .... Porretta
Ko-Ko .... Kelley
Pooh-Bah .... Beattie
Pish-Tush .... Metcalf
Yum-Yum .... Meister
Pitti-Sing .... Dussault
Peep-Bo .... Steffan
Katisha .... Kobart

October 1 (m)

THE MIKADO

Same cast as September 30

October 1

LA BOHÈME (Puccini)

Conductor .... Buckley

Mimi .... Carron
Musetta .... Leigh
Rodolfo .... Morell,
    (s, Verreau)
Marcello .... Ludgin
Schaunard .... Fredricks (d)
Colline .... Treigle
Benoit .... Merriman
Alcindoro .... Voketaitis
Parpignol .... Stern
Guards .... Dowlen,
    (s, Dennison), Yule

October 4

OEDIPUS REX (Stravinsky)

Conductor .... Rudel

Narrator .... Davis (d)
Oedipus .... Cassilly
Creon .... Voketaitis
Tiresias .... Macurdy,
    (s, Hecht)
Jocasta .... Sarfaty

Messenger .... Macurdy
Shepherd .... Stern

Followed by:

CARMINA BURANA (Orff)

Conductor .... Rudel

Soprano .... Messina (d)
Tenor .... Porretta
Baritone .... Reardon
Solo dancers ... de Lavallade,
    Mlakar; Taylor (d), Watts

October 5

ORFEO

Same cast as September 29

Followed by:

THE PRISONER

Same cast as September 29

October 6

THE PIRATES OF PENZANCE
(Sullivan)

Staged by .... Raedler
Costume designer .. Campbell
Conductor .... Irving

Major-General
    Stanley .... Chapman
Pirate King .... Voketaitis
Samuel .... Metcalf
Frederic .... Porretta
Police sergeant .... Beattie
Mabel .... Meister
Edith .... Clements
Kate .... Steffan
Isabel .... Metzger
Ruth .... Kobart

October 7

COSÌ FAN TUTTE (Mozart)
(English version by
Ruth and Thomas Martin)

Conductor .... Rudel

Fiordiligi .... Bower
Dorabella .... Bible
Guglielmo .... Reardon
Ferrando .... Alexander
Despina .... Raskin
Don Alfonso .... Pease

October 8 (m)

CARMEN (Bizet)

Conductor .... Krachmalnick

Carmen .... Lane
Don José .... Cassilly
Escamillo .... Treigle
Micaëla .... Yarick
Zuniga .... Voketaitis
Frasquita .... LeSawyer
Mercédès .... Steffan
Remendado .... Stern
Dancairo .... Metcalf
Morales .... Fredricks
Solo dancers ...... Martinet;
    Arpino

October 8

MADAMA BUTTERFLY (Puccini)

Staged by .... Gauld
Conductor .... Buckley

Butterfly .... Carron
Suzuki .... Sarfaty
Kate Pinkerton ..... Metzger
Pinkerton .... Alexander
Sharpless .... Ludgin
Goro .... Carolan (d)
Yamadori .... Frierson
The Bonze .... Voketaitis
Imperial
    Commissioner ..... Metcalf

October 9 (m)

LA TRAVIATA (Verdi)

Staged by .... Felmar (d)
Conductor .... Krachmalnick

Violetta .... Bower
Alfredo .... Porretta
Germont .... Quilico
Flora .... LeSawyer
Annina .... Steffan
Gaston .... Stern
Douphol .... Voketaitis
D'Obigny .... Metcalf
Dr. Grenvil .... Macurdy
Solo dancers ...... Martinet;
    Arpino

October 9

ORFEO

Same cast as September 29
except:

Euridice ...... DeCurtis (d),
    (s, Raskin)
Prosperina .... Ward (d)

Followed by:

THE PRISONER

Same cast as September 29

October 12

DER ROSENKAVALIER
(R. Strauss)

Staged by .... Herbert (d)
Conductor .... Rudel

Marschallin .... McKnight
Baron Ochs .... Pease
Octavian .... Bible
Faninal .... Ludgin
Sophie .... Raskin
Marianne .... Brooks (d)
Valzacchi .... Vellucci
Annina .... Sarfaty
Police
    Commissioner ... Voketaitis
Singer .... Alexander
Innkeeper .... Carolan
Major-Domo of the
    Marschallin ..Broadhurst (d)
Major-Domo of
    Faninal .... Stern
Attorney .... Macurdy
1st Orphan .... Andrea
2nd Orphan .... Metzger

3rd Orphan .... Steffan
Animal vendor ..... Carolan
Milliner .... Clements
Leopold .... Merriman

October 13

OEDIPUS REX

Same cast as October 4 except:

Oedipus .... McChesney
Tiresias .... Hecht

Followed by:

CARMINA BURANA

Same cast as October 4 except:

Baritone .... Ludgin

October 14

LA BOHÈME

Same cast as October 1 except:

Rodolfo .... Alexander
Marcello .... Chapman
Colline .... Hecht

October 15 (m)

THE PIRATES OF PENZANCE

Same cast as October 6 except:

Ruth .... Krebs

October 15

CARMEN

Same cast as October 8 (m)
except:

Micaëla .... DeCurtis

October 16 (m)

THE MIKADO

Same cast as September 30
except:

Conductor .... Saffir

Mikado .... Gaynes
Yum-Yum .... Clements
Pitti-Sing ...... Kroschell (d)
Katisha .... Krebs

October 16

COSÌ FAN TUTTE

Same cast as October 7

October 19

THE INSPECTOR GENERAL
(Egk)
American premiere
Performed in English

Staged by .... Ball
Scenic designer .. Weishar (d)
Costume designer .. Campbell
Conductor .... Egk (d)

Town mayor .... Beattie
Judge .... Macurdy

Charity
  commissioner ...... Ludgin
Postmaster .... Stern
Bobtschinskij ...... Carolyn
Dobtschinskij .... Merriman
Mishka .... Broadhurst
Anna .... Kobart
Marja .... Brooks
Avdotya .... Porter
Chlestakow .... Crain
Ossip .... Voketaitis
Waiter .... Herrick
Young widow ..... LeSawyer
Locksmith's wife ..... Sarfaty

October 21

CARMEN

Same cast as October 8 (m)
except:

Don José .... Crain,
                  (s, Cassilly)
Escamillo .... Chapman
Micaëla .... Mari

October 22 (m)

MADAMA BUTTERFLY

Same cast as October 8 except:

Suzuki .... Steffan
Kate Pinkerton .... LeSawyer
Pinkerton .... Poleri
Sharpless .... Herbert

October 22

LA TRAVIATA

Same cast as October 9 (m)
except:

Alfredo .... Alexander
Germont .... Ludgin

October 23 (m)

LA BOHÈME

Same cast as October 1 except:

Mimi .... Mari
Musetta .... Loraine (d)
Rodolfo .... Poleri
Marcello .... Chapman
Colline .... Hecht

October 23

DER ROSENKAVALIER

Same cast as October 12
except:

Marianne .... LeSawyer
Singer .... Williams (d)

October 25

THE INSPECTOR GENERAL

Same cast as October 19

October 26

DER ROSENKAVALIER

Same cast as October 12
except:

Marschallin .... Jung (d)
Octavian .... Leigh

Marianne .... LeSawyer
Singer .... Williams

October 27

COSÌ FAN TUTTE

Same cast as October 7

October 28

LA TRAVIATA

Same cast as October 9 (m)
except:

Violetta .... Di Gerlando
Flora .... Delmonte

October 29 (m)

THE MIKADO

Same cast as September 30
except:

Conductor .... Jonson

Mikado .... Gaynes
Ko-Ko .... Allen (d)
Yum-Yum .... Clements
Pitti-Sing .... Kroschell

October 29

MADAMA BUTTERFLY

Same cast as October 8 except:

Conductor .... Rudel

Butterfly .... Mari
Suzuki .... Steffan
Kate Pinkerton .... LeSawyer
Pinkerton .... Cassilly
Goro .... Stern

October 30 (m)

THE PIRATES OF PENZANCE

Same cast as October 6 except:

Pirate King .... Pease
Mabel .... Messina

October 30

RIGOLETTO (Verdi)

Staged by .... A. Fletcher (d)
Choreographer .... Joffrey
Conductor .... Buckley

Duke .... Alexander
Rigoletto .... Quilico
Gilda .... Witkowska
Sparafucile .... Hecht
Maddalena .... Ward,
                  (s, Steffan)
Giovanna .... LeSawyer
Monterone .... Voketaitis
Marullo .... Metcalf
Borsa .... Stern
Ceprano .... Fredricks
Countess Ceprano ... Metzger
Page .... Reynolds

November 3

THE INSPECTOR GENERAL

Same cast as October 19
except:

Conductor ...... Popper (d)

Waiter .... Warner
Locksmith's wife ..... Steffan

November 4

THE PIRATES OF PENZANCE

Same cast as October 6 except:

Conductor .... Saffir

Frederic .... Broadhurst
Mabel .... Messina
Ruth .... Krebs

November 5 (m)

COSÌ FAN TUTTE

Same cast as October 7 except:

Fiordiligi .... Jung
Guglielmo .... Metcalf
Despina .... Meister
Don Alfonso .... Hecht

November 5

RIGOLETTO

Same cast as October 30
except:

Duke .... Verreau
Sparafucile .... Macurdy
Maddalena .... Steffan
Page .... Stark

November 6 (m)

CARMEN

Same cast as October 8 (m)
except:

Conductor .... Rudel

Carmen .... Sanders
Don José .... Crain
Escamillo .... Chapman
Micaëla .... Clements

November 6

LA BOHÈME

Same cast as October 1 except:

Mimi .... Di Gerlando
Musetta .... Loraine
Rodolfo .... Poleri
Colline .... Hecht
Alcindoro .... Stern

Spring 1961 no season

Fall 1961 (OCTOBER 5 – NOVEMBER 12)

Female artists
Addison, Adele
Alberts, Eunice
Barrera, Giulia*
Bible, Frances
Bower, Beverly
Broadhurst, Janet*
Brooks, Patricia
Brown, Debria
Carron, Elisabeth
Ceniceros, Lorna*
Clements, Joy
Coulter, Dorothy*
Di Gerlando, Maria
Ebert, Joyce*
Evans, Beverly*
Ferriero, Maria*
Guile, Helen
Jung, Doris
Kawecka, Antonina*
Kelm, Joan*
Kokolska, Martha*
Kova, Marija*
Kriese, Gladys*
LeSawyer, Mary
Lipton, Martha
Owen, Joan
Povia, Charlotte
Raskin, Judith
Roy, Nancy
Sarfaty, Regina
Saunders, Arlene*
Schwering, Elizabeth

Sena, Joan
Smith, Carol
Steffan, Sophia
Turner, Claramae
Williams, Nancy*
Yarick, Doris

Male artists
Addy, Wesley
Alexander, John
Beattie, Herbert
Buckley, Richard*
Cassilly, Richard
Chapman, William
Cossa, Dominic*
Davis, J. B.*
Diard, William*
Dowlen, Glenn
Fredricks, Richard
Frierson, Andrew
Gaynes, George
Gibin, Giovanni*
Gramm, Donald
Grogan, Norman
Kelley, Norman
LoMonaco, Jerome*
Ludgin, Chester
Macurdy, John
Malas, Spiro*
Metcalf, William
Milstein, Fredric*
Neate, Ken*
Poleri, David

Porretta, Frank
Reardon, John
Shirley, George*
Stern, Maurice
Theyard, Harry
Treigle, Norman
Ukena, Paul
Voketaitis, Arnold
Williams, Robert

Conductors
Bamberger, Carl
Buckley, Emerson
Patané, Franco*
Popper, Felix
Rudel, Julius
Saffir, Kurt
Susskind, Walter*

Chorus master
Jonson, William

Dancers
de Lavallade, Carmen
Hinkson, Mary
Jackson, Mary Ann*
Martinet, Françoise
Ruiz, Brunhilda
Zide, Rochelle

Arpino, Gerald
Douglas, Scott
Rhodes, Lawrence*
Sutherland, Paul

* New artist   * New artist   * New artist

Tetley, Glen
Wilson, John

Choreographers
Butler, John
Joffrey, Robert

Directors
Ball, William
Browning, Kirk
Butler, John
Felmar, Albert
Fletcher, Allen
Gauld, Carlton
Raedler, Dorothy
Sylbert, Paul
West, Christopher

Designers
Campbell, Patton
Condell, H. A.
Fletcher, Robert
Micunis, Gordon*
Morley, Ruth
Oenslager, Donald
Sylbert, Paul
Ter-Arutunian, Rouben

* New artist

October 5

IL TRITTICO (Puccini)
First performance by The New
York City Opera Company

Staged by .... West
Designer ...... Ter-Arutunian
Conductor .... Rudel
IL TABARRO

Michele .... Chapman
Luigi .... Alexander
Tinca .... Stern
Talpa .... Macurdy
Giorgetta ...... Saunders (d)
Frugola .... Turner
Song vendor .... Theyard
Two lovers .... Kokolska (d),
                      Stern

Followed by:

SUOR ANGELICA

Suor Angelica ... Di Gerlando
La Principessa .... Turner
La Badessa .... Kriese (d)
La Suora Zelatrice ... Alberts
La Maestra
  delle Novizie .... Steffan
Suor Genovieffa ... Kokolska
Le due novizie .... Owen, Roy
Suor Dolcina .... Povia
Le due converse ... LeSawyer,
                      Evans (d)
La Cercatrice .... Brown

Boys Choir from the
Church of the Holy Apostles
George Hall, Choirmaster

Followed by:

GIANNI SCHICCHI

Gianni Schicchi ...... Treigle
Lauretta .... Yarick
Zita .... Turner

Rinuccio .... Porretta
Gherardo .... Stern
Nella .... LeSawyer
Gherardino ..... Buckley (d)
Betto .... Milstein (d)
Simone .... Macurdy
Marco .... Fredricks
La Ciesca .... Kelm (d)
Spinellocchio ..... Malas (d)
Nicolao .... Beattie
Pinellino .... Grogan
Guccio .... Dowlen

October 6

COSÌ FAN TUTTE (Mozart)
(English version by
Ruth and Thomas Martin)

Conductor .... Rudel

Fiordiligi .... Bower
Dorabella .... Bible
Guglielmo .... Metcalf
Ferrando .... Alexander
Despina .... Raskin
Don Alfonso ...... Macurdy,
                  (s, Beattie)

October 7

LA BOHÈME (Puccini)

Conductor .... Patané (d)

Mimi .... Addison
Musetta .... Brooks
Rodolfo .... Shirley (d)
Marcello .... Ludgin
Schaunard .... Fredricks
Colline .... Treigle
Benoit .... Malas
Alcindoro .... Malas
Parpignol .... Theyard
Guards ..... Dowlen, Grogan

October 8 (m)

THE MIKADO (Sullivan)

Conductor .... Buckley

Mikado .... Gaynes
Nanki-Poo .... Porretta
Ko-Ko .... Kelley
Pooh-Bah .... Beattie
Pish-Tush .... Metcalf
Yum-Yum .... Clements
Pitti-Sing .... Broadhurst (d)
Peep-Bo .... Steffan
Katisha .... Kriese

October 8

AIDA (Verdi)

Staged by .... Fletcher
Choreographer .... Joffrey
Conductor .... Patané

King .... Macurdy
Amneris .... Bible
Aida .... Barrera (d)
Radames .... Gibin (d)
Ramfis .... Treigle
Amonasro .... Ludgin

Messenger .... Theyard,
                  (s, Stern)
Priestess .... Kokolska
Solo dancers .... Jackson (d),
                  Martinet, Zide (this
                  performance and
                  Oct. 19 only);
                  Arpino, Rhodes (d)

October 12

THE WINGS OF THE DOVE
(Moore)
World premiere

Staged by .... West
Scenic designer .... Oenslager
Costume designer .. Campbell
Choreographer .... Joffrey
Conductor .... Rudel

Kate Croy .... Sarfaty
Homer Croy .... Ukena
Aunt Maud Lowder .. Lipton
Miles Dunster ...... Reardon
Milly Theale .... Coulter (d)
Susan Stringham ... LeSawyer
Lord Mark .... Kelley
Steffans .... Fredricks
Lecturer .... Stern
Giuliano .... Milstein
Janus ballet:
Janus .... Arpino, Sutherland
Goddess of spring ... Martinet
Goddess of winter ...... Ruiz

October 13

CARMEN (Bizet)
Boys Choir from the
Church of the Holy Apostles
George Hall, Choirmaster

Conductor .... Bamberger

Carmen .... Turner
Don José .... Neate (d)
Escamillo .... Chapman
Micaëla .... Saunders
Zuniga .... Gaynes
Frasquita .... Kokolska
Mercédès .... Steffan
Remendado .... Stern
Dancairo .... Metcalf
Morales .... Fredricks
Solo dancers ...... Martinet;
                      Arpino

October 14 (m)

COSÌ FAN TUTTE

Same cast as October 6 except:

Ferrando .... Porretta
Despina .... Clements

October 14

MADAMA BUTTERFLY (Puccini)
New production

Staged by .... Felmar
Designer .... Micunis (d)
Conductor .... Patané

Butterfly .... Carron
Suzuki .... Steffan

Kate Pinkerton .... Kokolska
Pinkerton .... Alexander
Sharpless .... Ludgin
Goro .... Theyard
Yamadori .... Milstein
The Bonze .... Davis (d)
Imperial
    Commissioner ..... Metcalf

October 15 (m)

H.M.S. PINAFORE (Sullivan)
First performance by The New
York City Opera Company

Staged by .... Fletcher
Designer .... Campbell
Conductor .... Popper

Sir Joseph Porter ..... Kelley
Captain Corcoran .. Chapman
Ralph Rackstraw .... Porretta
Dick Deadeye .... Ukena
Bill Bobstay .... Fredricks
Bob Becket .... Macurdy
Josephine .... Yarick
Cousin Hebe .... Steffan
Little Buttercup ...... Kriese

October 15

IL TABARRO

Same cast as October 5

Followed by:

SUOR ANGELICA

Same cast as October 5

Followed by:

GIANNI SCHICCHI

Same cast as October 5 except:

Rinuccio ..... LoMonaco (d)

October 18

THE MARRIAGE OF FIGARO
(Mozart)
(English version by
Ruth and Thomas Martin)

Staged by .... Browning
Scenery by .. Condell, Micunis
Choreographer .... Joffrey
Conductor ..... Susskind (d)

Almaviva .... Chapman
Countess .... Jung
Figaro .... Treigle
Susanna .... Raskin
Cherubino .... Bible
Bartolo .... Malas
Marcellina .... Alberts
Basilio .... Stern
Curzio .... Theyard
Antonio .... Fredricks
Barbarina .... Clements

October 19

AIDA

Same cast as October 8 except:

King .... Frierson
Amneris .... Smith
Ramfis .... Macurdy

October 20

LA BOHÈME

Same cast as October 7 except:

Marcello .... Fredricks
Schaunard .... Metcalf
Parpignol .... Stern

October 21 (m)

H.M.S. PINAFORE

Same cast as October 15 (m)
except:

Sir Joseph Porter .... Gramm

October 21

CARMEN

Same cast as October 13
except:

Don José .... Gibin
Escamillo .... Treigle
Mercédès .... Kova (d)

October 22 (m)

MADAMA BUTTERFLY

Same cast as October 14
except:

The Bonze .... Davis,
                    (s, Macurdy)

October 22

THE WINGS OF THE DOVE

Same cast as October 12

October 24

IL TABARRO

Same cast as October 5 except:

Giorgetta .... Sena

Followed by:

SUOR ANGELICA

Same cast as October 5 except:

La Maestra delle
    Novizie ... N. Williams (d)

Followed by:

GIANNI SCHICCHI

Same cast as October 5

October 25

COSÌ FAN TUTTE

Same cast as October 6 except:

Fiordiligi .... Jung
Dorabella .... Sarfaty
Don Alfonso .... Beattie

October 26

THE CRUCIBLE (Ward)
World premiere

Staged by .... Fletcher
Scenic designer ...... Sylbert
Costume designer .... Morley
Conductor .... Buckley

Betty Parris .... Ebert (d)
Rev. Samuel Parris .... Kelley
Tituba .... Brown
Abigail Williams .... Brooks
Ann Putnam ...... LeSawyer
Thomas Putnam ...... Ukena
Rebecca Nurse ...... Alberts
Francis Nurse .... Malas
Giles Corey .... Stern
John Proctor .... Ludgin
Rev. John Hale ...... Treigle
Elizabeth Proctor ...... Bible
Mary Warren ...... Clements
Ezekiel Cheever ..... Theyard
Judge Danforth .... Neate
Sarah Good .... Kelm
Ruth Putnam .. Ceniceros (d)
Susanna Walcott ...... Guile
Mercy Lewis .... Roy
Martha Sheldon ... Schwering
Bridget .... Evans

October 27

OEDIPUS REX (Stravinsky)
(English narration
translated by e.e. cummings)

Conductor .... Rudel

Narrator .... Addy
Oedipus .... Cassilly
Creon .... Voketaitis
Tiresias .... Macurdy
Jocasta .... Turner
Messenger .... Frierson
Shepherd .... Stern

Followed by:

CARMINA BURANA (Orff)

Conductor .... Rudel

Soprano .... Bower,
                (s, Kokolska)
Tenor .... Porretta
Baritone .... Reardon
Solo dancers ... de Lavallade,
                    Hinkson;
                Douglas, Tetley

October 28 (m)

CARMEN

Same cast as October 13
except:

Carmen .... Smith
Don José .... Cassilly,
                    (s, Neate)

Escamillo .... Treigle
Micaëla .... Yarick
Zuniga .... Davis
Mercédès .... Kova
Morales .... Cossa (d)

October 28

AIDA

Same cast as October 8 except:
King .... Malas
Aida .... Ferriero (d)
Ramfis .... Macurdy

October 29 (m)

THE MIKADO

Same cast as October 8 (m)
except:
Nanki-Poo .... Diard (d)
Pooh-Bah .... Malas
Peep-Bo .... Kova

October 29

LA BOHÈME

Same cast as October 7 except:
Mimi .... Saunders
Musetta .... Bower
Rodolfo .... Poleri
Colline .... Macurdy

October 31

THE CRUCIBLE

Same cast as October 26

November 1

THE WINGS OF THE DOVE

Same cast as October 12
except:
Lord Mark .... Diard

November 2

IL TABARRO

Same cast as October 5 except:
Michele .... Ludgin
Luigi .... Alexander,
                 (s, Poleri)
Followed by:

SUOR ANGELICA

Same cast as October 5 except:
Suor Angelica .... Jung
La Maestra
  delle Novizie .. N. Williams

Followed by:

GIANNI SCHICCHI

Same cast as October 5 except:
Lauretta .... Clements

November 3

THE MARRIAGE OF FIGARO

Same cast as October 18
except:
Countess .... Bower

November 4 (m)

THE MIKADO

Same cast as October 8 (m)
except:
Ko-Ko .... Theyard
Pooh-Bah .... Malas
Pish-Tush .... Fredricks
Peep-Bo .... Kova

November 4

MADAMA BUTTERFLY

Same cast as October 14
except:
Conductor .... Saffir
Butterfly .... Di Gerlando
Suzuki .... Kova
Pinkerton .... R. Williams
Sharpless .... Cossa
Goro .... Stern
The Bonze .... Malas

November 5 (m)

H.M.S. PINAFORE

Same cast as October 15 (m)
except:
Sir Joseph Porter .... Gramm
Josephine .... Broadhurst
Cousin Hebe .... Kova
Little Buttercup ...... Alberts

November 5

AIDA

Same cast as October 8 except:
Conductor .... Rudel
King .... Malas
Amneris .... Smith
Aida .... Kawecka (d)

November 8

THE CRUCIBLE

Same cast as October 26

November 9

OEDIPUS REX

Same cast as October 27

Followed by:

CARMINA BURANA

Same cast as October 27
except:
Soprano .... Kokolska
Baritone .... Ludgin

November 10

MADAMA BUTTERFLY

Same cast as October 14
except:
Conductor .... Buckley
Butterfly .... Di Gerlando
Suzuki .... Kova
Kate Pinkerton .... Evans
Pinkerton .... R. Williams
Sharpless .... Fredricks
Goro .... Stern
The Bonze .... Malas
Imperial
  Commissioner ..... Dowlen

November 11 (m)

H.M.S. PINAFORE

Same cast as October 15 (m)
except:
Bob Becket .... Davis
Josephine .... Clements
Cousin Hebe .... Kova

November 11

LA BOHÈME

Same cast as October 7 except:
Conductor .... Buckley
Mimi .... Saunders
Musetta .... Bower
Rodolfo .... Poleri
Marcello .... Fredricks
Schaunard .... Metcalf
Colline .... Macurdy

November 12 (m)

CARMEN

Same cast as October 13
except:
Conductor .... Popper
Carmen .... Smith
Micaëla .... Yarick
Zuniga .... Davis
Mercédès .... Kova

November 12

THE MARRIAGE OF FIGARO

Same cast as October 18
except:
Almaviva .... Ludgin
Figaro .... Gramm
Marcellina .... Kriese

Spring 1962 (MARCH 22–APRIL 8)

Female artists
Bible, Frances
Brice, Carol
Brooks, Patricia
Burton, Miriam*
Ceniceros, Lorna
Duquan, Doreese
Ebert, Joyce
Evans, Beverly
Farr, Michelle*
Farr, Naomi*
Foster, Leesa*
Foster, Nancy*
Goldsmith, Pearle
Guile, Helen
Kova, Marija
Kraft, Jean
Kriese, Gladys
LeSawyer, Mary
Marlo, Maria
Martin, Janice*
Morris, Wendy*
Neway, Patricia
Owen, Hanna
Pollak, Haya*
Povia, Charlotte
Racz, Teresa*
Ricks, Edna
Sachs, Evelyn
Schwering, Jane*
Sills, Beverly
Venora, Lee
Walters, Gwendolyn*
Webb, Alyce
Webb, Barbara*
Wynder, Gloria
Yarick, Doris

Male artists
Atkins, Norman
Barnes, Irving*
Bender, David*
Berberian, Jon
Bottcher, Ron*
Brice, Eugene
Cassilly, Richard
Chapman, William
Cossa, Dominic
Crain, Jon
Crawford, Jerry
Davis, Harris
De Lon, Jack
Del Monte, George
Dowlen, Glenn
DuPree, William
Fels, James
Fiorito, John*
Fredricks, Richard
Gaynes, George
Gibson, Scott
Graham, Arthur*
Grogan, Norman
Hoel, Edson
Hutcherson, Laverne*
Kaldenberg, Keith
Kelley, Norman
King, Walza

* New artist

Krause, Richard*
LoMonaco, Jerome
Ludgin, Chester
Macurdy, John
McWhorter, George
Malas, Spiro
Miller, Kellis
Milstein, Fredric
Morgan, Donald
Pierson, Harold
Randolph, James*
Smith, John
Spearman, Rawn*
Stern, Maurice
Turner, Clyde
Ukena, Paul
Williams, Arthur
Winters, Lawrence
Wright, Ned
Zahariades, Bruce*

Conductors
Buckley, Emerson
Jonson, William
Popper, Felix
Rudel, Julius
Saffir, Kurt
Torkanowsky, Werner

Chorus master
Jonson, William

Choreographer
Maslow, Sophie

Directors
Ball, William
Englander, Roger
Fletcher, Allen
Rosing, Vladimir

Designers
Armistead, Horace
Colt, Alvin*
Morley, Ruth
Oenslager, Donald
Polakov, Lester
Saxe, Stephen O.*
Simmons, Stanley*
Sylbert, Paul
Venza, Jac*

* New artist

March 22

THE GOLEM (Ellstein)
World premiere

Staged by .... Fletcher
Scenic designer ..... Polakov
Costume designer .... Morley
Choreographer ...... Maslow
Conductor .... Rudel

Rabbi
 Levi Bar Bezallel .... Crain
Avrom .... Fiorito (d)
The Golem .... Ludgin
Yacov .... DuPree
Isaac .... Cossa
Rabbi's wife .... Kriese
Deborah .... Venora
Reb Bashevi .... Macurdy
Four citizens .... Miller,
 Berberian,
 Dowlen, Crawford
Tanchum .... Stern
Hunchback .... Milstein
The Blind One .. Graham (d)
Peg-Leg .... Del Monte
The Tall .... Davis
The Short .... McWhorter
The Red .... Miller
The sick old
 woman .... Goldsmith
Four women beggars .. Owen,
 Schwering, Guile, Evans
Tadeus .... Ukena
Tadeus's men ..... D. Bender
 (d), Bottcher (d)
The old man .... Krause (d)

March 23 (m)

THE BALLAD OF BABY DOE
(Moore)
Student matinee

Conductor .... Buckley

An old silver miner .... Stern
Saloon bartender ... Fredricks
Horace Tabor ..... Chapman
Sam .... Kaldenberg
Bushy .... De Lon
Barney .... Milstein
Jacob .... Malas
Augusta .... Kriese
Baby Doe .... Yarick
Kate .... Schwering
Mag .... Guile
Samantha .... Owen
Hotel clerk ...... Kaldenberg
Albert .... Milstein
Sarah .... LeSawyer
Mary .... N. Foster (d)
Emily .... Evans
Effie .... Povia
McCourt family .. Schwering,
 Guile, Berberian, Grogan
Mama McCourt ... Racz (d)
Four Washington
 dandies ...... Hoel, Miller,
 Dowlen, Smith
Father Chapelle .... Stern
Hotel footman ..... Milstein
Chester A. Arthur .... De Lon
Elizabeth and
 Silver Dollar ..M. Farr (d),
 Morris (d)
Mayor of Leadville .... Stern
William
 Jennings Bryan ... Macurdy

Stage doorman .... Stern
Denver politician .. Fredricks
Silver Dollar
   (grown up) .... Guile

March 23

THE BALLAD OF BABY DOE

Same cast as March 23 (m)
except:

Augusta .... Bible
Baby Doe .... Sills

March 25 (m)

THE CRUCIBLE (Ward)

Conductor .... Buckley

Betty Parris .... Ebert
Rev. Samuel Parris .... Kelley
Tituba .... Wynder
Abigail Williams ..... Brooks
Ann Putnam .... N. Farr (d)
Thomas Putnam ...... Ukena
Rebecca Nurse .... Racz
Francis Nurse .... Malas
Giles Corey .... Stern
John Proctor .... Ludgin
Rev. John Hale ..... Macurdy
Elizabeth Proctor ...... Bible
Mary Warren ..... N. Foster
Ezekiel Cheever ...... Krause
Judge Danforth ...... De Lon
Sarah Good ...... Pollak (d)
Ruth Putnam ..... Ceniceros
Susanna Walcott ...... Guile
Mercy Lewis .... Kova
Martha Sheldon .. Schwering
Bridget .... Evans

March 25

THE TURN OF THE SCREW
(Britten)
First performance by The New
York City Opera Company

Staged by .... Fletcher
Scenic designer ... Venza (d)
Costume designer ... Colt (d)
Lighting .... Watson
Conductor .... Rudel

Prologue .... Krause
Governess .... Neway
Miles .... Zahariades (d)
Flora .... M. Farr
Mrs. Grose ...... Martin (d)
Quint .... Cassilly
Miss Jessel .... Kraft

March 27

THE GOLEM

Same cast as March 22 except:

The Golem .... Atkins
Yacov .... LoMonaco

March 28

THE CONSUL (Menotti)

Staged by .... Englander
Conductor .... Torkanowsky

John Sorel .... Fredricks
Magda Sorel .... Neway

The Mother .... Sachs
Secret Police Agent .. Chapman
1st plainclothesman .. Dowlen,
                       (s, Smith)
2nd plainclothesman .. Grogan
Secretary .... Kova
Mr. Kofner .... Gaynes
The Foreign Woman .. Marlo
Anna Gomez ..... LeSawyer
Vera Boronel .... Racz
*The Magician
   Magadoff* .... Kelley
Assan .... Milstein
*Voice on the
   record* ...... Mabel Mercer

March 29

THE CRUCIBLE

Same cast as March 25 (m)

March 30

THE CONSUL

Same cast as March 28 except:

1st plainclothesman .... Smith

March 31

PORGY AND BESS (Gershwin)
First performance by The New
York City Opera Company

Staged by .... Ball
Scenic designer ..... Saxe (d)
*Costume
   designer* ..... Simmons (d)
Conductor .... Rudel

Clara .... Walters (d)
Mingo .... Pierson
Sportin' Life .. Spearman (d)
Jake .... Barnes (d)
Serena .... B. Webb (d)
Robbins .... Wright
Jim .... Gibson
Peter .... Crawford
Lily .... Ricks
Maria .... C. Brice
Porgy .... Winters
Crown .... Randolph (d)
Bess .... L. Foster (d)
1st Policeman .... Dowlen
2nd Policeman .... Fels
Undertaker .... King
Annie .... A. Webb
Frazer .... E. Brice
Strawberry Girl .... Duquan
Detective .... Fredricks
Nelson .... Williams
Crabman .... Turner
Coroner .... Krause
Police Sergeant ...... Grogan

April 1 (m)

PORGY AND BESS

Same cast as March 31 except:

Conductor .... Jonson

Maria .... Burton (d)
Porgy .... Hutcherson (d)

April 1

PORGY AND BESS

Same cast as March 31

April 3

THE TURN OF THE SCREW

Same cast as March 25

April 4

THE GOLEM

Same cast as March 22 except:

Yacov .... LoMonaco

April 5

THE CONSUL

Same cast as March 28 except:

Conductor .... Popper

The Mother .... Kriese
1st plainclothesman .... Smith
Mr. Kofner .... Macurdy

April 6

PORGY AND BESS

Same cast as March 31 except:

1st Policeman .... Morgan

April 7 (m)

PORGY AND BESS

Same cast as March 31 except:

Conductor .... Jonson

Maria .... Burton
Porgy .... Winters,
                   (s, Hutcherson)

April 7

PORGY AND BESS

Same cast as March 31 except:

Porgy .... Hutcherson,
                   (s, Winters)
1st Policeman .... Morgan

April 8 (m)

THE BALLAD OF BABY DOE

Same cast as March 23 (m)
except:

Conductor .... Saffir

Augusta .... Bible
Baby Doe .... Sills
Horace Tabor .... Ludgin

April 8

THE CONSUL

Same cast as March 28 except:

Conductor .... Popper

The Mother .... Kriese
1st plainclothesman .... Smith
Mr. Kofner .... Macurdy

Fall 1962 (OCTOBER 4 – NOVEMBER 11)

Female artists
Barrera, Giulia
Bible, Frances
Brawner, Alpha*
Brooks, Patricia
Burton, Miriam
Carron, Elisabeth
Clements, Joy
Curtin, Phyllis
Di Gerlando, Maria
Endich, Sara*
Evans, Beverly
Farr, Michelle
Ferriero, Maria
Foster, Nancy
Goldsmith, Pearle
Grillo, Joann*
Guile, Helen
Heller, Bonnie*
Hepburn, Betsy
Jennings, Mary*
Jordan, Lynda
Kelm, Joan
Kleinman, Marlena*
Kokolska, Martha
Kolacz, Rita
Kova, Marija
Kraft, Jean
Lane, Gloria
Mari, Dolores
Neway, Patricia
Newman, Linda*
Owen, Hanna
Povia, Charlotte
Raskin, Judith
Sachs, Evelyn
Sarfaty, Regina
Saunders, Arlene
Sena, Joan
Sills, Beverly
Simon, Joanna*
Stevenson, Madeline*
Turner, Claramae
Witkowska, Nadja
Yarick, Doris

Male artists
Alexander, John
Atkins, Norman
Beattie, Herbert
Brice, Eugene
Bottcher, Ron
Buckley, Richard
Cassilly, Richard
Chapman, William
Clatworthy, David*
Cossa, Dominic
Craig, John*
Crain, Jon
Deis, Jean
Diard, William
Dowlen, Glenn
Fels, James
Fiorito, John
Fredricks, Richard
Frierson, Andrew

* New artist

Gibin, Giovanni
Graham, Arthur
Gramm, Donald
Harrold, Jack
Kelley, Norman
Krause, Richard
LoMonaco, Jerome
Ludgin, Chester
Malas, Spiro
Metcalf, William
Meyer, Jeffrey*
Miller, Kellis
Paul, Thomas*
Porretta, Frank
Quilico, Louis
Reardon, John
Smith, David*
Smith, John
Stuart, Roy
Theyard, Harry
Treigle, Norman
Ukena, Paul
Uppman, Theodor
Verreau, Richard
Voketaitis, Arnold
Williams, Robert
Yule, Don
Zahariades, Bruce

Conductors
Bamberger, Carl
Buckley, Emerson
Jonson, William
Morel, Jean
Patané, Franco
Popper, Felix
Rudel, Julius
Ryan, Dean*
Saffir, Kurt
Susskind, Walter
Wilson, Charles*

Chorus Master
Jonson, William

Solo dancers
Apinée, Irene*
Martinet, Françoise

Gotshalks, Jury*

Choreographers
Andrew, Thomas*
Joffrey, Robert

Directors
Browning, Kirk
Englander, Roger
Felmar, Albert
Fletcher, Allen
Janney, Ben*
Pollock, Michael
Raedler, Dorothy
West, Christopher

* New artist

Designers
Armstrong, Will Steven*
Campbell, Patton
Colt, Alvin
Condell, H. A.
Micunis, Gordon
Morley, Ruth
Oenslager, Donald
Ter-Arutunian, Rouben
Van Witsen, Leo
Venza, Jac

* New artist

October 4

LOUISE (Charpentier)
First performance by The New
York City Opera Company

Staged by	West
Designer	Micunis
Conductor	Morel

Louise	Saunders
Julien	Alexander
Mother	Turner
Father	Treigle
Young rag picker	Guile
Wood gatherer	Goldsmith
Sleepwalker	Porretta
Milk woman	Burton
Rag picker	Paul (d)
Junk man	Malas
1st Policeman	J. Smith
2nd Policeman	Fels
Street urchin	Hepburn
Street sweeper	Povia
Painter	Bottcher
Sculptor	Metcalf
Song writer	Miller
Poet	Krause
1st Philosopher	Clatworthy (d)
2nd Philosopher	Dowlen
Blanche	Kokolska
Marguerite	Guile
Suzanne	Kleinman (d)
Gertrude	Grillo (d)
Irma	Yarick
Camille	Heller (d)
Apprentice	Hepburn
Elise	Evans
Madeleine	Owen
Old clothes man	Graham
Forewoman	Kraft
King of Fools	Porretta
Chair mender	Grillo (d)
Artichoke vendor	Yarick
Bird food vendor	Kokolska
Carrot vendor	Miller
Green peas vendor	Krause

October 5

THE TURN OF THE SCREW
(Britten)

Conductor	Rudel
Prologue	Krause
Governess	Neway

Miles .... Zahariades
Flora .... Farr
Mrs. Grose .... Kova
Quint .... Cassilly
Miss Jessel .... Kraft

October 6

RIGOLETTO (Verdi)

Conductor .... Patané
Duke .... Verreau
Rigoletto .... Quilico
Sparafucile .... Treigle
Monterone .... Paul
Ceprano ...... D. Smith (d)
Marullo .... Fredricks
Borsa .... Krause
Gilda .... Witkowska
Maddalena .... Kova
Giovanna .... Povia
Countess
  Ceprano ..... Newman (d)
Page .... Evans

October 7 (m)

AIDA (Verdi)

Choreographers ...... Joffrey
  (Priestess's dance and
  Moorish dance); Andrew
  (d) (Triumphal
  Scene ballet)
Conductor .... Patané
King .... Malas
Amneris .... Bible
Aida .... Barrera
Radames .... Gibin
Ramfis .... Treigle
Amonasro .... Quilico
Messenger .... Krause
Priestess .... Kokolska
Solo dancers .... Apinée (d),
  Martinet (this
  performance only);
  Gotshalks (d)

October 7

MADAMA BUTTERFLY (Puccini)

Conductor .... Buckley
Butterfly .... Carron
Suzuki .... Kova
Kate Pinkerton .... Kokolska
Pinkerton .... Porretta,
  (s, Crain)
Sharpless .... Metcalf
Goro .... Miller
Yamadori .... D. Smith
The Bonze .... Paul
Imperial
  Commissioner ..... Dowlen

October 11

THE PASSION OF JONATHAN
  WADE (Floyd)
World premiere

Staged by .... Fletcher
Scenic
  designer ... Armstrong (d)
Costume designer .... Morley
Conductor .... Rudel
Judge Townsend ..... Treigle
Celia Townsend ...... Curtin
Young girl .... Newman

Young boy ...... Meyer (d)
Confederate
  soldier .... Fredricks
Lieut. Patrick ...... Theyard
Jonathan Wade .... Uppman
Nicey .... Burton
J. Tertius Riddle ..... Ukena
Lucas Wardlaw ..... Porretta
Ely Pratt .... Kelley
Amy Pratt .... Brooks
Union soldier ...... Bottcher
Rector .... Paul
Union leaguer ...... Graham
Senator .... Brice
Judge Bell .... Frierson
1st Carpetbagger .... Graham
2nd Carpetbagger .. D. Smith
Driver .... Scott

October 12

THE MARRIAGE OF FIGARO
  (Mozart)
(English version by
Ruth and Thomas Martin)

Choreographer ...... Andrew
Conductor .... Susskind
Almaviva .... Chapman
Countess .... Endich (d),
  (s, Kolacz)
Figaro .... Gramm
Susanna .... Raskin
Cherubino .... Bible
Bartolo .... Beattie
Marcellina .... Kraft
Basilio .... Krause
Curzio .... Graham
Antonio .... D. Smith
Barbarina .... Newman

October 13 (m)

THE MIKADO (Sullivan)

Conductor .... Jonson
Mikado .... Ukena
Nanki-Poo .... Diard
Ko-Ko .... Kelley
Pooh-Bah .... Malas
Pish-Tush .... D. Smith
Yum-Yum .... Clements
Pitti-Sing .... Evans
Peep-Bo .... Kova
Katisha .... Sachs

October 13

MADAMA BUTTERFLY

Same cast as October 7 except:

Conductor .... Patané
Butterfly .... Ferriero
Suzuki .... Grillo
Pinkerton .... Craig (d)
Goro .... Graham

October 14 (m)

LA BOHÈME (Puccini)

Stage director .... Janney (d)
Conductor .... Patané
Mimi .... Di Gerlando
Musetta .... Jennings (d)

Rodolfo .... Verreau
Marcello .... Fredricks
Schaunard .... Metcalf
Colline .... Voketaitis
Benoit .... Malas
Alcindoro .... Malas,
  (s, D. Smith)
Parpignol .... Graham
Guards .... Dowlen; Yule

October 14

CARMEN (Bizet)
New production

Staged by .... Englander
Scenic designer ..... Micunis
  (Costumes courtesy of the
  Lyric Opera of Chicago—
  except Carmen's Act IV
  costume: Van Witsen)
Choreographer ..... Andrews
Lighting .... Watson

Boys' choir from St. Thomas
Church, Westfield, New Jersey

Conductor .... Rudel
Carmen .... Turner
Don José .... Gibin
Escamillo .... Treigle
Micaëla .... Yarick
Zuniga .... Paul
Frasquita .... Kokolska
Mercédès .... Kova
Remendado .... Krause
Dancairo .... D. Smith
Morales .... Bottcher

October 16

LOUISE

Same cast as October 4

October 18

IL TRITTICO (Puccini)

Conductor .... Rudel

IL TABARRO

Michele .... Chapman
Luigi .... Gibin
Tinca .... Krause
Talpa .... Malas
Giorgetta .... Saunders
Frugola .... Turner
Song vendor .... Graham
Two lovers .... Kokolska

Followed by:

SUOR ANGELICA

Suor Angelica .... Carron
La Principessa .... Turner
La Badessa .... Grillo
La Suora Zelatrice ..... Kraft
La Maestra
  delle Novizie .... Kova
Suor Genovieffa .... Kokolska
Le due novizie .. Guile, Owen
Suor Dolcina .... Povia
Le due converse ... Newman,
  Evans
La Cercatrice .... Jordan

Followed by:

GIANNI SCHICCHI

Gianni Schicchi	Treigle
Lauretta	Yarick
Zita	Turner
Rinuccio	Porretta
Gherardo	Krause
Nella	Brooks
Gherardino	Buckley
Betto	D. Smith
Simone	Beattie
Marco	Fredericks
La Ciesca	Kelm
Spinellocchio	Malas
Nicolao	Fiorito
Pinellino	Yule
Guccio	Dowlen

October 19

CARMEN

Same cast as October 14
except:

Conductor	Popper
Escamillo	Chapman
Micaëla	Sena

October 20 (m)

THE MARRIAGE OF FIGARO

Same cast as October 12
except:

Bartolo	Malas

October 20

LA BOHÈME

Same cast as October 14 (m)
except:

Mimi	Carron
Musetta	Mari
Alcindoro	D. Smith

October 21 (m)

THE MERRY WIDOW (Lehár)
(Words by Adrian Ross)

Choreographer	Andrew
Conductor	Bamberger
Sonia	Saunders
Prince Danilo	Reardon
Baron Popoff	Harrold
Natalie	Foster
De Jolidon	Crain
Marquis de Cascada	D. Smith
St Brioche	Krause
Admiral Khadja	Paul
Mme. Khadja	Jordan
General Novikovich	Malas
Mme. Novikovich	Povia
Nish	Stuart
Head waiter	J. Smith
Lo-Lo	Guile
Solo dancers	Apinée; Gotshalks

October 21

AIDA

Same cast as October 7 (m)
except:

King	Frierson
Amneris	Grillo
Amonasro	Atkins

October 24

THE WINGS OF THE DOVE
(Moore)

Choreographer	Andrew
Conductor	Buckley
Kate Croy	Sarfaty
Homer Croy	Ukena
Aunt Maud Lowder	Kraft
Miles Dunster	Reardon
Milly Theale	Sills
Susan Stringham	Foster
Lord Mark	Kelley
Steffens	Bottcher
Lecturer	Krause
Giuliano	D. Smith
Madrigalist	Graham
Janus	Gotshalks
Maiden	Apinée

October 25

LOUISE

Same cast as October 4

October 26

MADAMA BUTTERFLY

Same cast as October 7 except:

Conductor	Patané
Butterfly	Di Gerlando
Pinkerton	Craig
Sharpless	Fredricks
Goro	Graham

October 27 (m)

CARMEN

Same cast as October 14
except:

Micaëla	Stevenson (d)

October 27

THE MERRY WIDOW

Same cast as October 21 (m)

October 28 (m)

RIGOLETTO

Same cast as October 6 except:

Sparafucile	Paul
Monterone	Bottcher

October 28

THE PASSION OF
JONATHAN WADE

Same cast as October 11

October 31

LOUISE

Same cast as October 4 except:

Louise	Sills
Julien	Alexander, (s, Crain)
Sleepwalker	Diard
King of Fools	Diard

November 1

THE TURN OF THE SCREW

Same cast as October 5

November 2

RIGOLETTO

Same cast as October 6 except:

Monterone	Bottcher
Gilda	Yarick
Countess Ceprano	Guile
Page	Newman

November 3 (m)

LA BOHÈME

Same cast as October 14 (m)
except:

Mimi	Sena
Musetta	Mari
Rodolfo	Deis
Schaunard	Clatworthy
Colline	Paul
Alcindoro	D. Smith

November 3

AIDA

Same cast as October 7 (m)
except:

Aida	Brawner (d)
Ramfis	Paul

November 4 (m)

THE MIKADO

Same cast as October 13 (m)
except:

Conductor	Ryan (d), (s, Jonson)

November 4

IL TABARRO

Same cast as October 18
except:

Michele	Ludgin
Luigi	Williams

Followed by:

SUOR ANGELICA

Same cast as October 18

Followed by:

GIANNI SCHICCHI

Same cast as October 18
except:

Rinuccio	LoMonaco

November 7

THE TURN OF THE SCREW

Same cast as October 5 except:
Conductor .... Wilson (d)

November 8

THE WINGS OF THE DOVE

Same cast as October 24

November 9

LA BOHÈME

Same cast as October 14 (m) except:

Conductor	Buckley
Mimi	Sena
Musetta	Brooks
Rodolfo	Deis
Schaunard	Bottcher
Colline ...:..........	Paul
Alcindoro	D. Smith

November 10 (m)

MADAMA BUTTERFLY

Same cast as October 7 except:

Conductor	Saffir
Butterfly	Di Gerlando
Pinkerton	Williams
Sharpless	Ludgin
Goro	Graham

November 10

CARMEN

Same cast as October 14 except:

Carmen	Lane, (s, Turner)
Don José	Cassilly
Escamillo	Chapman
Micaëla	Stevenson
Mercédès	Kleinman
Morales	Cossa

November 11 (m)

THE MERRY WIDOW

Same cast as October 21 (m) except:

Conductor	Popper
Prince Danilo	Metcalf
Natalie	Newman
De Jolidon	Porretta
Mme. Khadja	Povia
Mme. Novikovich	Jordan

November 11

THE MARRIAGE OF FIGARO

Same cast as October 12 except:

Almaviva	Ludgin
Countess	Kolacz
Figaro	Treigle
Cherubino	Simon (d)
Bartolo	Malas
Curzio	Miller
Barbarina	Clements, (s, Newman)

Spring 1963 (APRIL 25–MAY 12)

Female artists
Andrews, Theodora*
Anglin, Florence
Bower, Beverly
Brooks, Patricia
Burgess, Mary*
Carron, Elisabeth
Chookasian, Lili*
Clements, Joy
De Forest, Anthea
Fletcher, Julia*
Frierson, Andrea*
Greenspon, Muriel*
Guile, Helen
Heller, Bonnie
Jordan, Lynda
Kleinman, Marlena
Kobart, Ruth
Kova, Marija
Kraft, Jean
Lowe, Lenore
Lynch, Anita
Maier, Barbara*
Mari, Dolores
Mason, Marilyn
Precht, Donna*
Sills, Beverly
Simon, Joanna
Small, Neva*
Troyanos, Tatiana*
Venora, Lee
Willauer, Marguerite
Witkowska, Nadja
Wyckoff, Lou Ann
Wyman, Florence*
Zara, Meredith*

Male artists
Armbruster, Richard*
Berberian, Ara*

Bottcher, Ron
Buckley, Robert*
Cash, Charles*
Cassel, Walter
Cassilly, Richard
Clatworthy, David
Clements, L. D.*
Crain, Jon
Davis, Harris
Dowlen, Glenn
DuPree, William
Fiorito, John
Fried, Howard
Frierson, Andrew
Graham, Arthur
Harrold, Jack
Henderson, Don
Hindsley, Charles*
Hoel, Edson
Krause, Richard
Lewis, Albert
McDonald, William*
Malas, Spiro
Metcalf, William
Miller, Julian*
Miller, Kellis
Olsen, Carl*
Reardon, John
Shinall, Vern*
Smith, David
Theyard, Harry
Trehy, Robert
Treigle, Norman
Voketaitis, Arnold
Wentworth, Richard
Yule, Don

Conductors
Buckley, Emerson
Henderson, Skitch*

Jonson, William
LaMarchina, Robert*
Popper, Felix
Rudel, Julius
Ryan, Dean
Saffir, Kurt

Chorus Master
Jonson, William

Solo dancers
de Lavallade, Carmen
Hinkson, Mary
Lee, Sondra

Davis, Ralph*
Douglas, Scott
Marks, Bruce*
Naneris, Nikiforos*
Tone, Richard

Choreographers
Butler, John
Levine, Rhoda*
Tone, Richard
Weidman, Charles

Directors
Ball, William
Butler, John
Floyd, Carlisle*
Janney, Ben
Machiz, Herbert
Menotti, Gian Carlo
Rosing, Vladimir
Sylbert, Paul

Designers
Armistead, Horace
Condell, H. A.
Dobujinsky, Mstislav

* New artist

* New artist

* New artist

Fletcher, Robert
Morley, Ruth
Oenslager, Donald
Sylbert, Paul

* New artist

April 25

A MIDSUMMER NIGHT'S DREAM
(Britten)
First performance by The New
York City Opera Company

Staged by	Ball
Designer	Fletcher

Boys' choir from
Epiphany Church, New York

Lighting	Fisher
Conductor	Rudel
Oberon	McDonald (d)
Tytania	Witkowska
Puck	J. Miller (d)
Theseus	Voketaitis
Hippolyta	Troyanos (d)
Lysander	Hindsley (d)
Demetrius	Clatworthy
Hermia	Kleinman
Helena	Willauer
Bottom	Malas
Quince	Fiorito
Flute	Krause
Snug	Wentworth
Snout	Fried
Starveling	Smith

April 26

STREET SCENE (Weill)

Choreographer	Tone
Conductor	Henderson (d)
Abraham Kaplan	Fried
Greta Fiorentino	Mari
Carl Olsen	Voketaitis
Emma Jones	Kobart
Olga Olsen	Greenspon (d)
Shirley Kaplan	Anglin
Henry Davis	Andrew Frierson
Willie Maurrant	Buckley (d)
Anna Maurrant	Carron
Sam Kaplan	DuPree
Daniel Buchanan	L. D. Clements (d)
Frank Maurrant	Trehy
George Jones	Wentworth
Steve Sankey	Armbruster (d)
Lippo Fiorentino	Harrold
Jennie Hildebrand	Maier (d)
2nd Graduate	De Forest
3rd Graduate	Mason
Mrs. Hildebrand	Lynch
Charlie Hildebrand	Cash (d)
Mary Hildebrand	Small (d)
Grace Davis	Andrea Frierson (d)
Rose Maurrant	J. Clements
Harry Easter	Reardon
Mae Jones	Lee
Dick McGann	Tone
Vincent Jones	Lewis
Dr. Wilson	Dowlen
Officer Murphy	Smith

City Marshall	Graham
Fred Cullen	Yule
1st nursemaid	Guile
2nd nursemaid	Wyckoff

April 27

THE LOVE FOR THREE ORANGES
(Prokofiev)
(English translation by
Victor Seroff)

Choreographer	Weidman
Conductor	Rudel
King	Voketaitis
Prince	Crain
Princess Clarissa	Greenspon
Leandro	Berberian (d)
Pantalone	Metcalf
Truffaldino	Harrold
Celio	Fiorito
Fata Morgana	Andrews (d)
Princess Linetta	Kleinman
Princess Nicoletta	Burgess (d)
Princess Ninetta	J. Clements
Cook	Wentworth
Farfarello	R. Davis (d)
Smeraldina	Kova
Prologue	Trehy

April 28 (m)

THE BALLAD OF BABY DOE
(Moore)

Staged by	Janney
Conductor	Buckley
An old silver miner	Graham
Saloon bartender	Yule
Horace Tabor	Cassel
Sam	Graham
Bushy	Krause
Barney	Smith
Jacob	Bottcher
Augusta	Kobart
Baby Doe	Sills
Kate	Lowe
Mag	Guile
Samantha	Jordan
Hotel clerk	Graham
Albert	Dowlen
Sarah	Heller
Mary	Precht (d)
Emily	Lynch
Effie	Kleinman
McCourt family	Lowe, Guile, Yule, H. Davis
Mama McCourt	Greenspon
Four Washington dandies	Hoel, K. Miller, Dowlen, Henderson
Father Chapelle	Graham
Hotel footman	Bottcher
Chester A. Arthur	Krause
Elizabeth and Silver Dollar	Small, Fletcher (d)
Mayor of Leadville	H. Davis
William Jennings Bryan	Fiorito
Stage doorman	K. Miller
Denver politician	Yule
Silver Dollar (grown up)	Guile

April 28

A MIDSUMMER NIGHT'S DREAM
Same cast as April 25

May 1

OEDIPUS REX (Stravinsky)
(English narration translated
by e.e. cummings)

Conductor	Rudel
Narrator	Trehy
Oedipus	Cassilly
Creon	Bottcher
Tiresias	Berberian
Jocasta	Troyanos
Messenger	Andrew Frierson
Shepherd	Graham

Followed by:

CARMINA BURANA (Orff)

Conductor	Rudel
Soprano	Witkowska
Tenor	McDonald
Baritone	Reardon
Solo dancers	de Lavallade, Hinkson; Douglas, Marks (d)

May 3

SUSANNAH (Floyd)

Staged by	Floyd (d)
Choreographer	Levine (d)
Conductor	Rudel
Susannah	Venora
Sam Polk	Cassilly
Olin Blitch	Treigle
Little Bat McLean	Theyard
Elder McLean	Wentworth
Elder Gleaton	Krause
Elder Hays	Graham
Elder Ott	Shinall (d)
Mrs. McLean	Greenspon
Mrs. Gleaton	Kleinman
Mrs. Hays	Precht
Mrs. Ott	Kraft

May 4 (m)

THE BALLAD OF BABY DOE
Same cast as April 28 (m)
except:

An old silver miner	K. Miller
Horace Tabor	Trehy
Baby Doe	Brooks
William Jennings Bryan	Wentworth

May 4

STREET SCENE
Same cast as April 26

May 5 (m)

THE LOVE FOR THREE ORANGES
Same cast as April 27 except:

Fata Morgana	Wyman (d)
Smeraldina	Troyanos

May 5

AMELIA GOES TO THE BALL
(Menotti)
(English translation by
George Meade)

Conductor .... Popper

Amelia .... Bower
Husband .... Reardon
Lover .... Olsen (d)
Police
    Commissioner ... Voketaitis
Friend .... Kleinman
1st Maid .... Wykoff
2nd Maid .... Guile

Followed by:

THE MEDIUM (Menotti)

Staged by .... Menotti
Conductor .. LaMarchina (d)

Monica .... Venora
Toby .... Naneris (d)
Madame
    Flora ..... Chookasian (d)
Mrs. Gobineau .... Heller
Mr. Gobineau .... Smith
Mrs. Nolan .... Kleinman

May 7

OEDIPUS REX

Same cast as May 1

Followed by:

CARMINA BURANA

Same cast as May 1 except:

Soprano .... Zara (d)
Baritone .... Metcalf

May 8

A MIDSUMMER NIGHT'S DREAM

Same cast as April 25 except:

Hippolyta .... Simon

May 10

STREET SCENE

Same cast as April 26 except:

Conductor .... Jonson

Harry Easter .... Metcalf

May 11 (m)

THE LOVE FOR THREE ORANGES

Same cast as April 27 except:

Conductor .... Ryan

Princess Clarissa ...... Kraft
Leandro .... Shinall
Smeraldina .... Troyanos

May 11

SUSANNAH

Same cast as May 3 except:

Elder Ott .... Malas

May 12 (m)

AMELIA GOES TO THE BALL

Same cast as May 5

Followed by:

THE MEDIUM

Same cast as May 5 except:

Monica .... J. Clements
Mr. Gobineau ...... Dowlen

May 12

THE BALLAD OF BABY DOE

Same cast as April 28 (m)
except:

Conductor .... Saffir

An old silver miner..K. Miller
William
    Jennings Bryan ..Wentworth

Fall 1963 (OCTOBER 3 – NOVEMBER 10)

Female artists
Bendyk, Betty*
Bergey, Carol*
Bonelli, Olivia
Bower, Beverly
Brice, Carol
Brookes, Jacqueline*
Brooks, Patricia
Burgess, Mary
Card, June*
Carron, Elisabeth
Di Gerlando, Maria
Draper, Anne*
Endich, Sara
Evans, Beverly
Faull, Ellen
Ferriero, Maria
Ghostley, Alice*
Greenspon, Muriel
Grey, Gillian*
Guile, Helen
Hamilton, Patricia*
Heller, Bonnie
Hepburn, Betsy
Herbert, Lila
Jordan, Lynda
King, Juanita*
Kleinman, Marlena
Kokolska, Martha
Kova, Marija

* New artist

Kraft, Jean
Lynch, Anita
Miko, Joyce
Pilla, Candida
Povia, Charlotte
Precht, Donna
Raskin, Judith
Sachs, Evelyn
Sena, Joan
Saunders, Arlene
Sulka, Elaine*
Summers, Joan*
Sills, Beverly
Troyanos, Tatiana
Turner, Claramae
Willauer, Marguerite
Witkowska, Nadja
Wolff, Beverly

Male artists
Addison, Bernard*
Alexander, John
Atkins, Charles*
Berberian, Ara
Bottcher, Ron
Byrd, David*
Clatworthy, David
Converse, Frank*
Craig, John
Crawford, Jerry

* New artist

Davis, Harris
Devlin, John*
Diard, William
Dowlen, Glenn
Fels, James
Fiorito, John
Frierson, Andrew
Fredricks, Richard
Gorin, Igor*
Graham, Arthur
Gramm, Donald
Harrold, Jack
Henderson, Don
Hindsley, Charles
Kelley, Norman
Krause, Richard
Lampi, Mauro†
Ledbetter, William*
Lide, Miller*
LoMonaco, Jerome
Long, Avon*
Ludgin, Chester
McCollum, John*
McDonald, William

* New artist
† Mauro Lampi was a stage
name used by Maurice Stern.
Although shown as Lampi in the
programs, we are showing him as
Stern in these Annals for the sake
of consistency.

Malas, Spiro
Martin, Nicholas*
Mathews, Richard*
Metcalf, William
Miller, Kellis
Paul, Thomas
Porretta, Frank
Reardon, John
Scammell, Terence*
Shawn, Dick*
Smith, David
Smith, Geddeth*
Smith, John
Stern, Maurice
Treigle, Norman
Ukena, Paul
Voketaitis, Arnold
Watson, Douglas*
Webb, R. G.*
Worth, Coley
Yule, Don

Conductors
Bamberger, Carl
Barzin, Leon*
Buckley, Emerson
Jonson, William
Patané, Franco
Popper, Felix
Rudel, Julius
Ryan, Dean
Saffir, Kurt
Susskind, Walter
Wilson, Charles

Chorus master
Jonson, William

Solo dancers
Galan, Rosario*
Hardy, Michele*
Zide, Rochelle

Bernard, Bob*
Draper, Paul*
Ellis, Bob*
Russel, Rec*
Sequoio, Ron*
Tormey, John*

Choreographers
Andrew, Thomas
Draper, Paul*

Directors
Ball, William
Browning, Kirk
Fletcher, Allen
Hebert, Bliss*
Janney, Ben
Pollock, Michael
Raedler, Dorothy
Turoff, Robert*
West, Christopher

Designers
Armstrong, Will Steven
Campbell, Patton
Condell, H. A.
Fletcher, Robert
Heymann, Henry*
Micunis, Gordon
Morley, Ruth
Oenslager, Donald
Pitkin, William*

* New artist

October 3

THE NIGHTINGALE (Stravinsky)
First performance by The New
York City Opera Company
(sung in Russian)

Staged by .... Hebert (d)
Designer .... Micunis
Choreographer ...... Andrew
Conductor .... Susskind

Fisherman .... Graham
Nightingale .... Brooks
Cook .... Carron
Chamberlain .... Paul
The Bonze .... Fiorito
Emperor .... Gramm
Mechanical nightingale .. Zide
Three Japanese
 envoys ... Krause, Bottcher,
                        Miller
Death .... Kraft

Followed by:

JEANNE D'ARC AU BÛCHER
(Honegger)
First performance by The New
York City Opera Company
(English version by
Dennis Arundell)

Staged by .... Fletcher
Designer .... Armstrong
Boys' choir from
Epiphany Church, New York
Conductor ...... Barzin (d)

Singers:
The Virgin Mary ..... Carron
A Voice,
 St. Margaret ..... King (d)
St. Catharine ...... Troyanos
Cauchon (Porcus) ...... Stern,
                  (as Lampi)
A Priest, 1st Herald,
 Clerk .... Krause
2nd Herald, a Priest,
 a Voice .... Bottcher
A Priest .... Fiorito
Actors:
Joan .... Brookes (d)
Brother Dominic..Watson (d)
The King England,
 Grinder Trusty .. Converse
                        (d)
Mother
 Winebarrels .... Greenspon
The Ass, the Duke of
 Burgundy .... Byrd (d)
The Usher, the King
 of France ...... Lide (d)
A priest, a sheep, Death,
 2nd Peasant ... Devlin (d)
A sheep, Guillaume de
 Flavy, 1st Peasant..Mathews
                        (d)
A sheep, the Duke of
 Bedford, the
 Dauphin ...... Martin (d)
A sheep, Regnault de
 Chartres, Perrot .. G. Smith
                        (d)
A sheep, Jean de
 Luxembourg .... Scammell
                        (d)

1st Woman, Queen
 Lasciviousness .. A. Draper
                        (d)
2nd Woman, Queen
 Bombast .... Hamilton (d)
3rd Woman, Queen
 Stupidity ..... Bendyk (d)
4th Woman, Queen
 Avarice .... Sulka (d)

October 4

LA BOHÈME (Puccini)

Staged by .... Hebert
Boys' choir from
Epiphany Church, New York
Conductor .... Patané

Mimi .... Bonelli
Musetta .... Sena
Rodolfo .... Craig
Marcello .... Fredricks
Schaunard .... Metcalf
Colline .... Paul
Benoit .... Malas
Alcindoro .... D. Smith
Parpignol .... Miller
Guards .... Dowlen, Yule

October 5

RIGOLETTO (Verdi)

Choreographer ...... Andrew
Conductor .... Patané

Duke .... LoMonaco
Rigoletto .... Gorin (d)
Sparafucile .... Berberian
Monterone .... .Fiorito,
                  (s, Bottcher)
Ceprano .... D. Smith
Marullo .... Clatworthy
Borsa .... Krause
Gilda .... Witkowska
Maddalena .... Kleinman
Giovanna .... Lynch
Countess Ceprano ..... Guile
Page .... Evans

October 6 (m)

MADAMA BUTTERFLY (Puccini)

Staged by .... Raedler
Conductor .... Patané

Butterfly .... Di Gerlando
Suzuki .... Kova
Kate Pinkerton .... Kokolska
Pinkerton .... Porretta
Sharpless .... Fredricks
Goro .... Krause
Yamadori .... D. Smith
The Bonze .... Fiorito
Imperial
 Commissioner ..... Dowlen

October 6

LOUISE (Charpentier)

Conductor .... Rudel

Louise .... Saunders
Julien .... Alexander

Mother .... Turner
Father .... Treigle
Young rag picker ...... Guile
Wood gatherer .... Jordan
Sleepwalker .... Diard
Milk woman ..... Greenspon
Rag picker .... Paul
Junk man .... Malas
1st Policeman ...... J. Smith
2nd Policeman .... Fels
Street urchin .... Hepburn
Street sweeper .... Povia
Painter .... Bottcher
Sculptor .... Crawford
Song writer .... Miller
Poet .... Krause
1st Philosopher .... Yule
2nd Philosopher .... Dowlen
Blanche .... Kokolska
Marguerite .... Guile
Suzanne .... Kleinman
Gertrude .... Troyanos
Irma .... Bonelli
Camille .... Heller
Apprentice .... Hepburn
Elise .... Evans
Madeleine .... Herbert
Old clothes man .... Graham
Forewoman .... Kraft
King of Fools .... Diard
Chair mender ..... Troyanos
Artichoke vendor ... Bonelli
Bird food vendor .. Kokolska
Carrot vendor ...... Miller
Green peas vendor ... Krause

October 10

GENTLEMEN, BE SEATED!
(Moross)
World premiere

Stage director .... Turoff (d)
Scenic designer ... Pitkin (d)
Costume
  designer .... Heymann (d)
Choreographer ... Draper (d)
Conductor .... Buckley

Interlocutor ...... Shawn (d)
Mr. Tambo .... Long (d)
Mr. Bones ...... Atkins (d)
The comedienne..Ghostley (d)
The contralto .... Brice
Johnny Reb ...... McDonald
Billy Yank .... Fredricks
Southern girl ...... Card (d)
Northern girl ...... Burgess
Mr. Banjo ...... Addison (d)
The character actor .. Krause
Mr. Taps ..... P. Draper (d)
Ermyntrude .... Povia
Farmer McLean .... D. Smith
Miss
  Florida Cotton .. Hardy (d)
Two soldiers .... Miller,
  Henderson
Drill team ...... Bernard (d),
  Tormey (d), Russel (d),
  Ellis (d)
Horse .... Bernard, Russel
Two other
  soldiers ...... Miller, Yule
Two girls ...... Miko, Evans
Four nurses ..... Miko, Pilla,
  Evans, Povia

October 11

THE MARRIAGE OF FIGARO
(Mozart)
(English version by
Ruth and Thomas Martin)

Conductor .... Susskind

Almaviva .... Fredricks
Countess .... Endich
Figaro .... Gramm
Susanna .... Raskin
Cherubino .... Wolff
Bartolo .... Malas
Marcellina .... Kraft
Basilio ... Stern, (scheduled
  as Lampi, sang as Stern)
Curzio .... Miller
Antonio .... D. Smith
Barbarina ...... Bergey (d)

October 12 (m)

THE MIKADO (Sullivan)

Conductor .... Jonson

Mikado .... Ukena
Nanki-Poo .... Diard
Ko-Ko .... Kelley
Pooh-Bah .... Malas
Pish-Tush .... D. Smith
Yum-Yum .... Bergey
Pitti-Sing .... Burgess
Peep-Bo .... Kleinman
Katisha .... Greenspon

October 12

MADAMA BUTTERFLY

Same cast as October 6 (m)
except:
Suzuki .... Kleinman
Pinkerton .... Craig
Sharpless .... Bottcher

October 13 (m)

THE MERRY WIDOW (Lehár)
(Words by Adrian Ross)

Conductor ...... Bamberger

Sonia .... Saunders
Prince Danilo ..... Reardon
Baron Popoff ...... Harrold
Natalie .... Grey (d)
De Jolidon .... Porretta
Marquis
  de Cascada .... D. Smith
St. Brioche .... Krause
Admiral Khadja .... Paul
Mme. Khadja ...... Povia
General
  Novikovich .... Webb (d)
Mme. Novikovich .... Jordon
Nish .... Worth
Head waiter .... Davis
Clo-Clo .... Guile
Solo dancers .... Zide;
  Sequoio (d)

October 13

THE NIGHTINGALE

Same cast as October 3
Followed by:
JEANNE D'ARC AL BÛCHER
Same cast as October 3

October 17

THE NIGHTINGALE

Same cast as October 3 except:
Nightingale ...... Witkowska
Followed by:
JEANNE D'ARC AU BÛCHER
Same cast as October 3 except:
St. Catherine .... Kraft

October 18

GENTLEMEN, BE SEATED!
Same cast as October 10

October 19 (m)

RIGOLETTO

Same cast as October 5 except:
Sparafucile .... Paul
Gilda .... Brooks

October 19

THE MERRY WIDOW

Same cast as October 13 (m)

October 20 (m)

THE MARRIAGE OF FIGARO

Same cast as October 11
except:
Conductor .... Bamberger
Almaviva .... Bottcher
Bartolo .... Paul

October 20

LA TRAVIATA (Verdi)
New production

Staged by .... Browning
Designer .... Micunis
Choreographer ..... Andrew
Conductor .... Patané

Violetta .... Sills
Alfredo .... Craig
Germont .... Gorin
Flora .... Kleinman
Annina .... Kraft
Gaston .... Krause
Douphol .... D. Smith
D'Obigny .... Metcalf
Dr. Grenvil .... Fiorito
Giuseppe .... J. Smith
Solo dancer ...... Galan (d)

October 24

DON GIOVANNI (Mozart)
(English version by
Ruth and Thomas Martin)
New production

Staged by .... Ball
Designer .... Fletcher
Lighting .... Fisher
Choreographer ...... Andrew
Conductor .... Rudel

Don Giovanni .... Treigle
Leporello .... Gramm

Donna Elvira ...... Saunders
Commendatore .... Berberian
Donna Anna .... Bower
Don Ottavio .. McCollum (d)
Masetto .... Metcalf
Zerlina .... Raskin

October 25

LA TRAVIATA

Same cast as October 20

October 26 (m)

MADAMA BUTTERFLY

Same cast as October 6 (m)
except:

Conductor .... Saffir

Butterfly .... Ferriero
Kate Pinkerton .... Guile
Sharpless .... Metcalf
Goro .... Miller
*Imperial
  Commissioner* ... Crawford

October 26

LA BOHÈME

Same cast as October 4 except:

Mimi .... Di Gerlando
Musetta .... Sena,
                  (s, Brooks)
Rodolfo .... LoMonaco
Schaunard .... D. Smith
Colline .... Voketaitis
Alcindoro .... Fiorito

October 27 (m)

THE MIKADO

Same cast as October 12 (m)
except:

Nanki-Poo .... Krause
Katisha .... Sachs

October 27

RIGOLETTO

Same cast as October 5 except:

Duke .... Porretta
Rigoletto .... Ludgin
Monterone .... Frierson

Ceprano .... Dowlen
Marullo ...... Ledbetter (d)
Maddalena .... Troyanos
Giovanna .... Povia

November 1

LOUISE

Same cast as October 6 except:

Junk man .... Fiorito

November 2 (m)

THE MERRY WIDOW

Same cast as October 13 (m)
except:

Conductor .... Popper
Sonia .... Sills,
                  (s, Bower)
Prince Danilo .... Metcalf
Natalie .... Card
De Jolidon .... McDonald
General Novikovich .. Fiorito

November 2

LA TRAVIATA

Same cast as October 20
except:

Violetta .... Di Gerlando
Alfredo .... LoMonaco
D'Obigny .... Ledbetter
Giuseppe .... Dowlen

November 3 (m)

DON GIOVANNI

Same cast as October 24
except:

Zerlina .... Summers (d)

November 3

THE MARRIAGE OF FIGARO

Same cast as October 11
except:

Almaviva .... Reardon
Countess .... Faull
Figaro .... Voketaitis
Cherubino .... Kleinman
Bartolo .... Paul
Marcellina .... Greenspon
Basilio .... Krause

November 8

LA BOHÈME

Same cast as October 4 except:

Conductor .... Ryan

Rodolfo .... LoMonaco
Marcello .... Bottcher
Schaunard .... D. Smith
Alcindoro .... Fiorito

November 9 (m)

THE MIKADO

Same cast as October 12 (m)
except:

Conductor .... Popper

Mikado .... Voketaitis
Pooh-Bah .... Berberian
Yum-Yum .... Card

November 9

DON GIOVANNI

Same cast as October 24
except:

Don Giovanni ...... Reardon
Leporello .... Malas
Donna Elvira ...... Willauer
Commendatore .... Paul
Donna Anna .... King
Don Ottavio .... McCollum,
                  (s, Porretta)

November 10 (m)

GENTLEMEN, BE SEATED!

Same cast as October 10
except:

Conductor .... Wilson

Johnny Reb .... Hindsley
Southern girl .... Precht

November 10

THE MERRY WIDOW

Same cast as October 13 (m)
except:

Conductor .... Popper

Prince Danilo .... Metcalf
Natalie .... Card
De Jolidon .... McDonald
General Novikovich .. Fiorito

Spring 1964 no season

(Gilbert & Sullivan season, different Company)
(G&S seasons not included in NYCO Annals)

Fall 1964 (OCTOBER I – NOVEMBER I5)

Female artists
August, Joan*
Bayard, Carol*
Beaman, Barbara
Bergey, Carol
Bonelli, Olivia
Brooks, Patricia
Caplan, Joan*
Clements, Joy
Crader, Jeannine*
Curtin, Phyllis
Darling, Sandra*
De Forest, Anthea
Di Gerlando, Maria
Donn, Carol*
Dornya, Maria*
Elgar, Anne*
Evans, Beverly
Ferriero, Maria
Gavoorian, Joan*
Greenspon, Muriel
Guile, Helen
Jeffrey, Donna*
Kleinman, Marlena
Kokolska, Martha
Neway, Patricia
Newton, Norma*
Povia, Charlotte
Sills, Beverly
Tosini, Ivana*
Troyanos, Tatiana
Tyler, Veronica*
Verrett, Shirley†
Welting, Patricia*
Willauer, Marguerite
Witkowska, Nadja
Wolff, Beverly

Male artists
Berberian, Ara
Bottcher, Ron
Cass, Lee*
Cassilly, Richard
Chapman, William
Citarelli, Enzo*
Corder, Paul
Cossa, Dominic
Craig, Jack
Crain, Jon
Cross, Richard
Davis, Harris
Di Virgilio, Nicholas*
Dowlen, Glenn
DuPree, William

* New artist
† Shirley Verrett had previously appeared with the New York City Opera Company (spring 1958) under the name of Shirley Carter.

Duval, Pierre*
Fredricks, Richard
Gramm, Donald
Harrold, Jack
Henderson, Don
Hicks, David
Kelley, Norman
Krause, Richard
Ledbetter, William
Malas, Spiro
McCollum, John
Metcalf, William
Miller, Kellis
Milnes, Sherrill*
Molese, Michele*
Paul, Thomas
Rall, Thomas*
Reardon, John
Rudel, Anthony*
Safina, Anthony
Sevier, John*
Shirley, George
Smith, David
Smith, John
Stamford, John*
Treigle, Norman
Vellucci, Luigi
Voketaitis, Arnold
Worth, Coley
Yule, Don

Conductors
Bamberger, Carl
Jonson, William
Patané, Franco
Popper, Felix
Rudel, Julius
Ryan, Dean
Susskind, Walter
Wilson, Charles

Chorus Master
Jonson, William

Solo dancers
de Lavallade, Carmen
Galan, Rosario
Hinkson, Mary
Zide, Rochelle

Douglas, Scott
Maule, Michael*
Tetley, Glen

Choreographer
Andrew, Thomas
Butler, John

Directors
Ball, William
Browning, Kirk

* New artist

Butler, John
Fletcher, Allen
Herbert, Ralph
Pollock, Michael
Raedler, Dorothy
Ringland, Byron*
Rudel, Julius*
Strasfogel, Ian*
Sylbert, Paul

Designers
Armstrong, Will Steven
Bay, Howard
Campbell, Patton
Condell, H. A.
Fletcher, Robert
Heymann, Henry
Micunis, Gordon
Morley, Ruth
Pitkin, William
Sylbert, Paul
Waring, James D.*
Wittop, Freddy*

* New artist

October 1

BORIS GODUNOV (Mussorgsky)
First performance by The New York City Opera Company
(English translation by Joseph Machlis)

Staged by .... Fletcher
Scenic designer ... Armstrong
Costume
  designer .... Wittop (d)
Choreographer ...... Andrew
  Boys' choir from
  Epiphany Church, New York
Conductor .... Susskind

Boris .... Treigle
Feodor .... Kleinman
Xenia .... Bergey
Nurse .... Evans
Shuisky .... Kelley
Shchelkalov .... Bottcher
Pimen .... Paul
Dmitri (Gregori) ...... Crain
Marina .... Troyanos
Rangoni .... Chapman
Varlaam .... Malas
Missail .... Miller
Innkeeper .... Greenspon
Simpleton .... Krause
1st Guard .... Cossa
Boyar .... Davis

Lovitzky .... Yule
Tcherniakowsky .... D. Smith
Police Officer ...... Ledbetter
1st Peasant .... Beaman
2nd Peasant .... Povia
3rd Peasant .... Safina
4th Peasant .... J. Smith
Solo dancers .... Zide;
                      Maule (d)

October 2

THE MARRIAGE OF FIGARO
(Mozart)
(English version by
Ruth and Thomas Martin)

Conductor .... Susskind

Almaviva .... Reardon
Countess .... Jeffrey (d)
Figaro .... Gramm
Susanna .... Brooks
Cherubino .... Wolff
Bartolo .... Malas
Marcellina .... Greenspon
Basilio .... Vellucci
Curzio .... Miller
Antonio .... D. Smith
Barbarina .... Bergey

October 3

CARMEN (Bizet)
New production

Stage director ...... Fletcher
Scenery designed by
James D. Waring (d) for the
Opera Society of Washington
Costume designer .. Heymann
Choreographer ..... Andrew
Conductor .... Rudel

Carmen .... Verrett
Don José .... Cassilly
Escamillo .... Treigle
Micaëla .... Bayard (d)
Zuniga .... Paul
Frasquita .... Kokolska
Mercédès .... Kleinman
Remendado .... Krause
Dancairo .... D. Smith
Morales .... Ledbetter

October 4 (m)

MADAMA BUTTERFLY (Puccini)
Conductor .... Patané

Butterfly .... Ferriero
Suzuki .... Kleinman
Kate Pinkerton ...... Evans
Pinkerton .... Molese (d)
Sharpless .... Bottcher
Goro .... Miller
Yamadori .... D. Smith
The Bonze .... Malas
Imperial
  Commissioner .... Dowlen
Registrar .... Henderson

October 4

BORIS GODUNOV

Same cast as October 1

October 8

NATALIA PETROVNA (Hoiby)
World premiere

Staged by .... Ball
Scenic designer .... Bay
Costume designer .. Campbell
Lighting .... Fisher
Conductor .... Rudel

Mikhail Mikhailovitch .. Cross
Natalia Petrovna..Dornya (d)
Arkady Sergeitch .. McCollum
Kolia .... Rudel (d)
Vera .... Darling (d)
Anna .... Greenspon
Lisavetta .... Brooks
Alexei .... Reardon
Doctor .... Harrold
Bolisov .... Krause

October 9

LA TRAVIATA (Verdi)

Stage director .... Raedler
Conductor .... Patané

Violetta .... Tosini (d)
Alfredo .... Molese
Germont .... Cossa
Flora .... Kleinman
Annina .... Evans
Gaston .... Krause
Douphol .... D. Smith
D'Obigny .... Sevier (d)
Dr. Grenvil .... Paul
Giuseppe .... Hicks
Solo dancer .... Galan

October 10 (m)

LA BOHÈME (Puccini)

Stage director .... Raedler
Conductor .... Patané

Mimi .... Di Gerlando
Musetta .... Donn (d)
Rodolfo .... Craig
Marcello .... Bottcher
Schaunard .... Ledbetter
Colline .... Paul
Benoit .... Malas
Alcindoro .... D. Smith
Parpignol .... Miller
1st Guard .... Dowlen
2nd Guard .... J. Smith

October 10

THE MERRY WIDOW (Lehár)
(Words by Adrian Ross)

Conductor .... Bamberger

Sonia .... Witkowska
Prince Danilo ...... Reardon
Baron Popoff ...... Harrold
Natalie .... Welting (d)
De Jolidon .... Molese
Marquis de Cascada..D. Smith
St. Brioche .... Krause
Admiral Khadja .... Ledbetter
Mme. Khadja .... Povia
General Novikovich ... Malas
Mme. Novikovich ..... Evans
Nish .... Worth
Clo-Clo .... Guile
Solo dancers .... Zide; Maule

October 11 (m)

THE MARRIAGE OF FIGARO

Same cast as October 2 except:

Almaviva .... Chapman
Figaro .... Treigle
Susanna .... Tyler (d)
Basilio .... Krause

October 11

DIE FLEDERMAUS (J. Strauss)
New production
(English version by
Ruth and Thomas Martin)

Staged by .... Rudel (d)
Scenic designer ...... Pitkin
Costume designer .. Heymann
Choreographer ...... Andrew
Conductor .... Rudel

Eisenstein .... Reardon
Rosalinda .... Sills
Adele .... Elgar (d)
Alfred .... Crain
Falke .... Fredricks
Frank .... Cass (d)
Blind .... Miller
Prince Orlovsky .... D. Smith
Sally .... Evans
Frosch .... Worth
Ivan .... Dowlen
Solo dancers .... Zide; Maule

October 15

BORIS GODUNOV

Same cast as October 1 except:

1st Peasant ...... August (d)

October 16

DIE FLEDERMAUS

Same cast as October 11

October 17 (m)

MADAMA BUTTERFLY

Same cast as October 4 (m)
except:

Kate Pinkerton .... De Forest
Pinkerton .... Craig

October 17

LA TRAVIATA

Same cast as October 9 except:

Violetta .... Curtin
Alfredo .... DuPree
Annina .... Povia
Dr. Grenvil .... Yule
Giuseppe .... Dowlen

October 18 (m)

THE MERRY WIDOW

Same cast as October 10
except:

Conductor .... Rudel

Natalie .... Elgar
De Jolidon .... Craig

Mme. Novikovich ...... Guile
Clo-Clo .... Evans

October 18

FAUST (Gounod)

Stage director .. Ringland (d)
Choreographer ...... Andrew
Conductor .... Patané

Faust .... Molese
Méphistophélès ...... Treigle
Valentin .... Milnes (d)
Wagner .... Sevier
Marguerite ....·... Tosini
Siébel .... Wolff
Marthe .... Greenspon

October 22

SALOME (R. Strauss)

Stage director .... Herbert
Conductor .... Rudel

Herodes .... Kelley
Herodias .... Neway
Salome .... Curtin
Jochanaan .... Chapman
Narraboth .... Rall (d)
Page .... Kleinman
1st Jew .... Krause
2nd Jew .... Vellucci
3rd Jew .... Citarelli (d)
4th Jew .... Miller
5th Jew .... Malas
Cappadocian .... Dowlen
Slave .... Corder
1st Nazarene .... Treigle
2nd Nazarene .... Henderson
1st Soldier .... Paul
2nd Soldier .... D. Smith

October 23

LA BOHÈME

Same cast as October 10 (m)
except:

Mimi .... Tosini
Musetta .... Elgar
Rodolfo .... Molese
Schaunard .... Cossa

October 24 (m)

FAUST

Same cast as October 18
except:

Faust .... Duval (d)

October 24

THE MARRIAGE OF FIGARO

Same cast as October 2 except:

Almaviva .... Fredricks
Figaro .... Voketaitis
Susanna .... Tyler
Basilio .... Krause
Antonio .... Sevier

October 25 (m)

DIE FLEDERMAUS

Same cast as October 11
except:

Conductor .... Popper
Eisenstein ..... Stamford (d)
Adele .... Welting
Alfred .... Citarelli
Falke .... Metcalf

October 25

CARMEN

Same cast as October 3 except:

Escamillo .... Bottcher,
                      (s, Treigle)
Micaëla ...... Gavoorian (d)

October 29

SALOME

Same cast as October 22

October 30

MADAMA BUTTERFLY

Same cast as October 4 (m)
except:

Butterfly .... Di Gerlando
Kate Pinkerton .... Guile
Sharpless .... Cossa
Yamadori .... Hicks

October 31 (m)

DON GIOVANNI (Mozart)
(English version by
Ruth and Thomas Martin)

Stage director ..Strasfogel (d)
Conductor .... Rudel

Don Giovanni .... Treigle
Leporello .... Gramm
Donna Elvira ... Newton (d)
Commendatore .... Berberian
Donna Anna .... Sills
Don Ottavio ..... McCollum
Masetto .... Metcalf
Zerlina .... Brooks

October 31

LA BOHÈME

Same cast as October 10 (m)
except:

Mimi .... Tosini
Musetta .... Elgar
Colline .... Voketaitis
2nd Guard .... Yule

November 1 (m)

CARMEN

Same cast as October 3 except:

Don José .... Shirley
Escamillo .... Chapman

Micaëla .... Gavoorian
Remendado .... Miller

November 1

THE MERRY WIDOW

Same cast as October 10
except:

Conductor .... Jonson
Prince Danilo .... Metcalf

November 3

BORIS GODUNOV

Same cast as October 1 except:

Conductor .... Wilson

Feodor .... De Forest
Xenia .... Darling
Nurse .... Povia
Shuisky .... Krause
Pimen .... Malas
Varlaam .... Cass
Innkeeper .... Caplan (d)
Simpleton .... DuPree
1st Peasant .... August

November 4

OEDIPUS REX (Stravinsky)
(English narration by
e.e. cummings)

Conductor .... Rudel

Narrator .... D. Smith
Oedipus .... Cassilly
Creon .... Bottcher
Tiresias .... Paul
Jocasta .... Troyanos
Messenger .... Cossa
Shepherd .... Krause

Followed by:

CARMINA BURANA (Orff)

Conductor .... Rudel

Soprano .... Gavoorian,
                    (s, Witkowska)
Tenor .... DuPree
Baritone .... Milnes
Solo dancers ... de Lavallade,
      Hinkson; Douglas, Tetley

November 5

NATALIA PETROVNA

Same cast as October 8 except:

Lisavetta .... Elgar,
                        (s, Brooks)

November 6

DON GIOVANNI

Same cast as October 31 (m)
except:

Donna Elvira .... Crader (d)
Commendatore .... Paul

Don Ottavio .... Krause
Zerlina .... Bergey,
(s, Brooks)

November 7 (m)

LA TRAVIATA

Same cast as October 9 except:

Conductor .... Rudel

Germont .... Milnes
Flora .... Evans
Annina .... Povia
Gaston .... Davis
Giuseppe .... Dowlen

November 7

DIE FLEDERMAUS

Same cast as October 11
except:

Conductor .... Popper

Eisenstein .... Stamford
Falke .... Ledbetter
Frank .... Malas

November 8 (m)

THE MARRIAGE OF FIGARO

Same cast as October 2 except:

Conductor .... Bamberger

Almaviva .... Fredricks
Countess .... Newton
Susanna .... Clements,
(s, Brooks)
Cherubino .... Troyanos
Marcellina .... Evans
Basilio .... Miller
Curzio .... Corder
Antonio .... Sevier

November 8

SALOME

Same cast as October 22
except:

Narraboth .... DuPree

November 12

OEDIPUS REX

Same cast as November 4

Followed by:

CARMINA BURANA

Same cast as November 4
except:

Baritone .... Reardon

November 13

FAUST

Same cast as October 18
except:

Conductor .... Rudel

Valentin .... Cossa
Wagner .... Ledbetter
Marguerite .... Sills
Siébel .... Kleinman

November 14 (m)

CARMEN

Same cast as October 3 except:

Conductor .... Wilson

Carmen .... Wolff
Escamillo .... Bottcher
Micaëla .... Bonelli
Frasquita .... Bergey

Mercédès .... Evans
Remendado .... Miller

November 14

MADAMA BUTTERFLY

Same cast as October 4 (m)
except:

Conductor .... Ryan

Kate Pinkerton .... Guile
Pinkerton .... Di Virgilio (d)
Sharpless .... Cossa
The Bonze .... Sevier

November 15 (m)

LA BOHÈME

Same cast as October 10 (m)
except:

Conductor .... Popper

Musetta .... Elgar
Rodolfo .... Molese
Marcello .... Fredricks
2nd Guard .... Yule

November 15

DON GIOVANNI

Same cast as October 31 (m)
except:

Leporello .... Malas
Donna Elvira ...... Willauer
Donna Anna .... Sills,
(s, King)
Don Ottavio .... Krause
Zerlina .... Bergey,
(s, Brooks)

(Note: Juanita King was not
to sing with the New York
City Opera this season.)

Spring 1965 (MARCH 4 – APRIL 4)

Female artists
August, Joan*
Bash, Phyllis*
Bible, Frances
Brice, Carol
Brash, Marion*
Brooks, Patricia
Bryant, Joyce*
Burgess, Mary
Clements, Joy
Darian, Anita
Darling, Sandra
De Forest, Anthea
Di Gerlando, Maria
Dowdy, Helen*
Elgar, Anne
Evans, Beverly
Faull, Ellen
Goodman, Margaret
Greenspon, Muriel

Herbert, Lila
Hoefer, Anita*
Jeffrey, Donna
Jennings, Mary
Kenting, Jodell
Kleinman, Marlena
Kobart, Ruth
Lewis, Brenda
Lindsay, Claudia*
Likova, Eva
Morris, Wendy
Povia, Charlotte
Precht, Donna
Schauler, Eileen*
Schlamme, Martha*
Sena, Joan
Sills, Beverly
Skala, Lilia*
Small, Neva
Smith, Karen*

Smith-Conrad, Barbara*
Troyanos, Tatiana
Turner, Claramae
Webb, Alyce
Willauer, Marguerite
Witkowska, Nadja
Wolff, Beverly
Wyckoff, Lou Ann
Young, Marie

Male artists
Anden, Mathew*
Andor, Paul*
Attles, Joseph*
Beattie, Herbert
Bittner, Jack*
Brice, Eugene
Cass, Lee
Cassel, Walter
Cassilly, Richard

* New artist

* New artist

* New artist

Chapman, William
Cordy, Henry
Corder, Paul
Davis, Harris
Di Giuseppe, Enrico*
Donaldson, Robert*
Dowlen, Glenn
DuPree, William
Duval, Pierre
Frieder, Sol*
Frierson, Andrew
Fredricks, Richard
Garson, John*
Grier, Bill*
Hausserman, Michael*
Henderson, Don
Herbert, Ralph
Hindsley, Charles
Irving, George S.
James, Joseph
Jurgens, Claus*
Kasznar, Kurt*
Kelly, Robert Lee
Kenny, James*
Krause, Richard
Laws, Jerry*
Ledbetter, William
Lewis, Carrington*
LoMonaco, Jerome
Long, Avon
Lowens, Curt*
Malas, Spiro
Metcalf, William
Miller, Julian
Miller, Kellis
Mosley, Robert*
Park, Richard
Paul, Thomas
Perkins, Garwood
Pierson, Edward*
Porretta, Frank
Randolph, James
Reardon, John
Safina, Anthony
Santillana, Robert*
Schmorr, Robert*
Schnabel, Stefan*
Smith, David
Stamford, John
Sylan, Oscar*
Treigle, Norman
Ukena, Paul
Ventura, Clyde*
Voketaitis, Arnold
Watkins, Gordon*
Wentworth, Richard
Yule, Don

Conductors
Baustian, Robert*
Coppola, Anton*
La Selva, Vincent*
Popper, Felix
Rudel, Julius
Ryan, Dean
Wilson, Charles

Chrous master
Jonson, William

Solo dancers
de Lavallade, Carmen

* New artist

Hinkson, Mary
Van Scott, Glory*
Douglas, Scott
Tetley, Glen

Choreographers
Butler, John
Levine, Rhoda

Directors
Ball, William
Butler, John
Corsaro, Frank
Field, Bill
Gerber, Ella*
Healy, Mark *
Menotti, Gian Carlo
Psacharopoulos, Nikos*
Rott, Adolph*
Rudel, Julius
Sylbert, Paul
West, Christopher

Designers
Armstrong, Will Steven
Campbell, Patton
Fletcher, Robert
Morley, Ruth
Oenslager, Donald
Randolph, Robert*
Roth, Wolfgang
Saxe, Stephen O.
Sullivan, Roger*
Sylbert, Paul
Ter-Arutunian, Rouben
Wexler, Peter*
Zipprodt, Patricia*

* New artist

March 4

KATERINA ISMAILOVA
(Shostakovich)
First performance by The New
York City Opera Company
(English translation by
Julius Rudel)

Staged by .... Corsaro
Scenic designer ... Armstrong
Costume
  designer ..... Zipprodt (d)
Lighting .... Armstrong
Conductor .... Rudel

Katerina
  Ismailova .... Schauler (d)
Boris Ismailov ..... Chapman
Zinovy Ismailov ...... Krause
Mill workman ..... Ledbetter
Sergei .... Cassilly
Aksinya .... Darling
Coachman .... Davis
Village drunk ..... K. Miller
Porter .... Bittner (d)
Steward .... Park
A workman .... Kelly
Priest .... Cass
Police inspector .... D. Smith
Old convict .... Paul
Sentry .... Bittner
Sonyetka,
  a convict .... Troyanos
Female convict ..... Wyckoff
Sergeant .... Ledbetter

March 5

PORGY AND BESS (Gershwin)

Staged by .... Gerber (d)
Scenic designer .. Sullivan (d)
Conductor .... Ryan

Clara .... Lindsay (d)
Mingo .... Laws (d)
Sportin' Life .... Long
Jake .... Pierson (d)
Serena .... Bash (d)
Robbins .... Watkins (d)
Jim .... Perkins
Peter .... C. Lewis (d)
Lily .... Dowdy (d)
Maria .... C. Brice
Porgy .... Frierson
Crown .... Randolph
Bess .... Bryant (d)
Policeman .... Grier
Undertaker .... James
Annie .... Webb
Frazer .... E. Brice
Detective .... Bittner
Crabman .... Attles (d)
Coroner .... K. Miller
Scipio .... O. Sylvan (d)
Dancer .... Van Scott (d)

March 6 (m)

PORGY AND BESS

Same cast as March 5 except:

Porgy .... Mosley (d)
Bess ...... Smith-Conrad (d)

March 6

PORGY AND BESS

Same cast as March 5

March 7 (m)

THE BALLAD OF BABY DOE
(Moore)

Staged by .... Field
Conductor ..... Baustian (d)

An Old Silver
  Miner .... K. Miller
Saloon Bartender ...... Yule
Horace Tabor .... Casse
Sam .... Schmorr (d)
Bushy .... Krause
Barney .... D. Smith
Jacob .... Bittner
Augusta .... Kobart
            (s, Turner
Baby Doe .... Sills
Kate .... Kentin
Mag .... Augus
Samantha .... De Fores
Hotel clerk .... Schmorr (d)
Albert .... Dowle
Sarah .... Prech
Mary .... Darlin
Emily .... Evar
Effie .... Povi
McCourt family .. L. Herber
      De Forest, Davis, Yu
Mama McCourt .. Greenspo

Four Washington
  dandies . . K. Miller, Corder,
           Dowlen, Henderson
Father Chapelle..Schmorr (d)
Hotel footman .... Bittner
Chester A. Arthur .... Krause
Elizabeth and
  Silver Dollar .... Small,
              K. Smith (d)
Mayor of Leadville .... Davis
William
  Jennings Bryan..Wentworth
Stage doorman ..... K. Miller
Denver politician ...... Yule
Silver Dollar
  (grown up) .... August

March 7

KATERINA ISMAILOVA

Same cast as March 4 except:

Sergei .... Stamford
Sonyetka, a convict .... Evans

March 11

DIE DREIGROSCHENOPER
(Weill)
First performance by The New
York City Opera Company
(performed in German)

Directed by .... Rott (d)
Scenic designer .... Roth
Costume designer .... Morley
Conductor .... Rudel

Ansager .... Irving
Jonathan Jeremiah
  Peachum .... Schnabel (d)
Mrs. Peachum ..... Skala (d)
Polly Peachum ... Hoefer (d)
Macheath ...... Kasznar (d)
Brown .... R. Herbert
Lucy .... Brash (d)
Filch .... Anden (d)
Die Platte (the gang):
Hakenfingerjakob .... Frieder
                   (d)
Münzmatthias ... Garson (d)
Trauerweidenwalter ... Andor
                   (d)
Ede .... Hausserman (d)
Sägerobert ...... Jurgens (d)
Jimmy .... Lowens (d)
Spelunkenjenny ... Schlamme
                   (d)
Smith .... D. Smith
Pastor Kimball .... Cordy

March 12

A MIDSUMMER NIGHT'S DREAM
(Britten)

Stage director ..... Healy (d)
Conductor .... Wilson

Oberon .... Bible
Tytania .... Witkowska
Puck .... J. Miller
Theseus .... Voketaitis
Hippolyta .... Troyanos
Lysander .... Hindsley

Demetrius .... Metcalf
Hermia .... Kleinman
Helena .... Willauer
Bottom .... Malas
Quince .... Ukena
Flute .... Krause
Snug .... Wentworth
Snout .... Schmorr
Starveling .... D. Smith

March 13 (m)

PORGY AND BESS

Same cast as March 5 except:

Robbins ..... Donaldson (d)
Porgy .... Mosley

March 13

PORGY AND BESS

Same cast as March 5 except:

Clara .... Young
Robbins .... Donaldson
Bess .... Smith-Conrad

March 14 (m)

PORGY AND BESS

Same cast as March 5 except:

Clara .... Young
Robbins .... Donaldson

March 14

DIE DREIGROSCHENOPER

Same cast as March 11

March 17

A MIDSUMMER NIGHT'S DREAM

Same cast as March 12

March 18

THE SAINT OF BLEECKER STREET
(Menotti)
First performance by The New
York City Opera Company

Staged by .... Menotti
Designer ...... Randolph (d)
Conductor ..... La Selva (d)

Assunta .... Greenspon
Carmela .... Jennings
Maria Corona .... Darian
Her Son .... Ventura (d)
Don Marco .... Paul
Annina .... Sena
Michele .... Di Giuseppe (d)
Desideria .... Wolff
Salvatore .... D. Smith
Concettina .... Morris
Young man .... Safina
Young woman .... Povia
Woman .... De Forest
Bartender .... Henderson
Guests .... Krause, Ledbetter

March 19

THE BALLAD OF BABY DOE

Same cast as March 7 (m)
except:

Conductor .... Popper
Horace Tabor ..... Fredricks
Augusta .... Turner
Baby Doe .... Brooks

March 20

DIE DREIGROSCHENOPER

Same cast as March 11

March 21 (m)

DIE DREIGROSCHENOPER

Same cast as March 11 except:

Conductor .... Ryan

March 21

IL TRITTICO (Puccini)

Conductor .... Rudel

IL TABARRO

Michele .... Chapman
Luigi .... Porretta
Tinca .... Krause
Talpa .... Paul
Giorgetta .... Likova
Frugola .... Turner
Song vendor ...... K. Miller
Two lovers .. Darling, Krause

Followed by:

SUOR ANGELICA

Suor Angelica ... Di Gerlando
La Principessa .... Turner
La Badessa .... Greenspon
La Suora Zelatrice .... Evans
La Maestra
  della Novizie .... Troyanos
Suor Genovieffa .... Elgar
Le due novizie ... L. Herbert,
                 De Forest
Suor Dolcina .... Povia
Le due converse .... Darling,
                  August
La Cercatrice ...... Wyckoff
Le altre Suore ...... Kenting,
     Goodman, Goldsmith,
                 Beaman

Followed by:

GIANNI SCHICCHI

Gianni Schicchi ...... Treigle
Lauretta .... Elgar
Zita .... Turner
Rinuccio .... Duval
Gherardo .... Krause
Nella .... Darling
Gherardino ... Santillana (d),
                (s, Kenny)
Betto .... D. Smith
Simone .... Beattie
Marco .... Ledbetter
La Ciesca .... Wyckoff
Spinellocchio .... Paul
Nicolao .... Cass
Pinellino .... Yule
Guccio .... Dowlen

March 24

    KATERINA ISMAILOVA

Same cast as March 4

March 25

    LIZZIE BORDEN (Beeson)
      World premiere

Directed by .. Psacharopoulos
                  (d)
Scenic designer .. Wexler (d)
Costume designer .. Campbell
Conductor ...... Coppola (d)

Andrew Borden ...... Beattie
Abigail Borden .... Faull
Elizabeth Borden ... B. Lewis
Margaret Borden ...... Elgar
Reverend Harrington ..Krause
Capt. Jason
   MacFarlane ..... Fredricks

March 26

    DIE DREIGROSCHENOPER

Same cast as March 11

March 27 (m)

    DIE DREIGROSCHENOPER

Same cast as March 11 except:

Conductor .... Ryan

March 27

    IL TRITTICO

Same casts as March 21
except:

    GIANNI SCHICCHI

Rinuccio .... LoMonaco

March 28 (m)

THE SAINT OF BLEECKER STREET

Same cast as March 18

March 28

    SUSANNAH (Floyd)

Stage director .... Rudel
Conductor .... Rudel

Susannah .... Clements
Sam Polk .... Cassilly
Olin Blitch .... Treigle
Little
   Bat McLean ..... J. Miller
Elder McLean ...... Beattie
Elder Gleaton ..... Schmorr
Elder Hays .... Krause
Elder Ott .... Cass
Mrs. McLean .... Greenspon
Mrs. Gleaton .... Darling
Mrs. Hays .... Precht
Mrs. Ott .... Evans

March 31

    OEDIPUS REX (Stravinsky)
     (English narration by
      e.e. cummings)

Conductor .... Rudel

Narrator .... D. Smith
Oedipus .... Cassilly
Creon .... Voketaitis
Tiresias .... Paul
Jocasta .... Bible
Messenger .... Ledbetter
Shepherd .... Krause

Followed by:

    CARMINA BURANA (Orff)

Conductor .... Rudel

Soprano .... Elgar
Tenor .... DuPree
Baritone .... Reardon
Solo dancers ... de Lavallade,
    Hinkson; Douglas, Tetley

April 1

    SUSANNAH

Same cast as March 28 except:

Conductor .... Popper

April 2

    IL TRITTICO

Same casts as March 21 except:

    IL TABARRO

Giorgetta .... Sena

    SUOR ANGELICA

Suor Angelica .... Likova

    GIANNI SCHICCHI

Rinuccio .... LoMonaco
Gherardino ...... Kenny (d)

April 3 (m)

    KATERINA ISMAILOVA

Same cast as March 4 except:

Katerina .... Jeffrey
Sergei .... Stamford

April 3

    THE BALLAD OF BABY DOE

Same cast as March 7 (m)
except:

Augusta .... Bible
Baby Doe .... Brooks
Mary .... Goodman
Emily .... Burgess
William Jenning Bryan .. Paul

April 4 (m)

    LIZZIE BORDEN

Same cast as March 25

April 4

    OEDIPUS REX

Same cast as March 31

Followed by:

    CARMINA BURANA

Same cast as March 31

Fall 1965 (SEPTEMBER 22 – NOVEMBER 14)

Female artists
Amedeo, Edy*
August, Joan
Bala, Iris*
Bayard, Carol
Bergey, Carol
Bonazzi, Elaine*
Brooks, Patricia
Carson, Clarice*
Christiansen, Beverly*
Creed, Kay*
Darian, Anita

   * New artist

Di Gerlando, Maria
Elgar, Anne
Evans, Beverly
Faull, Ellen
George, Edna Mae*
Grant, Sylvia*
Greenspon, Muriel
Guile, Helen
Hepburn, Betsy
Herbert, Lila
Hupp, Rosalind*
Jeffrey, Donna

   * New artist

Jennings, Mary
Kenting, Jodell
Kleinman, Marlena
Kova, Marjia
Likova, Eva
Migenes, Julia*
Morris, Wendy
Povia, Charlotte
Precht, Donna
Reale, Marcella*
Schauler, Eileen
Shane, Rita*

   * New artist

FALL 1965

Sills, Beverly
Summers, Joan
Willauer, Marguerite
Wolff, Beverly

Male artists
Beattie, Herbert
Beck, William*
Berberian, Ara
Bittner, Jack
Bullard, Gene*
Cassilly, Richard
Castel, Nico*
Chapman, William
Citarelli, Enzo
Clatworthy, David
Consiglio, Giovanni*
Corder, Paul
Cossa, Dominic
Craig, John
Crain, Jon
Dembaugh, William*
Domingo, Placido*
DuPree, William
Finkelstein, Gary*
Gramm, Donald
Harrold, Jack
Henderson, Don
Hoekman, Guus*
James, Lester*
Kelley, Norman
Krause, Richard
Ledbetter, William
Lloyd, David
LoMonaco, Jerome
Maffeo, Gianni*
Malas, Spiro
Metcalf, William
Miller, Kellis
Milnes, Sherrill
Molese, Michele
Mosley, Robert
Park, Richard
Rayson, Benjamin*
Reardon, John
Roden, Jacob*
Smith, David
Smith, Malcolm*
Stamford, John
Theyard, Harry
Trehy, Robert
Treigle, Norman
Tyl, Noel*
Vellucci, Luigi
Ventura, Clyde
Wentworth, Richard
Worth, Coley
Yule, Don

Conductors
Coppola, Anton
La Selva, Vincent
Märzendorfer, Ernst*
Patané, Franco
Popper, Felix
Rudel, Julius
Ryan, Dean
Wilson, Charles
Zeller, Robert*

Solo dancers
Balestracci, Sandra*
Galan, Rosario

* New artist

Hennessey, Christina*
Kovach, Nora*
Peterson, Joan*
Terrell, Betty Ann*

Glassman, William*
Rabovsky, Istvan*

Choreographer
Andrew, Thomas

Directors
Ball, William
Capobianco, Tito*
Corsaro, Frank
Harrold, Jack*
Menotti, Gian Carlo
Moresco, Riccardo*
Psacharopoulos, Nikos
Raedler, Dorothy
Renan, Emile*
Ringland, Byron
Rizzo, Francis*
Rudel, Julius
Savoca, Carmen*
Strasfogel, Ian
West, Christopher

Designers
Armstrong, Will Steven
Bay, Howard
Campbell, Patton
Condell, H. A.
Evans, Lloyd*
Fletcher, Robert
Heymann, Henry
Maganini, Margaretta*
Micunis, Gordon
Nomikos, Andreas
Pitkin, William
Randolph, Robert
Waring, James D.
Wittstein, Ed*
Zipprodt, Patricia

* New artist

September 22

THE FLAMING ANGEL
(Prokofiev)
American premiere
(English translation by
Joseph Machlis)

Staged by .... Corsaro
Scenic designer ... Armstrong
Costume designer ... Zipprodt
Lighting .... Armstrong
Conductor .... Rudel

Renata .... Schauler
Ruprecht .... Milnes
Innkeeper .... Evans
Waiter .... Beck (d)
Fortune Teller .... Greenspon
Jacob Glock .... Vellucci
Agrippa .... Crain
Matthew .... Beck
Physician .... Krause
Tavernkeeper .... Bittner
Three men of
  Cologne .... Henderson,
                  Park, Yule
Potboy ...... Finkelstein (d)
Méphistophélès ...... Kelley
Dr. Faustus .... Trehy
Abbess .... Greenspon
Inquisitor ..... M. Smith (d)

Count Heinrich ... James (d)
Nuns ...... Bala (d), Bergey,
            Creed (d), Evans,
            Hupp (d), Kleinman,
            Precht, Summers

September 24

CARMEN (Bizet)

Stage director .... Renan (d)
Children's Chorus from
Epiphany School, New York

Conductor .... Coppola

Carmen .... Wolff
Don José .... Cassilly
Escamillo .... Treigle
Micaëla .... Bayard
Zuniga .... Beattie
Frasquita .... Bergey
Mercédès .... Kleinman
Remendado .... Krause
Dancairo .... Beck
Morales .... Ledbetter

September 25 (m)

DIE FLEDERMAUS (J. Strauss)
(English version by
Ruth and Thomas Martin)

Lighting .... Sondheimer
Conductor .... Rudel

Eisenstein .... Stamford
Rosalinda .... Sills
Frank .... Wentworth
Prince Orlofsky ... D. Smith
Alfred .... Crain
Falke .... Ledbetter
Blind .... Miller
Adele .... Elgar
Frosch .... Worth
Sally .... Evans
Ivan .... Yule
Solo dancers .... Kovach (d);
                  Rabovsky (d),
              Peterson (d), Terrell (d)

September 25

MADAMA BUTTERFLY (Puccini)

Conductor .... Patané

Butterfly .... Reale (d)
Suzuki .... Kleinman
Kate Pinkerton .... Guile
Pinkerton .... LoMonaco
Sharpless .... Clatworthy
Goro .... Krause
Yamadori .... Vellucci
The Bonze .... M. Smith
Imperial
  Commissioner .... Yule
Registrar .... Henderson

September 26 (m)

FAUST (Gounod)

Conductor .... Patané

Faust .... Molese
Méphistophélès ...... Treigle
Valentin .... Cossa
Wagner .... Beck
Marguerite .... Sills
Siébel .... Wolff
Marthe .... Greenspon

September 26

THE FLAMING ANGEL

Same cast as September 22
except:

Physician .... Vellucci

September 29

THE SAINT OF BLEECKER STREET
(Menotti)

Stage director ..... Rizzo (d)
Conductor .... La Selva

Assunta .... Greenspon
Carmela .... Jennings
Maria Corona ...... Darian
Her Son .... Ventura
Don Marco .... M. Smith
Annina .... Migenes (d)
Michele .... Theyard
Desideria .... Wolff
Salvatore .... Beck
Concettina .... Morris
Young man .... Safina
Young woman ..... Kenting
Bartender .... Henderson
Guests .... Krause, Ledbetter

September 30

THE MARRIAGE OF FIGARO
(Mozart)
(English version by
Ruth and Thomas Martin)
New production

Staged by .... West
Designer ...... Wittstein (d)
Choreographer ...... Andrew
Conductor .... Rudel

Almaviva .... Chapman
Countess .... Jeffrey
Figaro .... Treigle
Susanna .... Brooks
Cherubino .... Wolff
Bartolo .... Wentworth
Marcellina .... Greenspon
Basilio .... Vellucci
Curzio .... Miller
Antonio .... Bittner
Barbarina .... Bergey

October 1

MADAMA BUTTERFLY

Same cast as September 25
except:

Pinkerton .... Molese
Sharpless .... Cossa

October 2 (m)

THE MERRY WIDOW (Lehár)
(Words by Adrian Ross)

Stage director ... Harrold (d)
Conductor .... Wilson

Sonia .... Schauler
Prince Danilo ...... D. Smith
Nish .... Worth
Baron Popoff .... Harrold
Natalie .... Elgar
De Jolidon .... Craig
Marquis de Cascada .... Beck
St. Brioche .... Krause
Admiral Khadja ... Ledbetter

Mme. Khadja .... Evans
General Novikovich .. Bittner
Mme. Novikovich ..... Povia
Clo-Clo .... Guile
Solo dancers .... Kovach;
                        Rabovsky

October 2

LA BOHÈME (Puccini)

Stage director .... Savoca (d)
Conductor .... Patané

Mimi .... Amedeo (d)
Musetta .... Bayard
Rodolfo .... Molese
Marcello .... Maffeo (d)
Schaunard .... Beck
Colline .... M. Smith
Benoit .... Wentworth
Alcindoro .... Bittner
Parpignol .... Miller
Guards .... Park, Yule

October 3 (m)

DIE FLEDERMAUS

Same cast as September 25 (m)
except:

Conductor .... Popper
Rosalinda .... Jeffrey
Sally .... Herbert

October 3

DON GIOVANNI
(English version by
Ruth and Thomas Martin)

Conductor .... Rudel

Don Giovanni .... Treigle
Leporello .... Beattie
Donna Elvira ..... Shane (d)
Commendatore ... M. Smith
Donna Anna .... Sills
Don Ottavio .... DuPree
Masetto .... Metcalf
Zerlina .... Brooks

October 7

IL BARBIERE DI SIVIGLIA
(Rossini)
New production

Staged by ...... Moresco (d)
Designer .... Evans (d)
Conductor .... Patané

Figaro .... Milnes
Almaviva .... Crain
Rosina ..... Christiansen (d),
                        (s, Elgar)
Bartolo .... Wentworth
Basilio .... Tyl (d)
Berta .... Greenspon
Fiorello .... Ledbetter
Officer .... Beck

October 8

FAUST

Same cast as September 26 (m)
except:

Valentin .... Mosley
Siébel .... Creed

October 9 (m)

THE SAINT OF BLEECKER STREET

Same cast as September 29

October 9

LA TRAVIATA (Verdi)

Stage director ..... Strasfogel
Conductor .... Coppola

Violetta .... Reale
Alfredo .... Craig
Germont .... Maffeo
Flora .... Kleinman
Annina .... Povia
Gaston .... Krause
Douphol .... Wentworth
D'Obigny .... Beck
Dr. Grenvil .... M. Smith
Giuseppe .... Park
Solo dancer .... Galan

October 10 (m)

CARMEN

Same cast as September 24
except:

Micaëla .... Bayard,
                        (s, Elgar)
Frasquita .... Precht
Remendado .... Miller

October 10

CAVALLERIA RUSTICANA
(Mascagni)

*Stage
director* ... Psacharopoulos
Conductor .... Patané

Santuzza .... George (d)
Mamma Lucia .... Greenspon
Alfio .... Chapman
Turiddu .... Molese
Lola .... Kleinman

Followed by:

I PAGLIACCI (Leoncavallo)

Stage director .... Renan
Conductor .... Patané

Canio .... Consiglio (d)
Nedda .... Amedeo
Tonio .... Milnes
Beppe .... Krause
Silvio .... Cossa
Peasants ...... Corder, Park

October 14

LES CONTES D'HOFFMANN
(Offenbach)
New production

Staged by ... Capobianco (d)
Scenic designer .... Nomikos
*Costume
designer* .... Maganini (d)
Choreographer ...... Andrew
Conductor .... Rudel

Hoffmann .... Molese
Lindorff .... Treigle
Andrès .... Keller

Nicklausse .... Kleinman
Luther .... Ledbetter
Nathanaël .... Miller
Hermann .... Beck
Olympia .... Sills
Coppélius .... Treigle
Spalanzani .... Bittner
Cochenille .... Kelley
Giulietta .... Sills
Dappertutto .... Treigle
Schlémil .... Ledbetter
Pittichinaccio .... Kelley
Antonia .... Sills
Dr. Miracle .... Treigle
Crespel .... Berberian
Mother .... George
Frantz .... Kelley

(Note: Loaned by the
Cincinnati Summer Opera
Association.)

October 15

THE MERRY WIDOW

Same cast as October 2 (m)
except:
Natalie .... Christiansen,
(s, Elgar)

October 16 (m)

THE MARRIAGE OF FIGARO

Same cast as September 30
except:
Conductor .... Popper

Almaviva .... Clatworthy
Countess .... Carson (d)
Basilio .... Krause
Antonio .... Yule
Barbarina .... Summers

October 16

CAVALLERIA RUSTICANA

Same cast as October 10
except:
Alfio .... Rayson (d)
Lola .... Guile

Followed by:

I PAGLIACCI

Same cast as October 10
except:
Canio .... Roden (d)
Nedda .... Grant (d)

October 17 (m)

LA BOHÈME

Same cast as October 2 except:

Mimi .... Di Gerlando
Musetta .... Bayard,
(s, Elgar)
Rodolfo .... Craig
Schaunard .... Ledbetter,
(s, Beck)

October 17

MADAMA BUTTERFLY

Same cast as September 25
except:
Butterfly .... Amedeo
Pinkerton ..... Domingo (d),
(s, Molese)
Sharpless .... Ledbetter
Goro .... Miller
Kate Pinkerton ...... August

October 20

THE FLAMING ANGEL

Same cast as September 22
except:
Jacob Glock ...... Castel (d)
Agrippa .... Theyard

October 21

CARMEN

Same cast as September 24
except:
Conductor .... Rudel,
(s, Coppola)

Don José .... Domingo
Zuniga .... M. Smith,
(s, Beattie)
Frasquita .... Precht
Remendado .... Miller
Dancairo .... Bittner

October 22

IL BARBIERE DI SIVIGLIA

Same cast as October 7 except:
Rosina .... Elgar

October 23 (m)

FAUST

Same cast as September 26 (m)
except:
Valentin .... Mosley
Marguerite .... Likova
Siébel .... Creed

October 23

DIE FLEDERMAUS

Same cast as September 25 (m)
except:
Conductor .... Popper

Alfred .... Citarelli
Adele .... Christiansen,
(s, Elgar)
Sally .... Guile

October 24 (m)

LA TRAVIATA

Same cast as October 9 except:
Annina .... August

October 24

THE MARRIAGE OF FIGARO

Same cast as September 30
except:
Countess .... Carson
Figaro .... Malas
Basilio .... Krause
Curzio .... Corder
Barbarina .... Summers

October 27

CAPRICCIO (R. Strauss)
First performance by The New
York City Opera Company
(English translation by
Maria Pelikan)

Staged by .... West
Scenic designer .... Bay
Costume designer .. Campbell
Choreographer ...... Andrew
Conductor ..Märzendorfer (d)

Countess .... Jeffrey
Count .... Trehy
Flamand .... Lloyd
Olivier .... Reardon
LaRoche ..... Hoekman (d)
Clairon .... Kova
M. Taupe .... Castel
Italian singers .... Faull;
Citarelli
Major-Domo ..... Berberian
Dancer ...... Balestracci (d)

October 28

THE FLAMING ANGEL

Same cast as September 22
except:
Jacob Glock .... Castel

October 29

DON GIOVANNI

Same cast as October 3 except:
Zerlina .... Bergey

October 30 (m)

LES CONTES D'HOFFMANN

Same cast as October 14

October 30

THE MERRY WIDOW

Same cast as October 2 (m)
except:
Conductor .... Ryan

Prince Danilo .... Metcalf
Solo dancers ..Hennessey (d),
(s, Kovach); Glassman
(d), (s, Rabovsky)

October 31 (m)

CAVALLERIA RUSTICANA

Same cast as October 10 except:

Conductor .... La Selva

Mamma Lucia .... Povia
Turiddu .... Craig

Followed by:

I PAGLIACCI

Conductor .... La Selva

Tonio .... Maffeo
Beppe .... Miller
Silvio .... Ledbetter

October 31

CARMEN

Same cast as September 24 except:

Don José .... Domingo
Escamillo .... Clatworthy,
(s, Treigle)
Micaëla .... Elgar
Frasquita .... Precht
Mercédès .... Guile
Morales .... Cossa

November 3

CAPRICCIO

Same cast as October 27

November 4

MISS JULIE (Rorem)
World premiere

Staged by .... Psacharopoulos
Scenic designer ... Armstrong
Costume designer .. Campbell
Lighting .... Armstrong
Choreographer ...... Andrew
Conductor .... Zeller (d)

Miss Julie .... Willauer
John .... Gramm
Christine .... Bonazzi (d)
Niels .... Krause
Wildcat boy .... Hepburn
Stableboy .... Yule
Young couple ..... Summers;
Castel

November 5

LA BOHÈME

Same cast as October 2 except:

Conductor .... La Selva

Musetta .... Elgar
Schaunard .... Ledbetter
Benoit .... Malas

November 6 (m)

IL BARBIERE DI SIVIGLIA

Same cast as October 7 except:

Conductor .... Coppola

Figaro .... Cossa
Almaviva .... Bullard (d)
Bartolo .... Malas

November 6

LES CONTES D'HOFFMANN

Same cast as October 14 except:

Hoffmann .... Molese,
(s, Craig)
Lindorff .... Beattie
Andrès .... Castel
Olympia .... Brooks
Coppélius .... Beattie
Cochenille .... Castel
Giulietta .... Likova,
(s, Willauer)
Dappertutto .... Milnes
Pittichinaccio .... Castel
Antonia .... Jeffrey
Dr. Miracle .... Beattie
Crespel .... M. Smith
Frantz .... Castel

November 7 (m)

DIE FLEDERMAUS

Same cast as September 25 (m) except:

Conductor .... Wilson

Rosalinda .... Bayard
Frank .... Malas
Sally .... Guile

November 7

LA TRAVIATA

Same cast as October 9 except:

Violetta .... Likova
Alfredo .... Molese
Germont .... Cossa
Annina .... August
Douphol .... Bittner
Dr. Grenvil .... Yule

November 10

MISS JULIE

Same cast as November 4

November 11

CAPRICCIO

Same cast as October 27 except:

Flamand .... Stamford
Major-Domo .... Beattie

November 12

MADAMA BUTTERFLY

Same cast as September 25 except:

Conductor .... Coppola

Butterfly .... Likova
Sharpless .... Ledbetter
Yamadori .... Castel
Imperial
Commissioner .. Henderson
Registrar .... Yule
Kate Pinkerton ...... August

November 13 (m)

LA BOHÈME

Same cast as October 2 except:

Conductor .... La Selva

Mimi .... Di Gerlando
Marcello .... Cossa
Benoit .... Malas

November 13

IL BARBIERE DI SIVIGLIA

Same cast as October 7 except:

Conductor .... Coppola

Almaviva .... DuPree
Rosina .... Elgar
Bartolo .... Malas

November 14 (m)

DON GIOVANNI

Same cast as October 3 except:

Don Ottavio .. Dembaugh (d)

November 14

THE MERRY WIDOW

Same cast as October 2 (m) except:

Conductor .... Ryan

Natalie .... Christiansen
Solo dancers ..... Hennessey,
(s, Kovach);
Glassman,
(s, Rabovsky)

(Note: This was the last performance by the company in the New York City Center. Mr. Rudel appeared on stage as an extra in the final scene, and at the end, led the company, orchestra, and audience in "Auld Lang Syne.")

Spring 1966 (FEBRUARY 22–MARCH 27)

Female artists
Anglin, Florence
August, Joan
Azova, Ludmilla*
Babbs, Donna*
Bible, Frances
Bonazzi, Elaine
Brooks, Patricia
Carron, Elisabeth
Casado, Providenzia*
Christensen, Catherine*
Crader, Jeannine
Creed, Kay
Darling, Sandra
Elgar, Anne
Evans, Beverly
Farmer, Elisabeth*
Faull, Ellen
Grant, Sylvia
Greene, Harriet
Greenspon, Muriel
Guile, Helen
Hepburn, Betsy
Herbert, Lila
Jeffrey, Donna
Kenting, Jodell
Kobart, Ruth
Mari, Dolores
Monette, LaVergne*
Morris, Janet*
Morris, Wendy
Neway, Patricia
Povia, Charlotte
Precht, Donna
Sachs, Evelyn
Schauler, Eileen
Shane, Rita
Sille, Beverly
Summers, Joan
Tanzy, Jeanne*
Turner, Claramae
West, Maria
Willauer, Marguerite
Wisnofsky, Anne Marie*
Wyckoff, Lou Ann
Young, Marie

Male artists
Armbruster, Richard
Beattie, Herbert
Bittner, Jack
Brooke, Tom*
Bullard, Gene
Carlo, Don
Cassel, Walter
Cassilly, Richard
Castel, Nico
Chapman, William
Citarelli, Enzo
Clatworthy, David
Clements, L. D.
Corder, Paul
Davis, Harris
De Lon, Jack
Dembaugh, William
Devlin, Michael*

* New artist

Domingo, Placido
DuPree, William
Erikson, Philip
Henderson, Don
Hindsley, Charles
Irving, George S.
Kelly, Robert Lee
Krause, Richard
Ledbetter, William
Lewis, William
Malas, Spiro
Martin, Barney*
Metcalf, William
Miller, Kellis
Milnes, Sherrill
Mosley, Robert
Papa, Bruce*
Park, Richard
Petrak, Rudolf
Pierson, Edward
Puleo, Robert*
Reardon, John
Riggs, Seth
Safina, Anthony
Smith, David
Smith, Malcolm
Stamford, John
Stern, Maurice
  (as Lampi, Mauro)
Thaw, David*
Trehy, Robert
Tyl, Noel
Ukena, Paul
Wolff, William*
Yule, Don

Conductors
Buckley, Emerson
La Selva, Vincent
Lombard, Alain*
Märzendorfer, Ernst
Popper, Felix
Rudel, Julius
Ryan, Dean
Wilson, Charles

Solo dancers
Balestracci, Sandra
de Lavallade, Carmen
Hinkson, Mary
Lee, Sondra

Douglas, Scott
Gelfer, Steven B.*
Peterson, Alan*
Tetley, Glen

Choreographers
Andrew, Thomas
Butler, John
Tone, Richard
Weidman, Charles

Directors
Butler, John
Capobianco, Tito
Corsaro, Frank
Machiz, Herbert

* New artist

Menotti, Gian Carlo
Psacharopoulos, Nikos
Rott, Adolf
Rudel, Julius
Strasfogel, Ian
Sylbert, Paul
West, Christopher

Designers
Aldredge, Theoni V.*
Armistead, Horace
Armstrong, Will Steven
Bay, Howard
Campbell, Patton
Conklin, John*
Dobujinsky, Mstislav
Lee, Ming Cho*
Morley, Ruth
Oenslager, Donald
Roth, Wolfgang
Sylbert, Paul
Zipprodt, Patricia

* New artist

February 22

DON RODRIGO (Ginastera)
North American premiere
(sung in Spanish)

Staged by .... Capobianco
Scenic designer ...... Lee (d)
Costume
  designer ..... Aldredge (d)
Conductor .... Rudel

Florinda .... Crader
Fortuna .... Creed
Don Rodrigo ...... Domingo
Don Julian ...... Clatworthy
Teudisclo .... Malas
Ladies in waiting .... Guile,
                  Monette (d)
Bishop .... M. Smith
Pages .... Castel, Pierson
1st Locksmith .... Miller,
                (s, F. D. Mayer)
2nd Locksmith .... Park
Messengers ... Miller, Pierson
Young messenger ..... Evans
Young boy .... Puleo (d)
Young girl ...... Casado (d)
Hermit .... Devlin (d)
Voice of Sleep .... Tyl

(Note: Fredrick D. Mayer,
scheduled for 1st Locksmith,
was not to sing with the
company this season.)

February 24

STREET SCENE (Weill)

Conductor .... Wilson

Abraham Kaplan ..... Castel
Greta Fiorentino .... Mari

Carl Olsen .... Irving
Emma Jones .... Kobart
Olga Olsen ...... Greenspon
Shirley Kaplan .... Anglin
Henry Davis .... Pierson
Willie Maurrant .... Papa (d)
Anna Maurrant .... Schauler
Sam Kaplan .... DuPree
Daniel Buchanan ... Clements
Frank Maurrant ... Chapman
George Jones .... Bittner
Steve Sankey .... Armbruster
Lippo Fiorentino .... De Lon
Jennie Hildebrand .. Hepburn
2nd Graduate .. J. Morris (d)
3rd Graduate .... Herbert
Mrs. Hildebrand ..... Evans
Charlie Hildebrand ... Brooke
    (d), (s, C. Martin)
Mary Hildebrand .. Tanzy (d)
Grace Davis ...... Babbs (d)
Rose Maurrant .... Elgar
Harry Easter .... Riggs
Mae Jones .... Lee
Dick McGann .. Peterson (d)
Vincent Jones .... Martin (d)
Dr. Wilson .... Carlo
Officer Murphy .... D. Smith
City Marshall .... Yule
Fred Cullen .... Corder
1st Nursemaid .... Povia
2nd Nursemaid ...... Young

(Note: Charles Martin,
scheduled for Charlie
Hildebrand, was not to sing
with the company this
season.)

February 25

STREET SCENE

Same cast as February 24

February 26

STREET SCENE

Same cast as February 24
except:

Rose
    Maurrant .. Christensen (d)

February 27 (m)

THE BALLAD OF BABY DOE
(Moore)

Stage director ..... Strasfogel
Costume designer .. Campbell
Conductor .... Buckley

An old silver miner ... Miller
Saloon bartender .... Yule
Horace Tabor .... Cassel
Sam .... Krause
Bushy .... De Lon
Barney .... Ledbetter
Jacob .... Bittner
Augusta .... Bible
Baby Doe .... Sills

Kate .... Kenting
Mag .... August
Samantha .... Greene
Hotel clerk .... Miller
Albert .... Kelly
Sarah .... Darling
Mary .... Precht
Emily .... Evans
Effie .... Povia
McCourt family .... Herbert,
            West, Safina, Yule
Mama McCourt .. Greenspon
Four Washington
    dandies .... Corder,
    Henderson, Miller, Park
Father Chapelle ..... Krause
Hotel footman ...... Bittner
Chester A. Arthur ... De Lon
Elizabeth and Silver
    Dollar ..... Wisnofsky (d),
        (s, Pretzat); W. Morris
Mayor of Leadville .... Davis
William
    Jennings Bryan ... M. Smith
Stage doorman .... Miller
Denver politician ..... Beattie
Silver Dollar
    (grown up) .... August

February 27

DON RODRIGO

Same cast as February 22

March 2

THE BALLAD OF BABY DOE

Same cast as February 27 (m)
except:

Horace Tabor ..... Chapman
Baby Doe .... Brooks
Silver Dollar .... Wisnofsky,
            (s, Pretzat)
William
    Jennings Bryan ..... Irving

March 3

DIALOGUES OF THE CARMELITES
(Poulenc)
First performance by The New
York City Opera Company
(English text by
Joseph Machlis)

Staged by .... Psacharopoulos
Scenic designer .. Conklin (d)
Costume designer .... Morley
Lighting designer .. Elson (d)
Conductor .... Lombard (d)

Marquis .... Ledbetter
Blanche .... Jeffrey
The Chevalier ..... Thaw (d)
Madame de Croissy,
    Prioress .... Turner
Madame Lidoine,
    the new Prioress ..... Faull
Mother Marie of the
    Incarnation ...... Willauer
Sister Constance of
    Saint-Denis .... Elgar
Mother Jeanne of the
    Child Jesus .... Evans

Sister Mathilde .... Guile
Convent Chaplin .. Dembaugh
1st Commissioner ..... Castel
2nd Commissioner .... Bittner
Officer .... Clements
Jailer .... Bittner,
            (s, Krause)
Thierry .... Miller
Doctor .... Henderson

March 4

OEDIPUS REX (Stravinsky)
(English narration by
e.e. cummings)

Conductor .... Rudel

Narrator .... D. Smith
Oedipus .... Cassilly
Creon .... Clatworthy
Tiresias .... M. Smith
Jocasta .... Bible
Messenger .... Ledbetter
Shepherd .... Krause

Followed by:

CARMINA BURANA (Orff)

Conductor .... Rudel

Soprano .... Brooks
Tenor .... DuPree
Baritone .... Reardon
Solo dancers ... de Lavallade,
    Hinkson; Douglas, Tetley

March 5

STREET SCENE

Same cast as February 24
except:

Anna Maurrant ...... Carron
Mrs. Hildebrand ...... Creed
1st Nursemaid .... August
2nd Nursemaid ...... Kenting

March 6 (m)

STREET SCENE

Same cast as February 24
except:

Mrs. Hildebrand ...... Creed
Rose Maurrant .. Christensen,
            (s, Elgar)
Vincent Jones .... Papa,
            (s, Martin)
1st Nursemaid .... August
2nd Nursemaid ...... Kenting

March 6

DIALOGUES OF THE CARMELITES

Same cast as March 3

March 9

DANTON'S DEATH (Von Einem)
American premiere
(English version by
Ruth and Thomas Martin)

Staged by .... Rott
Scenic designer .... Roth
Costume designer .... Morley
Conductor .... Märzendorfer

George Danton ..... Reardon
Camille Desmoulins .. DuPree

Hérault de Séchelles .. Krause
Robespierre .... Stern
St. Just .... M. Smith
Herman .... Ledbetter
Simon .... Beattie
A young man .... Castel
Executioners .. Miller, Pierson
Julie .... Creed
Lucille .... Grant
A woman .... Guile
Simon's wife ..... Greenspon

March 10

DON RODRIGO

Same cast as February 22

March 11

THE LOVE FOR THREE ORANGES
(Prokofiev)
(English translation by
Victor Seroff)

Stage director .... Rudel
Conductor .... Rudel

King .... Tyl
Prince .... Thaw
Princess Clarissa .. Greenspon
Leandro .... Beattie
Truffaldino .... Castel
Pantalone .... Metcalf
Celio .... Ukena
Fata Morgana .... Faull
Princess Linetta .... Creed
Princess Nicoletta .. Summers
Princess Ninetta .... Elgar
Cook .... Irving
Farfarello .... Gelfer (d)
Smeraldina .... Evans
Prologue .... Trehy

March 12 (m)

THE LOVE FOR THREE ORANGES

Same cast as March 11 except:

Leandro .... Devlin

March 12

THE BALLAD OF BABY DOE

Same cast as February 27 (m)
except:

Augusta .... Kobart
William
  Jennings Bryan ..... Irving
Denver politician .... Beattie,
                      (s, Yule)

March 13 (m)

DANTON'S DEATH

Same cast as March 9

March 13

OEDIPUS REX

Same cast as March 4 except:

Oedipus .... Stamford
Creon .... Pierson
Tiresias .... Wolff (d)

Followed by:

CARMINA BURANA

Same cast as March 4 except:

Soprano .... Elgar
Tenor .... Bullard
Baritone .... Metcalf

March 16

DIALOGUES OF THE CARMELITES

Same cast as March 3 except:

Blanche .... Elgar
Madame Lidoine, the
  new Prioress .... Shane
Sister Constance of
  Saint-Denis .... Brooks

March 17

THE CONSUL (Menotti)

Staged by .... Menotti
Conductor .... La Selva

John Sorel .... Milnes
Magda Sorel .... Neway
The Mother .... Sachs
Secret Police Agent ... Beattie
1st Plainclothesman .. Erikson
2nd Plainclothesman .... Park
Secretary .... Evans
Mr. Kofner .... D. Smith
The Foreign Woman .. Carron
Anna Gomez ..... Azova (d)
Vera Boronel .... Farmer (d)
The Magician
  Magadoff .... Bullard
Assan .... Bittner
Voice on the
  record ...... Mabel Mercer

March 18

KATERINA ISMAILOVA
(Shostakovich)
(English translation by
Julius Rudel)

Conductor .... Rudel

Katerina Ismailova .. Schauler
Boris Ismailov ..... Chapman
Zinovy Ismailov ..... Krause
Mill workman .... Ledbetter,
                      (s, Riggs)
Sergei .... Cassilly
Aksinya .... Darling
Coachman .... Davis
Village drunk .... Miller
Porter .... Bittner
Steward .... Park
A workman .... Kelly
Priest .... M. Smith
Police inspector .... D. Smith
Old convict .... Malas
Sentry .... Bittner
Sonyetka, a convict ... Creed,
                      (s, Evans)
Female convict ..... Wyckoff
Sergeant .... Ledbetter,
                      (s, Riggs)

March 19 (m)

STREET SCENE

Same cast as February 24
except:

Henry Davis .... Mosley
Anna Maurrant ...... Carron
Sam Kaplan .... Lewis
Mrs. Hildebrand ..... Creed
Rose Maurrant ... Christensen
1st Nursemaid .... August
2nd Nursemaid ...... Kenting

March 19

OEDIPUS REX

Same cast as March 4 except:

Messenger .... Metcalf
Shepherd .... Stern

Followed by:

CARMINA BURANA

Same cast as March 4 except:

Soprano .... Elgar

March 20 (m)

THE LOVE FOR THREE ORANGES

Same cast as March 11 except:

Conductor .... Ryan

Pantalone .... Ledbetter
Fata Morgana .... Faull,
                      (s, Shane)

March 20

THE CONSUL

Same cast as March 17

March 22

CAPRICCIO (R. Strauss)
(English translation by
Maria Pelikan)

Conductor ..... Märzendorfer

Countess .... Jeffrey
Count .... Trehy
Flamand .... Thaw
Olivier .... Reardon
LaRoche .... Malas
Clairon .... Bonazzi
M. Taupe .... Castel
Italian singers .... Faull;
                      Citarelli
Major-Domo .... Beattie
Dancer .... Balestracci

March 23

THE CONSUL

Same cast as March 17

March 24

KATERINA ISMAILOVA

Same cast as March 18 except:

Katerina .... Jeffrey
Sergei .... Stamford

March 25

DON RODRIGO

Same cast as February 22

March 26 (m)

OEDIPUS REX

Same cast as March 4 except:

Oedipus .... Petrak
Creon .... Pierson
Messenger .... Metcalf

Followed by:

CARMINA BURANA

Same cast as March 4 except:
Soprano .... Elgar
Baritone .... Metcalf

March 26

KATERINA ISMAILOVA

Same cast as March 18 except:

Boris Ismailov .... Ukena
Sergei .... Stamford
Old convict .... Devlin

March 27 (m)

DON RODRIGO

Same cast as February 22

March 27

THE LOVE FOR THREE ORANGES

Same cast as March 11 except:

Conductor .... Ryan
Prince .... Hindsley
Pantalone .... Ledbetter
Fata Morgana .... Shane

Fall 1966 (SEPTEMBER 27 – NOVEMBER 13)

Female artists
August, Joan
Bible, Frances
Blackham, Joyce*
Brooks, Patricia
Clements, Joy
Crader, Jeannine
Creed, Kay
Elgar, Anne
Evans, Beverly
Forrester, Maureen*
George, Edna Mae
Goodman, Margaret
Grant, Sylvia
Greenspon, Muriel
Jeffrey, Donna
Migenes, Julia
Monette, LaVergne
Neway, Patricia
Newton, Norma
Patenaude, Joan*
Povia, Charlotte
Sachs, Evelyn
Schauler, Eileen
Sena, Joan
Shane, Rita
Sills, Beverly
Summers, Joan
Tyler, Veronica
Willauer, Marguerite
Witkowska, Nadja
Wolff, Beverly
Wyckoff, Lou Ann

Male artists
Alexander, John
Beattie, Herbert
Beck, William
Bittner, Jack
Bullard, Gene
Cassel, Walter
Castel, Nico
Clatworthy, David
Cossa, Dominic
Dembaugh, William
Devlin, Michael
Domingo, Placido
DuPree, William
Erikson, Philip
Fair, Joseph*

* New artist

Fischer, Stuart*
Freeman, Carroll*
Gramm, Donald
Harrold, Jack
Henderson, Don
Hindsley, Charles
Lankston, John*
Ledbetter, William
Lishner, Leon
LoMonaco, Jerome
Malas, Spiro
Mangin, Noel*
Metcalf, William
Miller, Kellis
Milnes, Sherrill
Molese, Michele
Moore, Christopher*
Novoa, Salvador*
Park, Richard
Paul, Thomas
Pierson, Edward
Reardon, John
Rounseville, Robert
Schwartzman, Seymour*
Smith, David
Smith, Malcolm
Stamford, John
Trehy, Robert
Treigle, Norman
Tyl, Noel
Van Way, Nolan*
Yule, Don

Conductors
Guadagno, Anton*
Märzendorfer, Ernst
Patané, Franco
Popper, Felix
Rudel, Julius
Ryan, Dean
Wilson, Charles

Solo dancers
Galan, Rosario
Gelfer, Steven B.

Choreographers
Andrew, Thomas
Weidman, Charles

* New artist

Directors
Ball, William
Capobianco, Tito
Corsaro, Frank
de Blasis, James*
Freedman, Gerald*
Harnick, Jay*
Hider, Ruth M.*
Menotti, Gian Carlo
Montresor, Beni*
Rizzo, Francis
Rudel, Julius
Savoca, Carmen
Strasfogel, Ian
West, Christopher

Designers
Armistead, Horace
Campbell, Patton
Dobujinsky, Mstislav
Evans, Lloyd
Fletcher, Robert
Heymann, Henry
Lee, Ming Cho
Maganini, Margaretta
Montresor, Beni*
Nomikos, Andreas
Oenslager, Donald
Waring, James D.
Wittstein, Ed
Varona, José*

* New artist

September 27

GIULIO CESARE (Handel)
First performance by The New York City Opera Company

Staged by .... Capobianco
Scenic designer .... Lee
Costume
   designer ...... Varona (d)
Conductor .... Rudel

Giulio Cesare .... Treigle
Curio .... Beck
Achilla .... Cossa
Cornelia ...... Forrester (d)
Sextus .... Wolff
Cleopatra .... Sills
Nireno .... Devlin
Tolomeo .... Malas

September 29

CARMEN (Bizet)

Stage director .. de Blasis (d)
Conductor .... Patané

Carmen .... Wolff
Don José .... Domingo
Escamillo ..... Van Way (d)
Micaëla .... Jeffrey
Zuniga .... D. Smith
Frasquita .... Wyckoff
Mercédès .... Creed
Remendado .... Miller
Dancairo .... Beck
Morales .... Ledbetter
Solo dancer .... Galan

September 30

DON GIOVANNI (Mozart)
(English version by
Ruth and Thomas Martin)

Conductor .... Rudel

Don Giovanni .... Treigle
Leporello .... Gramm
Donna Elvira .... Newton
Commendatore .... M. Smith
Donna Anna .... Sills
Don Ottavio .... Domingo
Masetto .... Metcalf
Zerlina .... Brooks

October 1

LA BOHÈME (Puccini)
New production

Staged by .... Savoca
Designer .... Evans
Conductor .... Märzendorfer

Mimi .... Elgar
Musetta .... Schauler
Rodolfo .... Molese
Marcello .... Cossa
Schaunard .... Beck
Colline .... M. Smith
Benoit .... Yule
Alcindoro .... Bittner
Parpignol .... Miller
Guards .... Henderson, Park

October 2 (m)

THE LOVE FOR THREE ORANGES
(Prokofiev)
(English translation by
Victor Seroff)

Conductor .... Ryan

King .... Tyl
Prince .... Rounseville
Princess Clarissa .. Greenspon
Leandro .... Devlin
Pantalone .... Ledbetter
Truffaldino .... Harrold
Celio .... Trehy
Fata Morgana ..... Wyckoff
Princess Linetta .... Creed
Princess Nicoletta .. Summers
Princess Ninetta .... Elgar
Cook .... Beattie
Farfarello .... Gelfer

Smeraldina .... Evans
Prologue .... D. Smith

October 2

GIULIO CESARE

Same cast as September 27

October 4

CARMEN

Same cast as September 29

October 6

THE CONSUL (Menotti)

Staged by .... Menotti
Conductor .... Wilson

John Sorel .... Clatworthy
Magda Sorel .... Neway
The Mother .... Sachs
Secret Police Agent .. Lishner,
                        (s, Fair)
1st Plainclothesman .. Erikson
2nd Plainclothesman .... Park
Secretary .... Evans
Mr. Kofner .... D. Smith
The Foreign Woman..Migenes
Anna Gomez .... Monette
Vera Boronel .... Povia
*The Magician
Magadoff* .... Bullard
Assan .... Bittner
*Voice on the
record* ...... Mabel Mercer

October 7

THE ABDUCTION FROM
THE SERAGLIO (Mozart)
(English translation by
John Bloch)

Stage director ... Harnick (d)
Conductor .... Rudel

Constanza .... Sills
Blonde .... Elgar
Belmonte .... Alexander
Padrillo .... Lankston (d)
Osmin .... Beattie
Pasha Selim .... D. Smith

October 8

THE MARRIAGE OF FIGARO
(Mozart)
(English version by
Ruth and Thomas Martin)

Stage director ..... Hider (d)
Conductor .... Märzendorfer

Almaviva .... Reardon
Countess .... Newton
Figaro .... Malas
Susanna .... Clements
Cherubino .... Bible
Bartolo .... M. Smith
Marcellina .... Greenspon
Basilio .... Castel
Curzio .... Miller
Antonio .... Bittner
Barbarina .... Summers
Solo dancer .... Galan

October 9 (m)

THE LOVE FOR THREE ORANGES

Same cast as October 2 (m)
except:

Prince .... Hindsley,
                    (s, Rounseville)

October 9

TOSCA (Puccini)
New production

Staged by .... Capobianco
Designer .... Oenslager
Conductor .... Guadagno (d)

Tosca .... Crader
Cavaradossi .... Molese
Scarpia .... Milnes
Angelotti .... D. Smith
Spoletta .... Miller,
                      (s, Castel)
Sacristan .... Beattie
Sciarrone .... Beck
Shepherd .... Fischer (d)
Jailer .... Bittner

October 13

THE MAGIC FLUTE (Mozart)
First performance by The New
York City Opera Company
(English translation by
Ruth and Thomas Martin)

*Designed and
directed by* ..Montresor (d)
Lighting .... Sondheimer
Choreographer ...... Andrew
Conductor .... Rudel

Tamino .... Molese
1st Lady .... Jeffrey
2nd Lady .... Grant
3rd Lady .... Evans
Papageno .... Reardon
Queen of the Night ..... Sills
Monostatos .... Castel
Pamina .... Tyler
1st Spirit ...... Freeman (d)
2nd Spirit .... Fischer
3rd Spirit .... Moore (d)
Priest .... Lankston
Sarastro .... Mangin (d)
Speaker .... Paul
Papagena .... Summers
1st Armored man .. Stamford
2nd Armored man ... Pierson

October 14

CARMEN

Same cast as September 29
except:

Don José .... DuPree
Escamillo .... Clatworthy
Micaëla ...... Patenaude (d)
Frasquita .... Monette
Mercédès .... Evans

October 15 (m)

IL BARBIERE DI SIVIGLIA
(Rossini)

Stage director ..Freedman (d)
Conductor .... Patané

Figaro .... Milnes
Almaviva .... Bullard
Rosina .... Elgar
Bartolo .... Malas
Basilio .... Tyl
Berta .... Greenspon
Fiorello .... Ledbetter
Officer .... Pierson

(Note: Director Gerald
Freedman chose to have
himself listed as Leonard
Bergmann for this production.)

October 15

THE CONSUL

Same cast as October 6 except:
The Mother ...... Greenspon
Secret Police Agent .. Fair (d)

October 16 (m)

LA BOHÈME

Same cast as October 1

October 16

THE MARRIAGE OF FIGARO

Same cast as October 8

October 18

THE MAGIC FLUTE

Same cast as October 13

October 19

THE MARRIAGE OF FIGARO

Same cast as October 8 except:
Almaviva .... Clatworthy
Countess .... Jeffrey
Bartolo .... Fair
Basilio .... Miller,
(s, Castel)

October 20

DON GIOVANNI

Same cast as September 30
except:
Donna Anna .... Shane
Don Ottavio ...... Dembaugh
Masetto .... Metcalf
Zerlina .... Summers

October 21

TOSCA

Same cast as October 9 except:
Spoletta .... Castel

October 22

THE ABDUCTION FROM
THE SERAGLIO

Same cast as October 7

October 23 (m)

IL BARBIERE DI SIVIGLIA

Same cast as October 15
except:

Conductor .... Popper

Almaviva .... DuPree
Rosina .... Witkowska
Basilio .... M. Smith

October 23

LA TRAVIATA (Verdi)
New production

Staged by .... Corsaro
Scenic designer ..... Fletcher
Costume designer .. Campbell
Lighting .... Sondheimer
Choreographer ...... Andrew
Conductor .... Patané

Violetta .... Brooks
Alfredo .... Domingo
Germont .... Cossa
Flora .... Greenspon
Annina .... Creed
Gaston .... Castel
Douphol .... Beck
D'Obigny .... Ledbetter
Dr. Grenvil .... Pierson
Giuseppe .... Park
Messenger .... Yule
Solo dancer .... Galan

October 26

LA BOHÈME

Same cast as October 1 except:
Marcello .... Ledbetter

October 27

LA TRAVIATA

Same cast as October 23
except:
Alfredo .... LoMonaco
D'Obigny .... Devlin

October 28

LES CONTES D'HOFFMANN

Lighting .... Sondheimer
Conductor .... Rudel

Hoffmann .... Molese
Nicklausse .... Creed
Lindorff .... Treigle
Luther .... Ledbetter
Nathanaël .... Miller
Hermann .... Beck
Andrès .... Castel
Olympia .... Sills
Coppélius .... Treigle
Spalanzani .... Bittner

Cochenille .... Castel
Giulietta .... Sills
Dappertutto .... Treigle
Schlémil .... Ledbetter
Pittichinaccio .... Castel
Antonia .... Sills
Dr. Miracle .... Treigle
Crespel .... M. Smith
Mother .... George
Frantz .... Castel

October 29 (m)

THE LOVE FOR THREE ORANGES

Same cast as October 2 (m)
except:
Truffaldino .... Harrold
Celio .... Pierson
Fata Morgana .... Grant
Princess Nicoletta .. Goodman

October 29

TOSCA

Same cast as October 9 except:
Cavaradossi ..... Novoa (d)

October 30 (m)

THE MAGIC FLUTE

Same cast as October 13
except:
2nd Lady .... Monette
Pamina .... Tyler,
(s, Newton)
Speaker .... Devlin

October 30

CARMEN

Same cast as September 29
except:
Carmen ...... Blackham (d)
Micaëla .... Elgar
Frasquita .... Monette
Mercédès .... Evans

November 1

LA TRAVIATA

Same cast as October 23
except:
Alfredo .... LoMonaco
D'Obigny .... Devlin

November 2

DON GIOVANNI

Same cast as September 30
except:
Conductor .... Märzendorfer

Donna Anna .... Shane
Don Ottavio ...... Dembaugh
Masetto .... Beck
Zerlina .... Summers

November 3

TOSCA

Same cast as October 9 except:

Conductor .... Rudel
Tosca .... Willauer
Cavaradossi ...... Domingo
Scarpia .... Cassel
Spoletta .... Castel

November 4

THE MARRIAGE OF FIGARO

Same cast as October 8 except:

Almaviva .... Van Way
Countess .... Jeffrey
Bartolo .... Fair
Antonio .... Yule

November 5 (m)

THE LOVE FOR THREE ORANGES

Same cast as October 2 (m) except:

Prince .... Hindsley
Truffaldino .... Castel
Celio .... Trehy
Smeraldina .... Povia

November 5

CARMEN

Same cast as September 29 except:

Conductor .... Märzendorfer
Carmen .... Blackham
Escamillo .... Clatworthy
Micaëla .... Patenaude
Zuniga .... Devlin
Frasquita ...., Monette
Mercedes .... Evans

November 6 (m)

LES CONTES D'HOFFMANN

Same cast as October 28

November 6

LA BOHÈME

Same cast as October 1 except:

Mimi .... Sena
Musetta .... Grant
Rodolfo .... LoMonaco
Schaunard .... Ledbetter
Colline .... Malas

November 8

GIULIO CESARE

Same cast as September 27

November 9

LES CONTES D'HOFFMANN

Same cast as October 28 except:

Hoffmann .... Domingo
Lindorff .... Beattie
Olympia .... Brooks
Coppélius .... Beattie
Giulietta .... Willauer
Dappertutto ..... Clatworthy
Antonia ....,,, Jeffrey
Dr. Miracle .... Beattie

November 10

DON GIOVANNI

Same cast as September 30 except:

Conductor .... Märzendorfer
Don Giovanni ..... Van Way
Leporello .... Malas,
 (s, Gramm)
Donna Elvira .... Crader
Commendatore ...... Devlin
Don Ottavio ..... Dembaugh
Masetto .... Beck
Zerlina .... Summers

November 11

THE MAGIC FLUTE

Same cast as October 13 except:

2nd Lady .... Monette
Papageno .... D. Smith
Sarastro .... M. Smith

November 12 (m)

LA TRAVIATA

Same cast as October 23 except:

Conductor .... Märzendorfer
Germont .. Schwartzman (d)
Annina .... August
D'Obigny .... Ledbetter,
 (s, Devlin)

November 12

IL BARBIERE DI SIVIGLIA

Same cast as October 15 (m) except:

Conductor .... Popper
Figaro .... Cossa
Almaviva .... DuPree
Bartolo .... Beattie

November 13 (m)

LA BOHÈME

Same cast as October 1 except:

Conductor .... Guadagno
Mimi ....,,,,,.... Monette
Marcello .... Ledbetter

November 13

GIULIO CESARE

Same cast as September 27

Spring 1967 (FEBRUARY 9 – MARCH 26)

Female artists

August, Joan
Bayard, Carol
Bible, Frances
Blackham, Joyce
Brooks, Patricia
Carron, Elisabeth
Clements, Joy
Crader, Jeannine
Creed, Kay
De Forest, Anthea
Elgar, Anne
Evans, Beverly

Evans, Edith
Grant, Sylvia
Grümmer, Elisabeth*
Guile, Helen
Heimall, Linda*
Herbert, Lila
Jeffrey, Donna
Kenting, Jodell
Lampropulos, Athena*
Monette, LaVergne
Owen, Donna
Owen, Hanna

Patenaude, Joan
Povia, Charlotte
Roberto, Francesca*
Sachs, Evelyn
Schauler, Eileen
Schuh, Audrey*
Sills, Beverly
Smith, Karen
Summers, Joan
Tourangeau, Huguette*
Turner, Claramae
Vergara, Mercedes*

* New artist   * New artist   * New artist

West, Maria
Willauer, Marguerite
Witkowska, Nadja
Wyckoff, Lou Ann

Male artists
Beck, William
Bentley, Ronald
Berberian, Ara
Bittner, Jack
Castel, Nico
Clatworthy, David
Cossa, Dominic
Davis, Harris
Devlin, Michael
Domingo, Placido
Fischer, Stuart
Hale, Robert*
Hecht, Joshua
Henderson, Don
Hindsley, Charles
Lankston, John
Ledbetter, William
LoMonaco, Jerome
Ludgin, Chester
McCollum, John
Malas, Spiro
Martí, Bernabé*
Miller, Kellis
Molese, Michele
Myers, Raymond*
Novoa, Salvador
Offley, Ronald*
Olsen, Alan
Park, Richard
Pease, James
Pierson, Edward
Porretta, Frank
Puleo, Robert
Rayson, Benjamin
Romaguera, Joaquin
Schwartzman, Seymour
Schnapka, Georg*
Smith, David
Smith, Malcolm
Treigle, Norman
Vellucci, Luigi
Yule, Don

Conductors
Effron, David*
Foss, Lucas*
Guadagno, Anton
Patané, Franco
Popper, Felix
Rudel, Julius
Ryan, Dean
Shaynen, Lee
Weisgall, Hugo*

Solo dancer
Alba, Maria

Choreographer
Andrew, Thomas

Directors
Capobianco, Tito
Corsaro, Frank
de Blasis, James
Erhardt, Otto
Harnick, Jay
Savoca, Carmen
West, Christopher

* New artist

Designers
Aldredge, Theoni V.
Campbell, Patton
Evans, Lloyd
Fletcher, Robert
Heymann, Henry
Lee, Ming Cho
Oenslager, Donald
Ter-Arutunian, Rouben
Varona, José
Waring, James D.
Wittstein, Ed

* New artist

February 9

DON RODRIGO (Ginastera)

Lighting .... Sondheimer
Conductor .... Rudel

Florinda .... Crader
Fortuna .... Creed
Don Rodrigo ...... Domingo
Don Julian ...... Clatworthy
Teudiselo .... Malas
Ladies in waiting ...... Guile,
                        Monette
Bishop .... M. Smith
Pages .... Castel, Beck
1st Locksmith .... Miller
2nd Locksmith .... Park
Messengers ..... Miller, Beck
Young messenger .. B. Evans
Young boy .... Puleo
Young girl .... K. Smith
Hermit .... Devlin
Voice of Sleep .... M. Smith

February 10

LA BOHÈME (Puccini)

Lighting .... Sondheimer
Conductor .... Patané

Rodolfo .... Molese
Mimi .... Schuh (d)
Marcello .... Cossa
Schaunard .... Ledbetter
Musetta .... Grant,
                      (s, Bayard)
Benoit .... Yule
Alcindoro .... Bittner
Colline .... M. Smith
Parpignol .... Miller
Guards .... Henderson, Park

February 11 (m)

THE ABDUCTION FROM
THE SERAGLIO (Mozart)
(English version by
Ruth and Thomas Martin)

Lighting .... Sondheimer
Conductor .... Rudel

Pasha Selim .... D. Smith
Constanza .... Sills
Blonde .... Elgar
Belmonte .... McCollum
Pedrillo .... Lankston
Osmin .... Berberian

February 11

THE MARRIAGE OF FIGARO
(Mozart)
(English version by
Ruth and Thomas Martin)

Lighting .... Sondheimer
Conductor .... Foss (d)

Figaro .... Malas
Susanna .... Clements
Bartolo .... M. Smith
Marcellina .... B. Evans
Cherubino .... Bible
Almaviva .... Clatworthy
Basilio .... Castel
Countess .... Jeffrey
Antonio .... Bittner
Curzio .... Miller
Barbarina .... Summers

February 12 (m)

CARMEN (Bizet)

Conductor .... Guadagno

Carmen .... Blackham
Don José .... Novoa
Escamillo .... Treigle
Micaëla .... Elgar
Zuniga .... D. Smith
Frasquita .... Monette
Mercédès .... Creed
Remendado .... Miller
Dancairo .... Beck
Morales .... Ledbetter
Solo dancer .... Alba

February 12

DON RODRIGO

Same cast as February 9
except:

Don Julian .... Pierson

February 15

TOSCA (Puccini)

Conductor .... Guadagno

Tosca .... Crader
Cavaradossi .... Molese
Scarpia .... Ludgin
Angelotti .... D. Smith
Spoletta .... Castel
Sacristan .... Bittner
Sciarrone .... Beck
Shepherd .... Fischer
Jailer .... Yule

February 16

LA TRAVIATA (Verdi)

Conductor .... Patané

Violetta .... Witkowska,
                  (s, Brooks)
Alfredo .... Domingo
Germont .... Cossa
Flora .... Povia
Annina .... Creed
Gaston .... Lankston
Douphol .... Beck
D'Obigny .... Devlin

Dr. Grenvil .... Pierson
Giuseppe .... Park
Messenger .... Olsen
Solo dancer .... Alba

February 17

DER ROSENKAVALIER
(R. Strauss)
New production

Staged by .... Erhardt
Scenic designer .... Oenslager
Costume designer .... Varona
Conductor .... Rudel

Marschallin ... Grümmer (d)
Baron Ochs ... Schnapka (d),
(s, Pease)
Octavian .... Bible
Faninal .... Clatworthy
Sophie .... Elgar
Marianne .... Wyckoff
Valzacchi .... Vellucci
Annina .... E. Evans
Police
Commissioner ... D. Smith
Major-domo of
the Marschallin ..... Davis
Major-domo of
Faninal .... Romaguera
Leopold .... Yule
Notary .... Bittner
Innkeeper .... Lankston
Singer .... Molese
Milliner .... Summers
Animal vendor .... Miller
1st Orphan .... Monette
2nd Orphan .... Kenting
3rd Orphan .... Creed
Mohamet .... Offley (d)

February 18 (m)

THE MARRIAGE OF FIGARO

Same cast as February 11
except:

Almaviva .... Ludgin

February 18

LA BOHÈME

Same cast as February 10
except:

Musetta .... Bayard

February 19 (m)

THE ABDUCTION FROM
THE SERAGLIO

Same cast as February 11 (m)

February 19

CARMEN

Same cast as February 12 (m)
except:

Don José .... Domingo
Escamillo .... Clatworthy
Micaëla .... Patenaude

February 22

DER ROSENKAVALIER

Same cast as February 17
except:

Singer .... LoMonaco

February 23

IL TRITTICO (Puccini)

Conductor .... Patané

IL TABARRO

Michele .... Ludgin
Luigi .... Martí (d)
Tinca .... Castel
Talpa .... M. Smith
Giorgetta .... Crader
Frugola .... B. Evans,
(s, Turner)
Song vendor .... Miller
Two lovers .... Lankston,
Summers

Followed by:

GIANNI SCHICCHI

Gianni Schicchi ...... Treigle
Lauretta .... Elgar
Zita .... B. Evans,
(s, Turner)
Rinuccio .... LoMonaco
Gherardo .... Castel
Nella .... Monette
Gherardino .... Puleo
Betto .... D. Smith
Simone .... M. Smith
Marco .... Ledbetter
La Ciesca .... Wyckoff
Spinellocchio .... Devlin
Nicolao .... Bittner
Pinellino .... Park
Guccio .... Henderson

Followed by:

SUOR ANGELICA

Suor Angelica .... Carron
La Principessa .... Sachs,
(s, Turner)
La Badessa .... Povia
La Suora Zelatrice .. B. Evans
La Maestra
della Novizie .... Creed
Suor Genovieffa .... Summers
Le due novizie ..... H. Owen,
De Forest
Le due converse .... Monette,
August
Suor Dolcina ...... D. Owen
La Cercatrice .... Wyckoff

February 24

LA TRAVIATA

Same cast as February 16
except:

Violetta .... Brooks
Alfredo .... Molese
Annina .... August

February 25 (m)

CARMEN

Same cast as February 12 (m)
except:

Conductor .... Shaynen

Escamillo .... Clatworthy
Micaëla .... Patenaude
Zuniga .... Devlin
Frasquita .... Wyckoff
Mercédès .... B. Evans
Remendado .... Castel
Dancairo .... Pierson

February 25

TOSCA

Same cast as February 15
except:

Cavaradossi .... Martí

February 26 (m)

THE MARRIAGE OF FIGARO

Same cast as February 11
except:

Conductor .... Shaynen

Susanna .... Summers
Marcellina .... Povia
Cherubino .... Creed
Antonio .... Yule
Barbarina .... Monette

February 26

LA BOHÈME

Same cast as February 10
except:

Mimi .... Elgar
Musetta .... Bayard
Colline .... Hale (d)

February 28

DER ROSENKAVALIER

Same cast as February 17

March 2

CARMEN

Same cast as February 12 (m)
except:

Conductor .... Shaynen

Carmen ..... Tourangeau (d)
Don José .... Molese
Escamillo .... Clatworthy
Micaëla .... Patenaude
Zuniga .... Devlin
Mercédès .... B. Evans

March 3

THE ABDUCTION FROM
THE SERAGLIO

Same cast as February 11 (m)
except:

Constanza .... Witkowska

March 4 (m)

Tosca

Same cast as February 15 except:

Conductor .... Popper
Cavaradossi .... Martí
Scarpia .... Hecht

March 4

La Traviata

Same cast as February 16 except:

Violetta .... Brooks
Alfredo .... Hindsley
Germont ...... Schwartzman
Douphol .... Bittner

March 5 (m)

La Bohème

Same cast as February 10 except:

Conductor .... Guadagno
Mimi .... Elgar
Marcello .... Ledbetter
Schaunard .... Beck

March 5

Madama Butterfly (Puccini)
New production

Staged by .... Corsaro
Designer .... Evans
Lighting .... Sondheimer
Conductor .... Patané

Butterfly .... Roberto (d)
Suzuki .... Creed
Pinkerton .... Domingo
Sharpless ...... Schwartzman
Goro .... Castel
Yamadori .... Lankston
The Bonze .... M. Smith
Imperial
  Commissioner .... Park
Registrar .... Henderson
Kate Pinkerton ...... August
Trouble .... Puleo

March 8

Il Trittico*

Same casts as February 23 except:

Il Tabarro

Michele .... Schwartzman
Luigi .... Domingo
Giorgetta .... Sills

Followed by:

Suor Angelica

Suor Angelica .... Sills
La Principessa .... Bible
Le due converse ..Heimall (d),
                  (for Monette),
                        August
La Cercatrice .... West

  * Order of operas changed
here and for the rest of the season

Followed by:

Gianni Schicchi

Lauretta .... Sills
Rinuccio .... Novoa
Nella .... Heimall (d)
Pinellino .... Yule,
                      (s, Park)

March 9

The Servant of
Two Masters (Giannini)
World premiere

Directed by ..... Capobianco
Designer .... Fletcher
Lighting .... Sondheimer
Conductor .... Rudel

Pantalone .... Devlin
Clarissa .... Jeffrey
Lombardi .... D. Smith
Silvio .... Hindsley
Beatrice .... Schauler
Florindo .... Porretta
Brighella .... Castel
Smeraldina .... Brooks
Truffaldino .... Myers (d)

March 10

The Marriage of Figaro

Same cast as February 11 except:

Figaro .... Treigle
Marcellina .... Povia
Countess .... Bayard

March 11 (m)

La Traviata

Same cast as February 16 except:

Germont ...... Schwartzman
Annina .... August
Giuseppe .... Henderson,
                     (s, Park)

March 11

Madama Butterfly

Same cast as March 5 except:

Pinkerton .... Porretta
Sharpless .... Ledbetter
Imperial
  Commissioner .. Henderson,
                     (s, Park)
Registrar .... Bentley,
                  (s, Henderson)

March 12 (m)

Don Rodrigo

Same cast as February 9 except:

Don Julian .... Pierson
2nd Locksmith ..... Devlin,
                      (s, Yule)

March 12

Der Rosenkavalier

Same cast as February 17 except:

Baron Ochs .... Pease
Sophie .... Brooks
Singer .... Novoa
1st Orphan .... Herbert
2nd Orphan ...... De Forest
3rd Orphan .... August

March 14

Madama Butterfly

Same cast as March 5 except:

Butterfly .... Schuh
Suzuki .... Creed,
                  (s, Vergara)
Pinkerton .... Porretta
Imperial
  Commissioner .. Henderson,
                      (s, Yule)
Registrar .... Bentley,
                  (s, Henderson)

March 15

Don Rodrigo

Same cast as February 9 except:

Don Julian ...... Clatworthy,
                   (s, Pierson)
2nd Locksmith .... Yule

March 16

Tosca

Same cast as February 15 except:

Tosca .... Schauler
Cavaradossi .... Novoa
Angelotti .... Pierson
Spoletta .... Miller

March 17

Il Trittico

Same casts as February 23 except:

Il Tabarro

Frugola .... Turner

Followed by:

Suor Angelica

Suor Angelica .... Schuh
La Principessa .... Turner

Followed by:

Gianni Schicchi

Zita .... Turner
Pinellino .... Yule,
                      (s, Park)

March 18 (m)

Madama Butterfly

Same cast as March 5 except:

Conductor .... Ryan

Suzuki .... B. Evans
Sharpless .... Ledbetter

Imperial
   Commissioner ...... Yule,
                              (s, Park)
Kate Pinkerton .... West

March 18

CARMEN

Same cast as February 12 (m)
except:

Conductor .... Shaynen
Carmen .... Tourangeau
Escamillo .... D. Smith
Micaëla .... Patenaude
Zuniga .... Devlin

March 19 (m)

DER ROSENKAVALIER

Same cast as February 17
except:

Baron Ochs .... Pease
Singer .... LoMonaco

March 19

THE SERVANT OF
TWO MASTERS

Same cast as March 9

March 21

THE SERVANT OF
TWO MASTERS

Same cast as March 9

March 22

LA TRAVIATA

Same cast as February 16
except:

Conductor ...... Weisgall (d)
Violetta .... Brooks
Germont ...... Schwartzman
Douphol .... Bittner
Giuseppe .... Henderson.
                              (s, Park)

March 23

MADAMA BUTTERFLY

Same cast as March 5 except:

Conductor .... Ryan
Pinkerton .... Molese
Sharpless .... Beck
Imperial
   Commissioner .... Yule
Kate Pinkerton ...... August,
                              (s, West)

March 24

DER ROSENKAVALIER

Same cast as February 17
except:

Octavian .... Willauer
Singer .... Martí

March 25 (m)

CARMEN

Same cast as February 12 (m)
except:

Conductor .... Shaynen
Carmen .... Tourangeau
Don José .... Molese
Escamillo .... Myers
Micaëla .... Patenaude
Zuniga .... Devlin
Frasquita .... Wyckoff
Mercédès .... B. Evans
Dancairo .... Pierson

March 25

LA BOHÈME

Same cast as February 10
except:

Conductor .... Popper
Rodolfo .... Domingo
Mimi .... Elgar

Marcello .... Rayson
Schaunard .... Beck
Musetta .... Bayard
Colline .... Malas

March 26 (m)

IL TRITTICO

Same casts as February 23
except:

Conductor .... Rudel,
                              (s, Patané)

IL TABARRO

Giorgetta .. Lampropulos (d)
Frugola .... Turner

Followed by:

SUOR ANGELICA

Suor Angelica .... Schuh
La Principessa .... Turner
La Badessa ..... Vergara (d)
Suor Genovieffa .. Patenaude

Followed by:

GIANNI SCHICCHI

Lauretta .... Summer
Zita .... Turner
Rinuccio .... Porretta
Pinellino .... Park,
                              (s, Yule)

March 26

LA TRAVIATA

Same cast as February 16
except:

Conductor .... Effron (d),
                              (s, Weisgall)
Violetta .... Brooks
Germont ...... Schwartzman
Giuseppe .... Park,
                              (s, Henderson)

Fall 1967 (SEPTEMBER 14 – NOVEMBER 12)

Female artists
Anderson, Rachel*
Anthony, Judith*
August, Joan
Bayard, Carol
Bible, Frances
Brooks, Patricia
Crader, Jeannine
Creed, Kay
De Forest, Anthea
Elgar, Anne
Evans, Beverly
Evans, Edith
Faull, Ellen
Greenspon, Muriel

Grümmer, Elisabeth
Heimall, Linda
Herbert, Lila
Jeffrey, Donna
Joanisse, Lisa*
Kenting, Jodell
Lampropulos, Athena
Lewis, Brenda
Monette, LeVergne
Niska, Maralin*
Papadaki, Zoe*
Patenaude, Joan
Povia, Charlotte
Roberto, Francesca
Schauler, Eileen

Shane, Rita
Sills, Beverly
Summers, Joan
Tourangeau, Huguette
Tyler, Veronica
Venora, Lee
West, Maria
Willauer, Marguerite
Witkowska, Nadja
Wolff, Beverly
Wyckoff, Lou Ann

Male artists
Ahearn, Michael*
Bardini, Gaetano*

* New artist

* New artist

* New artist

Beck, William
Bittner, Jack
Castel, Nico
Clatworthy, David
Cossa, Dominic
Davis, Harris
Devlin, Michael
Di Giuseppe, Enrico
Domingo, Placido
Fischer, Stuart
Fredricks, Richard
Hale, Robert
Henderson, Don
Lankston, John
Ledbetter, William
Lee, Christopher*
LoMonaco, Jerome
Malas, Spiro
Malone, Patrick*
Marsh, Calvin*
Martí, Bernabé
Metcalf, William
Miller, Kellis
Molese, Michele
Novoa, Salvador
Paige, Norman*
Park, Richard
Pierson, Edward
Rayson, Benjamin
Roma, Romano*
Romaguera, Joaquin
Schnapka, Georg
Schwartzman, Seymour
Slayton, Stephen*
Smith, David
Smith, Malcolm
Stewart, John*
Treigle, Norman
Tyl, Noel
Vellucci, Luigi
Yule, Don

Conductors
Alessandro, Victor*
Buckley, Emerson
Effron, David
Flagello, Nicholas*
Patané, Franco
Rudel, Julius
Ryan, Dean
Wilson, Charles

Solo dancers
Galan, Esperanza*
Galan, Rosario

Choreographer
Andrew, Thomas

Directors
Bamberger, David*
Capobianco, Tito
Corsaro, Frank
de Blasis, James
Erhardt, Otto
Montresor, Beni
Psacharopoulos, Nikos
Savoca, Carmen
West, Christopher
Zorina, Vera*

Designers
Campbell, Patton
Evans, Lloyd

* New artist

Fletcher, Robert
Heymann, Henry
Lee, Ming Cho
Montresor, Beni
Oenslager, Donald
Varona, José
Waring, James D.
Wexler, Peter
Wittstein, Ed

* New artist

September 14

THE MAGIC FLUTE (Mozart)
(English version by
Ruth and Thomas Martin)

Stage director . . Bamberger (d)
Conductor . . . . Rudel

Sarastro . . . . Schnapka
Tamino . . . . Molese
1st Lady . . . . Jeffrey
2nd Lady . . . . Monette
3rd Lady . . . . B. Evans
Speaker . . . . Hale
1st Priest . . . . Lankston
Queen of the Night . . . . . Sills
Pamina . . . . Tyler
1st Spirit . . . . Ahearn (d),
                    (s, Malone)
2nd Spirit . . . . Slayton (d)
3rd Spirit . . . . Fischer
Papageno . . . . Metcalf
Papagena . . . . Heimall
Monostatos . . . . Castel
*1st Armored
  man* . . . . Stewart (d)
*2nd Armored
  man* . . . . Pierson

September 15

LA TRAVIATA (Verdi)

Conductor . . . . Patané

Violetta . . . . Brooks
Alfredo . . . . Domingo
Germont . . . . Cossa
Flora . . . . B. Evans
Annina . . . . Creed
Gaston . . . . Lankston
Douphol . . . . Beck
D'Obigny . . . . Devlin
Dr. Grenvil . . . . Yule
Solo dancer . . . . E. Galan (d)
Messenger . . . . Park
Giuseppe . . . . Romaguera

September 16 (m)

CARMEN (Bizet)

Conductor . . . . Buckley

Carmen . . . . Tourangeau
Don José . . . . Martí
Escamillo . . . . Fredricks
Micaëla . . . . Patenaude
Zuniga . . . . D. Smith
Frasquita . . . . Monette
Mercédès . . . . Creed
Remendado . . . . Miller
Dancairo . . . . Beck
Morales . . . . Pierson
Solo dancer . . . . E. Galan

September 16

THE MARRIAGE OF FIGARO
(Mozart)
(English version by
Ruth and Thomas Martin)

Conductor . . . . Wilson

Figaro . . . . Treigle
Susanna . . . . Elgar
Marcellina . . . . Povia
Bartolo . . . . M. Smith
Cherubino . . . . Bible
Almaviva . . . . Clatworthy
Basilio . . . . Castel
Countess . . . . Niska (d)
Antonio . . . . Bittner
Curzio . . . . Miller
Barbarina . . . . Monette
Solo dancer . . . . E. Galan

September 17 (m)

THE MAGIC FLUTE

Same cast as September 14
except:

Queen of the Night . . . . Shane

September 17

LA TRAVIATA

Same cast as September 15

September 21

LE COQ D'OR
(Rimsky-Korsakov)
First performance by The New
York City Opera Company
(English version by Antal
Dorati and James Gibson)

Directed by . . . . . Capobianco
Scenic designer . . . . Lee
Costume designer . . . . Varona
Lighting . . . . Sondheimer
Conductor . . . . Rudel

King Dodon . . . . Treigle
Prince Guidon . . . . Castel
Prince Afron . . . . . . D. Smith
General Polkan . . . . Tyl
Amelfa . . . . Greenspon
Astrologer . . . . . . Di Giuseppe
Queen of Shemakha . . . . . Sills
Golden Cockerel . . . Summers

September 22

CARMEN

Same cast as September 16 (m)
except:

Zuniga . . . . Devlin

September 23 (m)

THE MAGIC FLUTE

Same cast as September 14
except:

Queen of the Night . . . . Shane
1st Spirit . . . . Malone (d)

Papageno .... D. Smith
Papagena .... Summers

September 23

IL BARBIERE DI SIVIGLIA
(Rossini)

Directed by .... de Blasis
Lighting .... Sondheimer
Conductor ... Allesandro (d)

Almaviva ...... Di Giuseppe
Bartolo .... Malas
Rosina .... Elgar
Basilio .... Tyl
Berta .... Povia
Figaro .... Cossa
Fiorello .... Ledbetter
Officer .... Pierson

September 24 (m)

LA TRAVIATA

Same cast as September 15
except:

Germont ...... Schwartzman
Annina .... August

September 24

LE COQ D'OR

Same cast as September 21

September 27

LA BOHÈME (Puccini)

Conductor .... Patané

Rodolfo .... LoMonaco
Mimi .... Elgar
Marcello .... Fredricks
Schaunard .... Ledbetter
Musetta .... Bayard
Benoit .... Yule
Alcindoro .... Bittner
Colline .... M. Smith
Parpignol .... Miller
Guards ..... Park, Henderson

September 28

CAVALLERIA RUSTICANA
(Mascagni)
New production

Directed by ...... Zorina (d)
Designer .... Evans
Lighting .... Sondheimer
Conductor .... Buckley

Santuzza ...... Papadaki (d)
Turiddu .... Molese
Alfio .... Clatworthy
Lola .... Creed
Mamma Lucia .... Povia

Followed by:

I PAGLIACCI (Leoncavallo)
New production

Directed by ...... Zorina (d)
Designer .... Evans
Lighting .... Sondheimer
Conductor .... Buckley

Nedda .... Brooks
Canio .... Domingo

Tonio .... Marsh (d)
Silvio .... Cossa
Beppe .... Paige (d)
Two villagers .... Romaguera,
Park

September 29

THE MARRIAGE OF FIGARO

Same cast as September 16
except:

Figaro .... Malas

September 30 (m)

MADAMA BUTTERFLY (Puccini)

Conductor .... Patané

Butterfly .... Venora
Suzuki .... Creed
Pinkerton .... Domingo
Sharpless ...... Schwartzman
Goro .... Castel
Yamadori .... Lankston
The Bonze .... Pierson
Imperial
Commissioner .... Park
Registrar .... Henderson
Kate Pinkerton ...... August
Trouble .... Lee (d)

September 30

CARMEN

Same cast as September 16 (m)
except:

Don José .... Novoa
Escamillo .... Hale
Micaëla ...., Joanisse (d)
Mercédès .... B. Evans

October 1 (m)

LE COQ D'OR

Same cast as September 21

October 1

CAVALLERIA RUSTICANA

Same cast as September 28
except:

Alfio .... Rayson,
(s, Clatworthy)

Followed by:

I PAGLIACCI

Same cast as September 28

October 3

CAVALLERIA RUSTICANA

Same cast as September 28
except:

Santuzza ...... Lampropulos
Turiddu .... Bardini (d)
Alfio .... Rayson
Lola .... Monette

Followed by:

I PAGLIACCI

Same cast as September 28
except:

Canio .... Martí
Silvio .... Ledbetter

October 4

THE MAGIC FLUTE

Same cast as September 14
except:

Sarastro .... M. Smith
Tamino .... Di Giuseppe
1st Lady .... Bayard
3rd Lady .... Creed
Speaker .... Malas
Queen of the Night ... Shane,
(s, Sills)
Pamina .... Elgar
1st Spirit .... Malone
Papageno .... D. Smith
Papagena .... Summers
Monostatos .... Miller

October 5

TOSCA (Puccini)

Conductor .... Buckley

Tosca .... Crader
Cavaradossi .... Domingo
Scarpia .... Fredricks,
(s, Roma)
Angelotti .... D. Smith
Spoletta .... Castel
Sacristan .... Bittner
Sciarrone .... Beck
Shepherd ....:..... Fischer
Jailer .... Yule

October 6

DER ROSENKAVALIER
(R. Strauss)

Stage director .... Bamberger
Conductor .... Rudel

Marschallin .... Schauler
Baron Ochs .... Schnapka
Octavian .... Bible
Faninal .... Clatworthy
Sophie .... Brooks
Marianne .... Wyckoff
Valzacchi .... Vellucci
Annina .... E. Evans
Police Commissioner ... Hale
Major-Domo of
the Marschallin ..... Davis
Major-Domo of
Faninal .... Romaguera
Leopold .... Yule
Attorney .... Bittner
Innkeeper .... Lankston
Singer .... Martí
Milliner .... Summers
Animal vendor .... Miller
1st Orphan .... Monette
2nd Orphan ...... Kenting
3rd Orphan .... Creed
Mohamet ..... Anderson (d)

October 7 (m)

LE COQ D'OR

Same cast as September 21

October 7

MADAMA BUTTERFLY

Same cast as September 30 (m)
except:

Sharpless .... Cossa
Kate Pinkerton .... West

October 8 (m)

CARMEN

Same cast as September 16 (m)
except:

Carmen .... Papadaki
Don José .... Molese
Escamillo .... Clatworthy
Micaëla .... Joanisse
Zuniga .... Devlin
Frasquita ...... Anthony (d)
Mercédès .... B. Evans

October 8

LA TRAVIATA

Same cast as September 15
except:

Alfredo .... LoMonaco
Germont ...... Schwartzman
Annina .... August
Gaston .... Castel
Douphol .... Bittner

October 11

CARMEN

Same cast as September 16 (m)
except:

Don José .... Molese
Escamillo .... Clatworthy
Zuniga .... Devlin
Frasquita .... Anthony
Mercédès .... B. Evans

October 12

GIULIO CESARE (Handel)

Conductor .... Rudel

Giulio Cesare .... Treigle
Curio .... Beck
Cornelia .... Bible
Sesto .... Wolff
Cleopatra .... Sills
Tolomeo .... Malas
Achilla .... Cossa
Nireno .... Devlin

October 13

LA BOHÈME

Same cast as September 27
except:

Rodolfo .... Domingo
Mimi .... Roberto
Marcello .... Ledbetter
Schaunard .... Beck

October 14 (m)

GIULIO CESARE

Same cast as October 12

October 14

DER ROSENKAVALIER

Same cast as October 6 except:

Octavian .... Willauer
Sophie .... Elgar
Singer .... LoMonaco

October 15 (m)

CAVALLERIA RUSTICANA

Same cast as September 28
except:

Conductor ...... Flagello (d)

Santuzza ...... Lampropulos
Alfio .... Fredricks
Lola .... Monette

Followed by:

I PAGLIACCI

Same cast as September 28
except:

Conductor ...... Flagello (d)

Nedda .... Bayard
Canio .... Martí
Tonio .... Marsh,
                (s, Roma)

October 15

MADAMA BUTTERFLY

Same cast as September 30 (m)
except:

Kate Pinkerton .... West

October 17

LA BOHÈME

Same cast as September 27
except:

Mimi .... Roberto
Schaunard .... Beck
Musetta .... Niska

October 18

MADAMA BUTTERFLY

Same cast as September 30 (m)
except:

Pinkerton .... LoMonaco

October 19

IL BARBIERE DI SIVIGLIA

Same cast as September 23
except:

Basilio .... M. Smith
Berta .... B. Evans

October 20

CAVALLERIA RUSTICANA

Same cast as September 28
except:

Santuzza ...... Lampropulos
Alfio .... Fredricks,
                (s, Clatworthy)
Lola .... Monette

Followed by:

I PAGLIACCI

Same cast as September 28
except:

Nedda .... Bayard
Canio .... Martí
Tonio .... Roma (d)
Silvio .... Ledbetter
Beppe .... Lankston

October 21 (m)

THE MARRIAGE OF FIGARO

Same cast as September 16
except:

Figaro .... Malas
Susanna .... Summers
Countess .... Jeffrey
Antonio .... Yule

October 21

TOSCA

Same cast as October 5 except:

Cavaradossi .... Novoa
Scarpia .... Fredricks,
                (s, Roma)
Angelotti .... Pierson,
                (s, D. Smith)
Sciarrone .... Ledbetter,
                (s, Beck)

October 22 (m)

GIULIO CESARE

Same cast as October 12

October 22

CARMEN

Same cast as September 16 (m)
except:

Carmen .... E. Evans
Don José .... Novoa
Escamillo .... Clatworthy
Zuniga .... Devlin

October 25

MADAMA BUTTERFLY

Same cast as September 30 (m)
except:

Conductor .... Ryan

Butterfly .... Roberto
Suzuki .... B. Evans
Pinkerton ...... Di Giuseppe

October 26

LIZZIE BORDEN (Beeson)

Conductor .... Patané
Andrew Borden .... D. Smith
Abigail Borden .... Faull
Elizabeth Borden ..... Lewis
Margaret Borden ...... Elgar
Reverend Harrington .. Castel
Capt. Jason
  MacFarlane ..... Fredricks

October 27

GIULIO CESARE

Same cast as October 12

October 28 (m)

LA BOHÈME

Same cast as September 27
except:

Mimi .... Venora
Marcello .... Ledbetter
Schaunard .... Beck
Colline .... Hale

October 28

DER ROSENKAVALIER

Same cast as October 6 except:

Marschallin .... Grümmer
Faninal .... Fredricks
Sophie .... Elgar
Marianne .... Bayard
Singer .... Di Giuseppe
Milliner .... Heimall
1st Orphan .... Herbert
2nd Orphan ...... De Forest
3rd Orphan .... August

October 29 (m)

THE MARRIAGE OF FIGARO

Same cast as September 16
except:

Figaro .... Malas
Susanna .... Summers
Cherubino .... Creed
Countess .... Jeffrey
Antonio .... Yule
Solo dancer ....R. Galan

October 29

TOSCA

Same cast as October 5 except:

Conductor .... Patané
Cavaradossi .... Novoa
Scarpia .... Rayson

October 31

MADAMA BUTTERFLY

Same cast as September 30 (m)
except:

Butterfly .... Roberto
Suzuki .... B. Evans

Pinkerton .... LoMonaco
Sharpless .... Cossa

November 1

TOSCA

Same cast as October 5 except:

Conductor .... Patané
Tosca .... Schauler
Cavaradossi .... Molese

November 2

LA TRAVIATA

Same cast as September 15
except:

Violetta .... Witkowska
Alfredo .... Novoa
Douphol .... Bittner
Solo dancer .... R. Galan

November 3

MADAMA BUTTERFLY

Same cast as September 30 (m)
except:

Conductor .... Ryan
Sharpless .... Ledbetter
Goro .... Miller,
                  (s, Castel)

November 4 (m)

LA BOHÈME

Same cast as September 27
except:

Mimi .... Roberto,
                  (s, Carron)
Schaunard .... Beck
Colline .... Hale

(Note: Elisabeth Carron was
not to appear with the
company this season.)

November 4

LA TRAVIATA

Same cast as September 15
except:

Conductor .... Effron
Violetta .... Niska
Germont ...... Schwartzman
Douphol .... Bittner
Solo dancer .... R. Galan

November 5 (m)

DER ROSENKAVALIER

Same cast as October 6 except:

Marschallin .... Grümmer
Sophie .... Elgar
Marianne .... Bayard
Valzacchi .... Castel
Singer .... LoMonaco

1st Orphan .... Herbert
2nd Orphan ...... De Forest
3rd Orphan .... August

November 5

IL BARBIERE DI SIVIGLIA

Same cast as September 23
except:

Rosina .... Witkowska
Basilio .... M. Smith

November 7

LIZZIE BORDEN

Same cast as October 26

November 8

GIULIO CESARE

Same cast as October 12

November 9

IL BARBIERE DI SIVIGLIA

Same cast as September 23
except:

Basilio .... M. Smith

November 10

DER ROSENKAVALIER

Same cast as October 6 except:

Marschallin .... Crader
Faninal .... Fredricks
Marianne .... Bayard
Valzacchi .... Castel
Annina .... B. Evans
Singer .... LoMonaco

November 11 (m)

TOSCA

Same cast as October 5 except:

Conductor .... Patané
Tosca .... Lampropulos
Scarpia .... Rayson

November 11

CARMEN

Same cast as September 16 (m)
except:

Conductor .... Ryan
Don José .... Novoa
Escamillo .... Hale
Zuniga .... Devlin
Frasquita .... Kenting
Mercédès .... B. Evans
Solo dancer .... R. Galan

November 12

LIZZIE BORDEN

Same cast as October 26

Spring 1968 (FEBRUARY 22– APRIL 21)

Female artists
Adler, Arlene*
Anthony, Judith
August, Joan
Bayard, Carol
Bergey, Carol
Bible, Frances
Brooks, Patricia
Carlson, Claudine*
Carron, Elisabeth
Crader, Jeannine
Crane, Lois*
Creed, Kay
De Forest, Anthea
Elgar, Anne
Evans, Beverly
Evans, Edith
Faull, Ellen
Greene, Harriet
Greenspon, Muriel
Guile, Helen
Herbert, Lila
Kehrig, Diana*
Lampropulos, Athena
Lueders, Mary Cross*
Martin, Colette*
Monette, LaVergne
Niska, Maralin
Norwood, Jacqueline*
Owen, Donna
Patenaude, Joan
Penagos, Isabel*
Povia, Charlotte
Pretzat, Anne
Randazzo, Arlene*
Roberto, Francesca
Sachs, Evelyn
Schauler, Eileen
Schmidt, Paulette*
Sills, Beverly
Simon, Joanna
Stanford, Caroline*
Summers, Joan
Swaine, Elizabeth*
Tourangeau, Huguette
Turner, Claramae
West, Maria
Witkowska, Nadja
Wolff, Beverly
Young, Marie

Male artists
Ahearn, Michael
Bañuelas, Roberto*
Beck, William
Bentley, Ronald
Bittner, Jack
Carlo, Don
Castel, Nico
Clatworthy, David
Cossa, Dominic
Crespo, Emilio*
DeLon, Jack
Devlin, Michael
Di Giuseppe, Enrico
Domingo, Placido
DuPree, William

* New artist

Folgar, Manuel*
Fredricks, Richard
Gibbs, Raymond*
Gregori, Robert*
Hale, Robert
Harwood, Robert*
Henderson, Don
Holmes, Eugene*
Hunniken, Douglas
Kelen, Tibor*
Kingman, Dan
Lankston, John
Ledbetter, William
Lee, Christopher
LoMonaco, Jerome
Ludgin, Chester
Malas, Spiro
Marsh, Calvin
Martí, Bernabé
Metcalf, William
Miller, Kellis
Molese, Michele
Moulson, Robert
Nichols, Clinton*
Novoa, Salvador
Paige, Norman
Papay, Raymond
Park, Richard
Patrick, Julian*
Pierson, Edward
Porras, Patricio*
Porretta, Frank
Romaguera, Joaquin
Roy, Will*
Ryan, Dean
Schwartzman, Seymour
Shinall, Vern
Shirley, George
Smith, Malcolm
Stamford, John
Stewart, John
Torigi, Richard
Treigle, Norman
Villechaize, Hervé*
Voketaitis, Arnold
Yule, Don

Conductors
Effron, David
Krachmalnick, Samuel
Patané, Franco
Rudel, Julius
Ryan, Dean
Wilson, Charles

Solo dancers
Bradley, Lisa*
Corkle, Francesca*
de Lavallade, Carmen
Mlakar, Veronika
Sandonato, Barbara*

Douglas, Scott
Fuente, Luis*
Miller, Buzz*
Moore, Charles*
Powell, Robert*
Uthoff, Michael*
Zomosa, Maximiliano*

* New artist

Choreographers
Butler, John
Cole, Jack*
Grandy, Maria*
Joffrey, Robert
Zaraspe, Hector*

Directors
Butler, John
Capobianco, Tito
Corsaro, Frank
de Blasis, James
Hicks, David*
Savoca, Carmen
Sylbert, Paul
West, Christopher

Special coach for Manon
Gauld, Carlton

Designers
Armstrong, Will Steven
Campbell, Patton
Eck, Marsha Louis*
Evans, Lloyd
Fletcher, Robert
Heymann, Henry
Lee, Ming Cho
Morley, Ruth
Oenslager, Donald
Sylbert, Paul
Varona, José
Waring, James D.
Wittstein, Ed

* New artist

February 22

OEDIPUS REX (Stravinsky)
(English narration by
e.e. cummings)

Lighting .... Sondheimer
Conductor .... Rudel

Narrator .... Trehy
Oedipus .... Shirley
Creon .... Pierson
Tiresias .... Smith
Jocasta .... Bible
Messenger .... Devlin
Shepherd .... Stewart,
(s, Paige)

Followed by:

CARMINA BURANA (Orff)

Lighting .... Sondheimer
Conductor .... Rudel

Soprano .... Elgar
Tenor .... Porretta
(s, Di Giuseppe)
Baritone .... Cossa
Solo dancers ... de Lavallade
Mlakar; Douglas
Powell (d)

February 23

TOSCA (Puccini)

Conductor	Patané
Tosca	Crader
Cavaradossi	Martí
Scarpia	Ludgin
Angelotti	Devlin
Spoletta	Castel
Sacristan	Bittner
Sciarrone	Beck
Shepherd	West
Jailer	Yule

February 24 (m)

MADAMA BUTTERFLY (Puccini)

Conductor	Patané
Butterfly	Carron
Suzuki	Creed
Pinkerton	Moulson
Sharpless	Schwartzman
Goro	Castel
Yamadori	Lankston
The Bonze	Pierson
Imperial Commissioner	Park
Registrar	Henderson
Kate Pinkerton	August
Trouble	Lee

February 24

CAVALLERIA RUSTICANA (Mascagni)

Directed by	Corsaro
Conductor	Rudel
Santuzza	Roberto
Turiddu	Di Giuseppe
Alfio	Fredricks
Lola	Tourangeau
Mamma Lucia	Greenspon

Followed by:

I PAGLIACCI (Leoncavallo)

Directed by	Corsaro
Conductor	Rudel
Nedda	Niska
Canio	Domingo
Tonio	Marsh
Silvio	Cossa
Beppe	Paige
Two villagers	Park, Davis
Picco	Villechaize (d)

February 25 (m)

LA TRAVIATA (Verdi)

Choreographer	Joffrey
Conductor	Patané
Violetta	Brooks
Alfredo	LoMonaco
Germont	Cossa
Flora	Greenspon
Annina	Creed
Gaston	Lankston
Douphol	Beck
D'Obigny	Devlin
Dr. Grenvil	Yule

Solo dancer	Fuente (d)
Messenger	Park
Giuseppe	Romaguera

February 25

OEDIPUS REX

Same cast as February 22 except:

Shepherd	Paige

Followed by:

CARMINA BURANA

Same cast as February 22 except:

Soprano	Witkowska, (s, Elgar)
Tenor	Di Giuseppe
Baritone	Metcalf

February 27

TOSCA

Same cast as February 23 except:

Spoletta	K. Miller

February 28

LA TRAVIATA

Same cast as February 25 (m) except:

Conductor	Effron
Alfredo	LoMonaco, (s, Di Giuseppe)
Germont	Marsh

February 29

LA BOHÈME (Puccini)

Conductor	Patané
Rodolfo	LoMonaco
Mimi	Elgar
Marcello	Clatworthy
Schaunard	Beck
Musetta	Bayard
Benoit	Yule
Alcindoro	Bittner
Colline	Smith
Parpignol	K. Miller
Guards	Park, Henderson

March 1

CARMEN (Bizet)

Choreographer	Zaraspe (d)
Conductor	Krachmalnick
Carmen	Tourangeau
Don José	Novoa
Escamillo	Fredricks
Micaëla	Crane (d), (s, Bayard)
Zuniga	Devlin
Frasquita	Anthony
Mercédès	Creed
Remendado	K. Miller
Dancairo	Beck
Morales	Bañuelas (d)
Solo dancer	Fuente

March 2 (m)

THE MARRIAGE OF FIGARO (Mozart)
(English version by Ruth and Thomas Martin)

Stage director	Hicks (d)
Choreographer	Joffrey
Conductor	Wilson
Figaro	Hale
Susanna	Summers
Marcellina	Greenspon
Bartolo	Smith
Cherubino	Bible
Almaviva	Clatworthy
Basilio	Paige
Countess	Niska
Antonio	Bittner
Curzio	K. Miller
Barbarina	Bergey

March 2

OEDIPUS REX

Same cast as February 22 except:

Oedipus	Nichols (d)
Tiresias	Roy (d)
Jocasta	E. Evans

Followed by:

CARMINA BURANA

Same cast as February 22 except:

Tenor	Di Giuseppe
Baritone	Metcalf
Solo dancers	Sandonato (d), (for Mlakar)

March 3 (m)

MADAMA BUTTERFLY

Same cast as February 24 (m) except:

Goro	Paige
Kate Pinkerton	West

March 6

OEDIPUS REX

Same cast as February 22 except:

Oedipus	Nichols

Followed by:

CARMINA BURANA

Same cast as February 22 except:

Soprano	Witkowska
Tenor	DuPree
Baritone	Metcalf
Solo dancers	Sandonato (for Mlakar)

March 7

MADAMA BUTTERFLY

Same cast as February 24 (m) except:

Butterfly	Carron, (s, Roberto)
Suzuki	B. Evans

Pinkerton ...... Di Giuseppe
Sharpless .... Cossa

March 8

THE CRUCIBLE (Ward)

Directed by .... Corsaro
Lighting .... Sondheimer
Conductor .... Krachmalnick

Betty Parris ...... Swain (d)
Rev. Samuel Parris .. De Lon
Tituba .... Norwood (d)
Abigail Williams .... Elgar
Ann Putnam .... Crane
Thomas Putnam ...... Devlin
Rebecca Nurse .... Povia
Francis Nurse .... Hale
Giles Corey .... Nichols
John Proctor .... Ludgin
Rev. John Hale .... Smith
Elizabeth Proctor ...... Bible
Mary Warren ...... Summers
Ezekiel .... K. Miller
Judge Danforth .... Stamford
Sarah Good .... Monette
Ruth Putnam .... Kehrig (d)
Susanna Walcott .. Adler (d)
Mercy Lewis .... Herbert
Sheldon .... Owen
Bridget .... Young

March 9 (m)

CAVALLERIA RUSTICANA

Same cast as February 24
Followed by:

I PAGLIACCI

Same cast as February 24
except:

Nedda .... Bayard
Canio .... LoMonaco

March 9

LA BOHÈME

Same cast as February 29
except:

Rodolfo .... Molese
Mimi .... Carron
Musetta ...... Randazzo (d)
Colline .... Malas

March 10 (m)

CARMEN

Same cast as March 1 except:
Don José .... Martí
Micaëla .... Patenaude

March 10

THE CRUCIBLE

Same cast as March 8

March 13

THE MARRIAGE OF FIGARO

Same cast as March 2 (m)
except:

Figaro .... Malas
Countess .... Crader
Antonio .... Yule

March 14

BOMARZO (Ginastera)
New York premiere

Directed by ..... Capobianco
Set designer .... Lee
Costume designer .... Varona
Choreographer ..... Cole (d)
Lighting .... Sondheimer
Conductor .... Rudel

Shepherd ...... Harwood (d)
Pier Francesco
  Orsini .... Novoa
Silvio de Narni .... Torigi
Nicolas Orsini ... Romaguera
Diana Orsini .... Turner
Pier Francesco,
  as a child ...... Porras (d)
Maerbale,
  as a child ...... Folgar (d)
Girolamo,
  as a child ..... Crespo (d)
Gian Corrado Orsini .. Devlin
Skeleton ...... B. Miller (d)
Messenger .... Castel
Pantasilea .... Simon
Abul .... Moore (d)
Girolamo .... Gregori (d)
Julia Farnese ... Penagos (d)
Maerbale .... Gibbs (d)
Alter ego of Pier
  Francesco ... B. Miller (d)
Solo dancers ... de Lavallade;
                          Powell

March 15

TOSCA

Same cast as February 23
except:

Tosca .... Lampropulos
Cavaradossi .... Molese
Scarpia .... Fredricks

March 16 (m)

OEDIPUS REX

Same cast as February 22
except:

Oedipus .... Nichols

Followed by:

CARMINA BURANA

Same cast as February 22
except:

Soprano .... Witkowska
Tenor .... DuPree

March 16

CARMEN

Same cast as March 1 except:

Conductor .... Ryan,
                (s, Krachmalnick)

Escamillo .... Hale
Micaëla .... Patenaude
Frasquita ...... Schmidt (d)
Mercédès .... Guile

March 17 (m)

THE CRUCIBLE

Same cast as March 8 except:

Tituba .... Stanford (d)
Giles Corey .... Stewart

March 17

CAVALLERIA RUSTICANA

Same cast as February 24
except:

Conductor .... Patané

Santuzza ...... Lampropulos
Turiddu .... LoMonaco
Mamma Lucia .... Povia

Followed by:

I PAGLIACCI

Same cast as February 24
except:

Conductor .... Patané
Nedda .... Bayard
Canio .... Martí
Beppe .... Romaguera

March 20

BOMARZO

Same cast as March 14

March 21

MANON (Massenet)
New production

Directed by ..... Capobianco
Set designer .... Eck (d)
Costume designer .... Varona
Choreographer .... Joffrey
Lighting .... Sondheimer
Special coach .... Gauld
Conductor .... Rudel

Des Grieux .... Molese
Count des Grieux ..... Smith
Lescaut .... Fredricks
Manon .... Sills
Guillot .... Castel
De Brétigny .... Hale
Pousette .... Bergey
Rosette .... Guile
Javotte .... Creed
Innkeeper .... Bittner
Prima ballerina .. Bradley (d)
Premier
  danseur .... Uthoff (d)
Ballet Master ... Zomosa (d)
Cupid .... Corkle (d)
Maid .... Greene
Guards ...... Papay, Yule
Seminary porter .... Carlo
Sergeant .... Yule
Gambler .... Kingman

March 22

THE CRUCIBLE

Same cast as March 8 except:

Tituba .... Stanford
Giles Corey .... Stewart
John Proctor .... Shinal

March 23 (m)

TOSCA

Same cast as February 23 except:

Tosca	Schauler
Cavaradossi	Di Giuseppe
Scarpia	Fredricks
Spoletta	K. Miller

March 23

LA TRAVIATA

Same cast as February 25 (m) except:

Alfredo	Kelen (d)
Germont	Schwartzman
Flora	B. Evans

March 24 (m)

LA BOHÈME

Same cast as February 29 except:

Mimi	Roberto
Marcello	Cossa
Schaunard	Ledbetter
Musetta	Niska
Colline	Hale

March 24

MANON

Same cast as March 21

March 27

MANON

Same cast as March 21 except:

Lescaut	Ledbetter

March 28

CARRY NATION (Moore)
New York premiere

Directed by	Corsaro
Set and lighting designer	Armstrong
Costume designer	Campbell
Choreographer	Grandy (d)
Conductor	Krachmalnick
Carry Nation	Wolff
Father	Voketaitis
Mother	Faull
Charles	Patrick (d)
Men in saloon	Kingman, Carlo
Piano player	Ryan
City marshall	Yule
Ben	K. Miller
Preacher	Pierson
Young man at hoedown	Stewart
Young girl at hoedown	Adler
Toaster at hoedown	Bittner
A boy	Ahearn

A girl	Martin (d)
Ladies of auxiliary	August, West, Herbert, Owen
Caretaker	Bittner

(Note: *2nd Young Man* at hoedown added to program of April 2)

March 29

BOMARZO

Same cast as March 14

March 30 (m)

GIULIO CESARE (Handel)

Lighting	Sondheimer
Conductor	Rudel
Giulio Cesare	Treigle
Curio	Beck
Cornelia	Sachs
Sesto	Creed, (s, Bible)
Cleopatra	Sills
Tolomeo	Malas
Achilla	Cossa
Nireno	Devlin

March 30

MADAMA BUTTERFLY

Same cast as February 24 (m) except:

Butterfly	Roberto
Suzuki	B. Evans
Pinkerton	Domingo

March 31 (m)

LA BOHÈME

Same cast as February 29 except:

Rodolfo	Molese
Marcello	Cossa
Schaunard	Ledbetter

March 31

THE MARRIAGE OF FIGARO

Same cast as March 2 (m) except:

Figaro	Malas
Marcellina	B. Evans, (s, Greenspon)
Cherubino	Creed
Almaviva	Fredricks
Basilio	Castel

April 2

CARRY NATION

Same cast as March 28 except:

Added to this program:

2nd Young man at hoedown	Bentley

April 3

LA TRAVIATA

Same cast as February 25 (m) except:

Violetta	Niska
Alfredo	LoMonaco, (s, Domingo)
Germont	Holmes (d)
Flora	B. Evans
Annina	August
Douphol	Bittner

April 4

BOMARZO

Same cast as March 14 except:

Silvio de Narni	Bañuelas

April 5

MANON

Same cast as March 21 except:

Des Grieux	Di Giuseppe
Manon	Brooks

April 6 (m)

BOMARZO

Same cast as March 14 except:

Pantasilea	Lueders (d)
Julia Farnese	Summers

April 6

CAVALLERIA RUSTICANA

Same cast as February 24 except:

Conductor	Patané
Santuzza	Lampropulos
Alfio	Bañuelas

Followed by:

I PAGLIACCI

Same cast as February 24 except:

Conductor	Patané
Canio	Martí
Tonio	Schwartzman
Silvio	Ledbetter
Beppe	Romaguera

April 7 (m)

CARRY NATION

Same cast as March 28

April 7

TOSCA

Same cast as February 23 except:

Cavaradossi	Domingo
Scarpia	Fredricks

April 9

MANON

Same cast as March 21 except:
Count des Grieux ..... Malas
Pousette .... Crane

April 10

MADAMA BUTTERFLY

Same cast as February 24 (m)
except:
Butterfly .... Niska,
        (s, Roberto)
Pinkerton .... LoMonaco

April 11

CAVALLERIA RUSTICANA

Same cast as February 24
except:
Conductor .... Patané
Santuzza ...... Lampropulos
Alfio .... Clatworthy
Lola .... Creed
Mamma Lucia .... Povia

Followed by:

I PAGLIACCI

Same cast as February 24
except:
Conductor .... Patané
Canio .... Martí,
        (s, Domingo)
Tonio .... Ludgin

April 12

LA TRAVIATA

Same cast as February 25 (m)
except:
Alfredo .... Kelen
Germont .... Holmes
Annina .... August

April 13 (m)

LA BOHÈME

Same cast as February 29
except:
Conductor .... Effron
Mimi .... Crane,
        (s, Roberto)
Marcello .... Fredricks
Musetta .... Niska
Colline .... Hale
2nd Guard .... Papay

April 13

THE MARRIAGE OF FIGARO

Same cast as March 2 (m)
except:
Conductor .... Ryan
Figaro .... Malas
Susanna .... Elgar
Marcellina .... B. Evans
Bartolo .... Yule
Basilio .... Castel
Countess .... Bayard

April 14 (m)

CARMEN

Same cast as March 1 except:
Carmen .... E. Evans
Don José .... Domingo
Escamillo .... Roy
Micaëla .... Bayard
Frasquita .... Monette
Mercédès .... Guile
Morales .... Gibbs

April 14

GIULIO CESARE

Same cast as March 30 (m)
except:
Sesto .... Bible

April 16

MADAMA BUTTERFLY

Same cast as February 24 (m)
except:
Conductor .... Ryan,
        (s, Patané)
Butterfly .... Niska
Suzuki .... B. Evans
Pinkerton ...... Di Giuseppe
Sharpless .... Cossa

April 17

THE MARRIAGE OF FIGARO

Same cast as March 2 (m)
except:
Figaro .... Malas
Susanna .... Elgar
Barbarina .... Pretzat

April 18

GIULIO CESARE

Same cast as March 30 (m)
except:
Cornelia .... Carlson (d)
Sesto .... Bible
Tolomeo .... Smith

April 19

TOSCA

Same cast as February 23
except:
Tosca .... Lampropulos
Cavaradossi .... Domingo
Scarpia .... Fredricks
Angelotti .... Beck
Sciarrone .... Ledbetter

April 20 (m)

LA TRAVIATA

Same cast as February 25 (m)
except:
Violetta .... Niska
Germont ...... Schwartzman
Annina .... De Forest

April 20

GIULIO CESARE

Same cast as March 30 (m)
except:
Tolomeo .... Smith

April 21 (m)

CAVALLERIA RUSTICANA

Conductor .... Patané
Santuzza ...... Lampropulos
Turiddu .... Domingo
Alfio .... Clatworthy
Lola .... Creed
Mamma Lucia .... Povia

Followed by:

I PAGLIACCI

Same cast as February 24
except:
Conductor .... Patané
Nedda .... Niska,
        (s, Bayard)
Canio .... Martí
Silvio .... Ledbetter
Beppe .... Romaguera

April 21

MANON

Same cast as March 21 except:
Des Grieux ..... Di Giuseppe
Count des Grieux ..... Malas
Manon .... Brooks
Pousette .... Crane
Gambler .... Henderson

Fall 1968 (SEPTEMBER 19– NOVEMBER 17)

Female artists
Adler, Arlene
Anthony, Judith
Armstrong, Marilyn
Bayard, Carol
Bible, Frances
Blanchard, Barbara*
Brooks, Patricia
Carlson, Claudine
Crader, Jeannine
Crane, Lois
Creed, Kay
De Forest, Anthea
Di Giglio, Maria*
Elgar, Anne
Evans, Beverly
Greene, Harriet
Greenspon, Muriel
Grillo, Joann
Guilet, Helene
Herbert, Lila
Kehrig, Diana
Lampropulos, Athena
Lueders, Mary Cross
Monette, LaVergne
Moody, Janette*
Niska, Maralin
Ottaviano, Anna*
Owen, Donna
Owen, Hanna
Pretzat, Anne
Randazzo, Arlene
Schauler, Eileen
Sills, Beverly
Simon, Joanna
Summers, Joan
Turner, Claramae
Tyler, Veronica
West, Maria
Winburn, Janet*
Wise, Patricia*

Male artists
Ahearn, Michael
Bañuelas, Roberto
Beck, William
Bentley, Ronald
Bittner, Jack
Brown, William*
Callio, Timo*
Carlo, Don
Castel, Nico
Clatworthy, David
Clements, David
Cossa, Dominic
Crespo, Emilio
Darius, Anthony
Davis, Harris
De Dio, Harry
Devlin, Michael
Di Giuseppe, Enrico
Domingo, Placido
Folgar, Manuel
Fredricks, Richard
Galiano, Joseph
Gibbs, Raymond

Goeke, Leo*
Gregori, Robert
Hale, Robert
Harwood, Robert
Hecht, Joshua
Hedlund, Ronald*
Henderson, Don
Huddleston, Paul
Hunniken, Douglas
Kelen, Tibor
Kingman, Dan
Krause, Karl Patrick
Lankston, John
Ledbetter, William
Lee, Christopher
LoMonaco, Jerome
Ludgin, Chester
Malas, Spiro
Miller, Kellis
Mitchell, Marc*
Molese, Michele
Morell, Barry
Nichols, Clinton
Novoa, Salvador
Paige, Norman
Papay, Raymond
Park, Richard
Patrick, Julian
Pierson, Edward
Porras, Patricio
Postrel, Leo
Puleo, Robert
Romaguera, Joaquin
Romeo, Bernard
Rouleau, Joseph*
Roy, Will*
Samuelsen, Roy*
Sardinero, Vincenzo*
Savoldi, Lino*
Schwartzman, Seymour
Smith, Malcolm
Stewart, John
Torigi, Richard
Trehy, Robert
Treigle, Norman
Yule, Don

Conductors
Dufallo, Richard*
Effron, David
Krachmalnick, Samuel
Meier, Gustav*
Rigacci, Bruno*
Rudel, Julius
Ryan, Byron Dean
Wilson, Charles
Zedda, Alberto*

Solo dancers
Bradley, Lisa
Corkle, Francesca
de Lavallade, Carmen

Fuente, Luis
Jorgensen, Nels
Miller, Buzz
Moore, Charles

Powell, Robert
Uthoff, Michael

Choreographers
Cole, Jack
Joffrey, Robert
Grandy, Maria

Directors
Bamberger, David
Capobianco, Tito
Corsaro, Frank
Habunek, Vlado*
Montresor, Beni
Savoca, Carmen
Strasfogel, Ian

Designers
Armstrong, Will Steven
Campbell, Patton
Eck, Marsha Louis
Evans, Lloyd
Fletcher, Robert
Greenwood, Jane*
Lee, Ming Cho
Montresor, Beni
Oenslager, Donald
Ter-Arutunian, Rouben
Varona, José

* New artist

† **September 19**

CAVALLERIA RUSTICANA
(Mascagni)

Conductor .... Zedda (d)

Santuzza ...... Lampropulos
Turiddu .... Di Giuseppe
Alfio .... Bañuelas
Lola .... Creed
Mamma Lucia .... Greenspon

Followed by:

I PAGLIACCI (Leoncavallo)

Conductor .... Zedda (d)

Nedda .... Bayard
Canio .... Domingo
Tonio .... Ludgin
Silvio .... Cossa
Beppe .... Paige
Two villagers .... Davis, Park

September 20

IL TRITTICO (Puccini)

Directed by .... Strasfogel
Lighting .... Sondheimer
Conductor .... Rudel

IL TABARRO

Michele .... Ludgin
Luigi .... Domingo
Tinca .... Castel

† Scheduled performances of
Il Trittico and *The Magic Flute*
on September 17 and 18 were canceled due to a musicians' strike

* New artist   * New artist

Talpa .... Smith
Giorgetta .... Crader
Frugola .... Turner
Song vendor .... K. Miller
Two lovers ... Blanchard (d);
                         Lankston

Followed by:

SUOR ANGELICA

Suor Angelica .... Niska
La Principessa .... Turner
La Badessa .... Winburn (d)
La Suora Zelatrice .... Evans
La Maestra
   delle Novizie .... Guilet
Suor Genovieffa ... Blanchard
Le due novizie .... H. Owen,
                         De Forest
Suor Dolcina ...... D. Owen
Le due converse .... Pretzat,
                         Armstrong
Le Cercatrice .... West

Followed by:

GIANNI SCHICCHI

Gianni Schicchi .... Malas
Lauretta .... Elgar
Zita .... Turner
Rinuccio .... LoMonaco
Gherardo .... Castel
Nella .... Crane
Gherardino .... Puleo
Betto .... Devlin
Simone .... Smith
Marco .... Ledbetter
La Ciesca .... Anthony
Spinellocchio .... Yule
Nicolao .... Bittner
Pinellino .... Park
Guccio .... Henderson

This performance was dedicated to the memory of conductor
Franco Patané, who was to have
conducted but who died in an
automobile accident on May 13,
1968

September 21 (m)

MADAMA BUTTERFLY (Puccini)

Conductor .... Wilson

Butterfly .... Niska
Suzuki .... Creed
Pinkerton ...... Di Giuseppe
Sharpless .... Clatworthy
Goro .... Castel
Yamadori .... Lankston
The Bonze .... Pierson
Imperial
   Commissioner .... Park
Registrar .... Henderson
Kate Pinkerton ..... Lueders
Trouble .... Lee

September 21

MANON (Massenet)

Conductor .... Rudel

Des Grieux .... Molese
Count des Grieux ...... Smith

Lescaut .... Fredricks
Manon .... Brooks
Guillot .... Castel
De Brétigny .... Hale
Pousette .... Crane
Javotte .... Guilet
Rosette .... Creed
Innkeeper .... Bittner
Prima ballerina ...... Bradley
Premier danseur ..... Uthoff
Ballet Master .... Jorgensen
Cupid .... Corkle
Maid .... Greene
Two guards .... Papay, Yule
Seminary porter .... Carlo
Sergeant .... Yule
Gambler .... Henderson

September 22 (m)

LA BOHÈME (Puccini)

Conductor .... Zedda

Rodolfo .... LoMonaco
              (Acts I and II);
      Molese (Acts III and IV)
Mimi .... Elgar
Marcello .... Ledbetter,
                    (s, Cossa)
Schaunard .... Beck,
                 (s, Ledbetter)
Musetta .... Crane
Benoit .... Yule
Alcindoro .... Bittner
Colline .... Smith
Parpignol .... K. Miller
Guards .... Park, Henderson

September 22

THE MAGIC FLUTE (Mozart)
(English version by
Ruth and Thomas Martin)

Conductor .... Ryan

Sarastro .... Hecht
Tamino .... Di Giuseppe
Speaker .... Hale
Priest .... Lankston
Queen of the
   Night .... Moody (d)
Pamina .... Tyler
1st Lady .... Bayard
2nd Lady .... Monette
3rd Lady .... Evans
1st Spirit .... Ahearn
2nd Spirit ...... Harwood
3rd Spirit ...... Mitchell (d)
Papageno .... Fredricks
Papagena .... Blanchard
Monostatos .... K. Miller
1st Armored man .... Stewart
2nd Armored man ... Pierson

September 25

IL TRITTICO

Same casts as September 20
except:

IL TABARRO

Frugola .... Greenspon

Followed by:

SUOR ANGELICA

La Principessa ... Greenspon

Followed by:

GIANNI SCHICCHI

Zita .... Greenspon
Rinuccio .... Di Giuseppe

September 26

BOMARZO (Ginastera)

Conductor .... Rudel

Shepherd .... Harwood
Pier Francesco Orsini ..Novoa
Silvio de Narni .... Torigi
Nicolas Orsini .... Romaguera
Diana Orsini .... Turner
Pier Francesco,
   as a child .... Porras
Maerbale, as a child .. Folgar
Girolamo, as a child .. Crespo
Gian Corrado Orsini .. Devlin
Skelton .... B. Miller
Messenger .... Castel
Pantasilea .... Simon
Abul .... Moore
Girolamo .... Gregori
Julia Farnese ...... Summers
Maerbale .... Gibbs
Alter ego of
   Pier Francesco ... B. Miller
Solo dancers ... de Lavallade;
                         Powell

September 27

CAVALLERIA RUSTICANA

Same cast as September 19

Followed by:

I PAGLIACCI

Same cast as September 19
except:

Beppe .... Romaguera

September 28 (m)

LA BOHÈME

Same cast as September 22 (m)
except:

Rodolfo .... Molese
Marcello .... Fredricks
Musetta .... Niska

September 28

THE MAGIC FLUTE

Same cast as September 22
except:

Sarastro .... Roy (d)
Papageno .... Ledbetter
Monostatos .... Castel

September 29 (m)

MADAMA BUTTERFLY

Same cast as September 21 (m)
except:

Butterfly .... Crader
Pinkerton ...... Savoldi (d)

September 29

BOMARZO

Same cast as September 26

October 1

IL TRITTICO

Same casts as September 20
except:

IL TABARRO

Luigi .... Savoldi
Tinca .... Clements (d)
Giorgetta ...... Lampropulos,
(s, Crader)
Followed by:

SUOR ANGELICA

Followed by:

GIANNI SCHICCHI

Lauretta ...... Di Giglio (d)
Gherardo ...... Clements (d)

October 2

MANON

Same cast as September 21
except:

Des Grieux ..... Di Giuseppe

October 3

IL TRITTICO

Same casts as September 20
except:

Conductor ...... Dufallo (d)

IL TABARRO

Luigi .... Savoldi
Tinca .... Clements
Giorgetta ...... Lampropulos
Frugola .... Greenspon
Followed by:

SUOR ANGELICA

Suor Angelica .... Elgar
La Principessa .... Bible
Followed by:

GIANNI SCHICCHI

Lauretta .... Di Giglio
Zita .... Greenspon
Gherardo .... Clements

October 4

MANON

Same cast as September 21
except:

Des Grieux ..... Di Giuseppe

October 5 (m)

CAVALLERIA RUSTICANA

Same cast as September 19
except:

Conductor .... Effron
Santuzza .... Crader
Turiddu .... Savoldi

Lola .... Lueders
Mamma Lucia .... Evans
Followed by:

I PAGLIACCI

Same cast as September 19
except:

Silvio .... Ledbetter
Beppe .... Goeke (d)

October 5

LA TRAVIATA (Verdi)

Conductor .... Zedda
Violetta .... Niska
Alfredo .... Kelen
Germont .... Cossa
Flora .... Evans,
(s, Greenspon)
Annina .... Creed
Gaston .... Lankston
Douphol .... Beck
D'Obigny .... Devlin
Dr. Grenvil .... Yule
Solo dancer .... Fuente
Messenger .... Park
Giuseppe .... Romaguera

October 6 (m)

BOMARZO

Same cast as September 26
except:

Messenger .... Clements

October 6

LA BOHÈME

Same cast as September 22 (m)
except:

Rodolfo .... LoMonaco
Marcello .... Fredricks
Schaunard .... Ledbetter
Colline .... Malas

October 8

BOMARZO

Same cast as September 26
except:

Silvio de Narni ..... Bañuelas
Messenger .... Clements
Pantasilea .... Leuders
Julia Farnese ...... Wise (d)

October 9

NINE RIVERS FROM JORDAN
(Weisgall)
World premiere

Directed by .... Habunek (d)
Scenic and lighting
designer .... Armstrong
Costume
designer .. Greenwood (d)
Choreography ...... Grandy
Conductor .... Meier (d)

Lt. Jean l'Aiglon ..Brown (d)
Father Matteo
Angelino .... Ledbetter
Sgt. Abe Goldberg .... Hecht
Maj. Mark Lyon ... Lankston

Capt. Rev. Lucius Bull ... Roy
Lance Cpl.
Don Hanwell ...... Patrick
Salt woman .... Schauler
Andrew .... Stewart
Copperhead
Kelly .... Huddleston
Otto Suder .... Clements
Pietà .... Schauler
Dead man ...... Romaguera
The Woman D. P. .. Schauler
Leader of the Bedouins .. Yule
Muezzin .... Romaguera
Little Jim Clap .... K. Miller
Peeper Johnny .... Gibbs
Tom Tosser .... Castel
Simple Simon .... Papay
Sgt. Pete Fisher ...... Devlin
Phil .... Goeke
Jim Gunner .... Kingman
Taddeo .... Darius
Bartolomeo .... Bentley
Giuda .... Henderson
Italian women. .Herbert, Adler
Italians .... Galiano,
Hunniken, Krause
Woman's Voice on
Radio .... Creed

October 10

LA BOHÈME

Same cast as September 22 (m)
except:

Rodolfo .... Molese
Mimi .... Ottaviano (d)
Marcello .... Cossa
Schaunard .... Ledbetter
Musetta .... Bayard

October 11

NINE RIVERS FROM JORDAN

Same cast as October 9

October 12 (m)

THE MAGIC FLUTE

Same cast as September 22
except:

Sarastro .... Roy
Speaker .... Devlin
Queen of the
Night .... Randazzo
Papagena .... Wise
Monostatos .... Castel
1st Armored man .. Clements

October 12

CAVALLERIA RUSTICANA

Same cast as September 19
except:

Turiddu .... Savoldi
Alfio .... Schwartzman
Followed by:

I PAGLIACCI

Same cast as September 19
except:

Nedda .... Niska
Silvio .... Ledbetter
Beppe .... Romaguera,
(s, Goeke)

October 13 (m)

LA TRAVIATA

Same cast as October 5 except:

Violetta .... Brooks
Flora .... Evans,
                    (s, Greenspon)
Douphol .... Bañuelas

October 13

IL TRITTICO

Came casts as September 20
except:

Conductor .... Dufallo

IL TABARRO

Michele .... Clatworthy
Luigi .... Savoldi
Giorgetta ...... Lampropulos

Followed by:

SUOR ANGELICA

Followed by:

GIANNI SCHICCHI

Gianni Schicchi .... Fredricks
Lauretta .... Di Giglio

October 16

MADAMA BUTTERFLY

Same cast as September 21 (m)
except:

Suzuki .... Evans
Pinkerton .... Savoldi
Sharpless ...... Schwartzman
*Imperial
    Commissioner* ..... Galiano

October 17

FAUST (Gounod)
New production

Directed by .... Corsaro
Scenic designer .... Lee
Costume designer .... Varona
Lighting .... Sondheimer
Choreographer .... Joffrey
Conductor .... Rudel

Marguerite .... Sills
Faust .... Molese
Méphistophélès ...... Treigle
Valentin .... Cossa
Siébel .... Bible
Marthe .... Greenspon
Wagner .... Beck
Juggler .... De Dio
Fire-eater .... Romeo
Acrobats .."Los Crackerjacks"

October 18

TOSCA (Puccini)

Conductor ...... Rigacci (d)

Tosca .... Schauler
Cavaradossi .... Morell
Scarpia .... Fredricks
Angelotti .... Devlin
Spoletta .... Castel
Sacristan .... Bittner

Sciarrone .... Bañuelas
Shepherd .... West
Jailer .... Yule

October 19 (m)

LA TRAVIATA

Same cast as October 5 except:

Conductor .... Effron
Germont .... Clatworthy
Flora .... Greenspon
Annina .... De Forest
Douphol .... Bañuelas

October 19

MANON

Same cast as September 21
except:

Des Grieux ..... Di Giuseppe

October 20 (m)

NINE RIVERS FROM JORDAN

Same cast as October 9 except:

*Lance Cpl.
    Don Hanwell* .... Trehy

October 20

FAUST

Same cast as October 17

October 22

IL BARBIERE DI SIVIGLIA
(Rossini)

Directed by ...... Bamberger
Conductor .... Krachmalnick

Almaviva .... Di Giuseppe
Bartolo .... Malas
Rosina .... Brooks
Basilio .... Hale
Berta .... Evans
Figaro .... Cossa
Fiorello .... Bañuelas
Officer .... Yule

October 23

GIULIO CESARE (Handel)

Conductor .... Rudel

Giulio Cesare .... Treigle
Curio .... Beck
Cornelia .... Carlson
Sesto .... Bible
Cleopatra .... Sills
Tolomeo .... Smith
Achilla .... Cossa
Nireno .... Devlin

October 24

TOSCA

Same cast as October 18
except:

Cavaradossi .... Molese
Scarpia .... Ludgin
Sacristan .... Yule
Jailer .... Park

October 25

IL BARBIERE DI SIVIGLIA

Same cast as October 22
except:

Almaviva .... Kelen
Rosina .... Randazzo
Figaro .... Sardinero (d)

October 26 (m)

MANON

Same cast as September 21
except:

Des Grieux ..... Di Giuseppe
Lescaut .... Ledbetter
Innkeeper .... Postrel,
                    (s, Roy)

October 26

FAUST

Same cast as October 17

October 27 (m)

CAVALLERIA RUSTICANA

Same cast as September 19
except:

Conductor .... Rigacci
Lola .... Lueders
Mamma Lucia .... Evans
Turiddu .... Savoldi

Followed by:

I PAGLIACCI

Same cast as September 19
except:

Conductor .... Rigacci

Tonio .... Schwartzman
Silvio .... Ledbetter
Beppe .... Romaguera

October 27

MADAMA BUTTERFLY

Same cast as September 21 (m)
except:

Butterfly .... Crader
Pinkerton .... LoMonaco
    (Act I); Molese (Act III)
Sharpless .... Beck
*Imperial
    Commissioner* .... Galiano
Kate .... De Forest

October 29

TOSCA

Same cast as October 18
except:

Tosca .... Crader
Cavaradossi .... Savoldi
Scarpia .... Ludgin
Sacristan .... Yule
Jailer .... Park

October 30

FAUST

Same cast as October 17
except:

Conductor .... Krachmalnick

Marguerite .... Brooks
Méphistophélès .. Rouleau (d)
Siébel .... Bible,
　　　　　　　　(s, Creed)

October 31

LA TRAVIATA

Same cast as October 5 except:

Conductor .... Rigacci

Germont ...... Schwartzman
Flora .... Greenspon
Annina .... De Forest
　　　　　　　　(s, Creed)
Douphol .... Bañuelas
D'Obigny .... Ledbetter,
　　　　　　　　(s, Devlin)

November 1

GIULIO CESARE

Same cast as October 23
except:

Giulio Cesare .... Devlin,
　　　　　　　　(s, Treigle)
Curio .... Pierson,
　　　　　　　　(s, Beck)
Nireno .... Beck,
　　　　　　　　(s, Devlin)

November 2 (m)

LA BOHÈME

Same cast as September 22 (m)
except:

Conductor .... Krachmalnick

Rodolfo .... Molese
Mimi .... Ottaviano
Marcello .... Hedlund (d)
Alcindoro .... Bañuelas
Colline .... Hale

November 2

CAVALLERIA RUSTICANA

Same cast as September 19
except:

Conductor .... Rigacci

Santuzza .... Crader
Turiddu .... Savoldi
Lola .... Lueders

Followed by:

I PAGLIACCI

Same cast as September 19
except:

Conductor .... Rigacci

Canio .... Nichols
Tonio .... Sardinero
Silvio .... Ledbetter
Beppe .... Clements

November 3 (m)

IL BARBIERE DI SIVIGLIA

Same cast as October 22
except:

Almaviva .... Kelen
Rosina .... Randazzo
Basilio .... Smith

November 3

LE COQ D'OR
(Rimsky-Korsakov)
(English version by Antal
Dorati and James Gibson)

Conductor .... Rudel

King Dodon .... Treigle
Prince Guidon .... Castel
Prince Afron .... Beck
General Polkan .... Pierson
Amelfa .... Greenspon
Astrologer ...... Di Giuseppe
Queen of Shemakha ..... Sills
Golden Cockerel .. Blanchard

November 5

FAUST

Same cast as October 17
except:

Marguerite .... Brooks
Méphistophélès ..... Rouleau

November 6

IL BARBIERE DI SIVIGLIA

Same cast as October 22
except:

Almaviva .... Kelen
Rosina .... Wise
Basilio .... Smith
Berta .... Winburn
Figaro .... Sardinero

November 7

LE COQ D'OR

Same cast as November 3

November 8

LA TRAVIATA

Same cast as October 5 except:

Conductor .... Rigacci

Germont .... Clatworthy
Flora .... Greenspon
Douphol .... Bañuelas

November 9 (m)

MANON

Same cast as September 21
except:

Lescaut .... Ledbetter
Innkeeper .... Postrel
Maid .... Kehrig,
　　　　　　　　(s, Greene)

November 9

IL BARBIERE DI SIVIGLIA

Same cast as October 22
except:

Bartolo .... Pierson
Rosina .... Wise
Basilio .... Roy
Berta .... Winburn

November 10 (m)

TOSCA

Same cast as October 18
except:

Tosca .... Crader
Cavaradossi .... Novoa,
　　　　　　　　(s, Savoldi)
Scarpia ...... Samuelsen (d)
Sacristan .... Yule
Jailer .... Park

November 10

LE COQ D'OR

Same cast as November 3

November 12

LE COQ D'OR

Same cast as November 3
except:

King Dodon .... Malas
General Polkan .... Roy
Astrologer .... Lankston,
　　　　　　　　(s, Di Giuseppe)
Golden Cockerel .... Wise

November 13

CAVALLERIA RUSTICANA

Same cast as September 19
except:

Conductor .... Rigacci

Santuzza .... Crader
Turiddu .... Savoldi
Lola .... Lueders
Mamma Lucia .... Evans

Followed by:

I PAGLIACCI

Same cast as September 19
except:

Conductor .... Rigacci

Canio .... Callio (d)
Tonio .... Schwartzman
Beppe .... Goeke

November 14

FAUST

Same cast as October 17
except:

Conductor .... Krachmalnick

Marguerite .... Niska
Valentin .... Schwartzman

November 15

IL BARBIERE DI SIVIGLIA

Same cast as October 22 except:

Almaviva .... Kelen
Bartolo .... Pierson
Berta .... Winburn
Figaro .... Sardinero

November 16 (m)

TOSCA

Same cast as October 18 except:

Conductor .... Meier

Cavaradossi .... Callio
Scarpia .... Samuelsen
Spoletta .... Davis

November 16

MADAMA BUTTERFLY

Same cast as September 21 (m) except:

Conductor .... Ryan
Suzuki .... Evans
Pinkerton .... Molese
Sharpless .... Cossa

November 17 (m)

GIULIO CESARE

Same cast as October 23 except:

Cornelia .... Grillo
Sesto .... Creed
Achilla .... Ledbetter

November 17

IL TRITTICO

Same casts as September 20 except:

Conductor .... Dufallo

IL TABARRO

Michele .... Clatworthy
Luigi .... Savoldi
Giorgetta ...... Lampropulos
Frugola .... Greenspon

Followed by:

SUOR ANGELICA

Suor Angelica .... Elgar
La Principessa .... Bible

Followed by:

GIANNI SCHICCHI

Lauretta .... Blanchard
Zita .... Greenspon
Rinuccio .... Di Giuseppe
Nella .... Pretzat

Spring 1969 (FEBRUARY 20– APRIL 20)

Female artists
Adler, Arlene
Anthony, Judith
Armstrong, Karan*
Armstrong, Marilyn
Augér, Arleen*
Bayard, Carol
Bible, Frances
Blanchard, Barbara
Bonini, Peggy
Brooks, Patricia
Clements, Joy
Crane, Lois
Creed, Kay
Darling, Sandra
Davidson, Joy*
De Forest, Anthea
Di Gerlando, Maria
Di Giglio, Maria
Elgar, Anne
Evans, Beverly
Evans, Nell*
Greene, Harriet
Greenspon, Muriel
Guilet, Helene
Herbert, Lila
Himmel, Michele*
Lampropulos, Athena
Ledur, Letitia
Lueders, Mary Cross
Martin, Colette
Moody, Janette
Mulvey, Marilyn*
Neblett, Carol*
Niska, Maralin
Ottaviano, Anna
Owen, Donna

Owen, Hanna
Roberto, Francesca
Schauler, Eileen
Sills, Beverly
Thomson, Heather*
Turner, Claramae
Tyler, Veronica
Vanni, Helen*
West, Maria
Wilson, Joemy
Winburn, Janet
Wise, Patricia
Wisnofsky, Anne Marie

Male artists
Alexander, John
Bañuelas, Roberto
Beck, William
Bentley, Ronald
Bittner, Jack
Callio, Timo
Carlo, Don
Castel, Nico
Chapman, William
Clatworthy, David
Clements, David
Cossa, Dominic
Darius, Anthony
Davis, Harris
De Dio, Harry
De Lon, Jack
Demon, Satani
Devlin, Michael
Di Giuseppe, Enrico
Domingo, Placido
Duval, Pierre

Fredricks, Richard
Friedman, Alan*
Galiano, Joseph
Gibbs, Raymond
Hale, Robert
Harwood, Robert
Hecht, Joshua
Henderson, Don
Hicks, David
Hoeler, William*
Huddleston, Paul
Imprescia, Richard*
Jamerson, Thomas*
Kelen, Tibor
Kingman, Dan
Krause, Karl Patrick
Lankston, John
Ledbetter, William
Lee, Christopher
LoMonaco, Jerome
Ludgin, Chester
Malas, Spiro
Martí, Bernabé
Molese, Michele
Murray, William*
Nagy, Robert*
Nichols, Clinton
Novoa, Salvador
O'Connell, Kevin*
Papay, Raymond
Park, Richard
Patrick, Julian
Pierson, Edward
Porretta, Frank
Postrel, Leo
Puleo, Robert
Quilico, Louis

* New artist

* New artist

* New artist

Romaguera, Joaquin
Roy, Will
Samuelsen, Roy
Savoldi, Lino
Schwartzman, Seymour
Smith, Malcolm
Stewart, John
Theyard, Harry
Trehy, Robert
Yule, Don

Conductors
Dufallo, Richard
Effron, David
Krachmalnick, Samuel
Meier, Gustav
Ötvös, Gabor*
Rudel, Julius
Ryan, Dean
Zedda, Alberto

Chorus master
David Effron

Solo dancers
Brayley, Sally*
Corkle, Francesca
Horne, Katharyn*

Fuente, Luis
Hoffman, Phil*
Sequoio, Ron
Uthoff, Michael
Villella, Edward*

Choreographers
Joffrey, Robert
Sequoio, Ron*

Directors
Bamberger, David
Capobianco, Tito
Corsaro, Frank
Habunek, Vlado
Montresor, Beni
Pollock, Michael
Savoca, Carmen
Strasfogel, Ian

Designers
Armstrong, Will Steven
Campbell, Patton
Eck, Marsha Louis
Evans, Lloyd
Fletcher, Robert
Lee, Ming Cho
Montresor, Beni
Oenslager, Donald
Ter-Arutunian, Rouben
Varona, José
Wittstein, Ed

* New artist

February 20

MANON (Massenet)

Conductor .... Rudel

Guillot .... Castel
De Brétigny .... Hale
Pousette .... Crane
Javotte .... Guilet
Rosette .... Lueders
Innkeeper .... Bittner
Lescaut .... Fredricks
Guards ...... Papay, Yule
Manon .... Sills
Des Grieux .... Domingo
Maid .... Greene

Count des Grieux ..... Smith
Prima ballerina .. Brayley (d)
Premier danseur ...... Uthoff
Ballet master ... Hoffman (d)
Cupid .... Corkle
Seminary porter ...... Carlo
Gambler .... Kingman
Sergeant .... Yule

February 21

MADAMA BUTTERFLY (Puccini)

Conductor .... Zedda

Butterfly .... Niska
Suzuki .... Winburn
Pinkerton .... Savoldi
Sharpless .... Cossa
Goro .... Castel
Yamadori .... Lankston
The Bonze .... Pierson
Imperial
  Commissioner .... Park
Registrar .... Henderson
Kate Pinkerton .... Guilet
Trouble .... Lee

February 22 (m)

CAVALLERIA RUSTICANA
(Mascagni)

Conductor .... Krachmalnick

Santuzza .... Roberto
Turiddu .... Di Giuseppe
Alfio .... Patrick
Lola .... Lueders
Mamma Lucia .... Greenspon

Followed by:

I PAGLIACCI (Leoncavallo)

Conductor .... Krachmalnick

Nedda .... Bayard
Canio .... Callio
Tonio .... Ludgin
Silvio .... Murray (d)
Beppe .... Huddleston
Peasants .... Park, Davis

February 22

MANON

Same cast as February 20
except:

Des Grieux ...... Alexander,
                (s, Domingo)

February 23 (m)

CAVALLERIA RUSTICANA

Same cast as February 22 (m)
except:

Santuzza .... Lampropulos
Turiddu .... Savoldi

Followed by:

I PAGLIACCI

Same cast as February 22 (m)
except:

Nedda .... Niska,
                (s, Bayard)
Canio .... Martí

February 23

LA BOHÈME (Puccini)

Conductor .... Zedda

Rodolfo .... Di Giuseppe
Marcello .... Clatworthy
Schaunard .... Ledbetter
Colline .... Hale
Mimi .... Tyler
Musetta .... Bonini,
                (s, Niska)
Benoit .... Yule
Alcindoro .... Bittner
Parpignol .... Romaguera
Guards ..... Park, Henderson

February 26

LA BOHÈME

Same cast as February 23
except:

Mimi .... Ottaviano,
                (s, Tyler)
Musetta .... Bonini,
                (s, Bayard)

February 27

PRINCE IGOR (Borodin)
First performance by The New
York City Opera Company
(English translation by
Robert K. Evans)

Directed by .... Corsaro
Designer .... Armstrong
Lighting .... Armstrong
Choreographer .. Sequoio (d)
Conductor .... Rudel

Eroshka .... De Lon
Skula .... Bittner
Vladimir
  Jaroslavich .... Samuelsen
Igor .... Patrick
Vladimir Igorevitch .. Stewart
Jarsoslavna .... Niska
Jaroslavna's nurse .. B. Evans
Polovetsian maiden ..... Wise
Kontchakovna ..Davidson (d)
Polovetsian chief..Villella (d)
Ovlour .... Lankston
Kontchak .... Chapman
Slave .... Horne (d)

February 28

CAVALLERIA RUSTICANA

Same cast as February 22 (m)
except:

Turiddu .... Savoldi
Alfio .... Fredricks
Lola .... Creed
Mamma Lucia ..... B. Evans

Followed by:

I PAGLIACCI

Same cast as February 22 (m)
except:

Nedda .... Anthony,
                (s, Bonini)
Silvio .... Jamerson (d)
Beppe .... D. Clements

March 1 (m)

LA TRAVIATA (Verdi)

Conductor .... Zedda

Violetta .... Brooks
Alfredo .... Kelen
Germont .... Murray
Flora .... B. Evans
Annina .... Creed
Gaston .... Lankston
Douphol .... Bañuelas
D'Obigny .... Devlin
Dr. Grenvil .... Yule
Giuseppe .... Davis
Messenger .... Park
Solo dancer .... Fuente

March 1

MANON

Same cast as February 20
except:

Guillot .... Lankston
De Brétigny .... Beck
Rosette .... Creed
Manon .... Bayard
Des Grieux ..... Di Giuseppe
Count des Grieux ..... Hecht

March 2 (m)

PRINCE IGOR

Same cast as February 27

March 2

LA TRAVIATA

Same cast as March 1 (m)
except:

Violetta .... Elgar

March 4

LA TRAVIATA

Same cast as March 1 (m)
except:

Annina .... Winburn

March 5

THE MAGIC FLUTE (Mozart)
(English version by
Ruth and Thomas Martin)

Conductor .... Meier

Sarastro .... Roy
Tamino .... Di Giuseppe
Speaker .... Hale
Priest .... Lankston
Queen of the Night ... Moody
Pamina .... Tyler
1st Lady .... Bayard
2nd Lady .... Winburn
3rd Lady .... B. Evans
1st Spirit ..... O'Connell (d)
2nd Spirit .... Harwood
3rd Spirit ..... Imprescia (d)
Papageno .... Fredricks
Papagena .... Blanchard
Monostatos ..... Romaguera,
(s, Huddleston)

1st Armored
man .... D. Clements
2nd Armored
man .... Pierson

March 6

LA TRAVIATA

Same cast as March 1 (m)
except:

Conductor .... Krachmalnick

Violetta .... Niska
Alfredo .... Stewart
Germont .... Cossa
Annina .... Winburn

March 7

THE BALLAD OF BABY DOE
(Moore)

Conductor .... Meier

An old silver
miner .... Huddleston
Bouncer at the saloon .. Yule
Horace Tabor .... Ludgin
Sam .... D. Clements
Bushy .... Lankston
Barney .... Ledbetter
Jacob .... Bittner
Augusta .... Bible
Baby Doe .... Elgar
Kate .... Wilson
Mag .... Lueders
Samantha .... De Forest
Hotel clerk ...... Huddleston
Albert .... Yule
Sarah .... Darling
Mary .... Anthony
Emily .... B. Evans
Effie .... Winburn
McCourt family .... Herbert,
West, Krause, Bentley
Mama McCourt .. Greenspon
Four Washington
dandies ..... Davis, Darius,
Henderson, Park
Father Chapelle ... Lankston
Hotel footman .... Bittner
Chester A.
Arthur .... D. Clements
Elizabeth and Silver
Dollar . . Martin, Himmel (d)
Mayor of Leadville .... Davis
William Jennings
Bryan .... Hecht
Stage doorman ... Huddleston
Denver politician .... Roy
Silver Dollar
(grown up) .... Lueders

March 8 (m)

LA BOHÈME

Same cast as February 23
except:

Conductor .... Krachmalnick

Marcello .... Cossa
Schaunard .... Gibbs
Colline .... Devlin
Musetta .... Neblett (d)

March 8

MADAMA BUTTERFLY

Same cast as February 21
except:

Sharpless ...... Schwartzman
Goro .... D. Clements
Imperial
Commissioner .... Yule
Registrar .... Lankston
Kate Pinkerton ...... Lueders

March 9 (m)

MANON

Same cast as February 20
except:

Guillot .... Lankston
Rosette .... Creed
Des Grieux .... Molese
Count des Grieux ..... Hecht

March 9

PRINCE IGOR

Same cast as February 27
except:

Jaroslavna .... Bonini,
(s, Niska)

March 12

PRINCE IGOR

Same cast as February 27
except:

Igor .... Clatworthy
Vladimir Igorevitch .. Theyard

March 13

THE BALLAD OF BABY DOE

Same cast as March 7 except:

Conductor .... Ryan

Augusta .... Greenspon
Mama
McCourt ... N. Evans (d)
William Jennings Bryan . . Hale

March 14

LA BOHÈME

Same cast as February 23
except:

Rodolfo .... Molese
Schaunard .... Beck
Mimi .... Ottaviano
Musetta .... Neblett
Guards ..... Galiano, Bentley

March 15 (m)

CAVALLERIA RUSTICANA

Same cast as February 22 (m)
except:

Turiddu .... Savolo
Alfio .... Fredrick

Followed by:

I PAGLIACCI

Same cast as February 22 (m)
except:

Nedda .... Anthony,
(s, Bayard)
Canio .... Martí
Tonio .... Chapman
Silvio .... Cossa
Beppe .... Romaguera

March 15

LA TRAVIATA

Same cast as March 1 (m)
except:

Violetta .... Niska
Annina .... Winburn

March 16 (m)

MANON

Same cast as February 20
except:

Guillot .... Lankston
Rosette .... Creed
Innkeeper .... Postrel
Manon .... Brooks
Des Grieux .... Molese

March 16

THE MAGIC FLUTE

Same cast as March 5 except:

Conductor .... Ryan

Tamino .... Stewart
Speaker .... Devlin
Queen of the
Night .... Augér (d)
1st Lady .... Crane,
(s, Bayard)
Papageno .... Ledbetter
Monostatos ..... Romaguera,
(s, Huddleston)

March 19

MADAMA BUTTERFLY

Same cast as February 21
except:

Suzuki .... B. Evans
Pinkerton ...... Di Giuseppe,
(s, Savoldi)
Sharpless .... Beck
Goro .... D. Clements
Kate Pinkerton ...... Lueders

March 20

RIGOLETTO (Verdi)
New production

Directed by .... Corsaro
Scenic designer .... Evans
Costume designer .... Varona
Choreographer .... Joffrey
Lighting .... Sondheimer
Conductor .... Ötvös (d)

Rigoletto .... Quilico
Monterone's daughter ..Horne
Duke .... Molese

Borsa .... D. Clements
Countess Ceprano ...... Wise
Ceprano .... Ledbetter
Marullo .... Beck
Monterone .... Pierson
Sparafucile .... Smith
Gilda .... Brooks
Giovanna .... Winburn
Page .... Crane
Maddalena .... Creed

March 21

CAVALLERIA RUSTICANA

Same cast as February 22 (m)
except:

Turiddu .... Savoldi
Alfio .... Fredricks

Followed by:

I PAGLIACCI

Same cast as February 22 (m)
except:

Nedda .... Niska
Canio .... Nichols
Tonio .... Chapman
Silvio .... Cossa
Beppe .... Romaguera

March 22 (m)

THE MAGIC FLUTE

Same cast as March 5 except:

Tamino .... Stewart,
(s, Di Giuseppe)
Queen of the Night ... Augér
Pamina .... Elgar
2nd Spirit ...... Hoeler (d)
3rd Spirit ...... Friedman (d)
Papagena .... Wise
Monostatos .... Romaguera,
(s, Huddleston)

March 22

LA BOHÈME

Same cast as February 23
except:

Rodolfo .... Kelen
Marcello .... Cossa
Colline .... Devlin
Mimi .... Di Gerlando
Musetta .... Neblett
Guards .... Galiano, Bentley

March 23 (m)

RIGOLETTO

Same cast as March 20

March 23

LE COQ D'OR
(Rimsky-Korsakov)
(English version by Antal
Dorati and James Gibson)

Conductor .... Rudel

Astrologer ..... Di Giuseppe
King Dodon .... Malas,
(s, Treigle)
Prince Guidon .. D. Clements
Prince Afron .... Beck

General Polkan ...... Pierson
Amelfa .... Greenspon
Golden Cockerel .. Blanchard
Queen of Shemakha ..... Sills

March 25

RIGOLETTO

Same cast as March 20 except:

Gilda .... Elgar

March 26

FAUST (Gounod)

Conductor .... Krachmalnick

Faust .... Di Giuseppe
Méphistophélès .... Hecht
Wagner .... Beck
Marguerite .... Niska
Valentin .... Cossa
Siébel .... Bible
Marthe .... Greenspon
Juggler .... De Dio
Fire-eater .... Demon
Acrobats .."Los Crackerjacks"

March 27

RIGOLETTO

Same cast as March 20 except:

Duke .... Duval
Gilda .... Elgar

March 28

FAUST

Same cast as March 26

March 29 (m)

PRINCE IGOR

Same cast as February 27
except:

Igor .... Clatworthy
Vladimir Igorevitch .. Theyard
Jaroslavna .... Bonini
Kontchakovna .... Creed
Polovetsian chief .... Sequoio

March 29

RIGOLETTO

Same cast as March 20 except:

Sparafucile .... Hale
Maddalena .... Lueders

March 30 (m)

THE BALLAD OF BABY DOE

Same cast as March 7 except:

Elizabeth .... Wisnofsky
William Jennings Bryan..Smith

March 30

FAUST

Same cast as March 26 except:

Méphistophélès .... Samuelsen
Marguerite .... Bayard

Valentin .... Jamerson,
(s, Cossa)
Siébel .... Creed

April 1

PRINCE IGOR

Same cast as February 27
except:

*Vladimir
Jaroslavich* ...... Chapman
*Vladimir
Igorevitch* .... Theyard
Polovetsian maiden .. Kehrig,
(s, Wise)

April 2

LE COQ D'OR

Same cast as March 23 except:

Prince Guidon .... Castel
Queen of Shemakha .... Wise

April 3

FAUST

Same cast as March 26 except:

Conductor .... Meier

Faust .... Molese
Méphistophélès .... Samuelsen
Wagner .... Hicks
Marguerite .... Thomson (d)
Valentin .... Jamerson

April 4

RIGOLETTO

Same cast as March 20 except:

Duke .... Duval
Sparafucile .... Hale
Giovanna .... B. Evans,
(s, Winburn)
Maddalena .... Lueders

April 5 (m)

IL TRITTICO (Puccini)

Directed by .... Pollock
Conductor .... Rudel

IL TABARRO

Giorgetta .... Schauler
Michele .... Ludgin
Luigi .... Theyard
Tinca .... Castel
Talpa .... Roy
Song vendor ..... Huddleston
Frugola .... Turner
Two lovers .... Crane;
Lankston

Followed by:

SUOR ANGELICA

Suor Angelica .... Niska
La Suora Zelatrice .. B. Evans
Le due Converse ...... Adler,
M. Armstrong
*La Maestra
della Novizie* .... Guilet
Suor Genovieffa ... Blanchard

Le due Novizie .... H. Owen,
De Forest
Suor Dolcina ...... D. Owen
La Cercatrice .... West
La Badessa ...... Greenspon,
(s, Winburn)
La Principessa .... Turner

Followed by:

GIANNI SCHICCHI

Zita .... Turner
Rinuccio .... Di Giuseppe
Gherardo .... Castel
Nella .... Crane
Gherardino .... Puleo
Betto .... Yule
Simone .... Smith
Marco .... Ledbetter
La Ciesca .... Anthony
Gianni Schicchi .... Fredricks
Lauretta .... Blanchard
Spinellocchio .... Pierson
Nicolao .... Bittner
Pinellino .... Park
Guccio .... Henderson

April 5

THE BALLAD OF BABY DOE

Same cast as March 7 except:

Baby Doe ...... Mulvey (d)
Mama McCourt ... N. Evans
Elizabeth .... Wisnofsky

April 6 (m)

LE COQ D'OR

Same cast as March 23 except:

King Dodon .... Devlin
Prince Guidon .... Castel
*Queen of
Shemakha* ... K. Armstrong
(d), (s, Wise)

April 6

RIGOLETTO

Same cast as March 20 except:

Countess Ceprano ..... Crane
Sparafucile .... Hale
Gilda .... Elgar
Page .... Ledur

April 8

IL TRITTICO

Same casts as April 5 (m)
except:

IL TABARRO

Luigi .... Savoldi

Followed by:

SUOR ANGELICA

Suor Angelica ... Di Gerlando
La Badessa .... Winburn

Followed by:

GIANNI SCHICCHI

Rinuccio .... Duval

April 9

LE COQ D'OR

Same cast as March 23 except:

King Dodon .... Devlin
Prince Guidon .... Castel
General Polkan .... Roy
*Queen of
Shemakha* ... K. Armstrong

April 10

THE MARRIAGE OF FIGARO
(Mozart)
(English version by
Ruth and Thomas Martin)

Directed by .... Habunek
Conductor .... Ötvös

Figaro .... Malas
Susanna .... J. Clements
Bartolo .... Smith
Marcellina .... B. Evans
Cherubino .... Bible
Almaviva .... Clatworthy
Basilio .... Castel
Countess .... Niska
Antonio .... Bittner
Curzio .... Lankston
Barbarina .... Blanchard

April 11

THE MAGIC FLUTE

Same cast as March 5 except:

Sarastro .... Hecht
*Queen of the
Night* ..... Moody (Act I);
Crane (Act II)
Pamina .... Elgar
2nd Spirit .... Hoeler
3rd Spirit .... Friedman
Papagena .... Wise
Monostatos .... Castel

April 12 (m)

IL TRITTICO

Same casts as April 5 (m)
except:

Conductor .... Dufallo

IL TABARRO

Giorgetta ...... Lampropulo
Luigi .... Savold
Tinca .... D. Clement
Frugola .... Greenspo

Followed by:

SUOR ANGELICA

Suor Angelica .... Niska
(s, Di Gerlando
La Badessa .... Winbur
La Principessa .... Greenspo

Followed by:

GIANNI SCHICCHI

Zita .... Greenspon
Rinuccio .... Duval
Gherardo .... D. Clements
Gianni Schicchi .... Malas
Lauretta .... Di Giglio

April 12

MADAMA BUTTERFLY

Same cast as February 21
except:

Conductor .... Effron

Butterfly .... Roberto
Suzuki .... Creed
Pinkerton .... Molese
Sharpless ...... Schwartzman
Imperial Commissioner .. Yule
Registrar .... Lankston
Kate Pinkerton ...... Lueders

April 13 (m)

LE COQ D'OR

Same cast as March 23 except:

Prince Guidon .... Castel
General Polkan ...... Pierson,
                         (s, Roy)
Queen of Shemakha .... Wise

April 13

THE MARRIAGE OF FIGARO

Same cast as April 10 except:

Figaro .... Hale

April 15

LA BOHÈME

Same cast as February 23
except:

Conductor .... Ötvös

Marcello .... Jamerson
Schaunard .... Gibbs

Colline .... Smith
Mimi .... Ottaviano
Musetta .... Bayard
Guards ..... Galiano, Bentley

April 16

THE MARRIAGE OF FIGARO

Same cast as April 10 except:

Countess .... Vanni (d)

April 17

FAUST

Same cast as March 26 except:

Conductor .... Meier

Méphistophélès .... Samuelsen
Wagner .... Hicks
Marguerite .... Thomson
Siébel .... Creed

April 18

MANON

Same cast as February 20
except:

Rosette .... Creed
Innkeeper .... Postrel
Lescaut .... Trehy
Manon .... Brooks
Des Grieux .... Molese

April 19 (m)

THE MARRIAGE OF FIGARO

Same cast as April 10 except:

Conductor .... Ryan

Figaro .... Hale
Bartolo .... Roy
Cherubino .... Creed
Countess .... Vanni
Antonio .... Yule
Curzio .... Romaguera

April 19

IL TRITTICO

Same casts as April 5 (m)
except:

Conductor .... Dufallo

IL TABARRO

Giorgetta ...... Lampropulos
Michele .... Chapman
Luigi .... Nagy (d)
Tinca .... D. Clements
Frugola .... Greenspon

Followed by:

SUOR ANGELICA

Suor Genovieffa ..... Mulvey
La Badessa .... Winburn
La Principessa .... Greenspon

Followed by:

GIANNI SCHICCHI

Zita .... Greenspon
Gherardo .... D. Clements
Gianni Schicchi .... Malas
Lauretta .... Di Giglio
Pinellino .... Papay

April 20 (m)

MADAMA BUTTERFLY

Same cast as February 21
except:

Conductor .... Effron

Pinkerton .... Stewart
Yamadori .... Hicks
Imperial Commissioner .. Yule
Registrar .... Hicks
Kate Pinkerton ...... Lueders

April 20

LE COQ D'OR

same cast as March 23 except:

Prince Guidon .... Castel
Queen of Shemakha .... Wise

Fall 1969 (SEPTEMBER 10 – NOVEMBER 16)

Female artists
Anthony, Judith
Armstrong, Karan
Bayard, Carol
Bible, Frances
Blanchard, Barbara
Brooks, Patricia
Clatworthy, Mary Ann*
Clements, Joy
Crane, Lois
Creed, Kay
Cruz-Romo, Gilda*
Darling, Sandra
Davidson, Joy*
De Forest, Anthea

Elgar, Anne
Evans, Beverly
Evans, Nell
Faull, Ellen
Greene, Harriet
Greenspon, Muriel
Guilet, Helene
Herbert, Lila
Himmel, Michele
Kern, Patricia*
Kleinman, Marlena
Ledur, Letitia
Lueders, Mary Cross
Meier, Johanna*
Neblett, Carol

Niska, Maralin
Ottaviano, Anna
Owen, Hanna
Roberto, Francesca
Rondelli, Barbara*
Sills, Beverly
Tyler, Veronica
Vanni, Helen
West, Maria
Winburn, Janet
Wise, Patricia

Male artists
Beattie, Herbert
Bentley, Ronald

* New artist

* New artist

* New artist

Bittner, Jack
Carlo, Don
Cassel, Walter
Castel, Nico
Citarelli, Enzo
Chapman, William
Clatworthy, David
Clements, David
Cletus, Douglas
Corbeil, Claude*
Cossa, Dominic
Crespo, Emilio
Darius, Anthony
Darrenkamp, John*
Davis, Harris
Demon, Satani
Devlin, Michael
Di Giuseppe, Enrico
Di Virgilio, Nicholas
Dunlap, John Robert*
DuPree, William
Duval, Pierre
Folgar, Manuel
Fredricks, Richard
Galiano, Joseph
Gibbs, Raymond
Hale, Robert
Henderson, Don
Hicks, David
Iglesias, Franco*
Jamerson, Thomas
Kingman, Dan
Krause, Karl Patrick
Lankston, John
Ledbetter, William
Lee, Christopher
LoMonaco, Jerome
McCray, James*
Malas, Spiro
Metcalf, William
Miller, Kellis
Molese, Michele
Nagy, Robert
Novoa, Salvador
Papay, Raymond
Park, Richard
Pierson, Edward
Pilley, Donald*
Porras, Patricio
Porretta, Frank
Puleo, Robert
Quilico, Louis
Riegel, Kenneth*
Romaguera, Joaquin
Roy, Will
Samuelsen, Roy
Schwartzman, Seymour
Sergi, Arturo*
Smith, Malcolm
Stewart, John
Torigi, Richard
Trehy, Robert
Treigle, Norman
Weeks, Larry
Yule, Don

Conductors
Albertini, Sergio*
Meier, Gustav
Ötvös, Gabor
Popper, Felix
Rudel, Julius
Wilson, Charles

* New artist

Chorus master
Nance, Chris*

Solo dancers
Brayley, Sally
Corkle, Francesca
de Lavallade, Carmen
Jones, Susan*
Kothera, Lynn*
Trammell, Sally*
Fuente, Luis
Miller, Buzz
Moore, Charles
Powell, Robert
Quinn, Michael*
Taylor, Burton*
Villella, Edward

Choreographers
Butler, John
Cole, Jack
Joffrey, Robert
Sequoio, Ron

Directors
Butler, John
Capobianco, Tito
Corsaro, Frank
Field, William
Hebert, Bliss
Hicks, David
Pollock, Michael
Savoca, Carmen
West, Christopher

Designers
Armstrong, Will Steven
Bay, Howard
Campbell, Patton
Eck, Marsha Louis
Evans, Lloyd
Fletcher, Robert
George, Hal*
Lee, Ming Cho
Mitchell, David*
Oenslager, Donald
Varona, José
Venza, Jac
Wittstein, Ed

* New artist

September 10

RIGOLETTO (Verdi)

Conductor .... Ötvös

Rigoletto .... Quilico
Monterone's
  daughter .... Brayley
Duke .... Molese
Borsa .... D. Clements
Countess Ceprano ...... Wise
Ceprano .... Ledbetter
Marullo .... Iglesias (d)
Monterone .... Pierson
Sparafucile .... Hale
Gilda .... Brooks
Giovanna .... Winburn
Page .... Crane
Maddalena .... Creed

September 11

FAUST (Gounod)

Conductor .... Meier

Faust .... Di Giuseppe
Méphistophélès ...... Treigle

Wagner .... Gibbs
Marguerite .... Sills
Valentin .... Cossa
Siébel .... Bible
Marthe .... Greenspon
Juggler .... Weeks
Fire-eater .... Demon
Acrobats .... Deighton Boyce,
        Ahmed Abdarrahman,
              Mustapha Ali,
              Clayton Blount,
              Maimon Sidah

September 12

RIGOLETTO

Same cast as September 10

September 13 (m)

LA BOHÈME (Puccini)

Conductor .... Wilson

Rodolfo .... LoMonaco,
        (s, Di Giuseppe)
Marcello .... Cossa
Schaunard .... Ledbetter
Colline .... Hale
Mimi .... Tyler
Musetta .... Neblett
Benoit .... Yule
Alcindoro .... Bittner
Parpignol .... Romaguera
Guards ..... Park, Henderson

September 13

THE MARRIAGE OF FIGARO
(Mozart)
(English version by
Ruth and Thomas Martin)

Conductor .... Ötvös

Figaro .... Malas
Susanna .... J. Clements
Bartolo .... Smith
Marcellina .... B. Evans
Cherubino .... Kern (d)
Almaviva ..... D. Clatworthy
Basilio .... Castel
Countess .... Niska
Antonio .... Yule
Curzio .... K. Miller
Barbarina .... Blanchard

September 14 (m)

MADAMA BUTTERFLY (Puccini)

Conductor .... Wilson

Butterfly .... Roberti
Suzuki .... Cree
Pinkerton .... Di Virgilio
Sharpless .... Dunlap (d
Goro .... D. Clements
Yamadori .... Lankston
The Bonze .... Pierson
Imperial Commissioner...Par
Registrar .... Henderso
Kate Pinkerton ...... Lueder
Trouble .... Le

September 14

FAUST

Same cast as September 11 except:

Faust .... Molese
Valentin .... Jamerson

September 17

LA BOHÈME

Same cast as September 13 (m) except:

Rodolfo .... Molese

September 18

MADAMA BUTTERFLY

Same cast as September 14 (m) except:

Pinkerton ...... Di Giuseppe

September 19

PRINCE IGOR (Borodin)
(English translation by Robert K. Evans)

Conductor .... Rudel

Eroshka .... Romaguera
Skula .... Bittner
Vladimir
  Jaroslavich ...... Chapman
Igor .... D. Clatworthy
Vladimir
  Igorevitch .... Porretta
Jaroslavna .... Niska
Jaroslavna's nurse .. Winburn
Polovetsian maiden ..... Wise
Kontchakovna ..Davidson (d)
Polovetsian chief ..... Villella
Ovlour .... Lankston
Kontchak .... Chapman
Slave .... Brayley

September 20 (m)

MADAMA BUTTERFLY

Same cast as September 14 (m) except:

Butterfly .... Rondelli (d)
Pinkerton ...... Di Giuseppe
Sharpless ... Darrenkamp (d)

September 20

THE MARRIAGE OF FIGARO

Same cast as September 13 except:

Figaro .... Hale
Susanna .... Elgar
Almaviva .... Samuelsen
Basilio .... D. Clements
Countess .... Vanni

September 21 (m)

PRINCE IGOR

Same cast as September 19 except:

Conductor .... Meier

September 21

MEFISTOFELE (Boito)
First performance by The New York City Opera Company

Directed by ..... Capobianco
Scenic designer .. Mitchell (d)
Costume designer ..George (d)
Choreographer .... Joffrey
Lighting .... Sondheimer
Conductor .... Rudel

Mefistofele .... Treigle
Faust .... Nagy
Wagner .... Lankston
Margherita .... Neblett
Marta .... B. Evans
Elena .... Neblett
Pantalis .... Lueders
Nereo .... Lankston

September 23

LA BOHÈME

Same cast as September 13 (m) except:

Rodolfo .... Molese
Colline .... Smith
Musetta .... Bayard
Benoit .... Roy

September 24

MEFISTOFELE

Same cast as September 21 except:

Wagner .... D. Clements

September 25

CAPRICCIO (R. Strauss)
(English translation by Maria Pelikan)

Directed by .... Hebert
Choreographer .... Joffrey
Lighting .... Sondheimer
Conductor .... Ötvös

Flamand .... Di Giuseppe
Olivier .... Metcalf
LaRoche .... Malas
Countess .... Vanni
Count .... Trehy
Clairon .... Creed
Dancer .... Brayley
Italian singers .... Faull;
                  Citarelli
Major-Domo .... Roy
M. Taupe .... Castel
Servants ...... D. Clements,
    Cletus, Lankston, Yule,
    Bittner, Romaguera,
    Davis, Henderson

September 26

THE MARRIAGE OF FIGARO

Same cast as September 13 except:

Figaro .... Hale
Almaviva .... Samuelsen
Antonio .... Bittner

September 27 (m)

PRINCE IGOR

Same cast as September 19 except:

Vladimir
  Igorevitch .... McCray (d)
Polovetsian chief ..Taylor (d),
             (s, Villella)

September 27

MEFISTOFELE

Same cast as September 21 except:

Wagner .... D. Clements

September 28 (m)

LA TRAVIATA (Verdi)

Conductor .... Meier

Violetta .... Brooks
Alfredo .... Molese
Germont .... Fredricks
Flora .... Lueders
Annina .... Winburn
Gaston .... Lankston
Douphol .... Iglesias
D'Obigny .... Devlin
Dr. Grenvil .... Yule
Giuseppe .... Davis
Messenger .... Park
Solo dancer .... Fuente

September 28

MADAMA BUTTERFLY

Same cast as September 14 (m) except:

Butterfly .... Rondelli
Pinkerton ...... Di Giuseppe
Sharpless .... Cossa
Goro .... Castel
The Bonze .... Roy
Imperial Commissioner .. Yule
Registrar .... Lankston

September 30

MEFISTOFELE

Same cast as September 21 except:

Faust .... Sergi (d)
Wagner .... D. Clements

October 1

MANON (Massenet)

Conductor .... Rudel

Guillot .... Castel
De Brétigny .... Hale
Pousette .... Crane
Javotte .... Kleinman
Rosette .... Creed
Innkeeper .... Bittner
Lescaut .... Fredricks
Guards .... Papay, Yule
Manon .... Sills
Des Grieux .... Molese
Maid .... Greene

Count des Grieux .... Smith
Prima ballerina ...... Brayley
Premier danseur ...... Taylor
Ballet master ..... Quinn (d)
Cupid .... Corkle
Seminary porter .... Carlo
Gambler .... Kingman
Sergeant .... Yule

October 2

THE MARRIAGE OF FIGARO

Same cast as September 13
except:

Figaro .... Hale
Bartolo .... Roy
Cherubino .... Creed
Countess .... Vanni
Antonio .... Bittner
Barbarina .... Crane

October 3

MADAMA BUTTERFLY

Same cast as September 14 (m)
except:

Butterfly .... Niska,
                  (s, Roberto)
Suzuki .... Winburn
Pinkerton .... Molese
Sharpless .... Cossa
The Bonze .... Roy
Imperial Commissioner .. Yule
Registrar .... Lankston

October 4 (m)

CAPRICCIO

Same cast as September 25
except:

M. Taupe ...... D. Clements,
                  (s, Castel)

October 4

THE BALLAD OF BABY DOE
(Moore)

Stage director .... Field
Conductor .... Meier

An old silver
  miner .... Romaguera
Bouncer at the saloon ... Yule
Horace Tabor ..... Chapman
Sam .... D. Clements
Bushy .... Lankston
Barney .... Ledbetter
Jacob .... Bittner
Augusta .... Bible
Baby Doe .... Elgar
Kate .... Owen
Mag .... Lueders
Samantha .... De Forest
Hotel clerk ...... Romaguera
Albert .... Yule
Sarah .... Darling
Mary .... Anthony
Emily .... B. Evans
Effie .... Winburn
McCourt family ..... Herbert,
          West, Krause, Bentley
Mama McCourt .. Greenspon

Four Washington
  dandies .... Davis, Darius,
          Henderson, Park
Father Chapelle .... Lankston
Hotel footman .... Bittner
Chester A.
  Arthur ...... D. Clements
Elizabeth and Silver
  Dollar..M. Clatworthy (d),
                  Himmel
Mayor of Leadville .... Davis
William Jennings Bryan..Smith
Stage doorman ... Romaguera
Denver politician .... Roy
Silver Dollar
  (grown up) .... Lueders

October 5 (m)

MEFISTOFELE

Same cast as September 21
except:

Faust .... Di Virgilio
                  (s, Sergi)
Wagner .... D. Clements
Margherita .. Cruz-Romo (d)
Elena ...... Cruz-Romo (d)
Pantalis .... B. Evans,
                  (s, Lueders)

October 5

PRINCE IGOR

Same cast as September 19
except:

Conductor .... Meier
Igor .... Pierson
Vladimir Igorevitch .. McCray
Kontchakovna ...... Lueders
Polovetsian chief ..... Taylor

October 8

PRINCE IGOR

Same cast as September 19
except:

Igor .... Darrenkamp
Jaroslavna .... Neblett
Kontchakovna ...... Lueders

October 9

LUCIA DI LAMMERMOOR
(Donizetti)
First performance by The New
  York City Opera Company

Directed by .... Capobianco
Scenic designer .... Eck
Costume designer .... Varona
Choreographer .... Joffrey
Lighting .... Sondheimer
Conductor .... Wilson

Alisa .... B. Evans
Edgardo .... Molese
Normanno ...... Romaguera
Enrico .... Cossa
Raimondo .... Hale
Lucia .... Sills
Arturo .... D. Clements

October 10

LA TRAVIATA

Same cast as September 28 (m)
except:

Alfredo .... Di Giuseppe
Solo dancer .... Taylor

October 11 (m)

THE MARRIAGE OF FIGARO

Same cast as September 13
except:

Conductor .... Wilson

Bartolo .... Roy
Cherubino .... Bible
Almaviva ..... D. Clatworthy
          (Acts I and II);
  Fredricks (Acts III and IV)
Antonio .... Bittner

October 11

LA BOHÈME

Same cast as September 13 (m)
except:

Conductor .... Rudel

Marcello .... Jamerson
Colline .... Devlin
Mimi .... Ottaviano
Benoit .... Roy
Guards ..... Bentley, Galiano

October 12 (m)

LUCIA DI LAMMERMOOR

Same cast as October 9

October 12

MANON

Same cast as October 1 except:

Manon .... Brooks
Des Grieux ..... Di Giuseppe

October 14

LUCIA DI LAMMERMOOR

Same cast as October 9

October 15

LA TRAVIATA

Same cast as September 28 (m)
except:

Violetta .... Niska
Alfredo .... LoMonaco
D'Obigny .... Ledbetter
Solo dancer .... Taylor

October 16

THE ABDUCTION FROM
THE SERAGLIO (Mozart)
(English version by
Ruth and Thomas Martin)

Directed by .... Pollock
Conductor .... Rudel

Belmonte .... Stewart
Osmin .... Beattie

Pedrillo .... Lankston
Constanza .... Sills
Pasha Selim .... Trehy
Blonde .... Elgar

October 17

CAPRICCIO

Same cast as September 25
except:

Conductor .... Popper
Countess .... Meier (d)

October 18 (m)

LA BOHÈME

Same cast as September 13 (m)
except:

Marcello .... Cossa,
          (s, D. Clatworthy)
Schaunard .... Gibbs
Colline .... Devlin
Mimi .... Ottaviano
Musetta .... Bayard
Benoit .... Roy
Guards ..... Bentley, Galiano

October 18

MANON

Same cast as October 1 except:

Manon .... Brooks
Cupid .... Jones (d),
               (s, Corkle)

October 19 (m)

BOMARZO (Ginastera)

Conductor .... Rudel

Shepherd .... Puleo
Pier Francesco Orsini ..Novoa
Silvio de Narni .... Torigi
Nicolas Orsini ... Romaguera
Diana Orsini ..... Greenspon
Pier Francesco,
  as a child .... Porras
Maerbale, as a child .. Folgar
Girolamo, as a child .. Crespo
Gian Corrado Orsini .. Devlin
Skeleton .... B. Miller
Messenger ...... D. Clements
Pantasilea .... Simon
Abul .... Moore
Girolamo .... Metcalf
Julia Farnese .... Wise
Maerbale .... Gibbs
Alter ego of Pier
  Francesco .... B. Miller
Solo dancer ... Trammell (d)

October 19

LUCIA DI LAMMERMOOR

Same cast as October 9 except:
Edgardo .... Di Virgilio

October 21

FAUST

Same cast as September 11
except:

Méphistophélès ... Samuelsen
Marguerite .... Bayard
Valentin .... Jamerson

October 22

LUCIA DI LAMMERMOOR

Same cast as October 9 except:

Enrico .... Fredricks

October 23

MEFISTOFELE

Same cast as September 21
except:

Nereo .... Romaguera

October 24

THE ABDUCTION FROM
THE SERAGLIO

Same cast as October 16
except:

Constanza .... Brooks

October 25 (m)

LUCIA DI LAMMERMOOR

Same cast as October 9 except:

Alisa .... Winburn,
            (s, B. Evans)
Enrico .... Fredricks
Raimondo .... Devlin

October 25

FAUST

Same cast as September 11
except:

Marguerite .... Niska
Valentin .... Jamerson
Siébel .... Creed

October 26 (m)

THE BALLAD OF BABY DOE

Same cast as October 4 except:

Horace Tabor .... Cassel
Mama McCourt .. Greenspon,
                (s, N. Evans)

October 26

BOMARZO

Same cast as October 19 (m)
except:

Gian Corrado Orsini ... Yule,
               (s, Devlin)
Pantasilea .... Lueders,
               (s, Simon)

October 29

FAUST

Same cast as September 11
except:

Wagner .... Hicks
Marguerite .... Niska
Siébel .... Creed

October 30

L'HEURE ESPAGNOLE (Ravel)

Directed by .... Hebert
Conductor .... Rudel

Torquemada .... Castel
Ramiro .... Fredricks
Concepcion ...... Armstrong
Gonzalve .... Riegel (d)
Don Inigo Gomez .... Malas

Followed by:

CATULLI CARMINA (Orff)
First performance by The New
York City Opera Company

Directed and
  choreographed by ... Butler
Designer .... Venza
Lighting .... Sondheimer
Conductor .... Rudel

Lesbia .... de Lavallade
Caelius .... B. Miller
Catullus .... Powell
Ipsitilla .... Kothera (d)
Soprano .... Wise
Tenor .... DuPree

October 31

MANON

Same cast as October 1 except:

Conductor .... Rudel,
               (s, Wilson)
Lescaut .... Trehy
Manon .... Brooks
Count des Grieux .... Devlin,
               (s, Smith)

November 1 (m)

LA TRAVIATA

Same cast as September 28 (m)
except:

Violetta .... Niska
Alfredo .... Di Giuseppe
Germont ...... Schwartzman
D'Obigny .... Ledbetter
Solo dancer .... Taylor

November 1

LUCIA DI LAMMERMOOR

Same cast as October 9 except:

Alisa .... Winburn
Edgardo .... Novoa
Enrico .... Fredricks
Raimondo .... Devlin

November 2 (m)

FAUST

Same cast as September 11 except:

Faust .... Molese
Wagner .... Hicks
Marguerite .... Bayard
Valentin .... Jamerson

November 2

THE ABDUCTION FROM
THE SERAGLIO

Same cast as October 16 except:

Constanza .... Brooks
Blonde .... Armstrong

November 4

THE ABDUCTION FROM
THE SERAGLIO

Same cast as October 16 except:

Pedrillo .... Riegel
Blonde .... Armstrong

November 5

RIGOLETTO

Same cast as September 10 except:

Conductor ..... Albertini (d)
Duke .... Pilley (d)
Sparafucile .... Smith
Gilda .... Elgar
Page .... Ledur,
(s, Crane)

November 6

MANON

Same cast as October 1 except:

Conductor .... Wilson
Pousette .... Wise,
(s, Crane)
Javotte .... Guilet
Manon .... Brooks
Count des Grieux . . Corbeil (d)

November 7

BOMARZO

Same cast as October 19 (m) except:

Silvio di Narni ...... Iglesias

November 8 (m)

MANON

Same cast as October 1 except:

Conductor .... Wilson
Pousette .... Wise,
(s, Crane)

Javotte .... Guilet
Des Grieux .... Duval
Count des Grieux .... Corbeil

November 8

RIGOLETTO

Same cast as September 10 except:

Conductor .... Albertini

Sparafucile .... Roy
Gilda .... Elgar

November 9 (m)

MADAMA BUTTERFLY

Same cast as September 14 (m) except:

Butterfly .... Niska
Suzuki .... B. Evans
Pinkerton .... Pilley
Sharpless .... Iglesias
Goro .... Castel
The Bonze .... Roy
Imperial Commissioner .. Yule
Registrar .... Lankston

November 9

L'HEURE ESPAGNOLE

Same cast as October 30

Followed by:

CATULLI CARMINA

Same cast as October 30

November 11

RIGOLETTO

Same cast as September 10 except:

Conductor .... Albertini

Sparafucile .... Smith
Maddalena .... Lueders

November 12

L'HEURE ESPAGNOLE

Same cast as October 30

Followed by:

CATULLI CARMINA

Same cast as October 30 except:

Tenor .... Lankston

November 13

THE BALLAD OF BABY DOE

Same cast as October 4 except:

Horace Tabor .... Cassel
Augusta .... Greenspon

Baby Doe .... Sills
Sarah .... Crane
Mama McCourt .... N. Evans
William Jennings Bryan...Roy
Denver politician .... Yule

November 14

RIGOLETTO

Same cast as September 10 except:

Duke .... Di Giuseppe
Borsa .... Lankston
Countess Ceprano ..... Crane
Marullo .... Bittner
Monterone .... Devlin
Gilda .... Elgar
Page .... Ledur
Maddalena .... Lueders

November 15 (m)

THE ABDUCTION FROM
THE SERAGLIO

Same cast as October 16 except:

Pedrillo .... Riegel
Blonde .... Armstrong

November 15

LA TRAVIATA

Same cast as September 28 (m) except:

Germont .... Cossa
D'Obigny .... Ledbetter
Solo dancer .... Taylor

November 16 (m)

L'HEURE ESPAGNOLE

Same cast as October 30 except:

Ramiro ...... D. Clatworthy
Concepcion ...... Blanchard

Followed by:

CATULLI CARMINA

Same cast as October 30 except:

Tenor .... Lankston

November 16

MADAMA BUTTERFLY

Same cast as September 14 (m) except:

Pinkerton ...... Di Giuseppe
Sharpless ...... Schwartzman
Goro .... Castel
The Bonze .... Roy
Imperial Commissioner .. Yule
Registrar .... Lankston

Spring 1970 (FEBRUARY 19–APRIL 19)

Female artists
Angela, June*
Anthony, Judith
Armstrong, Karan
Bible, Frances
Blanchard, Barbara
Brooks, Patricia
Carron, Elisabeth
Crane, Lois
Creed, Kay
Cruz-Romo, Gilda
Dal Piva, Milena*
Darling, Sandra
Elgar, Anne
Evans, Beverly
Faull, Ellen
Greene, Harriet
Greenspon, Muriel
Guilet, Helene
Hinds, Esther*
Hunt, Alexandra*
Kieffer, Deborah*
Lebrun, Louise*
Lueders, Mary Cross
Meier, Johanna
Moody, Janette
Nadler, Sheila*
Neblett, Carol
Niska, Maralin
Schauler, Eileen
Sills, Beverly
Winburn, Janet
Wise, Patricia

Male artists
Bass, Robert*
Beattie, Herbert
Bentley, Ronald
Bittner, Jack
Carlo, Don
Casellato-Lamberti, Giorgio*
Castel, Nico
Clatworthy, David
Clements, David
Cossa, Dominic
Darrenkamp, John
Davis, Harris
Demon, Satani
Devlin, Michael
Di Giuseppe, Enrico
Di Virgilio, Nicholas
DuPree, William
Fredricks, Richard
Galiano, Joseph
Garcia, Nino
Glaze, Gary*
Hale, Robert
Hecht, Joshua
Henderson, Don
Hicks, David
Iglesias, Franco
Jamerson, Thomas
Jennings, Jerry J.*
Jobin, André*
Kalfayan, Kris*

* New artist

Kingman, Dan
Krause, Karl Patrick
Lankston, John
Ledbetter, William
Lee, David*
LoMonaco, Jerome
Malas, Spiro
Molese, Michele
Morell, Barry
Moulson, Robert
Mundt, Richard*
Nagy, Robert
Papay, Raymond
Park, Richard
Pierson, Edward
Piso, Ion*
Polakoff, Abe*
Postrel, Leo
Puleo, Robert
Quilico, Louis
Riegel, Kenneth
Romaguera, Joaquin
Roy, Will
Schwartzman, Seymour
Sergi, Arturo
Shirley, George
Smith, David Rae
Smith, Malcolm
Stamford, John
Stein, Peter*
Stewart, John
Stilwell, Richard*
Townsend, Erik*
Treigle, Norman
Vega, Joseph*
Weeks, Larry
Wishner, Samuel
Yule, Don

Conductors
Marty, Jean-Pierre*
Meier, Gustav
Mester, Jorge*
Nance, Chris*
Rudel, Julius
Ryan, Dean
Singer, George*
Wilson, Charles

Chorus master
Nance, Chris

Solo dancers
Balestracci, Sandra
Fuerstner, Fiona*
Galan, Esperanza
Martin, Erin*
Menes, Rose Marie*
Morales, Hilda*
Sandonato, Barbara

Blankshine, Robert*
Browne, Richard*
Fata, Wesley*
Menchaca, Rudy*
Parkes, Ross*
Rodham, Robert*
Salatino, Anthony*

* New artist

Choreographers
Andrew, Thomas
Butler, John

Directors
Bamberger, David
Capobianco, Tito
Corsaro, Frank
Hicks, David
Lucas, James*
Mann, Theodore*
Montresor, Beni
Savoca, Carmen
Sylbert, Paul

Designers
Armstrong, Will Steven
Campbell, Patton
Colt, Alvin
Eck, Marsha Louis
Evans, Lloyd
Fletcher, Robert
George, Hal
Lee, Ming Cho
Mitchell, David
Montresor, Beni
Morley, Ruth
Sylbert, Paul
Ter-Arutunian, Rouben
Varona, José
Venza, Jac
Zipprodt, Patricia

* New artist

February 19

LUCIA DI LAMMERMOOR
(Donizetti)

Choreography ...... Andrew
Conductor .... Wilson

Alisa .... Evans
Edgardo .... Molese
Normanno .... Castel
Lucia .... Sills
Enrico .... Fredricks
Raimondo .... Hale
Arturo .... Clements

February 20

THE MAGIC FLUTE (Mozart)
(English version by
Ruth and Thomas Martin)

Conductor .... Meier

Sarastro .... Roy
Tamino .... Stewart
Speaker .... Devlin
Priest .... Lankston
Queen of the Night ... Moody
Pamina .... Meier
1st Lady .... Hinds (d)
2nd Lady .... Winburn
3rd Lady .... Evans

1st Spirit .... Bass (d)
2nd Spirit .... Vega (d)
3rd Spirit ...... Kalfayan (d)
Papageno .... Clatworthy
Papagena .... Blanchard
Monostatos .... Castel
1st Armored man .. Clements
2nd Armored man ... Pierson

February 21 (m)

LA TRAVIATA (Verdi)

Choreographer ...... Andrew
Conductor .... Meier

Violetta .... Niska
Alfredo .... LoMonaco
Germont ...... Schwartzman
Flora .... Lueders
Annina .... Winburn
Gaston .... Lankston
Douphol .... Iglesias
D'Obigny .... Devlin
Dr. Grenvil .... Yule
Giuseppe .... Romaguera
Messenger .... Postrel
Solo dancer .... Galan

February 21

MADAMA BUTTERFLY (Puccini)

Conductor .... Ryan

Butterfly .... Cruz-Romo
Suzuki .... Creed
Pinkerton .... Moulson
Sharpless .... Darrenkamp
Goro .... Castel
Yamadori .... Lankston
The Bonze .... Roy
Imperial Commissioner .. Park
Registrar .... Henderson
Kate Pinkerton ..... Lueders
Trouble .... Lee (d)

February 22 (m)

THE MAGIC FLUTE

Same cast as February 20

February 22

LUCIA DI LAMMERMOOR

Same cast as February 19

February 24

FAUST (Gounod)

Choreographer ...... Andrew
Conductor .... Wilson

Faust .... Di Virgilio
Méphistophélès ...... Treigle
Wagner .... Ledbetter
Marguerite .... Neblett
Valentin .... Darrenkamp
Siébel .... Creed
Marthe .... Greenspon
Juggler .... Weeks
Fire-eater .... Demon

Acrobats ... Deighton Boyce,
   Ahmed Abdarrahman,
      Mustapha Ali,
      Clayton Blount,
      Maimon Sidah

February 25

LUCIA DI LAMMERMOOR

Same cast as February 19
except:

Edgardo .... LoMonaco
   (Acts I and II);
   Di Virgilio (Act III)
Lucia .... Dal Piva (d)

February 26

FAUST

Same cast as February 24
except:

Faust .... Di Giuseppe,
   (s, Di Virgilio)

February 27

THE MAGIC FLUTE

Same cast as February 20
except:

Speaker .... Hale
Queen of the Night ... Moody
   (Act I); Crane (Act II)
Pamina .... Elgar
1st Lady .... Anthony
Papagena .... Wise

February 28 (m)

LA BOHÈME (Puccini)

Conductor .... Rudel

Rodolfo .... Di Giuseppe
Marcello ...... Polakoff (d)
Schaunard .... Ledbetter
Colline .... Devlin
Mimi .... Cruz-Romo
Musetta .... Neblett
Benoit .... Yule
Alcindoro .... Bittner
Parpignol .... Romaguera
Guards ..... Park, Henderson

February 28

LA TRAVIATA

Same cast as February 21 (m)
except:

Violetta .... Brooks
Alfredo .... Stewart
D'Obigny .... Ledbetter

March 1 (m)

RIGOLETTO (Verdi)

Choreographer ...... Andrew
Conductor .... Ryan

Rigoletto .... Quilico
Monterone's
   daughter ...... Balestracci

Duke .... Casellato-
   Lamberti (d)
Borsa .... Clements
Countess Ceprano ...... Wise
Ceprano .... Ledbetter
Marullo .... Iglesias
Monterone .... Pierson
Sparafucile .... Hale
Gilda .... Lebrun (d)
Giovanna .... Evans
Page .... Crane
Maddalena .... Creed

March 1

THE TURN OF THE SCREW
(Britten)

Directed by ...... Mann (d)
Lighting .... Sondheimer
Conductor .... Wilson

Prologue .... Lankston
Guardian .... DuPree
Governess .... Niska
Miles .... Puleo
Flora .... Angela (d)
Mrs. Grose .... Faull
Quint .... DuPree
Miss Jessel .... Crane

March 3

RIGOLETTO

Same cast as March 1 (m)
except:

Sparafucile .... Roy,
   (s, Hale)
Giovanna .... Winburn

March 4

THE MAGIC FLUTE

Same cast as February 20
except:

Tamino .... Di Giuseppe
Speaker .... Devlin,
   (s, Hale)
Queen of the Night .... Crane
Pamina .... Elgar
1st Lady .... Anthony
2nd Lady .... Kieffer (d)
Papageno .... Fredricks
Papagena .... Wise

March 5

THE TURN OF THE SCREW

Same cast as March 1

March 6

LUCIA DI LAMMERMOOR

Same cast as February 19
except:

Alisa .... Winburn
Edgardo .. Casellato-Lamberti
Normanno .... Glaze (d)
Lucia .... Dal Piva
Enrico .... Cossa
Raimondo .... Devlin

March 7 (m)

FAUST

Same cast as February 24 except:

Méphistophélès .... M. Smith
Valentin .... Jamerson

March 7

RIGOLETTO

Same cast as March 1 (m) except:

Duke .... Morell
Monterone .... Devlin
Sparafucile .... Roy
Gilda .... Elgar
Giovanna .... Winburn
Page .... Blanchard
Maddalena .... Lueders

March 8 (m)

MANON (Massenet)

Choreographer ...... Andrew
Conductor .... Rudel
Guillot .... Castel
De Brétigny .... Hale
Pousette .... Crane
Javotte .... Guilet
Rosette .... Creed
Innkeeper .... Bittner
Lescaut .... Fredricks
Guards .... Papay, Yule
Manon .... Brooks
Des Grieux ..... Di Giuseppe
Maid .... Greene
Count des Grieux ..... Hecht
Prima ballerina .. Menes (d)
Premier danseur..Salatino (d)
Ballet master .... Browne (d)
Cupid .... Balestracci
Seminary porter .... Carlo
Gambler .... Kingman
Sergeant .... Yule

March 8

LA BOHÈME

Same cast as February 28 (m) except:

Conductor .... Singer (d)
Rodolfo .... Shirley,
           (s, Casellato-Lamberti)
Marcello .... Cossa
Mimi .... Niska

March 10

RIGOLETTO

Same cast as March 1 (m) except:

Conductor .... Singer
Duke .... Di Giuseppe
Countess Ceprano ..Blanchard
Marullo .... Bittner
Monterone .... Devlin
Gilda .... Elgar
Giovanna .... Winburn
Page .... Evans,
                    (s, Crane)
Maddalena .... Lueders

March 11

THE TURN OF THE SCREW

Same cast as March 1 except:

Guardian .... Riegel
Mrs. Grose .... Anthony
Quint .... Riegel

March 12

MEFISTOFELE (Boito)

Choreographer ...... Andrew
Conductor .... Rudel
Mefistofele .... Treigle
Faust .... Di Virgilio
Wagner .... Clements
Margherita ...... Cruz-Romo
Marta .... Evans
Elena .... Cruz-Romo
Pantalis .... Lueders
Nereo .... Romaguera
Solo dancers .... Balestracci,
        Menes; Blankshine (d)

March 13

LUCIA DI LAMMERMOOR

Same cast as February 19 except:

Alisa .... Winburn
Normanno .... Castel,
                  (s, Glaze)
Enrico .... Cossa

March 14 (m)

MANON

Same cast as March 8 (m) except:

De Brétigny .... Jamerson
Manon .... Neblett
Des Grieux .... Piso (d)
Count des Grieux .... Devlin

March 14

RIGOLETTO

Same cast as March 1 (m) except:

Conductor .... Singer
Rigoletto .... Polakoff
Duke .... Di Giuseppe
Borsa .... Lankston,
               (s, Clements)
Countess Ceprano ..Blanchard
Marullo .... Bittner
Sparafucile .... Roy
Giovanna .... Winburn
Maddalena .... Lueders

March 15 (m)

FAUST

Same cast as February 24 except:

Marguerite .... Niska
Valentin .... Darrenkamp,
                  (s, Cossa)
Marthe .... Lueders
Fire-eater .... [omitted]
Added this performance:
Magician .... Wishner

March 15

PELLÉAS ET MÉLISANDE
(Debussy)
New production

Directed by .... Corsaro
Designer .... Evans
Lighting .... Sondheimer
Conductor .... Rudel

Mélisande .... Brooks
Golaud .... Quilico
Geneviève .... Bible
Arkel .... M. Smith
Pelléas .... Jobin (d)
Yniold .... Puleo
Shepherd .... Ledbetter
Physician .... Yule

March 17

MEFISTOFELE

Same cast as March 12

March 18

PELLÉAS ET MÉLISANDE

Same cast as March 15

March 19

MADAMA BUTTERFLY

Same cast as February 21 except:

Butterfly .... Cruz-Romo,
                  (s, Niska)
Pinkerton .... Stewart
Sharpless .... Cossa
Imperial Commissioner .. Yule
Registrar .... Lankston

March 20

RIGOLETTO

Same cast as March 1 (m) except:

Conductor .... Nance (d)
Duke .... Piso
Countess Ceprano ..Blanchard
Marullo .... Bittner
Sparafucile ...... Mundt (d)
Giovanna .... Winburn
Maddalena .... Lueders

March 21 (m)

LA BOHÈME

Same cast as February 28 (m) except:

Conductor .... Singer

Marcello .... Darrenkamp
Guards ..... Galiano, Bentley

March 21

LUCIA DI LAMMERMOOR

Same cast as February 19 except:

Lucia .... Dal Piva

March 22 (m)

LA TRAVIATA

Same cast as February 21 (m) except:

Alfredo .... Stewart
Germont ...... Schwartzman,
(s, Cossa)
Douphol .... Bittner,
(s, Iglesias)
D'Obigny .... Ledbetter
Dr. Grenvil .... Pierson,
(s, Yule)

March 22

PELLÉAS ET MÉLISANDE

Same cast as March 15

March 25

FAUST

Same cast as February 24 except:

Faust .... Molese
Wagner .... Hicks
Marguerite .... Sills
Valentin .... Darrenkamp,
(s, Cossa)

March 26

LA CENERENTOLA (Rossini)

Directed by ...... Lucas (d)
Choreographer .... Butler
Lighting .... Sondheimer
Conductor .... Mester (d)

Clorinda .... Crane
Tisbe .... Evans
Angelina .... Bible
Alidoro .... Ledbetter
Don Magnifico .... Malas
Prince Ramiro .. Di Giuseppe
Dandini .... Fredricks
Solo dancers .... Martin (d),
Fata (d)

March 27

PELLÉAS ET MÉLISANDE

Same cast as March 15 except:

Geneviève .... Greenspon
Arkel .... Roy

March 28 (m)

FAUST

Same cast as February 24 except:

Faust .... Molese
Méphistophélès .... Hale
Wagner .... Hicks
Marguerite .... Sills
Valentin .... Darrenkamp,
(s, Cossa)
Siébel .... Kieffer

March 28

LA CENERENTOLA

Same cast as March 26 except:
Don Magnifico ...... Pierson

March 29 (m)

MEFISTOFELE

Same cast as March 12 except:
Faust .... Nagy

March 29

OEDIPUS REX (Stravinsky)
(English narration by
e.e. cummings)

Stage director .... Hicks
Conductor .... Wilson

Narrator .... D. R. Smith
Oedipus .... Sergi
Creon .... Devlin
Tiresias .... M. Smith
Jocasta .... Bible
Messenger .... Ledbetter
Shepherd .... Glaze

Followed by:

CARMINA BURANA (Orff)

Conductor .... Rudel

Soprano .... Wise
Tenor .... Di Giuseppe
Baritone .... Darrenkamp
Solo dancers .. Fuerstner (d),
Sandonato; Parkes (d),
Rodman (d), Menchaca (d)
(and dancers of the
Pennsylvania Ballet)

March 31

LA CENERENTOLA

Same cast as March 26 except:

Alidoro .... Iglesias,
(s, Ledbetter)

April 1

PELLÉAS ET MÉLISANDE

Same cast as March 15 except:
Geneviève .... Greenspon

April 2

THE ABDUCTION FROM
THE SERAGLIO (Mozart)
(English version by
Ruth and Thomas Martin)

Directed by .... Hicks
Conductor .... Rudel

Belmonte .... Stewart
Osmin .... Beattie
Pedrillo .... Riegel
Constanza .... Sills
Pasha Selim ..... D. R. Smith
Blonde .... Wise

April 3

LA TRAVIATA

Same cast as February 21 (m) except:

Alfredo .... Molese
Germont .... Quilico
D'Obigny .... Ledbetter

April 4 (m)

OEDIPUS REX

Same cast as March 29 except:

Creon .... Pierson
Jocasta .... Nadler (d)
Shepherd .... Lankston
Followed by:

CARMINA BURANA

Same cast as March 29 except:

Conductor .... Wilson

Soprano .... Carron
Solo dancers ... Morales (d),
(for Sandonato)

April 4

THE ABDUCTION FROM
THE SERAGLIO

Same cast as April 2 except:

Conductor .... Meier

April 5 (m)

PELLÉAS ET MÉLISANDE

Same cast as March 15 except:

Conductor .... Marty (d)

Geneviève .... Greenspon

April 5

LA CENERENTOLA

Same cast as March 26 except:

Clorinda .... Darling
Alidoro .... Iglesias
Don Magnifico ...... Pierson
Don Ramiro ...... Riegel

April 7

PELLÉAS ET MÉLISANDE

Same cast as March 15 except:

Conductor .... Marty

Mélisande .... Crane
Geneviève .... Greenspon
Pelléas .... Stilwell (d)

April 8

MANON

Same cast as March 8 (m) except:

Guillot .... Lankston
Pousette .... Blanchard

Manon .... Sills
Des Grieux .... Molese
Count des Grieux ..... Devlin

April 9

PELLÉAS ET MÉLISANDE

Same cast as March 15 except:

Geneviève .... Greenspon

April 10

OEDIPUS REX

Same cast as March 29 except:

Creon .... Clatworthy
Tiresias .... Roy
Shepherd .... Lankston

Followed by:

CARMINA BURANA

Same cast as March 29 except:

Conductor .... Wilson

Soprano .... Carron
Tenor .... Riegel

April 11 (m)

THE ABDUCTION FROM
THE SERAGLIO

Same cast as April 2 except:

Belmonte ...... Jennings (d)
Osmin .... Roy

April 11

MANON

Same cast as March 8 (m)
except:

Conductor .... Wilson,
(Acts I and II);
Rudel (Acts III and IV)

Guillot .... Lankston
Rosette .... Lueders
Lescaut .... Darrenkamp
Count des Grieux .. M. Smith

April 12 (m)

THE ABDUCTION FROM
THE SERAGLIO

Same cast as April 2 except:

Conductor .... Meier

Belmonte .... Jennings
Pedrillo .... Lankston
Constanza .... Lebrun

April 12

KATERINA ISMAILOVA
(Shostakovich)
(English translation by
Julius Rudel)

Conductor .... Rudel

Katerina Ismailova .. Schauler
Boris Ismailov .... Pierson
Zinovy Ismailov .... Clements
Mill workman ..... Jamerson
Sergei .... Stamford
Coachman .... Davis
Aksinya .... Darling
Village drunk .... Romaguera
Porter .... Bittner
Steward .... Park
Workmen .... Krause, Garcia
Priest .... M. Smith
Police inspector .. D. R. Smith
Sergeant .... Jamerson
Sentry .... Bittner
Old convict .... Roy
Sonyetka, a convict .. Lueders
Female convict ..... Anthony

April 14

MADAMA BUTTERFLY

Same cast as February 21
except:

Pinkerton ...... Di Giuseppe
Sharpless .... Iglesias
Goro .... Clements
Imperial Commissioner .. Yule
Registrar .... Lankston
Trouble .... Stein (d)

April 15

KATERINA ISMAILOVA

Same cast as April 12

April 16

OEDIPUS REX

Same cast as March 29 except:

Creon .... Pierson
Tiresias .... Roy
Shepherd .... Lankston

Followed by:

CARMINA BURANA

Same cast as March 29 except:

Conductor .... Wilson

Tenor .... Riegel
Solo dancers .... Morales,
(for Sandonato)

April 17

MANON

Same cast as March 8 (m)
except:

Guillot .... Lankston
Pousette .... Blanchard
Innkeeper .... Postrel
Lescaut .... Darrenkamp
Manon .... Neblett
Des Grieux .... Piso
Count des Grieux .. M. Smith

April 18 (m)

LUCIA DI LAMMERMOOR

Same cast as February 19
except:

Edgardo .... Di Giuseppe
Normanno ...... Romaguera
Lucia .... Dal Piva
Enrico .... Cossa

April 18

THE ABDUCTION FROM
THE SERAGLIO

Same cast as April 2 except:

Osmin .... Roy
Pedrillo .... Lankston
Constanza .... Lebrun
Blonde .... Armstrong

April 19 (m)

KATERINA ISMAILOVA

Same cast as April 12 except:

Sergei .... Townsend (d)
Female convict .... Hunt (d)

April 19

MANON

Same cast as March 8 (m)
except:

Conductor .... Wilson,
(s, Rudel)

Guillot .... Lankston
De Brétigny .... Jamerson
Pousette .... Blanchard
Innkeeper .... Postrel
Lescaut .... Darrenkamp
Manon .... Neblett
Des Grieux .... Piso
Count des Grieux .... Devlin,
(s, M. Smith)

Fall 1970 (SEPTEMBER 9 – NOVEMBER 15)

Female artists
Anthony, Judith
Bible, Frances
Blanchard, Barbara
Bonazzi, Elaine
Brooks, Patricia
Ciraulo, Marianna*
Clatworthy, Mary Ann
Crader, Jeannine
Crane, Lois
Creed, Kay
Cruz-Romo, Gilda
Dal Piva, Milena
Evans, Beverly
Greene, Harriet
Greenspon, Muriel
Kehrig, Diana
Kieffer, Deborah
Lebrun, Louise
Lueders, Mary Cross
Marsee, Susanne*
Meier, Johanna
Neblett, Carol
Niska, Maralin
Sauler, Bianca*
Sills, Beverly
Winburn, Janet
Wise, Patricia
Wolff, Beverly

Male artists
Bentley, Ronald
Bittner, Jack
Carlo, Don
Castel, Nico
Clatworthy, David
Cossa, Dominic
Darrenkamp, John
Devlin, Michael
Demon, Satani
Di Giuseppe, Enrico
Di Virgilio, Nicholas
Domingo, Placido
Fitch, Bernard*
Fredricks, Richard
Galiano, Joseph
Glaze, Gary
Hale, Robert
Henderson, Don
Hicks, David
Jamerson, Thomas
Jennings, Jerry J.
Jobin, André
Kingman, Dan
Lankston, John
Lee, David
Ledbetter, William
Ludgin, Chester
Malamood, Herman*
Malas, Spiro
Molese, Michele
Montané, Carlos*
Novoa, Salvador
Papay, Raymond
Park, Richard
Perry, Douglas R.*
Pierson, Edward

* New artist

Postrel, Leo
Puleo, Robert
Quilico, Louis
Riegel, Kenneth
Romaguera, Joaquin
Roy, Will
Schwartzman, Seymour
Smith, David Rae
Smith, Malcolm
Stamford, John
Stein, Peter
Stewart, John
Stilwell, Richard
Theyard, Harry
Treigle, Norman
Weeks, Larry
Yule, Don

Conductors
Keene, Christopher*
Marty, Jean-Pierre
Mester, Jorge
Morelli, Giuseppe*
Nance, Chris
Ötvös, Gabor
Reimueller, Ross*
Rudel, Julius
Wilson, Charles

Chorus master
Nance, Chris

Assistant chorus master
Somogi, Judith

Solo dancers
Balestracci, Sandra
Barr, Lynn*
Galan, Esperanza
Glemby, Ellen*
Lombardi, Joan*
Martin, Erin
Menes, Rose Marie

Fata, Wesley
Roberts, Chester*
Salatino, Anthony

Choreographers
Andrew, Thomas
Butler, John
Denda, Elena*

Directors
Capobianco, Tito
Corsaro, Frank
Hicks, David
Lucas, James
Savoca, Carmen

Designers
Aldredge, Theoni V.
Ardolino, Emile*
Campbell, Patton
Compton, Gardner*
Eck, Marsha Louis
Evans, Lloyd
Fletcher, Robert
George, Hal
Lee, Ming Cho

* New artist

Mitchell, David
Ter-Arutunian, Rouben
Varona, José
Wittstein, Ed

· * New artist

September 9

MEFISTOFELE (Boito)

Conductor .... Rudel

Mefistofele .... Treigle
Faust .... Di Virgilio
Wagner .... Fitch (d)
Margherita .... Neblett
Marta .... Evans
Elena .... Neblett
Pantalis .... Lueders
Nereo .... Romaguera
Solo dancers .... Balestracci,
Menes; Salatino

September 10

LUCIA DI LAMMERMOOR
(Donizetti)

Conductor .... Wilson

Alisa .... Evans
Edgardo .... Molese
Normanno .... Castel
Lucia .... Sills
Enrico .... Cossa
Raimondo .... Hale
Arturo .... Glaze

September 11

LA BOHÈME (Puccini)

Conductor ...... Morelli (d)

Rodolfo .... Di Giuseppe
Marcello .... Fredricks
Schaunard .... Ledbetter
Colline .... Malas
Mimi .... Dal Piva
Musetta .... Meier
Benoit .... Yule
Alcindoro .... Bittner
Parpignol .... Romaguera
Guards ..... Galiano, Bentley

September 12 (m)

MADAMA BUTTERFLY (Puccini)

Conductor .... Morelli

Butterfly .... Cruz-Romo
Suzuki .... Bonazzi
Pinkerton .... Theyard
Sharpless .... Cossa
Goro .... Castel
Yamadori .... Romaguera
The Bonze .... Roy
Imperial Commissioner .. Yule
Registrar .... Romaguera
Kate Pinkerton ...... Lueders
Trouble .... Lee

September 12

MEFISTOFELE

Same cast as September 9

September 13 (m)

LA BOHÈME

Same cast as September 11

September 13

THE MARRIAGE OF FIGARO
(Mozart)
(English version by
Ruth and Thomas Martin)

Choreographer ...... Andrew
Conductor .... Wilson

Figaro .... Devlin
Susanna .... Wise
Bartolo .... M. Smith
Marcellina .... Evans
Cherubino .... Bible
Almaviva ..... D. Clatworthy
Basilio .... Castel
Countess .... Niska
Antonio .... Bittner
Curzio .... Lankston
Barbarina .... Blanchard
Solo dancer .... Galan

September 15

LA BOHÈME

Same cast as September 11
except:

Marcello ..... D. Clatworthy
Colline .... Hale
Musetta .... Neblett

September 16

MADAMA BUTTERFLY

Same cast as September 12 (m)
except:

Sharpless ...... Darrenkamp

September 17

LA TRAVIATA (Verdi)

Conductor .... Wilson

Violetta .... Niska
Alfredo .... Stewart
Germont .... Fredricks
Flora .... Lueders
Annina .... Winburn
Gaston .... Lankston
Douphol .... Bittner
D'Obigny .... Ledbetter
Dr. Grenvil .... Pierson
Giuseppe .... Romaguera
Messenger .... Kingman
Solo dancer .... Galan

September 18

THE MARRIAGE OF FIGARO

Same cast as September 13
except:

Countess .... Meier

September 19 (m)

LA BOHÈME

Same cast as September 11
except:

Marcello .... Darrenkamp
Colline .... Hale
Musetta .... Neblett
Benoit .... Roy

September 19

LA TRAVIATA

Same cast as September 17
except:

Germont ...... Schwartzman

September 20 (m)

LA CENERENTOLA (Rossini)

Conductor .... Mester

Clorinda .... Crane
Tisbe .... Evans
Angelina .... Bible
Alidoro .... Ledbetter
Don Magnifico .... Malas
Prince Ramiro .... Riegel
Dandini .... Fredricks
Solo dancers .... Martin, Fata

September 20

MADAMA BUTTERFLY

Same cast as September 12 (m)
except:

Pinkerton .... Malamood (d)
Sharpless ...... Darrenkamp

September 22

LUCIA DI LAMMERMOOR

Same cast as September 10
except:

Enrico .... Fredricks

September 23

THE MARRIAGE OF FIGARO

Same cast as September 13
except:

Figaro .... Treigle
Countess .... Meier

September 24

LA TRAVIATA

Same cast as September 17
except:

Alfredo .... Di Giuseppe
Germont .... Cossa

September 25

MANON (Massenet)

Conductor .... Rudel

Guillot .... Castel
De Brétigny .... Hale
Pousette .... Crane
Javotte .... Winburn
Rosette .... Creed
Innkeeper .... Bittner

Lescaut .... Darrenkamp
Guards .... Papay, Yule
Manon .... Sills
Des Grieux .... Molese
Maid .... Greene
Count des Grieux .. M. Smith
Prima ballerina .... Menes
Premier danseur .... Salatino
Ballet master .... Roberts (d)
Cupid .... Balestracci
Seminary porter .... Carlo
Gambler .... Kingman
Sergeant .... Yule

September 26 (m)

MADAMA BUTTERFLY

Same cast as September 12 (m)
except:

Suzuki .... Creed
Pinkerton .... Stewart
Sharpless ...... Schwartzman
Trouble .... Stein

September 26

MEFISTOFELE

Same cast as September 9

September 27 (m)

LA BOHÈME

Same cast as September 11
except:

Marcello .... Cossa
Guards .... Galiano,
(s, Park), Henderson

September 27

MANON

Same cast as September 25

September 29

THE MARRIAGE OF FIGARO

Same cast as September 13
except:

Figaro .... Treigle
Susanna .... Lebrun
Bartolo .... Roy
Cherubino .... Creed
Antonio .... Yule

September 30

LUCIA DI LAMMERMOOR

Same cast as September 10
except:

Normanno ...... Romaguera
Lucia .... Del Piva,
(s, Sills)
Enrico .... Fredricks
Raimondo .... M. Smith

October 1

LA TRAVIATA

Same cast as September 17
except:

Alfredo .... Di Giuseppe
Germont .... Cossa
Gaston .... Glaze
Dr. Grenvil .... Yule

October 2

MEFISTOFELE

Same cast as September 9 except:

Wagner .... Glaze
Margherita ...... Cruz-Romo
Elena .... Cruz-Romo

October 3 (m)

LA BOHÈME

Same cast as September 11 except:

Marcello .... Cossa
Colline .... Devlin
Guards ..... Park, Henderson

October 3

MANON

Same cast as September 25 except:

Conductor .... Marty
De Brétigny .... Jamerson
Manon .... Neblett

October 4 (m)

MADAMA BUTTERFLY

Same cast as September 12 (m) except:

Suzuki .... Creed
Pinkerton .... Stewart
Sharpless ...... Schwartzman
Kate Pinkerton ...... Kieffer
Trouble .... Stein

October 4

LUCIA DI LAMMERMOOR

Same cast as September 10 except:

Alisa .... Winburn
Edgardo .... Di Virgilio
Enrico .... Fredricks

October 7

DON RODRIGO (Ginastera)

Choreographer ... Denda (d)
Conductor .... Rudel

Don Rodrigo .... Novoa
Don Julian .... D. Clatworthy
Florinda .... Crader
Fortuna .... Creed
Teudiselo .... Malas
Bishop .... M. Smith
Ladies in waiting ...... Wise,
                       Lueders
Pages ...... Castel, Jamerson
Locksmiths ..Romaguera, Yule
Voice of Sleep .... Roy
Messengers ...... Romaguera,
                       Ledbetter
Young messenger ...... Evans
Young boy .... Puleo

Young girl .... M. Clatworthy
Hermit .... Devlin

October 8

MEFISTOFELE

Same cast as September 9 except:

Faust .... Theyard

October 9

LA BOHÈME

Same cast as September 11 except:

Marcello .... Cossa
Colline .... Devlin
Mimi .... Cruz-Romo
Benoit .... Roy
Guards ... Galiano, (s, Park),
                       Henderson

October 10 (m)

LUCIA DI LAMMERMOOR

Same cast as September 10 except:

Alisa .... Winburn
Normanno .... Romaguera
Enrico .... Fredricks

October 10

LA TRAVIATA

Same cast as September 17 except:

Conductor .... Morelli
Alfredo .... Montané (d)
Germont .... Cossa
Annina .... Kieffer
Dr. Grenvil .... Yule
Messenger .... Kingman,
                     (s, Park)

October 11 (m)

MANON

Same cast as September 25 except:

Conductor .... Marty
De Brétigny .... Jamerson
Javotte .... Kieffer
Rosette .... Lueders
Lescaut .... Fredricks
Manon .... Neblett
Des Grieux ..... Di Giuseppe

October 11

THE MARRIAGE OF FIGARO

Same cast as September 13 except:

Figaro .... Treigle
Susanna .... Sauler (d)
Bartolo .... Roy
Cherubino .... Creed
Almaviva ...... Darrenkamp
Basilio .... Perry (d)
Countess .... Meier

October 14

MEFISTOFELE

Same cast as September 9 except:

Faust .... Theyard
Wagner .... Glaze
Margherita ...... Cruz-Romo
Elena .... Cruz-Romo
Solo dancers ... Glemby (d),
                     Lombardi (d)

October 15

ROBERTO DEVEREUX
(Donizetti)
First performance by The New
York City Opera Company

Directed by ..... Capobianco
Set designer .... Lee
Costume designer .... Varona
Lighting .... Sondheimer
Conductor .... Rudel

Sara .... Wolff
Elizabeth .... Sills
Cecil .... Lankston
Page .... Bittner
Raleigh .... D. R. Smith
Robert Devereux ... Domingo
Duke of Nottingham .. Quilico
Servant .... Yule

October 16

LA CENERENTOLA

Same cast as September 20 (m) except:

Conductor ... Reimueller (d)

October 17 (m)

MADAMA BUTTERFLY

Same cast as September 12 (m) except:

Conductor .... Nance

Pinkerton .... Malamood
Sharpless .... Darrenkamp
Goro .... Perry
Yamadori .... Lankston
Registrar .... Henderson
Kate Pinkerton ...... Kieffer

October 17

FAUST (Gounod)

Conductor .... Ötvös

Faust .... Molese
Méphistophélès ...... Treigle
Wagner .... Ledbetter
Marguerite .... Niska
Valentin .... Cossa
Siébel .... Creed
Marthe .... Greenspon
Juggler .... Weeks
Fire-eater .... Demon

October 18 (m)

DON RODRIGO

Same cast as October 7 except:

Conductor .... Keene (d)

October 18

ROBERTO DEVEREUX

Same cast as October 15

October 20

DON RODRIGO

Same cast as October 7 except:

Florinda .... Ciraulo (d)

October 21

ROBERTO DEVEREUX

Same cast as October 15
except:

*Duke of
Nottingham* .... Fredricks,
(s, Quilico)

October 22

PELLÉAS ET MÉLISANDE
(Debussy)

Conductor .... Rudel

Mélisande .... Brooks
Golaud .... Quilico
Geneviève .... Greenspon
Arkel .... M. Smith
Pelléas .... Jobin
Yniold .... Puleo
Shepherd .... Ledbetter
Physician .... Yule

October 23

FAUST

Same cast as October 17
except:

Marguerite .... Neblett
Valentin .... Darrenkamp
Siébel .... Kieffer,
(s, Creed)

October 24 (m)

LA CENERENTOLA

Same cast as September 20 (m)

October 24

ROBERTO DEVEREUX

Same cast as October 15
except:

Sara .... Marsee (d)

October 25 (m)

PELLÉAS ET MÉLISANDE

Same cast as October 22
except:

Golaud .... Hale

October 25

FAUST

Same cast as October 17
except:

Valentin .... Darrenkamp
Siébel .... Kieffer,
(s, Creed)

October 27

DON RODRIGO

Same cast as October 7
except:

Florinda .... Ciraulo

October 28

FAUST

Same cast as October 17
except:

Méphistophélès .... Hale
Marguerite .... Meier
Valentin .... Jamerson
Siébel .... Marsee

October 29

RIGOLETTO (Verdi)

Conductor .... Ötvös

Rigoletto .... Quilico
*Monterone's
daughter* .... Barr (d)
Duke .... Di Giuseppe
Borsa .... Fitch
Countess Ceprano ..Blanchard
Ceprano .... Ledbetter
Marullo .... Bittner
Monterone .... Pierson
Sparafucile .... M. Smith
Gilda .... Lebrun
Giovanna .... Winburn
Page .... Kieffer
Maddalena .... Creed

October 30

LA CENERENTOLA

Same cast as September 20 (m)
except:

Clorinda .... Anthony

October 31 (m)

LA TRAVIATA

Same cast as September 17
except:

Violetta .... Brooks
Alfredo .... Montané
Germont ...... Schwartzman
Annina .... Kieffer
Dr. Grenvil .... Yule
Messenger .... Park

October 31

PELLÉAS ET MÉLISANDE

Same cast as October 22
except:

Mélisande .... Crane
Geneviève .... Bonazzi

November 1 (m)

LUCIA DI LAMMERMOOR

Same cast as September 10
except:

Enrico .... Fredricks

November 1

THE MAKROPOULOS AFFAIR
(Janáček)
First performance by The New
York City Opera Company
(English translation by
Norman Tucker)

Directed by .... Corsaro
Designer .... Campbell
*Film and slide
projections by* ... Compton
(d) and Ardolino (d)
*Kinetic and photographic
environment by* .. Compton
(d)
Lighting .... Sondheimer
Conductor .... Ötvös

Vitek .... Lankston
Albert Gregor ...... Theyard
Christa .... Blanchard
Emilia Marty .... Niska
Chauffeur .... D. R. Smith
Dr. Kolenaty .... Pierson
Jaroslav Prus .... Ludgin
Maid .... Anthony
Janek .... Glaze
Hauk-Sendorf .... Castel

November 3

THE MAKROPOULOS AFFAIR

Same cast as November 1

November 4

RIGOLETTO

Same cast as October 29
except:

Duke .... Molese
Monterone .... Devlin
Page .... Lueders

November 5

DON RODRIGO

Same cast as October 7 except:

Don Rodrigo ...... Stamford
Don Julian .... Pierson
Fortuna .... Kieffer
1st lady in waiting..Blanchard
Pages .... Fitch, Ledbetter

November 6

ROBERTO DEVEREUX

Same cast as October 15
except:

Sara .... Marsee
Robert Devereux ..Malamood
*Duke of
Nottingham* ..... Fredricks

November 7 (m)

PELLÉAS ET MÉLISANDE

Same cast as October 22
except:

Conductor .... Marty
Golaud .... Hale
Geneviève .... Bonazzi

Arkel .... Roy
Pelléas .... Stilwell

November 7

MANON

Same cast as September 25
except:

Conductor .... Wilson

Javotte .... Kieffer
Rosette .... Lueders
Innkeeper .... Postrel
1st Guard .... Galiano
Manon .... Neblett
Count des Grieux .... Devlin
Prima ballerina ..... Glemby
Cupid .... Lombardi

November 8 (m)

LA CENERENTOLA

Same cast as September 20 (m)
except:

Conductor .... Reimueller

Clorinda .... Anthony
Don Magnifico .... Bittner
Prince Ramiro ...... Jennings
Dandini .... Jamerson
1st Solo dancer .... Lombardi

November 8

ROBERTO DEVEREUX

Same cast as October 15
except:

Sara .... Marsee
Page .... Ledbetter
Robert Devereux .. Malamood

November 10

THE MAKROPOULOS AFFAIR

Same cast as November 1

November 11

LUCIA DI LAMMERMOOR

Same cast as September 10
except:

Enrico .... Fredricks
Arturo .... Fitch,
                  (s, Glaze)

November 12

RIGOLETTO

Same cast as October 29
except:

Marullo .... Hicks
Sparafucile .... Roy
Maddalena .... Lueders

November 13

MANON

Same cast as September 25
except:

Conductor .... Wilson

Javotte .... Kieffer
Rosette .... Lueders
Innkeeper .... Postrel
1st guard .... Galiano
Manon .... Neblett
Maid .... Kehrig,
                 (s, Greene)
Count des Grieux .... Devlin
Prima ballerina ..... Glemby
Cupid .... Lombardi

November 14 (m)

LA CENERENTOLA

Same cast as September 20 (m)
except:

Angelina .... Creed
Don Magnifico .... Bittner
Prince Ramiro ...... Jennings
Dandini .... Jamerson

November 14

LUCIA DI LAMMERMOOR

Same cast as September 10
except:

Edgardo .... Novoa
Enrico .... Fredricks
Arturo .... Glaze,
                  (s, Fitch)

November 15 (m)

THE MAKROPOULOS AFFAIR

Same cast as November 1
except:

Albert Gregor ...... Stamford
Jaroslav Prus .. D. Clatworthy

November 15

RIGOLETTO

Same cast as October 29
except:

Conductor .... Reimueller

Countess Ceprano ..... Sauler
Marullo .... Hicks
Monterone .... Devlin
Sparafucile .... Roy
Maddalena .... Lueders

Spring 1971 (FEBRUARY 17– APRIL 25)

Female artists
Adler, Arlene
Angela, June
Barker, Joyce*
Barnes, Dori
Bayard, Carol
Bible, Frances
Bonazzi, Elaine
Brooks, Patricia
Bruno, Joanna*
Chookasian, Lili
Ciraulo, Marianna
Clatworthy, Mary Ann
Craig, Patricia*
Creed, Kay
Cruz-Romo, Gilda
Dal Piva, Milena
Darling, Sandra
Doty, Myrna
Evans, Beverly
Faull, Ellen
Gonzalez, Carmen*
Greenspon, Muriel

Guilet, Helene
Hepburn, Betsy
Herbert, Lila
Jones, Delores*
Kieffer, Deborah
Lebrun, Louise
Lueders, Mary Cross
Makas, Maxine*
Marsee, Susanne
Meier, Johanna
Neblett, Carol
Niska, Maralin
Owen, Hanna
Pavlides, Frances
Queler, Elizabeth*
Sauler, Bianca
Schauler, Eileen
Shuttleworth, Barbara
Sills, Beverly
Welting, Ruth
West, Maria
Winburn, Janet
Wise, Patricia

Wolff, Beverly
Young, Marie
Young, Syble*

Male artists
Bentley, Ronald
Berberian, Ara
Bittner, Jack
Clatworthy, David
Cossa, Dominic
Darrenkamp, John
Davis, J. B.
Densen, Irwin*
Devlin, Michael
Di Amorim, Sergio*
Di Giuseppe, Enrico
Di Virgilio, Nicholas
Fitch, Bernard
Fredricks, Richard
Galiano, Joseph
Glaze, Gary
Hale, Robert
Hall, David*

* New artist   * New artist   * New artist

Harper, Talmage
Hicks, David
Holmes, Eugene
Jamerson, Thomas
Jennings, Jerry J.
Johnson, Robert*
Kingman, Dan
Lankston, John
Ledbetter, William
Lee, David
Liccioni, Georges*
Malamood, Herman
Malas, Spiro
Mason, Spencer*
Molese, Michele
Montané, Carlos
Novoa, Salvador
Perry, Douglas R.
Pierson, Edward
Puleo, Robert
Quilico, Louis
Riegel, Kenneth
Romaguera, Joaquin
Rouleau, Joseph
Roy, Will
Schwartzman, Seymour
Smith, David Rae
Stamford, John
Stein, Peter
Stewart, John
Stilwell, Richard
Theyard, Harry
Treigle, Norman
Yule, Don

Conductors
Bernardi, Mario*
Keene, Christopher
Mester, Jorge
Morelli, Giuseppe
Nance, Chris
Reimueller, Ross
Rudel, Julius
Singer, George
Wilson, Charles

Chorus master
Nance, Chris

Assistant chorus master
Somogi, Judith

Solo dancers
Balestracci, Sandra
Galan, Esperanza
Martin, Erin
Menes, Rose Marie
Fata, Wesley
Horvath, Juliu*

Choreographers
Andrew, Thomas
Butler, John
Denda, Elena

Directors
Besch, Anthony*
Capobianco, Tito
Corsaro, Frank
de Blasis, James
Denda, Elena*
Hicks, David
Hirsch, John*
Lucas, James
Mann, Theodore
Menotti, Gian Carlo

* New artist

Designers
Aldredge, Theoni V.
Campbell, Patton
Colt, Alvin
Eck, Marsha Louis
Evans, Lloyd
Fletcher, Robert
George, Hal
Lee, Ming Cho
Micunis, Gordon
Mitchell, David
Smith, Oliver
Sprott, Eoin*
Ter-Arutunian, Rouben
Thompson, Frank*
Varona, José
Venza, Jac
Wittstein, Ed

* New artist

February 17

LA CENERENTOLA (Rossini)

Conductor .... Mester

Clorinda .... Darling
Tisbe .... Evans
Angelina .... Marsee
Alidoro .... Ledbetter
Don Magnifico .... Malas
Prince Ramiro .... Riegel
Dandini .... Stilwell
Solo dancers ... Martin, Fata

February 18

MEFISTOFELE (Boito)

Stage director .... Denda (d)
Conductor .... Rudel

Mefistofele .... Treigle
Faust .... Di Virgilio
Wagner .... Fitch
Margherita .... Neblett
Marta .... Evans
Elena .... Neblett
Pantalis .... Lueders
Nereo .... Romaguera
Solo dancers ..... Balestracci,
Menes, Horvath (d)

February 19

MADAMA BUTTERFLY (Puccini)

Conductor .... Morelli

Pinkerton .... Malamood
Goro .... Fitch
Suzuki .... Creed
Sharpless .... Cossa
Butterfly .... Cruz-Romo
Imperial
Commissioner ... Jamerson
Registrar .... Lankston
The Bonze .... Pierson
Yamadori .... Lankston
Trouble .... Lee
Kate Pinkerton ...... Lueders

February 20 (m)

LA TRAVIATA (Verdi)

Conductor .... Morelli

Violetta .... Brooks
Flora .... Lueders

Douphol .... Hicks
D'Obigny .... Ledbetter
Dr. Grenvil .... Yule
Gaston .... Glaze
Alfredo .... Montané
Annina .... Kieffer
Giuseppe .... Romaguera
Germont ...... Schwartzman
Messenger .... Kingman
Solo dancer .... Galan

February 20

LA CENERENTOLA

Same cast as February 17
except:

Conductor .... Reimueller
Don Magnifico ...... Bittner

February 21 (m)

THE MARRIAGE OF FIGARO
(English version by
Ruth and Thomas Martin)

Conductor .... Rudel

Figaro .... Treigle
Susanna .... Wise
Bartolo .... Roy
Marcellina .... Evans
Cherubino .... Bible
Almaviva ...... Darrenkamp
Basilio .... Perry
Countess .... Meier
Antonio .... Yule
Curzio .... Lankston
Barbarina .. Shuttleworth (d)
Solo dancer .... Galan

February 21

MADAMA BUTTERFLY

Same cast as February 19
except:

Trouble .... Stein

February 23

LA TRAVIATA

Same cast as February 20 (m)
except:

Violetta .... Niska
Germont .... Cossa

February 24

MEFISTOFELE

Same cast as February 18
except:

Margherita ...... Cruz-Romo
Elena .... Cruz-Romo

February 25

LA CENERENTOLA

Same cast as February 17
except:

Dandini .... Fredricks

February 26

MADAMA BUTTERFLY

Same cast as February 19
except:

Trouble .... Stein

February 27 (m)

LA BOHÈME (Puccini)

Directed by .... Hicks
Conductor .... Mester

Rodolfo .... Di Giuseppe
Marcello ..... D. Clatworthy
Schaunard .... Ledbetter
Colline .... Hale
Mimi .... Dal Piva
Musetta .... Bayard
Benoit .... Yule
Alcindoro .... Bittner
Parpignol .... Romaguera
Guards ..... Galiano, Bentley

February 27

THE MARRIAGE OF FIGARO

Same cast as February 21 (m)
except:

Antonio .... Bittner

February 28 (m)

MADAMA BUTTERFLY

Same cast as February 19
except:

Goro .... Hall (d)
Sharpless .... Fredricks
Kate Pinkerton .... Kieffer

February 28

LOUISE (Charpentier)

Directed by .... Besch (d)
Choreographer ...... Andrew
Lighting .... Sondheimer
Conductor .... Wilson

Julien .... Liccioni (d)
Louise .... Neblett
Mother .... Bonazzi
Father .... Rouleau
Young rag picker ..... Guilet
Coal gatherer .... West
Sleepwalker .... Riegel
Milk woman .... Adler
Rag picker .... Roy
Junk man .... Densen (d)
Policemen ... Bittner, Bentley
Street urchin .... Puleo
Street sweeper ...... Winburn
Painter .... Fitch
Sculptor .... Ledbetter
Song writer .... Jamerson
Poet .... Lankston
Philosophers .... Romaguera,
                          Yule
Blanche .... Shuttleworth
Marguerite .... Guilet
Suzanne .... Doty
Gertrude .... Lueders
Irma .... Sauler
Camille .... Darling
Apprentice .... Hepburn

Elise .... Kieffer
Madeleine .... Owen
Old clothes man .... Glaze
Forewoman .... Evans
King of Fools .... Riegel
Solo dancer ...... Balestracci
Chair mender ...... Lueders
Clothing vendor .. Romaguera
Artichoke vendor ..... Sauler
Carrot vendor .... Fitch
Bird food vendor ... Darling
Barrel vendor ..... Ledbetter
Broom vendor ..... Jamerson
Potato vendors .... Hepburn,
                          Lankston
Green peas vendor .... Fitch
Watercress vendor ..... Evans

March 2

ROBERTO DEVEREUX
(Donizetti)

Stage director .... Denda
Conductor .... Rudel

Sara .... Marsee
Elizabeth .... Sills
Cecil .... Fitch
Page .... Ledbetter
Raleigh .... Smith
Robert Devereux .. Malamood
Duke of
Nottingham ..... Fredricks
Servant .... Yule

March 3

THE MARRIAGE OF FIGARO

Same cast as February 21 (m)
except:

Susanna .... Sauler
Cherubino .... Creed
Almaviva ..... D. Clatworthy
Antonio .... Bittner

March 4

LOUISE

Same cast as February 28

March 5

LA BOHÈME

Same cast as February 27 (m)
except:

Marcello .... Cossa

March 6 (m)

ROBERTO DEVEREUX

Same cast as March 2

March 6

MEFISTOFELE

Same cast as February 18
except:

Faust .... Novoa
Margherita ...... Cruz-Romo
Elena .... Cruz-Romo

March 7 (m)

LA BOHÈME

Same cast as February 27 (m)
except:

Marcello .... Cossa
Musetta .... Meier

March 7

THE MOST IMPORTANT MAN
(Menotti)
World premiere

Directed by .... Menotti
Set designer .... Smith
Costume
designer .... Thompson (d)
Lighting .... Sondheimer
Conductor .... Keene

Toimé Ukamba ..... Holmes
Dr. Otto Arnek .... Theyard
Leona .... Wolff
Eric Rupert .... Stilwell
Cora .... Bruno (d)
Professor Clement .. Lankston
Professor
  Risselberg .... Romaguera
Professor Bolental .. Jamerson
Professor
  Hisselman ...... Ledbetter
Professor Grippel ...... Yule
Undersecretary of
  State .... Bittner
Mrs. Adebda
  Akawasi .... Jones (d)

March 9

ROBERTO DEVEREUX

Same cast as March 2 except:

Sara .... Wolff
Duke of Nottingham .. Quilico

March 10

MEFISTOFELE

Same cast as February 18
except:

Faust .... Novoa
Margherita ...... Cruz-Romo
Elena .... Cruz-Romo

March 11

LUCIA DI LAMMERMOOR
(Donizetti)

Stage director .... Denda
Conductor .... Wilson

Alisa .... Evan
Edgardo .... Moles
Normanno ...... Romaguera
Lucia .... Sill
Enrico .... Fredrick
Raimondo .... Hal
Arturo .... Glaz

March 12

THE MOST IMPORTANT MAN

Same cast as March 7

March 13 (m)

THE MARRIAGE OF FIGARO

Same cast as February 21 (m) except:

Susanna .... Sauler
Cherubino .... Creed
Basilio .... Hall
Antonio .... Bittner
Barbarina ..... S. Young (d)

March 13

LUCIA DI LAMMERMOOR

Same cast as March 11 except:

Alisa .... Kieffer
Enrico .... D. Clatworthy

March 14 (m)

IL BARBIERE DI SIVIGLIA
(Rossini)

Directed by .... de Blasis
Conductor .... Morelli

Fiorello .... Ledbetter
Almaviva .... Jennings
Figaro .... Cossa
Bartolo .... Malas
Rosina .... Wise
Basilio .... Derberian
Berta .... Evans
Officer .... Yule

March 14

LA TRAVIATA

Same cast as February 20 (m) except:

Violetta .... Niska
Douphol .... Bittner
Gaston .... Lankston
Alfredo .... Di Giuseppe
Germont .... Quilico

March 16

IL BARBIERE DI SIVIGLIA

Same cast as March 14 (m) except:

Figaro .... Fredricks

March 17

LA CENERENTOLA

Same cast as February 17

March 18

THE MOST IMPORTANT MAN

Same cast as March 7

March 19

LA CENERENTOLA

Same cast as February 17 except:

Clorinda .... Shuttleworth
Dandini .... Fredricks

March 20 (m)

LOUISE

Same cast as February 28 except:

Mother .... Bible
Junk man .... Yule
2nd philosopher ...... Harper
Gertrude .... Pavlides,
(s, Lueders)
Irma .... Lebrun
Camille .... M. Young
Chair mender ...... Pavlides,
(s, Lueders)
Artichoke vendor .... Lebrun
Bird food vendor .. M. Young

March 20

MADAMA BUTTERFLY

Same cast as February 19 except:

Pinkerton .... Stewart
Suzuki .... Kieffer
Butterfly .... Niska
The Bonze .... Roy

March 21 (m)

THE MOST IMPORTANT MAN

Same cast as March 7

March 21

UN BALLO IN MASCHERA
(Verdi)
First performance by The New
York City Opera Company

Directed by ...... Hirsch (d)
Set designer ...... Sprott (d)
Costume designer .... Varona
Choreographer ...... Andrew
Lighting .... Sondheimer
Conductor .... Rudel

Count Horn .... Devlin
Count Ribbing .... Roy
Oscar .... Wise
Gustavo .... Di Giuseppe
Renato .... Quilico
Chief Justice .... Fitch
Ulrica .... Greenspon
Silvano .... Ledbetter
Servant .... Bittner
Amelia .... Cruz-Romo
Solo dancer .... Horvath

March 23

UN BALLO IN MASCHERA

Same cast as March 21

March 24

THE MARRIAGE OF FIGARO

Same cast as February 21 (m) except:

Susanna .... Sauler
Bartolo .... Pierson
Marcellina .... Kieffer
Almaviva ..... D. Clatworthy
Basilio .... Hall
Antonio .... Bittner
Barbarina .... S. Young

March 25

IL BARBIERE DI SIVIGLIA

Same cast as March 14 (m) except:

Fiorello .... Jamerson
Basilio .... Hale
Berta .... Winburn

March 26

LOUISE

Same cast as February 28 except:

Mother .... Bible
Junk man .... Davis
Blanche .... Ciraulo
Irma .... Lebrun
Artichoke vendor .... Lebrun

March 27 (m)

IL BARBIERE DI SIVIGLIA

Same cast as March 14 (m) except:

Fiorello .... Jamerson
Almaviva .... Johnson (d)
Figaro .... Fredricks
Bartolo .... Pierson
Rosina .... Marsee
Basilio .... Hale

March 27

LA CENERENTOLA

Same cast as February 17 except:

Conductor ...... Reimueller
Tisbe .... Winburn
Angelina .... Creed
Prince Ramiro .. Di Giuseppe

March 28 (m)

MEFISTOFELE

Same cast as February 18 except:

Mefistofele .... Devlin,
(s, Treigle)
Faust .... Theyard
Margherita ...... Cruz-Romo
Elena .... Cruz-Romo

March 28

LA TRAVIATA

Same cast as February 20 (m) except:

Conductor .... Wilson
Violetta .... Niska
Douphol .... Bittner
Gaston .... Lankston
Germont .... Quilico

March 30

UN BALLO IN MASCHERA

Same cast as March 21 except:

Ulrica .... Chookasian

March 31

LOUISE

Same cast as February 28 except:

Mother .... Bible
Junk man .... Davis
Blanche .... Ciraulo
Irma .... Makas (d)
Madeleine .... Herbert
Solo dancer .... Menes
Artichoke vendor ..Makas (d)

April 1

LA BOHÈME

Same cast as February 27 (m) except:

Rodolfo .... Malamood
Schaunard .... Jamerson
Mimi .... Niska
Musetta .... Meier

April 2

LA TRAVIATA

Same cast as February 20 (m) except:

Conductor .... Nance

Douphol .... Bittner
Gaston .... Lankston
Alfredo .... Stewart
Germont .... Cossa

April 3 (m)

UN BALLO IN MASCHERA

Same cast as March 21 except:
Ulrica .... Chookasian

April 3

LOUISE

Same cast as February 28 except:

Julien .... Theyard
Mother .... Bible
Junk man .... Davis
Blanche .... Ciraulo
Irma .... Makas
Madeleine .... Herbert
Solo dancer .... Menes
Artichoke vendor .... Makas

April 4 (m)

THE TURN OF THE SCREW
(Britten)

Conductor .... Wilson

Prologue .... Lankston
Guardian .... Riegel
Governess .... Niska
Miles .... Puleo
Flora .... Angela
Mrs. Grose .... Faull
Quint .... Riegel
Miss Jessel ..... Shuttleworth

April 4

LA BOHÈME

Same cast as February 27 (m) except:

Rodolfo .... Malamood
Marcello .... Cossa
Schaunard .... Jamerson
Mimi .... Craig (d)
Musetta .... Meier

April 6

DON RODRIGO (Ginastera)

Stage director .... Denda
Conductor .... Rudel

1st Lady in
  waiting ...... Shuttleworth,
                (s, Wise)
2nd Lady in waiting .. Lueders
Pages .... Fitch, Jamerson
Fortuna .... Kieffer
Florinda .... Schauler
Teudiselo .... Malas
Don Julian .... D. Clatworthy
Don Rodrigo ...... Stamford
Bishop .... Roy
Blacksmiths ..... Romaguera,
                  Yule
Voice of Sleep .... Roy
Messengers ...... Romaguera,
                Ledbetter
Young messenger ...... Evans
Young boy .... Puleo
Young girl .... M. Clatworthy
Hermit .... Devlin

April 7

ROBERTO DEVEREUX

Same cast as March 2 except:
Sara .... Creed
Robert
  Devereux .. Di Amorim (d)
Duke of Nottingham ..Quilico

April 8

UN BALLO IN MASCHERA

Same cast as March 21 xcept:

Renato .... D. Clatworthy
Ulrica .... Chookasian
Silvano .... Jamerson

April 9

ROBERTO DEVEREUX

Same cast as March 2 except:

Sara .... Gonzalez (d)
Cecil .... Lankston
Robert Devereux .. Di Virgilio
Duke of Nottingham ..Quilico

April 10 (m)

THE TURN OF THE SCREW

Same cast as April 4 (m) except:

Miles .... Mason (d)

April 10

UN BALLO IN MASCHERA

Same cast as March 21 except:

Count Horn .... Pierson
Renato .... Fredricks
Chief Justice ..... Romaguera
Ulrica .... Chookasian
Silvano .... Jamerson

April 11 (m)

ROBERTO DEVEREUX

Same cast as March 2 except:

Sara .... Gonzalez
Cecil .... Lankston
Robert Devereux .. Di Virgilio
          (Act I); Di Amorim
          (Acts II & III)
Duke of
  Nottingham .. Schwartzman

April 11

DON RODRIGO

Same cast as April 6 except:

Conductor .... Keene
1st Lady in waiting ..... Wise
Fortuna .... Creed

April 13

LUCIA DI LAMMERMOOR

Same cast as March 11 except:

Conductor .... Reimueller
Lucia .... Brooks

April 14

DON RODRIGO

Same cast as April 6 except:

Conductor .... Keene

1st Lady in waiting ..... Wise
2nd Page .... Ledbetter
Florinda .... Ciraulo
Don Julian .... Pierson
Don Rodrigo .... Novoa
Young girl .... Queler (d)

April 15

ROBERTO DEVEREUX

Same cast as March 2 except:

Conductor .... Wilson

Sara .... Gonzalez
Cecil .... Lankston
Robert Devereux ..Di Amorim

April 16

UN BALLO IN MASCHERA

Same cast as March 21 except:

Conductor .... Wilson

Count Horn .... Pierson
Gustavo .... Moles

Chief Justice ..... Romaguera
Ulrica .... Chookasian
Silvano .... Jamerson
Amelia .... Barker (d)

April 17 (m)

THE ABDUCTION FROM
THE SERAGLIO (Mozart)
(English version by
Ruth and Thomas Martin)

Conductor ..... Bernardi (d)

Belmonte .... Jennings
Osmin .... Malas
Pedrillo .... Hall
Constanza .... Lebrun
Pasha Selim .... Smith
Blonde .... Wise

April 17

MADAMA BUTTERFLY

Same cast as February 19
except:

Conductor .... Singer

Pinkerton ...... Di Giuseppe
Goro .... Hall
Suzuki .... Kieffer
The Bonze .... Roy

April 18 (m)

THE TURN OF THE SCREW

Same cast as April 4 (m)
except:

Guardian .... Glaze
Miles .... Mason
Quint .... Glaze

April 18

UN BALLO IN MASCHERA

Same cast as March 21 except:

Count Horn .... Pierson
Oscar .... Lebrun
Gustavo .... Molese
Renato .... Fredricks
Chief Justice ..... Romaguera
Silvano .... Jamerson
Amelia .... Barker

April 20

LA BOHÈME

Same cast as February 27 (m)
except:

Conductor .... Wilson

Rodolfo .... Molese
Marcello .... Fredricks
Schaunard .... Jamerson
Mimi .... Craig
Musetta .... Neblett

April 21

LA TRAVIATA

Same cast as February 20 (m)
except:

Conductor .... Keene

Douphol .... Bittner
D'Obigny .... Jamerson
Gaston .... Lankston
Germont .... Cossa

April 22

LOUISE

Same cast as February 28
except:

Julien .... Theyard
Louise .... Meier
Mother .... Greenspon
Sleepwalker .... Hall
Rag picker .... Densen
Junk man .... Davis
Sculptor .... Kingman
Blanche .... Ciraulo
Suzanne .... Barnes
Camille .... M. Young
Madeleine .... Herbert
King of Fools .... Hall
Solo dancer .... Menes
Bird food vendor .. M. Young
Barrel vendor ..... Kingman

April 23

THE ABDUCTION FROM
THE SERAGLIO

Same cast as April 17 (m)
except:

Belmonte .... Johnson
Blonde .... Welting (d)

April 24 (m)

LA TRAVIATA

Same cast as February 20 (m)
except:

Conductor .... Keene

Douphol .... Bittner
D'Obigny .... Jamerson
Gaston .... Lankston
Alfredo .... Di Giuseppe

April 24

UN BALLO IN MASCHERA

Same cast as March 21 except:

Count Horn .... Pierson
Oscar .... Lebrun
Gustavo .... Molese
Ulrica .... Chookasian
Silvano .... Jamerson

April 25 (m)

LOUISE

Same cast as February 28
except:

Julien .... Theyard
Louise .... Meier
Mother .... Greenspon
Father .... Hale
Sleepwalker .... Hall
Rag picker .... Davis
Sculptor .... Kingman
Songwriter .... Galiano
Blanche .... Ciraulo
Suzanne .... Barnes
Madeleine .... Herbert
King of Fools .... Hall
Solo dancer .... Menes
Barrel vendor ...... Kingman
Broom vendor ...... Galiano

April 25

THE ABDUCTION FROM
THE SERAGLIO

Same cast as April 17 (m)
except:

Osmin .... Roy
Pedrillo .... Lankston
Constanza .... Makas

Fall 1971 (SEPTEMBER 2 – NOVEMBER 14)

Herbert, Lila
Hirschl, Lana*
Kieffer, Deborah
Killebrew, Gwendolyn*
Lueders, Mary Cross
Marsee, Susanne
Meier, Johanna
Neblett, Carol
Niska, Maralin
Owen, Hanna
Sauler, Bianca
Schauler, Eileen
Shade, Nancy*
Shuttleworth, Barbara
Sills, Beverly
Welting, Ruth
West, Maria
Wise, Patricia
Young, Syble

Male artists
Alexander, John
Bass, Robert
Bentley, Ronald
Bittner, Jack
Castel, Nico
Chapman, William
Clatworthy, David
Cossa, Dominic
Darrenkamp, John
Davis, J. B.
Densen, Irwin
Devlin, Michael
Di Giuseppe, Enrico
Duffy, Colin*
Edwards, Ryan*
Fitch, Bernard
Fredricks, Richard
Galiano, Joseph
Gill, Richard T.*
Glaze, Gary
Hale, Robert
Hall, David
Harper, Talmage
Henderson, Don
Jamerson, Thomas
Jennings, Jerry J.
Johnson, Robert
Kingman, Dan
Lankston, John
Ledbetter, William
Malamood, Herman
Malas, Spiro
Marini, Franco*
Martí, Bernabé
McCray, James
Molese, Michele
Montané, Carlos
Park, Richard
Paul, Thomas
Pierson, Edward
Price, Perry*
Profanato, Gene*
Quilico, Louis
Riegel, Kenneth
Romaguera, Joaquin
Schwartzman, Seymour
Smith, David Rae
Stamford, John
Stewart, John
Stilwell, Richard
Theyard, Harry

* New artist

Treigle, Norman
Yule, Don

Conductors
Bernardi, Mario
Keene, Christopher
Mester, Jorge
Morelli, Giuseppe
Nance, Chris
Rudel, Julius
Susskind, Walter
Wilson, Charles

Chorus master
Nance, Chris

Assistant chorus master
Somogi, Judith

Solo dancers
Balestracci, Sandra
Galan, Esperanza
Menes, Rose Marie

Roberts, Chester

Choreographers
Andrew, Thomas
Denda, Elena

Directors
Besch, Anthony
Capobianco, Tito
Corsaro, Frank
de Blasis, James
Denda, Elena
Hicks, David
Hirsch, John
Lewis, Robert
Sherin, Edwin*

Designers
Ardolino, Emile
Campbell, Patton
Compton, Gardner
Evans, Lloyd
Fletcher, Robert
George, Hal
Lee, Ming Cho
Micunis, Gordon
Mitchell, David
Oenslager, Donald
Sprott, Eoin
Varona, José
Wittstein, Ed

* New artist

September 2

THE MAKROPOULOS AFFAIR
(Janáček)
(English translation by
Norman Tucker)

Conductor .... Susskind

Vitek .... Langston
Albert Gregor ...... Theyard
Christa .... Shuttleworth
Emila Marty .... Niska
Chauffeur .... Smith
Dr. Kolenaty .... Pierson
Jaroslav Prus .. D. Clatworthy
Maid .... Anthony
Janek .... Glaze
Hauk-Sendorf .... Castel

September 3

LOUISE (Charpentier)

Conductor .... Wilson

Julien .... Alexander
Louise .... Neblett
Mother .... Bible
Father .... Devlin
Young rag picker ..... Guilet
Coal gatherer .... West
Sleepwalker .... Riegel
Milk woman .... Adler
Rag picker .... Gill (d)
Junk man .... Densen
Policemen ... Bittner, Bentley
Street urchin .... Hepburn
Street sweeper ...... Anthony
Painter .... Fitch
Sculptor .... Ledbetter
Songwriter .... Jamerson
Poet .... Lankston
Philosophers .... Romaguera,
                           Yule
Blanche .... Ciraulo
Marguerite .... Guilet
Suzanne .... Doty
Gertrude .... Lueders
Irma .... Sauler
Camille .... Darling
Apprentice .... Hepburn
Elise .... Kieffer
Madeleine .... Owen
Old clothes man .... Glaze
Forewoman .... Evans
King of Fools .... Riegel
Solo dancer ...... Balestracci
Chair mender .... Lueders
Clothing vendor .. Romaguera
Artichoke vendor ..... Sauler
Carrot vendor .... Fitch
Bird food vendor .... Darling
Barrel vendor ...... Ledbetter
Broom vendor ..... Jamerson
Potato vendors .... Hepburn,
                      Lankston
Green peas vendor ..... Fitch
Watercress vendor .... Evans

September 4 (m)

LA TRAVIATA (Verdi)

Conductor .... Morelli

Violetta .... Brooks
Flora .... Lueders
Douphol .... Smith
D'Obigny .... Jamerson
Dr. Grenvil .... Yule
Gaston .... Glaze
Alfredo .... Montané
Annina .... Kieffer
Giuseppe .... Romaguera
Germont .... Fredricks
Messenger .... Kingman
Solo dancer .... Galan

September 4

LA BOHÈME (Puccini)

Conductor .... Morelli

Rodolfo .... Di Giuseppe
Marcello .... Cossa
Colline .... Hale

Schaunard .... Ledbetter
Benoit .... Yule
Mimi .... Cruz-Romo
Parpignol .... Romaguera
Musetta .... Meier
Alcindoro .... Bittner
Guards ..... Galiano, Bentley

September 5 (m)

THE MAKROPOULOS AFFAIR

Same cast as September 2

September 5

LOUISE

Same cast as September 3

September 7

LOUISE

Same cast as September 3
except:

Julien .... Theyard
Father .... Hale

(Note: *Potato vendors* changed
to *Potato vendor*: Lankston
only listed)

September 8

THE MARRIAGE OF FIGARO
(Mozart)
(English version by
Ruth and Thomas Martin)

Conductor .... Keene

Figaro .... Devlin
Susanna .... Wise
Bartolo .... Pierson
Marcellina .... Evans
Cherubino .... Creed
Almaviva ...... Darrenkamp
Basilio .... Fitch
Countess .... Meier
Antonio .... Bittner
Curzio .... Lankston
Barbarina .... Young
Solo dancer .... Galan

September 9

THE MAKROPOULOS AFFAIR

Same cast as September 2
except:

Albert Gregor ...... Stamford

September 10

LOUISE

Same cast as September 3
except:

Julien .... Theyard
Louise .... Meier
Mother .... Greenspon
Father .... Hale
Rag picker .... Densen
Junk man .... Yule
Street sweeper ... Hirschl (d)
2nd Philosopher ...... Harper

Blanche .... Shuttleworth
Suzanne .... Barnes
Irma .... Craig
Madeleine .... Herbert
Artichoke vendor ...... Craig

September 11 (m)

UN BALLO IN MASCHERA
(Verdi)

Conductor .... Morelli

Count Horn .... Pierson
Count Ribbing .... Gill
Oscar .... Wise
Gustavo .... Molese
Renato .... Quilico
Chief Justice .... Fitch
Ulrica .... Killebrew (d)
Silvano .... Ledbetter
Servant .... Bittner
Amelia .... Cruz-Romo

September 11

LA BOHÈME

Same cast as September 4
except:

Conductor .... Mester

Marcello .... Darrenkamp
Colline .... Devlin
Mimi .... Bruno
Musetta .... Bayard

September 12 (m)

LA TRAVIATA

Same cast as September 4 (m)
except:

Dr. Grenvil .... Pierson

September 12

THE MAKROPOULOS AFFAIR

Same cast as September 2
except:

Albert Gregor ...... Stamford

September 14

UN BALLO IN MASCHERA

Same cast as September 11 (m)

September 15

ALBERT HERRING (Britten)
First performance by The New
York City Opera Company

Directed by .... Besch
Designer .... Evans
Lighting .... Sondheimer
Conductor .... Bernardi

Florence .... Evans
Lady Billows .... Faull
Miss Wordsworth .... Darling
Mr. Gedge .... Jamerson
Mr. Upfold .... Lankston
Superintendent Budd .... Gill
Harry .... Duffy (d)
Emmie .... Glick (d)
Cis .... M. Clatworthy

Sid .... Cossa
Albert Herring ...... Stewart
Nancy .... Creed
Mrs. Herring ..... Greenspon

September 16

LA BOHÈME

Same cast as September 4
except:

Conductor .... Mester

Marcello .... Darrenkamp
Benoit .... Densen
Mimi .... Bruno
Musetta .... Bayard
Guards ..... Park, Henderson

September 17

LA TRAVIATA

Same cast as September 4 (m)
except:

Conductor .... Nance

Violetta .... Neblett
D'Obigny .... Ledbetter
Alfredo .... Stewart
Germont .... Cossa
Messenger .... Galiano

September 18 (m)

UN BALLO IN MASCHERA

Same cast as September 11 (m)
except:

Renato .... Fredricks
Chief Justice .... Romaguera,
                  (s, Fitch)
Amelia .... Barker

September 18

THE MAKROPOULOS AFFAIR

Same cast as September 2
except:

Conductor .... Keene

Vitek .... Lankston,
                  (s, Fitch)
Christa .... Young
Jaroslav Prus ... Edwards (d)
Maid .... Hirschl
Janke .... Hall

September 19 (m)

MADAMA BUTTERFLY (Puccini)

Conductor .... Morelli

Pinkerton .... Stewart
Goro .... Hall
Suzuki .... Creed
Sharpless ..... D. Clatworthy
Butterfly .... Cruz-Romo
Imperial
  Commissioner ... Jamerson
Registrar .... Lankston
The Bonze .... Densen
Yamadori .... Lankston
Trouble ...... Profanato (d)
Kate Pinkerton ..... Lueders

September 19
LA BOHÈME
Same cast as September 4 except:

Conductor	Mester
Schaunard	Jamerson
Benoit	Densen
Mimi	Craig
Musetta	Shade (d)

September 21
MADAMA BUTTERFLY
Same cast as September 19 (m)

September 22
LA TRAVIATA
Same cast as September 4 (m) except:

D'Obigny	Ledbetter
Alfredo	Marini (d)
Germont	Cossa
Messenger	Galiano

September 23
LOUISE
Same cast as September 3 except:

Julien	Theyard
Mother	Greenspon
Street sweeper	Hirschl
Blanche	Shuttleworth
Suzanne	Barnes
Irma	Craig
Madeleine	Herbert
Forewoman	Anthony
Artichoke vendor	Craig
Watercress vendor ..	Anthony

September 24
LA BOHÈME
Same cast as September 4 except:

Rodolfo	Molese
Marcello	Schwartzman
Schaunard	Jamerson
Benoit	Densen
Mimi	Craig
Musetta	Shade
Guards	Park, Henderson

September 25 (m)
MADAMA BUTTERFLY
Same cast as September 19 (m) except:

Conductor	Wilson
Pinkerton	Malamood
Goro	Fitch
Suzuki	Kieffer

September 25
THE MARRIAGE OF FIGARO
Same cast as September 8 except:

Bartolo	Densen, (s, Pierson)

September 26 (m)
TOSCA (Puccini)

Staged by	Denda
Lighting	Sondheimer
Conductor	Morelli
Angelotti	Smith
Sacristan	Bittner
Cavaradossi	Di Giuseppe
Tosca	Niska
Scarpia	Fredricks
Spoletta	Hall
Sciarrone	Ledbetter
Shepherd	Bass
Jailer	Yule

September 26
ALBERT HERRING
Same cast as September 15

September 28
TOSCA
Same cast as September 26 (m) except:

Tosca	Cruz-Romo
Scarpia	Pierson

September 29
UN BALLO IN MASCHERA
Same cast as September 11 (m) except:

Oscar	Welting
Renato	Fredricks
Chief Justice	Romaguera
Ulrica	Greenspon
Amelia	Barker

September 30
COSÌ FAN TUTTE (Mozart)
(English version by Ruth and Thomas Martin)

Directed by	Sherin (d)
Lighting	Sondheimer
Conductor	Mester
Ferrando	Jennings
Guglielmo	Darrenkamp
Don Alfonso	Devlin
Fiordiligi	Meier
Dorabella	Bible
Despina	Wise

October 1
ALBERT HERRING
Same cast as September 15 except:

Sid	Stilwell

October 2 (m)
MADAMA BUTTERFLY
Same cast as September 19 (m) except:

Conductor	Wilson
Pinkerton	Malamood
Goro	Hall, (s, Fitch)
Suzuki	Kieffer

October 2
TOSCA
Same cast as September 26 (m) except:

Tosca	Schauler

October 3 (m)
COSÌ FAN TUTTE
Same cast as September 30 except:

Conductor	Wilson

October 3
UN BALLO IN MASCHERA
Same cast as September 11 (m) except:

Oscar	Welting
Gustavo	Montané
Renato	Edwards
Amelia	Barker

October 5
COSÌ FAN TUTTE
Same cast as September 30

October 6
TOSCA
Same cast as September 26 (m) except:

Spoletta	Fitch

October 7
CARMEN (Bizet)
New production

Directed by	Capobianco
Designer	Varona
Choreographer	Andrew
Lighting	Sondheimer
Conductor	Rudel
Morales	Jamerson
Andrès	Yule
Zuniga	Smith
Micaëla	Brune
Don José	Molese
Carmen	Davidson
Frasquita	Shuttleworth
Mercédès	Marsee
Lillas Pastia	Romaguera
Escamillo	Hale
Remendado	Fitch
Dancairo	Pierson

October 8
ALBERT HERRING
Same cast as September 15 except:

Lady Billows	Anthony
Miss Wordsworth ...	Welting
Albert Herring	Glaze
Mrs. Herring	Alber

October 9 (m)

CARMEN

Same cast as October 7

October 9

THE MAKROPOULOS AFFAIR

Same cast as September 2
except:

Conductor	Keene
Christa	Young
Jaroslav Prus	Edwards
Maid	Hirschl
Janek	Hall

October 10 (m)

TOSCA

Same cast as September 26 (m)
except:

Cavaradossi	Montané
Tosca	Cruz-Romo
Spoletta	Fitch

October 10

THE MARRIAGE OF FIGARO

Same cast as September 8
except:

Susanna	Sauler
Bartolo	Densen
Marcellina	Kieffer
Almaviva	D. Clatworthy
Basilio	Hall
Antonio	Yule

October 12

MEFISTOFELE (Boito)

Conductor	Rudel
Mefistofele	Devlin,
	(s, Treigle)
Faust	Martí
Wagner	Fitch
Margherita	Neblett
Marta	Evans
Elena	Neblett
Pantalis	Lueders
Nereo	Romaguera
Solo dancers	Balestracci,
	Menes; Roberts

October 13

ROBERTO DEVEREUX
(Donizetti)

Conductor	Rudel
Sara	Marsee
Elizabeth	Sills
Cecil	Fitch
Page	Ledbetter
Raleigh	Smith
Robert Devereux	Di Giuseppe
Duke of	
Nottingham	Fredricks
Servant	Yule

October 14

CARMEN

Same cast as October 7 except:

Don José	McCray
Mercédès	Kieffer

October 15

ROBERTO DEVEREUX

Same cast as October 13
except:

Conductor	Rudel
	(s, Wilson)

October 16 (m)

THE MARRIAGE OF FIGARO

Same cast as September 8
except:

Figaro	Malas
Susanna	Sauler
Bartolo	Densen
Marcellina	Kieffer
Cherubino	Bible
Almaviva	D. Clatworthy
Basilio	Hall
Countess	Domanski (d)
Antonio	Yule

October 16

CARMEN

Same cast as October 7 except:

Don José	Theyard
Mercédès	Kieffer

October 17 (m)

ROBERTO DEVEREUX

Same cast as October 13
except:

Conductor	Wilson
Sara	Creed
Robert Devereux	Marini

October 17

MEFISTOFELE

Same cast as October 12
except:

Mefistofele	Treigle
Margherita	Cruz-Romo
Elena	Cruz-Romo

October 19

LE COQ D'OR
(Rimsky-Korsakov)
(English version by Antal
Dorati and James Gibson)

Staged and	
choreographed by	Denda
Conductor	Susskind
Astrologer	Di Giuseppe
General Polkan	Pierson
Prince Guidon	Glaze

Prince Afron	Smith
King Dodon	Malas
Golden Cockerel	Welting
Amelfa	Greenspon
Queen of Shemakha	Neblett

October 20

CARMEN

Same cast as October 7 except:

Zuniga	Densen
Micaëla	Craig
Carmen	Schauler
Mercédès	Kieffer
Escamillo	Devlin
Remendado	Glaze
Dancairo	Bittner

October 21

MEFISTOFELE

Same cast as October 12
except:

Conductor	Morelli
Mefistofele	Treigle
Margherita	Cruz-Romo
Elena	Cruz-Romo

October 22

GIULIO CESARE (Handel)

Staged and	
choreographed by	Denda
Conductor	Rudel
Giulio Cesare	Hale
Curio	Ledbetter
Cornelia	Gerber (d)
Sesto	Marsee
Achilla	Cossa
Cleopatra	Sills
Nireno	Smith
Tolomeo	Paul

October 23 (m)

CARMEN

Same cast as October 7 except:

Zuniga	Densen
Micaëla	Craig
Carmen	Schauler
Mercédès	Kieffer
Escamillo	Devlin
Remendado	Glaze
Dancairo	Bittner

October 23

COSÌ FAN TUTTE

Same cast as September 30
except:

Ferrando	Johnson
Guglielmo	Stilwell
Don Alfonso	Malas
Fiordiligi	Brooks
Dorabella	Creed
Despina	Welting

October 24 (m)

MEFISTOFELE

Same cast as October 12
except:

Conductor .... Morelli

Mefistofele .... Treigle
Margherita ...... Cruz-Romo
Elena .... Cruz-Romo

October 24

GIULIO CESARE

Same cast as October 22
except:

Cornelia .... Gerber (Act I);
      Bible (Acts II & III)

October 26

MEFISTOFELE

Same cast as October 12
except:

Conductor .... Morelli

Mefistofele .... Chapman
Faust .... Theyard,
       (s, Martí)

October 27

CARMEN

Same cast as October 7 except:

Morales .... Ledbetter
Micaëla .... Sauler
Frasquita .... Young
Escamillo .... Devlin,
       (s, Treigle)
Remendado .... Glaze
Dancairo .... Bittner

October 28

GIULIO CESARE

Same cast as October 22
except:

Cornelia .... Bible,
       (s, Gerber)
Sesto .... Creed

October 29

CARMEN

Same cast as October 7 except:

Morales .... Ledbetter
Micaëla .... Neblett
Frasquita .... Young
Escamillo .... Chapman
Remendado .... Glaze
Dancairo .... Bittner

October 30 (m)

GIULIO CESARE

Same cast as October 22
except:

Giulio Cesare .... Devlin
Cornelia .... Bible

Sesto .... Creed
Tolomeo .... Davis

October 30

IL BARBIERE DI SIVIGLIA
(Rossini)

Conductor .... Morelli

Fiorello .... Ledbetter
Almaviva .... Price (d)
Figaro .... Fredricks
Bartolo .... Pierson
Rosina .... Wise
Basilio .... Hale
Berta .... Evans
Officer .... Yule

October 31 (m)

LE COQ D'OR

Same cast as October 9

October 31

SUSANNAH (Floyd)
New production

Directed by .... Lewis
Set designer .... Lee
Costume designer .. Campbell
Choreographer ...... Andrew
Lighting .... Sondheimer
Conductor .... Rudel

Mrs. Gleaton ... Shuttleworth
Mrs. Hayes .... Darling
Mrs. McLean .... Lueders
Mrs. Ott .... Kieffer
Elder McLean .... Bittner
Elder Ott .... Yule
Elder Gleaton .... Fitch
Elder Hayes .... Lankston
Susannah .... Niska
Little Bat McLean ..... Hall
Olin Blitch .... Treigle
Sam Polk .... Theyard

November 2

SUSANNAH

Same cast as October 31

November 3

LE COQ D'OR

Same cast as October 19
except:

Astrologer .... Riegel
Queen of
     Shemakha ..... Armstrong

November 4

GIULIO CESARE

Same cast as October 22
except:

Giulio Cesare .... Treigle
Cornelia .... Bible
Achilla .... Stilwell
Tolomeo .... Davis

November 5

LE COQ D'OR

Same cast as October 19
except:

General Polkan .... Gill
Golden Cockerel ..... Young
Amelfa .... Evans
Queen of
     Shemakha ...... Armstrong

November 6 (m)

COSÌ FAN TUTTE

Same cast as September 30
except:

Conductor .... Wilson

Ferrando .... Johnson
Guglielmo .... Stilwell
Dorabella .... Creed
Despina .... Welting

November 6

IL BARBIERE DI SIVIGLIA

Same cast as October 30

November 7 (m)

ROBERTO DEVEREUX

Same cast as October 13
except:

Conductor .... Wilson

Duke of
     Nottingham .. Schwartzman

November 7

MEFISTOFELE

Same cast as October 12
except:

Mefistofele .... Treigle
Faust .... Theyard
       (s, Martí

November 9

LE COQ D'OR

Same cast as October 19
except:

Conductor .... Rudel

King Dodon .... Treigle
Golden Cockerel ..... Young
Queen of Shemakha ..... Sills

Telecast—Cable TV

November 10

MEFISTOFELE

Same cast as October 12
except:

Mefistofele .... Chapman
Faust .... Theyard

November 11

ROBERTO DEVEREUX

Same cast as October 13

November 12

IL BARBIERE DI SIVIGLIA

Same cast as October 30
except:

Figaro .... Stilwell
Bartolo .... Malas
Berta .... Lueders

November 13 (m)

MEFISTOFELE

Same cast as October 12
except:

Mefistofele .... Treigle
Faust .... Theyard

November 13

MADAMA BUTTERFLY

Same cast as September 19 (m)
except:

Pinkerton .... Malamood
Sharpless .... Cossa

November 14 (m)

SUSANNAH

Same cast as October 31
except:

Elder Ott .... Smith
Olin Blitch .... Treigle,
(s, Devlin)

November 14

COSÌ FAN TUTTE

Same cast as September 30
except:

Ferrando .... Johnson
Guglielmo .... Stilwell
Don Alfonso .... Malas

Spring 1972 (FEBRUARY 23 – APRIL 30)

Female artists
Angela, June
Anthony, Judith
Bayard, Carol
Bible, Frances
Brooks, Patricia
Ciraulo, Marianna
Clements, Joy
Craig, Patricia
Creed, Kay
Cruz-Romo, Gilda
Darling, Sandra
Davidson, Joy
Dunn, Mignon
Evans, Beverly
Faull, Ellen
French, Norma*
Galvany, Marisa*
Gerber, Joyce
Greene, Harriet
Greenspon, Muriel
Guilet, Helene
Hirschl, Lana
Kellogg, Riley*
Kieffer, Deborah
Killebrew, Gwendolyn
Leporska, Zoya*
Lueders, Mary Cross
Marsee, Susanne
Meier, Johanna
Neblett, Carol
Niska, Maralin
Peil, Mary Beth*
Roberto, Francesca
Sauler, Bianca
Schauler, Eileen
Shade, Nancy
Shuttleworth, Barbara
Sills, Beverly
Tinsley, Pauline*
Tyler, Veronica
Wells, Patricia*
Welting, Ruth
Wise, Patricia
Young, Syble

* New artist

Male artists
Bentley, Ronald
Bittner, Jack
Cade, James*
Carlo, Don
Carreras, José*
Castel, Nico
Chapman, William
Clatworthy, David
Cossa, Dominic
Darrenkamp, John
Davis, Harris
Davis, J. B.
Densen, Irwin
Devlin, Michael
Di Giuseppe, Enrico
Duffy, Colin
Fitch, Bernard
Fredricks, Richard
Galiano, Joseph
Gill, Richard T.
Glaze, Gary
Goeke, Leo
Hale, Robert
Hall, David
Henderson, Don
Hirst, Grayson*
Holloway, David*
Jamerson, Thomas
Johnson, Robert
Kingman, Dan
Lankston, John
Ledbetter, William
Ludgin, Chester
Malamood, Herman
Malas, Spiro
Manno, Robert
Marini, Franco
Miller, Michael*
Molese, Michele
Montané, Carlos
Novoa, Salvador
Papay, Raymond
Park, Richard
Pierson, Edward

* New artist

Presnell, Steve
Profanato, Gene
Quilico, Louis
Rampaso, Luciano*
Reardon, John
Romaguera, Joaquin
Schwartzman, Seymour
Smith, David Rae
Stamford, John
Stewart, John
Theyard, Harry
Titus, Alan*
Yule, Don

Conductors
Keene, Christopher
Morelli, Giuseppe
Nance, Chris
Reimueller, Ross
Rudel, Julius
Susskind, Walter
Wilson, Charles

Chorus master
Nance, Chris

Assistant chorus master
Somogi, Judith

Solo dancers
Balestracci, Sandra
Galan, Esperanza
Menes, Rose Marie

Roberts, Chester
Seetoo, Dennis*

Choreographers
Andrew, Thomas
Denda, Elena

Directors
Bakman, Patrick*
Capobianco, Tito
Corsaro, Frank
Denda, Elena
Hicks, David
Mann, Theodore

* New artist

Osterhaus, Carveth*
Sherin, Edwin

Designers
Ardolino, Emile
Campbell, Patton
Colt, Alvin
Compton, Gardner
Eck, Marsha Louis
Evans, Lloyd
Fletcher, Robert
George, Hal
Lee, Ming Cho
Mitchell, David
Oenslager, Donald
Varona, José
Venza, Jac
Wittstein, Ed

* New artist

February 23

ROBERTO DEVEREUX
(Donizetti)

Stage director .... Hicks
Conductor .... Rudel

Sara .... Marsee
Elizabeth .... Sills
Cecil .... Fitch
Page .... Ledbetter
Raleigh .... Smith
Robert Devereux. . Di Giuseppe
Duke of
 Nottingham ..... Fredricks
Servant .... Yule

February 24

CARMEN (Bizet)

Conductor .... Rudel

Morales .... Jamerson
Andrès .... Yule
Zuniga .... Smith
Micaëla .... Sauler
Don José .... Molese
Carmen .... Schauler,
                 (s, Davidson)
Frasquita ...... Shuttleworth
Mercédès .... Kieffer
Lillas Pastia,
 Guide .... Romaguera
Escamillo .... Chapman
Remendado .... Glaze
Dancairo .... Pierson

February 25

LA TRAVIATA (Verdi)

Conductor .... Morelli

Violetta .... Brooks
Flora .... Lueders
Douphol .... Bittner
D'Obigny .... Ledbetter
Dr. Grenvil .... Densen
Gaston .... Glaze
Alfredo .... Stewart
Annina .... Kieffer
Giuseppe .... Romaguera
Germont .... Cossa
Messenger .... Galiano
Solo dancer .... Galan

February 26 (m)

THE MARRIAGE OF FIGARO
(Mozart)
(English version by
Ruth and Thomas Martin)

Conductor .... Keene

Figaro .... Devlin
Susanna .... Wise
Bartolo .... Gill
Marcellina .... Evans
Cherubino .... Creed
Almaviva ...... Darrenkamp
Basilio .... Hall
Countess .... Meier
Antonio .... Bittner
Curzio .... Lankston
Barbarina .... Young
Solo dancer .... Galan

February 26

CARMEN

Same cast as February 24
except:

Carmen .... Dunn,
               (s, Davidson)

February 27 (m)

MADAMA BUTTERFLY (Puccini)

Conductor .... Morelli

Pinkerton .... Stewart
Goro .... Fitch
Suzuki .... Kieffer
Sharpless .... Clatworthy
Butterfly .... Niska
Imperial
 Commissioner ... Jamerson
Registrar .... Lankston
The Bonze .... Densen
Yamadori .... Lankston
Trouble .... Profanato
Kate Pinkerton ...... Hirschl

February 27

ROBERTO DEVEREUX

Same cast as February 23

February 29

CARMEN

Same cast as February 24
except:

Carmen .... Dunn
Escamillo .... Hale

March 1

MEFISTOFELE (Boito)

Conductor .... Rudel

Mefistofele .... Devlin
Faust .... Theyard
Wagner .... Fitch
Margherita .... Neblett
Marta .... Evans
Elena .... Neblett
Pantalis .... Fitch
Nereo .... Romaguera
Solo dancers ..... Balestracci,
               Menes; Roberts

March 2

ROBERTO DEVEREUX

Same cast as February 23
except:

Cecil .... Lankston

March 3

MADAMA BUTTERFLY

Same cast as February 27 (m)
except:

Pinkerton .... Malamood
Suzuki .... Creed

March 4 (m)

MEFISTOFELE

Same cast as March 1 except:

Conductor .... Morelli

Mefistofele .... Chapman
Margherita ...... Cruz-Romo
Elena .... Cruz-Romo

March 4

LA TRAVIATA

Same cast as February 25
except:

Conductor .... Wilson

Alfredo .... Montané
Annina .... Hirschl

March 5 (m)

THE MARRIAGE OF FIGARO

Same cast as February 26 (m)
except:

Susanna .... Sauler

March 5

CARMEN

Same cast as February 24
except:

Conductor .... Keene

Micaëla .... Wells (d)
Escamillo .... Hale
Dancairo .... Bittner

March 7

MARIA STUARDA (Donizetti)
First performance by The New
York City Opera Company

Directed by ..... Capobianco
Scenic designer .... Lee
Costume designer .... Varona
Lighting .... Sondheimer
Conductor .... Wilson

Herald .... Galian
Elisabetta .... Tinsley (d)
Talbot .... Fredrick
Cecil .... Devlin
Roberto Dudley .... Stewart
Maria Stuarda .... Sills
Anna Kennedy .... Kieffer

March 8

MEFISTOFELE

Same cast as March 1 except:

Conductor .... Morelli

Mefistofele .... Chapman
Margherita .... Shade
Elena .... Shade

March 9

THE MARRIAGE OF FIGARO

Same cast as February 26 m)
except:

Susanna .... Sauler
Marcellina .... Lueders
Cherubino .... Marsee
Almaviva .... Clatworthy
Countess .... Neblett

March 10

COSÌ FAN TUTTE (Mozart)
(English version by
Ruth and Thomas Martin)

Stage director .. Osterhaus (d)
Conductor .... Wilson

Ferrando .... Johnson,
                  (s, Jennings)*
Guglielmo ...... Darrenkamp
Don Alfonso .... Malas
Fiordiligi .... Meier
Dorabella .... Bible
Despina .... Wise

(Note: Jerry J. Jennings was
not to appear with the company
this season.)

March 11 (m)

CARMEN

Same cast as February 24
except:

Conductor .... Keene

Micaëla .... Wells
Don José .... Theyard
Mercédès .... Marsee
Remendado .... Fitch
Dancairo .... Bittner

March 11

MADAMA BUTTERFLY

Same cast as February 27 (m)
except:

Butterfly .... Cruz-Romo

March 12 (m)

LA TRAVIATA

Same cast as February 25
except:

Conductor .... Reimueller

Violetta .... Neblett
Douphol .... Bittner,
                  (s, Smith)
Dr. Grenvil .... Yule

Gaston .... Lankston
Alfredo .... Di Giuseppe
Annina .... Hirschl
Germont ...... Schwartzman

March 12

RIGOLETTO (Verdi)

Conductor .... Morelli

Rigoletto .... Fredricks
Monterone's daughter .. Galan
Duke .... Molese
Borsa .... Fitch
Countess Ceprano .... Young
Ceprano .... Ledbetter
Marullo .... Jamerson
Monterone .... J. B. Davis
Sparafucile .... Gill
Gilda .... Brooks
Giovanna .... Evans
Page .... Kieffer
Maddalena .... Lueders

March 14

MARIA STUARDA

Same cast as March 7

March 15

MADAMA BUTTERFLY

Same cast as February 27 (m)
except:

Pinkerton ...... Carreras (d)
Suzuki .... Creed
Sharpless .... Darrenkamp
Butterfly .... Shade

March 16

MARIA STUARDA

Same cast as March 7 except:

Elisabetta ...... Galvany (d)
Roberto
  Dudley ...... Rampaso (d)
Anna Kennedy ...... Hirschl

March 17

CARMEN

Same cast as February 24
except:

Conductor .... Keene

Morales .... Ledbetter
Zuniga .... J. B. Davis
Micaëla .... Craig
Carmen .... Dunn
Frasquita .... Young
Mercédès .... Marsee
Escamillo .... Hale
Remendado .... Fitch
Dancairo .... Bittner

March 18 (m)

TOSCA (Puccini)

Conductor .... Morelli

Angelotti .... Smith
Sacristan .... Bittner
Cavaradossi .... Montané
Tosca .... Niska

Scarpia .... Quilico
Spoletta .... Hall
Sciarrone .... Ledbetter
Shepherd .... Kieffer
Jailer .... Yule

March 18

LA TRAVIATA

Same cast as February 25
except:

Conductor .... Wilson

Flora .... Evans,
                  (s, Lueders)
Douphol .... Smith
Dr. Grenvil .... Yule
Gaston .... Lankston
Alfredo ...... Di Giuseppe
Annina .... Hirschl
Messenger .... Kingman
Germont ...... Schwartzman

March 19 (m)

SUSANNAH (Floyd)

Directed by .... Bakman (d)
Conductor .... Keene

Mrs. Gleaton .. Shuttleworth
Mrs. Hayes .... Darling
Mrs. McLean .... Evans
Mrs. Ott .... Lueders
Elder McLean .... J. B. Davis
Elder Ott .... Yule
Elder Gleaton .... Fitch
Elder Hayes .... Lankston
Susannah .... Clements
Little Bat McLean ..... Hall
Olin Blitch .... Devlin
Sam Polk .... Theyard

March 19

SUMMER AND SMOKE (Hoiby)
New York premiere

Directed by .... Corsaro
Designer .... Evans
Lighting .... Sondheimer
Conductor .... Rudel

Alma, as a child ..Kellogg (d)
John, as a child ...... Duffy
Alma Winemiller .... Peil (d)
Rev. Winemiller .. J. B. Davis
Mrs. Winemiller .... Leporska
                        (d)
John Buchanan, Jr. .. Reardon
Dr. Buchanan .... Smith
Rosa Gonzales ...... Lueders
Papa Gonzales ... Cade (d)
Nellie Ewell .... Shuttleworth
Mrs. Bassett .... Anthony
Roger Doremus .... Lankston
Rosemary .... Kieffer
Vernon .... Krause
Archie Kramer .... Titus (d)

March 21

MARIA STUARDA

Same cast as March 7 except:

Talbot .... Darrenkamp
Cecil .... J. B. Davis
Roberto Dudley .... Rampaso

March 22
SUSANNAH
Same cast as March 19 (m)
Sam Polk .... Stamford

March 23
SUMMER AND SMOKE
Same cast as March 19

March 24
GIULIO CESARE (Handel)
Conductor .... Rudel

Giulio Cesare .... Hale
Curio .... Ledbetter
Cornelia .... Killebrew
Sesto .... Marsee
Achilla .... Cossa
Cleopatra .... Sills
Nireno .... Smith
Tolomeo .... Pierson

March 25 (m)
COSÌ FAN TUTTE
Same cast as March 10 except:
Ferrando .... Goeke
Don Alfonso .... Devlin
Fiordiligi .... Brooks
Dorabella .... Creed

March 25
MEFISTOFELE
Same cast as March 1 except:
Conductor .... Morelli
Mefistofele .... Chapman
Faust .... Novoa

March 26 (m)
TOSCA
Same cast as March 18 (m) except:
Scarpia .... Fredricks

March 26
CARMEN
Same cast as February 24 except:
Conductor .... Keene
Morales .... Ledbetter
Zuniga .... J. B. Davis
Micaëla .... Craig
Don José .... Theyard
Carmen .... Davidson
Frasquita .... Young
Escamillo .... Hale
Remendado .... Fitch
Dancairo .... Bittner

March 28
GIULIO CESARE
Same cast as March 24

March 29
MEFISTOFELE
Same cast as March 1 except:
Conductor .... Morelli
Mefistofele .... Chapman
Faust .... Novoa
Wagner .... Glaze

March 30
CARMEN
Same cast as February 24 except:
Conductor .... Keene
Zuniga .... J. B. Davis
Micaëla .... Craig
Don José .... Theyard
Frasquita .... Young
Mercédès .... Marsee
Lillas Pastia,
  Guide .... Presnell,
            (s, Romaguera)
Escamillo ...... Darrenkamp
Remendado ..... Romaguera,
            (s, Glaze)

March 31
RIGOLETTO
Same cast as March 12 except:
Rigoletto .... Quilico
Monterone .... Densen

April 1 (m)
GIULIO CESARE
Same cast as March 24 except:
Giulio Cesare .... Devlin
Cornelia .... Greenspon
Sesto .... Creed
Tolomeo .... J. B. Davis

April 1
SUSANNAH
Same cast as March 19 (m) except:
Little Bat
  McLean ...... Romaguera
Olin Blitch .... Chapman

April 2 (m)
THE TURN OF THE SCREW (Britten)
Conductor .... Wilson
Prologue .... Lankston
Guardian .... Glaze
Governess .... Schauler
Miles .... Miller (d)
Flora .... Angela
Mrs. Grose .... Faull
Quint .... Glaze
Miss Jessel ..... Shuttleworth

April 2
TOSCA
Same cast as March 18 (m) except:
Cavaradossi .... Molese
Scarpia .... Fredricks

April 4
CARMEN
Same cast as February 24 except:
Conductor .... Keene
Zuniga .... J. B. Davis
Micaëla .... Craig
Don José .... Novoa
Carmen .... Killebrew,
            (s, Davidson)
Frasquita .... Young
Mercédès .... Marsee
Escamillo ...... Darrenkamp

April 5
RIGOLETTO
Same cast as March 12 except:
Borsa .... Lankston
Sparafucile .... Hale
Gilda .... Wise
Page .... Hirschl
Maddalena .... Creed

April 6
MEFISTOFELE
Same cast as March 1 except:
Conductor .... Morelli
Mefistofele .... Chapman
Faust .... Novoa

April 7
THE TURN OF THE SCREW
Same cast as April 2 (m) except:
Mrs. Grose .... Anthony

April 8 (m)
MADAMA BUTTERFLY
Same cast as February 27 (m) except:
Conductor .... Nance
Pinkerton .... Malamood
Goro .... Hal
Suzuki .... Creed
Sharpless .... Cossa
Butterfly .... Shade

April 8
TOSCA
Same cast as March 18 (m) except:
Sacristan .... Densen
Cavaradossi .... Theyard
Tosca .... Galvan

April 9 (m)

MEFISTOFELE

Same cast as March 1 except:

Faust .... Novoa

April 9

CAVALLERIA RUSTICANA
(Mascagni)

Conductor .... Morelli

Mamma Lucia .... Greenspon
Santuzza .... Roberto
Turiddu .... Di Giuseppe
Lola .... Creed
Alfio .... Ludgin

Followed by:

I PAGLIACCI (Leoncavallo)

Conductor .... Morelli

Tonio .... Chapman
Canio .... Molese
   (performance was
   finished by Malamood)
Nedda .... Bayard
Beppe .... Glaze
Peasants .... Manno, H. Davis
Silvio .... Jamerson

April 11

CAVALLERIA RUSTICANA

Same cast as April 9 except:

Mamma Lucia .... Evans,
   (s, Greenspon)
Santuzza .... Ciraulo
Turiddu .... Theyard
Alfio .... Darrenkamp

Followed by:

I PAGLIACCI

Same cast as April 9 except:

Tonio .... Ludgin
Canio .... Malamood,
   (s, Molese)
Beppe .... Fitch
Silvio .... Titus

April 12

GIULIO CESARE

Same cast as March 24 except:

Giulio Cesare .... Devlin
Cornelia .... Gerber
Achilla .... Jamerson

April 13

CAVALLERIA RUSTICANA

Same cast as April 9 except:

Mamma Lucia .... Evans,
   (s, Greenspon)
Santuzza .... Ciraulo,
   (s, Roberto)
Turiddu .... Marini

Lola .... Lueders
Alfio .... Darrenkamp

Followed by:

I PAGLIACCI

Same cast as April 9 except:

Canio .... Stamford,
   (s, Molese)
Beppe .... Glaze,
   (s, Fitch)
Silvio .... Titus

April 14

GIULIO CESARE

Same cast as March 24 except:

Sesto .... Creed
Achilla .... Jamerson

April 15 (m)

COSÌ FAN TUTTE

Same cast as March 10 except:

Ferrando .... Goeke
Guglielmo ..... Holloway (d)
Don Alfonso .... Devlin
Despina .... Welting

April 15

LA TRAVIATA

Same cast as February 25 except:

Flora .... Evans,
   (s, Lueders)
Douphol .... Smith
Dr. Grenvil .... Yule
Gaston .... Lankston
Alfredo .... Stewart,
   (s, Montane)
Annina .... Hirschl
Germont .... Darrenkamp
Messenger .... Kingman

April 16 (m)

THE MAKROPOULOS AFFAIR
(Janáček)
(English translation by
Norman Tucker)

Conductor .... Keene

Vitek .... Lankston
Albert Gregor ...... Theyard
Christa .... Shuttleworth
Emilia Marty .... Niska
Chauffeur .... Smith
Dr. Kolenaty .... Pierson
Jaroslav Prus .... Ludgin
Maid .... Anthony
Janek .... Glaze
Hauk-Sendorf .... Castel

April 16

SUMMER AND SMOKE

Same cast as March 19 except:

Papa Gonzales .... Bittner

April 18

THE MAKROPOULOS AFFAIR

Same cast as April 16 (m) except:

Chauffeur .... Yule
Dr. Kolenaty .... Smith

April 19

RIGOLETTO

Same cast as March 12 except:

Rigoletto .... Quilico
Duke .... Montané
Borsa .... Lankston
Countess
 Ceprano ..... Shuttleworth
Monterone .... Devlin
Sparafucile ...... J. B. Davis
Gilda .... French (d)
Page .... Hirschl
Maddalena .... Creed

April 20

COSÌ FAN TUTTE

Same cast as March 10 except:

Ferrando .... Goeke
Dorabella .... Creed
Despina .... Welting

April 21

MANON (Massenet)

Staged by .... Denda
Conductor .... Wilson

Guillot .... Castel
De Brétigny .... Jamerson
Pousette .... Shuttleworth
Javotte .... Guilet
Rosette .... Kieffer
Innkeeper .... Bittner
Lescaut .... Darrenkamp
Guards .... Papay, Yule
Manon .... Brooks
Des Grieux .... Molese
Maid .... Greene
Count des Grieux .... Devlin
Prima ballerina .... Menes
Premier danseur .. Seetoo (d)
Ballet master .... Roberts
Cupid .... Balestracci
Seminary porter ...... Carlo
Gambler .... Kingman
Sergeant .... Yule

April 22 (m)

LA BOHÈME (Puccini)

Conductor .... Reimueller

Rodolfo .... Di Giuseppe
Marcello .... Cossa
Colline .... Malas
Schaunard .... Ledbetter
Benoit .... Densen
Mimi .... Niska
Parpignol .... Romaguera
Musetta .... Meier

Alcindoro .... Bittner
Guards ..... Bentley, Galiano

April 22

CAVALLERIA RUSTICANA

Same cast as April 9 except:

Turiddu .... Marini,
                (s, Theyard)
Lola .... Lueders

Followed by:

I PAGLIACCI

Same cast as April 9 except:

Canio .... Malamood
Nedda .... Shade

April 23 (m)

MANON

Same cast as April 21 except:

Conductor .... Rudel,
                (s, Wilson)

April 23

LA BOHÈME

Same cast as April 22 (m)

April 25

LA BOHÈME

Same cast as April 22 (m)
except:

Conductor .... Morelli

Rodolfo .... Montané
Marcello .... Darrenkamp

Colline .... Hale
Mimi .... Tyler,
                (s, Niska)
Musetta .... Shade
Guards ..... Park, Henderson

April 26

MANON

Same cast as April 21 except:

Lescaut .... Fredricks
Manon .... Neblett
Count des Grieux .... Gill

April 27

THE TURN OF THE SCREW

Same cast as April 2 (m)
except:

Guardian .... Hirst (d)
Governess .... Meier
Quint .... Hirst (d)
Miss Jessel .... Young

April 28

THE MAKROPOULOS AFFAIR

Same cast as April 16 (m)
except:

Conductor .... Susskind

Vitek .... Fitch
Albert Gregor ..... Stamford
Christa .... Young
Jaroslav Prus .... Clatworthy
Maid .... Hirschl
Janek .... Hall
Hauk-Sendorf .... Romaguera

April 29 (m)

LA BOHÈME

Same cast as April 22 (m)
except:

Conductor .... Morelli
Marcello .... Darrenkamp
Benoit .... Yule
Mimi .... Tyler
Musetta .... Shade
Guards ..... Park, Henderson

April 29

MADAMA BUTTERFLY

Same cast as February 27 (m)
except:

Pinkerton .... Malamood
Sharpless ...... Schwartzman
Butterfly .... Ciraulo
Kate Pinkerton .... Evans

April 30 (m)

CARMEN

Same cast as February 24
except:

Zuniga .... J. B. Davis
Don José .... Theyard,
                (s, Molese)
Carmen .... Killebrew
Mercédès .... Marsee
Escamillo .... Hale

April 30

COSÌ FAN TUTTE

Same cast as March 10 except:
Ferrando .... Goeke
Don Alfonso .... Devlin
Fiordiligi .... Brooks

Fall 1972 (AUGUST 30 – NOVEMBER 12)

Female artists
Adler, Arlene
Anderson, Sylvia*
Anthony, Judith
Bayard, Carol
Brooks, Patricia
Carey, Patricia*
Carron, Elisabeth
Craig, Patricia
Creed, Kay
Cruz-Romo, Gilda
Curry, Diane*
Darling, Sandra
Evans, Beverly
Galvany, Marisa
Gerber, Joyce
Guilet, Helene
Hebert, Pamela*
Hirschl, Lana
Howard, Ann*

Jung, Doris
Kieffer, Deborah
Killebrew, Gwendolyn
Marsee, Susanne
Meier, Johanna
Neblett, Carol
Niska, Maralin
Robinson, Faye*
Sauler, Bianca
Schauler, Eileen
Shade, Nancy
Shuttleworth, Barbara
Sills, Beverly
Stapp, Olivia*
Tinsley, Pauline
Turofsky, Ricki*
Tyler, Veronica
Wells, Patricia
Welting, Ruth
Wildes, Rose*

Wise, Patricia
Young, Syble

Male artists
Beattie, Herbert
Best, Michael*
Billings, James*
Brennan, Tommy*
Carreras, José
Castel, Nico
Chapman, William
Clatworthy, David
Cossa, Dominic
Darrenkamp, John
Davis, Harris
Davis, J. B.
Densen, Irwin
Devlin, Michael
Di Giuseppe, Enrico
Fitch, Bernard

* New artist   * New artist   * New artist

Fredricks, Richard
Galiano, Joseph
Gill, Richard T.
Goeke, Leo
Hale, Robert
Hall, David
Henderson, Don
Jamerson, Thomas
Lagger, Peter*
Lankston, John
Ledbetter, William
Ludgin, Chester
Malamood, Herman
Malas, Spiro
Martinoiu, Vasile*
Molese, Michele
Montané, Carlos
Mosley, Jeffrey*
Novoa, Salvador
Park, Richard
Pierson, Edward
Powers, William*
Riegel, Kenneth
Romaguera, Joaquin
Ronson, David*
Roy, Will
Schwartzman, Seymour
Siena, Jerold*
Smith, David Rae
Stamford, John
Stewart, John
Stilwell, Richard
Terranova, Vittorio*
Theyard, Harry
Treigle, Norman
Tucker, Thomas*
Yule, Don

Conductors
Bernardi, Mario
Keene, Christopher
Maderna, Bruno*
Morelli, Giuseppe
Nance, Chris
Nelson, John*
Reimueller, Ross
Rudel, Julius
Wilson, Charles

Chorus master
Nance, Chris

Assistant chorus master
Somogi, Judith

Solo dancers
Galan, Esperanza
Gardella, Toni-Ann*
Itow, Candace*
Menes, Rose Marie
Roberts, Chester
Rubino, Michael*

Choreographer
Andrew, Thomas

Directors
Bakman, Patrick
Capobianco, Tito
Corsaro, Frank
Denda, Elena
Hicks, David
Osterhaus, Carveth
Sherin, Edwin
Yannopoulos, Dino*

* New artist

Designers
Ardolino, Emile
Campbell, Patton
Compton, Gardner
Eck, Marsha Louis
Evans, Lloyd
Fletcher, Robert
George, Hal
Lee, Ming Cho
Mitchell, David
Oenslager, Donald
Varona, José
Wittstein, Ed

* New artist

August 30
MARIA STUARDA (Donizetti)

Staged by	Denda
Conductor	Wilson
Herald	Galiano
Elisabetta	Tinsley
Talbot	Fredricks
Cecil	Devlin
Roberto Dudley	Di Giuseppe
Maria Stuarda	Sills
Anna Kennedy	Hirschl

August 31
MEFISTOFELE (Boito)

Stage director	Hicks
Conductor	Rudel
Mefistofele	Chapman
Faust	Novoa
Wagner	Fitch
Margherita	Cruz-Romo
Marta	Evans
Elena	Cruz-Romo
Pantalis	Evans
Nereo	Romaguera
Solo dancers	Itow (d), Menes; Roberts

September 1
MADAMA BUTTERFLY (Puccini)

Conductor	Morelli
Pinkerton	Stewart
Goro	Fitch
Suzuki	Kieffer
Sharpless	Cossa
Butterfly	Shade
Imperial Commissioner	Ledbetter
Registrar	Lankston
The Bonze	Densen
Yamadori	Lankston
Trouble	Tucker (d)
Kate Pinkerton	Hirschl

September 2 (m)
MARIA STUARDA

Same cast as August 30 except:

Talbot .... Darrenkamp

September 2
CARMEN (Bizet)

Stage director	Bakman
Conductor	Keene
Morales	Jamerson
Andrès	Yule
Zuniga	J. B. Davis
Micaëla	Craig
Don José	Molese
Carmen	Killebrew
Frasquita	Shuttleworth
Mercédès	Kieffer
Lillas Pastia, Guide	Romaguera
Escamillo	Hale
Remendado	Lankston
Dancairo	Pierson

September 3 (m)
LA TRAVIATA (Verdi)

Conductor	Morelli
Violetta	Brooks
Flora	Evans
Douphol	Smith
D'Obigny	Ledbetter
Dr. Grenvil	Densen
Gaston	Lankston
Alfredo	Riegel
Annina	Hirschl
Giuseppe	Romaguera
Germont	Cossa
Messenger	Galiano
Solo dancer	Galan

September 3
SUSANNAH (Floyd)

Conductor	Rudel
Mrs. Gleaton	Shuttleworth
Mrs. Hayes	Darling
Mrs. McLean	Evans
Mrs. Ott	Kieffer
Elder McLean	J. B. Davis
Elder Ott	Yule
Elder Gleaton	Fitch
Elder Hayes	Lankston
Susannah	Niska
Little Bat McLean	Romaguera
Olin Blitch	Chapman
Sam Polk	Theyard

September 5
MARIA STUARDA

Same cast as August 30 except:

Talbot .... Fredricks, (s, Darrenkamp)

September 6
MEFISTOFELE

Same cast as August 31 except:

Conductor .... Morelli

September 7
MARIA STUARDA

Same cast as August 30 except:

Talbot .... Darrenkamp

September 8

MEFISTOFELE

Same cast as August 31 except:

Conductor .... Morelli
Faust .... Theyard,
                        (s, Novoa)
Wagner .... Lankston

September 9 (m)

CARMEN

Same cast as September 2

September 9

THE MAKROPOULOS AFFAIR
(Janáček)
(English translation by
Norman Tucker)

Conductor .... Keene

Vitek .... Lankston
Albert Gregor ...... Theyard
Christa .... Shuttleworth
Emilia Marty .... Niska
Chauffeur .... Yule
Dr. Kolenaty .... Pierson
Jaroslav Prus .... Clatworthy
Maid .... Anthony
Janek .... Hall
Hauk-Sendorf .... Castel

September 10 (m)

COSÌ FAN TUTTE (Mozart)
(English version by
Ruth and Thomas Martin)

Conductor .... Wilson

Ferrando .... Riegel
Guglielmo .... Stilwell
Don Alfonso .... Devlin
Fiordiligi .... Meier
Dorabella .... Creed
Despina .... Welting

September 10

RIGOLETTO (Verdi)

Conductor .... Morelli

Rigoletto .... .Fredricks
Monterone's daughter .. Galan
Duke .... Molese
Borsa .... Lankston
Countess Ceprano .. S. Young
Ceprano .... Ledbetter
Marullo .... Jamerson
Monterone .... Densen
Sparafucile .... Gill
Gilda .... Wise
Giovanna .... Evans
Page .... Hirschl
Maddalena .... Creed,
                        (s, Carey)

September 12

SUSANNAH

Same cast as September 3
except:

Conductor .... Reimueller

Susannah .... Shade
*Little Bat
   McLean* .... Hall
Olin Blitch .... Devlin

September 13

MARIA STUARDA

Same cast as August 30 except:

Elisabetta .... Galvany
Cecil .... J. B. Davis
Roberto Dudley ...... Riegel
Anna Kennedy .... Kieffer

September 14

MADAMA BUTTERFLY

Same cast as September 1
except:

Sharpless .... Darrenkamp
Butterfly .... Carron

September 15

DON GIOVANNI (Mozart)
New production

Directed by .... Corsaro
Designer .... Evans
Choreographer .... Agnew
Lighting .... Sondheimer
*Film and laser
   effects* .... Compton
Conductor ..... Maderna (d)

(Italian series)

Leporello .... Malas
Don Giovanni .... Hale
Donna Anna .... Niska
Commendatore .... Roy
Don Ottavio .... Di Giuseppe
Donna Elvira .... Brooks
Zerlina .... Wise
Masetto .... Clatworthy

September 16 (m)

MEFISTOFELE

Same cast as August 31 except:

Faust .... Theyard
Margherita .... Shade
Elena .... Shade
1st Solo dancer ..Gardella (d)

September 16

LA TRAVIATA

Same cast as September 3 (m)
except:

Violetta .... Neblett
Alfredo .... Stewart

September 17 (m)

MARIA STUARDA

Same cast as August 30 except:

Elisabetta .... Galvany
Cecil .... J. B. Davis

Roberto Dudley ...... Riegel
Anna Kennedy ...... Kieffer

September 17

DON GIOVANNI
(Italian series)

Same cast as September 15

September 19

MARIA STUARDA

Same cast as August 30 except:

Elisabetta .... Galvany
Talbot .... Darrenkamp
Cecil .... J. B. Davis
Anna Kennedy ...... Kieffer

September 20

DON GIOVANNI
(English series: translation by
Ruth and Thomas Martin)

Same cast as September 15
except:

Don Giovanni ..... Fredricks
Donna Anna .... Meier
Commendatore .... Gill
Don Ottavio .... Stewart
Donna Elvira .... Niska
Zerlina .... Tyler
Masetto .... Darrenkamp

September 21

LA TRAVIATA

Same cast as September 3 (m)
except:

Douphol .... J. B. Davis
Alfredo .... Carreras
Germont ...... Schwartzman

September 22

LUCIA DI LAMMERMOOR
(Donizetti)

Conductor .... Wilson

Alisa .... Evans
Edgardo .... Molese
Normanno .... Lankston
Lucia .... Sills
Enrico .... Clatworthy
Raimondo .... Hale
Arturo .... Siena (d)

September 23 (m)

TOSCA (Puccini)

Stage director .... Hicks
Conductor .... Morelli

Angelotti .... Smith
Sacristan .... Densen
Cavaradossi .... Montané
Tosca .... Galvany
Scarpia .... Pierson
Spoletta .... Fitch
Sciarrone .... Ledbetter
Shepherd .... Hirsch
Jailer .... Yul

September 23

DON GIOVANNI
(English series)

Same cast as September 15
except:

Don Giovanni ..... Fredricks
Donna Anna .... Meier
Commendatore .... Gill
Don Ottavio .... Stewart
Donna Elvira .... Niska
Zerlina .... Tyler
Masetto .... Darrenkamp

September 24 (m)

RIGOLETTO

Same cast as September 10
except:

Rigoletto ..... Martinoiu (d)
Maddalena .... Carey (d)

September 24

MARIA STUARDA

Same cast as August 30 except:

Talbot .... Schwartzman
Cecil .... J. B. Davis
Anna Kennedy ...... Kieffer

September 26

DON GIOVANNI
(Italian series)

Same cast as September 15

September 27

LUCIA DI LAMMERMOOR

Same cast as September 22
except:

Enrico .... Fredricks
Raimondo .... Devlin
Arturo .... Fitch

September 28

MADAMA BUTTERFLY

Same cast as September 1
except:

Pinkerton .... Carreras
Suzuki .... Creed
Sharpless ...... Darrenkamp

September 29

MEFISTOFELE

Same cast as August 31 except:

Conductor .... Morelli

Margherita .... Neblett
Elena .... Neblett
1st Solo dancer ..... Gardella

September 30 (m)

THE MAKROPOULOS AFFAIR

Same cast as September 9
except:

Conductor .... Wilson
Maid .... Hirschl

September 30

LA BOHÈME (Puccini)

Conductor .... Morelli
Rodolfo .... Carreras
Marcello .... Stilwell
Colline .... Malas
Schaunard .... Jamerson
Benoit .... Yule
Mimi .... Carron
Parpignol .... Romaguera
Musetta .... Shade
Alcindoro .... Ronson (d)
Guards ..... Bentley, Galiano

October 1 (m)

COSÌ FAN TUTTE

Same cast as September 10 (m)
except:

Guglielmo ..... Darrenkamp

October 1

LUCIA DI LAMMERMOOR

Same cast as September 22
except:

Conductor .... Reimueller
Lucia .... Brooks
Enrico .... Fredricks
Raimondo .... Devlin,
(s, Hale)
Arturo .... Siena,
(s, Fitch)

October 3

DON GIOVANNI
(English series)

Same cast as September 15
except:

Conductor .... Wilson

Leporello .... Powers (d)
Don Giovanni ..... Fredricks
Donna Anna .... Meier
Commendatore .... Gill
Don Ottavio .... Stewart
Donna Elvira .... Niska
Zerlina .... S. Young
Masetto .... Darrenkamp

October 4

LES CONTES D'HOFFMANN
(Offenbach)
New production

Directed by ..... Capobianco
Scenic designer .... Lee
Costume designer .... Varona
Lighting .... Sondheimer
Conductor .... Rudel

Lindorff .... Treigle
Andrès .... Lankston

Luther .... Densen
Nathanaël .... Fitch
Hermann .... Jamerson
Nicklausse .... Creed
Hoffmann .... Molese
Stella .... Sills
Olympia .... Sills
Spalanzani ...... Billings (d)
Cochenille .... Lankston
Coppélius .... Treigle
Giulietta .... Sills
Pittichinaccio ...... Lankston
Schlémil .... Ledbetter
Dappertutto .... Treigle
Antonia .... Sills
Crespel .... Pierson
Frantz .... Lankston
Dr. Miracle .... Treigle
Mother .... Gerber

October 5

CARMEN

Same cast as September 2
except:

Conductor .... Nelson (d)

Zuniga .... Smith
Micaëla .... Sauler
Don José .... Theyard
Carmen .... Schauler
Escamillo .... Chapman
Remendado .... Fitch

October 6

DON GIOVANNI
(English series)

Same cast as September 15
except:

Conductor .... Wilson

Don Giovanni ..... Fredricks
Donna Anna .... Meier
Commendatore .... Gill
Don Ottavio .... Stewart
Donna Elvira .... Niska
Zerlina .... S. Young
Masetto .... Darrenkamp

October 7 (m)

LES CONTES D'HOFFMANN

Same cast as October 4

October 7

MEFISTOFELE

Same cast as August 31 except:

Conductor .... Morelli

Mefistofele .... Devlin
Faust .... Stamford
Margherita .... Neblett
Elena .... Neblett
1st Solo dancer ..... Gardella

October 8 (m)

LUCIA DI LAMMERMOOR

Same cast as September 22
except:

Conductor .... Reimueller

Alisa .... Kieffer
Edgardo .... Carreras

Lucia .... Brooks
Enrico .... Fredricks,
                 (s, Clatworthy)

October 8

COSÌ FAN TUTTE

Same cast as September 10 (m)
except:

Ferrando .... Goeke
Don Alfonso .... Malas
Despina .... Welting,
                 (s, Wise)

October 10

LES CONTES D'HOFFMANN

Same cast as October 4

October 11

DON GIOVANNI
(English series)

Same cast as September 15
except:

Conductor .... Wilson

Don Giovanni .... Stilwell
Donna Anna ..... Hebert (d)
Commendatore .... Gill
Don Ottavio ...... Best (d)
Donna Elvira .... Niska
Zerlina .... Wildes (d)
Masetto .... Darrenkamp

October 12

LES CONTES D'HOFFMANN

Same cast as October 4

October 13

LA BOHÈME

Same cast as September 30
except:

Marcello .... Cossa
Colline .... Hale
Mimi .... Niska

October 14 (m)

THE MARRIAGE OF FIGARO
(Mozart)
(English version by
Ruth and Thomas Martin)

Conductor .... Rudel

Figaro .... Malas
Susanna .... Wise
Bartolo .... Pierson
Marcellina .... Evans
Cherubino .... Creed
Almaviva ...... Darrenkamp
Basilio .... Hall
Countess .... Meier
Antonio .... Yule
Curzio .... Lankston
Barbarina .... S. Young
Solo dancer .... Galan

October 14

RIGOLETTO

Same cast as September 10
except:

Countess
  Ceprano .... Shuttleworth
Monterone .... Powers
Gilda .... Welting
Maddalena .... Carey

October 15 (m)

LUCIA DI LAMMERMOOR

Same cast as September 22
except:

Conductor .... Reimueller,
                (s, Wilson)
Alisa .... Kieffer
Edgardo .... Carreras
Normanno .... Romaguera
Lucia .... Brooks

October 15

LA TRAVIATA

Same cast as September 3 (m)
except:

Violetta .... Neblett
Flora .... Guillet
Douphol .... J. B. Davis
Gaston .... Hall

October 17

LES CONTES D'HOFFMANN

Same cast as October 4

October 18

LA BOHÈME

Same cast as September 30
except:

Marcello .... Cossa
Colline .... Hale
Mimi .... Niska
Alcindoro .... Billings

October 19

LES CONTES D'HOFFMANN

Same cast as October 4 except:

Nicklausse .... Marsee
Crespel .... Gill
Mother .... Curry (d)

October 20

DER ROSENKAVALIER
(R. Strauss)

Directed by..Yannopoulos (d)
Lighting .... Sondheimer
Conductor .... Bernardi

Octavian ...... Anderson (d)
Marschallin .... Meier
Mohamet ...... Mosley (d)
Baron Ochs ..... Lagger (d)
Major-Domo of
  the Marschallin .. H. Davis

1st Orphan .... S. Young
2nd Orphan .... Kieffer
3rd Orphan .... Hirschl
Animal vendor .... Hall
Milliner ...... Shuttleworth
Valzacchi .... Fitch
Annina .... Creed
Hairdresser ..... Rubino (d)
Singer .... Riegel
Notary .... Ronson
Leopold .... Yule
Faninal .... Clatworthy
Major-Domo of
  Faninal .... Romaguera
Sophie .... Wise
Marianne .... Anthony
Innkeeper .... Lankston
Police
  Commissioner .. J. B. Davis

October 21 (m)

THE MAKROPOULOS AFFAIR

Same cast as September 9
except:

Conductor .... Wilson

Albert Gregor .... Stamford
Christa .... S. Young
Jaroslav Prus .... Ludgin

October 21

LA TRAVIATA

Same cast as September 3 (m)
except:

Flora .... Guilet
Gaston .... Hall
Alfredo .... Carreras

October 22 (m)

CARMEN

Same cast as September 2
except:

Conductor .... Nelson

Micaëla .... Wells
Don José .... Novoa
Carmen .... Stapp (d)
Frasquita .... S. Young
Dancairo .... Ledbetter

October 22

LES CONTES D'HOFFMANN

Same cast as October 4 except:

Lindorff .... Chapman
Andrès .... Fitch
Nathanaël ...... Romaguera
Nicklausse .... Marsee
Hoffmann .... Theyard
Olympia .... Welting
Cochenille .... Fitch
Coppélius .... Chapman
Giulietta .... Schauler
Pittichinaccio .... Fitch
Dappertutto .... Chapman
Antonia .... Bayard
Crespel .... Gill
Frantz .... Fitch
Dr. Miracle .... Chapman
Mother .... Curry

October 24

LA BOHÈME

Same cast as September 30 except:

Marcello .... Cossa
Colline .... Gill
Schaunard .... Ledbetter
Benoit .... Densen
Mimi .... Niska
Alcindoro .... Billings
Guards ..... Henderson, Park

October 25

LES CONTES D'HOFFMANN

Same cast as October 4 except:

Lindorff .... Beattie
Andrès .... Lankston,
(s, Fitch)
Nathanaël ...... Romaguera
Nicklausse .... Marsee
Cochenille .... Lankston,
(s, Fitch)
Coppélius .... Beattie
Pittichinaccio ..... Lankston,
(s, Fitch)
Dappertutto .... Darrenkamp
Crespel .... Gill
Frantz .... Lankston,
(s, Fitch)
Dr. Miracle .... Beattie
Mother .... Curry

October 26

DON GIOVANNI
(Italian series)

Same cast as September 15 except:

Conductor .... Wilson,
(s, Maderna)
Don Giovanni ..... Fredricks
Don Ottavio .... Best
Donna Elvira .... Neblett
Zerlina .... Welting
Masetto .... Darrenkamp

October 27

CARMEN

Same cast as September 2 except:

Conductor .... Rudel
Micaëla .... Wells
Don José .... Theyard
Carmen .... Howard (d)
Frasquita ..... Turofsky (d)
Mercédès .... Hirschl
Escamillo .... Chapman
Remendado .... Fitch
Dancairo .... Ledbetter

October 28 (m)

DER ROSENKAVALIER

Same cast as October 20 except:

Singer .... Terranova (d)
Sophie .... Wildes

October 28

COSÌ FAN TUTTE

Same cast as September 10 (m) except:

Fiordiligi .... Brooks
Dorabella .... Marsee

October 29 (m)

DON GIOVANNI
(Italian series)

Same cast as September 15 except:

Conductor .... Wilson

Donna Anna .... Hebert
Don Ottavio .... Goeke
Donna Elvira .... Neblett
Zerlina .... S. Young
Masetto .... Darrenkamp

October 29

TOSCA

Same cast as September 23 (m) except:

Cavaradossi .... Molese
Tosca .... Niska
Scarpia .... Fredricks

October 31

LA TRAVIATA

Same cast as September 3 (m) except:

Douphol .... J. B. Davis
Alfredo .... Montané
Servant .... Henderson

November 1

MADAMA BUTTERFLY

Same cast as September 1 except:

Pinkerton .... Malamood
Suzuki .... Creed
Sharpless ...... Darrenkamp
Kate Pinkerton .... Evans

November 2

LUCIA DI LAMMERMOOR

Same cast as September 22 except:

Alisa .... Kieffer
Normanno ...... Romaguera
Lucia .... Brooks
Enrico .... Fredricks

November 3

THE MARRIAGE OF FIGARO

Same cast as October 14 (m) except:

Susanna .... Sauler
Bartolo .... Gill
Countess .... Neblett

November 4 (m)

DER ROSENKAVALIER

Same cast as October 20 except:

Marschallin .... Jung

November 4

TOSCA

Same cast as September 23 (m) except:

Sacristan .... Ronson
Scarpia .... Fredricks

November 5 (m)

CARMEN

Same cast as September 2 except:

Conductor .... Nance
Zuniga .... Densen
Micaëla .... Robinson (d)
Carmen .... Howard
Frasquita .... Turofsky
Remendado .... Fitch
Dancairo .... Ledbetter

November 5

MADAMA BUTTERFLY

Same cast as September 1 except:

Pinkerton .... Malamood
Goro .... Hall
Butterfly .... Cruz-Romo
Kate Pinkerton .... Evans

November 7

THE MARRIAGE OF FIGARO

Same cast as October 14 (m) except:

Figaro .... Devlin
Susanna .... Sauler
Bartolo .... Gill
Marcellina .... Kieffer
Almaviva .... Clatworthy
Countess .... Meier,
(s, Neblett)
Barbarina ...... Shuttleworth

November 8

DER ROSENKAVALIER

Same cast as October 20 except:

Octavian .... Marsee
Annina .... Curry
Faninal .... Jamerson
Marianne .... Adler

November 9

LA BOHÈME

Same cast as September 30 except:

Rodolfo .... Molese
Marcello .... Cossa
Colline .... Gill

Schaunard .... Ledbetter
Benoit .... Densen
Mimi .... Brooks
Musetta .... Bayard
Alcindoro .... Billings
Guards ..... Henderson, Park

November 10

TOSCA

Same cast as September 23 (m)
except:

Sacristan .... Ronson
Cavaradossi ...... Malamood
Tosca .... Cruz-Romo

November 11 (m)

CARMEN

Same cast as September 2
except:

Conductor .... Rudel

Zuniga .... Smith
Micaëla .... Robinson
Carmen .... Anderson
Frasquita .... Turofsky
Mercédès .... Hirschl
Escamillo ...... Darrenkamp
Remendado .... Fitch
Dancairo .... Ledbetter

November 11

CARMEN

Same cast as September 2
except:

Conductor .... Rudel
Zuniga .... Smith
Micaëla .... Sauler
Don José .... Theyard
Carmen .... Howard
Frasquita .... S. Young
Mercédès .... Marsee
Remendado .... Fitch

November 12 (m)

MADAMA BUTTERFLY

Same cast as September 1
except:

Pinkerton .... Malamood
Goro .... Hall
Sharpless .... Fredricks
Butterfly .... Carron
Trouble .... Brennan (d)

November 12

THE MARRIAGE OF FIGARO

Same cast as October 14 (m)
except:

Conductor .... Wilson
Figaro .... Devlin
Bartolo .... Gill
Marcellina .... Kieffer
Almaviva .... Clatworthy
Countess .... Neblett

Spring 1973 (FEBRUARY 21 – APRIL 29)

Female artists
Allen, Betty
Anderson, Sylvia
Anthony, Judith
Bayard, Carol
Bible, Frances
Brooks, Patricia
Carron, Elisabeth
Craig, Patricia
Curry, Diane
Derr, Emily*
Evans, Beverly
French, Norma
Galvany, Marisa
Gerber, Joyce
Greene, Harriet
Greenspon, Muriel
Guilet, Helene
Harris, Hilda*
Hebert, Pamela
Hirschl, Lana
Hocher, Barbara*
James, Carolyne*
Jung, Doris
Kehrig, Diana
Kieffer, Deborah
Killebrew, Gwendolyn
Kitsopoulos, Antonia*
Little, Gwenlynn*
Marsee, Susanne
Meier, Johanna
Neblett, Carol
Niska, Maralin
Parker, Louise
Robinson, Faye
Sauler, Bianca
Saunders, Arlene
Schauler, Eileen
Shade, Nancy

Shuttleworth, Barbara
Sills, Beverly
Stapp, Olivia
Tinsley, Pauline
Wells, Patricia
Welting, Ruth
Wildes, Rose
Wise, Patricia
Yauger, Margaret*
Young, Syble

Male artists
Alexander, John
Bentley, Ronald
Billings, James
Bing, Sir Rudolf*
Brennan, Tommy
Byers, Reginald*
Cañas, Juan*
Carlo, Don
Carreras, José
Chapman, William
Clatworthy, David
Cossa, Dominic
Darrenkamp, John
Davis, Harris
Davis, J. B.
De Dio, Harry
Densen, Irwin
Devlin, Michael
Díaz, Justino*
Di Giuseppe, Enrico
Duffy, Colin
Fitch, Bernard
Fran, Adam*
Fredricks, Richard
Frizell, Cornelius
Gibbs, Raymond
Gill, Richard T.

Glaze, Gary
Goeke, Leo
Gonzalez, Ernesto*
Griffith, David*
Grosselfinger, Burt
Hale, Robert
Hall, David
Holloway, David
Jamerson, Thomas
King, Patrick
Lankston, John
Ledbetter, William
Lowery, Melvin*
Malamood, Herman
Malas, Spiro
Manno, Robert
Marini, Franco
Martinoiu, Vasile
Molese, Michele
Morell, Barry
Mosley, Jeffrey
Papay, Raymond
Pierson, Edward
Presto*
Quilico, Louis
Ramey, Samuel*
Riegel, Kenneth
Romaguera, Joaquin
Ronson, David
Roy, Will
Schnapka, Georg*
Schwanbeck, Bodo*
Schwartzman, Seymour
Sergi, Arturo
Siena, Jerold
Sims, Jack
Smith, David Rae
Stamford, John
Stewart, John

* New artist   * New artist   * New artist

Terranova, Vittorio
Theyard, Harry
Timberlake, Samuel*
Titus, Alan
Tobin, Robert L. B.*
Townsend, Erik
Turp, André*
Voketaitis, Arnold
Waymann, Mark*
Yule, Don

Conductors
Bernardi, Mario
Keene, Christopher
Morelli, Giuseppe
Nance, Chris
Nelson, John
Reimueller, Ross
Rudel, Julius
Susskind, Walter
Wendelken-Wilson, Charles

Chorus master
Nance, Chris

Assistant chorus master
Somogi, Judith

Solo dancers
Balestracci, Sandra
Calzada, Alba*
Fuerstner, Fiona
Galan, Esperanza
Itow, Candace
Morales, Hilda
Pradera, Rebeka*

Martin, Keith*
Rhodes, Lawrence
Roberts, Chester
Rubino, Michael
Seetoo, Dennis

Choreographers
Andrew, Thomas
Butler, John
Trisler, Joyce*

Directors
Bakman, Patrick
Butler, John
Caldwell, Sarah*
Capobianco, Tito
Corsaro, Frank
Denda, Elena
Freedman, Gerald
Hicks, David
Osterhaus, Carveth
Sherin, Edwin
Yannopoulos, Dino

Designers
Aldredge, Theoni V.
Campbell, Patton
Conklin, John
Eck, Marsha Louis
Evans, Lloyd
Fletcher, Robert
George, Hal
Kleiber, Eleonore*
Lee, Ming Cho
Mitchell, David
Morley, Ruth
Oenslager, Donald
Senn, Herbert*
Sylbert, Paul
Varona, José
Wittstein, Ed

* New artist

February 21

DER ROSENKAVALIER
(R. Strauss)

Stage director ..... Osterhaus
Lighting .... Sondheimer
Conductor .... Bernardi

Octavian .... Anderson
Marschallin .... Meier
Mohamet .... Mosley
Baron Ochs..Schwanbeck (d)
Major-Domo of
  the Marschallin .. H. Davis
1st Orphan .... Kehrig
2nd Orphan .... Kieffer
3rd Orphan .... Hirschl
Animal vendor .... Hall
Milliner .... S. Young
Valzacchi .... Fitch
Annina .... Curry
Hairdresser .... Rubino
Singer .... Terranova
Notary .... Billings
Leopold .... Yule
Faninal .... Jamerson
Major-Domo of
  Faninal .... Romaguera
Sophie .... Wise
Marianne .... Anthony
Innkeeper .... Lankston
Police Commissioner ..Densen

February 22

LES CONTES D'HOFFMANN
(Offenbach)

Conductor .... Rudel

Lindorff .... Hale
Andrès .... Lankston
Luther .... Densen
Nathanaël .... Fitch
Hermann .... Jamerson
Nicklausse .... Marsee
Hoffmann .... Turp (d)
Stella .... Sills
Olympia .... Sills
Spalanzani .... Billings
Cochenille .... Lankston
Coppélius .... Hale
Giulietta .... Sills
Pittichinaccio ...... Lankston
Schlémil .... Ledbetter
Dappertutto .... Hale
Antonia .... Sills
Crespel .... Pierson
Frantz .... Lankston
Dr. Miracle .... Hale
Mother .... Gerber

February 23

DER ROSENKAVALIER

Same cast as February 21

February 24 (m)

CARMEN (Bizet)

Conductor .... Rudel

Morales .... Jamerson
Andrès .... Yule
Zuniga .... Densen,
                    (s, Smith)
Micaëla .... Wells
Don José .... Theyard

Carmen .... Killebrew
Frasquita .... S. Young
Mercédès .... Kieffer
Lillas Pastia,
  Guide .... Romaguera
Escamillo ...... Darrenkamp
Remendado .... Siena
Dancairo .... Pierson

February 24

LUCIA DI LAMMERMOOR
(Donizetti)

Conductor .... Reimueller

Alisa .... Evans
Edgardo .... Carreras
Normanno ....Siena
Lucia .... Brooks
Enrico .... Fredricks
Raimondo .... Malas
Arturo .... Griffith (d)

February 25 (m)

MADAMA BUTTERFLY (Puccini)

Conductor .... Nance

Pinkerton .... Byers (d)
Goro .... Fitch
Suzuki .... Kieffer
Sharpless .... Cossa
Butterfly .... Niska
Imperial
  Commissioner ... Ledbetter
Registrar .... Lankston
The Bonze .... Densen
Yamadori .... Lankston
Trouble .... Brennan
Kate Pinkerton .... Guilet

February 25

LES CONTES D'HOFFMANN

Same cast as February 22

February 27

LES CONTES D'HOFFMANN

Same cast as February 22
except:

Lindorff .... Chapman
Nicklausse ....Kieffer
Hoffmann .... Theyard
Stella .... Schauler,
                    (s, Sills)
Olympia .... Welting,
                    (s, Sills)
Coppélius .... Chapman
Giulietta .... Schauler,
                    (s, Sills)
Dappertutto .... Chapman
Antonia .... Brooks,
                    (s, Sills)
Dr. Miracle .... Chapman

February 28

OEDIPUS REX (Stravinsky)
(English narration by
e.e. cummings)

Conductor .... Susskind

Narrator .... Smith
Oedipus .... Stamford

Creon .... Pierson
Tiresias .... Roy
Jocasta .... Killebrew
Messenger .... Ledbetter
Shepherd .... Fitch

Followed by:

CARMINA BURANA (Orff)

Conductor .... Susskind

Soprano .... Welting
Tenor .... Terranova
Baritone .... Cossa
Dancers .... The Pennsylvania
    Ballet, with Calzada (d),
    Fuerstner, Morales;
    Martin (d), Rhodes,
    and corps de ballet

March 1

COSÌ FAN TUTTE (Mozart)
(English text by
Ruth and Thomas Martin)

Conductor ...... Wendelken-
                    Wilson

Ferrando .... Goeke
Guglielmo .... Holloway
Don Alfonso .... Malas
Fiordiligi .... Brooks
Dorabella .... Marsee
Despina .... Wise

March 2

MARIA STUARDA (Donizetti)

Stage director .... Hicks
Conductor ...... Wendelken-
                    Wilson
Herald .... Bentley,
                    (s, Manno)
Elisabetta .... Manno
Talbot .... Darrenkamp
Cecil .... Gill
Roberto Dudley .. Di Giuseppe
Maria Stuarda .... Sills
Anna Kennedy ...... Kieffer

March 3 (m)

RIGOLETTO (Verdi)

Conductor .... Rudel

Rigoletto .... Martinoiu
Monterone's daughter .. Galan
Duke .... Carreras
Borsa .... Lankston
Countess Ceprano .. S. Young
Ceprano .... Ledbetter
Marullo .... Jamerson
Monterone .... Densen
Sparafucile .... Gill
Gilda .... Wise
Giovanna .... Evans
Page .... Hirschl
Maddalena .... Marsee

March 3

CARMEN

Same cast as February 24 (m)
except:

Zuniga .... Smith
Micaëla .... Robinson,
                    (s, Wells)

Carmen .... Anderson
Escamillo .... Hale

March 4 (m)

OEDIPUS REX

Same cast as February 28
except:

Jocasta .... Stapp,
                    (s, Killebrew)

Followed by:

CARMINA BURANA

Same cast as February 28

March 4

MARIA STUARDA

Same cast as March 2 except:

Herald .... Bentley,
                    (s, Manno)
Talbot .... Schwartzman,
                    (s, Darrenkamp)

March 6

OEDIPUS REX

Same cast as February 28
except:

Creon .... Clatworthy

Followed by:

CARMINA BURANA

Same cast as February 28
except:

Soprano .... Brooks
Tenor .... Terranova,
                    (s, Reigel)
Baritone .... Holloway

March 7

ROBERTO DEVEREUX
(Donizetti)

Conductor .... Rudel

Sara .... Marsee
Elizabeth .... Sills
Cecil .... Lankston
Page .... Billings
Raleigh .... Smith
Robert Devereux .. Di Giuseppe
Duke of
    Nottinghom ..... Fredricks
Servant .... Yule

March 8

L'INCORONAZIONE DI POPPEA
(Monteverdi)
First performance by The New
York City Opera Company

Directed by .... Freedman
Scenic designer .... Evans
Costume designer .... Varona
Choreographer ...... Andrew
Lighting .... Sondheimer
Conductor .... Nelson

Fortuna .... Robinson,
                    (s, French)
Virtù .... Hebert

Amor .... S. Young
Ottone .... Cossa
Soldiers ..... Lankston, Siena
Poppea .... Neblett
Nerone .... Titus
Arnalta .... Greenspon
Ottavia .... Bible
Drusilla .... Robinson,
                    (s, French)
Valetto .... Lankston
Seneca .... Gill
Pallade .... Hebert
Liberto and
    Littore .... Ledbetter
Damigella .... S. Young
Lucano .... Siena

March 9

MADAMA BUTTERFLY

Same cast as February 25 (m)
except:

Conductor ...... Wendelken-
                    Wilson
Pinkerton .... Carreras
Sharpless .... Jamerson
Trouble .... Fran (d)

March 10 (m)

ROBERTO DEVEREUX

Same cast as March 7 except:

Sara .... Stapp,
                    (s, Marsee)
Robert Devereux .. Terranova

March 10

DER ROSENKAVALIER

Same cast as February 21
except:

Marschallin .... Jung
Baron Ochs .... Schnapka
Singer .... Riegel
Sophie .... Wildes
Police
    Commissioner .. J. B. Davis

March 11 (m)

LA TRAVIATA (Verdi)

Stage director .... Bakman
Conductor ...... Wendelken-
                    Wilson
Violetta .... Brooks
Flora .... Evans
Douphol .... J. B. Davis
D'Obigny .... Ledbetter
Dr. Grenvil .... Densen
Gaston .... Siena
Alfredo .... Carreras
Annina .... Kieffer
Giuseppe .... Romaguera
Germont ...... Schwartzman
Messenger .... Manno
Solo dancer .... Galan

March 11

CARMEN

Same cast as February 24 (m)
except:

Zuniga .... Ramey (d)
Micaëla .... Robinson

Don José .... Malamood
Mercédès .... Kieffer,
　　　　　　　(s, Kitsopoulos)
Escamillo .... Hale
Remendado .... Fitch
Dancairo .... Ledbetter

March 13

ROBERTO DEVEREUX

Same cast as March 7 except:

Conductor ...... Wendelken-
　　　　　　　　　　Wilson
Sara .... Stapp
Robert Devereux .. Terranova
Duke of
Nottingham .. Schwartzman

March 14

BEATRIX CENCI (Ginastera)
First performance by The New
York City Opera Company

Directed by .... Freedman
Scenic designer ..... Conklin
Costume designer ... Aldredge
Choreographer ... Trisler (d)
Lighting .... Sondheimer
Conductor .... Rudel

Francesco Cenci .... Díaz (d)
Andrea .... Densen
Beatrix Cenci ...... Saunders
Lucrecia .... Killebrew
Bernardo .... Duffy
Orsino .... Glaze
Giacomo .... J. B. Davis
Olimpio .... Gonzalez (d)
Marzio .... Cañas (d)
Guard .... Bentley

March 15

TOSCA (Puccini)

Conductor .... Keene

Angelotti .... J. B. Davis
Sacristan .... Billings
Cavaradossi .... Morell
Tosca .... Galvany
Scarpia .... Fredricks
Spoletta .... Siena
Sciarrone .... Ledbetter
Shepherd .... Kieffer
Jailer .... Yule

March 16

OEDIPUS REX

Same cast as February 28
except:

Conductor ...... Wendelken-
　　　　　　　　　　Wilson
Oedipus .... Sergi
Tiresias .... Gill
Jocasta .... Stapp
Shepherd .... Siena

Followed by:

CARMINA BURANA

Same cast as February 28
except:

Conductor ...... Wendelken-
　　　　　　　　　　Wilson
Soprano .... Brooks
Tenor .... Riegel
Baritone .... Holloway

March 17 (m)

LES CONTES D'HOFFMANN

Same cast as February 22
except:

Lindorff .... Voketaitis
Hoffmann .... Theyard
Olympia .... Welting
Coppélius .... Voketaitis
Giulietta .... Meier
Dappertutto .... Voketaitis
Antonia .... Meier
Dr. Miracle .... Voketaitis

March 17

MADAMA BUTTERFLY

Same cast as February 25 (m)
except:

Conductor ...... Wendelken-
　　　　　　　　　　Wilson
Pinkerton .... Stewart
Suzuki .... Curry
Sharpless ...... Schwartzman
Butterfly .... Carron
Imperial
Commissioner .... Billings
Trouble .... Fran

March 18 (m)

CARMEN

Same cast as February 24 (m)
except:

Conductor .... Keene
Zuniga .... Ramey
Micaëla .... Robinson
Don José .... Malamood
Frasquita .... Wildes
Mercédès .... Kitsopoulos (d)
Escamillo .... Martinoiu
Remendado .... Fitch

March 18

RIGOLETTO

Same cast as March 3 (m)
except:

Rigoletto .... Fredricks
Duke .... Morell
Giovanna .... Kieffer

March 20

BEATRIX CENCI

Same cast as March 14

March 21

TOSCA

Same cast as March 15 except:

Cavaradossi ...... Malamood
Tosca .... Niska
Shepherd .... Guilet,
　　　　　　　　　(s, Kieffer)

March 22

L'INCORONAZIONE DI POPPEA

Same cast as March 8

March 23

COSÌ FAN TUTTE

Same cast as March 1 except:

Ferrando .... Griffith
Don Alfonso .... Ramey

March 24 (m)

BEATRIX CENCI

Same cast as March 14

March 24

MADAMA BUTTERFLY

Same cast as February 25 (m)
except:

Conductor .... Morelli
Pinkerton .... Stewart
Suzuki .... Curry
Sharpless ...... Schwartzman
Trouble .... Fran

March 25 (m)

LA BOHÈME (Puccini)

Conductor .... Morelli
Rodolfo .... Malamood
Marcello .... Timberlake (d)
Colline .... Hale
Schaunard .... Ledbetter
Benoit .... Yule
Mimi .... Carron
Parpignol .... Romaguera
Musetta .... Shade
Alcindoro .... Billings
Guards ...... Manno, Bentley

March 25

OEDIPUS REX

Same cast as February 28
except:

Oedipus .... Sergi
Tiresias .... Gill
Jocasta .... Stapp
Shepherd .... Siena

Followed by:

CARMINA BURANA

Same cast as February 28
except:

Conductor ...... Wendelkin-
　　　　　　　　　　Wilson
Soprano .... Derr (d)
Tenor .... Riegel

March 27

L'INCORONAZIONE DI POPPEA

Same cast as March 8 except:

Fortuna .... French
Amor .... Wildes
Ottone .... Jamerson
1st Soldier .... Hall
Arnalta .... Parker
Drusilla .... French
Valetto .... Hall
Seneca .... Roy
Damigella .... Wildes

March 28

THE YOUNG LORD (Henze)
First performance by The New
York City Opera Company
(*Der junge Lord*; English
translation by Eugene Walter,
revised by Julius Rudel)

Directed by .... Caldwell (d)
Scenic designer .... Senn (d)
Costume designer ..Kleiber (d)
Choreographer ..... Andrew
Lighting .... Sondheimer
Conductor .... Rudel

M. La Truiare .... Rubino
Herr Voightlander ..... Sims
Town comptroller .... Ronson
Chief magistrate ..... Billings
Burgomaster .... Gill
Prof. von Mucker .. Lankston
Frau von Hoofnail .... Curry
Frau
  Harethrasher .. Hocher (d)
Luise .... Wise
Ida .... Welting
Wilhelm .... Glaze
Schoolmaster .... Yule
Three
  young men .... Romaguera
    Lowery (d), Ledbetter
Baroness .... Greenspon
Parlormaid .... Kehrig
Jeremy .... Waymmann
Meadows .... Frizell
Begonia .... Allen
Sir Edgar's
  secretary .... Fredricks
Sir Edgar .... Bing (d)
Amintore la Rocca ..Stamford
Vulcano .... Presto (d)
Bombilla .... De Dio
Rosita .... Galan
Lamplighter ...... J. B. Davis
Lord Barrat .... Riegel

March 29

BEATRIX CENCI

Same cast as March 14 except:

Conductor .... Keene

Orsino .... Stamford
Giacomo .... J. B. Davis,
          (s, Pierson)

March 30

COSÌ FAN TUTTE

Same cast as March 1 except:

Conductor .... Reimueller,
     (s, Wendelken-Wilson)

Ferrando .... Griffith
Guglielmo ..... Darrenkamp
Don Alfonso .... Devlin
Fiordiligi .... Meier
Dorabella .... Kieffer

March 31 (m)

LA TRAVIATA

Same cast as March 11 (m)
except:

Conductor .... Morelli

Violetta .... Neblett
Alfredo .... Gibbs
Annina .... Kitsopoulos
Germont .... Fredricks

March 31

LA BOHÈME

Same cast as March 25 (m)
except:

Colline .... Gill
Mimi .... Derr

April 1 (m)

LES CONTES D'HOFFMANN

Same cast as February 22
except:

Lindorff .... Devlin
Andrès .... Fitch
Nathanaël .... Romaguera
Nicklausse .... Kieffer
Hoffmann .... Theyard
Olympia .... Welting
Cochenille .... Fitch
Coppélius .... Devlin
Giulietta .... Schauler
Pittichinaccio .... Fitch
Dappertutto .... Devlin
Antonia .... Brooks
Frantz .... Fitch
Dr. Miracle .... Devlin
Mother .... Curry

April 1

BEATRIX CENCI

Same cast as March 14 except:

Conductor .... Keene

Orsino .... Stamford
Giacomo .... J. B. Davis,
          (s, Pierson)

April 3

MANON (Massenet)

Conductor .... Rudel

Guillot .... Billings
De Brétigny .... Jamerson
Pousette .... Wildes
Javotte .... Guilet
Rosette .... Kieffer
Innkeeper .... Densen
Lescaut .... Darrenkamp
Guards .... Papay, Yule

Manon .... Sills
Des Grieux .... Alexander
Maid .... Greene
Count des Grieux ...... Gill
Prima ballerina .. Pradera (d)
Premier danseur ..... Seetoo
Ballet master .... Rubino
Cupid .... Balestracci
Seminary porter ...... Carlo
Gambler .... Bentley
Sergeant .... Yule

April 4

MEFISTOFELE (Boito)

Conductor .... Morelli

Mefistofele .... Devlin
Faust .... Theyard
Wagner .... Fitch
Margherita .... Neblett
Marta .... Evans
Elena .... Neblett
Pantalis .... Evans
Nereo .... Romaguera
Solo dancers .... Balestracci,
          Itow; Roberts

April 5

THE YOUNG LORD

Same cast as March 28 except:

Baroness .... James (d)

April 6

LES CONTES D'HOFFMANN

Same cast as February 22
except:

Lindorff .... Chapman
Andrès .... Fitch
Nathanaël .... Romaguera
Nicklausse .... Harris (d)
Cochenille .... Fitch
Coppélius .... Chapman
Pittichinaccio .... Fitch
Dappertutto .... Chapman
Crespel .... Gill
Frantz .... Fitch
Dr. Miracle .... Chapman
Mother .... Curry

April 7 (m)

TOSCA

Same cast as March 15 except:

Sacristan .... Billings,
          (s, Densen)
Cavaradossi .... Carreras
Tosca .... Schauler

April 7

LA TRAVIATA

Same cast as March 11 (m)
except:

Conductor .... Morelli

Dr. Grenvil .... Yule,
          (s, Densen)

Alfredo .... Riegel
Germont .... Cossa

April 8 (m)

LES CONTES D'HOFFMANN

Same cast as February 22
except:

Lindorff .... Devlin
Andrès .... Fitch
Luther .... Yule,
(s, Densen)
Nathanaël .... Romaguera
Nicklausse .... Harris
Olympia .... Welting
Cochenille .... Fitch
Coppélius .... Devlin
Giulietta .... Meier
Pittichinaccio .... Fitch
Dappertutto .... Devlin
Antonia .... Meier
Crespel .... Gill
Frantz .... Fitch
Dr. Miracle .... Devlin
Mother .... Curry

April 8

THE MARRIAGE OF FIGARO
(Mozart)
(English version by
Ruth and Thomas Martin)

Conductor .... Keene

Figaro .... Malas
Susanna .... Little (d)
Bartolo .... Gill
Marcellina .... Evans
Cheurbino .... Stapp
Almaviva .... Clatworthy
Basilio .... Hall
Countess .... Niska
Antonio .... Yule
Curzio .... Lankston
Barbarina ...... Shuttleworth
Solo dancer .... Galan

April 10

TOSCA

Same cast as March 15 except:

Cavaradossi .... Carreras
Tosca .... Niska
Scarpia .... Martinoiu

April 11

MANON

Same cast as April 3 except:

Innkeeper .... J. B. Davis
1st Guard .... Ledbetter

April 12

THE YOUNG LORD

Same cast as March 28 except:

Ida .... S. Young
Jeremy .... King
Meadows ...... Grosselfinger
Sir Edgar's
secretary .... Fredricks,
(s, Jamerson)

Sir Edgar .... Tibon (d)
Amintore .... Townsend

April 13

LUCIA DI LAMMERMOOR

Same cast as February 24
except:

Conductor .... Nance
Edgardo .... Malamood
Lucia .... Welting
Raimondo .... Hale

April 14 (m)

THE MARRIAGE OF FIGARO

Same cast as April 8 except:

Susanna .... Sauler
Cherubino .... Marsee
Basilio .... Fitch
Countess .... Jung

April 14

CAVALLERIA RUSTICANA
(Mascagni)

Conductor .... Morelli

Mamma Lucia .... Greenspon
Santuzza .... Galvany
Turiddu .... Marini
Lola .... Harris
Alfio .... Darrenkamp

Followed by:

I PAGLIACCI (Leoncavallo)

Conductor .... Morelli

Tonio .... Martinoiu
Canio .... Malamood
Nedda .... Bayard
Beppe .... Fitch
Peasants ... Manno, H. Davis
Silvio .... Jamerson

April 15 (m)

DON GIOVANNI (Mozart)
(English translation by
Ruth and Thomas Martin)

Conductor .... Keene

Leporello .... Malas
Don Diovanni ..... Fredricks
Donna Anna .... Meier
Commendatore .... Gill
Don Ottavio .... Griffith
Donna Elvira .... Niska
Zerlina .... Little
Masetto .... Darrenkamp

April 15

MEFISTOFELE

Same cast as April 4 except:

Conductor .... Rudel
Wagner .... Lankston
Margherita .... Shade
Elena .... Shade

April 17

MANON

Same cast as April 3 except:

Pousette .... S. Young
Lescaut .... Fredricks
1st Guard .... Ledbetter
Count des Grieux .... Devlin

April 18

CARMEN

Same cast as February 24 (m)
except:

Conductor .... Keene
Morales .... Ledbetter
Zuniga .... Ramey
Micaëla .... Sauler
Don José .... Molese
Carmen .... Stapp
Frasquita .... Shuttleworth
Escamillo .... Martinoiu
Dancairo .... Billings

April 19

DON GIOVANNI

Same cast as April 15 (m)
except:

Don Ottavio .... Stewart

April 20

THE YOUNG LORD

Same cast as March 28 except:

Baroness .... James,
(s, Greenspon)
Jeremy .... King
Meadows ...... Grosselfinger
Begonia .... Parker
Sir Edgar's
secretary .... Jamerson
Amintore .... Townsend
Lord Barrat .... Hall

April 21 (m)

MEFISTOFELE

Same cast as April 4

April 21

THE MARRIAGE OF FIGARO

Same cast as April 8 except:

Susanna .... Sauler
Bartolo .... Pierson
Cherubino .... Marsee

April 22 (m)

RIGOLETTO

Same cast as March 3 (m)
except:

Rigoletto .... Quilico
Countess
Ceprano ..... Shuttleworth
Page .... Kieffer
Maddalena ...... Yauger (d)

April 22

CAVALLERIA RUSTICANA

Same cast as April 14

Followed by:

I PAGLIACCI

Same cast as April 14 except:

Tonio	Chapman
Canio	Molese
Beppe	Lowery
Silvio	Cossa

April 24

L'INCORONAZIONE DI POPPEA

Same cast as March 8 except:

Fortuna	French
Drusilla	French

April 25

CAVALLERIA RUSTICANA

Same cast as April 14 except:

Santuzza	Schauler
Turiddu	Theyard
Alfio	Chapman

Followed by:

I PAGLIACCI

Same cast as April 14 except:

Canio	Molese
Nedda	Shade
Beppe	Lowery

April 26

RIGOLETTO

Same cast as March 3 (m) except:

Rigoletto	Quilico
Countess Ceprano	Shuttleworth
Page	Kieffer

April 27

CARMEN

Same cast as February 24 (m) except:

Conductor	Keene
Morales	Ledbetter
Zuniga	Ramey
Micaëla	Robinson
Don José	Molese
Carmen	Stapp
Frasquita	Shuttleworth
Escamillo	Martinoiu
Dancairo	Billings

April 28 (m)

LUCIA DI LAMMERMOOR

Same cast as February 24 except:

Conductor	Wendelken-Wilson
Normanno	Lankston, (s, Siena)

Enrico	Clatworthy
Raimondo	Hale
Arturo	Siena, (s, Griffith)

April 28

THE MARRIAGE OF FIGARO

Same cast as April 8 except:

Figaro	Devlin
Bartolo	Pierson
Marcellina	James
Cherubino	Harris
Almaviva	Darrenkamp
Basilio	Fitch
Countess	Meier
Barbarina	S. Young

April 29 (m)

LA BOHÈME

Same cast as March 25 (m) except:

Rodolfo	Di Giuseppe
Marcello	Cossa
Colline	Gill
Schaunard	Jamerson
Mimi	Craig

April 29

DON GIOVANNI

Same cast as April 15 (m) except:

Donna Anna	Hebert
Don Ottavio	Stewart

Fall 1973 (AUGUST 2 9 – NOVEMBER I I)

Female artists
Adler, Arlene
Albanese, Cecilia*
Anderson, Sylvia
Angela, June
Anthony, Judith
Bayard, Carol
Bible, Frances
Brooks, Patricia
Carron, Elisabeth
Cooper, June*
Craig, Patricia
Curry, Diane
Derr, Emily
Evans, Beverly
Galvany, Marisa
Greene, Harriet
Greenspon, Muriel
Guilet, Helene
Harris, Hilda
Hebert, Pamela
Hocher, Barbara
Kehrig, Diana
Kieffer, Deborah

Killebrew, Gwendolyn
Lynn, Judith*
Marsee, Susanne
Meier, Johanna
Neblett, Carol
Niska, Maralin
Piland, Jeanne*
Robinson, Faye*
Schauler, Eileen
Sills, Beverly
Soviero, Diana*
Stapp, Olivia
Tyler, Veronica
Wells, Patricia
Welting, Ruth
Wildes, Rose
Wise, Patricia
Yauger, Margaret
Yoes, Janice*
Young, Syble

Male artists
Alexander, John
Aquino, Paul*

Bentley, Ronald
Billings, James
Bohachevsky, George
Campora, Giuseppe*
Carlo, Don
Castel, Nico
Clatworthy, David
Cossa, Dominic
Darrenkamp, John
Davis, Harris
De Dio, Harry
Densen, Irwin
Devlin, Michael
Di Giuseppe, Enrico
Di Stefano, Filippo*
Duffy, Colin
Fazah, Adib*
Forsmo, Ronald*
Fredricks, Richard
Gibbs, Raymond
Gill, Richard T.
Glaze, Gary
Griffith, David
Hale, Robert

* New artist   * New artist   * New artist

Harper, Talmage
Hilferty, Robert*
Holloway, David
Jamerson, Thomas
Khanzadian, Vahan*
Lankston, John
Ledbetter, William
Ledbetter, William, Jr.*
Li-Paz, Michael*
Livings, George*
Lowery, Melvin
Malamood, Herman
Marini, Franco
Martinoiu, Vasile
Molese, Michele
Ortiz, Francisco*
Park, Richard
Patterson, Roger*
Pierson, Edward
Ramey, Samuel
Rampaso, Luciano
Romaguera, Joaquin
Ronson, David
Roy, Will
Sharkey, Mickey
Shinall, Vern
Siena, Jerold
Smith, David Rae
Stamford, John
Stewart, John
Stilwell, Richard
Termine, Robert*
Terranova, Vittorio
Theyard, Harry
Timberlake, Samuel
Titus, Alan
Townsend, Erik
Voketaitis, Arnold
Weston, Robert*
Yule, Don

Conductors
Bernardi, Mario
Domingo, Placido*
Keene, Christopher
Morelli, Giuseppe
Nelson, John
Rudel, Julius
Wendelken-Wilson, Charles

Chorus master
Nance, Chris

Assistant chorus master
Somogi, Judith

Solo dancers
Balestracci, Sandra
Galan, Esperanza
Pradera, Rebeka

Rubino, Michael
Seetoo, Dennis

Choreographer
Andrew, Thomas

Directors
Auvray, Jean-Claude*
Bakman, Patrick
Caldwell, Sarah
Capobianco, Tito
Corsaro, Frank
Denda, Elena

* New artist

Freedman, Gerald
Hicks, David

Designers
Aldredge, Theoni V.
Campbell, Patton
Chase, Ronald*
Eck, Marsha Louis
Evans, Lloyd
Fletcher, Robert
Lee, Ming Cho
Montresor, Beni
Oenslager, Donald
Pond, Helen*
Senn, Herbert
Varona, José

* New artist

August 29

ROBERTO DEVEREUX
(Donizetti)

Conductor .... Rudel

Sara .... Marsee
Elizabeth .... Sills
Cecil .... Lankston
Page .... Billings
Raleigh .... Smith
Robert Devereux..Di Giuseppe
Duke of
  Nottingham ..... Fredricks
Servant .... Yule

August 30

LES CONTES D'HOFFMANN
(Offenbach)

Conductor ...... Wendelken-
                    Wilson

Lindorff .... Devlin
Andrès .... Castel
Luther .... Densen
Nathanaël .... Lowery
Hermann .... Jamerson
Nicklausse .... Harris
Hoffmann .... Molese
Olympia .... Welting
Spalanzani .... Billings
Cochenille .... Castel
Coppélius .... Devlin
Giulietta .... Meier
Pittichinaccio .... Castel
Schlémil .... Ledbetter
Dappertutto .... Devlin
Antonia .... Meier
Crespel .... Ramey
Frantz .... Castel
Dr. Miracle .... Devlin
Mother .... Curry

August 31

LA TRAVIATA (Verdi)

Conductor .... Morelli

Violetta .... Brooks
Flora .... Evans
Douphol .... Smith
D'Obigny .... Ledbetter
Dr. Grenvil .... Densen
Gaston .... Siena

Alfredo .... Stewart
Annina .... Kieffer
Giuseppe .... Lowery
Germont .... Cossa
Messenger .... Harper
Solo dancer .... Galan

All performances scheduled
between September 1 (m) and
September 29 (m) were
canceled due to a strike.
Tosca, scheduled for October 2,
was also canceled, and the
performances of *Don Giovanni*
announced for October 6
and 12 were replaced by
performances of *A Village
Romeo and Juliet*.

September 29

LA TRAVIATA

Same cast as August 31 except:

Violetta .... Galvany
Giuseppe .... Romaguera
Germont .... Fredricks

September 30 (m)

L'INCORONAZIONE DI POPPEA
(Monteverdi)

Conductor .... Nelson

Fortuna .... Robinson
Virtù .... Hebert
Amor .... Wildes
Ottone .... Cossa
Soldiers ..... Lankston, Siena
Poppea .... Neblett
Nerone .... Titus
Arnalta .... Greenspon
Ottavia .... Bible
Drusilla .... Robinson
Valetto .... Lankston
Seneca .... Gill
Pallade .... Hebert
Liberto and Littore..Ledbetter
Damigella .... Wildes
Lucano .... Siena

September 30

CAVALLERIA RUSTICANA
(Mascagni)

Conductor .... Morelli

Mamma Lucia .... Greenspon
Santuzza .... Yoes (d)
Turiddu .... Theyard
Lola .... Yauger
Alfio .... Darrenkamp

Followed by:

I PAGLIACCI (Leoncavallo)

Conductor .... Morelli

Tonio .... Fazah (d)
Canio .... Molese
Nedda .... Bayard
Beppe .... Lowery
Peasants .... Davis,
              Bohachevsky (d)
Silvio .... Holloway

October 3

ANNA BOLENA (Donizetti)

(Note: Billed as the New York stage premiere, the opera had actually been performed here as early as August 2, 1843.)

Directed by ..... Capobianco
Scenic designer .... Lee
Costume designer .... Varona
Lighting .... Sondheimer
Conductor .... Rudel

Giovanna .... Marsee
Anna .... Sills
Smeton .... Harris
Enrico .... Hale
Percy .... Di Giuseppe
Lord Rochefort ...... Ramey
Sir Hervey .... Siena

October 4

ARIADNE AUF NAXOS
(R. Strauss)
New production
(English translation of prologue and opera by Lewis Sydenham, revised by Julius Rudel)*

Directed by .... Caldwell
Scenic designers .... Pond (d) and Senn
Costume designer ..... Evans
Choreographer ...... Andrew
Lighting .... Sondheimer
Conductor .... Rudel

Major-Domo .... Smith
Music Master .... Devlin
Composer .... Niska
Wigmaker .... Romaguera
Echo .... Hocher
Najade .... Derr
Dryade .... Curry
Lackey .... Densen
Dancing Master .... Lankston
Zerbinetta .... Wise
Tenor, Bacchus ... Alexander
Officer .... Ledbetter
Primadonna,
  Ariadne .... Neblett
Harlequin .... Cossa
Scaramuccio .... Lankston
Truffaldin .... Ramey
Brighella .... Livings (d)

* Note: The prologue and *commedia dell'arte* sections were performed in English; the *opera seria* sections between *Ariadne* and *Bacchus* were sung in German

October 5

MADAMA BUTTERFLY (Puccini)

Conductor .... Morelli

Pinkerton .... Theyard
Goro .... Romaguera
Suzuki .... Curry
Sharpless .... Timberlake
Butterfly .... Carron

Imperial
  Commissioner ... Ledbetter
Registrar .... Smith
The Bonze .... Densen
Yamadori .... Smith
Trouble ... Ledbetter, Jr. (d)
Kate Pinkerton .... Guilet

October 6 (m)

L'INCORONAZIONE DI POPPEA

Same cast as September 30 (m) except:

Virtù .... Hocher
Ottone .... Jamerson
2nd Soldier .... Lowery
Poppea .... Hebert
Nerone .... Griffith
Pallade .... Hocher
Lucano .... Lankston

October 6

A VILLAGE ROMEO AND JULIET
(Delius)
New York stage premiere

Directed by .... Corsaro
Production
  conceived by ...... Corsaro and Chase (d)
Costume designer ... Aldredge
Films and
  projections by ... Chase (d)
Choreographer ...... Andrew
Lighting .... Sondheimer
Conductor .... Bernardi

Marti .... Gill
Sali, as a child .... Duffy
Vreli, as a child ..... Angela
Manz .... Jamerson
Dark Fiddler ...... Holloway
Sali .... Stewart
Vreli .... Wells
Wild girl .... Wildes
Stoned girl .... Yauger
Doll and
  puppet man ..... Townsend
Knick knack man .... Ronson
Wheel of fortune
  woman .... Lynn (d)
Fruit man .... Densen
Pastry woman .... Wildes
Cheap jewelry
  woman .... Yauger
Three women .... Kehrig, Adler, Evans
Two men .... Ledbetter, Yule
Poor horn player .. Townsend
Hunchbacked bass
  fiddle player ..... Billings
Bargemen .... Jamerson, Ledbetter, Griffith

October 7 (m)

LA TRAVIATA

Same cast as August 31 except:

Conductor .... Domingo (d)

Gaston .... Lankston
Alfredo .... Patterson (d)
Annina .... Piland (d)
Giuseppe .... Romaguera

October 7

ANNA BOLENA

Same cast as October 3

October 9

FAUST (Gounod)

Conductor .... Keene

Faust .... Rampaso
Méphistophélès ...... Devlin
Wagner .... Ledbetter
Marguerite .... Meier
Valentin .... Cossa
Siébel .... Kieffer, (s, Yauger)
Marthe .... Evans
Juggler .... De Dio
Fire eater ...... Sharkey (d)

October 10

ANNA BOLENA

Same cast as October 3 except:

Giovanna .... Anderson
Sir Hervey .... Lankston

October 11

TOSCA (Puccini)

Conductor .... Keene

Angelotti .... Smith
Sacristan .... Billings
Cavaradossi .... Theyard
Tosca .... Schauler, (s, Niska)
Scarpia .... Shinall
Spoletta .... Romaguera, (s, Siena)
Sciarrone .... Ledbetter
Shepherd .... Kieffer
Jailer .... Yule

October 12

A VILLAGE ROMEO AND JULIET

Same cast as October 6 except:

Fruit man .... Billings, (s, Densen)

October 13 (m)

ANNA BOLENA

Same cast as October 3 except:

Giovanna .... Anderson
Smeton .... Piland
Percy .... Terranova
Sir Hervey .... Lankston

October 13

CAVALLERIA RUSTICANA

Same cast as September 30

Followed by:

I PAGLIACCI

Same cast as September 30 except:

Tonio .... Martinoi
Canio .... Malamoo

October 14 (m)

ARIADNE AUF NAXOS

Same cast as October 4 except:

Prima Donna,
Ariadne .... Meier

October 14

LA BOHÈME (Puccini)

Conductor .... Morelli

Rodolfo .... Malamood
Marcello .... Fredricks
Colline .... Gill
Schaunard .... Ledbetter
Benoit .... Yule
Mimi .... Tyler
Parpignol .... Romaguera
Musetta .... Bayard
Alcindoro .... Billings
Guards .... Park, Bentley

October 16

ARIADNE AUF NAXOS

Same cast as October 4 except:

Composer .... Marsee
Echo .... Cooper (d)
Najade .... Wildes
Dryade .... Yauger
Dancing Master ...... Livings
Harlequin .... Jamerson
Truffaldin .... Yule
Brighella .... Lowery

October 17

LA BOHÈME

Same cast as October 14
except:

Rodolfo .... Malamood,
(s, Carreras)
Marcello .... Cossa
Mimi .... Niska

(Note: José Carreras was not
to appear with the company
this season.)

October 18

ANNA BOLENA

Same cast as October 3 except:

Giovanna .... Stapp
Smeton .... Piland
Percy .... Terranova
Lord Rochefort .... Yule
Sir Hervey .... Lankston

October 19

RIGOLETTO (Verdi)

Conductor ...... Weldenken-
Wilson

Rigoletto .... Fredricks
(Act I); Martinoiu
(Acts II & III)
Monterone's daughter .. Galan
Duke .... Khanzadian (d)
Borsa .... Lankston

Countess Ceprano .. S. Young
Ceprano .... Ledbetter
Marullo .... Billings
Monterone .... Pierson
Sparafucile .... Gill
Gilda .... Wise
Giovanna .... Evans
Page .... Kehrig
Maddalena .... Marsee

October 20 (m)

CAVALLERIA RUSTICANA

Same cast as September 30
except:

Santuzza .... Schauler
Turiddu .... Marini

Followed by:

I PAGLIACCI

Same cast as September 30
except:

Tonio .... Martinoiu
Canio .... Stamford
(through first scene);
Malamood (finished
performance)
Nedda .... Soviero (d)
Beppe .... Siena
Silvio .... Cossa

October 20

FAUST

Same cast as October 9 except:

Faust .... Di Stefano (d),
(s, Byers)
Valentin .... Stilwell
Siébel .... Yauger

(Note: Reginald Byers was not
to appear with the company
this season.)

October 21 (m)

CARMEN (Bizet)

Conductor .... Keene

Morales .... Jamerson
Andrès .... Yule
Zuniga .... Smith
Micaëla .... Robinson
Don José .... Malamood
Carmen .... Stapp
Frasquita .... S. Young
Mercédès .... Piland
Lillas Pastia,
Guide .... Romaguera
Escamillo ...... Darrenkamp
Remendado .... Siena
Dancairo .... Pierson

October 21

MANON (Massenet)

Conductor ...... Wendelken-
Wilson

Guillot .... Billings
De Brétigny ...... Jamerson
Pousette .... Wildes
Javotte .... Guilet

Rosette .... Kieffer
Innkeeper .... Densen
Lescaut ...... Darrenkamp
Guards ..... Ledbetter, Yule
Manon .... Brooks
Des Grieux .... Campora (d)
Maid .... Greene
Count des Grieux .... Gill
Prima ballerina ...... Pradera
Premier danseur ...... Seetoo
Ballet master .... Rubino
Cupid .... Balestracci
Seminary porter .... Carlo
Gambler .... Bentley
Sergeant .... Yule

October 23

MADAMA BUTTERFLY

Same cast as October 5 except:

Pinkerton .... Malamood
Goro .... Forsmo (d)
Suzuki .... Kieffer
Sharpless .... Clatworthy

October 24

ARIADNE AUF NAXOS

Same cast as October 4 except:

Composer .... Anderson
Echo .... Cooper
Najade .... Wildes
Dryade .... Yauger
Dancing Master ..... Livings
Harlequin .... Jamerson
Truffaldin .... Yule

October 25

MANON

Same cast as October 21

October 26

CARMEN

Same cast as October 21 (m)
except:

Morales .... Ledbetter
Micaëla .... Craig
Don José .... Theyard
Carmen .... Anderson
Frasquita .... Wildes

October 27 (m)

RIGOLETTO

Same cast as October 19
except:

Duke .... Marini
Sparafucile .... Roy
Maddalena .... Yauger

October 27

FAUST

Same cast as October 9 except:

Faust .... Di Stefano,
(s, Byers)
Valentin .... Stilwell
Siébel .... Marsee

October 28 (m)

LA BOHÈME

Same cast as October 14
except:

Rodolfo .... Rampaso
Marcello .... Darrenkamp
Mimi .... Wells

October 28

THE MAGIC FLUTE (Mozart)
(English version by
Ruth and Thomas Martin)

Directed by .... Bakman
Conductor .... Keene

Tamino .... Stewart
1st Lady .... Bayard
2nd Lady .... Curry
3rd Lady .... Yauger
Papageno .... Cossa
Queen of the Night ..S. Young
1st Spirit .... Duffy
2nd Spirit .... Weston (d)
3rd Spirit ...... Hilferty (d)
Pamina .... Tyler
Monostatos .... Siena
Speaker .... Aquino (d)
Sarastro .... Roy
Priest .... Lankston
Papagena .... Wildes
1st Armored man .... Griffith
2nd Armored man ... Pierson

October 30

THE MAGIC FLUTE

Same cast as October 28

October 31

MADAMA BUTTERFLY

Same cast as October 5 except:

Pinkerton .... Marini
Goro .... Forsmo
Sharpless .... Clatworthy
Butterfly .... Craig

November 1

MANON

Same cast as October 21
except:

Des Grieux .... Molese

November 2

CAVALLERIA RUSTICANA

Same cast as September 30
except:

Turiddu .... Ortiz (d)
Lola .... Piland

Followed by:

I PAGLIACCI

Same cast as September 30
except:

Tonio .... Martinoiu
Canio .... Malamood
Beppe .... Siena
Silvio .... Cossa

November 3 (m)

IL BARBIERE DI SIVIGLIA
(Rossini)

Directed by ..... Auvray (d)
Conductor .... Morelli

Fiorello .... Ledbetter
Almaviva .... Terranova
Figaro .... Stilwell
Bartolo .... Li-Paz (d)
Rosina .... Welting
Basilio .... Voketaitis
Berta .... Evans
Officer .... Yule

November 3

RIGOLETTO

Same cast as October 19
except:

Duke .... Molese,
                      (s, Byers)
Monterone .... Densen
Gilda .... Albanese (d)
Giovanna .... Curry
Maddalena .... Yauger

November 4 (m)

FAUST

Same cast as October 9 except:

Faust .... Molese
Méphistophélès .... Hale
Valentin .... Jamerson
Siébel .... Harris

November 4

CARMEN

Same cast as October 21 (m)
except:

Morales .... Termine (d)
Zuniga .... Ramey
Micaëla .... Craig
Don José .... Theyard
Carmen .... Killebrew
Frasquita .... Wildes

November 6

RIGOLETTO

Same cast as October 19
except:

Duke .... Molese,
                      (s, Byers)
Monterone .... Densen
Sparafucile .... Roy
Gilda .... Albanese,
                      (s, Welting)
Giovanna .... Curry
Maddalena .... Greenspon

November 7

THE MAGIC FLUTE

Same cast as October 28
except:

Tamino .... Glaze
1st Lady .... Derr
3rd Lady .... Evans
Queen of the Night .... Lynn
Pamina .... Meier

Sarastro .... Gill
Papagena .... Kehrig
2nd Armored man ..... Yule

November 8

IL BARBIERE DI SIVIGLIA

Same cast as November 3 (m)
except:

Rosina .... Albanese

November 9

FAUST

Same cast as October 9 except:

Faust .... Molese
Méphistophélès .... Hale
Marguerite .... Bayard
Valentin .... Darrenkamp
Siébel .... Harris

November 10 (m)

THE MAGIC FLUTE

Same cast as October 28
except:

Tamino .... Glaze
1st Lady .... Derr
3rd Lady .... Evans
Papageno .... Jamerson
Queen of the Night .... Lynn
Pamina .... Meier
Sarastro .... Gill
Papagena .... Kehrig
2nd Armored man ..... Yule

November 10

LA TRAVIATA

Same cast as August 31 except:

Flora .... Guilet
Douphol .... Ramey,
                      (s, Smith)
Alfredo .... Gibbs
Giuseppe .... Romaguera
Germont .... Fredricks

November 11 (m)

CAVALLERIA RUSTICANA

Same cast as September 30
except:

Turiddu .... Marini
Lola .... Piland

Followed by:

I PAGLIACCI

Same cast as September 30
except:

Tonio .... Martinoiu
Canio .... Malamood
Nedda .... Anthony
Silvio .... Cossa

November 11

IL BARBIERE DI SIVIGLIA

Same cast as November 3 (m)
except:

Fiorello .... Termine
Basilio .... Ramey

Spring 1974 (FEBRUARY 21 – APRIL 28)

Female artists
Allen, Betty
Anderson, Shari*
Bayard, Carol
Bible, Frances
Brobyn, Virginia*
Brooks, Patricia
Chamorro, Angeles*
Craig, Patricia
Curry, Diane
De Rosa, Judith*
Derr, Emily
Evans, Beverly
Falcon, Ruth*
Fowles, Glenys*
French, Norma
Galvany, Marisa
Giancotti, Anna*
Greenspon, Muriel
Guilet, Helene
Harris, Hilda
Hebert, Pamela
Hegierski, Kathleen*
Hocher, Barbara
Ito, Yoshi*
James, Carolyne
Jung, Doris
Kehrig, Diana
Kessler, Irene*
Killebrew, Gwendolyn
Marsee, Susanne
Meier, Johanna
Niska, Maralin
Parker, Louise
Piland, Jeanne
Robinson, Faye
Rogers, Noëlle*
Schauler, Eileen
Shade, Nancy
Sills, Beverly
Skarimbas, Carol Bergey†
Soviero, Diana
Stapp, Olivia
Toro, Puli*
Walker, Sandra*
Welting, Ruth
Wildes, Rose
Wise, Patricia
Yauger, Margaret
Yoes, Janice

Male artists
Alexander, John
Barbieri, Saverio*
Bentley, Ronald
Berberian, Ara
Billings, James
Bohachevsky, George
Brennan, Thomas
Bullard, Gene
Byers, Reginald

* New artist
† She previously appeared with the company under the name of Carol Bergey.

Cañas, Juan
Carreras, José
Castel, Nico
Clatworthy, David
Cossa, Dominic
Darrenkamp, John
Davis, Harris
Densen, Irwin
Devlin, Michael
Díaz, Justino
Di Giuseppe, Enrico
Duffy, Colin
DuPree, William
Duval, Pierre
Eddleman, Jack*
Ellis, Brent*
Elvira, Pablo*
Fazah, Adib
Fisher, Robert*
Fredricks, Richard
Fried, Howard
Gibbs, Raymond
Gill, Richard T.
Glaze, Gary
Gonzalez, Ernesto
Griffith, David
Hale, Robert
Harper, Talmage
Holloway, David
Jamerson, Thomas
Justus, William*
Lankston, John
Ledbetter, William
Ledbetter, William, Jr.
Li-Paz, Michael
Livings, George
Lowery, Melvin
Malamood, Herman
Martinoiu, Vasile
Mazzieri, Maurizio*
Nagy, Robert
Ortiz, Francisco
Pane, Tullio*
Park, Richard
Patterson, Roger
Paul, Robert*
Pierson, Edward
Poll, Melvyn*
Ramey, Samuel
Rampaso, Luciano
Reece, Arley*
Romaguera, Joaquin
Shinall, Vern
Siena, Jerold
Sims, Jack
Stahl, Friedrich
Stamford, John
Stewart, John
Stilwell, Richard
Taylor, Richard*
Termine, Robert
Titus, Alan
Townsend, Erik
Van Orden, Ray
White, Willard*

* New artist

Wilder, Dean*
Yule, Don

Conductors
Bernardi, Mario
Choset, Franklin*
Keene, Christopher
Köpe, Karoly*
Martelli, Luigi*
Morelli, Giuseppe
Nance, Chris
Nelson, John
Pallo, Imre*
Popper, Felix
Reimueller, Ross
Rudel, Julius
Somogi, Judith*

Chorus master
Nance, Chris

Assistant chorus master
Somogi, Judith

Solo dancers
Galan, Esperanza
Pradera, Rebeka

Lopez, Miguel*
Rubino, Michael

Choreographers
Andrew, Thomas
Eddleman, Jack*
Trisler, Joyce

Directors
Auvray, Jean-Claude
Bakman, Patrick
Caldwell, Sarah
Capobianco, Tito
Corsaro, Frank
Denda, Elena
Eddleman, Jack*
Freedman, Gerald
Getke, Richard*
Hicks, David
Justesen, Joel*
Menotti, Gian Carlo
Osterhaus, Carveth
Presnell, Steve*

Designers
Aldredge, Theoni V.
Armistead, Horace
Campbell, Patton
Conklin, John
Eck, Marsha Louis
Evans, Lloyd
Fletcher, Robert
Lee, Ming Cho
Oenslager, Donald
Pond, Helen
Senn, Herbert
Toms, Carl*
Varona, José
Wittstein, Ed

* New artist

February 21

I PURITANI (Bellini)
First performance by The New
York City Opera Company
in New York

Directed by ..... Capobianco
Designer .... Toms (d)
Choreographer ...... Andrew
Lighting .... Sondheimer
Conductor .... Rudel

Riccardo .... Fredricks
Bruno .... Siena
Elvira .... Sills
Enrichetta .... Curry
Giorgio .... Gill
Gualtiero .... Ramey
Arturo .... Di Giuseppe

February 22

LA BOHÈME (Puccini)

Stage director ... Presnell (d)
Conductor .... Morelli

Rodolfo .... Carreras
Marcello .... Jamerson
Colline .... Ramey,
      (s, Gill)
Schaunard .... Paul (d)
Benoit .... Yule
Mimi .... Brooks
Parpignol .... Romaguera
Musetta .... Bayard
Alcindoro .... Billings
Guards .... Park, Bentley

February 23 (m)

CARMEN (Bizet)

Conductor .... Keene

Morales .... Ledbetter
Andrès .... Yule
Zuniga .... Ramey
Micaëla .... Fowles (d)
Don José .... Malamood
Carmen .... Stapp
Frasquita .... Wildes
Mercédès .... Piland
Lillas Pastia,
 Guide .... Romaguera
Escamillo ...... Darrenkamp
Remendado .... Lankston
Dancairo .... Pierson

February 23

LA TRAVIATA (Verdi)

Conductor .... Bernardi

Violetta .... Galvany
Flora .... Evans
Douphol .... Fisher (d)
D'Obigny .... Ledbetter
Dr. Grenvil .... Yule
Gaston .... Lowery
Alfredo .... Byers
Annina .... Guilet
Giuseppe .... Romaguera
Germont .... Cossa
Messenger .... Harper
Solo dancer .... Galan

February 24 (m)

I PURITANI

Same cast as February 21

February 24

TOSCA (Puccini)

Conductor .... Morelli
Angelotti .... Paul
Sacristan .... Billings
Cavaradossi .... Carreras
Tosca .... Schauler
Scarpia .... Shinall
Spoletta .... Siena
Sciarrone .... Ledbetter
Shepherd .... Piland
Jailer .... Yule

February 26

TOSCA

Same cast as February 24
except:

Tosca .... Galvany,
    (s, Schauler)

February 27

I PURITANI

Same cast as February 21

February 28

ARIADNE AUF NAXOS
(R. Strauss)
(English translation of
prologue and opera by
Lewis Sydenham, revised by
Julius Rudel)

Stage director ..... Getke (d)
Conductor .... Rudel

Major-Domo .... Yule
Music Master ..... Justus (d)
Composer .... Niska
Wigmaker .... Romaguera
Echo .... Hocher
Najade .... Derr
Dryade .... Curry
Lackey .... Densen
Dancing Master ... Lankston
Zerbinetta .... Wise
Tenor, Bacchus .... Alexander
Officer .... Ledbetter
Prima donna, Ariadne .. Meier
Harlequin .... Cossa
Scaramuccio .... Lankston
Truffaldin .... Ramey
Brighella .... Livings

March 1

RIGOLETTO (Verdi)

Stage director ..... Osterhaus
Conductor .... Morelli

Rigoletto .... Martinoiu,
    (s, Fredricks)
Monterone's daughter .. Galan
Duke .... Alexander
Borsa .... Siena
Countess Ceprano .... Kehrig
Ceprano .... Ledbetter
Marullo .... Billings
Monterone .... Pierson
Sparafucile .... Gill
Gilda .... Welting
Giovanna .... Evans
Page .... Toro (d)
Maddalena .... Yauger

March 2 (m)

LA TRAVIATA

Same cast as February 23
except:

Alfredo .... Gibbs
Germont .... Elvira (d)

March 2

LA BOHÈME

Same cast as February 22
except:

Rodolfo .... Rampaso
Marcello .... Cossa
Colline .... Ramey,
     (s, Gill)

March 3 (m)

CARMEN

Same cast as February 23 (m)
except:

Mercédès .... Walker (d)

March 3

ANNA BOLENA (Donizetti)

Stage director .... Denda
Conductor .... Rudel

Giovanna .... Marsee
Anna .... Sills
Smeton .... Piland
Enrico .... Hale
Percy .... Di Giuseppe
Lord Rochefort ...... Ramey
Sir Hervey .... Siena

March 5

LA TRAVIATA

Same cast as February 23
except:

Alfredo .... Patterson
Germont .... Darrenkamp
Messenger .... Stahl
    (s, Harper)

March 6

ANNA BOLENA

Same cast as March 3

March 7

MEDEA (Cherubini)
First performance by The New
York City Opera Company

Directed by .... Corsaro
Designer .... Evans
Lighting .... Sondheimer
Conductor .... Morel

Glauce .... Derr
Glauce's
 attendants ... Kehrig, Toro
Creon .... Gill
Jason .... Wilder (d)
Medea's
 children ..... Ledbetter, Jr.
     Brenna
Neris .... Bible
Medea .... Niska

Medea's
attendants ..... Lopez (d),
Rubino

March 8

ARIADNE AUF NAXOS

Same cast as February 28
except:

Composer .... Hebert

March 9 (m)

MADAMA BUTTERFLY (Puccini)

Stage director ..... Osterhaus
Conductor .... Morelli

Pinkerton .... Rampaso
Goro .... Romaguera
Suzuki .... Curry
Sharpless .... Fazah
Butterfly .... Craig
Imperial
Commissioner ... Ledbetter
Registrar .... Fried
The Bonze .... Densen
Yamadori .... Fried
Trouble .... Ledbetter, Jr.
Kate Pinkerton .... Guilet

March 9

CARMEN

Same cast as February 23 (m)
except:

Micaëla .... Robinson
Mercédès ...... Hegierski (d)
Escamillo .... Justus

March 10 (m)

ANNA BOLENA

Same cast as March 3 except:

Sir Hervey .... Lankston,
(s, Siena)

March 10

MEDEA

Same cast as March 7

March 12

ARIADNE AUF NAXOS

Same cast as February 28
except:

Composer .... Hebert
Zerbinetta .... Welting
Harlequin .... Jamerson

March 13

ANNA BOLENA

Same cast as March 3 except:

Percy .... Bullard
Sir Hervey .... Lankston

March 14

LA BOHÈME

Same cast as February 22
except:

Rodolfo .... Rampaso
Marcello .... Cossa
Colline .... White (d)
Schaunard .... Ledbetter
Mimi .... Anderson (d)
Musetta .... Rogers (d)

March 15

ANNA BOLENA

Same cast as March 3 except:

Giovanna .... Stapp
Anna .... Galvany
Percy .... Patterson
Lord Rochefort .... Yule
Sir Hervey .... Lankston

(Note: Act II, scene 3, the
Tower of London scene,
omitted from this and
subsequent performances)

March 16 (m)

LA TRAVIATA (s, MEDEA,
due to the illness of
Maralin Niska)

Same cast as February 23
except:

Conductor .... Rudel

Violetta .... Brooks
Douphol .... Barbieri (d)
Dr. Grenvil .... Densen
Gaston .... Lankston
Alfredo .... Stewart
Messenger .... Stahl

March 16

TOSCA

Same cast as February 24
except:

Sacristan .... Densen,
(s, Billings)
Cavaradossi ...... Malamood
Tosca .... Meier
Scarpia .... Fredricks
Shepherd .... Toro

March 17 (m)

THE MIKADO (Sullivan)

Directed and choreographed
by .... Eddleman (d)
Lighting .... Sondheimer
Conductor ...... Somogi (d)

Pooh-Bah .... Berberian
Pish-Tush .... Jamerson
Nanki-Poo .... Glaze
Ko-Ko .... Billings
Yum-Yum .... Fowles
Pitti-Sing .... Piland
Peep-Bo .... Toro
Katisha .... Allen
Mikado .... Pierson

March 17

ANNA BOLENA

Same cast as March 3 except:

Enrico .... Gill
Percy .... Bullard
Sir Hervey .... Lankston

March 19

IL BARBIERE DI SIVIGLIA
(Rossini)

Stage director ... Justesen (d)
Conductor .... Morelli

Fiorello .... Termine
Almaviva .... Livings
Figaro .... Stilwell
Bartolo .... Li-Paz
Rosina .... Wise
Basilio .... Ramey
Berta .... Evans
Officer .... Yule

March 20

LA TRAVIATA (s, MEDEA,
due to Maralin Niska's
continued illness)

Same cast as February 23
except:

Conductor .... Rudel

Violetta .... Sills
Alfredo .... Stewart
Messenger .... Stahl

March 21

I PURITANI

Same cast as February 21
except:

Enrichetta .... Yauger
Giorgio .... Hale
Arturo .... DuPree

March 22

ARIADNE AUF NAXOS

Same cast as February 28
except:

Conductor .... Popper

Composer .... Hebert
Lackey .... Fisher
Zerbinetta .... Welting
Tenor, Bacchus ... Reece (d)
Prima donna, Ariadne ... Jung
Harlequin .... Jamerson
Brighella .... Lowery

March 23 (m)

MIKADO (s, MEDEA)

Same cast as March 17 (m)
except:

Nanki-Poo .... Griffith
Katisha .... James

March 23

MADAMA BUTTERFLY

Same cast as March 9 (m)
except:

Conductor .... Köpe (d)
Pinkerton .... Malamood
Suzuki .... Evans
Butterfly .... Shade

March 24 (m)

I PURITANI

Same cast as February 21
except:

Enrichetta .... Yauger
Giorgio .... Hale
Gualtiero .... Densen
Arturo .... Duval,
(s, DuPree)

March 24

L'INCORONAZIONE DI POPPEA
(Monteverdi)

Conductor .... Nelson

Fortuna .... Hocher
Virtù ....:...... Derr
Amor .... Wildes
Ottone .... Cossa
Soldiers .... Lankston, Siena
Poppea .... Rogers
Nerone .... Griffith
Arnalta .... Killebrew
Ottavia .... Bible
Drusilla .... Hocher
Valetto .... Lankston
Seneca .... Gill
Pallade .... Derr
Liberto and
Littore .... Ledbetter
Damigella .... Wildes
Lucano .... Siena

March 26

MADAMA BUTTERFLY

Same cast as March 9 (m)
except:

Pinkerton .... Poll (d)
Suzuki .... Evans,
(s, Curry)

March 27

THE CONSUL (Menotti)

Conductor .... Keene

John Sorel ..... Darrenkamp
Magda Sorel .... Stapp
The Mother ...... Greenspon
Secret Police Agent .. Pierson
1st Plainclothesman ..... Sims
2nd
Plainclothesman..Van Orden
Secretary .... Walker
Mr. Kofner .... Yule
The Foreign
Woman ...... De Rosa (d)
Anna Gomez .... Hocher
The Magician
Magadoff .... Castel
Vera Boronel .... Brobyn (d)
Assan .... Ledbetter
Voice on the
record ..... Mabel Mercer

March 28

CARMEN

Same cast as February 23 (m)
except:

Morales .... Fisher
Zuniga .... Barbieri

Micaëla .... Falcon (d)
Carmen .... Killebrew
Mercédès .... Hegierski
Escamillo .... Hale

March 29

LA BOHÈME

Same cast as February 22
except:

Rodolfo .... Rampaso
Marcello .... Fazah
Colline .... Gill
Schaunard .... Ledbetter
Mimi .... Anderson
Musetta .... Rogers

March 30 (m)

THE MARRIAGE OF FIGARO
(Mozart)
(English version by
Ruth and Thomas Martin)

Conductor .... Keene

Figaro .... Devlin
Susanna .... Wise
Bartolo .... Pierson
Marcellina .... James
Cherubino .... Harris
Almaviva .... Clatworthy
Basilio .... Fried
Countess .... Meier
Antonio .... Billings
Curzio .... Lankston
Barbarina .... Kehrig
Solo dancer .... Galan

March 30

CAVALLERIA RUSTICANA
(Mascagni)

Conductor .... Rudel

Mamma Lucia .... Greenspon
Santuzza .... Stapp
Turiddu .... Ortiz
Lola .... Piland
Alfio .... Justus

Followed by:

I PAGLIACCI (Leoncavallo)

Conductor .... Rudel

Tonio .... Martinoiu
Canio .... Malamood
Nedda .... Brooks
Beppe .... Lowery
Peasants ..Davis, Bohachevsky
Silvio .... Holloway

March 31 (m)

LA TRAVIATA

Same cast as February 23
except:

Violetta ...... Chamorro (d)
Dr. Grenvil .... Densen
Alfredo .... Taylor (d)
Germont .... Elvira
Messenger .... Stahl

March 31

TOSCA

Same cast as February 24
except:

Cavaradossi .... Rampaso
Tosca .... Meier
Scarpia .... Fredricks

April 2

CARMEN

Same cast as February 23 (m)
except:

Morales .... Fisher
Zuniga .... Barbieri
Micaëla .... Falcon
Carmen .... Killebrew
Frasquita .... Ito (d)
Escamillo .... Justus
Remendado .... Fried
Dancairo .... Pierson,
(s, Billings)

April 3

L'INCORONAZIONE DI POPPEA

Same cast as March 24
except:

Ottone .... Jamerson

April 4

LA BOHÈME

Same cast as February 22
except:

Rodolfo .... Rampaso
Marcello .... Fazah
Colline .... White
Schaunard .... Ledbetter
Benoit .... Densen
Mimi .... Derr
Musetta .... Rogers

April 5

CAVALLERIA RUSTICANA

Same cast as March 30

Followed by:

I PAGLIACCI

Same cast as March 30 except:

Canio .... Nagy

April 6 (m)

IL BARBIERE DI SIVIGLIA

Same cast as March 19 except:

Figaro .... Fazah
Rosina .... Marsee

April 6

MADAMA BUTTERFLY

Same cast as March 9 (m)
except:

Conductor .... Pallo (d)

Pinkerton .... Gibbs
Goro .... Fried
Suzuki .... Walker

Sharpless .... Jamerson
Butterfly .... Shade
Registrar .... Lankston
Yamadori .... Lankston

April 7 (m)

RIGOLETTO

Same cast as March 1 except:

Rigoletto .... Fredricks
Duke .... Pane (d)
Monterone .... Barbieri

April 7

THE MIKADO

Same cast as March 17 (m)
except:

Katisha .... James
Mikado .... Densen

April 9

LUCIA DI LAMMERMOOR
(Donizetti)

Conductor .... Reimueller

Alisa .... Curry
Edgardo .... Bullard
Normanno .... Lankston
Lucia .... Sills
Enrico .... Fazah,
                (s, Cossa)
Raimondo .... Hale
Arturo .... Griffith

April 10

CARMEN

Same cast as February 23 (m)
except:

Morales .... Termine
Micaëla .... Craig
Carmen .... Killebrew
Frasquita .... Ito
Remendado .... Fried
Dancairo .... Billings

April 11

LA TRAVIATA

Same cast as February 23
except:

Violetta .... Brooks
Flora .... Guilet
Dr. Grenvil .... Densen
Alfredo .... Stewart
Annina .... Toro
Messenger .... Stahl

April 12

LUCIA DI LAMMERMOOR

Same cast as April 9

April 13 (m)

MADAMA BUTTERFLY

Same cast as March 9 (m)
except:

Conductor ...... Martelli (d)
Pinkerton .... Poll
Goro .... Fried

Suzuki .... Walker
Butterfly .... Niska
Registrar .... Lankston
Yamadori .... Lankston

April 13

THE MARRIAGE OF FIGARO

Same cast as March 30 (m)
except:

Bartolo .... Li-Paz
Solo dancer .... Pradera,
                (s, Galan)

April 14 (m)

THE MIKADO

Same cast as March 17 (m)

April 14

THE CONSUL

Same cast as March 27

April 16

LUCIA DI LAMMERMOOR

Same cast as April 9 except:

Conductor .... Nance

Edgardo .... Poll
Normanno .... Fried
Lucia .... Brooks
Raimondo ...... Mazzieri (d)

April 17

IL BARBIERE DI SIVIGLIA

Same cast as March 19 except:

Conductor .... Martelli

Almaviva .... Pane
Rosina .... Welting
Berta .... Curry

April 18

BEATRIX CENCI (Ginastera)

Conductor .... Keene

Count Francesco Cenci ..Díaz
Andrea .... Densen
Beatrix Cenci ...... Schauler
Lucrecia .... Killebrew
Bernardo .... Duffy
Orsino .... Stamford
Giacomo .... Pierson
Olimpio .... Gonzalez
Marzio .... Cañas
Guard .... Bentley

April 19

THE CONSUL

Same cast as March 27

April 20 (m)

THE MIKADO

Same cast as March 17 (m)

Pish-Tush .... Ledbetter
Nanki-Poo .... Griffith

Ko-Ko .... Eddleman (d)
Yum-Yum .... Soviero
Pitti-Sing .... Hegierski
Peep-Bo .... Kehrig

April 20

THE MARRIAGE OF FIGARO

Same cast as March 30 (m)
except:

Figaro .... Hale
Susanna .... Fowles
Bartolo .... Li-Paz
Cherubino .... Piland
Barbarina .... Wildes

April 21 (m)

CAVALLERIA RUSTICANA

Same cast as March 30 except:

Conductor .... Nance

Santuzza .... Yoes
Lola .... Yauger
Alfio .... Darrenkamp

Followed by:

I PAGLIACCI

Same cast as March 30 except:

Conductor .... Nance

Nedda .... Bayard
Beppe .... Siena

April 21

LA TRAVIATA

Same cast as February 23
except:

Violetta .... Chamorro
Flora .... Guilet
Dr. Grenvil .... Densen
Alfredo .... Taylor
Annina .... Toro
Germont .... Fredricks
Messenger .... Stahl

April 23

BEATRIX CENCI

Same cast as April 18

April 24

LUCIA DI LAMMERMOOR

Same cast as April 9 except:

Alisa .... Hegierski
Normanno .... Fried
Lucia .... Welting

April 25

CAVALLERIA RUSTICANA

Same cast as March 30 except:

Mamma Lucia .... Evans
Santuzza .... Yoes
Lola .... Yauger
Alfio .... Darrenkamp

Followed by:

I PAGLIACCI

Same cast as March 30 except:

Nedda .... Bayard
Beppe .... Siena
Silvio .... Jamerson

April 26

L'INCORONAZIONE DI POPPEA

Same cast as March 24 except:

Fortuna .... Skarimbas
Amor .... French
Ottone .... Jamerson
Nerone .... Titus
Arnalta .... Greenspon
Ottavia .... Killebrew
Drusilla .... Skarimbas
Damigella .... French

April 27 (m)

MEDEA (s, THE MIKADO)

Same cast as March 7 except:

Glauce .... Giancotti (d)
*Glauce's 1st
  attendant* ...... Kessler (d)
Creon .... Ramey
Jason .... Townsend
Neris .... Curry

April 27

RIGOLETTO

Same cast as March 1 except:

Conductor .... Choset (d)
*Monterone's
  daughter* .... Pradera,
         (s, Galan)

Duke .... Pane
Maddalena .... Greenspon

April 28 (m)

THE CONSUL

Same cast as March 27

April 28

L'INCORONAZIONE DI POPPEA

Same cast as March 24 except:

Fortuna .... Skarimbas
Amor .... French
Ottone .... Ellis (d)
Nerone .... Titus
Arnalta .... Parker
Ottavia .... Killebrew
Drusilla .... Skarimbas
Damigella .... French

Fall 1974 (AUGUST 28 – NOVEMBER 10)

Female artists
Adler, Arlene
Allen, Betty
Angela, June
Anthony, Judith
Bayard, Carol
Bible, Frances
Bonazzi, Elaine
Brooks, Patricia
Craig, Patricia
Curry, Diane
Derr, Emily
Fowles, Glenys
Galvany, Marisa
Haley, Elizabeth*
Harris, Hilda
Hebert, Pamela
Hegierski, Kathleen
Hinds, Esther
Hocher, Barbara
Ito, Yoshi
James, Carolyne
Jones, Betty*
Kehrig, Diana
Kessler, Irene
Killebrew, Gwendolyn
Malfitano, Catherine*
Marsee, Susanne
Meier, Johanna
Neblett, Carol
Niska, Maralin
Patenaude, Joan
Piland, Jeanne
Pisacano, Claudia*
Randazzo, Arlene
Robinson, Faye
Rogers, Noëlle
Schauler, Eileen
Shade, Nancy
Sills, Beverly
Skarimbas, Carol Bergey
Soviero, Diana

Stapp, Olivia
Talarico, Rita*
Toro, Puli
Walker, Sandra
Wells, Patricia
Welting, Ruth
Wildes, Rose
Wise, Patricia

Male artists
Alexander, John
Barasorda, Antonio*
Bentley, Ronald
Berberian, Ara
Billings, James
Brennan, Thomas
Bullard, Gene
Carreras, José
Clatworthy, David
Cossa, Dominic
Darrenkamp, John
De Dio, Harry
Densen, Irwin
Devlin, Michael
Di Giuseppe, Enrico
Di Loreto, Gregory*
Domingo, Placido
Duval, Pierre
Eddleman, Jack
Elvira, Pablo
Fazah, Adib
Fisher, Robert
Fredricks,. Richard
Fried, Howard
Glaze, Gary
Griffith, David
Hale, Robert
Hamilton, Brett*
Harper, Talmage
Holloway, David
Jamerson, Thomas
Justus, William

Kness, Richard*
Lankston, John
Ledbetter, William
Ledbetter, William, Jr.
Li-Paz, Michael
Livings, George
Lowery, Melvin
Malamood, Herman
Malas, Spiro
Marek, Dan*
Mazzieri, Maurizio
McDonald, William
Molese, Michele
Pane, Tullio
Park, Richard
Patterson, Roger
Paul, Robert
Pierson, Edward
Poll, Melvyn
Presto
Ramey, Samuel
Rampaso, Luciano
Reece, Arley
Riegel, Kenneth
Roe, Charles*
Romaguera, Joaquin
Ronson, David
Roy, Will
Scano, Gaetano*
Siena, Jerold
Sims, Jack
Smith, David Rae
Stewart, John
Stilwell, Richard
Taylor, Richard
Termine, Robert
Titus, Alan
Townsend, Erik
Weston, Robert
White, Willard
Worth, Coley
Yule, Don

* New artist   * New artist   * New artist

Conductors
Bernardi, Mario
Domingo, Placido
Keene, Christopher
Martelli, Luigi
Morelli, Giuseppe
Plasson, Michel*
Rudel, Julius
Somogi, Judith

Chorus master
Gray, George Branson

Assistant chorus master
Somogi, Judith

Solo dancers
Galan, Esperanza

Horvath, Juliu
Lopez, Miguel
Rubino, Michael

Choreographers
Andrew, Thomas
Trisler, Joyce

Directors
Bakman, Patrick
Caldwell, Sarah
Capobianco, Tito
Corsaro, Frank
Denda, Elena
Eddleman, Jack
Freedman, Gerald
Getke, Richard
Hicks, David
Presnell, Steve
Porter, Stephen*

Designers
Aldredge, Theoni V.
Campbell, Patton
Chase, Ronald
Eck, Marsha Louis
Evans, Lloyd
Fletcher, Robert
Lee, Ming Cho
Oenslager, Donald
Pond, Helen
Senn, Herbert
Sprott, Eoin
Toms, Carl
Varona, José

* New artist

August 28

LUCIA DI LAMMERMOOR
(Donizetti)

Conductor .... Martelli

Alisa .... Curry
Edgardo .... Carreras
Normanno ...... Romaguera
Lucia .... Sills
Enrico .... Elvira
Raimondo .... Mazzieri
Arturo .... Griffith

August 29

MADAMA BUTTERFLY (Puccini)

Stage director .... Getke
Conductor .... Morelli

Pinkerton .... Poll
Goro .... Fried
Suzuki .... Walker

Sharpless .... Darrenkamp
Butterfly .... Shade
Imperial
Commissioner ... Ledbetter
Registrar .... Lankston
The Bonze .... Densen
Yamadori .... Lankston
Trouble ...... Ledbetter, Jr.
Kate Pinkerton .... Hegierski

August 30

CARMEN (Bizet)

Conductor ...... Plasson (d)

Morales .... Termine
Andrès .... Yule
Zuniga .... Smith
Micaëla .... Robinson
Don José .... Malamood
Carmen .... Stapp
Frasquita .... Wildes
Mercédès .... Hegierski
Lillas Pastia,
  Guide .... Romaguera
Escamillo .... Justus
Remendado .... Lankston
Dancairo .... Pierson

August 31 (m)

LUCIA DI LAMMERMOOR

Same cast as August 28

August 31

LA TRAVIATA (Verdi)

Conductor .... Bernardi

Violetta .... Brooks
Flora .... Walker
Douphol .... Fisher
D'Obigny .... Ledbetter
Dr. Grenvil .... Yule
Gaston .... Lankston
Alfredo .... Taylor
Annina .... Toro
Giuseppe .... Romaguera
Germont .... Cossa
Messenger .... Harper
Solo dancer .... Galan

September 1 (m)

THE MIKADO (Sullivan)

Conductor .... Somogi

Pooh-Bah .... Berberian
Pish-Tush .... Termine
Nanki-Poo .... Glaze
Ko-Ko .... Billings
Yum-Yum .... Fowles
Pitti-Sing .... Piland
Peep-Bo .... Toro
Katisha .... Allen
Mikado .... Pierson

September 1

LA BOHÈME (Puccini)

Conductor .... Morelli

Rodolfo .... Pane
Marcello .... Jamerson

Colline .... White
Schaunard .... Paul
Benoit .... Densen
Mimi .... Niska
Parpignol .... Romaguera
Musetta .... Rogers
Alcindoro .... Billings
Guards .... Park, Bentley

September 3

ANNA BOLENA (Donizetti)

Conductor .... Rudel

Giovanna .... Marsee
Anna .... Sills
Smeton .... Harris
Enrico .... Hale
Percy .... McDonald
Lord Rochefort ..... Fisher
Sir Hervey .... Lankston

September 4

THE MIKADO

Same cast as September 1 (m)

September 5

CARMEN

Same cast as August 30 except:

Escamillo .... Justus,
              (s, Mazzieri)

September 6

ANNA BOLENA

Same cast as September 3
except:

Smeton .... Piland

September 7 (m)

LA BOHÈME

Same cast as September 1
except:

Mimi .... Malfitano (d)

September 7

LUCIA DI LAMMERMOOR

Same cast as August 28 except:

Edgardo .... Bullard
Lucia .... Welting
Arturo .... Marek

(Note: As a member of the
chorus, Marek had frequently
appeared in very minor parts.
This was his first significant
role and the company
considered it his official debut.)

September 8 (m)

ANNA BOLENA

Same cast as September 3
except:

Giovanna .... Stapp
Anna .... Galvany
Enrico .... Ramey
Percy .... Patterson

September 8

MANON LESCAUT (Puccini)
New production

Directed by	Corsaro
Designer	Eck
Choreographer	Andrew
Lighting	Sondheimer
Conductor	Martelli

Edmondo	Barasorda (d)
Lescaut	Holloway
Des Grieux	Molese
Innkeeper	Ronson
Geronte	Malas
Manon Lescaut	Niska
Hairdresser	Rubino
Musician	Piland
Dancing master	Lankston
Sergeant	Yule
Lamplighter	Siena
Officer	Densen

September 10

MANON LESCAUT

Same cast as September 8

September 11

MARIA STUARDA (Donizetti)

Stage director	Denda
Conductor	Martelli

Herald	Bentley
Elisabetta	Galvany
Talbot	Darrenkamp
Cecil	Densen
Roberto Dudley	Pane
Maria Stuarda	Sills
Anna Kennedy	Hegierski

September 12

MADAMA BUTTERFLY

Same cast as August 29 except:

Sharpless	Jamerson
Butterfly	Craig

September 13

LA TRAVIATA

Same cast as August 31 except:

Alfredo	Pane

September 14 (m)

MANON LESCAUT

Same cast as September 8

September 14

MEDEA (Cherubini)

Conductor	Morelli

Glauce	Hocher
Glauce's attendants	Kehrig, Toro
Creon	Ramey
Jason	Taylor
Medea's children	Ledbetter, Jr., Brennan

Neris	Bible
Medea	Galvany
Medea's attendants	Lopez, Rubino

September 15 (m)

LUCIA DI LAMMERMOOR

Same cast as August 28 except:

Alisa	Hegierski
Edgardo	Bullard
Normanno	Fried
Lucia	Welting, (s, Sills)
Enrico	Fazah
Arturo	Marek

September 15

THE MIKADO

Same cast as September 1 (m) except:

Pish-Tush	Jamerson
Yum-Yum	Soviero
Katisha	Bonazzi

September 17

LA TRAVIATA

Same cast as August 31 except:

Violetta	Talarico (d)
Gaston	Lowery
Germont	Darrenkamp

September 18

DIE FLEDERMAUS (J. Strauss)
New production
(English version by
Ruth and Thomas Martin)

Directed by	Freedman
Scenic designer	Evans
Costume designer	Aldredge
Choreographer	Trisler
Lighting	Sondheimer
Conductor	Bernardi

Alfred	Glaze
Adele	Welting
Rosalinda	Meier
Eisenstein	Titus
Blind	Fried
Falke	Cossa
Frank	Malas
Sally	Kehrig
Ivan	Sims
Prince Orlofsky	Smith
Frosch	Worth
Solo dancers	Galan, Horvath

September 19

I PURITANI (Bellini)

Conductor	Rudel

Riccardo	Elvira
Bruno	Siena
Elvira	Sills
Enrichetta	Curry
Giorgio	Hale

Gualtiero	Densen
Arturo	Duval, (s, Di Giuseppe)

September 20

FAUST (Gounod)

Conductor	Keene

Faust	Riegel
Méphistophélès	Ramey
Wagner	Hamilton (d)
Marguerite	Bayard
Valentin	Jamerson
Siébel	Marsee
Marthe	Walker
Juggler	De Dio
Fire-eater	Presto

September 21 (m)

DIE FLEDERMAUS

Same cast as September 18 except:

Falke	Holloway, (s, Cossa)

September 21

LA BOHÈME

Same cast as September 1 except:

Marcello	Fazah
Benoit	Yule
Mimi	Malfitano

September 22 (m)

CARMEN

Same cast as August 30 except:

Conductor	Keene
Zuniga	Li-Paz
Mercédès	Piland

September 22

I PURITANI

Same cast as September 19

September 24

MEDEA

Same cast as September 14 except:

Jason	Townsend

September 25

TOSCA (Puccini)

Stage director	Dend
Conductor	Morell

Angelotti	Fishe
Sacristan	Billing
Cavaradossi	Scano (d
Tosca	Meie
Scarpia	Justu
Spoletta	Romaguer
Sciarrone	Ledbette
Shepherd	Tor
Jailer	Yul

September 26

I PURITANI

Same cast as September 19 except:

Riccardo .... Fredricks
Bruno .... Griffith
Elvira .... Brooks
Giorgio .... White

September 27

DIE FLEDERMAUS

Same cast as September 18 except:

Rosalinda .... Bayard
Falke .... Holloway

September 28 (m)

ARIADNE AUF NAXOS
(R. Strauss)
(English translation of prologue and opera by Lewis Sydenham, revised by Julius Rudel)

Conductor .... Rudel

Major-Domo .... Yule
Music Master .... Justus
Composer .... Niska
Wigmaker .... Romaguera
Echo .... Hocher
Najade .... Derr
Dryade .... Curry
Lackey .... Densen
Dancing Master,
  Scaramuccio .... Lankston
Zerbinetta .... Wise
Tenor, Bacchus .... Reece
Officer .... Ledbetter
Prima Donna,
  Ariadne .... Neblett
Harlequin .... Jamerson
Truffaldin .... Ramey
Brighella .... Livings

September 28

I PURITANI

Same cast as September 19 except:

Elvira .... Brooks
Enrichetta .... Hegierski

September 29 (m)

DIE FLEDERMAUS

Same cast as September 18 except:

Blind .... Romaguera
Falke .... Holloway
Prince Orlofsky .... Lankston

September 29

ROBERTO DEVEREUX
(Donizetti)

Stage director .... Denda
Conductor .... Rudel

Sara .... Marsee
Elizabeth .... Sills
Cecil .... Siena
Page .... Billings
Raleigh .... Fisher
Robert Devereux . . Di Giuseppe
Duke of
  Nottingham ..... Fredricks
Servant .... Yule

October 1

FAUST

Same cast as September 20 except:

Valentin .... Elvira

October 2

LA BOHÈME

Same cast as September 1 except:

Rodolfo .... Malamood
Benoit .... Yule
Mimi .... Derr
Musetta .... Bayard

October 3

LA TRAVIATA

Same cast as August 31 except:

Conductor .... Somogi
Flora .... Hegierski
Gaston .... Lowery
Alfredo .... Stewart

October 4

DON GIOVANNI (Mozart)

New staging by ... Porter (d)
Conductor .... Rudel

Leporello .... Malas
Don Giovanni .... Hale
Donna Anna .... Meier
Commendatore .... Roy
Don Ottavio .... Taylor
Donna Elvira .... Hinds
Zerlina .... Fowles
Masetto .... Jamerson

October 5 (m)

MADAMA BUTTERFLY

Same cast as August 29 except:

Sharpless .... Fazah
Butterfly .... Anthony

October 5

TOSCA

Same cast as September 25 except:

Conductor .... Keene
Cavaradossi ...... Malamood
Tosca .... Schauler
Spoletta .... Siena

October 6 (m)

MANON LESCAUT

Same cast as September 8 except:

Conductor .... Morelli
Edmondo .... Griffith
Lescaut .... Fredricks
Geronte .... Li-Paz
Lamplighter .... Lowery
Officer .... Termine

October 6

DIE FLEDERMAUS

Same cast as September 18 except:

Prince Orlofsky .... Lankston

October 8

MANON LESCAUT

Same cast as September 8 except:

Conductor .... Morelli
Edmondo .... Griffith
Lescaut .... Fredricks
Geronte .... Li-Paz
Musician .... Toro
Lamplighter .... Lowery
Officer .... Termine

October 9

L'INCORONAZIONE DI POPPEA
(Monteverdi)

Conductor .... Keene

Fortuna .... Hocher
Virtù .... Derr
Amor .... Wildes
Ottone .... Cossa
Soldiers ..... Lankston, Siena
Poppea .... Hebert
Nerone .... Roe (d)
Arnalta .... Bonazzi
Ottavia .... Bible
Drusilla .... Hocher
Valetto .... Lankston
Seneca .... Ramey
Pallade .... Derr
Liberto and Littore . . Ledbetter
Damigella .... Wildes
Lucano .... Siena

October 10

MADAMA BUTTERFLY

Same cast as August 29 except:

Goro .... Romaguera
Suzuki .... Curry
Sharpless .... Holloway
Butterfly .... Craig
Registrar, Yamadori ... Fried

October 11

ARIADNE AUF NAXOS

Same cast as September 28 (m) except:

Conductor .... Keene
Music Master .... Devlin

434   ANNALS, *1944–1981*

October 12 (m)

THE MIKADO

Same cast as September 1 (m)
except:

Pooh-Bah .... Malas
Pish-Tush .... Jamerson
Nanki-Poo .... Griffith
Ko-Ko .... Lankston
Yum-Yum .... Skarimbas
Peep-Bo .... Kehrig
Katisha .... James
Mikado .... Densen

October 12

TOSCA

Same cast as September 25
except:

Cavaradossi .... Molese
Tosca .... Schauler
Scarpia .... Fredricks
Spoletta .... Siena

October 13 (m)

DON GIOVANNI

Same cast as October 4

October 13

DIE FLEDERMAUS

Same cast as September 18
except:

Alfred .... McDonald
Adele .... Randazzo
Rosalinda .... Bayard
Eisenstein .... Roe
Blind .... Romaguera
Falke .... Holloway
Frank .... Densen
Sally .... Toro
Prince Orlofsky .... Lankston

October 15

DIE FLEDERMAUS

Same cast as September 18
except:

Alfred .... McDonald
Adele .... Haley (d)
Eisenstein .... Roe
Blind .... Romaguera
Sally .... Toro
Prince Orlofsky .... Lankston
Frosch .... Billings,
                  (s, Worth)

October 16

CARMEN

Same cast as August 30 except:

Conductor .... Keene

Zuniga .... Li-Paz
Micaëla .... Fowles
Don José .... Domingo
Carmen .... Killebrew
Frasquita .... Kessler
Escamillo ...... Darrenkamp
Remendado .... Siena

October 17

A VILLAGE ROMEO AND JULIET
(Delius)

Conductor .... Bernardi

Marti .... Roy
Sali, as a child ...... Weston
Vreli, as a child ...... Angela
Manz .... Jamerson
Dark Fiddler ...... Holloway
Sali .... Stewart
Vreli .... Wells
Wild girl .... Wildes
Stoned girl .... Piland
Doll and puppet
  man .... Townsend
Knick knack man .... Ronson
Wheel of fortune
  woman .... Hocher
Fruit man .... Densen
Pastry woman .... Wildes
Cheap jewelry
  woman .... Hegierski
Three women .... Kehrig,
                  Adler, Toro
Two men .... Ledbetter, Yule
Poor horn player .. Townsend
Hunchbacked bass
  fiddle player ...... Billings
Bargemen .... Jamerson,
          Ledbetter, Griffith

October 18

LA BOHÈME

Same cast as September 1
except:

Rodolfo .... Molese
Marcello ...... Darrenkamp
Schaunard .... Hamilton
Benoit .... Yule
Mimi .... Craig
Musetta .... Randazzo

October 19 (m)

DIE FLEDERMAUS

Same cast as September 18
except:

Adele .... Haley
Rosalinda .... Bayard
Falke .... Holloway
Sally .... Toro
Prince Orlofsky .. Romaguera

October 19

ARIADNE AUF NAXOS

Same cast as September 28 (m)
except:

Conductor .... Keene

Music Master .... Devlin
Composer .... Stapp
Tenor, Bacchus ... Kness (d)
Prima Donna,
  Ariadne .... Meier
Harlequin .... Cossa
Brighella .... Lowery

October 20 (m)

MADAMA BUTTERFLY

Same cast as August 29 except:

Goro .... Romaguera
Suzuki .... Curry,
                  (s, Walker)
Sharpless .... Fazah
Butterfly .... Craig
Registrar, Yamadori ... Fried
The Bonze .... Li-Paz
Kate Pinkerton .... Toro

October 20

I PURITANI

Same cast as September 19
except:

Riccardo .... Fredricks
Enrichetta .... Hegierski
Arturo .... McDonald

October 22

MEDEA

Same cast as September 14
except:

Conductor .... Keene

Glauce .... Derr
Creon .... White
Neris .... Curry
Medea .... Niska

October 23

DON GIOVANNI

Same cast as October 4 except:

Don Ottavio .... Glaze
Masetto .... Fazah

October 24

TOSCA

Same cast as September 25
except:

Conductor .... Domingo

Angelotti .... Ramey
Cavaradossi ...... Malamood
Tosca .... Schauler
Scarpia .... Fredricks

October 25

LA TRAVIATA

Same cast as August 31 except:

Conductor .... Somog

Violetta .... Patenaud
Flora .... Hegiersk
Germont .... Elvir

October 26 (m)

PELLÉAS ET MÉLISANDE
(Debussy)

Conductor .... Rud

Mélisande .... Brook
Golaud .... Devli
Geneviève .... Killebre
Arkel .... Berberia

Pelléas .... Stilwell
Yniold .... Pisacano
Shepherd .... Ledbetter
Physician .... Yule

October 26

MANON LESCAUT

Same cast as September 8 except:

Conductor .... Morelli

Lescaut .... Fredricks
Des Grieux ...... Malamood
Manon .... Craig
Musician .... Toro
Lamplighter .... Marek

October 27 (m)

MADAMA BUTTERFLY

Same cast as August 29 except:

Conductor .... Keene

Pinkerton .... Rampaso
Goro .... Romaguera
Suzuki .... Curry
Sharpless .... Clatworthy
Butterfly .... Anthony
Registrar, Yamadori ... Fried
The Bonze .... Li-Paz
Kate Pinkerton .... Toro

October 27

LA BOHÈME

Same cast as September 1 except:

Rodolfo .... Poll
Marcello .... Cossa
Colline .... Roy
Schaunard .... Hamilton
Benoit .... Yule
Mimi .... Derr

October 29

UN BALLO IN MASCHERA
(Verdi)

New staging by .... Hicks
Conductor .... Morelli

Count Horn .... Li-Paz
Count Ribbing .... White
Oscar .... Fowles
Gustavo .... Molese
Renato .... Fredricks
Chief Justice .... Romaguera
Ulrica .... Killebrew
Silvano .... Fisher
Servant .... Termine
Amelia .... Galvany

October 30

LA BOHÈME

Same cast as September 1 except:

Rodolfo .... Rampaso
Marcello .... Darrenkamp
Benoit .... Yule

October 31

PELLÉAS ET MÉLISANDE

Same cast as October 26 (m)

November 1

UN BALLO IN MASCHERA

Same cast as October 29 except:

Ulrica .... James

November 2 (m)

DON GIOVANNI

Same cast as October 4 except:

Don Giovanni .... Ramey
Donna Anna .... Hebert
Commendatore ...... Densen
Zerlina .... Skarimbas
Masetto ...... Fazah (Act I);
           Ledbetter (Act II)

November 2

THE MIKADO

Same cast as September 1 (m) except:

Nanki-Poo .... Griffith
Ko-Ko .... Eddleman
Yum-Yum .... Soviero
Pitti-Sing .... Hegierski

November 3 (m)

FAUST

Same cast as September 20 except:

Faust .... Poll
Méphistophélès .... Hale
Wagner .... Fisher
Marguerite .... Brooks
Valentin .... Stillwell
Siébel .... Harris

November 3

CARMEN

Same cast as August 30 except:

Conductor .... Keene
Morales .... Fisher
Zuniga .... Li-Paz
Micaëla .... Fowles
Carmen .... Killebrew
Frasquita .... Ito
Escamillo .... Devlin
Remendado .... Fried

November 5

A VILLAGE ROMEO AND JULIET

Same cast as October 17 except:

Manz, 1st Bargeman .... Roe

November 6

FAUST

Same cast as September 20 except:

Méphistophélès .... Hale
Wagner .... Fisher

Marguèrite .... Brooks
Valentin .... Stillwell
Siébel .... Harris

November 7

DIE FLEDERMAUS

Same cast as September 18 except:

Eisenstein .... Roe
Falke .... Holloway
Sally .... Toro
Frosch .... Billings

November 8

DON GIOVANNI

Same cast as October 4 except:

Leporello .... Li-Paz
Don Giovanni .... Ramey
Donna Anna .... Hebert
Don Ottavio .... Stewart
Zerlina .... Skarimbas
Masetto .... Jamerson,
              (s, Fazah)

November 9 (m)

CARMEN

Same cast as August 30 except:

Conductor .... Keene
Morales .... Fisher
Zuniga .... Densen
Micaëla .... Craig
Frasquita .... Ito
Mercédès .... Piland
Escamillo ...... Darrenkamp
Remendado .... Fried

November 9

THE MIKADO

Same cast as September 1 (m) except:

Nanki-Poo .... Griffith
Pitti-Sing .... Hegierski
Peep-Bo .... Kehrig
Mikado .... Densen

November 10 (m)

A VILLAGE ROMEO AND JULIET

Same cast as October 17 except:

Sali, as a child..Di Loreto (d)
Vreli, as a child Pisacano (d)
Manz .... Roe
Dark Fiddler ...... Jamerson
Vreli .... Soviero
1st Man .... Fisher,
              (s, Ledbetter)
1st Bargeman .... Roe
2nd Bargeman ...... Ronson,
              (s, Ledbetter)

November 10

UN BALLO IN MASCHERA

Same cast as October 29 except:

Gustavo .... Bullard
Renato .... Fredricks,
              (s, Elvira)
Amelia .... Jones (d)

Spring 1975 (FEBRUARY 20 – APRIL 27)

Female artists
Allen, Betty
Anthony, Judith
Ballard, Earline*
Bergquist, Eleanor*
Bible, Frances
Brooks, Patricia
Ciraulo, Marianna
Costa-Greenspon, Muriel
Craig, Patricia
Curry, Diane
De Rosa, Judith
Derr, Emily
Fowles, Glenys
Grillo, Joann
Haley, Elizabeth
Hegierski, Kathleen
Hocher, Barbara
Ito, Yoshi
Kehrig, Diana
Malfitano, Catherine
Marsee, Susanne
Mathes, Rachel*
Meier, Johanna
Neblett, Carol
Niska, Maralin
Piland, Jeanne
Randazzo, Arlene
Robinson, Faye
Schauler, Eileen
Shade, Nancy
Sills, Beverly
Soviero, Diana
Stapp, Olivia
Steffan, Sofia
Thomson, Heather
Toro, Puli
Tyler, Veronica
Walker, Sandra
Wells, Patricia
Wildes, Rose
Wise, Patricia
Yarmat, Karen*

Male artists
Alexander, John
Barasorda, Antonio
Barrett, Tom
Bentley, Ronald
Billings, James
Bini, Carlo*
Blanton, Joseph*
Bohachevsky, George
Carreras, José
Cossa, Dominic
Crofoot, Alan*
Darrenkamp, John
Davis, Harris
De Dio, Harry
Densen, Irwin
Di Giuseppe, Enrico
Di Loreto, Gian*
Duval, Pierre
Eddleman, Jack
Elvira, Pablo

Fazah, Adib
Fisher, Robert
Fredricks, Richard
Gill, Richard T.
Glaze, Gary
Griffith, David
Hale, Robert
Harper, Talmage
Hensel, Howard*
Holloway, David
Jamerson, Thomas
Justus, William
Kness, Richard
Lankston, John
Ledbetter, William
Ledbetter, William, Jr.
Li-Paz, Michael
Livings, George
Lowery, Melvin
Malas, Spiro
Marek, Dan
Mauro, Ermanno*
McDonald, William
McKee, Richard*
Nagy, Robert
Novick, Melvyn*
Palay, Elliot*
Pane, Tullio
Park, Richard
Patterson, Roger
Paul, Robert
Pierson, Edward
Poll, Melvyn
Presto
Quilico, Louis
Ramey, Samuel
Rampaso, Luciano
Rinaldi, Walter*
Roe, Charles
Romaguera, Joaquin
Ronson, David
Scano, Gaetano
Siena, Jerold
Sims, Jack
Smith, David Rae
Steele, Philip*
Stilwell, Richard
Taylor, Richard
Termine, Robert
Titus, Alan
White, Willard
Worth, Coley
Yule, Don

Conductors
Gray, George Branson*
Hauser, Alexis*
Keene, Christopher
Martelli, Luigi
Morelli, Giuseppe
Pallo, Imre
Rudel, Julius
Somogi, Judith

Chorus master
Gray, George Branson

Associate chorus master
Somogi, Judith

Solo dancers
Balestracci, Sandra
Galan, Esperanza

Horvath, Juliu
Rubino, Michael
Seetoo, Dennis

Choreographers
Andrew, Thomas
Birch, Patricia*
Eddleman, Jack
Leporska, Zoya*

Directors
Capobianco, Tito
Corsaro, Frank
Denda, Elena
Eddleman, Jack
Freedman, Gerald
Getke, Richard
Hicks, David
Menotti, Gian Carlo
Presnell, Steve
Rizzo, Francis
Strasfogel, Ian
Yannopoulos, Dino

Designers
Aldredge, Theoni V.
Armistead, Horace
Barcelo, Randy*
Campbell, Patton
Chase, Ronald
Eek, Marcho Louis
Evans, Lloyd
Fletcher, Robert
Larkey, Joan*
Lee, Ming Cho
Montresor, Beni
Oenslager, Donald
Schmidt, Douglas W.*
Toms, Carl
Varona, José
Wittstein, Ed

* New artist

February 20

I PURITANI (Bellini)

Conductor .... Rude
Riccardo .... Elvira
        (s, Fredricks)
Bruno .... Siena
Elvira .... Sills
Enrichetta .... Curry
Giorgio .... Hale
Gualtiero .... Densen
Arturo .... Duval
        (s, Di Giuseppe)
        (Act I); Patterson
        (s, Di Giuseppe) (Act III)

(Performance dedicated to the
memory of Norman Treigle)

February 21

TURANDOT (Puccini)
New production

Directed by	Yannopoulos
Stage director	Presnell
Designer	Montresor
Choreographer	Andrew
Lighting	Sondheimer
Conductor	Rudel

Mandarin	Densen
Liù	Malfitano
Calaf	Mauro (d)
Timur	Gill
Turandot	Mathes (d)
Ping	Jamerson
Pang	Griffith
Pong	Lankston
Emperor	Romaguera

February 22 (m)

MANON LESCAUT (Puccini)

Conductor	Martelli
Edmondo	Barasorda
Lescaut	Holloway
Des Grieux	Bini (d)
Innkeeper	Ronson
Geronte	Malas
Manon Lescaut	Niska
Hairdresser	Rubino
Musician	Hegierski
Dancing master	Lankston
Sergeant	Yule
Lamplighter	Lowery
Officer	Densen

February 22

THE MARRIAGE OF FIGARO
(Mozart)
(English version by
Ruth and Thomas Martin)

Conductor	Keene
Figaro	Ramey
Susanna	Fowles
Bartolo	Pierson
Marcellina	Walker
Cherubino	Piland
Almaviva	Darrenkamp
Basilio	Siena
Countess	Wells
Antonio	Billings
Curzio	Romaguera
Barbarina	Wildes
Solo dancer	Galan

February 23 (m)

CARMEN (Bizet)

Stage director	Presnell
Conductor	Keene
Morales	Fisher
Andrès	Yule
Zuniga	Densen
Micaëla	Craig
Don José	Kness
Carmen	Stapp
Frasquita	Ito
Mercédès	Hegierski
Lillas Pastia, guide	Romaguera

Escamillo	Justus
Remendado	Siena
Dancairo	Ledbetter

February 23

I PURITANI

Same cast as February 20
except:

Riccardo	Fredricks
Arturo	Di Giuseppe

February 26

I PURITANI

Same cast as February 20
except:

Riccardo	Fredricks, (s, Quilico)
Arturo	Duval

February 27

MANON LESCAUT

Same cast as February 22 (m)
except:

Manon Lescaut	Craig
Lamplighter	Siena

February 28

LA TRAVIATA (Verdi)

Conductor	Pallo
Violetta	Thomson
Flora	Walker
Douphol	Fisher
D'Obigny	Ledbetter
Dr. Grenvil	Yule
Gaston	Marek
Alfredo	Scano
Annina	Toro
Giuseppe	Romaguera
Germont	Quilico
Messenger	Harper
Solo dancer	Galan

March 1 (m)

I PURITANI

Same cast as February 20
except:

Conductor	Keene
Arturo	Patterson, (s, Duval)

March 1

TOSCA (Puccini)

Stage director	Presnell
Conductor	Martelli
Angelotti	Fisher
Sacristan	Billings
Cavaradossi	Rampaso
Tosca	Schauler
Scarpia	Fredricks
Spoletta	Romaguera
Sciarrone	Ledbetter
Shepherd	Toro
Jailer	Yule

March 2 (m)

TURANDOT

Same cast as February 21

March 2

SALOME (R. Strauss)
New production (joint
production with the Opera
Society of Washington)

Directed by	Strasfogel
Sets and projections designed by	Schmidt (d)
Costume designer	Barcelo (d)
Choreographer	Birch (d)
Lighting	Sondheimer
Conductor	Rudel

Narraboth	Blanton (d)
Page	Piland
1st Soldier	White
2nd Soldier	Densen
Cappadocian	Fisher
Salome	Niska
Slave	Romaguera
Jochanaan	Justus
Herodes	Crofoot (d)
Herodias	Bible
1st Jew	Siena
2nd Jew	Lankston
3rd Jew	Lowery
4th Jew	Griffith
5th Jew	Steele (d)
1st Nazarene	Ramey
2nd Nazarene	Marek

March 4

ANNA BOLENA (Donizetti)

Conductor	Rudel
Giovanna	Stapp
Anna	Sills
Smeton	Piland
Enrico	Ramey
Percy	Patterson
Lord Rochefort	Fisher
Sir Hervey	Lankston

March 5

CARMEN

Same cast as February 23 (m)
except:

Morales	Termine
Zuniga	McKee (d)
Micaëla	Robinson
Don José	Scano, (s, Kness)
Escamillo	Darrenkamp

March 6

I PURITANI

Same cast as February 20
except:

Conductor	Keene
Bruno	Griffith
Elvira	Brooks
Giorgio	Gill
Arturo	McDonald

March 7

ANNA BOLENA

Same cast as March 4 except:

Giovanna .... Marsee

March 8 (m)

SALOME

Same cast as March 2

March 8

I PURITANI

Same cast as February 20
except:

Riccardo .... Elvira,
                 (s, Quilico)
Bruno .... Griffith
Elvira .... Randazzo
Giorgio .... Gill
Arturo .... Di Giuseppe

March 9 (m)

THE MIKADO (Sullivan)

Conductor .... Somogi

Pooh-Bah .... McKee
Pish-Tush .... Jamerson
Nanki-Poo .... Glaze
Ko-Ko .... Billings
Yum-Yum .... Fowles
Pitti-Sing .... Hegierski
Peep-Bo .... Toro
Katisha .... Allen
Mikado .... Densen

March 9

LA TRAVIATA

Same cast as February 28
except:

Germont .... Cossa

March 12

ANNA BOLENA

Same cast as March 4 except:

Giovanna .... Marsee
Enrico .... Gill
Percy .... Di Giuseppe
Sir Hervey .... Siena

March 13

SALOME

Same cast as March 2 except:

2nd Soldier .... Yule
Salome .... Schauler
Herodias .... Stapp

March 14

TURANDOT

Same cast as February 21
except:

Mandarin .... Fisher
Calaf .... Kness
Turandot .... Ballard (d)
Emperor .... Lowery

March 15 (m)

THE MIKADO

Same cast as March 9 (m)
except:

Nanki-Poo .... Griffith
Ko-Ko .... Eddleman

March 15

MADAMA BUTTERFLY (Puccini)

Conductor .... Martelli

Pinkerton .... Rampaso
Goro .... Billings
Suzuki .... Walker
Sharpless .... Elvira
Butterfly .... Anthony
Imperial
  Commissioner ... Ledbetter,
                 (s, Termine)
Registrar, Yamadori .. Marek
The Bonze .... Densen
Trouble ...... Di Loreto (d)
Kate Pinkerton .... Toro

March 16 (m)

MANON LESCAUT

Same cast as February 22 (m)
except:

Lescaut .... Holloway,
               (s, Fredricks)
Des Grieux .... Scano
Geronte .... McKee
Manon Lescaut ...... Craig
Officer .... Termine

March 16

IDOMENEO (Mozart)
First performance by The New
York City Opera Company

Directed by ...... Freedman
Scenic designer .... Lee
Costume designer .. Aldredge
Choreographer ...... Andrew
Lighting .... Sondheimer
Conductor .... Rudel

Ilia .... Tyler
Idamante .... Glaze
Elektra .... Niska
Idomeneo .... Taylor
Arbace .... Lankston
High Priest .... Hensel
Voice of Neptune .... Densen

March 18

DIE FLEDERMAUS (J. Strauss)
(English version by
Ruth and Thomas Martin)

Choreographer ...... Andrew
Conductor .... Rudel

Alfred .... Glaze
Adele .... Haley
Rosalinda .... Meier
Eisenstein .... Titus
Blind .... Romaguera
Falke .... Holloway

Frank .... McKee
Sally .... Toro
Ivan .... Sims
Prince Orlofsky .... Lankston
Frosch .... Worth
Solo dancers ... Balestracci,
               Galan; Horvath

March 20

TURANDOT

Same cast as February 21
except:

Liù .... Robinson
Timur .... Ramey
Turandot .... Ballard
Ping .... Fazah
Pang .... Marek
Pong .... Siena
Emperor .... Lowery

March 21

TOSCA

Same cast as March 1 except:

Conductor .... Morelli
Cavaradossi .... Carreras
Tosca .... Meier

March 22 (m)

THE MIKADO

Same cast as March 9 (m)
except:

Yum-Yum .... Soviero
Pitti-Sing .... Piland
Peep-Bo .... Kehrig
Mikado .... Pierson

March 22

THE CONSUL (Menotti)

Stage director .... Rizzo
Conductor .... Keene

John Sorel ..... Darrenkamp
Magda Sorel .... Stapp
The Mother ..Costa-Greenspon
Secret Police Agent .. Pierson
Plainclothesmen..Sims, Barrett
Secretary .... Walker
Mr. Kofner .... Yule
The Foreign Woman..De Rosa
Anna Gomez .... Hocher
The Magician
  Magadoff .... Lankston
Vera Boronel .... Steffan
Assan .... Ledbetter
Voice on the
  record ...... Mabel Mercer

March 23 (m)

IDOMENEO

Same cast as March 16

March 23

LUCIA DI LAMMERMOOR
(Donizetti)

Conductor .... Morelli

Alisa .... Curr
Edgardo .... Carreras

Normanno ...... Romaguera
Enrico .... Elvira
Lucia .... Wise
Raimondo .... Hale
Arturo .... Griffith

March 25

TOSCA

Same cast as March 1 except:

Conductor .... Morelli

Cavaradossi .... Carreras
Tosca .... Meier
Scarpia .... Justus,
(s, Fredricks)
Spoletta .... Siena
Sciarrone .... Termine

March 27

IDOMENEO

Same cast as March 16 except:

Ilia .... Hocher
Idamante .... Livings
Elektra .... Wells
Idomeneo .... Taylor,
(s, Blanton)

March 28

SALOME

Same cast as March 2 except:

Narraboth .... Taylor
1st Soldier .... Steele
Salome .... Schauler
Jochanaan .... Justus,
(s, Clatworthy)
Herodias .... Stapp
5th Jew .... Yule

(Note: David Clatworthy was
not to appear with the
company this season.)

March 29 (m)

LA BOHÈME (Puccini)

Conductor .... Morelli

Rodolfo .... Pane
Marcello .... Elvira
Colline .... Ramey
Schaunard .... Paul
Benoit .... Yule
Mimi .... Wells
Parpignol .... Romaguera
Musetta .... Meier
Alcindoro .... Billings
Guards .... Park, Bentley

March 29

LA TRAVIATA

Same cast as February 28
except:

Douphol .... Termine
Alfredo .... Poll
Germont .... Cossa

March 30 (m)

CARMEN

Same cast as February 23 (m)
except:

Morales .... Termine,
(s, Fisher)
Zuniga .... McKee
Micaëla .... Fowles
Don José .... Scano
Frasquita .... Derr
Mercédès .... Piland

March 30

LUCIA DI LAMMERMOOR

Same cast as March 23 except:

Lucia .... Wise,
(s, Brooks)

April 2

DIE TOTE STADT (Korngold)
First performance by The New
York City Opera Company

Directed by .... Corsaro
Films and
projections by ...... Chase
Scenic designer ... Larkey (d)
Costume designer ... Aldredge
Choreographer ...... Andrew
Choreographer of Marietta's
dances ...... Leporska (d)
Lighting .... Porcher
Conductor .... Pallo

Brigitta .... Curry
Frank .... Roe
Paul .... Alexander
Marietta .... Neblett
Victorin .... Lankston
Albert .... Siena
Juliette .... Wildes
Lucienne .... Toro
Fritz .... Cossa
Gaston .... Seetoo

April 3

THE MARRIAGE OF FIGARO

Same cast as February 22
except:

Susanna .... Wise
Cherubino .... Marsee
Almaviva .... Fredricks
Countess .... Meier,
(s, Wells)
Barbarina .... Kehrig

April 4

DIE TOTE STADT

Same cast as April 2

April 5 (m)

DIE FLEDERMAUS

Same cast as March 18 except:

Conductor .... Hauser (d)

Sally .... Kehrig
Prince Orlofsky ...... Smith

April 5

FAUST (Gounod)

Conductor .... Keene

Faust .... Taylor,
(s, Poll)
Méphistophélès .... Hale
Wagner .... Ledbetter
Marguerite .... Wells
Valentin .... Stilwell
Siébel .... Marsee
Marthe .... Walker
Juggler .... De Dio
Fire-eater .... Presto

April 6 (m)

SALOME

Same cast as March 2 except:

Conductor .... Keene

Narraboth .... Taylor
1st Soldier .... Steele
Herodes .... Nagy
3rd Jew .... Marek
4th Jew .... Hensel
5th Jew .... Yule
2nd Nazarene ...... Ledbetter

April 6

THE CONSUL

Same cast as March 22

John Sorel .... Roe

April 8

LA BOHÈME

Same cast as March 29 (m)
except:

Colline .... Hale
Musetta .... Bergquist (d)

April 9

SALOME

Same cast as March 2 except:

Conductor .... Keene

Page .... Yarmat (d)
1st Soldier .... Steele
4th Jew .... Hensel
5th Jew .... Yule

April 10

CAVALLERIA RUSTICANA
(Mascagni)

Conductor .... Martelli

Mamma Lucia ...... Walker
Santuzza .... Stapp
Turiddu .... Kness
Lola .... Piland
Alfio .... Fredricks

Followed by:

I PAGLIACCI (Leoncavallo)

Conductor .... Martelli

Tonio .... Fredricks
Canio .... Nagy

Nedda .... Craig
Beppe .... Siena
Peasants ..Davis, Bohachevsky
Silvio .... Cossa

April 11

THE MARRIAGE OF FIGARO

Same cast as February 22
except:

Susanna .... Wise
Cherubino .... Marsee
Almaviva .... Justus
Countess .... Meier
Antonio .... Yule

April 12 (m)

FAUST

Same cast as April 5 except:

Faust .... Poll
Marguerite .... Fowles
Valentin .... Elvira
Siébel .... Piland

April 12

DIE FLEDERMAUS

Same cast as March 18 except:

Conductor .... Pallo

Adele .... Randazzo
Rosalinda .... Craig
Eisenstein .... Roe
Falke .... Cossa
Frank .... Densen
Sally .... Kehrig
Prince Orlofsky ...... Smith

April 13 (m)

IL BARBIERE DI SIVIGLIA
(Rossini)

Directed by ...... Eddleman
Conductor .... Morelli

Fiorello .... Termine
Almaviva .... Pane
Figaro .... Stilwell
Bartolo .... Li-Paz
Rosina .... Wise
Basilio .... Ramey
Berta .... Walker
Officer .... Yule

April 13

MADAMA BUTTERFLY

Same cast as March 15 except:

Pinkerton .... Scano
Suzuki .... Curry
Sharpless .... Holloway
Imperial
  Commissioner .... Termine
Registrar,
  Yamadori .... Lankston
Trouble .... Ledbetter, Jr.,
               (s, Di Loreto)

April 15

DIE TOTE STADT

Same cast as April 2 except:

Paul .... Alexander,
                 (s, Kness)
Marietta .... Shade

April 16

DIE FLEDERMAUS

Same cast as March 18 except:

Conductor .... Hauser

Alfred .... McDonald
Adele .... Randazzo
Eisenstein .... Roe
Frank .... Malas
Prince Orlofsky ...... Smith
Frosch .... Billings

April 17

LA TRAVIATA

Same cast as February 28
except:

Conductor .... Somogi

Violetta .... Brooks
Douphol .... Termine
Gaston .... Lowery
Alfredo .... Pane
Germont .... Fredricks

April 18

CAVALLERIA RUSTICANA

Same cast as April 10 except:

Santuzza .... Ciraulo
Alfio .... Justus

Followed by:

I PAGLIACCI

Same cast as April 10 except:

Tonio .... Elvira
Canio .... Palay (d)
Beppe .... Lowery

April 19 (m)

LA BOHÈME

Same cast as March 29 (m)
except:

Marcello .... Fredricks
Colline .... Malas
Musetta .... Bergquist

April 19

LUCIA DI LAMMERMOOR

Same cast as March 23 except:

Alisa .... Hegierski
Edgardo .... Scano
Enrico .... Fazah
Raimondo .... Ramey
Arturo .... Novick (d)

April 20 (m)

DIE TOTE STADT

Same cast as April 2

April 20

CARMEN

Same cast as February 23 (m)
except:

Zuniga .... Steele
Micaëla .... Fowles
Carmen .... Grillo
Frasquita .... Derr
Mercédès .... Piland
Escamillo ..... Darrenkamp
Remendado .... Marek
Dancairo .... Billings

April 22

SALOME

Same cast as March 2 except:

Conductor .... Keene
Page .... Yarmat
1st Soldier .... Steele
Herodias .... Stapp
5th Jew .... Yule

April 23

DIE TOTE STADT

Same cast as April 2 execept:

Juliette .... Derr
Fritz .... Jamerson

April 24

FAUST

Same cast as April 5 except:

Conductor .... Gray (d)
Mephistophélès ...... Ramey
Siébel .... Piland

April 25

MADAMA BUTTERFLY

Some cast as March 15 except:

Pinkerton .... Scano
Goro .... Romaguera
Suzuki .... Curry
Sharpless .... Fredricks
Butterfly .... Niska
Imperial
  Commissioner .... Termine
Registrar,
  Yamadori .... Lankston

April 26 (m)

DIE TOTE STADT

Same cast as April 2 except:

Paul .... Kness
Juliette .... Derr
Fritz .... Jamerson

April 26

IL BARBIERE DI SIVIGLIA

Same cast as April 13 (m)

April 27 (m)

CAVALLERIA RUSTICANA

Same cast as April 10 except:

Turiddu .... Rinaldi (d

Followed by:

I PAGLIACCI

Same cast as April 10 except:

Tonio .... Elvira
Nedda .... Soviero
Silvio .... Jamerson

April 27

CARMEN

Same cast as February 23 (m) except:

Zuniga .... Steele
Micaëla .... Malfitano
Don José .... Scano

Carmen .... Grillo
Frasquita .... Derr
Mercédès .... Piland
Lillas Pastia,
  Guide .... Harper,
     (s, Romaguera)
Escamillo ...... Darrenkamp
Remendado .... Marek
Dancairo .... Billings

Fall 1975 (AUGUST 27 – NOVEMBER 9)

Female artists
Adler, Arlene
Armstrong, Karan
Arroyo, Martina†
Ballard, Earline
Bergquist, Eleanor
Bible, Frances
Brooks, Patricia
Christos, Marianna*
Ciraulo, Marianna
Colt, Ethel Barrymore
Costa-Greenspon, Muriel
Craig, Patricia
Curry, Diane
Curtin, Phyllis†
Dale, Clamma*
Dean, Laura*
De Rosa, Judith
Derr, Emily
Dunn, Mignon
Faull, Ellen
Fowles, Glenys
Haley, Elizabeth
Harris, Hilda
Hegierski, Kathleen
Hocher, Barbara
Ito, Yoshi
Kehrig, Diana
Lee, Sung Sook*
Malfitano, Catherine
Mathes, Rachel
Meier, Johanna
Neblett, Carol
Niska, Maralin
Palmer, Roberta*
Piland, Jeanne
Randazzo, Arlene
Randazzo, Maria*
Robinson, Faye
Rolandi, Gianna*
Schauler, Eileen
Shade, Nancy
Sills, Beverly
Soviero, Diana
Stapp, Olivia
Tatum, Nancy*
Thomson, Heather
Toro, Puli
Walker, Sandra
Wells, Patricia
Wildes, Rose

Male artists
Alexander, John
Bailey, Norman*

Baker, Alan*
Bentley, Ronald
Billings, James
Carreras, José
Clatworthy, David
Collins, Kenneth*
Cossa, Dominic
Crofoot, Alan
Darrenkamp, John
Densen, Irwin
Diaz, Justino†
Di Giuseppe, Enrico
Di Loreto, Gian
Elvira, Pablo
Fazah, Adib
Fekula, Peter*
Fisher, Robert
Fredricks, Richard
Gill, Richard T.
Glaze, Gary
Griffith, David
Hale, Robert
Harper, Talmage
Hensel, Howard
Holloway, David
Jamerson, Thomas
Justus, William
Kness, Richard
Lankston, John
Ledbetter, William
Lowery, Melvin
Malamood, Herman
Malas, Spiro
Marek, Dan
Mauro, Ermanno
McDonald, William
McGrath, Matthew*
McKee, Richard
Nagy, Robert
Neill, William*
Novick, Melvyn
Palay, Elliot
Pane, Tullio
Park, Richard
Paul, Robert
Pierson, Edward
Poll, Melvyn
Price, Henry*
Ramey, Samuel
Roe, Charles
Romaguera, Joaquin
Ronson, David
Roy, Will
Scano, Gaetano
Sandor, John*

Sergi, James*
Siena, Jerold
Sims, Jack
Smith, David Rae
Steele, Philip
Taylor, Richard
Theyard, Harry†
Titus, Alan
Ukena, Paul
White, Willard
Worth, Coley
Yule, Don

Conductors
Effron, David
Hauser, Alexis
Irving, Robert†
Keene, Christopher
Martelli, Luigi
Pallo, Imre
Rudel, Julius
Somogi, Judith
Wendelken-Wilson, Charles

Chorus master
Gray, George Branson

Associate chorus master
Somogi, Judith

Solo dancers
Balestracci, Sandra
Galan, Esperanza
Gregory, Cynthia†

Horvath, Juliu
Martins, Peter†
Rubino, Michael
Seetoo, Dennis

Choreographers
Andrew, Thomas
Balanchine, George†
Birch, Patricia
Leporska, Zoya

Directors
Auerbach, Cynthia*
Bakman, Patrick
Caldwell, Sarah
Capobianco, Tito
Corsaro, Frank
Cox, John*
Denda, Elena
Donnell, Bruce*

* New artist
† Guest artist at the Norman Treigle Memorial Concert, October 27, 1975.

* New artist

* New artist

Eddleman, Jack
Freedman, Gerald
Getke, Richard
Hicks, David
Mann, Theodore
Mansouri, Lofti*
Presnell, Steve
Strasfogel, Ian
Yannopoulos, Dino

Designers
Aldredge, Theoni V.
Barcelo, Randy
Campbell, Patton
Chase, Ronald
Colt, Alvin
Eck, Marsha Louis
Evans, Lloyd
Fletcher, Robert
Larkey, Joan
Lee, Ming Cho
Montresor, Beni
Pond, Helen
Schmidt, Douglas W.
Senn, Herbert
Toms, Carl
Varona, José
Venza, Jac
Wittstein, Ed

* New artist

August 27

SALOME (R. Strauss)

Conductor .... Rudel

Narraboth .... Taylor
Page .... Piland
1st Soldier .... McKee
2nd Soldier .... Densen
Cappadocian .... Fisher
Salome .... Niska
Slave .... Romaguera
Jochanaan .... Justus
Herodes .... Neill (d)
Herodias .... Bible
1st Jew .... Siena
2nd Jew .... Lankston
3rd Jew .... Lowery
4th Jew .... Griffith
5th Jew .... Steele
1st Nazarene .... Ramey
2nd Nazarene .... Marek

August 28

I PURITANI (Bellini)

Conductor .... Rudel

Riccardo .... Elvira
Bruno .... Siena
Elvira .... Sills
Enrichetta .... Curry
Giorgio .... Hale
Gualtiero .... Densen
Arturo .... Di Giuseppe

August 29

DIE FLEDERMAUS (J. Strauss)
(English version by
Ruth and Thomas Martin)

Stage director .... Getke
Conductor .... Hauser

Alfred .... Glaze
Adele .... A. Randazzo

Rosalinda .... Meier
Eisenstein .... Titus
Blind .... Romaguera
Falke .... Holloway
Frank .... Malas
Sally .... Toro
Ivan .... Sims
Prince Orlofsky ...... Smith
Frosch .... Worth
Solo dancers .... Balestracci,
                  Galan; Horvath

August 30 (m)

TURANDOT (Puccini)

Conductor .... Rudel

Mandarin .... Densen
Liù .... Robinson
Calaf .... Mauro
Timur .... Ramey
Turandot .... Ballard
Ping .... Jamerson
Pang .... Griffith
Pong .... Lankston
Emperor .... Romaguera

August 30

LA TRAVIATA (Verdi)

Conductor .... Martelli

Violetta .... Armstrong
Flora .... Walker
Douphol .... Fisher
D'Obigny .... Ledbetter
Dr. Grenvil .... Yule
Gaston .... Lowery
Alfredo .... Scano
Annina .... Toro
Giuseppe .... Romaguera
Germont .... Fredricks
Messenger .... Harper
Solo dancer .... Galan

August 31 (m)

I PURITANI

Same cast as August 28

August 31

DIE FLEDERMUS

Same cast as August 29 except:

Adele .... Haley

September 2

TURANDOT

Same cast as August 30 (m)

September 3

I PURITANI

Same cast as August 28 except:

Conductor .... Keene

Riccardo .... Fredricks
Elvira .... A. Randazzo
Enrichetta .... Hegierski
Arturo .... Sandor (d)

September 4

SALOME

Same cast as August 27

September 5

DIE FLEDERMAUS

Same cast as August 29 except:

Conductor .... Pallo

September 6 (m)

LA TRAVIATA

Same cast as August 30 except:

Gaston .... Marek

September 6

CARMEN (Bizet)

Conductor .... Pallo

Morales .... Jamerson
Andrès .... Yule
Zuniga .... McKee
Micaëla .... Robinson
Don José .... Collins (d)
Carmen .... Stapp
Frasquita .... Ito
Mercédès .... Piland
Lillas Pastia,
  Guide .... Romaguera
Escamillo ...... Darrenkamp
Remendado .... Marek
Dancairo .... Ledbetter

September 7 (m)

LA BOHÈME (Puccini)

Conductor .... Martelli

Rodolfo .... Pane
Marcello .... Cossa
Colline .... Hale
Schaunard .... Jamerson
Benoit .... Yule
Mimi .... Niska
Parpignol .... Romaguera
Musetta .... Bergquist
Alcindoro .... Billings
Guards .... Park, Bentley

September 7

THE DAUGHTER OF THE
REGIMENT (Donizetti)
First performance by The New
York City Opera Company
(*La Fille du régiment*;
English version by
Ruth and Thomas Martin)

Directed by ... Mansouri (d)
Stage director ... Donnell (d)
Designer .... Montreso
Lighting .... Sondheime
Conductor ...... Wendelken
                       Wilso

Hortensius .... Ronso
Marquise ... Costa-Greenspo
Peasant .... Sergi (d
Sulpice .... Mala
Marie .... Sil
Tonio .... Di Giusepp
Corporal .... Ledbette
Dancing master ..... Rubin
Duchess .... Co
Notary .... Lower

September 9

THE DAUGHTER OF THE
REGIMENT

Same cast as September 7

September 10

TURANDOT

Same cast as August 30 (m)
except:

Liù .... Malfitano
Timur .... Gill

September 11

LES CONTES D'HOFFMANN
(Offenbach)

Stage director .... Denda
Conductor .... Rudel

Lindorff .... Ramey
Andrès .... Siena
Luther .... Steele
Nathanaël .... Lowery
Hermann .... Jamerson
Nicklausse .... Harris
Hoffmann .... Scano
Olympia .... Rolandi (d)
Spalanzani .... Billings
Cochenille .... Siena
Coppélius .... Ramey
Giulietta .... Shade
Pittichinaccio .... Siena
Schlémil .... Ledbetter
Dappertutto .... Ramey
Antonia .... Craig
Crespel .... Densen
Frantz .... Siena
Dr. Miracle .... Ramey
Mother .... Curry

September 12

THE DAUGHTER OF THE
REGIMENT

Same cast as September 7

September 13 (m)

SALOME

Same cast as August 27 except:

Herodes .... Nagy
5th Jew .... Yule
1st Nazarene .... Steele

September 13

CARMEN

Same cast as September 6

September 14 (m)

ARIADNE AUF NAXOS
(R. Strauss)
(English translation of
prologue and opera by
Lewis Sydenham,
revised by Julius Rudel)

Conductor .... Rudel

Major-Domo .... Smith
Music Master ...... Holloway
Composer .... Stapp

Wigmaker .... Romaguera
Echo .... Hocher
Najade .... Derr
Dryade .... Curry
Lackey .... Densen
Dancing Master,
  Scaramuccio ..... Lankston
Zerbinetta .... Rolandi
Tenor, Bacchus ... Alexander
Officer .... Ledbetter
Prima donna,
  Ariadne .... Meier
Harlequin .... Jamerson
Truffaldin .... McKee
Brighella .... Lowery

September 14

LA BOHÈME

Same cast as September 7 (m)
except:

Mimi .... Malfitano

September 16

MADAMA BUTTERFLY (Puccini)

Conductor .... Martelli

Pinkerton .... Poll
Goro .... Billings
Suzuki .... Walker
Sharpless .... Jamerson
Butterfly .... Craig
Imperial
  Commissioner ... Ledbetter
Registrar,
  Yamadori .... Lankston
The Bonze .... Densen
Trouble .... Di Loreto
Kate Pinkerton .... Hegierski

September 17

THE DAUGHTER OF THE
REGIMENT

Same cast as September 7
except:

Conductor .... Somogi
Tonio .... McDonald

September 18

DIE FLEDERMAUS

Same cast as August 29 except:

Conductor .... Pallo

Alfred .... Griffith
Falke .... Cossa
Sally .... Kehrig
Prince Orlofsky ... Baker (d)
Frosch .... Billings

September 19

SALOME

Same cast as August 27 except:

Page .... Hegierski
Jochanaan .... Pierson
Herodes .... Crofoot
5th Jew .... Yule
1st Nazarene .... Steele

September 20 (m)

DIE TOTE STADT (Korngold)

Conductor .... Pallo

Brigitta .... Curry
Frank .... Roe
Paul .... Alexander
Marietta .... Neblett
Victorin .... Lankston
Albert .... Siena
Juliette .... Wildes
Lucienne .... Toro
Fritz .... Cossa
Gaston .... Seetoo

September 20

LES CONTES D'HOFFMANN

Same cast as September 11

September 21 (m)

TURANDOT

Same cast as August 30 (m)
except:

Liù .... Malfitano
Timur .... Gill
Turandot .... Tatum (d)

September 21

CARMEN

Same cast as September 6
except:

Micaëla .... Fowles
Don José .... Malamood,
                (s, Collins)
Carmen .... Dunn

September 23

THE DAUGHTER OF THE
REGIMENT

Same cast as September 7
except:

Conductor .... Somogi

Marquise .... Walker
Sulpice .... McKee
Tonio .... McDonald

September 24

DIE TOTE STADT

Same cast as September 20 (m)

September 25

MADAMA BUTTERFLY

Same cast as September 16
except:

Butterfly .... Niska

September 26

LA BOHÈME

Same cast as September 7 (m)
except:

Marcello .... Elvira
Schaunard .... Paul
Mimi .... Malfitano

September 27 (m)

H.M.S. PINAFORE (Sullivan)

Directed by .... Eddleman
Choreographer ...... Andrew
Lighting .... Sondheimer
Conductor .... Effron

Captain Corcoran ...... Roe
Bill Bobstay .... Ledbetter
Bob Becket .... Densen
Little Buttercup ...... Costa-
Greenspon
Dick Deadeye .... Ukena
Ralph Rackstraw ...... Glaze
Josephine .... Soviero
Sir Joseph Porter .... Billings
Cousin Hebe .... Toro

September 27

ARIADNE AUF NAXOS

Same cast as September 14 (m)
except:

Major-Domo .... Yule
Tenor, Bacchus .... Kness

September 28 (m)

LA TRAVIATA

Same cast as August 30 except:

Violetta .... Niska,
(s, Tourné)
Gaston .... Marek
Alfredo .... Price (d)
Germont .... Fazah,
(s, Elvira)

(Note: Teresa Tourné was
not to sing with the company
this season.)

September 28

TURANDOT

Same cast as August 30 (m)
except:

Turandot .... Tatum
Emperor .... Lowery

September 30

LES CONTES D'HOFFMANN

Same cast as September 11
except:

Lindorff .... Hale
Luther .... Yule
Olympia .... Haley
Coppélius .... Hale
Dappertutto .... Hale
Antonia .... Dale (d)
Crespel .... Steele
Dr. Miracle .... Hale

October 1

MADAMA BUTTERFLY

Same cast as September 16
except:

Registrar,
Yamadori .... Marek
Trouble .... McGrath (d)

October 2

SALOME

Same cast as August 27 except:

Narraboth .... Lankston
Page .... Hegierski
Salome .... Ciraulo
Herodes .... Nagy
Herodias .... Stapp
2nd Jew .... Novick
5th Jew .... Yule
1st Nazarene .... Steele

October 3

DIE TOTE STADT

Same cast as September 20 (m)
except:

Marietta .... Shade
Fritz .... Jamerson

October 4 (m)

CARMEN

Same cast as September 6
except:

Zuniga .... Steele
Frasquita .... Wildes
Escamillo .... Justus

October 4

H.M.S. PINAFORE

Same cast as September 27 (m)

October 5 (m)

LES CONTES D'HOFFMANN

Same cast as September 11
except:

Conductor .... Effron

Luther .... Yule
Nicklausse .... Piland
Hoffmann .... Scano
(s, Taylor)
Giulietta .... Dale
Crespel .... Steele

October 5

THE MARRIAGE OF FIGARO
(Mozart)
(English version by
Ruth and Thomas Martin)

Conductor .... Keene

Figaro .... Malas
Susanna .... Fowles
Bartolo .... McKee
Marcellina .... Walker
Cherubino .... Harris
Almaviva .... Clatworthy
Basilio .... Siena
Countess .... Niska
Antonio .... Yule
Curzio .... Romaguera
Barbarina .... Wildes
Solo dancer .... Galan

October 7

MANON LESCAUT (Puccini)

Stage director .. Auerbach (d)
Conductor .... Martelli

Edmondo .... Griffith
Lescaut .... Fredricks
Des Grieux .... Collins
Innkeeper .... Ronson
Geronte .... Malas
Manon Lescaut ...... Craig
Hairdresser .... Rubino
Musician .... Piland
Dancing master .... Lankston
Sergeant .... Yule
Lamplighter .... Lowery
Officer .... Densen

October 8

LA TRAVIATA

Same cast as August 30 except:

Violetta .... Niska
Flora .... Hegierski
Gaston .... Marek
Alfredo .... Poll
Germont .... Elvira

October 9

A VILLAGE ROMEO AND JULIET
(Delius)

Stage director ...... Bakman
Conductor .... Keene

Marti .... Roy
Sali, as a child ... Fekula (d)
Vreli, as a child .... Dean (d)
Manz .... Roe
Dark Fiddler ...... Holloway
Sali .... Taylor
Vreli .... Soviero
Stoned girl .... Piland
Wild girl .... Wildes
Doll and puppet man .. Hensel
Knick knack man .... Ronson
Wheel of fortune
woman .... Hocher
Fruit man .... Paul
Pastry woman .... Wildes
Cheap jewelry
woman .... Hegierski
Three women .... Kehrig,
Adler, Toro
Two men .... Ledbetter, Yule
Poor horn player ..... Hensel
Hunchbacked bass
fiddle player .... Billings
Bargemen .... Roe,
Ledbetter, Lowery

October 10

CARMEN

Same cast as September 6
except:

Morales .... Fisher
Zuniga .... Steele
Micaëla .... Derr
Frasquita .... Wildes
Remendado .... Lankston,
(s, Marek)

October 11 (m)

H.M.S. PINAFORE

Same cast as September 27 (m) except:

Josephine .... Fowles

October 11

MADAMA BUTTERFLY

Same cast as September 16 except:

Goro .... Romaguera
Sharpless .... Fredricks
Butterfly .... Niska

October 12 (m)

DIE FLEDERMAUS

Same cast as August 29 except:

Conductor .... Pallo

Alfred .... McDonald
Adele .... Haley
Rosalinda .... Armstrong
Falke .... Cossa
Sally .... Kehrig

October 12

LUCIA DI LAMMERMOOR
(Donizetti)

Stage director ..... Auerbach
Conductor .... Martelli

Alisa .... Hegierski
Edgardo .... Scano
Normanno .... Romaguera
Lucia .... Brooks
Enrico .... Elvira
Raimondo .... Hale
Arturo .... Griffith,
                (s, Marek)

October 14

A VILLAGE ROMEO AND JULIET

Same cast as October 9

October 15

LA BOHÈME

Same cast as September 7 (m) except:

Conductor .... Pallo

Rodolfo .... Poll
Schaunard .... Paul
Benoit .... Densen

October 16

CARMEN

Same cast as September 6 except:

Morales .... Fisher
Zuniga .... Steele
Micaëla .... Derr,
                (s, Fowles)
Don José .... Scano
Carmen .... Curry
Frasquita .... De Rosa
Mercédès .... Hegierski

October 17

LA TRAVIATA

Same cast as August 30 except:

Violetta .... Thomson
Flora .... Hegierski
Dr. Grenvil .... Densen
Gaston .... Novick
Alfredo .... Poll
Germont .... Elvira

October 18 (m)

THE MARRIAGE OF FIGARO

Same cast as October 5 except:

Figaro .... Hale
Almaviva .... Fredricks
Countess .... Meier

October 18

MANON LESCAUT

Same cast as October 7 except:

Lescaut .... Holloway
Des Grieux ...... Malamood
Manon Lescaut .... Niska

October 19 (m)

DIE TOTE STADT

Same cast as September 20 (m) except:

Paul .... Neill
Marietta .... Shade

October 19

MADAMA BUTTERFLY

Same cast as September 16 except:

Pinkerton .... Scano
Goro .... Romaguera
Sharpless .... Fazah
Butterfly .... Lee (d)
Trouble .... McGrath

October 21

THE MARRIAGE OF FIGARO

Same cast as October 5 except:

Figaro .... Hale
Cherubino .... Piland
Almaviva .... Fredricks
Barbarina .... De Rosa

October 22

CARMEN

Same cast as September 6 except:

Conductor .... Somogi
Morales .... Fisher
Zuniga .... Steele
Micaëla .... Fowles
Frasquita .... De Rosa
Mercédès .... Hegierski

October 23

DIE MEISTERSINGER (Wagner)
New production
(English text by John Gutman)

Directed by .... Cox (d)
Designer .... Toms
Choreographer ...... Andrew
Lighting .... Sondheimer
Conductor .... Rudel

Walther .... Alexander
Eva .... Meier
Magdalene .... Curry
David .... Glaze
Pogner .... Gill
Beckmesser .... Billings
Vogelgesang .... Hensel
Nachtigall .... Fisher
Hans Sachs .... Bailey (d)
Kothner .... Holloway
Ortel .... McKee
Zorn .... Romaguera
Moser .... Lowery
Eisslinger .... Marek
Foltz .... Densen
Schwarz .... Steele
Night Watchman .... Paul

October 24

A VILLAGE ROMEO AND JULIET

Same cast as October 9 except:

Vreli, as a
    child .... M. Randazzo (d)
Dark Fiddler ...... Jamerson
Sali .... Griffith

October 25 (m)

TURANDOT

Same cast as August 30 (m) except:

Liù .... Christos (d)
Calaf .... Collins
Timur .... White
Turandot .... Mathes
Emperor .... Lowery

October 25

DIE FLEDERMAUS

Same cast as August 29 except:

Conductor .... Pallo

Alfred .... McDonald
Adele .... Haley
Rosalinda .... Armstrong
Eisenstein .... Roe
Blind .... Siena
Falke .... Coșsa
Frank .... McKee

October 26 (m)

DIE MEISTERSINGER

Same cast as October 23

October 26

MADAMA BUTTERFLY

Same cast as September 16 except:

Pinkerton .... Scano
Goro .... Romaguera
Sharpless .... Fredricks
Butterfly .... Lee
Trouble .... McGrath

October 27

A memorial tribute to Norman Treigle, for the benefit of the Norman Treigle Memorial Fund. All artists volunteered their services.

Director .... Patrick Bakman
Lighting
  by ...... Hans Sondheimer
Narration
  devised by .. Rosanne Klass,
                Martin Sokol
Narrator .... Beverly Sills
Conductor ..... Julius Rudel

THE MARRIAGE OF FIGARO

Overture .... Orchestra

LA BOHÈME

Addio dolce
  svegliare .... Craig, Shade,
              Malamood, Cossa

DON GIOVANNI

Or sai chi l'onore ..... Meier

CARMEN

Je vais danser
  en votre honneur ... Stapp,
                Harry Theyard

RIGOLETTO

Bella figlia
  dell'amore .. Brooks, Costa-
    Greenspon, Di Giuseppe,
                    Fredricks

SUSANNAH

The trees on the
  mountains ... Phyllis Curtin

GIULIO CESARE

Tal di
  ciascuno .. Norman Treigle
            (on RCA records)
PAS DE DEUX (Tschaikovsky)
Choreographed
  by ..... George Balanchine
Conducted by .. Robert Irving
Dancers ... Gregory, Martins

AIDA

Fu la sorte .. Martina Arroyo,
                    Dunn
LES CONTES D'HOFFMANN
Une poupee aux yeux ... Bible

LOUISE

Depuis le jour .... Sills

FAUST

Anges purs, anges
  radieux! ..Niska, Alexander,
                Justino Diaz

MEFISTOFELE

Salve Regina! .... Chorus

(Note: All the singers who participated were currently members of The New York City Opera Company except Martina Arroyo, Phyllis Curtin, Justino Diaz, and Harry Theyard. Neither of the dancers was associated with City Opera (although both subsequently joined the company), and they, Balanchine, and Irving furnished their services as a tribute to Treigle's overwhelming talent.)

October 28

DIE MEISTERSINGER

Same cast as October 23

October 29

THE TURN OF THE SCREW
(Britten)

Conductor .... Keene

Prologue .... Siena
Guardian .... Lankston
Governess .... Schauler
Miles .... Fekula
Flora .... Dean
Mrs. Grose .... Faull
Quint .... Lankston
Miss Jessel .... Derr

October 30

LA BOHÈME

Same cast as September 7 (m) except:

Conductor .... Pallo

Rodolfo .... Carreras
Marcello ...:...... Fredricks
Colline .... Roy
Musetta .... Palmer (d)
Alcindoro .... Ronson

October 31

DIE MEISTERSINGER

Same cast as October 23 except:

Eva .... Bergquist
Magdalene .... Walker
Pogner .... Roy

November 1 (m)

H.M.S. PINAFORE

Same cast as September 27 (m) except:

Captain Corcoran .. Fredricks
Ralph Rackstraw .... Hensel
Josephine .... Fowles

November 1

DIE FLEDERMAUS

Same cast as August 29 except:

Conductor .... Pallo

Alfred .... McDonald
Adele .... Haley
Rosalinda .... Craig
Eisenstein .... Roe
Blind .... Siena
Falke .... Cossa
Frank .... McKee
Sally .... Kehrig
Frosch .... Yule,
                (s, Worth)

November 2 (m)

LUCIA DI LAMMERMOOR

Same cast as October 12 except:

Edgardo .... Carreras
Normanno .... Siena,
              (s, Romaguera)
Enrico .... Fazah
Arturo .... Marek

November 2

DIE MEISTERSINGER

Same cast as October 23 except:

Walther .... Palay

November 4

LA BOHÈME

Same cast as September 7 (m) except:

Conductor .... Pallo

Rodolfo .... Malamood
Marcello .... Fredricks
Colline .... Roy
Mimi .... Craig
Parpignol .... Davis,
              (s, Romaguera)
Musetta .... Palmer

November 5

DIE MEISTERSINGER

Same cast as October 23 except:

Eva .... Bergquist
Magdalene .... Walker
David .... Griffith
Pogner .... Roy
Kothner .... Paul
Zorn .... Lankston,
              (s, Romaguera)
Night Watchman .... Yule

November 6

LUCIA DI LAMMERMOOR

Same cast as October 12 except:

Normanno .... Siena,
              (s, Romaguera)
Lucia .... A. Randazzo
Raimondo .... Ramey
Arturo .... Marek

November 7

DIE MEISTERSINGER

Same cast as October 23
except:
Walther .... Palay
Zorn .... Lankston,
(s, Romaguera)

November 8 (m)

THE TURN OF THE SCREW

Same cast as October 29

November 8

MANON LESCAUT

Same cast as October 7 except:
Edmondo .... Siena
Geronte .... Densen
Officer .... Fisher

November 9 (m)

H.M.S. PINAFORE

Same cast as September 27 (m)
except:
Little Buttercup ..... Walker
Ralph Rackstraw ..... Hensel

Josephine .... Hocher
Sir Joseph Porter ...... Baker

November 9

I PURITANI

Same cast as August 28 except:
Conductor .... Keene

Giorgio .... Ramey
Arturo .... Sandor,
(s, Di Giuseppe)
Broadcast performance

Spring 1976 (FEBRUARY 19– APRIL 25)

Female artists
Armstrong, Karan
Ballard, Earline
Bergquist, Eleanor
Bible, Frances
Brooks, Patricia
Campbell, Joan
Clark, Arin*
Colt, Ethel Barrymore
Conrad, Barbara†
Costa-Greenspon, Muriel
Craig, Patricia
Curry, Diane
Dale, Clamma
Daly, Pegge*
Derr, Emily
Faull, Ellen
Fowles, Glenys
Goodman, Margaret*
Haley, Elizabeth
Harris, Hilda
Hegierski, Kathleen
Hynes, Elizabeth*
Ito, Yoshi
Jones, Betty
Kehrig, Diana
Lee, Sung Sook
Little, Gwenlynn
Lynn, Joyce*
Malfitano, Catherine
Marsee, Susanne
Mathes, Rachel
Meier, Johanna
Metzger, Rita
Niska, Maralin
Orlando, Valeria
Piland, Jeanne
Randazzo, Arlene
Randazzo, Maria
Reynolds, Myrna*
Robinson, Faye
Rolandi, Gianna
Schauler, Eileen
Shaulis, Jane*

Shields, Alice*
Sills, Beverly
Smith, Alethia*
Stapp, Olivia
Tomanec, Joyce
Toro, Puli
Von Stade, Frederica*
Walker, Sandra
Welting, Ruth
Wildes, Rose
Young, Marie

Male artists
Alexander, John
Baker, Alan
Bartolini, Lando*
Bentley, Ronald
Berberian, Ara
Billings, James
Bohachevsky, George
Castel, Nico
Clark, Lester
Cossa, Dominic
Cowan, Sigmund*
Darrenkamp, John
Davis, Harris
Densen, Irwin
Di Giuseppe, Enrico
Dovel, Kenn
Elvira, Pablo
Farone, Dominick
Fazah, Adib
Fisher, Robert
Fredricks, Richard
Gill, Richard T.
Glaze, Gary
Green, Jay
Griffith, David
Hale, Robert
Harness, William*
Harper, Talmage
Hensel, Howard
Holloway, David
Jamerson, Thomas
Justus, William
Kingman, Dan
Lankston, John

Ledbetter, William
Lloyd, David
Lowery, Melvin
Ludgin, Chester
Malamood, Herman
Malas, Spiro
Marek, Dan
Mauro, Ermanno
McDonald, William
McGrath, Matthew
McKee, Richard
Morrison, Ray*
Nagy, Robert
Nelson, Richard
Novick, Melvyn
Palay, Elliot
Pane, Tullio
Park, Richard
Paul, Robert
Pierson, Edward
Poll, Melvyn
Pool, Gary*
Presto
Price, Henry
Ramey, Samuel
Roe, Charles
Romaguera, Joaquin
Ronson, David
Roy, Will
Sandor, John
Scano, Gaetano
Sergi, James
Siena, Jerold
Smith, David Rae
Steele, Philip
Stilwell, Richard
Taylor, Richard
Ukena, Paul
Vega, Robert
Voketaitis, Arnold
Williams, Ralph*
Worth, Coley
Yule, Don

Conductors
Bernardi, Mario
Bertini, Gary*
Effron, David

* New artist
† Barbara Conrad had previously appeared with the company under the name of Barbara Smith-Conrad.

* New artist

* New artist

Gray, George Branson
Martelli, Luigi
Miner, John*
Pallo, Imre
Rudel, Julius
Somogi, Judith
Wendelken-Wilson, Charles

Chorus master
Gray, George Branson

Director for electronic sound
Maronn, Eckhard*

Solo dancers
Balestracci, Sandra
Galan, Esperanza

Anthony, Steve*
Calvert, John*
Horvath, Juliu
Mann III, Fred*
Mattson, Wayne*
Nolfi, Ed*
Rubino, Michael
Swanson, Don*

Choreographers
Andrew, Thomas
Birch, Patricia
Field, Ron*

Directors
Auerbach, Cynthia
Bakman, Patrick
Capobianco, Tito
Corsaro, Frank
Cox, John
Eddleman, Jack
Freedman, Gerald
Getke, Richard
Hicks, David
Mansouri, Lotfi
Presnell, Steve
Prince, Harold*
Psacharopoulos, Nikos
Strasfogel, Ian
Yannopoulos, Dino

Designers
Aldredge, Theoni V.
Barcelo, Randy
Bardon, Henry*
Campbell, Patton
Evans, Lloyd
Fletcher, Robert
Greenwood, Jane
Hall, Peter J.*
Lee, Eugene*
Lee, Franne*
Montresor, Beni
Oenslager, Donald
Schmidt, Douglas W.
Sprott, Eoin
Toms, Carl
Varona, José
Wexler, Peter
Wittstein, Ed

    * New artist

February 19

DIE MEISTERSINGER (Wagner)
(English text by John Gutman)

Conductor .... Rudel

Walther .... Alexander
Eva .... Meier

Magdalene .... Curry
David .... Griffith
Pogner .... Gill
Beckmesser .... Billings
Vogelgesang .... Hensel
Nachtigall .... Fisher
Hans Sachs ...... Berberian
Kothner .... Holloway
Ortel .... McKee
Zorn .... Romaguera
Moser .... Lowery
Eisslinger .... Marek
Foltz .... Densen
Schwarz .... Steele
Night Watchman ...... Paul

February 20

MADAMA BUTTERFLY (Puccini)

Conductor .... Martelli

Pinkerton .... Scano
Goro .... Siena
Suzuki .... Walker
Sharpless ...... Darrenkamp
Butterfly .... Niska
Imperial
  Commissioner ... Ledbetter
Registrar,
  Yamadori ...... Lankston
The Bonze .... Densen
Trouble .... McGrath
Kate Pinkerton .... Toro

February 21 (m)

CARMEN (Bizet)

Conductor .... Pallo

Morales .... Jamerson
Andrès .... Yule
Zuniga .... Steele
Micaëla .... Lee
Don José .... Malamood
Carmen .... Curry,
           (s, Stapp)
Frasquita .... Wildes
Mercédès .... Hegierski
Lillas Pastia,
  guide .... Romaguera
Escamillo .... Justus
Remendado .... Lankston
Dancairo .... Baker

February 21

LA TRAVIATA (Verdi)

Conductor .... Martelli

Violetta .... Brooks
Flora .... Walker
Douphol .... Fisher
D'Obigny .... Ledbetter
Dr. Grenvil .... Yule
Gaston .... Lowery
Alfredo .... Sandor
Annina .... Toro
Giuseppe ...... Romaguera
Germont .... Elvira
Messenger .... Harper
Solo dancer .... Galan

February 22 (m)

DIE MEISTERSINGER

Same cast as February 19
except:

Conductor .... Pallo

Magdalene .... Walker
Ortel .... Ronson

February 22

H.M.S. PINAFORE (Sullivan)

Conductor .... Miner (d)

Captain Corcoran .. Fredricks
Bill Bobstay ...... Ledbetter
Bob Becket .... Steele
Little Buttercup ...... Costa-
           Greenspon
Dick Deadeye ...... Densen
Ralph Rackstraw ...... Price
Josephine .... Fowles
Sir Joseph Porter .... Billings
Cousin Hebe .... Toro

February 25

DIE MEISTERSINGER

Same cast as February 19
except:

Conductor .... Pallo

Walther .... Palay
Eva .... Bergquist
David .... Glaze
Pogner .... Roy
Beckmesser ..... D. R. Smith
Ortel .... Ronson

February 26

MADAMA BUTTERFLY

Same cast as February 20

February 27

CARMEN

Same cast as February 21 (m)
except:

Don José .... Mauro
Carmen .... Stapp

February 28 (m)

LA TRAVIATA

Same cast as February 21

February 28

LA BOHÈME (Puccini)

Stage director ..... Auerbach
Conductor .... Martelli

Rodolfo .... Pane
Marcello .... Fredricks
Colline .... Hale
Schaunard .... Fisher
Benoit .... Yule

Mimi .... Craig
Parpignol .... Romaguera
Musetta .... Bergquist
Alcindoro .... Billings
Guards .... Park, Bentley

February 29 (m)

DIE FLEDERMAUS (J. Strauss)
(English version by
Ruth and Thomas Martin)

Conductor .... Pallo

Alfred .... Glaze
Adele .... Haley
Rosalinda .... Armstrong
Eisenstein .... Roe
Blind .... Romaguera
Falke .... Cossa
Frank .... Malas
Sally .... Toro
Ivan .... Sims
Prince Orlofsky .... Baker
Frosch .... Billings
Solo dancers ..... Balestracci,
Galan; Horvath

February 29

IL RITORNO D'ULISSE IN PATRIA
(Monteverdi—
realized and orchestrated by
Raymond Leppard)
New York premiere

Directed by .... Strasfogel
Scenic designer ..... Schmidt
Costume designer . . Greenwood
Lighting .... Sondheimer
Conductor .... Bernardi

L'Umana
Fragilità ...... Shields (d)
Il Tempo .... Densen
La Fortuna .... Curry
Amore .... Wildes
Penelope ..... Von Stade (d)
Ericlea .... Walker
Nettuno .... Berberian
Giove .... Griffith
Ulisse .... Stilwell
Minerva .... Harris
Melanto .... Hegierski
Eurimaco .... Hensel
Eumete .... Lloyd
Iro .... Castel
Telemaco .... Price
Artinoro .... Roy
Pisandro .... Lankston
Amfinomo .... Lowery

March 3

DIE MEISTERSINGER

Same cast as February 19
except:

Conductor .... Pallo

Walther .... Palay
David .... Griffiths,
(s, Glaze)
Pogner .... Roy
Kothner .... Paul

Ortel .... Ronson
Night Watchman .... Yule

March 2

THE DAUGHTER OF THE
REGIMENT (Donizetti)
(English version by
Ruth and Thomas Martin)

Stage director .... Presnell
Conductor .... Somogi,
(s, Wendelken-Wilson)

Hortensius .... Ronson
Marquise ... Costa-Greenspon
Peasant .... Sergi
Sulpice .... Malas
Marie .... Sills
Tonio .... Di Giuseppe
Corporal .... Ledbetter
Dancing master ...... Rubino
Duchess .... Colt
Notary .... Lowery

March 4

MADAMA BUTTERFLY

Same cast as February 20
except:

Butterfly .... Lee
The Bonze .... Steele

March 5

H.M.S. PINAFORE

Same cast as February 22

March 6 (m)

THE DAUGHTER OF THE
REGIMENT

Same cast as March 3 except:

Conductor ...... Wendelken-
Wilson

March 6

TURANDOT (Puccini)

Conductor .... Rudel

Mandarin .... Densen
Liù .... Robinson
Calaf .... Mauro
Timur .... Gill
Turandot .... Ballard
Ping .... Jamerson
Pang .... Griffith
Pong .... Lankston
Emperor .... Romaguera

March 7 (m)

DIE MEISTERSINGER

Same cast as February 19
except:

Pogner .... Roy,
(s, Gill)
Kothner .... Paul
Ortel .... Ronson
Night Watchman .... Yule

March 7

LA BOHÈME

Same cast as February 28
except:

Mimi .... Niska
Musetta .... Dale
Alcindoro .... Ronson,
(s, Billings)

March 9

MADAMA BUTTERFLY

Same cast as February 20
except:

Pinkerton .... Malamood
Goro .... Romaguera
Suzuki .... Curry
Sharpless .... Fazah
The Bonze .... Steele
Kate Pinkerton .... Hegierski

March 10

IL RITORNO D'ULISSE IN PATRIA

Same cast as February 29

March 11

THE DAUGHTER OF THE
REGIMENT

Same cast as March 3 except:

Conductor ...... Wendelken-
Wilson

Tonio .... Harness (d)

March 12

CARMEN

Same cast as February 21 (m)
except:

Micaëla .... Derr
Don José .... Scano
Carmen .... Conrad
Escamillo .... Hale

March 13 (m)

UN BALLO IN MASCHERA
(Verdi)

Conductor .... Rudel

Count Horn .... Pierson
Count Ribbing .... Densen
Oscar .... Fowles
Gustavo .... Mauro
Renato .... Elvira
Chief Justice .... Hensel
Ulrica .... Bible
Silvano .... Fisher
Servant .... Baker
Amelia .... Meier

March 13

SALOME (R. Strauss)

Stage director .... Getke
Conductor .... Rudel

Narraboth .... Taylor
Page .... Piland
1st Soldier .... McKee

2nd Soldier .... Densen
Cappadocian .... Fisher
Salome .... Niska
Slave .... Romaguera
Jochanaan .... Justus
Herodes .... Nagy
Herodias .... Bible
1st Jew .... Siena
2nd Jew .... Lankston
3rd Jew .... Lowery
4th Jew .... Griffith
5th Jew .... Yule
1st Nazarene .... Steele
2nd Nazarene .... Marek

March 14 (m)

H.M.S. PINAFORE

Same cast as February 22
except:

Conductor .... Effron
Little Buttercup ...... Walker
Ralph Rackstraw ...... Glaze
Josephine .... Wildes

March 14

THE MARRIAGE OF FIGARO
(Mozart)
(English version by
Ruth and Thomas Martin)

Conductor .... Effron

Figaro .... Ramey
Susanna .... Fowles
Bartolo .... McKee
Marcellina .... Walker
Cherubino .... Marsee
Almaviva .... Darrenkamp
Basilio .... Siena
Countess .... Jones
Antonio .... Yule
Curzio .... Romaguera
Babarina .... Wildes
Solo dancer .... Galan

March 16

DIE FLEDERMAUS

Same cast as February 29 (m)
except:

Alfred .... McDonald
Falke .... Holloway

March 18

LUCREZIA BORGIA (Donizetti)
First performance by The New
York City Opera Company
in New York

Directed by ..... Capobianco
Scenic designer .. Bardon (d)
Costume designer ... Hall (d)
Choreographer ...... Andrew
Lighting .... Sondheimer
Conductor .... Rudel

Apostolo Gazella ..... Fisher
Ascanio Petrucci .... Yule
Maffio Orsini .... Marsee
Gubetta .... McKee

Oloferno Vitellozzo ... Hensel
Jeppo Liverotto ...... Lowery
Gennaro .... Scano
Lucrezia Borgia .... Sills
Alfonso .... Fredricks
Rustighello .... Siena
Astolfo .... Baker
Servant .... Vega
Princess Negroni ..... Young

March 19

TURANDOT

Same cast as March 6 except:

Timur .... Berberian

March 20 (m)

MADAMA BUTTERFLY

Same cast as February 20
except:

Conductor .... Gray
Pinkerton .... Poll
Goro .... Romaguera
Suzuki .... Curry
Sharpless .... Fazah
Butterfly .... Lee
The Bonze .... Steele
Kate Pinkerton .... Hegierski

March 20

LA BOHÈME

Same cast as February 28
except:

Marcello .... Elvira
Colline .... Roy
Musetta .... Dale

March 21 (m)

DIE FLEDERMAUS

Same cast as February 29 (m)
except:

Alfred .... McDonald
Falke .... Jamerson

March 21

THE DAUGHTER OF THE
REGIMENT

Same cast as March 3 except:

Conductor ..... Wendelken-
                  Wilson
Marquise .... Walker
Sulpice .... McKee
Tonio .... Harness

March 23

CARMEN

Same cast as February 21 (m)
except:

Micaëla .... Fowles
Don José .... Scano
Carmen .... Stapp

March 25

DIE FLEDERMAUS

Same cast as February 29 (m)
except:

Adele .... A. Randazzo
Sally .... Kehrig
Prince Orlofsky .. D. R. Smith
Frosch .... Worth

March 26

IL RITORNO D'ULISSE IN PATRIA

Same cast as February 29
except:

Giove .... Hensel,
                 (s, Griffith)

March 27 (m)

LUCREZIA BORGIA

Same cast as March 18 except:

Conductor .... Pallo,
                   (s, Rudel)
Gennaro .... Price

March 27

CAVALLERIA RUSTICANA
(Mascagni)

Stage director .... Getke
Conductor .... Martelli
Mamma Lucia .... Curry
Santuzza .... Stapp
Turiddu .... Di Giuseppe
Lola .... Piland
Alfio .... Darrenkamp

Followed by:

I PAGLIACCI (Leoncavallo)

Stage director .... Getke
Conductor .... Martelli
Tonio .... Elvira
Canio .... Malamood
Nedda .... Dale
Beppe .... Siena
Peasants .... Davis,
              Bohachevsky
Silvio .... Jamerson

March 28 (m)

LA TRAVIATA

Same cast as February 21
except:

Alfredo .... Pane
Annina .... A. Smith (d)
Giuseppe .... Davis
Germont .... Cossa

March 28

CARMEN

Same cast as February 21 (m)
except:

Morales .... Fisher
Zuniga .... McKee

Micaëla .... Fowles
Don José .... Scano
Carmen .... Conrad
Frasquita .... Ito
Mercédès .... Piland
Lillas Pastia,
    Guide .... Vega
Remendado .... Siena
Dancairo .... Billings

March 31

LUCREZIA BORGIA

Same cast as March 18 except:

Gennaro .... Price
Alfonso .... Fazah

April 1

ASHMEDAI (Tal)
American premiere
(English version by
Alan Marbe)

Directed by ...... Prince (d)
Scenic designer ... E. Lee (d)
Costume designer ..F. Lee (d)
Choreographer .... Field (d)
Director for electronic
    sound .... Maronn (d)
Lighting ..... Billington (d)
Conductor .... Bertini (d)

Sergeant .... Nolfi (d)
Army .... Anthony (d),
    Calvert (d), Mann
    (d), Mattson (d)
Fire-eater .... Presto
Knife thrower .... Rubino
Juggler .... Green
Ashmedai .... Lankston
Counsellors .... Griffith,
    Jamerson, Ronson
Firechief .... Baker
Prince .... Taylor
Queen .... Schauler
Executioner .... Steele
King .... Ukena
Tailor .... Siena
Daughter .... Rolandi
Mistress of the
    inn .... Craig
Citizen .... Yule
Soldier .... Hensel
Townspeople ..... Daly (d),
    Lynn (d), Metzger
Trumpeter .... Kingman
Drummer ...... Williams (d)
Officer .... Fisher
Runner .... Pool (d)
Rooster .... Swanson (d)

April 2

TURANDOT
Same cast as March 6 except:

Liù .... Malfitano
Calaf .... Malamood
Timur .... Ramey
Emperor .... Lowery

April 3 (m)

LA BOHÈME

Same cast as February 28
except:

Marcello .... Cossa
Colline .... Ramey
Schaunard .... Jamerson
Mimi .... Niska
Parpignol .... Lowery
Musetta .... Dale
Alcindoro .... Ronson

April 3

H.M.S. PINAFORE

Same cast as February 22
except:

Conductor .... Effron

Captain Corcoran .... Roe
Dick Deadeye .... Yule

April 4 (m)

ASHMEDAI

Same cast as April 1

April 4

LUCREZIA BORGIA

Same cast as March 18 except:
Maffio Orsini .... Harris

April 6

ASHMEDAI

Same cast as April 1

April 7

CAVALLERIA RUSTICANA

Same cast as March 27 except:
Turiddu .... Bartolini (d)
Lola .... Toro
Alfio .... Pierson

Followed by:

I PAGLIACCI

Same cast as March 27 except:

Tonio .... Fredricks
Nedda .... Niska
Silvio .... Cossa

April 8

LUCREZIA BORGIA

Same cast as March 18 except:

Apostolo Gazella .. Ledbetter,
    (s, Fisher)
Maffio Orsini .... Piland
Gennaro .... Price
Alfonso .... Fazah

April 9

IL BARBIERE DI SIVIGLIA
(Rossini)

Conductor .... Martelli
Fiorello .... Ledbetter,
    (s, Fisher)

Almaviva .... Pane
Figaro .... Elvira
Bartolo .... McKee
Rosina .... Rolandi
Basilio .... Ramey
Berta .... Walker
Officer .... Yule

April 10 (m)

TURANDOT

Same cast as March 6 except:

Liù .... Lee
Calaf .... Malamood
Timur .... Berberian
Turandot .... Mathes
Emperor .... Lowery

April 10

THE MARRIAGE OF FIGARO

Same cast as March 14 except:

Susanna .... Little
Cherubino .... Harris
Countess .... Dale
Curzio .... Novick

April 11 (m)

SALOME

Same cast as March 13 except:

Narraboth .... Lankston
Slave .... Dovel
2nd Jew .... Novick

April 11

UN BALLO IN MASCHERA

Same cast as March 13 (m)
except:

Renato .... Fredricks
Servant .... Paul
Amelia .... Jones

April 13

IL BARBIERE DI SIVIGLIA

Same cast as April 9 except:

Fiorello .... Fisher
Basilio .... Hale

April 14

CARMEN

Same cast as February 21 (m)
except:

Morales .... Fisher
Zuniga .... McKee
Micaëla .... Robinson
Don José .... Mauro,
    (s, Kness)
Carmen .... Stapp
Frasquita .... Ito
Mercédès .... Piland
Escamillo .... Ramey

Remendado .... Novick
Dancairo .... Billings

April 15

THE BALLAD OF BABY DOE
(Moore)

Directed by .... Bakman
Lighting .... Sondheimer
Conductor .... Somogi

An old silver miner ... Billings
Saloon bouncer .... Yule
Kate .... Orlando
Mag .... Tomanec
Horace Tabor ..... Fredricks
Sam .... Siena
Bushy .... Lankston
Barney .... Jamerson
Jacob .... Steele
Augusta .... Bible
Sarah .... Wildes
Mary .... Goodman (d)
Emily .... Toro
Effie .... Walker
Baby Doe .... Welting
Samantha .... Campbell
Hotel clerk .... Lowery
Albert .... Yule
Mama McCourt .. Shaulis (d)
McCourt
family .. Bohachevsky, Daly,
Reynolds (d), L. Clark,
Sergi, Farone
Four Washington
dandies .. Nelson, Kingman,
Morrison, Bentley
Hotel footman .... Yule
Father Chapelle ...... Hensel
Chester A. Arthur .... Griffith
Elizabeth and
Silver Dollar .. M. Randazzo,
A. Clark (d)
Mayor of Leadville .... Davis
William Jennings
Bryan .... McKee
Stage doorman ...... Billings
Denver politician .... Paul
Silver Dollar
(grown up) ...... Hegierski

April 16

LA BOHÈME

Same cast as February 28
except:

Conductor .... Rudel

Rodolfo .... Mauro
Marcello .... Cossa
Colline .... Ramey
Schaunard .... Jamerson
Mimi .... Malfitano
Parpignol .... Lowery
Musetta .... Dale
Alcindoro .... Ronson

April 17 (m)

THE MARRIAGE OF FIGARO

Same cast as March 14 except:

Figaro .... Hale
Susannah .... Little
Bartolo .... Densen
Cherubino .... Harris
Almaviva .... Justus
Antonio .... Billings,
(s, Yule)
Barbarina .... Ito

April 17

DIE FLEDERMAUS

Same cast as February 29 (m)
except:

Alfred .... McDonald
Adele .... A. Randazzo
Rosalinda .... Craig
Eisenstein .... Griffith
Falke .... Holloway
Frank .... McKee
Prince Orlofsky .. D. R. Smith
Frosch .... Billings,
(s, Worth)

April 18 (m)

LA TRAVIATA

Same cast as February 21
except:

Violetta .... Niska
Dr. Grenvil .... Densen,
(s, Yule)
Gaston .... Novick
Alfredo .... Pane
Germont .... Fredricks

April 18

TURANDOT

Same cast as March 6 except:

Liù .... Malfitano
Timur .... Berberian
Turandot .... Mathes
Emperor .... Lowery

April 20

UN BALLO IN MASCHERA

Same cast as March 13 (m)
except:

Oscar .... Rolandi
Ulrica .... Costa-Greenspon
Servant .... Paul
Amelia .... Jones,
(s, Meier)

April 21

THE BALLAD OF BABY DOE

Same cast as April 15

Telecast

April 22

LIZZIE BORDEN (Beeson)

Lighting .... Sondheimer
Conductor .... Pallo

Andrew Borden ...... Pierson
Abigail Borden .... Faull
Elizabeth Borden ... Schauler
Margaret Borden .. Hynes (d)
Reverend Harrington ... Siena
Capt. Jason
MacFarlane .. Darrenkamp

April 23

IL BARBIERE DI SIVIGLIA

Same cast as April 9 except:

Fiorello .... Fisher
Figaro .... Cowan (d)
Rosina .... Rolandi,
(s, Haley)
Basilio .... Voketaitis

April 24 (m)

CARMEN

Same cast as February 21 (m)
except:

Morales .... Fisher
Zuniga .... McKee
Micaëla .... Derr
Carmen .... Stapp
Frasquita .... Ito
Mercédès .... Piland
Remendado .... Siena
Dancairo .... Billings

April 24

I PAGLIACCI

Same cast as March 27 except:

Canio .... Mauro
Nedda .... Niska
Beppe .... Lowery
Silvio .... Cossa

Followed by:

CAVALLERIA RUSTICANA

Same cast as March 27 except:

Santuzza .... Niska
Turiddu .... Bartolini
Lola .... Toro

April 25 (m)

THE BALLAD OF BABY DOE

Same cast as April 15 except:

Horace Tabor .... Ludgin
Augusta .... Costa-Greenspon
Baby Doe .... Haley,
(s, Welting)

April 25

LIZZIE BORDEN

Same cast as Aprli 22

Fall 1976 (SEPTEMBER 1 – NOVEMBER 14)

Female artists
Armstrong, Karan
Ballard, Earline
Battle, Kathleen*
Bergquist, Eleanor
Brisebois, Danielle*
Brooks, Patricia
Campbell, Joan
Claveau, Sharon*
Conrad, Barbara
Costa-Greenspon, Muriel
Craig, Patricia
Curry, Diane
Curtin, Phyllis
De Rosa, Judith
Derr, Emily
Farley, Carole*
Fowles, Glenys
Goodman, Margaret
Grof, Vicki*
Haley, Elizabeth
Harris, Hilda
Hegierski, Kathleen
Herbert, Lila*
Hynes, Elizabeth
Jones, Betty
Kehrig, Diana
Lee, Sung Sook
Malfitano, Catherine
Meier, Johanna
Mines, Madeleine
Niska, Maralin
Orlando, Valeria
Palmer, Roberta
Piland, Jeanne
Reynolds, Myrna
Robinson, Faye
Rolandi, Gianna
Schauler, Eileen
Shaulis, Jane
Sills, Beverly
Simon, Ilona*
Soviero, Diana
Stapp, Olivia
Tatum, Nancy
Thyssen, Charlott*
Tomanec, Joyce
Toro, Puli
Walker, Sandra

Male artists
Alexander, John
Baker, Alan
Bartolini, Lando
Bentley, Ronald
Berberian, Ara
Billings, James
Bohachevsky, George
Boucher, Ron*
Brown, Melvin*
Bunger, Reid*
Carlo, Don
Castel, Nico
Clatworthy, David
Clemmons, François*
Collins, Kenneth

Cossa, Dominic
Darrenkamp, John
Davis, Harris
Densen, Irwin
Devlin, Michael
Di Giuseppe, Enrico
Dovel, Kenn
Elvira, Pablo
Evans, Joseph*
Fazah, Adib
Foss, Harlan*
Fredricks, Richard
Gill, Richard T.
Glaze, Gary
Gramm, Donald
Griffith, David
Guettel, Adam*
Hale, Robert
Harness, William
Harper, Talmage
Henderson, Don
Hensel, Howard
Holloway, David
Jamerson, Thomas
Justus, William
Kelley, Ronald*
Lankston, John
Ledbetter, William
Lowery, Melvin
Malas, Spiro
Mauro, Ermanno
McGrath, Matthew
McKee, Richard
Muni, Nicholas*
Munkittrick, Mark*
Nagy, Robert
Novick, Melvyn
Paul, Robert
Pierson, Edward
Pool, Gary
Price, Henry
Ramey, Samuel
Roe, Charles
Romaguera, Joaquin
Ronson, David
Sandor, John
Sarabia, Guillermo*
Scano, Gaetano
Sergi, James
Siena, Jerold
Sims, Jack
Smith, David Rae
Stavola, Charlie*
Steele, Philip
Stilwell, Richard
Taylor, Richard
Titus, Alan
Unruh, Stan*
Worth, Coley
Yule, Don

Conductors
Caldwell, Sarah*
Campanino, Gigi*
Charry, Michael*
Effron, David

Gray, George Branson
Kellogg, Cal Stewart*
Klippstatter, Kurt*
Miner, John
Morelli, Giuseppe
Pallo, Imre
Rudel, Julius
Somogi, Judith
Walser, Lloyd*

Chorus master
Gray, George Branson

Assistant chorus master
Ballard, Conoley*

Solo dancers
Balestracci, Sandra
Galan, Esperanza

Fogarty, John*
Horvath, Juliu
Korogodsky, Mikhail*
Rubino, Michael

Choreographer
Andrew, Thomas

Directors
Auerbach, Cynthia
Caldwell, Sarah
Capobianco, Tito
Corsaro, Frank
Cox, John
Darling, Robert E.*
Eddleman, Jack
Freedman, Gerald
Getke, Richard
Hicks, David
Presnell, Steve
Rizzo, Francis
Yannopoulos, Dino

Designers
Aldredge, Theoni V.
Ardolino, Emile
Campbell, Patton
Compton, Gardner
Darling, Robert E.*
Evans, Lloyd
Fletcher, Robert
Luiken, Carol*
Montresor, Beni
Pond, Helen
Salzer, Beeb*
Senn, Herbert
Skalicky, Jan*
Toms, Carl
Varona, José
Wittstein, Ed

* New artist

September 1

TURANDOT (Puccini)

Conductor .... Rudel
Mandarin .... Densen
Liù .... Malfitano
Calaf .... Mauro
Timur .... Ramey

Turandot .... Ballard
Ping .... Jamerson
Pang .... Griffith
Pong .... Lankston
Emperor .... Romaguera

September 2

DIE MEISTERSINGER (Wagner)
(English text by John Gutman)

Stage director ..... Auerbach
Conductor .... Rudel

Walther .... Alexander
Eva .... Meier
Magdalene .... Curry
David .... Griffith
Pogner .... Gill
Beckmesser .... Billings
Vogelgesang .... Hensel
Nachtigall .... Jamerson
Hans Sachs ..... Bunger (d)
Kothner .... Holloway
Ortel .... McKee
Zorn .... Romaguera
Moser .... Lowery
Eisslinger .... Brown (d)
Foltz .... Densen
Schwarz .... Steele
Night Watchman .... Paul

September 3

H.M.S. PINAFORE (Sullivan)

Conductor .... Miner

Captain Corcoran .. Fredricks
Bill Bobstay .... Ledbetter
Bob Becket .... Steele
Little Buttercup ...... Costa-
Greenspon
Dick Deadeye .... Densen
Ralph Rackstraw ...... Hale
Josephine .... Fowles
Sir Joseph Porter .... Billings
Cousin Hebe .... Toro

September 4 (m)

LA BOHÈME (Puccini)

Conductor .... Morelli

Rodolfo .... Bartolini
Marcello .... Cossa
Colline .... Hale
Schaunard .... Paul
Benoit .... Yule
Mimi .... Malfitano
Parpignol .... Romaguera
Musetta .... Palmer
Alcindoro .... Ronson
Guards. .Bentley, Bohachevsky

September 4

TURANDOT

Same cast as September 1
except:

Liù .... Lee

September 5 (m)

MADAMA BUTTERFLY (Puccini)

Conductor .... Morelli

Pinkerton .... Scano
Goro .... Siena

Suzuki .... Walker
Sharpless .... Justus
Butterfly .... Craig,
(s, Lee)
*Imperial
Commissioner* ... Ledbetter
Registrar, Yamadori .... Sergi
The Bonze .... McKee
Trouble .... McGrath
Kate Pinkerton .... Hegierski

September 5

LA TRAVIATA (Verdi)

Stage director ..... Auerbach
Conductor .... Somogi

Violetta .... Brooks
Flora .... Hegierski
Douphol .... Baker
D'Obigny .... Ledbetter
Dr. Grenvil .... Ronson
Gaston .... Lowery
Alfredo .... Sandor
Annina .... Toro
Giuseppe .... Romaguera
Germont .... Fredricks
Messenger .... Harper
Solo dancer .... Galan

September 7

THE MARRIAGE OF FIGARO
(Mozart)
(English version by
Ruth and Thomas Martin)

Conductor .... Effron

Figaro .... Hale
Susanna .... Battle (d)
Bartolo .... Densen
Marcellina .... Walker
Cherubino .... Harris
Almaviva .... Justus
Basilio .... Siena
Countess .... Meier
Antonio .... Yule
Curzio .... Novick
Barbarina .... Goodman,
(s, Kehrig)
Solo dancer .... Galan

September 8

H.M.S. PINAFORE

Same cast as September 3

September 9

TURANDOT

Same cast as September 1
except:

Ping .... Fazah

September 10

THE MAKROPOULOS AFFAIR
(Janáček)
(English translation by
Norman Tucker)

Conductor .... Pallo

Vitek .... Lankston
Albert Gregor .... Taylor

Christa .... Hynes
Emilia Marty .... Niska
Chauffeur .... Smith
Dr. Kolenaty ...... Pierson
Jarsoslav Prus .... Clatworthy
Maid .... Toro
Janek .... Pool
Hauk-Sendorf .... Castel

September 11 (m)

LA BOHÈME

Same cast as September 4 (m)

September 11

DIE FLEDERMAUS (J. Strauss)
(English version by
Ruth and Thomas Martin)

Conductor .... Pallo

Alfred .... Glaze
Adele .... Rolandi
Rosalinda .... Meier
Eisenstein .... Roe
Blind .... Siena
Falke .... Jamerson
Frank .... Malas
Sally .... Kehrig
Ivan .... Sims
Prince Orlofsky ...... Smith
Frosch .... Billings
Solo dancers ..... Balestracci,
Galan; Horvath

September 12 (m)

MADAMA BUTTERFLY

Same cast as September 5 (m)
except:

Butterfly .... Lee

September 12

CAVALLERIA RUSTICANA
(Mascagni)

Conductor .... Morelli

Mamma Lucia .... Curry
Santuzza .... Niska
Turiddu .... Bartolini
Lola .... Hegierski
Alfio .... Darrenkamp

Followed by:

I PAGLIACCI (Leoncavallo)

Conductor .... Morelli

Tonio .... Elvira
Canio .... Mauro
Nedda .... Craig
Beppe .... Lowery
Peasants ..Davis, Bohachevsky
Silvio .... Holloway
Acrobats .... Fogarty (d)
Horvath

September 14

CARMEN (Bizet)

Conductor .... Pallo

Morales .... Jamerson
Andrès .... Ronson
Zuniga .... McKee
Micaëla .... Fowles

Don José .... Mauro
Carmen .... Conrad
Frasquita .... Hynes
Mercédès .... Walker
Lillas Pastia,
  Guide .... Romaguera
Escamillo .... Ramey
Remendado .... Lankston
Dancairo .... Baker

September 15

LA BOHÈME

Same cast as September 4 (m)

September 16

LA TRAVIATA

Same cast as September 5
except:

Conductor .. Klippstatter (d)

September 17

MADAMA BUTTERFLY

Same cast as September 5 (m)
except:

Butterfly .... Craig,
  (s, Niska)

September 18 (m)

DIE FLEDERMAUS

Same cast as September 11
except:

Sally .... Toro

September 18

H.M.S. PINAFORE

Same cast as September 3
except:

Little Buttercup ...... Shaulis
DickDeadeye .... Yule
Ralph Rackstraw ..... Glaze,
  (s, Price)
Josephine .... Hynes
Sir Joseph Porter ..... Baker

September 19 (m)

CAVALLERIA RUSTICANA

Same cast as September 12
except:

Santuzza ....Stapp
Turiddu .... Di Giuseppe

followed by:

I PAGLIACCI

Same cast as September 12
except:

Canio .... Nagy

September 19

THE MAKROPOULOS AFFAIR

Same cast as September 10

September 21

LA BELLE HÉLÈNE (Offenbach)
First performance by The New
York City Opera Company
(English version by Geoffrey
Dunn, revised by Julius Rudel)

Directed by .... Eddleman
Scenic designer .... Evans
Costume designer .. Campbell
Choreographer ...... Andrew
Lighting .... Sondheimer
Conductor .... Rudel

Calchas .... McKee
Philocomos ...... Romaguera
Young ladies ...... Campbell,
  Reynolds
Euthycles .... Yule
Helen .... Armstrong
Daphne .... Toro
Orestes .... Griffith
Jocanthis .... Grof (d)
Anthea .... Orlando
Phantis .... Mines
Chloe .... Tomanec
Paris .... Price
Ajax I .... Siena
Ajax II .... Lowery
Achilles .... Lankston
Menelaus .... Billings
Agamemnon ...... Holloway
Living statues .... Balestracci;
  Korogodsky (d)

September 22

LA TRAVIATA

Same cast as September 5
except:

Violetta .... Niska
Alfredo .... Harness
Annina .... Goodman

September 23

CARMEN

Same cast as September 14
except:

Don José .... Collins
Carmen .... Stapp
Dancairo .... Ledbetter

September 24

MADAMA BUTTERFLY

Same cast as September 5 (m)
except:

Goro .... Romaguera
Sharpless .... Cossa
Butterfly .... Niska
The Bonze .... Steele
Kate Pinkerton .... Toro

September 25 (m)

LA BELLE HÉLÈNE

Same cast as September 21
except:

Ajax I .... Brown

September 25

DIE MEISTERSINGER

Same cast as September 2
except:

Eva .... Jones
  (s, Meier)
Beckmesser .... Baker

September 26 (m)

TURANDOT

Same cast as September 1
except:

Liù .... Robinson
Turandot .... Tatum
Ping .... Fazah

September 26

H.M.S. PINAFORE

Same cast as September 3
except:

Conductor .... Walser (d)
Ralph Rackstraw ...... Price

(Note: All performances
scheduled from September 28
to October 18 were canceled
due to a musicians' strike.
Some program changes were
put into effect for the
remainder of the season.)

October 19

LA BELLE HÉLÈNE

Same cast as September 21
except:

Helen .... Farley (d)
Orestes .... Hensel
Ajax I .... Brown,
  (s, Siena)

October 22

DER FLIEGENDE HOLLÄNDER
(Wagner)
New production

Directed and
  designed by ... Darling (d)
Lighting .... Sondheimer
Conductor .... Rudel

Daland .... Malas
Steersman .... Siena
Dutchman ...... Sarabia (d)
Mary .... Curry
Senta .... Meier
Erik .... Colilns

October 23 (m)

DER FLIEGENDE HOLLÄNDER

Same cast as October 22
except:

Daland ..... Munkittrick (d)
Steersman .... Clemmons (d)
Mary .... Walker
Senta .... Jones,
  (s, Ballard)
Erik .... Unruh (d)

October 24 (m)

LA BOHÈME

Same cast as September 4 (m)
except:

Rodolfo .... Mauro
Colline .... Malas
Schaunard .... Jamerson
Mimi .... Derr
Musetta .... Bergquist
Alcindoro .... Billings

October 24

IL BARBIERE DI SIVIGLIA
(Rossini)
New production

Directed by .... Caldwell
Scenic
  designers ... Pond and Senn
Costume
  designer ..... Skalicky (d)
Lighting .... Sondheimer
Conductor ..... Caldwell (d)

Fiorello .... Ledbetter
Almaviva .... Harness
Figaro .... Titus
Rosina .... Sills
Bartolo .... Gramm
Basilio .... Ramey
Berta .... Curry
Ambrogio .... Muni (d)
Officer .... Yule
Notary .... Rubino

October 26

LA BELLE HÉLÈNE

Same cast as September 21
except:

Conductor .... Miner

Orestes .... Hensel
Paris .... Evans (d)

October 27

IL BARBIERE DI SIVIGLIA

Same cast as October 24

October 28

CARMEN

Same cast as September 14
except:

Morales .... Foss (d)
Zuniga .... Steele
Micaëla .... Robinson
Frasquita .... Goodman
Mercédès .... Piland
Escamillo .... Hale
Dancairo .... Billings

October 29

LA BELLE HÉLÈNE

Same cast as September 21
except:

Conductor .... Miner

Paris .... Sandor

October 30 (m)

IL BARBIERE DI SIVIGLIA

Same cast as October 24

October 30

MADAMA BUTTERFLY

Same cast as September 5 (m)
except:

Conductor ... Campanino (d)

Pinkerton .... Mauro
Goro .... Romaguera
Sharpless .... Fredricks
Butterfly .... Niska
The Bonze .... Steele
Kate Pinkerton .... Toro

October 31 (m)

RIGOLETTO (Verdi)

Conductor .... Charry (d)

Rigoletto .... Elvira
Monterone's daughter .. Galan
Duke .... Di Giuseppe
Borsa .... Hensel
Countess Ceprano ... Kehrig
Ceprano .... Ledbetter
Marullo .... Jamerson
Monterone .... McKee
Sparafucile .... Densen
Gilda .... Robinson
Giovanna .... Toro
Page .... Mines
Maddalena .... Walker,
                  (s, Curry)
Clown .... Fogarty

October 31

PELLÉAS ET MÉLISANDE
(Débussy)

Conductor .... Rudel

Mélisande .... Fowles
Golaud .... Devlin
Geneviève .... Curry
Arkel .... Berberian
Pelléas .... Stilwell
Yniold .... Guettel (d)
Shepherd .... Ledbetter
Physician .... Yule

November 2

CAVALLERIA RUSTICANA

Same cast as September 12
except:

Conductor .... Gray

Mamma Lucia .... Walker
Turiddu .... Collins
Lola .... Piland

Followed by:

I PAGLIACCI

Same cast as September 12
except:

Conductor .... Gray

Nedda .... Soviero
Beppe .... Brown
Silvio .... Roe

November 3

IL BARBIERE DI SIVIGLIA

Same cast as October 24
except:

Almaviva .... Price

Televised performance

November 4

RIGOLETTO

Same cast as October 31 (m)
except:

Duke .... Bartolini
Marullo .... Paul

November 5

THE SAINT OF BLEECKER
STREET (Menotti)
New production

Directed by .... Rizzo
Scenic designer ..... Salzer (d)
Costume designer..Luiken (d)
Choreographer ...... Andrew
Lighting .... Sondheimer
Conductor ...... Kellogg (d)

Assunta .... Shaulis
Young man .... Hensel
Maria Corona ...... De Rosa
Her son ...... Boucher (d)
Carmela .... Soviero
Young woman .... Kehrig
Don Marco .... Densen
Annina .... Malfitano
Michele .... Di Giuseppe
Girl at the
  window ...... Herbert (d)
Concettina .... Brisebois (d)
Desideria .... Piland
Guests .... Siena, Baker
Salvatore .... Ledbetter
Bartender .... Henderson
Nun .... Thyssen (d)
Young priest .... Kelley (d)
Neighbors ...... Dovel, Sergi

November 6 (m)

IL BARBIERE DI SIVIGLIA

Same cast as October 24
except:

Figaro .... Fredricks
Bartolo .... Malas

November 6

DIE FLEDERMAUS

Same cast as September 11
except:

Alfred .... Sandor
Adele .... Hale
Rosalinda .... Simon (d)
Eisenstein .... Lanksto
Falke .... Hollowa
Frank .... McKe
Sally .... To
Frosch .... Stavola (d

November 7 (m)

THE SAINT OF
BLEECKER STREET

Same cast as November 5

November 7

DIE FLEDERMAUS

Same cast as September 11
except:

Conductor .... Rudel

Alfred .... Price
Falke .... Holloway
Sally .... Toro
Frosch .... Worth

Broadcast performance

November 9

IL BARBIERE DI SIVIGLIA

Same cast as October 24
except:

Almaviva .... Price
Figaro .... Fredricks
Bartolo .... Malas

November 10

THE SAINT OF
BLEECKER STREET

Same cast as November 5

November 11

CARMEN

Same cast as September 14
except:

Morales .... Sergi
Zuniga .... Steele
Don José .... Scano
Carmen .... Curry
Frasquita .... Goodman
Mecédès .... Hegierski
Escamillo ..... Darrenkamp
Dancairo .... Billings

November 12

RIGOLETTO

Same cast as October 3 (m)
except:

Rigoletto .... Fredricks
Duke .... Sandor
Countess Ceprano .. Goodman
Marullo .... Paul
Monterone .... Steele
Gilda .... Rolandi
Giovanna .... Hegierski
Page .... Claveau (d)

November 13 (m)

THE MARRIAGE OF FIGARO

Same cast as September 7
except:

Conductor .... Somogi

Figaro .... Ramey
Bartolo .... McKee
Cherubino .... Piland

Countess .... Curtin
Barbarina .... Kehrig

November 13

CAVALLERIA RUSTICANA

Same cast as September 12
except:

Conductor .... Gray

Mamma Lucia .... Walker
Santuzza .... Schauler
Turiddu .... Di Giuseppe
Lola .... Piland

Followed by:

I PAGLIACCI

Same cast as September 12
except:

Conductor .... Gray

Nedda .... Soviero
Beppe .... Siena
1st Peasant .... Carlo
Silvio .... Roe

November 14 (m)

PELLÉAS ET MÉLISANDE

Same cast as October 31

November 14

LA TRAVIATA

Same cast as September 5
except:

Violetta .... Robinson
Gaston .... Novick
Alfredo .... Bartolini

Spring 1977 (FEBRUARY 23 – MAY 1)

Female artists
Allison, Patti*
Arrauzau, Francine*
Ballard, Earline
Belling, Susan*
Bible, Frances
Blackett, Joy*
Brooks, Patricia
Campbell, Joan
Carron, Elisabeth
Costa-Greenspon, Muriel
Craig, Patricia
Curry, Diane
Dale, Clamma
Daniels, Sharon*
De Rosa, Judith
Ehrlich, Judith*
Ellington, Mercedes*
Evans, Beverly
Faulkner, Geanie*
Fiske, June*
Fowles, Glenys
Freni, RoseMarie*
Gregory, Susan*
Grof, Vicki

Haley, Elizabeth
Hazzan, Atarah*
Hegierski, Kathleen
Howard, Ann
Hynes, Elizabeth
Kehrig, Diana
Little, Gwenlynn
Luxemburg, Leslie
Malfitano, Catherine
Marsee, Susanne
McCarty, Victoria*
Meier, Johanna
Mines, Madeleine
Morein, Donna*
Niska, Maralin
Orlando, Valeria
Palmer, Roberta
Piland, Jeanne
Reynolds, Myrna
Robinson, Faye
Rolandi, Gianna
Schauler, Eileen
Seibel, Paula*
Shaulis, Jane
Sills, Beverly
Soviero, Diana

Thigpen, Martha*
Tisch, Rosalie
Tomanec, Joyce
Toro, Puli
Vergara, Victoria*
Walker, Sandra
West, Maria
Young, Syble
Zannoth, Sherry*

Male artists
Alexander, John
Baker, Alan
Bartolini, Lando
Berberian, Ara
Billings, James
Bohachevsky, George
Bostwick, Barry*
Brewer, James
Castel, Nico
Clatworthy, David
Darrenkamp, John
Davis, Harris
Densen, Irwin
Di Giuseppe, Enrico

* New artist   * New artist   * New artist

Elvira, Pablo
Evans, Joseph
Foss, Harlan
Fredricks, Richard
Griffith, David
Guettel, Adam
Guss, John Galt*
Hale, Robert
Harper, Talmage
Hartman, Vernon*
Hensel, Howard
Holloway, David
Jamerson, Thomas
Justus, William
Lankston, John
Ledbetter, William
Long, Charles*
Lowery, Melvin
Malamood, Herman
Malas, Spiro
Manno, Robert*
Matthews, Benjamin*
Mauro, Ermanno
McGrath, Matthew
McKee, Richard
Morales, Abram*
Muni, Nicholas
Munkittrick, Mark
Novick, Melvyn
Parker, Moises*
Paul, Robert
Pierson, Edward
Pool, Gary
Price, Henry
Ramey, Samuel
Roe, Charles
Romaguera, Joaquin
Ronson, David
Roy, Will
Sandor, John
Sapolsky, Robert*
Sarabia, Guillermo
Scano, Gaetano
Seetoo, Dennis*
Sergi, James
Shirley, George
Siena, Jerold
Sims, Jack
Smith, David Rae
Stavola, Charlie
Steele, Philip
Taylor, Richard
Walser, Lloyd*
Worth, Coley
Yule, Don

Conductors
Caldwell, Sarah
Campanino, Gigi
Charry, Michael
Effron, David
Kirchner, Leon*
Klippstatter, Kurt
Morelli, Giuseppe
Pallo, Imre
Rosenthal, Manuel*
Rudel, Julius
Somogi, Judith
Walser, Lloyd

Director for electronic sound
Tcherepnin, Ivan*

Chorus master
Gray, George Branson

* New artist

Assistant chorus master
Ballard, Conoley

Solo dancers
Balestracci, Sandra
Galan, Esperanza
Itow, Candace*
Thuesen, Nancy*

Dunne, James*
Horvath, Juliu
Korogodsky, Mikhail
Rhodes, Lawrence*
Romero, Rafael*
Rubino, Michael
Wayne, Dennis*

Choreographers
Andrew, Thomas
Butler, John
Compton, Gardner*

Directors
Auerbach, Cynthia
Butler, John
Caldwell, Sarah
Capobianco, Tito
Compton, Gardner*
Corsaro, Frank
Darling, Robert E.
Eddleman, Jack
Freedman, Gerald
Getke, Richard
Hicks, David
O'Horgan, Tom*
Presnell, Steve
Rudel, Julius

Designers
Aldredge, Theoni V.
Barcelo, Randy
Campbell, Patton
Capecce, Vittorio*
Darling, Robert E.
Evans, Lloyd
Fletcher, Robert
George, Hal
Micunis, Gordon
Mitchell, David
Moore, John J.*
Morley, Ruth
Pond, Helen
Rodolitz, Lynda*
Senn, Herbert
Skalicky, Jan
Stabile, Bill*
Sylbert, Paul
Varona, José
Wittstein, Ed

* New artist

February 23

IL BARBIERE DI SIVIGLIA
(Rossini)

Stage director .... Presnell
Conductor .... Caldwell

Fiorello .... Ledbetter
Almaviva .... Price
Figaro .... Fredricks
Rosina .... Sills
Bartolo .... Malas
Basilio .... Ramey
Berta .... Curry
Arbrogio .... Muni
Officer .... Yule
Notary .... Rubino

February 24

DER FLIEGENDE HOLLÄNDER
(Wagner)

Conductor .... Rudel

Daland .... Berberian
Steersman .... Siena
Dutchman .... Sarabia
Mary .... Curry
Senta .... Meier
Erik .... Taylor

February 25

LA BOHÈME (Puccini)

Conductor .... Morelli

Rodolfo .... Mauro
Marcello .... Elvira
Colline .... Roy
Schaunard .... Paul
Benoit .... Yule
Mimi .... Soviero
Parpignol .... Lowery
Musetta .... Palmer
Alcindoro .... Ronson
Guards ..Brewer, Bohachevsky

February 26 (m)

IL BARBIERE DI SIVIGLIA

Same cast as February 23

February 26

DIE FLEDERMAUS (J. Strauss)
(English version by
Ruth and Thomas Martin)

Conductor .... Pallo

Alfred .... Griffith
Adele .... Rolandi
Rosalinda .... Fiske (d)
Eisenstein .... Roe
Blind .... Siena
Falke .... Holloway
Frank .... McKee
Sally .... Torc
Ivan .... Sims
Prince Orlofsky ...... Baker
Frosch .... Billing
Solo dancers ..... Balestracci
Galan; Horvath

February 27 (m)

THE MARRIAGE OF FIGARO
(Mozart)
(English version by
Ruth and Thomas Martin)

Conductor .... Charr

Figaro .... Hal
Susanna .... Littl
Bartolo .... Dense
Marcellina .... Shauli
Cherubino .... Marse
Almaviva .... Clatworth
Basilio .... Sien
Countess .... Dal
Antonio .... Yul
Curzio .... Novic
Barbarina ...... Thigpen (d
Solo dancer .... Gala

February 27

LA BELLE HÉLÈNE (Offenbach)
(English version by Geoffrey
Dunn, revised by Julius Rudel)

Conductor	Rudel, (s, Effron)
Calchas	McKee
Philocomos	Romaguera
1st Young lady	Luxemburg
2nd Young lady	Campbell
Euthycles	Yule
Helen	Daniels (d)
Daphne	Kehrig
Orestes	Hensel
Jocanthis	Grof
Anthea	Orlando
Phantis	Mines
Chloe	Tomanec
Paris	J. Evans
Ajax I	Siena
Ajax II	Lowery
Achilles	Lankston
Menelaus	Billings
Agamemnon	Holloway
Living statues	Balestracci, Korogodsky

March 1

IL BARBIERE DI SIVIGLIA

Same cast as February 23

March 3

LA BELLE HÉLÈNE

Same cast as February 27
except:

Conductor	Effron
Paris	Price
Agamemnon	Baker

March 4

CARMEN (Bizet)

Conductor	Pallo
Morales	Ledbetter
Andrès	Ronson
Zuniga	McKee
Micaëla	Fowles
Don José	Scano
Carmen	Arrauzau (d)
Frasquita	Hynes
Mercédès	Hegierski
Lillas Pastia, Guide	Romaguera
Escamillo	Holloway
Remendado	Lankston
Dancairo	Baker

March 5 (m)

MADAMA BUTTERFLY (Puccini)

Conductor	Morelli
Pinkerton	Di Giuseppe
Goro	Siena
Suzuki	Walker
Sharpless	Darrenkamp
Butterfly	Niska

Imperial Commissioner	Ledbetter
Registrar, Yamadori	Sergi
The Bonze	Steele
Trouble	McGrath
Kate Pinkerton	Hegierski

March 5

LA TRAVIATA (Verdi)

Conductor	Pallo
Violetta	Robinson
Flora	Walker
Douphol	Baker
D'Obigny	Ledbetter
Dr. Grenvil	Ronson
Gaston	Lowery
Alfredo	Bartolini
Annina	Morein (d)
Giuseppe	Davis
Germont	Fredricks
Messenger	Harper
Solo dancer	Galan

March 6 (m)

LA BOHÈME

Same cast as February 25

March 6

LOUISE (Charpentier)

Directed by	Rudel
Conductor	Rudel
Julien	Alexander
Louise	Sills
Mother	Bible
Father	Hale
Young ragpicker	Hegierski
Coal gatherer	Tisch
Paper girl	Tomanec
Noctambulist	Taylor
Milk woman	West
Ragpicker	Roy
Junk man	Densen
Policemen	Ronson, Manno (d)
Street Arab	Kehrig
Street sweeper	Curry
Painter	Griffith
Sculptor	Ledbetter
Songwriter	Hensel
Poet	Pool
Philosophers	Romaguera, Yule
Blanche	De Rosa
Marguerite	Campbell
Suzanne	Reynolds
Gertrude	Shaulis
Irma	Hynes
Camille	Thigpen
Apprentice	Kehrig
Elise	Hegierski
Madeleine	Orlando
Old clothes man	Siena
Forewoman	B. Evans
King of fools	Taylor
Solo dancer	Balestracci
Bird food boy	Guettel
Chair mender	Shaulis
Clothing vendor	Romaguera
Artichoke vendor	Hynes
Carrot vendor	Griffith
Bird food vendor	Thigpen

Barrel vendor	Ledbetter
Broom vendor	Hensel
Potato vendors	Kehrig, Pool
Green peas vendor	Griffith
Watercress vendor	B. Evans

March 8

LOUISE

Same cast as March 6

March 9

LA BELLE HÉLÈNE

Same cast as February 27
except:

Conductor	Effron
Helen	Brooks

March 10

DER FLIEGENDE HOLLÄNDER

Same cast as February 24

March 11

THE MARRIAGE OF FIGARO

Same cast as Fabruary 27 (m)
except:

Figaro	Holloway
Almaviva	Fredricks
Barbarina	Kehrig

March 12 (m)

LOUISE

Same cast as March 6

March 12

MADAMA BUTTERFLY

Same cast as March 5 (m)
except:

Pinkerton	Bartolini
Butterfly	Carron

March 13 (m)

LA BOHÈME

Same cast as February 25

March 13

CARMEN

Same cast as March 4

March 15

LOUISE

Same cast as March 6

March 16

DER FLIEGENDE HOLLÄNDER

Same cast as February 24
except:

Daland	Munkittrick
Steersman	Griffith
Mary	Shaulis
Senta	Ballard

March 17

LA TRAVIATA

Same cast as March 5 except:

Gaston .... Novick
Annina .... Toro
Germont .... Elvira

March 18

LOUISE

Same cast as March 6 except:

Ragpicker .... Steele
Street sweeper .... Morein
Irma .... Haley
Camille .... Gregory (d)
Bird food boy .. Sapolsky (d),
                    (s, Guettel)
Artichoke vendor ...... Haley
Bird food
    vendor .... Gregory (d)

March 19 (m)

CAVALLERIA RUSTICANA
(Mascagni)

Stage director .... Presnell
Conductor .... Morelli

Santuzza .... Freni (d)
Mamma Lucia .... Curry
Turiddu .... Bartolini
Lola .... Hegierski
Alfio .... Long (d)

Followed by:

I PAGLIACCI (Leoncavallo)

Stage director .... Presnell
Conductor .... Morelli

Tonio .... Elvira
Canio .... Malamood
Nedda .... Dale
Beppe .... Siena
Peasants ..Davis, Bohachevsky
Silvio .... Jamerson
Acrobats ... Rubino, Horvath

March 19

LA BOHÈME

Same cast as February 25
except:

Rodolfo .... Scano
Marcello .... Justus
Colline .... Malas
Mimi .... Malfitano
Parpignol .... Romaguera
Musetta .... Zannoth (d)
Alcindoro .... Billings

March 20 (m)

CARMEN

Same cast as March 4 except:

Morales .... Jamerson
Zuniga .... Steele
Don José .... Parker (d)
Escamillo .... Hale

March 20

MEFISTOFELE (Boito)

Staged by .... Hicks
Conductor .... Rudel

Mefistofele .... Ramey
Faust .... Mauro
Wagner .... Griffith
Margherita .... Meier
Marta .... B. Evans
Elena .... Meier
Pantalis .... Walker
Nereo .... Romaguera
Solo dancers ..... Balestracci,
        Itow (d); Korogodsky,
                        Horvath

March 22

THE MARRIAGE OF FIGARO

Same cast as February 27 (m)
except:

Susanna .... Fowles
Bartolo .... McKee
Cherubino .... Piland
Almaviva .... Fredricks

March 23

CAVALLERIA RUSTICANA

Same cast as March 19 (m)
except:

Alfio .... Justus

Followed by:

I PAGLIACCI

Same cast as March 19 (m)
except:

Nedda .... Niska
Silvio .... Hartman (d)

March 24

MEFISTOFELE

Same cast as March 20

March 25

CARMEN

Same cast as March 4 except:

Morales .... Jamerson
Zuniga .... Steele
Frasquita .... Gregory
Escamillo .... Justus

March 26 (m)

THE PIRATES OF PENZANCE
(Sullivan)
New production

Directed by .... Eddleman
Scenic designer ...... Evans
Costume designer .. Campbell
Lighting ...... Sondheimer
Conductor .... Somogi

Samuel .... Ledbetter
Pirate King .... McKee
Frederic .... Price
Ruth ...... Costa-Greenspon
Edith .... Kehrig

Kate .... Walker
Isabel .... Mines
Mabel .... Rolandi
Major-General
    Stanley .... Billings
Police sergeant .... Densen
Solo dancer ..... Korogodsky

March 26

LA BELLE HÉLÈNE

Same cast as February 27
except:

Conductor .... Walser
Helen .... Marsee
Daphne .... Toro
Paris .... Sandor
Ajax II .... Novick
Menelaus .... Foss
Agamemnon .... Baker

March 27 (m)

MEFISTOFELE

Same cast as March 20

March 27

DIE FLEDERMAUS

Same cast as February 26
except:

Conductor ...... Klippstatter

Adele .... Haley
Rosalinda .... Allison (d)
Eisenstein .... Lankston
Falke .... Jamerson
Frank .... Malas

March 29

MADAMA BUTTERFLY

Same cast as March 5 (m)
except:

Conductor ...... Campanino
Pinkerton .... Bartolini
Suzuki .... Curry
Sharpless .... Fredricks
Kate Pinkerton .... Toro

March 30

LA TRAVIATA

Same cast as March 5 except:

Conductor ...... Klippstatter
Violetta .... Brooks
Flora .... Hegierski
Douphol .... Foss
D'Obigny .... Paul
Dr. Grenvil .... Densen
Gaston .... Novick
Alfredo .... Price
Annina .... Toro
Giuseppe .... Romaguera
Germont .... Elvira

March 31

MEFISTOFELE

Same cast as March 20 except:

Margherita ...... Ehrlich (d)
Elena .... Ehrlich (d)

April 1

LA BOHÈME

Same cast as February 25
except:

Conductor	Campanino
Rodolfo	Di Giuseppe, (s, Poll)
Marcello	Justus
Colline	Malas
Schaunard	Jamerson
Mimi	Niska
Musetta	Zannoth
Alcindoro	Billings

(Note: Melvyn Poll was not to
appear with the company
this season.)

April 2 (m)

CARMEN

Same cast as March 4 except:

Morales	Foss
Zuniga	Steele
Micaëla	Robinson
Carmen	Howard
Frasquita	Gregory
Mercédès	Walker
Escamillo	Hale
Dancairo	Billings

April 2

RIGOLETTO (Verdi)

Conductor	Campanino
Rigoletto	Fredricks
Monterone's daughter	Galan
Clown	Horvath
Duke	Di Giuseppe
Borsa	Hensel
Countess Ceprano	Kehrig
Ceprano	Ledbetter
Marullo	Jamerson
Monterone	Steele
Sparafucile	Densen
Gilda	Malfitano
Giovanna	Toro
Page	Gregory
Maddalena	Walker

April 3 (m)

THE PIRATES OF PENZANCE

Same cast as March 26 (m)

April 3

DIE FLEDERMAUS

Same cast as February 26
except:

Adele	Haley
Blind	Romaguera
Frank	Malas
Prince Orlofsky	Smith
Frosch	Stavola

April 6

LOUISE

Same cast as March 6 except:

Noctambulist	Sandor
Ragpicker	Steele

Street sweeper	Morein
Irma	Thigpen, (s, Haley)
Camille	Gregory
King of Fools	Sandor
Artichoke vendor	Thigpen, (s, Haley)
Bird food vendor	Gregory

April 7

MEFISTOFELE

Same cast as March 20

April 8

OEDIPUS REX (Stravinsky)
(English narration by
e.e. cummings)

Conductor	Rosenthal (d)
Narrator	Roe
Oedipus	Taylor
Creon	Pierson
Tiresias	Roy
Jocasta	Freni, (s, Bible)
Messenger	Ledbetter
Shepherd	Griffith

Followed by:

CARMINA BURANA (Orff)

Conductor	Rosenthal (d)
Soprano	Haley
Baritone	Roe
Tenor	Morales (d)
Dancers	Dennis Wayne's Dancers, with soloists Balestracci, Thuesen (d); Dunne (d), Rhodes (d), Wayne (d)

April 9 (m)

THE PIRATES OF PENZANCE

Same cast as March 26 (m)
except:

Samuel	Sergi
Frederic	Hensel
Edith	Thigpen
Kate	Hegierski
Mabel	Haley
Major-General Stanley	Foss
Police sergeant	Munkittrick

April 9

ARIADNE AUF NAXOS
(R. Strauss)
(English translation of
prologue and opera by
Lewis Sydenham,
revised by Julius Rudel)

Conductor	Rudel
Major-Domo	Smith
Music Master	Holloway
Composer	Niska
Wigmaker	Romaguera
Echo	Little
Najade	Fowles

Dryade	Shaulis
Dancing Master	Lankston
Lackey	Foss
Zerbinetta	Rolandi
Tenor, Bacchus	Alexander
Officer	Ledbetter
Prima Donna, Ariadne	Meier
Harlequin	Jamerson
Scaramuccio	Lankston
Truffaldin	McKee
Brighella	Lowery

April 10 (m)

RIGOLETTO

Same cast as April 2 except:

Sparafucile	Roy

April 10

MEFISTOFELE

Same cast as March 20 except:

Margherita	Ehrlich
Elena	Ehrlich

April 12

CARMEN

Same cast as March 4 except:

Conductor	Klippstatter
Morales	Foss
Zuniga	Steele
Micaëla	Robinson
Carmen	Howard
Frasquita	Gregory
Mercédès	Walker
Escamillo	Ramey

April 13

DIE FLEDERMAUS

Same cast as February 26
except:

Alfred	Price
Blind	Romaguera
Falke	Jamerson
Frank	Densen
Sally	Kehrig
Frosch	Stavola

April 14

LILY (Kirchner)
World premiere

Directed by	O'Horgan (d)
Scenic designer	Stabile (d)
Scenic supervisor	Moore (d)
Media designer	Rodolitz (d)
Costume designer	Barcelo
Director for electronic sound	Tcherepnin (d)
Lighting	Nelson (d)
Conductor	Kirchner (d)
Gene Henderson	Berberian
Romilayu	Shirley
Princess Mtalba	Faulkner (d)
Queen Willatale	Blackett (d)
Lily	Belling (d)

Pianist .... Walser (d)
Frances .... McCarty (d)
Prince Itelo ... Matthews (d)
Lily's mother .... Walker
Voice on
  tape .... Gertrude Kirchner

April 15

CAVALLERIA RUSTICANA

Same cast as March 19 (m)
except:

Conductor .... Rudel

Mamma Lucia .... Walker
Santuzza .... Hazzan (d)
Turiddu .... Scano
Lola .... Vergara (d)
Alfio .... Darrenkamp

Followed by:

I PAGLIACCI

Conductor .... Rudel

Tonio .... Fredricks
Beppe .... Lowery
1st peasant .... Carlo,
                (s, Davis)

April 16 (m)

OEDIPUS REX

Same cast as April 8 except:
Jocasta .... Bible

Followed by:

CARMINA BURANA

Same cast as April 8

April 16

CARMEN

Same cast as March 4 except:

Morales .... Jamerson
Zuniga .... Steele
Micaëla .... Fowles,
               (s, Robinson)
Don José .... Parker
Carmen .... Freni
Frasquita .... Thigpen
Mercédès .... Walker
Escamillo .... Ramey

April 17 (m)

THE PIRATES OF PENZANCE

Same cast as March 26 (m)
except:

Ruth .... Shaulis
Kate .... Hegierski
Solo dancer .... Romero (d),
             (s, Korogodsky)

April 17

LILY

Same cast as April 14

April 19

DIE FLEDERMAUS

Same cast as February 26
except:

Rosalinda .... Allison
Blind .... Romaguera
Falke .... Jamerson
Frank .... Densen
Prince Orlofsky ...... Smith
Frosch .... Worth

April 20

LA BELLE HÉLÈNE

Same cast as February 27
except:

Conductor .... Effron

Paris .... Price
Ajax I .... Novick
Agamemnon .... Baker
Male living statue ... Horvath,
            (s, Korogodsky)

April 21

MADAMA BUTTERFLY

Same cast as March 5 (m)
except:

Conductor ...... Campanino

Pinkerton .... Scano
Goro .... Romaguera
Sharpless .... Jamerson
Butterfly .... Craig
The Bonze .... McKee
Trouble .... Guss (d)
Kate Pinkerton .... Toro

April 22

THE IMPRESARIO (Mozart)
New production
(*Der Schauspieldirektor*;
English adaptation by
Giovanni Cardelli)

Directed by .... Corsaro
Designer .... Evans
Lighting .... Sondheimer
Conductor .... Pallo

Mr. Scruples .... Smith
Mr. Bluff .... Billings
Mr. Angel .... Castel
Madame Goldentrill .. Brooks
Miss Silverpeal ... Seibel (d),
             (s, S. Young)

Followed by:

THE VOICE (Poulenc)
First performance by The New
York City Opera Company
(*La Voix Humaine;* English
translation by Joseph Machlis)

Directed by .... Corsaro
Designer .... Evans

Lighting .... Sondheimer
Conductor .... Pallo
The Woman .... Niska

Followed by:

A SOLDIER'S TALE (Stravinsky)
New production
(*L'Histoire du Soldat;*
new English version by
Frank Corsaro)

Directed by .... Corsaro
              and Compton (d)
Designer .... Capecce (d)
Choreographer ..Compton (d)
Lighting .... Billington
Conductor .... Pallo

Devil .... Lankston
Voice .... Smith
Joseph .... Bostwick (d)
Reporter .... Seetoo (d),
               (s, McMahon)
Princess .... Ellington (d)

(Note: Jim-Patrick McMahon,
scheduled for debut, was not
to appear with the company
this season.)

April 23 (m)

OEDIPUS REX

Same cast as April 8 except:

Jocasta .... Bible

Followed by:

CARMINA BURANA

Same cast as April 8

April 23

LA TRAVIATA

Same cast as March 5 except:

Conductor ...... Campanino

Flora .... Hegierski
Douphol .... Foss
D'Obigny .... Paul
Dr. Grenvil .... Yule
Alfredo .... Price
Annina .... Toro
Giuseppe .... Romaguera
Germont .... Elvira

April 24 (m)

THE IMPRESARIO,
THE VOICE
A SOLDIER'S TALE

Same casts as April 22

April 24

RIGOLETTO

Same cast as April 2 except:

Rigoletto .... Elvira
Monterone ..... Munkittrick
Sparafucile .... Roy
Gilda .... Roland
Maddalena .... Vergara

April 26

THE IMPRESARIO,
THE VOICE
A SOLDIER'S TALE

Same casts as April 22

April 27

MADAMA BUTTERFLY

Same cast as March 5 (m)
except:

Conductor .... Campanino
Pinkerton .... Scano
Goro .... Romaguera
Suzuki .... Hegierski
Sharpless .... Jamerson
Butterfly .... Craig
Kate Pinkerton .... Toro

April 28

LILY

Same cast as April 14

April 29

THE IMPRESARIO

Same cast as April 22 except:

Madame Goldentrill .... Little
Miss Silverpeal .... S. Young

Followed by:

THE VOICE

Same cast as April 22

Followed by:

A SOLDIER'S TALE

Same cast as April 22

April 30 (m)

DIE FLEDERMAUS

Same cast as February 26
except:

Conductor ...... Klippstatter
Alfred .... Price
Adele .... Haley
Rosalinda .... Craig
Frank .... Malas
Prince Orlofsky .... Smith
Frosch .... Worth

April 30

OEDIPUS REX

Same cast as April 8 except:

Creon .... Densen
Tiresias .... Steele
Messenger .... Foss
Shepherd .... Lowery

Followed by:

CARMINA BURANA

Same cast as April 8 except:

Soprano .... Brooks
Baritone .... Jamerson
Tenor .... Novick

May 1 (m)

THE IMPRESARIO

Same cast as April 22 except:

Madame Goldentrill .... Little
Miss Silverpeal ..... S. Young

Followed by:

THE VOICE

The Woman .... Schauler

Followed by:

A SOLDIER'S TALE

Same cast as April 22

May 1

ARIADNE AUF NAXOS

Same cast as April 9

Fall 1977 (AUGUST 31– NOVEMBER 13)

Female artists
Allison, Patti
Armstrong, Karan
Arrauzau, Francine
Ballard, Earline
Bible, Frances
Brooks, Patricia
Brustadt, Marilyn*
Campbell, Joan
Carron, Elisabeth
Clarey, Cynthia*
Costa-Greenspon, Muriel
Craig, Patricia
Curry, Diane
Daniels, Sharon
Ehrlich, Judith
Esham, Faith*
Evans, Beverly
Fowles, Glenys
Freni, RoseMarie
Greene, Harriet
Haley, Elizabeth
Hegierski, Kathleen
Howard, Ann
Hynes, Elizabeth
Kehrig, Diana
Lee, Sung Sook
Lindsley, Celina*
Little, Gwenlynn
Lynn, Joyce
Malfitano, Catherine

Meier, Johanna
Metzger, Rita
Mines, Madeleine
Niculescu, Mariana*
Niska, Maralin
Orlando, Valeria
Robinson, Faye
Rolandi, Gianna
Schauler, Eileen
Seibel, Paula
Shaulis, Jane
Sheil, Martha*
Sills, Beverly
Soviero, Diana
Tatum, Nancy
Thigpen, Martha
Toro, Puli
Vergara, Victoria
Walker, Sandra
Wallis, Delia*
Wyner, Susan Davenny*
Zannoth, Sherry

Male artists
Bartolini, Lando
Billings, James
Bohachevsky, George
Brewer, James
Carlo, Don
Castel, Nico

Chapman, William
Collins, Kenneth
Cossa, Dominic
Davis, Harris
Densen, Irwin
Di Giuseppe, Enrico
Elvira, Pablo
Fekula, Peter
Foss, Harlan
Fran, Ethan
Fredricks, Richard
Gill, Richard T.
Green, Jay
Green, Jonathan*
Griffith, David
Guettel, Adam
Guss, John Galt
Hale, Robert
Harper, Talmage
Hartman, Vernon
Hensel, Howard
Holloway, David
Hyman, Adam*
Jamerson, Thomas
Justus, William
Kays, Alan*
Kingman, Dan
Lankston, John
Ledbetter, William
Long, Charles
Lowery, Melvin

* New artist   * New artist   * New artist

Malamood, Herman
Mauro, Ermanno
McKee, Richard
Meade, Christopher*
Molese, Michele
Munkittrick, Mark
Novick, Melvyn
Paul, Robert
Presto
Price, Henry
Ramey, Samuel
Roe, Charles
Romaguera, Joaquin
Roy, Will
Schwartzman, Seymour
Sergi, James
Shinall, Vern
Siena, Jerold
Sims, Jack
Smith, Andrew*
Smith, David Rae
Steele, Philip
Taylor, Richard
Theyard, Harry
Trussel, Jacque*
Ukena, Paul
Winston, Lee*
Worth, Coley
Yule, Don

Conductors
Bertini, Gary
Comissiona, Sergiu*
Effron, David
Kellogg, Cal Stewart
La Selva, Vincent
Mauceri, John*
Mester, Jorge
Morelli, Giuseppe
Musgrave, Thea*
Noll, William*
Pallo, Imre
Rudel, Julius
Somogi, Judith
Walser, Lloyd

Chorus master
Walser, Lloyd

Assistant chorus master
Hillmer, Leann*

Solo dancers
Balestracci, Sandra
Galan, Esperanza
Gardella, Toni-Ann*
Itow, Candace

Anthony, Steve
Calvert, John
Horvath, Juliu
Korogodsky, Mikhail
Mann III, Fred
Mattson, Wayne
Nolfi, Ed
Osbon, John*
Romero, Rafael
Rubino, Michael

Choreographers
Andrew, Thomas
Field, Ron
Nolfi, Ed*

Directors
Auerbach, Cynthia
Capobianco, Tito

* New artist

Copley, John*
Corsaro, Frank
Eddleman, Jack
Freedman, Gerald
Getke, Richard
Graham, Colin*
Hicks, David
Karp, Barbara*
Presnell, Steve
Prince, Harold
Rudel, Julius
Yannopoulos, Dino

Designers
Aldredge, Theoni V.
Campbell, Patton
Eck, Marsha Louis
Evans, Lloyd
Fletcher, Robert
George, Hal
Lee, Eugene
Lee, Franne
Mess, Suzanne*
Mitchell, David
Montresor, Beni
O'Hearn, Robert*
Ter-Arutunian, Rouben
Toms, Carl
Varona, José

* New artist

August 31

MEFISTOFELE (Boito)

Conductor .... Rudel

Mefistofele .... Ramey
Faust .... Mauro
Wagner .... Griffith
Margherita .... Meier
Marta .... Evans
Pantalis .... Walker
Elena .... Meier
Nereo .... Romaguera
Solo dancers .... Balestracci,
                    Itow; Horvath

September 1

TURANDOT (Puccini)

Conductor .... Rudel

Mandarin .... Densen
Liù .... Malfitano
Calaf .... Collins
Timur .... Gill
Turandot .... Ballard,
                    (s, Tatum)
Ping .... Jamerson
Pang .... Griffith
Pong .... Lankston
Emperor .... Romaguera

September 2

DIE FLEDERMAUS (J. Strauss)
(English version by
Ruth and Thomas Martin)

Conductor .... Rudel

Alfred .... Price
Adele .... Sills
Rosalinda .... Meier
Eisenstein .... Roe
Blind .... Lowery
Falke .... Holloway

Frank .... McKee
Sally .... Toro
Ivan .... Sims
Prince Orlofsky .. D. R. Smith
Frosch .... Worth
Solo dancers .... Balestracci,
                    Galan; Horvath

September 3 (m)

LA TRAVIATA (Verdi)

Conductor .... Pallo

Violetta ...... Niculescu (d)
Flora .... Hegierski
Douphol .... Steele
D'Obigny .... Ledbetter
Dr. Grenvil .... Densen
Gaston .... Lowery
Alfredo .... Trussel (d)
Annina .... Toro
Giuseppe .... Romaguera
Germont .... Fredricks
Messenger .... Harper
Solo dancer .... Galan

September 3

CAVALLERIA RUSTICANA
(Mascagni)

Conductor .... Kellogg

Mamma Lucia .... Shaulis
Santuzza .... Niska
Alfio .... Justus
Turiddu .... Di Giuseppe
Lola .... Vergara

Followed by:

I PAGLIACCI (Leoncavallo)

Conductor .... Kellogg

Tonio .... Elvira
Canio .... Malamood
        (finished by Collins)
Nedda .... Soviero
Beppe .... Kays (d)
Peasants ..Davis, Bohachevsky
Silvio .... Roe
Acrobats ... Horvath, Rubino

(Note: Herman Malamood lost
his voice halfway through the
opera; Kenneth Collins sang the
rest of the performance from the
orchestra pit while Malamood
mimed the role.)

September 4 (m)

MADAMA BUTTERFLY (Puccini)

Conductor .... Morelli

Pinkerton .... Molese
Goro .... Siena
Suzuki .... Walker
Sharpless .... Cossa
Butterfly .... Craig
*Imperial
 Commissioner* ... Ledbetter
Registrar, Yamadori .... Sergi
The Bonze .... Steele
Trouble .... Gust
Kate Pinkerton .... Toro

September 4

DIE FLEDERMAUS

Same cast as September 2

September 7

DIE FLEDERMAUS

Same cast as September 2

September 8

CARMEN (Bizet)

Production director .. Auerbach
Conductor .... Pallo

Morales .... Jamerson
Zuniga .... McKee
Micaëla .... Robinson
Don José .... Trussel
Carmen .... Howard
Frasquita .... Thigpen
Mercédès .... Walker
Lillas Pastia,
 Guide .... Romaguera
Escamillo .... Holloway
Remendado .... Lankston
Dancairo .... Foss

September 9

LA BOHÈME (Puccini)

Conductor .... Morelli

Rodolfo .... Di Giuseppe
Marcello .... Elvira
Colline .... Hale
Schaunard .... Jamerson
Benoit .... Yule
Mimi .... Soviero
Parpignol .... Romaguera
Musetta .... Zannoth
Alcindoro .... Billings
Guards .. Brewer, Bohachevsky

September 10 (m)

LA TRAVIATA

Same cast as September 3 (m)

September 10

TURANDOT

Same cast as September 1
except:

Turandot .... Tatum

September 11 (m)

MADAMA BUTTERFLY

Same cast as September 4 (m)
except:

Pinkerton .... Taylor
Suzuki .... Hegierski

September 11

MANON (Massenet)

Conductor .... Rudel

Guillot .... Castel
De Brétigny .... Hale
Rousette .... Hynes
Javotte .... Fowles
Rosette .... Walker
Innkeeper .... Foss

Lescaut .... Fredricks
Guards .... Sergi, Yule
Manon .... Sills
Des Grieux .... Molese
Maid .... Greene
Count Des Grieux .... Gill
Prima ballerina .. Gardella (d)
Premier danseur .. Korogodsky
Ballet master .... Rubino
Cupid .... Balestracci
Seminary porter .... Carlo
Gambler .... Kingman
Sergeant .... Yule

September 13

MEFISTOFELE

Same cast as August 31 except:

Faust .... Molese

September 14

CAVALLERIA RUSTICANA

Same cast as September 3
except:

Santuzza .... Freni,
                     (s, Niska)
Alfio .... Long,
                     (s, Justus)

Followed by:

I PAGLIACCI

Same cast as September 3
except:

Canio .... Malamood

September 15

MANON

Same cast as September 11

September 16

DIE FLEDERMAUS

Same cast as September 2
except:

Conductor .... Pallo

Alfred .... Griffith
Adele .... Haley
Eisenstein .... Hensel
Falke .... Cossa

September 17 (m)

TURANDOT

Same cast as September 1
except:

Liù .... Niculescu
Turandot .... Tatum

September 17

CARMEN

Same cast as September 8

September 18 (m)

MANON

Same cast as September 11
except:

Javotte .... Little

September 18

MADAMA BUTTERFLY

Same cast as September 4 (m)
except:

Pinkerton .... Taylor
Suzuki .... Curry
Butterfly .... Niska

September 20

MANON

Same cast as September 11
except:

Javotte .... Little
Des Grieux .... Price

September 22

THE MARRIAGE OF FIGARO
(Mozart)
New production
(English version by
Ruth and Thomas Martin)

Directed by ...... Copley (d)
Designer .... Toms
Lighting .... Sondheimer
Conductor .... Rudel

Figaro .... Ramey
Susanna .... Malfitano
Bartolo .... McKee
Marcellina .... Shaulis
Cherubino .... Wallis (d)
Almaviva .... Justus
Basilio .. Jonathan Green (d)
Countess .... Meier
Antonio .... Foss
Curzio .... Lowery
Barbarina .... Thighpen
Peasant girls ...... Campbell,
                      Orlando

September 23

LA TRAVIATA

Same cast as September 3 (m)
except:

Violetta .... Robinson
Germont .... Cossa

September 24 (m)

RIGOLETTO (Verdi)

Stage director .... Presnell
Conductor .... Pallo

Rigoletto .... Elvira
Monterone's daughter .. Galan
Clown .... Horvath
Duke .... Di Giuseppe
Borsa .... Hensel
Countess Ceprano .... Kehrig
Ceprano .... Ledbetter
Marullo .... Jamerson
Monterone .... Densen
Sparafucile .... Roy
Gilda .... Rolandi
Giovanna .... Toro
Page .... Mines
Maddalena .... Walker

September 24

LA BOHÈME

Same cast as September 9
except:

Rodolfo .... Bartolini
Marcello .... Justus
Benoit .... Densen
Mimi .... Niculescu
Alcindoro .... Yule

September 25 (m)

CAVALLERIA RUSTICANA

Same cast as September 3
except:

Mamma Lucia .... Curry
Santuzza .... Schauler
Alfio .... Long
Turiddu .... Malamood

Followed by:

I PAGLIACCI

Same cast as September 3
except:

Tonio .... Fredricks
Canio .... Collins

September 25

MADAMA BUTTERFLY

Same cast as September 4 (m)
except:

Pinkerton .... Taylor
Goro .... J. Green
Suzuki .... Curry
Butterfly .... Niska

September 27

TURANDOT

Same cast as September 1
except:

Liù .... Niculescu
Calaf .... Mauro
Timur .... Roy

September 29

THE MARRIAGE OF FIGARO

Same cast as September 22

September 30

THE VOICE OF ARIADNE
(Musgrave)
American premiere

Directed by .... Graham (d)
Designer .... Toms
Lighting .... Billington
Conductor .... Musgrave (d)

Gualtiero .... Gill
Giovanni .... Lowery
Marchesa Bianca
  Bianchi .... Walker
Mrs. Tracy .... Bible
Countess .... Clarey (d)
Baldovino .... Griffith
Mr. Lamb .... Jamerson

Count Marco
  Valerio .... Holloway
Voice of Ariadne ... Voice of
                    Joan Davies

October 1 (m)

LA TRAVIATA

Same cast as September 3 (m)
except:

Alfredo .... Di Giuseppe
Germont .... Cossa

October 1

MEFISTOFELE

Same cast as August 31

October 2 (m)

TURANDOT

Same cast as September 1
except:

Timur .... Roy
Ping .... Ledbetter

October 2

THE VOICE OF ARIADNE

Same cast as September 30

October 4

CAVALLERIA RUSTICANA

Same cast as September 3
except:

Conductor .... Effron

Mamma Lucia .... Curry
Turiddu .... Bartolini
Lola .... Hegierski

Followed by:

I PAGLIACCI

Same cast as September 3
except:

Conductor .... Effron

Canio .... Collins
Beppe .... Lowery
1st Peasant .... Carlo
Silvio .... Jamerson

October 5

CARMEN

Same cast as September 8
except:

Micaëla .... Hynes
Don José .... Malamood
Carmen .... Arrauzau
Mercédès .... Hegierski

October 6

MADAMA BUTTERFLY

Same cast as September 4 (m)
except:

Conductor .... Noll (d)

Pinkerton .... Bartolini
Goro .... J. Green

Sharpless .... Elvira
Butterfly .... Carron,
                    (s, Lee)

October 7

RIGOLETTO

Same cast as September 24 (m)
except:

Rigoletto .... Fredricks
Maddalena .... Vergara

October 8 (m)

THE MARRIAGE OF FIGARO

Same cast as September 22
except:

Barbarina .... Kehrig

October 8

LA BOHÈME

Same cast as September 9
except:

Conductor .... La Selva

Rodolfo .... Mauro
Marcello .... Cossa
Colline .... Roy
Benoit .... Densen
Musetta .... Allison
Alcindoro .... Yule

October 9 (m)

THE MAGIC FLUTE (Mozart)
(English version by
Ruth and Thomas Martin)

Directed and
  conducted by ...... Rude

Tamino .... Price
1st Lady .... Thigpe
2nd Lady .... Curry
3rd Lady .... Shauli
Papageno .... Ro
Queen of the Night .. Roland
1st Spirit .... Fekul
2nd Spirit .... Guette
3rd Spirit .... Hyman (d
Pamina .... Robinso
Monostatos .... Fos
Speaker .... Steel
Sarastro .... Ro
1st Priest .... Lanksto
2nd Priest .... Yul
Papagena .... Littl
1st Armored man .... Hens
2nd Armored man .... Dense

October 9

CARMEN

Same cast as September 8
except:

Conductor .... Somo

Micaëla .... Hyn
Don José .... Colli
Carmen .... Arrauza
Frasquita .... Kehr
Mercédès .... Hegiers
Escamillo .... Fredric

October 11

LA BOHÈME

Same cast as September 9
except:

Conductor	Mester
Rodolfo	Mauro
Marcello	Cossa
Colline	Ramey
Parpignol	Lowery
Musetta	Allison

October 12

MADAMA BUTTERFLY

Same cast as September 4 (m)
except:

Conductor	Noll
Pinkerton	Bartolini
Goro	J. Green
Sharpless	Elvira
Butterfly	Carron, (s, Lee)
Trouble	Guss

(Note: Ethan Fran announced as
replacement for Guss, but Guss
performed. Fran was not to
appear this season.)

October 13

RIGOLETTO

Same cast as September 24 (m)
except:

Rigoletto	Fredricks
Duke	Price
Borsa	Lowery
Gilda	Malfitano
Maddalena	Vergara

October 14

DIE FLEDERMAUS

Same cast as September 2
except:

Conductor	Pallo
Alfred	Sandor, (s, Griffith)
Adele	Haley
Rosalinda	Allison
Eisenstein	Lankston
Falke	Cossa
Frosch	Billings

October 15 (m)

THE MARRIAGE OF FIGARO

Same cast as September 22
except:

Figaro	Holloway
Susanna	Little
Marcellina	Hartman
Countess	Sheil (d)
Barbarina	Kehrig, (s, Thigpen)

October 15

MEFISTOFELE

Same cast as August 31 except:

Conductor	Mauceri (d)
Faust	Collins
Margherita	Ehrlich
Marta	Walker
Elena	Ehrlich

October 16 (m)

CARMEN

Same cast as September 8
except:

Morales	Sergi
Zuniga	Steele
Micaëla	Craig
Don José	Theyard
Carmen	Freni
Mercédès	Hegierski
Escamillo	Fredricks
Remendado	J. Green

October 16

LA FANCIULLA DEL WEST
(Puccini)
First performance by The New
York City Opera Company

Directed by	Corsaro
Scenic designer	O'Hearn (d)
Costume designer	Mess (d)
Lighting	Sondheimer
Conductor	Comissiona (d)
Nick	Lankston
Jack Rance	Long, (s, Chapman)
Larkens	Ledbetter
Billy	Yule
Joe	Hensel
Bello	Sergi
Harry	Griffith
Happy	Densen
Sid	Foss
Sonora	Jamerson
Trin	Lowery
Jake	A. Smith (d)
Ashby	McKee
Minnie	Niska
Post rider	Romaguera
Johnson	Mauro
Castro	Billings
Wowkle	Hegierski

(Note: Chapman was not to
appear this season.)

Broadcast

October 18

MANON

Same cast as September 11
except:

Javotte	Little
Des Grieux	Price
Count des Grieux	Ramey

Televised broadcast

October 19

THE VOICE OF ARIADNE

Same cast as September 30

October 20

THE MAGIC FLUTE

Same cast as October 9 (m)
except:

Sarastro	Gill
Papagena	Kehrig, (s, Little)

October 21

MEFISTOFELE

Same cast as August 31 except:

Faust	Collins
Marta	Walker

October 22 (m)

MANON

Same cast as September 11
except:

De Brétigny	Jamerson
Javotte	Fowles, (s, Little)
Des Grieux	Taylor

October 22

LA FANCIULLA DEL WEST

Same cast as October 16
except:

Jack Rance	Long (Act I); Shinall (Acts II & III)

October 23 (m)

DIE FLEDERMAUS

Same cast as September 2
except:

Conductor	Pallo
Alfred	Griffith
Adele	Rolandi
Rosalinda	Allison
Eisenstein	Hensel
Sally	Kehrig
Prince Orlofsky	Foss
Frosch	Billings

October 23

L'INCORONAZIONE DI POPPEA
(Monteverdi)

Conductor	Mauceri
Fortuna	Rolandi
Virtù	Curry
Amor	Haley
Ottone	Cossa
Soldiers	Lankston, Griffith
Poppea	Wyner (d)
Nerone	Roe
Arnalta	Shaulis
Ottavia	Bible

Drusilla .... Rolandi
Valetto .... Lankston
Seneca .... Gill
Pallade .... Walker
Liberto and Littore . . Ledbetter
Damigella .... Haley
Lucano .... Griffith

Broadcast

October 25

LA FANCIULLA DEL WEST

Same cast as October 16
except:

Jack Rance .... Shinall,
                      (s, Long)
Trin .... Novick,
                     (s, Lowery)

October 26

THE VOICE OF ARIADNE

Same cast as September 30

October 27

L'INCORONAZIONE DI POPPEA

Same cast as October 23

October 28

RIGOLETTO

Same cast as September 24 (m)
except:

Borsa .... Lowery
Monterone .... Steele
Sparafucile .... Densen
Gilda .... Malfitano

October 29 (m)

THE PIRATES OF PENZANCE
(Sullivan)

Conductor .... Somogi

Samuel .... Ledbetter,
                   (s, Sergi)
Pirate King .... McKee
Frederic .... Hensel
Ruth .... Costa-Greenspon
Edith .... Kehrig
Kate .... Walker
Isabel .... Luxemburg
Mabel .... Rolandi
Major-General
  Stanley .... Billings
Police sergeant .... Densen
Solo dancer .... Romero

October 29

LA TRAVIATA

Same cast as September 3 (m)
except:

Violetta .... Robinson
D'Obigny .... Paul
Dr. Grenvil .... Yule
Gaston .... Novick
Germont .... Cossa

October 30 (m)

THE MAGIC FLUTE

Same cast as October 9 (m)
except:

Conductor .... Pallo
1st Lady .... Thigpen,
                      (s, Sheil)
2nd Lady .... Zannoth
3rd Lady .... Walker
Queen of the
  Night .... Lindsley (d)
Monostatos .... Billings
Pamina .... Wyner
Papagena .... Rolandi

October 30

THE MARRIAGE OF FIGARO

Same cast as September 22
except:

Conductor .... Somogi

Cherubino .... Esham (d)
Almaviva .... Hartman
Basilio .... Lankston,
                      (s, J. Green)
Countess .... Sheil,
                       (s, Meier)

Broadcast

November 1

DIE FLEDERMAUS

Same cast as September 2
except:

Conductor .... Pallo

Adele .... Rolandi
Rosalinda .... Armstrong
Eisenstein .... Hensel
Falke .... Cossa
Sally .... Kehrig
Prince Orlofsky .... Foss
Frosch .... Billings

November 2

LA BOHÈME

Same cast as September 9
except:

Conductor .... Mester

Rodolfo .... Bartolini
Marcello .... Holloway
Colline .... Ramey
Schaunard .... Ledbetter
Mimi .... Carron
Parpignol .... Lowery
Musetta .... Daniels

November 3

CAVALLERIA RUSTICANA

Same cast as September 3
except:

Conductor .... Effron

Mamma Lucia .... Curry

Santuzza .... Freni
Alfio .... Long
Lola .... Hegierski

Followed by:

I PAGLIACCI

Same cast as September 3
except:

Conductor .... Effron

Tonio .... Fredricks
Canio .... Malamood
Nedda .... Zannoth
Beppe .... Lowery
Silvio .... Jamerson

Broadcast

November 4

ASHMEDAI (Tal)
(English version by
Alan Marbe)

Choreography .... Ron Field
Restaged by .... Nolfi (d)
Conductor .... Bertini

Sergeant .... Nolfi
Army ..... Anthony, Calvert,
              Mann, Mattson
Fire-eater .... Presto
Knife thrower .... Rubino
Juggler .... Jay Green
Ashmedai .... Lankston
Counsellors .... Romaguera,
              Ledbetter, Densen
Firechief .... Foss
Prince .... Griffith
Queen .... Schauler
Executioner .... Steele
King .... Ukena
Tailor .... Lowery
                     (s, J. Green)
Daughter .... Rolandi
Mistress of the inn ..... Craig
Citizen .... Yule
Soldier .... Hense
Townspeople ...... Campbell,
              Lynn, Metzger
Trumpeter .... Kingman
Drummer .... Meade (d),
                     (s, Dovel)
Officer .... D. R. Smith
Runner .... Winston (d
Rooster .... Osbon (d

(Note: Kenn Dovel appeared
only with the chorus this
season.)

November 5 (m)

L'INCORONAZIONE DI POPPEA

Same cast as October 23
except:

Fortuna .... Litt
Ottone .... Hollow
Drusilla .... Litt
Seneca .... R

November 5

CARMEN

Same cast as September 8
except:

Conductor	Walser
Morales	Sergi
Zuniga	Densen, (s, Steele)
Micaëla	Fowles
Carmen	Freni
Mercédès	Hegierski
Escamillo	Fredricks
Remendado	Novick
Dancairo	Ledbetter, (s, Foss)

November 6 (m)

THE PIRATES OF PENZANCE

Same cast as October 29 (m)
except:

Samuel	Sergi
Frederic	Price
Mabel	Haley
Police sergeant	Munkittrick

November 6

ASHMEDAI

Same cast as November 4
except:

Firechief	Paul, (s, Foss)
Tailor	Lowery, (s, J. Green)

November 8

LA FANCIULLA DEL WEST

Same cast as October 16

November 9

L'INCORONAZIONE DI POPPEA

Same cast as October 23
except:

Fortuna	Little
Virtù	Hegierski

Ottone	Holloway
Poppea	Fowles
Nerone	Hensel
Ottavia	Curry
Drusilla	Little
Seneca	Roy
Pallade	Hegierski

November 10

THE IMPRESARIO (Mozart)
(English adaptation by
Giovanni Cardelli)

Conductor	Pallo
Mr. Scruples	D. R. Smith
Mr. Bluff	Billings
Mr. Angel	Castel
Madame Goldentrill	Brooks
Miss Silverpeal	Seibel

Followed by:

THE VOICE (Poulenc)
(La Voix Humane: English
translation by Joseph Machlis)

Conductor	Pallo
The Woman	Niska

Followed by:

L'HEURE ESPAGNOLE (Ravel)
(English translation by
Katharine Wolff)

Director	Auerbach
Conductor	Pallo
Torquemada	Castel
Ramiro	Fredricks
Concepcion	Daniels
Gonzalve	Lowery
Don Inigo Gomez	McKee

November 11

LA FANCIULLA DEL WEST

Same cast as October 16
except:

Sonora	Paul
Jake	Hartman
Ashby	Steele
Minnie	Armstrong
Johnson	Malamood

November 12 (m)

MADAMA BUTTERFLY

Same cast as September 4 (m)
except:

Conductor	Effron
Pinkerton	Malamood
Goro	Romaguera
Suzuki	Curry
Sharpless	Schwartzman
Butterfly	Carron
Kate Pinkerton	Hegierski

November 12

LA TRAVIATA

Same cast as September 3 (m)
except:

Violetta	Craig
D'Obigny	Paul
Dr. Grenvil	Yule
Gaston	Novick
Alfredo	Bartolini
Annina	Thigpen

November 13 (m)

LA BOHÈME

Same cast as September 9
except:

Conductor	Mester
Rodolfo	Mauro
Marcello	Holloway
Colline	Ramey
Schaunard	Ledbetter
Mimi	Fowles
Parpignol	Lowery
Musetta	Daniels

November 13

THE MAGIC FLUTE

Same cast as October 9 (m)
except:

1st Lady	Sheil
2nd Lady	Zannoth
Papageno	Jamerson
Queen of the Night	Brustadt (d)
3rd Spirit	Sapolsky
Monostatos	Billings
Papagena	Rolandi

Broadcast

Spring 1978 (FEBRUARY 23 – APRIL 30)

Hill, Eunice*
Hinds, Esther
Howard, Ann
Little, Gwenlynn
Malfitano, Catherine
Meier, Johanna
Mercer-White, Rebecca*
Mines, Madeleine
Murphy, Kathleen*
Niculescu, Mariana
Orlando, Valeria
Randazzo, Maria
Reynolds, Myrna
Robinson, Faye
Rogers, Noëlle
Rolandi, Gianna
Saunders, Arlene
Schauler, Eileen
Seibel, Paula
Shaulis, Jane
Sheil, Martha
Sills, Beverly
Smith, Alanna*
Soviero, Diana
Spacagna, Maria*
Thigpen, Martha
Thomson, Heather
Thyssen, Charlott
Tomanec, Joyce
Toro, Puli
Verdejo, Awilda*
Walker, Sandra
Wallis, Delia
Zannoth, Sherry
Zschau, Marilyn*

Male artists
Bailey, Dennis*
Baker, Alan
Bartolini, Lando
Berberian, Ara
Billings, James
Bohachevsky, George
Boucher, Ron
Brewer, James
Burchinal, Frederick*
Collins, Kenneth
Cossa, Dominic
Davis, Harris
Densen, Irwin
Di Giuseppe, Enrico
Dovel, Kenn
Elvira, Pablo
Embree, Marc*
Fekula, Peter
Foldi, Andrew*
Foss, Harlan
Fredricks, Richard
Gill, Richard T.
Grahame, Gerald*
Green, Jonathan
Griffith, David
Guss, John Galt
Harper, Talmage
Hartman, Vernon
Henderson, Don
Hensel, Howard
Holloway, David
Hunsberger, Herbert*
Jamerson, Thomas
Justus, William
Kays, Alan

* New artist

Lankston, John
Ledbetter, William
Lima, Luis*
Long, Charles
Lowery, Melvin
Malamood, Herman
Mauro, Ermanno
McKee, Richard
Morales, Abram
Norman, Jerold*
Paul, Robert
Perry, Louis
Price, Henry
Ramey, Samuel
Reed, Bruce*
Rendall, David*
Roe, Charles
Sandor, John
Sapolsky, Robert
Scalese, Bobby*
Sergi, James
Shinall, Vern
Sims, Jack
Smith, David Rae
Steele, Philip
Taylor, Richard
Titus, Alan
Trussel, Jacque
Wildermann, William
Worth, Coley
Yule, Don

Conductors
De Renzi, Victor*
Effron, David
Keene, Christopher
Kellogg, Cal Stewart
La Selva, Vincent
Mauceri, John
Minde, Stefan*
Pallo, Imre
Queler, Eve*
Rudel, Julius
Somogi, Judith
Walser, Lloyd

Chorus master
Walser, Lloyd

Assistant chorus master
Hillmer, Leann

Solo dancers
Ettlin, Emilietta*
Galan, Esperanza
Gardella, Toni-Ann
Itow, Candace
McBride, Patricia*

Horvath, Juliu
Rubino, Michael

Choreographers
Andrew, Thomas
Denda, Gigi

Directors
Auerbach, Cynthia
Bamberger, David
Capobianco, Tito
Copley, John
Corsaro, Frank
Denda, Gigi
Eddleman, Jack

* New artist

Freedman, Gerald
Getke, Richard
Hicks, David
Mann, Theodore
Rizzo, Francis
Smith, Christian*

Designers
Aldredge, Theoni V.
Campbell, Patton
Colt, Alvin
Evans, Lloyd
Fletcher, Robert
George, Hal
Lee, Ming Cho
Luiken, Carol
Mess, Suzanne
Mitchell, David
Oenslager, Donald
O'Hearn, Robert
Salzer, Beeb
Toms, Carl
Varona, José
Venza, Jac

* New artist

February 23

LA TRAVIATA (Verdi)

Assistant to
  Corsaro .... Lesenger
Conductor .... Pallo

Violetta .... Niculescu
Flora ..... Mercer-White (d)
Douphol .... Baker
D'Obigny .... Ledbetter
Dr. Grenvil .... Densen
Gaston .... Hensel
Alfredo .... Di Giuseppe,
                   (s, Price)
Annina .... Toro
Giuseppe .... Lowery
Germont .... Elvira
Messenger .... Harper
Solo dancer .... Galan

February 24

MEFISTOFELE (Boito)

Conductor .... Rudel
Mefistofele .... Ramey
Faust .... Collins
Wagner .... Griffith
Margherita .... Ehrlich
Marta .... Evans
                   (s, Walker)
Elena .... Ehrlich
Pantalis .... Evans
                   (s, Walker)
Nereo .... Lowery
Solo dancers .... Gardella
                   Itow; Horvath

February 25 (m)

CAVALLERIA RUSTICANA
(Mascagni)

Stage director ..... Smith (d
Conductor .... Kellogg

Mamma Lucia .... Shaulis
Santuzza .... Fredi

Alfio .... Justus
Turiddu .... Di Giuseppe
Lola .... Hill (d)

Followed by:

I PAGLIACCI (Leoncavallo)

Stage director ..... Smith (d)
Conductor .... Kellogg

Tonio .... Fredricks
Acrobats ... Horvath, Rubino
Canio .... Malamood
Nedda .... Zannoth
Beppe .... Kays
Peasants ..Davis, Bohachevsky
Silvio .... Jamerson

February 25

MADAMA BUTTERFLY (Puccini)

Conductor .... Somogi

Pinkerton .... Sandor
Goro .... Green
Suzuki .... Shaulis,
                (s, Walker)
Sharpless .... Holloway
Butterfly .... Hinds
Imperial
 Commissioner ... Ledbetter
Registrar, Yamadori .... Sergi
The Bonze .... Steele
Trouble .... Guss
Kate Pinkerton .... Toro

February 26 (m)

MEFISTOFELE

Same cast as February 24
except:

Marta .... Hegierski,
                (s, Walker)
Pantalis .... Hegierski
                (s, Walker)

February 26

LA TRAVIATA

Same cast as February 23
except:
Alfredo .... Price
Broadcast performance

March 1

LA BOHÈME (Puccini)

Conductor .... Mauceri

Rodolfo .... Di Giuseppe
Marcello .... Holloway
Colline .... Gill
Schaunard .... Jamerson
Benoit .... Foss
Mimi .... Niculescu
Parpignol .... Kays
Musetta .... Daniels

Alcindoro .... Yule
Guards ..Brewer, Bohachevsky

March 2

IL BARBIERE DI SIVIGLIA
(Rossini)

Directed by .... Eddleman
Designer .... Evans
Lighting .... Sondheimer
Conductor .... Mauceri

Fiorello .... Sergi
Almaviva .... Price
Figaro .... Elvira
Bartolo .... Foldi (d)
Rosina .... Rolandi
Basilio .... Ramey
Berta .... Shaulis
Officer .... Yule

March 3

LA FANCIULLA DEL WEST
(Puccini)

Conductor .... Keene

Nick .... Lankston
Jack Rance .... Shinall
Larkens .... Ledbetter
Billy .... Yule
Joe .... Hensel
Bello .... Sergi
Harry .... Green
Happy .... Densen
Sid .... Foss
Sonora .... Jamerson
Trin .... Lowery
Iake .... Hartman
Ashby .... McKee
Minnie .... Zschau (d)
Post rider .... Kays
Johnson .... Mauro
Castro .... Baker
Wowkle .... Hill

March 4 (m)

LA BOHÈME

Same cast as March 1 except:

Rodolfo .... Bartolini
Mimi .... Clarey

March 4

RIGOLETTO (Verdi)

Assistant to
 Corsaro .... Bentley
Conductor .... Pallo

Rigoletto .... Elvira
Monterone's daughter .. Galan
Clown .... Horvath
Duke .... Collins
Borsa .... Hensel
Countess Ceprano ... Thigpen
Ceprano .... Ledbetter
Marullo .... Paul
Monterone .... Steele
Sparafucile .... Densen
Gilda .... Robinson
Giovanna .... Toro
Page .... Mines
Maddalena .... Hill

March 5 (m)

CARMEN (Bizet)

Conductor .... Pallo

Morales .... Jamerson
Zuniga .... Embree (d)
Micaëla .... Fowles
Don José .... Trussel
Carmen .... Howard
Frasquita .... Thigpen
Mercédès ...... Mercer-White
Lillas Pastia, Guide .... Baker
Escamillo .... Fredricks
Remendado .... Lankston
Dancairo .... Ledbetter

March 5

LA FANCIULLA DEL WEST

Same cast as March 3

March 7

RIGOLETTO

Same cast as March 4 except:

Monterone .... Densen
Sparafucile .... Gill

March 8

DIE FLEDERMAUS (J. Strauss)
(English version by
Ruth and Thomas Martin)

Stage director .... Smith
Conductor .... Pallo

Alfred .... Price
Adele .... Rolandi
Rosalinda .... Allison
Eisenstein .... Roe
Blind .... Lowery
Falke .... Jamerson
Frank .... McKee
Sally .... Thigpen
Ivan .... Sims
Prince Orlofsky .... Foss
Frosch .... Worth
Solo dancers .... Galan,
        McBride (d); Horvath

March 9

CARMEN

Same cast as March 5 (m)
except:

Escamillo .... Holloway

March 10

CAVALLERIA RUSTICANA

Same cast as February 25 (m)
except:

Santuzza .... Schauler
Alfio .... Long
Turiddu .... Bartolini

Followed by:

I PAGLIACCI

Same cast as February 25 (m)
except:

Canio .... Collins
Silvio .... Roe

March 11 (m)

LA FANCIULLA DEL WEST

Same cast as March 3 except:

Jack Rance ... Burchinal (d)
Jake .... Holloway
Ashby .... Steele
Minnie .... Saunders
Post rider .... Perry,
(s, Kays)
Johnson .... Trussel

March 11

IL BARBIERE DI SIVIGLIA

Same cast as March 2 except:

Almaviva .... Kays,
(s, Price)
Basilio .... Berberian

March 12 (m)

MADAMA BUTTERFLY

Same cast as February 25 except:

Pinkerton .... Lima (d)
Suzuki .... Curry
Butterfly .... Craig
Kate Pinkerton .. Murphy (d)

March 12

TOSCA (Puccini)

Staged by .... Hicks
Conductor .... Kellogg

Angelotti .... Long
Sacristan .... McKee
Cavaradossi .... Mauro
Tosca .... Galvany
Scarpia .... Justus
Spoletta .... Green
Sciarrone .... Ledbetter
Shepherd .... Grof
Jailer .... Yule

Broadcast performance

March 14

MEFISTOFELE

Same cast as February 24 except:

Conductor .... Mauceri

Marta .... Walker
Pantalis .... Hill

March 15

CAVALLERIA RUSTICANA

Same cast as February 25 (m) except:

Alfio .... Long

Followed by:

I PAGLIACCI

Same cast as February 25 (m) except:

Tonio .... Long,
(s, Fredricks)
Canio .... Mauro

Nedda .... Thomson
Silvio .... Roe

March 16

LA TRAVIATA

Same cast as February 23 except:

Violetta .... Robinson
Dr. Grenvil .... Yule
Gaston .... Kays
Alfredo .... Lima
Annina .... Shaulis
Germont .... Burchinal

March 17

THE TURN OF THE SCREW
(Britten)

Conductor .... Keene

Prologue .... Hensel
Guardian .... Lankston
Governess .... Schauler
Miles .... Fekula
Flora .... Randazzo
Mrs. Grose .... Faull
Quint .... Lankston
Miss Jessel .... Thigpen

March 18 (m)

Same cast as March 5 (m) except:

Don José .... Bailey (d)
Frasquita ..... Spacagna (d)
Mercédès .... Walker

March 18

TOSCA

Same cast as March 12

March 19 (m)

LA FANCIULLA DEL WEST

Same cast as March 3 except:

Jack Rance .... Burchinal
Harry .... Griffith
Sonora .... Paul
Minnie .... Saunders
Johnson .... Trussel
Wowkle .... Tomanec

March 19

MADAMA BUTTERFLY

Same cast as February 25 except:

Pinkerton ...... Di Giuseppe
Goro .... Lowery
Suzuki .... Walker
Butterfly .... Craig
Kate Pinkerton ...... Murphy

March 22

MEFISTOFELE

Same cast as February 24 except:

Conductor .... Mauceri

Faust .... Mauro
Marta .... Walker
Pantalis .... Hill

March 23

MADAMA BUTTERFLY

Same cast as February 25 except:

Conductor .... La Selva

Pinkerton ...... Di Giuseppe
Goro .... Lowery
Suzuki .... Walker
Sharpless .... Burchinal
Butterfly .... Craig

March 24

CARMEN

Same cast as March 5 (m) except:

Don José ...... Norman (d)
Frasquita .... Spacagna
Mercédès .... Walker

March 25 (m)

LA BOHÈME

Same cast as March 1 except:

Rodolfo .... Bartolini
Schaunard .... Paul
Mimi .... Clarey
Musetta .... Thigpen

March 25

DIE FLEDERMAUS

Same cast as March 8 except:

Alfred .... Sandor,
(s, Griffith)
Adele .... Little
Sally .... Toro
Solo dancer .... Ettlin (d)
(for McBride)

March 26 (m)

RIGOLETTO

Same cast as March 4 except:

Conductor .... Effron

Rigoletto .... Fredricks
Borsa .... Lowery
Marullo .... Jamerson
Sparafucile .... Gill
Gilda .... Rolandi

March 26

LE COQ D'OR
(Rimsky-Korsakov)
(English version by Antal
Dorati and James Gibson)

Stage director .... Bamberger
Choreographer ...... Andrew
Conductor .... Pallo

Astrologer .... Morales
King Dodon .... Wildermann
Prince Guidon ...... Hensel
General Polkan ...... Denser
Prince Afron .... Foss
Golden Cockerel ...... Seibe
Amelfa ..... Costa-Greenspon
Queen of
Shemakha .... Robinson

March 29

CARMEN

Same cast as March 5 (m)
except:

Zuniga .... McKee
Don José .... Norman
Frasquita .... Spacagna
Mercédès .... Walker

March 30

THE MARRIAGE OF FIGARO
(Mozart)
(English version by
Ruth and Thomas Martin)

Stage director .... Smith
Conductor .... Rudel

Figaro .... Ramey
Susanna .... Malfitano
Bartolo .... McKee
Marcellina .... Shaulis
Cherubino .... Wallis
Almaviva .... Justus
Basilio .... Green
Countess .... Sheil
Antonio .... Foss
Curzio .... Lowery
Barbarina .... Thigpen
Bridesmaids .... Campbell,
                    Orlando

March 31

MADAMA BUTTERFLY

Same cast as February 25
except:

Conductor .... La Selva
Suzuki .... Curry
Sharpless .... Burchinal
Butterfly .... Verdejo (d)

April 1 (m)

LE COQ D'OR

Same cast as March 26

April 1

CAVALLERIA RUSTICANA

Same cast as February 25 (m)
except:

Mamma Lucia .... Curry
Santuzza .... Ehrlich
Alfio .... Long
Turiddu .... Bartolini
Lola .... Esham

Followed by:

I PAGLIACCI

Same cast as February 25 (m)
except:

Tonio .... Elvira
Canio .... Collins
Nedda .... Soviero
Beppe .... Grahame (d)
Silvio .... Hartman

April 2 (m)

RIGOLETTO

Same cast as March 4 except:

Rigoletto .... Fredricks
Duke .... Di Giuseppe
Marullo .... Jamerson
Sparafucile .... Gill
Gilda .... Robinson,
              (s, Malfitano)

April 2

THE MERRY WIDOW (Lehàr)
New production
(San Diego Opera version
by Tito Capobianco)
(English translation and
dialogue by Ursula Eggers and
Joseph de Rugeris;
lyrics by Sheldon Harnick)

Directed by .... Capobianco
Stage director and
  choreographer ...... Denda
Designer .... Toms
Lighting .... Billington
Conductor .... Rudel

Baron Mirko
  Zeta .... D. R. Smith
Valencienne .... Fowler
Count Danilo .... Titus
Anna Glawari .... Sills
Camille
  de Rosillon ...... Reed (d)
Vicomte Cascada ...... Foss
Raoul St. Brioche .... Hensel
Bogdanovitch ...... Lankston
Sylviane .... Shaulis
Kromov .... Ledbetter
Olga .... Walker
Pritchitch .... Green
Praskovia .... Toro
Njegus .... Billings
Lolo .... Itow
Dodo .... Shaulis
Jou-Jou .... Walker
Frou-Frou .... Gardella
Clo-Clo .... Toro
Margot .... Ettlin

Broadcast performance

April 4

TOSCA

Same cast as March 12 except:

Scarpia .... Fredricks
Shepherd .... Toro
Jailer .... Steele

April 5

THE MERRY WIDOW

Same cast as April 2

April 6

CAVALLERIA RUSTICANA

Same cast as February 25 (m)
except:

Santuzza .... Ehrlich
Alfio .... Long
Lola .... Esham

Followed by:

I PAGLIACCI

Same cast as February 25 (m)
except:

Tonio .... Elvira
Canio .... Mauro
Nedda .... Soviero
Beppe .... Grahame
Silvio .... Hartman

April 7

THE MERRY WIDOW

Same cast as April 2

April 8 (m)

THE TURN OF THE SCREW

Same cast as March 17

April 8

LE COQ D'OR

Same cast as March 26 except:

King Dodon .... McKee
Queen of Shemakha .. Rolandi

April 9 (m)

THE MERRY WIDOW

Same cast as April 2 except:

Count Danilo .... Hensel,
               (s, Titus)
Raoul St. Brioche ...... Kays,
              (s, Hensel)

April 9

MEFISTOFELE

Same cast as February 24
except:

Margherita ... Hernandez (d)
Marta .... Walker
Elena .... Hernandez (d)
Pantalis .... Hill
Nereo .... Kays

Broadcast performance

April 11

DIE FLEDERMAUS

Same cast as March 8 except:

Conductor .... Minde (d)
Alfred .... Griffith
Rosalinda .... Rogers
Eisenstein .... Hensel
Blind .... Green
Falke .... Holloway
Frank .... Densen
Frosch .... Billings

April 12

THE MERRY WIDOW

Same cast as April 2 except:

Sylviane .... Murphy
Olga .... Reynolds
Dodo .... Murphy
Jou-Jou .... Reynolds

April 13

THE SAINT OF
BLEECKER STREET (Menotti)

Conductor .... Kellogg

Assunta .... Shaulis
Young man .... Kays
Maria Corona ...... De Rosa
Her son .... Scalese (d)
Carmela .... Soviero
Young woman ...... Thigpen
Don Marco .... Densen
Annina .... Malfitano
Michele .... Di Giuseppe
Girl at the window .. Herbert
Concettina ..... A. Smith (d)
Desideria .... Walker
Guests .... Kays, Baker
Salvatore .... Ledbetter
Bartender .... Dovel
Nun .... Thyssen
Young priest .... Boucher
Neighbors .... Henderson,
                    Davis

April 14

THE MERRY WIDOW

Same cast as April 2 except:

Sylviane .... Murphy
Olga .... Reynolds
Dodo .... Murphy
Jou-Jou .... Reynolds

April 15 (m)

CARMEN

Same cast as March 5 (m)
except:

Conductor .... Effron

Zuniga .... McKee
Micaëla .... Daniels
Don José .... Norman
Carmen .... Freni
Remendado .... Green

April 15

MEFISTOFELE

Same cast as February 24
except:

Faust .... Taylor
Margherita .... Hernandez
Marta .... Walker
Elena .... Hernandez
Pantalis .... Hill
Nereo .... Kays

April 16 (m)

THE MARRIAGE OF FIGARO

Same cast as March 30 except:

Figaro .... Holloway
Susanna .... Little
Bartolo .... Densen
Almaviva .... Hartman
Countess .... Brinkerhoff (d)
Curzio .... Kays

April 16

IL BARBIERE DI SIVIGLIA

Same cast as March 2 except:

Bartolo .... McKee
Basilio .... Berberian

Broadcast performance

April 18

THE MERRY WIDOW

Same cast as April 2 except:

Conductor .... Walser

Baron Mirko Zeta ..... Baker
Valencienne .... Haley
Count Danilo .... Hensel
Anna Glawari ...... Daniels
Camille de Rosillon ... Price
Raoul St. Brioche ..... Kays
Bogdanovitch ..... Lankston
   (Act I); Hunsberger (d)
            (Acts II & III)
Sylviane .... Murphy
Olga .... Reynolds,
               (s, Walker)
Praskovia .... Delery-
        Whedon (d), (s, Toro)
Dodo .... Murphy
Jou-Jou .... Reynolds,
               (s, Walker)
Clo-Clo .... Delery-
        Whedon (d), (s, Toro)

April 19

THE SAINT OF
BLEECKER STREET

Same cast as April 13

Telecast

April 20

LA BOHÈME

Same cast as March 1 except:

Rodolfo .... Rendall (d)
Marcello .... Fredricks
Colline .... Ramey
Musetta .... Zannoth
Alcindoro .... Billings

April 21

MADAMA BUTTERFLY

Same cast as February 25
except:

Conductor .... La Selva

Pinkerton .... Bartolini
Suzuki .... Curry
Sharpless .... Burchinal

April 22 (m)

THE MARRIAGE OF FIGARO

Same cast as March 30 except:

Conductor .... Queler (d)

Susanna .... Little
Marcellina .... Shaulis,
               (s, Curry)

Countess .... Meier
Antonio .... Yule
Curzio .... Kays,
               (s, Lowery)
Barbarina .... Mines,
               (s, Thigpen)

April 22

CARMEN

Same cast as March 5 (m)
except:

Conductor .... Effron

Zuniga .... McKee
Micaëla .... Daniels
Don José .... Norman
Carmen .... Freni
Frasquita .... Spacagna
Mercédès .... Hill
Remendado .... Green

April 23 (m)

LA TRAVIATA

Same cast as February 23
except:

Conductor ..... De Renzi (d)

Violetta .... Thomson
Flora .... Murphy
Douphol .... Steele
Dr. Grenvil .... Yule
Gaston .... Kays
Alfredo .... Price
Germont .... Cossa

April 23

THE SAINT OF
BLEECKER STREET

Same cast as April 13

April 25

LA BOHÈME

Same cast as March 1 except:

Rodolfo .... Rendall
Marcello .... Cossa
Colline .... Ramey
Mimi .... Fowles
Musetta .... Zannoth
Alcindoro .... Billings

April 26

THE MARRIAGE OF FIGARO

Same cast as March 30 except:

Cherubino .... Walker
Almaviva .... Hartman
Countess .... Meier
Antonio .... Yule
Barbarina .... Mines

April 27

THE MERRY WIDOW

Same cast as April 2 except:

Conductor .... Walser

Baron Mirko
   Zeta .... D. R. Smith
               (s, Baker)
Valencienne .... Haley

Count Danilo .... Hensel
Anna Glawari .... Daniels
Camille de Rosillon .... Price
Raoul St. Brioche ...... Kays
Bogdanovitch .... Hunsberger
Olga .... Reynolds
Jou-Jou .... Reynolds

April 28

LA TRAVIATA

Same cast as February 23
except:

Conductor .... De Renzi

Flora .... Murphy
Douphol .... Steele
Dr. Grenvil .... Yule
Gaston .... Kays
Alfredo .... Rendall
Germont .... Cossa

April 29 (m)

LE COQ D'OR

Same cast as March 26 except:

Conductor .... Effron
Astrologer .... Morales,
                  (s, Novick)
Golden Cockerel ... Spacagna
Amelfa .... Shaulis

April 29

IL BARBIERE DI SIVIGLIA

Same cast as March 2 except:

Figaro .... Holloway
Bartolo .... McKee
Rosina .... French
Berta .... Curry

April 30 (m)

TOSCA

Same cast as March 12 except:

Angelotti .... Foss
Cavaradossi .... Bartolini
Tosca .... Meier
Scarpia .... Fredricks
Sciarrone .... Sergi,
                  (s, Baker)
Shepherd .... Toro
Jailer .... Steele

April 30

THE TURN OF THE SCREW

Same cast as March 17 except:

Miles .... Sapolsky
Miss Jessel .... Sheil

Fall 1978 (AUGUST 31 – NOVEMBER 12)

Female artists
Adoff, Denise*
Anderson, June*
Barnes, Sheila*
Bartolini, Dela*
Cohen, Lynn*
Costa-Greenspon, Muriel
Curry, Diane
Daniels, Sharon
Delery-Whedon, Susan
Dickison, Judith*
Donaldi, Maria
Ehrlich, Judith
Esham, Faith
Fowles, Glenys
Freni, Rosemarie
Hegierski, Kathleen
Hill, Eunice
Hinds, Esther
Howard, Ann
Hynes, Elizabeth
Lambert, Sally*
Little, Gwenlynn
Lovelace, Kimara*
Luxemburg, Leslie
Malfitano, Catherine
Marsee, Susanne
Meier, Johanna
Metzger, Rita
Murphy, Kathleen
Orloff, Penny*
Putnam, Ashley*
Reynolds, Myrna
Robinson, Faye
Rolandi, Gianna
Schauler, Eileen
Schoenfeld, Kay*
Shade, Nancy
Shaulis, Jane
Sheil, Martha
Sills, Beverly
Simon, Joanna
Soviero, Diana

Spacagna, Maria
Thigpen, Martha
Toro, Puli
Verdejo, Awilda
Walker, Sandra
Williams, Vanessa*
Young, Marie
Zannoth, Sherry
Zschau, Marilyn

Male artists
Albert, Donnie Ray*
Baker, Alan
Bartolini, Lando
Bassett, Ralph*
Berberian, Ara
Billings, James
Bohachevsky, George
Brewer, James
Brubaker, Robert*
Carlo, Don
Castel, Nico
Chapman, William
Clark, James*
Cossa, Dominic
Davis, Harris
Densen, Irwin
Devlin, Michael
Di Giuseppe, Enrico
Dovel, Kenn
Eaton, Timothy*
Elvira, Pablo
Embree, Marc
Foss, Harlan
Fredricks, Richard
Gill, Richard T.
Grahame, Gerald
Gramm, Donald
Green, Jonathan
Guss, John Galt
Hale, Robert
Hartman, Vernon
Hensel, Howard

Herndon, Bill*
Holloway, David
Hunsberger, Herbert
Jamerson, Thomas
Jones, Ted C.*
Justus, William
Kays, Alan
Kingman, Dan
Lankston, John
Large, Norman*
Ledbetter, William
Lima, Luis
Long, Charles
Malas, Spiro
Mauro, Eramanno
McKee, Richard
McNulty, Aidan*
Morales, Abram
Morton, Brooks*
Novick, Melvyn
Paglialunga, Augusto*
Paul, Robert
Perry, Douglas*
Perry, Louis
Postrel, Leo
Price, Henry
Ramey, Samuel
Reed, Bruce
Roe, Charles
Rowen, Glenn
Sandor, John
Sapolsky, Robert
Seabury, John*
Sergi, James
Sims, Jack
Smith, Andrew
Smith, David Rae
Steele, Philip
Stell, Ian*
Straney, Paul*
Taylor, Richard
Thacker, Russ*
Titus, Alan
Trussel, Jacque

* New artist   * New artist   * New artist

Vaughan, Edward
Wechsler, Mitchell*
Wildermann, William
Yule, Don

Conductors
Buckley, Emerson
Comissiona, Sergiu
De Renzi, Victor
Mauceri, John
Pallo, Imre
Rudel, Julius
Salesky, Brian*
Somogi, Judith
Walser, Lloyd

Chorus master
Walser, Lloyd

Assistant chorus master
Hillmer, Leann

Solo dancers
Galan, Esperanza
Gardella, Toni-Ann
Itow, Candace
Pradera, Rebeka
Thomas, Bronwyn*
Wilkinson, Raven*

Bourbon, José*
Kalba, Terence*
Levans, Daniel*
Rubino, Michael

Choreographers
Andrew, Thomas
Birch, Patricia
Daniele, Graciela*
Denda, Gigi
Leporska, Zoya
Redel, Jessica*

Directors
Auerbach, Cynthia
Bentley, Ronald*
Capobianco, Tito
Copley, John
Corsaro, Frank
Freedman, Gerald
Jaworski, Antoni*
Lesenger, Jay*
Merrill, Nathaniel*
O'Brien, Jack*
Rudel, Julius
Smith, Christian

Designers
Aldredge, Theoni V.
Campbell, Patton
Chase, Ronald
Conklin, John*
Evans, Lloyd
Fletcher, Robert
Hemsley, Gilbert V., Jr.*
Larkey, Joan
Lee, Ming Cho
Mess, Suzanne
Montresor, Beni
Oenslager, Donald
O'Hearn, Robert
Potts, Nancy*
Smith, Oliver
Sylbert, Paul
Toms, Carl
Varona, José
Zipprodt, Patricia

* New artist

August 31

NAUGHTY MARIETTA (Herbert)
First performance by The New
York City Opera Company
(New book and additional
lyrics by Frederick S. Roffman,
based on the 1910 original
of Rida Johnson Young)

Production
 conceived by ..... Roffman
Directed by ...... Freedman
Musical numbers
 staged by ..... Daniele (d)
Scenic designer .... Smith
Costume designer ... Zipprodt
Lighting .... Billington
Conductor .... Mauceri

Marietta d'Altena ... Rolandi
Captain Richard
 Warrington .... Trussel
Etienne Grandet .... Titus
Adah Le Clercq ...... Simon
Private Silas
 Slick .... Thacker (d)
Acting Governor
 Grandet .... Billings
Florenze .... Morton (d)
Sir Harry Blake .... Yule
Rudolfo .... Foss
Pierre La Farge ...... McKee
Sister Domenique ... Metzger
Pirates ...... Kingman, Sergi
Ranger .... Hunsberger
Town crier .... Vaughan
Flower girls .... Delery-
 Whedon, Lambert (d)
Flower vendor .. Bohachevsky
Bird vendor .... L. Perry
Fruit vendor ... Brubaker (d)
Sugar cane vendor ..... Davis
Thomas Bailey .... Sergi
Giovanni ...... Bourbon (d)
Gambler .... Carlo
Pierre .... Dovel
Robillard .... Hunsberger
Plauche .... Brewer
Beaurivage .... Davis
Major-Domo .... Rowen
Spanish dancer .... Galan
Bordenave .... Sergi
Durand .... L. Perry
La Fourche .... Kingman
San Domingo ladies. . Gardella,
 Itow, Pradera

September 1

NAUGHTY MARIETTA

Same cast as August 31

September 2 (m)

NAUGHTY MARIETTA

Same cast as August 31 except:

Marietta d'Altena ..... Hynes
Captain Richard
 Warrington .... Hensel
Etienne Grandet .... Roe
Adah Le Clercq ..... Marsee

September 2

NAUGHTY MARIETTA

Same cast as August 31 except:

Thomas Bailey ..... Omitted

September 3 (m)

NAUGHTY MARIETTA

Same cast as August 31 except:

Marietta d'Altena ..... Hynes
Captain Richard
 Warrington .... Hensel
Etienne Grandet .... Roe
Adah Le Clercq ...... Marsee

September 3

NAUGHTY MARIETTA

Same cast as August 31

Broadcast performance

September 6 (m)

NAUGHTY MARIETTA

Same cast as August 31 except:

Conductor .... Walser,
 (s, Mauceri)

September 6

NAUGHTY MARIETTA

Same cast as August 31 except:

Conductor .... Walser

Mariette d'Altena ..... Hynes
Captain Richard
 Warrington .... Hensel
Etienne Grandet .... Roe
Adah Le Clercq ...... Marsee

September 7

NAUGHTY MARIETTA

Same cast as August 31 except:

Conductor .... Walser

Mariette d'Altena ..... Hynes
Captain Richard
 Warrington .... Hensel
Etienne Grandet .... Roe
Adah Le Clercq ..... Marsee

September 8

NAUGHTY MARIETTA

Same cast as August 31 except:

Conductor .... Walser

Marietta d'Altena ..... Hynes
Captain Richard
 Warrington .... Hensel
Etienne Grandet .... Roe
Adah Le Clercq ..... Marsee

September 9 (m)

NAUGHTY MARIETTA

Same cast as August 31

September 9

NAUGHTY MARIETTA

Same cast as August 9 except:

Conductor ...... Salesky (d)

Marietta d'Altena ..... Hynes
Captain Richard
   Warrington .... Hensel
Etienne Grandet .... Roe
Adah Le Clercq ..... Marsee

September 10 (m)

NAUGHTY MARIETTA

Same cast as August 31

September 10

NAUGHTY MARIETTA

Same cast as August 31 except:

Conductor .... Salesky

Marietta .... Hynes
Captain Richard
   Warrington .... Trussel,
              (s, Hensel)
Etienne .... Roe
Adah .... Marsee

September 13

THE MARRIAGE OF FIGARO
(Mozart)
(English version by
Ruth and Thomas Martin)

Conductor .... Rudel

Figaro .... Holloway
Susanna .... Malfitano
Bartolo .... McKee
Marcellina .... Shaulis
Cherubino .... Esham
Almaviva .... Devlin
Basilio .... Green
Countess .... Hinds
Antonio .... Foss
Curzio .... Kays
Barbarina .... Thigpen
Bridesmaids ..... Luxemburg,
           Schoenfeld (d)

September 14

ANDREA CHÉNIER (Giordano)
New production

Directed by ...... Merrill (d)
Scenic designer ..... O'Hearn
Costume designer ...... Mess
Choreographer ...... Andrew
Lighting .... Hemsley, Jr. (d)
Conductor .... Buckley

Major-Domo, Schmidt .. Yule
Gérard .... Fredricks
Maddalena .... Zschau
Bersi .... Walker
Contessa di Coigny ... Shaulis
Fléville .... Foss
Flando Fiorinelli .. Jones (d)
Chénier .... Mauro
L'Abate .... Green
Mathieu .... Densen
Incredible .... Lankston
Roucher .... Jamerson
Madelon .... Curry
Child .... Stell (d)

Dumas .... Steele
Fouquier-Tinville .... Embree

September 15

LA TRAVIATA (Verdi)

Assistant to
  Mr. Corsaro ..Jaworski (d)
Conductor .... Pallo

Violetta .... Putnam (d)
Flora .... Hegierski
Douphol .... Steele
D'Obigny .... Ledbetter
Dr. Grenvil .... Yule
Gaston .... Kays
Alfredo .... H. Price
Annina .... Hill
Giuseppe .... Novick
Germont .... Cossa
Messenger ...... Bohachevsky
Solo dancer .... Galan

September 16 (m)

RIGOLETTO (Verdi)

Stage director .. Lesenger (d)
Conductor .... Somogi

Rigoletto .... Elvira
Monterone's daughter .. Galan
Clown .... Kalba (d)
Duke .... Di Giuseppe
Borsa .... Large (d)
Countess Ceprano ... Thigpen
Ceprano .... Ledbetter
Marullo .... Jamerson
Monterone .... Embree
Sparafucile .... Gill
Gilda .... Robinson
Giovanna .... Shaulis
Page .... Donaldi,
       (s, Schoenfeld)
Maddalena .... Hegierski

September 16

CARMEN (Bizet)

Conductor .... Pallo

Morales .... Jamerson
Zuniga .... McKee
Micaëla .... Fowles
Don José .... Trussel
Carmen .... Howard
Frasquita .... Thigpen
Mercédès .... Hill
Lillas Pastia, Guide ..... Sims
Escamillo .... Holloway
Remendado .... Lankston
Dancairo .... Ledbetter

September 17 (m)

THE MERRY WIDOW (Lehár)
San Diego Opera version by
Tito Capobianco
(English translation and
dialogue by Ursula Eggers and
Joseph de Rugeriis; English
lyrics by Sheldon Harnick)

Stage director .. Jaworski (d)
Choreography
  staged by .... Redel (d)
Conductor ....:...... Pallo

Baron
  Mirko Zeta ... D. R. Smith

Valencienne .... Soviero
Count Danilo .... Hensel
Anna Glawari .... Meier
Camille de Rosillon .... Reed
Vicomte Cascada ...... Foss
Raoul St. Brioche ...... Kays
Bogdanovitch .... Hunsberger
Sylviane .... Murphy
Kromov .... Ledbetter
Olga .... Reynolds
Pritchitch .... L. Perry
Praskovia .... Delery-Whedon
Njegus .... Billings
Lolo .... Itow
Dodo .... Murphy
Jou-Jou .... Reynolds
Frou-Frou .... Gardella
Clo-Clo ...... Delery-Whedon
Margot ...... Wilkinson (d)

September 17

ANDREA CHÉNIER

Same cast as September 14

Broadcast

September 19

LA TRAVIATA

Same cast as September 15

September 20

ANDREA CHÉNIER

Same cast as September 14

September 21

TOSCA (Puccini)

Stage director .... Bentley (d)
Conductor .... Pallo

Angelotti .... Foss
Sacristan .... McKee
Cavaradossi .... Trussel
Tosca .... Meier
Scarpia .... Justus
Spoletta .... Clark (d)
Sciarrone .... Sergi
Shepherd .... Hill
Jailer .... Steele

September 22

RIGOLETTO

Same cast as September 16 (m)
except:

Page .... Schoenfeld

September 23 (m)

ANDREA CHÉNIER

Same cast as September 14

September 23

THE MERRY WIDOW

Same cast as September 17 (m)

September 24 (m)

CARMEN

Same cast as September 16

September 24

THE TURK IN ITALY (Rossini)
First performance by The New
York City Opera Company
(*Il Turco in Italia;* English
translation by Andrew Porter)

Directed by ..... Capobianco
Designer .... Conklin
Choreographer .... Denda
Lighting .... Hemsley, Jr.
Conductor .... Rudel

Selim .... Gramm
Fiorilla .... Sills
Geronio .... Billings
Narciso .... H. Price
Prosdocimo .... Titus
Zaida .... Marsee
Albazar .... Green

September 26

THE TURK IN ITALY

Same cast as September 24

September 27 (m)

THE MERRY WIDOW

Same cast as September 17 (m)

September 28

LA BOHÈME (Puccini)

Conductor .... Mauceri

Rodolfo .... Di Giuseppe
Marcello .... Holloway
Colline .... Gill
Schaunard .... Hartman
Benoit .... Foss
Mimi .... Fowles
Parpignol .... Kays
Musetta .... Zannoth
Alcindoro .... Yule
Guards ..Brewer, Bohachevsky

September 29

THE TURK IN ITALY

Same cast as September 24
except:

Narciso .... Kays,
                 (s, H. Price)

September 30 (m)

DIE TOTE STADT (Korngold)

Conductor .... Pallo

Brigitta .... Curry
Frank .... Hartman
Paul .... Taylor
Marietta .... Shade
Victorin .... Lankston
Albert .... Kays
Juliette .... Thigpen
Lucienne .... Toro
Fritz .... Jamerson
Gaston .... Rubino

September 30

MADAMA BUTTERFLY (Puccini)

Stage director .... Smith
Conductor .... Somogi

Pinkerton .... Trussel
Goro .... Green
Suzuki .... Hegierski
Sharpless .... Justus
Butterfly .... Verdejo
Imperial
  Commissioner ... Ledbetter
Registrar, Yamadori .... Sergi
The Bonze .... Steele
Trouble .... Guss
Kate Pinkerton .... Hill

October 1 (m)

THE MARRIAGE OF FIGARO

Same cast as September 13
except:

Countess .... Sheil,
                 (s, Hinds)

October 1

THE TURK IN ITALY

Same cast as September 24
Broadcast

October 4

THE TURK IN ITALY

Same cast as September 24
Telecast

October 5

TOSCA

Same cast as September 21

October 6

THE MARRIAGE OF FIGARO

Same cast as September 13
except:

Figaro .... Ramey
Almaviva .... Hartman
Countess .... Sheil
Antonio .... Yule
Barbarina .... Orloff (d)

October 7 (m)

MADAMA BUTTERFLY

Same cast as September 30
except:

Butterfly .... Zschau

October 7

DIE TOTE STADT

Same cast as September 30 (m)

October 8 (m)

THE TURK IN ITALY

Same cast as September 24
except:

Prosdocimo .... Hartman

October 8

PELLÉAS ET MÉLISANDE
(Débussy)

Conductor .... Rudel

Mélisande .... Fowles
Golaud .... Devlin
Geneviève .... Curry
Arkel .... Berberian
Pelléas .... Titus
Yniold .... Sapolsky
Shepherd .... Ledbetter
Physician .... Yule

October 11

THE MAGIC FLUTE (Mozart)
(English version by
Ruth and Thomas Martin)

Conductor .... Rudel

Tamino .... Grahame
1st Lady .... Sheil
2nd Lady .... Zannoth
3rd Lady .... Shaulis
Papageno .... Jamerson
Queen of the
  Night .... Dickison (d)
1st Spirit .... Sapolsky
2nd Spirit ...... McNulty (d)
3rd Spirit .... Stell
Monostatos .... Foss
Pamina .... Robinson
Speaker .... Embree
Sarastro .... Berberian
1st Priest .... Kays
2nd Priest .... Embree
Papagena .... Little
1st Armored man ..... Hensel
2nd Armored
  man .... Seabury (d)

October 12

THE TURK IN ITALY

Same cast as September 24
except:

Prosdocimo .... Hartman

October 13

PELLÉAS ET MÉLISANDE

Same cast as October 8

October 14 (m)

THE MERRY WIDOW

Same cast as September 17 (m)

October 14

LA BOHÈME

Same cast as September 28
except:

Rodolfo .... Lima
Marcello .... Elvira
Benoit .... Yule
Mimi .... Malfitano
Parpignol .... Green
Musetta .... Thigpen
Alcindoro .... Billings

October 15 (m)

LE COQ D'OR
(Rimsky-Korsakov)
(English version by Antal
Dorati and James Gibson)

Stage director .... Bentley
Conductor .... Pallo

Astrologer .... Morales
King Dodon .... Windermann
Prince Guidon .... Hensel
General Polkan ...... Embree
Prince Afron .... Foss
Golden Cockerel ... Spacagna
Amelfa ..... Costa-Greenspon
Queen of Shemakha ..Rolandi

Broadcast performance

October 15

THE MARRIAGE OF FIGARO

Same cast as September 13
except:

Figaro .... Malas
Susanna .... Little
Cherubino .... Hegierski
Almaviva .... Hartman
Antonio .... Yule
Barbarina .... Orloff

October 17

RIGOLETTO

Same cast as September 16 (m)
except:

Rigoletto .... Fredricks
Duke .... Lima
Countess Ceprano .... Orloff
Ceprano .... Yule
Marullo .... Paul
Monterone ...... Straney (d)
Gilda .... Rolandi
Page .... Schoenfeld
Maddalena .... Hill

October 18

CARMEN

Same cast as September 16
except:

Morales .... Sergi
Zuniga .... Embree
Micaëla .... Little
Frasquita .... Spacagna
Mercédès .... Hegierski
Escamillo .... Long,
                (s, Chapman)
Remendado .... Green

October 19

LA BOHÈME

Same cast as September 28
except:

Rodolfo .... Lima
Marcello .... Elvira
Colline .... Malas
Benoit .... Yule
Mimi .... Malfitano

Parpignol .... Green
Musetta .... Daniels
Alcindoro .... Billings

October 20

THE MAGIC FLUTE

Same cast as September 11
except:

Sarastro .... Gill

October 21 (m)

LA FANCIULLA DEL WEST
(Puccini)

Stage director .... Smith
Conductor .... Comissiona

Nick .... Large
Jack Rance .... Long
Larkens .... Ledbetter
Billy .... Yule
Joe .... Clark
Bello .... Sergi
Harry .... Green
Happy .... Seabury
Sid .... Foss
Sonora .... Paul
Trin .... D. Perry (d)
Jake .... A. Smith
Ashby .... Steele
Minnie .... Zschau
Post rider .... L. Perry
Castro .... Baker
Johnson .... Trussel
Wowkle .... Hegierski

October 21

RIGOLETTO

Same cast as September 16 (m)
except:

Rigoletto .... Fredricks
Duke .... Lima
Countess Ceprano ..... Orloff
Ceprano .... Yule
Marullo .... Paul
Monterone .... Straney
Gilda .... Rolandi
Giovanna .... Hill
Page .... Schoenfeld
Maddalena .... Hill

October 22 (m)

THE MERRY WIDOW

Same cast as September 17 (m)
except:

Baron Mirko Zeta ..... Baker
Valencienne .... Thigpen
Anna Glawari .... Daniels
Camille de Rosillon .... Kays
Raoul St. Brioche ...... Large

October 22

LA TRAVIATA

Same cast as September 15
except:

Conductor .... De Renzi

Flora .... Shaulis
Alfredo .... Sandor

October 24

TOSCA

Same cast as September 21
except:

Sacristan .... Billings
Cavaradossi ..... L. Bartolini
Tosca .... Ehrlich

October 25 (m)

CARMEN

Same cast as September 16
except:

Morales .... Sergi
Zuniga .... Embree
Micaëla .... Daniels
Don José .... Mauro
Frasquita .... Spacagna
Escamillo .... Chapman

October 26

THE MAGIC FLUTE

Same cast as October 11
except:

*Queen of the
 Night* .... Anderson (d)
Papagena .... Spacagna

October 27

LA FANCIULLA DEL WEST

Same cast as October 21 (m)
except:

Conductor .... De Renzi
Jake .... Albert (d)

October 28 (m)

STREET SCENE (Weill)

Directed by ..... O'Brien (d)
Costume designer .. Potts (d)
Choreographer .... Birch
Lighting .... Hemsley, Jr.
Conductor .... Mauceri

Greta Fiorentino .... Thigpen
Emma Jones .... Curry
Olga Olsen .... Freni
Carl Olsen ...... Bassett (d)
Shirley Kaplan ... Cohen (d)
Abraham Kaplan ...... Castel
Henry Davis .... A. Smith
Willie Maurrant .... Sapolsky
Anna Maurrant ... Schauler
Sam Kaplan .... Kays
Daniel Buchanan ...... Clark
Frank Maurrant .... Chapman
George Jones .... Paul
Steve Sankey ...... Ledbetter
Lippo Fiorentino ...... Green
Mrs. Hildebrand .... Lambert
Jenny Hildebrand .. Hegierski
Graduates .... Adoff (d),
                Williams (d)
*Charlie
 Hildebrand* ..... Eaton (d)
*Mary Hilde-
 brand* .... D. Bartolini (d)
Grace Davis .... Lovelace (d)
Rose Maurrant .... Malfitano
Harry Easter .... Titus
Dick McGann ... Levans (d)

Mae Jones ... B. Thomas (d)
Vincent Jones .. Herndon (d)
Dr. Wilson .... Carlo
Officer Murphy ...... Dovel
Milkman .... Brubaker
James Henry .... Yule
Fred Cullen .... Baker
Nursemaids .. Young, Metzger

October 28

ANDREA CHÉNIER

Same cast as September 14
except:

Conductor .... De Renzi
Gérard .... Elvira
Maddalena .... Ehrlich
Bersi .... Hegierski
Mathieu .... Bassett
Roucher .... Paul
Madelon .... Shaulis

October 29 (m)

LE COQ D'OR

Same cast as October 15

October 29

CARMEN

Same cast as September 16
except:

Conductor .... Somogi
Morales .... Sergi
Zuniga .... Embree
Micaëla .... Robinson
Don José .... Paglialunga (d)
Frasquita .... Spacagna
Escamillo .... Long

October 31

MADAMA BUTTERFLY

Same cast as September 30
except:

Pinkerton .... L. Bartolini
Goro .... Clark
Suzuki .... Shaulis
Sharpless .... Fredricks
The Bonze .... Seabury
Trouble .... Wechsler (d)

November 1

LA TRAVIATA

Same cast as September 15
except:

Violetta .... Soviero
Douphol .... Embree
Dr. Grenvil .... Bassett
Germont .... Elvira

November 2

ANDREA CHÉNIER

Same cast as September 14
except:

Conductor .... De Renzi
Maddalena .... Ehrlich
Bersi .... Hegierski
Mathieu .... Bassett
Roucher .... Paul
Madelon .... Shaulis

November 3

THE MAGIC FLUTE

Same cast as October 11
except:

Tamino .... Reed
Papageno .... Cossa
Monostatos .... Billings
Pamina .... Little
1st priest .... Lankston
Papagena .... Orloff

November 4 (m)

THE TURK IN ITALY

Same cast as September 24
except:

Selim .... Malas
Narciso .... Kays
Zaida .... Hegierski

November 4

LA FANCIULLA DEL WEST

Same cast as October 21 (m)
except:

Minnie .... Schauler
Johnson .... Mauro
Wowkle .... Hill

November 5 (m)

LA BOHÈME

Same cast as September 28
except:

Rodolfo .... L. Bartolini
Marcello .... Cossa
Colline .... Seabury
Schaunard .... Jamerson
Mimi .... Verdejo
Parpignol .... Davis,
            (s, Kays)
Musetta .... Barnes (d)

November 5

STREET SCENE

Same cast as October 28 (m)
Broadcast

November 7

LA TRAVIATA

Same cast as September 15
except:

Violetta .... Robinson
Douphol .... Embree
Dr. Grenvil .... Bassett
Annina .... Toro,
            (s, Hill)
Germont .... Elvira

November 8 (m)

MADAMA BUTTERFLY

Same cast as September 30
except:

Pinkerton .... L. Bartolini
Goro .... Clark
Suzuki .... Shaulis
Sharpless .... Fredricks
Butterfly .... Zschau
The Bonze .... Seabury
Trouble .... Wechsler

November 9

CARMEN

Same cast as September 16
except:

Zuniga .... Embree
Micaëla .... Little
Don José .... Mauro
Carmen .... Freni
Frasquita .... Orloff
Mercédès .... Hegierski
Escamillo .... Hale
Dancairo .... Foss

November 10

STREET SCENE

Same cast as October 28 (m)
except:

Abraham Kaplan .... Postrel
Anna Maurant ...... Zannoth
Jenny Hildebrand .. Hegierski,
            (s, Hill)
Rose Maurrant ...... Daniels
Harry Easter .... Foss

November 11 (m)

THE MAGIC FLUTE

Same cast as October 11
except:

Conductor .... Pallo
Tamino .... Reed
Papageno .... Cossa
Queen of the
   Night .... Anderson
Monostatos .... Billings
Pamina .... Hynes
1st Priest .... Lankston
Papagena .... Spacagna

November 11

THE MERRY WIDOW

Same cast as September 17 (m)
except:

Baron Mirko Zeta ..... Baker
Valencienne .... Thigpen
Count Danilo .... Titus
Camille de Rosillon .... Kays
Raoul St. Brioche ..... Large

November 12 (m)

STREET SCENE

Same cast as September 28 (m)
except:

Rose Maurrant ...... Daniels

November 12

LA BOHÈME

Same cast as September 28
except:

Rodolfo .... Mauro
Marcello .... Cossa
Colline .... Malas
Schaunard .... Jamerson
Mimi .... Verdejo
Parpignol .... Green
Musetta .... Barnes

Spring 1979 (FEBRUARY 22 – APRIL 29)

Female artists
Anderson, June
Bonazzi, Elaine
Browne, Sandra*
Christos, Marianna
Coronada, Maria*
Costa-Greenspon, Muriel
Curry, Diane
Daniels, Sharon
Davidson, Joy
Delery-Whedon, Susan
Esham, Faith
Falcon, Ruth
Faull, Ellen
Fowles, Glenys
Freni, RoseMarie
Greene, Harriet
Haley, Elizabeth
Hall, Janice*
Harth, Laura*
Hegierski, Kathleen
Hill, Eunice
Hynes, Elizabeth
Jarosz, Judith-Mari*
Little, Gwenlynn
Long, Zola*
Luxemburg, Leslie
Malfitano, Catherine
Marsee, Susanne
Meier, Johanna
Nelson, Nelda*
Niculescu, Mariana
Orloff, Penny
Putnam, Ashley
Rawn, Jean
Robinson, Faye
Rolandi, Gianna
Schoenfeld, Kay
Shane, Rita
Shaulis, Jane
Sheil, Martha
Sills, Beverly
Thigpen, Martha
Toro, Puli
Verdejo, Awilda
Walker, Sandra
Wallach, Lorna*
Zannoth, Sherry
Zschau, Marilyn

Male artists
Bartolini, Lando
Bassett, Ralph
Billings, James
Bohachevsky, George
Booth, Philip*
Brewer, James
Burchinal, Frederick
Carlo, Don
Castel, Nico
Clark, James
Cole, Vinson*
Cossa, Dominic
Cross, Richard

Davis, Harris
De Dio, Harry
Densen, Irwin
Di Giuseppe, Enrico
Elvira, Pablo
Embree, Marc
Fazah, Adib
Fredricks, Richard
Gonzalez, Dalmacio*
Grahame, Gerald
Green, Jonathan
Hale, Robert
Hartman, Vernon
Holloway, David
Holmes, Eugene
Hunsberger, Herbert
Jamerson, Thomas
Jones, Ted C.
Kays, Alan
Kingman, Dan
Lankston, John
Large, Norman
Ledbetter, William
Lima, Luis
Long, Charles
Macurdy, John
Malas, Spiro
Mauro, Ermanno
McKee, Richard
Morales, Abram
Novick, Melvyn
Paglialunga, Augusto
Paul, Robert
Peyton, J. Randolph
Presto
Price, Henry
Ramey, Samuel
Reed, Bruce
Sandor, John
Sapolsky, Robert
Seabury, John
Sergi, James
Sims, Jack
Steele, Philip
Stell, Ian
Sullivan, Dan*
Taylor, Richard
Thomas, John Henry
Tippie, Frank
Titus, Alan
Trussel, Jacque
Ukena, Paul
Wechsler, Mitchell
Yule, Don

Conductors
De Renzi, Victor
Effron, David
Keene, Christopher
Kellogg, Cal Stewart
Mauceri, John
Pallo, Imre
Rudel, Julius
Salesky, Brian
Shapirra, Elyakum*

Chorus master
Walser, Lloyd

Assistant chorus master
Hillmer, Leann

Dancers
Galan, Esperanza
Gardella, Toni-Ann
Itow, Candace
Kaufhold, Barbara*
McBride, Patricia
Pradera, Rebeka
Redel, Jessica*
Rinaldi, Victoria*
Rzasa, Laura*
Williams, Patricia*

Bonnefous, Jean-Pierre*
Bourbon, José
Cousins, Scott*
Delgado, Alberto*
Iracledes, Vasilis*
Kalba, Terence
Kokich, Jerry*
Medina, Roberto*
Nureyev, Rudolf*
Romero, Rafael
Rubino, Michael

Choreographers
Andrew, Thomas
Balanchine, George
Danner, Dorothy Frank*
Denda, Gigi
Martins, Peter*
Robbins, Jerome*

Directors
Auerbach, Cynthia
Balk, H. Wesley*
Bentley, Ronald
Capobianco, Tito
Copley, John
Corsaro, Frank
Denda, Gigi
Eddleman, Jack
Lesenger, Jay
Merrill, Nathaniel
Smith, Christian

Designers
Campbell, Patton
Conklin, John
Eck, Marsha Louis
Evans, Lloyd
Fletcher, Robert
George, Hal
Hemsley, Gilbert V., Jr.
Lee, Ming Cho
Mess, Suzanne
Mitchell, David
Montresor, Beni
Oenslager, Donald
O'Hearn, Robert
Ter-Arutunian, Rouben
Toms, Carl
Varona, José

* New artist   * New artist   * New artist

February 22

ANDREA CHÉNIER (Giordano)

Stage director ..... Auerbach
Conductor .... Keene

Major domo .... Yule
Gérard .... Fredricks
Maddalena .... Zschau
Bersi .... Hegierski
Contessa di Coigny ... Shaulis
Fléville .... Sergi
Flando Fiorinelli ...... Jones
Chénier .... Mauro
L'Abate .... Green
Mathieu .... Densen
Incredible .... Lankston
Roucher .... Jamerson
Madelon .... Curry
Child .... Stell
Dumas .... Seabury
Fouquier-Tinville .... Embree
Schmidt .... Yule

February 23

LA BOHÈME (Puccini)

Conductor .... Mauceri

Rodolfo .... Lima
Marcello .... Cossa
Colline .... Embree
Schaunard .... Jamerson
Benoit .... Bassett
Mimi .... Fowles
Parpignol .... Davis
Musetta .... Daniels
Alcindoro .... Yule
Guards ..Peyton, Bohachevsky

February 24 (m)

MADAMA BUTTERFLY (Puccini)

Conductor .... Pallo

Pinkerton ...... Di Giuseppe
Goro .... Clark
Suzuki .... Hegierski
Sharpless .... Fazah
Butterfly .... Verdejo
Imperial
  Commissioner ... Ledbetter
Registrar .... Sergi
The Bonze .... Densen
Yamadori .... Sergi
Trouble .... Wechsler
Kate Pinkerton .... Hill

February 24

THE MARRIAGE OF FIGARO
(Mozart)
(English version by
Ruth and Thomas Martin)

Conductor .... Rudel

Figaro .... Hale
Susanna .... Little
Bartolo .... Bassett
Marcellina .... Shaulis
Cherubino .... Esham
Almaviva .... Hartman
Basilio .... Large

Countess .... Falcon
Antonio .... Yule
Curzio .... Novick
Barbarina .... Thigpen
Bridesmaids .... Luxemburg,
                  Schoenfeld

February 25 (m)

CARMEN (Bizet)

Conductor ..... Shapirra (d)

Morales .... Ledbetter
Zuniga .... Seabury
Micaëla .... Robinson
Don José .... Trussel
Carmen .... Davidson
Frasquita .... Thigpen
Mercédès .... Hill
Lillas Pastia, Guide ..... Sims
Escamillo .... C. Long
Remendado .... Lankston
Dancairo .... Sergi

February 25

ANDREA CHÉNIER

Same cast as February 22
except:

Maddalena .... Coronada (d)
Madelon .... Shaulis

February 28

MADAMA BUTTERFLY

Same cast as February 24 (m)

March 1

CARMEN

Same cast as February 25 (m)

March 2

LUCIA DI LAMMERMOOR
(Donizetti)

Assistant to
  Mr. Capobianco .. Lesenger
Conductor .... Pallo

Alisa .... Shaulis
Edgardo .... Mauro
Normanno .... Clark
Lucia .... Rolandi
Enrico .... Burchinal
Raimondo .... Hale
Arturo .... Green

March 3 (m)

LA BOHÈME

Same cast as February 23

March 3

THE MARRIAGE OF FIGARO

Same cast as February 24

March 4 (m)

LA TRAVIATA (Verdi)

Conductor .... Pallo

Violetta .... Putnam
Flora .... Hegierski

Douphol .... Seabury
D'Obigny .... Jamerson
Dr. Grenvil .... Bassett
Gaston .... Green
Alfredo .... Gonzalez (d)
Annina .... Thigpen
Giuseppe .... Hunsberger
Germont .... Burchinal
Messenger ...... Bohachevsky
Solo dancer .... Galan

March 4

RIGOLETTO (Verdi)

Conductor .... De Renzi

Rigoletto .... Elvira
Monterone's daughter .. Galan
Clown .... Kalba
Duke .... Di Giuseppe
Borsa .... Large
Countess
  Ceprano ... Delery-Whedon
Ceprano .... Ledbetter
Marullo .... Paul
Monterone .... Bassett,
                  (s, Embree)
Sparafucile .... Densen
Gilda .... Robinson
Giovanna .... Toro
Page .... Rawn
Maddalena .... Hill

Broadcast

March 6

LUCIA DI LAMMERMOOR

Same cast as March 2

March 8

LA TRAVIATA

Same cast as March 4 (m)
except:

Douphol .... Steele,
                  (s, Seabury)

March 9

FAUST (Gounod)

Conductor .... Keene

Faust .... Lima
Méphistophélès ...... Ramey
Wagner .... Sergi
Marguerite .... Niculescu
Valentin .... Cossa
Siébel .... Esham
Marthe .... Shaulis
Juggler .... De Dio
Fire-eater .... Presto

March 10 (m)

RIGOLETTO

Same cast as March 4 except:

Rigoletto .... Holmes
Monterone .... McKee
Gilda .... Fowles

March 10

CARMEN

Same cast as February 25 (m) except:

Morales .... Jamerson
Zuniga .... McKee
Micaëla .... Daniels
Don José .... Mauro
Frasquita .... Orloff
Mercédès .... Hegierski
Escamillo .... Holloway
Remendado .... Lankston,
(s, Green)
Dancairo .... Ledbetter

March 11 (m)

LA BOHÈME

Same cast as February 23 except:

Rodolfo .... Cole (d)
Marcello .... Cossa,
(s, C. Long)
Colline .... Seabury
Schaunard .... Hartman
Benoit .... Billings
Mimi .... Christos
Musetta .... Thigpen

March 11

FAUST

Same cast as March 9

March 13

THE MARRIAGE OF FIGARO

Same cast as February 24 except:

Bartolo .... McKee
Count .... Hartman,
(s, C. Long)
Countess .... Sheil
Curzio .... Kays

March 14 (m)

FAUST

Same cast as March 9 except:

Wagner .... Ledbetter
Siébel .... Hegierski

March 16

CARMEN

Same cast as February 25 (m) except:

Morales .... Jamerson
Zuniga .... McKee
Micaëla .... Daniels
Don José .... Mauro
Frasquita .... Orloff
Mercédès .... Hegierski
Escamillo .... Holloway
Dancairo .... Ledbetter

March 17 (m)

LE COQ D'OR
(Rimsky-Korsakov)
(English version by Antal Dorati and James Gibson)

Conductor .... Pallo

Astrologer .... Morales
King Dodon .... Malas
Prince Guidon .... Kays
Genueral Polkan .. Booth (d)
Prince Afron .... Sergi
Golden Cockerel ...... Little
Amelfa .... Costa-Greenspon
Queen of
Shemakha ...... Robinson

March 17

THE MARRIAGE OF FIGARO

Same cast as February 24 except:

Susanna .... Hynes
Bartolo .... McKee
Almaviva .... Hartman,
(s, C. Long)
Curzio .... Kays

March 18 (m)

FAUST

Same cast as March 9 except:

Faust .... Taylor
Marguerite .... Fowles

Broadcast performance

March 18

ANDREA CHÉNIER

Same cast as February 22 except:

Maddalena .... Coronada
Fouquier-Tinville ..... Bassett

March 21

LUCIA DI LAMMERMOOR

Same cast as March 2 except:

Arturo .... Kays

March 22

MISS HAVISHAM'S FIRE
(Argento)
World premiere

Directed by .... Balk (d)
Designer .... Conklin
Lighting .... Hemsley, Jr.
Choreographer ... Danner (d)
Conductor .... Rudel

Aurelia Havisham ..... Shane
Aurelia Havisham,
as a young woman ..Rolandi
Estella Drummle ..... Marsee
Estelle Drummle, as a
young girl .... Wallach (d)
Phillip Pirrip,
known as Pip .... Titus

Phillip Pirrip, as a
young boy .... Sapolsky
Grace-Helen
Broome .... Bonazzi
Grace-Helen Broome,
as a young woman .... Sheil
Jaggers .... Cross
Examiner .... Bassett
Bentley Drummle ... Lankston
Old Orlick .... Ukena
Old Orlick, as a
young man .... Brewer
Pumblechook ...... Ledbetter
Sarah Pocket .... Freni
Camilla Pocket ..... Thigpen
Georgiana Pocket .. Hegierski
Raymond Pocket ...... Green
Reflections of
Miss Havisham. .Harth (d),
Jarosz (d), Z. Long (d)
Maids .... Little, Hill

March 23

MADAMA BUTTERFLY

Same cast as February 24 (m) except:

Pinkerton .... Trussel
Suzuki .... Walker
Sharpless .... Cossa
Kate Pinkerton ... Schoenfeld

March 24 (m)

LUCIA DI LAMMERMOOR

Same cast as March 2 except:

Lucia .... Robinson
Raimondo .... Macurdy
Arturo .... Kays

March 24

MEFISTOFELE (Boito)

Sage director .... Denda
Conductor .... Rudel

Mefistofele .... Ramey
Faust .... Di Giuseppe
Wagner .... Clark
Margherita .... Meier
Marta .... Hegierski
Elena .... Meier
Pantalis .... Hill
Nereo .... Large
Solo dancers .... Gardella,
Itow, Delgado (d)

March 25 (m)

MISS HAVISHAM'S FIRE

Same cast as March 22

March 25

LE COQ D'OR

Same cast as March 17 (m) except:

King Dodon .... McKee
Amelfa .... Shaulis
Queen of
Shemakha ...... Anderson

March 27

MEFISTOFELE

Same cast as March 24

March 28 (m)

LA BOHÈME

Same cast as February 23 except:

Rodolfo .... Cole
Colline .... Hale
Schaunard .... Hartman
Mimi .... Christos
Musetta .... Thigpen

March 29

RIGOLETTO

Same cast as March 4 except:

Rigoletto .... Fredricks
Duke .... Sandor
Monterone .... McKee
Sparafucile .... Bassett
Gilda .... Fowles
Giovanna .... Hill
Maddalena .... Walker

March 30

LA TRAVIATA

Same cast as March 4 (m) except:

Violetta .... Shane
Flora .... Shaulis
D'Obigny .... Ledbetter
Dr. Grenvil .... Yule
Germont .... Cossa

March 31 (m)

MEFISTOFELE

Same cast as March 24

March 31

MADAMA BUTTERFLY

Same cast as February 24 (m) except:

Conductor .... De Renzi
Pinkerton .... Bartolini
Suzuki .... Curry
Butterfly .... Zschau
Kate Pinkerton ... Schoenfeld

April 1 (m)

THE DAUGHTER OF
THE REGIMENT (Donizetti)
(English version by
Ruth and Thomas Martin)

Directed by .... Auerbach
Conductor .... Mauceri

Hortensius .... Ledbetter
Marquise ... Costa-Greenspon
Peasant .... Tippie
Sulpice .... McKee
Marie .... Putnam

Tonio .... Reed
Corporal .... Seabury
Major domo .... Rubino
Duchess .... Faull
Notary .... Sims

(Note: *Henry Jean-Paul
Krackenthorp* added to
program of April 11 [m])

Broadcast performance

April 1

THE TURK IN ITALY (Rossini)
(English translation by
Andrew Porter)

Stage director .... Denda
Conductor .... Rudel

Selim .... Malas
Fiorilla .... Sills
Geronio .... Billings
Narciso .... Kays
Prosdocimo .... Titus
Zaida .... Hegierski,
                (s, Marsee)
Albazar .... Green

April 4

MISS HAVISHAM'S FIRE

Same cast as March 22

April 5

MADAMA BUTTERFLY

Same cast as February 24 (m) except:

Conductor .... De Renzi
Pinkerton .... Bartolini
Suzuki .... Curry
Sharpless .... Fredricks
Butterfly .... Zschau
The Bonze .... McKee
Kate Pinkerton ... Schoenfeld

April 6

CARMEN

Same cast as February 25 (m) except:

Conductor .... Pallo

Micaëla .... Hynes
Don José .... Taylor
Carmen .... Walker
Frasquita .... Orloff
Mercédès .... Hegierski
Remendado .... Green

April 7 (m)

THE DAUGHTER OF
THE REGIMENT

Same cast as April 1 (m) except:

Marquise .... Shaulis
Sulpice .... Sulliivan (d)
Marie .... Rolandi
Tonio .... Kays

April 7

THE DAUGHTER OF
THE REGIMENT

Same cast as April 1 (m)

April 8 (m)

THE TURK IN ITALY

Same cast as April 1 except:

Zaida .... Marsee

April 8

DIDO AND AENEAS (Purcell)
First performance by The New
York City Opera Company
(Realized and edited by
Benjamin Britten and
Imogen Holst)

Directed by .... Corsaro
Designer ...... Ter-Arutunian
Lighting .... Hemsley, Jr.
Choreographer .. Martins (d)
Conductor .... Kellogg
Pantomime scenes directed in
collaboration with Balanchine

Dido .... Browne (d)
Aeneas .... Holloway
Belinda .... Hall (d)
Lady-in-Waiting .... Little
Sorceress .... Freni
Witches .... Thigpen, Hill
Spirit .... Sapolsky
Sailor .... Lankston
Witches (dancers) .. Gardella,
    Pradera, Itow, Kaufold (d),
    Redel (d), Rinaldi (d),
    Williams (d), Rzasa (d)
Sailors (dancers) .... Rubino,
    Romero, Bourbon, Kalba,
    Iracledes (d), Medina (d),
    Cousins (d), Kokich (d)

Followed by:

LE BOURGEOIS GENTILHOMME
(R. Strauss)
World premiere of this version

Designer ...... Ter-Arutunian
Lighting .... Hemsley, Jr
Choreographers .. Balanchine
    and Robbins (d)
Conductor .... Kellogg

Lucile .... McBride
M. Jourdain .. Bonnefous (d)
Cleonte .... Nureyev (d)

With additional dancers
trained at the School of
American Ballet

April 10

DIDO AND AENEAS

Same cast as April 8

Followed by:

LE BOURGEOIS GENTILHOMME

Same cast as April 8

April 11 (m)

THE DAUGHTER OF THE REGIMENT

Same cast as April 1 (m)

Added to this program:

Henry Jean Paul
Krackenthorp ..... Thomas

April 12

CARMEN

Same cast as February 25 (m) except:

Conductor .... Effron

Morales .... Jamerson
Micaëla .... Fowles
Carmen .... Freni
Frasquita .... Orloff
Mercédès .... Hegierski
Remendado .... Green
Dancairo .... Ledbetter

April 13

DIDO AND AENEAS

Same cast as April 8

Followed by:

LE BOURGEOIS GENTILHOMME

Same cast as April 8

April 14 (m)

LA BOHÈME

Same cast as February 23 except:

Rodolfo .... Bartolini
Colline .... Hale
Schaunard .... Sergi
Benoit .... Billings
Mimi .... Christos
Musetta .... Zannoth

April 14

TOSCA (Puccini)

Conductor .... Kellogg

Angelotti .... Bassett
Sacristan .... Billings
Cavaradossi .... Trussel
Tosca .... Meier
Scarpia .... Burchinal
Spoletta .... Clark
Sciarrone .... Sergi
Shepherd .... Hill
Jailer .... Seabury

April 15 (m)

LE COQ D'OR

Same cast as March 17 (m) except:

Conductor .... Effron

Astrologer .... Novick
Golden Cockerel .... Christos

April 15

LA TRAVIATA

Same cast as March 4 (m) except:

Conductor .... Salesky

D'Obigny .... Ledbetter,
                 (s, Jamerson)
Dr. Grenvil .... Yule
Alfredo .... Paglialunga
Germont .... Fredricks

April 17

MADAMA BUTTERFLY

Same cast as February 24 (m) except:

Conductor .... De Renzi

Pinkerton .... Trussel
Goro .... Green
Suzuki .... Walker
Sharpless .... Fredricks
Butterfly .... Zschau
The Bonze .... McKee
Kate Pinkerton ... Schoenfeld

April 18

DIDO AND AENEAS

Same cast as April 8

Followed by:

LE BOURGEOIS GENTILHOMME

Same cast as April 8

April 19

IL BARBIERE DI SIVIGLIA (Rossini)

Conductor .... Effron

Fiorello .... Jamerson
Almaviva .... Kays
Figaro .... Elvira
Bartolo .... McKee
Ambrogio .... Thomas
Berta .... Curry
Rosina .... Rolandi
Basilio .... Hale
Officer .... Bassett

April 20

MANON (Massenet)

Conductor .... Rudel

Guillot .... Castel
De Brétigny .... Hartman
Pousette .... Daniels
Javotte .... Little
Rosette .... Hegierski
Innkeeper .... Sergi
Lescaut .... Holloway
Guards ..... Ledbetter, Yule
Manon .... Malfitano
Des Grieux .... Price
Maid .... Greene
Count des Grieux .... Embree

Prima ballerina .... Rzasa
Premier danseur ..... Romero
Ballet master .... Rubino
Cupid .... Gardella
Seminary porter .... Carlo
Gambler .... Kingman
Sergeant .... Yule

April 21 (m)

DIDO AND AENEAS

Same cast as April 8 except:

Belinda .... Hynes

Followed by:

LE BOURGEOIS GENTILHOMME

Same cast as April 8

April 21

LA TRAVIATA

Same cast as March 4 (m) except:

Conductor .... Salesky

Dr. Grenvil .... Yule
Alfredo .... Paglialunga
Germont .... Fredricks

April 22 (m)

TOSCA

Same cast as April 14

April 22

MANON

Same cast as April 20 except:

Des Grieux .... Taylor,
                  (s, Price)

Broadcast performance

April 24

MANON

Same cast as April 20 except:

De Brétigny .... Jamerson
Manon .... Fowles
Des Grieux .... Taylor

April 25 (m)

IL BARBIERE DI SIVIGLIA

Same cast as April 19

April 25

DIDO AND AENEAS

Same cast as April 8 except:

Dido .... Nelson (d)
Aeneas .... Titus
Belinda .... Hynes
Lady-in-Waiting .... Orloff
Sorceress .... Shaulis

Followed by:

LE BOURGEOIS GENTILHOMME

Same cast as April 8

April 27

MANON

Same cast as April 20 except:

Lescaut .... Fredricks

April 28 (m)

IL BARBIERE DI SIVIGLIA

Same cast as April 19 except:

Fiorello .... Ledbetter
Almaviva .... Grahame
Figaro .... Holloway
Bartolo .... Billings
Rosina .... Haley
Officer .... Yule

April 28

DIDO AND AENEAS

Same cast as April 8 except:

Dido .... Nelson
Aeneas .... Titus
Lady-in-Waiting ..... Orloff
Belinda .... Hynes
Sorceress .... Shaulis

Followed by:

LE BOURGEOIS GENTILHOMME

Same cast as April 8

April 29 (m)

TOSCA

Same cast as April 14

April 29

MISS HAVISHAM'S FIRE

Same cast as March 22 except:

Jaggers .... McKee

Broadcast performance

(Note: This was the last performance of Julius Rudel's regime as director of The New York City Opera Company. At the end of the performance, hundreds of company members, past and present, filed to the stage and sang "For He's a Jolly Good Fellow.")

Fall 1979 (AUGUST 30 – NOVEMBER II)

Female Artists
Aaronson, Cindy Lynn
Adoff, Denise
Anderson, June
Bartolini, Dela
Bouleyn, Kathryn*
Christos, Marianna
Costa-Greenspon, Muriel
Curry, Diane
Davidson, Joy
Delery-Whedon, Susan
de los Angeles, Victoria*
Esham, Faith
Fowles, Glenys
Freni, RoseMarie
Greene, Harriet
Hall, Janice
Hegierski, Kathleen
Hill, Eunice
Hynes, Elizabeth
Krueger, Dana*
Lambert, Sally
Lerner, Mimi*
Little, Gwenlynn
Lovelace, Kimara
Luxemburg, Leslie
Malfitano, Catherine
Marsee, Susanne
Metzger, Rita M.
Murray, Ann*
Niculescu, Mariana
Orloff, Penny
Pelle, Nadia*
Putnam, Ashley
Rawn, Jean
Rogers, Noelle
Rolandi, Gianna
Rosenfeld, Carol
Schauler, Eileen
Schoenfeld, Kay
Shaulis, Jane
Sheil, Martha
Sills, Beverly
Simon, Joanna
Soviero, Diana
Thigpen, Martha

Thomas, Bronwyn
Tisch, Rosalie
Toro, Puli
Vaness, Carol*
Verdejo, Awilda
Wilkinson, Raven
Williams, Vanessa
Young, Marie
Zannoth, Sherry
Zschau, Marilyn

Male Artists
Bartolini, Lando
Bassett, Ralph
Billings, James
Blake, Rockwell*
Bohachevsky, George
Bröcheler, John*
Brown, Maurice*
Brubaker, Robert
Calleo, Riccardo*
Carl, Barry
Carlo, Don
Castel, Nico
Chapman, William
Clark, James
Cole, Vinson
Cossa, Dominic
Crook, Mervin
Davis, Harris
Densen, Irwin
Dietrich, Gary
Di Giuseppe, Enrico
Eaton, Timothy
Elvira, Pablo
Embree, Marc
Evans, Joseph
Foss, Harlan
Fredricks, Richard
Gately, David
Gramm, Donald
Green, Jonathan
Hadley, Jerry*
Hale, Robert
Hartman, Vernon
Hecht, Joshua

Hensel, Howard
Herndon, Bill
Holloway, David
Hunsberger, Herbert
Jamerson, Thomas
Jones, Reed*
Kays, Alan
Lankston, John
Large, Norman
Ledbetter, William
Long, Charles
Mauro, Ermanno
McGrath, Matthew
McKee, Richard
Molese, Michele
Moser, Thomas*
Paul, Robert
Perry, Louis
Peyton, J. Randolph
Postrel, Leo
Price, Henry
Ramey, Samuel
Reed, Bruce
Roe, Charles
Rowen, Glenn
Seabury, John
Serbo, Rico*
Sergi, James
Smith, David Rae
Teeter, Lara*
Thomas, John Henry
Tippie, Frank
Titus, Alan
Trussel, Jacque
Wechsler, Mitchell
Woodley, Arthur*
Yule, Don
Zimmerman, Edward

Principal Conductor
Rudel, Julius

Conductors
Caldwell, Sarah
Crosby, John*

    * New artist   * New artist   * New artist

Holt, Henry*
Keene, Christopher
Kellogg, Cal Stewart
Mauceri, John
Pallo, Imre
Salesky, Brian
Somogi, Judith
Wendelken-Wilson, Charles

Chorus Master
Walser, Lloyd

Assistant Chorus Master
Krieger, Mitchell

Director of Children's Chorus
Hohner, Mildred

Dancers
Farrell, Suzanne*
Itow, Candace
Galan, Esperanza
Gardella, Toni-Ann
Pradera, Rebeka
Rzasa, Laura
Wilkinson, Raven

Bourbon, José
Delgado, Alberto
Kalba, Taras
Martins, Peter*
Ohman, Frank*
Romero, Rafael
Rubino, Michael

Choreographers
Andrew, Thomas
Balanchine, George
Birch, Patricia
Danner, Dorothy Frank
Denda, Gigi
Martins, Peter
Robbins, Jerome

Directors
Alden, Christopher*
Auerbach, Cynthia
Caldwell, Sarah
Capobianco, Tito
Copley, John
Corsaro, Frank
Eddleman, Jack
Mirdita, Federick*
O'Brien, Jack

Designers
Abrams, Don*
Billington, Ken
Collins, Patricia*
Eck, Marsha Louis
Evans, Lloyd
Hemsley, Gilbert V., Jr.
Lee, Ming Cho
Mess, Suzanne
Montresor, Beni
Oenslager, Donald
Pond, Helen
Potts, Nancy
Senn, Herbert
Smith, Oliver
Sondheimer, Hans
Steinberg, Paul*
Sylbert, Paul
Ter-Arutunian, Rouben
Toms, Carl
Vanarelli, Mario*
Varona, José
Zipprodt, Patricia

* New artist

August 30

NAUGHTY MARIETTA (Herbert)

Adapted by ...... Eddleman
Conductor .... Mauceri

Marietta d'Altena .... Hynes
Captain
   Richard Warrington..Hensel
Etienne Grandet ...... Titus
Adah Le Clercq ..... Marsee
Private
   Silas Slick ..... Teeter (d)
Lizette .... Krueger (d)
Acting Governor
   Grandet .... Billings
Florenze .... Gately (d)
Sir Harry Blake .... Yule
Rudolfo .... Foss
Pirates .... Kalba, Rubino
Town crier .... Zimmerman
Flower girls ..Delery-Whedon,
                        Lambert
Nanette .... Aaronson
Felice .... Lambert
Fanchon .... Luxemburg
Knife grinder .... Carl
Flower vendor .. Bohachevsky
Bird vendor .... Perry
Fruit vendor ...... Brubaker
Sugar cane vendor .... Davis
Indian .... Carlo
Pierrot .... Bourbon
Graziella .... Gardella
Major-domo .... Rowen
Spanish dancer .... Galan
San Domingo
   ladies ..... Gardella, Itow,
                        Pradera
Quadroon waiters .... Kalba,
      Rubino, Romero, Bourbon
Man at auction ...... Crook
Turk .... Carl

August 31

NAUGHTY MARIETTA

Same cast as August 30 except:

Mariette d'Altena ... Rolandi
Captain Richard
   Warrington .... Trussel
Etienne Grandet .... Roe
Adah Le Clercq ..... Simon

September 1 (m)

NAUGHTY MARIETTA

Same cast as August 30

September 1

NAUGHTY MARIETTA

Same cast as August 30 except:

Conductor .... Salesky

Marietta d'Altena ... Rolandi
Captain Richard
   Warrington .... Trussel
Etienne Grandet .... Roe
Adah Le Clercq ..... Simon

September 2 (m)

NAUGHTY MARIETTA

Same cast as August 30

September 2

NAUGHTY MARIETTA

Same cast as August 30 except:

Conductor .... Salesky

Marietta d'Altena ... Rolandi
Captain Richard
   Warrington .... Trussel
Etienne Grandet .... Roe
Adah Le Clercq ...... Simon

September 5

THE MERRY WIDOW (Lehár)

(English translation and
dialogue by Ursula Eggers and
Joseph De Rugeriis; English
lyrics by Sheldon Harnick)

Conductor .... Pallo

Baron Mirko Zeta .... Smith
Valencienne .... Christos
Count Danilo
   Danilovitch .... Titus
Anna Glawari ...... Soviero
Camille de Rosillon .... Reed
Vicomte Cascada ...... Foss
Raoul St. Brioche ..... Kays
Bogdanovitch ... Hunsberger
Sylviane .... Shaulis
Kromov .... Ledbetter
Olga .... Orloff
Pritchitch .... Perry
Praskovia ... Delery-Whedon
Njegus .... Billings
Lolo .... Itow
Dodo .... Shaulis
Jou-Jou .... Orloff
Frou-Frou .... Gardella
Clo-Clo ..... Delery-Whedon
Margot .... Wilkinson

September 6

THE MERRY WIDOW

Same cast as September 5

September 7

THE MERRY WIDOW

Same cast as September 5
except:

Conductor .... Somogi

Valencienne .... Bouleyn (d)
Count Danilo
   Danilovitch .... Hensel
Anna Glawari .... Fowles
Camille de Rosillon .... Price
Vicomte Cascada .. Jamerson
Kromov .... Sergi
Olga .... Toro
Jou-Jou .... Toro

September 8 (m)

THE MERRY WIDOW

Same cast as September 5

September 8

THE MERRY WIDOW

Same cast as September 5
except:

Conductor .... Somogi
Valencienne .... Bouleyn
Count Danilo
  Danilovitch .... Hensel
Anna Glawari .... Fowles
Camille de Rosillon .... Price
Vicomte Cascada .. Jamerson
Kromov .... Sergi
Olga .... Toro
Jou-Jou .... Toro

September 9 (m)

THE MERRY WIDOW

Same cast as September 5

September 9

THE MERRY WIDOW

Same cast as September 5
except:

Conductor .... Somogi
Valencienne .... Bouleyn
Count Danilo
  Danilovitch .... Hensel
Anne Glawari .... Fowles
Camille de Rosillon .... Price
Vicomte Cascada .. Jamerson
Kromov .... Sergi
Olga .... Toro
Jou-Jou .... Toro

September 11

TOSCA (Puccini)

Conductor .... Kellogg

Cesare Angelotti ..... Bassett
A Sacristan .... Billings
Mario Cavaradossi ... Mauro
Tosca .... Zschau
Scarpia .... Hecht
Spoletta .... Lankston
Sciarrone .... Sergi
A Shepherd .... Hill
A Jailer .... Seabury

September 13

FAUST (Gounod)

Conductor .... Keene

Faust .... Serbo (d)
Méphistophélès ...... Ramey
Wagner .... Ledbetter
Marguerite .... Niculescu
Valentin .... Cossa
Siébel .... Esham
Marthe .... Shaulis

September 14

LUCIA DI LAMMERMOOR
(Donizetti)

Conductor .... Pallo

Alisa .... Shaulis
Edgardo .... Mauro
Normanno .... Clark
Lucia .... Rolandi
Enrico .... Fredricks
Raimondo .... Hale
Lord Arturo
  Bucklaw ...... Hadley (d)

September 15 (m)

MADAMA BUTTERFLY (Puccini)

Conductor ...... Crosby (d)

Pinkerton ...... Di Giuseppe
Goro .... Clark
Suzuki .... Hegierski
Sharpless .... Long
Madama Butterfly ... Zschau
Imperial
  Commissioner ... Ledbetter
Registrar .... Sergi
Bonze .... Seabury
Yamadori .... Sergi
Trouble .... Wechsler
Kate Pinkerton ... Schoenfeld

September 15

FAUST

Same cast as September 13

September 16 (m)

LUCIA DI LAMMERMOOR

Same cast as September 14

September 16

LA LOCA (Menotti)

First performance by The New
York City Opera Company

Devised and
  directed by .... Capobianco
Sets and costumes
  designed by .. Vanarelli (d)
Lighting
  designed by ... Abrams (d)
Conductor .... Mauceri

Dona Manuela ..... Marsee
Ladies-in-waiting ..... Orloff,
                  Schoenfeld
Juana (La Loca) .... Sills
Nurse .... Krueger
Miguel de Ferrera .... Evans
Felipe .... Bröcheler (d)
Chaplain .... Foss
Ximenes de Cisneros ... Hale
Fernando ..... Bröcheler (d)
Carlos V
  as a young boy .... Eaton
Marques de Denia .. Seabury

Catalina .... Block
Emperor Carlos
  (adult) ..... Bröcheler (d)
Broadcast performance

September 19

LA LOCA

Same cast as September 16

September 20

LUCIA DI LAMMERMOOR

Same cast as September 14
except:

Alisa .... Hill
Raimondo .... Seabury

September 21

FAUST

Same cast as September 13

September 22 (m)

CARMEN (Bizet)

Conductor ...... Wendelken-
                  Wilson

Morales .... Jamerson
Zuniga .... Embree
Micaëla .... Soviero
Don José .... Calleo (d)
Carmen .... Davidson
Frasquita .... Thigpen
Mercédès .... Krueger
Lillas Pastia .... Dietrich
Escamillo .... Long
Remendado .... Green
Dancairo .... Foss
A Guide .... Dietrich

September 22

TOSCA

Same cast as September 11
except:

Scarpia ...... Hecht (Act 1),
            Fredricks (Act 2)

September 23 (m)

LA LOCA

Same cast as September 16

September 23

COUNT ORY (Rossini)
(Le Comte Ory; English
version by Tom Hammond)
First performance by The New
York City Opera Company

Director .... Alden (d
Scenery and costumes
  designed by .. Steinberg (d
Lighting
  designed by ...... Hemsle
Conductor .... Pall

Raimbaud .... Hollowa
Alice .... Thigpe

Ragonde .... Shaulis
Count Ory .... Blake (d)
Tutor .... Ramey
Countess Adèle ..... Putnam
Courtiers ... Davis, Brubaker
Lady-in-waiting .... Tisch

(Note: The scenic concept for this production was originally created for the Opera Theatre of Saint Louis.)

Broadcast performance

September 25

COUNT ORY

Same cast as September 23

September 26

LA LOCA

Same cast as September 16

September 27

MADAMA BUTTERFLY

Same cast as September 15 (m) except:

Bonze .... Bassett

September 28

COUNT ORY

Same cast as September 23

September 29 (m)

LA LOCA

Same cast as September 16

September 29

LUCIA DI LAMMERMOOR

Same cast as September 14 except:

Alisa .... Hill
Edgardo .... Di Giuseppe
Enrico .... Cossa
Raimondo .... Seabury

September 30 (m)

COUNT ORY

Same cast as September 23 except:

Countess Adèle ...... Hynes,
(s, Putnam)

September 30

CARMEN

Same cast as September 22 (m)

Note: A strike by the musicians caused the cancellation of all performances scheduled for October 2 through October 10 inclusive, as well as that of October 17 (m). In addition, there were changes of programming on October 19, October 30, November 1, and November 9. The scheduled performances that were canceled were:

October 2
  THE MARRIAGE OF FIGARO
October 3
  MADAMA BUTTERFLY
October 4
  LA LOCA
October 5
  FALSTAFF
October 6 (m)
  DIDO AND AENEAS
  followed by
  LE BOURGEOIS
  GENTILHOMME
October 6
  CARMEN
October 7 (m)
  FALSTAFF
October 7
  RIGOLETTO
October 9
  FALSTAFF
October 10 (m)
  DIDO AND AENEAS
  followed by
  LE BOURGEOIS
  GENTILHOMME
October 17 (m)
  RIGOLETTO)

October 11

FALSTAFF (Verdi)
(English translation by Andrew Porter)
New Production

Director .... Caldwell
Scenic designers .. Pond, Senn
Costume supervision .. Joseph
Lighting designer ... Hemsley
Choreographer ...... Andrew
Conductor .... Caldwell

Dr. Caius .... Lankston
Sir John Falstaff .... Gramm
Bardolph .... Billings
Pistol .... Bassett
Mistress Page ..... Hegierski
Mistress Ford ...... Fowles
Dame Quickly .... Costa-
                   Greenspon
Nanetta .... Hynes
Ford .... Fredricks
Fenton .... Reed

October 12

CARMEN

Same cast as September 22 (m) except:

Morales .... Sergi
Micaëla .... Little

October 13 (m)

STREET SCENE (Weill)

Conductor ...., Mauceri

Greta Fiorentino ... Thigpen
Emma Jones .... Curry
Olga Olsen .... Freni

Carl Olsen .... Bassett
Shirley Kaplan .... Rosenfeld
Abraham Kaplan ... Postrel,
                 (s, Castel)
Henry Davis ... Woodley (d)
Willie Maurrant ...... Eaton
Anna Maurrant .... Schauler
Sam Kaplan .... Kays
Daniel Buchanan ...... Large
Frank Maurrant ... Chapman
George Jones .... Paul
Steve Sankey ...... Ledbetter
Lippo Fiorentino ..... Green
Mrs. Hildebrand ... Lambert
Jenny Hildebrand .. Hegierski
Graduates ... Adoff, Williams
Charlie Hildebrand..McGrath
Mary Hildebrand..D. Bartolini
Grace Davis .... Lovelace
Rose Maurrant ... Malfitano
Harry Easter .... Foss
Mae Jones ...... B. Thomas
Dick McGann .... Jones (d)
Vincent Jones ..... Herndon
Dr. Wilson .... Carlo
Officer Murphy .. Zimmerman
Milkman .... Brubaker
James Henry .... Yule
Fred Cullen .... Densen
Nursemaids .... Young,
                   Metzger

October 13

RIGOLETTO (Verdi)

Conductor .... Salesky

Rigoletto .... Elvira
Monterone's daughter .. Galan
A Clown .... Kalba
The Duke of Mantua..Molese
Borsa .... Clark
Countess
  Ceprano .. Delery-Whedon
Ceprano .... Yule
Marullo .... Sergi
Monterone .... Embree
Sparafucile .... Bassett
Gilda .... Niculescu
Giovanna .... Shaulis
A Page .... Rawn
Maddalena .... Hill

October 14 (m)

FALSTAFF

Same cast as October 11

Broadcast performance

October 14

CARMEN

Same cast as September 22 (m) except:

Morales .... Sergi
Zuniga .... Seabury
Micaëla .... Little
Carmen .. de los Angeles (d)
Frasquita .... Orloff
Mercédès .... Hill
Escamillo .... Hale
Remendado .... Lankston
Dancairo .... Ledbetter

October 16

STREET SCENE

Same cast as October 13 (m)

October 18

THE MARRIAGE OF FIGARO
(Mozart)
(In Italian)

Conductor	Rudel
Figaro	Holloway
Susanna	Little
Dr. Bartolo	Bassett
Marcellina	Shaulis
Cherubino	Esham
Count Almaviva	Hartman, (s, Hale)
Don Basilio	Large
Countess Almaviva	Sheil, (s, de los Angeles)
Antonio	Yule
Don Curzio	Kays
Barbarina	Thigpen
Bridesmaids	Luxemburg, Schoenfeld

October 19

FALSTAFF
(s, DIDO AND AENEAS and
LE BOURGEOIS GENTILHOMME)

Same cast as October 11
except:

Mistress Ford .... Sheil

October 20 (m)

LA BOHÈME (Puccini)

Conductor	Holt (d)
Rodolfo	Cole
Marcello	Cossa
Colline	Embree
Schaunard	Jamerson
Benoit	Billings
Mimi	Soviero
Parpignol	Green
Musetta	Rogers
Alcindoro	Yule
Guards	Peyton, Bohachevsky

October 20

MADAMA BUTTERFLY

Same cast as September 15 (m)
except:

Pinkerton	L. Bartolini
Suzuki	Curry
Sharpless	Hartman
Madama Butterfly	Verdejo
The Bonze	Bassett

October 21 (m)

CARMEN

Same cast as September 22 (m)
except:

Morales	Sergi
Zuniga	Seabury

Micaëla	Little
Frasquita	Orloff
Mercédès	Hill
Escamillo	Hale
Remendado	Lankston
Dancairo	Ledbetter

Broadcast performance

October 21

MANON (Massenet)

Conductor	Mauceri
Guillot	Lankston
De Brétigny	Hartman
Pousette	Thigpen
Javotte	Zannoth
Rosette	Pelle (d)
Innkeeper	Foss
Lescaut	Fredricks
Guards	Ledbetter, Yule
Manon	Malfitano
Des Grieux	Molese
Maid	Greene
Comte Des Grieux	Brown (d)
Prima Ballerina of the Paris Opera	Rzasa
Premier Danseur of the Paris Opera	Romero
Ballet master	Rubino
Cupid	Gardella
Seminary porter	Carlo
Gambler	Zimmerman
Sergeant	Yule

October 24

MANON

Same cast as October 21

October 25

LA CLEMENZA DI TITO
(Mozart)
First performance by The New
York City Opera Company

Director	Mirdita (d)
Scenic and Costume designer	Evans
Lighting designer	Hemsley
Conductor	Rudel
Titus	Moser (d)
Vitellia	Vaness (d)
Sextus	Murray (d)
Annius	Pelle
Servilia	Hall
Publius	Seabury

October 26

THE MARRIAGE OF FIGARO

Same cast as October 18
except:

Count Almaviva .... Hale

October 27 (m)

LA CLEMENZA DI TITO

Same cast as October 25

October 27

STREET SCENE

Same cast as October 13 (m)

Televised performance

October 28 (m)

MANON

Same cast as October 21

October 28

LA BOHÈME

Same cast as October 20 (m)

October 30

FALSTAFF, (s, CARMEN)

Same cast as October 11
except:

Mistress Ford .... Sheil

October 31

STREET SCENE

Same cast as October 13 (m)
except:

Abraham Kaplan ..... Castel

November 1

LA LOCA,
(s, LA CLEMENZA DI TITO)

Same cast as September 16

(Note: This was Beverly Sills's
last operatic performance with
The New York City Opera.
Her official farewell, which
would take place almost a
year later, was a gala concert,
rather than an opera.)

November 2

THE DAUGHTER OF
THE REGIMENT (Donizetti)
(La Fille du Regiment:
English version by
Ruth and Thomas Martin)

Conductor	Wendelken-Wilson
Hortensius	Ledbetter
The Marquise of Berkenfeld	Costa-Greenspon
A Peasant	Tippie
Sulpice	McKee
Marie	Roland
Tonio	Reed
Corporal	Seabury
Major-Domo	Rubino
Duchess of Krackenthorp	Krueger
Henry Jean-Paul Krackenthorp	J. Thomas
Notary	Dietrich

November 3 (m)

RIGOLETTO

Same cast as October 13
except:

Rigoletto .... Fredricks
The Duke of Mantua .. Serbo
Ceprano .... Ledbetter
Sparafucile .... Densen
Gilda .... Anderson
Maddalena .... Hegierski

November 3

LA BOHÈME

Same cast as October 2 (m)
except:

Conductor .... Pallo

Rodolfo .... Mauro
Colline .... Hale
Musetta .... Zannoth

November 4 (m)

LA CLEMENZA DI TITO

Same cast as October 25

Broadcast performance

November 4

MANON

Same cast as October 21
except:

Guillot .... Castel
De Brétigny ...... Jamerson
Des Grieux .... Price
Le Comte
   Des Grieux .... Embree

November 6

LA CLEMENZA DI TITO

Same cast as October 25
except:

Vitellia .... Sheil
Sextus .... Lerner (d)
Annius .... Hill
Publius .... Bassett
Servilia .... Hynes

November 7 (m)

TOSCA

Same cast as September 11

November 8

THE DAUGHTER OF
THE REGIMENT

Same cast as November 2

November 9

DIDO AND AENEAS (Purcell),
(s, LA BOHÈME)

Conductor .... Kellogg

Dido .... Curry
Aeneas .... Hartman
Belinda .... Hynes
Lady-in-waiting .... Orloff
Sorceress .... Freni
Witches .... Thigpen, Hill
Spirit .... Sloan
Sailor .... Lankston

Followed by:

LE BOURGEOIS GENTILHOMME
(R. Strauss)

Conductor .... Kellogg

Lucile .... Farrell (d)
M. Jourdain .... Ohman (d)
Cleonte .... Martins (d)

November 10 (m)

MADAMA BUTTERFLY

Same cast as September 15 (m)
except:

Pinkerton .... L. Bartolini
Suzuki .... Shaulis
Sharpless .... Hartman
Madama Butterfly ... Verdejo
The Bonze .... Bassett

November 10

STREET SCENE

Same cast as October 13 (m)

November 11 (m)

THE DAUGHTER OF
THE REGIMENT

Same cast as November 2

November 11

TOSCA

Same cast as September 11

Spring 1980 (FEBRUARY 21 – APRIL 27)

Female Artists
Aaronson, Cindy Lynn
Anderson, June
Bonazzi, Elaine
Bouleyn, Kathryn
Claveau, Sharon
Christos, Marianna
Costa-Greenspon, Muriel
Curry, Diane
Davidson, Joy
Dickison-Rhodus, Judith
Esham, Faith
Falcon, Ruth
Fowles, Glenys
Freni, RoseMarie
Greene, Harriet
Gutknecht, Carol*
Hall, Janice
Harris, Hilda
Hegierski, Kathleen
Hill, Eunice
Hinds, Esther
Hynes, Elizabeth

James, Judith*
Krueger, Dana
Lambert, Sally
Little, Gwenlynn
Marsee, Susanne
Myers, Pamela*
Nielsen, Inga*
Niska, Maralin
Orloff, Penny
Pelle, Nadia
Rolandi, Gianna
Schoenfeld, Kay
Shaulis, Jane
Sheil, Martha
Simon, Joanna
Soviero, Diana
Sundine, Stephanie*
Terzian, Anita*
Thigpen, Martha
Thomson, Heather
Tisch, Rosalie
Toro, Puli
Vaness, Carol

Verdejo, Awilda
Zannoth, Sherry
Zschau, Marilyn

Male Artists
Albert, Donnie Ray*
Arnold, David*
Bartolini, Lando
Bassett, Ralph
Billings, James
Blake, Rockwell
Bohachevsky, George
Brown, Maurice
Brubaker, Robert
Calleo, Riccardo
Carlo, Don
Chausson, Carlos*
Clark, James
Cossa, Dominic
De Dio, Harry
Densen, Irwin
Diaz, Justino

* New artist   * New artist   * New artist

Dietrich, Gary J.
Di Giuseppe, Enrico
Ellis, Brent
Embree, Marc
Evans, Joseph
Farone, Dominick
Foss, Harlan
Grahame, Gerald
Gramm, Donald
Green, Jay
Green, Jonathan
Grey, Joel*
Hadley, Jerry
Hale, Robert
Hall, David
Harrold, Jack
Hartman, Vernon
Holloway, David
Hunsberger, Herbert
Jamerson, Thomas
Kelley, Ronald
Lankston, John
Large, Norman
Ledbetter, William
Long, Charles
McCauley, Barry*
McDonald, William
McFarland, Robert*
McKee, Richard
Molese, Michele
Neill, William
Perry, Douglas
Peyton, J. Randolph
Poplaski, William*
Porter, Richard L.
Presto
Price, Henry
Ramey, Samuel
Reed, Bruce
Rippon, Michael*
Roe, Charles
Serbo, Rico
Sergi, James
Smith, David Rae
Thomas, John Henry
Tippie, Frank
Titus, Alan
Trussel, Jacque
Wechsler, Mitchell
Yule, Don
Zimmerman, Edward

Principal Conductor
Rudel, Julius

Conductors
Caldwell, Sarah
Crosby, John
Dufallo, Richard
Keene, Christopher
Mauceri, John
Meltzer, Andrew*
Pallo, Imre
Salesky, Brian
Scott, William Fred, III
Wendelken-Wilson, Charles

Chorus Master
Walser, Lloyd

Assistant Chorus Master
Krieger, Mitchell

Director of Children's Chorus
Hohner, Mildred

* New artist

Solo Dancers
Galan, Esperanza
Gardella, Toni-Ann
Gregory, Cynthia*
Itow, Candace
Rzasa, Laura

Chryst, Gary*
Delgado, Alberto
Kalba, Taras
Romero, Rafael
Rubino, Michael
Sewell, James

Choreographers
Andrew, Thomas
Denda, Gigi
Fuller, Larry*
Nahat, Dennis*
Redel, Jessica*

Directors
Alden, Christopher
Auerbach, Cynthia
Bentley, Ronald
Caldwell, Sarah
Capobianco, Tito
Copley, John
Corsaro, Frank
Cox, John
Denda, Gigi
Freedman, Gerald
Galterio, Lou*
Prince, Harold
Smith, Christian

Designers
Abrams, Don
Aldredge, Theoni V.
Annals, Michael*
Billington, Ken
Campbell, Patton
Eck, Marsha Louis
Evans, Lloyd
Fletcher, Robert
George, Hal
Hemsley, Gilbert V., Jr.
Joseph, J. Edgar
Lee, Ming Cho
Lutgenhorst, Manuel*
Mann, Jack
Mitchell, David
Montresor, Beni
Pond, Helen
Senn, Herbert
Sondheimer, Hans
Steinberg, Paul
Ter-Arutunian, Rouben
Toms, Carl
Vanarelli, Mario
Varona, José

* New artist

February 21

COUNT ORY (Rossini)
(*Le Comte Ory*: English
version by Tom Hammond)

Conductor .... Pallo

Raimbaud .... Holloway
Alice .... Thigpen
Ragonde .... Shaulis
Count Ory .... Blake
Tutor .... Ramey

Isolier .... Esham
Countess Adèle ..... Rolandi
Courtiers ... Davis, Brubaker
Lady-in-waiting .... Tisch

February 22

LA TRAVIATA (Verdi)

Choreography
re-staged by .... Redel
Conductor ...... Meltzer (d)

Violetta .... Soviero
Flora .... Hegierski
Baron Douphol ..... Embree
Marquis d'Obigny ...... Sergi
Dr. Grenville .... Yule
Gaston .... Hadley
Alfredo .... Serbo
Annina .... Pelle
Giuseppe .... Hunsberger
Germont .... Ellis
Messenger ..... Bohachevsky
Solo dancer .... Galan

February 23 (m)

DIE FLEDERMAUS (J. Strauss)
(English version by
Ruth and Thomas Martin)

Choreography
re-staged by .... Redel
Miss Gregory's
solo choreographed
by .... Nahat (d)
Conductor .... Pallo

Alfred .... Grahame
Adele .... Nielsen (d)
Rosalinda .... Niska
Eisenstein .... Roe
Dr. Blind .... Large
Falke .... Cossa
Frank .... McKee
Sally .... Torc
Ivan .... Dietrich
Prince Orlofsky ..... Smith
Frosch .... Harrold
Solo dancers .. Galan, Kalba
Special Guest ... Gregory (d)

February 23

COUNT ORY

Same cast as February 21

February 24 (m)

LA TRAVIATA

Same cast as February 22

February 24

DIE FLEDERMAUS

Same cast as February 23 (m)

Broadcast performance

February 26

COUNT ORY

Same cast as February 21
except:

Raimbaud .... Jamerso
Alice .... Orlo

Ragonde .... Krueger
Count Ory ...... McDonald
Tutor .... Ramey
(s, Bassett)
Isolier .... Hill
Countess Adèle .... Hynes

February 27

LA TRAVIATA

Same cast as February 22

February 28

DIE FLEDERMAUS

Same cast as February 23 (m)

February 29

MADAMA BUTTERFLY (Puccini)

Conductor .... Crosby

Pinkerton ...... Di Giuseppe
Goro .... Jonathan Green
Suzuki .... Hegierski
Sharpless .... Cossa
Madama Butterfly ... Zschau
Imperial
Commissioner ... Ledbetter
Registrar .... Sergi
Bonze .... Bassett
Yamadori .... Sergi
Trouble .... Wechsler
Kate Pinkerton .... Hill

March 1 (m)

THE MARRIAGE OF FIGARO
(Mozart)
(Le Nozze di Figaro:
English version by
Ruth and Thomas Martin)

Conductor .... Rudel

Figaro .... Hale
Susanna .... Little
Dr. Bartolo .... McKee
Marcellina .... Shaulis
Cherubino .... Marsee
Count Almaviva .... Long
Basilio .... Large
Countess .... Thomson
Antonio .... Yule
Curzio .... Clark
Barbarina .... Thigpen
Bridesmaids ...... Aaronson,
Schoenfeld

March 1

DIE FLEDERMAUS

Same cast as February 23 (m)

March 2 (m)

FALSTAFF (Verdi)

Choreography
re-staged by .... Redel
Conductor .... Salesky,
(s, Caldwell)

Robin .... Sewell
Dr. Caius ... Jonathan Green

Sir John Falstaff .... Gramm
Bardolph .... Large
Pistol .... Bassett
Mistress Page ..... Hegierski
Mistress Ford .... Fowles
Dame Quickly ...... Costa-
Greenspon
Nanetta .... J. Hall
Ford .... Holloway
Fenton .... Reed
Young men of
Windsor .. Delgado, Sewell

March 2

LA TRAVIATA

Same cast as February 22

March 5

FALSTAFF

Same cast as March 2 (m)
except:

Conductor .... Salesky,
(s, Caldwell)

March 6

DON GIOVANNI (Mozart)
New Production

Director .... Cox
Scenery and Costumes
designed by .... Annals (d)
Choreography .... Redel (d)
Conductor .... Rudel

Leporello .... Rippon (d)
Don Giovanni ...... Ramey
Donna Anna .... Vaness
Commendatore ..Chausson (d)
Don Ottavio .... Blake
Donna Elvira .... Hinds
Zerlina ,,,, ... Esham
Masetto .... Embree

March 7

THE MARRIAGE OF FIGARO

Same cast as March 1 (m)

March 8 (m)

FALSTAFF

Same cast as March 2 (m)
except:

Conductor .... Caldwell

March 8

DON GIOVANNI

Same cast as March 6

March 9 (m)

MADAMA BUTTERFLY

Same cast as February 29

March 9

THE MARRIAGE OF FIGARO

Same cast as March 1 (m)

March 11

MADAMA BUTTERFLY

Same cast as February 29
except:

Pinkerton .... Bartolini,
(s, Di Giuseppe)
Madama Butterfly .. Verdejo,
(s, Zschau)

March 12

FALSTAFF

Same cast as March 2 (m)
except:

Conductor .... Caldwell

Mistress Page .... Pelle
Mistress Ford .... Sheil
Dame Quickly ...... Shaulis
Nanetta .... Nielsen
Ford .... Long
Fenton .... Hadley

March 14

DON GIOVANNI

Same cast as March 6

March 15 (m)

FALSTAFF

Same cast as March 2 (m)
except:

Conductor .... Caldwell

Mistress Page .... Pelle
Mistress Ford .... Sheil
Dame Quickly .... Sheil
Nanetta .... Nielsen
Ford .... Long
Fenton .... Hadley

March 15

MANON (Massenet)

Choreography
re-staged by .... Redel
Conductor .... Mauceri

Guillot .... Perry
De Brétigny ..... Arnold (d)
Pousette .... Thigpen
Javotte .... Toro
Rosette .... Pelle
Innkeeper .... Sergi
Lescaut .... Cossa
Guards ..... Ledbetter, Yule
Manon .... Fowles
Des Grieux .... Price
Maid .... Greene
Comte Des Grieux ... Embree
Prima Ballerina of
the Paris Opera ..... Rzasa
Premier Danseur of
the Paris Opera ... Romero
A Ballet Master ..... Rubino
Cupid .... Gardella
A Seminary Porter ... Carlo
A Gambler ..... Zimmerman
A Sergeant .... Yule

March 16 (m)

CARMEN (Bizet)

Choreography
  re-staged by .... Redel
Conductor .... Pallo

Morales .... Jamerson
Zuniga .... Bassett
Micaëla .... Bouleyn
Don José .... Molese
Carmen .... Davidson
Frasquita .... Thigpen
Mercédès .... Hill
Lillas Pastia .... Dietrich
Escamillo .... Holloway
El Remendado .... Large
El Dancairo .... Sergi
A Guide .... Dietrich

March 16

DON GIOVANNI

Same cast as March 6

March 18

MANON

Same cast as March 15

March 19

DON GIOVANNI

Same cast as March 6 except:

Leporello .... Brown
Donna Anna .... Falcon
Commendatore ...... Bassett
Don Ottavio .... Evans
Donna Elvira ..... Anderson
Zerlina .... Little
Masetto .... Jamerson

March 20

SILVERLAKE (Weill)
(*Der Silbersee*: Lyrics by
Lys Symonette with selections
of Weill's incidental music
integrated by Symonette)
First performance by The New
  York City Opera Company

Director .... Prince
Choreographer ... Fuller (d)
Scenic and Costume
  designer .. Lutgenhorst (d)
Lighting
  designed by .... Billington
Sound designed by . . Mann (d)
Conductor .... Rudel

Johann .... Foss
Dietrich ..... McFarland (d)
Severin .... Neill
Heckler .... Zimmerman
Klaus .... Clark
Hans .... Large
Hunger .... Chryst (d)
Salesgirls ..... Orloff, Shaulis
Handke .... Smith
Officer Olim ...... Grey (d)
City Inspector .. Poplaski (d)

Lottery Agent ...... Harrold
Doctor .... Porter
Baron Laur .... Harrold
Fennimore .... Hynes
Liveried footman ... Dietrich
Frau von Luber ..... Bonazzi

(Note: Two chefs added to
program of March 23 (m))

March 21

MANON

Same cast as March 15

March 22 (m)

THE BARBER OF SEVILLE
(Rossini)
(*Il Barbiere di Siviglia*:
English translation by
Ruth and Thomas Martin)

Conductor .... Scott (d)

Fiorello .... Ledbetter
Count Almaviva ..... Hadley
Figaro .... Holloway
Doctor Bartolo ..... McKee
Rosina .... Rolandi
Basilio .... Albert
Berta .... Curry
Ambrogio .... Thomas
An Officer .... Yule
A Notary .... Kelley

March 22

DON GIOVANNI

Same cast as March 6 except:

Leporello .... Brown
Donna Anna .... Falcon
Commendatore ...... Bassett
Don Ottavio .... Evans
Donna Elvira ..... Anderson
Zerlina .... Little
Masetto .... Jamerson

Broadcast performance

March 23 (m)

SILVERLAKE

Same cast as March 20 except:

Chefs ...... Rubino, Romero
           (added to program)

March 23

CARMEN

Same cast as March 16 (m)
except:

Escamillo .... Ramey

March 25

SILVERLAKE

Same cast as March 20 except:

Chefs ...... Rubino, Romero
           (added to program)

March 27

SILVERLAKE

Same cast as March 20 except:

Chefs ...... Rubino, Romero
           (added to program)

March 28

MEFISTOFELE (Boito)

Choreography
  re-staged by .... Redel
Conductor .... Mauceri

Mefistofele .... Diaz
Faust .... Trussel
Wagner .... Lankston
Margherita ...... Myers (d)
Marta .... Krueger
Elena .... Myers (d)
Pantalis .... Hill
Nereo .... Lankston
Solo dancers ...... Gardella,
                    Itow, Sewell

March 29 (m)

SILVERLAKE

Same cast as March 20 except:

Chefs ...... Rubino, Romero
           (added to program)

March 29

CARMEN

Same cast as March 16 (m)
except:

Escamillo .... Ramey

March 30 (m)

MEFISTOFELE

Same cast as March 28

March 30

THE BARBER OF SEVILLE

Same cast as March 22 (m)

April 3

MEFISTOFELE

Same cast as March 28

April 4

SILVERLAKE

Same cast as March 20 except:

Salesgirls ...... Orloff, Pelle
                 (s, Shaulis
Chefs ...... Rubino, Romere
           (added to program

April 5 (m)

MEFISTOFELE

Same cast as March 28 except:

Faust .... Calle
Margherita ..... Sundine (d
Elena .... Sundine (d

April 5

THE BARBER OF SEVILLE

Same cast as March 22 (m)

April 6 (m)

THE LOVE FOR THREE ORANGES
(*L'Amour des Trois Oranges*:
English translation by
Walter Decloux)
New Production

Devised and Directed
  by .... Capobianco
Scenery and
  Costumes designed
  by .... Vanarelli
Lighting
  designed by ...... Abrams
Choreography .... Denda
Conductor .... Keene
Production originally presented
  by the San Diego Opera

The Herald .... Yule
The King of Clubs ... McKee
Pantalone .... Foss
Truffaldino .... D. Hall
Leandro .... Billings
Celio .... Bassett
Fata Morgana .... Curry
Clarissa .... Costa-Greenspon
Smeraldina .... Hegierski
The Prince .... Evans
Farfarello .... Lankston
The Cook .... Densen
Linetta .... Lambert
Nicoletta .... Claveau
Ninetta ...... Gutknecht (d)
Master of Ceremonies .. Clark

Broadcast performance

April 6

LA BOHÈME (Puccini)

Conductor .... Pallo
Rodolfo .... Trussel
Marcello .... Hartman
Colline .... Ramey
Schaunard .... Jamerson
Benoit .... Yule
Mimi .... Christos
Parpignol .... Clark
Musetta .... Zannoth
Alcindoro .... Ledbetter
Guards ..Peyton, Bohachevsky

April 8

THE LOVE FOR THREE ORANGES

Same cast as April 6 (m)

April 10

THE LOVE FOR THREE ORANGES

Same cast as April 6 (m)

April 11

LA CENERENTOLA (Rossini)
English version by Gimi Beni)

Director .... Galterio (d)
Conductor .... Salesky

Clorinda .... Rolandi
Tisbe .... Freni
Cinderella
  (Angelina) .... Marsee
Alidoro .... Bassett
Don Magnifico ...... Billings
Ramiro .... Blake
Dandini .... Titus

April 12 (m)

THE LOVE FOR THREE ORANGES

Same cast as April 6 (m)

April 12

LA BOHÈME

Same cast as April 6

April 13 (m)

LA CENERENTOLA

Same cast as April 11

Broadcast performance

April 13

FAUST (Gounod)

Choreography
  re-staged by .... Redel
Conductor .... Keene

Faust .... McCauley (d)
Méphistophélès .... Diaz
Wagner .... Ledbetter
Marguerite .... Soviero
Valentin .... Ellis
Siébel .... Hegierski
Marthe .... Krueger
An Acrobat .... Delgado
A Juggler .... De Dio
A Fire-eater .... Presto

April 16

LA CENERENTOLA

Same cast as April 11

April 17

FAUST

Same cast as April 13 except:

A Juggler .... Jay Green

April 18

LES CONTES D'HOFFMANN
(Offenbach)

Conductor .... Dufallo

Lindorff .... Ramey
Andrès .... Lankston
Luther .... Bassett
Nathanaël .... Clark
Hermann .... Jamerson
Nicklausse .... Harris
Hoffmann .... Calleo
Olympia .... Anderson
Spalanzani .... Billings
Cochenille .... Lankston

Coppélius .... Ramey
Giulietta .... Simon
Pittichinaccio ..... Lankston
Schlémil .... Ledbetter
Dappertutto .... Ramey
Antonia .... Anderson
Crespel .... Brown
Franz .... Lankston
Dr. Miracle .... Ramey
The Mother .... Shaulis

April 19 (m)

CARMEN

Same cast as March 16 (m)
except:

Conductor ..... Wendelken-
                    Wilson

Zuniga .... Embree
Micaëla .... James (d)
Carmen .... Terzian (d)
Mercédès .... Pelle
El Remendado .... Lankston

April 19

FAUST

Same cast as April 13 except:

A Juggler .... Jay Green

April 20 (m)

THE DAUGHTER OF
THE REGIMENT (Donizetti)
(*La Fille du Regument*:
English version by
Ruth and Thomas Martin)

Conductor ...... Wendelken-
                    Wilson

Hortensius .... Ledbetter
The Marquise of
  Berkenfeld .... Costa-
                    Greenspon
A Peasant .... Tippie
Sulpice .... McKee
Marie .... Rolandi
Tonio .... Reed
A Corporal .... Sergi
Major Domo .... Rubino
Duchess of
  Krackenthorp .... Krueger
Henry Jean-Paul
  Krackenthorp .... Thomas
Notary .... Dietrich

April 20

LES CONTES D'HOFFMANN

Same cast as April 18

Broadcast performance

April 22

FAUST

Same cast as April 13 except:

A Juggler .... Jay Green

April 23

LA BOHÈME

Same cast as April 6 except:
Marcello .... Holloway
Colline .... Embree
Schaunard ...... McFarland
Mimi .... Myers
Musetta .... Sundine
Alcindoro .... Yule

April 24

LES CONTES D'HOFFMANN

Same cast as April 18

April 25

THE DAUGHTER OF
THE REGIMENT

Same cast as April 20 (m)

April 26 (m)

CARMEN

Same cast as March 16 (m) except:
Conductor ...... Wendelken-
                              Wilson
Zuniga .... Embree
Micaëla .... James
Carmen .... Terzian
Mercédès .... Pelle
El Remendado ..... Lankston

April 26

LES CONTES D'HOFFMANN

Same cast as April 18 except:
Olympia .... Dickison-
                              Rhodus

April 27 (m)

LA BOHÈME

Same cast as April 6 except:
Marcello .... Holloway
Colline .... Embree
Schaunard ...... McFarland
Mimi .... Myers
Musetta .... Sundine
Alcindoro .... Yule

April 27

THE DAUGHTER OF
THE REGIMENT

Same cast as April 20 (m)

Fall 1980 (AUGUST 29 – NOVEMBER 9)

Female Artists
Anderson, June
Bouleyn, Kathryn
Carter, Barbara*
Christos, Marianna
Costa-Greenspon, Muriel
Craig, Patricia
Curry, Diane
Davidson, Joy
Esham, Faith
Evans, Beverly
Fowles, Glenys
Freni, RoseMarie
Gutknecht, Carol
Hall, Janice
Hegierski, Kathleen
Hynes, Elizabeth
Krueger, Dana
Lerner, Mimi
Little, Gwenlynn
Marsee, Susanne
McCaffrey, Patricia*
Munro, Leigh*
Myers, Pamela
Nielsen, Inga
Niska, Maralin
Orloff, Penny
Pelle, Nadia
Rhodus, Judith
Rolandi, Gianna
Shaulis, Jane
Sheil, Martha
Simon, Joanna
Sonnenschein, Suzanne*
Soviero, Diana
Stapp, Olivia
Sundine, Stephanie
Thigpen, Martha
Thomson, Heather
Toro, Puli
Vaness, Carol
Wallis, Delia

Wright, Barbara*
Yorke, Sylvia*
Zschau, Marilyn

Male Artists
Albert, Donnie Ray
Arnold, David
Bassett, Ralph
Beattie, Herbert
Billings, James
Blake, Rockwell
Bohachevsky, George
Brown, Maurice
Burchinal, Frederick
Burt, Michael*
Calleo, Riccardo
Castel, Nico
Chausson, Carlos
Clark, James
Cole, Vinson
Corsaro, Andrew
Cossa, Dominic
Crook, Mervin
Cross, Richard
Daniels, Phillip*
Davis, Harris
Diaz, Justino
Dickson, Stephen*
Dietrich, Gary
Elvira, Pablo
Evans, Joseph
Foss, Harlan
Fredericks, Richard
Glassman, Allen*
Hadley, Jerry
Hale, Robert
Hall, David
Harrold, Jack
Jamerson, Thomas
Kays, Alan
Kelley, Ronald

Lankston, John
Large, Norman
Ledbetter, William
Long, Charles
Malas, Spiro
McCauley, Barry
McFarland, Robert
McKee, Richard
Molese, Michele
Neill, William
Nelson, Richard
Opalach, Jan*
Perry, Douglas
Perry, Louis
Peyton, J. Randolph
Poor, Harris*
Poplaski, William
Price, Henry
Ramey, Samuel
Reed, Bruce
Roe, Charles
Seabury, John
Sergi, James
Smith, Andrew
Smith, David Rae
Sullivan, Dan
Thomas, John Henry
Titus, Alan
Trussel, Jacque
White, Lewis*
Wildermann, William
Williams, Steven Alexus*
Yule, Don
Zimmerman, Edward

**Special guests (other than
company members) who
appeared at Beverly Sills's
farewell, October 27, 1980**
Alexander, John
Burnett, Carol
Caldwell, Sarah

* New artist   * New artist   * New artist

Carlisle, Kitty
Cronkite, Walter
Domingo, Placido
Farrell, Eileen
Field, Ron
Galway, James
Gregory, Cynthia
Johnson, Lady Bird
Knight, Eric
Koch, The Hon. Edward J.
Lipton, James
Martin, Mary
Martins, Peter
Matz, Peter
Mehta, Zubin
Merman, Ethel
Milnes, Sherrill
Price, Leontyne
Reynolds, Burt
Scotto, Renata
Shore, Dinah
Short, Bobby
Wadsworth, Charles
Watts, Heather

Principal Conductor
Rudel, Julius

Conductors
Effron, David
Mauceri, John
Meltzer, Andrew
Pallo, Imre
Salesky, Brian
Scott, William Fred, III
Simmons, Calvin*
Somogi, Judith
Weikert, Ralph*
Wendelken-Wilson, Charles

Chorus Master
Walser, Lloyd

Assistant Chorus Master
Krieger, Mitchell

Director of Children's Chorus
Hohner, Mildred

Solo Dancers
Galan, Esperanza
Gregory, Cynthia
Chryst, Gary
Kalba, Taras
LaFosse, Robert*
Romero, Rafael
Rubino, Michael

Choreographers
Andrew, Thomas
Denda, Gigi
Fuller, Larry
Nahat, Dennis
Norman, Jay*
Redel, Jessica
Saddler, Donald*

Directors
Auerbach, Cynthia
Capobianco, Tito
Corsaro, Frank
Cox, John
Eddleman, Jack
Foreman, Richard*
Freedman, Gerald

* New artist

Galterio, Lou
Hofsiss, Jack*
Lesenger, Jay*
Prince, Harold

Designers
Aldredge, Theoni V.
Annals, Michael
Billington, Ken
Campbell, Patton
Conklin, John
Evans, Lloyd
Hemsley, Gilbert V., Jr.
Jenkins, David*
Lee, Ming Cho
Lutgenhorst, Manuel
Sondheimer, Hans
Ter-Arutunian, Rouben
Varona, José

* New artist

August 29

THE STUDENT PRINCE
(Romberg)
First performance by The New
York City Opera Company

Director .... Hofsiss (d)
Choreographer .. Saddler (d)
Scenic Designer ..Jenkins (d)
Lighting Designer .. Hemsley
Costume Designer .. Campbell
Conductor .... Meltzer

Lackeys .... Zimmerman,
L. Perry, Davis, Crook
Dr. Engel .... Cossa
Count von Mark..D. R. Smith
Prince Karl Franz ... Trussel
Lutz .... Billings
Gretchen .... Thigpen
Ruder .... Sullivan (d)
Nicholas .... LaFosse (d)
Toni .... Harrold
Hubert .... Foss
Detlef .... Lankston
von Asterberg ..... Jamerson
Lucas .... Bassett
Freshman .... L. Perry
Kathie .... Munro (d)
Grand Duchess
Anastasia ..Costa-Greenspon
Princess Margaret ... Bouleyn
Captain Tarnitz .... J. Evans
Countess Leydon .... Shaulis

August 30 (m)

THE STUDENT PRINCE
Same cast as August 29 except:
Dr. Engel .... Roe
Prince Karl Franz ..... Price
Lutz .... Harrold
Toni .... Billings
Kathie .... Hynes

August 30

THE STUDENT PRINCE
Same cast as August 29

August 31 (m)

THE STUDENT PRINCE
Same cast as August 29 except:
Dr. Engel .... Roe
Prince Karl Franz ..... Price
Lutz .... Harrold
Toni .... Billings
Kathie .... Hynes

August 31

THE STUDENT PRINCE
Same cast as August 29

September 2

THE STUDENT PRINCE
Same cast as August 29

September 3

THE STUDENT PRINCE
Same cast as August 29 except:
Dr. Engel .... Roe
Prince Karl Franz ..... Price
Lutz .... Harrold
Toni .... Billings
Kathie .... Hynes

September 4

THE STUDENT PRINCE
Same cast as August 29

September 5

THE STUDENT PRINCE
Same cast as August 29 except:
Dr. Engel .... Roe
Prince Karl Franz ..... Price
Lutz .... Harrold
Toni .... Billings
Kathie .... Hynes

September 6 (m)

THE STUDENT PRINCE
Same cast as August 29

September 6

THE STUDENT PRINCE
Same cast as August 29 except:
Dr. Engel .... Roe
Prince Karl Franz ..... Price
Lutz .... Harrold
Toni .... Billings
Kathie .... Hynes

September 7 (m)

THE STUDENT PRINCE
Same cast as August 29

September 7

THE STUDENT PRINCE
Same cast as August 29 except:
Dr. Engel .... Roe
Prince Karl Franz ..... Price

Lutz .... Harrold
Toni .... Billings
Kathie .... Hynes

September 11

ANNA BOLENA (Donizetti)

Newly staged
by ...... Jay Lesenger (d)
Conductor ...... Wendelken-
Wilson

Giovanna .... Marsee
Anna .... Stapp
Smeton .... Lerner
Enrico .... Ramey
Lord Riccardo Percy .. Blake
Lord Rochefort ..... Bassett
Sir Hervey .... Clark

September 12

DIE FLEDERMAUS (J. Strauss)
(English version by
Ruth and Thomas Martin)

Conductor .... Pallo

Alfred .... Price
Adele .... Nielsen
Rosalinda .... Niska
Eisenstein .... Titus
Dr. Blind .... Large
Dr. Falke .... Fredricks
Frank .... Foss
Sally .... Toro
Ivan .... Dietrich
Prince Orlofsky .... Billings
Frosch .... Harrold
Solo dancers .. Galan, Kalba
Special guest .... Gregory

September 13 (m)

IL BARBIERE DI SIVIGLIA
(Rossini)

Conductor .... Scott

Fiorello .... Jamerson
Count Almaviva .... J. Evans
Figaro .... Elvira,
(s, Ellis)
Dr. Bartolo .... Malas
Rosina .... Rolandi
Basilio .... Albert
Berta .... Shaulis
Ambrogio .... Thomas
An Officer .... Yule
A Notary .... Kelley

(Note: Brent Ellis was not to
appear with The New York
City Opera this season.)

September 13

CARMEN (Bizet)

Conductor ...... Wendelken-
Wilson

Morales .... Sergi
Zuniga .... McKee
Micaëla .... Hynes
Don José .... Calleo
Carmen .... Freni,
(s, Davidson)

Frasquita .... Orloff
Mercédès .... Pelle
Lillas Pastia .... Dietrich
Escamillo .... Long
Remendado ...... Lankston
Dancairo .... Ledbetter
A Guide .... Dietrich

September 14 (m)

DIE FLEDERMAUS

Same cast as September 12

September 14

ANNA BOLENA

Same cast as September 11

September 16

IL BARBIERE DI SIVIGLIA

Same cast as September 13 (m)

September 17

DIE FLEDERMAUS

Same cast as September 12
except:

Alfred .... Hadley
Adele .... Rolandi
Frank .... McKee

September 18

ANNA BOLENA

Same cast as September 11

September 19

CARMEN

Same cast as September 13
except:

Carmen .... Davidson

September 20 (m)

MADAMA BUTTERFLY (Puccini)

Conductor .... Somogi

Pinkerton .... J. Evans
Goro .... Clark
Suzuki .... Hegierski
Sharpless .... Arnold
Madama Butterfly .... Craig
Imperial
Commissioner ... Ledbetter
Registrar .... Sergi
The Bonze .... Chausson
Yamadori .... Sergi
Trouble .... Daniels (d)
Kate Pinkerton .... Pelle

September 20

DIE FLEDERMAUS

Same cast as September 12
except:

Special Guest .. omitted from
this performance

September 21 (m)

IL BARBIERE DI SIVIGLIA

Same cast as September 13 (m)

September 21

CARMEN

Same cast as September 13

September 23

ANNA BOLENA

Same cast as September 11
except:

Giovanna .... McCaffrey (d)
Smeton .... Hegierski
Lord Riccardo Percy..Molese

September 25

LES PÊCHEURS DE PERLES
(Bizet)
First performance by The New
York City Opera Company

Director .... Auerbach
Scenic and Costume
Designer .... O'Hearn
Lighting Designer .. Hemsley
Choreographer .. Norman (d)
Conductor .... Simmons (d)

Leïla .... Soviero
Nadir .... McCauley
Zurga .... Cossa
Nourabad .... Seabury

(Note: This production was
originally presented by the
Greater Miami Opera
Association.)

September 26

IL BARBIERE DI SIVIGLIA

Same cast as September 13 (m)
except:

Almaviva .... Hadley
Figaro .... McFarland
Dr. Bartolo .... McKee
Basilio .... Chausson

September 27 (m)

LA BOHÈME (Puccini)

Conductor .... Mauceri

Rodolfo .... Cole
Marcello .... Fredricks
Colline .... Hale
Schaunard .... Foss
Benoit .... Yule
Mimi .... Myers
Parpignol .... Large
Musetta .... Gutknecht
Alcindoro .... Ledbetter
Guards ..Peyton, Bohachevsky

September 27

MADAMA BUTTERFLY

Same cast as September 20 (m)

September 28 (m)

ANNA BOLENA

Same cast as September 11
except:

Giovanna .... McCaffery
Smeton .... Hegierski
Lord Riccardo Percy . . Molese

September 28

LES PÊCHEURS DE PERLES

Same cast as September 25

October 1

LES PÊCHEURS DE PERLES

Same cast as September 25
except:

Leïla .... Christos
Nadir .... J. Evans
Zurga .... Arnold
Nourabad .... Bassett

October 2

DON GIOVANNI (Mozart)

Conductor .... Mauceri
Leporello .... Ramey
Don Giovanni .... Diaz
Donna Anna .... Vaness
Commendatore ...... Bassett
Don Ottavio .... Kays
Donna Elvira ...... Thomson
Zerlina .... Little
Masetto .... Foss

October 3

LES PÊCHEURS DE PERLES

Same cast as September 25
except:

Leïla .... Christos
Nadir .... J. Evans
Zurga .... Arnold
Nourabad .... Bassett

October 4 (m)

DON GIOVANNI

Same cast as October 2

October 4

LA BOHÈME

Same cast as September 27 (m)

October 5 (m)

LES PÊCHEURS DE PERLES

Same cast as September 25

October 5

MADAMA BUTTERFLY

Same cast as September 20 (m)
except:

Trouble .... Corsaro

October 7

DON GIOVANNI

Same cast as October 2

October 9

AN AMERICAN TRILOGY
consisting of:
MADAME ADARE (Silverman)
World Premiere

Director .... Foreman (d)
Scenic and Costume
  Designer .... Evans
Lighting Designer .. Hemsley
Conductor .... Salesky

Madame Adare ... Gutknecht
Dr. Hoffman .... Cross
The Agent .... Billings
The Devil .... Poor (d)
Diaghilev .... Castel
The Interviewer . . D. R. Smith
The Director ..... White (d)

Followed by:

BEFORE BREAKFAST (Pasatieri)
World Premiere

Director .... Corsaro
Scenic and Costume
  Designer .... Evans
Lighting Designer .. Hemsley
Conductor .... Pallo

The Woman .... Zschau

Followed by:

THE STUDENT FROM
SALAMANCA (Jan Bach)
World Premiere

Director .... Eddleman
Scenic and Costume
  Designer .... Evans
Lighting Designer .. Hemsley
Conductor .... Somogi

Cristina .... B. Evans
Craccio .... Lankston
Mariana .... Marsee
Gonzalo .... D. Hall
Nicolas .... Opalach (d)
Stephano ..... Glassman (d)

October 10

DON GIOVANNI

Same cast as October 2

October 11 (m)

SILVERLAKE (Weill)
(Der Silbersee: English lyrics
  by Symonette, with Weill's
  incidental music integrated
  by Symonette)

Conductor .... Rudel

Johann .... Foss
Dietrich .... McFarland
Severin .... Neill
Heckler .... Zimmerman

Klaus .... Clark
Hans .... Large
Hunger .... Chryst
Salesgirls .... Orloff, Shaulis
Handke .... D. R. Smtih
Officer Olim ..... Lankston
City Inspector ..... Poplaski
Lottery Agent ...... Harrold
Doctor .... Nelson
Baron Laur .... Harrold
Fennimore .... Hegierski
Liveried footman ... Dietrich
Frau von
  Luber ... Costa-Greenspon
Chefs ...... Rubino, Romero

October 11

LA BOHÈME

Same cast as September 27 (m)
except:

Marcello .... Burchinal
Schaunard ...... McFarland
Mimi .... Soviero
Musetta .... Anderson

October 12 (m)

MADAMA BUTTERFLY

Same cast as September 20 (m)
except:

Goro .... D. Perry
Suzuki .... Shaulis
Sharpless .... A. Smith
Madama
  Butterfly . . Sonnenschein (d)

October 12

AN AMERICAN TRILOGY

Same casts as October 9

October 14

SILVERLAKE

Same cast as October 11 (m)

October 15

AN AMERICAN TRILOGY

Same casts as October 9

October 17

SILVERLAKE

Same cast as October 11 (m)

October 18 (m)

AN AMERICAN TRILOGY

Same casts as October 9

October 18

MADAMA BUTTERFLY

Same cast as September 20 (m)
except:

Pinkerton .... McCauley
Goro .... D. Perry
Suzuki .... Shaulis

Sharpless .... A. Smith
Madama
    Butterfly .... Sonnenschein
Trouble .... Corsaro

October 19 (m)

SILVERLAKE

Same cast as October 11 (m)

October 19

LA BOHÈME

Same cast as September 27 (m)
except:

Marcello .... Burchinal
Schaunard ...... McFarland
Mimi .... Soviero
Parpignol .... Clark
Musetta .... Anderson

October 22

DON GIOVANNI

Same cast as October 2 except:

Leporello .... Chausson
Donna Anna ..... Yorke (d)
Commendatore .... Burt (d)
Don Ottavio .... J. Evans
Donna Elvira .... Sheil
Zerlina .... Esham
Masetto .... McFarland

October 23

THE MERRY WIVES OF WINDSOR
    (Nicolai)
(Die Lustigen Weiber von
Windsor: English version by
Joseph Blatt)
New Production

Director .... Galterio
Scenic and Costume
    Designer .... Conklin
Lighting Designer .. Hemsley
Choreographer .... Redel
Conductor .... Rudel

Mrs. Ford .... Vaness
Mrs. Page .... Freni
Page .... Sullivan
Slender .... Large
Dr. Cajus .... Foss
Ford .... Dickson (d)
Fenton .... Cole
Sir John
    Falstaff ...... Wildermann
Anne Page .... J. Hall
Innkeeper .... Thomas

October 24

LA BOHÈME

Same cast as September 27 (m)
except:

Rodolfo .... Molese
Marcello .... Burchinal
Schaunard ...... McFarland
Mimi .... Soviero
Musetta .... Anderson

October 25 (m)

THE MERRY WIVES OF WINDSOR

Same cast as October 23

October 25

DON GIOVANNI

Same cast as October 2 except:

Leporello .... Chausson
Donna Anna .... Yorke
Commendatore .... Burt
Don Ottavio .... J. Evans
Donna Elvira .... Sheil
Zerlina .... Esham
Masetto .... McFarland

October 27

BEVERLY SILLS FAREWELL
    PERFORMANCE

Consisted of Act II of Johann
Strauss's Die Fledermaus
excluding the Czardas. Many
guest celebrities appeared in
the ballroom scene.

Cast of
DIE FLEDERMAUS (Act II):
Devised and Directed
    by ...... Gerald Freedman
Director for
    Beverly Sills's
    performance .. Capobianco
Conductor .... Rudel

Rosalinda .... Sills
Adele .... Rolandi
Orlofsky .... Carlisle
Sally .... Toro
Blumentein .... Titus
Dr. Falke .... Fredricks
Frank .... Malas
Ivan .... Billings

Guests at the Gala Sequence
Mistress of
    Ceremonies .. Carol Burnett
Special lyrics
    by .... Betty Comden,
        Adolph Green,
        Martin Charnin
Musical Staging
    and Choreography
    by .... Ron Field
Produced and Directed
    by .... James Lipton
Conductors .... Julius Rudel,
        Eric Knight, Peter Matz

"It's Today" from
    GYPSY (with new
    words) .... Burnett
"Maria" from WEST
    SIDE STORY .... Milnes
"Nashville Nightingale"
    (Gershwin) .... Short
"I Got the World on a
    String" (Arlen) .... Farrell
    (accompanied by Short)
"Blues in the Night"
    (Arlen) .... Shore

"I Want What I Want"
    from MLLE. MODISTE
    (with new words).. Gramm
"What I Did for Love"
    from A CHORUS
    LINE .... L. Price
"Granada" (Lara).. Domingo
"My Heart Belongs
    to Daddy" from
    LEAVE IT TO ME ... Martin
"Somewhere Over the
    Rainbow" (Arlen) .. Scotto
"Wien, du Stadt
    Meiner Träume"
    (Sieczynski) ... Alexander
"There's No Business
    Like Show Business"
    from ANNIE GET
    YOUR GUN ...... Merman
"O Danny Boy"
    (Traditional London-
    derry air) .... Galway
"Fledermaus
    Ballet" .... Gregory
"Du bist die Ruh"
    (Schubert) .... Cossa
    (accompanied by
    Wadsworth), danced
    by Heather Watts
    and Peter Martins
Musico-comic routine:
    Opera vs. pop
    music .... Sills and Burnett

At this point, several well-
known personalities appeared
on stage to pay homage to,
and dance a few turns with
Miss Sills. They included Zubin
Mehta, The Hon. Edward
I. Koch, Sarah Caldwell
Walter Cronkite, Lady Bird
Johnson, and Burt Reynolds.
The festivities concluded with
"Tell Me Why"
    (Portuguese folk-song,
    arranged by Estelle
    Liebling) .... Sill
    (accompanied b
    Wadsworth

Televised performance

October 28

THE MERRY WIVES OF WINDSO

Same cast as October 23

October 29

LA CENERENTOLA (Rossini)
(English version by Gimi Beni

Conductor .... Salesk

Clorinda .... Anderso
Tisbe .... Kruege
Angelina
    (Cenerentola) ..... Mars
Alidoro .... Basse
Don Magnifico ...... Billin
Ramiro .... Bla
Dandini .... Tit

October 31

LES CONTES D'HOFFMANN
(Offenbach)

Conductor	Effron
Lindorff	Diaz
Andrès	D. Perry
Luther	Yule
Nathanaël	Large
Hermann	Jamerson
Nicklausse	Pelle
Hoffmann	Molese
Olympia	Rhodus
Spalanzani	Billings
Cochenille	D. Perry
Coppélius	Diaz
Giulietta	Simon
Pittichinaccio	D. Perry
Schlémil	Sergi
Dappertutto	Diaz
Antonia	Vaness
Crespel	Brown
Frantz	D. Perry
Dr. Miracle	Diaz
The Mother	Shaulis

November 1 (m)

LA CENERENTOLA

Same cast as October 29

November 1

THE MERRY WIVES OF WINDSOR

Same cast as October 23
except:

Mrs. Ford	Fowles
Mrs. Page	Costa-Greenspon

Page	Bassett
Fenton	Reed
Sir John Falstaff	Beattie
Ann Page	Gutknecht

November 2 (m)

LES CONTES D'HOFFMANN

Same cast as October 31

November 2

GIULIO CESARE (Handel)
(Performance Edition by
Julius Rudel)

Conductor	Weikert (d)
Giulio Cesare	Hale
Curio	Ledbetter
Cornelia	Curry
Sesto	Wallis
Achilla	Cossa
Cleopatra	Rolandi
Nireno	Williams (d)
Tolomeo	Albert

November 4

GIULIO CESARE

Same cast as November 2

November 5

LES CONTES D'HOFFMANN

Same cast as October 31
except:

Nicklausse	Hegierski
Hoffmann	Price
Olympia	Carter (d)
Giulietta	Sundine
Antonia	Christos

November 6

LA CENERENTOLA

Same cast as October 29
except:

Clorinda	Rolandi
Tisbe	Freni

Televised performance

November 7

GIULIO CESARE

Same cast as November 2

November 8 (m)

THE MERRY WIVES OF WINDSOR

Same cast as October 23
except:

Mrs. Ford	Fowles
Mrs. Page	Costa-Greenspon
Page	Bassett
Fenton	Reed
Sir John Falstaff	Beattie
Ann Page	Gutknecht

November 8

LES CONTES D'HOFFMANN

Same cast as October 31
except:

Nicklausse	Hegierski
Hoffmann	Price
Olympia	Carter
Giulietta	Sundine
Antonia	Christos

November 9 (m)

GIULIO CESARE

Same cast as November 2

Spring 1981 (FEBRUARY 19 – APRIL 26)

Blake, Rockwell
Bohachevsky, George
Brown, Maurice
Brubaker, Robert
Busse, Barry*
Byars, Christopher*
Calleo, Riccardo
Clark, James
Cole, Vinson
Corsaro, Andrew
Cross, Richard
Daniels, Phillip
Densen, Irwin
Diaz, Justino
Dickson, Stephen
Dietrich, Gary
Di Giuseppe, Enrico
Embree, Marc
Evans, Joseph
Foss, Harlan
Fredericks, Richard
Grice, Garry*
Hadley, Jerry
Hale, Robert
Hall, David
Harrold, Jack
Jaffe, Monte*
Jamerson, Thomas
Justus, William*
Lankston, John
Large, Norman
Ledbetter, William
Ludgin, Chester
Malas, Spiro
Martinovich, Boris*
McCauley, Barry
McFarland, Robert
McKee, Richard
Moser, Thomas
Novick, Melvyn
Opalach, Jan
Perry, Douglas
Peyton, J. Randolph
Ramey, Samuel
Reed, Bruce
Reeve, Scott*
Renfrew, Owen*
Roe, Charles
Schmorr, Robert
Seabury, John
Serbo, Rico
Sergi, James
Smith, Andrew
Smith, David Rae
Sullivan, Dan
Titus, Alan
Tramon, Carl*
Trussel, Jacque
Van Buskirk, Eliot
Wilderman, William
Yule, Don

Conductors
Bergeson, Scott*
Bernardi, Mario
Comissiona, Sergiu
de Almeida, Antonio*
Effron, David
Keene, Christopher
Mark, Peter*
Mauceri, John
Pallo, Imre
Salesky, Brian

* New artist

Simmons, Calvin
Thomas, Michael Tilson*
Weikert, Ralph
Wendelken-Wilson, Charles

Chorus Master
Walser, Lloyd

Assistant Chorus Master
Krieger, Mitchell

Director of Children's Chorus
Hohner, Mildred

Solo Dancers
Galan, Esperanza

Kalba, Taras

Choreographers
Andrew, Thomas
Hilton, Wendy*
Norman, Jay
Redel, Jessica
Sappington, Margo*

Directors
Auerbach, Cynthia
Bentley, Ronald
Caldwell, Sarah
Corsaro, Frank
Farrar, David*
Galterio, Lou
Lesenger, Jay
Mansouri, Lotfi
Melano, Fabrizio*
Mirdita, Federick

Designers
Abrams, Don
Annals, Michael
Campbell, Patton
Conklin, John
Evans, Lloyd
Feldman, Steven*
George, Hal
Hemsley, Gilbert V., Jr.
Jampolis, Neil Peter*
Joseph, J. Edgar
Lee, Ming Cho
Oenslager, Donald
O'Hearn, Robert
Pond, Helen
Reid, Alex*
Romero, Miguel*
Sendak, Maurice*
Senn, Herbert
Sondheimer, Hans
Vanarelli, Mario
Varona, José

* New artist

February 19

THE MERRY WIVES OF WINDSOR
(Nicolai)
(*Die Lustigen Weiber von
Windsor*: English version by
Joseph Blatt)

Conductor ...... Wendelken-
                        Wilson

Mrs. Ford .... Vaness
Mrs. Page .. Costa-Greenspon
Page .... Sullivan
Slender .... Large
Dr. Cajus .... Jamerson
Ford .... Dickson

Fenton .... Reed
Sir John Falstaff .. Wildermann
Ann Page .... J. Hall
Innkeeper .... Ledbetter

February 20

DON GIOVANNI (Mozart)

Conductor .... Mauceri

Leporello .... Diaz
Donna Anna ...... Thomson
Don Giovanni .... Ramey
Commendatore ...... Bassett
Don Ottavio .... Aler (d)
Donna Elvira ..... Shade (d)
Zerlina .... Haddon (d)
Masetto .... McFarland

February 21 (m)

CARMEN (Bizet)

Conductor .... Salesky

Morales .... Jamerson
Zuniga .... Brown
Micaëla .... Zannoth
Don José .... Trussel
Carmen .... Davidson
Frasquita ..... Aaronson (d)
Mercédès ...... Hegierski
Lillas Pastia .... Dietrich
Escamillo .... Fredricks
Remendado .... Lankston
Dancairo .... Sergi
A Guide .... Dietrich

(Note: Cynthia Aaronson
appeared with the chorus for
several seasons under the name
of Cindy Lynn Aaronson.)

February 21

LES PÊCHEURS DE PERLES
(Bizet)

Conductor .... Simmons

Zurga .... Arnold
Nadir .... J. Evans
Nourabad .. Martinovich (d)
Leila .... Vaness

February 22 (m)

LES CONTES D'HOFFMANN
(Offenbach)

Conductor .. de Almeida (d)

Lindorff .... Hal
Andrès .... Schmor
Luther .... Yule
Nathanaël .... Clar
Hermann .... Jamerson
Nicklausse .... Pell
Hoffmann .... Calle
Olympia .... Anderson
Spalanzani .... Billing
Cochenille .... Schmor
Coppélius .... Hal
Giulietta .... Simo
Pittichinaccio ...... Schmo
Schlémil .... Ledbette
Dappertutto .... Hal
Antonia .... Christe

Crespel .... Brown
Franz .... Schmorr
Dr. Miracle .... Hale
The Mother .... Shaulis

February 22

DON GIOVANNI

Same cast as February 20
except:

Don Ottavio ...... J. Evans,
(s, Aler)

February 24

DON GIOVANNI

Same cast as February 20

February 27

LES PÊCHEURS DE PERLES

Same cast as February 21

February 28 (m)

DON GIOVANNI

Same cast as February 20

February 28

LES CONTES D'HOFFMANN

Same cast as February 22 (m)
except:

Conductor .... Salesky,
(s, de Almeida)

March 1 (m)

THE MERRY WIVES OF WINDSOR

Same cast as February 19

March 1

MARY, QUEEN OF SCOTS
(Musgrave)
First performance by The New
York City Opera Company

Director .... Farrar (d)
Scenic Designer ..Romero (d)
Costume Designer .. Reid (d)
Lighting Designer ... Hemsley
Choreographer ... Hilton (d)
Conductor .... Mark (d)

Cardinal Beaton .... Bell (d)
James Stewart,
Earl of Moray .. Fredricks
Mary, Queen of Scots..Putnam
James Hepburn,
Earl of Bothwell..Busse (d)
Earl of Morton .. McFarland
Earl of Ruthven ... Lankston
Lord Gordon .... Seabury
David Riccio ...... Bell (d)
Henry, Lord Darnley .. Serbo
Mary Seton ...... Woods (d)
Mary Beaton .... Pelle
Mary Fleming .... Hegierski
Mary Livingstone ... Shaulis

March 3

MARY, QUEEN OF SCOTS

Same cast as March 1

March 6

LA BOHÈME (Puccini)

Conductor ...... Wendelken-
Wilson

Rodolfo .... McCauley
Marcello .... Titus
Colline .... Martinovich
Schaunard .... Jamerson
Benoit .... Yule
Mimi .... Vaness
Parpignol .... Clark
Musetta .... Poston (d)
Alcindoro .... Sullivan
Guards ..Peyton, Bohachevsky

March 7 (m)

LES CONTES D'HOFFMANN

Same cast as February 22 (m)
except:

Nicklausse .... Hegierski
Stella ..... Anderson (added
for this performance)
Giulietta .... Anderson
Antonia .... Anderson

March 7

MARY, QUEEN OF SCOTS

Same caset as March 1

March 8 (m)

DON GIOVANNI

Same cast as February 20
except:

Leporello .... Ramey
Donna Anna .... Shade
Don Giovanni .... Diaz
Commendatore ..... Seabury
Don Ottavio .... J. Evans
Donna Elvira .... Sheil
Zerlina .... J. Hall
Masetto .... Jamerson

March 8

LES PÊCHEURS DE PERLES

Same cast as February 21
except:

Nadir .... McCauley
Leila .... Christos

March 11

THE MERRY WIVES OF WINDSOR

Same cast as February 19
except:

Conductor .... Bergeson (d),
(s, Wendelken-Wilson)

Mrs. Ford .... Sheil
Mrs. Page .... Freni
Page .... Opalach

Slender .... Novick
Dr. Cajus .... Foss
Ford .... McFarland
Fenton .... Hadley
Sir John Falstaff ..... Malas
Ann Page .... Woods

March 12

LA BOHÈME

Same cast as March 6 except:

Conductor .... Pallo,
(s, Wendelken-Wilson)

March 13

ATTILA (Verdi)
First performance by The New
York City Opera Company

Director .... Mansouri
Scenic Designer .... Lee
Costume Designer ... George
Lighting Designer .. Hemsley
Choreographer .. Sappington
(d)
Conductor ...... Comissiona

Attila .... Ramey
Uldino .... Clark
Odabella .... Zschau
Ezio .... Fredricks
Foresto .... Di Giuseppe
Leone .... Sullivan

March 14 (m)

MADAMA BUTTERFLY (Puccini)

Conductor .... Effron

Pinkerton .... Calleo
Goro .... Clark
Suzuki .... Shaulis
Sharpless .... A. Smith
Madama Butterfly .... Craig
Imperial
Commissioner ... Ledbetter
Registrar .... Sergi
The Bonze .... Brown
Yamadori .... Sergi
Trouble .... Corsaro
Kate Pinkerton .... Pelle

March 14

MARY, QUEEN OF SCOTS

Same cast as March 1

March 15 (m)

GIULIO CESARE (Handel)
(Performance Edition by
Julius Rudel)

Conductor .... Weikert

Giulio Cesare .... Diaz
Curio .... Ledbetter
Cornelia .... Curry
Sesto .... Forst (d)
Achilla .... Roe

Cleopatra .... Rolandi
Nireno .... Foss
Tolomeo .... Albert

March 15

ATTILA

Same cast as March 13 except:

Odabella .... Galvany
Ezio .... Justus
Foresto .... J. Evans

March 17

ATTILA

Same cast as March 13

March 18

MADAMA BUTTERFLY

Same cast as March 14 (m)
except:

Trouble .... Daniels

March 19

CARMEN

Same cast as February 21 (m)
except:

Morales .... Foss
Zuniga .... Sullivan
Micaëla .... Nielsen
Don José .... Grice (d)
Carmen .... Forst
Frasquita .... Orloff
Mercédès .... Pelle
Escamillo .... Hale

March 20

ATTILA

Same cast as March 13

March 21 (m)

THE MERRY WIVES OF WINDSOR

Same cast as February 19
except:

Conductor .... Bergeson
Mrs. Ford .... Sheil
Mrs. Page .... Freni
Page .... Opalach
Slender .... Novick
Dr. Cajus .... Foss
Ford .... McFarland
Fenton .... Hadley
Sir John Falstaff ..... Malas
Ann Page .... Woods

March 21

GIULIO CESARE

Same cast as March 15 (m)

March 22 (m)

ATTILA

Same cast as March 13

March 22

MARIA STUARDA (Donizetti)

Director .... Melano (d)
Conductor .... Pallo
Herald .... Brubaker
*Elisabetta, Queen of
   England* .... Galvany
*Talbot, Earl of
   Shrewsbury* .... Justus
*Cecil, Lord
   Burleigh* .... Seabury
*Roberto Dudley,
   Earl of Leicester* . . McCauley
Maria Stuarda ..... Putnam
Anna Kennedy ...... Shaulis

March 25

GIULIO CESARE

Same cast as March 15 (m)
except:

Cornelia .... Shaulis
Sesto .... Lerner
Cleopatra .... Anderson
Tolomeo .... Seabury

March 26

MARIA STUARDA

Same cast as March 22

March 27

FALSTAFF (Verdi)
(English tranlation by
Andrew Porter)

Conductor .... Salesky
Dr. Caius .... Lankston
Sir John Falstaff ...... Malas
Bardolph .... Foss
Pistol .... Opalach
Mistress Page ..... Hegierski
Mistress Ford .... Sheil
Dame Quickly .... Costa-
                  Greenspon
Nanetta .... J. Hall
Ford .... Titus
Fenton .... Reed

March 28 (m)

MADAMA BUTTERFLY

Same cast as March 14 (m)
except:

Goro .... Perry
Suzuki .... Curry
Sharpless .... McFarland
*Madama
   Butterfly* .... Sonnenschein

March 28

MARIA STUARDA

Same cast as March 22

March 29 (m)

CARMEN

Same cast as February 21 (m)
except:

Morales .... Foss
Zuniga .... Sullivan

Micaëla .... Nielsen
Don José .... Grice
Carmen .... Forst
Frasquita .... Orloff
Mercédès .... Pelle
Escamillo .... Hale

March 29

LA BOHÈME

Same cast as March 6 except:

Rodolfo .... Cole
Colline .... Reeve (d)
Schaunard ...... McFarland
Mimi .... Soviero
Parpignol .... Large
Musetta .... Hynes
Alcindoro .... Ledbetter

March 31

MARIA STUARDA

Same cast as March 22 except:

Elisabetta .... Niska
Talbot .... Fredricks
Cecil .... Jaffe (d)
Roberto Dudley .... J. Evans

April 1

TOSCA (Puccini)

Director .... Bentley
Conductor .... Pallo
Angelotti .... Reeve
A Sacristan .... McKee
Mario Cavaradossi ... Trussel
Tosca .... Zschau
Scarpia .... Diaz
Spoletta .... Large
Sciarrone .... Foss
A Shepherd ..... Schoenfeld
A Jailer .... Yule

April 3

FALSTAFF

Same cast as March 27

April 4 (m)

TOSCA

Same cast as April 1

April 4

MADAMA BUTTERFLY

Same cast as March 14 (m)
except:

Goro .... Perr
Suzuki .... Curr
Sharpless .... McFarlan
*Madama
   Butterfly* .... Sonnenschei
Trouble .... Danie

April 5 (m)

LA BOHÈME

Same cast as March 6 except:

Rodolfo .... Co
Colline .... Reev

Schaunard ...... McFarland
Mimi .... Soviero
Parpignol .... Large
Musetta .... Hynes
Alcindoro .... Ledbetter

April 5

MARIA STUARDA

Same cast as March 22 except:

Elisabetta .... Niska
Talbot .... Fredricks
Cecil .... Jaffe
Roberto Dudley .... J. Evans

April 7

TOSCA

Same cast as April 1

April 8

ANNA BOLENA (Donizetti)

Conductor ...... Wendelken-
Wilson
Giovanna .... Marsee
Anna .... Stapp
Smeton .... Lerner
Enrico .... Ramey
Lord Riccardo Percy .. Blake
Lord Rochefort ..... Bassett
Sir Hervey .... Clark

April 9

THE CUNNING LITTLE VIXEN
(Janáček)
(English translation by
Robert T. Jones and
Yveta Synek Graff)
First performance by The New
York City Opera Company

Director .... Corsaro
Scenic Designer ..Jampolis (d)
Costume
Designer .... Feldman (d)
Lighting
Designer .... Jampolis (d)
Choreographer .... Redel
Conductor ..... Thomas (d)

Bartos .... Cross
The Cricket ...... Rosoff (d)
The
Grasshopper ..Cassaday (d)
The
Mosquito ..Van Buskirk (d)
The Frog .... Byars (d)
Baby Sharp-Ears..Fogarty (d)
Mrs. Bartos .... B. Evans
Vixen Sharp-Ears ... Rolandi
Catcher .... Shaulis
Joey .... Blaber (d)
Frank .... Tramon (d)
The Rooster .... Orloff
Chocholka .... Mines
The Badger .... Billings
Father Alois .... Beattie
The Schoolmaster .. Lankston
Terynka .... Jarosz
Mr. Pasek .... Yule
Golden-stripe .... Pelle
The Owl .... Shaulis

The Jay .... Bellaver
The Woodpecker ...... Toro
Hypolit Harasta ..... Densen
Mrs. Pasek .... Hegierski

(Note: This performance
was erroneously listed as
Madeleine Mines's debut. She
had, in fact, previously sung
roles with the company,
including Barbarina in THE
MARRIAGE OF FIGARO.)

April 10

MADAMA BUTTERFLY

Same cast as March 14 (m)
except:

Goro .... Perry
Suzuki .... Hegierski
(s, Farone)
Sharpless .... McFarland
Madama
Butterfly .... Sonnenschen
Trouble .... Daniels
Kate Pinkerton .. Schoenfeld

April 11 (m)

ANNA BOLENA

Same cast as April 8

April 11

THE CUNNING LITTLE VIXEN

Same cast as April 9

April 12 (m)

THE LOVE FOR THREE ORANGES
(Prokofiev)
(L'Amour des Trois Oranges:
English translation by
Walter Ducloux)

Conductor .... Keene
The Herald .... Reeve
The King of Clubs .. McKee
Pantalone .... Foss
Truffaldino .... D. Hall
Leandro .... Billings
Celio .... Bassett
Fata Morgana .... Curry
Princess Clarissa ..... Costa-
Greenspon
Smeraldina .... Hegierski
The Prince .... J. Evans
Farfarello .... Lankston
The Cook .... Densen
Linetta .... Lambert
Nicoletta .... Claveau
Ninetta .... Gutknecht
Master of Ceremonies .. Clark

April 12

TOSCA

Same cast as April 1 except:

Conductor .... La Selva
Spoletta .... Clark

April 14

THE CUNNING LITTLE VIXEN

Same cast as April 9

April 15

CARMEN

Same cast as February 21 (m)
except:

Morales .... Ledbetter
Micaëla .... Hynes
Don José .... Grice
Remendado .... Large

April 16

THE CUNNING LITTLE VIXEN

Same cast as April 9

April 17

ANNA BOLENA

Same cast as April 8 except:

Enrico .... Hale

April 18 (m)

THE LOVE FOR THREE ORANGES

Same cast as April 12 (m)

April 18

THE CUNNING LITTLE VIXEN

Same cast as April 9 except:

Frank .... Renfrew (d),
(s, Tramon)

April 19 (m)

LA BOHÈME

Same cast as March 6 except:

Rodolfo .... Calleo
Marcello .... Fredricks
Colline .... Malas
Schaunard ...... McFarland
Mimi .... Soviero
Parpignol .... Large
Musetta .... Sheil
Alcindoro .... Ledbetter

April 19

THE MAKROPOULOS AFFAIR
(Janáček)
(English translation by
Norman Tucker)

Conductor .... Mauceri

Vitek .... Lankston
Albert Gregor .. Di Giuseppe
Christa .... Hynes
Emilia Marty .... Niska
Chauffeur ...... D. R. Smith
Dr. Kolenaty ...... Embree
Jaroslav Prus .... Ludgin
Miss Marty's maid ..... Toro
Janek .... Reed
Hauk-Sendorf ...... Harrold

April 21

THE LOVE FOR THREE ORANGES
Same cast as April 12 (m)

April 22

LA CLEMENZA DI TITO
(Mozart)

Conductor	Bernardi
Vitellia	Vaness
Sextus	Marsee
Annius	Pelle
Publius	Bassett
Titus	Moser
Servilia	J. Hall

April 23

THE MAKROPOULOS AFFAIR
Same cast as April 19

April 24

LA CLEMENZA DI TITO
Same cast as April 22

April 25 (m)

LA BOHÈME
Same cast as March 6 except:

Rodolfo	Calleo
Marcello	Fredricks, (Acts 1 & 2); Titus, (Acts 3 & 4)
Colline	Reeve
Schaunard	McFarland
Mimi	Soviero
Parpignol	Large
Musetta	Sheil
Alcindoro	Ledbetter

April 25

CARMEN
Same cast as February 21 (m) except:

Morales	Ledbetter
Micaëla	Hynes
Don José	Grice
Escamillo	Embree, (s, Fredricks)
Remendado	Large

April 26 (m)

THE MAKROPOULOS AFFAIR
Same cast as April 19

April 26

LA CLEMENZA DI TITO
Same cast as April 22

Bibliography

This bibliography has been divided into two parts—the first dealing with books, the second with magazines and periodicals. Omitted from both categories are generalized reference works such as the *Encyclopaedia Britannica,* newspapers, and such magazines as *Time* and *Newsweek.* Periodicals pertaining primarily to music, however, have been included. Also omitted are many books to which I referred, but which failed to disclose the particular information being sought. Thus, all of the works listed below have provided some information that has been incorporated into this book.

My primary references consisted of unpublished material: Morton Baum's notes and correspondence files, as well as those of the New York City Opera, minutes of board of directors' meetings, etc. As for the published sources, It is hoped that the reader will find the following list both interesting and useful.

BOOKS

Alberti, Luciano. *Music of the Western World.* New York: Crown Publishers, Inc., 1974.

Arditi, Luigi. *My Reminiscences.* New York: Dodd, Mead & Co., 1896.

Arendt, Hannah. *The Origins of Totalitarianism.* New York: Harcourt, Brace and Co., 1951.

Bateson, F. W. *English Comic Drama, 1700–1750.* Oxford, England: Clarendon Press, 1929.

Bing, Sir Rudolf. *Five Thousands Nights at the Opera.* Garden City, N.Y.: Doubleday & Co., Inc., 1972.

Bloomfield, Arthur. *Fifty Years of the San Francisco Opera.* San Francisco, Calif.: San Francisco Book Co., 1972.

———. *The San Francisco Opera, 1923–1961.* New York: Appleton-Century-Crofts, 1961.

Blum, Daniel. *Opera World.* New York: G. P. Putnam's Sons, 1955.

———. *A Pictorial Treasury of Opera in America.* New York: Greenberg, 1954.

507

Brockway, Wallace, and Weinstock, Herbert. *The Opera: A History of Its Creation and Performance, 1600–1941*. New York: Simon & Schuster, 1941.

Champlin, John Denison, Jr. *Cyclopedia of Music and Musicians*. New York: Charles Scribner's Sons, 1893.

Clément, Félix. *Dictionnaire des Opéras*. Paris: Larousse, 1905.

Dalrymple, Jean. *From the Last Row*. Clifton, N.J.: James T. White & Co., 1975.

———. *September Child*. New York: Dodd, Mead & Co., 1963.

Davis, Ronald. *Opera in Chicago*. New York: Appleton-Century, 1966.

Dent, Edward J. *Opera*. Middlesex, England: Penguin Books, 1940.

Drummond, Andrew H. *American Opera Librettos*. Metuchen, N.J.: Scarecrow Press, 1973.

Eaton, Quaintance. *Opera Caravan*. New York: Farrar, Straus & Cudahy, 1957.

Edwards, Henry Sutherland. *History of the Opera*. New York: Da Capo Press, 1977.

Elson, Louis C. *The Book of Musical Knowledge*. Boston: Houghton Mifflin Co., 1927.

———. *The History of American Music*. New York: Macmillan Publishing Co., 1925.

Ewen, David. *Complete Book of the American Musical Theater*. New York: Henry Holt & Co., 1958.

———. *The New Encyclopedia of the Opera*. New York: Hill & Wang, 1971.

Freedly, George, and Reeves, John A. *A History of the Theatre*. New York: Crown Publishers, 1941.

Garret, Charles. *The La Guardia Years*. New Brunswick, N.J.: Rutgers University Press, 1961.

Goddard, Joseph. *The Rise and Developmeunt of Opera*. London, England: W. Reeves, 1912.

Green, Stanley. *The World of Musical Comedy*. New York: Grosset & Dunlap, 1962.

Grout, Donald Jay. *A Short History of Opera*. New York: Columbia University Press, 1947.

Harewood, The Earl of. *The New Kobbe's Complete Opera Book*. New York: G. P. Putnam's Sons, 1976.

Hipsher, Edward E. *American Opera and Its Composers*. Philadelphia: T. Presser, 1927.

Holderness, Marvin. *Curtain Time in Forest Park*. St. Louis, Mo.: St. Louis Municipal Theatre Association, 1960.

Howard, John Tasker, and Bellows, George Kent. *A Short History of Music in America*. New York: Thomas Y. Crowell Co., 1967.

Hughes, Rupert (rev. by Deems Taylor and Russell Kerr). *The Biographical Dictionary of Musicians*. Garden City, N.Y.: Garden City Pub. Co., 1939.

Johnson, H. Earle. *Operas on American Subjects*. New York: Coleman-Ross Co., 1964.

Karp, Theodore. *Dictionary of Music*. New York: Dell Publishing Co., 1973

Kirstein, Lincoln. *The New York City Ballet*. New York: Alfred A. Knopf, 1973.

Kolodin, Irving. *The Metropolitan Opera, 1883–1938*. New York: Oxford University Press, 1939.

Lahee, Henry C. *Annals of Music in America*. Boston: Marshall Jones Co., 1922.

Leinsdorf, Erich. *Cadenza*. Boston: Houghton Mifflin Co., 1976.

Levine, Faye. *The Culture Barons.* New York: Thomas Y. Crowell Co., 1976.
Loewenberg, Alfred. *Annals of Opera, 1597–1940.* Cambridge, England: W. Heffer, 1943.
McSpadden, Joseph Walker. *Operas and Musical Comedies.* New York: Thomas Y. Crowell Co., 1946.
Maretzek, Max. *Revelations of an Opera Manager in 19th-Century America.* New York: Dover Publications, 1968.
Martens, Frederick Herman. *A Thousand and One Nights of Opera.* New York: D. Appleton, 1926.
Martin, George. *The Opera Companion to Twentieth-Century Opera.* New York: Dodd, Mead & Co., 1979.
Martin, Ralph G. *Lincoln Center for the Performing Arts.* Englewood Cliffs, N.J.: Prentice-Hall, 1971.
Mattfeld, Julius. *A Handbook of American Operatic Premieres, 1731–1962.* Detroit, Mich.: Information Service, Inc., 1963.
———. *A Hundred Years of Grand Opera in New York.* New York: New York Public Library, 1927.
Moore, Edward C. *Forty Years of Opera in Chicago.* New York: Horace Liveright, 1930.
Mordden, Ethan. *Opera in the Twentieth Century.* New York: Oxford University Press, 1978.
Read, Oliver, and Welch, Walter L. *From Tin Foil to Stereo.* Indianapolis, Ind.: Bobbs-Merrill Co., 1959.
Reis, Claire R. *American Composers of Today.* New York: New York International Society for Contemporary Music, 1930.
———. *Composers in America.* New York: Macmillan Publishing Co., 1938; rev. 1947.
———. *Composers, Conductors and Critics.* New York: Oxford University Press, 1955.
Rich, Maria. *Who's Who in Opera.* New York: Arno Press, 1976.
Rockefeller Panel Report. *The Performing Arts: Problems and Prospects.* New York: McGraw-Hill Book Co., 1965.
Rodman, Bella. *Fiorello La Guardia.* New York: Hill & Wang, 1962.
Rosenthal, Harold. *Opera Annual,* nos. 1–7. London: John Calder Ltd., 1954–1960.
———, and Warrack, John. *Concise Oxford Dictionary of Opera.* London: Oxford University Press, 1964.
Schmidgall, Gary. *Literature as Opera.* New York: Oxford University Press, 1977.
Seltsam, William H. *Metropolitan Opera Annals,* 1947; First Supplement, 1957; Second Supplement, 1968. New York: H. W. Wilson Co.; Third Supplement, compiled by Mary Ellis Peltz and Gerald Fitzgerald. Clifton, N.J.: James T. White & Co., 1978.
Sills, Beverly. *Bubbles: A Self-Portrait.* Indianapolis, Ind.: Bobbs-Merrill Co., 1976.
Sonneck, Oscar. *Catalogue of Opera Librettos Printed Before 1800.* Washington, D. C.: Government Printing Office, 1914.
Spaeth, Sigmund. *Music & Dance in New York State.* New York: Bureau of Musical Research, 1952.
Spencer, Janet, and Turner, Nolanda. *The National Directory for the Performing Arts and Civic Centers.* Dallas, Texas: Händel & Co., 1973.
Stuckenschmidt, H. H. *Twentieth-Century Composers.* New York: Holt, Rinehart & Winston, 1970.

Teasdale, May Silva. *Twentieth-Century Opera at Home and Abroad*. New York: E. P. Dutton & Co., 1938.

Thompson, Oscar. *International Cyclopedia of Music and Musicians*. New York: Dodd, Mead & Co., 1940.

Thomson, Virgil. *American Music Since 1910*. New York: Holt, Rinehart & Winston, 1971.

Towers, John. *Dictionary-Catalogue of Operas & Operettas*. New York: Da Capo Press, 1967.

Weisstein, Ulrich. *The Essence of Opera*. New York: W. W. Norton & Co., 1969.

MAGAZINES AND PERIODICALS

About the House. London, England: Friends of Covent Garden.

Central Opera Service bulletins (and transcripts of Central Opera Service conferences of 1973, 1974, 1976). New York: Central Opera Service.

The Gramophone. Middlesex, England: General Gramophone Publications, Ltd.

High Fidelity. New York: ABC Leisure Magazines.

Musical America. Great Barrington, Mass.: ABC Leisure Magazines.

Opera. London, England: Opera.

Opera News. New York: Metropolitan Opera Guild.

Quarter Notes (later: *City Opera Spotlight*). New York: New York City Opera Guild.

Record Collector. Suffolk, England: Record Collectors' Shop.

Schwann Record Catalogues. Boston: ABC Schwann Publications.

Stereo Review. New York: Ziff-Davis Pub. Co.

In addition to the above, many references were made to articles in New York City Opera programs, press releases of both City Opera and City Center, and annual reports of City Center.

Index to the Annals

This index consists of two sections. The first part is a listing of every work performed by the New York City Opera from its inception through the Spring 1981 season. The second part deals with performing artists. In both parts, references are made to seasons rather than to pages.

In general, there have been two seasons yearly, one in Spring and one in Fall. Exceptions occurred in 1944, which had three seasons (Winter, Spring, and Fall); and in 1957, 1961, and 1964, each of which had a Fall season only.

Within the first section of the index, we have attempted to list operatic titles in their most familiar forms. This, of necessity, introduced certain inconsistencies. American audiences tend to think of *The Gypsy Baron* rather than *Der Zigeunerbaron,* but they also tend to think of *Die Fledermaus* rather than *The Bat,* even though it is always produced in English. We felt that ease of reference was the most important factor, and it is hoped that no reader is disturbed by this tabulation. Cross-referencing has been provided between various forms of titles and between operas and composers.

City Opera has performed works in English, French, German, Italian, Japanese, Latin, Russian, and Spanish. Certain works have been done at times in one language, at times in another (e.g., *Die Meistersinger* and *Don Giovanni*), while others have been done in more than one language within a given performance (e.g. *Ariadne auf Naxos*). The language of performance is indicated in parentheses after the title of each opera. Where two languages are shown, they are either separated by a semicolon (indicating different languages at different times) or joined by an ampersand (indicating multilingual performances).

NP indicates "New Production," meaning that new scenery and/or new costumes were introduced at that performance.

Within the artist section, each name is associated with a coded entry, according to the following key:

sop	soprano
m-s	mezzo-soprano
ten	tenor
bar	baritone
bs	bass
dan	dancer
act	actor or actress
ch	child
mus	musician (onstage pianist, violinist, etc.)
spe	special (fire-eaters, jugglers, acrobats, etc.)
con	conductor
dir	director
chor	choreographer
des	designer (scenic, costume, lighting, electronic sound)
ch. mas.	chorus master (or assistant)
adv	adviser (including language, acting, and stylistic coaches)

When an artist functioned in more than one capacity (e.g., Placido Domingo appeared as a tenor and as a conductor) separate listings for each category have been provided.

I INDEX OF OPERAS
AND COMPOSERS LISTED
IN THE ANNALS

Abduction from the Seraglio, The
(Mozart) (E; E&G)
F57; F58; F66–S67; F69–S70; S71
Aida (Verdi) (I)
F48–F49; F50–F51; F52–S53; F54;
F61; F62
Albert Herring (Britten) (E)
F71
Amahl and the Night Visitors
(Menotti) (E)
S52–S53; S54
Amelia al Ballo. See Amelia Goes to
the Ball
Amelia Goes to the Ball (Menotti) (E)
S48–F48; S63
American Trilogy, An. See Before
Breakfast; Madame Adare; Student
from Salamanca, The
Amor Brujo, El (Falla) (S)
F57
Andrea Chénier (Giordano) (I)
S47; S52; F78–S79.
NP F78
Anna Bolena (Donizetti) (I)
F73–S75; F80–S81
Argento, Dominick. See Miss Havisham's
Fire
Ariadne auf Naxos (Strauss, R.) (G&E)
F46–F47; F49; F73–F74; F75; S77.
NP F73
Ashmedai (Tal) (E)
S76; F77
Attila (Verdi) (I)
S81

Bach, Jan. See Student from Salamanca,
The

Ballad of Baby Doe, The (Moore) (E)
S58–S59; S60; S62; S63; S65; S66;
S69–F69; S76.
NP S59
Ballo in Maschera, Un (Verdi) (I)
S71–F71; F74; S76
Barber of Seville, The (Rossini) (I; E)
F47; F65; F66; F67; F68; S71–F71;
F73–S74; S75; S76–S77; S78; S79;
S80–F80.
NP F65; F76
Barbiere di Siviglia, Il. See Barber of
Seville, The
Bartered Bride, The (Smetana) (E)
F45–F46; F55
Bartók, Bela. See Bluebeard's Castle
Beatrix Cenci (Ginastera) (S)
S73; S74
Beeson, Jack. See Lizzie Borden
Before Breakfast (Pasatieri) (E)
F80
Belle Hélène, La (Offenbach) (E)
F76–S77
Bellini, Vincenzo. See Puritani, I
Berg, Alban. See Wozzeck
Bernstein, Leonard. See Trouble in Tahiti
Bizet, Georges. See Carmen; Pearl
Fishers, The
Blitzstein, Marc. See Cradle Will Rock,
The; Regina
Bluebeard's Castle (Bartók) (E)
F52–S53
Bohème, La (Puccini) (I)
S44–F46; F47–F57; F58; F59;
F60–F61; F62; F63–F64; F65;
F66–S81.
NP F56; S66

II INDEX OF ARTISTS
LISTED IN THE ANNALS

Aaronson, Cindy Lynn (sop)
F79–S80; S81
Aaronson, Cynthia (sop). *See* Aaronson,
Cindy Lynn
Abbot, Adelaide (sop)
S44
Abdarrahman, Ahmed (spe)
F69–S70
Abilena, Mia (dan)
S45
Able, Will B. (act)
S59
Abrams, Don (des)
F79–S80; S81
Addison, Adele (sop)
S55–F57; F58; F61
Addison, Bernard (act)
F63
Addy, Wesley (act)
F59; F61
Adler, Arlene (sop)
S68–S69; S71–F71; F72; F73; F74; F75
Adler, Peter Herman (con)
F57–F58
Adoff, Denise (ch)
F78; F79
Ahearn, Michael (ch)
F67–F68
Aiken, David (bar)
S53; S55
Alba, Maria (dan)
S67
Albanese, Cecilia (sop)
F73
Albert, Donnie Ray (bar)
F78; S80–S81
Albertini, Sergio (con)
F69
Alberts, Eunice (m–s)
F51; F61; F71

Albertson, Jack (act)
S54
Aldaba, Dalisay (sop)
F47–S48; S50–S51
Alden, Christopher (dir)
F79–S80
Aldredge, Theoni V. (des)
S66; S67; F70–S71; S73–F80
Aler, John (ten)
S81
Alessandro, Victor (con)
F67
Alexander, Carlos (bar)
S47
Alexander, John (ten)
F57–F58; F59; F60–F61; F62; F63;
F66; S69; F71; S73; S74–S77;
Special guest F80
Ali, Mustapha (spe)
F69–S70
Allen, Betty (m–s)
F54; S73; S74–S75
Allen, Chet (ch)
S52; S53
Allen, Raymond (ten)
F60
Allers, Franz (con)
F57
Allison, Patti (sop)
S77–S78
Alpert, Anita (m–s)
S58
Alvary, Lorenzo (bs)
F49–S50
Ambros, Edwin (dir)
S47
Amedeo, Edy (sop)
F65
Amundsen, Monte (sop)
F58

Anden, Mathew (act)
S65
Anderson, Frances (sop)
S46–F46
Anderson, June (sop)
F78–S81
Anderson, Rachel (ch)
F67
Anderson, Ray (ten)
F47
Anderson, Robert (bs)
F52–S54
Anderson, Shari (sop)
S74
Anderson, Sylvia (m–s)
F72–F73
Andor, Paul (act)
S65
Andrea, Jennie (sop)
F53–S56; F57–F60
Andrew, Thomas (chor)
F62; F63–F64; F65–F67; S70–F77;
F78–S81
Andrews, Theodora (sop)
S63
Angela, June (ch)
S70; S71; S72; F73; F74
Anglin, Florence (act)
S59–F59; S63; S66
Annaloro, Antonio (ten)
S48
Annals, Michael (des)
S80–S81
Annovazzi, Napoleone (con)
F59
Anthony, Judith (sop)
F67–F68; F69–F70; F71–F73; F74–S75
Anthony, Mary (dan)
F52–S53
Anthony, Steve (dan)
S76; F77
Apinée, Irene (dan)
F62
Archambault, Blanche (m–s)
F44–F45
Ardelli, Norbert (ten)
W44–F44
Ardolino, Emile (des)
F70; F71–F72; F76
Argyris, Vasso (ten)
F46–F47; F50
Arie, Raffaele (bs)
F50; F51
Armbruster, Richard (act)
S63; S66
Armistead, Horace (des)
F52–F53; S58; S59; S60; S62; S63;
S66–F66; S74; S75
Armstrong, Karan (sop)
S69–S70; F71; F75–F76; F77
Armstrong, Marilyn (m–s)
F68–S69
Armstrong, Will Steven (des)
F62; F63–S66; S68–S70

Arnold, David (bar)
S80–S81
Aronovich, Sura (m–s)
S44; S45
Arpino, Gerald (dan)
F57; F58; F60–F61
Arrauzau, Francine (m–s)
S77–F77
Arroyo, Martina (sop)
special guest F75
Arshansky, Michael (act)
S53–S54; F59
Arthur, Donald (bs)
S59
Asaro, Josephine (sop)
S55; S56
Atherton, Robert (bar)
F56; S58–S59
Atkins, Charles (act)
F63
Atkins, Norman (bar)
F59–S60; S62–F62
Atkinson, David (bar)
S58; S59; S60
Attles, Joseph (ten)
S65
Auerbach, Cynthia (dir)
F75–S81
Augér, Arleen (sop)
S69
August, Joan (m–s)
F64–S68
Austin, Patti (act)
S58
Auvray, Jean-Claude (dir)
F73–S74
Ayars, Ann (sop)
S47–F53
Azova, Ludmilla (sop)
S66

Babbs, Donna (ch)
S66
Baccaloni, Salvatore (adv)
S55
Bailey, Dennis (ten)
S78
Bailey, John (bs)
F47; F48
Bailey, Norman (bar)
F75
Bain, Conrad (act)
S58
Baisley, Helen (m–s)
S55–S59
Baker, Alan (bar)
F75–S77; S78–F78
Bakman, Patrick (dir)
S72–F74; F75–S76
Bala, Iris (sop)
F65
Balanchine, George (chor)
F48–S49; S79–F79; special guest F75
Balestracci, Sandra (dan)
F65–S66; S70–S72; S73–F73; S75–F77

Forst, Judith (m–s)
S81
Foss, Harlan (bar)
F76–F78; F79–S81
Foss, Lucas (con)
S67
Foster, Leesa (sop)
S62
Foster, Nancy (sop)
F62
Foster, Naomi (sop)
S62
Fowles, Glenys (sop)
S74–F80
Fran, Adam (ch)
S73
Fran, Ethan (ch)
F77
Frank, David (bar)
S59
Frank, Phyllis (sop)
F57
Fratesi, Gino (ten)
F46
Fredericks, Walter (ten)
S50; S51; S53–S55; S56; F59
Fredricks, Richard (bar)
F60–F62; F63–S65; F67–F79;
F80–S81
Freedman, Gerald (dir)
F66; S73–F78; S80–F80
Freeman, Carroll (ch)
F66
French, Norma (sop)
S72; S73; S74; S78
Freni, Rosemarie (m–s)
S77–S81
Freyhan, Irene (sop)
S46
Fried, Howard (ten)
S56; S58; S59; S60; S63; S74–F74
Frieder, Sol (act)
S65
Friedman, Alan (ch)
S69
Frierson, Andrea (ch)
S63
Frierson, Andrew (bar)
S58; S59–F61; F62–F63; S65
Frigerio, Claudio (bar)
F53
Frizell, Cornelius (act)
S73
Fry, Cleo (sop)
F56–F57
Fuente, Luis (dan)
S68–F69
Fuerstner, Fiona (dan)
S70; S73
Fuller, Larry (chor)
S80–F80

Gainey, Andrew (bar)
S48–S50; S52; S54

Galan, Esperanza (dan)
F67; S70–F71; F72–S81
Galan, Rosario (dan)
F63–F64; F65; F66; F67; S72
Galiano, Joseph (bar)
F68–F72
Gallagher, Gil (bar)
F45
Gallagher, Robert (act)
S54–F54
Galli, Gianna (sop)
F58; F59
Galterio, Lou (dir)
S80–S81
Galvany, Marisa (sop)
S72–F74; S78–S81
Galway, James (mus)
special guest F80
Gamboni, Frank (bar)
F49
Gamson, Arnold (con)
S58
Gannon, Teresa (sop)
F53–S55
Garcia, Nino (ten)
S70
Gardella, Toni-Ann (dan)
F77–S80
Garen, David (ten)
S49–S50
Gari, Giulio (ten)
S45–F47; S49–F52; F55
Gari, Madeleine (m–s)
S50
Garnell, Grant (bar)
S45–S47
Garson, John (act)
S65
Gaston, Conchita (m–s)
F49
Gately, David (act)
F79
Gateson, Marjorie (m–s)
S54
Gauld, Carlton (bs)
F44; F45; S48–S53; F54–F55; F57;
F58
Gauld, Carlton (adv)
S68
Gauld, Carlton (dir)
F57; F58; F59; F60–F61
Gavoorian, Joan (sop)
F64
Gaynes, George (bar)
S52–S54; F59; F60–S62
See also Jongeyans, George
Gbur, Jan (bs)
S52
Geiger-Torel, Herman (dir)
F53–F54
Gelfer, Steven B. (dan)
S66–F66
Genia, Panna (sop)
F47

Poplaski, William (act)
S80–F80
Popper, Felix (con)
F60–S67; F69; S74
Porras, Patricia (ch)
S68–F68; F69
Porretta, Frank (ten)
F56; S58–F61; F62; F63; S65; S67;
S68; S69
Porter, Joan (act)
F60
Porter, Richard L. (act)
S80
Porter, Stephen (dir)
F74
Portnoy, Lenore (sop)
F46–S48
Poston, Karon (sop)
S81
Postrel, Leo (bar)
F68–S69; S70–F70; F78; F79
Potts, Nancy (des)
F78; F79
Povia, Charlotte (m–s)
F61–F62; F63–S68
Powell, Robert (dan)
S68–F68; F69
Powell, Thomas (bar)
S49–S50; S51–F56
Powers, Marie (m–s)
S48–F49
Powers, William (bs)
F72
Pradera, Rebeka (dan)
S73–S74; F78–F79
Precht, Donna (sop)
S63–F63; S65–S66
Preminger, Otto (dir)
F53
Presnell, Steve (act)
S72; S76
Presnell, Steve (dir)
S74–F77
Pressman, David (dir)
F56
Presto (spe)
S73; F74–S75; S76; F77; S79; S80
Pretzat, Anne (sop)
S68–F68
Price, Henry (ten)
F75–F80
Price, Leontyne (sop)
special guest F80
Price, Perry (ten)
F71
Primm, John (act)
F49–S50; S51
Prince, Harold (dir)
S76; F77; S80–F80
Profanato, Gene (ch)
F71–S72
Protti, Aldo (bar)
S56
Psacharopoulos, Nikos (dir)
S65–S66; F67; S76

Puleo, Robert (ch)
S66; S67; F68–S71
Putnam, Ashley (sop)
F78–F79; S81

Queler, Elizabeth (ch)
S71
Queler, Eve (con)
S78
Quilico, Louis (bar)
F55–S56; F57; F60; F62; F69–S72;
S73; S75
Quinn, Michael (bs)
S56
Quinn, Michael (dan)
F69
Quintero, José (dir)
S58; S59

Rabovsky, Istvan (dan)
F65
Racz, Teresa (m–s)
S62
Raedler, Dorothy (dir)
F59; F60–F61; F62; F63–F64; F65
Rael, Eduardo (bar)
S44–F44
Rall, Thomas (ten)
F64
Ramey, Samuel (bs)
S73–S81
Rampasso, Luciano (ten)
S72; F73–S75
Randall, Carl (chor)
F45
Randazzo, Arlene (sop)
S68–F68; F74–S76
Randazzo, Maria (ch)
F75–S76; S78
Randolph, James (bar)
S62; S65
Randolph, Jess (bs)
F47–S48
Randolph, Robert (des)
S65–F65
Raskin, Judith (sop)
F59–F61; F62; F63
Rawn, Jean (sop)
S79–F79
Ray, Nadine (sop)
F45
Rayson, Benjamin (bar)
F65; S67–F67
Reale, Marcella (sop)
F65
Reardon, John (bar)
F54–S56; F57–F59; F60–F61;
F62–F66; S72
Redding, Earl (bar)
F53
Redel, Jessica (chor)
F78; S80–S81
Redel, Jessica (dan)
S79
Reece, Arley (ten)
S74–F74

Treigle, Norman (bs)
S53–S55; S56–F57; F58; S60–F61;
F62–F65; F66–F68; F69–F71; F72
Triana, Antonio (chor)
F57
Triana, Antonio (dan)
F57
Trisler, Joyce (chor)
S73; S74–F74
Troyanos, Tatiana (m–s)
S63–S65
Trussel, Jacque (ten)
F77–S81
Tucker, Thomas (ch)
F72
Turcano, Lucia (sop)
S50–F50
Turner, Claramae (m–s)
S53–F53; S58; S59–F59; F61; F62;
F63; S65; S66; S67; S68–S69
Turner, Clyde (act)
S62
Turner, Douglas (act)
S58
Turoff, Robert (dir)
F63
Turofsky, Ricki (sop)
F72
Turp, André (ten)
S73
Turrini, Roberto (ten)
F52
Tyers, John (bar)
F48–S51
Tyl, Noel (bar)
F65–F66; F67
Tyler, Veronica (sop)
F64; F66; F67; F68–F69; S72–F72;
F73; S75
Tynes, Margaret (sop)
S52–F53; F55

Ukena, Paul (bs)
S58–S60; F61–F62; F63; S65; S66;
F75–S76; F77; F79
Ulisse, Arthur (ten)
F44
Underwood, Willabelle (sop)
F51–F54
Unruh, Stan (ten)
F76
Uppman, Theodor (bar)
S48; F62
Urhausen, Roy (bs)
F54
Uthoff, Michael (dan)
S68–S69

Valdengo, Giuseppe (bar)
F46–S48
Vanarelli, Mario (des)
F79–S80; S81
Van Buskirk, Eliot (ch)
S81
Vandenburg, Howard (ten)
S52

Vaness, Carol (sop)
F79–S81
Vanni, Helen (sop)
S69–F69
Vanoff, Nick (dan)
F49–S50
Van Orden, Ray (act)
S74
Van Scott, Glory (dan)
S65
Van Way, Nolan (bar)
F66
Van Witsen, Leo (des)
F56; F62
Varona, José (des)
F66–S81
Vaughan, Edward (bs)
F78–S79
Vega, Joseph (ch)
S70
Vega, Rita (dan)
F57
Vega, Robert (ten)
S76
Vellucci, Luigi (ten)
F48–F55; F60; F64; F65; S67–F67
Venora, Lee (sop)
S58–S59; S62; S63; F67
Ventura, Clyde (ch)
S65–F65
Venza, Jac (des)
F61; F62; F69–S70; S71; S72; F75; S78
Verdejo, Awilda (sop)
S78–S80
Vergara, Mercedes (m–s)
S67
Vergara, Victoria (m–s)
S77–F77
Verreau, Richard (ten)
F56; F59; F60; F62
Verrett, Shirley (m–s)
F64
See also Carter, Shirley
Vertecchi, Giuseppe (ten)
S53
Villechaize, Hervé (act)
S68
Villella, Edward (dan)
S69–F69
Vinay, Ramon (ten)
F45–F46; F48; S54
Vincent, George (ten)
F47–F48
Viracola, Fiddle (sop)
S59; S60
Virga, Rose (m–s)
F54
Visca, Edward (ten)
S44–S45
Voketaitis, Arnold (bs)
F58–F61; F62–S65; S68; S73–F73; S76
Von Stade, Frederica (m–s)
S76
Vroons, Frans (ten)
S49; S50; F51

Williams, Camilla (sop)
S46–S54
Williams, David (ten)
F57
Williams, Grant (ten)
S58–S60
Williams, Lee (act)
S52
Williams, Lee (dir)
F52–F53; F54
Williams, Mary (m–s)
F54–S55
Williams, Nancy (m–s)
F61
Williams, Patricia (dan)
S79
Williams, Ralph (act)
S76
Williams, Robert (ten)
F60–F61; F62
Williams, Sharon (ch)
S59–F59
Williams, Steven Alexus (bs)
F80
Williams, Vanessa (sop)
F78–F79
Wilson, Charles (con)
F62; F63–S65, S66–F66; F67 F68;
F69–F72
See also Wendelken-Wilson, Charles
Wilson, Joemy (m–s)
S69
Winburn, Janet (m–s)
F68–S71
Winston, Alan (bar)
F45–F46; F49–S50
Winston, Lee (ten)
F77
Winston, Shirley (m–s)
F56
Winter, Ethel (dan)
F54
Winters, Lawrence (bar)
F48–S56; S58; S62
Wise, Patricia (sop)
F68–S75
Wishner, Samuel (spe)
S70
Wisnofsky, Anne Marie (ch)
S66; S69
Witkowska, Nadja (sop)
S55; F60; F62–S65; F66–S68
Wittop, Freddy (des)
F64
Wittstein, Ed (des)
F65; F66–S68; S69–F69; F70–S73;
S74; S75–S77
Wolff, Beverly (m–s)
S58; F63–F65; F66; F67–S68; F70–S71
Wolff, Greta (m–s)
F58–S59
Wolff, William (bs)
S66
Wolmut, Hans (dir)
W44–S44

Woodley, Arthur (bar)
F79
Woods, Sheryl (sop)
S81
Worth, Coley (act)
F53; F54–F57; F58; F63–F64; F65;
F74–S78
Wright, Ned (ten)
S62
Wright, Richard (ten)
F49–F50
Wyckoff, Lou Ann (m–s)
S63; S65; S66–F67
Wyman, Florence (sop)
S63
Wymetal, William (dir)
F44
Wynder, Gloria (m–s)
S54–F54; S62
Wyner, Susan Davenny (sop)
F77
Wysor, Elizabeth (m–s)
F44

Yamaguchi, Kazuko (bs)
F53
Yancy, Alexander (ten)
S58
Yannopoulos, Dino (dir)
F72–S73; S75–F76; F77
Yarick, Doris (sop)
F60–F62
Yarmat, Karen (m–s)
S75
Yauger, Margaret (m–s)
S73–S74
Yearsley, Charles (bs)
S44
Yeend, Frances (sop)
S48–S53; S54–F57; F58; F59
Yoes, Janice (sop)
F73–S74
Yorke, Sylvia (sop)
F80
Young, Marie (sop)
S65; S66; S68; S71; S76; F78; F79; F80
Young, Norman (bar)
F46–F49
Young, Syble (sop)
S71–S73; S77
Yule, Don (bs)
S60–F60; F62–S81

Zahariades, Bruce (ch)
S62–F62
Zakariesen, William (ten)
S58–S60
Zambrana, Margarita (sop)
S49–F49; F50; S53; S60
Zannoth, Sherry (sop)
S77–S80; S81
Zara, Meredith (sop)
S63
Zaraspe, Hector (chor)
S68

General Index

558 GENERAL INDEX

Herbert, Ralph, 64, 71, 78
Herbert, Victor, 191
L'Heure Espagnole (Ravel), 190
Hewitt, James, 18
High School of Music and Art, 4
Hippodrome Opera Company, 39
L'Histoire du Soldat (Stravinsky), 188, 190
Hoiby, Lee, 161, 173, 175, 184
Homer, Louise, 30
Hopkinson, Francis, 19
Horne, William, 62
Hughes, Langston, 66
Hull, Mrs. Lytle, 7, 9, 33, 139
Hurok, Sol, 62, 66
Hutcheson, Ernest, 7, 9
Hynds, Reed, 36–37

Idomeneo (Mozart), 187
Impellitteri, Vincent, 119, 120
Impresario, The (Mozart), 190
L'Incantesimo (Montemezzi), 55–56
L'Incoronazione di Poppea (Monteverdi), 15n
Italian Opera House, 24
Iturbi, José, 149–152

Jagel, Frederick, 30
Janáček, Leoš, 184
Jobin, André, 184
Jobin, Raoul, 44, 184
Johnson, Edward, 33
Johnson, H. Earle, 162
Johnson, Harriet, 59, 152, 160–161
Johnson, Horace, 5, 31
Johnston, Denis, 159
Jordan, Irene, 152
Joseph, J. Edgar, 197
Juilliard Foundation, 31
Julius Caesar (Handel), 177–178

Kasznar, Kurt, 175
Kay, Hershy, 157
Kelley, Norman, 157, 160, 162
Kern, Jerome, 126
Kerz, Leo, 135, 136
Ketcham, Ben, 13
Kiepura, Jan, 33
Kingsley, Sidney, 29
Kirchner, Leon, 189
Kirk, Florence, 33, 43
Kirstein, Lincoln, 107, 115–117, 123–129, 153, 154, 167, 170–172
Kirsten, Dorothy, 60–61
Klemperer, Otto, 40, 112
Knapp, Eleanor, 41
Knight, Felix, 40, 41, 46
Kobart, Ruth, 165
Kodály, Zoltán, 35, 39, 40
Korngold, Erich Wolfgang, 33, 187
Kozakevich, Stefan, 41
Kravitt, Harold, 41
Kreste, Mary, 72–76, 88, 109
Kurka, Robert, 157, 165

La Guardia, Achille Luigi Carlo, 4

La Guardia, Fiorello, 1–9, 11–13, 31, 34, 50, 54, 61, 172
La Guardia, Irene Coen, 4
La Mance, Eleanor, 42
Laciar, Samuel, 37
Laikind, Jeffrey, 188
Lankston, John, 189
Lauri-Volpi, Giacomo, 30
Lawrence, Gertrude, 29
Lawrence, Marjorie, 37, 38, 43, 44
Lazarus, Reuben, 120
Lee, Sondra, 159
Leinsdorf, Erich, 7, 131–139, 143, 147, 152
Leoncavallo, Ruggiero, 43–45
Leonidoff, Leon, 116
Leonora (Fry), 19, 24
Lert, Ernst, 37–39
Lewis, Brenda, 63, 160
Liebling, Estelle, 194, 195
Likova, Eva, 71
Lily (Kirchner), 189–190
Limón, José, 33
Lincoln Center, 166–173, 181
Lipkin, Seymour, 156
Lipton, Martha, 33, 55, 58, 155
Litvinne, Felia, 27
Loca, La (Menotti), 193
Long, Charles, 190
Long-playing records, 47
Longone, Elen, 42
Lost in the Stars (Weill), 156
Love for Three Oranges, The (Prokofiev), 66
Lowry, W. McNeil, 154
Lucca, Pauline, 27
Lucia di Lammermoor (Donizetti), 183, 184, 189
Lucrezia Borgia (Donizetti), 189
Ludgin, Chester, 165, 173
Lully, Jean-Baptiste, 15
Lustig, Ludwig, 72
Lynch, Dominick, 21

Macbeth (Verdi), 152
McBride, Patricia, 192
McCormack, John, 28
McGoldrick, Joseph D., 4, 7, 9
McGrath, J. Howard, 115, 116
MacNeil, Cornell, 59, 143
MacNeil, Dorothy, 78
Macurdy, John, 163
MacWatters, Virginia, 33, 64
Madame Butterfly (Puccini), 46, 67
Magic Flute (Mozart), 178
Mahler, Fritz, 32
Makropoulos Affair, The (Janáček), 184
Malibran, Maria, 20–23
Manhattan Opera Company, 28
Manon (Massenet), 45, 69, 71–72, 182
Manon Lescaut (Puccini), 61, 62, 187
Mapleson, James Henry, 27, 28
Marazzoli, Marco, 15
Maretzek, Max, 24–27
Maria Golovin (Menotti), 159, 160
Maria Stuarda (Donizetti), 184

Wittrisch, Marcel, 30
Wolf-Ferrari, Ermanno, 78
Wolff, Beverly, 156, 182
Works Progress Administration (WPA), 5, 31, 32, 39
Wozzeck (Berg), 114, 115, 117
Wuthering Heights (Floyd), 159–160

Yeend, Frances, 63, 78
Young Lord, The (Henze), 184

Zenatello, Giovanni, 28
Ziegler, Edward, 32
Ziliani, Alessandro, 30
Zschau, Marilyn, 191